RISE OF THE AMERICAN NATION

HERITAGE EDITION

VOLUME 2
1865 TO THE PRESENT
WITH READINGS

LEWIS PAUL TODD
MERLE CURTI

EDITORIAL CONSULTANTS

ELIZABETH CONNOR Supervisor of Social Studies,
Detroit, Michigan

PEGGY WEBSTER HAYS Head of Social Studies, Lexington High School,
Lexington, Virginia

WESLEY J. JONES, JR. Director of Social Studies, Toledo, Ohio

FLOYD B. PITTS Assistant Director of Social Studies,
Dallas Independent School District, Dallas, Texas

FRANKLIN SMITH Assistant Principal of Social Studies,
Benjamin Franklin High School, New York, New York

MARIA C. VIRAMONTES Teacher, La Canada High School,
La Canada, California

RICHARD WILSON Supervisor of Social Studies,
Montgomery County, Maryland

HARCOURT BRACE JOVANOVICH

New York   Chicago   San Francisco   Atlanta   Dallas   *and*   London

RISE OF THE AMERICAN NATION

HERITAGE EDITION

VOLUME 2

1865 TO THE PRESENT

WITH READINGS

LEWIS PAUL TODD

MERLE CURTI

LEWIS PAUL TODD has acquired national distinction as a teacher and writer on American history and related subjects. He taught American history for many years and was head of the Department of Social Studies at Bound Brook High School, Bound Brook, New Jersey. He also has taught American history, historical geography of the United States, American government, and related courses at Queens College, New York, at Western Connecticut State College, Danbury, Connecticut, and at New York University.

Dr. Todd is widely known among social studies teachers for his textbook writing and for his many articles and editorials in social studies journals. He has contributed to the Yearbooks and other publications of the National Council for the Social Studies (NCSS). From 1947 to 1969 he was editor of *Social Education,* the official journal of the NCSS. Dr. Todd also has served as editorial writer for *Civic Leader.* In addition to his collaboration on *Rise of the American Nation,* he co-authored two series of social studies textbooks for elementary schools.

MERLE CURTI is Frederick Jackson Turner Professor of American History, Emeritus, at the University of Wisconsin (Madison) and has been Visiting Professor of History at the University of Tokyo. He has lectured at many American colleges and at Cambridge University. He also has served as honorary consultant in American cultural history, Library of Congress. Dr. Curti was formerly Professor of American History at Teachers College, Columbia University, where he and Dr. Todd began their collaboration on instructional materials for American history classrooms.

Professor Curti has been president of the American Historical Association, the highest honor a historian in the United States can receive. He also received the award of the American Council of Learned Societies for particularly distinguished scholarship. His long list of distinguished historical writings includes *The Social Ideas of American Educators, The Making of an American Community, The American Paradox: The Conflict of Thought and Action,* and *The Growth of American Thought,* for which he won the Pulitzer prize for history.

ACKNOWLEDGMENTS: For permission to reprint copyrighted material, grateful acknowledgment is made to Joan Daves Literary Agency for an excerpt from "I Have a Dream," an address by Martin Luther King, Jr., © 1963 by Martin Luther King, Jr., and to Harper & Row, Publishers, Inc. for an excerpt from *The Big Change* by Frederick Lewis Allen.

Cover: The American bald eagle; illustration by Robert Goldstein, based on a 19th century woodcut
Text Maps: Harold K. Faye
Drawings: Samuel H. Bryant

ISBN   0-15-376055-9

Printed in the United States of America

CONTENTS

READINGS

UNIT SEVEN: THE CHALLENGES OF A NEW ERA (1945–1970's)

SPECIAL FEATURES

SOURCES

TEXT MAPS AND CHARTS

HISTORICAL ATLAS
OF THE UNITED STATES

INTRODUCTION

Washington, D.C. in the 1830's

FROM 1607 TO 1865

The roots of American culture

Not one of the men and women who settled in the American colonies landed on these shores empty-handed. To be sure, some arrived with little more than the clothing they wore. Others, even less fortunate, came as indentured servants who had sold their labor for a period of several years to pay for their passage across the ocean. And some, the tragic victims of slavery, arrived in chains to be sold to the highest bidder. But rich or poor, free or slave, every one of them brought along some part of the culture of their former homelands. Each person, regardless of his or her position in society, made a contribution to American culture.

What is culture?

Culture, simply defined, is the whole way of life of a people or a nation. It is the sum of all the things that distinguish one group of people or one nation from another.

Culture includes language, religion, laws, forms of government, methods of educating the young, means of communicating, ways of earning a living, games and recreation, habits and customs, and the organization of family and community life.

Culture is always changing. It develops and grows. It is the product of an endless interaction between human beings and their environment. Each greatly influences the other. The environment shapes in part the way a nation or a people lives. People, in turn, alter the environment. People who have an advanced science and technology are, of course, able to alter and control their environment far more effectively than men and women who must depend upon hand labor, simple tools, and traditional methods of working.

Europeans' advantages over the Indians

The culture that Europeans brought with them to the Americas gave them a decisive advantage over the Indians. As a result, European ways of living became firmly established in North America and in parts of Central and South America.

The *material* culture the Europeans brought with them included instruments of navigation, guns and gunpowder, iron and steel tools, plows, wheels, and a variety of domestic animals. Their *nonmaterial* culture included the alphabet, books and printing, the concept of the nation-state, and mathematics. These cultural developments, unknown to the Indians, gave the Europeans enormous advantages over the original inhabitants of the Americas. Because of their more advanced technology, the Europeans also had a great advantage in warfare. Equally important, they were conditioned by their culture to want to make use of America's natural resources and to reshape the environment to make it serve their own needs.

The European struggle for control

From the beginning, it was evident that the American continents were a rich prize for the nation that had the courage, enterprise, and ability to seize them. For more than 200 years the colonial nations of Europe took part in a fierce struggle—diplomatic, religious, economic, and military—for control of one part or another of the Americas. The

The women who arrived at Jamestown in 1619 played a significant role in building the first European settlements in America.

major powers in this conflict were Spain, France, and England, but Portugal and the Netherlands also took part, and Sweden, too, was involved.

By 1763 the contest had for the most part been settled. Portugal remained in possession of Brazil. The Spanish flag flew over all the rest of South America; over nearly all of Central America; over a number of islands in the Caribbean Sea; over the city of New Orleans, east of the Mississippi River, and over the plains and mountains west of the Mississippi. France and the Netherlands retained only a few islands in the Atlantic Ocean and the Caribbean Sea. Great Britain controlled all of Canada and (with the exception of New Orleans) all of the area east of the Mississippi River. Thus by 1763 Great Britain had not only retained control over the 13 colonies it had planted along the Atlantic seaboard, but had also greatly expanded the area that it claimed in North America.

British culture in the colonies

All of the European nations shared a common background. All had inherited knowledge and skills from the past—from a past that reached far back into the beginnings of human history. The European ways of life had been shaped by contributions from primitive people, from the peoples of Egypt and Mesopotamia, from the Hebrews and Greeks and Romans, and from many peoples whom the Romans regarded as "barbarians." Europeans, like all peoples in all times, were part of the endless stream of history.

But each of the European nations reshaped this common heritage in its own way. Each developed its own variation of European civilization; each carried its own way of life, its own culture, to the colonies overseas.

The British carried the English language, English law, and English political and economic and social institutions to the 13 colonies that were later to become the United States of America. The British also carried to their colonies a distinctive set of values and beliefs.

Especially important was the British emphasis on the rights of the individual. This emphasis helped to shape British law and British political institutions.

British law protected an individual against arbitrary arrest. It guaranteed each person a fair trial by a jury of that person's equals.

British law also included the right of an individual to be represented in government. The colonial assemblies were, in most ways, smaller versions of the Parliament that governed the people of England and Scotland.

There were, of course, many other traditions, practices, and beliefs that the British settlers carried overseas. They brought, for example, the institution of the established church, that is, an official church supported by public funds. They brought the class system—a system that designated individuals at birth as members of the aristocracy and various lower classes. But neither the established church nor the class system was peculiarly British. Both were part of the European way of life, and both were transferred to the colonies throughout the Americas.

But it was the emphasis on the importance of the individual that was a special feature of British culture. The men and women who settled the British colonies jealously guarded what they called "their rights as English subjects."

Greater importance of the individual

In North America, however, many aspects of British culture that the early settlers brought to the colonies were changed. Climate, geography, and the influence of the Indians and of immigrants from other countries all helped to bring about changes.

From the beginning, the individual settler enjoyed increasing freedom in the colonies. For one thing, the English government did not itself establish any of the colonies along the Atlantic coast. Instead, it granted this right, in the form of charters, to private companies, to groups of persons, or even to individuals to build colonies overseas.

Moreover, the conditions of life in the colonies gave added importance to the individual. The colonists on the frontier had to clear the land, build their houses, and plant crops to provide their own food. Since the wilderness was vast, extending from the Atlantic Ocean to the Pacific Ocean, there were never enough men and women to do all the necessary work. Thus individual initiative and inventiveness were nourished and strengthened by the conditions of life in colonial America.

Breakdown of the class system

The growing importance of the individual greatly weakened the class system. It is true that in all the colonies except Rhode Island, Connecticut, and Pennsylvania the governors and their associates continued to represent the aristocracy of the mother country. But it was impossible to maintain the rigid class lines that separated the aristocracy and the lower classes in Great Britain. Poor settlers in the colonies could save their money and buy farms or could obtain free land on the frontier. With initiative and hard work they could prosper and become "independent." Even indentured servants, who were required to serve their masters for several years, could secure free or cheap land when their terms ended, and become prosperous farmers. African slaves were the only group unable to share these opportunities.

Nor was farming the only way for poor colonists to improve their lives. They could start their own businesses as skilled workers—bakers, shoemakers, tailors, gunsmiths, blacksmiths, silversmiths. They could build or buy fishing boats, start shipyards or sawmills, or become merchants. And, more easily than in England, young men could attend one of the colonial colleges or become apprentices to gain enough training and education to enter the professions of medicine, law, and the ministry.

Social mobility, or the opportunity to improve one's position in society, was a distinctive feature of colonial life from the beginning. And many colonists took advantage of opportunities to achieve success. Benjamin Franklin, for example, started life as a poor boy and became one of the most distinguished men of his time, honored in Europe as well as in America.

Contributions of the Indians

The *environment* of the American colonies included far more than the climate and the land itself—the soil, forests, rivers and streams, rolling hills and sheltered valleys. It included the people—the Indians, the British settlers, the Africans, and the immigrants from many countries.

One of the major contributions of the Indians was food. Long before the first Europeans arrived, the Indians had learned how to make use of a large variety of plants unknown in Europe. The list of these plants

The Indian tribes in the colonies had well-developed cultures. The Eastern Woodland Indians, shown here, and other tribes helped the early European settlers to survive.

is long and impressive—corn, white and sweet potatoes, many varieties of beans, tomatoes, squash, pumpkins, blackberries, blueberries, cranberries, crab apples, chestnuts, peanuts, maple syrup.

The discovery of these foodstuffs created a revolution in Europe's eating habits. It provided both Europe and the Americas with food for their constantly growing population. The amazing truth is that more than half of all the agricultural goods produced in the world today have come from plants first discovered and cultivated by the Indians.

The Indians, moreover, helped to feed the first settlers in Jamestown, in Plymouth, and in other new and struggling settlements. They also provided the colonists with seed and taught them how to plant, fertilize, and cultivate their crops. They taught the settlers hunting skills and forest lore.

It was also skillful Indian hunters who provided furs for the colonies' important fur trade with Europe. And the Indians gave many new words and phrases to the English language.

Not least important, the presence of Indian tribes in the colonies forced the English settlers to join together and to organize for their own defense. In this respect, the Indians indirectly helped to strengthen the colonists' exercise of initiative, responsibility, and local government in the colonies.

Contributions of the Africans

Africans also contributed to the distinctive way of life that was developing in the American colonies. They were among the first newcomers other than the English to arrive in the British colonies. The earliest group landed in Virginia in 1619. For a number of years they worked as indentured servants, as did many of the early European settlers. But by the middle 1600's, Africans were being transported to America as slaves. Even in slavery, however, the Africans adopted many American customs and contributed to the American way of life.

As workers—whether indentured servants, free individuals, or slaves —black Americans contributed their labor and their skill to the task of conquering the wilderness and transforming it into a productive land. As individuals—men and women from another continent and another way of life—they introduced new cultural traits into the colonies.

And, like the Indians, black Americans by their very presence in the colonies forced the settlers to develop new social arrangements. Slavery compelled the colonists to create methods of controlling the labor and the lives of other human beings. It confronted all the colonists but particularly the slave owners with a moral problem that they were unable to solve except by the irrational declaration that Africans were inferior people.

The inhuman institution of slavery and the moral issue it posed had far-reaching effects upon American society. As the years passed, it increasingly troubled the conscience of Americans. ("I tremble for my country when I reflect that God is just," Thomas Jefferson wrote.) It became an issue that deeply divided the nation and later contributed to a bloody war that nearly destroyed it. To this day practices adopted during the slavery era, as well as attitudes developed in the effort to justify the system, continue to haunt American society. Traditions from the past continue to hamper efforts to eliminate discrimination and to provide the full equality to which black Americans are entitled under the law and as human beings. Thus, both directly and indirectly, people from Africa have had an incalculable influence upon American life.

Contributions of non-English immigrants

In the colonies, British culture was also greatly modified by settlers from many different countries. Swedes and Finns, who settled along the Delaware River, left their mark in many place names, such as Christiana and Hockessin, and in building what soon became known as the American log cabin. The Dutch in New Netherland had an even more lasting influence. They brought to the colonies a tradition of religious toleration and a belief in the value of elementary education. They brought interesting customs and architectural styles; and Dutch names of persons, places, and things soon became familiar—Roosevelt, Van Buren, Harlem, Brooklyn, cruller, boss, St. Nicholas.

By the late 1600's other immigrants from many countries were arriving in ever-growing numbers. The largest groups were those from Germany, Scotland, and Ireland. Many of these newcomers settled in the Quaker colony of Pennsylvania, but soon the stream of settlers flowed down the valleys into Virginia and the Carolinas.

All of the immigrants brought to America the language, clothing, customs, and ways of thinking and behaving of their mother countries. They tried to continue these everyday ways of life in their new homeland, but this proved to be impossible. As a result, they soon adapted the material aspects of their lives—houses, clothing, food, tools, weapons—to meet the needs of their new environment. More slowly, but just as surely, these groups of immigrants began to change and to modify the ideas and the ways of behaving that they had brought with them to the colonies.

Americans—a new people

From the earliest times America was regarded by Europeans as a "melting pot." Out of the mingling of peoples from many different lands, a "new people" and a new way of life were being fashioned.

"What," a French settler asked in the 1770's—"what then is the American, this new person?" And then Michel-Guillaume de Crèvecoeur answered his own question: "I could point out to you a family whose grandfather was English, whose wife was Dutch, whose son married a French woman, and whose present four sons now have four wives from four different nations. Americans are those who, leaving behind all their long-held prejudices and manners, acquire new ones from the new kind of life they have embraced, the new government they obey, and the new rank they hold . . . . Here individuals of all nations are melted into a new people, whose labors and posterity will one day cause great changes in the world."

Growth of religious toleration

The mingling of people of many different religious faiths encouraged the growth of toleration. Roger Williams in Rhode Island, Lord Baltimore in Maryland, and William Penn in Pennsylvania led the way by providing religious freedom in their colonies. In other colonies as the years passed, Quakers, Baptists, Presbyterians, Catholics, and Jews secured freedom to worship in their own way. By the end of the colonial period the principle of an established church had been abandoned except in Connecticut and Massachusetts. When the new nation was being born, the First Amendment to the Constitution forbade Congress to make any law establishing or favoring a particular religion.

"Flax Scutching Bee," Linton Park, National Gallery of Art, Washington, Gift of Edgar William and Bernice Chrysler Garbisch

Colonial families often worked together to build their homes and settlements. They also found time to enjoy themselves, as shown in this painting of a flax-making party.

Growth of cooperation

Hand in hand with the growing emphasis on the rights of the individual was the growth of the spirit and practice of cooperation. From the beginning the shortage of labor compelled neighboring families to help each other. They gathered together to clear land, to build cabins, to harvest crops. They banded together for self-protection.

As the frontier moved westward, colonists cooperated in establishing new settlements, and in building roads, schools, and churches. The government was far away and often weak; and since the work had to be done, colonial men and women accomplished things by using their own initiative and joining together to do it. Visitors from foreign countries were amazed at the extent to which the colonists relied upon their own cooperative efforts.

Creating a distinctive American culture

During the colonial period there was, in the words of historian Frederick Jackson Turner, "a steady movement away from Europe, a steady growth of independence on American lines." Faced with the challenge of a new environment, the colonists became increasingly self-reliant.

Long before they broke with Great Britain the colonists had created a distinctively American way of life. They had moved toward the principle of religious freedom, had laid the foundations of free public education, and had strengthened the institution of representative government.

As late as 1776 most of the colonists insisted that they were loyal citizens of the British empire. But the fact was that during the colonial period they had been growing away from the mother country. They had begun to think of the colonies as *their* land, as a place apart from Great Britain.

In 1776 the colonists, recognizing their growing need for independence, declared their intention of separating from Great Britain. In 1789, following the victorious ending of the Revolutionary War and the ratification of the Constitution, the new nation was born. But in 1789, the United States was a nation in name only.

A national language

Among the striking evidences of the new nation's spirit of independence were the efforts to mold a national "American" language distinct from English. "America," Noah Webster declared in 1783, "must be as independent in *literature* as it is in *politics,* as famous for *arts* as for *arms.*" With this in mind, Webster labored at the tremendous task of preparing a dictionary—*An American Dictionary of the English Language*—in which the British spelling of many words was simplified. The dictionary, finally published in 1828, helped to establish a standardized American language.

Noah Webster also prepared a spelling book. First published in 1783, it was used in nearly every elementary school in America. By the time Webster died in 1843, more than 15 million copies had been sold, and before the book went out of use nearly 100 million copies had been sold. Like the dictionary, the spelling book helped to develop a uniform national language.

American history and geography

In addition to his work on the dictionary and the spelling book, Noah Webster edited a famous school reader, *An American Selection of Lessons in Reading and Speaking.* One of the major purposes of this textbook was to arouse Americans' feeling of national pride by focusing attention on the nation's heroes. In order to realize this purpose, Webster devoted more than half of his school reader to material from American history. He later wrote other books devoted entirely to American history.

Meanwhile, another scholar, Jedidiah Morse, was instructing American students about their country's geography. Morse, like Webster, stated that one of his purposes was to teach American history, and his geographies were largely devoted to the story of American life.

American art

American artists also contributed to the growing spirit of nationalism —the people's feeling of pride and loyalty to the new nation. There were, for instance, the architects who designed the nation's capital. Although a French engineer, Major Pierre L'Enfant, planned the city of Washington, American architects played a large part in its design and construction. Benjamin Banneker, a free Negro from Maryland, helped to survey and lay out the final plan for the District of Columbia. Thomas Jefferson drew up plans for the Capitol Building, and although they were not used the architects did accept his proposal for the locations of the Capitol and the White House. Another American, William Thornton, and Benjamin Latrobe, an English citizen whose mother was born in Pennsylvania, designed the Capitol. As the city of Washington grew, it helped to give the American people a growing conviction that the new nation was solidly planted and destined to endure.

During this same period, artists like Charles Willson Peale, Gilbert Stuart, and John Trumbull began to devote much of their time to painting portraits of the nation's leaders. Their influence is shown by the fact that even today copies of their portraits of Washington, Jefferson, Franklin, and other leaders of the United States hang on the walls of public buildings all across America.

American literature

Literature as well as art helped to unite the American people. During the early 1800's a number of writers began to depict American heroes and themes. Some, such as Mason Locke Weems (better known as Parson Weems), who published a biography of George Washington, wrote in glowing terms about the founders of the nation.

Other writers, among them Washington Irving and James Fenimore Cooper, began to write about America itself. Irving turned chiefly to the Dutch society of the Hudson Valley, producing such works as "The Legend of Sleepy Hollow," "Rip Van Winkle," and the *Knickerbocker History of New York.* In his early novels Cooper wrote about the Indians and the frontier. *The Leather-Stocking Tales,* a series of novels, are only a few of the many books that he produced.

America's culture-heroes

America's culture-heroes also helped to unite the American people. Every country has such figures—men and women, usually real but sometimes legendary—who represent the hopes and beliefs of the people and who serve as models of conduct in war and peace.

There were naval heroes like John Paul Jones and John Barry. The independence, courage, and skills of America's pioneers were represented by such frontiersmen as Daniel Boone and Davy Crockett. In later years, riverboat crews celebrated the deeds of Mike Fink, while lumber cutters told and retold the fabulous feats of the legendary Paul Bunyan and "Babe," his blue ox.

Black Americans, who contributed so much to the building of the nation but were denied their share in the American dream, had their own culture-heroes, among them Harriet Tubman. As a young woman, she escaped from slavery by fleeing to the North. Once free, she worked at any job she could get in order to earn the money she used to rescue more than 300 men, women, and children from slavery. As one of the leaders of the "underground railroad," she repeatedly risked her own life to free others.

Benjamin Franklin, another of the nation's leading culture-heroes, symbolized the "self-made" individual, that is, the person who achieves success solely through intelligence and hard work. Franklin strengthened the deeply rooted belief that every American, no matter what background he or she came from, no matter how deprived or poor, might rise to a position of wealth, fame, and influence.

Franklin also became a symbol of the American spirit of ingenuity and inventiveness. And he demonstrated the value of learning by making a series of memorable inventions, among them the lightning rod, improved eyeglasses, and the Franklin stove.

National Gallery of Art, Washington, Andrew W. Mellon Collection

George Washington, portrait by Gilbert Stuart

America's leading culture-hero was, of course, George Washington. People looked up to him as "the father of our country." At the close of the Revolutionary War he had helped to defeat a plot to make the new nation a monarchy by refusing to accept the title of king. Although he would have preferred to remain at Mount Vernon and run his plantation there, he could not refuse his nation's call to duty: He presided over the Constitutional Convention, and then served two terms as President of the new nation. Patriotism, self-sacrifice, and devotion to the common welfare made Washington a great hero to the American people. In their eyes he stood above party factions and quarrels. Washington, indeed, became a symbol of the nation itself.

America's value system

The aspirations and beliefs widely held by the people throughout the growing nation made up what is known as a *value system.* Most Americans, like their European ancestors and contemporaries, shared a common heritage of Judeo-Christian teachings. These included the belief that individuals were responsible to God for their conduct, and would be rewarded or punished in a future life for their behavior on earth. Individuals had a duty to be kind and helpful to others, especially to those who were needy or suffering. Slavery and injustice thus were opposed to these beliefs, and this deeply troubled many Americans.

Americans believed in government based on law. They believed their nation was superior to any other on earth. They believed that theirs was a land of limitless opportunity in which all individuals could improve their position in life if they were hardworking, honest, and thrifty.

Closely related to faith in the United States as a land of opportunity was the conviction of most Americans that progress was inevitable. The future was certain to be better than the past. Education was important, not only because it was the means by which individuals could improve their position in life, but also because it was necessary for the progress of the nation as a whole. The system of free public schools that Americans developed reflected their belief in the importance of education.

Although Americans believed that thrift and planning were important in their personal lives, they did not have this same attitude toward the nation's natural resources. On this subject Americans gave little if any thought to the future. Most Americans assumed their nation's resources were inexhaustible. But European visitors were shocked by Americans' reckless misuse of their forests and soil.

Benjamin Franklin, portrait by Charles Willson Peale

Improvements in transportation and communication

Even with their widely shared beliefs, Americans could not have achieved unity as a nation without improvements in transportation and communication. The National Road, running from Maryland to central Illinois, was built between 1811 and 1853 with aid from the federal government. The Erie Canal, completed in 1825, connected the Great Lakes with the Atlantic Ocean. Soon a large system of roads and canals was established throughout much of the nation.

Steamboats on the rivers and, after 1830, a growing network of railroad tracks also helped to bind together the different parts of the nation. The telegraph strengthened these links of transportation and communication among Americans. All of these developments contributed to the growth of a national market and a national culture.

Labor-saving machines

The invention of labor-saving machines also contributed to the development of a national culture and a national market. Immigrants brought with them the tools, weapons, and skills of their homelands. In America, however, they modified and improved the European tools and machines to meet the needs of the new environment. For example, German gunsmiths who settled in Pennsylvania greatly improved the accuracy of rifles, which were so effective as weapons against the Indians and in hunting for food and furs.

Faced with a vast continent to be conquered and a shortage of labor, Americans were forced to depend in large part upon what they could accomplish through their own efforts. The American environment required the colonists to develop individual initiative and inventiveness.

The skilled hands of women workers were used to develop the important textile industry in New England.

Detail, Barfoot, "Progress of Cotton," No. 6: "Spinning," Yale University Art Gallery, Mabel Brady Garvan Collection

"Yankee ingenuity," as it came to be called, was one of the striking characteristics of the new nation. Shortly after the Revolutionary War, a young English mechanic named Samuel Slater built for his American employer the first power-driven textile mill in North America. Although Slater copied machinery he had worked on in England, he greatly improved it. At about the same time, Oliver Evans, an American inventor, built a grist mill that could be operated by one worker, who fed the grain in at one end and took out the ground flour at the other.

Another American, Eli Whitney, invented the cotton gin and, even more important, developed the principle of using interchangeable parts in the manufacture of new products. Other Americans made major contributions to the development of the steamboat, the steam railroad, steampowered factories, labor-saving appliances for the home, and agricultural machinery. By the mid-1800's the United States was well on its way to becoming one of the world's leading industrial nations.

Divisions in the national culture

However, by the mid-1850's the United States was still far from being a completely unified nation. There were sharp divisions in the national culture. Americans were divided in matters of religion and on the issue of slavery.

Many Protestants who were descended from English-speaking colonial ancestors resented the ever-growing number of immigrants, especially those of the Roman Catholic faith. In the name of "Americanism," they demanded restrictions on immigration and were opposed to persons who were foreign-born serving in government jobs. Religious differences also led many Americans to persecute the Mormons, who belonged to the Church of Latter-day Saints. During the 1840's and 1850's, these religious differences became major political issues.

Even more serious were the differences rooted in sectionalism. The North, with its growing industries and factories and cities, was developing along very different lines from the West and especially the South.

By the early 1800's the South was developing what in certain respects was a national culture of its own. Climate, geography, and an agricultural economy based largely on the growth of cotton, tobacco, and rice gave the southern states a distinctive way of life. So, too, did the fact that relatively few European immigrants settled there. But the most critical difference between the North and the South concerned the issue of slavery.

As the forces of sectionalism grew stronger, they became increasingly serious. By 1861, when war broke out, the differences between the cultures of the North and the South had become so great that the future of the nation itself was at stake.

The shaping of American democracy

Nothing is more crucial in any society than the power to make decisions. The person or persons who have this power are the real rulers of the society. The process by which decisions are made both reflects and determines the kind of society that develops in a nation. In an authoritarian society a single ruler or a small group of persons makes the major decisions. Through most of human history people have lived in such authoritarian societies. Because they were subjected to the will of their rulers, the people were known—and thought of themselves—as *subjects.* Their freedom and their rights as individuals were drastically limited.

The roots of American democracy

In a democratic society the power to make decisions is widely shared. The people in a democracy are considered citizens, not subjects. The extent to which citizens enjoy freedom of choice and are able and willing to participate effectively in the process of government is the true measure of democracy.

Democracy as we know it today did not exist in England or in colonial America. To be sure, the people of England enjoyed greater freedom than the subjects of any of the other major colonial nations. Although the right to vote was limited, those who could vote had the right to elect representatives to Parliament. And in 1688, as a result of the "Bloodless Revolution," the principle that the politically active people, through their elected representatives, should possess the final governing authority was firmly established in English law.

The English men and women who settled in the American colonies brought with them the principle of representative government. Here, nourished in a new environment, it flourished. Steadily, through the years, individuals secured increasing freedom to make decisions—in the family, the local community, the state, and eventually at the national level.

Changing nature of the family

When the American colonies were founded, family life in Europe was highly authoritarian. By tradition and by law, the husband was, at least in theory, absolute ruler of the family. This pattern of family life was carried to the colonies, and it continued to exist all through the colonial period and well into the 1800's. The husband was expected to make all important decisions. The wife was subject to his authority, as were their children. Legally, he controlled any wages his children or his wife might earn, as well as any property they might inherit. His daughters—and sometimes his sons—could not marry without his consent. As late as the 1850's, a father might have the right to claim the wages of his sons until they were 21 years old.

There was a major exception to this pattern of family life. The owner of slaves completely controlled the lives of all members of a slave family. The weakness of the family in slavery was one of the system's most inhuman aspects.

Like all other aspects of European culture, however, the character of family life was modified in the American environment. The wife's influence increased as she worked side by side with her husband on the pioneer farm, and in many cases helped to defend their home and village during conflicts with the Indians. The influence of the sons also increased. Opportunities for them to become self-supporting and therefore independent were much greater in America than in Europe. They could leave home and get jobs in nearby towns, or find work on sailing ships, or move west and establish their own farms on the frontiers.

By the 1830's, 1840's, and 1850's, women were demanding—and beginning to win—changes in the laws to enable them to control their own wages and property. Some were even starting to demand the right to vote.

As a result of these and other changes, the authoritarian nature of the family began to break down. More and more, every member of

In the colonies, all members of the family, young and old alike, helped to provide the family's food, clothing, and shelter.

the family began to share in the process of making decisions. This growth of democracy in family life not only meant increased personal freedom, it also helped to prepare Americans to take a more active part in the government of their communities, states, and nation.

Growing vitality of local government

Local communities, too, furnished fertile soil for the roots of democracy in America. The colonies were separated from England by a vast ocean, which even the fastest sailing ships needed about six weeks to cross. And as the colonies grew, more and more of the villages were located far from the seats of the colonial governments. As a result, villagers and townspeople were required to take an active part in regulating their own affairs.

Citizens in the New England Colonies (Plymouth, Massachusetts Bay, Rhode Island, Connecticut, New Hampshire) had a greater part than any of the other colonists in making the decisions that affected their local communities. Of course, even in those colonies only white male settlers could take part in government. In New England, men who owned a certain amount of property and who were church members gathered at least once a year in town meetings. At these meetings they discussed local problems, elected town officials, and voted to levy taxes for support of schools and other community activities. Later, church membership as a requirement for voting was abandoned. Although the ownership of property remained a requirement for voting, land was cheap, and thus a majority of the townsmen had the right to take an active part in town meetings.

The situation in the Southern Colonies (Virginia, Maryland, the Carolinas, Georgia) was somewhat different. In contrast to the compact villages of New England, southern farms and plantations were widely scattered. The town meeting type of government was therefore not practical. But farmers and planters did gather on "Court Days" at cross-road settlements to hear—and sometimes to approve or protest—decisions that affected them. These decisions were made by justices of the peace and county lieutenants, who were appointed by the royal governors from among the prominent plantation owners.

The Middle Colonies (New York, New Jersey, Pennsylvania, Delaware) developed their own system of local government adapted from those practiced in New England and the Southern Colonies.

As the population moved westward, the settlers carried one or another of these types of local government to their new communities on the frontier. From the beginning, therefore, Americans acquired practice in self-government in their villages and towns. Long before the United States was created as a nation, most Americans had won a large measure of freedom in making decisions that affected their daily lives.

Growing power of the colonial assemblies

The distance between Great Britain and the American colonies also served to increase the amount of freedom enjoyed by the colonists. The colonies were simply too far away to be governed in every detail by the directors of the chartered companies, by the wealthy owners of the propri-etary colonies, or by the king. But even if communications had been bet-ter, conditions in the colonies were so different from those in Great Brit-ain that it would have been impossible—and foolish—for the British rulers to make all decisions affecting their colonies. Moreover, English colonists jealously guarded their "rights as English subjects"—includ-ing the right to take part in government through elected representatives.

As early as 1619, the London Company gave the colonists in Jamestown the right to take part in their own government. In July of that year 22 burgesses, or representatives, 2 from each of the settled districts along the James River, met in Jamestown. Each of the burgesses had been elected by the voters of his own district. The creation of the House of Burgesses, as the elected group was called, marked a significant step toward representative government in the British colonies.

Representative government in the Massachusetts Bay Colony developed in a different way. In 1629 a number of prominent Puritans in England secured a charter from the king and organized the Massachusetts Bay Company. Fortunately for the Puritans, the charter did not name the place where the directors of the company were to hold their yearly meeting. The directors, who were shrewd men, took advantage of this fact. They did so by voting to take the charter and move to North America, where they would be free to run the company as they pleased. In this way Massachusetts became, in effect, a self-governing colony, for many years almost independent of the English king and Parliament. At first only a few settlers were allowed any voice in the government. Soon, however, some of the newly settled towns demanded and secured the right to send representatives to Boston to meet with the governor and other officials and to help make the laws.

In the other colonies, as well as in Virginia and Massachusetts, elected representatives took part in the decision-making process. At first the governors of the royal colonies and the proprietary colonies could veto the actions of these assemblies, or groups of representatives. As the years went by, however, the colonial assemblies gained more and more influence. They had the power to vote taxes and to appropriate money for salaries and other expenses of government. Since they controlled all spending, they often refused to grant money unless the governing officials in the colony did as they wished. The colonial assemblies' experience in self-government proved invaluable to the colonists when the time came to create a new nation.

Written covenants and constitutions

During the colonial period Americans developed another extremely important check against the arbitrary use of power by appointed or elected officials. This was the written covenant, or agreement, voluntarily accepted by the people of the colony.

The earliest example of such an agreement was, of course, the Mayflower Compact. On November 11, 1620, shortly after the *Mayflower* had anchored off what is now Provincetown, the Pilgrim leaders gathered in the ship's cabin. There they wrote and signed an agreement to obey all laws that they themselves would adopt in the future.

Some years later, in 1639, settlers in the Connecticut Valley took an even more important step. Faced with the need to join together for certain common purposes, including self-defense, the settlers decided to adopt an official, written plan of government. The Fundamental Orders of Connecticut, as the document was called, was the first written constitution in America. In contrast to the Mayflower Compact, which was a general agreement in favor of majority rule, the Fundamental Orders set up a detailed plan of government.

The use of the written covenant, setting forth specific rules by which the people were to be governed, or to govern themselves, marked another significant step in the development of self-government in America. After the colonies declared their independence, each of the states as well as the national government adopted written constitutions.

Protest and rebellion

The right of people to protest and even to rebel against what they considered arbitrary use of power by the government also was strengthened during the colonial period. The victory of John Peter Zenger, who was brought to trial in 1735 for publishing articles criticizing the royal governor of New York, helped to establish the principle of freedom of speech as one of the foundations of democracy. This was only the most famous example of the colonists' demanding the right to protest. Throughout the colonial period they did not hesitate to speak out when they believed it necessary to defend their interests.

When verbal or written protests failed, groups of colonists sometimes moved to unsettled areas where they were free to govern themselves in their own way. Roger Williams did just that when he fled from Massachusetts Bay Colony and founded what was to become Rhode Island. Through the years other groups followed his example. As late as 1847 the Mormons, fleeing persecution for their religious beliefs,

Americans often moved to new, unsettled areas seeking greater freedom and opportunity. Thus the Mormons crossed the plains of the West to establish their church in Salt Lake City.

crossed the plains of the West and built Salt Lake City, laying the foundations for the state of Utah. This method of securing the right to self-government was of course only possible in a country with an abundance of unsettled land.

As a last effort, some groups of colonists turned to direct action in their struggle against what they believed was oppressive authority. For example, in 1676 farmers in the less settled areas of Virginia, led by Nathaniel Bacon, rebelled against the government headed by Sir William Berkeley. Although the rebellion was put down, the government did make some concessions. In much the same way, in the 1760's frontiersmen in North Carolina, known as the Regulators, rebelled against the government in that colony, which was dominated by well-to-do planters.

These and other attempts at rebellion when all other efforts failed provided precedents for the American Revolution itself. In the Declaration of Independence, Thomas Jefferson declared that when "a long train of abuses" threatens people with "absolute despotism, it is their right, it is their duty, to throw off such government, and to provide new guards for their future security."

The experiment with a league of states

As part of the British empire, the colonies had operated under the central authority of the British government. This authority was exercised by the king, by Parliament, and by agencies that the king and Parliament created to manage the affairs of the colonies. The final power to make decisions remained in London.

Early in 1775, more than a year before the colonists declared their independence, the colonial governments began to crumble. British officials began to leave the colonies. The Tories, or those who remained loyal to the British king and Parliament, began to flee to Canada, the British West Indies, and Great Britain. By 1776 the Americans faced the problem of creating new state governments and a new central government.

The state constitutions that Americans wrote during the Revolutionary War reflected the people's deep-felt desire for a voice in their own government. All of the new governments were based upon written constitutions. These new constitutions also contained bills of rights guaranteeing to every citizen freedom from arbitrary government.

During the Revolutionary War, Americans also tackled the problem of building a central government. In their first efforts to govern themselves at the national level, the leaders of the 13 new states wrote the Articles of Confederation. However, this experiment with a league of more or less independent states was only partially successful.

There were two basic problems. First, there was the problem of dividing powers between the states and the central government. The Confederation was never able to provide a successful answer to this

The signers of the Declaration of Independence proposed a new and revolutionary form of government—a democracy based on "the consent of the governed."

problem. Second, the Confederation could not establish common, uniform laws for the states and the people of the states.

Even before 1787, a number of leaders in America had become convinced that only a strengthened central government could remedy these weaknesses and secure order in the new nation.

Acting on this conviction, delegates from the various states met in Philadelphia in 1787. There they wrote the Constitution that, when ratified, became "the supreme law of the land," binding on both the states and the people of the states. (The Constitution appears on pages 647-75.)

Establishing the federal union

The Constitution of the United States created a federal union. It granted many important powers to the central government. Thus the central government now had the power and authority that it needed to deal with matters of common concern to all the states. By granting all other powers to the states, the Constitution guaranteed each state a large amount of independence in governing itself.

A federal system of government

This division of authority between the states and the central government, called federalism, provided a strong and effective system of government. Even so, disputes over where the final authority rested continued to arise. The issue reached the breaking point in 1861 when 11 southern states decided to withdraw from the Union and establish a Confederacy in which the ultimate power would be reserved to the states. Although the victory of the Union armies ended this greatest test of the federal system, the tug of war between the central government and the states continues to this day. Nevertheless, the principle of federalism written into the Constitution has proven to be one of the nation's greatest sources of strength. This principle has worked as well with a federal union of 50 states as it did with the original 13.

James Madison, a leading member of the Constitutional Convention

Distributing power within the federal government

Those who wrote the Constitution believed in government under law, that is, government with written rules that must be applied equally to all citizens. They were aware that a misguided majority could be as great a danger to a government under law as a privileged ruling class or an all-powerful executive. Therefore, they were determined to protect the new nation from tyranny in any form.

Fear of tyranny by the central government was one of the major reasons for dividing power between the states and the federal government. This same fear prompted the founders of the nation to distribute the decision-making power *within* the federal government itself.

In an effort to prevent any one branch of the federal government from becoming too strong, the framers of the Constitution agreed that the executive, legislative, and judicial powers must be separated. To carry out this principle, they established three separate branches of the government, each having certain specified powers. To Congress, they gave the power to legislate, or make the laws (Article 1). To the Chief Executive, or President, they granted the power to execute, or carry out, the laws (Article 2). To the judiciary—the federal courts—they gave the power to interpret or rule on the meaning of the laws (Article 3).

Creating a system of checks and balances

But even these safeguards against tyranny did not satisfy the framers of the Constitution. As an additional protection, they wrote into the Constitution a system of *checks and balances.*

In order to prevent any one branch of the government from becoming too powerful, the Constitution provides checks on its power by the other two branches. For example, Congress has the power to enact laws, but the President has the power to veto them. However, Congress can by a two-thirds vote override the President's veto. The judiciary also has the power to check Congress. Ever since the famous decision of *Marbury v. Madison* in 1803, the Supreme Court has had the power to declare a law unconstitutional.

This is only a leading example of the carefully planned system of checks and balances written into the Constitution.

In practice, the exact powers of each branch of government have never been as clear as the framers of the Constitution intended. From time to time—and even today—there have been disagreements over which branch has the authority to take certain actions. In general, however, the system has worked remarkably well. It is a system that neatly balances effective government and freedom.

Identifying the source of final authority

In 1776 Thomas Jefferson outlined what was then a new and revolutionary theory of government. In the Declaration of Independence (see pages 644-45), Jefferson clearly and simply stated the basic principles of what today we call democracy: ". . . all men ° are cre- ated equal," he wrote. ". . . they are endowed by their Creator with certain unalienable rights; . . . among these are life, liberty, and the pursuit of happiness." Governments exist in order to secure these rights, and the authority of all governments must be based on "the consent of the governed."

Those who wrote the Constitution made these ideals "the supreme law of the land." The Preamble makes this fact clear and beyond dispute. "We, the people of the United States, in order to form a more perfect Union, establish justice, insure domestic tran- quility, provide for the common defense, promote the general welfare, and secure the blessings of liberty to ourselves and our posterity, do ordain and establish this Constitution for the United States of America."

In addition to defining the purposes of the Constitution, the Preamble makes it clear that the government is established by consent of the

Thomas Jefferson, author of the Declaration of Independence

° The term "men" used in the Declaration, the Constitution, and many other documents in American history really means "people" and refers to women and children as well as men.

governed. "We, the people . . . ordain and establish" the government. This means that we, the people, have the final authority, the supreme power, in our nation.

Guaranteeing the rights of individuals

The separation of powers with checks and balances is one way in which the Constitution protects the rights of each individual. And there are others.

Among the important guarantees of civil liberty in the Constitution as it was adopted in 1789 are prohibitions against ex post facto laws and bills of attainder. An ex post facto law—that is, a law passed "after the deed"—is one that sets forth a penalty for committing some action that was not illegal at the time that action was committed. A bill of attainder is a law, or legislative measure, that punishes a person by fine, imprisonment, or confiscation of property without a trial in court.

The Constitution also guarantees that "The privilege of the writ of habeas corpus shall not be suspended, unless when in cases of rebellion or invasion the public safety may require it." The writ of habeas corpus is a legal document that requires that a person be released from prison unless that person has been formally charged with, or found guilty of committing, a crime.

The Constitution gives special protection to an individual accused of treason. The framers of the Constitution knew that the charge of treason often was used by all-powerful rulers to get rid of persons those rulers did not like. Moreover, the Constitution gives protection to innocent relatives of persons accused of treason. Only the persons guilty of treason can be punished. No penalty can be imposed upon their families or relatives.

These are only a few of the guarantees of personal rights that the founders wrote into the Constitution. They are important examples of the way in which the Constitution establishes a common standard of law for every American citizen, old and young, rich and poor alike.

The Bill of Rights

Despite the safeguards written into the Constitution, a number of states at first refused to ratify, or approve, it. They refused in part because they believed that it did not offer strong enough protection to the rights of individuals. They finally ratified it after they had been promised that a bill of rights would be added to the Constitution when Congress met.

In 1789–90 the first Congress of the United States drafted the first 10 amendments to the Constitution. Among the guarantees of liberty in these 10 amendments, known as the Bill of Rights, several are especially important. The First Amendment guarantees each American freedom of religion, speech, press, assembly, and petition. The Fourth Amendment upholds the principle of each citizen's right to privacy by prohibiting unlawful searches. The Fifth, Sixth, and Eighth Amendments protect accused persons from arbitrary arrest and from punishment by officials of the federal government.

The test of time

In their effort to protect the nation against tyranny by either a majority or a minority, the framers of the Constitution distributed the decision-making power throughout the government. Time has proven the wisdom of this provision. The Constitution has endured for nearly two centuries as the supreme law of the land. In general, it works as well today in a large industrialized nation of 50 states and 215 million people as it once did in a small agricultural nation of 13 states and 4 million people.

The compromise on representation

The Constitution was the product of a number of important compromises. If the delegates to the Constitutional Convention in 1787 had refused to compromise their differences, the writing of the Constitution would have been impossible.

One of the most serious conflicts of the Convention was the struggle between the large and small states over representation in Congress. The small states, fearful of being outvoted, insisted upon equal representation. The large states, unwilling to form the new federal union on this basis, insisted that the size of each state's population should determine the number of representatives it had in Congress. After a month of debate, the delegates agreed to accept a compromise. Each state, large or small, was to be represented by two Senators. Thus each state would have equal power in the Senate. In the House, however, each state's representation was to be based upon population.

The compromise on tariffs

Another source of conflict at the Constitutional Convention was the different economic interests of the North and South. Northern merchants wanted the central government to regulate commerce with foreign nations and among the states. Southern planters opposed this idea because they feared that the government would pass tariff laws and other legislation unfavorable to their interests. For example, if Congress imposed tariffs, or taxes, on exports, this would increase the cost of American tobacco to overseas buyers, and the planters' income might decline. Moreover, tariffs on imported goods might increase the price of the products the planters purchased.

The members of the Convention solved the problem by a compromise that gave Congress power "to regulate commerce with foreign nations, and among the several states," including the power to levy tariffs on *imports.* But Congress was denied the power to levy tariffs on *exports.*

Compromises concerning slavery

The tragic contradiction between slavery and the noble principles outlined in the Declaration of Independence was not reconciled in the Constitution. In addition, two issues involving slavery caused bitter argument among the delegates.

One dispute arose over whether slaves should be included in counting population. Southerners wanted to count slaves in determining the number of representatives to be elected to the House of Representatives, but they did not want to count slaves for purposes of direct taxation. Northerners, on the other hand, thought that slaves should be counted for purposes of taxation, but not for representation. As a compromise, northerners and southerners agreed to count only three fifths of the total slave population for purposes of both representation and taxation.

There were also strong differences about regulating the slave trade. Southern planters were fearful that after Congress was given the power "to regulate commerce" and to tax imports, it would be able to prohibit the slave trade by law or by taxing the importation of slaves. As a compromise, the delegates agreed that until 1808 Congress should be denied the power to forbid the importation of any persons, such as slaves. Meanwhile no import tax could be levied in excess of $10 per person. By this compromise southerners won the right to import slaves for 20 more years and northerners secured the right to regulate the slave trade in the future.

The growth of the new nation

The new nation was created as a result of compromises. In the case of slavery, the compromises were unfortunate because they denied the principles of freedom upon which the nation was founded. Without them, however, it is doubtful that the Constitution could have been written.

Compromise as a solution to problems

As the years passed, the American people's ability to compromise made it possible for them to resolve serious conflicts or sometimes to put off the need to solve problems until some future time. In many other countries, the refusal or inability to reach compromise solutions often led to revolutions.

In the United States the use of compromise proved to be a substitute for revolution. By reconciling conflicting values and interests, the nation's leaders managed to resolve crises that might have destroyed the federal union.

The Missouri Compromise of 1820

The first serious clash between the North and the South developed early in 1819. Congress was about to admit Alabama as the eleventh slave state. With the entry of Alabama, power in the Senate would be equally divided. The North and the South each would have 22 Senators. This was the situation when the Territory of Missouri, in which slavery already existed, asked to be admitted. If Congress accepted Missouri as a slave state, the balance of power in the Senate would be upset, with the South having 24 votes to the North's 22.

At this point Representative James Tallmadge of New York presented an amendment to Missouri's application. Tallmadge proposed that no more slaves be allowed to enter Missouri. He also proposed to free all children born into slavery in Missouri after its admission as a state. This, however, was to be done gradually; the children of slaves were to become free only when they reached their twenty-fifth birthday.

Tallmadge's amendment touched off a bitter debate. At times the controversy became so heated that some political leaders talked boldly of "disunion" and "civil war." The issue had reached a deadlock when a group led by Senator Henry Clay of Kentucky proposed a compromise. At this time the people of Maine also applied to Congress to become a state. The admission of Maine would increase the number of free states in the Union. Clay therefore proposed that both Maine and Missouri be admitted together —one as a free state and the other without restrictions on slavery. As Clay pointed out, if this were done the balance of power between the North and the South in the Senate would not be changed. With Alabama, Missouri, and Maine in the Union, each section would have 24 votes.

Congress agreed to Clay's compromise proposal in 1820. As part of this compromise, however, slavery was prohibited in all other parts of the

Vice-President
John C. Calhoun

Louisiana Purchase north of latitude 36° 30′. Southern members of Congress accepted this ban because cotton could not be grown profitably on most farmland north of latitude 36° 30′.

In this way the crisis of 1819–20 had passed. But thoughtful people realized that a period of grave danger lay ahead of the young nation. John Quincy Adams wrote in his diary that the conflict over Missouri was "a mere preamble—a title page to a great, tragic volume."

The Compromise of 1833

Only a few years later Congress was faced with another very serious crisis. Once again, powerful groups in the North and the South clashed. This time the issue was the right of Congress to pass protective tariffs.

The issue arose in 1828 when the industrial interests of the North, joined by the agricultural interests of the West, succeeded in getting Congress to adopt a high protective tariff on imports. South Carolina and other southern states, led by Vice-President John C. Calhoun, bitterly opposed this so-called "Tariff of Abominations" on the grounds that it would force them to pay higher prices for goods manufactured in Europe.

The conflict smoldered for several years. Then, in 1832, Congress adopted a new tariff law. The Tariff Act of 1832 provided somewhat lower rates than the 1828 act. But the new law was still a protective tariff, and therefore from the southern point of view it was no better than the old. South Carolina was convinced that the states that favored a protective tariff now controlled Congress. Therefore, it decided to take action.

Portrait by Thomas Sully, National Gallery of Art, Washington, Andrew W. Mellon Collection

In a convention called to act on the issue South Carolina adopted the Ordinance of Nullification. The ordinance declared that the tariff acts of 1828 and 1832 were "null, void, and no law," and that they were not "binding upon this state, its officers, or citizens." It also contained a solemn warning that if the federal government tried to enforce the tariff law, South Carolina would leave, or secede from, the Union and become an independent nation.

President Andrew Jackson responded promptly. In "off-the-record" statements he warned that he was prepared to "hang every leader" who defied the authority of the federal government. For the public record, however, Jackson was more moderate, expressing his firm belief in the Union and his determination as President to enforce the law.

The crisis finally was resolved when both northerners and southerners agreed to another compromise proposed by Henry Clay. The Tariff Act of 1833 provided for a gradual reduction of tariff rates. At the same time, however, Congress passed the Force Bill, giving the President power to use federal forces, if necessary, to collect tariffs.

President Andrew Jackson

A new crisis develops

During the next 15 years Congress admitted six new states to the Union—three from the South, three from the North. In 1848 the uneasy balance still existed, with 15 slave states and 15 free states. But during these same years the differences between the North and the South had been growing increasingly serious, with slavery the most bitter issue.

This was the situation in 1849 when California applied for admission to the Union. Southerners refused to consider the application because California's constitution prohibited slavery. If California entered as a free state, the balance between the sections would be upset in favor of the North.

Another issue before Congress was the controversy between the state of Texas and the newly acquired but still unorganized territory of New Mexico. Texas, where slavery was permitted, claimed that its boundary extended westward into an area that the federal government had recognized as belonging to New Mexico. Anti-slavery forces in Congress naturally tried to keep Texas' boundaries to the smallest possible limits. Southerners just as naturally were opposed to northern attempts to limit the area of Texas.

Arguments over other issues grew louder in both houses of Congress. Southerners sternly resisted a proposal to abolish slavery in the District of Columbia. They also resisted a northern proposal that New Mexico and Utah be organized into Territories without any provision for slavery.

Many northerners were just as strongly opposed to a southern proposal to pass a new and more effective fugitive slave law. According to the original Fugitive Slave Law, adopted in 1793, state and local officials were responsible for capturing runaway slaves and returning them to their owners. In 1842, however, the Supreme Court had ruled that state law enforcement officers were not required to help federal officials to capture and return runaway slaves to their southern owners. The proposed new law now required that state officials assist in capturing runaway slaves.

All of these issues were loaded with political dynamite. Any one of them could lead to a showdown between the North and South. In the opening months of 1850, many people felt that the United States was on the brink of disunion—perhaps on the brink of war.

The Compromise of 1850

Such was the situation when Henry Clay of Kentucky rose on the floor of the Senate to offer a compromise proposal. Clay, whose compromises had saved the Union from great danger in 1820 and again in 1833, was known and respected as "the Great Compromiser." Now, in 1850, ill and weary from years of devoted effort to hold the Union together, he stood before the Senate to plead once more for reason and moderation.

Senator Henry Clay

Clay's proposals included: (1) The admission of California as a free state. (2) The organization of the land acquired from Mexico (except California) into Territories on the basis of "popular sovereignty," so that the settlers in each of the Territories might decide for themselves whether or not they wanted slavery in their Territory. (3) The payment of $10 million by the United States to Texas in return for Texas' abandoning all claim to New Mexico east of the Rio Grande. (4) The abolition of the slave trade—that is, of the buying and selling of slaves—but not of slavery itself in the District of Columbia. (5) The enactment of a more effective fugitive slave law, one that would compel state and local law enforcement officials to cooperate with federal officials in the capture and return of runaway slaves.

Clay's proposals provoked one of the most important and heated debates in American history, one that lasted more than six months. In the end, Congress adopted all of Clay's measures by substantial majorities. Compromise had once again saved the day. Throughout the nation

Americans gathered in public meetings and hailed the Compromise of 1850 as a great triumph for national unity.

The Compromise of 1850 lasted about four years. As it turned out, this period of relative calm proved to be merely the lull before the storm.

The Kansas-Nebraska Act

In 1854 Senator Stephen A. Douglas of Illinois sponsored and guided through Congress the Kansas-Nebraska Act. This act created two new organized Territories in the West—Kansas and Nebraska. Both Territories were north of the 36° 30′ line established by the Missouri Compromise and therefore closed to slavery. But the Kansas-Nebraska Act abolished this dividing line, stating that the Territories were now "perfectly free to form and regulate their domestic institutions in their own way . . . ."

The right of people in the Territories to decide for themselves whether they wanted slavery or not was known as "popular sovereignty." Douglas had argued in favor of this procedure because he believed it was democratic. He had assumed that the people of Kansas would choose slavery and those of Nebraska would oppose it. He also had assumed that since the balance between the sections would be maintained, the measure would meet with approval in both the North and the South.

Douglas soon realized that his plan could not succeed. The Kansas-Nebraska Act immediately stirred up new arguments over the slavery question all across the nation. Throughout the North the issue of slavery again became the subject of heated discussion. The Fugitive Slave Law became increasingly difficult to enforce. And "Anti-Nebraska" meetings in northern cities denounced Douglas for reopening the slavery dispute.

"Bleeding Kansas"

Senator Charles Sumner of Massachusetts was one of many extreme anti-slavery people who believed that the Kansas-Nebraska Act would plunge the nation into serious trouble. "It puts freedom and slavery face to face and bids them grapple," he declared.

And grapple they did on the plains of the new Territory of Kansas. Northerners and southerners began to pour weapons and ammunition into the Territory. Soon fighting broke out between the anti-slavery and the pro-slavery groups. At least 200 citizens lost their lives in the bitter strife. In the end it was necessary to send in federal troops to restore order.

Meanwhile, the settlers were trying to draw up a constitution and organize a Territorial government. Hopelessly divided, they ended with *two* constitutions—one pro-slavery, one anti-slavery. Congress, also hopelessly divided over the issue, could reach no decision as to which constitution to recognize.

Fateful changes in the political parties

The Kansas-Nebraska Act and the struggle for control of Kansas widened the gap between the pro-slavery and anti-slavery groups within the two major political parties, the Whigs and the Democrats. Faced with this situation, anti-slavery forces in both parties decided to organize a new, purely sectional party. The Republican Party, as it was called, pledged itself to prevent the further expansion of slavery into the Territories. Although its Presidential candidate failed to win the 1856 election, he did receive the electoral votes of 11 states, all in the North.

The growing split within the two major political parties into northern

The issue of slavery increasingly divided the South and the North despite efforts at compromise. Here, newly purchased slaves are being sent to their owners.

and southern wings and the formation of the purely sectional Republican Party were alarming developments. Other serious developments were to follow.

The Dred Scott decision

On March 6, 1857, the Supreme Court handed down the explosive Dred Scott decision, ruling that the Missouri Compromise was unconstitutional because Congress had no power to exclude slavery from the Territories. The Court based its ruling on the Fifth Amendment, which prohibited Congress from depriving any person of ". . . property, without due process of law." The Dred Scott decision was a clear victory for the pro-slavery South and a bitter blow for the anti-slavery forces in the North. It reinforced the belief of many northerners that southern slave owners were determined to force their will on the entire nation.

John Brown's raid

Some two years later, in the fall of 1859, John Brown undertook to start a rebellion of slaves in Virginia. With money obtained from a number of New England and New York abolitionists, Brown armed a group of 18 men. On October 16 he seized the federal arsenal at Harpers Ferry in what is now West Virginia. He planned to seize the guns stored in the arsenal and give them to the slaves nearby. He would then lead the slaves in what he hoped would be a widespread rebellion.

It was a wild idea, certain to fail. Brown and his followers were captured. And after a trial that Brown admitted was more fair than he had reason to expect, he was hanged for "murder, criminal conspiracy, and treason against the Commonwealth of Virginia."

Many southerners believed that Brown's action represented northern opinion. They concluded therefore that slavery was no longer safe from direct attack. As a matter of fact, northern politicians and the majority of northerners were shocked at the news of the raid and quickly condemned it. But extreme abolitionists regarded Brown as a heroic martyr. Ralph Waldo Emerson went so far as to declare that Brown was a "new saint" who would "make the gallows glorious like the cross."

Southern newspapers reported this small minority of abolitionist opinion as typical of northern thinking. To southerners John Brown's raid was convincing evidence that the North was determined to abolish slavery.

The breakup of the Union

By 1860 most of the ties binding the North and the South had been broken. The issue of slavery had split several churches—the Methodist, the Baptist, and one branch of the Presbyterian. Although many business ties still existed, the older political parties were divided and the new Republican Party was a purely sectional organization.

The final failure of compromise

The breakup of the Whig and Democratic parties into sectional groups and the election of the Republican candidate, Abraham Lincoln, to the Presidency did not make the breakup of the Union inevitable. There was still a genuine love of the Union in the South. However, the election of the Republicans strengthened southern extremists. They insisted that the Republicans, who now controlled the federal government, would not only confine slavery to the areas where it already existed, but would also try to abolish slavery altogether. Lincoln denied this.

In an effort to put such fears to rest, moderate leaders on both sides suggested a compromise that would guarantee slavery in the states where it was already established. But southern extremists demanded much more than this. They demanded guarantees of the right to extend slavery into the Territories. Since the Republican Party was pledged to prevent the spread of slavery, the southern demands were completely unacceptable. So the last-minute efforts at compromise failed.

The steps toward war

South Carolina was the first state to leave the Union. Others soon followed its example, and early in 1861 delegates from six southern states met at Montgomery, Alabama, and drafted a constitution for the Confederate States of America. The Confederate Constitution resembled the Constitution of the United States. It created a federal government. But there were some crucial differences. The Confederate Constitution stressed "the sovereign and independent character" of each state. It also guaranteed the right to own slaves.

The next, fateful step was now up to the government in Washington. Unless it was content to let the southern states depart in peace, armed conflict was only a matter of time. When President Lincoln sent reinforcements to Fort Sumter at Charleston, South Carolina, Confederate forces opened fire on the fort. Thus began, in the early morning of April 12, a terrible struggle that was to last for four long and bloody years.

Union advantages

The northern and western states—24 in number before the war ended —held clear advantages over the 11 states in the Confederacy. The North had a population of some 22 million, the South only about 9 million, of whom 3½ million were slaves. The North was also greatly superior in manufacturing, in agriculture, in natural resources, in finance, and in transportation facilities. For example, when the war started, the North controlled 92 percent of the nation's industries and almost all of the known supplies of coal, iron, copper, and gold. The wealth of the Confederacy, by contrast, was largely in land and slaves. Moreover, at least during the early period of the conflict, the North was more united than it had ever been.

Confederate advantages

Considering the advantages enjoyed by the North, why did the Confederacy enter the conflict with confidence and why was it able to fight so effectively for four years? There are several answers to this question.

First, the South needed only to fight a defensive war to protect its own territory until the North grew tired of the struggle—whereas the North had to invade and conquer the South, an area as large as Western Europe.

Boston symbolized the North's growing industrial and financial power. This strong, prosperous economy gave the North important advantages during the Civil War.

Cotton and other agricultural products formed the basis of the South's economy on the eve of the Civil War, as shown in this plantation scene.

Second, southerners were fighting for the things all people cherish most —their homes, their independence, and the right to govern themselves in their own way. Northerners, by contrast, were fighting for something much more abstract, the idea of the preservation of the Union. After September 1862, however, when President Lincoln issued a preliminary Emancipation Proclamation, ° northerners were also fighting to free the slaves.

Third, the armies of the Confederacy were led by able officers, men trained at West Point who knew the country they were defending. Probably the greatest military commander of the war was General Robert E. Lee, a Virginian, who resigned from the United States Army and supported his state when it joined the Confederacy.

Finally, the South hoped for support from other nations. Southerners believed that the textile mills of Great Britain and France were so dependent on southern cotton that those countries would come to the aid of the Confederacy.

Why the war broke out

None of this explains why efforts to compromise the differences between the two sections finally broke down and the Union was torn apart by armed conflict. There is no simple answer to this question.

At the heart of the matter, however, is the fact that during the first half of the 1800's the North and the South and the West had developed

° The final Emancipation Proclamation was issued on January 1, 1863.

along different lines. The increasingly industrialized North with its growing factories and towns; the agricultural South with its increasing dependence on its major crop, cotton; the new, growing West, with its restless pioneers moving toward ever-new frontiers—here were three radically different ways of life and different sets of values.

The rapid development of railroads linking the Northeast and the West during the 1850's and the growing dependence of each section on the other's food products and industrial output were among the important reasons why these two sections stood together when war came. Both also had a free labor system; both regarded slavery as evil and as a denial of the American dream of equality and freedom.

But the differences between the North and the South were not limited to slavery. The rural South and the rapidly developing industrial North held different views in regard to tariffs, federally financed public improvements, the control of money and banking, the disposal of public lands, and the issue of states' rights.

All of these factors helped to divide the nation and lead it down the road to armed conflict. For this reason, thoughtful historians do not attempt to give a short, simple explanation of why the North and the South went to war. Instead, they explain why northern extremists and southern extremists, a minority in each section, felt and acted as they did. Historians point out that the great majority of the people in the North loved the Union and believed in it so strongly that they could not permit it to be destroyed. And historians also point out that many in the South who loved the Union and would have preferred to remain a part of it supported the Confederacy because they were determined to defend the principle of states' rights, to protect their homes, and to support the position taken by their relatives, neighbors, and friends.

A reunited nation faces the future

In 1865 the nation's terrible trial by fire and sword came to an end. The conflict had cost the American people billions of dollars. Far worse, large areas of the South lay in ruins, and hundreds of thousands of Americans had been killed or wounded. Not counting the wounded, the North had lost 359,000 people, the South about 258,000. Memories of these losses were to hang over the nation like a dark shadow for years to come.

The war had many far-reaching consequences. It ended the doctrine of secession. It strengthened the Union by increasing the power of the federal government at the expense of the states. It strengthened democracy by showing that a representative form of government could operate successfully in wartime. And, by freeing the slaves, it gave the American people a new opportunity to demonstrate that they were committed without any exceptions to the principle that all individuals are equal under the law and are entitled to the "unalienable rights" of "life, liberty, and the pursuit of happiness."

Not least important, the victory of the North marked the triumph, not just of one section over another, but of city and factory over a rural, agricultural society. This victory insured the development of America as a powerful industrial nation.

In the spring of 1865, the people of the United States stood at the beginning of a new era. Great new opportunities were opening before them. But, of course, they could not know this at the time. They could look only into the immediate future. And the big problem they faced, northerners and southerners alike, was "to bind the nation's wounds" and to join hands as a reunited people.

PART ONE

THE NATION REUNITED

Theodore Roosevelt was six years old when Lincoln was shot by an assassin in 1865. During his rich and full life Roosevelt saw the reunited nation grow from 36 to 48 states, expand overseas, and fight a war "to make the world safe for democracy." During Roosevelt's boyhood the United States was still a predominantly agricultural country. Before he died in 1919, the United States had become one of the leading industrial nations of the world.

UNIT ONE
Rebuilding the Nation
1865-1900

CHAPTER 1

RESTORING THE SOUTH
TO THE UNION

1865-1900

After the Civil War came to an end, bitterness between the North and the South continued for many years. In part this was the inevitable result of a terrible conflict in which most people on each side believed that their cause was right and just.

But equally important as a cause of resentment was the decade of *reconstruction,* or rebuilding the Union, that followed the war. During this period, bitter feelings arose over the stubborn political and constitutional problems involved in bringing the southern states back into the Union. There were also the grave economic problems of rebuilding devastated southern industries and reopening normal trade relations among the states. Finally there was the continuing social problem of bringing black Americans into the mainstream of national life.

As you will read in this and the next chapter, the problems of reconstruction had to be dealt with at a time when both the North and the South faced a breakdown of public morality, with graft and corruption reaching into every level of government—local, state, and national. This breakdown was due not only to the war, which had dislocated long-established ways of life in every section of the country. It was brought about also by the changes taking place in the United States during the latter half of the 1800's—the rapid development of industry, a flood of immigration, and the phenomenal growth of cities.

THE CHAPTER IN OUTLINE

1. A lenient plan of reconstruction under President Lincoln.

2. Attempts to establish order in the war-ravaged South.

3. A severe program of reconstruction under the Radical Republicans.

4. The short-lived era of Radical control in the South.

5. Advances in agriculture, industry, and education in the New South.

6. The struggle of black southerners to find their place in the New South.

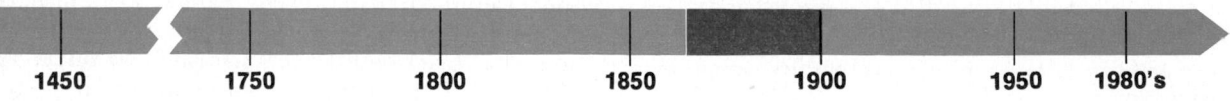

1450   1750   1800   1850   1900   1950   1980's

1 A lenient plan of reconstruction under President Lincoln

On March 4, 1865, near the end of the war, President Lincoln stated his policy of reconstruction for the South. The roar of cannon fire at Richmond would soon be stilled but Lincoln's Second Inaugural Address was destined to live on.

"With malice toward none," he said; "with charity for all; with firmness in the right, as God gives us to see the right; let us strive on to finish the work we are in; to bind up the nation's wounds; to care for him who shall have borne the battle, and for his widow, and his orphan—to do all which may achieve and cherish a just and lasting peace among ourselves and with all nations."

Lincoln's program

Lincoln's were not idle words. He had already begun to develop a program of reconstruction based upon "charity for all," and he fully intended to carry out that program.

As early as December 8, 1863, Lincoln outlined his program for restoring the South to the Union in his Proclamation of Amnesty° and Reconstruction. It was a practical, flexible program rather than one based on rigid and theoretical ideas about the Constitution. The program rested on Lincoln's theory that the Confederate states had never succeeded in leaving the Union. They had for a time left the "family circle," but they were still part of the family, and the immediate problem was to get them back into the circle quickly.

First, he offered full pardon to all southerners who would take an oath of allegiance to the Union and promise to accept federal laws and proclamations dealing with slavery. The only southerners excluded from this offer were those who had resigned civil and military positions in the federal government to serve in the Confederacy, members of the Confederate government, high-ranking Confederate army and naval officers, and Confederates who had mistreated Negro or white prisoners of war.

Second, Lincoln declared that a state could draw up a new constitution, elect new officials, and return to the Union on a basis of full equality with all other states when it met certain conditions. A minimum number of persons (at least 10 percent of those who had voted in the election of 1860) must take the oath of allegiance. Each person taking the oath must have been a quali-

° *amnesty:* a broad pardon for offenses against a government.

fied voter in the state before its secession from the Union.

In 1863 this program applied only to areas conquered by Union armies. Lincoln intended to apply it to all other Confederate areas as soon as they were in Union hands. But he did not insist that this proposal was the only acceptable one. He agreed that Congress must give final approval to admitting members of Congress from the reconstructed states. Moreover, as time passed Lincoln revealed flexibility in his own thinking. For example, in a letter written in 1864 he stated that the restoration of the southern states to the Union "must rest upon the principle of civil and political equality of both races; and it must be sealed by a general amnesty." And in his last public address, delivered on April 11, 1865, only four days before his death, he declared that he favored giving the vote to those Negroes who had fought for the Union and to those with some educational qualifications.

Opposition to Lincoln's policy

Not all Republican leaders agreed with Lincoln's ideas on reconstruction. Many opposed the idea of pardoning former Confederates and allowing them to vote and hold office. These Republican leaders doubted the loyalty of former Confederates. They also doubted whether, if given political power, the former Confederates would permit black Americans to enjoy legal and political rights.

The Republicans who were most opposed to Lincoln's speedy and lenient reconstruction policy were called Radicals. The Radical Republicans were by no means a well-defined group. Different Radicals took different positions on political and economic issues and on methods of readmitting the former Confederate states to the Union. The public at the time, and some historians since, often overlooked these differences. They incorrectly assumed that the two most outspoken Congressional Radicals—Senator Charles Sumner of Massachusetts and Representative Thaddeus Stevens of Pennsylvania—expressed the views of all Radical Republicans.

Senator Sumner insisted on measures to guarantee the political and legal equality of black Americans and to educate them so that they could carry out the responsibilities of freedom. Representative Stevens wanted to punish the South for all the injustices and discriminations that black southerners had suffered under white rule. Stevens also wanted to do everything possible to make sure that in the future the freed slaves would be treated justly. Believing that political and legal rights for former slaves would be meaningless if they did not have economic independence, Stevens urged that the estates of "rebel traitors" be divided up and given to the freed slaves. Few Radical Republicans accepted so extreme a policy.

While the war was being fought and in the months following Confederate surrender, a majority of Republican leaders, more moderate in their views, lined up with Lincoln's reconstruction policies. But many moderates agreed with the Radicals on one point. They believed that President Lincoln, in exercising his war powers, had encroached upon the constitutional powers of the legislative branch. They all felt that Congress, not the President, was responsible for laying down the rules for restoring the southern states to the Union.

Some Republicans frankly admitted that their thinking about reconstruction was influenced by practical political considerations. They had every reason to believe that, when the war ended, white southerners would reject the wartime Republican Party and flock to the Democratic Party. Southern Democrats returning to Congress would probably support northern Democrats, thus making the Republicans a minority party. Such a combination might endanger measures that had the support of many, though not all, Republicans—a high tariff, national banks, free land, and federal aid to railroads.

The Republicans could keep the Democrats from gaining majority power in state as well as federal governments in two ways. First, they could give voting rights to the former slaves, who would support the Republicans at the polls in gratitude for emancipation. Second, they could keep former Confederate leaders from voting and holding public office.

Political considerations of this kind played some part in shaping attitudes of many Republicans toward reconstruction—historians disagree as to how large a part. However, it should also be emphasized that many Republican members of Congress approached the very difficult problems of reconstruction with a genuine desire to help the freed slaves and guarantee them fair opportunities in American life.

The Wade-Davis Bill

Opposition to President Lincoln's plan for reconstruction found expression in the Wade-Davis Bill. Although some Radical Republican members of Congress thought the bill was too mild, enough moderate Republicans supported it so that the bill was passed by a slender majority in early July 1864.

The Wade-Davis Bill provided for readmitting the southern states into the Union under harsher conditions than those favored by President Lincoln. The bill was intended to give political power to southerners who had remained loyal to the Union. It was also intended to insure that the new constitutions of the southern states would recognize the freedom of black southerners. Finally, the bill was intended to insure that Confederate war debts were *repudiated,* or not paid.

President Lincoln refused to sign the Wade-Davis Bill. He felt that its rigid provisions would

The fateful and lonely decisions that American Presidents sometimes have to make are reflected in this brooding photograph of President Lincoln. It was taken at the White House by Mathew Brady in 1862.

THE NATION MOURNS.

THE DEATH OF ABRAHAM LINCOLN

On the evening of Friday, April 14, 1865, the President and Mrs. Lincoln left the White House and went with friends to Ford's Theater. They were going to see an English play called *Our American Cousin.* Lincoln watched the play from an armchair in a box overlooking the stage. Shortly after ten o'clock John Wilkes Booth, a former actor, entered the box and fastened the door behind him. Armed with a Derringer pistol and a dagger, he rested the pistol on the back of the chair and shot President Lincoln through the head. An officer named Major Rathbone rushed to the President's aid, but Booth slashed at Rathbone with the dagger and leaped to the stage, tripping and injuring himself as he fled.

Witnesses disagreed as to what Booth shouted as he escaped. Some thought he cried "Sic semper tyrannus!" ("Thus be it ever to tyrants!" spoken in Latin). Others thought he said "The South is avenged!"

A young army doctor came to the aid of the President, but Lincoln never regained consciousness. He was carried to a house across the street, where he died the next morning.

Booth was eventually found hiding in a barn in Virginia. He refused to give himself up, and shots were fired, but whether he died by his own hand or was killed by a Union soldier is not known.

The entire nation mourned the President's death. Carl Sandburg, poet and Lincoln biographer, has described the slowly moving funeral train that carried Lincoln's body to its final resting place at Springfield, Illinois: "There was a funeral," he wrote. "It took long to pass its many given points. Many millions of people saw it and personally moved in it and were part of its procession. . . . Nothing like it had ever been attempted before."

restrict him when the time came to rebuild the Union. He also believed that Congress did not have the constitutional authority to compel a state to abolish slavery. Abolition of slavery, he believed, would require an amendment to the Constitution.

Lincoln's assassination

Whether or not Lincoln's tact and moderation could have won acceptance of his policy must remain unanswered. On April 14, 1865, he was assassinated by John Wilkes Booth, a former actor.

Sorrow and anger gripped the nation—South as well as North, black as well as white. White southerners had despised Lincoln during the war. Yet many had now come to feel that he was a wise, compassionate leader who offered their best hope for a workable program of reconstruction.

But Lincoln was gone. Flags flew at half-mast, bells tolled, and weeping crowds filed through the funeral train as it stopped in cities between Washington, D.C., and Lincoln's burial place in Springfield, Illinois. Meanwhile, Vice-President Andrew Johnson became President.

President Johnson

Andrew Johnson was a self-educated man. Without any formal schooling, he had spent his boyhood as a tailor's apprentice. Later his devoted wife had helped him to improve his meager writing ability. While still a young man, he was elected mayor of his community, a small mountain village in eastern Tennessee. This was the beginning of a political career in the Democratic Party that took him in 1857 to the Senate of the United States. Although he owned a few slaves, Johnson disliked the large planters who were so influential in the South, and he had resisted the secession of Tennessee in 1861.

Johnson's service for the Union during the war won him an appointment as military governor of Tennessee, responsible for controlling those areas of his state occupied by Union troops. When the Republicans, including Lincoln himself, feared that they might lose the Presidential election in 1864, Johnson, a Democrat, was placed on the "Union" ticket in the hope that he would draw votes for Lincoln.

Andrew Johnson had many good qualities, among them a stubborn fighting spirit and the moral courage to act according to his convictions. Unfortunately, he was not a flexible man. Whereas Lincoln always tried to understand the positions of his political opponents, Johnson tended to insist upon the rightness of his own point of view. Johnson lacked sufficient patience, tact, and political skill to be an effective leader at this critical time.

Johnson and reconstruction

One of Johnson's first decisions as President was to offer rewards for the arrest of Jefferson Davis and other former Confederate leaders. Most Radical Republicans were pleased with Johnson's action, for they thought he would help them carry out their program.

President Johnson soon disappointed the Radicals, however, by adopting a more conciliatory attitude toward the South and by claiming that he intended to follow Lincoln's program. For a time he seemed to be doing so. He officially recognized the reconstructed governments of Tennessee, Arkansas, Louisiana, and Virginia. He kept all of Lincoln's cabinet.

In several ways, however, Johnson did not follow Lincoln's program—neither in details nor in general approach. Lincoln had kept an open mind about the best method of reconstructing the Union. Johnson refused to consider any plan but his own. His stubbornness antagonized the Radical Republicans, as did his policy of pardoning former Confederates. When the Radicals objected to his policies, Johnson further angered them by answering their arguments with name-calling and personal abuse.

Johnson managed even to antagonize the moderate Republicans. Most moderates shared with the Radicals the conviction that any program of reconstruction must provide civil and political equality for both races. Johnson opposed this viewpoint.

End of the first stage of reconstruction

In spite of strong differences of opinion, the reconstruction program proceeded for a time along the lines laid down by Lincoln and modified by Johnson. Within a few months all the former Confederate states except Texas had adopted new constitutions and organized new governments.

When Congress assembled on December 4, 1865, Senators and Representatives from the southern states, most of whom had been leaders in the Confederacy, were waiting outside the doors to take their seats in the national legislature. To many observers it looked as though the long and dreadful war was finally ended and the restored nation was about to start anew.

SECTION SURVEY

IDENTIFY: amnesty, freed slaves, Wade-Davis Bill; John Wilkes Booth, Charles Sumner, Thaddeus Stevens, Andrew Johnson; April 14, 1865.

1. (a) What did Lincoln mean when he said, "With malice toward none; with charity for all"? (b) By referring to the terms of Lincoln's reconstruction plan, show that he intended to practice what he preached in his Second Inaugural Address.
2. Outline the opposition to Lincoln's reconstruction plan. Be sure to include the reasoning of those who opposed him.
3. (a) State the provisions of the Wade-Davis Bill. (b) What were Lincoln's objections to this bill?
4. Compare the ideas of Lincoln, Johnson, and the Radical Republicans on reconstruction.

2 Attempts to establish order in the war-ravaged South

A new chapter in American history opened when Congress assembled on December 4, 1865, but it was not the chapter outlined by either Lincoln or Johnson. It was, instead, one of the most troubled chapters in the nation's history.

Economic chaos in the South

The scene in the South at the end of the war was one of utter poverty. Crumbling chimneys rose from the ashes of once lovely mansions, grass grew in the roads, broken bridges lay in ruins, and two thirds of the railroads were destroyed.

The devastation in the cities was especially grim. A visitor reported that Columbia, South Carolina, was "a wilderness of crumbling walls, naked chimneys, and trees killed by flames." The business section of Richmond, Virginia, one of the great southern manufacturing centers, lay in ruins. The scene in Atlanta, Georgia, was one of devastation. City and country alike, wherever armies had fought, were largely in ruins.

Social chaos

The southern economy, as well as southern property, had been torn apart by the war. A citizen of Mississippi wrote in April 1865 that "our fields everywhere lie untilled. Naked chimneys and charred ruins all over the land mark the spots where happy homes . . . once stood. Their former inhabitants wander in poverty and exile, wherever chance or charity affords them shelter or food. Childless, old age widows, and helpless orphans beggared and hopeless, are everywhere." Conditions were not everywhere so bad as this, but they were bad enough.

The plight of some 4 million freed slaves was far worse. The former slaves were at last free, at least in name, but free to do what? Most of them had never been given an opportunity to learn how to read and write. None had owned land. Few knew what it was like to work for their own wages. Nor could most of their former owners pay them wages, for Confederate money was worthless and United States currency was scarcely to be found in the South. The land itself remained, but seeds and farm tools had almost disappeared.

Disease, always the companion of hunger and lack of sanitation, swept across the South. It was especially serious in the cities and their outskirts, where uprooted people struggled to survive in makeshift shelters. Thousands died during the summer and winter of 1865–66. In some crowded urban areas, as many as one quarter to one third of the black population died of disease. And the death rate among the white population was almost as grim.

Relief efforts for freed slaves

Even while the war was being fought, some abolitionists tried to relieve the plight of freed slaves who had fled into areas controlled by Union forces. When white planters abandoned their plantations on islands off the coast of South Carolina, black people there were left helpless and destitute. With support from religious groups and anti-slavery northerners, idealistic men and women, white and black, helped the freed slaves to operate these plantations and also established schools there. Outstanding among the volunteers was Laura Towne of Massachusetts, who looked after the health of former slaves, helped them with legal problems, and established the Penn School. This school later became a teacher-training institution with vocational as well as academic programs.

Elsewhere, relief societies financed by northern religious and charitable groups tried to fill the needs of freed slaves for food, shelter, jobs, and schooling. Washington, D.C., became a magnet for thousands of hopeful but destitute black people. Their need for relief soon became desperate. Josephine Griffing, an Ohio abolitionist and women's rights leader of the 1850's, set up in the capital city a program that provided food, clothing, shelter, and job training for freed blacks. She was assisted by her daughters and by financial donors. Josephine Griffing also urged Congress to undertake a program to find places to live in the North and West for homeless black people and to help them become self-supporting citizens. She herself helped thousands find homes and jobs in many localities.

The Freedmen's Bureau

During the war, the United States Army provided food and clothing for impoverished southerners, black and white, in areas under its control. Once the war was over, it was clear that neither the Army nor the voluntary relief societies could meet the pressing needs of southerners, especially the freed slaves. At the urging of Josephine Griffing and others, Congress in 1865 created the Freedmen's Bureau, making it responsible for looking after "refugees, freedmen°, and abandoned lands." This was the first important example in the nation's history of federal support

° *freedmen* was the term used in these years to refer to former slaves—women and children as well as men.

for needy and underprivileged people. The Freedmen's Bureau was headed by General Oliver Otis Howard of Maine. In 1867, General Howard also founded Howard University in Washington, D.C., with the primary purpose of offering higher education to the freed slaves.

Northerners and southerners differed in their attitude toward the Freedmen's Bureau. Most northerners regarded it as an honest effort to help the South bring order out of chaos. Most white southerners, on the other hand, resented the bureau. They charged that many bureau agents deliberately encouraged the freed slaves to look upon their former owners as enemies, and were therefore responsible for creating racial friction.

White southerners also charged the bureau with raising false hopes among the freed slaves, thereby making the process of readjustment increasingly difficult. One of these "false hopes" was the former slaves' belief that they would all receive farms. During the summer and fall of 1865 the rumor circulated that every former slave would get "forty acres and a mule" as a Christmas gift from the federal government. This rumor was based on the vague promise in the Freedmen's Bureau bill that land which had been abandoned, or for which taxes had not been paid, would eventually be distributed among the former slaves. But many freed slaves accepted the rumor as truth. Overjoyed at the prospect of soon owning farms, and understandably associating freedom with the right to choose where and how they worked, some freed slaves decided not to work for white southerners.

Restrictions on freed slaves

Faced with such a new situation, southern leaders began to take steps to restore life as they had known it. One step was the adoption of laws to regulate the conduct of the freed slaves.

Laws of this kind, known as "slave codes," had existed before the war. The new black codes, which varied from state to state, contained many of the same provisions as the old slave codes. As white southerners pointed out, however, they also included certain improvements in civil rights for the former slaves. Under the new codes, former slaves were permitted to own personal property, to sue and be sued in court, to act in court cases involving one or more black persons, and legally to marry members of their own race.

But in general, the black codes denied Negroes their basic civil rights. Mississippi, for example, using its old code, merely substituted the word "Negro" for "slave." Black southerners were forbidden to possess firearms unless licensed

This sewing school was established in Richmond, Virginia, by the Freedman's Bureau. The bureau was created to aid refugees, freed slaves, and poverty-stricken people after the Civil War.

to do so. They were forbidden to assemble unless white southerners were present. Nor could Negroes appear on the streets after sunset or travel without permits. Above all, the codes established white control over black labor. They prohibited black southerners from starting businesses, and provided for tight labor contracts, including severe apprenticeship regulations and stern punishments if contracts were broken. Some codes also restricted black southerners from renting or leasing farm land. The black codes indicated the widespread determination of white southerners to confine the freed slaves to a clearly defined, subordinate way of life.

Such was the situation in December 1865 when the newly elected Senators and Representatives from all the former Confederate states except Texas appeared in Washington to take their seats in Congress. The former Confederate states had taken some, but not all, of the steps required by both President Lincoln and President Johnson for readmission to the Union. The new Senators and Representatives fully expected to take their seats in Congress and to share with northern members of Congress the task of rebuilding the Union.

Congress, however, refused to admit the southern Senators and Representatives. What motives prompted Congress to reject the South's newly elected representatives? Why did Congress refuse to accept Lincoln's and Johnson's programs for restoring the South to the Union?

Reasons behind rejection

From the time Lincoln's program began to take shape, as you know, Radical Republicans had argued that southern leaders could not be trusted. Now, in December 1865, they pointed to the legal restrictions placed on freed slaves as evidence that white southerners were unwilling to recognize the complete freedom of black Americans.

The Radical Republicans also disagreed with the Lincoln and Johnson theory about the nature of the war. Both Lincoln and Johnson had argued that the conflict was *a rebellion of individuals*. This being so, the President could use his pardoning power, granted him by the Constitution, to restore the South to the Union.

Charles Sumner, leader of the Radical Republicans in the Senate, opposed Lincoln's theory with the "state suicide" argument. According to Sumner, the southern states, as complete political organizations, had committed "state suicide" when they seceded from the Union. Now, with the war over, they were in the same position as any other unorganized Territory of the United States. This being the case, Congress alone had the constitutional right to establish the terms for admitting them to the Union.

Thaddeus Stevens, majority leader of the House, held an even more drastic point of view. According to Stevens, the former Confederate states did not exist even as Territories. In Stevens' opinion they were "conquered provinces," and should be treated as such.

The historian cannot be sure of the motives that led Radical Republicans to take the positions they did. Some Radicals, as you have read, were influenced by economic and political considerations. But a good many Republicans, both Radicals and moderates, were strongly influenced by a sincere feeling of obligation to the freed slaves. They genuinely wanted to make sure that white southerners did not deprive black southerners of their freedom and reduce them to a permanently inferior way of life.

Many moderate Republicans shared Lincoln's attitude toward the South. If Johnson had been less insistent upon having his own way, if he had been willing to work with the moderate Republicans, they and the Democratic members of the House and Senate might have carried through a reconstruction program acceptable to white southern leaders. But President Johnson would not change his views. As a result, control of Congress passed into the hands of the Radicals.

SECTION SURVEY

IDENTIFY: "forty acres and a mule," "state suicide" theory, "conquered provinces" theory, black codes; Josephine Griffing, General O. O. Howard.

1. If you had been living in the South in 1865, what would have been the most pressing problems you and your family would have had to face?
2. (a) Describe the work of the Freedmen's Bureau. (b) Contrast northern and southern opinion of this bureau.
3. (a) List the restrictions placed on black southerners by white southern leaders. (b) How did the new black codes differ from the old slave codes?
4. What reasons led Congress to reject (a) new southern members of Congress, (b) Lincoln's and Johnson's reconstruction programs?
5. How did Andrew Johnson contribute to the problems of reconstruction?

3 A severe program of reconstruction under the Radical Republicans

By refusing in December 1865 to seat the southern members of Congress, the Radical Republicans practically guaranteed their own control of both houses of Congress. Within a few months they restored military rule in the South, thereby sowing seeds of bitterness that were to live for many years.

The first steps

Congress immediately appointed a joint committee of six Senators and nine Representatives to study the entire question of reconstruction. While Congress waited for the committee's report, it proceeded to safeguard the rights of the freed slaves.

As one step in this direction, Congress passed a bill enlarging the powers of the Freedmen's Bureau. The new law gave the bureau power to prosecute in military courts, rather than in civil courts, any person accused of depriving freed slaves of their civil rights. President Johnson promptly vetoed the bill, arguing (1) that trial by military courts violated the Fifth Amendment of the Constitution, and (2) that Congress had no power to pass *any* laws with 11 states unrepresented. Johnson's veto infuriated the Radical Republicans. After long debate they finally gathered enough votes to pass the bill over the President's veto.

In the meantime, Congress passed a civil rights bill, the first in a series of federal acts designed to give black Americans full citizenship and guarantee them complete equality of treatment with all other citizens. Johnson also vetoed this bill on the ground that it was an unconstitutional invasion of states' rights. Enough moderate Republicans joined the Radicals in Congress to pass this measure, the Civil Rights Act, over Johnson's veto.

Johnson's vetoes of the Freedmen's Bureau bill and the Civil Rights Act had two immediate results. First, the vetoes cost him the support of moderate Republicans who, without any desire to "punish" white southerners, believed that Congress should protect the rights of former slaves, which the black codes endangered. Second, the vetoes strengthened the influence of Thaddeus Stevens and other Radical Republicans. The Radicals argued that Johnson, the Democrats, and the old ruling white class in the South were making the North's victory meaningless.

The Fourteenth Amendment

Congress, fearing that the Supreme Court might declare the Civil Rights Act unconstitutional, decided to write the provisions of the act into the Constitution by amendment. This amendment, the Fourteenth, was the outcome of compromise between moderate and Radical Republicans. Some Radicals had hoped to outlaw all forms of racial segregation and discrimination. That objective does not seem to have been shared by the moderates, nor even by all Radicals who shaped the Amendment.

The Fourteenth Amendment (page 667) made black Americans citizens of the United States and of the states in which they lived. It forbade states to deprive citizens of the rights of life, liberty, and property without due process of law, or to deny any citizen "the equal protection of the laws." It went further and excluded former Confederate leaders from holding public office, state or federal. It provided for reduction of Congressional representation of states that deprived black Americans of their rights as citizens. It also forbade southern states to repay Confederate war debts or to compensate former slaveowners for their loss of slaves.

Radical Republicans in control

Tennessee ratified the Fourteenth Amendment in July 1866 and was immediately readmitted to the Union. But, on the advice of President Johnson, all of the other southern states rejected the amendment by overwhelming votes.

What would Congress do next? The answer depended in part on the Congressional elections in the fall of 1866. If the Democrats won control of Congress, they might return to Lincoln's and Johnson's programs, or some modification of them. If the Radical Republicans won, the nation might expect further restrictions on the political role of the former Confederates and stronger guarantees of the rights and opportunities of the freed slaves.

At this point several events helped to swing voters toward the Radical Republicans. Violent race riots were especially influential in shaping public opinion. In Memphis, Tennessee, 46 black Americans were killed, and 12 Negro schools and 4 Negro churches were burned. In a riot at New Orleans about 200 people, mostly black, were killed or wounded. Many northerners, shocked by such violence, began to feel that perhaps the Radical Republicans were right in demanding further federal protection for the freed slaves.

In the late summer of 1866 President Johnson made a trip to Chicago, stopping along the way to make election speeches. When opponents heckled him, Johnson's answers often seemed to reflect a lack of understanding of the election issues, as well as bitter hatred of Radical Republicans. His language, often blunt and uncouth, antagonized many voters.

More important, however, as a reason for Radical Republican strength was the memory of the war itself. During the terrible conflict, both sides had suffered immense casualties. Voters who did not want to risk losing the fruits of hard-won military victory voted for Radical Republican candidates.

In the election the Radical Republicans increased their hold on both houses of Congress. With more than a two-thirds majority in both the Senate and the House, the Republicans, if they held together, could override Presidential vetoes.

Reconstructing the South

In March 1867 a combination of Radical and moderate Republicans passed, over Johnson's vetoes, a number of measures that provided a complete program for reconstruction. The new program, which the majority in Congress was determined to force upon the South, contained five major provisions.

First, Congress divided the 10 southern states that had rejected the Fourteenth Amendment into five military districts. Each district was under a military governor, with federal troops to maintain law and order while the states drafted new constitutions and organized new governments.

Second, Congress deprived most former Confederate leaders of the right to vote and hold

The impeachment trial of President Andrew Johnson was held in the Senate in 1868. The final vote was 35 to 19, one vote short of the two-thirds majority required to remove him from office.

office. The restrictions were the same as those Congress had earlier written into the Fourteenth Amendment.

Third, Congress gave the freed slaves the right to vote and hold office.

Fourth, Congress authorized the states to write new constitutions which guaranteed freed slaves the right to vote.

Fifth, Congress required the states to ratify the Fourteenth Amendment.

The white southern governments that had been formed under the Presidential plan of reconstruction now had no choice but to accept the new Congressional program. One by one, the states held conventions, drafted new constitutions, organized new governments, and entered the Union under the terms laid down by Congress.

Johnson's impeachment and trial

By the summer of 1868 all but three southern states had returned to the Union on the terms laid down by Congress. (Mississippi, Texas, and Virginia finally accepted the terms and were readmitted in 1870.) Meanwhile, the Radical Republicans determined to remove their hated "enemy," President Johnson, from office.

Several things led the Radical Republicans to this decision. They certainly were affected by the emotional hatreds and tensions of the times. But more important, the Radicals knew that the success of their reconstruction program depended heavily on its enforcement. They were convinced that President Johnson would not enforce Congressional policy. And Johnson confirmed their suspicions when, by executive order, he restricted the power of commanding military officers in the South and removed commanders known to be sympathetic to Radical programs.

To find grounds for impeachment and to reduce the President's power, Congress in 1867 adopted the Tenure of Office° Act over Johnson's veto. Under this law the President could not dismiss important civil officers without the Senate's consent. Believing the law unconstitutional, Johnson decided to put it to a test. In February 1868 he demanded the resignation of Secretary of War Edwin M. Stanton, who had consistently cooperated with Johnson's enemies, the Radical Republicans.

° *tenure of office:* the period during which an individual has the right to continue in office.

The House immediately adopted a resolution that "Andrew Johnson, President of the United States, be impeached of high crimes and misdemeanors in office." Having passed the resolution, the Radicals then hunted for other charges to bolster their case against the President.

The Radicals charged that Johnson, ". . . unmindful of the . . . harmony and courtesies which ought to exist and be maintained between the executive and legislative branches of the government . . . did attempt to bring into disgrace, ridicule, contempt, and reproach the Congress of the United States. . . ." The Radicals cited various occasions when the President publicly made "with a loud voice certain intemperate, inflammatory, and scandalous harangues" against Congress, "and did therein utter loud threats and bitter menaces."

Under the Constitution, a President may be impeached on grounds of "treason, bribery, or high crimes and misdemeanors" (pages 649 and 658). On these grounds, the controversial charges brought by the House against President Johnson were of doubtful legality. Nevertheless, he was impeached.

Johnson's trial before the Senate, presided over by Chief Justice Salmon P. Chase, lasted about two months. After prolonged debate it became clear that Johnson was not guilty of any offense for which he could legally be removed from office. Nevertheless, when the Senate vote was counted, it stood 35 to 19 against Johnson, just one vote short of the necessary two-thirds majority required for removal from office. Johnson continued to serve as President until his term expired on March 4, 1869, almost a year after his trial. But his influence as President was at an end.

Decline of Radical power

It soon became apparent, however, that the Radical Republicans had overreached themselves by attacking the President, even though much of his behavior had been provocative. For two years, with some support from other Republicans, the Radicals had been able to ignore the moderate program of reconstruction and to override Johnson's repeated vetoes of their own program. But when they tried to remove the President from office, they lost the support of many moderate Republicans. Moreover, public opinion finally began to turn against them.

The election of 1868

As the election of 1868 approached, the Republicans realized they were in trouble. In hopes of winning the election, they unanimously nominated Ulysses S. Grant for the Presidency. Grant had no political experience. He did not share the moral conviction of many Radical Republicans of the need to protect the freed slaves. Nevertheless, he was popular with the public as a war hero.

The Democrats chose as their Presidential candidate Horatio Seymour, a wealthy New Yorker and former governor of his state. The Democratic platform denounced the Radical Republican program of reconstruction, declaring it unconstitutional. It condemned the Radicals for their attempt to remove President Johnson from office.

Economic issues were also important in the election of 1868. The platform of the Democratic Party, for example, contained a plank advocating a "cheap money" policy. During the war the government had issued $450 million in paper money which were called "greenbacks." After the war, in 1866, the Republican Congress had provided for the gradual withdrawal of the greenbacks from circulation. By 1868 nearly $100 million had been withdrawn. In their 1868 platform

This 1868 campaign poster shows Republican Presidential candidate Ulysses S. Grant. Why do you think Grant is shown in military uniform?

the Democrats promised, if elected, to reverse this policy and reissue the paper money. They proposed to use the greenbacks to redeem those war bonds not specifically redeemable in gold.

The Democrats knew that this "cheap money" plank would antagonize wealthy bondholders, who fully expected that the money they had lent the government would be repaid in gold. But they also knew that the proposal would appeal to many less well-to-do voters, particularly those who owed money, for with more currency in circulation they could more easily pay off their debts.

Republican candidate Ulysses S. Grant barely squeaked through to victory. Although he won by an overwhelming electoral vote of 214 to 80, capturing 24 of the 36 states, his popular majority was only 309,000 out of almost 6 million votes. A shift of only a few thousand votes in a handful of states would have swung the election to Horatio Seymour, the Democratic candidate.

The Radical Republicans studied the election returns with growing concern. They realized that many voters had turned against the Republicans because of their "hard money" policy. They also realized that the black vote had made possible their thin majority of the popular vote.

The Fifteenth Amendment

With this disturbing conclusion in mind, the Radicals drew up the Fifteenth Amendment and submitted it to the states for ratification. The Fifteenth Amendment was short and to the point: "The right of citizens of the United States to vote shall not be denied or abridged by the United States or any state on account of race, color, or previous condition of servitude."

The Fifteenth Amendment was ratified by the necessary three fourths of the states and became part of the Constitution in 1870. Mississippi, Texas, and Virginia—the last three southern states to return to the Union—were required to ratify the amendment as a condition for readmission.

Women, you recall, made many contributions to Union victory in the Civil War. Leaders of the women's rights movement expected, in return, that women would now receive the same legal protections and voting rights as blacks. Despite their vigorous protests, women were not included in the Fourteenth and Fifteenth Amendments.

SECTION SURVEY

IDENTIFY: due process of law, equal protection of the laws; Ulysses S. Grant.

1. (a) Explain how the new Freedmen's Bureau law and the Civil Rights Act aimed to protect the freed slaves. (b) Why did Johnson veto both? (c) What were the results of Johnson's vetoes?
2. (a) Why did Congress propose the Fourteenth Amendment? (b) Read the Fourteenth Amendment on pages 667–68 and summarize the main ideas in each of its sections.
3. Describe the five major provisions of the Congressional plan for reconstruction.
4. What were the reasons for Johnson's impeachment?
5. Read the Fifteenth Amendment on page 669. (a) What does it provide? (b) Why was it passed?

4 The short-lived era of Radical control in the South

The Radical Republican program of reconstruction brought far-reaching changes to the South, but only for a relatively short time. For varying periods—as long as 10 years in only three states—Radical Republicans and their allies controlled the former Confederate states.

Help from the North

In the 10 years after the surrender of the Confederacy, the main concern of the federal government was the restoration of the Union. Providing aid to the war-ravaged South and to needy southerners took second place. The Freedmen's Bureau was severely limited by lack of funds and by opposition from most southerners and many northerners. Its work was supplemented, however, by teachers and missionaries, black as well as white. Most of the northern volunteers were motivated by humanitarian and democratic ideals. Many were successful in winning the confidence of the men, women, and children whom they had come to help. Others, equally well-meaning but unfamiliar with southern ways of life and perhaps less tactful, antagonized the people with whom they tried to work.

Carpetbaggers and scalawags

White southerners especially resented the arrival in the South of northerners whom they jeeringly called "carpetbaggers." This nickname implied, wrongly, that the newcomers were all fly-by-night adventurers who carried everything they owned in suitcases made of carpeting material, which were common at the time.

The carpetbaggers came for many different reasons. Some sincerely wanted to help the freed slaves exercise their newly acquired rights. Some hoped to get themselves elected to political office.

Several black southerners served in Congress after the Civil War. Shown here are Senator Hiram Revels of Mississippi (far left) and members of the House of Representatives.

Some came to make their fortunes, as Americans had long been doing, by acquiring farm land or by starting new businesses.

But some carpetbaggers came for reasons of pure greed or fraud. Horace Greeley, editor of the *New York Tribune,* wrote that such carpetbaggers were "stealing and plundering, many of them with both arms around the Negroes, and their hands in their rear pockets, seeing if they cannot pick a paltry dollar out of them."

Most white southerners and some northerners scorned the northern carpetbaggers who moved into the South. Special scorn, however, was heaped upon native-born southerners who cooperated with northern authorities. Some of these native-born southerners were prompted by the best of motives. Having opposed slavery and secession, they had sympathized with the Union during the war; now they believed that the best way to restore peace and prosperity to the South and to the nation was to forgive and forget. But others were selfish and ambitious individuals who seized any opportunity to advance their own fortunes at the expense of their neighbors.

Whatever the motives of these native-born southerners, most were held in contempt by other white southerners, who referred to them as "renegades," "mangy dogs," and "scalawags," a word used to describe scoundrels.

Reconstruction governments

Such were the individuals—scalawags and carpetbaggers, good and bad alike—who largely controlled southern state governments during part of the Radical reconstruction period. Northerners held most of the important political offices, at least during the early years. They were able to get themselves elected partly because they persuaded the freed slaves to vote for them, and partly because many white southerners were deprived of the right to vote and others refused to take part in political activities.

The enormous influence of northerners in southern politics can be seen by examining the election results in the seven southern states readmitted to the Union by 1868. As a result of the first postwar elections held in these states, 4 of the 7 governors, 10 of the 14 United States Senators, and 20 of the 35 United States Representatives were carpetbaggers. In general, southern scalawags and freed slaves had to be content with the less important state and federal offices.

Black southerners in public life

Negroes were elected to the southern "carpetbag" governments, and they played an important role in some of them. In recent years, however, some historians have pointed out that the Negro's role in these governments has often been exaggerated. Only one black American served briefly as a southern governor. In only one southern state—South Carolina—did black members for a time hold a majority in the state legislature. Only Mississippi sent black Senators, two of them, to Washington. One was Hiram Revels, a native of North Carolina who, after studying at Knox

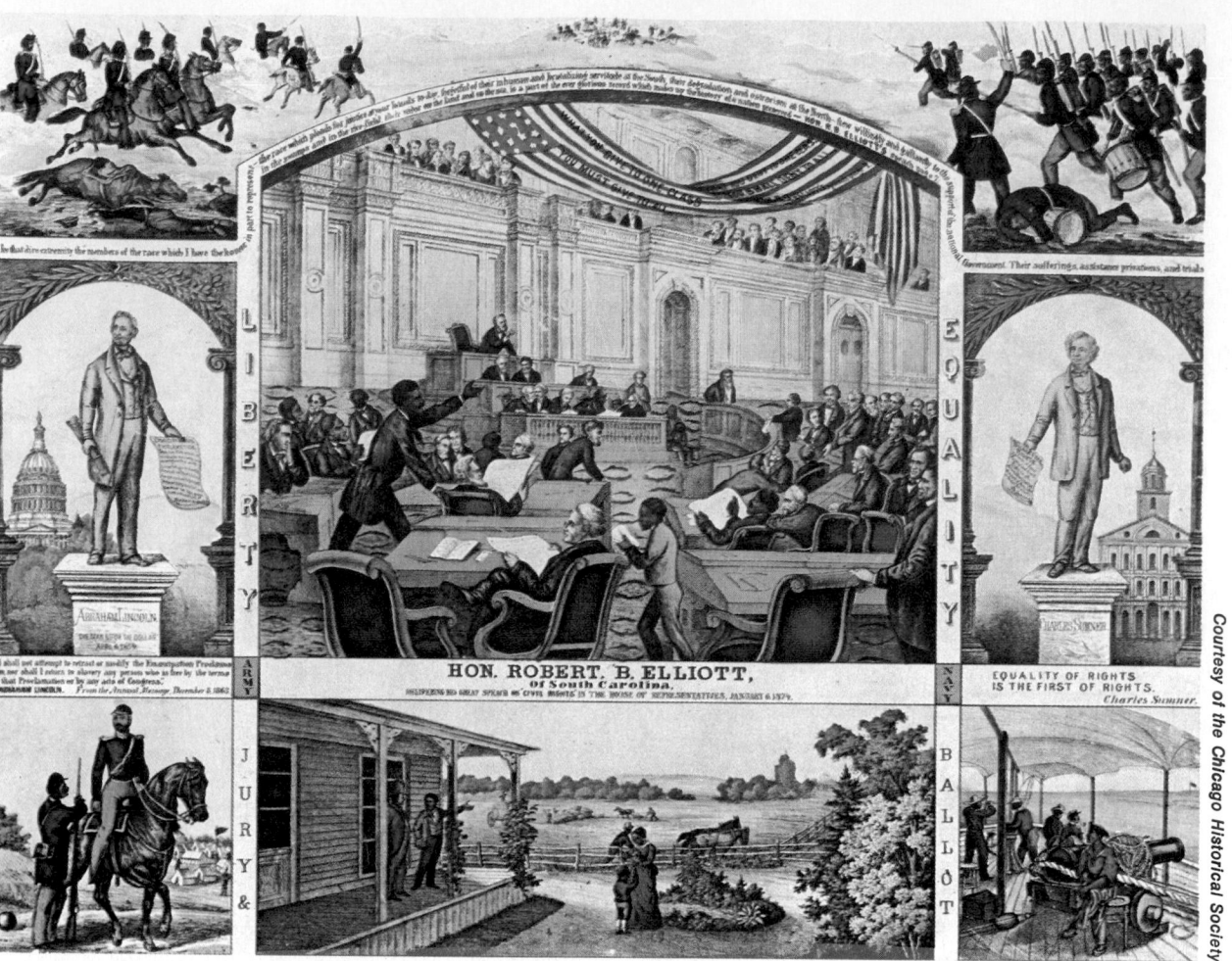

Robert Brown Elliott was a brilliant lawyer, scholar, and member of Congress. He is shown in the center illustration speaking on civil rights before the House of Representatives in 1874.

College in Illinois, had been a teacher and minister. The other was Blanche K. Bruce, who had escaped from slavery in Virginia and who had also been a teacher.

The record of black citizens in reconstruction politics also has often been misrepresented, according to recent historians. Many Negroes, to be sure, who had been denied an education and experience in public life through no fault of their own, were victimized by clever carpetbaggers and scalawags, whose leadership they followed. Others showed independence and political skill, among them Robert Brown Elliott of South Carolina, a brilliant lawyer and scholar, and P. B. S. Pinchback of Louisiana, son of a Mississippi planter and a black mother.

The Negroes in public life during reconstruction did not demand revenge upon white southerners. In fact, most black leaders favored returning the right to vote to their former white masters. The records of those elected to the United States Congress compared well with the records of many of their white colleagues.

The record of reconstruction governments

White southerners who had once dominated public life rightly deplored large expenditures for needless luxuries authorized by legislators, white and black, in some reconstruction governments. They also rightly denounced some reconstruction legislators for outright corruption and graft.

Some of the new legislators were all too willing to enrich themselves while granting favorable railroad and corporation charters to business groups, often northern, who wanted to develop southern enterprises. But southern Democrats who briefly controlled southern legislatures in the first years after the war had followed some of the same corrupt practices. And, as you will read later, public morality in all sections of the United States sank to an extremely low level during the years following the Civil War.

The southern reconstruction legislatures, controlled by carpetbaggers, scalawags, and freed slaves, did increase the debts of their states. But this was often the result of borrowing for much needed and long overdue public improvements. The new legislatures, for example, strengthened public education and, for the first time, made it available to large numbers of black children.

The reconstruction governments also pushed forward other constructive programs. They spread the tax burden more equitably. They introduced overdue reforms in local government and the judicial system. Imprisonment for debt was abolished. The legal rights of women were extended. Laws were passed to protect homes and farms against illegal foreclosures—that is, against unjustified seizure by dishonest officials. And most of the southern state constitutions drafted during the period of reconstruction continued in effect for many years.

Secret societies

Whatever the merits and demerits of the reconstruction governments may have been, most white southerners resented them. Since many former Confederate leaders were denied the vote and since others chose to boycott politics, some white southerners expressed their opposition by defying the law through intimidation and violence. By 1867 some white southerners were attacking carpetbaggers, scalawags, and politically active black southerners through a number of secret societies. The best known were the Knights of the White Camellia and the Ku Klux Klan.

These secret organizations tried to frighten black southerners and their white leaders into staying out of politics. Bands of hooded members clad in ghostly white costumes rode through the countryside at night, stopping now and then at a house to issue warnings. When warnings failed, cabins and churches were burned, and some freed slaves were beaten or killed. White sympathizers and friends of Negroes sometimes received the same treatment. Moderate white southerners, disgusted with the brutality and fearful of northern reaction, disapproved of these actions. But for a time they were unable to prevent these acts of terror and brutality.

Congress tried to end the lawlessness by passing a series of Military Enforcement Acts, sometimes called the Force Acts (1870–71). These acts gave the President power to use federal military forces to control the secret societies, to call upon the state militias when necessary, to suspend the writ of habeas corpus, and to provide for federal supervision of southern elections.

To many white southerners, the Force Acts seemed unduly harsh. Yet compared with the treatment of the losers in civil wars elsewhere, the former Confederates were not severely punished. There were never more than 25,000 federal troops in the occupied states after the war. No political or military leader was executed. Few were imprisoned. President Johnson made liberal use of his pardoning power. Jefferson Davis was released from prison within two years. Except for the loss of slaves, property was seldom seized as punishment for what many northerners regarded as treason.

Further leniency prevailed in 1872, when Congress passed the Amnesty Act. This act restored political rights, including the right to vote, to about 160,000 former Confederates. After 1872 only about 500 white southerners were still barred from political activity.

The Force Acts, the withdrawal of many southerners from the secret societies, and finally the Amnesty Act virtually ended the power of the Ku Klux Klan and other such groups at that time. As most white southerners began to vote again, and as white southern leadership reemerged, the reconstruction governments in several states were replaced by governments representing traditional white southern rule.

The end of Radical reconstruction

During the early 1870's northerners began to lose interest in the problems of southern reconstruction. Radical Republican power was reduced, and its leadership diminished, by the death of Thaddeus Stevens in 1868 and of Charles Sumner in 1874. More northerners began to believe that political chaos in the South would continue as long as former southern leaders were kept out of power.

At first many northerners had championed the cause of the freed slaves. Now they became disillusioned at reports, often exaggerated, of the political ineptness of black southerners. Some northerners seemed to ignore the fact that the former slaves had little, if any, education and no political experience. Other northerners grew weary of the problems of black southerners and less willing to press for an effective program to help them learn their new political roles as citizens.

Weary of tensions in the South, many northerners began to say that perhaps the freed slaves *did* need the supervision of white southern leaders. Perhaps it would be better, they now said, to let southerners work out their own problems of government and race relations. Northerners justified their retreat by referring to the federal system embodied in the Constitution, which left many powers in the hands of the states. No doubt many northerners, sincere enough earlier in demanding equal rights for the freed slaves, now became increasingly and uncomfortably aware that black Americans were not treated as equal citizens in most northern states. Thus many northerners now found it easier to concentrate on strengthening national unity and to give less attention to the place of black Americans in national life.

This attitude was stimulated by a growing number of northern businesses that wanted to stop the Radical program of reconstruction. A disorganized, poverty-stricken South was not good for business on either side of the Mason-Dixon line.

In 1877, shortly after the inauguration of President Rutherford B. Hayes, the last of the federal troops of occupation were withdrawn from the southern states.

The era of reconstruction left many major problems unsolved and created a number of new and equally urgent problems. This was true even though many forces in the North and the South continued working for the reconciliation of the two sections of the Union.

SECTION SURVEY

IDENTIFY: Knights of the White Camellia, Ku Klux Klan, Force Acts, Amnesty Act; Horace Greeley, Hiram Revels.

1. (a) Define carpetbagger and scalawag. (b) Why did the carpetbaggers go south?
2. Why is the period of reconstruction sometimes called the "tragic era"?
3. (a) What was the record of the reconstruction governments? (b) How did white southerners express their opposition to these governments? (c) Was their opposition justified? Explain. (d) What was the attitude of black southern leaders toward white southerners?
4. How did the federal government react to the secret societies and the violence that developed in the South during this period?
5. How did racial prejudice in the North influence the attitudes of some northerners toward reconstruction?

5 Advances in agriculture, industry, and education in the New South

During the 1880's many southerners began to speak of the "New South." Those who used this term, including editor Henry W. Grady of the Atlanta *Constitution*, urged their fellow citizens to abandon the one-crop system of agriculture and develop all the resources of a rich land —the minerals and the forests as well as the soil. Above all, Grady and others who shared his beliefs urged southerners to convert the region's raw materials into manufactured goods in southern mills and factories.

Breakup of plantations

One characteristic of the postwar South was the breakup of many, though by no means all, of the large plantations. This process started in 1865, immediately after the war ended. Planters, who had little if any cash to hire farm laborers, began to sell portions of their plantations to the more prosperous independent farmers. Because of the breakup of the large plantations and the opening of new lands, between 1865 and 1880 the number of small farms more than doubled, while the size of the average southern farm decreased.

Some black southerners, who had emerged from slavery without education, without land, and almost without clothes, also benefited from the breakup of the large plantations. As the years passed, a small but growing number of former slaves acquired small farms.

Tenant farming and sharecropping

While some poor white southerners and a few black southerners became owners of small farms, many others became *tenant farmers*. Under the tenant relationship, which had existed even before the war, a planter usually rented portions of the plantation land to several tenants, who supplied their own seed, mules, and provisions. The owner managed the scattered tenant holdings much as if these made up the old-time plantation, thus retaining some advantages of large-scale production. Many tenants remained tenants all their lives. Others saved enough money to buy a plot of land and become small landowners.

Less fortunate was the *sharecropper*. This farm worker furnished nothing but labor, getting a cabin, seed, tools, a mule, and a plot of land from the owner. In return for farming this land, the sharecropper received a percentage of the crop. Since sharecroppers did not get paid until harvest time, they had to buy provisions for their families on credit. To obtain credit, they had to give a "lien," or mortgage, on the crops they expected to plant and harvest. The debts they could not pay at harvest time were added to the bill to be paid a year later.

When the crops were harvested, almost all of the sharecroppers' share of the money usually went to pay their bills. Because they also had to pay interest on this debt, sharecroppers found it very difficult to get out of debt. And as long as they were in debt, they were practically bound to the soil, since the law forbade them to leave the state until their bills were paid. Frequently the owner of the land also owned the store where the sharecroppers bought their provisions and where they could buy on credit. Since the sharecroppers were seldom free from debt and almost never had any cash, they had to buy at the owner's store.

Many sharecroppers raised only cotton or tobacco since the landowner insisted on cultivating these crops exclusively. The owner argued that the sharecroppers did not know anything about other crops and that cotton and tobacco were the only dependable cash crops.

Although tenant farming and sharecropping existed in other parts of the country, these practices were especially widespread in the South. Indeed, tenant farming and sharecropping provided a workable solution to the frequently desperate economic situation confronting southerners in the postwar years. But tenant farming and sharecropping also made it difficult for the South to abandon its traditional one-crop system and develop diversified farming.

Agricultural progress

Despite the problems facing southern farmers, the South made considerable progress during the postwar years. Southerners, like farmers elsewhere in the nation, benefited from new developments in science and technology. During the 1870's and 1880's improved machines for sowing, cultivating, fertilizing, and reaping were introduced. In 1872 Alabama and Virginia established agricultural colleges; by 1900 the other southern states had followed their example. Because of these institutions and the development of scientific agriculture in other parts of the country, the cultivation of traditional crops was improved and some new plants were introduced.

Cotton continued to be the most important single crop. Indeed, by 1871 the South was growing more cotton than it had in 1860. The older states increased their yield per acre by using commercial fertilizers and improved farming methods. Much of the total increase, however, came from the opening of new cotton lands in the Southwest. By 1900 Texas alone produced one third of all the nation's cotton.

Improved farming methods led to greatly increased production of tobacco, rice, sugar, corn, and other traditional crops. But the most important change in southern agricultural life was the development of truck farming and fruit growing.

Because of railroad expansion and the invention of the refrigerator car, fresh vegetables and fruit could be shipped to northern urban centers. The long growing season in the South and an abundance of cheap labor also stimulated truck farming. As early as 1900 thousands of refrigerator cars were rolling northward, hauling welcome supplies of green vegetables, watermelons, strawberries, oranges, apples, and peaches to northern cities.

Industrial development

An even more remarkable development in the New South was the growth of industry. In industry, as in agriculture, the South responded to forces that were transforming economic life in other regions of the United States and, for that matter, in most of Europe.

Southern industrial development actually started before the outbreak of the Civil War. By 1860 about 10 percent of the manufactured wealth of the United States came from southern textile mills, iron works, lumber projects, and sugar refineries. But the war and reconstruction ruined many southern industries, and for nearly 20 years the South made little industrial progress.

By the late 1870's, however, more and more southerners were concluding that southern progress depended upon industrialization. The development of industry would enable the South to take fuller advantage of its rich natural resources.

Money to build factories, mines, steel mills, railroads, and other industries came in part from northern investors, in still larger part from the South itself. Profits from expanding agriculture were poured into new industrial ventures. In community after community the people themselves gathered in mass assemblies to plan a factory, often a textile mill, and to raise the necessary capital. By 1900 more than 400 cotton textile mills had been built. Throughout the South farming villages were transformed into mill towns within a few short years. The labor force for the new factories was supplied in large part by poorer white people. Black laborers were almost entirely excluded from the new industrial development.

Many early mills were controlled by a single family or a small group of persons, who owned the houses in which the workers lived, the stores where they bought their goods, and the other town buildings. The men and women who worked in these mills depended on the owners for their jobs and had to spend their wages to rent company-owned dwellings and to buy provisions from company-owned stores. As a result, the labor organizations that were developing rapidly

Industrial development in the New South helped to spur the growth of large cities. This picture shows Atlanta, Georgia, in the 1880's, already a busy manufacturing and commercial city.

in the North during these years made little headway in the South.

The growth of southern industry depended not only on local and northern capital, natural resources, and a cheap labor supply, but also on improvements and extensions of southern railroads. The war left southern railroads in terrible condition. But old railroads were quickly rebuilt, and new lines constructed. By 1890 the southern railroad system was twice as large as in 1860.

Industrial development in the New South led to the growth of cities. Between 1870 and 1890 Durham, North Carolina, developed from a small village to a flourishing tobacco center. Richmond, Virginia, and Nashville, Tennessee, became leading urban centers. The population of Atlanta, Georgia, increased from 37,000 to 65,000 between 1880 and 1890. Birmingham, Alabama, founded in 1871 on the site of a former cotton field, within a few years became a bustling iron and steel center, often called "the Pittsburgh of the South."

By 1900 southern manufactured products were worth four times as much as in 1860. With its growing industrial cities, its factories and mills and mines, and its developing transportation system, the South was beginning to be more and more like other regions of the United States. But with all its industrial progress, the New South had a long way to go to catch up industrially with other sections of the country.

Educational developments

During the closing years of the 1800's, able and far-seeing leaders urged southerners to improve their educational system and thus make better use of their human resources. Southern education did improve, but every forward step was taken in the face of tremendous handicaps. Southern leaders had to deal with widespread poverty despite improving economic conditions and traditional reluctance to support public education by adequate taxation. They also had to pay the high cost of maintaining separate schools for white and black children.

Among the outstanding contributions to southern education were the gifts of northern philanthropists. Especially noteworthy were the gifts of George Peabody and John F. Slater, both northern millionaires. The Peabody Fund was created in 1867, the Slater Fund in 1882. Money from these funds helped to provide educational opportunities for white and black southerners alike in the post-war years.

The money provided by private sources, however, was only a fraction of what was needed. Most of the burden of rebuilding schools and opening up educational opportunities for white as well as black southerners had to be shouldered by the southern states. Slowly, as the economic situation improved, the South was able to provide more opportunities.

The "Solid South"

Most southerners belonged to the Democratic Party. There were southern Republicans, to be sure, but they were completely outnumbered in local, state, and national elections. For example, when the Presidential elections rolled around, the former Confederate states cast all their electoral votes for the Democratic candidates. Thus people began to refer to the southern states as the "Solid South."

The "Solid South" was born during reconstruction days when Radical Republican governments composed largely of carpetbaggers, scalawags, and freed slaves controlled the southern states. In their determination to rid themselves of Radical Republican rule, white southerners poured into the Democratic Party. After 1877, when the last federal troops were withdrawn from the South, most white southerners continued to support the Democratic Party.

SECTION SURVEY

IDENTIFY: New South, one-crop agriculture, "the Pittsburgh of the South," philanthropist, "Solid South."

1. (a) Define tenant farming and sharecropping. (b) Explain why these types of farming were widespread in the postwar South.
2. Show how science and technology contributed to agricultural progress in the postwar South.
3. (a) Give three reasons for southern industrial development. (b) What were some results of industrial growth?
4. (a) Summarize the factors which influenced the development of education in the South. (b) What handicaps hindered this development?

6 The struggle of black southerners to find their place in the New South

Black southerners had hoped to share in the agricultural, industrial, and educational progress of the New South, and in the nation's ideals of freedom and equality. Their hopes did not materialize for several reasons. First, the federal government suspended its program for helping black southerners make the transition from slavery to freedom. Second and equally important, white Americans in both the North and the South continued to think of black Americans not as equals but as inferiors. And third, since so many Negroes lived in the South, white southerners feared that the white southern way of life would be threatened if black southerners were not firmly "kept in their place."

Disenfranchisement of the Negro

For more than a decade after white southern Democrats regained control of southern governments in 1877, many Negroes continued to vote, and a few even held public office.

Early in the 1890's, however, the Populist Party, a radical third-party movement, began to threaten the power of both the Democratic and Republican parties (Chapter 2). In the South, Populist organizers had their greatest success among poor and disadvantaged white people, but they also worked hard to win the support of black voters. Southern Democrats, alarmed by this development, tried to prevent Negroes from voting.

Beginning with Mississippi in 1890, the southern states began to adopt laws and to frame new constitutions that excluded most black southerners from the polls, or voting places, on grounds other than "race, color, or previous condition of servitude." By the early 1900's the guarantees of civil rights in the Fourteenth and Fifteenth Amendments had become largely ineffec-

tive in the South. In many southern areas few Negroes voted and fewer still held public office, even in minor positions.

A number of states adopted a *poll tax*—a fixed tax imposed on every person as a requirement for voting, and a *literacy test*—an examination to determine whether a person can read or write or has a certain amount of education. Since

Black Americans took part in municipal elections held in Washington, D.C., in 1867. This sketch of the scene appeared in a contemporary magazine report on the long lines of black citizens who began to assemble early on election day.

many black southerners had little money and little if any education, these laws kept large numbers from voting.

But the poll tax and the literacy test also deprived many "poor whites" of the vote. To remedy this situation, several states, starting with Louisiana in 1898, added a "grandfather clause" to their constitutions. This clause declared that, even if a man could not pay the poll tax or pass the educational test, he could still vote if he had been eligible to do so on January 1, 1867, or if he were the son or the grandson of a man who had been eligible to vote on January 1, 1867. Under this clause many "poor whites" were allowed to vote, but Negroes, whose fathers or grandfathers had not had the suffrage at that time, could not.

The "grandfather clause" was declared unconstitutional by the Supreme Court in 1915. But while it was in force many black southerners were effectively deprived of their right to vote.

Segregation of the races

Meanwhile, a pattern of segregation, or separation, of white and black southerners was taking shape.

Except in a few instances, the Radical Republicans had not tried to bring white and black children together in southern public schools. But black and white southerners used the same transportation facilities and other public services. The Civil Rights Act of 1875 had declared that "all persons within the jurisdiction of the United States shall be entitled to the full and equal enjoyment of the accommodations, advantages, facilities, and privileges of inns, public conveyances on land or water, theaters and other places of public amusement; subject only to the conditions and limitations established by law and applicable alike to citizens of every race and color, regardless of any previous condition of servitude."

Even after white southern rule was restored in 1877, southerners of both races often used the same transportation facilities and other public services. But in 1883 the Supreme Court ruled against the Civil Rights Act of 1875 on the ground that the Fourteenth Amendment forbade states, not individuals or corporations (such as railroads), from discriminating against black citizens. However, black and white southerners in many places continued to use the same public accommodations.

In 1881 Tennessee passed the first of the so-called "Jim Crow" laws. Under this law, white southerners and black southerners were required to ride in separate railway cars. Other states followed Tennessee's example. By the 1890's all southern states required such separation, not only in schools but in streetcars, railroads, and railroad stations. Within a few years this pattern of separation, or segregation, spread to parks, playgrounds, and other public facilities.

Then, in 1896, the Supreme Court added legal support to segregation. In the case of *Plessy v. Ferguson,* the Court ruled that it was not a violation of the Fourteenth Amendment to provide "separate but equal" facilities for black Americans. This 1896 ruling by the Supreme Court was a serious blow to the efforts of black Americans to improve their lives.

Black southerners' reactions

Confronted by segregation and denied their political and civil rights, some black Americans became disheartened and migrated to other nearby states, such as Oklahoma and Kansas, or moved to the growing northern cities. Most, however, stayed in the South, and worked to develop their own black communities. Black southerners strengthened their own churches, lodges, and mutual aid societies, developed their own businesses, and, against handicaps, tried to secure an education. Their efforts began to produce results. In 1865 only about 5 percent of all Negro adults could read and write; by 1900 more than 50 percent had achieved these basic skills.

Southern Negro leaders also protested the growing pattern of segregation and discrimination, and the denial of civil rights guaranteed by the Fourteenth Amendment. On the lecture platform, in churches, in the press, and in conventions, they demanded recognition of their constitutional rights. In 1889 the former black abolitionist Frederick Douglass, now an old man, asked whether "American justice, American liberty, American civilization, American law, and American Christianity could be made to include and protect alike and forever all American citizens in the rights which have been guaranteed to them by the organic and fundamental laws of the land."

In Baltimore E. J. Waring, a black lawyer, urged Negroes to fight discrimination by law suits against officials and citizens guilty of violating their rights. In Memphis Ida Wells Barnett, teacher and publisher, was dismissed from teaching for denouncing the inferior, segregated schools for black children. She then launched a single-handed crusade against black lynchings—that is, the murder of black people by white mobs. Even after a mob broke into her newspaper office and threatened her life, she persisted in exposing the evils of "lynch law," including the misleading justifications for it that were commonly voiced by white opponents of black civil rights.

Booker T. Washington

Alongside such protests, the leading Negro voice from 1890 to 1915, Booker T. Washington, followed a different course. Washington, the son of a slave mother and a white father, received a vocational education at Hampton Institute in Virginia. He then founded and built Tuskegee Institute in Alabama. Washington believed that if Negroes were to survive and improve their lives, they must have job skills and training. He was convinced that vocational education, not the classical or liberal education then widely taught, was necessary to provide black people with the skills they needed to earn a living. He felt that such education would prepare black Americans for jobs in the skilled trades, small businesses, farming, and in household work.

Washington also spoke out against lynching and illegal discrimination, especially in the years just before his death in 1915. Generally, however, he remained convinced that black southerners would achieve more immediate progress by avoiding protests and emphasizing vocational training, farm and home ownership, and the development of small businesses.

W. E. B. Du Bois

Booker T. Washington's views met a strong challenge from a much younger Negro, W. E. B. Du Bois. Born and reared in western Massachusetts, Du Bois studied in German universities and earned his Ph.D. at Harvard. At first he believed that if white southerners and northerners came to understand past Negro achievements and present Negro conditions and problems, their attitudes toward black Americans would change for the better. His pioneer sociological studies of Negroes in Philadelphia and in the South, which he pursued at Atlanta University, were directed toward this end.

Gradually, however, Du Bois came to believe that only vigorous and continuous protests against inequalities and injustices, and effective appeals to black pride, could change existing conditions. *The Souls of Black Folk,* a book of eloquently written essays, criticized Booker T. Washington's exclusive emphasis on vocational training. It urged broader educational opportunities, particularly for talented young Negroes. Liberal education, leading to professional careers in all fields, as well as special job training and other kinds of education, should be open to black Americans. And Du Bois urged black Americans to demand their rights to have whatever kind of education they needed to achieve full equality and opportunity in American life. With a few like-minded black leaders, Du Bois organized a meeting in 1905 at Niagara Falls which demanded an end to all unequal treatment based on race and color.

The appeals and demands of the Niagara Movement, which included criticisms of Booker T. Washington's program, aroused many Americans, white as well as black. One outcome was the formation of the National Association for the Advancement of Colored People (NAACP). The NAACP worked through the courts to end disenfranchisement and other civil injustices. In time it succeeded in winning Supreme Court decisions which declared unconstitutional the "grandfather clause" in southern state constitutions, jury trials conducted under mob pressure, and segregation by local law of housing for black people. The Urban League, likewise organized by both black and white Americans, concentrated on securing equal job opportunities for black workers and fought discrimination in urban housing.

The work of the NAACP and the Urban League brought some progress for black citizens

The Crisis, the official publication of the NAACP, was first edited by W. E. B. Du Bois. Its object was "to set forth those facts and arguments which show the danger of race prejudice."

THE CRISIS

A RECORD OF THE DARKER RACES

Volume One   NOVEMBER, 1910   Number One

Edited by W. E. BURGHARDT DU BOIS, with the co-operation of Oswald Garrison Villard, J. Max Barber, Charles Edward Russell, Kelly Miller, W. S. Braithwaite and M. D. Maclean

CONTENTS

Along the Color Line   3
Opinion   7
Editorial   10
The N. A. A. C. P.   12
Athens and Brownsville   13
   By MOORFIELD STOREY
The Burden   14
What to Read   15

PUBLISHED MONTHLY BY THE
National Association for the Advancement of Colored People
AT TWENTY VESEY STREET   NEW YORK CITY

ONE DOLLAR A YEAR   TEN CENTS A COPY

in the North and West. These national organizations were also represented in the South, but they made less progress there. Most black southerners continued to experience discrimination, segregation, and denial of equal rights.

SECTION SURVEY

IDENTIFY: "Jim Crow" laws, *Plessy v. Ferguson*, "separate but equal," NAACP, Urban League; Booker T. Washington, W. E. B. Du Bois.

1. Why did black southerners not share in the progress of the New South?
2. Show how each of the following affected the right of black southerners to vote: (a) poll tax, (b) literacy test, (c) "grandfather clause."
3. (a) Why did southern states pass laws barring Negroes from voting? (b) How did this affect black southerners?
4. (a) How was a new pattern of segregation established in the South? (b) How did the Supreme Court contribute to the separation of the races?
5. How did black Americans react to discrimination?

CHAPTER SURVEY

INQUIRING INTO HISTORY

1. To what extent do you think revenge was the motivating factor in the behavior of the Radical Republicans in Congress?
2. (a) Compare the Presidential plan of reconstruction with the Congressional plan, as to purpose and provisions. (b) Why do you think the Presidential plan was more lenient than the Congressional plan?
3. The experience of losing the war and of Congressional reconstruction was so bitter and humiliating that white southerners found it hard to forgive and even harder to forget. Discuss.
4. What, in your opinion, is the historical significance of the impeachment of President Andrew Johnson?
5. Compare the ideas of Booker T. Washington and W. E. B. Du Bois. Why did each regard education as the key to survival and progress by black Americans?
6. If Lincoln had lived to carry out his plan of reconstruction, do you think he would have encountered the same difficulties that President Andrew Johnson did? Explain.
7. How did the Supreme Court decision in the case of *Plessy v. Ferguson* reflect the spirit of the times?
8. (a) How did northern attitudes serve to encourage the South's segregation practices? (b) How did the attitudes of the federal government encourage segregation and discrimination in the nation?
9. How were the conflicts of the reconstruction period rooted in the issue of slavery?
10. If you had been a northerner in Congress during the period 1850–70, what would have been your position on the South and reconstruction?
11. Did the black codes and "Jim Crow'" laws reestablish slavery in the South? Explain.

RELATING PAST TO PRESENT

1. Black Americans have striven to achieve equality, not dominance. Comment.
2. Both the North and the South missed the opportunity after 1865 to bring the former slaves into the mainstream of American life. In the 1970's, there is new hope that black Americans, as well as other minority groups, will for the first time participate fully in the life of the nation. Do you think this hope is well founded? If the opportunity of the 1970's is missed, do you think there will be another opportunity in the future? Explain your answers.
3. Compare the federal government's attitude toward minorities during reconstruction and today.
4. During reconstruction only the South was prejudiced against black Americans; today, there is little difference in the various sections of the nation regarding racial prejudice. Do you agree or disagree with this statement? Explain.

DEVELOPING SOCIAL SCIENCE SKILLS

1. If Lincoln had lived, do you think he could have avoided the mistakes that were made during the reconstruction period? Why? What do you think would have been a wise reconstruction policy? Why?
2. Make a time line for the years 1865 to 1877, for classroom display, showing the major events in the restoration of the South to the Union.
3. Were any of the problems that caused the Civil War solved by the war? Which ones and how? Were any of these problems left unsolved by the war? Were any new problems created as a result of the war? How effective is war in solving a nation's problems?

CHAPTER 2

SEVERE TRIALS

FOR DEMOCRACY

1865-1897

Courtesy of the Chicago Historical Society.

Change is often disturbing, and in no period of American history was change more disturbing than in the generation following the Civil War. You have read how drastic changes came to the South during reconstruction and how white and black southerners struggled to adjust to these changes. Equally striking changes were occurring in the Northeast, the Middle West, and the West during these years.

The major cause of these changes was the rapid growth of industry after the war. New power-driven machinery was invented and installed in large factories, giant corporations were organized, and new methods of mass production were adopted. These exciting developments made many new products and services available to more and more Americans and helped to raise their standard of living.

But there were dark shadows in this bright picture. As industries grew, cities grew and became overcrowded, creating new problems—problems of sanitation, disease, fire, and transportation.

In order to see this dramatic and disturbing period of American history clearly, it is necessary to take several looks at it. In later chapters you will see how the growth of "big business" created complex problems, not only for many business people, large and small, but also for farmers, miners, and wage earners. In this chapter you will see how graft and corruption plagued American political life during the postwar years, and how repeated efforts were made to root out this dishonesty in government.

THE CHAPTER IN OUTLINE

1. Similarities and differences between the two major political parties.

2. The spread of graft and corruption in the postwar years.

3. Initial moves toward restoring honesty to government.

4. Increasing political reforms in government despite setbacks.

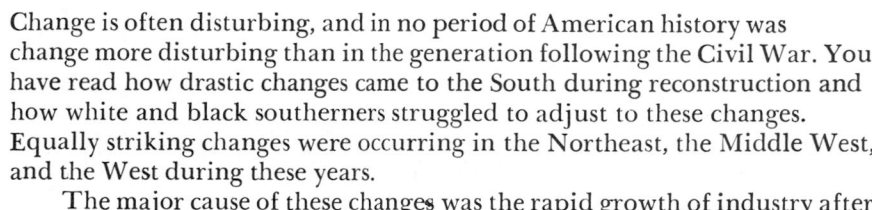

| 1450 | 1750 | 1800 | 1850 | 1900 | 1950 | 1980's |

1 Similarities and differences between the two major political parties

Political behavior is an important and complicated aspect of every modern society. In the United States, for example, the political behavior of American voters often stems from habit and tradition. Americans sometimes cross party lines to cast their vote, but more often they vote for candidates of one party—the party they have "always" supported.

The political behavior of American leaders is also complex—as complex, in fact, as human nature itself. Why do people seek political office? Some do so out of a genuine desire to make a contribution to American life. Some are motivated by the competitive spirit, the satisfaction of winning out over others. Some run to win prestige and power, which can be used either to enrich the lives of all Americans or to enrich only the lives of the officeholders.

In the years from 1865 to 1897, the character and structure of the Democratic and Republican parties reflected these and other characteristics of American political behavior. The make-up of the political parties, in turn, explains a good deal about political leadership and election contests during these years. The problems and functions of the political parties at this time were also related to the political corruption that shocked many Americans and led to a demand for reform.

Similarities between the parties

The Republican and Democratic parties in the years between 1865 and 1897 shared many common features. Each party counted on the votes of thousands of men whose fathers and even grandfathers had preferred that party, and who voted for it more or less from habit.

In terms of votes cast in national elections, the parties were fairly evenly matched. This meant that in spite of—or perhaps because of—a good deal of public indifference to politics, competition between the two parties was sharp. Eagerness to win when the race was close led each party to criticize the other with slogans and name-calling. Sometimes these slogans and names appealed to the American sense of humor, but often they also were unfair and emotionally charged.

Each party was made up of members from many different areas of the country. Thus the members often had conflicting regional and economic interests. In order to win elections, each party had to play down these conflicts. The result was that neither party was able or wanted to face squarely some of the most serious issues of the time.

In each party, factional rivalries centered around the rival ambitions of the leaders, or "bosses," of the several organizations, or "machines," making up the party. These personal rivalries often led to the selection of undistinguished "compromise" candidates.

The Republican Party

The Republican Party after the Civil War continued to enjoy the support of a great many northern and western farmers, who had been important pillars of Republican strength in the party's early years. These farmers voted, almost out of habit, for the Republican Party because they believed that the Republicans, by supporting the free homestead policy, had opened the frontier areas of the West to settlement.

But the Republicans also increasingly attracted industrialists. The influence of manufacturers and other business people became more and more important as the Republicans encouraged the growth of business and industry and refrained from trying to control business enterprises. In an age of industrial growth and the rise of huge new fortunes in business, many Americans seemed to approve such success no matter how it had been achieved. Operators of railroads, mines, and other businesses often did not hesitate to ask politicians for favors or to return such favors with cash payments or other rewards. Many of these operators sought favors from both political parties. As it happened, the Republicans dominated the federal government for much of the period between 1865 and 1897.

Since victory at the polls depended on the voting support of both business people and farmers, and since farmers and business people often differed on such economic issues as currency, banking, and tariffs, Republican leaders tried to keep the support of both groups by not taking a firm stand on important issues when party platforms were written.

In addition to support from farmers and business people, the Republicans could count upon other voters. Most of the 1 million northern Civil War veterans, appreciative of the Republican Party's role in the war and of its liberal pension policy for "old soldiers," voted Republican. By identifying the Democratic Party as the party of secession and defeatism in the war, the Republicans successfully used the political tactic that came to be known as "waving the bloody shirt"—appealing to American patriotism. Finally, as the party of emancipation, the Republicans could count on the votes of most black

Americans when and wherever they could vote.

The Democratic Party

The Democratic Party was also made up of various groups with conflicting interests. After 1877 the party could count on the support of the "Solid South," which was still primarily agricultural. Democratic leadership, however, passed to people engaged in banking and importing interests in northern cities, and to the lawyers who served them.

While bankers and importers favored low tariffs and "sound money," southern and western farmers generally wanted "easy credit," a plentiful money supply, and decentralized banking. Thus the Democrats tried to avoid taking clear-cut positions on these important issues. Moreover, while a great many Democrats favored low tariffs, some did not. For example, Pennsylvania Democrats who developed the steel industry, and Louisiana sugar planters and processors, both wanted tariffs to protect their special interests against competing foreign producers. In general, however, the Democratic Party did not favor government measures to promote industrial growth. It clung to the traditional doctrine of *laissez faire,* meaning that the federal government should not interfere with business and industry.

A chief source of Democratic strength was the immigrant vote in the northern cities. The newcomers were helped in various ways by the Democratic Party organizations—the so-called political "machines"—in the cities, such as Tammany Hall in New York City. At a time when city governments provided little or no help to needy people, the "machines" performed a necessary function. They did so, of course, for political reasons—they wanted the immigrants' votes at election time.

The Democratic city "machines," like those in the Republican Party, made profitable deals with contractors eager to get bids for public buildings and concessions for street lighting, streetcars, sewers, and other public services. Thus, when Democrats pointed to the Republican corruption in the nation's government during these years, they ignored their own record in the northern cities.

Third parties

Many honest people in both parties opposed political corruption. However, these reformers often were unable to make much progress inside their own parties. Moreover, many Americans were dissatisfied because the two major parties refused to take clear-cut stands on many serious issues. Thus the way was opened to third-party movements.

The Boss

In the Republican Party and in the Democratic Party, factional rivalries centered around the ambitions of the "bosses" of the several "machines" making up each party. These bosses used their influence to deliver large blocs of votes to candidates they favored.

Third-party movements also were confronted by many problems. They faced the opposition of well-financed, powerful "machines" in the two major parties. Third parties also had to face the reluctance of many Americans to risk "throwing away" their votes on a new party which had slight chance of winning elections. As you will read, however, third parties sometimes caused the two older parties to take a stand on important election issues or even to change their policies.

SECTION SURVEY

IDENTIFY: "waving the bloody shirt," *laissez faire*, party "machines."

1. Make a chart listing the similarities between the two major political parties in the period from 1865 to 1897.
3. (a) Who supported the Republican Party? Why? (b) Who supported the Democratic Party? Why?
3. What is meant by the statement that government should not interfere with business and industry?
4. Describe how the character and structure of the Democratic and Republican parties from 1865 to 1897 reflected certain characteristics of American political behavior.

2 The spread of graft and corruption in the postwar years

It was Ulysses S. Grant's unhappy destiny to occupy the White House during the period in which graft and corruption infected every level of American government—federal, state, and local.

President Grant

In 1868, when he won the election for the Presidency on the Republican ticket, Grant enjoyed the respect of millions of Americans. His well-earned reputation rested upon his success as commander of the Union armies during the latter years of the Civil War. Had he never served as President, Grant would have lived and died a popular hero. Unfortunately, his lack of political experience was a serious handicap, and his eight-year administration proved to be a dark page in the history of the Presidency.

Grant himself was honest and upright. His great weakness—which could have been a virtue if tempered by reason—was his total loyalty to friends. Being honest himself, he could not believe that his associates were any less honest, and he stubbornly refused to admit that some of his "friends" used him to advance their own fortunes.

The Crédit Mobilier scandal

Even before Grant took office, the federal government was involved in an unsavory scandal.

In 1862 Congress had granted a charter to the Union Pacific Railroad and to the Central Pacific Railroad to build a transcontinental railroad. The Union Pacific was to build westward from the Missouri River at Omaha, in Nebraska Territory. Meanwhile, the Central Pacific was to build eastward from Sacramento, California.

Building such a railroad was extremely expensive and risky. But since the completed railroad would be important to national development, the federal government gave various subsidies to the railroad companies, as you will read later.

The small group of shareholders who controlled the Union Pacific Railroad saw a chance to make enormous profits. They organized a construction company called the Crédit Mobilier (kray·DEE moh·bee·LYAY), to which they awarded construction contracts. These contracts were paid for by other stockholders of the Union Pacific Railroad at several times what the job actually cost. As a result, much of the money invested by stockholders in the Union Pacific, as well as a large share of the government subsidies, enriched a small group of greedy speculators.

When Congressional committees finally investigated, they discovered that some members of Congress had owned stock in the Crédit Mobilier company. The company owners had given these members stock, or had sold it to them at half price, in an effort to bribe them and to block investigations.

The "salary grab"

The Crédit Mobilier scandal was occupying the attention of Congress when the Senators and Representatives voted themselves a 50 percent increase in salaries—from $5,000 to $7,500 per year. Congress pushed the salary bill through on the last day of the session, March 3, 1872. To make matters worse, it made the measure retroactive for two years, meaning that each member of Congress would receive two years' back pay, or $5,000, besides this future salary increase. The public was so outraged at this "salary grab" that Congress hastily repealed the act at the opening of its next session. Although the "salary grab" was perfectly legal, it does indicate the "something for nothing" philosophy of many public figures—Democrats and Republicans alike—during these unsettled years.

The Treasury Department scandal

Public resentment had hardly died when another scandal made newspaper headlines. Secretary of the Treasury William A. Richardson signed a contract with a private citizen, John D. Sanborn, giving Sanborn authority to collect some overdue federal taxes, with the right to keep half of all he could collect. By various devious methods, Sanborn collected $427,000, keeping about $213,000 for himself.

When called to explain the affair, Sanborn swore that he had kept only a small part of the "commission," having been forced to give $156,000 to his "assistants"! These "assistants" were politicians who had used their influence to swing the tax-collection contract to Sanborn. But the contract was legal, and the "commission" was paid in full. A new law prevented the situation from recurring, however, and Richardson resigned.

The "Whisky Ring"

The new Secretary of the Treasury, Benjamin H. Bristow, was an honest official who promptly discovered other corrupt practices in his department. Investigation disclosed that taxes were not being collected on about seven eighths of the liquor distilled in the United States. Further investigation revealed that high public officials were guilty of blackmail and fraud.

According to the tax law, a distiller who

Thomas Nast (1840–1902), one of the greatest political cartoonists of all time, came to the United States from Germany when he was only 6 years old. By the time he was 20, Nast had demonstrated his amazing skill. In the early 1870's, while attacking the Tammany Hall political machine, he was offered $500,000 to drop his work and move abroad.

It was during his anti-Tammany campaign that Nast drew one of his most famous cartoons, "The Tammany Tiger Loose." In this cartoon he showed a ravenous beast in an arena surrounded by the bodies of its victims. The beast was about to devour the "Republic" pictured as a helpless young woman. The corrupt political boss, "Emperor Tweed," was seated in the stands with his supporters. Under the cartoon Nast asked readers, "What are you going to do about it?" Aroused New York citizens took such vigorous action that Tweed and his associates fled the country. But they could not escape Nast. Several years later, in Spain, Boss Tweed was identified by a person who recognized him from one of Nast's drawings, and Tweed was returned to New York and sent to prison.

The "Tammany Tiger" is only one of many famous symbols created by Thomas Nast. He invented the Republican elephant and the Democratic donkey. But his most popular creation was the lovable image of Santa Claus. It was Thomas Nast who first portrayed Santa Claus as the merry old gift bringer with the long white beard.

AMERICA'S MASTER CARTOONIST

---

failed to pay revenue taxes on distilled liquor would be compelled, if caught, to pay a double tax. Any informer who revealed to the government that a company had failed to pay its taxes received 10 percent of the tax penalty as a reward. Informers soon saw, however, that they could collect more by blackmailing the tax-evading company than by reporting the evasion.

The Secretary of the Treasury discovered that a ring, or group, of whisky distillers and blackmailers had been defrauding the federal government of a million dollars annually. The Supervisor of Internal Revenue in St. Louis, who was involved in the conspiracy, went to prison for a year, but not before the trail of corruption was traced even to President Grant's private secretary.

Other scandals

Meanwhile, it was discovered that Secretary of War William W. Belknap had accepted $24,500 in bribes from a trader at Fort Sill in what is now Oklahoma. Belknap had decided to give the profitable and exclusive trading concession to a New York friend. But the trader who had the contract was making a huge profit from the Indians around Fort Sill. Therefore, he agreed to pay Belknap and his friend each $6,000 a year if he could keep this concession.

When evidence of this bribery was presented, the House of Representatives voted unanimously to impeach Secretary Belknap, who then hastily resigned. Despite all the evidence, the Senate's impeachment trial failed to convict the ex-Secretary of War. The Senators who voted "not guilty" claimed that because Belknap had resigned he was no longer subject to trial by the Senate.

There were still other evidences of graft in the federal government. The Secretary of the Navy "sold" business to builders and suppliers of ships. The Secretary of the Interior was involved with land speculators. President Grant himself had no part in these illegal activities, but many people felt that he was at fault for allowing his "friends" to hide behind his good name.

Corruption in state governments

Corruption was as bad, if not worse, in the state governments. In 1868 when the Erie Railroad, which was controlled by Daniel Drew, James ("Jim") Fisk, Jr., and Jay Gould, wanted to sell $10 million worth of additional stock, Gould, to smooth the way, went to the New York state capital at Albany with a trunk full of money to bribe lawmakers to legalize the stock sale. Evidence suggested that the governor of New York sold his influence for $20,000 and that state senators got $15,000.

The Tweed Ring

Perhaps worst of all was the corruption in municipal, or city, government. William M. Tweed, an uneducated chairmaker, rose in 15 years to be a multimillionaire "dictator" of New

York City in the 1860's and 1870's. Working with Tammany Hall—the Democratic political "machine" of the city—"Boss" Tweed completely controlled the city government.

Tweed gained control very simply. He or some of his followers met immigrant families when they landed, fed them, found them jobs and housing, left them baskets of food at Thanksgiving and Christmas. After they secured the right to vote, the newcomers returned Tweed's "friendship" by voting for candidates he favored. Moreover, when election outcomes seemed doubtful, the ballot boxes were "stuffed" with votes in favor of Tweed's candidates. That is, Tammany supporters voted several times, using different names and addresses each time.

How did Tweed use his power? He gave city jobs to many of his friends. He demanded "kickbacks" from people who wanted city jobs. He demanded bribes from companies that wanted to provide city services. A courthouse, started in 1868, was to cost $250,000; three years later, still uncompleted, it had cost $8 million. In three years Tweed and his crooked "ring" stole from New York City an estimated $20 million. It is further estimated that between 1868 and 1871 Boss Tweed's "ring" and his business friends cost the city close to $100 million.

Reasons for corruption

Why was public morality at such a low level in the years following the Civil War?

The war itself was partly responsible. In the crisis of wartime the all-important consideration is to get things done quickly. Cost is secondary to national survival, and money flows freely into war industries. During the war years, with business booming, unscrupulous business interests and legislators had a rare opportunity to engage in dishonest practices. These practices were continued in the postwar years.

A related and equally significant explanation of the postwar graft was the rapid growth of large-scale industry, about which you will read in Chapter 4. In earlier times, when factories and businesses were small, their owners were well known. If their practices were dishonest, they were apt to lose their neighbors' good will. But the new large corporations were impersonal. The people who controlled them were hardly known even by many of their own stockholders. Within the corporations, it was easier for dishonest individuals to get away with questionable practices.

SECTION SURVEY

IDENTIFY: Crédit Mobilier, "salary grab," Whisky Ring, Tammany Hall, Tweed Ring; William Belknap, Jay Gould, "Boss" Tweed.

1. Ulysses S. Grant's administration was a dark page in the history of the American Presidency. Describe four scandals that support this conclusion.
2. Although Grant was not personally involved in these scandals, people blamed him for them. Why?
3. Show that graft and corruption also existed on the state and local levels.
4. Why was public morality at such a low level in the postwar years?

3 Initial moves toward restoring honesty to government

Newspapers in the late 1860's and the early 1870's were filled with stories and cartoons attacking government graft among federal, state, and local officials. The most famous American cartoonist was Thomas Nast of New York, whose powerful cartoons in *Harper's Weekly* helped to reveal to the public the abuses of "Boss" Tweed and his friends.

These revelations of corruption stimulated a widespread demand for reform. No reform movement aroused greater interest than the proposal to appoint persons to government jobs on the basis of merit. Under the "spoils system," which Andrew Jackson had helped to extend, government jobs were given to political favorites. Under the proposed "merit system," those who received the highest grades in competitive examinations would get the jobs, whether they were Republi-cans or Democrats. All these public jobs in the federal, state, and local governments would be called *civil service* jobs.

Growth of the reform movement

A half-hearted attempt by Congress and President Grant to reform the civil service failed. In 1875 the head of the recently appointed civil service commission resigned in disgust, and the commission was discontinued.

Meanwhile, in 1872, a varied group of reform-minded Republicans, who called themselves the Liberal Republican Party, nominated Horace Greeley, the editor of the *New York Tribune,* as their Presidential candidate to run against the regular Republican candidate, President Grant. The Democrats, meeting two months later, also nominated Greeley, hoping by this means to benefit from the split in the Republican Party.

The Liberal Republican platform included a pledge to fight corruption in public life and a specific plank, or section, urging civil service reform. But Grant was re-elected President by an overwhelming electoral vote—286 to 66.

The defeat at the polls in 1872 was a disheartening blow to the reformers. Within a year, however, they began to gather strength. For one thing, new public scandals drove more Americans into the reform movement. Although the two major parties were evenly matched at the national level, growing dissatisfaction with Grant's Republican administration enabled the Democrats to win control of the House of Representatives in the Congressional elections of 1874.

The election of 1876

The Democrats, heartened by the growing demand for reform, approached the 1876 elections confident of victory. They chose as their Presidential candidate Governor Samuel J. Tilden of New York. Governor Tilden had won national attention by helping to break up the Tweed Ring in New York. The Democratic platform demanded civil service reform and an end to graft in public life.

The Republicans, who were "running scared," nominated a man well known as a reformer, Governor Rutherford B. Hayes of Ohio. Hayes promised to work for civil service reform in the federal government. He also promised to end the troubled and troublesome period of reconstruction.

Both Tilden and Hayes were wealthy men. Both were closely associated with industrialists and business groups. Tilden's one big asset was the fact that he was running against a party that for eight years had been identified with scandal after scandal.

Disputed election returns

The election gave Tilden 250,000 more popular votes than Hayes received. The first count of the electoral votes, based on early returns, also gave Tilden an advantage over Hayes—184 to 165. As a result, most newspapers at first said Tilden had won.

But the papers had jumped to the wrong conclusion. Tilden with his 184 electoral votes was one short of the necessary majority. Ordinarily, when no Presidential candidate has a clear majority of the electoral vote, the House of Representatives chooses the President. But this was

In 1876 Americans celebrated the 100th anniversary of their nation. Here, a crowd is gathered to enjoy patriotic speeches and a fireworks display.

no ordinary election. Four states—South Carolina, Florida, Louisiana, and Oregon—had each sent in *two* different sets of returns. In all, 20 electoral votes from these four states were claimed by both the Republicans and the Democrats. Tilden needed only one of these disputed votes to win. Hayes, however, needed all 20.

The single disputed vote from Oregon was quickly settled in favor of Hayes. But the remaining 19 votes from the three southern states aroused a storm of controversy. The Republicans claimed all three states for Hayes, but the Democrats insisted that, since these states were still under carpetbag rule, the will of the majority had not been expressed. For a time the controversy threatened to plunge the nation into violence.

Settling the dispute

Unfortunately, the Constitution provided no explicit procedures for solving this complicated situation. According to the Constitution, the votes had to be counted, but by whom? If the Republican-controlled Senate counted the votes, the Senators would throw out the Democratic returns and give the election to Hayes. If the Democratic-controlled House counted the votes, the Representatives would throw out the Republican returns and give the election to Tilden.

In order to break the apparently hopeless deadlock, Congress created an Electoral Commission of 15 members—five Senators, five Representatives, and five Supreme Court Justices. By previous arrangement the Senate chose three Republicans and two Democrats; the House, two Republicans and three Democrats. Four Justices —two Republicans and two Democrats—were to name a fifth member of the commission—an independent voter without ties to either party.

It was generally understood that the one "independent" member of the Electoral Commission would be Justice David Davis. At the last minute, however, Davis resigned from the Supreme Court because of his election to the Senate, and his place on the Electoral Commission went to a Republican. It was not surprising, therefore, that when the disputed votes were counted, the returns from South Carolina, Florida, and Louisiana went to the Republicans by a "straight" party vote of eight Republicans as opposed to the seven Democrats on the commission.

Thus it was that Hayes, who had received a minority of the popular votes, entered the White House as President on March 5, 1877. The controversial election of 1876–77, however, had a larger significance. It represented a victory for compromise and for the process of orderly government. It showed that violence and bloodshed could be avoided even in an extremely close and hotly contested election.

Difficulties for Hayes

President Hayes had four difficult years in the White House. Throughout his administration the Democrats controlled the House, and for two years, from 1879 to 1881, the Senate as well. Although the Democrats did not try to upset the decision of the Electoral Commission, they called Hayes "His Fraudulency" and "Old Eight to Seven" to remind him that they questioned his right to the Presidency.

Hayes also faced opposition from his own party. The election of 1876 split the Republicans into two groups—the "Stalwarts" and the "Half-Breeds." The Stalwarts, led by Senator ("Boss") Roscoe Conkling of New York, included most of the Radical Republicans who had created and for a time enforced the program of southern reconstruction. The Stalwarts, sometimes called "Old Guard" Republicans, were against reform and reformers, including the President himself, whom they called "Granny Hayes." The "Half-Breeds," led by James G. Blaine of Maine and John Sherman of Ohio, agreed with Hayes that at least some reform was needed.

To fulfill his promise of ending reconstruction, President Hayes named a former Confederate leader to his cabinet and withdrew what were left of federal occupation troops from the South. As the remaining reconstruction, or "carpetbag," governments lost power, southern Democrats were free to manage state affairs in their own way. Southern Democrats elected to Congress from the "Solid South," in alliance with northern Democrats, now broke the power of the Radical Republicans who had controlled Congress during the years of reconstruction.

Hayes' battle for reform

The opposition he faced did not prevent President Hayes from fighting for reform legislation. He was the first President to take serious steps to reform the civil service. He refused to follow the practice of many earlier Presidents of discharging thousands of officeholders and replacing them with political favorites. He also insisted that all persons recommended by members of Congress for jobs should be carefully investigated.

One of Hayes' cabinet members, Carl Schurz, a German-born Republican, introduced the merit system into the Department of the Interior. And the President himself courageously removed a prominent Republican leader, Chester A. Arthur, from his job as Collector of Customs in New York because of his undue political activity.

Many "Old Guard," or Stalwart, Republicans were furious, but Hayes stood his ground.

The election of 1880

Well before the nominating conventions for the 1880 elections, President Hayes announced that he would not run for re-election. The Stalwart wing of the Republican Party, fed up with talk of reform and eager to return to the "good old days," tried to win the nomination for former President Ulysses S. Grant. But the Half-Breed wing of the party managed to block this attempt. Finally, the Republican convention nominated a war veteran, General James A. Garfield of Ohio. To win the support of the disappointed Stalwarts, the convention nominated for Vice-President Chester A. Arthur, a leading Stalwart.

The Democrats also pinned their hopes for the Presidency on a war veteran, General Winfield S. Hancock of Pennsylvania.

Divided into groups with conflicting interests and eager to win elections, neither the Democrats nor the Republicans faced up to basic problems of the new industrial age—labor legislation, regulation of railroads and other "big business," the money issue, and an income tax. Thus it was a third party, the Greenback-Labor Party, as you will read, that squarely faced the new and controversial issues of the time.

The election of 1880 was a close one. Garfield won with an electoral vote of 214 to Hancock's 155. But the popular vote totaled 4,449,053 for the Republicans, 4,442,035 for the Democrats.

Civil service reform

On July 2, 1881, President Garfield was shot by Charles J. Guiteau, a disappointed—and mentally unbalanced—government job seeker. Garfield died in September.

The President's tragic death shocked the country into seeing the evils of the old spoils system. Chester A. Arthur, the new President, responded to the widespread demand for reform and supported the Pendleton Civil Service Act.

The Pendleton Act, which became law in 1883, set up a *bipartisan* commission, on which both parties were represented, to give competitive examinations to those seeking government jobs. The first examinations were to include only about 12 percent of federal jobs, but the President was given authority to broaden the list. The Pendleton Act also forbade the party in power to ask for campaign contributions from federal officeholders. President Arthur appointed as head of the commission a well-known champion of civil service reform and extended the list of "classified" federal positions—positions for which civil service examinations had to be taken.

Thus after years of agitation, reformers at last managed to write into law the principle that federal jobs below the policy-making level should be filled by "merit," using competitive examinations. A long step had been taken toward making government more honest and efficient.

Presidential candidates in 1884

When the election year of 1884 rolled around, Chester A. Arthur made it clear that he wanted to run for the Presidency. But his

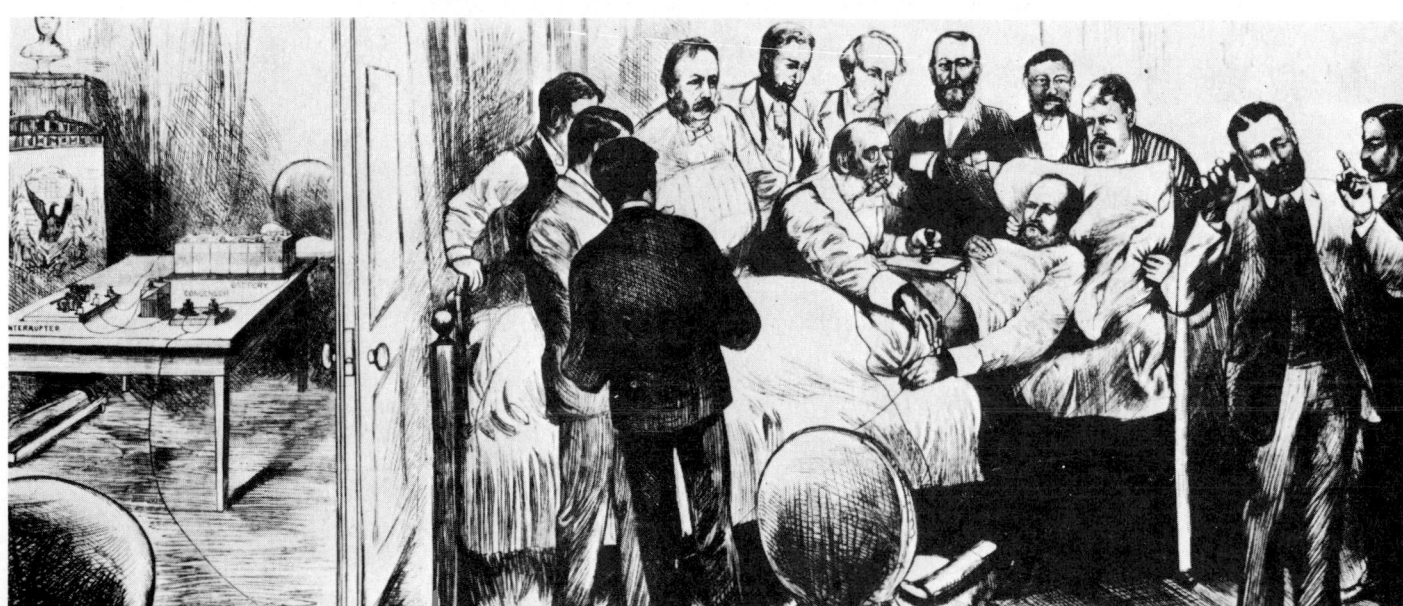

After President Garfield was shot, a device invented by Alexander Graham Bell was used to find the exact location of the assassin's bullet. But Garfield's life could not be saved.

Republican Stalwart supporters had lost faith in him because of his reform activities. Instead, the leader of the Half-Breed wing of the Republican Party, James G. Blaine, won the nomination.

Blaine was a handsome, colorful, and persuasive candidate. But during his long political career he had made many enemies, including the reformers in his own party. These enemies now accused Blaine of having used his political influence to secure favors for big business—at a generous profit for himself. Unhappy with his nomination, a large group of Republicans, nicknamed "Mugwumps," bolted the party and voted for the Democratic candidate.

The Democrats made the most of Blaine's reputation as "a tool of the special interests" by choosing a reformer for their Presidential nominee. Grover Cleveland, who had been governor of New York, was known to be thoroughly honest, courageous, independent—and stubborn when fighting for a principle. His reform activities also had provoked strong opposition within his own party.

Democratic victory

In the campaign the big issues of the day were almost forgotten as the politicians heaped abuse upon the rival candidates. Each party raked over the personal life of the opposition candidate, searching for misconduct that could be held against him.

Throughout the election campaign the two candidates, Blaine and Cleveland, ran neck and neck. And then, on the very eve of the election, at a reception given for Blaine by a group of Protestant clergy, a speaker called the Democrats the party of "Rum, Romanism, and Rebellion."

The speaker's use of the word "rum" was a deliberate attempt to "smear" the Democrats. His use of the word "rebellion" referred to the alliance between northern Democrats and the "Solid South" Democrats. Both references were bad enough, but the speaker's reference to "Romanism"—the Roman Catholic religion—was fatal. It was generally agreed that Blaine's failure to rebuke the speaker for this insult to Roman Catholic voters cost him the election. Cleveland won the Presidency, squeaking through with 219 electoral votes to Blaine's 182.

The election of 1884 was the first Presidential victory for the Democrats in 28 years. It was one sign that memories of the Civil War were beginning to fade.

SECTION SURVEY

IDENTIFY: civil service, "Old Guard" Republicans, "Mugwumps"; Samuel Tilden, Rutherford Hayes, "Boss" Conkling, James Blaine, James Garfield, Chester Arthur, Thomas Nast.

1. Contrast the "spoils system" with the "merit system" of appointment to government jobs.
2. In what ways was the election of 1876 one of the most unusual in American history?
3. What position did each of the following take concerning reform: (a) Liberal Republicans, (b) Stalwarts, (c) Half-Breeds?
4. Explain the provisions and the significance of the Pendleton Act of 1883.
5. Discuss the factors that led to Cleveland's election in 1884.

4 Increasing political reforms in government despite setbacks

When President Cleveland entered the White House in 1885, the movement for political reform entered a new phase.

Cleveland's firm stand

President Cleveland, who strongly believed that "a public office is a public trust," took a firm stand on important issues even though he knew that his action would antagonize influential members of his own party.

He supported civil service reform by doubling the number of federal offices on the classified list. He took a step toward conserving the nation's natural resources by recovering more than 80 million acres (32.4 million hectares) of public land illegally held by railroads, lumber companies, and cattle interests. He signed a bill in 1887 creating a federal Division of Forestry.

One of his most courageous acts was his attempt to block pension "grabs" by veterans of the Union army. For many years the Pension Bureau had been very generous in handing out pensions. Now and then, however, requests for pensions were based on such flimsy grounds that even the bureau rejected them. Often, when this happened, the disappointed pension seeker asked his representative in Congress to get the pension for him by pushing a special bill through Congress. President Cleveland vetoed more than 200 of these bills. He thus antagonized many ex-soldiers, who were united in the politically powerful veterans' organization the Grand Army of the Republic, known as the G.A.R.

Important laws

In addition to Cleveland's personal accomplishments, Congress adopted several important laws during the years from 1885 to 1889.

The Presidential Succession Act of 1886 provided that, if both the President and the Vice-President died or were disabled, the cabinet officers would succeed to the Presidency in the order in which their offices had been created.

The Electoral Count Act of 1887 was designed to prevent another disputed election similar to the election of 1876. The act provided that, if a state sent in more than one set of electoral returns, Congress had to accept the returns approved by the governor of the state.

In 1887 Congress, in an effort to quiet the clamor of small business people and farmers against unfair business practices by the railroads, passed the Interstate Commerce Act. For some time the act did not achieve its stated objectives, but it did start what was to become a far-reaching policy change in relations between government and business (Chapter 5).

Congress refused, however, to accept President Cleveland's strong recommendation that tariff rates be lowered. Despite the President's urging, high-tariff supporters in the Senate blocked the administration bill providing lower tariff rates.

The election of 1888

President Cleveland's reform activities, and especially his campaign for lower tariffs, antagonized political leaders in his own party. Nevertheless, in 1888 the Democrats nominated him for a second term.

Although Cleveland won nearly 100,000 more popular votes than his opponent, Benjamin Harrison, he lost the election by an electoral count of 233 to 168. The Republicans won the Presidency and control of both houses of Congress.

Cleveland's policies reversed

Benjamin Harrison was a successful lawyer, a veteran of the Union army, and the grandson of former President William Henry Harrison. He was not, however, a "strong" President. In his opinion, his duty as Chief Executive was to follow the wishes of the Senators and Representatives, who in turn had the responsibility of carrying out the wishes of the people.

During President Harrison's administration the Republicans reversed many of President Cleveland's policies. They did little to change the spoils system, and replaced Democratic office-holders (except those on the classified list) with Republicans. Congress passed the Dependent Pension Act that almost doubled the number of pensioners and their dependents. Congress also adopted the highest protective tariff the country had had up to that time. The McKinley Tariff of 1890, introduced by William McKinley of Ohio, raised rates from an average of about 38 percent to an average of close to 50 percent.

But "Old Guard" Republicans did not have everything their way. In an effort to appeal to farmers, laborers, miners, small business people, and the American public in general, Congress passed two important laws in 1890. The Sherman Silver Purchase Act was intended to appeal to western mining interests and to increase the amount of money in circulation as a benefit to farmers, wage earners, and small business interests. The Sherman Antitrust Act was intended to protect the public at large from monopoly practices and other abuses of free enterprise that had arisen with the growth of industry. You will read about these two laws in the next unit.

Growing dissatisfaction

Neither the Sherman Silver Purchase Act nor the Sherman Antitrust Act stopped the growing dissatisfaction with President Harrison's Republican administration. Wage earners, united in the newly organized A. F. of L., had no reason to hope their demands would be met by Republicans. Many farmers, abandoning hope of help from either party, began to take steps with the support of organized labor to try to win control of the government and bring about long-sought reforms. And Americans in general, struggling to make ends meet at a time of rising prices, blamed their troubles on the Republican-sponsored McKinley Tariff.

Of course, the problems Americans faced in the 1890's could not be explained simply in terms of a tariff act or the policies of a political party. Basic to everything else was the fact that a new industrial civilization was being born. Enterprising business leaders were creating new industries; technology was creating new jobs and opportunities—and, in the process, displacing men and women from older lines of work; and the entire economy was growing ever more rapidly. American wage earners on the whole were better off than workers in industrial Europe; some wage earners were doing very well indeed; and the large middle class was growing. But there was poverty, too, and insecurity for millions of American workers. And many large problems were clamoring for attention.

Need for reform

Two widely read books expressed growing dissatisfaction with the concentration of wealth in the hands of the few. Henry George's *Progress and Poverty,* first published in 1879, contrasted the wealth of the few with the poverty of many people. George thought that this inequality was due to the fact that a few persons had monopoly control over the nation's choicest land sites and other natural resources. George proposed a new system of land taxation which, he thought, would abolish great fortunes and provide a good standard of living for everyone.

In 1894 the book *Wealth Against Commonwealth* by Henry Demarest Lloyd was published. The author concluded that the giant new corporations and business enterprises were running the new industrial economy for their own gain.

Lloyd's book expressed the deep discontent of millions of Americans. It was not industrialism that people feared and hated. They agreed with Lloyd that the new industrial age held the promise of a brighter future for people everywhere. What concerned many Americans was that the new industrialism had created extremes of poverty and wealth. Expanding industries brought vast wealth to a few owners, while the majority of workers lived in poverty. For a solution to this problem, many Americans turned to government—whether controlled by Republicans or Democrats.

By 1892 the demand for government action had reached clamorous proportions. Owners of small businesses, wage earners in every section of the country, and especially the western farmers, were calling for reform.

The election of 1892

Rising discontent turned the election of 1892 into a spirited three-way contest. Both the Republicans and the Democrats realized that they had to do something about reform. They were prodded into action by the strength of a new party, the Populist Party, which had been created in 1891. The Populist Party, which you will read about later, was organized by farmers. But it also attracted wage earners and many other voters who were discontented with the two major parties.

The Republicans were on the defensive. President Harrison and the Republican Party received widespread criticism. The President himself had almost completely abandoned civil service reform. Congress had opened the door to a flood of pensions for disabled veterans. Congress had also passed the McKinley Tariff Act, the highest protective tariff in history. Despite criticism, the Republicans decided to stand on their record, and nominated President Harrison for a second term.

The Democrats, eager to take advantage of the demands for reform from both workers and farmers, nominated Grover Cleveland, who was already known as a champion of honest politics.

The Democrats won, with Cleveland gathering 277 electoral votes to Harrison's 145. The Democrats also won control of Congress. But the new Populist Party—an out-and-out reform party—made a remarkable showing. Although the Populist candidate, James B. Weaver, collected only 22 electoral votes, his popular vote totaled more than 1 million. And the Populist Party elected three governors and numerous representatives to state legislatures and to Congress.

Cleveland in trouble

From the beginning President Cleveland was in trouble. He antagonized wage earners with his labor policy, and farmers with his money policy, as you will see later. People in general blamed him for a depression that hit the country shortly after he took office. In the Congressional elections of 1894, the voters expressed their dissatisfaction by electing enough Republican Senators and Representatives to give the Republicans control of Congress.

The Wilson-Gorman Tariff Act

Cleveland's election had stemmed in part from his promise to lower the McKinley Tariff. Acting on the President's recommendations, in December 1893 Representative William L. Wilson of West Virginia introduced a bill that provided substantial reductions in existing tariff rates. The bill passed the House without great difficulty. In the Senate, however, high-tariff forces, led by Senator Gorman of Maryland, added more than 600 amendments to the original bill.

The Wilson-Gorman bill, as it was called, provided lower average tariff rates than the act it was designed to replace—39.9 percent to the McKinley Tariff's 48.4 percent. But it was still a high protective tariff, and President Cleveland was furious. He did not veto the bill, for he thought it was better than the McKinley Tariff. But he refused to endorse it by signing it, preferring instead to leave it on his desk for 10 days, after which it automatically became law without his signature.

Dissatisfaction with the tariff

During the tariff debates in the Senate, powerful *lobbies,* or pressure groups, tried in every way possible to influence the votes of doubtful Senators. Producers of iron, steel, wool, glass, and hundreds of other commodities demanded tariff protection.

One of the most active lobbies was the Amer-

On May 5, 1893, only two months after Cleveland took office, a financial panic began. The value of stocks on the New York Stock Exchange, shown here, suddenly plunged downward.

ican Sugar Refining Company, usually called "the sugar trust."° The original House bill had completely removed the tariff on raw and refined sugar. The sugar trust, determined to get the tariff restored, immediately went to work on the Senate. After a long and heated debate, the trust won, and the tariff on sugar was restored.

The Wilson-Gorman Tariff cost the Democrats the support of millions of Americans who were convinced that the Democrats had broken their campaign promise to do away with a high protective tariff.

Decision against an income tax

The original tariff bill introduced by Representative Wilson would have sharply lowered the tariff rates. Expecting a loss in government revenue because of the lower rates, the House Ways and Means Committee added a clause to the tariff bill providing for a 2 percent tax on all incomes of more than $4,000.

The income tax clause provoked violent debate, but it finally became law. Opponents of the

° **trust:** a group of companies centrally controlled to regulate production, reduce production costs, and eliminate competition.

income tax immediately tested the new measure in the courts, and in 1895 the Supreme Court declared it unconstitutional. The Supreme Court ruled against the income tax because it was a direct tax not apportioned among the states according to population, as required by the Constitution (page 655).

The Democratic administration could by no stretch of the imagination be held responsible for the Supreme Court's negative decision on the income tax. Nevertheless, millions of Americans considered this decision as merely one more example of how the government favored "big business." Thus the Supreme Court's rejection of the income tax helped to fan the flame of protest sweeping the country.

Financial panic and depression

On May 5, 1893, only two months after Cleveland took office, a financial panic began as the value of stocks on the New York Stock Exchange suddenly plunged downward. As the weeks passed, the situation rapidly became worse. Thousands of businesses failed. Factories closed their doors. Perhaps as many as 4 million workers were unemployed. The prices of farm produce dropped so low that farmers could not afford the cost of shipping it. By the end of the year, the

American nation was in the grip of one of the worst depressions in its history.

There were a number of reasons for the depression that hit the country in 1893, but, as the depression deepened, money became the central issue. In the Republican convention of 1896 the Republicans, favoring a money policy demanded by business owners and industrialists, nominated William McKinley of Ohio as their candidate. The Democrats, adopting the money policy of the Populist Party, nominated William Jennings Bryan of Nebraska. You will read a full account of this dramatic Presidential election in Chapter 5. McKinley won the election, and the Populist Party died out. But the forces of reform soon rallied, in the early 1900's, to a new and more powerful banner—the Progressive movement.

SECTION SURVEY

IDENTIFY: pension "grabs," McKinley Tariff of 1890, Populist Party, lobbies, trust, panic of 1893; Benjamin Harrison.

1. What did Grover Cleveland mean by saying that "a public office is a public trust"?
2. Explain how each of the following laws helped to solve an important national problem: (a) Presidential Succession Act of 1886, (b) Electoral Count Act of 1887, (c) Interstate Commerce Act of 1887.
3. Between 1890 and 1896 workers and farmers felt that the government favored "big business" and the well-to-do. What events made them feel this way?
4. What was the significance of the writings of Henry Demarest Lloyd and Henry George?
5. Why was the income tax declared unconstitutional in 1895?

CHAPTER SURVEY

INQUIRING INTO HISTORY

1. (a) What, in your opinion, are the causes of political corruption? (b) Why were graft and corruption so widespread after the Civil War?
2. (a) Explain the Pendleton Act's significance regarding democratic government. (b) Why has the act been called the "Magna Carta of civil service reform"?
3. Compare and explain the positions of the Republican and Democratic parties concerning the tariff issue during the period 1865–96. Refer to specific tariff laws.
4. According to some historians, the Hayes-Tilden election of 1876 is an example of a secret political bargain. Search historical sources to find out what various historians say about this issue. What evidence do these historians use to support their positions?

RELATING PAST TO PRESENT

1. What in your opinion is the function of the news media regarding government policies and practices?
2. Has civil service reform fulfilled the expectations of those who proposed it? Do you think the civil service has contributed to bureaucracy and red tape in government today? Explain your answers.

3. Does the word "reform" have a different meaning today from the one it had during the period just studied? Explain.
4. Compare the present Presidential Succession Law of 1967 (Amendment 25) with the one enacted in 1886.
5. What groups of people made up the majority of Republican and Democratic party members during the period 1865–97? What major groups make up both parties' majorities today? Compare and comment.
6. Would any military man elected to the Presidency in 1868 have encountered the same difficulties that Grant did? Explain.

DEVELOPING SOCIAL SCIENCE SKILLS

1. Historians have rated American Presidents by the following categories: great, near great, average, below average, and failure. Make a list of the Presidents elected between 1865 and 1896 and evaluate them according to these categories. What things did you consider in making your judgments?
2. Study the cartoons on pages 59 and 61. (a) Identify the characters shown in the cartoons. (b) What is the point of view of each cartoon? (c) How effective do you think each cartoon is?
3. Make a time line for classroom display for the years 1865 to 1897. Using drawings or pictures, show the Presidents elected in these years and some important events that took place in their administrations.

CHAPTER 3
CONQUERING THE "LAST FRONTIER"
1865-1900

Thomas Gilcrease Institute of American History and Art, Tulsa, Oklahoma.

Chief Joseph, leader of the Nez Percé (NAY per·SAY) Indians, stood before his conquerors. "I am tired of fighting," he said. "Our chiefs are killed. . . . It is cold and we have no blankets. The little children are freezing to death. . . . My heart is sick and sad. From where the sun now stands I will fight no more, forever."

The year was 1877. The place, the plains of Montana, near the Canadian border.

The Nez Percé Indians had dwelt in peace for half a century in the Oregon country. But in the years after 1865, pioneers looked with greedy eyes on the Nez Percé hunting grounds, and soon a federal order arrived: The Indians were to be removed to a reservation—a tract of land set aside by the federal government as a dwelling place for the tribe.

As the tribe was preparing to leave, white settlers stole several hundred Nez Percé horses. Young Indian warriors demanded revenge. Federal troops were called out. After first outmaneuvering the troops, Chief Joseph tried to lead his people to safety in Canada. With 200 warriors and 600 women and children, the tribe traveled more than 1,300 miles (2,092 kilometers) in two months, fighting off pursuing troops along the way. Finally, Chief Joseph and his people were forced to surrender. They were within sight of the Canadian border.

Thus, in 1877, Chief Joseph faced his conquerors on the last frontier of the West, the Great Plains. This vast area, stretching from the Canadian border to Texas, had been the Indians' land from earliest times. Now it was being claimed by people from the North and South and from distant Europe.

This is the story of the conquest of the Indians. It is also the story of the West itself and of new ways of life on the "last frontier."

THE CHAPTER IN OUTLINE

1. Troubled relations with the American Indians.

2. The short-lived Cattle Kingdom on the plains.

3. The rapid settlement of the "last frontier" by pioneering farmers.

4. The discovery of mineral treasures in the western mountains.

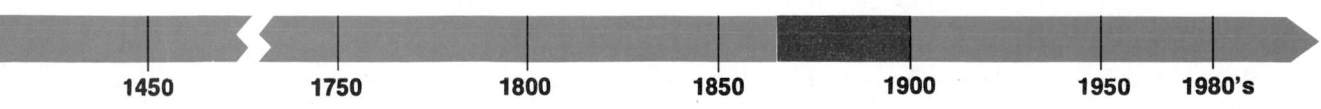

| 1450 | 1750 | 1800 | 1850 | 1900 | 1950 | 1980's |

1 Troubled relations with the American Indians

On their western edge the prairies of the Middle West merge into the Great Plains. Although no sharp line separates the prairies from the plains, the 100th meridian is usually accepted as the dividing line. As one travels westward from the 100th meridian to the Rocky Mountains, the rainfall gradually decreases and the grass gets shorter.

Obstacles to settlement

It was along the 100th meridian that the westward advance halted for at least a generation during the early 1800's. The reluctance of the pioneers to settle on the Great Plains arose in part from misinformation. Earlier explorers, accustomed to wooded country with abundant rainfall, had established the idea that the Great Plains were mainly uninhabitable desert. Maps of the time called the plains the "Great American Desert." By the 1850's, however, this notion was being dispelled. Traders and pioneers who crossed the plains on their way to California and the Pacific Northwest reported that much of the plains country was good for settlement.

When the Civil War ended, the Great Plains began to attract increasing numbers of land speculators, engineers, miners, ranchers, farmers, and town builders. But a tremendous obstacle to settlement remained—the Plains Indians. Even during the war, you recall, there had been serious Indian trouble in Minnesota and Colorado.

Failure of the peace policy

Some members of Congress, disturbed over the likelihood of continued and expanding conflict between settlers and Indians, hoped to prevent it, or at least to limit it, in the years ahead. A Congressional investigating commission reported that white settlers' aggression was largely responsible for Indian attacks. A second commission, with the encouragement of President Grant, negotiated treaties for the settlement of Plains Indians on reservations, chiefly in South Dakota and in Indian Territory. Under the new "peace policy," church groups, including peace-committed Quakers, were invited to choose government agents who might have less trouble with the Indians than army officers or the frequently corrupt civilian agents of the Bureau of Indian Affairs. Some of the new agents were wise and skillful; some were not. Many Indians, resenting the restrictions and frequent injustices of reservation life, decided to leave the reservations and resume their lives as hunters on the Great Plains.

With this breakdown of the new peace policy, the United States Army took over. Its mission was to keep the Plains Indians on the reservations or to compel the return of those who fled, to protect Indians against the worst injustices, and to provide security for white settlers.

A long period of conflict began between the Plains Indians and the ranchers, miners, farmers, and other settlers on the Great Plains. The basic reason for the conflict, as in the past, was the determination of the white settlers, on the one hand, to possess the land and, on the other hand, the resistance by the Indians to the destruction of their hunting grounds. The Indians also objected to the restrictions and alien ways of life imposed on them on the reservations. As in the past, treaties were broken, and the better lands of the reservations were reallocated to greedy settlers. Also, as in the past, each side often sought indiscriminate revenge when the other side violated its code of conduct. But in the many skirmishes and major conflicts for control of the Great Plains, new forces were also at work.

Bows and arrows against long rifles

The Plains Indians had learned what the white settlers would have to learn—how to adapt to the plains environment. The buffalo, or bison, provided the Indians with food, clothing, and shelter.

The Indians were powerful adversaries. They rode horses with superb ease. Before they secured rifles, they fought with spears and with short bows, from which they could drive their arrows with amazing rapidity and penetrating force. They were protected by shields of buffalo hide, which they coated with glue made from horses' hooves and hardened over the fire to an almost iron-like consistency. A favorite Indian tactic was to gallop around the enemy, hiding behind horses and shields, deliberately drawing enemy fire. When the enemy's ammunition was exhausted, the Indians darted in to strike with arrows and long spears.

Faced with these weapons and tactics, white settlers at first were at a great disadvantage. Their long rifles could be reloaded and fired only with great difficulty from the back of a galloping horse.

A new weapon

The invention of the revolver in the late 1830's soon ended the Indians' temporary superiority in weapons. The revolver could be reloaded easily at full gallop, and several bullets could be fired in rapid succession without reloading. Armed with this new weapon, settlers in the 1850's began to move out onto the plains with more confidence.

Here, artist George Catlin shows Plains Indians hunting buffaloes. When white settlers slaughtered the buffaloes, they destroyed the Indians' main source of food, clothing, and shelter.

New transportation

The early pioneers who crossed the plains on their way west depended upon horses and oxen for transportation. A rider on horseback, however, could not transport goods in bulk. To fill this need, caravans of covered wagons set out upon the plains, forming circles around campfires at night for protection against Indian attack. As time passed, stagecoach lines provided speedier transportation.

But it was the railroad that finally provided adequate transportation. Construction of the first transcontinental railroad to the Pacific coast began in 1866. Chinese workers were imported to do most of the physical labor on the Central Pacific. Most of the workers on the Union Pacific, building from Omaha, in Nebraska Territory, were recent Irish immigrants. All work was done under the eyes of scouts, who protected the railroad builders from hostile Indians. The meeting of the rails of the Central Pacific and the Union Pacific at Promontory in what is now Utah (see map, page 77) in 1869 was an occasion of jubilation. Silk-hatted gentlemen, surrounded by workers, drove a golden spike to hold the last rails in place while the news was telegraphed to Americans everywhere.

The first transcontinental railroad contributed enormously to the nation's economic growth. It brought the Atlantic and the Pacific seaboards within a week's journey of each other, and opened a route to the rich resources of the West.

The railroad carried northerners and southerners alike into the untamed West. It also destroyed the vast buffalo herds. The herds were split again and again as new railroad lines crept across the grasslands. The completion of the Northern Pacific Railway in 1883 sealed the fate of the final, northernmost buffalo herd (see map, page 77).

Slaughter of the buffalo

Government agents and army officers, knowing that the Plains Indians depended mainly on the buffalo for their living, sometimes encouraged the destruction of the great herds as a means of confining Indians to reservations. Parties of hunters debarked from trains with horses and equipment, killed the buffalo at will, and loaded the hides on trains bound for eastern markets. It has been estimated that between 1871 and 1874 hunters killed nearly 3 million buffalo each year. By 1875 buffalo hides were selling from 65¢ to $1.15 apiece. The waste was frightful. Buffalo carcasses were abandoned, and for every hide taken, four were left on the plains.

The disappearance of the buffalo doomed the Plains Indians, who had built their hunting culture upon the buffalo herds. In destroying the buffalo, white hunters destroyed the Indians' only source of food, clothing, and shelter. Almost the last of the free Indians in the United States were driven on to remote reservations, where they lived as wards—that is, under the protection and control—of the federal government.

Thus the revolver and the railroad, both products of the Industrial Revolution, helped to sweep the Indians from the Great Plains and to open the way for white settlement.

The Indian wars

Despite their advantages over the Indians, white settlers and the army had to fight long and hard to drive the Plains Indians from their hunting grounds. Between 1865 and 1886 the United States conducted a costly and brutal campaign against the Plains Indians. In all the engagements of this campaign, former soldiers who had fought for the South or the North in the Civil War now fought together against the Indians.

In 1866 Congress decided to recruit four all-black regiments—the 24th and 25th Infantries, and the 9th and 10th Cavalries—to fight in the Indian wars. One fifth of the army's soldiers on horseback in the western campaigns were enrolled in the 9th and 10th Cavalries.

During the 30-odd years of the Indian wars, the Indians fought back against white and black military forces in an effort to hold on to their lands and to keep their distinctive ways of life. As in earlier conflicts with settlers, the Indians were not always united in their struggle. Traditional tribal rivalries explain in part why the federal regiments were often able to enlist Indians as highly useful scouts.

Still, Indian resistance was remarkable. The smaller the area into which the Indians were driven, the more desperately they fought back. There was brutality on both sides. And army leaders fought not only with guns but also with broken promises. In 1877, the same year in which Chief Joseph made his heroic attempt to lead his people to freedom in Canada, President Hayes himself told Congress, "Many, if not most, of our Indian wars have their origin in broken promises and acts of injustice on our part."

Custer's "last stand"

Just the year before, one broken promise had brought disaster. The Sioux had been promised as a permanent home the Black Hills in what are now South Dakota and Wyoming, which they considered sacred. But after gold was discovered in the Black Hills, the 7th Cavalry, in 1876, was ordered to remove the Indians to a less desirable area. The removal operation was under the command of General George Custer, an experienced Indian fighter who, several years earlier, had attacked a peaceful Indian village on the Washita River in Oklahoma, killing unarmed women and children as well as warriors. In June of 1876, General Custer attacked a large camp of Sioux and Cheyenne near the Little Big Horn River in Montana. The Sioux and Cheyenne warriors had two outstanding leaders. One was Sitting Bull, able, honest, idealistic. The other was Crazy Horse, uncompromising, reckless, a military genius and the most honored hero of the Sioux.

In fierce fighting along the Little Big Horn, Custer and his whole detachment of 264 troops were killed and their bodies mutilated. General Custer's "last stand" provoked long controversy, but none could deny that it was a major humiliation for the United States government. Still, the action at the Little Big Horn for a time marked the end of major fighting on the northern Great Plains. Troops pursued and harried the Sioux and Cheyenne until Crazy Horse and Sitting Bull were defeated and the Indians forced onto reservations.

Final resistance

The Sioux soon became restless again as a result of poor food rations and the further whittling away of their reservation. They expressed their feelings in a religious revival called the Ghost Dance, which foresaw a return to the old ways of free-roaming Indian life. Alarmed miners and settlers on the northern plains demanded further action by the army against the restless Sioux. At Wounded Knee, South Dakota, in December 1890, a unit of the 7th Cavalry arrested a band of Sioux men, women, and children who were moving toward the Pine Ridge Reservation in search of food and protection. Although the Sioux men had been disarmed, a scuffle took place in a further search for hidden arms. A shot was fired. The cavalry opened deadly machine-gun fire on the unprotected Sioux, killing or mortally wounding 90 men and 200 women and children.

Many Americans were horrified at such brutality. Others felt that, at last, General Custer had been avenged. Organized Indian resistance on the northern plains was ended. It had ended even earlier on the southern plains and in the Southwest. For some time, Comanches and Apaches had resisted efforts to keep them on reservations. Led by Victorio and Geronimo, the Apaches raided white communities in Arizona until Geronimo surrendered in 1886.

The reservations

The reservations where the Indians were forced to live were often far away from their original homelands, with terrain and climate different from those they were used to. When they

The Plains Indians were conquered during the Indian Wars from 1865 to 1886. The photograph shows the Pine Ridge Indian Reservation, established by the government as a home for the conquered tribes.

tried to escape they were pursued, captured, punished, and sent back to the reservation. To make matters worse, just when some of the Indians were beginning to adjust to their new environments, the government would move them to different reservations.

Legally, the reservation Indians were *wards* of the government, like minor children without parents. In return for the lands they had given up, they were supposed to receive certain supplies, such as blankets, seed corn, and basic food. These supplies were often poor in quality and quantity, and slow in reaching the Indians. Some agents in charge of the reservations were honest and well disposed toward the Indians, but many profited from corrupt deals with traders and with those who provided the supplies. The Indians were commonly treated with contempt or, at best, as children might be treated.

"Americanizing" the Indians

Even with the Indians confined to the reservations, there was still a serious "Indian problem" in the view of most white Americans. Most white Americans believed that it was necessary for the Indians to be "Americanized," that is, to be assimilated into the American way of life and to accept the culture of the dominant majority. To the Indians—between 200,000 and 300,000 of them at that time—this idea meant giving up many of their deeply held values and customs. These might include the collective or tribal ownership and use of land; a belief that work was

only a means of providing food and shelter, not an end in itself; marriage traditions, including having more than one wife; many religious beliefs; even clothing styles and adornments. Indian men, for example, resented efforts to make them cut their long, braided hair. Nor did Indian men and boys accept the idea that they were supposed to plant and cultivate the soil; that had always been women's work.

The vast majority of white Americans neither understood nor appreciated the Indian cultures. They were unaware of the importance of these cultures to the Indians' sense of identity and self-respect.

Reform activities

Some Americans, however, were deeply troubled by the long history of the white settlers' injustice to the Indians. Helen Hunt Jackson in her book *A Century of Dishonor* (1881) provided documentary evidence of the government's broken promises. The reformers were also profoundly disturbed by the corruption, inefficiency, and lack of leadership in the Bureau of Indian Affairs.

Sarah Winnemucca, daughter of a Nevada Piute chief, played a unique role in reform circles. She was a scout, a guide, an interpreter at army posts, a teacher of Indian children, the widow of one army officer and the wife of another. In lectures at Boston, San Francisco, and elsewhere, she spoke out against the injustices to her people, denounced the corruption of agents of the Bureau of Indian Affairs, and called for better distribution of lands to Indians. General O. O. Howard, for whom she was a scout and interpreter, declared that she "should have a place beside the name of Pocahontas in the history of our country."

One reform group, the National Indian Defense Organization, argued that the deep-rooted cultures of the Indians could not be rapidly changed without grave consequences. Members of this group argued that the Indians should be allowed to retain their own traditions and customs. Most other reform organizations, however, believed that the Indians could and should be speedily "Americanized" by persuading them to adopt Christianity, American forms of education, and individual land ownership.

Reformers who urged Americanization of the Indians through individual land ownership actually strengthened, without intending to, the more selfish interests of land speculators, miners, ranchers, and farmers who were already occupying the unsettled areas of the West. These groups, who wanted the more valuable parts of Indian reservations, supported the reformers' policy of individual Indian ownership, since this would open remaining reservation lands to white occupation.

Writing the policy into law

Responding to such pressures, the federal government in the Dawes Act of 1887 made a general policy of what it had been trying to do in a piecemeal fashion. With the Dawes Act, Congress hoped to hasten the time when the Indians living on reservations would be "Americanized."

The Dawes Act provided that each male head of an Indian family could, if he wished, claim 160 acres (64.8 hectares) of reservation land as his own. Bachelors, women, and children were to be entitled to lesser amounts. Legal ownership of the property was to be held in trust by the federal government for 25 years. During this period the Indians could neither sell their land nor use it as security for a mortgage. This restriction was intended to protect the Indians from unscrupulous land speculators. The Burke Act of 1906 modified this provision. It gave the Secretary of the Interior authority to reduce the 25-year period in cases where the Secretary was convinced that the Indians were capable of handling their own affairs.

The Dawes Act and the Burke Act also provided that Indians who accepted the land and abandoned their tribal way of life were to be given citizenship, including the right to vote. Meanwhile, Congress voted larger but still inad-

equate funds for the education of Indian children in regular day schools or in boarding schools far from their homes. In these schools the children were taught, often by poorly trained and unsympathetic teachers, to look down on Indian ways of life as inferior and degraded.

Failure of the "Americanization" policy

The new laws persuaded and enabled some Indians to adopt the way of life of the white majority and to become American citizens. Even so, Indians who left the reservations to live in American towns and cities often met with discrimination in jobs and unfair treatment. Most Indians remained on the reservations, clinging as best they could to their tribal customs, and living as wards of the federal government. The government policy of encouraging individual land ownership and individual farming among the Indians largely failed when land speculators found loopholes in the Dawes Act. Between 1887 and the 1920's much of the reservation land was, in one way or another, taken from the Indians. What remained was generally eroded and inferior. Moreover, provisions for safeguarding the health of the Indians were neglected. Malnutrition and disease were widespread.

Thus the lot of the Indians became more and more desperate. The late 1800's and early 1900's were in many ways the Indians' darkest period. Yet their vitality and spirit were reflected even then in the continuing insistence by many of them that they be regarded as separate, self-respecting peoples with worthy ways of viewing human relationships, of understanding their part in the environment, and of sensing their place in the universe.

SECTION SURVEY

IDENTIFY: Great Plains, prairies, buffalo, reservations, Little Big Horn, Wounded Knee, Dawes Act of 1887; General George Custer, Chief Joseph, Helen Hunt Jackson, Sarah Winnemucca.

1. (a) In combat, what advantages did the Indians at first have over the settlers? (b) How did the following contribute to the defeat of the Indians—the revolver, the railroads, the destruction of the buffalo?
2. President Hayes said, "Many, if not most, of our Indian wars have their origin in broken promises and acts of injustice on our part." Explain.
3. What part did each of the following play in the "Americanization" of the Indians: (a) government policies, (b) reformers?
4. Give arguments for and against the policy of Americanization.

2 The short-lived Cattle Kingdom on the plains

Cattle raisers began to move out onto the Great Plains in the 1860's, long before the Indians were conquered. By the 1890's the cattle industry had become "big business," its products passing from the western ranges through the stockyards, slaughterhouses, and packing plants to become major items of domestic and world trade.

Rise of the "Cattle Kingdom"

Many of the animals for the cattle industry came from the ranches in southeastern Texas formerly operated by Spaniards and Mexicans. These ranches were occupied by the Texans, who also took over the huge herds of wild cattle, called longhorns, estimated in 1865 to number about 5 million head. The wild herds sprang from cattle lost by the Spaniards and by the American wagon trains crossing the plains in earlier days.

It was no easy task for the first Texans to learn how to handle the cattle, wild or tame. A writer in the 1870's warned that "the wild cattle of Texas . . . animals miscalled tame, are fifty times more dangerous . . . than the fiercest buffalo."

In learning how to handle cattle, the Texans owed a good deal to Mexican *vaqueros*° (vah‧KAIR‧ohs), and to Indians. These men helped to train many slaves in the dangerous business of handling cattle. After emancipation, freed slaves comprised perhaps one third of those working in cattle raising. With the aid of the horse, the saddle, the rope, and the revolver, white and Negro cowboys learned how to handle the longhorns on the open grasslands. Cattle ranching became a

° *vaquero:* the Spanish word for cowboy.

WESTERN RAILROADS AND CATTLE TRAILS

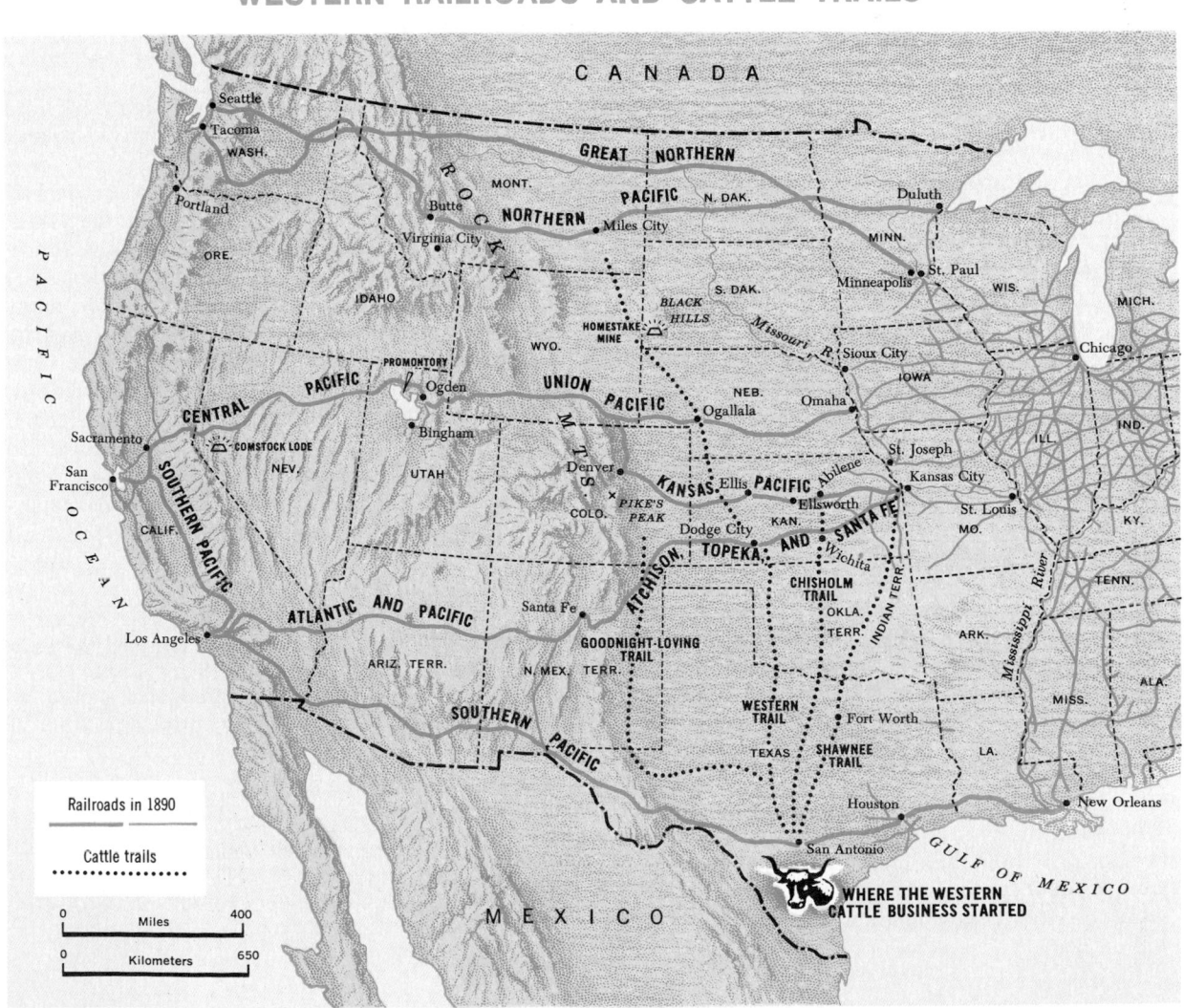

Railroads in 1890

Cattle trails

WHERE THE WESTERN CATTLE BUSINESS STARTED

These cowboys in this 1898 photograph have stopped their difficult, dusty work for a quick meal served off the back of a chuck wagon.

profitable occupation and a distinctive way of life.

The "long drive"

People in the nation's growing cities needed enormous quantities of beef. The problem was to find a means of transporting the steers to urban markets. Transportation was provided by the railroads, which in the 1860's began to push out upon the Great Plains.

As the steel rails moved westward, enormous herds of steers were driven from Texas north on "long drives" to towns that grew up along the railroads. By 1870 Kansas cattle towns like Abilene, Ellsworth, and Ellis (all on the Kansas Pacific Railroad) and Dodge City and Wichita (on the Atchison, Topeka, and Santa Fe Railway) had become roaring, riotous, lawless communities (see map, page 77).

During the early years of the long drives, nearly all the steers driven from Texas were sold in the cattle towns at good prices. In time, however, the number of cattle began to exceed the demand, and Texans who arrived in late fall were either unable to sell their steers or had to sell them at a loss.

The open range

At this point, enterprising cattle raisers began to winter their surplus steers on the open range, or unfenced grazing lands, near the cattle towns. After fattening them during the winter, they sold them at high prices in the towns before the new cattle drives from Texas arrived to glut the market.

This was not the first time that cattle had been pastured on the short grass of the Great Plains. Pioneers crossing the plains to the Southwest and to the Pacific Northwest in the 1830's had watched buffalo grazing. In addition, many wagon trains had wintered on the plains, and the pioneers had discovered that their horses and cattle grew fat on the short and thin, but nutritious, grass. The great freight carriers and stagecoach companies regularly pastured their stock on the open range. The open-range cattle industry did not develop, however, until the railroads provided access to markets, and the Texans provided the cattle.

The cattle rush

News that quick money could be made in the open-range cattle business soon reached the eastern seaboard and spread to Europe. The cattle rush that followed was similar to the gold rush that had populated California in 1849–50. Prices for land and steers soared as newcomers on the Great Plains staked out their claims.

People rushed to the cattle country to make their fortunes. They built dugouts, sod huts, or simple ranch houses, and pastured their herds on the open grasslands. Some, though by no means all, did become wealthy.

Until the 1880's the cattle ranchers ruled the Great Plains. This was the period of the long drive, the open range, the roundup, and the picturesque roving cowboy.

End of the open range

The open-range cattle industry ended, however, almost as quickly as it had started. As the supply of steers rapidly increased, beef prices fell disastrously low. In 1885 a severe drought burned up the grasses on the overstocked range, and cattle starved by the thousands.

Even more disastrous for the cattle raisers was the arrival of sheepherders and farmers in the 1880's. Sheep cropped the grass so close that little was left for the cattle. Farmers broke up the open range with their farms and barbed-wire fences (page 81). The cattle ranchers fought desperately to keep the range open. But they fought a hopeless battle. By the late 1880's the open, unfenced range was fast becoming a thing of the past.

Ranches and fences

By the 1890's the western cattle industry centered in the high plains running through eastern Montana, Wyoming, Colorado, the New Mexico Territory, and western Texas. Most ranchers by now owned their grazing land and fenced it in with barbed wire.

Ranches varied in size from about 2,000 to 100,000 acres (about 800 to 40,500 hectares). To an easterner, accustomed to small farms of a few hundred acres at most, western ranches seemed enormous. But the ranches had to be large since each steer required a grazing area of 15 to 75 acres (or about 6 to 30 hectares), depending upon the amount of rainfall and the resulting growth of grass.

With the invention of better instruments for drilling into the ground and the improvement of windmills for pumping water, many cattle raisers watered their stock from wells scattered over their ranches. In years of abundant rainfall, cattle ranchers might prosper, since their herds could fatten on the natural grasses. But in years of drought they were forced to feed their cattle hay or cottonseed cake, a costly practice which often wiped out their profits.

Growth and specialization

The development of the railroads revolutionized the cattle industry, which tended to become more and more specialized. Many ranchers on the plains began to concentrate on breeding and raising cattle. The steers were then sold to farmers in the rich corn and pasture lands of the prairies. After being fattened for market, the cattle were shipped to nearby stockyards in Omaha,

In the latter half of the 1800's, states, railroads, and privately owned land companies advertised western lands in glowing colors to attract settlers.

Kansas City, St. Joseph, Sioux City, St. Paul–Minneapolis, and Chicago (see map, page 77). There they were slaughtered and transported in refrigerator cars to eastern cities and sometimes from there to Europe.

Ranchers used the prairies, the semiarid plains, the high plateaus, and the mountain valleys of the West for cattle grazing lands. On these lands they produced a substantial portion of the nation's meat and wool. By the 1890's the western livestock industry had become an organized, specialized business, closely tied to the nation's economic life.

IDENTIFY: Cattle Kingdom, longhorns, roundup, ranch, vaqueros.

1. What was the relationship between the railroads and the "long drive"?

2. Explain how cattle raisers used the open range of the Great Plains.
3. Give the reason for the cattle rush of the 1870's.
4. Why did the open range disappear?
5. Show how the development of the railroads helped to bring about specialization in the cattle industry.

3 The rapid settlement of the "last frontier" by pioneering farmers

Farm families, single men, and some single women followed the cattle ranchers out on the prairies and plains. From 1870 to 1900, American pioneers settled more land than had all previous generations combined.

In the 263 years from the first tiny settlement at Jamestown in 1607 until 1870, Americans transformed nearly 408 million acres (165.1 million hectares) of wilderness into farm land. Mighty though this achievement was, its pace was leisurely compared to the speed with which later settlers conquered the prairies and the plains. In the 30 years between 1870 and 1900 pioneers settled an additional 430 million acres (174 million hectares)—an area roughly equal to the combined areas of Norway, Sweden, Denmark, the Netherlands, Belgium, Germany, and France.

What was happening in America to make possible this rapid settlement of the last frontier?

Free land for settlers

One attraction of the West was free land. In 1862 Congress enacted the Homestead Act, which granted 160 acres (64.8 hectares) to any individual who wished to settle a farm, or, as it was called, a "homestead."

Farmers, as well as land speculators, rushed to accept the offer. Thousands were ex-soldiers who sought new homes in the West. Thousands of others came from worn-out farms in the East, particularly from New England, in the hope of finding more fertile land. Still other thousands came from Europe. In many areas of the Middle West, more than half of the pioneers were immigrants—Germans, Norwegians, Swedes, Danes, Czechs, Finns, and Russians.

The railroads and settlement

Without the railroad, however, the free land in the West, no matter how attractive, would have remained unpopulated. During the 1870's and the 1880's four great transcontinental railroads crossed the prairies and the plains. These railroads along with their branch lines opened up the western country for settlement.

The rail lines into and through the wild western country were built only at enormous cost.

Moreover, the investment was extremely risky. Investors did not know when, if ever, the new railroads would begin to make a profit and reward them for their risks. Thus the government, which was eager to have the railroads built, encouraged the pioneer railroad companies with cash subsidies and grants of land. The companies used the cash subsidies and money raised from the sale of some of the land to lay the rails, build the bridges and stations, and buy the engines and cars.

At the time the grants were made to the railroads, the land itself was almost worthless. Before the railroad companies could profit from their grants, they had to persuade people to move into the unsettled areas. Because the land was close to the railroads and therefore would be valuable, the railroad companies could hope to sell it, even though free land was available in more remote areas. But more important was the fact that once the land was settled, the railroads would gain revenue from passengers and freight. In addition, any land that the railroads could not sell immediately would rise in value as settlers built farms, villages, and towns along the right of way.

With such things in mind, the railroads started extensive advertising campaigns, sending literature and agents all over the United States and even into Europe. Life on the plains was pictured in glowing colors. As an added lure prospective purchasers were frequently offered free railroad transportation to any land they might buy. The transatlantic steamship lines, always eager to obtain passengers and freight, also began advertising campaigns in Europe.

The problem of houses and fences

Despite such efforts, settlers did not at first pour into the plains. For one thing, many still believed the old myth of the "Great American Desert." An even more important factor was the scarcity of wood.

Pioneer families solved the problem of housing, as people have always done, by making use of whatever building material was available. On the plains this was sod. Cut out of the soil, brick-

This farm family had its picture taken outside its sod home in Custer County, Nebraska, in 1888. Why was this house not made of wood?

like chunks of sod formed the walls of shelters. With a few precious pieces of wood the settlers framed the roof, finishing it with a layer of sod to keep out wind and rain and snow.

Fencing presented an even more difficult problem. Pioneer families could not farm without fences to protect their crops, and on the plains there was no material for fences.

During the 1870's nearly every newspaper on the edge of the plains carried long articles on the problem of fencing. The first pioneers tried everything, even mud walls, but without success. Ordinary wire strung between a few precious wooden posts was not effective, for cattle could get their heads through the smooth strands of wire and gradually work an opening in the fence.

The problem of fencing was finally solved by a New Hampshire-born Yankee, Joseph Glidden, who had moved to De Kalb, Illinois. His solution was barbed wire—that is, wire with sharp, projecting points. Glidden took out his patent in 1874. Barbed-wire fences proved effective as a barrier to cattle, and within 10 years the open range was criss-crossed by a network of barbed-wire fences.

The problem of water

Scarcity of water, like scarcity of wood, was a problem that pioneer farm families had never had to face in the eastern part of the United States or in the European countries from which they had migrated. Eastern farmers secured their water from springs bubbling to the surface or from shallow wells. They hauled well water to the surface in buckets or pumped it up easily by hand; later, in the 1900's, they pumped it by gasoline-driven or electric pumps. But on the Great Plains, where the water was much deeper underground, machinery was needed to drill deeper wells. And once the well shafts had reached the water, the farmers needed mechanical pumps to draw the water to the surface.

In a search for oil during the 1860's, petroleum companies developed new drilling machinery capable of penetrating farther beneath the surface than ever before. This machinery speedily found its way to the Great Plains, where it was used to tap water supplies deep underground.

Barbed-wire Fence. On the Great Plains, which were largely treeless, farmers could not build fences from tree stumps or boards. "Barbed wire," which cattle learned to avoid, was finally the answer. Fence posts were made from scrap lumber or from branches of the few trees that grew on the plains.

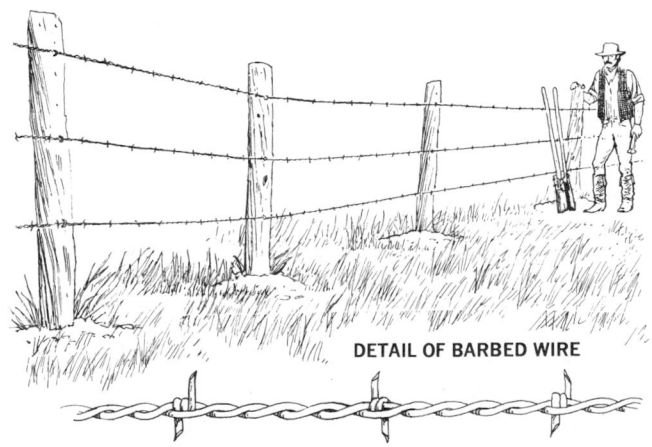

DETAIL OF BARBED WIRE

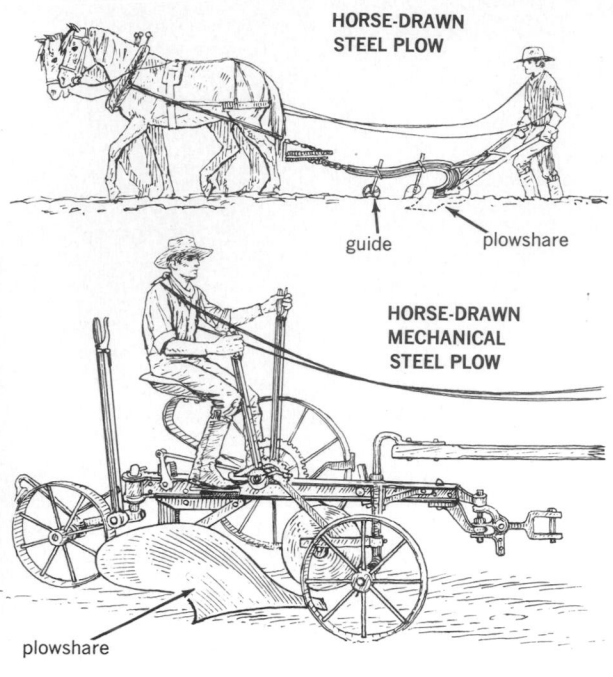

HORSE-DRAWN STEEL PLOW

guide   plowshare

HORSE-DRAWN MECHANICAL STEEL PLOW

plowshare

Improved Farm Implements. Steel "plowshares" (above) were developed to turn in furrows the tough sod of the prairie. Better implements (below) were also developed for breaking the furrows and pulverizing the soil.

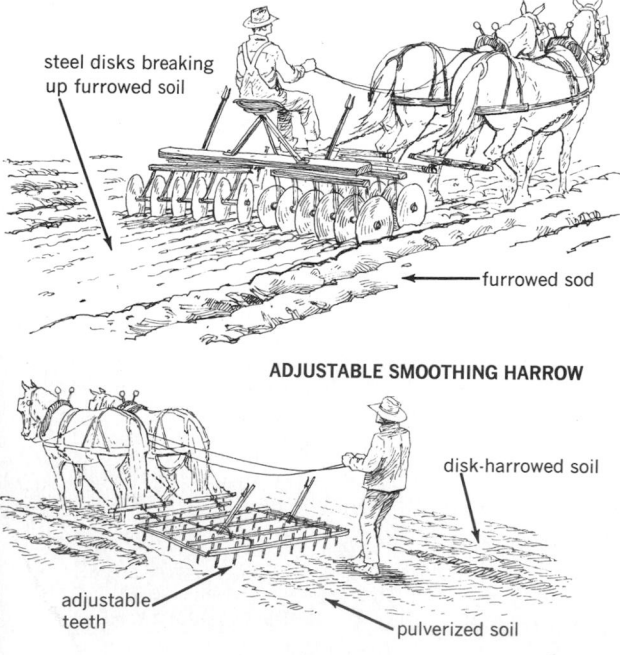

DOUBLE-DISK HARROW

steel disks breaking up furrowed soil

furrowed sod

ADJUSTABLE SMOOTHING HARROW

disk-harrowed soil

adjustable teeth

pulverized soil

Meanwhile, other inventors were developing windmills capable of operating pumps to draw water to the surface. Another New Englander, Daniel Halladay of Connecticut, developed the self-governing windmill that automatically adjusted itself to wind pressure, and thus operated at a uniform speed.

Windmills were first used on the Great Plains by cattle ranchers to provide water for their stock and in steam locomotives crossing the plains. But the windmill really came into its own when farmers began to settle on the semiarid lands. Factories producing windmills were soon doing a thriving business.

Other problems of the settlers

Railroads, barbed wire, factory-made windmills—all products of the new industrial age—helped farmers conquer the Great Plains. So, too, did the development of "dry farming," a better method for farming areas with limited amounts of rainfall. "Dry farming" involved deep plowing and careful cultivation to keep the surface of the soil pulverized and thus conserve as much precious moisture as possible. The development of improved farm machinery also helped to lighten the farmers' work.

But the pioneer farm families had other problems to solve, problems for which inventors, manufacturers, and agricultural experts had no ready answers. For one thing, the cattle ranchers resented the settlers who broke up the open range with their fences. Bitter fights raged in the early days between ranchers and farmers, and many unmarked graves soon dotted the plains. But it was an unequal struggle, for by sheer force of numbers the farmers eventually won.

Nature also contributed to the settlers' difficulties. Until men and women learned how to deal with the plains environment, life was sometimes extremely harsh. The unrelieved round of daily labor impressed writers who tried to describe the life of the farmers on the Great Plains. The novels of O. E. Rölvaag (ROHL·vagh), *Giants in the Earth* and *Peder Victorious,* give a picture of empty plains and lives spent beneath a burning sun, of grasshopper plagues, of drought, of ruined crops, of bitter cold and blinding blizzards. Many pioneers gave up the struggle and moved back east. But others remained and forced the plains to yield their treasures.

In addition to the same problems faced by the early settlers, farm families in the 1880's and 1890's encountered many new problems created by industrialism. In the new industrial age, as you will read, farmers became increasingly concerned with freight and shipping charges, prices fixed in distant markets, the cost of farm machinery, interest rates on mortgages, and many other factors they could not control.

The Oklahoma "Sooners"

After the Civil War, many Plains Indians were moved to western portions of Indian Territory, leaving a large area of unoccupied land in the central part of present-day Oklahoma. Several treaties had reserved these lands for the Five Civilized tribes—the Cherokees, Creeks, Chicasaws, Choctaws, and Seminoles. When white intruders moved onto this land, federal troops at first drove them off. In 1885, however, the government negotiated with the Creeks and Seminoles to open the vacant land to white settlement.

In March 1889 President Benjamin Harrison issued a proclamation that set in motion a wild rush to the "District of Oklahoma." The President announced that free homesteads of 160 acres (64.8 hectares) would be available "at and after the hour of twelve o'clock noon, on the twenty-second day of April." The army immediately set up patrols along the district boundaries to guard against premature entry, and waited for the rush to begin.

It was a short wait. By April 22 almost 100,-000 land-hungry pioneers—some in wagons, some on horseback—were packed solidly along the boundary line. Exactly at noon the officer in charge fired a shot, and the wild stampede began.

But even the swiftest riders discovered that they were not there "soon" enough. Despite army precautions, many "Sooners" had evaded the patrols, slipped across the boundary, and staked out claims before the area was officially opened.

Within a few hours of the deadline, every inch of "Oklahoma District" was occupied. Thousands of disappointed landseekers started back along the roads they had eagerly traveled earlier.

But more land was soon available—again at the expense of the Indians. In 1889 1 million acres (404,700 hectares) of land previously reserved for the Sac, Fox, and Pottawatami, and a large area assigned to the Cheyenne and Arapaho were thrown open to white settlement. In the years that followed, the huge Cherokee Strip and reservations assigned to the Kickapoo, Iowa, Comanche, Apache, and Wichita were also opened to settlement. All told, the Indians lost more than 11 million acres (nearly 4.5 milion hectares) of land to white settlers.

The last frontier

The roll call of states entering the Union in the half-century after 1865 is an impressive one—Nebraska in 1867; Colorado in 1876; North Dakota, South Dakota, Montana, and Washington in 1889; Idaho and Wyoming in 1890; Utah in 1896; Oklahoma in 1907; and New Mexico and Arizona in 1912.

In 1890 the Superintendent of the Census Bureau made a significant statement: "Up to and including 1880," he declared, "the country had a frontier of settlement, but at present the unsettled area has been so broken into by isolated bodies of settlement that there can hardly be said to be a frontier line."

SECTION SURVEY

IDENTIFY: sod houses, "dry farming," Oklahoma "Sooners," the last frontier; Joseph Glidden, Daniel Halladay.

1. How was western settlement speeded by (a) the Homestead Act, (b) the railroads?
2. How did the farmers on the plains solve the problems of housing and fencing?
3. Discuss the importance of the windmill to the Great Plains farmers.
4. If you had been living on the Great Plains in the late 1800's, what problems and pleasures might you have experienced?

4 The discovery of mineral treasures in the western mountains

Developments of the new industrial age made it possible for the farmer to conquer the last western frontiers. But the West in turn helped to speed the Industrial Revolution. From western farms came unending food supplies for the growing city populations. From western mines came an apparently limitless supply of gold and silver to provide capital to build industries. From other western mines came a steadily swelling volume of iron, copper, and other metals.

From "Forty-Niners" to "Fifty-Niners"

The discovery of gold in California drew fortune hunters by the tens of thousands to the Pacific coast in 1849–50. Some of the "Forty-Niners" made fortunes, but most were disappointed. Refusing to admit defeat, prospectors began to explore the valleys and slopes of the mountainous regions between the Pacific Ocean and the Great Plains. The development of mining communities again put pressure on the government to force Indians onto reservations.

In 1859 prospectors discovered gold near Pikes Peak in the unorganized territory of Colorado. More than 100,000 "Fifty-Niners" rushed to the scene to stake their claims. Caravans of covered wagons lumbered across the plains with the slogan "Pikes Peak or bust" lettered on the white canvas. Some shouldered packs and crossed the plains on foot. Others pulled handcarts behind them. Perhaps half of the fortune hunters returned the way they had come, with their slogan changed to "Busted, by gosh!" Nevertheless, enough remained to organize the Territory of Colorado in 1861.

Even more valuable than the Colorado deposits were the discoveries of silver in 1859 in the western part of the Territory of Utah. Within a decade nearly $150 million worth of silver and gold had been extracted from the famous Comstock Lode in what is now Nevada (see map, page 77), and by 1890 the total had reached $340 million. Enough of the early prospectors stayed after the stampede of 1859 to organize the Territory of Nevada, which became a state in 1864.

Gold in the Black Hills

In 1874, as you have read, prospectors found gold in the Black Hills of South Dakota (see map, page 77), and another gold rush followed. This

As this painting shows, the lack of women in western mining camps did not prevent the miners from holding dances. "Ladies" at the dance were designated by a patch on their clothing or a handkerchief on their sleeves.

area, as you have read, was Indian territory, the Sioux Reservation, which the federal government was supposed to preserve for the Indians. But the government made only half-hearted efforts to keep prospectors out of the region. The lure of gold was too strong, however, and the government soon completely abandoned its efforts to protect the Indians. In 1877 the government opened the entire area to white settlers.

Early mining communities

During and after the Civil War, mining communities sprang up in many areas of the West. Life in these mining camps has been described vividly in *The Luck of Roaring Camp* by Bret Harte and in *Roughing It* by Mark Twain. These and other contemporary accounts present a picture of wild, lawless communities of tents, rough board shacks, and smoke-filled saloons strung along a muddy street.

Each mining camp passed through several stages of development. At first, people made their own laws, relying for safety upon fists or guns to protect themselves and their families. Then some citizens began to organize private police forces, often called "vigilantes" (vij·i·LAN·tees), in an effort to maintain order. Soon men and women built schools and churches—crude shacks, but important steps toward civilized living. With the schools and churches came organized local government. Then came the appeal to Congress for recognition as a United States Territory, and eventually the adoption of a constitution and admission to the Union as a state.

Today the mountain regions, the valleys, and the high plateaus of the West are dotted with abandoned mining communities—ghost towns, as they are called. The abandoned mine shafts and the sagging, windowless cabins stand as mute testimony to the fact that prospectors and miners once pioneered on this vast frontier.

Systematic exploration

The early discoveries of gold and silver acted like magnets, drawing adventuresome prospectors into the unexplored mountainous regions of the West. Before long, however, exploration was conducted on a more systematic basis, partly through federal efforts. Between 1865 and 1879 the federal government sent many expeditions into the mountains, and in 1879 the United States Geological Survey was organized. Private industry also sent out carefully organized expeditions. The picturesque prospector with pack horse and hand tools continued to roam the mountains, but long before the end of the 1800's an increasing number of the mineral deposits were being discovered by expeditions equipped with the latest technological devices and knowledge of geology.

Minerals for industry

The development of the nation's industries brought a growing demand for metals of all kinds. The list of minerals discovered in the western mountains is impressive. Copper, needed when the electrical industry developed, was found in enormous quantities around Butte, Montana; Bingham, Utah; and in Nevada and Arizona. Lead and zinc were discovered in the same area. These and other metals have helped the United States to become the leading industrial nation in the world.

Mining as big business

The systematic exploration for mineral wealth was paralleled by other developments that brought about great changes in mining. New methods of extracting the metal from the ore were discovered, colleges of mining engineering were opened, powerful machinery was invented, great corporations were organized, and armies of skilled technicians and engineers moved into the mining regions. New equipment and the growing knowledge of chemistry and metallurgy enabled companies to work low-grade ores with profit.

By the 1890's mining had become "big business." Engineers, equipped with the latest tools of science and technology, were converting the West into a region of enormous value to the industrial development of the nation.

SECTION SURVEY

IDENTIFY: "Pikes Peak or bust," Comstock Lode, vigilantes, ghost towns; Bret Harte, Mark Twain.

1. Who were the "Fifty-Niners"?
2. Describe life in the early mining communities and the stages of development they went through.
3. How and why was the picturesque prospector replaced by systematic exploration?
4. Why did mining become "big business" by 1890?
5. What is the connection between the West and the Industrial Revolution?

CHAPTER SURVEY

INQUIRING INTO HISTORY

1. (a) Which of the reform groups concerned with the Indians best understood their problems? Explain the reasons for your choice. (b) Should the question of how to "Americanize" the Indians ever have arisen? Why or why not?
2. Technological developments such as railroads, barbed wire, and factory-made windmills helped the farmer to conquer the Great Plains. Explain.
3. The last frontier disappeared by 1890. (a) Explain how this occurred. (b) What in your opinion is the significance of the frontier in American history?
4. (a) How well do you think western stories and movies show life as it really was in the West between 1870 and 1890? (b) Which aspects of western life are overstressed? (c) Which are neglected?
5. Why does the life of the open range and the mining camps still appeal to the imaginations of millions of Americans?
6. In what ways did the federal government encourage the settlement and development of the West?

RELATING PAST TO PRESENT

1. What part has racial prejudice played in the history of American Indians? What part has lack of understanding and acceptance of a different culture played?
2. Compare early government policies regarding the Indians with the policies of today. Are they different? Explain.
3. Is scarcity of water still a problem in the West? Cite evidence to support your answer.
4. President John F. Kennedy named the reform program of his administration the "New Frontier." What historical appeal was he making to Americans?

DEVELOPING SOCIAL SCIENCE SKILLS

1. Study the photographs on pages 78 and 81, then compare the ways of life shown in each. (a) What is the subject of each photograph? (b) What details does each emphasize? (c) What is the general feeling each gives you?
2. Read the advertisement on page 79. (a) What is being advertised? (b) Whom do you think this advertisement is aimed at? (c) What methods of persuasion does it use? (d) Compare it with modern advertisements.
3. Compare the problems that miners, cattle raisers, and farmers faced in settling the land west of the Mississippi River. What solutions did each find for their problems? Were these solutions effective?
4. The United States tried to solve "the Indian problem" by getting rid of the Indians. Do you agree or disagree? Give evidence to support your opinion.

UNIT TWO
The Rise of Industrialism
1860's-1890's

CHAPTER 4
BUSINESS PIONEERS AND THE GROWTH OF AMERICAN INDUSTRY

In the 1870's a large majority of Americans lived in the country or in small rural villages and towns. This was the age of dirt roads; of carriages and wagons; and of covered bridges, their wooden sides plastered with circus posters and notices of county fairs. It was the age of oil lamps; woodstoves; the handpump or the open well; and the Saturday-evening bath in a washtub in the center of the kitchen floor.

This was the age of sewing circles and spelling bees; the one-room schoolhouse; and the country store with its tubs of butter and pickles, its cracker barrel, and its clutter of groceries and clothing and household articles hanging from the ceiling and spilling over the shelves. Symbols of the age were the small family-owned factory and the blacksmith shop at the crossroads with its charcoal fire, its huge bellows, and its burly smith in grimy leather apron shaping and fitting new shoes to a neighbor's horse.

But a new age was coming into being. Symbols of the new age were the rapidly growing cities, large factories with smoke pouring from their towering stacks, long lines of railroad cars rumbling across the countryside, and a growing number of farm machines standing outside barns or operating in the fields. In brief, life in the new industrial age was being transformed in many ways.

This, then, is the story of how America began to change from a rural, agricultural economy to an urban, industrial way of life.

THE CHAPTER IN OUTLINE

1. Binding the nation with systems of transportation and communication.

2. Creating more products for more people through expanding business.

3. Developing new forms of business organization for expanding industry.

4. The rise of business pioneers in the new industrial society.

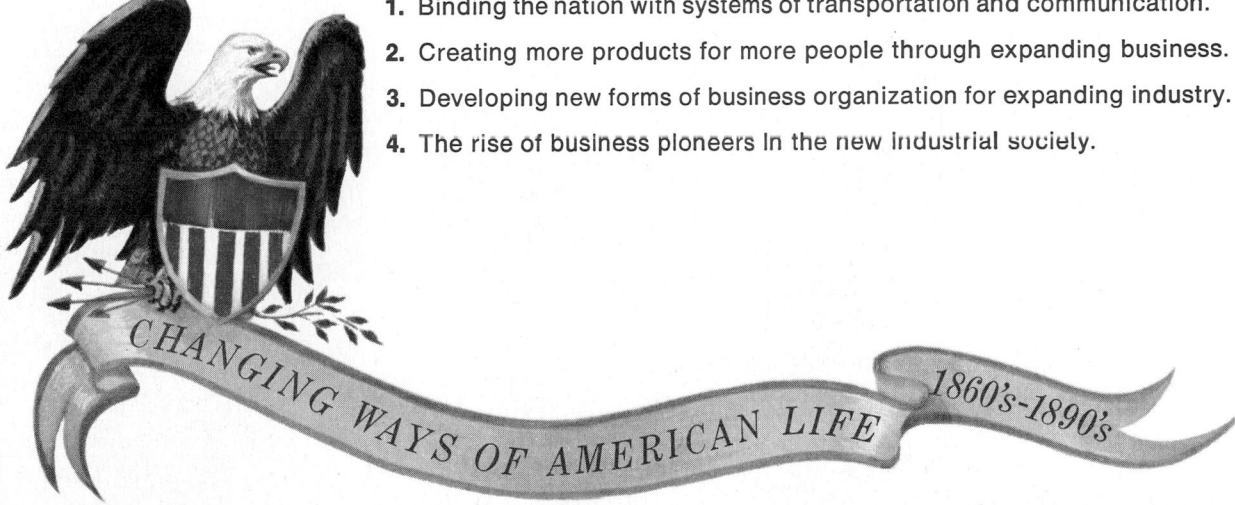

CHANGING WAYS OF AMERICAN LIFE   1860's-1890's

1 Binding the nation with systems of transportation and communication

The heart of an industrial society is the city. It is here that most factories and workers are concentrated and that most raw materials are fashioned into finished products. It is also here that most goods and services are bought and sold.

If the city is the heart of an industrial society, the routes of transportation are the veins and arteries. Into the city flow the vital resources gathered from farm and mine and forest and sea. Out of the city flow the unending supplies of manufactured articles, moving day and night over a vast transportation network to every corner of the land and overseas to other lands.

Just as the human body cannot function without heart and veins and arteries, so an industrial economy cannot function without its urban manufacturing centers and an efficient system of transportation and communication.

The growth of cities

One of the most striking developments during the years between 1865 and 1900 was the rise of the modern city with its busy railroad yards, its smoking factories, its factory workers, and its office workers. During these years, scores of American cities grew from sprawling towns to huge urban centers. In 1870, for example, about 75 percent of the people lived in the country or in communities of fewer than 2,500 inhabitants. By 1900 only about 60 percent of all Americans lived on farms or in small rural communities. The urban population had skyrocketed. While in 1870 only about 10 million of the nation's total population of 40 million were urban dwellers, by 1900 more than 30 million of America's 76 million people were living in urban areas.

The growth of cities was the result of many revolutionary developments, including the discovery of new sources of power, the application of hundreds of new inventions and new processes, and the enormous expansion of the nation's transportation and communication network.

The growth of railroads

Between 1870 and 1900 railway mileage in the United States increased from 53,000 miles (85,293 kilometers) to more than 190,000 miles (305,767 kilometers). During these same years the railroads improved in speed, comfort, and safety. Double sets of tracks replaced single sets, allowing streams of traffic to flow in two directions at once. Iron rails, which had shattered beneath heavy loads, were replaced by steel rails. Bridges of iron and later of steel replaced wooden

The years from 1865 to 1900 saw the rise of the modern city in America. Chicago, the largest city in the Middle West, is shown here as it appeared in the 1890's.

bridges. Coal, a more efficient fuel, replaced wood in the tenders of locomotives. In 1869 George Westinghouse patented the air brake, a system of power braking more efficient than the old hand brake.

Railroad passenger comfort increased. In the 1850's railroad cars had been overcrowded wooden boxes, but during the next 20 years George M. Pullman and others invented and placed in operation sleeping cars, dining cars, and parlor cars.

A nationwide network of steel

The success of the first transcontinental line (page 73) quickly led to the construction of several others. By 1893 a half-dozen major, or trunk, lines crossed the plains and mountains to the Far West, while north of the Canadian border the Canadian Pacific furnished an additional route to the Pacific coast. All over the United States, feeder, or branch, lines were also built to link the trunk lines with surrounding areas. Presently a network of steel rails served every part of the country, however remote from the major centers of industry and transportation.

Financing the construction of railroads

The construction of railroads, especially of lines reaching into the still unsettled West, was enormously expensive. To encourage the building of new lines, the government provided grants of land and loans of money.

The original land grants set aside large areas of land within which the railroad could claim a specified amount. Until the railroads exercised their claim, none of the land could be sold to the public. Some railroads ran into construction or other difficulties and did not exercise their choice for 10 years or more. Others never exercised the right, and the land reverted to the government. In round figures, the national government turned over 131 million acres (53 million hectares) of land to the railroads. At the time, this land was worth a total of approximately $123 million.

But that is only one side of the story. In return, the land-grant railroads and their competitors carried government troops and military freight for one half the standard rates for many decades (until October 1, 1946). In addition, the railroads carried United States mail for four fifths of the standard rates. In 1945 a Congressional committee reported that the railroads had already "contributed over $900 million in payment of the lands which were transferred to them under the Land Grant Act."

The government also provided subsidies in the form of bonds loaned to the railroads. These bonds bore interest at 6 percent. The railroads eventually repaid the original loans of close to $65 million with payments of interest and principal totaling about $168 million.

Importance of steamships

While land transportation was being improved, traffic on the sea lanes and inland waterways was also being developed. After 1850 sailing ships on the oceans and on the Great Lakes were replaced by steam-driven, steel-hulled freighters and sleek passenger liners. These ocean-going vessels carried millions of emigrants from Europe to the rest of the world, mostly to the United States. They also carried raw materials and manufactured goods to and from the expanding world markets.

Urban transportation

Meanwhile, in the growing urban areas new methods of transportation enabled people to move quickly within the crowded cities. By the late 1800's electric trolleys were rapidly replacing horse-drawn cars. Steam-driven and, later, electric-powered elevated trains rumbled along above crowded city streets. By the early 1900's subway trains carried passengers below the streets of New York and Boston.

As steel-framed skyscrapers climbed higher into the air, elevators, powered first by steam and then by electricity, began to carry passengers and freight from story to story. Indeed, without the elevator, skyscrapers could not have been used.

From telegraph to telephone

Equally important developments came in the field of communications. Until the 1870's the telegraph had been the most significant advance in communication since the invention of printing from movable type. From the 1870's on, however, new inventions appeared one after another.

The telegraph had been first successfully developed in the United States by Samuel F. B. Morse and in England by Charles Wheatstone during the late 1830's and the early 1840's—just as the new steam railroads began to appear. The telegraph moved across the country with the railroads—indeed, without the telegraph the railroads could not have operated safely.

In 1866, about 25 years after Morse's invention, Cyrus W. Field succeeded in laying a transatlantic telegraph cable. During the next few years additional underwater cables connected North America with other continents, giving Americans almost instantaneous communication with the rest of the world.

In 1876 Alexander Graham Bell, a teacher of the deaf in Boston, applied for a patent on a telephone he had invented. Bell's telephone quickly

The typewriter created many new job opportunities for American women in business offices throughout the nation. How do you think these job opportunites helped change women's lives?

captured the public's imagination, and in 1885 the American Telephone and Telegraph Company was organized to put the new invention into widespread use. The first crude instrument was rapidly improved, benefiting from Thomas Alva Edison's work in the field of electricity. Soon there were webs of telephone wires throughout the nation's cities, and telephone lines began to reach out into rural areas.

Other influential inventions

The telegraph, the underwater cable, and the telephone were landmarks in the history of communications. But in the late 1800's other important inventions and developments also began to reshape American life.

In the 1860's Christopher Sholes of Wisconsin developed the typewriter, which was improved by others until it became an essential part of all business operations. An improved postal system, without which modern business could not function, was also developed.

The improvement of machines for making cheap paper from wood pulp and for printing newspapers, books, and magazines also played a vital part in developing more effective means of communication. And then, of course, there was the camera, which later provided new forms of recreation as well as new techniques for industry and research.

By 1900 improvements in transportation and communications were binding all parts of the United States into a single complex economic unit. Specialized business enterprises, both agricultural and industrial, were springing up in all parts of the land, each playing its part in the ever-expanding, interlocking economic system.

SECTION SURVEY

IDENTIFY: urban center; George M. Pullman, Samuel F. B. Morse, Cyrus W. Field, Alexander Graham Bell, Thomas Alva Edison, Christopher Sholes.

1. "If the city is the heart of an industrial society, the routes of transportation are the veins and arteries." Explain.
2. (a) Why did the federal government help finance the building of the railroads? (b) What methods did it use?
3. The communications revolution at this time bridged space and time. Explain.

2 Creating more products for more people through expanding business

"Which came first, the chicken or the egg?" is a good question to keep in mind when thinking about the Industrial Revolution. For example, did improvements in transportation and communications come first, and then the big factories and mass production? Or was it the other way around?

The answer, of course, is that the Industrial Revolution was the product of many different developments in many different fields, all going on at the same time, and all combining to transform, or "revolutionize," the older ways of life. These developments included new sources of power, new machines, new and bigger industries, and new ways of selling.

In the late 1800's two entirely new sources of power—oil and electricity—were developed.

Power from petroleum

From the earliest times people had known about the dark, thick substance that oozed from the earth in certain places and that is now called "petroleum," or "oil." In the early 1850's it was discovered that kerosene, an efficient and inexpensive fuel for lamps, could be refined from petroleum. The growing demand for kerosene prompted Edwin L. Drake, a retired railroad conductor, to try to drill an "oil well" near Titusville, Pennsylvania. This was in 1859. While he was drilling, people thought he was crazy. When the oil began to flow, however, people quickly began sinking wells of their own.

Kerosene rapidly replaced whale oil as an efficient fuel for lamps. In every American city, peddlers carted kerosene through the streets, selling their product from door to door. And as the years passed, oil was used more and more as a lubricant for the nation's many new machines.

It was the development of the internal combustion engine, which burned gasoline or, later, diesel fuel, that finally turned oil into one of the nation's major sources of power. In Chapter 10 you will read how oil as a source of power virtually revolutionized American life.

Power from electricity

Electricity, like oil, was known long before it was put to practical use. The work of two Italians, Galvani and Volta, led in the late 1700's and early 1800's to the invention of the storage battery. The storage battery, which supplied small amounts of electric current at low "voltages," greatly aided Americans and Europeans who were experimenting with the uses of electricity. Even more far-reaching in their consequences were the dis-

This early oil well was one of the many drilled in the United States after 1859. First used to make fuel for lamps, oil became a source of power that virtually revolutionized American life.

coveries of the principles governing the electric motor and the dynamo. Although many persons contributed to these discoveries, a major share of the credit belongs to England's Michael Faraday and America's Joseph Henry.

Thousands of Americans first learned about

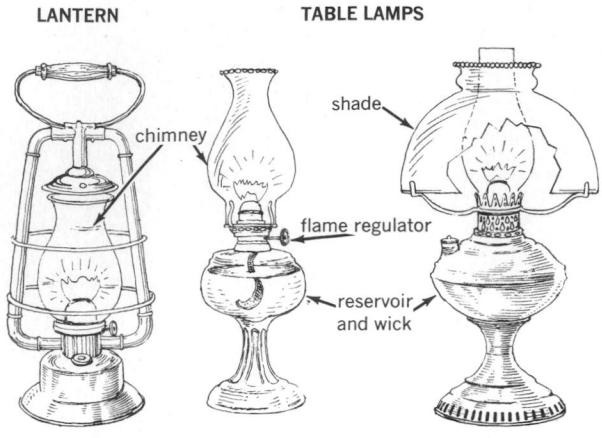

LANTERN

TABLE LAMPS

chimney

shade

flame regulator

reservoir and wick

Kerosene Lighting. A "wick" soaked in kerosene extended upward from the "reservoir" through the "flame regulator" to the point where it could be lighted. The glass "chimneys" had to be cleaned frequently because soot from the flame accumulated inside.

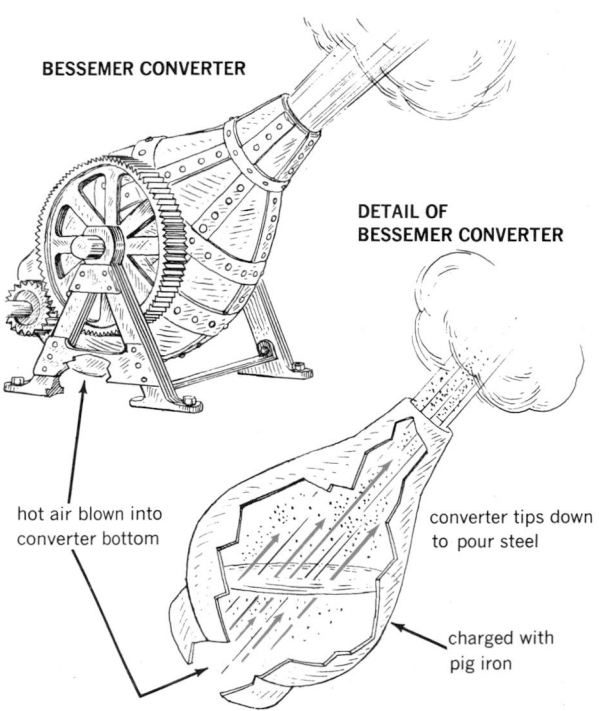

BESSEMER CONVERTER

DETAIL OF BESSEMER CONVERTER

hot air blown into converter bottom

converter tips down to pour steel

charged with pig iron

Bessemer Converter. Steel is made by removing impurities from "pig iron" which previously has been made in an iron furnace. In this Bessemer converter of 1863, a very strong blast of hot air was forced through the molten pig iron, blowing away the impurities and leaving molten steel. The steel could then be poured out and shaped into various forms.

the dynamo at the Centennial Exhibition at Philadelphia in 1876, where they saw one in operation converting mechanical energy into electrical energy. Six years later, in 1882, Thomas Edison built in New York City the first large central power plant in the United States for generating electricity. Edison drove his dynamos with steam engines. Other steam-powered electric generating plants soon appeared in other cities. Another giant stride forward was made in 1895 with the opening at Niagara Falls of the first large hydroelectric plant for producing electricity from water power. In spite of these developments, by 1900 only about 2 percent of America's manufacturing industries were powered by electricity. The revolutionary impact of this new source of power was to come after 1900.

Steel for the new industries

Behind the story of new sources of power lies still another story—the discovery of new ways of producing steel.

The United States had an abundance of the raw materials vital to the new industrial age—iron ore and coal. Immense deposits of iron ore lay near the western shores of Lake Superior. Nearly one half of the world's known coal deposits were waiting to be tapped, the largest of them in Pennsylvania.

Steel, a hard, tough metal containing iron, carbon, and other elements, was not a new material. People had made it for centuries and fashioned it into weapons, tools, and utensils. But until the mid-1800's no one knew how to produce steel cheaply and in large quantities.

In the 1850's Henry Bessemer in England, and William Kelly in the United States, independently discovered a new process for making large quantities of steel cheaply by burning out impurities in molten iron with a blast of air. During the next few years the "Bessemer process," as it was called, was steadily improved and other even more effective processes were developed.

The annual production of steel in the United States soared steadily upward. In 1870, for example, the United States produced only about 68,000 tons (61,690 metric tons) of steel. By 1900, however, Americans produced more than 10 million tons (9,072,000 metric tons) of steel annually, and by 1918 production had increased to 44 million tons (39.9 million metric tons).

Without steel—as well as copper and other materials—the Industrial Revolution would not have occurred the way it did in the United States. Steel, power, rapidly growing factories, efficient transportation and communications—these were the keys to the new industrial age.

The growth of mass production

Much of the growing steel production at this time was going into the construction of railroads, bridges, heavy machinery, factories, mills, and other industrial enterprises. American businesses were laying the foundations of an industrial system that eventually would make the United States the most productive country in the world and would provide Americans with the highest national standard of living in history.

As businesses expanded and factories grew larger, their owners and managers continually developed more efficient methods of production. During the first half of the 1800's, Eli Whitney had developed interchangeable parts. This development in turn called for a division of labor. For instance, a shoemaker no longer made an entire shoe. Instead, in large shoe factories—mostly in New England—parts of shoes were cut and shaped by workers using machines that performed only a single operation at a time. The different parts—heel, sole, lining—were then brought together at a central location in the factory and assembled into a shoe. In this way, vast quantities of shoes could be made quickly and cheaply.

This division of labor was soon adopted by most American factories in every industry, making possible the *mass production* of products of every kind.

New ways of selling products

The small general store, as well as the small family-owned factory, became less important in America during the late 1800's. Completely new types of stores appeared to handle the ever-growing quantities of products pouring forth from the nation's factories.

The *specialty store* concentrated upon a single line of goods—hardware, clothing, groceries, shoes, and so forth.

The *department store* combined many specialty stores under one roof. John C. Wanamaker opened one of the first department stores in the United States in Philadelphia in 1876. Marshall Field opened another in Chicago in 1881. Other merchants opened department stores in other cities.

Chain stores—stores with branches in many cities—also began to appear. Pioneers in this field of selling were the Great Atlantic and Pacific Tea Company (A&P), founded in 1859, and the chain of stores started by Frank Woolworth in 1879. Chain stores, like department stores, sold goods at lower prices because they bought the goods they sold in large quantities at low prices. Since women were commonly paid less than men

In 1879 F. W. Woolworth opened a "5 & 10¢ store" in Lancaster, Pennsylvania. It was the first in a chain of stores that sold only goods at a low price. By 1899 Woolworth owned 54 such stores.

for the same work, managers welcomed women clerks.

Manufacturers in the 1880's also began to develop large-scale, professional advertising. Such advertising introduced new products, promoted mass purchasing, and helped create large national markets for new streams of manufactured products.

Mail-order houses

Specialty stores, department stores, and chain stores were all part of the urban scene. In 1872, however, Aaron Montgomery Ward started in Chicago a mail-order business aimed at the rural market. A few years later the Sears, Roebuck mail-order business was started. Montgomery Ward and Sears, Roebuck used the same business methods. Customers placed orders and paid for them by mail; their goods were shipped to them by mail or railway express. Catalogs from these two mail-order houses became prized possessions in every rural household and in many a cattle raiser's or sheepherder's bunkhouse or camp. They helped to bring the outside world to isolated farms and speeded the transformation of farm life.

SECTION SURVEY

IDENTIFY: "Bessemer process," division of labor (specialization), mass production; Edwin L. Drake, Michael Faraday, Joseph Henry, Marshall Field.

1. Of what significance was the revolution in power to (a) workers, (b) manufacturers?
2. Relate an abundance of natural resources and advanced technological techniques to the growth of a nation as an industrial power.
3. What basic premise or idea did the following have regarding the merchandising of goods: (a) Frank Woolworth, (b) John Wanamaker, (c) Montgomery Ward?
4. Why did changes in selling methods take place at this time?

3 Developing new forms of business organization for expanding industry

Most of America's factories and stores in the 1860's and 1870's were *individual proprietorships* —small enterprises owned by individuals or families. The individual or the family members who owned a small factory knew all the workers— often by their first names. Most wage earners in the 1860's lived in small towns, worked in small factories, and took part in community activities with their employers.

During the next 30 years much of this small-town, personal relationship began to disappear. It was crowded out by the huge industrial plant located in or on the outskirts of a large city and employing hundreds, even thousands, of wage earners, who were often strangers to one another and even more remote from those who owned the business.

Partnerships

As businesses grew in size, business owners had to find ways of sharing expanding costs and responsibilities. The *partnership* as a form of business organization became more common. The partnership, even then, was an old form of business organization.

When two or more persons go into partnership, they have the advantage of greater capital and greater skill than one person can provide, for generally each partner invests both money and time in the enterprise. But partnerships have one major weakness for the partners. Each partner is completely liable, or responsible, for anything that happens to the business.

Corporations

As industries grew larger in the 1800's, another form of business organization, the *corporation,* became more common. It gradually became the leading form of business organization in the United States.

To start a corporation, three or more persons must apply to a state legislature for a *charter,* or license, to start a specific business enterprise. Once granted, this charter allows the in-terested persons to organize a corporation and sell shares of *stock,* or certificates of ownership, to raise the capital needed to carry on the enterprise. The *stockholders* or *shareholders*—those who invest their money in the enterprise—may periodically receive *dividends,* that is, a share of the corporation's profits. Legally, a corporation is regarded as an individual—an "artificial person" entirely separate from its owners—possessing certain rights, such as the right to make contracts, to buy and sell property, and to sue and be sued in court.

The corporation has important advantages over the individual proprietorship and the partnership. Two advantages are especially important to the corporation itself. First, the corporation can draw upon very large supplies of capital because it can sell shares of stock to many people. Second, the charter gives the corporation "perpetual life"; that is, the corporation is not ended by the death or resignation of one or several of its owners.

For the owners, or investors, the corporation also offers two important advantages. First, stockholders can sell all or part of their stock whenever they choose. Second, investors have only "limited liability." That is, if the corporation fails, they lose only the money they have invested in its stocks; they cannot be made to pay any debts owed by the bankrupt corporation. This makes the corporation a far safer investment than, say, a partnership, in which each partner has "unlimited liability" and may lose everything he or she owns if the business fails.

Corporations after 1860

During the first half of the 1800's only a few large American industries were organized as corporations, and these were usually owned by only a handful of persons. By the 1860's, however, business owners needed increasing amounts of capital to build, equip, and operate the new manufacturing enterprises that utilized the vast resources of America's forests, soils, mines, and waters. Because corporations proved ideal for gathering large amounts of capital, they became very common after 1860.

Business consolidation

During the latter half of the 1800's there was also a growing trend toward business combination, or consolidation. Corporations in the same type of business joined together to create large combinations.

Economists have pointed out that these combinations were, in many ways, a stronger form of business organization. Several corporations, when banded together, could save some of the costs of production and distribution. They could eliminate competing salespeople and advertising. They could purchase larger quantities of raw materials at lower prices and make better use of by-products. They could arrange better bargains with banks, transportation companies, and workers. It was thought, too, that they could put an end to "cutthroat competition," in which rival companies kept undercutting prices until none was earning any profits. In short, through consolidation, businesses could substitute cooperation for competition and thus reduce waste, costs, and risky losses.

But these large enterprises sometimes presented dangers to important principles of freedom in the American economic system. Through consolidation, a group of corporations might gain monopoly control over a particular field of business. Monopoly control could lead to great economic evils by operating "in restraint of trade." That is, it could reduce competition, which lies at the heart of a free enterprise economy.

For example, a business combination might have so much power that it could "freeze out" competitors by undercutting prices until the competitors failed. Then the combination could raise prices to make up its losses. Or if a consolidated enterprise gained monopoly control of an entire business field, it could charge any price it chose, denying purchasers their right to shop around for the best bargains. These and other economic evils stemming from monopoly control presently became problems, as you will read, for the government, for businesses, and for the American people.

Corporation pools

One of the earliest ways in which corporations combined was by organizing *pools*. To form a pool, several corporations simply agreed to divide all their business opportunities among themselves. For example, several railroads serving the same city might agree on what percentage of local business each would handle. Or they might agree to charge uniform freight rates so that none would gain a price advantage. Or a group of manufacturing corporations might agree to divide the country into several market areas, each reserved for the sales force of one of the corporations in the pool and "off limits" to all the others.

Unlike the corporation, which operated

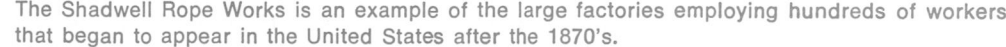

The Shadwell Rope Works is an example of the large factories employing hundreds of workers that began to appear in the United States after the 1870's.

under a legal charter, a pooling agreement had no legal standing. For that reason, courts refused to judge cases in which a member of a pool violated such an agreement with the other members. However, in 1887 pools were declared illegal in interstate commerce, and practically disappeared.

Powerful trusts

Meanwhile, other business owners developed a second form of business consolidation called the *trust.*

Business owners who wanted to organize a trust first had to reach an agreement with the major stockholders in the several corporations involved. The promise of greater profits from a larger organization was often all that was needed to persuade stockholders to enter a trust.

Under the trust agreement, the promoters of the trust, called the "trustees," gained control of the stock in all the corporations and thus of the corporations themselves. In exchange, the trustees gave the stockholders of the corporations "trust certificates" on which dividends were paid out of the profits of the trust.

With control of the stock in their hands, the trustees could run several corporations as a single giant business enterprise. If the trustees could get control of enough corporations they could secure monopoly control of an entire business field and charge whatever prices or rates they desired. They could, for example, lower prices temporarily in one area to drive a competitor out of business, while raising prices everywhere else.

During the 1870's and the 1880's giant trusts swallowed up corporations in many of the nation's largest industries, including oil, steel, sugar refining, and whisky distilling. When a trust did get control of enough corporations to secure a monopoly and end competition, it often raised prices on the products it controlled. The consumers who purchased and used these products complained bitterly about the high prices. The smaller competing businesses complained even more bitterly as the trusts closed in on them.

Magazines and newspapers of the time were filled with articles, letters, and editorials pointing out the evils of the "all-powerful monopolies," and pleading with the government to step in and restore freedom of enterprise. But local, state, and federal governments were powerless. There were no laws that said trusts and monopolies were illegal, although under the *common law,*°

° **common law:** a system of law based upon custom, tradition, and precedents established by courts of law.

which courts might or might not enforce, "conspiracies in restraint of trade" were forbidden.

The Sherman Antitrust Act

Finally, in 1890, during the administration of President Benjamin Harrison, Congress passed the Sherman Antitrust Act. The public assumed that the act was intended to restore a larger measure of free competition by breaking up giant "trusts"—a term that had come to mean any monopoly or near-monopoly of an industry. This also seemed to be what Congress intended, for Section 1 of the act declared: "Every contract, combination in the form of trust or otherwise, or conspiracy, in restraint of trade or commerce among the several states or with foreign nations is hereby declared to be illegal. . . ." The act further stated that individuals and corporations found guilty of violating the law would be liable to legal penalties.

Weakness of the Sherman Antitrust Act

Actually, few Americans, including even corporation lawyers and members of Congress, understood precisely what the new law did and did not prohibit. The act failed to define such words as "trust," "combination," "conspiracy," and "monopoly."

Because of its loose wording, the Sherman Antitrust Act was extremely difficult to enforce. The government lost seven out of the first eight cases that it brought against giant business combinations, or trusts.

In 1895 the Supreme Court handed down a decision in the case of *U.S. v. E. C. Knight Company* that made the antitrust law almost meaningless. The Court ruled that the company, which had secured control of 98 percent of the sugar refining business, was not guilty of violating the antitrust law because its control of the refining process alone did not involve restraint of interstate trade. A monopoly itself was not illegal, the Court stated. It became illegal only when it served to restrain interstate trade.

This and other decisions by the Supreme Court convinced businesses that they were free to consolidate. Thus the movement to form business consolidations actually speeded up in the years after the Sherman Antitrust Act was passed.

And yet, despite its glaring weakness, the Sherman Antitrust Act was a major attempt by the federal government to make rules for the conduct of big business. It established an important precedent for later and more effective laws.

Holding companies

After 1890 some of the nation's business leaders abandoned the trust for another form of business consolidation—the *holding company.*

This famous cartoon of 1889 pictures giant trusts looming over the Senate floor. Notice that there is an open entrance for monopolists, but that the "people's entrance" is closed.

To form such a consolidation, it was necessary to get a charter from one of the states. The directors of the holding company then issued stock in the holding company itself. With the money raised by selling this stock, the directors bought controlling shares of stock in two or more corporations that were actually engaged in producing goods or services, such as manufacturing companies, mining companies, or transportation companies. The holding company did not itself produce either goods or services. But the company did control all the corporations whose stock it held.

After the 1890's the holding company became very popular. It was legal. It was reponsible for its actions because, unlike the trust, it operated under a charter that could be revoked if the terms were violated. And when a holding company threatened to monopolize an industry, it was liable, like a trust, to prosecution under the Sherman Antitrust Act, although conviction was unlikely.

Other forms of consolidation

Another form of consolidation that often defied prosecution was the *interlocking directorate*. In an interlocking directorate some or all of the directors of one company served as directors of several other companies. Thus they could develop a uniform policy for the entire industry.

There were, of course, other ways to establish a uniform policy. Directors of different companies could simply meet and make secret agreements on prices they would charge and other matters.

Business leaders who tried to establish uniform policies for an entire industry—either through interlocking directorates or through secret understandings—were subject to prosecution under the Sherman Antitrust Act. But, as you have seen, it was difficult to prove that a monopoly existed. And it was especially difficult to prove when the monopoly had been created by means of interlocking directorates and secret agreements.

4 The rise of business pioneers in the new industrial society

Those who presided over the new world of throbbing machines, noisy factories, and crowded cities were the business leaders and the financiers. And their influence was reflected in local, state, and national politics.

Growing influence of business leaders

Between 1789 and 1860 thirteen Presidents had been elected—seven from the South, six from the North. Between 1860 and 1900 each of the seven Presidents elected was from the industrial regions of the Northeast or from the Middle West. On nearly all essential issues, moreover, the major differences between the Republicans and Democrats diminished during these years.

The business leaders of this period were not all of a single type. They varied greatly in personalities, abilities, and methods of doing business. They were pioneers, possessing the virtues as well as the shortcomings of pioneers. Some were rough, some were refined. All were eager to seize the unlimited opportunities of the new industrial world emerging around them. Some were fabulously successful. Others, the small business owners, never amassed fortunes or won great power. But all—"big" business leaders and "small" business owners alike—shared the ideal of self-reliant individualism. This ideal was also shared by the few women who took active parts in business. Among them were Nettie Fowler McCormick in farm machinery, Lydia Pinkham in patent medicines, and Kate Gleason in machine tools.

Cornelius Vanderbilt

"Commodore" Cornelius Vanderbilt was born in 1794, when George Washington was President of the United States. By 1865 Vanderbilt, who had started life as a poor boy, had accumulated great wealth and owned a fleet of steamships worth $10 million. When he died in 1877 at age 82, he was worth $105 million.

Even in his seventies Commodore Vanderbilt was an energetic man, with a defiant bearing. He could hardly write, his spelling was impossible, and his temper won him many enemies. He seemed to act on impulse, following his own hunches, or even consulting astrologers or fortunetellers, in his business affairs.

What did Vanderbilt contribute to American life? For one thing, he consolidated the railroad companies that provided service between New York and Chicago. Before he secured control of the different lines, passengers and freight had to be transferred 17 times between the two cities during a 50-hour trip. When he had completed the consolidation, one train made the entire trip in about 24 hours. He replaced iron rails and wooden bridges with steel rails and steel bridges. He built double tracks to make two-way traffic safe and speedy. He constructed new locomotives and terminals. Achievements such as these made possible the rapid development of America's industrial economy.

Andrew Carnegie

Andrew Carnegie was another fabulous business leader during the early decades of industrialism. Born in 1835 in Scotland, Carnegie came to America at age 12 and settled with his parents in Allegheny, now a part of Pittsburgh. At 14 he was working 12 hours a day as a bobbin boy in a cotton mill for $1.20 a week. He studied hard, and at 16 was a telegraph clerk earning about $4.00 a week—a fair salary in those days. A likable lad, at 17 Carnegie became private secretary to the president of the Pennsylvania Railroad.

In 1850 Carnegie bought an oil well, and he made money in the new oil industry. But he soon turned to the steel industry, and it was here that he spent the rest of his business life.

Carnegie frankly admitted that he knew nothing about steel manufacturing. His success lay in his ability as a seller and promoter. He knew how to gather around him people who were specialists. He was a relentless driver, never satisfied with himself or with others. One day he received a telegram from one of his plant superintendents: "We broke all records for making steel last week." Carnegie wired back: "Congratulations. Why not do it every week?"

Carnegie, however, also recognized the achievements of others. People he liked rose rapidly up the ladder to financial success. Charles M. Schwab, for instance, who entered one of Carnegie's plants as a stake driver at a dollar a day, became president of the Carnegie Steel Company at age 34. Schwab's share of profits in 1896 was $1.3 million. Similar stories are told of Carnegie's friendship for Henry Phipps, Henry C. Frick, and others.

By 1900 Andrew Carnegie, who began as a poor immigrant boy, was said to be the second richest man in the world. He owned all the types of property and equipment necessary for the mass production of steel, including deposits of iron ore, limestone, and coal; ships and railways to carry the raw material to smelters and mills; and huge steel plants from which the finished products poured forth. Carnegie sold his steel property in 1901 for $225 million. This tremendous financial deal was negotiated by J. P. Morgan, the most famous investment banker of the time. Out of the negotiations, in which 11 steel companies were merged, was born the mighty United States Steel Corporation, then the largest corporation in the world. Many economic historians have regarded this event as a critical point in the development of American capitalism. It marked a shift from "industrial capitalism," in which corporations were controlled by their industrial owners, to "finance capitalism," in which whole industries were dominated by bankers.

Carnegie retired in 1901. He spent much of the rest of his life giving away his money for education and other causes. "I started life as a poor man," he once said, "and I wish to end it that way." Before his death he had disposed of more than $350 million. Many public libraries stand today as monuments to Carnegie's generosity, while foundations created by his money still support causes such as education, world peace, and medical research.

John D. Rockefeller

Even richer than Carnegie was John D. Rockefeller, born in 1839, who started life as a poor boy and accumulated the world's greatest fortune. One of five children, Rockefeller left high school after one year to work as a clerk for about $3 a week. In 1858, at age 19, he went into the wholesale food business. The Civil War brought large profits to the new company. Rockefeller promptly invested his money in oil refineries, and from this point on oil became his major interest. He pioneered in developing the trust as a form of

Some of the business pioneers in the new industrial society amassed enormous fortunes. "Commodore" Cornelius Vanderbilt, for example, was worth $105 million when he died. His grandson later built a summer "cottage" for $4 million. The mansion's dining room, with its two crystal chandeliers, is shown here.

© Arnold Newman

The dangerous, back-breaking labor in early steel mills is vividly shown in this painting done in 1877 by John Ferguson Weir. The workers are guiding a shaft of steel out of a heating furnace.

big business organization. Although ruthless in forcing competitors to choose between joining him or going down to ruin, Rockefeller is credited with bringing order and efficiency to the highly chaotic and wasteful oil industry.

By 1900, however, Rockefeller's interests had broadened. He owned controlling stock in the gigantic Standard Oil Company, in railway lines, in steamship lines, in iron ore deposits in Colorado and in the Lake Superior region, in steel mills, and in many other enterprises. When the United States Steel Corporation was being organized by J. P. Morgan, Rockefeller sold to the newly formed corporation his iron ore deposits and Great Lakes steamers, receiving $80 million for the iron ore deposits alone.

Like Carnegie, Rockefeller later gave away many millions, and the foundations created with his money today continue to foster research and promote the welfare of the American people.

Pioneers of industrialism

These were only a few of the many pioneers of the new industrial society. Like other pioneers —cattle raisers, prospectors, frontier farmers, and wage earners—they helped to develop the resources of a new land. They were endowed with great energy and rare ability. They were gamblers, willing to take chances in the hope of gain. They were highly competitive people in a highly competitive society, at a time when few laws had been passed to bring order into the mad rush of business enterprise. They were absorbed in the excitement of building a new industrial world, of creating huge fortunes, of securing power.

These business leaders have often been condemned as "robber barons" for their selfishness and ruthless business methods, for exploiting their workers and forcing their rivals out of business. At the same time, their critics have acknowledged that they built new industries, introduced efficient organization, and provided opportunities that enabled many people to invest their savings profitably in the new industries springing up all over the nation.

Leaders of this type were the products of their time. It is unlikely that they will ever again appear in American life. But during these years they played an important part in an important period of the nation's development, and they helped to give new directions to American life.

SECTION SURVEY

IDENTIFY: industrial capitalism, finance capitalism, Standard Oil Company; J. P. Morgan.

1. Draw up a list of characteristics which entitle Vanderbilt, Carnegie, and Rockefeller to be called (a) "pioneers of industrial society," (b) "robber barons."
2. What important contributions did the business pioneers of the late 1800's make to American economic life?
3. Business leaders of the late 1800's had different personalities but used the same methods to achieve success. Comment.

CHAPTER SURVEY

INQUIRING INTO HISTORY

1. What is meant by the statement that America has changed from a rural, agricultural economy to an urban, industrial economy?
2. The Civil War helped speed up industrial expansion. Comment.
3. Technological changes often meet with resistance. Why do you think this is so?
4. Would you rather live and work in a rural, agricultural society or in an urban, industrial society? Why?
5. Did the Industrial Revolution change the relationship between people and their environment? Explain.

RELATING PAST TO PRESENT

1. Should industries in the United States bear responsibility for what happens to the environment as a result of their activities? Why or why not?

2. What methods are used by business today to consolidate and control vast economic enterprises?
3. Are today's objections to business monopolies comparable to the objections raised during the period just studied? Explain.

DEVELOPING SOCIAL SCIENCE SKILLS

1. Make a list of the discoveries or inventions before 1900 that you think did the most to encourage America's industrial growth. Explain how each affected the growth of industry.
2. Study the pictures on pages 91 and 95. (a) What evidence do they provide about the effects of industrialization? (b) What do you think is the viewpoint of each artist about industrialization? Explain.
3. Make a chart showing the ratio of rural and urban population in the United States in 1790, 1850, 1870, and 1900. What change do you observe? What were some causes of this change? How did this change transform the nation?

CHAPTER 5

THE REVOLT OF AMERICAN FARMERS AGAINST BIG BUSINESS PRACTICES

After 1865 American farmers stood on the threshold of the new industrial age. To be sure, neither the farmers nor the great majority of other Americans were aware of the sweeping developments that were about to transform life in America, in Western Europe, and eventually throughout the world.

Even by 1870, however, the symbols of the new industrial age were beginning to appear everywhere. Steel rails were being laid on the prairies, across the plains, and through remote mountain valleys, opening up new farm lands and bringing older farm lands in closer touch with the cities. Farm machines had begun to appear on some of the nation's more prosperous farms, enabling the farmer to produce more with less labor. The rapidly growing industrial cities were opening up ever-larger markets for farm products. As a result of these and other related developments, the farmer was becoming an increasingly important part of the new industrial economy.

In the 1870's farm families had every reason to assume that better times lay ahead for the nation's rural population. Better times did come, but not in the 1880's and 1890's. Instead, as industrialism swung into full stride, American farmers in general were confronted with a host of new problems.

THE CHAPTER IN OUTLINE

1. A simple but laborious life for farmers up to the 1870's.

2. Complex new problems for farmers in the industrial age.

3. The farmers' increasing influence on government.

4. The farmers' failure to win control of the national government.

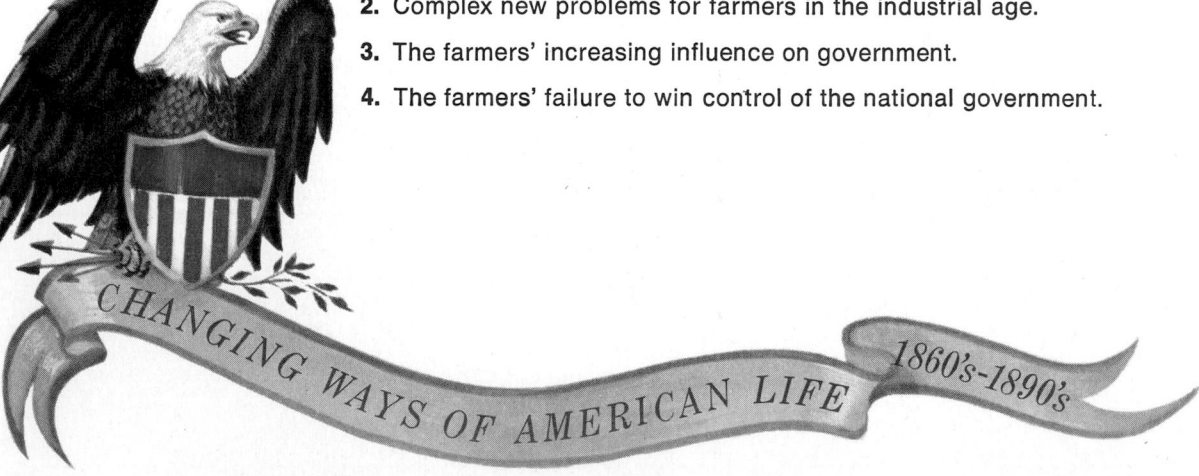

CHANGING WAYS OF AMERICAN LIFE   1860's-1890's

1 A simple but laborious life for farmers up to the 1870's

Every 10 years, in accordance with the requirement laid down in the Constitution, a federal census has been taken all across America. Occupations, income, and other information have been recorded and these records sent to the nation's capital, where they have been compiled and published.

The farm population in 1870

The returns from the 1870 census showed that the nation's urban population was growing more rapidly than the rural population. Whereas in 1860 about 80 percent of all Americans had lived in rural areas, by 1870 only about 75 percent lived on farms or in small towns and villages. Even so, the United States was still predominantly a farm country.

The 2.7 million farms that the census takers visited in 1870 varied greatly. Some were large, others small. Some farmers were prosperous; others just managed to earn a living. But regardless of size or degree of prosperity, the farms of 1870 shared certain characteristics.

The day of hand tools

Manual labor and a few simple hand tools characterized work on most farms in 1870. It is easier, perhaps, to visualize the typical farm of 1870 by starting with things the farm family did not have.

No farmers, for instance, had gasoline-driven machines or machines powered by electricity. Farmers pumped water by hand, lifted it in buckets from open wells, or, if they were fortunate, ran a pipe from a hilltop spring and allowed the water to flow to the barn and the farmhouse. There were no electric or gas stoves. Farm women usually cooked on iron, wood-burning stoves; only a few had the newly developed kerosene stoves. There were no gas or electric lights; for lighting farmers used smoky kerosene lamps and lanterns. There was no central heating; there were only stoves and, in the milder climate of the South, open fireplaces. There were no mail-order catalogs from which farm families could order ready-made clothing, tools, or equipment. In 1870 none of these "modern" conveniences had yet been developed.

On some of the nation's large and more prosperous farms, improved machines were becoming increasingly important. Steel plows were in general use. More horse-drawn corn planters, mowers, hayrakes, reapers, and threshers were being manufactured and bought. But in 1870 relatively few farmers could afford this equipment.

In 1870 farmers depended almost entirely upon hand tools—axes, saws, spades, pitchforks, sickles, scythes, and rakes. For power they relied on their muscles and on horses, mules, or oxen.

There was nothing new in this situation. For many farmers, American life in 1870 was not essentially different from American farm life in, say, 1770 or 1820.

The self-reliant farm family

Farming was not an easy way of life. The family rose at daybreak—or even earlier in winter—to milk the cows, bring in firewood, feed the hens and chickens, and fill the water trough for the livestock. When night fell—and long after dark in winter—the family was still busy with its unending chores.

But this hard life had its compensations. The family was its own boss. The land, and the labor of the farmer, his wife, and their children, provided most of life's necessities—food, clothing, and shelter. A farm family that had to rely on its own efforts developed a spirit of independence that wage earners could not hope to enjoy.

But not all American farmers in 1870 shared this feeling of independence. Nearly one fourth of the families living on farms at this time did not

Heating and Cooking. The parlor stove for heating and the kitchen range for cooking and heating were commonly used by city and country families until the development of central heating, the gas stove, and the electric stove. Coal or wood was burned, and ashes had to be removed frequently.

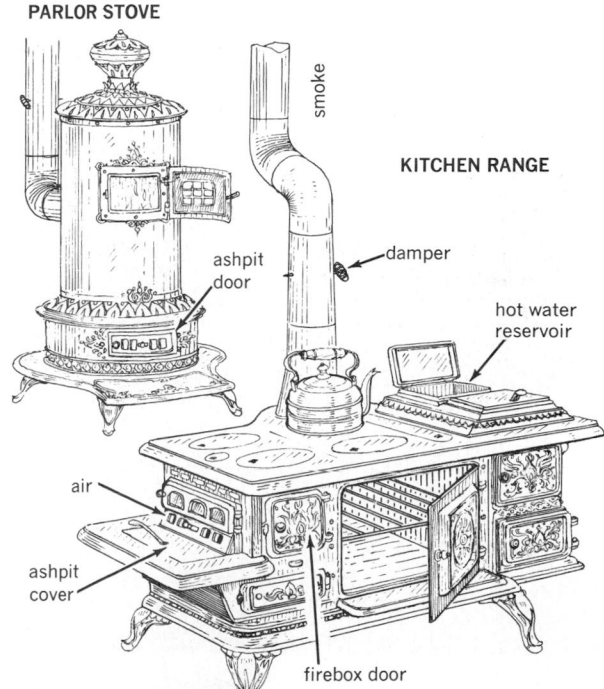

PARLOR STOVE

smoke

ashpit door

KITCHEN RANGE

damper

hot water reservoir

air

ashpit cover

firebox door

own the land they worked. They either rented farms as tenants or operated them as sharecroppers. Sharecropping, as you have read, was especially common among black farmers in the South.

Social life

Except for farmers who lived close to a growing city or a large town, opportunities for social activities in 1870 were limited. Most farm families had only three centers of social activity—the nearest town, the church, and the school.

The Saturday drive to town in a wagon or buggy behind "Old Dobbin" was a big weekly event. Even a 10-mile (16.1-kilometer) trip meant about 4 hours on the road. As for the "town," it might be nothing more than a country store at the crossroads, with a blacksmith shop on the opposite corner. Or it might be a sizable village, or even a county seat with a courthouse, a railroad station, several stores, a bank, a doctor's office, a lawyer's office, and a cluster of houses, including the homes of a handful of retired farmers.

These Saturday trips combined business with pleasure. While the farm women shopped, and while the farmers arranged for the sale of their cash crops or settled accounts at the bank or the store, the children played with their friends. But the shopping and the business gave families a chance to chat with neighbors, to watch some horse trading in front of the blacksmith shop, and to hear the latest news.

The Sunday trip to church was another bright spot in the week. Once again "Old Dobbin" was hitched to the wagon or buggy, and the entire family, freshly scrubbed and dressed in their best clothes, drove to church. There they sang, listened to the sermon, and afterward gathered in front of the church for leisurely talk before driving home.

The local school

On weekdays the children attended a one-room elementary school. To reach it, some of the boys and girls walked several miles each way along the country roads. School terms were short, for the children had to help with spring planting and fall harvesting. The teacher, usually a young woman, taught all grades. The emphasis in 1870, as in earlier times, was on "readin', 'ritin', and 'rithmetic." During the school term the

Winslow Homer painted this picture of a group of boys playing "Snap the Whip." Their one-room country school is shown in the background.

teacher often lived in the homes of the pupils, staying a month in one home, then a month in another, and so on throughout the term.

The school was also a community center. Graduation day was a big occasion, and now and then there were spelling bees and other events for parents as well as for their children.

Loneliness of farm life

For most farm families, however, farming in 1870 was a hard, lonely way of life. It was especially hard and lonely for the pioneers living on the prairies and plains.

Hamlin Garland, who spent his boyhood on farms in Wisconsin, Iowa, and the Dakotas, pictured in his books and short stories the dreary loneliness in isolated farming communities. In his famous collection of tales, *Main-Traveled Roads,* Garland wrote:

"The main-traveled road in the West (as everywhere) is hot and dusty in summer, and desolate and drear with mud in fall and spring, and in winter the winds sweep the snow across it; but it does sometimes cross a rich meadow where the songs of the larks and bobolinks and blackbirds are tangled. Follow it far enough, it may lead past a bend in the river where the water laughs eternally over its shallows.

"Mainly it is long and wearyful, and has a dull little town at one end and a home of toil at the other. Like the main-traveled road of life, it is traversed by many classes of people, but the poor and the weary predominate."

Special difficulties were faced by immigrant farmers from Europe who, by 1870, were moving out onto the western prairies and plains. These immigrant pioneers had to adjust not only to a strange physical environment but also to a strange and bewildering social environment. Churches were different, schools were different, life in nearly every way was different from what they had known in the Old World. At first they did not understand the language and customs of their neighbors. Nor did their neighbors understand the language and customs of the newcomers.

Hardest of all, perhaps, was the life of black settlers who ventured into the new areas of the prairies and plains. One "great exodus" of about 15,000 Negroes from the southern states arrived in Kansas in 1879, where they hoped to start new lives free from discrimination. These black newcomers—penniless, wearing patched and tattered clothing, weary and often ill from their long journey—took up homesteads in the new and unfamiliar lands. To buy a calf, a pig, a few chickens, or a plow, the men worked for wages on nearby farms, on railroads, or in mines. Despite these hardships, many of the black settlers managed to carve out homes for their families in Kansas. Smaller groups of Negroes settled in other parts of the West. Most of them endured some form of discrimination from their white neighbors.

New problems

Most American farmers of the 1870's were not unhappy with their lot. They expected to work hard, and they expected to live more or less apart from their neighbors.

The most troublesome problems confronting America's farmers in the late 1800's were not the age-old problems of hard manual labor and the loneliness of farm life. The problems that troubled them most were new problems growing out of the new industrial economy that was bringing changes to every part of American life.

SECTION SURVEY

1. Explain why the life of farm families in 1870 was not very different from farm life in 1770 or 1820.
2. Although farm life in 1870 was not easy, it had compensations. Explain.
3. (a) Describe the social life of a farm family on the plains or the prairies in the 1870's. (b) How different was this social life from that back east?
4. Compare the adjustments of immigrants in the 1870's settling on the plains and prairies with the adjustments of immigrants in the 1700's who settled along the eastern seaboard.
5. Do you think the reasons for the exodus of Negroes to Kansas in 1879 parallel the reasons for the exodus of Europeans to the New World? Explain.

2 Complex new problems for farmers in the industrial age

For American farmers in general, the last 25 or 30 years of the 1800's brought new problems. Not all farm families were equally affected by these problems. Farmers who remained self-sufficient continued to live much as their parents had lived before them. And many farmers living near city markets, especially farmers concentrating on truck gardening and dairying, were fairly well off. In fact, many wheat growers and other single-crop farmers turned to dairying in the 1870's and 1880's.

Most of the nation's farmers, however, were

in serious trouble during the last quarter of the 1800's. What were the new problems farm families faced?

Overproduction and falling prices

The fundamental causes of agricultural discontent—overproduction and falling prices—were rarely understood by most farmers.

From 1865 to about 1900, farmers produced more food than people could afford to buy. This increase of food in the American markets was the result of (1) the rapid opening of new farm lands on the prairies and plains, and (2) the development of new farm machinery and improved methods of farming.

Why did American farmers not sell their surplus products to other countries? They did. But competing agricultural countries such as Russia, Canada, Argentina, and Australia were also seeking customers abroad and often had the same products that American farmers wanted to export. Thus there was an increased amount of certain kinds of food on the world market as well as in the United States.

In an open-market economy, whenever the supply of any commodity is greater than the demand for that commodity, prices fall. Starting in the 1930's, as you will read later, the federal government tried to "support" farm prices in the United States, but in the late 1800's nobody even suggested such a possibility. Thus farm prices kept falling.

Wheat, which had sold for $2.50 a bushel (35.2 liters) in 1868, dropped to about 78 cents a bushel in the late 1880's. Because of high transportation costs and for other reasons, however, the farmers actually often got only 30 cents a bushel. Corn fell to 15 cents a bushel and, being cheaper than coal, was often used for fuel. Cotton, which in the late 1860's had sold for 65 cents a pound (.45 kilogram), dropped to 5 cents a pound in 1895. Thus growers of these important staple crops were farming at a loss.

High farm costs

The situation was even more desperate than these figures indicate. To add to their difficulties, farm families had to pay high prices for their shoes, clothing, kerosene, furniture, farm machinery, household equipment, and other goods. In many instances prices were high because cheaply made European goods had been kept out of American markets by the high tariffs put on imports to protect American manufacturers. And in some instances prices were high because they had been artificially raised by monopolies.

Mortgages and increased debts

To make matters worse, farm families almost always owed money. Many had borrowed money in the form of mortgages to pay for their land, homes, and barns. They had added to this burden of debt by borrowing money to pay for fences, livestock, seed, and machinery. As prices for farm products fell with overproduction, the farmers could not pay their debts. To ward off disaster, they increased their mortgages by borrowing more money, thus adding to their burden of debt.

The 1880's were often called "the decade of mortgages." Of the total number of farms in the country, 43 percent were mortgaged. In Kansas the number reached 60 percent.

Of course, these mortgages often were necessary. By means of mortgages, families with little or no money could borrow the capital they needed to buy a farm, purchase farm machinery, or make improvements on existing farms. It was not mortgages themselves, but hard times and high interest rates that troubled the farmers.

High interest rates

During the late 1800's interest rates on western farm loans ran from 8 to 20 percent. These rates were higher than interest rates charged to industrial and commercial enterprises. Bankers and other money lenders justified the higher rates on farm loans on the ground that farming was a riskier business than industry or commerce. In addition to these high interest rates, money brokers charged a commission for arranging farm loans. In several farm states loan brokers, starting with nothing, became millionaires within a few years.

The problem of money

The farmers blamed their troubles on the shortage of money, which was only part of the problem, but an important part. To understand the farmers' point of view, it is necessary to see how money affected their everyday lives.

The first thing to remember is that money is a *medium of exchange*—that is, something of value given in exchange for goods or services. Its value is determined by the goods or services it will buy. A flour miller might say, "One dollar will buy one bushel of wheat." A farmer might say, "One bushel of wheat will buy one dollar." The miller and the farmer are saying the same thing; both are stating the value of a dollar *and* the value of a bushel of wheat.

The second thing to remember is that there are two ways to change the value of a dollar *and* the value of a bushel of wheat. All other things being equal, if you *increase the amount of wheat,* for example say double it, then "one dollar will buy two bushels of wheat" or "two bushels of wheat will buy one dollar." If you *decrease the number of dollars in circulation,* say by one half, you can accomplish the same result, for one half as many dollars will now buy just as much wheat. That is, "50 cents will buy one bushel of wheat" and "one dollar will buy two bushels of wheat"; or again, "two bushels of wheat will buy one dollar."

In actual practice, the problem of money value is not this simple. But the illustration may help to clarify the problem of western farmers in the late 1800's.

Falling farm prices

Between 1865 and 1900 the price, or value, of farm products fell lower and lower. In other words, the value of money rose higher and higher. Consider a specific example. In 1868 Olaf Erickson sold 1,000 bushels (35,238 liters) of wheat at $2.50 a bushel. In 1868, then, his wheat brought him $2,500. Since his interest payments that year amounted to $250, Olaf could pay this interest with the income from 100 bushels (3,524 liters) of wheat, or one tenth of his income. Each year from 1868 on, Olaf continued to grow and sell 1,000 bushels (35,238 liters) of wheat. But by 1890 wheat was bringing only 75 cents a bushel. Olaf's income in 1890, therefore, was only $750. Since his interest payments were still $250, he now had to pay his debt with the income from 334 bushels (11,769 liters) of wheat, or one third of his total income.

As far as Olaf could tell, he had done nothing to cause this state of affairs. He owned the same farm. He and his family worked just as hard every day from sunup to sundown. Yet his income had dropped from $2,500 to $750 a year. Something was wrong. Olaf and his family were working as hard and raising as much wheat as ever. Clearly,

For farm families in the late 1800's, the country store was an important institution. Here, farm people gather to buy and sell, to get mail, to exchange gossip, and to discuss politics.

Olaf reasoned, the *value of money* had changed. Money was harder to get. Money was scarce. Money was "tight" or "expensive." It had gone up in value. That was why, Olaf thought, the same amount of wheat brought him fewer dollars each year.

Olaf, of course, forgot that there were many more farmers in 1890, both in the United States and in other countries, than there had been in 1868, and that most of these farmers were producing far more wheat than they had produced in 1868.

Although Olaf did not understand the whole complex problem, he did have his finger upon one key to his difficulties. The supply of money in the United States was not expanding rapidly enough during the late 1800's to meet the needs of the new industrial economy. The answer, as Olaf saw it, was simple enough: Let the government increase the amount of money in circulation. This would "cheapen" the dollar and raise the price of farm products. Olaf could pay his debts, buy what his family needed, and enjoy a decent standard of living.

The distributors

Farmers also blamed many of their difficulties on the distributors who bought from the farmers and sold to wholesalers and retailers. The services performed by these distributors—brokers, produce buyers, grain-elevator operators, and stockyard owners—were important in the distribution of farm products. But farmers believed that the distributors were taking too large a share of the wealth produced on farms and ranches.

Many distributors no doubt did take advantage of the farmers. Farmers, having little cash and credit, and needing money to pay their debts, had to sell their goods at harvest time even if prices were disastrously low. The distributors, backed by considerable capital, could afford to store what they bought from the farmers until prices went up. Of course, prices did not always go up, and distributors were sometimes ruined when prices fell.

The railroads

Farmers, especially on the prairies and plains, reserved their chief hatred, however, for the railroads. Like other Americans, including small business owners, farmers had at first welcomed the railroad with enthusiasm. They believed that it would open distant markets to them and increase the value of their farm lands by bringing more farmers into the community. Farmers who could afford to do so often bought a few shares of railroad stock. And the governments of small farming communities often invested money in railroad stocks and bonds in return for the railroad's promise to build a branch line to the community.

Unfortunately, events did not always develop as the farmers expected. In the first place, the railroad stock that farmers owned was so small a part of all the stock sold that the farmers had little voice in determining railroad policies.

In the second place, the farmers expected that competition among the railroads would keep freight rates low. In this hope they were also disappointed because the railroads charged "differential freight rates." The different railroads were competitors only at terminal points in the major cities, not in the towns and villages along any given stretch of track. To state it differently, railroad officials bid against each other for "long-haul" shipments between two distant cities served by two or more lines, sometimes cutting their rates so low that they operated at actual losses. They made up these losses, however, by charging much higher rates for "short-haul" shipments to communities served by only one railroad.

Farmers and other small shippers protested, of course, against this so-called "long-haul, short-haul abuse" on the part of the railroads. But it was very difficult for them to do anything about the situation.

Many of the problems that farmers faced in the late 1800's were new, strange, and complicated. Most farmers did not at first understand the new problems of overproduction, falling prices, "tight" money, high interest rates, distributors, and high shipping costs. Like all other Americans, the farmers had to grope their way into the industrial age.

SECTION SURVEY

IDENTIFY: medium of exchange, "tight" money, differential freight rates, long-haul shipments.

1. Explain the connection between overproduction and declining farm prices in the period following the Civil War.
2. The 1880's were often called the decade of mortgages. Why?
3. Describe the reasoning of farmer Olaf Erickson when he blamed the shortage of money for the decline in farm prices.
4. What were the farmers' grievances against (a) distributors, (b) railroads?
5. The new problems faced by farmers were related to the industrial age. Explain.

3 The farmers' increasing influence on government

One of the first lessons that farmers learned as they began to tackle the problems facing them in the late 1800's was the need for cooperative action.

The Grange

The first national farm organization, started in 1867, was called the Grange, or the Patrons of Husbandry. Its founder, Oliver Hudson Kelley, was familiar with the hardships and loneliness of farm life. He proposed, therefore, to establish a national organization with a local chapter in every farm community, where farm families could meet for recreation and listen to discussions on better ways of farming.

At first Kelley fought an uphill battle in organizing the Grange. By 1872, however, farm prices were falling rapidly, and the farmers, bewildered and disturbed, joined the Grange in growing numbers. By 1875 some 1.5 million farmers, most of them in the Middle West, were Grange members.

Farmers' cooperatives

Kelley had started the Grange primarily to combat social isolation and lack of educational opportunity. The farmers who joined in the 1870's, however, were more interested in economic problems and in the slogans "Cooperation" and "Down with monopoly."

Working together in the Grange and in many local farm organizations, farmers organized cooperative associations, usually called *cooperatives.* A farm cooperative owned and managed by the farmers themselves could bypass distributors by (1) selling the produce of a group of farmers directly to big city markets and (2) buying farm machines, clothing, and household goods in large quantities at wholesale prices. Before long, farmers began to set up not only cooperative stores but also cooperative grain storage elevators, creameries, and even factories to manufacture their own farm machines and equipment.

Some of these early cooperative ventures were successful, but most failed, partly because farmers often lacked business experience, partly because the farmers did not have enough capital to compete successfully with established businesses. But the farmers did not give up, for they still had the possibility of political action.

Influence in state politics

As early as 1870 farmers in Illinois forced the state legislature to investigate unfair practices by the railroads. As a result, in 1871 the Illinois legislature created a commission to fix maximum freight rates, and made it illegal for a railroad to charge "differential freight rates." Encouraged by the passage of these so-called "Granger laws" in Illinois, farmers in Minnesota, Iowa, and Wisconsin persuaded their legislatures to adopt similar laws.

The railroads opposed these laws, of course, and sometimes refused to obey them. But in 1876 and 1877 the Supreme Court, in a series of decisions known as the "Granger cases," of which the most far-reaching case was *Munn v. Illinois,* ruled that state legislatures had the right to regulate businesses that affected the public, including grain elevators and railroads.

Unfortunately for the farmers, the railroads either evaded the laws or exerted enough pressure on the legislators to get the laws repealed. The most serious blow for the farmers, however, came in 1886, when the Supreme Court qualified its decision in the "Granger cases" by ruling that state legislatures had no power to regulate traffic that moved across state boundaries. Thus, the Court ruled, only the federal government had the

SOURCES

MUNN v. ILLINOIS (1877)

Property does become clothed with a public interest when used in a manner to make it of public consequence, and affect the community at large. When, therefore, one devotes his property to a use in which the public has an interest, he, in effect, grants to the public an interest in that use, and must submit to be controlled by the public for the common good, to the extent of the interest he has thus created. He may withdraw his grant by discontinuing the use; but, so long as he maintains the use, he must submit to the control. . . .

—*United States Supreme Court*

power to regulate interstate activities of railroads.

The Interstate Commerce Act

The 1886 Supreme Court decision led Congress to pass the Interstate Commerce Act of 1887. This act was needed to correct a number of unfair practices.

"Pooling" arrangements by the railroads were one of the practices opposed by farmers and by the public at large. Several railroads operating in the same area and across state borders would get together in order to form a pool. All members of the pool then agreed not to compete, but instead to charge certain agreed-upon rates. As a result, farmers and others using the railroads often had to pay exorbitant rates.

Another practice the public wanted corrected was the granting of special favors. In order to get business, competing railroads often gave large corporations especially low rates. Or instead of actually lowering the rates, the railroads sometimes agreed to grant *rebates,* that is, to refund, or return, part of the shipping charges.

Farmers, small businesses, and the public also complained, as you know, that railroads sometimes charged more for a short haul than for a long haul. It sometimes cost more to send goods a few miles than to send the same goods from, say, Chicago to New York.

Provisions of the act

The Interstate Commerce Act, adopted in 1887 and applying to all railroads passing through more than one state, made it illegal for railroads to (1) make pooling arrangements, (2) give special favors in the form of lower rates or rebates, (3) charge more for a short haul than for a long haul over the same line, or (4) charge unjust or unreasonable rates. The act also required railroads to print and display their rates, and give a minimum of 10 days' public notice before changing rates.

Finally, the Interstate Commerce Act created an Interstate Commerce Commission (ICC) of five members appointed by the President and confirmed by the Senate. The commission had authority to (1) investigate complaints against railroads, (2) summon witnesses, (3) examine a railroad's accounts and correspondence, and (4) require railroads to file annual reports of operations and finances and to adopt a uniform system of accounting.

The commission, however, had no real authority to fix rates and to enforce its orders. If a railroad refused to accept the commission's proposals, the commission had to appeal to the courts for an order compelling the railroads to obey. In some instances the courts refused to grant such orders. In other instances the courts reversed the commission's decision. Some big business leaders regarded the Interstate Commerce Act as a sop to disgruntled farmers and small business owners, who, however, soon demanded more effective legislation.

And yet, despite its limitations, the Interstate Commerce Act was highly significant. It was the first important attempt by the federal government to regulate transportation and to create a federal "regulatory commission." Because the act set a precedent for more sweeping measures later adopted by Congress, it marked a turning point in the history of the relations between government and business.

Politics and paper money

While struggling with railroad legislation, farmers also turned to a more serious problem— the problem of falling prices for farm produce. Ignoring the facts of (1) overproduction and (2) competition from farmers overseas, they blamed low farm prices solely on the scarcity of money.

The farmers' analysis of their problem was partly right, for during the late 1860's and the 1870's money was becoming increasingly scarce. In 1865, for example, the amount of "currency," or money of all kinds, in circulation in the United States averaged $31.18 per person. By 1878 the average had dropped to $17.08.

Faced with growing hardship, farmers demanded that the government increase the supply of currency in circulation. When neither the Republicans nor the Democrats promised to help them, farmers began to join the Greenback-Labor Party, commonly called the Greenback Party.

The Greenback Party took its name from the paper money known as "greenbacks" which had been issued by the government during the Civil War. After the war the government began to withdraw the greenbacks from circulation. Farmers and other "cheap money" advocates protested. They wanted *more,* not fewer, greenbacks in circulation.

Greenbacks redeemed in gold

But the "cheap money" people did not get what they wanted. Instead, in 1875 Congress adopted the Resumption Act. This act ordered the Secretary of the Treasury to redeem *in gold* all greenbacks presented to the Treasury on or after January 1, 1879. As a result of this action, by January 1, 1879, greenbacks were worth their full, or face, value in gold. Under these circumstances, owners of greenbacks did not bother to redeem them, and Congress decided to allow 346 million of them to remain in circulation as a permanent part of United States currency.

Detail from A. Logan's "The Circus," 1874. Oil on Canvas. Gift of Edgar William and Bernice Chrysler Garbisch. Collection Whitney Museum of American Art, New York

The circus, the Fourth of July, and the county fair—these were the big events of the year for farm children and their parents. Most exciting of all was the circus, and the most famous circus was that operated by Phineas T. Barnum.

Barnum started his circus in 1871, calling it "The Greatest Show on Earth." Ten years later he joined with his major rival, J. A. Bailey, to form the famous Barnum and Bailey Circus.

Every spring the circus started its tour, traveling from town to town in wagon trains over dusty country roads. Agents traveled ahead of the show, pasting colorful posters on the sides of barns, on fence posts, and in the windows of general stores. For weeks in advance farm girls and boys from miles around saved every penny they could get their hands on in anticipation of the big event.

Under the big tent young Americans saw a strange and exciting world. They saw "Jumbo, the King of Elephants," trained bears, snarling tigers and roaring lions, giants and dwarfs, fat men and bearded ladies, sword swallowers and clowns, acrobats and jugglers and other entertainers who performed feats unlike any the audience had ever seen.

When the show was over, many young people dreamed of leaving home and following the circus. A few did run away, but most were content to live with their memories and to begin counting off the months until the circus appeared again.

THE GREATEST SHOW ON EARTH

Meanwhile, in 1875, dismayed by Congress' decision to redeem the greenbacks in gold, the "cheap money" advocates decided to take their case to the people at the polls. That was when they organized their own political party. Although the newly organized Greenback Party did not win a significant number of votes in the 1876 election, the Greenbackers continued their battle for "cheap money."

The silver issue

President Rutherford B. Hayes, who entered the White House in 1877, successfully opposed the pressure of the Greenbackers to get more paper money into circulation. But he was unable to block another move by the "cheap money" people to increase the volume of currency in circulation.

Back in 1834 the government had adopted a law providing for the coinage of both gold and silver, at a ratio of about 16 to 1. That is, the government offered to buy 16 ounces (453.6 grams) of silver for the same price it paid for one ounce (28.3 grams) of gold. At the time silver was relatively scarce, and silver producers could sell 16 ounces of silver to private buyers for *more than* one ounce of gold. As a result, they did not take silver to the United States Mint to be coined into silver dollars.

In the 1870's however, this situation changed. With the discovery of huge silver deposits in parts of Colorado and Nevada, the supply of silver increased tremendously and the value of silver *bullion,* or uncoined metal, began to fall. In 1874, for the first time in more than 30 years, 16 ounces of silver bullion were sold on the open market for *less than* one ounce of gold.

Faced with falling prices, silver producers remembered the government's offer to buy silver at the ratio of 16 to 1. But in trying to sell their silver bullion to the Treasury Department, they discovered that in 1873 Congress had passed a law removing silver dollars from the list of standard coins.

Furious at the loss of a profitable market for their bullion, silver producers denounced Congress for what they called the "Crime of '73." Actually Congress had passed the law because for more than 30 years the silver producers had not wanted to sell their bullion to the government.

But the "Crime of '73" became a rallying cry for those who demanded that the government buy silver. This demand came mostly from the West. But the silver people were also supported by other Americans, including farmers, who wanted more currency in circulation.

The Bland-Allison Act

In 1877 Representative Richard P. Bland of Missouri introduced a bill calling for free and unlimited coinage of silver dollars at a ratio of 16 silver dollars to 1 gold dollar. When this bill

Harvey T. Dunn (1884–1952), American. "The Homesteader's Wife" (detail). South Dakota State University, gift of the artist to the people of South Dakota

Starting in 1886, a 10-year series of droughts on the Great Plains turned farm lands into arid desert. This picture reflects the hard life of farm women on the Great Plains during these years.

reached the Senate, it was modified by Senator William B. Allison of Iowa to become the Bland-Allison bill.

The Bland-Allison bill authorized the Treasury Department to buy and to mint not less than $2 million and not more than $4 million worth of silver each month. President Hayes vetoed the bill, but Congress passed it over his veto in 1878. The new law was a partial victory for the silver interests, the Greenbackers, and other "cheap money" people.

Failure of the Greenback movement

The Greenback Party reached its high-water mark in 1878, when it polled 1 million votes and elected members to Congress. This was a shock to the two major parties. But the triumph was short-lived. Two years later the Greenback Presidential candidate, General J. B. Weaver, received only 300,000 votes.

Although it failed to achieve its goal, the Greenback movement, like the Grange movement, taught the farmers several valuable lessons. The farmers learned from their experience with the Grange that they could, if united, gain influence in state legislatures. They learned from the Greenback movement that their influence might be felt even in the national legislature. And, above all, they learned that the secret of power lay in organization.

Farmers' Alliances

Even before the Greenback Party began to break up, farmers began to form organizations called "alliances." During the early 1880's the different state alliances in the North and Northwest organized a loose federation called the Northern, or Northwestern, Farmers' Alliance. The southern groups joined in a much more tightly knit organization known as the Southern Alliance.

Like the Grange, the alliances experimented with cooperative buying and selling organizations. They were prepared to take action to protect the farmers from the exploitation of manufacturers, railroads, and distributors.

Hard times in the late 1880's transformed the alliances into influential political organizations. By 1890, for example, the Southern Alliance had 3 million white members, while 1 million southern black farmers were enrolled in an affiliated Colored Alliance. A proposal to merge the Southern Alliance and the Northwestern Farmers' Alliance failed, however, because southerners insisted upon separate white and black lodges in the merged alliance. Northern leaders refused to accept this arrangement.

Desperate conditions for farmers

Starting in 1886, a 10-year series of droughts on the Great Plains turned farm lands into arid desert. Driven to desperation, thousands of farmers finally gave up and moved back east. But others remained and continued to fight the land and those they held responsible for much of their trouble—the owners of railroads and factories, the directors of banks and insurance companies that held farm mortgages, and the distributors who bought and sold farm produce. The farmers also continued their pressure, along with other "cheap money" interests, to get the government to put more money into circulation.

The Sherman Silver Purchase Act

During the administration of President Benjamin Harrison, the Republicans in Congress were eager, you recall, to increase tariff rates. They succeeded when the McKinley Tariff Act became law in 1890. However, in order to get enough votes to pass this tariff act, the Republican had to make a deal with the "cheap money" people.

In 1889 and 1890 six new states entered the Union—North Dakota, South Dakota, Montana, Washington, Idaho, and Wyoming. These states, all in the West, greatly increased the political strength of the farmers and the silver mining interests in Congress. Members of Congress representing farming and silver mining areas agreed to vote for the McKinley Tariff Act if the high-tariff members voted for a "cheap money" bill.

As a result of this "deal," the Sherman Silver Purchase Act became law in 1890. This act required the United States Treasury to purchase 4.5 million ounces (127.6 million grams) of silver each month at the prevailing market price and to pay for this silver with paper money that could be redeemed in gold or silver.

Silver miners hoped that the law would raise the price of silver, and farmers hoped that, by increasing the supply of money, it would raise the prices of farm produce. These expectations were not realized. The purchased silver was not coined; the money in circulation did not greatly increase.

New farm leaders

Leaders of the Farmers' Alliances were active in securing passage of the Sherman Silver Purchase Act and other legislation favorable to farmers. Some of the leaders became national figures by reason of their powerful oratory, their vigor, and the depth of their convictions. Among the nationally famous leaders was Ignatius Donnelly of Minnesota, a spellbinder on the platform and a pamphleteer with a biting literary style. In Kansas there was "Sockless Jerry" Simpson, who denounced the rich eastern monopolists. Kansas also produced two influential women leaders—Mary Elizabeth Lease, a colorful and dynamic orator, and Annie Diggs, an editor and an effective behind-the-scenes political worker.

In the South a new group of political leaders representing the poorer farmers arose to challenge the traditional leaders of the Democratic Party. Among the more picturesque and eloquent of the new leaders were Governor James Hogg of Texas, Tom Watson of Georgia, and "Pitchfork Ben" Tillman of South Carolina.

The big question

By 1890 American farmers were facing a major question: Should they form a third party?

Many northern farmers favored a third party; most southern farmers opposed it. The opposition of southern farmers arose from a split within the southern Democratic ranks.

Since reconstruction days, prosperous, white, conservative southerners, called "Bourbon"° Democrats, had regained major political strength in the South. They were opposed by agrarian reformers within the Democratic Party who were demanding greater economic opportunity and justice for poor white farmers. The voices of these southern Democratic reformers and their followers were strong within the Southern Alliance of farmers.

In 1890 many black southerners were still permitted to vote. As a rule, the Bourbon Democrats were less determined than poorer white farmers in discriminating against black southerners. Thus many black tenant farmers voted for Bourbon candidates.

Leaders of the southern Democratic reformers had differing opinions on the issue of Negro suffrage. A few, recognizing the common economic interests of the poorer farmers, white and black, favored an effort to enlist black voters on their side. But the majority feared that competition with the Bourbons for black votes would endanger white supremacy in the South. They especially feared that a third political party would divide the southern white vote and thereby enable Negroes to become a political power again in the South, as they had been during reconstruction. Thus most leaders of the Southern Alliance were opposed to a new farmers' political party. These leaders preferred to continue their efforts to capture control of the southern Democratic Party from the Bourbon Democrats.

° **Bourbon:** in politics, an extremely conservative or reactionary person, named after France's Bourbon family of rulers.

SECTION SURVEY

IDENTIFY: the Grange, rebates, pooling, "cheap money," ratio of 16 to 1, bullion, "Crime of '73," Sherman Silver Purchase Act of 1890; Oliver H. Kelley.

1. (a) What was the original purpose of the Grange? (b) Why were farmers' cooperatives formed?
2. Discuss the strengths, limitations, and significance of the Interstate Commerce Act of 1887.
3. Explain the reasons for the formation of (a) the Greenback Party, (b) Farmers' Alliances.
4. Farmers learned that one way to power was through organization. Discuss.
5. In the political struggle in the South, black southerners were caught in the middle. Comment.

4 The farmers' failure to win control of the national government

Should the farmers form their own national political party? This was the question that farmers discussed in schoolhouses and Grange halls during the summer of 1890.

Birth of the Populist Party

The Congressional elections in the fall of 1890 drew farm men and women into what seemed to be a fiery crusade. Speakers such as Mary Elizabeth Lease bluntly stated the farmers' grievances. In a powerful speech she proclaimed: "Wall Street ° owns the country. It is no longer a government of the people, by the people, and for the people, but a government of Wall Street, by Wall Street, and for Wall Street. The great common people of this country are slaves, and monopoly is the master. The West and South are bound and prostrate before the manufacturing East. . . . There are thirty men in the United States whose aggregrate wealth is over one and one-half billion dollars. There are half a million looking for work. . . . We want money, land, and transportation. . . . We will stand by our homes and stay by our firesides by force if necessary, and we will not pay our debts to the loanshark companies until the government pays its debts to us. The people are at bay, let the bloodhounds of money who have dogged us thus far beware."

Fired by this new militant spirit, Republican and Democratic farmers decided in 1891 to forget their political differences and form a third party. A meeting made up chiefly of Farmers' Alliance leaders from the West and Middle West launched the People's Party, or the Populist Party, at Cincinnati, Ohio, in 1891. In Omaha, Nebraska, the following year, the Populists drew up a platform and nominated James B. Weaver of Iowa for President of the United States.

Farmers' "Declaration of Independence"

On July 4, 1892, the Populists adopted their platform, demanding far-reaching reforms.

"We meet in the midst of a nation brought to the verge of moral, political, and material ruin," stated the platform. "The people are demoralized. . . . The newspapers are largely subsidized or muzzled; public opinion silenced; business prostrated; our homes covered with mortgages; labor impoverished; and the land concentrating in the hands of the capitalists. . . . We have witnessed for more than a quarter of a century the struggles

of the two great political parties for power and plunder, while grievous wrongs have been inflicted upon the suffering people. We charge that the controlling influences dominating both these parties have permitted the existing dreadful conditions to develop without serious effort to prevent or restrain them. Neither do they now promise us any substantial reform. . . . They propose to sacrifice our homes, lives, and children on the altar of Mammon.° . . ."

Specific Populist demands

The Populist platform then listed the specific demands of the farmers: (1) an increase in the currency, to be secured by the "free and unlimited coinage of silver at a ratio of 16 to 1"; (2) government ownership of railroads, telegraphs, and telephones; (3) the return to the government of all land held by railroads and other corporations in excess of their needs; (4) a graduated income tax, requiring people with higher incomes to pay a proportionally higher tax; (5) a system of national warehouses where farm produce could be stored until market conditions improved, with the government providing loans on each deposit by a farmer; (6) political reforms, including the direct election of United States Senators, and the adoption of the secret ballot, the initiative, and the referendum.

The Populist Party had strong support from many industrial wage earners, as well as from farmers. Thus the Populist platform also demanded shorter working hours and restrictions on immigration, which many workers held responsible for unemployment and low wages.

The election of 1892

In the campaign of 1892, great crowds of farmers in the Middle West gathered at outdoor meetings and picnics to listen to eloquent Populist speakers. James B. Weaver, the Populist Presidential candidate, traveled widely and spoke to enthusiastic audiences in the Middle West.

In the South, however, the story was different because of the racial situation. Conservative Democrats and Populists alike were willing to let black southerners vote—but only if it seemed certain that they could control the black vote. Populist leaders, however, urged poor farmers, white and black, to vote together against their "exploiters," the well-to-do planters and business people of the Democratic Party. This angered many white

---

° **Wall Street:** a street in New York City's financial district, the nation's principal financial center; often used as a symbol of large banking and business interests.

° **Mammon:** an ancient god, used to symbolize wealth, greed, and materialism, to whom human sacrifices were made.

In the election of 1892, a Republican and a Democrat in Chicago promised each other that the supporter of the losing candidate would pull the supporter of the winning candidate through the streets in a wagon. The Democrat won the bet. The painter, Joseph Klir, included in this picture a number of immigrants who, like him, had come to the United States from Czechoslovakia.

southerners, rich and poor alike, who feared that the Populist bid for black support might endanger white supremacy. Populist speakers in the South were greeted with howls and jeers.

The Populist bid for southern Negro votes was not very successful. The Populists did not attempt to build a strong or lasting alliance between poor white and black southerners. They did not support a move toward federal supervision of elections, which would have guaranteed the right of black southerners to vote. Nor did the Populists support other efforts of southern Negroes to overcome their grievances. Thus Populist candidates in the election of 1892 were generally defeated in the South.

President Benjamin Harrison, running for reelection on the Republican ticket, was defeated, as you know, by the Democratic candidate, Grover Cleveland. The Democratic victory was a sweeping one. But the Populists made an impressive showing in the nation as a whole, despite their failure in the South. They polled more than 1 million popular votes, won 22 electoral votes for their Presidential candidate, and gained seats in state legislatures and in Congress. No third party had ever shown such strength in its first year. Democrats and Republicans alike realized that the Populist movement was much more than the protest of a few discontented Americans.

Depression and growing resentment

For the two older political parties, however, the Populist movement was only the beginning of their problems. In 1893 the country sank into a serious economic depression. Farm prices plunged downward. Factories closed their doors, and thousands of unemployed workers walked the streets, desperately looking for jobs.

Farmers and wage earners blamed the depression on "tight money." They demanded that the government increase the amount of currency in circulation by the "free and unlimited coinage of silver at a ratio of 16 to 1."

President Cleveland blamed the crisis on the Sherman Silver Purchase Act of 1890. He believed that it was not "tight money" that had led to the depression, but rather uncertainty over the "value of money." Cleveland insisted that the only way to end the depression was to accept gold as the single standard of value for the nation's currency. This was an oversimplified explanation, for the depression was worldwide. But there was some truth in the President's analysis.

Reviewing the money problem

As you have read, during the 1870's and 1880's farmers blamed their difficulties, in part at least, on the government's refusal to increase the supply of money, or currency, in circulation. Farmers and other *debtors* wanted "cheap money" with which to pay their overwhelming debts. On the other hand, *creditors* and business people in general wanted to be paid back in dollars worth at least as much as the dollars they had lent or invested. Creditors and business people wanted, therefore, to restrict the amount of money in circulation. They wanted what they called "sound money."

Acting under the authority of the Sherman Silver Purchase Act, the Treasury had begun in 1890 to buy silver in large quantities. Mine owners now had a sure market for almost the entire output of their mines, but the price of silver continued to drop. Farmers and other "cheap money" people considered the new law merely a halfway measure. What they demanded in the Populist platform of 1892 was the "free and unlimited coinage of silver at a ratio of 16 to 1."

The shrinking gold reserves

By 1893, however, the Treasury Department was becoming deeply concerned about the policy of *bimetallism*—meaning that two metals, gold and silver, furnished the security for all the nation's currency. The value of silver had fallen until the actual silver in a silver dollar was worth only 60 cents. Since silver as well as gold provided the "backing," or security, for the nation's currency, more Americans began to grow uneasy about this situation. As a result, many people began to exchange their silver bank notes for gold coins, rather than for silver coins. By the time Cleveland entered the White House in March 1893, the gold reserves had shrunk to only a little more than $100 million.

The shrinkage in gold reserves created a serious government crisis. If the gold reserves completely disappeared, the government would no longer be able to keep its promise with gold

coins. It would, instead, have to pay with silver. And, since by mid-summer of 1893 the value of the silver in a silver dollar had fallen to 49 cents, prices would soar in a runaway inflation, and the nation would head toward economic disaster.

Repeal of the Sherman Silver Purchase Act

President Cleveland acted promptly. He called a special session of Congress to repeal the Sherman Silver Purchase Act. The President's recommendation provoked violent debate. Representatives of silver mines, farmers, and "cheap money" people in general refused to consider repeal. But in the late fall the administration finally secured enough votes to push the repeal bill through Congress.

Repeal of the Sherman Silver Purchase Act stopped the flow of silver into the Treasury. But the gold reserves continued to shrink, for there were still many millions of silver bank notes in circulation and the Treasury kept on redeeming them in gold. By 1895 the gold reserves had dropped to only $41 million. It seemed to be only a question of time before the United States would go off the gold standard—that is, would stop redeeming its paper currency with gold—and runaway inflation would start.

Cleveland aided by bankers

At this critical point President Cleveland accepted the recommendation of a group of bankers headed by J. P. Morgan. The bankers offered to lend gold to the government, receiving government bonds as security.

The arrangement worked. When people heard that J. P. Morgan and other leading bankers were behind the government, confidence returned and the run on the gold reserves ended. Many Americans, those with "sound money" views, felt that President Cleveland and the bankers had acted wisely and had saved the nation from disaster. But "cheap money" Americans were furious. Pointing out that the bankers had charged a generous commission for their services, they insisted that the President had made a "deal with Wall Street."

Battle lines drawn

By the time of the Presidential election of 1896, both major parties were split between the "sound money," gold-standard people and the "cheap money," silver people.

The Republicans chose as their Presidential candidate William McKinley of Ohio. Although McKinley tried to straddle the money issue, he came to be regarded as the leader of those people who favored the gold standard.

The Democratic convention opened with a bitter struggle between the "sound money" wing of the party and the "silver" wing. The "sound money" delegates were soon howled down, and "cheap money" delegates adopted a platform demanding "free and unlimited coinage of both gold and silver. . . ."

The battle lines were drawn, with the Republicans on the "sound money" side and the majority of Democrats on the "cheap money" side. But the Democrats had not yet selected a Presidential candidate. Rejecting President Cleveland, the "silver" Democrats began to look for someone who could lead them to victory.

William Jennings Bryan

The field was wide open when a handsome young lawyer stepped forward to address the convention. Only 36 years old, William Jennings Bryan of Nebraska had served in the House of Representatives for four years. This was his only political experience in the national capital. But when he began to speak at the convention, people listened.

"We do not come as aggressors," Bryan cried. "Our war is not a war of conquest; we are fighting in the defense of our homes, our families, and prosperity. We have petitioned, and our petitions have been scorned; we have entreated, and our entreaties have been disregarded; we have begged, and they have mocked when our calamity came. We beg no longer; we petition no more. We defy them! . . .

"You come to us and tell us that the great cities are in favor of the gold standard; we reply that the great cities rest upon our broad and fertile prairies. Burn down your cities and leave our farms, and your cities will spring up again as if by magic; but destroy our farms and the grass will grow in the streets of every city in the country. . . .

"Having behind us the producing masses of this nation and the world, supported by the commercial interests, the laboring interests, and the toilers everywhere, we will answer their demand for a gold standard by saying to them: You shall not press down upon the brow of labor this crown of thorns, you shall not crucify mankind upon a cross of gold!"

With the closing words of Bryan's "Cross of Gold" speech, wild tumult broke out at the convention. Here was the Democratic standard-bearer. Here was a fitting leader for a crusade to seize power from the big business, "sound money" groups.

The Democratic nomination of Bryan and the adoption of a platform demanding free and unlimited coinage of silver left the Populists in an awkward position. The Democrats had stolen

William Jennings Bryan was the Democratic candidate for President in the elections of 1896 and 1900. This campaign poster refers to Bryan's famous "Cross of Gold" speech of 1896.

their thunder. When they met in convention, the Populists decided to support Bryan as their Presidential candidate, but they tried to preserve their party identity by nominating Tom Watson of Georgia for the Vice-Presidency rather than Arthur Sewall of Maine, the Democratic nominee.

Bryan's crusade

Bryan turned the election campaign into a crusade. In 14 exhausting weeks traveling vast distances by railroad, Bryan accomplished the almost superhuman feat of making 600 speeches to 5 million people in 27 states. Bryan's speeches roused his supporters to frenzies of enthusiasm.

The "sound money" people threw all their energy and resources into defeating Bryan. Under the leadership of Mark Hanna of Ohio, McKinley's campaign manager and a wealthy business leader, the Republicans raised at least $3.5 million to offset Bryan's $300,000 campaign fund. Nearly every influential newspaper in the country backed the

Republicans. Many factories paid their workers on the Saturday before election with the warning that they would have no jobs if William Jennings Bryan won the election.

McKinley's victory

Bryan lost with 176 electoral votes to McKinley's 271. But the popular vote was much closer—7 million for the Republicans, 6.5 million for the Democrats. Although the country had decided in favor of the gold standard, the farmers and other "cheap money" advocates had come close to winning the Presidency and control of Congress.

Defeat in the 1896 election and the arrival of better times for the farmers ended the power of the Populist Party. As you will read, however, during the early 1900's a new third party, the Progressive Party, as well as progressive Democrats and Republicans, won many of the reforms that the Populists had demanded.

SECTION SURVEY

IDENTIFY: Populists, free and unlimited coinage of silver, "sound money," bimetallism, "Cross of Gold" speech; James B. Weaver, William McKinley, William Jennings Bryan, Mark Hanna.

1. In your opinion, which four planks in the Populist Party platform of 1892 would have aided the farmers most at that time?
2. Which ideas in Bryan's "Cross of Gold" speech were most effective in winning him the nomination?
3. If all the underprivileged people in the nation in the 1890's had been able to form an alliance or had been able to organize, what do you think might have been the result?

CHAPTER SURVEY

INQUIRING INTO HISTORY

1. Third parties in national politics have never won a Presidential election. What then has been their function in our political system?
2. (a) Discuss the reasons why farmers wanted cheap money (greenbacks) and free and unlimited coinage of silver. (b) To what extent were farmers successful in achieving this goal?
3. Explain why you would have felt as you did about cheap money vs. sound money, if you had been a (a) debtor farmer, (b) creditor business owner, (c) retired person living on a fixed income, (d) banker, (e) worker.
4. How did each of the following complicate the farm problem: (a) railroads, (b) interest on mortgages, (c) protective tariff?
5. Why was the Populist Party so fiercely opposed to the banks, railroads, and corporate businesses of the United States?
6. By referring to the "Cross of Gold" speech, explain why William Jennings Bryan came to be known as "the voice of populism."

RELATING PAST TO PRESENT

1. Search current newspapers and magazines for articles on migrant farm workers in the United States.

Compare the difficulties these migrant workers have with the problems faced by early Grange members.
2. Do groups with differing views need a crisis in order to mobilize behind one leader and one platform? Does a society have to be confronted with a crisis or an emergency before it listens to those who are in need? Explain your answers.
3. Does mechanization continue to bring about change in our society today? Explain.

DEVELOPING SOCIAL SCIENCE SKILLS

1. Examine the pictures on pages 107 and 112. (a) What is the mood of each picture? (b) What details does each artist emphasize? (c) What do you think is the viewpoint of each artist about farm life? What makes you think so?
2. Find accounts or books written by or about people who lived on farms on the Great Plains between 1860 and 1890. How do these accounts compare with your ideas about life on farms in those years?
3. Read the Populist Party Platform of 1892 and answer the following: (a) What were the problems facing Americans according to the Platform? (b) Based on your reading so far, can you find evidence to support or refute the claims made in the Platform? (c) What solutions were offered for these problems?

CHAPTER 6

THE STRUGGLE OF AMERICAN WORKERS TO ORGANIZE

On April 14, 1865, when President Lincoln was shot in Ford's Theater in the nation's capital, the United States was still a predominantly agricultural country. By 1900 it had become the leading industrial and manufacturing nation in the world.

America's amazing industrial growth was possible only because of immense improvements in transportation, notably the railroad and the steamship; the development of power-driven machines; the organization of business into large corporations; the construction of giant factories and other industrial plants; the development of more efficient production techniques; and the rapid growth in the number of workers.

The workers—women and children as well as men—came from farms and rural areas. They also came from Europe, in a mighty flood of immigration numbering hundreds of thousands every year.

Both the older Americans and the newcomers entered a new world when they moved into America's growing industrial communities. In the early days of power-driven machines and mass production, they were as much pioneers as the men and the women who had earlier pushed America's frontiers westward to the Pacific. And, like pioneers in every age, wage earners in the late 1800's faced complex problems.

THE CHAPTER IN OUTLINE

1. Complex new problems for wage earners in the industrial age.

2. The influence of immigrant workers in American society.

3. The role of labor organizations in dealing with workers' grievances.

4. Opposition to organized labor's early efforts to win reforms.

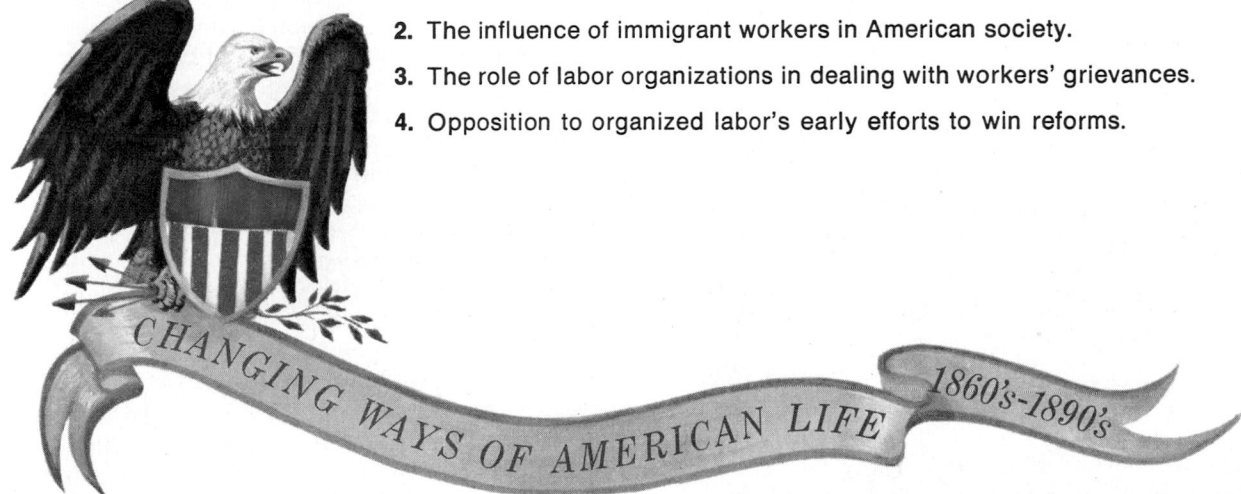

CHANGING WAYS OF AMERICAN LIFE   1860's-1890's

1 Complex new problems for wage earners in the industrial age

The industrial developments that were transforming the United States from 1865 to 1900 created new problems as well as new opportunities for wage earners. Like all other Americans, wage earners had to adapt themselves to a rapidly changing industrial society.

New owner-worker relations

For one thing, large corporations hiring thousands of workers changed the old-time relations between owners and employees. In earlier days when factories were small, the owner knew the workers and often took a personal interest in their welfare. But in the huge factories workers seldom saw the owners, most of whom were stockholders living in widely separated parts of the country.

Nor did many owners know at first hand what working conditions were like in their factories and mines. They bought shares of stock as an investment. They hired managers to run the plants.

Moreover, the workers themselves often were less interested in the new, large, impersonal corporations. As the factories grew larger, the workers, as individuals, became less important.

One effect of the growth of industry was the crowding of workers and their families in big-city slums. This photograph was taken during the early 1900's.

If a worker objected to the way a factory was run, he or she could easily be replaced. Thus individual workers could not hope to change or improve their working conditions. Nor could they reasonably hope to become an owner beyond, perhaps, buying a few shares of stock. To be sure, some workers did become supervisors and managers, and a few rose to positions of wealth and power.

But in general, as factories grew larger and more impersonal, it became harder for individual workers or groups of workers to "bargain" with employers over wages and working conditions.

Company towns

Workers in so-called "company towns" labored under the greatest disadvantages. There were mining districts in Pennsylvania and West Virginia and textile-mill regions in the South where companies owned entire towns—all the houses, stores, and other buildings. The companies employed the teachers and the doctors. The local magistrates and the police owed their jobs to the company. In these towns workers did not dare to protest the rent they paid for their company-owned houses or the prices they paid in the company-owned store. Frequently, the workers received part of their wages not in cash but in credit at the company store.

Effects of mechanization

The use of power-driven machines in factories also created new problems for wage earners. For one thing, work became increasingly specialized and increasingly monotonous. Moreover, the new machinery often did the work of several wage earners. Indeed, the new machines might produce much more than the displaced wage earners. Thus the installation of new machines often caused *technological unemployment* by throwing workers out of jobs. Of course, new and different jobs were often created because workers were needed to build and repair the machines. Further, the higher output of the machines increased the nationwide production of goods and thereby created new jobs of many kinds. But displaced workers often found it difficult to learn new skills and get new jobs.

Machines were also physically dangerous. Until about 1910 little was done to safeguard workers from accidents. When an accident occurred, the worker was usually blamed. If disabled, he or she received no compensation to pay the costs of doctors and hospitalization. When a worker was killed, the worker's family was usually left without an income, for employers did not insure the lives of wage earners. Yet industrial hazards were a problem of primary importance. Between 1900 and 1910, for example, 3 percent of all employed workers in the United States were killed or injured annually in industrial accidents. In 1911 a fire in the unsafe Triangle Building in New York City brought death to 146 women textile workers. In a strike just the year before, the women had protested against their unsafe working conditions.

Effect of the railroads

Before the nationwide network of railroads was built, American manufacturers usually sold their products only in nearby market areas, without competition from other areas. With the railroad network, however, a manufacturer could sell products anywhere in the country, provided the manufacturer's prices were as low as those elsewhere.

This creation of a competitive national market for goods also created a competitive national market for labor. For example, if cotton goods were being made cheaper in southern mills because of lower wage rates, then New England manufacturers of cotton goods were inclined to lower their wage rates to compete with the lower-priced output of the southern mills.

The business cycle and unemployment

Like other citizens, workers were greatly influenced by what economists call the *business cycle*—the expansion of business and industry during periods of prosperity and their contraction during periods of depression. Business leaders and government officials had not yet learned how to cushion the effects of depression. Workers lived in constant dread of being laid off or having their wages sharply reduced whenever business conditions took a downturn. Even when business was good, unemployment brought misery to many industrial workers.

Between 1870 and 1900 hundreds of thousands of jobless persons searched for work. In 1889, a fairly typical year, about 19 percent of the workers in manufacturing and transportation were jobless.

The closed frontier

As long as the frontier remained open, farmers on worn-out eastern land could choose between migration to the frontier or migration to the city. Many chose to continue farming and moved west. After about 1900, however, as eastern farm families had fewer and fewer opportunities to find good cheap western land, they turned to the cities for work. Thus they helped to swell the population of the cities and to drive down the wages of the industrial worker.

Low wages and long hours

During the last quarter of the 1800's, many wage earners complained with increasing bitterness about their low wages. Unskilled male workers might earn no more than $10 a week. Skilled male workers—those whose jobs required a certain amount of training and education—might earn no more than $20 a week. In both skilled and unskilled jobs, the wage scale for women workers was even lower. In 1903, for example, a woman might receive $2.16 for a 62-hour work week in a cap factory. Still, industrial expansion brought higher *real wages*° to workers as a whole. Nevertheless, large numbers of workers believed that they were not receiving a fair share of the profits from the country's industrial growth.

Wages tended to be low for several reasons: the increasing power of employers over employees; the creation of a competitive national labor market; depressions; and the flooding of the labor market by new workers.

Wage earners also complained about their long working hours. After 1865 an 11-hour day was common in American industry. Yet even in the 1880's textile workers in many places toiled from 12 to 14 hours daily.

From 1900 to 1920 working hours began to be shortened. The average working hours in factories decreased from 57 per week in 1909 to 50 per week in 1919. But even as late as this, the 12-hour day prevailed in the steel industry, for example.

It was indeed a new and rapidly changing world with which the American wage earner wrestled in the late 1800's. The problems of wage earners were complex ones, and neither the workers, the owners of the industries, nor Americans in general had any ready answers.

° *real wages:* wages measured in terms of actual purchasing power, or what the money will buy.

SECTION SURVEY

IDENTIFY: "company town," technological unemployment, Triangle Building fire, business cycle, real wages.

1. Compare relations between owners and workers in the small, privately owned mills and the huge, corporation-owned factories.
2. Discuss the problems faced by workers as a result of increasing mechanization.
3. How did each of the following affect workers: (a) railroads, (b) business cycle, (c) end of the frontier?
4. What were two of the most common complaints of workers in the 1880's and 1890's?

2 The influence of immigrant workers in American society

Immigrants played an essential part in the amazing industrial development of the United States from 1865 to 1900. Immigrants came seeking jobs and new opportunities. In trying to find places for themselves in their new homeland and in the industrial age, the immigrants were often greeted with distrust and suspicion.

The problem of numbers

Part of the difficulty was the overwhelming number of immigrants who poured into the country. During the 29 years from 1870 to 1899, more than 11 million women, men, and children entered the United States.

The changing character of immigration

The changing character of immigration, as well as the swelling tide, alarmed many Americans. Until the early 1880's most immigrants came from northwestern Europe—Great Britain, Ireland, Scandinavia, Germany, and the Netherlands. But after 1890 an increasingly large number came from southern and eastern Europe—Russia (including Poland), Greece, Austria-Hungary, and Italy. The languages, customs, and ways of living of these immigrants were quite different from those of immigrants from northwestern Europe.

Effect of immigration on labor

The immigrants had an enormous influence on American life. Although some settled on farms, the great majority moved to the densely crowded slum areas of the cities. Here they competed with native-born Americans for housing, thereby driving up housing costs.

Most immediate of all, however, was their effect upon established workers. Immigrants competed with established American wage earners for jobs, thereby lowering wages. To be sure, immigrants helped to stimulate the economy by creating new demands for factory and farm products. But most wage earners were more disturbed by the job competition of the immigrants than they were impressed with the stimulating effects of large-scale immigration.

Tension on the Pacific Coast

Chinese workers on the Pacific Coast, particularly in California, were the first victims of the

Many Chinese laborers, after helping to build the western railroad, stayed on as track workers, or "gandy dancers." In this painting, Chinese workers are waving as a Central Pacific train puffs along between snowsheds built as a protection against avalanches. The painting was made by artist Joseph Becker in 1869.

rising distrust against all immigrants. By the terms of the Burlingame Treaty of 1868, Chinese people had the right to immigrate to the United States. For some years Chinese laborers had been welcome additions to the labor supply. They had been forced to accept the hardest and least desirable jobs for very low wages. They were the backbone of the construction gangs that built the western section of the first transcontinental railroad. By the 1870's nearly 75,000 Chinese workers had settled in California, where they made up about 20 percent of the labor force.

Such was the situation in 1873 when a depression hit the country. As unemployment mounted, California workers feared that the Chinese would take their jobs at low wages. Fear and insecurity were intensified because the Chinese, for reasons not always of their own choosing, lived entirely to themselves. Thus they did not have an opportunity to learn and adapt to the ways of living accepted by most Californians.

Restrictions on Chinese immigrants

Ill feeling, already running high, was fanned into violence by crowds of unemployed California workers who gathered on street corners and sand lots. The "sand lotters" soon attacked the unfortunate Chinese, killing some and burning the property of others.

In cooperation with distressed farmers, California workers were able to influence the writing of a new state constitution in 1879. California's new constitution discriminated against the Chinese by prohibiting them from owning property or working at certain jobs.

The opponents of Chinese immigration also succeeded in getting Congress to pass an "exclusion bill" in 1879. This bill prohibited all but a few Chinese from settling in the United States in any year. Because this bill violated the Burlingame Treaty of 1868, President Hayes vetoed it. But under pressure the Chinese government agreed not to object if the United States regulated immigration, and in 1882 Congress enacted a new Chinese Exclusion Act which, with several extensions, continued in effect until World War II. The Chinese Exclusion Act forbade the immigration of Chinese laborers and denied American citizenship to Chinese born in China. Only students and a few other groups of Chinese could enter the United States.

Other immigration restrictions

The Chinese Exclusion Act of 1882 was the first of a long series of restrictions on immigration, enacted mainly because of pressure from worker groups. The second was the repeal in 1885 of the Contract Labor Law.

The Contract Labor Law had been adopted by Congress in 1864, when booming wartime industries were in desperate need of workers. This law permitted American employers to recruit laborers in Europe. Under the law it was legal for employers to have workers abroad sign contracts agreeing to come to the United States to work for a specified employer for specified wages for a specified time. It was illegal for the workers to leave their jobs while the contract was in force. American workers objected to the law because (1) it came dangerously close to setting up a slave-labor system and (2) it subjected American workers to the unfair competition of cheap foreign labor.

After the repeal of the Contract Labor Law, American wage earners pressured Congress to pass other restrictive measures. One bill that kept coming up for 30 years would have forbidden entry to any immigrant who could not read and write. Congress actually did pass this law on several occasions, but each time the President then in office vetoed the bill. In 1917, however, Congress passed a "literacy test" bill over President Woodrow Wilson's veto, and the door to immigration was shut a little further.

The role of immigrants

From 1865 to 1900 the restrictions placed on immigration were relatively minor. And without the more than 11 million immigrants who poured into the United States between 1870 and 1900, America's industrial progress would have been much slower. Immigrant muscles and brains helped to transform the United States from a predominantly agricultural country into a giant industrial power.

SECTION SURVEY

IDENTIFY: immigrants, slums, "sand lotters," "literacy test" bill.

1. Describe the changing character of immigration after 1880.
2. Discuss three ways in which immigration affected American workers.
3. (a) Give the reasons for the passage of the Chinese Exclusion Act of 1882. (b) How would you feel about this if you were Chinese?
4. Why was the Contract Labor Law of 1864 repealed?
5. "Immigrant muscles and brains helped to transform the United States." Explain.
6. Is there any irony in the fact that the United States, a nation of immigrants, restricted immigration? Comment.

3 The role of labor organizations in dealing with workers' grievances

Faced with numerous problems in the new industrial age, wage earners, like farmers, began increasingly to seek solutions for their problems through organization.

The National Labor Union

Labor organizations were not new. During the war years 1861–65, however, as industry boomed and the cost of living soared, the labor movement gained new momentum.

In 1866 the National Labor Union was launched under the leadership of William Sylvis, an experienced and able organizer of iron molders. In 1868 the National Labor Union helped push through Congress a law establishing an 8-hour working day for laborers and mechanics employed by or in behalf of the federal government. But after unsuccessfully supporting a third-party movement in the election of 1872, this union faded away.

The Knights of Labor

Far more important than the National Labor Union was the Knights of Labor, founded in 1869 in Philadelphia by Uriah S. Stephens, a tailor. The Knights of Labor tried to unite all American workers into one great union—foreign born and native born, blacks and whites, skilled and unskilled, women as well as men. Several women headed local units or "assemblies" and a few became national leaders. The Knights aimed "to secure to the toilers a proper share of the wealth that they create; more of the leisure that rightfully belongs to them." Among other things, they favored an 8-hour work day.

The Knights of Labor also tried to organize and operate their own cooperative stores and manufacturing plants, as some farmers already had done. They hoped by this means to save for themselves the profits that normally went to manufacturers and distributors and at the same time to produce lower-priced goods. However, most of their cooperative enterprises failed, largely because they did not have enough money to buy good machinery and to hire qualified managers.

Reasons for the Knights' success

In some of their efforts the Knights of Labor were more successful. They were influential, for

In the new industrial age, wage earners, like farmers, were faced with serious problems. This painting, showing steelworkers on their lunch break, was made about 1890.

example, in causing Congress to pass the Chinese Exclusion Act in 1882 and to repeal the Contract Labor Law in 1885.

The Knights of Labor officially frowned on strikes, preferring to settle disputes between managers and laborers through industrial *arbitration*.° However, a successful railroad strike in 1885 did much to boost the group's membership. For the first time in American labor history, railroad operators met strike leaders on equal terms and agreed to labor's chief demands. When the railroad strike occurred, the Knights numbered about 500,000 members, and by 1886 their membership had reached 700,000. This remarkable growth also owed much to the idealism and enthusiasm of Terence V. Powderly, who succeeded Uriah S. Stephens as leader of the Knights of Labor.

Reasons for decline

The decline of the Knights was almost as rapid as their rise. In 1888 only 260,000 members were enrolled and by 1890 this figure had dropped to about 100,000.

There were several reasons for this decline in membership. For one thing, the Knights lost an important railroad strike in 1886 against the southwestern railroad system controlled by financier Jay Gould. This strike antagonized the public because of violence accompanying it and because of shortages of food and coal resulting from it. In the second place, the Knights included too many opposing groups to develop real strength. Skilled workers especially disliked the Knights' policy of taking in unskilled workers, with whom they felt they had little or nothing in common.

Finally, Terence V. Powderly's aims came to be too general to satisfy numerous workers. Many wage earners were now convinced that a strong labor movement must avoid political crusades and concentrate instead on improving working conditions for specific groups of workers. This conviction accounted for the rise of a rival organization of workers, the American Federation of Labor (A. F. of L.).

Rise of the A. F. of L.

Started in 1881 under another name and reorganized in 1886, the A. F. of L. quickly replaced the Knights of Labor as the leading American labor organization.

Unlike the Knights of Labor, the A. F. of L. was a federation of separate national *craft unions*, each representing a group of skilled workers in a separate trade, or craft, such as carpentry, welding, or typography. It sought to organize all skilled workers by their craft rather than by the industry in which they worked. However, the A. F. of L. did include a few *industrial unions* which tried to organize all workers in a single industry, unskilled as well as skilled.

Each A. F. of L. union was free to bargain collectively for all its members, to call strikes, and to manage its own affairs.

The A. F. of L. also differed from the Knights of Labor in keeping itself aloof from general reform movements and from independent or third-party political activities. The A. F. of L. was an economic organization of workers emphasizing craft unionism—"pure and simple unionism."

Program of the A. F. of L.

The A. F. of L. program called for an 8-hour working day and a 6-day working week; for legislation protecting workers on dangerous jobs and compensating them and their families in case of injury or death; for higher wages and for generally better working conditions. The A. F. of L. threw its weight in political contests to whichever party or candidate came closest to representing its aims.

The A. F. of L. accepted the capitalistic free-enterprise system. It did insist, however, on controlling the skilled labor market, on getting a larger share of the output of industry through higher wages and shorter hours, and on improving labor conditions.

With the exception of a single year, the president of the A. F. of L. from 1886 to 1924 was its principal founder, Samuel Gompers. Under Gompers' leadership the A. F. of L. grew rapidly. In 1890 it had only 100,000 members, but by 1900 membership had climbed to 500,000.

° *arbitration:* the judging of a dispute by an impartial person accepted by both sides to act as referee.

SECTION SURVEY

IDENTIFY: National Labor Union, skilled worker, unskilled worker, arbitration, craft union, industrial union; Uriah Stephens, Terence Powderly, Samuel Gompers.

1. Why did American workers decide to organize unions?
2. Describe the (a) purpose, (b) successes, and (c) reasons for the decline of the Knights of Labor.
3. How did the A. F. of L. differ from the Knights of Labor?
4. What is meant by the statement that the A. F. of L. was "job-conscious rather than class-conscious"?

4 Opposition to organized labor's early efforts to win reforms

When American workers began to organize during the late 1880's, they encountered numerous obstacles in their efforts to improve labor conditions. Their attempts to form unions and to seek recognition of their unions' right to bargain for them met widespread opposition.

Public opposition to unions

During the late 1880's Americans in general, as well as government, usually supported employers in any conflicts between employers and unions or between employers and workers striking for union recognition.

This opposition to unions is not hard to understand. Most Americans had grown up in the older, rural America where individual workers had more control over their fates than they now had in the giant corporations. And most believed that employers had the right to hire and fire as they pleased.

Many Americans resented union demands for the closed shop. Businesses that had closed-shop agreements with a union could hire only union members. Employers resented this restriction on what they considered their right to hire anyone they pleased. Many workers also resented closed-shop agreements, which forced them to join a union whether they wanted to or not.

Moreover, many Americans believed that most workers were quite content with their lot.

Nothing during the 1880's did more to turn public opinion against organized labor than the Haymarket affair. For many years large numbers of Americans continued to identify organized labor with anarchy and radicalism.

And the fact that as late as 1914 only about one worker out of ten belonged to a labor organization seemed to support this belief. Many Americans held that the best workers could still rise to become managers and even owners. Most Americans blamed the entire labor problem, as well as industrial conflict itself, on "power-hungry" labor leaders interested in their own personal advancement.

The Haymarket affair

On May 4, 1886, a large group of workers gathered in Haymarket Square in Chicago. They were there to protest an attack on strikers in which, on May 3, one striker had been killed and a number of others wounded.

The meeting was orderly and the crowd was just beginning to leave when nearly 200 police officers appeared. Suddenly, without warning, a bomb burst in the midst of the police, killing one and wounding many others.

No one ever identified the bomb thrower. Nevertheless, eight "radicals," who on earlier occasions had advocated violence, were arrested. Seven were sentenced to death, the eighth to 15 years in prison.

No evidence was ever produced to indicate that organized labor was responsible for the violence in Haymarket Square. Yet nothing during the 1880's did more to turn public opinion against organized labor than the tragic Haymarket affair.

Immigrants and labor unions

Many union leaders were of foreign birth. In several labor organizations, especially in the textile and coal mining industries, immigrant workers were a source of strength. On the other hand, however, a great many immigrants opposed labor unions. Coming from rural backgrounds in the Old World, most immigrants had no previous experience with labor organizations. Bewildered by their new and strange environment, they often did not feel a need to join with native-born American workers to promote common interests by presenting a united front.

Many immigrants had left Europe partly to be as free as possible from all sorts of restrictions. Thus they did not like labor unions, with their dues, their rules, and their insistence that no one work for less than a certain wage. Many immigrants felt that, however bad working conditions in the United States might be, they were better than conditions in the Old World.

Most immigrants, also, were unskilled workers. Thus the A. F. of L. made little or no effort to admit them to the craft unions. Finally, there

Attention Workingmen!

GREAT

MASS-MEETING

TO-NIGHT, at 7.30 o'clock,

AT THE

HAYMARKET, Randolph St., Bet. Desplaines and Halsted.

Good Speakers will be present to denounce the latest atrocious act of the police, the shooting of our fellow-workmen yesterday afternoon.

Workingmen Arm Yourselves and Appear in Full Force!

THE EXECUTIVE COMMITTEE

The near exclusion of Negroes from the American labor movement weakened the movement. Here, black workers who had been denied union membership take temporary jobs as strike-breakers during a 1905 dispute between the teamsters and Chicago employers.

was widespread prejudice among native-born American workers toward immigrant workers. This prejudice was deepened when foreign-born workers were recruited by business managers to break strikes.

Women and the unions

Many unions did not admit women to membership, but in a few craft unions women played important roles. Most notable was the International Ladies Garment Workers Union, in which Rose Schneiderman and Leona O'Reilly were leaders. The A. F. of L. expressed interest in organizing women but did not vigorously pursue this aim.

The National Women's Trade Union League, founded largely by middle class women in 1903, assisted the organization of women workers in several ways, especially by providing financial support during strikes. The league stressed voting rights for women as a means for advancing their economic equality, and promoted minimum, or "living," wages for women.

Black workers and the unions

Because of the racial prejudice of many white workers, Negroes were excluded from most labor organizations. A notable exception was the Knights of Labor, which, proclaiming the solidarity of all wage earners, enrolled black workers without discrimination, at least until the organization's later years.

At first the leaders of the A. F. of L. favored including skilled black workers in their craft unions. They believed that if this was not done, black workers might undermine the purposes of the federation by accepting lower wages. But when the machinists' union and others refused to admit Negroes, Samuel Gompers, by now the dominant power in the A. F. of L., backed down. He insisted that union constitutions should not specifically exclude black members, but he admitted that in practice the unions might do so. The United Mine Workers and a few other A. F. of L. unions admitted black members on equal terms with white members. Most other unions insisted, however, that any black workers admitted to A. F. of L. membership be organized in separate unions.

Most northern Negroes were unskilled workers. Thus after the decline of the Knights of Labor, the A. F. of L. policy of organizing only skilled workers meant, in effect, that black wage earners were excluded from northern labor organizations. In the South, where there were many skilled black workers, the labor market in the skilled trades was controlled by all-white A. F. of L. unions. As a result, many skilled black workers were forced into the ranks of unskilled labor.

By 1902, in both the North and the South, 43 national labor unions had not a single black member, and 27 others had only a handful. Gompers tried to argue that Negroes had only themselves to blame for their exclusion because few were skilled workers and fewer still were willing to accept the self-discipline and cooperation necessary in trade unionism. Booker T. Washington, however, declared in 1897 that the union movement was holding back the economic progress of black workers by refusing to admit them as apprentices and by making no effort to organize them.

The virtual exclusion of Negroes from the American labor movement closed off to the great mass of black Americans an important opportunity to be included in the mainstream of American life. It also weakened the effectiveness of the labor movement itself.

Division in the ranks of labor

The mechanization of industrial plants also weakened the power of wage earners to unite. When factories were small, skilled workers could see that the work of unskilled workers, however minor, was an essential part of the production process. But when factories grew large and workers became strangers, skilled workers came to look down on unskilled workers.

Thus the wage earners themselves divided into two groups: (1) a small number of skilled workers who gained more and more bargaining power with employers; and (2) a large number of unskilled, unorganized laborers whose voices and interests counted very little.

Industry against the unions

With a majority of Americans generally distrustful of unions, huge industrial enterprises did not find it difficult to influence public opinion and government in their own favor. They hired lawyers to fight their battles in the courts. They spent money on advertising and publicity to win public sympathy. They paid skillful lobbyists to get favorable laws passed or to defeat bills that employers did not like. Some corporations contributed to the political party most likely to win an election, hoping to secure government favors.

To discourage workers from joining unions, employers also developed more direct methods. For example, employers' associations, made up of several manufacturers, compiled *black lists,* or lists of certain workers considered as undesirable—sometimes because the workers were incompetent, sometimes because they were labor organizers, sometimes merely because they belonged to a union. The black list was circulated throughout an entire industry, all over the country. No person whose name appeared on such a black list could get a job in that industry, at least under her or his own name.

Many employers also required workers applying for a job to sign a written agreement not to join a union. The workers called these agreements *yellow-dog contracts.* A worker who violated such a contract was fired.

Employers used still other methods to prevent workers from organizing. Sometimes private detectives, posing as workers, joined unions and reported strike plans to employers, as well as names of union leaders. Sometimes when strikes broke out, unscrupulous employers actually paid agents to commit acts of violence, which were then blamed on labor. At other times, of course, the workers themselves resorted to violence. Such violence provided employers with a good excuse for calling in the local police, the state militia, or even federal troops to restore order and break the strike.

Sometimes employers fought strikes with another weapon—the *lockout.* They closed their plants, thus "locking out" the workers. Then they brought in "strikebreakers"—nonunion workers hired to do the work of those on strike—and the plant was reopened despite the angry strikers outside its gates. On other occasions owners simply locked their plants and waited until the hungry, impoverished strikers were willing to work on any terms.

State support of industry

With public opinion on their side, employers counted on government aid in conflicts with workers. There were, it is true, some exceptions to this general rule.

In most serious labor disputes, however, governors sent the state militia to the scene, where their presence worked to the employers' advantage. Whenever they sent the militia, the governors argued that the troops were needed to protect property, prevent violence, and maintain order. Since the governors were sworn to uphold law and order, this seemed reasonable. On the other hand, the arrival of the state militia often made it impossible for the workers to continue to strike.

Federal support of industry

In the last quarter of the 1800's, the Presidents of the United States in general followed the example of the state governors in ordering troops to a scene of trouble. Thus during a series of railroad strikes in Pennsylvania and Maryland in 1877, when state troops could not restore order, President Hayes sent federal soldiers to keep the trains running. The strikes collapsed.

A famous case of federal intervention occurred near Chicago in 1894 when a strike was called against the Pullman Palace Car Company by the American Railway Union led by Eugene V. Debs. The strike was supported by railway workers around Chicago and elsewhere, who refused to handle trains which included Pullman cars. When Governor Altgeld of Illinois refused to call out the state militia or ask for federal help, President Cleveland sent federal troops anyway. Cleveland declared that such action was justified in order to guarantee mail delivery, although mail trains were in fact running and the mails were being delivered. Whatever the merits of the arguments over the use of troops in the Pullman strike, organized labor was bitter about their use.

Court support of industry

In the late 1800's the courts, no less than governors and Presidents, generally used their powers in behalf of management. For example, during the Pullman strike the railroad owners asked a federal court in Chicago to issue an injunction, or court order, forbidding Debs and other labor leaders to continue the strike. The court issued the injunction. It justified this action on the ground that the strikers had entered into "a conspiracy in restraint of trade" and were therefore violating the Sherman Antitrust Act of 1890, which declared such conspiracies illegal.

Debs defied the court order. He was promptly arrested, and sentenced to six months in jail for refusing to obey the injunction. Labor denounced this conviction as "government by injunction." But the Supreme Court in 1895 upheld the ruling, Debs was jailed, and the strike was broken.

President Cleveland's role in strikes consistently aroused the opposition of organized labor. Thus organized workers vigorously supported the Populist Party during the early 1890's, and favored William Jennings Bryan in the election of 1896.

After 1895 the injunction became a powerful weapon against organized labor since employers often secured injunctions to prevent or break up strikes. Labor leaders complained bitterly, but their only possible relief was (1) that the Supreme Court would reverse its decision of 1895, or (2) that Congress would modify the Sherman Antitrust Act so that it could not be used against labor unions.

Radical movements

After the Haymarket affair of 1886, many Americans, believing that organized labor was filled with anarchists, began to identify the labor movement with radicalism. But most Americans in the 1880's and 1890's did not distinguish among the three major radical movements—anarchism, Communism, and socialism.

The anarchists believed that people could work and live happily together in voluntary associations if they could be freed from the restraints of government. They believed that the idealistic society they advocated could be achieved only by the violent overthrow of the government and of capitalism—the economic system under which industry is owned and controlled by private individuals. Although the anarchists were few in number, their reputation for violence deeply alarmed the nation. The best known anarchist, and the most feared and hated, was Emma Goldman, an immigrant from Russia. She was a tough and fighting champion of working people, of free speech, and of greater freedom for women. Emma Goldman was also an uncompromising foe of militarism and the use of police force in what she regarded as the exploitation of ordinary people.

The followers of Karl Marx believed that, under capitalism, wage earners would always be exploited. They argued that capitalism must be replaced by an economic system in which the workers would own and control the means of production.

In time, the followers of Marx developed into two separate groups. One group, known as Communists, insisted that the only way to build the new society of workers was by means of revolution and the violent seizure of power.

The other group, known as socialists, did not advocate revolution. The socialists believed that the workers, organized in a political party, could vote themselves into power and by democratic means could reconstruct the economic and social foundations of society. Socialist leaders included Morris Hillquit, Kate Richards O'Hare, and Eugene V. Debs.

The influence of the radical movements upon American labor organizations was never as strong as it became in some parts of Europe. Union members, by and large, continued to support Republicans, Democrats, or third party candidates and policies according to the union members' personal judgment of issues and of their own best interests.

Influence of organized labor

As you have read, the labor movement of the late 1800's faced much opposition. But despite setbacks, organized labor continued to fight for its aims and for public recognition and support. By the early 1900's the lot of American workers was beginning to improve.

SECTION SURVEY

IDENTIFY: closed shop, Haymarket affair, Pullman strike, "government by injunction," capitalism, anarchism, socialism, Communism; Eugene Debs, Emma Goldman.

1. (a) Explain why public opinion in the late 1800's usually supported employers over workers. (b) What role did prejudice play in this attitude?
2. Why did many immigrants oppose the labor movement?
3. (a) Why were black workers excluded from the labor movement? (b) What have been the long-term effects of this discrimination? (c) How were women workers treated by the labor movement?
4. Show how employers used each of the following against organized labor: (a) publicity, (b) lobbyists, (c) political contributions, (d) black lists, (e) yellow-dog contracts, (f) lockouts.
5. What evidence is there to support the belief that in the late 1800's government, federal and state, was on the side of industry?

CHAPTER SURVEY

INQUIRING INTO HISTORY

1. How did the Haymarket affair help turn public opinion against the labor unions?
2. In human terms, what did the United States lose in becoming an industrialized nation? What advantages did it gain?
3. During the period just studied, there was a shortage of skilled labor. How did this encourage manufacturers to mechanize as much as possible?
4. The majority of immigrants coming to the United States during the period just studied were between the ages of 14 and 45. What significance for the nation's economy can you derive from this fact?
5. In the period 1870–1900, what were the major grievances of working people against (a) employers, (b) state governments, and (c) the federal government?
6. Machines widened the gap between skilled and unskilled wage earners. Comment.
7. What democratic "safety valves" prevented a political revolution in the United States during the economic conflicts of the Industrial Revolution?

RELATING PAST TO PRESENT

1. Compare the power of labor unions during the period 1865–1900 with their power today.
2. Compare the demands labor unions make today with the demands made during the period 1865–1900.
3. In recent years, have American labor unions changed their policies regarding the admission of minority groups? Support your answer with evidence found in news stories or encyclopedia articles dealing with present-day labor unions.
4. Do you think most Americans today can distinguish radical activities from lawful dissent? Explain.
5. Radical political movements were not able to gain control of the labor movement during the period just studied. Do you think that they could today? Explain.

DEVELOPING SOCIAL SCIENCE SKILLS

1. Find accounts written by immigrants between 1860 and 1900 telling about their lives in America. (a) What reasons do they give for coming to America? (b) How do these reasons compare with the reasons people had for coming during the colonial period? (c) What attracted immigrants to America in the late 1800's? (d) Were immigrants able to fulfill their goals in America?
2. Find a record or a book of songs about the labor movement between 1860 and 1900. (a) What ideas are expressed in the songs? (b) What is the mood of each song? (c) What feelings or ideas are common to most of the songs? (d) What techniques are used in the songs to persuade people to join a union?
3. Find and read three or four original eyewitness accounts of the Haymarket riot. Compare these accounts on the factual details: (a) date, (b) strikers injured, (c) strikers killed, (d) policemen killed, (e) group responsible for starting violence. Are there differences in the facts in the accounts? How do you account for these differences?

CHAPTER 7

CHANGING WAYS OF LIFE
IN THE NEW INDUSTRIAL AGE

"We cannot all live in cities," Horace Greeley once remarked, "yet nearly all seem determined to do so." Greeley, the famous newspaper editor, was speaking of a new phenomenon in American life—the movement of many people away from the rural areas and into the great urban centers—the trend toward "urbanization" in America. From 1865 to 1900, growing numbers of young men and women and a considerable number of older people left the farms and country villages and headed cityward. The majority of these people moved to the larger cities, those having populations of 25,000 to 50,000 or more.

What was the compelling attraction of the growing cities? The answer was "opportunity"—opportunity for adventure, opportunity to win fame and fortune. The city offered jobs in offices and factories, work in the building trades, employment for skilled and unskilled alike, the chance to carve out a successful career in any of hundreds of lines of enterprise. Many people, especially young people, were eager to share in the excitement of the new age, and they found the attractions of urban life irresistible.

For a number of years ways of life in the city and the countryside drew far apart, and terms like "city slicker" and "country hick" were often heard. As the years passed, however, the differences between life in rural and urban areas became less marked.

THE CHAPTER IN OUTLINE

1. Changing life patterns in American cities in the industrial age.

2. Changes in American education in response to changing life patterns.

3. Reflections of the industrial age in new styles of American writing.

4. New trends in architecture and other fine arts in a changing society.

5. The enrichment of American life through new forms of recreation.

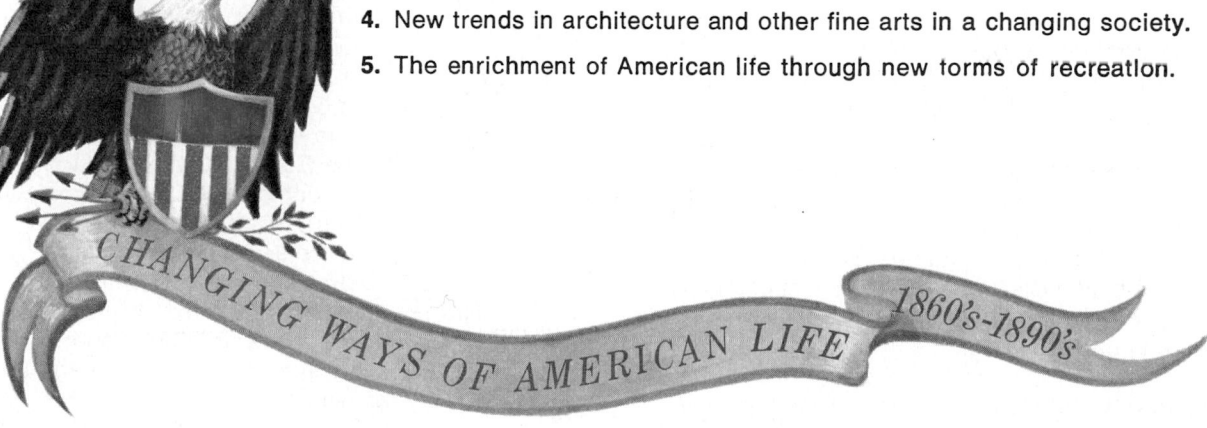

CHANGING WAYS OF AMERICAN LIFE   1860's-1890's

1 Changing life patterns in American cities in the industrial age

The city had many faces. It was stores and banks and offices, museums and libraries and theaters, churches and schools. It was freight yards—and, in seaports, waterfronts—ringed by factories, warehouses, stockyards, and wholesale markets. It was slum areas with drab tenement buildings crowded along narrow, dirty streets and alleys littered with rubbish. It was row after row of houses arranged, in newer cities, in a neat pattern of "blocks" or "squares." It was pretentious mansions, the costly show places of the self-appointed leaders of "society."

But mainly the city was people—rich people, people with modest incomes, poor people—all affected, more or less, by the new power-driven machines and new methods of mass production steadily transforming the world around them.

Concentration of wealth

One of the most obvious characteristics of this new industrial age was the concentration of wealth in relatively few hands. To be sure, some Americans had always been rich while others had been poor, but the gap between the richest and the poorest had never been as great as it was in the late 1800's.

Many of the new, self-educated millionaires built huge mansions, filled with expensive and gaudy furnishings. They bought race horses, yachts, and summer estates. They traveled abroad. Sometimes they gave parties costing tens of thousands of dollars.

The rich as public benefactors

As time went on, however, the newly rich, and especially their college-educated children, smoothed off the rougher edges. Many successful business leaders began to accept the responsibility for using their money to improve their communities. They increasingly gave money to build and support churches, colleges, art galleries, opera houses, and libraries.

For example, during his lifetime Andrew Carnegie, a self-made man, gave $60 million to help towns and cities establish free public libraries. Men of enormous wealth, such as Ezra Cornell, Leland Stanford, John D. Rockefeller, Sr., Jonas Clark, Matthew Vassar, and Cornelius Vanderbilt, founded or gave endowments to colleges and universities. J. P. Morgan, Henry C. Frick, Andrew W. Mellon, and dozens of others built up costly and valuable art collections, many of which were in time opened to the public. Others gave financial support to American symphony orchestras. Wealthy women also gave large sums for the support of education, social welfare, and the arts.

Thus American education and arts began to benefit from fortunes made in railroads, the stock market, and industry. Some of the new business "magnates" and their wives and daughters became patrons of art and culture much as the kings, queens, princes, and princesses of the Renaissance had helped artists of their day.

The middle-income group

Lower down on the economic ladder were the professional people, the smaller business people, the clerks, the managers, and the more successful skilled workers. These people raised their standard of living and enjoyed the new "modern conveniences," such as gas and electric lighting, modern plumbing, and new household appliances. They went to the theater, used libraries, bought magazines and books, and increasingly sent their children, not only through high school, but also to college.

Women in religion and welfare

In activities such as religion and social welfare, several women achieved international reputations. Mary Baker Eddy founded Christian Science and contributed to its growth with her inspirational leadership and administrative ability. At a time when traditional Protestantism was losing its appeal for some people, Christian Science affirmed the ability of men and women, "with divine help and right thinking," to triumph over disease, misfortune, and evil. Several women were active in church missionary work abroad, establishing training schools, colleges, and hospitals in Turkey, Japan, India, and other countries.

A number of Catholic women founded religious orders. The most famous was Mother Frances Xavier Cabrini. After emigrating from Italy in 1889, she established hospitals, orphanages, and schools in the Italian-American communities of New York, Chicago, and other cities. Mother Cabrini was the first American citizen to become a saint in the Roman Catholic Church.

The tireless and competent Clara Barton, after her contributions to nursing in the Civil War, went on to establish and develop the American Red Cross. Despite opposition and indifference, she broadened its purposes to include not only aid to soldiers in wartime but also help to civilians in such disasters as floods, earthquakes, major fires, and epidemics.

Opportunities for women

The continuing development of coeducational universities in the Middle West and the West, and the establishment in the East of such women's colleges as Mount Holyoke, Wellesley, Vassar, and Smith, meant that more young women could obtain an education equal to that once enjoyed only by young men. The battle for the higher education of women was a real one, for many people doubted that girls had the physical and mental ability to do college work. But the experiment proved successful. Women college graduates became increasingly active in civic affairs. Some became business executives, and others entered the professions. By 1900 there were 1,000 women lawyers, 3,000 women ministers, and 7,500 women doctors in the United States. Maria Mitchell, an astronomer on the faculty of Vassar College, discovered a comet that was named for her.

Girls who did not go to college but who wanted careers found new opportunities in business, especially as stenographers in offices, banks, and industrial plants. The development of the typewriter was a tremendous benefit to business as well as to women eager or compelled by circumstances to work outside the home. Tradition and prejudice, however, blocked opportunities for most women to advance into management positions.

In addition to these new activities, a great many women of the white middle class joined the women's clubs which rapidly multiplied after the Civil War. These clubs at first concentrated mainly on discussions of literary and cultural topics, but before 1900 they were also fighting political corruption, working for better health and recreational conditions, and in some instances battling for women's suffrage.

Black women also established clubs, which concentrated on social welfare. Leaders in this movement were Josephine Ruffin and Mary Church Terrell, who also led in founding the National Federation of Afro-American Women and the National Association of Colored Women.

Toward women's suffrage

After the Civil War, you recall, women did not receive voting rights and other rights under the Fourteenth and Fifteenth Amendments. Differences over the stand to be taken on this issue contributed to a division in the women's rights movement. Elizabeth Cady Stanton and Susan B. Anthony refused to support the amendments. In 1869 they organized the National Woman Suffrage Association, which excluded men from membership and adopted as its goal a women's

Mother Cabrini was the first American woman to be recognized as a saint by the Catholic Church.

suffrage amendment to the Constitution. Lucy Stone, her husband Henry Blackwell, Mary A. Livermore, and Julia Ward Howe launched the more conservative American Woman Suffrage Association, which sought voting rights for women by working for amendments to state constitutions. In 1890, after many years of rivalry, the two organizations were merged in the National American Woman Suffrage Association.

Such veterans of the women's rights movement as Elizabeth Cady Stanton, Susan B. Anthony, and Lucy Stone continued active in the new association, while younger leaders also appeared. Abigail Duniway of Oregon, a vigorous opponent of women's legal disabilities, became an effective speaker and lobbyist. Anna Howard Shaw, a graduate of Boston University in both theology and medicine, became a forceful speaker and untiring campaigner. Carrie Chapman Catt was a brilliant orator and skilled administrator.

Under the steady efforts of these leaders and others, resistance to women's participation in public affairs began to soften. But progress was slow. The woman suffragists were ridiculed and opposed by many women as well as men, by professional politicians, and by some religious

Jane Addams became famous for her work among the poor in Chicago. Hull House, which she established there, became the model for settlement houses in many large cities.

groups. They also were opposed by the liquor industry, which feared that voting women might succeed in outlawing the manufacture and sale of alcoholic drinks.

Although by 1900 only a few western states had given women the right to vote, in the next 15 years the number grew. Meanwhile, in states which gave them limited suffrage, women took part increasingly in school board elections and local politics.

Jane Addams

Jane Addams (1860–1935) was one of America's most influential women—a social reformer, humanitarian, and crusader for peace. Searching for a meaningful mission in life and horrified by the suffering she saw in sprawling city slums, Jane Addams decided to dedicate her life to helping the poor. She purchased a building called Hull House in the slums of Chicago and opened it to the public in 1889.

At Hull House Jane Addams provided kindergartens for the children of working mothers, classes in child care, and recreational facilities for youth and adults. She also insisted on the collection of garbage from slum streets and fought incompetent, dishonest, and corrupt politicians and city officials. For a time many business and political leaders opposed her as a dangerous meddler. Eventually, however, even her most bit-

ter critics admitted that she was performing a great service. Social workers from all parts of the United States and from foreign countries visited Hull House, and then returned to their own communities to apply what they had learned.

Jane Addams was also influential in securing child-labor laws and funds for public parks. In 1931 she received the Nobel peace prize for her active work in the cause of world peace. But her most enduring memorial was the growing recognition by people in all walks of life that they shared a responsibility for helping to reduce poverty and suffering.

The lower-income groups

On the lower rungs of the economic ladder in American life were the very poor people, including large numbers of immigrants, and almost all black Americans. The people in these lower-income groups enjoyed only a few of the advantages of the new urban culture. They could not afford to send their children to school beyond the elementary grades. Frequently, in fact, children from poor families had to take jobs in factories even before they finished elementary school. Nor could most of the poorer people afford adequate medical care or go to hospitals when they were sick.

Yet improvements in urban living affected at least a few of the poor. In the late 1880's a group of high-minded men and women founded social "settlement houses" in some of the worst slum areas of the major cities. Jane Addams' Hull House in Chicago was one of the most famous of these. These centers for recreation, education, and decent living affected only a small part of the slum population, but they were nevertheless important. In addition, the Salvation Army, a religious group founded in England, provided food, shelter, and some hope to many of the most poverty-stricken urban citizens. And by 1900 some cities were building a few playgrounds in the poorest areas.

Moreover, opportunities to climb the economic ladder existed, even for the poor, and the opportunities far surpassed those in the Old World. These opportunities drew immigrants to the American cities in an ever-swelling volume. And a determination to increase the opportunities and to provide a better way of life for all Americans motivated the numerous reform programs and the development of more and better schools in the late 1800's and early 1900's. Finally, these opportunities caused many poorer people to exert strenuous efforts to acquire an education and to rise above the environment into which they had been born.

The establishment of coeducational universities and women's colleges meant that more young women could obtain higher education. Here, students work in a science laboratory.

One group remained a notable exception. Negroes found their opportunities limited because of racial prejudice, which set the great mass of black Americans apart from even the most disadvantaged white Americans. Their struggle was yet to come.

SECTION SURVEY

IDENTIFY: suffrage, settlement house, Salvation Army; Mary Baker Eddy, Mother Cabrini, Clara Barton, Jane Addams, Susan B. Anthony, Mary Church Terrell.

1. Explain what is meant by the statement, "The city had many faces."
2. "American education and arts began to benefit from fortunes made in railroads, the stock market, and industry." Why was this so?
3. What social class divisions existed in the United States by 1890?
4. What is the relationship between the nation's industrialization and the emancipation of American women?
5. (a) Whose responsibility is it to try to improve the condition of the poor in the United States? Explain. (b) Who took the responsibility in 1890?

2 Changes in American education in response to changing life patterns

Like almost every other aspect of American life, education was transformed by the rising force of industrialism. Most obvious were (1) increased school enrollments, (2) new methods of teaching, and (3) new courses of study.

Expansion of the schools

In 1870 about 7 million children were enrolled in American schools, most of them in the lower grades. Only 30 years later, in 1900, the number had more than doubled. During this same period the number of high schools multiplied 10 times. And still the demand for education grew.

Between 1900 and 1920 the growth in enrollment and the increase in construction of school buildings were even more striking. In 1900 about 16 million children attended American schools; by 1920 the number had risen to about 23 million. This growth reflected the increasing throngs of children in America's cities, but it also testified to the rapid accumulation of wealth that could be taxed to support education.

From old ways to new

The character of the schools—including courses of study and methods of teaching—was also changing.

Pupils in the earlier rural classrooms were all too familiar with the sharp sting of the hickory stick, wielded by teachers on the theory "spare the rod and spoil the child." This earlier education emphasized the memorization of facts that were often unrelated to meaningful ideas. Children learned reading, writing, and arithmetic and memorized a few more or less related facts about geography and history. The few students who went to high school or to a private "academy" spent much time learning Latin, Greek, and mathematics. Most educators believed that these subjects provided mental training and therefore fully equipped students for later life.

As science and industry began to transform American life and as the urban population grew, some reformers demanded a new program of education better suited to the industrial age. A few educational pioneers, such as Colonel Francis W. Parker of Chicago, began to stress the idea that education is not just the memorization of facts, but also the broadening of a child's experience. Education, Parker insisted, must prepare children to live in an expanding and complex world of science and industry. John Dewey was another educational pioneer who stressed the idea that education is not something apart from the rest of life but an essential part of life itself. By the 1890's Dewey's experimental school in Chicago was attracting attention for its program of "learning by doing" and for its emphasis upon making children physically sound, intellectually competent, socially well adjusted, and able to work with other people. Ella Flag Young, head of the Chicago school system, worked closely with Parker and Dewey. This able and influential educator was the first woman to serve as head of a major school system.

Most schools, it is true, continued along more traditional lines, but the influence of Colonel Parker, John Dewey, and other pioneers began to cause changes in American education.

Direct influence of industrialism

The needs of the new industrial society were also reflected in new courses of study in elementary and secondary schools. By 1900 educational programs were being broadened to include the natural sciences and such "practical" and "useful" subjects as industrial designing, business arithmetic, bookkeeping, typing, stenography, shopwork, home economics, and manual arts.

Many school administrators also reflected the growing influence of business and industry. Superintendents and principals became more and more businesslike in their emphasis upon efficiency and organization.

New trends in higher education

The colleges and universities no less than the elementary and the secondary schools responded to the needs of the new age. New technical schools, such as the Columbia University School of Mines, the Massachusetts Institute of Technology, and the Case School of Applied Science, turned out growing numbers of graduates prepared to take important jobs in railroad building, in mining, and in other engineering projects. The state universities and land-grant colleges especially reflected the newer emphasis on practical training for a wide variety of fields.

Even the older colleges which emphasized the classics often felt obliged to add more scientific and "practical" subjects to their traditional courses of study. Under the influence of President Charles W. Eliot of Harvard, President Andrew D. White of Cornell, and other educational leaders, the colleges modified the old, rigid curriculum in which students studied mainly Latin, Greek, and mathematics.

Colleges and universities also enriched their educational programs by adding courses in the social sciences and modern languages, as well as in the natural sciences. It was no longer possible for every student to take all the subjects in the curriculum. To meet individual differences, the "elective" system was introduced.

At the same time marked progress was made in the professional studies of medicine and law. This was especially important, for people living in urban centers increasingly needed the services of good lawyers and doctors.

In these and many other ways, education responded to the changing patterns of everyday life after 1865.

SECTION SURVEY

IDENTIFY: "learning by doing," elective system; Colonel Francis W. Parker, John Dewey, Ella Flag Young.

1. How did the rise of industrialism influence American education in the late 1800's?
2. (a) What changes were made in the courses of study in public schools to meet the needs of the new industrial society? (b) Do you agree with these changes?
3. Describe the ways in which colleges and universities responded to the needs of the new age.
4. Do you think education should provide you with the means of making a living or should it enable you to understand yourself and your society? Explain.

3 Reflections of the industrial age in new styles of American writing

Newspapers, magazines, and novels also revealed the influence of the new urban industrial way of life. Most obvious was an enormous increase in circulation of printed material. Only slightly less obvious were changes in appearance and content.

Growth of newspapers and magazines

Between 1870 and 1900 the number of daily newspapers in the country increased from 600 to nearly 2,500. Their circulation multiplied six times—a jump far greater than the growth in population. This huge expansion reflected gains in the reading ability of many Americans and a growing interest in the world beyond the local community. It also reflected a new trend in journalism.

Several important mechanical inventions enabled publishers to print more newspapers, magazines, and books at lower costs. Most important of these inventions were the typewriter, improved printing presses, and the linotype, a fast and efficient typesetting machine invented by Ottmar Mergenthaler in 1885.

Mass circulation was also stimulated by the rapidly developing art of advertising. Businesses were ready to advertise, but only in newspapers and magazines that had mass circulation. The desire to secure advertising stimulated publishers to capture an ever-wider reading public. Thus the publishers used more and more "popular" articles written in a "catchy" style to attract the largest possible number of readers.

New "titans of the press"

Three of the outstanding leaders of the new trend in journalism were Charles A. Dana, Joseph Pulitzer, and William Randolph Hearst.

Dana, publisher of the New York *Sun,* dug up sensational news and gave it prominent space on the front pages of his paper. Pulitzer, publisher of the New York *World,* followed much the same technique. His paper appealed to the general reader because it contained human interest stories and many articles on the scandalous activities of the rich and the tragedies of the poor. Stories by Elizabeth Seaman, who succeeded in defying the prejudice against women reporters, were especially popular. Under the name "Nelly Bly," she reported what she found when she worked in a factory, entered a mental institution by pretending to be insane, or got herself jailed. Pulitzer also developed the comic strip, the sports page, and a section with columnists, puzzles, and advice to readers.

Hearst, who was Pulitzer's chief rival, outdid Pulitzer at his own game. Hearst bought the New York *Journal* in 1895 and raised its circulation beyond that of any other paper. By denouncing the irresponsibility and selfishness of some of the well-to-do, Hearst appealed to the masses of people. But his special success rested on his ability to hire gifted feature writers, able sports reporters, and popular comic artists. He also was able to get the most sensational news before anyone else and to play it up for all it was worth—frequently far more than it was worth.

Journalism as big business

Well before 1900 journalism began to adopt the methods of other big business enterprises. Leading publishers began to buy up small papers and to consolidate great newspaper chains. Large chains could use the same feature articles, the same comic strips, and even the same editorials. This was especially true as the different parts of the nation and the world became increasingly interdependent, with public interest reaching out beyond the local community to national and world affairs. Moreover, the newspaper chains subscribed to great news-reporting services, or "syndicates," such as the Associated Press (AP) and the United Press (UP), which collected news items from every corner of the earth.

Even the newspapers that remained independent were influenced by the trend toward standardized practices in journalism. Many of them also subscribed to the big news-reporting services and bought columns, comic strips, and other features from syndicates.

By 1900 there also were numerous foreign language newspapers for immigrants and about 150 newspapers for black Americans. Although these publications had limited resources, they served important functions. They gave their readers a "sense of identity" with other people of the same national origin or racial background. Most of them, also, were uncompromising in opposing discrimination and in supporting the rights and interests of their readers.

Mass circulation magazines

Magazines, like newspapers, adapted themselves to the changing times. To be sure, some of the older magazines, such as the *Atlantic Monthly, Harper's, Scribner's,* and others, continued to appeal to the better educated. Even before the Civil War, however, a new type of low-priced, popular magazine began to appear, which contained material aimed at mass circulation among "average" readers. The *Ladies' Home*

Journal, established in 1883, was one of the most successful. It provided reading material that interested millions of women, and it further built up its circulation by setting its price at 10 cents. Under the editorship of a Dutch immigrant, Edward Bok, the *Ladies Home Journal* sponsored many crusades to raise standards of living and improve community life.

Literature about urban life

American literature—no less than schools, newspapers, and magazines—reflected the growing influence of urban industrialism. Extremely popular were the success stories for boys which Horatio Alger, Jr., and W. T. Adams (under the name of Oliver Optic) turned out by the dozens. These stories in a sense glorified an urban society in which a hard-working boy, no matter how humble his beginnings, could climb to the top by sheer pluck—and luck.

William Sydney Porter (O. Henry) struck a very different note with short stories that presented realistic pictures of American life, both urban and rural. Different again were the novels of Edith Wharton, which pictured the conflicts between the newly rich and older well-to-do families of New York in the 1880's. Henry James suggested the tensions of members of America's leisure class who chose to live in the sophisticated urban centers of Europe.

One of the best-known novels of the period was *The Gilded Age,* written by Samuel L. Clemens (Mark Twain) and Charles Dudley Warner. In a humorous but biting manner, the writers described the corrupt activities of many politicians and land speculators operating in the nation's capital. Edward Bellamy's *Looking Backward: 2000–1887,* another widely read book, described an imaginary society in which poverty and corruption had been eliminated and people lived in freedom and dignity.

One of the ablest writers was William Dean Howells, whose realistic stories furnished a faithful picture of middle-class life in America. Howells, in *The Rise of Silas Lapham,* was especially successful in telling of the triumphs and tragedies of a self-made man.

Notable exceptions

There were, of course, many authors whose work was in no way influenced by the changing times. Emily Dickinson, for example, was one of a number of authors interested in literature for its own sake. A sheltered New England writer, Emily Dickinson created many thought-provoking short poems that have since been recognized as poetry of great distinction and originality.

Even many of the books written for the general public had no apparent relation to the new issues of industrialism. For instance, General Lew Wallace's *Ben-Hur,* a widely read novel, dealt with the conflict between paganism and Christianity in the early days of the Roman Empire. The growing reading public also enjoyed highly romantic and sentimental novels, as well as colorful Wild West adventure stories which enterprising publishers put out in paper covers for only 10 cents—the famous "dime novels."

"Local-color" writers

Partly in reaction against the more or less standardized ways of city life, another group of writers concentrated upon describing those regions of the United States that were still largely under the influence of the older, rural ways of living. One of these writers, Edward Eggleston, touched a "folksy" note in describing life in rural Indiana in his book *The Hoosier Schoolmaster.*

The greatest of these "local-color" writers was Samuel L. Clemens (Mark Twain), the first important writer from west of the Atlantic seaboard states. His *Life on the Mississippi* dramatized the crude, vigorous, racy aspects of the American steamboat era. *The Adventures of Tom Sawyer* and *The Adventures of Huckleberry Finn* were landmarks in the literary and psychological representation of the adolescent American boy. At the same time, these books satirized the middle-class values and racial prejudices of a rural community in Missouri. Twain's *Roughing It* vividly portrayed the raw life of western mining camps.

The colorful and heroic verses of Joaquin (hwah·KEEN) Miller and the realistic stories of mining camps written by Bret Harte brought the Far West into the nation's literature. Helen Hunt Jackson also did much to increase the awareness of the Far West with her stories of Spanish missions and of Indian life in old California. Hamlin Garland, in *Main-Traveled Roads* and other books, wrote of the harsh conditions endured by pioneers on the northern prairies.

The South, too, had its share of local-color writers. George Washington Cable, Kate Chopin, and Grace King presented life among the French-speaking Creoles of Louisiana. Thomas Nelson Page popularized a romantic image of master-slave relations on Virginia plantations before the Civil War. Joel Chandler Harris of Georgia won fame for his "Uncle Remus" tales, folk stories brought from Africa by slaves.

The writings of black authors also partly reflected the influence of the local-color school of writing. Local color distinguished *My Southern Home,* the last book of the pioneer black novelist

William Wells Brown. Another important Negro writer, Paul L. Dunbar, was hailed by a leading white critic as the first black American writer "to feel the Negro life esthetically and express it lyrically." Some of the novels and tales of Charles W. Chestnutt, a black writer of North Carolina, also reflected the local-color school of writing.

New England, like other regions, excited the imaginations of local-color authors, among them Mary E. Wilkins Freeman and Sarah Orne Jewett. These writers pictured the changes in rural life in New England as young people abandoned the rocky, unproductive family farms to seek their fortunes in the growing cities.

SECTION SURVEY

IDENTIFY: journalism, dime novels, local color; Horatio Alger, O. Henry, Mark Twain, William Wells Brown, Paul L. Dunbar, Bret Harte, Emily Dickinson.

1. New developments made possible the mass circulation of newspapers and magazines. Of what significance is this fact?
2. Indicate the contributions of each of the following to journalism: (a) Dana, (b) Pulitzer, (c) Hearst.
3. (a) What is meant by the statement that newspaper publishing became big business? (b) How would this affect the reading public?
4. How did magazines adapt to the changing times?
5. Show how some novels of this period reflected the "growing influence of urban industrialism."

4 New trends in architecture and other fine arts in a changing society

Architecture and art, no less than journalism and literature, revealed the influence of urban life and the growth of industry after 1865.

Decline and revival of architecture

For a number of years after the Civil War, American architecture reached what many have regarded as a low level. During the 1870's and the 1880's many successful business leaders and financiers poured fortunes into huge, gaudy mansions. These overdone show places, as well as many equally tastless public buildings and smaller houses, were a far cry from the dignified and beautiful structures Americans had designed and built along simple classical lines in the late 1700's and early 1800's.

Toward the end of the 1800's, however, a number of architects, notably Henry Hobson Richardson and Richard Morris Hunt, began to design more pleasing, practical houses and public buildings in a dignified, restrained style.

The World's Columbian Exposition, or World's Fair, held in Chicago in 1893, helped to quicken public interest in good architecture. Many of the buildings that housed the exhibits were designed in the simple classical style. Thousands of visitors carried back to their home communities memories of beautiful structures with noble pillars and clean, direct lines.

New trends in architecture

One structure at the Chicago World's Fair, the Transportation Building, heralded a really new day in architecture. Its architect, Louis H. Sullivan, taught that "form follows function," meaning that the best-designed building is one that has a style and uses materials perfectly suited to the purposes of the building. Gradually this idea was adopted by more and more archi-

tects, among them Frank Lloyd Wright, who started to practice his profession in Chicago in 1893 and became one of the world's foremost architects.

The availability of such new building materials as steel, concrete, and plate glass, plus the

The 21-story Flatiron Building, New York City's first skyscraper, towered above nearby buildings when it was completed in 1903.

necessities of urban life, did much to stimulate a new type of business structure.

The "invention" of skyscrapers

As city business districts became more crowded and as real-estate values soared, architects tried to solve the problem by building upward. How could they erect taller buildings? Ingenious architects provided the answer by constructing huge steel frames and filling the spaces with stone, brick, concrete, and glass. The Home Insurance Building, built in Chicago in 1884, set the example for these towering structures. During the next few years, in both Chicago and New York, builders erected taller and taller skyscrapers.

But the new towering buildings turned the narrow streets below into dark, gloomy canyons. To solve this problem, the governing authorities of New York City finally adopted an ordinance requiring architects to "set back" the higher stories of all tall buildings so that more light would reach the streets. This ordinance accomplished its purpose. It also relieved the rectangular lines of the boxlike skyscraper and accounted for the magically beautiful and unique character of the New York sky line. Like many other activities of American life, architecture began to reveal more and more the influence of new times and new ways of living.

Painting and sculpture

The new industrial age had less influence on painters and sculptors than it did on architects. Between 1865 and 1900 the most important development in the fine arts was the increasing skill of American artists who had studied in European art centers. The improving standards in American art also rested in part on the ability and the willingness of wealthy Americans to collect masterpieces, to establish art schools, and to buy the works of American artists.

The themes that painters and sculptors chose often seemed to have little to do with the growing urban industrial society. Gifted sculptors created great statues of Lincoln and other national heroes. One outstanding creation was the "Adams Monument" in Rock Creek Cemetery in Washington, D.C., made by Augustus Saint-Gaudens (saynt-GAW·d'nz). This brooding, hooded figure, sometimes referred to as "The Peace of God," suggests the mystery of life and death.

A number of painters did equally outstanding work. George Inness captured on canvas the beauties of woodland scenes. Winslow Homer's brilliantly colored seascapes suggested the strength and primitive force of the sea. Mary Cassatt, influenced by the new French impressionist style and by Japanese art, painted portraits notable for lively charm and for exquisite tone and color.

The influence of industrialism on art

The work of a number of artists, however, did reveal the influence of industrial and urban America. Thomas Eakins, for example, painted famous and wealthy Americans with such frank realism that they would not buy his works. But Eakins refused to change his style for the sake of immediate popularity and profit, and continued to paint life as he saw it. In a painting designed to reveal the surgeon's scientific skill, the "Clinic of Dr. Gross," Eakins suggested very concretely the new scientific trend of the age.

SECTION SURVEY

IDENTIFY: architecture, fine arts; Frank Lloyd Wright, Augustus Saint-Gaudens, Winslow Homer, Mary Cassatt, Thomas Eakins.

1. What did Louis Sullivan mean by the statement that in architecture "form follows function"?
2. Describe the themes that inspired the noted American sculptors and painters of this period.
3. How do skyscrapers reflect the American spirit?

5 The enrichment of American life through new forms of recreation

Recreation, like all other aspects of everyday living, was transformed by the new urban industrial age. The well-to-do, having time and money, enjoyed such new and, at first, exclusive sports as tennis and golf. Gradually, however, the middle-income groups also began to enjoy such forms of recreation.

New types of rural recreation

For many thousands of American children and their parents in the early 1900's, one of the most memorable events of the year was the arrival of the circus. P. T. Barnum's tent circus, started in Brooklyn in 1871, was called "the greatest show on earth."

Equally awaited was the arrival of the Chautauqua. The Chautauqua movement was an educational enterprise started in 1874 on the shores of Chautauqua Lake in upper New York state. Each year thousands of Americans from all over the United States traveled to Chautauqua Lake

The following report of the Yale-Princeton game of 1884 appeared in the New York *Evening Post*. Although the reporter probably exaggerated, the account does remind us that football in the 1880's was still a rough-and-tumble game with only a few basic rules.

"The spectators could see the elevens hurl themselves together and build themselves in kicking, writhing heaps. They had a general vision of threatening attitudes, fists shaken before noses, dartings hither and thither, throttling, wrestling, and the pitching of individuals headlong to earth; and all this was an exceedingly animated picture which drew from them volley after volley of applause. Those inside the lines, the judges, reporters, and so on, were nearer and saw something more. They saw real fighting, savage blows that drew blood, and falls that seemed as if they must crack all the bones and drive the life from those who sustained them."

to enjoy a summer vacation and to benefit intellectually and spiritually from the lectures and sermons provided for them. Study groups using Chautauqua publications were organized in many towns and villages. As the years passed, the program at Chautauqua Lake became increasingly varied, adding illustrated travel talks, stage presentations, and humorous acts to the more serious lectures and the religious services. Other enterprising leaders also organized traveling tent programs similar to those earlier developed on the shores of Chautauqua Lake. By the early 1900's the traveling Chautauquas were bringing a glimpse of the outside world into many rural communities.

New types of urban recreation

During the 1880's the bicycle changed from a clumsy, high-wheeled, dangerous contraption into something like the machine we know today. As a result, bicycling became a popular fad, as well as a means of getting to and from work for many people.

The theater also gained popularity, particularly for middle-income groups. At its best the theater in this period offered admirable plays performed by great actors, American and foreign-born. Some of the most appealing programs, however, were the melodramas that reminded city dwellers of their own rural background. Such plays as *Way Down East* and *The Old Homestead* attracted large audiences. There was also an equally popular series of melodramas on significant urban themes, such as *Bertha, the Sewing-Machine Girl*. Vaudeville shows, providing a variety of singing, dancing, and gymnastic acts, also attracted large audiences.

By 1900 amusement parks were attracting crowds of city people and making fortunes for their owners. In many cases trolley car companies built amusement parks just outside the city, thereby reaping profits from the parks as well as from trolley fares.

Physical exercise and American sports

During the last quarter of the 1800's an increasing number of middle-class city dwellers became aware of the need for physical exercise, especially for youth. One answer was gymnasiums, which appeared in growing numbers in cities and towns as well as in schools and colleges.

These same years also saw the rapid development of three major spectator sports—baseball, football, and basketball.

Baseball in various forms had been played long before the first professional team, the Cincinnati Red Stockings, was formed in 1869. Seven years later, in 1876, the National League was organized. In 1900 the American League was formed. Well before 1900 urban dwellers in growing numbers were packing ball parks to watch what was becoming one of America's favorite spectator sports.

Football, which evolved from the English game of rugby, also became increasingly popular. The first intercollegiate football contest, played between Rutgers and Princeton in 1869, had 25 players on each side. Within a few years intercollegiate contests were being held in the West as well as in the East. Played mostly by college men, football in the early days was a rough-and-tumble game, so rough, in fact, that some people protested against its "brutality" and demanded its abolition. As the years passed, however, new rules were developed, and the game became better organized.

Basketball, which also became a typically American sport, was first played in 1892 by students at the Y.M.C.A. college in Springfield, Massachusetts. Its inventor, Dr. James Naismith, then an instructor in physical education, created the game to provide the same opportunities for recreation in the winter that baseball provided in the summer, and football in the autumn. Within a few years the game was being played all over the country.

The older rural forms of recreation—picnics, amateur baseball, horseshoe pitching—continued to be popular. Increasingly, however, the ways in which people relaxed and amused themselves were being transformed in the new industrial age.

SECTION SURVEY

1. Show how the circus and the Chautauqua movement affected rural and urban recreation.
2. What three major spectator sports were developed in the late 1800's?
3. How do recreational activities reflect people and their values?

CHAPTER SURVEY

INQUIRING INTO HISTORY

1. Show how architecture and art were affected by urban life and the growth of industry.
2. Explain how each of the following terms reflects the changing ways of American life during the period just studied: (a) concentration of wealth, (b) settlement house, (c) elective system, (d) mass circulation of magazines, (e) skyscrapers, (f) spectator sports.
3. Examine the pictures on pages 135 and 139 and indicate how they help to show the changes taking place during the period just studied.
4. What is the relationship between education and an effective democracy?
5. To what extent should the press be "free"? Why?
6. What is the relationship between functionalism in architecture and an industrialized society?
7. What accounts for the emphasis on reform during the period just studied?

RELATING PAST TO PRESENT

1. Does education today reflect the needs of our society? What changes, if any, would you recommend be made in the high schools and colleges today?
2. What in your opinion is the role of newspapers today?
3. Do you think the federal government should be involved in the support of the arts? Explain.

DEVELOPING SOCIAL SCIENCE SKILLS

1. Jacob Riis, a journalist and photographer, described life in the tenements of New York City. Find excerpts from the book *How the Other Half Lives* or pictures taken by Riis and answer the following: (a) What was life like for the poor in the cities? (b) Compare the lives of the workers and the industrialists. (c) How effective do you think writers such as Riis were in changing conditions?
2. From primary and secondary sources find out more about the women's rights movement between 1860 and 1900. (a) Who were the leaders? (b) What gains were made by women in these years? (c) What obstacles did women still have to work to overcome? (d) What techniques were most effective in promoting women's rights?

UNIT THREE
The Arrival of Reform
1897-1920

CHAPTER 8

THE START OF REFORMS UNDER THE "SQUARE DEAL"

1897-1909

The fortunes of nations as well as of individuals sometimes change with bewildering speed. But people have no certain ways of foreseeing when such change will come or of predicting its directions.

The administration of President McKinley, from 1897 to 1901, is a good example here.

Who on McKinley's inauguration day could have foreseen that within little more than a year the nation would be at war with Spain in a conflict called the Spanish-American War, and that before McKinley's four years in office were over the United States would become a great colonial power with possessions in the Pacific and the Caribbean? (You will read about these striking international developments in Unit Four.)

And who, looking at the solid triumph of big business in the election of 1896, would have dared to predict that within six years a new reform movement, the Progressive movement, would begin to sweep the country, and that a progressive President and Congress would draw up new rules for the conduct of business?

The reform movements of the early 1900's were really a continuation, on a broader front, of earlier efforts to preserve and strengthen democracy in the new industrial age. As you will read, however, the progressives also tackled other problems, including the increasingly serious issue of the conservation of the nation's natural resources.

THE CHAPTER IN OUTLINE

1. Reforms in government as a result of the Progressive movement.

2. A "square deal" under President Theodore Roosevelt's leadership.

3. Conservation of natural resources under Theodore Roosevelt.

1450   1750   1800   1850   1900   1950   1980's

1 Reforms in government as a result of the Progressive movement

To many Americans, the victory of William McKinley and the Republicans in the Presidential election of 1896 spelled the doom of the reform movement. In 1897 the conservative Republicans seemed to have a clear road before them. Having just defeated William Jennings Bryan in his bid for the White House, their leaders in Congress now passed the Dingley Tariff of 1897, which raised average tariff rates to a new high of 57 percent.

In the meantime the depression of 1893–96 gave way to prosperity. New corporations sprang up, and older corporations merged to form giant trusts and industrial concerns. Even the short-lived Spanish-American War of 1898 did not interrupt the nation's economic growth.

Surrounded by prosperity and caught up in the fervor of war and overseas expansion, many Americans in the late 1890's began to forget the demands of the Populists and other reform groups. Yet by 1900 a new reform impulse, known as the Progressive movement, was underway. Many historians regard the Progressive movement as a successor to the Populist movement. But they have held different views regarding its aims, its significance, and its achievements.

Aims of the Progressives

The Progressive movement cut across party lines. It included people from the Bryan wing of the Democratic Party as well as discontented Republicans.

Leaders of the Progressive movement had specific aims. (1) They wanted to restore control of the government to the rank and file of people. (2) They wanted to correct the abuses and injustices that had crept into American life in the age of urban industrialism. (3) They wanted to restore greater equality of economic opportunity by drawing up new rules for the conduct of business.

The progressives were optimists. They believed that these reforms would create a more prosperous and a more democratic country. They hoped to set new standards of honesty for both business and government.

Robert M. La Follette

Robert M. "Fighting Bob" La Follette of Wisconsin was one of the outstanding leaders of the Progressive movement. After graduating from the University of Wisconsin in 1879, La Follette

Election campaigning was a colorful event in towns and cities across America. A crowd gathers here to listen to a candidate's speech.

By 1900 four states had granted full voting rights to women. Here, women line up at the polls in Wyoming.

fought his way upward in local and state politics. He won victories over the opposition of the Republican political machine that dominated Wisconsin, and in doing so won a reputation for fearless honesty. An excellent speaker, he sought support from the farmers and working people, and won the governorship of Wisconsin in 1900.

As governor, La Follette helped to break the power of the political "machine" that had been running the state, and restored control of the government to the majority of the people. He persuaded hesitant legislators to levy heavier taxes on the railroads and on the newer public utilities—the gas, electric, and streetcar companies. He also persuaded the legislators to create commissions to regulate the public-utility companies. In cooperation with Charles Van Hise, president of the University of Wisconsin, La Follette inaugurated a movement for the conservation of Wisconsin's forests and water-power sites, which had largely come under the control of large industrial corporations.

The La Follette administration also promoted good government in Wisconsin by using university scholars to help legislators find needed facts and draft laws that the courts could not easily set aside. He also appointed scholars to serve on the new state regulatory commissions. The "Wisconsin Idea," as the La Follette movement was called, attracted nationwide attention.

Other progressive leaders

Encouraged by La Follette's example, other governors and public officials began to attack corrupt government and powerful corporations. Joseph W. Folk became governor of Missouri in 1906 largely as a result of his success in prosecuting a ring of corrupt politicians in St. Louis. Charles Evans Hughes became governor of New York in 1907 chiefly because of his success in uncovering the highly questionable business practices of certain insurance companies. Hiram Johnson became governor of California in 1910 after fighting the political "bosses" and powerful railroads that had so great an influence in the state.

Women reformers

Even though most women still lacked the vote, some of them took part in reforms whose purpose was to influence government. The National Consumers League, in which Florence Kelley was a leader, brought unfavorable publicity to stores and companies that paid women less than men for equal work and that maintained unhealthful working conditions. The league urged the public to boycott consumer goods produced by child labor and by women who were unfairly treated. With the cooperation of the National Child Labor Committee, the league also secured legislation in the interests of women and children.

The Women's Christian Temperance Union (W.C.T.U.), founded in 1879, carried on a widespread campaign in churches, schools, and public meetings urging that people not use intoxicating beverages and that their manufacture and sale be prohibited. The W.C.T.U. stressed the physical, psychological, and social dangers of alcohol and revealed the menace posed by alcoholics to the well-being of their families. Frances Willard, president of the W.C.T.U. for 20 years, persuaded the organization to support women's suffrage as a means to attain prohibition. The W.C.T.U was committed to educational methods of influence on government. It did not approve the militant tactics of Carrie Nation of Kansas, who invaded saloons with a hatchet to smash mirrors and bottles.

Many women also took part in the work of the Anti-Saloon League, which supported political candidates who pledged opposition to the liquor interests and opposed those who did not.

The "muckrakers"

The Progressive movement also included many scholars, journalists, preachers, and novelists. Theodore Roosevelt applied the name "muckrakers" to the writers who exposed the evils and corruption they found in politics and the business world. Although Roosevelt used the term in an unfavorable sense, the writers accepted it with pride, and it came into popular use.

The "muckraking" movement as such, however, is usually dated from an article, "Tweed Days in St. Louis," written by Lincoln Steffens and Claude H. Wetmore for the October 1902 issue of *McClure's Magazine*. The following month *McClure's* began the serial publication of Ida M. Tarbell's critical *History of the Standard Oil Company*. Many other magazines also began publishing attacks on abuses in American life.

Muckraking novelists as well as journalists attacked many of the evils of their day. Upton Sinclair in his sensational novel *The Jungle* exposed unsanitary practices in the meat-packing industry—and, incidentally, turned many of his readers into vegetarians. Frank Norris's novel *The Octopus* exposed the railroads' control over rural political and economic life. And Jack London in *The War of the Classes, The Iron Heel,* and *Revolution* warned of a revolution that could wipe out private capitalism.

A few, though not many, of the muckrakers called attention to the plight of American Negroes. The most impressive work was *Following the Color Line* by Ray Stannard Baker, a series of magazine articles published as a book in 1908.

Following the Color Line was a competent and honest report of segregation in the South and of racial discrimination in the North. As such, it put the problem of white-black relations in a nation-wide context. In general, Baker favored Booker T. Washington's gradual approach to the difficult problems facing black Americans. In so doing, he reflected the optimistic faith that all people of good will, once aware of the facts, could be counted upon to support policies to help Negroes improve their lives and enjoy greater opportunities.

The root of the problem

The muckrakers brought to light many abuses in American life. Lincoln Steffens, however, pinpointed the basic problem in a series of articles later published as a book entitled *The Shame of the Cities*. Years later, in his *Autobiography*, Steffens summarized his conclusions. The basic problem facing Americans was not the development of industrialism or of business, large or small. The source of the evil was "privilege"—the understandably human demand for special privileges from government. This had to be controlled, according to Steffens, or abuses and cor-

ruption were sure to be the results.

Millions of Americans in the late 1800's and the early 1900's shared Steffens' views. They also agreed that one way to combat the evils of special privilege was to restore control of government to the people.

The Australian ballot

One of the first steps in the direction of more democratic government was the adoption of the *Australian ballot,* or secret vote. Until about 1890 voting had not been done in secret. Each political party printed its own ballots in a distinctive color. Thus when a man cast his ballot—as he did in open view of anybody who cared to watch—it was easy to determine how he had voted. The secret ballot, developed in Australia and adopted in the United States, made this open voting impossible by placing the names of all candidates on a single sheet of paper, printing all ballots at public expense, and requiring voters to mark and cast their ballots in secrecy.

The initiative, referendum, and recall

In trying to secure a more democratic government the progressives supported the use of the initiative, referendum, and recall. All of these reform measures had been advocated by the Populists in the 1890's.

The *initiative* enabled voters in a state to initiate, or introduce, legislation at any time. Suppose, for instance, that a group of citizens wanted to increase the amount of state money spent for public schools. They would draw up a bill and attach to it a petition containing the signatures of a certain percentage of the voters in the state (usually from 5 to 15 percent, depending upon state law). When the petition was presented to the state legislature, the representatives were required by law to debate the bill openly.

The *referendum* was a logical companion to the initiative. Suppose that a bill was pending before a state legislature to give excessive privileges to a public utility company. By securing a specified number of signatures to a petition, voters could compel the legislature to place the bill before *all* the voters of the state for their approval or disapproval. In effect, the referendum enabled every qualified voter to act as a legislator.

The *recall* enabled voters to remove an elected government official before the official's term expired. When a specified number of voters, usually 25 percent, presented a petition, a special election had to be held. In this election all of the voters had an opportunity to vote for or against allowing the official to continue in office.

South Dakota, in 1898, was the first state to

adopt the initiative and the referendum. Eventually 20 states adopted initiative and referendum procedures, and 12 states adopted the recall.

The direct primary

In trying to make government more responsive to the people's wishes, the progressives also advocated the *direct primary*.

Under long-established custom, all candidates for government office were nominated in political conventions. Since the conventions were easily controlled by professional politicians, rank and file voters had little opportunity to express a preference for any candidate.

The direct primary remedied this situation by providing "a nominating election" well in advance of the regular election. Individuals who wanted to run for office could, by securing a specified number of signatures to a petition, have their names printed on the primary ballot of any one of the political parties. On the day of the primary election, the registered voters of each party then marked their ballots for their candidate.

First adopted by Wisconsin in 1903, the direct primary soon spread to almost every state.

Women's suffrage

The vote for women also became part of the progressive program. By 1900 four states—Wyoming, Utah, Colorado, and Idaho—had granted full voting rights to women. As a result of vigorous campaigns by women suffragists and progressive efforts, between 1910 and 1914 seven other states, all west of the Mississippi, gave women the right to vote. Still seeking a Constitutional amendment, women's rights organiza-

tions kept up pressure with parades, demonstrations, and political activity. Public support of the movement increased, especially as a result of women's contributions to the defeat of Germany in World War I. Finally, in 1920, with the ratification of the Nineteenth Amendment, the right of women to vote throughout the United States was written into the Constitution.

Direct election of Senators

Another reform advocated by the progressives was the direct election of United States Senators. According to the Constitution, Senators were chosen by state legislatures. During the early 1900's, however, progressive members of the House of Representatives urged the adoption of an amendment that would allow the people to vote directly for Senators. But the Senate, which was often criticized as a "rich man's club" and which included many politicians who owed their jobs to political bosses and political "machines," blocked every attempt to get this amendment before the states.

In the end, however, the rising power of the progressives proved too much for the "machine" politicians. In 1913, in the Seventeenth Amendment, the right to choose Senators was taken from the state legislatures and given to the voters at large.

Reform of city government

While winning victories at the state and federal level, the progressives were also trying to reform corrupt city governments. Most municipal governments consisted of a mayor and a large city council, elected by the voters and given com-

Thirty thousand demonstrators marched in this suffragette parade in 1912. But most American women could not vote until 1920 when the Nineteenth Amendment was adopted.

plete responsibility for running city affairs. This system made it relatively easy for a well-organized political "machine," using corrupt election procedures, to win control of city government and use its power as it saw fit.

Galveston, Texas, led the way to a new type of government in 1900 after a disastrous hurricane and tidal wave killed one sixth of the city's people and destroyed a third of its property. To meet the emergency, Galveston gave a commission of five persons extraordinary power to run the city. The experiment proved so successful that the *commission* form of government soon spread to other cities.

By 1912 more than 200 American communities had adopted the commission form of government. Supporters argued that it was simpler, more efficient, and less expensive than older types of city government. Also, since each elected commissioner was directly responsible for a separate function of the city government, such as the police, the fire department, sanitation, and public works, it was easier to fix responsibility for the proper conduct of city affairs.

In 1908 Staunton, Virginia, led the way in developing another effective innovation in city government—the *city manager* plan. The plan received national attention in 1914 when it was adopted by Dayton, Ohio, after the mayor and council were unable to cope effectively with a flood emergency. The city manager, an expert in municipal administration, without political connections, is appointed by an elected city council or board of commissioners to run the city as efficiently and economically as possible. After 1914 city manager government spread to numerous cities.

The progressives were, indeed, a powerful force in American life in the early 1900's. In the remaining pages of this chapter you will see how a progressive President, Theodore Roosevelt, and a progressive-minded Congress used their power to bring about long-demanded changes in the relations between government and business.

SECTION SURVEY

IDENTIFY: Progressive movement, National Consumers League, W.C.T.U., "muckrakers," "Wisconsin Idea," Australian ballot, initiative, referendum, recall, direct primary, the Seventeenth and Nineteenth Amendments, city manager plan; Florence Kelley, Lincoln Steffens, Upton Sinclair, Ida Tarbell.

1. In what ways did La Follette reform the government of Wisconsin?
2. (a) Muckrakers exposed many abuses in American life. Explain. (b) How did the mass circulation of newspapers and magazines relate to the muckrakers' influence?
3. (a) Was reform of the Negroes' plight a major progressive concern? Why or why not? (b) Why were Booker T. Washington's views accepted by many white Americans?
4. (a) In the early 1900's there was extensive need for reform in many areas of American society. Why was this so? (b) To what did critics attribute the abuses that existed at this time?

2 A "square deal" under President Theodore Roosevelt's leadership

President McKinley and the Republicans entered the elections of 1900 confident of victory. The Democrats, who had again nominated William Jennings Bryan, tried to make free silver a major campaign issue. But Americans in general, including most farmers, were enjoying prosperity, and they returned President McKinley to the White House with an electoral vote of 292 to 155.

Six months after his second inauguration, on September 6, 1901, McKinley was shot by a half-crazed assassin. He died a few days later and, to the dismay of conservative Republicans, Vice-President Theodore Roosevelt became the nation's Chief Executive.

Theodore Roosevelt's background

Theodore Roosevelt was born in 1858 into a well-to-do New York family. He studied at Harvard, where he acquired a taste for history and politics. After graduation he served a two-year term, from 1882 to 1884, as a member of the New York state legislature. Part of the next two years he lived on a cattle ranch in the Dakota Territory. Returning home in 1886, he unsuccessfully ran for mayor of New York City. He devoted the following three years to the study and writing of history, a task that had occupied much of his spare time since his college days.

In 1889 President Harrison appointed Roosevelt to the Civil Service Commission, where he served effectively for six years. In 1895 he became president of the New York City Police Commission, leaving this job in 1897 to become Assistant Secretary of the Navy. When war with Spain broke out in 1898, he resigned his Navy post to organize, with Leonard Wood, a volunteer cavalry regiment known as the "Rough Riders." After the war he became the Republican governor of New York, but his vigorous, independent actions so alarmed the Republican political bosses that in 1900 they decided to get him out of active politics by "kicking him upstairs" into the Vice-Presidency.

Such was the man who at age 42 became the youngest President the United States had ever had—and, as the conservative Republicans had rightly feared, one of the most independent.

Roosevelt as a progressive

Roosevelt had a gift for sensing public opinion and expressing it in telling phrases. A man of immense energy, he fought zealously for things he believed to be right.

Theodore Roosevelt was also a good politician. That is, he was ready to compromise, taking half a loaf when the whole loaf could not be had. He did not start the Progressive movement. Nor did he go as far as many progressives felt he could and should go. But he gave the Progressive movement dramatic national leadership. His general popularity, his enthusiasm, his ability as a speaker, and his position enabled him to promote a number of reforms. One notable exception was government policy toward Indians, whose needs were largely ignored.

The election of 1904

Roosevelt's progressive ideas antagonized many Republicans leaders. When election year 1904 rolled around, the Republican political leaders would have abandoned him in favor of a more conservative candidate had they dared. But by this time "Teddy" Roosevelt enjoyed widespread popularity. No other Republican candidate had a chance of winning the nomination.

Roosevelt went on to win a resounding victory at the polls—336 electoral votes to 140 for his Democratic opponent, Judge Alton B. Parker of New York.

What was the secret of Roosevelt's popularity with the rank and file of voters? During the campaign, he had announced that he was "unhampered by any pledge, promise, or understanding of any kind, save my promise, made openly to the American people, that so far as my power lies I shall see to it that every man has a square deal, no less and no more." This promise carried weight because Roosevelt convinced voters that he meant what he said.

Settling a coal strike

Less than a year after succeeding McKinley as President, Roosevelt showed where he stood on the question of organized labor. In the spring of 1902 a strike broke out in Pennsylvania in the coal mines owned largely by railroad companies serving the region. The miners worked long hours, lived in company towns, bought from company stores, and because of low wages found it hard to make ends meet. Organized as part of the United Mine Workers Union, they had asked for a 9-hour day, a 20 percent wage increase, improved working conditions, and recognition of their right to bargain as a union. The mineowners refused to negotiate with the union, whereupon the miners went out on strike.

By autumn the country faced a coal-less winter with factories closed and homes without heat.

In Theodore Roosevelt's era, working conditions in American coal mines were grim. Young boys as well as men mined long hours for low wages. This photo of boy miners was taken in the early 1900's.

The mineowners demanded that the President send federal troops into the area to break the strike. Roosevelt refused. Instead, he summoned representatives of the owners and of the union to a White House conference.

At this conference the mineowners refused to listen to a proposal for impartial arbitration. Furious at this lack of cooperation, Roosevelt let it be known that he might send the army to take over the mines in the name of the government. Faced with this prospect, the mineowners agreed to accept the decision of a board of arbitration.

After four months of study, the board gave its decision. The miners won a 9-hour day and a 10 percent wage increase. But the board did not grant the miners the right to negotiate as a union.

Although the miners won only part of their demands, the case was a landmark in the history of organized labor. For the first time the federal government had stepped into a labor controversy with the idea of protecting the interests of all concerned—wage earners, owners, and, by no means least important, the public.

The Danbury Hatters' case

Organized labor was not pleased, however, with the outcome of another labor dispute that began in 1902. In that year the hatters' union started a nationwide effort to boycott, or to halt the purchase of, the hats produced by a hat manufacturer of Danbury, Connecticut. The hat company claimed that the boycott restrained trade and was therefore illegal under the Sherman Antitrust Act. After a long delay, in 1908 the Supreme Court decided in favor of the hat manufacturer. As a result, the members of the hatters' union were held liable for three times the damages suffered by the hat manufacturer.

Theodore Roosevelt was in no way responsible for the Supreme Court ruling. But organized labor, thoroughly alarmed at the outcome of the Danbury Hatters' case, held the government responsible for failing to draft laws that gave reasonable protection to labor unions.

Roosevelt and black Americans

Some progressives fought the exploitation of black workers, established settlement houses for Negroes, and organized national societies to protect the legal rights of black citizens. But the progressives, on the whole, did not focus attention on the plight of black Americans. Many progressive leaders, to be sure, spoke out against racial injustice, but most of them believed that this problem could, at that time, be dealt with realistically only at state and local levels.

Theodore Roosevelt, too, did little to try to

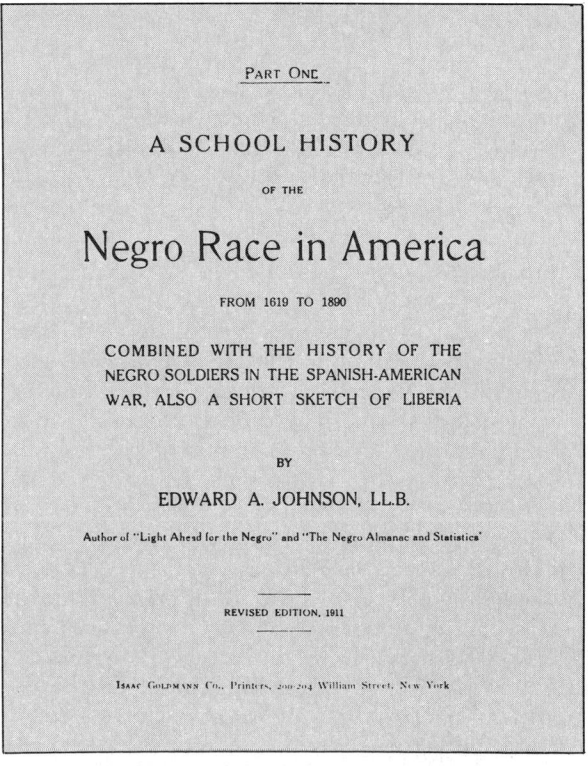

PART ONE

A SCHOOL HISTORY

OF THE

Negro Race in America

FROM 1619 TO 1890

COMBINED WITH THE HISTORY OF THE
NEGRO SOLDIERS IN THE SPANISH-AMERICAN
WAR, ALSO A SHORT SKETCH OF LIBERIA

BY

EDWARD A. JOHNSON, LL.B.

Author of "Light Ahead for the Negro" and "The Negro Almanac and Statistics"

REVISED EDITION, 1911

Isaac Goldmann Co., Printers, 200-204 William Street, New York

Edward A. Johnson, a black textbook author, is shown here, with a page from his *School History of the Negro Race in America*. Studies such as this were part of a growing literature on black Americans.

President Theodore Roosevelt liked to hunt big game. In this political cartoon by Clifford Berryman, hunter Roosevelt has shot down harmful trusts and tamed other trusts by means of "restraint."

improve the condition of black Americans. But Roosevelt did become involved in southern politics, where questions of segregation and black leadership were important issues. Especially during his first term, he wanted to strengthen his influence in southern Republican organizations. Thus, against the opposition of segregated southern Republican organizations, Roosevelt sometimes supported the claims of black politicians to federal office and to participation as delegates at Republican national conventions.

In such matters Roosevelt often used Booker T. Washington as his adviser. Once, after a conference with Washington, Roosevelt invited the black leader to lunch with him at the White House. When the episode became known, a storm of criticism swept the South. Roosevelt did not repeat the invitation.

Roosevelt's failure to include Negroes in his "square deal," except when politically expedient to do so, reflected the attitudes and prejudices of most white Americans, including most of the progressives, during these years.

Roosevelt as "trust buster"

During Roosevelt's administration the federal government took a number of steps toward regulating business practices in the interests of the public welfare. Before this time, as you recall, the federal government, with few exceptions, had not become much involved in business affairs.

Early in his first term Roosevelt directed his Attorney General to bring suit under the Sherman Antitrust Act against the Northern Securities Company. This was a holding company that controlled the three leading railroads serving the country between Lake Michigan and the Pacific Northwest. "We do not wish to destroy corporations," Roosevelt announced, "but we do wish to make them subserve the public good." In 1904 the Supreme Court held that the Northern Securities Company did restrain trade and was illegal under the Sherman Antitrust Act.

Early in 1903, while the Northern Securities Company case was still pending in the courts, Congress passed two important laws. The first measure, the Expedition Act, speeded up antitrust cases by giving them a priority over the other cases in federal courts. The second measure created the Department of Commerce and Labor, with a Secretary in the President's cabinet. The new department included a Bureau of Corporations, authorized to investigate and report on corporation activities.

After 1904, encouraged by the Supreme Court decision in the Northern Securities Company case and by his own victory at the polls, Roosevelt started action against a number of other trusts. Altogether, 44 suits against trusts were started during Roosevelt's administration.

But even when the Supreme Court ordered a trust to dissolve, the business executives who had controlled the various corporations in the trust often continued to run them as a unit by meeting informally and sharing in the decisions of the separate corporations. By secret arrangements of this kind—often called "communities of interest"—the corporations continued to do informally what they had previously done as a trust. The possible advantages of large-scale operations, both for the consumer and for the corporations, were obviously very great. Moreover, big business was so tied together that any attempt to break up a monopoly was like trying to unscramble the eggs in an omelet. The trend of the times was toward larger and larger business combinations, and neither Roosevelt nor anyone else could reverse this trend.

"Good" and "bad" combinations

Before leaving office in 1909, Roosevelt concluded that the problem of trusts was not simply one of size. What really mattered was whether a business combination, regardless of size, was "good" or "bad" for the public as a whole. He asked Congress to pass laws defining "good" and "bad" practices, but Congress refused.

Finally, in 1911, two years after Roosevelt left office, the Supreme Court adopted his point of view. In two cases involving business combinations, the Court ruled that the Sherman Antitrust Act's prohibition of "all combinations in restraint of trade" should mean "all *unreasonable* combinations in restraint of trade." In applying the "rule of reason," as it was called, the Supreme Court from then on decided whether a large business combination was "reasonable" or "unreasonable" by looking not merely at its size, but also at its effect upon the public.

Important railroad legislation

The Roosevelt administration had much better success in regulating railroads than in breaking up trusts. Following the President's recommendations, Congress adopted two laws which put teeth into the Interstate Commerce Act of 1887 and strengthened the Interstate Commerce Commission.

The Elkins Act of 1903 made it illegal for a shipper to accept a rebate, just as the Interstate Commerce Act had made it illegal for a railroad company to give one. Many railroads approved of this act, for it freed them from the necessity of giving special privileges to large shippers.

The Hepburn Act of 1906 provided for more thorough regulation over railroads by giving the Interstate Commerce Commission authority (1) to regulate express and sleeping-car companies, oil pipelines, bridges, railroad terminals, and ferries doing business across state lines; (2) to fix "just and reasonable" rates, subject to approval by the federal courts; (3) to restrict the granting of free passes; and (4) to require that railroads use uniform methods of accounting.

In 1910, after President Roosevelt had left office, Congress also passed the Mann-Elkins Act, which placed telephone, telegraph, cable, and wireless companies under the control of the Interstate Commerce Commission.

Laws protecting public health

President Roosevelt also gave leadership to a movement to protect public health.

Government chemists had long known that the products of some distilleries, drug companies, and meat-packing plants were endangering public health. Many canned foods were spoiled or were treated with poisonous preservatives. Patent medicines often contained harmful habit-forming drugs or ingredients that could not possibly relieve any ailments. And, as Upton Sinclair had pointed out in his book *The Jungle,* meats in the packing houses were often from diseased animals.

Against the powerful opposition of the meat-packing interests, Roosevelt and the progressives in Congress secured passage in 1906 of the Meat Inspection Act, requiring government approval of all meat shipped from one state to another. Also under pressure from reform groups, including a women's letter-writing campaign, Congress passed the Pure Food and Drug Act of 1906, forbidding the manufacture, sale, or transportation of adulterated or poisonous patent medicines and foods. It also required the makers of patent medicines to put labels on containers indicating their exact contents. Five years later, in 1911, Congress supplemented this law by making it illegal to use false or misleading labels.

These acts helped to strengthen the developing theory that the federal government had a responsibility for protecting the public welfare.

SOURCES

THEODORE ROOSEVELT'S "NEW NATIONALISM" SPEECH (1910)

Our country—this great republic—means nothing unless it means the triumph of a real democracy, the triumph of popular government, and, in the long run, of an economic system under which each man shall be guaranteed the opportunity to show the best that there is in him. . . .

I stand for the square deal. But when I say that I am for the square deal, I mean not merely that I stand for fair play under the present rules of the game, but that I stand for having those rules changed so as to work for a more substantial equality of opportunity and of reward for equally good service. . . .

IDENTIFY: "square deal," Danbury Hatters' case, Northern Securities Company case, "communities of interest," "rule of reason."

1. Explain why organized labor was pleased with Roosevelt's handling of the 1902 coal strike.
2. How did Roosevelt's attitude toward black Americans reflect the attitudes and prejudices of most white Americans of the time?
3. Do the facts support Roosevelt's claim to the title of "trust buster"? Why or why not?
4. The Elkins Act, the Hepburn Act, the Meat Inspection Act, and the Pure Food and Drug Act were important steps toward a new interpretation of government responsibility and of the general welfare clause in the preamble to the Constitution. Do you agree or disagree with this interpretation? Explain.

3 Conservation of natural resources under Theodore Roosevelt

"The first work I took up when I became President," Roosevelt wrote in his *Autobiography,* "was the work of reclamation." This, the job of reclaiming and conserving the nation's natural resources, proved to be one of his greatest contributions.

Wasted natural resources

Before Theodore Roosevelt became President almost nothing had been done to safeguard the nation's resources. Indeed, Americans had always used their natural resources without regard for the future. Pioneer farmers had cut and burned their way westward, with ax and fire transforming forest lands into farm lands. With careless generosity the federal and state governments had encouraged waste, especially during the latter half of the 1800's, handing over to private individuals and to corporations priceless natural resources—agricultural and grazing lands, forest regions, mineral deposits, oil fields, and water-power sites.

By 1900 only 200 million acres (80.9 million hectares) of the nation's original 800 million acres (323.8 million hectares) of virgin forest were still standing, and four fifths of the timber was privately owned. The executives who controlled the nation's corporations were, in general, no more concerned about waste than the pioneer settlers had been. Lumber companies destroyed forests without regard for wildlife, flood control, fire protection, replanting, or the preservation of young trees. Cattle raisers and sheepherders overgrazed semiarid lands, stripping them of their protective covering of grass and often converting them into dust bowls.

Coal companies worked only the richest and most accessible veins, leaving the bulk of the coal buried in abandoned mines. Oil companies allowed natural gas to escape unused into the air. The growing cities polluted rivers and streams with sewage and industrial wastes, destroying fish and creating a menace to public health. The only excuse for these wasteful practices was that Americans had been accustomed to thinking that their natural resources were inexhaustible.

Early conservation efforts

By the late 1800's the situation was becoming increasingly serious. A rapidly growing population was making heavier and heavier demands upon the nation's resources. The growing industries were devouring raw materials in ever larger quantities. A few thoughtful Americans realized that the nation's resources could not last forever.

As early as 1873 the American Association for the Advancement of Science demanded some action to prevent the waste of natural resources. Because of these efforts and the efforts of other

Arizona's Roosevelt Dam, which was in operation by 1911, created an enormous reservoir. Water from this reservoir flowed through irrigation canals and ditches to transform a vast desert area into rich farm land.

In 1903 Theodore Roosevelt and John Muir (at Roosevelt's right), a famous naturalist, camped for four days at Yosemite Park in California, where they discussed conservation.

farsighted people, Congress in 1887 established the Forest Bureau in the Department of Agriculture. And in 1891 Congress authorized the President to withdraw timberlands from public sale. Acting under this law, President Harrison set aside a national forest reserve of 17 million acres (6.9 million hectares), and Presidents Cleveland and McKinley more than doubled this area.

A small beginning toward the conservation of natural resources had been made. But the public as a whole had not yet learned to think of the need for conservation as a serious national problem.

Roosevelt's leadership

During his administration President Roosevelt awakened public interest to the need for conservation, aroused Congress to action, and managed to get the federal and the state governments to adopt new policies.

In 1901, the year he became President, Roosevelt warned Americans that "The forest and water problems are perhaps the most vital internal problems of the United States." In a special message to Congress he reminded the legislators that "The mineral wealth of this country, the coal, iron, oil, gas, and the like, does not reproduce itself. . . . If we waste our resources today," he warned, "our descendants will feel that exhaustion a generation or two before they otherwise would. . . ."

But Theodore Roosevelt was never content with mere talk. During his administration he withdrew from public sale 150 million acres (60.7 million hectares) of forest land—an area substantially larger than France. He also withdrew millions of acres of coal and phosphate lands and potential water-power sites. In response to his urging, Congress created wildlife sanctuaries and national parks. Needless to say, in all of these activities Roosevelt met strong opposition from private interests.

The Newlands Reclamation Act

For one of the most important acts of his administration, however, President Roosevelt received considerable support, especially from western members of Congress. Early in his Presidency he supported the Newlands Reclamation Act, which provided that money from the sale of public lands in 16 western states and Territories was to be used to build irrigation projects that would reclaim wasteland—that is, make it suitable for farming. Money from the sale of water to farmers who settled on the reclaimed land was to go into a revolving fund that would finance additional irrigation projects.

Reclamation work started at once. Within four years 28 different irrigation projects were under way. By 1911 the Shoshone (shoh·SHOH·nee) Dam in Wyoming and the Roosevelt Dam in Arizona were in operation. Water from the enormous reservoir created by the Roosevelt Dam flowed through irrigation canals and ditches to transform 200,000 acres (80,940 hectares) of desert into rich farm land. As other projects were completed, additional thousands of acres of wasteland were brought under cultivation.

The White House Conference

In 1907 Roosevelt took another important step when he created the Inland Waterways Commission. After studying nearly every aspect of the conservation program, the commission urged the President to organize a national conference to publicize the need for conservation.

Roosevelt immediately issued invitations for a White House meeting in May 1908. Those invited included state governors, members of Congress, Supreme Court justices, leading scientists, and scores of prominent citizens.

The White House Conservation Conference was a great success. One result was the appointment of a 50-member National Conservation Commission made up of nearly equal numbers of scientists, business executives, and political leaders. This commission went to work at once on a systematic study of the country's mineral, water, forest, and soil resources.

Another important outgrowth of the White House Conference was the appointment of state conservation agencies in 41 of the states by governors convinced of the need for them.

Thus Theodore Roosevelt succeeded in arousing public opinion to the need for conservation. Equally important, he established the foundations of a solid conservation program for the future.

SECTION SURVEY

IDENTIFY: conservation, reclamation, natural resources.

1. Show how Theodore Roosevelt tried to arouse the nation to the need for conservation.
2. What was the significance of the Newlands Reclamation Act of 1902?
3. Why was there opposition to the concept of conservation proposed by Roosevelt?
4. In what ways did Roosevelt establish "the foundations of a solid conservation program for the future"?
5. Pioneers, corporations, state and federal governments, and Americans in general were and are responsible for the waste of America's natural resources and the pollution of the natural environment. Comment on why this was true in the early 1900's and why it is still true today.

CHAPTER SURVEY

INQUIRING INTO HISTORY

1. How did the role of government change during the period just studied?
2. To what extent did Roosevelt's domestic policies follow the goals of his "square deal" program?
3. Theodore Roosevelt's main goal was not to "bust the trusts" but rather to assert the power of the federal government over big business. Do you agree or disagree with this statement? Explain.
4. Was reform necessary for the preservation of American business and the free enterprise system in the United States? Why or why not?
5. Did the ideals of Progressivism agree with the ideals expressed in the Declaration of Independence and the preamble to the Constitution? Explain.

RELATING PAST TO PRESENT

1. In what ways did Theodore Roosevelt extend the powers of the Presidency?
2. In *Following the Color Line* (1908), Ray Stannard Baker stated that the plight of the Negro was more white America's problem than black America's problem. Comment.
3. How does today's federal government protect the American public from unfair business practices?
4. Which critics in our society today might qualify for the title "muckraker"? What are they criticizing?

DEVELOPING SOCIAL SCIENCE SKILLS

1. Americans tend to elect Presidents who reflect the spirit of the times. Gather evidence to support or refute this hypothesis, using Theodore Roosevelt as an example. Can you think of other Presidents who reflected the spirit of their times? Explain.
2. Make a chart showing the social, educational, economic, and political reforms that were made in the Progressive era (1895–1917). Which of these reforms do you consider the most important? Why?

CHAPTER 9
THE EXTENSION OF REFORMS UNDER THE "NEW FREEDOM"
1909-1920

From 1901 to 1921 the White House opened its doors to three different Presidents. From 1901 to 1909 "Teddy" Roosevelt—colorful, dynamic, forceful—promised to give Americans a "square deal" and, on the whole, did much to fulfill this promise. From 1909 to 1913 William Howard Taft—a huge man, genial, highly intelligent, thoroughly competent, but without "Teddy's" ability to capture the public's imagination—made important contributions to the reform program. From 1913 to 1921 Woodrow Wilson—scholar, idealist, in his own quieter way sharing Theodore Roosevelt's conviction that the President's job was to lead Congress and the country—promised Americans a "New Freedom" and took important steps toward fulfilling that promise before World War I interrupted his program.

Each of the three Presidents had to grapple with one basic issue—the role of government in the new industrial age. Should government try to guarantee vigorous competition by breaking up the giant industries? This was what the reformers of the 1880's and 1890's had demanded, and this was what they thought they had secured with the passage of the Sherman Antitrust Act of 1890.

Or should government accept the trend toward larger and larger industrial combinations and be content to make rules under which "good" combinations could prosper and "bad" combinations could be broken up? This was the view that Theodore Roosevelt came to accept.

THE CHAPTER IN OUTLINE

1. Gains and losses of the Progressive movement under President Taft.

2. Expanded opportunities under Woodrow Wilson's "New Freedom."

| 1450 | 1750 | 1800 | 1850 | 1900 | 1950 | 1980's |

1 Gains and losses of the Progressive movement under President Taft

Despite a financial panic and depression in 1907, President Roosevelt's popularity with the public was at its peak in 1908. It was clear that the Republican nomination for another term was his for the asking. But Roosevelt stood by an earlier announcement that he would not run again.

The election of 1908

At the Republican convention in Chicago, Roosevelt threw his support to his close friend and associate William Howard Taft of Ohio, who won the nomination on the first ballot. Roosevelt also played a leading role in drafting the Republican platform. The platform called for strengthening the Interstate Commerce Act of 1887 and the Sherman Antitrust Act of 1890, for conserving the nation's resources, developing an improved highway system, and revising the tariff.

The Democrats again chose William Jennings Bryan as their Presidential candidate. The Democratic platform condemned the Republican Party as the party of "privileges and private monopolies." It called for a lower tariff, new antitrust laws, and a federal income tax.

One unusual feature of the election campaign was the action taken by the American Federation of Labor. Until 1908 the A. F. of L. had consistently refused to throw its support behind any political party, choosing instead to support friends of organized labor in both parties. In 1908, however, the A. F. of L. abandoned this traditional policy and came out for Bryan and the entire Democratic ticket.

Despite the support of organized labor, the Democrats lost by a considerable margin, with Taft receiving 321 electoral votes to Bryan's 162. The Republicans also retained control of both houses of Congress.

Reforms under Taft

William Howard Taft, a Cincinnati lawyer and judge, had served the Roosevelt administration in the Philippines and in the War Department. Taft was a cautious man. Both his legal training and his temperament led him to stress the legalistic restrictions on his Presidential power. As one commentator put it, the transfer of the Presidency from Roosevelt to Taft was like changing from an automobile to a horse-drawn carriage. Despite his conservative nature, however, Taft recognized the force of the Progressive movement and supported a number of important reform measures.

Taft's administration chalked up an impressive list of accomplishments which progressives had favored. Taft's Attorney General started 90 antitrust suits against big corporations compared with 44 suits started under President Roosevelt. Following Taft's recommendation, Congress strengthened the Interstate Commerce Act by passing the Mann-Elkins Act of 1910. This new legislation placed telephone, telegraph, cable, and wireless companies under the jurisdiction of the Interstate Commerce Commission. Congress also established a Bureau of Mines in the Department of the Interior, and created a new department with cabinet rank—the Department of Labor. In response to the growing attack upon the evils of child labor, Congress established a Children's Bureau in the Department of Labor. It also established an 8-hour day for all workers on projects contracted for by the federal government.

In addition to its antitrust measures and efforts to improve the lot of wage earners, the Taft administration also took steps to create a healthier political climate. President Taft himself added a considerable number of federal jobs to the civil service list, and Congress adopted the Publicity Act requiring political parties to make public the sources and amounts of money spent in political campaigns.

Taft's administration was also partly responsible for the adoption of a constitutional amendment to make possible a federal income tax. The Sixteenth Amendment, which had been recommended by Taft and proposed in July 1909, was ratified by the required number of states by February 1913.

Progressive opposition to the tariff

In spite of these impressive reform measures, President Taft early began to lose the support of the progressives in the Republican Party. As a result, he relied more and more on conservative members of the party.

The split between President Taft and the progressives appeared as early as April 1909, when Congress adopted the Payne-Aldrich Tariff. The progressives had worked for lower tariff rates, and at first Taft had supported their position. Then he switched to the high tariff point of view, and swung his influence behind the Payne-Aldrich measure. In the new act some reductions were in fact made, but rates on many thousands of items were actually increased.

Taft's conservation policy

In the midst of the tariff controversy, Taft was also violently attacked for his stand on conservation. Indeed, some of his most bitter critics charged that he had undermined Theodore

Roosevelt's conservation program. Although this was an unfair charge, it is true that the conservation movement suffered a setback during the opening months of Taft's administration.

Taft's Secretary of the Interior, Richard A. Ballinger, was a cautious lawyer. After examining the timber law of 1891, he concluded that the President's authority to withdraw land from sale extended only to timber lands. He therefore restored to public sale valuable water-power sites that President Roosevelt had previously withdrawn. Gifford Pinchot, head of the Forest Service under both Roosevelt and Taft, promptly protested. Taft sided with Pinchot, and the lands in question were returned to the forest reserve. But Pinchot, an ardent conservationist, was convinced that Ballinger was on the side of private interests and opposed to the conservation program.

Pinchot's fears were strengthened when Ballinger allowed extensive coal lands and timber lands in Alaska to pass into private hands. This action aroused a storm of controversy throughout the country. In the midst of the storm, Taft removed Pinchot from office.

Although Ballinger resigned in 1911 and the new Secretary of the Interior restored the Alaskan lands to the federal forest reserve, the damage had been done. Taft's stand on the Ballinger controversy cost the Republicans large numbers of votes in the Congressional elections of 1910. For the first time in 16 years the Republicans lost control of the House of Representatives.

Actually, Taft did a great deal to advance the conservation program. After receiving authorization from Congress, he withdrew almost 59 million acres (23.9 million hectares) of coal lands from public sale. He also signed the Appalachian Forest Reserve Act, which enabled the government to add large tracts of land in the southern Appalachians and in the White Mountains of New Hampshire to the federal reserves.

A political victory for progressives

Early in 1910 the progressive wing of the Republican Party launched an attack upon the Speaker of the House. Since 1903 Speaker Joseph G. "Uncle Joe" Cannon of Illinois had been one of the most powerful officers in the government. As Speaker, he appointed all House committees and selected their leadership. He appointed himself head of the powerful Committee on Rules, which determined the order of business in the House. Acting in this capacity, he could prevent any bill to which he objected from coming out of committee for debate on the floor of the House. Moreover, as presiding officer of the House he could determine who should speak during debate by recognizing or refusing to recognize anyone he pleased. As a result of these powers, "Uncle Joe" was able to rule the House with an iron hand.

President William Howard Taft was conservative by nature. Yet he recognized the force of the Progressive movement and supported a number of important reform measures.

The progressives charged that Cannon, a conservative, had used his great power to block progressive legislation. Determined to put an end to Cannon's control, in March 1910 Representative George W. Norris of Nebraska proposed an amendment to the House rules. He moved that in the future the Committee on Rules be elected by the members of the House instead of being chosen by the Speaker, and that the Speaker be excluded from membership on the Rules Committee.

Speaker Cannon, solidly supported by the conservatives, fought desperately to maintain his power. After a heated debate, about 40 progressive Republicans voted with the Democrats in favor of Norris' motion and stripped the Speaker of his traditional powers over the Committee on Rules. A year later the House deprived the Speaker of his power to appoint members of the remaining committees. The Speaker remained an extremely influential figure, but the Speaker's power was diminished.

Split in the Republican Party

By 1912 the Republican Party was split wide open, with the "old guard" on one side and the progressives on the other. Theodore Roosevelt, by now dissatisfied with Taft's leadership, decided to run again for the Presidency. To do so, Roosevelt had to brush aside the obvious candidate of the progressive forces, Robert M. La Follette of Wisconsin. Roosevelt also had to line up enough delegates to the nominating convention to insure his own nomination.

But President Taft had the advantage that a President always has at a political convention. When the Republican convention began to organize, the Roosevelt supporters claimed that many of their delegates were refused seats by the steamroller methods of the Taft forces. The convention named Taft as its candidate. Disgruntled at this turn of affairs, Roosevelt's supporters called another convention, which nominated him for the Presidency and launched a new third party—the Progressive Party, sometimes called the "Bull Moose" Party.°

The "Bull Moose" Republicans with "Teddy" Roosevelt at their head adopted a platform calling for numerous reforms. The platform favored legislation in the interest of labor; it advocated tariff reform; it endorsed the initiative, referendum, and recall; and it declared that it stood for government control over unfair business practices. In a spirited campaign, full of an almost frenzied zeal, Roosevelt popularized his "New Nationalism" program. By the phrase "New Nationalism" he meant the extension of the powers of the federal government so that it might become an effective instrument in the battle for progressive measures and social reform.

Wilson as the Democratic candidate

The Democrats had every reason to believe that the split in the Republican Party would insure their own victory. As their standard bearer, they chose Governor Woodrow Wilson of New Jersey. The Democratic platform called for tariff

reduction, banking reform, laws on behalf of workers and farmers, and the enforcement of stronger antitrust laws. Both the platform and the nomination of Wilson indicated that the Democratic Party was under the influence of its progressive wing.

Wilson, the son of a southern Presbyterian minister, had been educated at Princeton, the University of Virginia, and Johns Hopkins University. In 1902 he became president of Princeton University. His writings emphasized the idea that the President of the United States ought to be the real leader of the government, taking the initiative and interpreting the will of the people.

Not until Wilson became governor of New Jersey in 1910 did he favor the newer progressive ideas. As governor he fought the political "machine" bosses of his party, showing a remarkable independence. He also took the lead in pushing through the legislature laws designed to reform the lax corporation laws of the state. And he showed more and more interest in other progressive measures. Thus he became the logical choice of the progressives in the Democratic Party.

An idealist and a man of convictions, Wilson was determined, courageous, and independent. He sensed the popular discontent in the country, and his neatly turned phrases about establishing a "New Freedom" for ordinary Americans greatly appealed to those who were convinced that special privilege menaced the nation.

Democratic victory

The election proved to be a clear-cut victory for the progressives, a defeat for the conservatives. Wilson received 435 electoral votes to 88 for Roosevelt and 8 for Taft.

Despite his overwhelming electoral vote, Wilson was a "minority" President. He received only 6 million popular votes out of a total of more than 15 million. Nevertheless, he could count upon widespread public support for his progressive "New Freedom" program.

SECTION SURVEY

IDENTIFY: Department of Labor, Publicity Act, Sixteenth Amendment, "Bull Moose" Party, "New Nationalism."

1. Make a chart comparing the parties, candidates, issues, and results of the 1908 and 1912 elections.
2. (a) What were the reasons for the revolt against "Uncle Joe" Cannon? (b) What were the results?
3. "Taft's administration chalked up an impressive list of accomplishments which progressives had favored." Explain.

° The party adopted as its emblem the powerful bull moose as a tribute to Roosevelt, who often used the term to describe a person's strength and vigor.

2 Expanded opportunities under Woodrow Wilson's "New Freedom"

With his "New Freedom" program President Wilson hoped to restore the equality of opportunity that many Americans had enjoyed when the frontier was still open to settlers. Wilson believed that this equality of opportunity had for the most part been destroyed by the closing of the frontier, by great corporations, and by the often corrupt alliance between government and business.

Wilson's plea for the "New Freedom"

President Wilson at once recommended to Congress a positive program to promote the public welfare. Opposed by pressure groups and lobbies representing special business interests, Wilson used all his skills as a speaker to win popular support.

The legislation enacted during Wilson's first administration did not fully realize the President's ideal of economic freedom and equality for ordinary Americans. But it was more than a step in that direction.

Tariff reform

Like most Democrats, Wilson believed that high protective tariffs benefited the trusts by excluding from the country products which foreign manufacturers could make and market more cheaply. It was also true, of course, that tariffs protected jobs and helped workers maintain higher wages than foreign workers received.

To check the trend toward monopoly and reduce the cost of living, the Wilson administration pushed through Congress the Underwood Tariff Act of 1913. This act did not establish *free trade*,° but it went further toward reducing tariffs than had any act adopted in the past 50 years. It lowered duties on almost a thousand items,

° *free trade:* the exchange of goods between countries unhampered by regulations or high protective tariffs aimed to keep out foreign goods.

This 1912 election campaign poster shows the Democratic candidate, Woodrow Wilson, against an American flag in the background.

including cotton and woolen goods, iron, steel, coal, wood, agricultural tools, and many agricultural products. The average of all duties was reduced from 41 to 29 percent.

To make up for the revenue thus lost, the Underwood Tariff Act took advantage of the recently ratified Sixteenth Amendment to the Constitution by including a section providing for an income tax. The new law provided for a "graduated" tax ranging from 1 to 6 percent on incomes over $3,000 per year.

The Underwood Tariff was passed against strong opposition. Its opponents claimed that it would seriously harm American business. Whether these claims were justified, however, remained unanswered, for in 1914 war broke out

SOURCES

WILSON'S "NEW FREEDOM" SPEECH (1912)

I take my stand absolutely, where every progressive ought to take his stand, on the proposition that private monopoly is indefensible and intolerable. And there I will fight my battle. . . . I am for big business, and I am against trusts. Any man who can survive by his brains, any man who can put the others out of the business by making the thing cheaper to the consumer at the same time that he is increasing its intrinsic value and quality, I take off my hat to, and I say: "You are the man who can build up the United States, and I wish there were more of you." . . .

in Europe and many normal trade relations were shattered. During World War I American business boomed, and American manufacturers did not need a tariff to protect them from foreign competition.

But the Underwood Tariff did answer the widespread cry for tariff reform. Moreover, in its income tax provision it laid down the principle that those with more income must bear a heavier share of the expenses of government. This rule is sometimes called the "ability-to-pay" principle of taxation.

Demand for a new banking system

The second important achievement of Wilson's "New Freedom" administration was in the field of money and banking. Almost everyone was dissatisfied with the existing banking system. But people disagreed on how to reform it. Some favored a strong centralized banking system under *private* control, and others wanted the *government* to exercise greater control over money and banking.

In general, the more conservative business groups wanted greater private control over the existing banking system. They argued that this control would enable the stronger banks to help the less favored banks in times of financial crisis.

On the other side were the Bryan Democrats and the progressive Republicans. They believed that the existing banking system was already too much under the control of the great bankers and financiers—the "money trust." They wanted the government, not private bankers, to control the banking system. This control, they argued, would enable the government to regulate the amount of currency in circulation and thus help to stabilize prices.

The Federal Reserve System

The Federal Reserve Act of 1913 was a compromise between these two proposals. It provided for the establishment of 12 Federal Reserve districts, each with a Federal Reserve Bank. The operations of these district banks were to be supervised and coordinated by a Federal Reserve

Artist George Bellows painted this scene of crowded, urban America, teeming with life. The painting, which he titled "Cliff Dwellers," was done in 1913.

Board in Washington, D.C. All national banks were to be members of a Federal Reserve Bank, and all of the state banks which met certain requirements were invited to join.

The Federal Reserve Banks were strictly "bankers' banks," established to provide services only for member banks, not for business concerns or private citizens. In times of crisis, when weak banks were on the point of failing, the Federal Reserve Banks could transfer money reserves and thus help to prevent failure and the loss of people's savings.

The Federal Reserve System also provided a more "elastic" currency by making it possible to put more money into circulation or to withdraw some from circulation according to the needs of the time. It provided this elastic currency by controlling the amount of lending that member banks could do.

Antitrust laws strengthened

The third great achievement of Wilson's "New Freedom" program was its effort to strengthen the antitrust laws. The Clayton Antitrust Act of 1914 helped to put teeth in the older Sherman Antitrust Act.

The Clayton Act was aimed at business practices that until then had not been illegal. (1) It prohibited business organizations from selling at lower prices to certain favored purchasers *if* such price discrimination helped to create a monopoly. (2) It prohibited "tying contracts"—that is, contracts requiring a purchaser to agree not to buy or sell the products of a competitor. (3) It declared interlocking directorates illegal in companies with capital investments of $1 million or more. (4) It prohibited corporations from acquiring the stock of another company *if* the purchase tended to create a monopoly.

The Clayton Act also attempted to protect the farmer and the wage earner. As you may remember, the Sherman Antitrust Act of 1890 had been used on a number of occasions against labor unions. The Clayton Act, on the other hand, declared that labor unions and farm organizations had a legal right to exist and could not "be held or construed to be illegal combinations or conspiracies in restraint of trade, under the antitrust laws."

The Clayton Act also prohibited the granting of an injunction in a labor dispute *unless* the court decided that an injunction was necessary "to prevent irreparable injury to property." This act also declared that strikes, peaceful picketing, and boycotts were legal under federal jurisdiction.

Organized labor hailed the Clayton Act as a great victory. But as you will read, the courts tended to interpret the act in such a way that the injunction continued to be used as a weapon against strikes.

The Federal Trade Commission

The Federal Trade Commission, created by Congress in 1914 as part of President Wilson's "New Freedom" program, was authorized to advise and regulate industries engaged in interstate and foreign trade. The commission was to be a bipartisan body of five members.

The commission was authorized to (1) require annual and special reports from corporations; (2) investigate the business activities of persons and most corporations; (3) publish reports on its findings; and (4) order corporations to stop unfair methods of competition. Among the unfair practices investigated by the commission were mislabeling, adulteration of products, and false claims to patents. If a corporation refused to obey an order to "cease and desist" such practices, the commission could appeal to the courts to enforce its ruling. But the law protected the corporation by providing that it also could appeal to the courts if it considered the "cease and desist" order to be unfair.

The Federal Trade Commission was intended to prevent the growth of monopolies and to help bring about a better understanding between big business and the government.

SOURCES

WILSON ON AMERICAN IDEALS (1914)

My dream is that, as the years go on and the world knows more and more of America, it will also drink at these fountains of youth and renewal; that it also will turn to America for those moral inspirations which lie at the basis of all freedom; that the world will never fear America, unless it feels that it is engaged in some enterprise which is inconsistent with the rights of humanity; and that America will come into the full light of the day when all shall know that she puts human rights above all other rights and that her flag is the flag not only of America, but of humanity.

Other "New Freedom" measures

The tariff, money and banking, regulation of trusts—these were the major problems tackled by Congress during Wilson's first administration. Much more reform legislation might have been adopted if the outbreak of World War I in Europe in the summer of 1914 had not interfered. Even so, Congress found time to pass several other important measures.

In 1914 Congress adopted the Smith-Lever Act. Among other things, this act provided federal funds for rural education. The educational programs were to be carried on by the Department of Agriculture in cooperation with the land-grant colleges. Federal grants of money were to be matched by similar grants from the states receiving this aid. Three years later, in 1917, just before the United States entered World War I, Congress adopted the Smith-Hughes Act. This additional measure provided federal funds for vocational education in both rural and urban areas of the country. You will learn more about these acts in Chapter 10.

The Federal Farm Loan Act of 1916 made it easier for farmers to borrow money. This act divided the country into 12 agricultural districts. It established a Farm Loan Bank for each district where farmers could get mortgages at rates lower than those available at regular banks.

Negroes and the "New Freedom"

During the election campaign of 1912 Woodrow Wilson promised an officer of the National Association for the Advancement of Colored People (NAACP) that, if elected, he would promote the interests of black Americans in every way possible. Such was not the case, however. As President, Wilson seemed to agree with most white Americans that segregation was in the best interests of black Americans and white Americans alike.

During Wilson's administration, which was largely dominated by white southerners, white employees and black employees in government offices in Washington, D.C., were segregated. And many black office workers were dismissed in southern cities. A Negro journalist expressed the bitterness of black people when he remarked that Wilson had given black Americans no part in the "New Freedom."

Presidential candidates in 1916

By 1916 President Wilson had established himself as a vigorous leader. The delegates to the Democratic convention pointed with pride to his solid list of achievements and enthusiastically renominated him for a second term.

The Republicans chose Supreme Court Justice Charles Evans Hughes, former governor of New York, as their standard bearer. The Progressive Party nominated Theodore Roosevelt. But Roosevelt, unwilling to split the Republican vote again, refused the nomination and supported Hughes. The Progressive Party, deprived of Roosevelt, decided not to nominate another candidate. As a result the Republicans, once more united, entered the campaign hopeful of victory.

Wilson's victory

Debate during the campaign of 1916 centered not only upon Wilson's record on domestic issues, but also upon America's relation to the war which, as you will read later, had broken out in Europe in 1914. During the campaign Hughes toured the country, criticizing the Democrats for the Underwood Tariff and for their handling of foreign affairs. Wilson, on the other hand, contented himself with delivering a number of speeches from the front porch of his summer home in New Jersey. Speakers for the Democratic Party adopted the slogan "He kept us out of war."

The election itself turned out to be one of the closest in American history. The final electoral vote was 277 for Wilson, 254 for Hughes.

Black Americans were not allowed to take part in Wilson's "New Freedom" and continued to live in a segregated environment. This photograph of a black teacher with his class was taken in the early 1900's.

California proved to be the decisive state—the Democrats won in California by a margin of only 3,773 popular votes! And yet, despite the closeness of the vote, Wilson had won against a united Republican Party, as had not been true in the election of 1912. Even more reassuring, he had collected nearly 600,000 more popular votes than Hughes.

Wilson seemed to feel that his first term in office had accomplished his goals, though many progressives held that much remained to be done. In any event, it was not the "New Freedom" that occupied the President during his second administration. As you will read later, within a month of Wilson's second inauguration on March 4, 1917, the United States entered World War I.

SECTION SURVEY

IDENTIFY: "New Freedom," Underwood Tariff, Federal Farm Loan Act, free trade, elastic currency, "ability-to-pay" principle of taxation.

1. (a) Why did Wilson institute the "New Freedom" program? (b) What did this program reveal about his view of the role and purpose of government?
2. How did the Clayton Antitrust Act of 1914 "put teeth in the older Sherman Antitrust Act"?
3. What was the function of the Federal Trade Commission?
4. Why can the Federal Reserve Act of 1913 be considered a victory for the progressives?

CHAPTER SURVEY

INQUIRING INTO HISTORY

1. The basic issue with which Presidents Roosevelt, Taft, and Wilson had to grapple was the role of government in the new industrial age. Explain.
2. Compare Theodore Roosevelt's "Square Deal" and Woodrow Wilson's "New Freedom" in regard to (a) aims, (b) legislative accomplishments, and (c) influence upon later history.
3. Do you agree or disagree with the basic principle of the income tax—the "ability-to-pay" principle? Why?
4. Black Americans were not included in Wilson's "New Freedom" program. Why? From what other reform programs had black Americans been excluded previously? Why?
5. Woodrow Wilson made the following statement: "Democratic institutions are never done—they are, like the living tissue, always a-making." Comment on this statement with regard to the events dealt with in this chapter.

RELATING PAST TO PRESENT

1. Has the attitude of the American public toward the graduated income tax changed from what it was during the period just studied? Explain.
2. What reforms are currently being proposed by the national government to help remedy the ills of our society? How do the problems of today compare with those of the period just studied?
3. Will black Americans and other minorities benefit from reform measures being proposed or enacted by the national government today? Explain.

DEVELOPING SOCIAL SCIENCE SKILLS

1. Theodore Roosevelt is remembered as a great President. Taft, on the other hand, is remembered as weak and ineffectual. Compare their actual accomplishments in office. Which President got more done in the areas of "trust busting" and progressive reforms? How much of a President's reputation do you think is based on public image? On accomplishments?
2. How would you have voted in the election of 1912 if you were (a) a farmer, (b) a banker, (c) a black American, (d) an Italian immigrant, (e) a factory worker? Give reasons for your choice.

CHAPTER **10**

"THE BIG CHANGE" IN
AMERICAN WAYS OF LIFE

As the United States approached the middle of the twentieth century, Frederick Lewis Allen wrote a book reviewing and interpreting 50 years of American history. He called his book *The Big Change,* and added the subtitle *America Transforms Itself, 1900–1950.* Note that Allen did not say "America *was* transformed," but chose instead to emphasize that Americans were themselves responsible in part for "the big change."

The transformation, as Allen saw it, was "in the character and quality of American life by reason of what might be called the democratization of our economic system, or the adjustment of capitalism to democratic ends." It was, he went on to say, "the way in which an incredible expansion of industrial and business activity, combined with a varied series of political, social, and economic forces, has altered the American standard of living and with it the average American's way of thinking and his status as a citizen."

In 1900 the United States was in full process of passing from a predominantly rural economy to a predominantly industrial economy. Americans as a whole were struggling to adjust their daily lives and institutions to the new world created by the Industrial Revolution. It was a world of crowded cities, of new sources of power, of machines, of mass production, and of an economy that each year was providing more and more people with more of the necessities and the luxuries of life.

During the years from 1900 to 1920 a growing number of Americans, including business owners and managers, became increasingly aware of the need to modify some of the attitudes and practices carried over from the early days of the Industrial Revolution. In 1920 there were still many large and difficult problems that remained unsolved. But "the big change" was already beginning to have an important influence on the direction of American life.

THE CHAPTER IN OUTLINE

1. A revolution in American industry through new inventions and ideas.

2. Improvements in the life of the American farmer in the early 1900's.

3. Improving conditions for American industrial workers.

CHANGING WAYS OF AMERICAN LIFE 1900-1920

1 A revolution in American industry through new inventions and ideas

In 1900 America was still in the horse-and-buggy age. But that age would not last much longer. Great changes were transforming the country, and even greater changes lay ahead.

Older ways of living

In 1900 Americans still rode in horsedrawn streetcars; hitching posts for horses were common sights; livery stables and blacksmith shops were centers of activity in every town; at nightfall the lamplighter turned on the gas lamps that still lighted most American streets.

It is easier, perhaps, to picture the America of 1900 by listing the things that people did not have and did not know. There were no rock groups, no supermarkets, no income taxes. No one had heard of vitamins or antibiotics. Women could vote in only four states—Wyoming, Colorado, Utah, and Idaho. Boy Scouts, Girl Scouts, and 4-H Clubs did not exist. Neither did motion pictures, radios, television, or airplanes. Automobiles were still curiosities; people often called them "horseless carriages."

Signs of change

And yet, in 1900, Americans stood on the threshold of a new way of life. Indeed, much of the new life was already apparent. By 1900 railroad builders had constructed 192,566 miles (309,896 kilometers) of track. All the great trunk lines had been built across the continent. Day and night, long lines of freight cars rumbled across the country loaded with products of America's farm lands, mines, mills, and factories. New railroad lines were being built—by 1920 the nation's railroad mileage reached its high mark of 260,000 miles (418,418 kilometers) of track.

Automobiles and highways

While railroad builders were feverishly building their network of steel rails, inventors in Europe and America were experimenting with a new source of power—the "internal combustion"

In 1900 America was still in the horse-and-buggy age, but changes were beginning to come with ever-increasing rapidity. This painting shows an elevated railway in New York City.

DEVIL WAGONS OF THE EARLY 1900's

Until about 1905 automobiles were luxuries that only wealthy people could afford, and expensive toys for mechanically minded individuals. To the average person they were public nuisances, noisy machines that frightened horses and sometimes caused accidents. Some people called them "devil wagons." Others joked about how often they failed to run. Typical of these jokes was this one that appeared in *Life* magazine in 1904:

"Do you enjoy your automobile?"

"Yes, I enjoy my automobile immensely."

"But I never see you out."

"Oh, I haven't got that far yet. I am just learning to make my own repairs."

engine, in which fuel, usually gasoline, was converted into a vapor and exploded within the engine walls. Among the American experimenters were Charles E. Duryea, George B. Selden, Elwood Haynes, Alexander Winton, and Henry Ford. These inventors and others developed the gasoline engine.

By 1900 "horseless carriages" were appearing on the roads. At first the automobile was an expensive toy for wealthy people. Mass production soon lowered costs, however, bringing the automobile within reach of people with modest incomes. Whereas in 1900 there were only 8,000 automobiles in the United States, by 1920 there were 8 million passenger cars and 1 million trucks.

The development of the automobile depended, of course, upon other inventions and developments. One was the discovery by Charles Goodyear of the process for vulcanizing, or hardening, rubber, for which he obtained his first patent in 1844. Other inventions led to improvements in refining petroleum into gasoline, and in developing batteries, generators, and other electrical devices.

The development of the automobile also depended upon—and helped to stimulate—the construction of paved roads. In 1904, for example, nearly all rural roads were little better than dirt lanes, although some were "surfaced" with gravel, clay, or crushed oyster shells. By 1924, however, 472,000 miles (759,590 kilometers) of rural highways had paved surfaces. By 1924 older roads were being widened, graded, and paved at the rate of about 40,000 miles (64,372 kilometers) a year, at an annual cost of approximately $1 billion.

The airplane

By 1900 Europeans and Americans were experimenting with powered flight. Samuel P. Langley of Washington invented the first power-driven airplane. But it was the Wright brothers, Orville and Wilbur, who on December 17, 1903, first put such a machine in the air. Their first flight went only about 120 feet, and did not attract much attention. Within a few years, however, the first crude flying machines were being replaced by more effective planes, and air pioneers were making longer and longer flights. In 1919 a Navy seaplane crossed the Atlantic by way of the Azores, and two English fliers, John Alcock and A. W. Brown, flew nonstop from Newfoundland to Ireland.

Wired and wireless communications

Equally revolutionary were developments in communications. Europeans and Americans were barely getting used to the idea of the telephone when, in 1895, a 21-year-old Italian inventor, Guglielmo (goo·LYEL·moh) Marconi, gave the first demonstration of wireless telegraphy. Eight years later, from a station at Cape Cod, Massachusetts, he transmitted a message across the ocean to England and received a reply.

Within a few years wireless equipment had been installed on all large vessels, and wireless messages were being sent over land and sea by powerful transmitters. Meanwhile, scientists and engineers were experimenting with the transmission of the spoken word through the air, as distinguished from mere signals. But commercial radio broadcasting did not become a reality until the 1920's.

One of the most significant inventions in the field of communications was the three-element vacuum tube, invented by Lee De Forest in 1906. The telegraph and the telephone, as well as wireless communication, benefited from this invention, which could be used to relay electric impulses over long distances. By 1915 New York and San Francisco were linked by telephone.

The motion picture

Several inventors, American, British, and French, contributed to the development of the motion picture. In 1895 two Americans, Thomas Armat and Woodville Latham, successfully used their projector in public showings.

In the early days, films ran only a few minutes. Then, in 1903, a pioneer "picture story" called *The Great Train Robbery* demonstrated the possibilities of the motion picture. Soon directors and producers, among them D. W. Griffith, who won fame in 1914 for his film *The Birth of a Nation,* were proving to ever larger audiences that the motion picture could do a great deal that was impossible on the stage. Night after night people crowded into the "nickelodeons," as the early movie theaters were called, and for the usual admission of five cents watched such popular stars as Mary Pickford, Douglas Fairbanks, and Charlie Chaplin.

New methods of production

The new world that was coming into being in the early 1900's depended upon the development of an old source of power—steam—and the even faster development of new power sources—oil and electricity. Between 1900 and 1920 oil production in the United States jumped from 63 million to about 443 million barrels annually. By 1914 nearly one third of the nation's factory machines were driven by electricity, and the use of electric power was rapidly increasing. High-voltage transmission lines carried the pulsing energy of dynamos—steam-driven or water-driven—to widely scattered cities. Smaller transmission lines, or "feeders," carried electricity to small towns and villages and even to some isolated farms.

Productivity of America's factories was greatly increased not only by the use of new sources of power, but also by the development of the *assembly line.* On an assembly line, individual parts were moved from station to station along a slowly moving track, or "conveyor belt." At each station, workers added a new part to the product on the track. Finally, a steady succession of finished products came off the end of the as-

Gas Lighting. Inflammable gas was led through walls to fixtures. Some fixtures used an "open fishtail flame" (left). Others used "mantles" made of heat-resisting material which glowed when a flame burned inside of them (right).

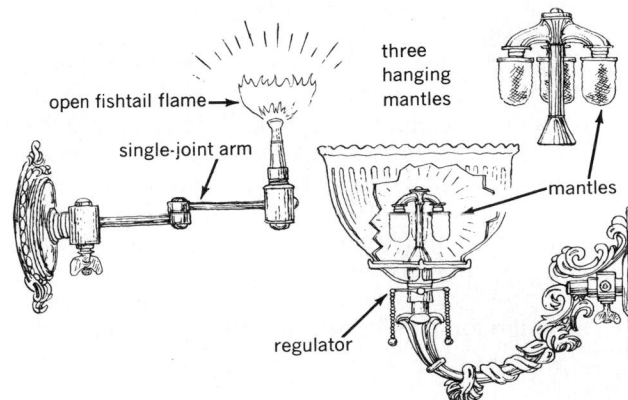

open fishtail flame

single-joint arm

three hanging mantles

mantles

regulator

sembly line. Developed in the early 1900's by Henry Ford in the manufacture of automobiles, the assembly line soon became an essential part of America's developing industrial economy.

Increasing efficiency

Efficiency engineering also increased the productivity of America's factories. Among the several contributors to this development, major credit is usually given to Frederick W. Taylor.

Taylor wanted to secure greater efficiency from machines and from the workers operating the machines. In an effort to do this, he developed "time-and-motion" studies of plant operation. Using a stop watch, Taylor carefully watched workers operating machines and counted the number of motions each worker made to complete a particular operation. Then he worked out ways to reduce the number of movements of the workers' hands and feet. Sometimes workers were trained to use their hands and feet more effectively. Sometimes the machine was redesigned, and its controls placed in more convenient locations.

The development of Taylor's methods made great economies possible in every stage of mass production. Each process in the mechanized industrial plant was simplified and speeded up along the assembly line. Each worker performed a highly specialized task, working with the least possible effort to produce the maximum output.

The "Ford idea"

Henry Ford had made a major contribution to American industry in developing the assembly line. But he made perhaps an even more fundamental contribution by introducing a revolutionary new theory of wages.

On January 5, 1914, Ford announced that he was nearly doubling the wages of the workers in his plants. Beginning immediately, he said, his 13,000 employees would receive a minimum wage of $5 for an 8-hour day. This announcement swept almost all other news off the front pages of America's newspapers. The New York *Herald* called it "an epoch in the world's industrial history."

Ford was both warmly applauded and sharply criticized for his action. But the criticism did not prevent the "Ford idea" from spreading to other industries. Rising wages gave American workers greater purchasing power. They could buy more and more of the products of America's expanding industry. As the years passed, more people came to understand that mass production and mass purchasing power are mutually interdependent. This understanding was an essential part of what Frederick Lewis Allen called "the big change" transforming America in the opening years of the twentieth century.

SECTION SURVEY

IDENTIFY: nickelodeons, assembly line, efficiency engineering; Charles Goodyear, Samuel Langley, Wright brothers, Guglielmo Marconi, Frederick Taylor.

1. Why was transportation vital to the creation of a modern America?
2. Henry Ford made an important contribution to the American economic system. Comment.
3. In 1900 the United States was in full process of passing from a rural to an industrial economy. (a) What changes were taking place in the "new world" created by the revolution in American industry? (b) What conflicts did these changes create? (c) Why was it difficult for people to adjust to these changes?

2 Improvements in the life of the American farmer in the early 1900's

The life of the farmer, like the lives of other Americans, was being transformed during the years between 1900 and 1920.

Growing demand for farm produce

One of the most significant developments in the early 1900's was the startling growth of America's city population. Between 1900 and 1920 the urban population increased by about 24 million, the rural population by only about 6 million. Between 1900 and 1920 urban dwellers increased from about 40 percent of the total population to more than 50 percent.

The swelling urban population came in part from the nation's farms as many farm youths left home to seek their fortunes in the cities. But it came in much larger part from the more than 14 million immigrants who poured into the United States between 1900 and 1920. Regardless of the source, however, the growing urban population meant more mouths to feed and a growing demand for farm products.

Rising prices and prosperity

The rapidly growing demand for farm products enabled farmers to receive higher prices. Indeed, between 1900 and 1920 farm prices increased threefold.

"Cheaper" money, as well as the increased demand for farm products, helped to raise prices.

Just as the Republicans had firmly planted the nation on the gold standard, new discoveries of gold in the Klondike region of Canada and in Alaska in 1897, and the invention of more efficient methods of extracting gold from ore, greatly increased the gold supply. As the supply of gold increased, the value of gold fell. And as the value of gold fell—making money "cheaper"—the prices of all other products rose.

Moreover, the value of farm lands increased, rising on the average fourfold between 1900 and 1920. As a result, many farmers were able to sell their surplus acres for a handsome profit and either retire or buy new farm machines.

Laborsaving machines

Farmers had been using laborsaving machines long before the turn of the century. Not until after 1900, however, did the shift from hand tools to power-driven machines begin to transform the farming industry. According to census records, in 1870 the total value of all farm implements and machinery in the United States amounted to $271 million. By 1900 the figure had risen to $750 million, by 1920 to $3.6 billion.

Whereas in 1900 farmers still carted their produce to market in wagons, by 1920 many were using trucks. Census figures show that in 1910 farmers spent $32 million for motor vehicles; in 1920, $392 million.

Even more revealing as a measure of the machine age was the use of tractors. In 1910 there were only 1,000 tractors on American farms; by 1920 there were 246,000.

Gasoline and electricity—these new sources of power were revolutionizing rural as well as urban life in the early 1900's. Power-driven machinery—pumps, plows, seeders, harvesters, milking machines, trucks, and tractors—began to ease the farmers' burden of labor, enabling them to produce far more products with much less toil.

This advertisement reflects the changes that were transforming the life of American farmers during the years between 1900 and 1920.

Have you placed a Sentimental Value on your Horses out of proportion to the work they are able to perform?

BAILOR MOTOR CULTIVATORS

The growth of scientific agriculture

Scientific knowledge, as well as power-driven machinery, helped to revolutionize farming. Chemists discovered secrets of the soil, enabling farmers to use new fertilizers and better methods of cultivation to stop soil exhaustion and replenish worn-out land. Biologists improved the life span and the productivity of livestock, plants, grains, and fruits. Bacteriologists discovered ways to check blights and diseases in both plants and animals.

Scientists also began to develop new grains and fruits resistant to disease and better adapted to varying climatic conditions. One of their most important discoveries was that of vitamins.

Federal aid to farmers

Much of the new research and experimentation was carried on by the federal government or in state institutions created with the aid of federal grants. As you may recall, in 1862 a Republican Congress adopted three measures of great importance for farmers: (1) it enacted the Homestead Act, granting farmers free land; (2) it passed the Morrill Act, granting land to the states for the establishment of "land grant" colleges of agriculture and mechanical arts; and (3) it created the Department of Agriculture.

In later years the federal government greatly expanded this program of aid to farmers. The Hatch Act of 1887, for example, provided money for agricultural experiment stations and farms in each state. The Smith-Lever Act of 1914 provided additional money for the employment of "county extension agents" who were to carry "useful and practical information on subjects relating to agriculture and home economics" to the farmers of each county. The Smith-Hughes Act of 1917 provided money for the support of vocational education in the public schools, including education in agriculture, industries, trade, home economics, and the training of teachers.

Rise of commercial farming

By the early 1900's the farmer had become an important part of the nation's industrial economy. To be sure, on thousands of small farms tucked away in mountain valleys and in other remote areas, farm families lived much as farmers had lived 100 years earlier. But these more or less self-sufficient farms were exceptions. Most of the nation's farm produce was raised by farmers who, whether they liked it or not, had in many respects become owners of a business.

The commercial farmers specialized in one or two or three crops, or in dairy farming, or in raising livestock. They needed money, or capital, to buy machinery and to hire labor. They had to keep careful accounts and to pay careful attention to market conditions. They were, in brief, one part of an abstract thing known as the "nation's economy." When the economy prospered, farmers could hope to prosper; when the economy went into a depression, farmers were certain to suffer.

Changing ways of living

Equally revolutionary was the impact of the new industrial age on the everyday lives of farm families. By 1920 loneliness and social isolation were becoming memories to many of the nation's farmers. The slender threads of telephone wires were spinning a net of communications across the countryside. The automobile—notably Henry Ford's "Tin Lizzie"—was bringing the farm closer to the town and the city. Whereas a five-mile (8-kilometer) drive to town had once meant a one- or two-hour trip behind "Old Dobbin," by 1920 the same trip could be made in the family car in half an hour or less. This meant more trips to town, often for an evening at the movies.

With better communication and transportation and with more money in their pockets, farm families enjoyed better living conditions and could provide better education for their children. The one-room school continued to dominate the rural educational scene, but more and more farm children began to come from miles around to enjoy the advantages of "consolidated schools," and many were able to continue their education at the state university. For farm children, no less than for their parents, life "down on the farm" in the early 1900's was far more comfortable and interesting than it had ever been before.

SECTION SURVEY

IDENTIFY: self-sufficient farming, commercial farming, "consolidated schools."

1. Explain how each of the following affected and changed farm life in the years from 1900 to 1920: (a) urbanization, (b) mechanization, (c) scientific agriculture, (d) federal aid.
2. How did the social life of farm families change as a result of mechanization?
3. By having a national, rather than a local, transportation system, farmers had wider markets as well as more competition. Comment on how this would affect their economic freedom.
4. By 1920 many farmers had become owners of businesses, who wanted to make money rather than to subsist, or merely make a living, from the land. Comment.

3 Improving conditions for American industrial workers

Conditions for the industrial worker as well as for the farmer improved considerably during the early 1900's. First, as you have read, wage earners benefited from the fast-increasing productivity of America's economic system. Second, through organization, wage earners were beginning to gain enough strength to exert real influence on state legislatures and on Congress. Third, many Americans, including some industrialists, were beginning to realize that the industrial age had raised serious problems—problems that had to be solved if democracy itself was to survive. Fourth, through articles in popular magazines and in the daily newspapers, the general public was becoming increasingly aware of the need for eliminating many of the wage earners' grievances.

Early social legislation

In an effort to improve the conditions of wage earners, European and American legislators began to pass laws commonly referred to as "social legislation." In the United States these laws mainly were passed by the northern and western states; the South, with its newer industrial development and its special problems, did little during this period to promote the welfare of workers through state laws.

In general, the first state laws limited hours of work and improved working conditions. As early as 1879 a Massachusetts law prohibited women and children from working more than 60 hours a week. Oregon enacted a similar law in 1903, and other states followed suit. Meanwhile, New York state initiated a series of laws protecting workers as well as consumers.

The recognition that certain types of work involved special risk led Utah in 1896 to pass a law limiting the working day of miners to 8 hours. In 1902 Maryland passed the first law to compensate workers for accidents that took place on the job. This law was declared unconstitutional, but New York passed a successful compensation law in 1910, as did Wisconsin in 1911.

In 1912 Massachusetts set a precedent by passing the first "minimum-wage law." The Massachusetts act established a minimum-wage rate —employers could not ask a wage earner to work below this rate. These early laws represented a new approach to the problems of wage earners in the emerging industrial society.

Early Supreme Court objections

Much of the early social legislation was declared unconstitutional by the Supreme Court. The Court argued that such laws deprived owners of the property rights guaranteed them by the Constitution. The Court said that a law limiting owners' control over their businesses, including employment policies, actually deprived them of part of their property without the "due process of law" guaranteed in the Fifth and Fourteenth Amendments.

The Supreme Court also objected to social legislation on the ground that it violated people's rights to enter into any contract they wished. According to the Court, when workers accepted employment and an employer agreed to pay them, a "contract" had been made even though the terms were not written down. Following this "freedom-of-contract" line of reasoning, the Supreme Court declared unconstitutional in 1905 a New York law which had fixed a maximum working day of 10 hours for New York bakers.

Changing Court attitudes

Many people objected that such an interpretation of the Constitution was unjust to labor. They argued that it was unrealistic to assume that the individual worker could actually bargain with a corporation that employed thousands of people. They insisted that, in reality, the Supreme Court was depriving all workers of freedom to bargain with their employers.

Supreme Court justices, like many other Americans, gradually changed their attitude toward social legislation. Like other citizens, they were influenced by the progressive temper of the times. The justices found other clauses in the Constitution that enabled states to limit people's right to do as they pleased with their property. The Court increasingly held that the Constitution had reserved to each state the power to enact laws necessary to protect the health and well-being of all its citizens. On these grounds the Supreme Court, in the case of *Muller v. Oregon* (1908), upheld an Oregon law that provided a 10-hour day for women, thereby setting a precedent for the Court's approval of other social legislation.

Federal laws in favor of labor

The states rather than the federal government enacted most of the early social legislation. But workers found state laws unsatisfactory since certain states, especially in the South, lagged behind others. This situation prompted organized labor and its champions to seek relief through federal laws.

Except for its constitutional power "to promote the general welfare" and "to regulate interstate commerce," the federal government had

During the early 1900's, social legislation was needed to improve the working conditions of wage earners by regulating hours and minimum-wage rates, and by correcting the abuses of child labor.

little power to control labor relations. To be sure, the federal government did have the power—and used it—to control working conditions for its own employees. In 1868, you recall, Congress established an 8-hour day for laborers and mechanics employed by or in behalf of the United States government. In 1892 all federal government employees were given an 8-hour day.

Later, in 1906, acting under its power "to regulate interstate commerce," Congress enacted an Employers' Liability Act protecting railroad workers from bearing all the costs of accidents that occurred on the job. Although this law was ruled unconstitutional, later legislation met the Court's objections. And in 1916, when the railroad workers' unions, known as the railroad brotherhoods, threatened to strike for an 8-hour day, Congress passed the Adamson Act. This act gave railroad workers the same pay for an 8-hour day that they had been getting for a 10-hour day.

During President Wilson's administration Congress also granted labor's request that it be exempt from the charge of conspiring "to restrain trade." As you have read, the Clayton Antitrust Act of 1914 helped to modify some of the clauses in the Sherman Antitrust Act of 1890 to which labor had objected.

By the time World War I broke out in Europe in 1914, labor still had many grievances, and it was still far from its goals. But it could look back upon a number of reforms gained through 50 years of struggle. And perhaps most important, organized labor enjoyed a small but steadily growing measure of support from public opinion.

SECTION SURVEY

IDENTIFY: social legislation, minimum wage, freedom of contract, *Muller v. Oregon,* Employers' Liability Act.

1. Why did the conditions of wage earners begin to improve in the early 1900's?
2. Describe the various kinds of social legislation passed by the states to aid workers.
3. (a) On what grounds did the Supreme Court declare this early social legislation unconstitutional? (b) How do Supreme Court decisions sometimes reflect the times in which they are made?
4. (a) Why was it that for many years the federal government did not enact social legislation? (b) Why did it become necessary for the federal government to become involved in social legislation?

CHAPTER SURVEY

INQUIRING INTO HISTORY

1. Industrialization strengthened the existing belief that America was the land of opportunity. Comment.
2. In general, whom do you respect more, people who inherit their money or people who "make it" on their own? Explain how your answer relates to your belief about America and opportunity.
3. (a) What is meant by "the American dream"? (b) Do you think this concept originated during the period just studied? Why or why not?
4. Comment on how the automobile affected the American way of life with regard to (a) where people worked, (b) where people lived, (c) individual freedom.
5. (a) Compare American transportation in 1900 and 1920. (b) What do these figures tell you about change in the United States during the period 1900–1920?
6. In what ways did the revolution in communication help initiate reform movements and the growth of political democracy?
7. Why was it necessary for farmers to receive federal aid during the period just studied?

RELATING PAST TO PRESENT

1. Explain why you agree or disagree with the following statement: In America, if an individual tries hard enough, he or she is bound to succeed.
2. Are we still making what Frederick Lewis Allen called "the adjustment of capitalism to democratic ends"? Explain.
3. American citizens increasingly look toward the federal government to meet the needs of our modern society. Do you think that the state and local governments could deal more effectively with some of our modern problems? Explain.

DEVELOPING SOCIAL SCIENCE SKILLS

1. Study a Sears, Roebuck or a Montgomery Ward catalog published during the period 1900 to 1920. What evidence do the ads provide about American life at that time? Name some things that have changed greatly since that period. Name some things that have remained much the same.
2. Consult an almanac to find out what the average family income was in 1900 and what it is now. Then examine old newspapers or magazines from 1900. Compare the prices of food and clothing in the ads with current prices. Do you think it was easier or more difficult to support a family in 1900?

PART TWO

THE NATION AS A WORLD LEADER

How thirteen colonies on the fringe of a vast untamed wilderness eventually became a powerful nation and world leader—such is the dramatic story of the United States. This story has unfolded in just 200 years.

One way to visualize the swift rise of the American nation is to think of Jefferson, Lincoln, and Theodore Roosevelt. Each of these men lived through a distinct period in the rapidly developing life of the nation.

Theodore Roosevelt, the last of the three, was born before the Civil War. He lived to see the reunited country grow from 36 to 48 states; acquire Alaska, Hawaii, Puerto Rico, and other far-flung territories; fight in World War I; and develop into the leading industrial power of the world.

Part Two of this book begins with the Spanish-American War of 1898 and comes down to the present. This period in the nation's history is marked by the rise of the United States to a position of leadership in the world.

Millions of Americans living today have vivid memories of the "Golden Twenties"; the Great Depression of the 1930's; the excitement and tragedy of World War II; and the momentous years since 1945, years filled with great changes and challenges for all Americans.

In Part Two, present-day Americans are writing their own history and adding still another chapter to the dramatic story of the American nation.

UNIT FOUR
Becoming a World Power
1898-1920

CHAPTER 11

AMERICAN EXPANSION OVERSEAS

1898-1914

From 1823 until the 1890's, Americans devoted most of their energy to the settlement and development of the continental United States. To be sure, Americans traveled to Europe and Europeans traveled to America. The two-way flow of people and ideas across the Atlantic never ceased. And always, of course, there was vigorous trade between the two continents. But it was the conquest of the West and, after 1865, the development of industry that engaged the major energy of the American people.

By the 1890's, however, a revolution was taking place in American opinion. With the Middle West becoming a major industrial area, an increasing number of Americans became interested in securing overseas markets where they could sell the surplus products of farm and factory. Some Americans even became interested in acquiring or controlling lands beyond their continental boundaries.

In this chapter you will learn how Americans acquired a new interest in world affairs, and how they emerged from the Spanish-American War of 1898 in possession of the Philippine Islands and other islands in the Pacific Ocean. You will learn how this growing Pacific empire created new problems for the United States, and how it forced America's leaders to develop new policies for dealing with the nations of the Far East.

THE CHAPTER IN OUTLINE

1. Reasons behind the nation's growing interest in overseas expansion.

2. Deepening American involvement overseas after the war with Spain.

3. Establishing American control over the Philippines, Hawaii, and Samoa.

4. The increasing influence of the United States in the Far East.

1450   1750   1800   1850   1900   1950   1980's

1 Reasons behind the nation's growing interest in overseas expansion

Great Britain, France, the Netherlands, Spain, Portugal—these were the old colonial powers. They had started their policies of *imperialism*—of establishing colonies and building empires—back in the 1500's and 1600's. Now, in the mid-1800's, they owned and controlled a large portion of the world. But huge areas of the earth still remained unclaimed by any colonial nation.

The race for empire

During the latter half of the 1800's there was a mad rush to gain ownership or control of the remaining uncolonized lands of the earth. Nations previously little interested in expansion joined the race—among them Belgium, Germany, Italy, Japan, and Russia. Within a few years the rival colonial powers seized control over almost all of Africa and sliced off large portions of China and other areas in the Far East. By the early 1900's nearly all of the underdeveloped regions of the world had been divided among the rival colonial empires.

Reasons for the New Imperialism

The Industrial Revolution was to a great extent responsible for the mounting interest in colonies. Factories needed raw materials in ever-growing quantities. Manufacturers, to keep their factories operating, had to find new markets for their finished products. Improvements in transportation, especially in the steamship, enabled businesses to buy and sell in a truly worldwide market. And as trade increased and profits accumulated, business executives and bankers began to look overseas for opportunities to invest savings. More than any other single factor, the growth of industry speeded up the race to secure colonies and to control underdeveloped lands.

It is not surprising that Great Britain, the world's leading industrial power before 1900, built the largest empire. Right behind Britain were France, Belgium, and the Netherlands. Industrialization in each of these countries was in full swing by the late 1800's.

Nor is it surprising that the countries that were late in achieving national unity or in industrializing were also late in entering the race for empire. Germany, Italy, and Japan were among these countries. As a result, when they began to look around for colonial possessions they found most of the world divided up, and they became jealous rivals for the territory that remained.

There were still other reasons for the growth of worldwide imperialism in the late 1800's and the early 1900's. One was the invention of new instruments of warfare, notably repeating rifles and machine guns. By 1900 these new weapons were becoming standard army equipment, enabling small bands of professional soldiers to conquer and control people in underdeveloped regions who did not have similar weapons.

Public support for imperialism

Another reason for the growth of imperialism was the attitude of people in the colonial powers. No government could have built an empire without public support. There were objectors in every country, but, in general, ordinary people were as eager for empire as were leaders of government and business. English factory workers, French shopkeepers, German farmers—these and other solid citizens of the colonial powers were all proud of their country's empires. Supported by their own citizens, the governments of the colonial nations were able to spend the huge sums of money needed for armies to occupy the colonial territories and for navies to guard the ever-lengthening sea lanes to and from the colonies.

End of the American frontier

Americans, with a few exceptions, had never been interested in acquiring colonies. Indeed, Americans had cast off their own colonial status in the American Revolution. Thus American sympathies were with colonial peoples, not with the colonizing powers.

America's lack of interest in acquiring colonies is easy to understand. For 300 years the undeveloped American West was, in a sense, an American "colony." Even as late as 1867, when Secretary of State Seward bought Alaska from Russia for just over $7 million, Americans referred to Alaska as "Seward's folly" and "Seward's icebox." It was not until 30 years later, in 1897, when gold was discovered in Alaska, that Americans began to realize what a great bargain they had made. But in 1867 when Alaska was purchased, it was not unreasonable for people to ask, "What does the United States want with more land?"

In 1890, however, the Census Bureau announced that a frontier line separating settled areas from wilderness could no longer be drawn between the Canadian and Mexican boundaries. There was still, to be sure, plenty of good land waiting to be settled. But the best land was becoming more expensive, and an important phase of American development was ending.

The expanding American business economy

During the late 1800's the United States became the world's leading exporter of agricultural products. By 1890, however, it was beginning to feel the competition of such agricultural nations as Canada and Argentina. American growers and processors of grain, livestock, and cotton, as well as the manufacturers of agricultural machinery, were eager to sell their products abroad. It was not surprising, therefore, that America's agricultural interests in general supported vigorous government efforts to open up new markets overseas.

Moreover, by 1890 the United States was rapidly becoming one of the world's leading industrial nations. American manufacturers, like manufacturers in Europe, needed a continuous flow of raw materials. They also needed markets for the products of their factories.

There was, to be sure, a big difference between American and European businesses. Euro-

peans, lacking sufficient raw materials and markets at home, were under considerable pressure to get firm control of new sources of raw materials and new markets. American businesses, operating in a young and only partly developed country, were not under the same pressure. The country as a whole, and especially the great American West, still offered large supplies of raw materials and almost limitless opportunities for the sale of manufactured goods and investment of surplus money.

But some American business leaders realized that the existing situation would not last forever. For this reason, by 1890 a growing number of American business groups as well as the nation's agricultural interests were pleased to have the United States pursue an active race for overseas economic opportunities, if not for actual colonies.

During the Alaskan gold rush, thousands of prospectors landed at Juneau, Alaska, and headed inland through the treacherous, snow-covered Chilkoot Pass, shown here.

American expansionists

Until 1898, at least, American interest in colonies was stimulated not so much by big business leaders as by preachers, scholars, politicians, and military leaders.

One influential advocate of American expansion was Josiah Strong, a Congregational minister and social reformer. His widely read book *Our Country,* written in 1885, argued that the American branch of the efficient and freedom-loving "Anglo-Saxon race" was destined to ex-

tend its civilizing influence in Latin America, Asia, and Africa.

An even more influential book was written by Captain Alfred Mahan in 1890 under the title *The Influence of Sea Power upon History, 1660–1783.* Mahan's book attempted to show that the world's greatest nations had risen largely because of their sea power, and that greatness depended upon sea power. Therefore, he argued, the United States must strengthen its navy and must also secure colonies overseas. Mahan claimed that colonies were needed as naval bases and as refueling stations, or "coaling stations." He also pointed out that colonies would provide raw materials and markets. Colonies would thereby strengthen the industrial organization on which a modern sea power is forced to rely.

Strengthening the navy

Even before Captain Mahan's book appeared, Congress had taken steps to strengthen the navy. These steps were needed. In 1880, for example, the United States had fewer than 100 "seagoing vessels"—and many were "seagoing" in name only, with rusty boilers and planking rotted beyond repair.

The situation began to change in 1882, however, when Congress authorized the construction of "two steam-cruising vessels of war." Three years later the Navy Department created the Naval War College at Newport, Rhode Island. About this time the Bethlehem Steel Corporation began to build a plant for the manufacture of "armor plate"—tough steel sheets to protect the hulls and superstructures of warships. By 1895 the "White Squadron," sometimes called the "Great White Fleet," was under construction.

Ready for a new role

In 1895 the United States had not yet really entered the race for empire. But the ground had been prepared. For various reasons, Americans were becoming increasingly interested in colonies. Some business leaders were becoming uneasy at the prospect that their European competitors might gain control of the markets of underdeveloped areas. The nation's industrial system was rapidly becoming one of the most productive in the world. And a new navy, small but modern and efficient, was ready for action. For these reasons and others, more and more Americans came to believe that the United States was destined to play a leading role in world affairs.

SECTION SURVEY

IDENTIFY: imperialism, colonial empire; Alfred Mahan, Josiah Strong.

1. The Industrial Revolution was responsible for the mounting interest in acquiring colonies by nations which had become industrialized. Explain.
2. How did the transportation and communication revolutions encourage the quest for colonies?
3. Why was the United States not interested in acquiring colonies before the late 1800's?
4. Show how each of the following affected American interest in colonies: (a) closing of the frontier, (b) industrial development, (c) growing power in world affairs.
5. Why were the industrial nations able to maintain control over the nonindustrialized areas of the world?

2 Deepening American involvement overseas after the war with Spain

The Spanish-American War of 1898 marked a turning point in American history. Before the war, which lasted only a few weeks in the spring and summer of 1898, the Midway Islands—occupied in 1867 in the name of the United States—and Alaska were the only lands that the United States owned beyond its immediate boundaries. Within a few years after the war ended, the American flag was flying over a number of islands in the Pacific Ocean, the United States was deeply involved in the Far East, and American influence was being strongly exerted in the lands bordering the Caribbean Sea.

Trouble in Cuba

Cuba and Puerto Rico, both in the Caribbean, were the last remnants of Spain's once mighty empire in the New World. Spaniards had once called Cuba "the Ever Faithful Isle." In 1868, however, when a violent revolution broke out, the Cubans proved to be something less than faithful to their Spanish rulers. It took Spain 10 years to crush this uprising, and even then Spain did so only with a promise to provide long-awaited reforms. But discontent continued to smolder.

The trouble was that most Cubans worked at starvation wages for extremely wealthy landowners. To make matters worse, the Spanish government in Madrid exploited the Cubans, antagonizing landowners as well as landless workers.

Spanish misrule plus an economic crisis finally plunged Cuba into another revolution. The United States was partly responsible for the economic crisis. In 1890, you recall, Congress adopted the McKinley Tariff Act. This act allowed Cuban sugar, the major crop of the island, to enter the United States free of duty. As a result, trade between the United States and Cuba prospered, reaching a total of more than $100 million a year. However, in 1894 the United States adopted the Wilson-Gorman Tariff Act, which placed a 40 percent duty on all raw sugar imported into the United States. When the 1894 tariff went into effect, sugar piled up in Cuban warehouses, plantations closed down, and thousands of Cubans lost their jobs.

Revolution in Cuba

Driven to desperation by the economic crisis and angry at Spain's failure to provide the long-promised reforms, the Cubans rose in revolution in 1895, one year after the Wilson-Gorman tariff went into effect. Bands of revolutionists roamed the countryside, killing, burning, and plundering.

The Spaniards, led by General Valeriano Weyler, nicknamed "The Butcher," retaliated with a policy of savage repression. General Weyler ordered all people living in territory controlled by the revolutionists into concentration camps, or prison camps, run by the Spaniards. Spanish soldiers then marched through the abandoned countryside, destroying buildings and putting to death all persons found in the area without permission. What the revolutionists had not destroyed, the Spaniards did. Large areas of Cuba were reduced to utter ruin. Starvation and disease plagued the land.

The revolution's effects on America

In a strictly legal sense, the revolution in Cuba was no concern of the United States. Spain was a sovereign, independent nation, free to do as it pleased with its own colonies. This was freely admitted by the American government, which officially adopted a policy of neutrality.

But the effects of the revolution could not be confined to Cuba. The revolutionists themselves did everything possible to win American sympathy and support. Despite Spanish protests, the revolutionists waged a vigorous propaganda campaign in America. They also bought American arms and ammunition which they smuggled into Cuba.

The revolution also affected some American pocketbooks. Before the uprising began, Americans had invested more than $50 million in Cuban plantations, transportation projects, and business establishments. Moreover, trade between Cuba and the United States was crippled by the revolution.

As months passed, more and more Americans expressed their sympathy for the revolutionists. They recalled their own efforts to win independence from the British during the American Revolution.

Sensation and sympathy in the press

American newspapers helped to inflame public opinion. Two New York papers—William Randolph Hearst's New York *Journal* and Joseph Pulitzer's New York *World*—were especially active in supporting the revolutionists. The owners of these papers discovered that sales skyrocketed when they published sensational stories and pictures of Spanish atrocities in Cuba.

Newspapers in other towns and cities quickly copied the financially successful methods of Hearst and Pulitzer. Before long, many Americans, feeding on the sensational stories and pictures, began to clamor for United States intervention in Cuba.

By 1898 even the more conservative newspapers, including weekly religious journals, insisted that the United States had a moral responsibility to restore order in Cuba.

McKinley's attempts to avoid war

When President William McKinley was inaugurated on March 4, 1897, he was strongly opposed to war. The United States was just emerging from the depression that had started in 1893, and the President, many of his advisers, and business leaders in general were fearful that war, or even the threat of war, would throw the country back into a depression.

For nearly a year the President managed to maintain the official policy of neutrality. But early in 1898 several events forced his hand.

On February 9, 1898, American newspapers headlined a letter written by the Spanish minister to the United States. In the letter, Señor De Lôme (LOH·may) characterized President McKinley as "weak and a bidder for the admiration of the crowd," and as a "would-be politician." The Spanish minister had written the letter to a friend in Havana. It was not intended for publication. Indeed, it had been stolen from the mails and sold to the press. But the harm was done. Unthinking Americans concluded that the uncomplimentary remark reflected the attitude of all Spaniards.

A few days later, on February 16, Americans read even more startling news in their papers. The night before, the United States battleship *Maine,* which had been sent to Cuba in January to protect American lives and property, had gone down in Havana harbor with the loss of more than 250 American lives. Captain Charles D. Sigsbee, commander of the *Maine,* stated that the disaster followed an explosion of unknown origin and urged that "public opinion should be suspended until further report." In Havana flags were flown at half-mast, theaters and places of business were closed, and expressions of sorrow and sympathy were forwarded to Washington. All of this was brushed aside by the public. People jumped to the conclusion that the Spaniards had destroyed the ship. "Remember the *Maine!*" became a national slogan.

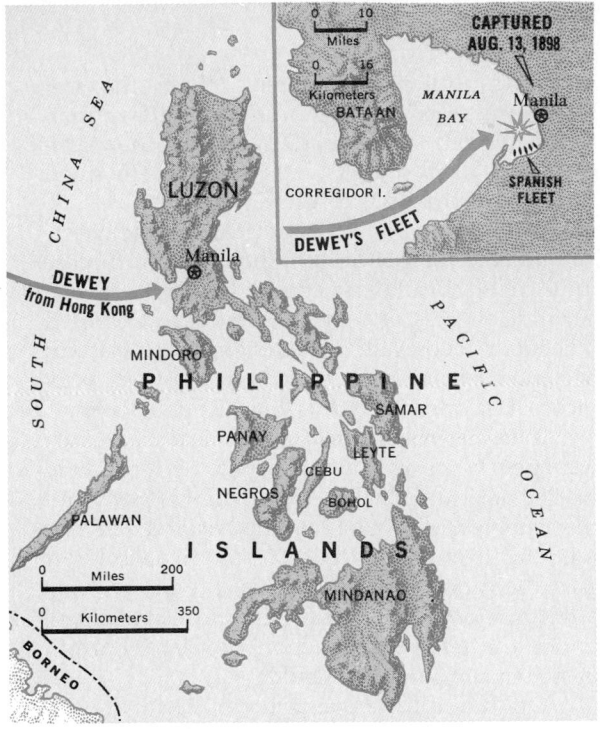

SPANISH-AMERICAN WAR: 1
(PHILIPPINE ISLANDS)

Despite these incidents, President McKinley refused to declare war. Assistant Secretary of the Navy Theodore Roosevelt declared that the President "has no more backbone than a chocolate eclair." But McKinley still hoped for a peaceable solution.

Spanish concessions

Late in March, with the President's approval, the Department of State sent an *ultimatum°* to Spain. In the ultimatum the United States demanded (1) that Spain immediately cease all fighting in Cuba and grant an armistice to the revolutionists, and (2) that the Spanish forces in Cuba immediately abolish the concentration camps.

On April 9 the Spanish government accepted the ultimatum. The Spaniards, however, hedged on the question of Cuban independence, which in the American view could alone bring peace to the island. But the American minister in Madrid felt that, with patience, independence for Cuba could be achieved. In cabling the good news to President McKinley, he added, "I hope that nothing will now be done to humiliate Spain. . . ."

° ultimatum: in diplomatic language, a final statement of terms whose rejection may lead to the breaking off of diplomatic relations or to war.

War declared

Despite the Spanish concession, on April 11, 1898, President McKinley asked Congress to intervene in Cuba. What was his reason for doing so?

The most likely explanation seems to be that the war spirit had proved too strong for the President to resist.

On April 19, after a week of debate, Congress by large majorities voted to use the land and naval forces of the United States to secure the full independence of Cuba. But Congress also adopted the Teller Resolution. This resolution stated that the United States claimed no "sovereignty, jurisdiction, or control" over Cuba except for *pacifying,* or bringing peace to, the island and promised that once Cuba was free the United States would "leave the government and control of the island to its people."

Victory in the Pacific

Curiously enough, fighting in the "war for Cuban liberty" started not in Cuba but in the Pacific. For weeks before Congress declared war, Theodore Roosevelt, the Assistant Secretary of the Navy, had been preparing for any developments. Roosevelt had sent orders to Commodore George Dewey, then in command of a fleet anchored at Hong Kong, to prepare his ships for action. When Dewey received word that war had been declared, he promptly headed for the Philippine Islands, the center of Spanish power in the Pacific.

On the night of April 30, 1898, Dewey's six ships slipped past the fortress of Corregidor and into the harbor of Manila, capital of the Philippines (see map, this page). At daybreak on May 1 the American warships opened fire. Their guns outranged those of the Spanish vessels, and by noon the one-sided battle was over. The Spaniards lost nearly 170 men and all their vessels. The Americans lost one man—who died of heatstroke.

Although Commodore Dewey controlled Manila harbor, he did not have a large enough force to land and seize the city. While he waited for a landing force to arrive from the United States, he sent arms and ammunition to a band of Filipinos led by Emilio Aguinaldo (ay·MEE·lyo ah·ge·NAHL·do). The Filipinos, eager to throw off Spanish rule and win their independence, began to organize for an attack on Manila.

Two months passed. Then, early in August, American transports arrived with a strong landing party. The position of the Spanish garrison was hopeless. Cut off by Dewey's warships from all hope of relief, surrounded on the land side

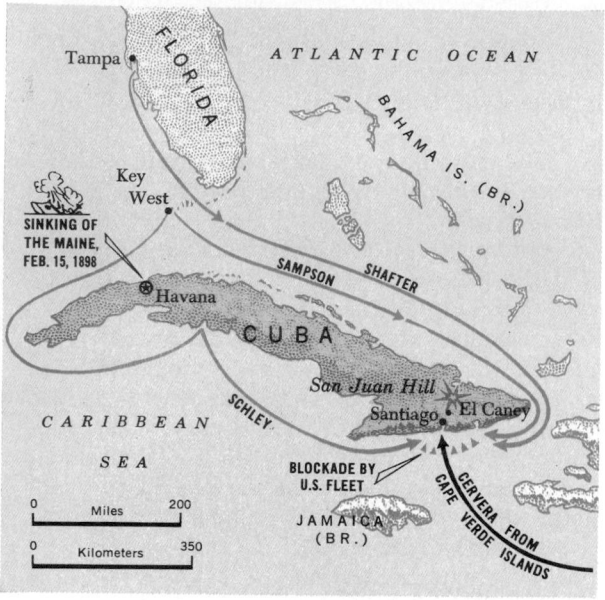

SPANISH-AMERICAN WAR: 2
(CUBA)

by the Filipino revolutionists, and faced with an attack by an American army, Manila surrendered on August 13, 1898.

Victory in the Atlantic

Meanwhile, Spain's Atlantic fleet under Admiral Cervera (sehr·VEH·rah) on April 29 had sailed westward from the Cape Verde Islands.

News that Admiral Cervera's fleet was steaming toward America threw Americans living in coastal areas into a panic. One coastal town after another begged for naval protection.

The alarm was unwarranted. Cervera's fleet was hopelessly inadequate for the task assigned to it, and the gallant admiral sailed only with the thought of saving the honor of Spain, not with the hope of victory. Instead of attacking, the Spaniards slipped into the harbor at Santiago, Cuba, for refueling. Here they were bottled up by an American squadron commanded by Admiral William T. Sampson and Commodore W. S. Schley.

On Sunday morning, July 3, 1898, Cervera's fleet made a wild dash for the open sea. But the American ships were waiting, and as the Spanish fleet raced out of the harbor and steamed along the coast, it was met by murderous fire (see map, this page). Within four hours the battle was over. Not a single Spanish vessel escaped.

Land fighting in Cuba

In contrast to the United States Navy, which moved swiftly and efficiently, the War Department was quite unprepared. When the war began, the regular army, numbering fewer than 30,000 officers and troops, including four regiments of black soldiers, was scattered in small contingents over the country.

More than 200,000 Americans immediately volunteered for war service, including four more units of black soldiers recruited under a special act of Congress. The volunteers also included Theodore Roosevelt, who resigned as Assistant Secretary of the Navy to lead a volunteer regiment of cavalry known as the "Rough Riders."

The first American troops to arrive in Cuba were poorly trained and equipped. Many of them carried antiquated rifles. The food was poor, and the army was without adequate hospital and sanitary facilities. Hundreds of American soldiers died needlessly from dysentery, typhoid, malaria, and yellow fever. The American Red Cross, under the personal direction of Clara Barton, provided such aid as it could.

On June 24 the two armies clashed. Slowly, fighting hard, the Americans under General William Shafter pushed the enemy back through the fortified village of El Caney and across San Juan Hill (see map, this page). By July 2 American forces had advanced to within a mile and a half of Santiago. It was this fact that led Admiral Cervera to make his desperate attempt to escape with the Spanish fleet. The destruction of the Spanish navy was the final blow. The Spanish commander at Santiago surrendered his forces on July 17.

Black soldiers, who had not been allowed to mix with white troops on the ships carrying them to Cuba, fought well in several engagements of the war. Frank Knox, later to be Secretary of the Navy, became separated from the Rough Riders at San Juan Hill and joined a troop of the all-black Tenth Cavalry. After the battle he wrote home that he had never seen "braver men anywhere," and he added, "Some of those who rushed up the hill will live in my memory forever."

Meanwhile another American army, under General Nelson A. Miles, landed on the Spanish island of Puerto Rico, east of Cuba. The Americans encountered no opposition, and by the end of July were in control of the island.

The fruits of victory

The United States entered the war with the argument that it was fighting merely to free the oppressed Cubans. It ended the war with an empire on its hands.

American and Spanish commissioners met in Paris in October 1898 to negotiate a peace treaty. By the terms of the treaty, Spain agreed to sur-

Members of a black signal corps that served in the Spanish-American War are shown here. Commenting on race relations during the war, one American officer wrote, "White regiments, black regiments, regulars, and Rough Riders, representing the young manhood of the North and the South, fought shoulder to shoulder, unmindful of race or color, unmindful of whether commanded by an ex-Confederate or not, and mindful only of their common duty as Americans."

render all claim to Cuba. In addition, Spain agreed to cede to the United States the following territories: (1) Puerto Rico; (2) the Pacific island of Guam; and (3) the Philippines—in exchange for which the United States agreed to pay Spain $20 million.

As a result of the war, the United States also acquired Wake Island in the Pacific. American armed forces had landed on Wake on July 4, 1898, and raised the American flag. Congress later annexed Wake.

Until 1898, except for the Midway Islands, the United States owned no overseas possessions. When the Senate ratified the peace treaty, however, the United States became a colonial power.

The expansionists—followers of Alfred Mahan, Theodore Roosevelt, and others—were delighted. But many Americans were deeply troubled. Was it wise and proper for the United States to join the European powers in the race for empire? Did the United States want to assume responsibility for a colonial empire scattered over the Pacific Ocean and the Caribbean Sea?

SECTION SURVEY

IDENTIFY: ultimatum, "Rough Riders," Teller resolution; Joseph Pulitzer, William Randolph Hearst, Commodore Dewey, Emilio Aguinaldo, Admiral Cervera; 1898.

1. (a) What were the causes of the Cuban revolt against Spain? (b) Why did this revolt affect the United States?
2. To what extent did each of the following help bring about the Spanish-American War: (a) sensational press coverage, (b) the De Lôme letter, (c) destruction of the *Maine*, (d) American investments and trade with Cuba?
3. Describe briefly the highlights of the fighting in (a) the Pacific, (b) Cuba.
4. The Spanish-American War marked a turning point in American history. Explain.

3 Establishing American control over the Philippines, Hawaii, and Samoa

The Philippine Islands presented Americans with an immediate and difficult problem: Should the United States set the islands free, just as it intended to set Cuba free? Or should it now turn on the Filipinos and force them to accept American rule?

American dilemma

President McKinley was one of countless

In 1898 Hawaii became a Territory of the United States; in 1959 it became the fiftieth state in the Union. This photograph of Kauai Island shows some of Hawaii's natural beauty.

Americans who wrestled with this problem. Finally he decided to establish American rule in the Philippine Islands.

As he later explained to a group of Americans, the United States could not return the Philippines to Spain, for "that would be cowardly and dishonorable." It could not give them to France, Germany, or Great Britain, for "that would be bad business and discreditable." It could not turn them over to the Filipinos, for they were "unfit for self-government."

". . . There was nothing left for us to do," McKinley concluded, "but to take them all, and to educate the Filipinos, and uplift and civilize and Christianize them. . . ."

President McKinley's motives were good, but his knowledge of the facts was incomplete. Indeed, he later confessed that when he had first heard of Dewey's victory, he had had to look for the islands on the map. As for "Christianizing" the Filipinos, they had long since been converted to Catholicism, except the Moros, a group of people who were Moslems.

Divided public opinion

Many Americans agreed with McKinley that it was America's duty to "educate" and "uplift and civilize and Christianize" the Filipinos. These Americans believed that the strong and wealthy nations shared the moral responsibility to assume what the British poet Rudyard Kipling had referred to as the white race's burden. Others hoped to profit economically by following the path of world empire. Still others, mostly military leaders, believed that America needed the islands as strategic bases.

But opponents of imperialism viewed the

decision with serious misgivings. They argued that, in taking the Philippines, the United States was violating its own Declaration of Independence and the principle that people had the right to live under a government of their own choice. "It will be only the old tale of a free people seduced by false ambitions and running headlong after riches and luxuries and military glory," warned Carl Schurz, a prominent Republican. A few opponents, including some Negro leaders, argued that American imperialism was based in part on the false assumption of white racial superiority. They argued that American expansion abroad could only work to the disadvantage of black Americans seeking to improve their lives in the United States.

Conquest and early rule

The conquest of the Philippines turned out to be more difficult than the defeat of Spain. The Filipinos were no more willing to accept American rule than they had been to endure Spanish rule. For three years 70,000 American troops fought in the islands at a cost of $175 million, and with a casualty list as high as that of the Spanish-American War. By 1902, however, the American forces were victorious.

Despite this unhappy beginning the United States tried to live up to McKinley's promise "not to exploit, but to develop; to civilize, to educate, to train in the science of self-government." In the Philippine Government Act of 1902, Congress created a government for the islands under which they were to be ruled by a governor and a small legislative body—an elected assembly and an appointed upper house. The United States Congress had the power to veto all legislation. The plan did not go into effect until 1907. Meanwhile, William Howard Taft, the first governor, ruled wisely. He cooperated closely with the Filipinos, and included many Filipinos in the new government.

Filipino dissatisfaction

But many Filipinos wanted full self-government nothing less. Their dissatisfaction became apparent in 1907 when the elected lower house met for the first time. Three quarters of the representatives were pledged to work for independence. Their hopes rose high in 1913 when Woodrow Wilson became President of the United States. Leading Democrats had opposed the conquest of the Philippines, and the Democratic Party had pledged itself to grant independence at the earliest possible date.

These hopes, however, were soon dashed. Although the Jones Act of 1916 did give the Filipinos the right to elect the members of both houses of the legislature, Congress did not grant independence, but merely promised it "as soon as a stable government can be established."

Independence granted

Meanwhile the islands prospered. Highways, railroads, telegraph and telephone lines were built. Education reduced illiteracy from 85 percent in 1898 to 37 percent in 1921. Disease was greatly reduced and Filipino health steadily improved. Exports and imports swelled in volume as the result of an American tariff policy which, in 1902, gave a 25 percent tariff reduction to products from the Philippines and, in 1913, removed all tariffs on many articles traded between the islands and the United States.

Most important of all, the United States eventually kept its promise to set the islands free, as you will read later.

Early relations with Hawaii

In 1898 Hawaii also occupied American attention. United States interest in the Hawaiian Islands went back many years.

Before 1865 about the only relations that the United States had with these central Pacific islands were through traders and missionaries. But after 1865 American businesses began to develop the resources of Hawaii—chiefly sugar cane and pineapples. In 1875 Hawaii signed a treaty with the United States. In return for the right to sell sugar in the United States without payment of any duty, the Hawaiians promised not to sell or lease territory to any foreign power. In 1887, when this treaty was renewed, the United States leased Pearl Harbor as a naval base.

The Hawaiians became increasingly alarmed as the wealth and power of the islands passed into foreign hands. Finally, led by Queen Liliuokalani (le·LEE·wo·kah·LAH·ne), they announced their intentions to end foreign influence.

Foreign seizure and control

The American businesses in Hawaii, aided by influential Hawaiians, met this challenge with prompt action. They started a revolution.

At this critical moment the American minister to Hawaii intervened. Claiming that he was acting only to protect American lives and property, he requested the aid of the marines who were conveniently at hand on a nearby warship. The Hawaiian soldiers, concluding that the marines had come to help the revolutionists, refused to fight. The new government, controlled by the foreign business interests and missionaries, asked to be annexed to the United States. The American minister promptly raised the Stars and Stripes, and on February 1, 1893, marines began to patrol the islands.

Refusal to annex Hawaii

When news of these events reached the United States, furious protests poured into Congress. Many Americans did not want island territory. They were indignant at the manner in which American marines had been used. They were afraid that overseas expansion would lead to heavy military expenditures.

Queen Liliuokalani of Hawaii led her people in an unsuccessful attempt to end the influence of American business groups and missionaries in the islands. She was forced from her throne in 1893.

President Cleveland sent a commission to Hawaii to investigate. The commission ordered the American flag hauled down and heard evidence from both sides. In its report, the commission stated that the revolution had been started largely by American business groups, aided by the American minister and the marines.

After studying the report, Cleveland concluded that the only way to make amends was to apologize to Queen Liliuokalani and to re-store her to her throne. But this would have required the exercise of force against the new government. By now Congress was fed up with the whole affair, and in 1894 it adopted a resolution refusing to interfere further in Hawaii.

Annexation of Hawaii

Then came the Spanish-American War, which, you recall, generated a new spirit in America. The question of Hawaii once again was brought up on the floor of Congress. This time, in 1898, by an overwhelming vote the islands were annexed to the United States and given Territorial status.

American control of Samoa

As in Hawaii, American interests in the Samoan Islands were of long standing. In 1878 the United States secured from a Samoan chief the right to use the harbor of Pago Pago (PAHN·goh PAHN·goh) on the island of Tutuila (too·too·EE·lah) as a naval base. The Samoans granted similar privileges to Germany and Great Britain.

The three countries—Great Britain, Germany, and the United States—then became involved in a scramble to control the islands. At one point, in 1889, a naval clash among the three powers was narrowly avoided, largely because a typhoon blew the rival squadrons out to sea.

Finally, in 1899, the British withdrew and the islands were divided between Germany and the United States. Germany lost control of its share of the islands when it was defeated in World War I. But Tutuila, with its excellent anchorage in the harbor of Pago Pago, remained in the hands of the United States, which developed it into a major naval base in the Pacific.

SECTION SURVEY

IDENTIFY: Jones Act; William Howard Taft, Queen Liliuokalani.

1. Do you agree or disagree with the anti-imperialists who argued that, in taking the Philippines, the United States violated the Declaration of Independence? Explain.
2. How did the United States finally acquire Hawaii?
3. The intense rivalry among nations to acquire colonies was demonstrated in the scramble for the Samoan Islands. Explain.
4. Some anti-imperialists argued that American imperialist policy worked to the disadvantage of black Americans at home. (a) Why did they feel this way? (b) Do you agree or disagree with their argument? Why? (c) What was the position of black Americans at home in the 1890's? (Review pages 127 and 151.)

4 The increasing influence of the United States in the Far East

By 1900 United States territory in the Pacific included Hawaii, Midway, Guam, Wake, the Philippine Islands, and part of Samoa. With this new territory the American people assumed heavy responsibilities. These new responsibilities, plus events taking place in the Far East, led the United States in 1899–1900 to proclaim the *Open Door policy* for China. This policy formed the basis for American action in the Far East, and involved the United States in the affairs of Russia and Japan. To understand the Open Door policy, it is necessary to review American relations with China during the 1800's.

The China trade

America's interest in China began back in 1784, when the *Empress of China* sailed from New York with a cargo intended for the Chinese seaport of Canton. The venture proved profitable, and enterprising Yankees were quick to seize the new trading opportunity.

Most of the Orient trade started in Philadelphia, New York, and New England ports. After a long voyage around South America, the ships anchored in the Pacific Northwest. There they traded with the Indians, exchanging blankets, axes, guns, and other goods for furs. When they had a full cargo, the Yankee skippers then headed out across the Pacific Ocean for China.

Early diplomatic relations

Despite this growing trade, the word "China" did not appear in a public or Presidential message or paper until 1831. In the 1840's however, relations between the United States and China grew closer.

As time passed, China's rulers began to fear the influence that foreigners were exerting in their country. When China began placing restrictions on British traders, however, Great Britain waged a successful war (1839–42) and forced the Chinese to open certain "treaty ports" to British trade.

Americans demanded and secured similar privileges when the American envoy to China, Caleb Cushing, negotiated a treaty which gave the United States all trading privileges granted by China to other nations and extended to Americans the right of *extraterritoriality*. This meant that American citizens in China who were charged with violations of China's civil or criminal laws had the right to be tried in American courts in China. Other foreign nations also secured trading privileges and extraterritorial rights in China.

These concessions from China encouraged foreign traders to settle there. As time passed, outsiders, including missionaries from the United States and other countries, began to exercise growing influence. Many of China's leaders strongly opposed this interference but were powerless to prevent it.

Among all the imperialistic powers interested in the Far East, the United States seemed least eager to grab Chinese territory. As a result, relations between the two countries remained friendly through the 1800's.

Crisis in China

In the 1890's, however, a major crisis developed. Japan entered the race for colonies with an attack upon China in the Sino-Japanese War of 1894–95. In this war Japan won the large island of Formosa, certain territory on the Shantung Peninsula, and control of Korea (see map, page 330).

While China was helpless as a result of the Japanese attack, Germany, Russia, Great Britain, and France rushed in to seize their share of the booty. It appeared for a time that China would soon share the fate of Africa, which had already been carved up and divided among the European imperial powers.

The crisis in China posed a problem for the United States. Americans did not want Chinese territory. On the other hand, Americans did not intend to be squeezed out of the growing trade in Chinese markets.

The Open Door policy

John Hay, who became Secretary of State in 1898, had a solution for the problem. He sent a note to all the powers concerned asking them to assure the United States (1) that they would keep open all "treaty ports"; and (2) that they would guarantee to all nations engaged in trade with China equal railroad, harbor, and tariff rates. In short, Hay asked for an Open Door policy that would insure American businesses the opportunity to compete on equal terms with other traders in China. Although the response to his note was not encouraging, Hay announced on March 20, 1900, that the Open Door policy was in effect.

The Boxer Rebellion

Naturally enough, the Chinese deeply resented the efforts by Japan, Russia, and the European powers to control their country. On the rising tide of resentment, the Chinese launched a movement to drive all "foreign devils" from their country. The movement was led by members of

A Japanese artist painted this picture of United States troops marching through Peking after the Boxer Rebellion in 1900.

a Chinese secret society whom westerners called "the Boxers."°

In the spring of 1900 the Boxers suddenly attacked. They killed about 300 foreigners in northern China. Then they surrounded the foreign settlement in Tientsin (TIN·TSIN) and the foreign legations in Peking, where men and women from many nations had gathered for protection.

The foreign powers promptly rushed troops to relieve the besieged people. The joint expeditionary force included 2,500 American troops from the Philippines as well as military units from Japan and several European nations. By August 14 the expeditionary force had relieved the foreigners in Tientsin and Peking, but not before 65 of the besieged had been killed.

The Boxer Rebellion provided the colonial powers with an excellent excuse to seize additional Chinese territory. But John Hay took a firm stand in opposition. On July 3, even while the expeditionary force was fighting its way inland to Peking, Hay announced that the United States wanted to "preserve Chinese territorial and administrative entity . . . and safeguard for the

° *the Boxers:* the Chinese name for this society literally meant "righteous harmonious band." But westerners wrongly translated the Chinese name to "righteous harmonious *fists*" and hence called the society the "Boxers."

world the principle of equal and impartial trade with all parts of the Chinese Empire."

Largely because of American influence, China did not lose any territory as a result of the Boxer Rebellion. China did, however, have to pay the foreign powers an indemnity of $333 million as compensation for loss, damage, and injury. The American share of the indemnity amounted to about $24 million, half of which the United States government turned over to American citizens to compensate them for losses of personal property in China. The American government then returned the remainder of the money to China.

Grateful for this American action, the Chinese government put the money into an educational fund to send Chinese students to the United States. This fund enabled thousands of China's ablest youth to study in American colleges and universities. These students helped to build closer understanding between the two countries.

The Open Door policy in China had other far-reaching results. It immediately involved the United States in the affairs of Russia and Japan, both of whom were expanding in the Far East.

The opening of Japan

Before 1853 the Japanese had lived in almost complete isolation from the rest of the world. Japan's rulers forbade foreigners to enter Japan;

only the Dutch had won the right to carry on a limited amount of trade through one small Japanese port. In 1853, however, Japan's isolation was abruptly shattered when Commodore Matthew C. Perry arrived in Japanese waters with a squadron of American naval vessels and demanded an audience with the Japanese rulers.

The exchange of presents that took place between the Americans and Japanese during a conference in 1854 symbolized the difference between the two countries. The United States received gifts of silk, brocades, lacquer ware, and other fine handmade articles; the Japanese received tokens of the new industrial world—a telegraph set, guns, and model railroad trains.

As a result of this conference and a later one, the United States and Japan signed the Treaty of Kanagawa. With this treaty both countries expressed a desire for peace, friendship, and developing trade. Japan also agreed to open two ports to United States trading vessels. Later, Japan opened other ports.

Japan and the race for empire

Few events in modern history have had such far-reaching effects as the opening by the United States of the doors of Japan. Two major developments followed at once. First, American and other traders started a lively commerce with Japan that grew to large proportions in the 1900's. Second, Japanese leaders were convinced that they should adopt the industrial techniques of the western nations. And once started, the process of modernization in Japan went on at an astonishingly rapid rate.

By the late 1800's Japan was a transformed country. But the "new" Japan faced new problems. Knowledge of science, medicine, and sanitation had reduced the death rate—a welcome development. But the lower death rate also meant a larger population—and this created difficulties, for Japan was a small country without enough farm land to feed all of its people adequately. The Japanese also needed raw materials for their new factories and markets for their products.

Faced with these problems, Japan started upon a program of imperialism similar to that being followed by the other industrial nations of the world. Japan needed colonies to secure food for its surplus population and to provide raw materials and markets for its growing industries. Thus Japan entered the race for empire and became one of the rivals for control of the Far East.

As you have seen, Japan started its career as an imperial power with an attack upon China in the Sino-Japanese War of 1894–95. Ten years later Japan plunged into war with Russia.

The United States in the Pacific

Although the Russo-Japanese War of 1904–05 took place on land nearly half a world away from the continental boundaries of the United States, Americans were immediately concerned. Their new commitments in the Pacific had given Americans a direct interest in the affairs of the Far East. The war between Russia and Japan, fought on Chinese soil and in Pacific waters, threatened to interfere with American trading and missionary interests in China. It also threatened to weaken, if not destroy, the Open Door policy.

Acting on his own authority, President Theodore Roosevelt warned Germany and France that, if they aided Russia, the United States would side with Japan. With Roosevelt acting as mediator, representatives from Russia and Japan met at Portsmouth, New Hampshire, during the summer of 1905 and worked out terms for settling the conflict. In 1906, for his efforts, Roosevelt received the Nobel peace prize.

The Treaty of Portsmouth transferred Russia's interest in Korea and Manchuria to Japan. The treaty also gave Japan the southern half of Sakhalin Island (see map, page 330). But the Russians refused to grant Japan's demand for a cash indemnity, and Roosevelt persuaded the Japanese, against their will, to drop this demand.

Roosevelt was delighted with the results of his efforts to end the Russo-Japanese War. The Treaty of Portsmouth left the Open Door policy intact. It maintained for a time the balance of power in the Far East. Neither Japan nor Russia nor any other colonial power had a dominant position in China. The doors of China remained open to American business and trade.

SECTION SURVEY

IDENTIFY: extraterritoriality, Boxer Rebellion, Treaty of Portsmouth, Nobel peace prize; John Hay, Commodore Perry.

1. (a) Describe the circumstances which led to the Open Door policy. (b) State the provisions of this policy.
2. Give the reasons for Chinese-American friendship during this period.
3. (a) Why did Japan become imperialistic? (b) Why were Americans concerned about Japanese imperialism?
4. Japan won the 1904–05 war against Russia. Why do you think this was significant?

CHAPTER SURVEY

INQUIRING INTO HISTORY

1. Why did the foreign policy of the United States change from one of isolationism to one of expansionism?
2. What arguments did the expansionists use to defend their position?
3. In your opinion, does expansionism contradict the ideals of self-government expressed in the Declaration of Independence? Why or why not?
4. Do you think the American people were in agreement with the statement by John Hay that "[The Spanish-American War] has been a splendid little war; begun with the highest motives, carried on with magnificent intelligence and spirit, favored by that fortune which loves the brave"? Why or why not?
5. (a) How did the areas acquired by the United States in 1898 differ from those acquired through the Louisiana Purchase and the Mexican Cession? (b) What problems of government do you think these new areas presented? (Remember that the Northwest Ordinance of 1787 was intended to serve as a plan of government for possessions in the continental United States.)
6. Recall American attitudes toward mercantilism before the American Revolution. What was our attitude toward our "mother country," Great Britain? Do you think you can generalize and say that most colonies feel this way about their mother country? Why or why not?
7. Was there a contradiction in the United States' favoring the Open Door policy for China and the policy of the Monroe Doctrine for the Western Hemisphere? Explain.

8. By moving into the Pacific and the Far East, the United States embarked upon a policy that was to have lasting consequences for foreign affairs and domestic conditions. Explain.

RELATING PAST TO PRESENT

1. Until World War II, the United States had friendly relations with China. The foundation for this friendship was established during the period just studied. Explain.
2. Is the United States involved overseas today for the same reasons it was involved during the period just studied? Explain.
3. Compare the role of the press today with the "yellow press" of Hearst and Pulitzer during the Spanish-American War.

DEVELOPING SOCIAL SCIENCE SKILLS

1. Make a list of the reasons why the United States became involved in the affairs of other nations between 1898 and 1914. Which of these reasons were the main causes of American involvement? Do you think that American involvement was justified? Was it right in some cases and wrong in others? Why?
2. Examine the picture on page 190. (a) What details has the artist emphasized? (b) Do you think that the Japanese artist has painted American troops as they actually appeared? (c) What do you think influenced the artist to paint the picture in this particular way?

CHAPTER 12

AMERICAN EXPANSION IN THE CARIBBEAN 1898-1914

On August 12, 1898, the Spaniards signed the armistice that brought the Spanish-American War to an end. For both the United States and Spain this event was a turning point.

By the terms of the armistice, Spain agreed (1) to leave Cuba, (2) to cede Puerto Rico and Guam to the United States, and (3) to allow American troops to occupy the Philippine Islands until a peace treaty could be drawn up and signed.

August 12, 1898, was a sad day for the Spanish nation. The Spaniards had reason for sorrow, for the Spanish-American War struck the final blow to the once mighty Spanish empire.

For the American people, however, the Spanish-American War marked a crucial step on the path of empire and world power. After 1898, as you know, the United States rapidly became a major power in the Pacific and in the Far East. And between 1898 and 1914, as you will read in this chapter, the course of events turned the Caribbean Sea into what was sometimes called "an American lake."

THE CHAPTER IN OUTLINE

1. The start of an American empire in the Caribbean area.

2. Intervention in Latin America under a modified Monroe Doctrine.

3. The outbreak of conflict between the United States and Mexico.

| 1450 | 1750 | 1800 | 1850 | 1900 | 1950 | 1980's |

1 The start of an American empire in the Caribbean area

With the Spanish-American War in 1898, the United States began to move into the Caribbean area. Less than 20 years later the American flag was flying not only over Puerto Rico, but also over the Panama Canal Zone and the Virgin Islands; American advisers were helping to govern small countries in and around the Caribbean; and the United States had developed a revised foreign policy for the Western Hemisphere.

"Does the Constitution follow the flag?"

The acquisition of overseas possessions caused the American government to face an important question: Were the people who lived in these areas entitled to all the rights guaranteed by the Constitution to citizens of the United States? Or, as the question was often stated, "Does the Constitution follow the flag?"

This question began to bother many members of Congress. Millions of people in the newly acquired territories had little understanding of the word "democracy." But if the Constitution did "follow the flag," these people were entitled to the rights of American citizenship. Many in Congress rejected such reasoning, however.

The Supreme Court's answer

In the Insular Cases of 1901 the Supreme Court settled the issue. It ruled that there are two kinds of possessions—"incorporated" and "unincorporated." The "incorporated" possessions—Hawaii and Alaska—were destined for statehood, and the citizens of these possessions were therefore entitled to all the constitutional rights guaranteed to United States citizens. The "unincorporated" possessions—Puerto Rico, the Philippines, Samoa, and others—were not destined for statehood, and the people of these areas were *not,* therefore, entitled to all constitutional guarantees. The people of the "unincorporated" possessions

This political cartoon criticized the growing imperialism of American foreign policy. Here, President Theodore Roosevelt is shown acting as the "police officer of the world."

THE WORLD'S CONSTABLE.

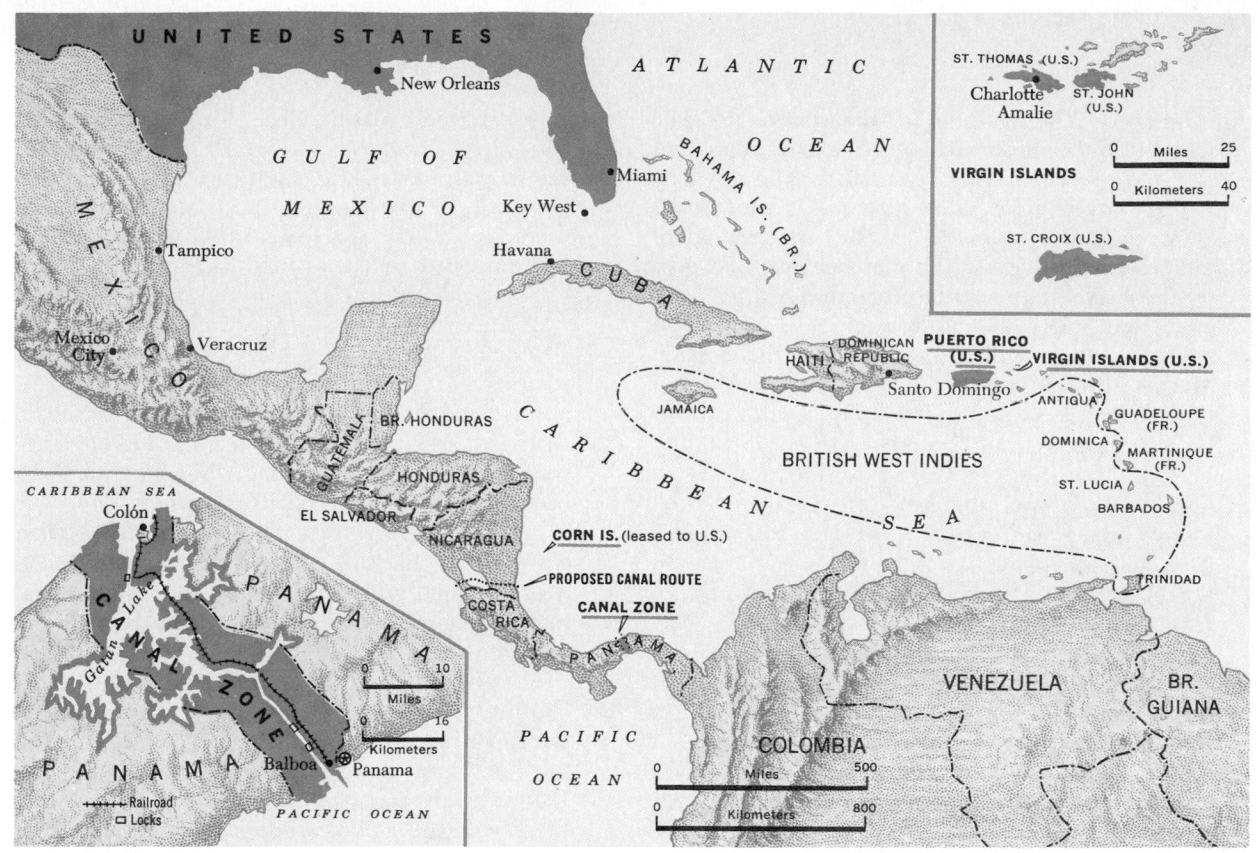

UNITED STATES EXPANSION IN THE CARIBBEAN, 1898-1917

were, however, entitled to certain fundamental rights, such as the guarantee that they would not be deprived of life, liberty, or property without due process of law.

The Insular Cases, and several similar Supreme Court decisions between 1901 and 1922, helped to develop an American colonial policy. However, it was Congress that passed the laws ruling America's growing colonial empire, subject only to certain broad limitations derived from the Constitution of the United States.

A government for Puerto Rico

In 1900, with the Foraker Act, Congress provided for the government of Puerto Rico. The new government consisted of a governor and an executive council appointed by the President of the United States, and a lower house elected by the Puerto Ricans.

Discontented Puerto Ricans, however, continued to demand a larger voice in their own government. In 1917, shortly after the Filipinos won a similar victory in the Jones Act of 1916, the United States adopted a second Jones Act making Puerto Rico a United States Territory and making the Puerto Ricans American citizens. Puerto Ricans were also granted the right to elect members of both houses of their legislature. Finally, in 1950, Congress gave Puerto Ricans the power to write their own constitution.

In 1952, after the constitution had been ratified by popular vote, Puerto Rico became a Commonwealth. As a Commonwealth, Puerto Rico is self-governing. It makes its own laws and controls its own finances. The United States, however, provides for the island's defense, includes Puerto Rico within its tariff system, and places no restrictions on immigration from Puerto Rico to the United States.

Strings on Cuban independence

Although Cuba was never considered an American colony, American influence over Cuban affairs remained strong after the Spanish-American War.

The Teller Resolution, which Congress adopted in 1898 when it declared war on Spain, pledged that the Cubans would be given their independence. But for three years after the war, while Congress was deciding what to do about the island, Cuba was ruled by an American army of occupation under General Leonard Wood.

In 1901 Congress finally decided to turn Cuba over to the Cuban people, but to do so with certain conditions. These conditions, incorporated in the Army Act of 1901 as the Platt Amendment, declared: (1) The Cuban government must never enter into any foreign agreements that might endanger Cuban independence. (2) The Cuban government must never incur debts that it could not repay in a reasonable time. (3) The Cuban government must give the United States "The right to intervene for the preservation of Cuban independence, the maintenance of a government adequate for the protection of life, property, and individual liberty." (4) The Cuban government must place naval bases at the disposal of the United States. Congress also announced that the United States would not withdraw its military forces until the Platt Amendment had been written into the Cuban constitution.

This was not the kind of "independence" many Cubans had expected, yet they had to agree to American demands. Therefore, they accepted the Platt Amendment, and in 1902 the American forces were withdrawn.

An American protectorate

Actually, Cuba became a "protectorate" of the United States. That is, the United States, a strong nation, attempted to protect Cuba, a weaker nation, by keeping partial control over Cuban affairs. Cubans were not happy with this relationship because of their experience under Spanish rule.

On three different occasions between 1906 and 1920, American troops landed in Cuba to maintain order and to protect American business and property. Moreover, American diplomatic pressure frequently forced the Cubans to accept policies favored by the United States.

In 1934, as you will see, Congress abolished the Platt Amendment, thus ending America's role as "protector" of Cuba.

Growing interest in a canal

In the years following the Spanish-American War, the United States was being pulled along a path of empire. As the empire grew, people began to say the United States needed two navies—one to protect its interests in the Pacific, the other to safeguard the Atlantic and the Caribbean.

But there was an alternative to a two-ocean navy. That was a canal across the narrow Isthmus of Panama separating the Atlantic and the Pacific oceans. Indeed, a French company in the 1880's had tried but had failed to build such a canal. Another possible canal route was through Nicaragua (see map, page 195). A canal in either place would enable a fleet to pass easily and quickly from one ocean to the other. It would also be of enormous commercial value to the United States, as well as to the merchant fleets of the world.

When the Spanish-American War began, the U.S. battleship *Oregon,* then in California waters, started to sail around South America in an effort to reach the Atlantic fleet. Public imagination was stirred, and for six weeks daily reports of the ship's progress appeared in every newspaper. The *Oregon's* voyage convinced many Americans that a canal was needed and that the canal must be controlled by the United States.

Withdrawal of British canal rights

Talk about building a canal through the Isthmus of Panama had gone on for many years. As early as 1850 the United States and Great Britain had agreed in the Clayton-Bulwer Treaty that, if a canal were built, they would together control it and guarantee that it be unfortified and open to all nations, even in wartime.

By 1898, however, the United States had changed its thinking. Americans had concluded that the canal was so important to their national interests that the United States must have exclusive control over it.

Negotiations with Great Britain resulted, in 1901, in the Hay-Pauncefote Treaty. In this treaty Great Britain gave up all rights to share in the building and management of the canal. The United States was now free to build and operate the canal. But it was understood that the canal would be open to all nations, even in time of war.

Difficulties encountered

The next step was to secure a right of way either through Nicaragua or across the Isthmus of Panama. The United States decided in favor of the Isthmus, which was then a province of Colombia. And Secretary of State John Hay immediately opened negotiations with the foreign minister of the Colombian government, Pedro Herrán. Soon the Hay-Herrán Treaty was ready for ratification. In return for a 99-year lease to a 16-mile (25.7-kilometer) strip of land across the province of Panama, the United States agreed to pay Colombia $10 million and a yearly rental of $250,000.

Matters stood at this promising point when the legislators of Colombia adjourned without taking action. They hoped to secure better terms through further negotiations. But many Americans, including President Theodore Roosevelt, were furious because Colombia's delay effectively blocked the entire canal project.

Revolution in Panama

Fortunately for the United States, many leaders in the province of Panama also were angry at Colombia's delay. These leaders had dreamed of a canal that would place Panama at a crossroads of world commerce. For years the people of Panama had resented control by Colombia. Colombia's delay was the last straw.

In Panama a group began secretly to organize a revolution. They were encouraged by

The building of the Panama Canal was an enormous undertaking, requiring the leveling of mountains and the conquest of tropical diseases. The canal was finally completed in 1914, at a cost of approximately $400 million.

representatives of the French company that had earlier tried to build a canal and now wanted to recover as much as possible of its investment.

One of the Panamanian leaders secretly traveled to Washington and asked the American government for assistance. Although open aid was refused, the Panamanian left Washington convinced that the United States would not interfere once the revolution began.

According to rumors, the revolution was to begin on November 4, 1903. On November 2 an American gunboat, the *Nashville*. arrived at Colón (see inset map, page 195). Hardly had it landed when a Colombian ship arrived with Colombian soldiers. The Colombian generals commanding the expedition immediately proceeded to the city of Panama, leaving orders for the troops to follow. Shortly after they arrived in Panama, however, the Colombian generals were seized and jailed.

The arrest of the Colombian generals was a signal for the outbreak of the revolution. The city of Panama quickly fell under the control of the revolutionists.

Meanwhile, during a dispute that broke out in Colón, Colombian soldiers and naval officers threatened to kill every American in the city. At this point United States marines landed. Colombian authorities demanded to know what right the Americans had to interfere. The Americans replied that in a treaty between the United States and Colombia signed back in 1846 the United States had guaranteed free passage through the Isthmus. The United States govern-

ment also added that no Colombian troops would be permitted to land within 50 miles of Panama. By this time enough American naval strength had arrived to make its warning effective.

Right of way through Panama

Largely because of American aid, the revolution in Panama was a success. On November 4, 1903, the new government took control in Panama. Two days later the United States recognized Panama's independence.

Two weeks later, on November 18, Panama granted the United States the long-sought canal right of way across the Isthmus. In the Hay-Bunau-Varilla (boo·NOH vah·REE·yah) Treaty, Panama gave the United States a perpetual lease to a 10-mile (16.1-kilometer) strip of land between the Atlantic and the Pacific. In return the United States agreed to pay Panama $10 million and a yearly rental of $250,000.

Did the United States help to start the revolution in Panama? President Theodore Roosevelt once boasted, "I took Panama." At other times he denied that the United States had in any way helped to carry out the revolution. But no matter how the revolution started, one fact is certain: It worked to the advantage of the United States, and Roosevelt made the most of the situation to advance American interests in Central America and the Caribbean.

Compensation for Colombia

Colombia was furious, of course, and the affair did much to stimulate the fear and distrust of the "Yankee" that was already strong in Latin America. In later years the United States tried to pacify the Colombian people. In 1921 the United States Senate ratified an agreement giving Colombia $25 million as partial compensation for the loss of the province of Panama.

Building the canal

Meanwhile, work on the canal progressed under the direct supervision of the United States Army Corps of Engineers. One of the first and most difficult tasks was to conquer malaria, yellow fever, and other tropical diseases. Until these diseases were brought under control, workers from the United States found it almost impossible to live in the Canal Zone.

Dr. Walter Reed and his colleagues working in Cuba discovered that yellow fever was transmitted by a certain mosquito, the *Stegomyia*. Using this and other medical discoveries, Dr. William C. Gorgas, the surgeon in charge of the American health program in Panama, was able to turn a deadly, steaming tropical jungle into a relatively healthful region.

By 1914 the canal was completed (see inset map, page 195) at a cost of approximately $400 million. Its completion was a major triumph of engineering and a personal triumph for the engineer in charge, Colonel George W. Goethals (GOH·thalz). The first traffic moved through the canal just as World War I broke out in Europe. During both world wars, the canal added immeasurably to the naval strength of the United States. And its value as a peacetime artery of trade and commerce has been almost incalculable.

SECTION SURVEY

IDENTIFY: Insular Cases, protectorate, Hay-Pauncefote Treaty, Hay-Bunau-Varilla Treaty; Walter Reed, George Goethals.

1. How did the Supreme Court answer the question, "Does the Constitution follow the flag"?
2. What provisions did Congress make for the government of Puerto Rico?
3. Why has it been said that the Platt Amendment made Cuba an American protectorate?
4. Give the economic and military reasons for American interest in a canal through Central America.
5. American policies helped to stimulate the fear and distrust of the "Yankee" that was already strong in Latin America. Comment.

2 Intervention in Latin America under a modified Monroe Doctrine

During the early 1900's, as you have read, the United States on a number of occasions intervened in the internal affairs of the smaller countries in the Caribbean area. On what grounds did the United States justify this interference?

Reasons for interference

Intervention was necessary, Americans argued, to maintain law and order in countries bordering on the United States. In the first place, the United States government had a duty to protect the lives and properties of its own citizens living in other countries. Second, the United States was determined as a matter of self-interest and self-defense to prevent European nations from intervening in the political affairs of the Western Hemisphere, and there would be less chance for such intervention if law and order prevailed. Third, the United States was concerned about the defense of the canal it was then building across the Isthmus of Panama.

Americans developed the argument of self-defense into a well-defined foreign policy. This foreign policy consisted of the Monroe Doctrine strengthened, as you will see, by Theodore Roosevelt's interpretation of the doctrine, called the Roosevelt Corollary.

The Monroe Doctrine of 1823

As you may recall, the original Monroe Doctrine of 1823 warned the European powers (1) not to attempt any further colonization in the Americas, and (2) not to interfere with independent nations in the Western Hemisphere.

When this warning was first issued and for many years after, the United States lacked enough naval strength to enforce the policy. But the support of Latin Americans and the backing of the British navy gave weight to Monroe's words.

The first major test

The first major test of the Monroe Doctrine came during the 1860's, when Emperor Napoleon III of France tried to establish a French empire in Mexico.

Napoleon III's effort to seize control of Mexico had the support of many people in France, including military leaders, those seeking adventure, and business groups seeking trade. It began when Napoleon III, together with Great Britain and Spain, sent an expedition to Mexico, supposedly to force Mexico to repay some of its debts. After Mexico repaid its debts, Great Britain and Spain withdrew. But Napoleon III refused to pull out his troops. Instead, aided by Mexicans opposed to President Benito Juárez

During the Venezuelan crisis of 1902, the United States warned European nations not to violate the Monroe Doctrine. In a cartoon of that year, Uncle Sam warns Great Britain and Germany, "That's a live wire, gentlemen."

(HWAH·res), the French troops installed Maximilian of Austria as emperor of Mexico. President Juárez fled to El Paso del Norte near the United States border.

The United States immediately protested that French occupation of Mexico was a clear violation of the Monroe Doctrine. But the United States was fighting the Civil War, and until 1865 was unable to take firm action. Then, with the war ended, the United States prepared to send an American army to the Mexican border—farther, if necessary.

But the American army was not needed. Napoleon, faced with the danger of war in Europe and convinced that he could not hold Mexico, withdrew his forces. Juárez and his followers destroyed Maximilian's army and executed Maximilian in 1867.

Thus ended a difficult situation. However, by upholding the Monroe Doctrine, the American government had shown its firm resolve to the rest of the world.

A second major test

A second major test of the Monroe Doctrine came in 1895. The immediate issue was a boundary dispute between Venezuela and British Guiana (see map, page 195).

This dispute originated when Great Britain acquired British Guiana back in 1814. Despite the protests of Venezuela, Great Britain had time and again pushed the western boundary of British Guiana on to territory claimed by Venezuela. Finally, in 1882, Venezuela demanded that Great Britain submit the controversy to arbitration, meaning that the British would have to agree in advance to accept the decision of a neutral party.

The British refused to submit the boundary controversy to arbitration. In 1895 Venezuela asked the United States to intervene. President Cleveland decided to act. In an extremely strong message, Secretary of State Richard Olney warned Great Britain that the United States would not tolerate any further interference with Venezuela and demanded an immediate settlement of the problem by arbitration.

Great Britain angrily rejected Olney's demands. In the first place, the British retorted, the Monroe Doctrine had not been violated. Second, the Monroe Doctrine was not a recognized part of international law. And third, the United States had no business interfering.

President Cleveland refused to accept this explanation. When the British refusal to arbitrate reached him, he appointed an American commission to investigate the controversy and reach a decision. This was a direct challenge to British imperial power.

Realizing that war between Great Britain and the United States was a real possibility, responsible leaders in both countries urged moderation.

Partly because of their efforts and partly because of British difficulties in South Africa at the time, the British government suddenly reversed its position and agreed to arbitrate the boundary dispute. It even offered to help the American commission with its investigation.

Once more the Monroe Doctrine had been successfully upheld by the United States. And on this occasion the United States could claim that it had used its foreign policy to protect a weak nation against a great power. Even more important, perhaps, was the fact that the British, desiring American friendship, now in effect recognized that the United States had special interests in the Caribbean area.

A third major test

In 1902, seven years later, Venezuela again became involved in a dispute with European countries. Venezuela was unable to repay debts owed to Great Britain, Germany, and Italy. After their demands for repayment produced no results, the three countries took joint action. They withdrew their diplomatic representatives, blockaded the Venezuelan coast, and seized several small gunboats.

At this point President Theodore Roosevelt warned the European powers that any attempt to seize territory in the Western Hemisphere would violate the Monroe Doctrine. Then he urged the countries involved to submit the dispute to arbitration. They did, and the matter was settled.

The Drago Doctrine

In the case of Mexico and in both of the Venezuelan controversies, the United States had intervened in the name of the Monroe Doctrine to warn European nations to keep out of the politics of the Western Hemisphere. In all of these controversies the United States had helped to protect its militarily weaker neighbors.

By 1902, however, many Americans were eager to promote their own interests in Latin America. The United States had gone into the Spanish-American War in 1898 to help the oppressed Cubans. It had come out of the war controlling Cuba and owning Puerto Rico. Moreover, by the early 1900's Americans in growing numbers were investing money in Caribbean countries.

Latin-American leaders were becoming alarmed at the growing influence of the United States. In 1902 one of these leaders, Luis M. Drago, Argentine Minister of Foreign Affairs, announced a policy for Latin America that came to be known as the Drago Doctrine.

Drago declared that Argentina could not agree that any European nation had the right to use force to collect debts from a Latin-American nation. He argued that when individuals or nations lent money they did so at their own risk.

Nearly all of Latin America's leaders, as well as many United States citizens, agreed with Drago. But in 1904, when trouble broke out in the Dominican Republic, President Roosevelt announced a policy that exempted the United States from the principle that foreign debts concerned only the debtor country and foreign investors.

The Roosevelt Corollary

The Dominican Republic (see map, page 195) owed long-overdue debts to several European countries as well as to American investors. When the European countries threatened to use armed force to collect the money, President Roosevelt at once intervened.

Roosevelt boldly announced in 1904 that if it became necessary for any nation to interfere in the affairs of a Latin-American country, the United States must do so, not a European government. Roosevelt declared that ". . . in the Western Hemisphere the adherence of the United States to the Monroe Doctrine may force the United States, however reluctantly, in flagrant cases of . . . wrongdoing or impotence, to the exercise of an international police power."

The new policy laid down in 1904 by President Roosevelt came to be known as the Roosevelt Corollary to the Monroe Doctrine. With this policy the United States assumed the role of "police officer" in the Western Hemisphere. On several occasions during the next two decades the United States used the Roosevelt Corollary to justify its intervention in the affairs of several Latin American nations.

There was, of course, another side to the Roosevelt Corollary. It aimed to improve conditions in the Latin-American countries so that European governments would have no excuse for intervention. In this sense the Roosevelt Corollary helped all of the American countries. But Latin Americans could not forget that it was also a weapon that could be used against them and was thus an insult to their national pride.

Dominican Republic as a protectorate

The United States first exercised its "international police power" by intervening in the affairs of the Dominican Republic. As part of an agreement with the Dominican government in 1905, President Roosevelt promised to guarantee the Republic's *territorial integrity*. That is, he promised to use American armed forces, if necessary, to prevent any European country from seizing Dominican territory. In exchange for this guarantee, the Dominican government agreed to allow an American agent to collect its customs duties, to turn over 45 percent of the duties to the Dominican government, and to use the rest of the money to pay foreign creditors.

Although customs duties doubled under American supervision and the financial position of the Dominican Republic improved, the Dominican people resented United States control. Finally, in 1916, during President Wilson's administration, the Dominican government announced it intended to end the protectorate.

The United States answered this challenge by landing marines and suspending the Dominican legislature. For eight years, until 1924, the Dominican Republic was ruled by a Dominican military dictatorship under the American government. The United States withdrew its military forces in 1924, but did not end its role of "protector" until 1940.

A protectorate over Haiti

The same general methods used to secure control of the Dominican Republic were applied to Haiti (see map, page 195).

When in 1914, during Wilson's administration, revolutions shook the debt-ridden Haitian republic, the United States landed marines.

The Haitians were then asked to ratify a treaty prepared by the United States Department of State. This treaty gave the United States the right to (1) supervise Haiti's finances, (2) intervene to maintain order, and (3) control the Haitian police force. After considerable American pressure, the legislature of Haiti ratified the treaty, which went into effect early in 1916.

Unfortunately, neither the treaty nor the continued presence of an American military force was sufficient to restore order completely. During the next four or five years nearly 2,000 Haitians were killed in riots and other outbreaks of violence.

Nevertheless, some improvements did come to Haiti during the years of United States control. Some Americans, however, agreed with those Haitians who argued that better sanitation, health, and education, and increased prosperity, were not worth the loss of freedom.

Despite continued resentment in Haiti and growing pressure from the American public to end military occupation of the island, the treaty permitting American control was renewed in 1926, as you will see. But in 1930 President Herbert Hoover announced that all American troops would be withdrawn when the treaty expired in 1936. Two years before that date, in 1934, President Franklin D. Roosevelt withdrew all military forces and gave the Haitian government a greater share of authority over the republic's finances.

The United States purchased three of the Virgin Islands from Denmark in 1917. This purchase helped to guarantee American control over the Caribbean and the approaches to the Panama Canal.

American interference in Central America

Twice between 1900 and 1920 American military forces were used in Nicaragua and Honduras to gain a large measure of control over these republics. In addition, the United States exercised a large amount of influence over the governments of Colombia, Costa Rica, and Guatemala (see map, page 195). This influence was secured by a policy labeled by its critics "dollar diplomacy."

Under the so-called "dollar diplomacy," American bankers, sometimes by invitation of the Department of State, lent money to Caribbean governments. When the debtors failed to repay their debts or the interest on their loans, the United States government intervened to protect American investments. This intervention took various forms, including the landing of marines, the supervision of elections, and support to the political group that favored the United States.

Purchase of the Virgin Islands

By purchase of three of the Virgin Islands

from Denmark, the United States completed its colonies in the Caribbean (see map, page 195).

Back in 1868 Secretary of State Seward had tried to get Congress to buy the Virgin Islands. Congress had refused; it refused again in 1902.

In 1917, however, with World War I raging in Europe, the United States was fearful that Germany might secure control of these strategic bases, and it renewed the offer to buy the islands. This time negotiations were completed. With the payment of $25 million to Denmark, the islands became outposts of America's Caribbean empire.

As the map on page 195 shows, the Virgin Islands lie at the eastern edge of the West Indies. United States naval bases on the islands, in Puerto Rico, and at Guantánamo Bay in Cuba help to guarantee American control over the Caribbean Sea and the approaches to the Panama Canal.

SECTION SURVEY

IDENTIFY: Drago Doctrine, territorial integrity, "dollar diplomacy"; Napoleon III, Benito Juárez, Richard Olney.

1. (a) How did the United States justify its intervention in Latin-American affairs? (b) Do you agree that this intervention was justified? Explain.
2. (a) What were the provisions of the original Monroe Doctrine of 1823? (b) Describe two occasions on which the Monroe Doctrine was tested and upheld.
3. (a) In what way did the Roosevelt Corollary modify the original Monroe Doctrine? (b) Cite examples of the application of the Roosevelt Corollary.
4. Latin Americans had strong reactions to events in the Caribbean resulting from United States policy. Comment.

3 The outbreak of conflict between the United States and Mexico

American investments south of the Rio Grande in time involved the United States in conflict with Mexico. By the time Woodrow Wilson became President in 1913, American citizens had invested nearly $1 billion in Mexican oil wells, mines, railroads, and ranches. Most of Mexico's trade was with the United States.

Dictatorship and revolution

Mexico was closely tied to the United States, and Mexico's President Porfirio Díaz was largely responsible for this fact. Díaz, although called "president," was actually a dictator who had ruled Mexico since 1877. During his long rule he had brought peace and order to Mexico and had helped to develop the country's resources. But, to develop Mexico's resources, he had encouraged foreign investors to finance and operate mines, factories, and other industries by offering them special privileges. Given this encouragement, foreign capital, much of it from American investors, had poured into Mexico. As a result, foreign investors and the privileged friends of dictator Díaz enjoyed most of the material benefits of Mexico's developing economy.

Finally, in 1910, the Mexicans staged a successful revolution. Díaz resigned and left for Europe. A sincere reformer, Francisco Madero, then became president—but only for a short time. Early in 1913 Madero was assassinated and Victoriano Huerta (WAIR·tah) seized the government.

Huerta had many enemies, including the friends of the late President Madero. The struggle between Huerta and his enemies, led by Venustiano Carranza, plunged Mexico into more bloodshed.

Wilson's policy of "watchful waiting"

Americans with investments in Mexico were deeply troubled by the situation. And millions of people throughout the Americas were dis-

Mexican leader "Pancho" Villa was thought of by many people in his country as a modern Robin Hood. In Mexico today he is still remembered in stories and songs.

mayed because Huerta had risen to power as the result of a cold-blooded murder.

Some Americans therefore wanted President Wilson to send an armed force into Mexico to protect American investments and to restore law and order. Wilson chose instead to follow a policy that he hoped would preserve the independence of the Mexican people.

Wilson outlined his policy in a speech given shortly after his election. "The United States will never again seek one additional foot of territory by conquest," he declared. "We have seen material interests threaten constitutional freedom in the United States," he went on to say. "Therefore we will now know how to sympathize with those in the rest of America who have to contend with such powers, not only within their borders but from outside their borders also." He then urged the Latin-American countries to settle the Mexican problem in their own way.

Although a number of European countries promptly recognized the Huerta government, Wilson refused to do so. He pointed out that Huerta had gained power not by the will of the Mexican people, but by force and murder. Moreover, he was convinced that the Mexicans themselves would soon get rid of Huerta. Meanwhile, Wilson announced, the United States would follow a policy of "watchful waiting."

Wilson's refusal to intervene pleased most Latin Americans. But many American businesses with Mexican investments harshly attacked the President as they saw American lives and property destroyed in Mexico.

American intervention

As the months passed, however, even President Wilson began to lose patience. Hundreds of small revolutionary bands roamed Mexico. But they were not organized, and Huerta remained in power. American citizens in Mexico were killed, and there were rumors that Huerta might try to confiscate, or seize, American property.

The final crisis came in April 1914 when a Mexican official arrested several American sailors near Tampico, Mexico, which was under martial law. The sailors were soon released, but Huerta refused to apologize for the incident. To make matters worse, a German ship arrived at Veracruz with machine guns and other military supplies for Huerta. President Wilson then ordered United States marines to seize Veracruz. Emboldened by America's action, the anti-Huerta forces in Mexico began to gain strength.

The "ABC mediation"

The United States was now in a position to dictate who should be chosen as the new Mexican president. But Wilson refused to do this. Instead he accepted an invitation from Argentina, Brazil, and Chile—sometimes called the "ABC powers"—for United States representatives to meet with Mexican leaders and those of the other nations to try to reach a solution. Huerta, too, now had to accept this invitation, and the conference was held at Niagara Falls, Canada. As a result of the "ABC mediation," Huerta resigned.

Venustiano Carranza then established himself in power in Mexico, and American forces were withdrawn from Veracruz. And in 1915, after Carranza guaranteed that Mexico would respect foreign lives and property, the United States recognized him as leader of the Mexican government.

American troops in Mexico

But trouble still continued, for the people Carranza chose to help him rule began to quarrel among themselves. One of those who turned against Carranza was Francisco (Pancho) Villa (VEE·yah). Angry at the United States for helping Carranza and hoping to force American troops to intervene in Mexico, Villa and his followers in 1916 seized 18 Americans in northern Mexico and deliberately put them to death. Later, he crossed the border and raided Columbus, New Mexico, killing 17 Americans.

General John J. Pershing led the American troops sent into Mexico in 1916 in an unsuccessful effort to capture "Pancho" Villa.

President Wilson immediately declared that he intended to send an expedition into Mexico to capture Villa, "dead or alive." Carranza reluctantly agreed, and General John J. Pershing led an initial force of some 5,000 troops across the border. But the deeper Pershing pushed into Mexican territory, the more hostile the Mexicans became. For a time the shadow of war hung over both countries. Finally, in January 1917, American troops withdrew from Mexico, without having captured Villa.

President Wilson had tried sincerely to respect the independence and freedom of the Mexican people. In the end, however, he felt he had to use force to maintain law and order and protect American lives and property. During these troubled years in Mexican-United States relations, Wilson learned that it was not easy for the United States to keep aloof from a nearby country where disorder threatened Americans.

SECTION SURVEY

IDENTIFY: confiscate, ABC powers; Porfirio Diaz, Victoriano Huerta, Venustiano Carranza, "Pancho" Villa, John J. Pershing.

1. Show how the economic interests of the United States and Mexico were closely interwoven.
2. (a) Describe the circumstances that led to Wilson's policy of "watchful waiting." (b) Explain this policy.
3. Why did Wilson abandon "watchful waiting"?
4. What important lesson did Americans learn from their experiences with Mexico during the years 1910–17?

CHAPTER SURVEY

INQUIRING INTO HISTORY

1. Theodore Roosevelt once boasted: "I took Panama." (a) What did he mean? (b) What does this say about the power of the Presidency? (c) Why did the United States pay Colombia $25 million in 1921?
2. If, during the period just studied, the Canadian ambassador to the United States had said to the Mexican ambassador to the United States, "We have a common problem between us," what do you think this might have meant?
3. What is your opinion of "dollar diplomacy"? Explain.
4. (a) How would you justify Theodore Roosevelt's policies in the Carribbean? (b) How would you criticize them?
5. The Panama Canal created new commitments for the United States. Explain.
6. Do you think Puerto Rico has benefited from its relationship with the United States? Explain.

RELATING PAST TO PRESENT

1. In the 1970's, Panama and the United States began negotiations to give Panama greater influence and control over the Panama Canal. Why, do you think, these negotiations were undertaken?
2. Compare the attitudes of two Latin-American countries toward the United States during the period just studied and in recent years.
3. Some have said that the Monroe Doctrine protected Latin America from Europe but not from the United States. Do you agree or disagree? Explain the reasons for your opinion.

DEVELOPING SOCIAL SCIENCE SKILLS

1. Examine the cartoons on pages 194 and 199. (a) What is the subject of each cartoon? (b) What is the viewpoint of each cartoon? (c) Which cartoon do you feel is most successful in attacking or supporting American foreign policy? Explain.
2. Do you think that the Roosevelt Corollary was a policy of imperialism or a policy to prevent imperialism? Give evidence to support your opinion. Was it a wise policy? Explain.
3. Make a time-line for classroom display for the years 1898 to 1914. Using drawings or pictures, show the major events in America's new role as a world power.

CHAPTER 13
AMERICA'S ENTRY INTO WORLD WAR I
1914-1920

On the morning of July 28, 1914, Americans opened their newspapers with shocked surprise. In huge headlines the New York *Tribune* reported: "AUSTRIA DECLARES WAR, RUSHES VAST ARMY INTO SERBIA; RUSSIA MASSES 80,000 MEN ON BORDER." All other American papers that day also carried this same news.

In general, the reaction of the American public was one of both stunned disbelief and withdrawal. Europeans could not be so reckless. But if they were, well, then they alone must suffer the consequences. Americans wanted no part of this European madness.

The summer of 1914 ushered in a new age—an age of violence, bloodshed, and revolution. Within the course of a few fateful months world peace went up in flames, and many nations were swept into one of the most terrible wars in history.

The conflict that started in the summer of 1914 spread rapidly. Before it ended four years later, 30 nations on six continents were involved; more than 8 million members of these nations' armed forces had been killed; an equal number of civilians had lost their lives; and property worth countless billions of dollars had gone up in flames.

But before looking at the war itself, it is necessary to answer several important questions: Why did the news of war come as such a surprise to Americans? Why did Americans think that the war was no concern of theirs? And, finally, what at last drew the United States into the conflict?

THE CHAPTER IN OUTLINE

1. American efforts to encourage international cooperation.

2. The outbreak of World War I in Europe despite efforts toward peace.

3. The failure of American attempts to remain neutral.

4. Mobilizing American strength for the war effort.

5. The role of American troops and ideals in helping to win the war.

1450　　1750　　1800　　1850　　1900　　1950　　1980's

1 American efforts to encourage international cooperation

During the late 1800's and the early 1900's the leading nations of the world had taken important steps toward international cooperation. By 1914 millions of men and women in both Europe and America were convinced that major wars would never again occur.

The peace movement

For nearly 100 years a movement for international peace had been steadily gaining strength. During the early 1900's anti-war societies in both Europe and America prepared numerous anti-war pamphlets. The pamphlets emphasized that war was wasteful and failed to solve the problems it was intended to solve—that even the victors paid too high a price.

Growing interdependence

It was obvious to everyone that industrial technology was rapidly breaking down the barriers of space and time and bringing the peoples of the earth closer together. Railway trains rumbled across national boundaries. Liners and freighters sailed back and forth across the oceans. The telegraph, the telephone, and underwater cables enabled people in all parts of the world to communicate almost instantaneously.

These and other technological developments greatly increased the number, variety, and importance of activities that people of different nations could and did carry on together. Many businesses now bought and sold in worldwide markets and built industries in many different countries. Humanitarian associations, among them the Red Cross, organized on an international basis. Professional groups—scientists, engineers, doctors, and scholars—formed international societies and pooled their knowledge for the benefit of all peoples.

International agencies

Governments as well as individual citizens were also engaged in a growing number of activities requiring international cooperation. By 1914, 30 different international agencies of government had been organized to deal with problems shared by many nations, such as transportation, communication, disease and sanitation, weights and measures, postal regulations, and maritime rules.

By bringing the nations of the world together in such cooperative efforts, all of these agencies seemed to strengthen international understanding.

The Pan-American Union

Meanwhile the governments of the leading nations of the world had been making new efforts to prevent war. On several occasions during the late 1800's and the early 1900's delegates from many different nations met to discuss the issues

During the early 1900's, anti-war societies were formed in both Europe and America. The women shown here belong to a "Peace Party" that urged Americans to stay out of foreign wars.

of war and peace. The First International Conference of American States of 1889–90 was one of these early meetings. Delegates from the Latin-American countries and the United States met in Washington, D.C., and organized the International Union of American Republics.

Secretary of State Blaine told the delegates, "We hold up this new Magna Carta, which abolishes war and substitutes arbitration between the American republics, as the first and great fruit of the International American Conference."

In 1910 the name of the International Union of American Republics was changed to the Pan-American Union. Under that name it continued to hold periodic meetings to discuss common problems. (Later, in 1948, the members of the Pan-American Union created the Organization of American States, known as the O.A.S.)

In the early 1900's United States expansion and interference in the Caribbean area angered many Latin-American countries and thus weakened the influence of the Pan-American Union. Nevertheless, to people throughout the Americas the Pan-American Union was the symbol of a new, more peaceful world that was coming into being.

The Hague Conferences

Millions of people in both Europe and the Americas had also taken hope from two conferences held in Europe.

The First Hague Conference, called by the tsar of Russia, met at The Hague in the Netherlands in 1899. Twenty-six nations sent delegates. The delegates strongly urged nations to try to settle disputes through mediation or arbitration. In cases involving mediation, two or more nations engaged in a dispute would ask a disinterested third party or nation to "recommend" a solution. In cases involving arbitration, two or more nations engaged in a dispute would agree in advance to accept the decision of a neutral party. To encourage nations to submit their disputes to arbitration, the First Hague Conference organized the Permanent Court of Arbitration with headquarters at The Hague. The conference also tried to lessen the horrors of warfare by outlawing certain weapons and by drawing up rules for the conduct of war.

The Second Hague Conference, called by the tsar of Russia and President Theodore Roosevelt, met at The Hague in 1907. This time 44 nations sent delegates. The conference drafted additional "rules" for the conduct of war. It also adopted the Drago Doctrine, which stated that no nation should use force to collect debts "unless the debtor country refused arbitration, or having accepted arbitration, failed to submit to the award."

The first two Hague Conferences encouraged those who were working to promote peace. A third conference was being planned when war broke out in Europe.

Individual efforts to promote peace

American citizens, both in public office and private life, took an active part in the search for ways to prevent war. Edward Ginn, a well-known Boston publisher, provided a grant of money to establish the World Peace Foundation. Andrew Carnegie set up the Carnegie Endowment for International Peace, donated money to construct the building for the Permanent Court of Arbitration at The Hague, and gave a grant to help construct the Pan-American Union building in Washington, D.C.

Although President Theodore Roosevelt believed that some wars were necessary, he played a leading role in the peace movement. He was responsible, as you know, for the 1905 peace conference held at Portsmouth, New Hampshire, at which Japan and Russia reached an agreement ending the Russo-Japanese War. President Roosevelt and his successor, President Taft, also played an active part in other international negotiations.

President Wilson, who entered the White House in 1913, was an even stronger champion of international understanding. He supported his Secretary of State, William Jennings Bryan, who negotiated anti-war treaties with 21 nations in 1913 and 1914. These treaties declared that every dispute must be submitted to a joint commission for investigation and recommendation. The nations signing these treaties promised not to go to war until the commissions had made their reports.

By 1914 such efforts had built what seemed to be a solid and enduring structure of peace. Why, then, did war break out?

SECTION SURVEY

IDENTIFY: interdependence, mediation, arbitration.

1. Describe the factors which led to the peace movement of the early 1900's.
2. Why did many people think that the Pan-American Union held bright promise for the future?
3. Why did the first two Hague Conferences greatly encourage those who were working to promote peace?
4. Describe briefly the efforts made by individuals to promote peace and international understanding in the years preceding World War I.

2 The outbreak of World War I in Europe despite efforts toward peace

War broke out in 1914 because the elaborate safeguards that had been built to prevent war were less strong than the forces pulling nations apart. Despite the many efforts made to preserve peace in the early 1900's, the European nations during these years were standing on a powder keg. When a spark was struck to the powder, the hopes and plans for peace of peoples everywhere exploded.

The "spark" that led to war

The spark was struck in the Balkan Peninsula of Europe (see map, this page) in the early summer of 1914 by Serbian nationalists who were pledged to free all Slavs° living under the rule of the Austro-Hungarian empire. The Serbian

---

° *Slavs:* a people widely spread over central, eastern, and southeastern Europe whose languages come from the same basic root. The Slavs under Austro-Hungarian rule were called **South Slavs**.

---

nationalists assassinated the Archduke Franz Ferdinand, heir to the throne of Austria-Hungary, and his wife as they rode through the streets of Sarajevo (SAH·rah·yeh·vo), capital of the province of Bosnia. Bosnia had only recently become part of the Austro-Hungarian empire.

The Serbian conspirators were caught and brought to trial. But Franz Joseph, the 83-year-old emperor of Austria-Hungary, and his advisers decided to use this opportunity to destroy Serbia's power completely. Thus Austria-Hungary made certain harsh demands against Serbia, which Serbia refused to meet.

As tension grew, European diplomats struggled to solve the differences between Austria-Hungary and Serbia. But Austria lined up the support of its main ally, Germany, and prepared for war. Austria-Hungary declared war on Serbia on July 28, 1914, and Austrian armies began to move southward across the border.

WORLD WAR I IN EUROPE

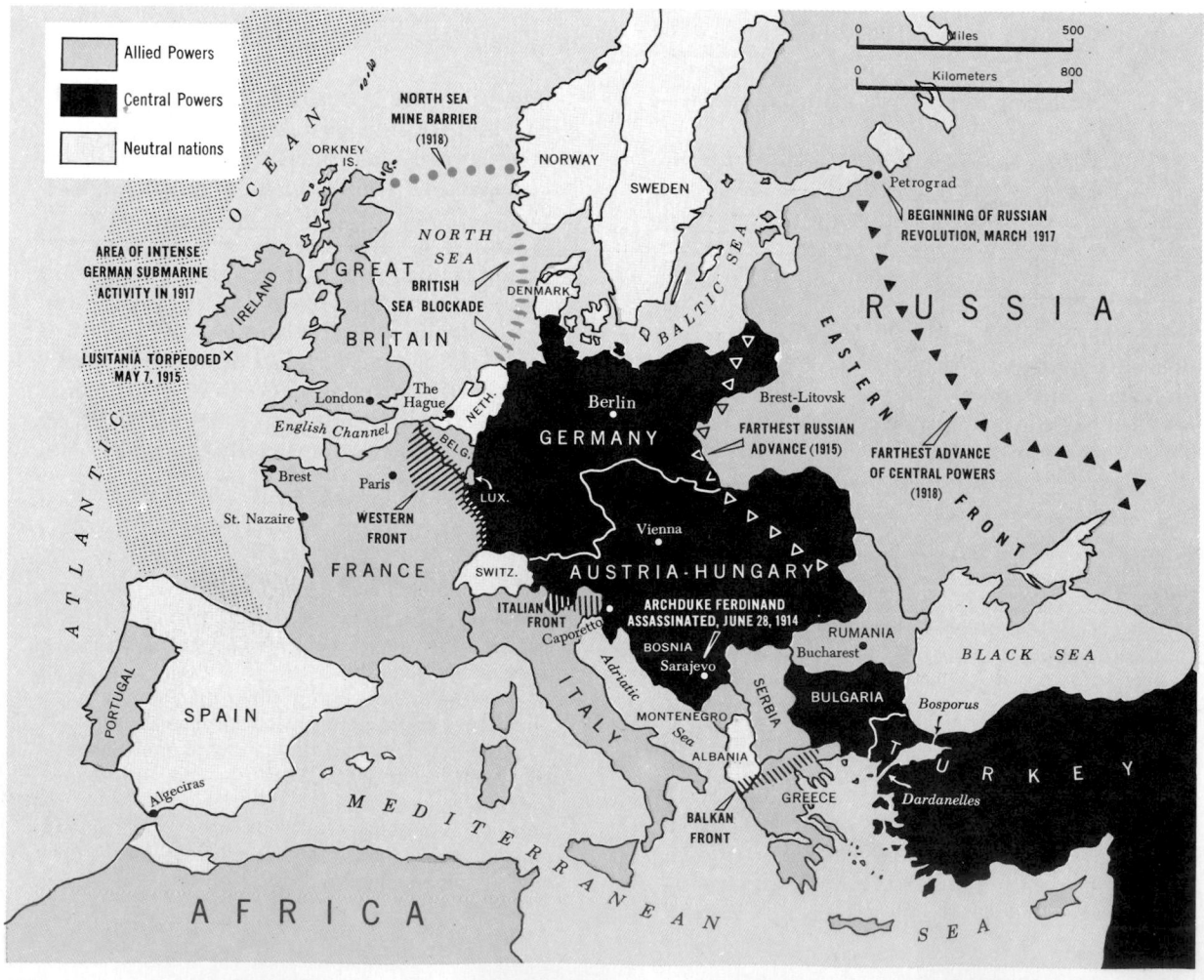

The spark that set off World War I was only minutes away on June 28, 1914, when Archduke Franz Ferdinand and his wife, both fated for assassination, drove away from the Senate House at Sarajevo.

The spread of war

The action of Austria-Hungary set off a chain of explosive events. Russia, a Slavic country sometimes called the "Protector of the Slavs," immediately prepared to go to Serbia's aid. Germany promptly declared war on Russia on August 1. When France, an ally of Russia, refused to declare its neutrality, Germany on August 3 declared war on France. Great Britain, an ally of France, then declared war on Germany on August 4 and on Austria on August 12.

A week after Austria-Hungary's attack on Serbia, then, five major European nations were at war. Before the conflict ended it had engulfed 30 nations on six continents. The nations siding with Austria-Hungary and Germany were known as the Central Powers. Those allying themselves with Russia, France, and Great Britain were referred to as the Allied Powers, or simply as the Allies.

Did the tragic incident at Sarajevo really start World War I? Yes and no. It was the immediate cause, the spark that touched off the explosion. But there were deep, underlying causes which help to explain why the war came and why it spread so rapidly and so widely.

Nationalism as a cause

An intense spirit of nationalism was one of the underlying sources of tension. The term *nationalism* often refers to the strong feeling people have for their own country, but it may also refer to the desire of people ruled by others to throw off this foreign rule and create their own nation. As you have read, it was a desire to free certain Slavs from Austro-Hungarian rule that prompted the Serbian conspirators to assassinate the heir to the throne of Austria-Hungary. And Austria-Hungary declared war on Serbia in order to crush the rising spirit of nationalism among the Slavic people and to hold the Austro-Hungarian empire together. But the spirit of nationalism was not confined to the Balkan Peninsula. In almost every country of Europe, as well as in the colonies overseas, people ruled by other nations longed for independence.

Imperialism as a cause

Another disruptive force was imperialism—the struggle for colonies. As you may recall, during the late 1800's and the early 1900's the major powers of the world were engaged in a race for empire. By 1914, so far as colonies were concerned, the nations of Europe could be grouped into two classes: the "have" nations and the "have-not" nations.

Great Britain and France, each with huge colonial empires, were among the "have" powers. Although Russia owned no colonies, it did possess immense areas of underdeveloped land, and thus was also a "have" nation.

Germany, on the other hand, was a "have-not" nation. It did own colonies in Africa and in the Pacific, but its colonial empire was relatively small, and Germany wanted additional territory. Italy was in a similar situation—and one of the reasons that finally brought Italy into the war on the Allied side was a promise of colonies when the war ended.

International rivalries

Rivalry among nations was not, however, confined to the race for colonies. Austria-Hungary attacked Serbia partly to strengthen its hold on the Slavic peoples and to increase its influence in the Balkan Peninsula. Russia, on the other hand, came to Serbia's aid to prevent Austria-Hungary from increasing its influence.

France supported Russia not only because it was Russia's ally, but also because it wanted to recover Alsace-Lorraine, a former French area which the Germans had conquered in 1871. Italy desired nearby territories within the Austro-Hungarian empire. Every Balkan country looked greedily at territory belonging to its neighbors. Russia longed for ice-free harbors in the Baltic Sea and for an outlet through the Dardanelles and the Bosporus into the Mediterranean Sea. Germany, the major Baltic Sea power, and Turkey, which controlled the Dardanelles, feared and distrusted Russia.

Search for a system of alliances

The mounting tensions with their accompanying plots and intrigues led inevitably to an armament race, or race for military power. Long before 1914 the relative sizes of navies and armies occupied a major part of the attention of every European government.

Besides building up their military forces, European nations tried to gain security with the *balance-of-power system*. This meant that every nation tried to increase its own strength by securing as many allies as possible. Thus Germany, Austria-Hungary, and Italy joined in what became known as the Triple Alliance. And to maintain a balance of power, Great Britain, France, and Russia formed what became known as the Triple Entente (ahn·TAHNT). Both of these rival alliances had been completed by 1907.

Austria's declaration of war on Serbia immediately set the whole system of alliances into motion. Of all the nations, only Italy failed to live up to its treaty obligations, which pledged Italy to support Austria-Hungary and Germany. Waiting to see which side would promise the most, Italy did not enter the war until 1915, and then it fought on the Allied side.

Peace or war?

During the early 1900's, as you may recall, strong forces pulled peoples and nations in two directions at the same time. With one hand, governments tried to strengthen the bonds between nations and build a solid structure of peace. With the other hand, governments plotted and schemed against one another and desperately planned for war or for the protection of their national interests in case war broke out.

SECTION SURVEY

IDENTIFY: Slavs, nationalism, imperialism, balance-of-power system, "have" and "have-not" nations, Central Powers, Allied Powers; 1914.

1. Why is the incident at Sarajevo considered the spark that set off World War I?
2. Discuss how the following factors help to explain why World War I came and why it spread so rapidly and so widely: (a) nationalism, (b) imperialism, (c) international rivalries, (d) the balance-of-power system.
3. How are the four factors listed in question 2 interrelated?
4. How do you think a nation prepares itself psychologically for war?

3 The failure of American attempts to remain neutral

America's first reaction to the outbreak of war in Europe, as you have read, was one of shocked surprise and withdrawal. The war seemed unreal, a nightmare that would not last.

American neutrality

But the war was all too real, and on August 19, 1914, President Wilson urged the American people to be "neutral in fact as well as in name" and "impartial in thought as well as in action." Americans did not find it easy to follow President Wilson's advice. From the beginning they were torn between the desire to avoid war and their sympathy for one side or the other.

Millions of recently naturalized Americans

had friends and relations in Europe. Men and women of German origin—or of Austrian or Turkish origin—wanted the Central Powers to win. Those of Irish origin saw in the war a chance for Ireland to win independence from Great Britain.

On the other hand, most Americans were sympathetic to the Allied Powers. The ties of language, similar democratic governments, and deep-rooted traditions bound Americans to Great Britain. The ties with France were also strong. After all, the French back in 1778 had come to the aid of Americans fighting for their independence. As World War I went on, this sympathy for the Allies led thousands of young Americans to enlist in the British, Canadian, and French armies. A special unit of volunteer American fliers, called the Lafayette Escadrille, was created as part of the new French flying force.

Although in 1914 American sympathies were divided, the great majority of Americans hoped for an Allied victory. However, most Americans supported the President's policy of neutrality and prayed for an early end to the war.

The German plan of attack

The Central Powers, under the leadership of the German High Command, had every intention of ending the war quickly. They intended to conquer France before the Russians could fully mobilize. With France at their mercy, they could then turn against Russia.

Long before the war the French, fearful of German attack, had built powerful fortifications along the entire Franco-German frontier. But the French had not fortified the border between France and Belgium. The French counted on an international agreement, which the Germans had signed, that in the event of war Belgium would be respected as a neutral nation.

The German Chancellor, however, declared that the international agreement respecting Belgium's neutrality was merely "a scrap of paper." And the German High Command launched an offensive against neutral Belgium and Luxembourg, intending to reach the borders of France in six days. As shown on the map on page 212, seven powerful German armies were to strike in a great wheeling action at northern France.

During the long stalemate along the battlefront in Western Europe, both sides used trench warfare. Here, British soldiers leave their trenches to undertake a surprise raid against the Germans.

Failure of the German plan

The German plan failed, largely because Belgium resisted. Fighting gallantly, the small Belgian army compelled the Germans to take 18 days to cross Belgium, not the six called for in the German timetable. This delay gave General Joffre, commander of the French armies, time to rush troops to the Belgian border. It also gave the British time to transport an army of about 90,000 to northern France.

The French and the British arrived too late to save Belgium. Nor were they able to stop the Germans at the Belgian frontier. Crushed by the superior might of the Germans, the French and British retreated to the Marne River, where Joffre hastily prepared his main defense.

Fighting against seemingly hopeless odds, the French and British stopped the German offensive early in September 1914 at the Marne River in the First Battle of the Marne. The Germans then fell back to the Aisne (AYN) River, where they dug a line of trenches and checked an Allied counteroffensive.

The First Battle of the Marne was one of the decisive battles of the war. If the Germans had won, they might have crushed all remaining French and British resistance in a few weeks.

Stalemate on the Western Front

By 1915 the war in Western Europe had reached a stalemate. Both sides were dug in along a 600-mile (965.6-kilometer) line reaching from the Swiss border to the English Channel. During the next three years both the Germans and the Allies, with only a thin strip of land called "no man's land" separating their trenches, fought desperately to gain control of the Western Front. But neither side was able to break through the enemy line or to end the trench warfare. Thousands died in this bloody struggle, but until the spring of 1918 neither side made a significant gain.

There were, to be sure, other fronts—and on all of them, as well as in Western Europe, troops were fighting and dying. The Central Powers and Russia were locked in combat along the entire Eastern Front. Turkish troops defended a precarious line that reached southward through Palestine as far as Medina, in Arabia, against the British and French and their allies. Fighting forces of Austria-Hungary and Italy faced each other in the area of their common boundary north of the Adriatic Sea (see map, page 208).

British interference with American trade

The prospect of a long war was bad news indeed for Americans who hoped to remain neutral. It meant, among other things, that warfare on the high seas would be intensified as Great Britain and Germany tried to prevent supplies from the United States and other neutral countries from reaching the other side.

The British fleet, which controlled the seas, at least during the opening months of the war, blockaded the German coast (see map, page 208) and laid explosive mines in the North Sea. To the angry astonishment of Americans, the British navy also blockaded neutral countries, such as Norway, Sweden, Denmark, and the Netherlands, through which American goods flowed into Germany. American anger increased when the British began to examine American mail bound for Europe and ordered all neutral ships to stop at British ports, where their cargoes were searched.

The United States vigorously protested that Great Britain's actions were "illegal" and a flagrant violation of the "rights of neutrals" to travel the high seas provided they were not carrying war materials.

Submarine warfare

American anger at Great Britain subsided, however, in the face of German submarine warfare.

According to international law, naval vessels of countries at war had the right to stop and search a neutral ship. If the neutral ship carried weapons, munitions, and other materials useful in war, known as *contraband*, the naval vessel had the right to seize the neutral ship and take it into port as a prize of war. If it were impossible to take the neutral vessel into port, the warship was required to take its passengers and crew to a safe place before sinking the prize.

Submarines, however, could not take seized

WESTERN FRONT: 1914-1917

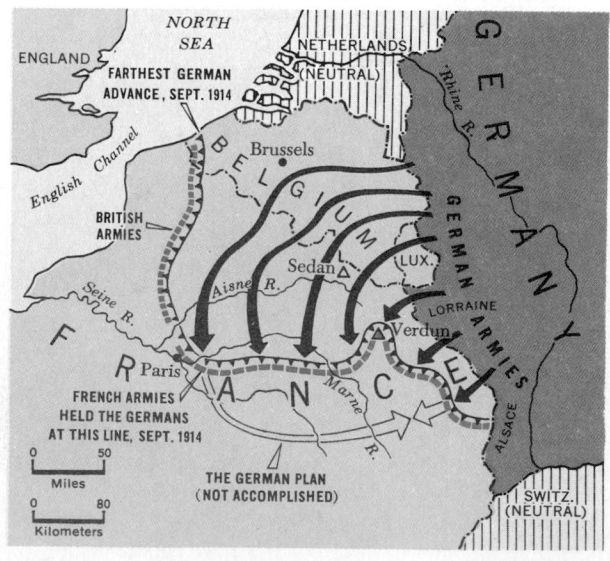

The sinking of the *Lusitania* in May 1915 marked the turning point in American feeling about the war. Most Americans still hoped that war could be avoided, but they now realized that the United States might be forced to fight.

vessels into port because they were not armed to defend themselves against enemy warships while on the surface. Nor could submarines take the passengers and crew of a large vessel on board. Least of all could they surface and search neutral ships, for the moment that they rose to the surface they were "sitting ducks" for even one well-aimed shot from a naval gun. By their very nature, submarines were designed to lurk in the ocean depths, to strike suddenly without warning at an enemy ship, and to get away before a counterattack.

German submarines unleashed

The German surface fleet, although powerful, was still no match for the British navy. The Germans, therefore, had concentrated on building submarines, called U-boats. Early in the war the Germans notified President Wilson that they intended to turn their submarines loose in the Atlantic. President Wilson promptly replied that the United States would hold Germany responsible for any acts that endangered American property and lives on the high seas.

Sinking of the *Lusitania*

The Germans were convinced that their submarine blockade would ruin Great Britain. They therefore ignored President Wilson's warning and ordered their U-boats to patrol the Atlantic shipping lanes. On March 28, 1915, a British steamer was torpedoed and sunk near Ireland, carrying to death more than 100 persons, including an American.

This and other incidents were the prelude to the sinking of the British liner *Lusitania* off the southern coast of Ireland on May 7, 1915, with the loss of 1,198 lives, including 128 Americans. Since the *Lusitania* was carrying war materials bound for England, the Germans believed that their action was justified.

In three strongly worded messages to the German government in Berlin, the American State Department protested against the sinking of the *Lusitania* and warned that any repetition of such action would lead to serious consequences. American anger at the *Lusitania* affair was still at the boiling point when on August 19, 1915 another U-boat sank the *Arabic*, a British liner, with the loss of two American lives.

Alarmed at the furious indignation of the American people, Germany on September 1 gave a written promise that in the future "Liners will not be sunk by our submarines without warning . . . provided that the liners do not try to escape or offer resistance." Americans had to be content with this promise.

The sinking of the *Lusitania* marked a turning point in American feeling about the war. Increasing numbers of Americans began to realize that the conflict in Europe was not far off but close at hand. They began to understand that neutrality might become impossible. Nevertheless, in 1915 most Americans continued to hope that the United States could avoid war.

SECTION SURVEY

IDENTIFY: trench warfare, contraband, U-boats, *Lusitania*.

1. The United States, Wilson asserted, must be "neutral in fact as well as in name" and "impartial in thought as well as in action." Why did Americans find it difficult to heed President Wilson's appeal?
2. America's neutral rights were violated by Great Britain and Germany. Explain.
3. How did Americans react to submarine warfare? Why?
4. Wilson was faced with the dilemma of keeping the United States out of war while making sure that the nation's neutral rights were protected. Comment.

4 Mobilizing American strength for the war effort

From the summer of 1914 to the spring of 1917 the United States moved slowly toward war. As time passed, more and more Americans came to believe that neutrality was impossible.

More sinkings, more promises

In March 1916 the Germans broke their promise and attacked a French passenger vessel, the *Sussex*. Lives were lost and several Americans were injured. President Wilson promptly threatened to break off diplomatic relations with Germany unless it agreed to abandon its methods of submarine warfare.

In what became known as the "*Sussex* pledge," Germany renewed its earlier promise not to sink liners without warning and without providing for the safety of the passengers. But the Germans added an important reservation. They would keep the promise on condition that the United States would persuade the Allies to modify the food blockade of Germany, which, according to Berlin, was inflicting hunger and even starvation on the German people. The United States replied that the British blockade had nothing to do with German violation of American neutral rights on the high seas.

A rising war spirit

American opinion was divided over Wilson's efforts to enforce neutrality. Some people, including former President Theodore Roosevelt, felt that the United States was not firm enough. Others believed that the American government was unwisely going too far in its threatening demands on Berlin. Secretary of State Bryan, for example, resigned during the *Lusitania* crisis. In Bryan's opinion, the United States should forbid American citizens to travel on British and French ships. Bryan also believed that Congress should stop Americans from selling war materials to belligerents.

Preparing for war

President Wilson refused to follow the advice of Bryan and others who shared Bryan's views. Instead, Wilson helped to arouse the public to support a program for strengthening the army and the navy. The National Defense Act, passed in June 1916, increased America's regular army from 106,000 to 175,000 soldiers and provided for officers' training camps. A three-year naval program, begun in 1916, was carried out vigorously. In 1916 the government also created the Council of National Defense and the United States Shipping Board. These agencies planned the mobilization of the country's resources in case of war and began a huge shipbuilding program.

The war preparations did not mean that either the administration or the American public had abandoned all hope of remaining neutral. Indeed, many Americans voted for the re-election of Wilson in November 1916 on the ground that "he kept us out of war."

But six months later, under the leadership of the President and Congress, the American people entered the conflict, millions of them with considerable enthusiasm. What happened to lead the administration to take this momentous step?

Diplomatic relations broken

On February 1, 1917, Germany renewed its unrestricted submarine warfare, thus going back on the "*Sussex* pledge." A German proposal to permit only one American passenger ship to sail to England each week added insult to injury.

The German High Command decided to renew unrestricted submarine warfare, fully aware that this decision would almost certainly bring the United States into the war. The High Command took the calculated risk that submarines could destroy Great Britain's power and will to fight before the United States could provide effective help.

Wilson met the new challenge promptly. On February 3 he broke off diplomatic relations with the German government.

Moving toward war

On February 24 British naval intelligence

agents handed to the American ambassador to Great Britain a German message they had intercepted and decoded. The message had been sent from Germany by Foreign Secretary Arthur Zimmermann to the German minister in Mexico. It contained instructions about what to do in case war broke out between Germany and the United States. In this event, the German minister was to offer Mexico an alliance with Germany. With German support Mexico was to attack the United States and "reconquer the lost territory in New Mexico, Texas, and Arizona." President Wilson released the Zimmermann note to the Associated Press on March 1. Americans were shocked and angry.

On March 12 President Wilson, through the State Department, announced that all American merchant vessels sailing through war zones would be armed for defense against German submarines. The public received this announcement with mixed reactions, but in general approved.

Still other and deeper forces moved American sympathies toward the Allies and toward war with Germany. For one thing, American ties with Great Britain and France were traditionally closer than those with Germany. Not least important, American shipments of munitions to the Allied Powers had risen from $6 million in 1914 to nearly $500 million in 1916, and by April 1917 American bankers had lent about $2 billion to the Allies. Naturally, these American investors wanted an Allied victory. But historians have found no evidence to indicate that economic interests influenced President Wilson's conduct in the critical weeks before the war.

The President's "War Message"

As the weeks passed, President Wilson reluctantly concluded that America's entrance into the war was inevitable. On March 20 he called an emergency cabinet meeting. He and his official advisers gravely considered the entire situation, from the long-standing grievances against Germany to the recent disturbing incidents. Supported by his entire cabinet, the President on March 21 called a special session of Congress for April 2. On April 2, 1917, a solemn and hushed group of Senators, Representatives, and a number of distinguished guests gathered to hear President Wilson present his "War Message."

The President condemned Germany's submarine warfare as "the wanton and wholesale destruction of the lives of noncombatants, men, women, and children, engaged in pursuits which have always, even in the darkest periods of modern history, been deemed innocent and legitimate. Property can be paid for; the lives of peaceful

and innocent people cannot be. . . . The challenge is to all mankind. . . . We will not choose the path of submission and suffer the most sacred rights of our Nation and our people to be ignored or violated," the President declared. "The wrongs against which we now array ourselves are no common wrongs; they cut to the very roots of human life."

Making the world "safe for democracy"

But Wilson was too great an idealist to rest his case upon the evils of unrestricted submarine warfare alone. He also summoned the American people to rise in a crusade for a better world: "We are glad, now that we see the facts with no veil of false pretense about them, to fight thus for the ultimate peace of the world and for the liberation of its peoples, the German peoples in-

The United States entered World War I in April 1917. Before the year ended, nearly 2 million Americans were at military training camps. Here, new soldiers, not yet in uniform, are taught how to salute.

cluded: for the rights of nations great and small and the privilege of men everywhere to choose their way of life and of obedience. The world must be made safe for democracy. Its peace must be planted upon the tested foundations of political liberty. We have no selfish ends to serve. We desire no conquest, no dominion. We seek no indemnities for ourselves, no material compensation for the sacrifices we shall freely make."

War declared

Congress promptly declared war. The Senate approved a war declaration on April 4, the House on April 6, 1917.

America's entry into the conflict had an immediate effect upon other neutral countries. Between April 1917 and July 1918 a number of Latin-American states declared war. Most of the other American countries, although unwilling to enter the war, severed diplomatic relations with Germany.

These soldiers attending a radio class were among the 371,000 black Americans who served in World War I. As in earlier wars, black Americans often faced prejudice and discrimination and were put in separate units.

Raising an army

As soon as war was declared the United States began a vast mobilization of its work force, its industries, and its natural resources. On May 18 Congress adopted the Selective Service Act, which provided for the registration of all men between the ages of 21 and 30. The act was amended on August 31, 1918, to include all men between 18 and 45. Before the war ended more than 24 million Americans were registered by their local draft boards, and 2.8 million of this group were drafted into the army. Before the war ended more than 4.7 million Americans served in the armed forces.

Even before the draft began to operate, construction had been started on training camps. During the summer and fall of 1917 nearly 2 million Americans poured into these camps to begin military training.

Black Americans in uniform

About 371,000 black Americans served in World War I, but, as in earlier wars, they often met prejudice and discrimination. They were restricted to separate units, recreation centers, and living accommodations. Most of the 200,000 black troops sent to Europe served in noncombat battalions, though many of them requested combat duty. All of the 10,000 Negroes who served in the navy were assigned to noncombat duties.

As the war progressed, the bravery and courage of black units under fire were plain to see. The first Allied unit to drive through to the River Rhine was the 369th, a Negro regiment attached to the Ninety-third Division. For outstanding courage in battle, Henry Johnson and Needham Roberts of the 369th became the first black Americans to receive the *Croix de Guerre,* or "cross of war," a coveted French military honor.

Financing the war

To secure money to finance the war, Congress decided to raise approximately two thirds by borrowing, the remaining one third by taxing current income.

The government borrowed money by selling war bonds. Through four "Liberty Loan Drives" and a "Victory Loan Drive," the government borrowed more than $21 billion. The government also raised money by boosting income-tax rates and by levying excise taxes on railroad tickets, telegraph and telephone messages, alcoholic beverages, tobacco, and certain amusements.

Mobilizing industry

Materials were as important as workers and money. The big problem was to stimulate production and prevent waste. To achieve this goal,

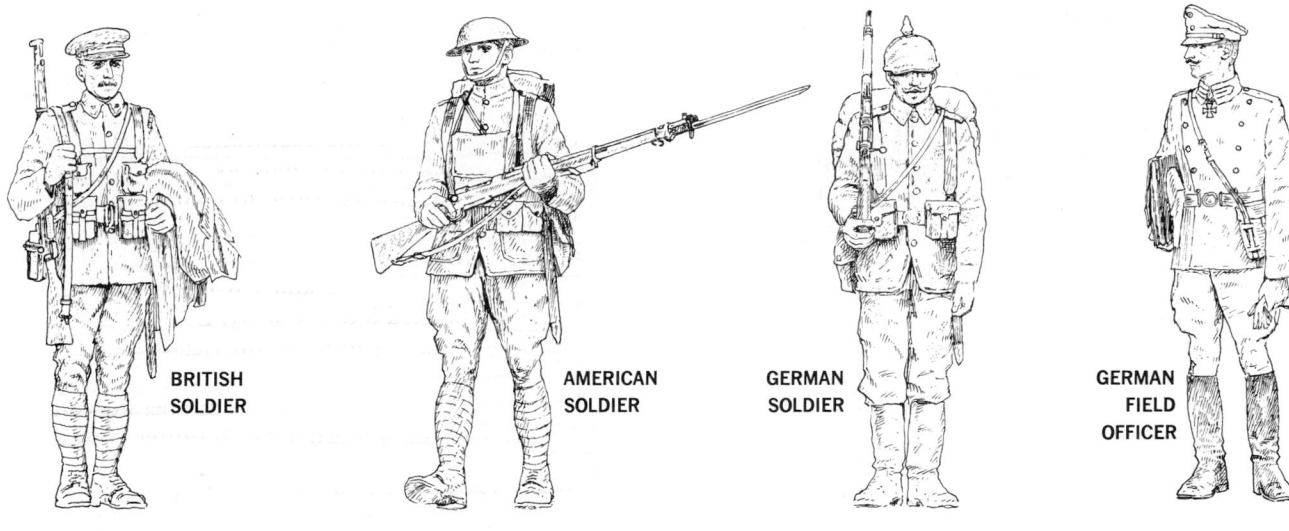

BRITISH
SOLDIER

AMERICAN
SOLDIER

GERMAN
SOLDIER

GERMAN
FIELD
OFFICER

Uniforms of World War I

Congress gave President Wilson sweeping wartime powers. He was authorized to set prices on many commodities, including food and fuels. He was also authorized to regulate, or even to take possession of, factories, mines, meat-packing houses, food-processing plants, and all transportation and communication facilities. The President exercised these vast powers through a number of wartime agencies, or boards.

The War Industries Board, established in 1917, became the virtual dictator of manufacturing. It developed new industries needed in the war effort. It regulated business to eliminate waste and nonessential goods. Before the war's end, the War Industries Board was regulating the production of some 30,000 commodities.

Other federal agencies also took an active part in planning the war program. The War Finance Corporation lent public funds to businesses needing aid in manufacturing war materials. The Emergency Fleet Corporation built ships faster than German submarines could destroy them. The Railroad Administration took over the operation of the railroads, reorganized the lines, and controlled rates and wages in the interest of war efficiency. The Fuel Administration stimulated a larger output of coal and oil, and encouraged economies in their use.

Mobilizing labor

The successful mobilization of industry depended, of course, upon the full cooperation of labor. In an effort to deal with labor disputes, President Wilson in April 1918 appointed the National War Labor Board. This board was

authorized to arbitrate disputes between workers and employers. In June Wilson appointed the War Labor Policies Board. This board was authorized to establish general policies affecting wages, hours, and working conditions. These measures and the cooperation of organized labor reduced labor disputes to a minimum during the war years.

As war-related industries expanded and more and more men entered the armed forces, women helped ease the labor shortages. They worked in shops, factories, the construction industry, even in steel mills. Some became conductors on trolley cars and engineers on trains.

Conserving food

The problem of food was equally critical. Late in 1917, in part to help conserve grain, which is used in making alcohol, Congress adopted and submitted to the states an amendment to the Constitution prohibiting the manufacture, sale, or transportation of alcoholic liquors. This Eighteenth Amendment was ratified by the necessary three fourths of the states in 1919, and went into effect on January 16, 1920.

The government also made other moves to guarantee food for the American people and their allies. Herbert Hoover, who had successfully managed food relief in war-stricken Belgium, was placed in charge of the Food Administration. Hoover brought about a vast expansion of agriculture, reduced the hoarding and waste of food, encouraged people to plant "victory gardens," and urged them to observe "wheatless" and "meatless" days. The sale of sugar and other commodities was limited. All this took place without rationing. Instead the Food Administration, with the crucial help of women's groups, used publicity and persuasion to get people to co-operate in conserving food.

Mobilizing public opinion

The government also undertook to gain the cooperation of all Americans in the war effort.

The Committee on Public Information circulated millions of leaflets describing in glowing language America's official war aims and denouncing the German government. Colleges, schools, the press, churches, fraternal lodges, women's organizations, and civic groups all cooperated with the government's campaign "to sell the war to the American people." In all sorts of public gatherings, the war aims were publicized in brief speeches delivered by well-known people.

Colleges, schools, the press, churches, fraternal lodges, women's organizations, and civic groups all cooperated with the government's campaign "to sell the war to the American people." This poster illustrates some of the roles of American women during the war.

Controlling dissent

From the beginning most Americans enthusiastically supported the war. There were, however, some dissenters, who, in greater or lesser measure, were not in sympathy with the war effort.

To deal with these people, Congress in June 1917 adopted the Espionage Act. This act was aimed at treasonable and disloyal activities. In May 1918 Congress strengthened the Espionage Act by an amendment, often called the Sedition Act. This act provided penalties of up to $10,000 in fines and 20 years' imprisonment, or both, for anyone found guilty of interfering with the sale of war bonds, attempting to curtail production, or using "disloyal, profane, scurrilous, or abusive language" about the American form of government or any of its agencies.

Operating under these laws, the Department of Justice arrested at least 1,597 persons. Of these, 41 received prison sentences of from 10 to 20 years. In addition, newspapers and periodicals that criticized the government's conduct of the war were deprived of their mailing privileges.

Many loyal Americans, themselves thoroughly in sympathy with the war effort, objected to the Espionage Act and the Sedition Act. They held that the constitutional rights of citizens should not be interfered with, even in wartime.

For the most part, however, Americans did not need persuasive arguments or restrictive laws to secure their loyalty. Americans entered the war on a great wave of enthusiasm, convinced, as Wilson had put it, that this was indeed a crusade "to make the world safe for democracy."

SECTION SURVEY

IDENTIFY: "*Sussex* pledge," Zimmermann note, unrestricted submarine warfare, Selective Service Act, Espionage Act; Henry Johnson; April 1917.

1. In his War Message, President Wilson asked Congress to declare war on Germany. (a) What reasons did he give? (b) Why did he view the war as a crusade?
2. How did the United States mobilize (a) workers, (b) industries, (c) natural resources, (d) public opinion?
3. In the crusade "to make the world safe for democracy," black members of the armed forces often faced discrimination. How do you explain this contradiction?
4. During wartime, the right to dissent should be curtailed by the federal government. Do you agree or disagree? Explain.

5 The role of American troops and ideals in helping to win the war

America's declaration of war came none too soon. In the spring of 1917 the Allies were facing a grim situation, and by the end of the year their position was desperate.

The military situation in 1917

By early 1917 the Allies, who had suffered enormous losses, were war weary and discouraged. In March they were further disturbed by news that the tsar of Russia had been deposed and a new revolutionary government established.

America's entry into the conflict in April was one of the few bright spots in a year during which Allied fortunes sank lower and lower.

In the fall Germany threw a number of crack divisions into the Austrian campaign, and on October 24 a combined force of Austrians and Germans crashed through the Italian lines at Caporetto (see map, page 208). French and British troops, rushed from the Western Front, helped to stop the rout and saved Italy from collapse.

Most serious of all, however, was the news from Russia. On November 7 the Bolsheviks, a party of radical Communists, seized power. A month later the Bolsheviks signed an armistice with Germany. Almost three months later, in March 1918, they concluded the peace treaty of Brest-Litovsk (BREST lih·TOFSK). Meanwhile Rumania, unable to stand alone against the Central Powers in eastern Europe, had sued for peace and in 1918 signed a peace treaty at Bucharest.

Thus by the end of 1917 the Germans were free to concentrate most of their forces on the Western Front. General Ludendorff, commander of the German armies, prepared for an offensive intended to end the war before American troops could play an important role.

American naval forces

Meanwhile the United States Navy, which had been rapidly building its strength since 1916, went into action. Before the war ended, Admiral William S. Sims, Commander of the United States Naval Forces Operating in European Waters, had established 45 naval bases, which were located as far north as Murmansk, in Russia, and as far south as Greece.

In cooperation with the British navy, American naval forces patrolled the North Sea and effectively bottled up the German fleet. They also laid most of a 230-mile (370.1-kilometer) barrier of mines that stretched across the North Sea from Norway to the Orkney Islands (see map, page 208). This barrier greatly increased the hazards for German submarines seeking to reach the open waters of the Atlantic Ocean or to return to their bases in Germany.

Meanwhile other naval vessels helped to convoy merchant ships and troop transports through the submarine-infested waters of the Atlantic Ocean. The Anglo-American convoy system was so effective that 2 million soldiers or more were transported to Europe with the loss of only a few hundred lives. It was a remarkable tribute to naval efficiency. It was also a severe blow to the German High Command.

Arrival of the A.E.F. in France

While the United States Navy was busy on the high seas, American land forces were being organized.

President Wilson appointed General John J. Pershing as Commander of the American Expeditionary Forces (the A.E.F.). Pershing, a West Point graduate, had served in Cuba, in the Philippines, and in 1916 as commander of the expedition sent into Mexico to capture Pancho Villa.

Pershing landed in France early in June 1917. By the end of June the first regiments of the First Division arrived, and on July 4 several thousand "Yanks" marched through Paris amid the heartfelt cheers of the French people.

American troops arrived in ever-swelling numbers. By May 1918 they were pouring in at the rate of 10,000 a day. By the fall of 1918 more than 2 million had landed in France. To supply and maintain this huge army, the Americans built huge docks and railroads as well as vast networks of telephone and telegraph lines in Europe. They landed 17,000 freight cars and more than 40,000 trucks. The Americans also built training camps, hospitals, storage houses, and ammunition dumps.

Germany's last bid for victory

On March 21, 1918, the Western Front exploded into violent action as the Germans, reinforced by seasoned troops released from the Russian front, launched a powerful campaign, or "peace offensive," to end the war. At the end of two weeks the Germans had gained a large area of land and inflicted 160,000 casualties. By the end of May they were at the River Marne, only 37 miles (59.5 kilometers) from Paris.

Pershing's original plans had called for a period of training behind the lines before his troops went into action. He had also insisted that American troops fight as a separate army under their own top command. But in the spring of 1918 he consented to putting every available sol-

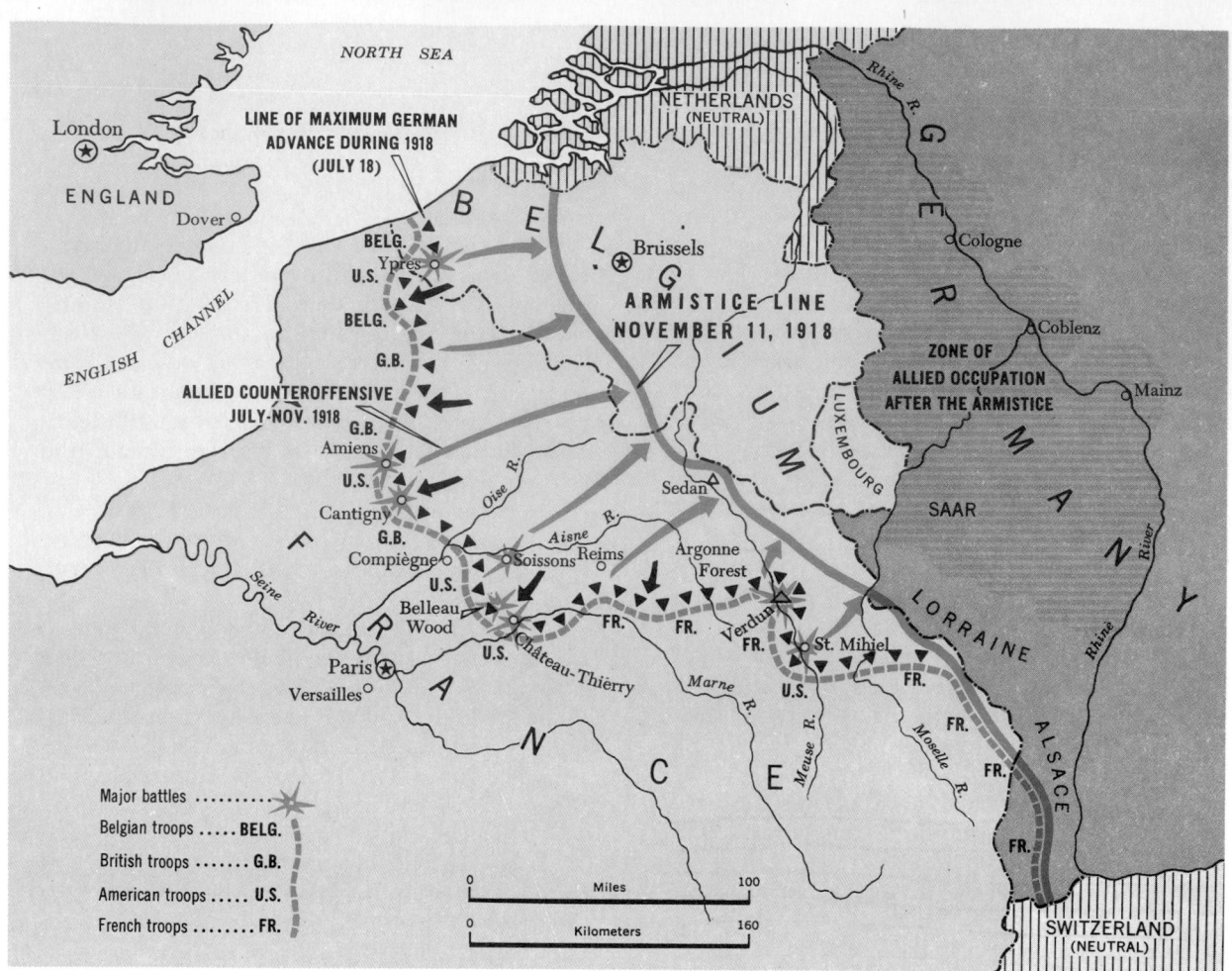

NORTH SEA

London ⊛

ENGLAND

Dover ○

ENGLISH CHANNEL

LINE OF MAXIMUM GERMAN ADVANCE DURING 1918 (JULY 18)

NETHERLANDS (NEUTRAL)

BEL. G. I U M

Brussels ○

ARMISTICE LINE NOVEMBER 11, 1918

BELG.

Ypres ○

U.S.

BELG.

G.B.

ALLIED COUNTEROFFENSIVE JULY–NOV. 1918

G.B.

Amiens ○

U.S.

Cantigny ○

G.B.

Compiègne ○

Soissons ○

Aisne R.

Reims

Argonne Forest

Sedan ○

Cologne ○

G E R M A N Y

Coblenz ○

ZONE OF ALLIED OCCUPATION AFTER THE ARMISTICE

Mainz ○

LUXEMBOURG

SAAR

Rhine R.

U.S.

Belleau Wood

FR.

FR.

FR.

Verdun ○

St. Mihiel ○

LORRAINE

U.S.

Château-Thierry

Marne R.

U.S.

Meuse R.

FR.

FR.

FR.

Moselle R.

Rhine River

ALSACE

FR.

SWITZERLAND (NEUTRAL)

Paris ⊛

Versailles ○

Seine River

F R A N C E

Major battles .... ✳

Belgian troops ..... BELG.

British troops .... G.B.

American troops ..... U.S.

French troops .... FR.

Miles 0 ——— 100

Kilometers 0 ——— 160

ALLIED VICTORY IN WORLD WAR I

dier into the lines immediately. French, British, and American troops fought under a unified Allied command directed by the French military leader, Marshal Foch (FOSH).

Stopping the German advance

Fighting desperately, French, British, Belgian, and American troops finally stopped the Germans. On May 28 the First Division of the United States Army took Cantigny (kahn·tee·NYEE). Three days later the Third Division, in a last ditch defense of Paris, only 40 miles (64.4 kilometers) away, helped the French hold the Germans at Château-Thierry (shah·TOH teh·REE). At Belleau (BEL·loh) Wood the Second Division, strengthened by the 4th Marine Brigade, held back the Germans in six days of fighting (see map, this page).

Then, on July 15, the Germans threw everything they could into one final ferocious assault around Reims (REEMZ). In this action, the beginning of the Second Battle of the Marne, the Allied lines held. And on July 18 Marshal Foch ordered

a counterattack spearheaded by the First and Second American Divisions and the First French Morocco Division. The Germans began to fall back. The tide at last had turned.

The Allied victory drive

The Allies now took the initiative. In July Foch launched a terrific offensive along the entire length of the line. The Germans were driven back.

Fighting as a separate American army under General Pershing's command, the American troops, 500,000 strong and supported by French troops and British planes, launched a powerful attack on the area around St. Mihiel (SAN mee·YEL) in September 1918. After three days of savage fighting, this section of the southern front was under American control.

Then, against withering artillery and machinegun fire, the Americans drove toward Sedan, the highly fortified position that the Germans had held since 1914. For 47 days the United States troops pushed toward their objective. The fighting in this tremendous Meuse-Argonne (MYOOZ ahr·GUN) offensive involved 1.2 million combatants. The Americans alone suffered 120,-000 casualties. But they pushed the German line back 30 miles (48.3 kilometers) and captured 28,000 prisoners and large supplies of war materials.

Important though they were, the American victories represented only part of the tremendous offensive against the crumbling German lines. Belgians, British, and French, confident of victory, were fighting fiercely against the enemy along the entire front.

Under these hammer blows German morale began to sag, and Germany's allies lost heart. In September the Turkish armies in Palestine and Arabia suffered crushing blows, and Bulgaria surrendered unconditionally. On November 3 the crews of the German ships at Kiel, a German naval base, mutinied rather than go to sea. Army units also mutinied, and riots broke out in German cities. On November 3 Austria signed an armistice with the Italians.

Convinced at last that the war was lost, Kaiser Wilhelm II, ruler of Germany, fled to the Netherlands, leaving his country in the hands of revolutionists, who signed an armistice with the Allies on November 11, 1918.

The armistice terms

The armistice was signed in a railroad car in the forest of Compiègne (kon·PYEN·y) in France on the eleventh hour of the eleventh day of the eleventh month of 1918. The Germans signed grimly, for the terms of the armistice were severe.

The Germans agreed to evacuate France, Belgium, Luxembourg, and Alsace-Lorraine without delay. They agreed to surrender to the Allies an enormous amount of war materials, including most of Germany's naval vessels, and to return prisoners, money, and all valuables taken from the occupied countries. They agreed to renounce the Treaty of Brest-Litovsk with Russia and the Treaty of Bucharest with Rumania.

In addition, the Allies reserved the right to occupy all German territory west of the Rhine as well as a strip of territory about 18 miles (29 kilometers) wide along the east bank of the Rhine (see map, page 220).

Wilson's Fourteen Points

An American expression of idealism, as well as American fighting strength, played a large part in breaking the Central Powers' will to fight. This important part of the story of World War I goes back to the early winter of 1917–18.

As you recall, in November 1917 the Bol-sheviks seized control of Russia and shortly thereafter signed a peace treaty with Germany. At this time the Bolsheviks published a number of secret treaties that the Allies had drawn up at the beginning of the war. These secret treaties outlined in detail how the Allies planned to divide the spoils of war if they were successful in defeating the Central Powers.

President Wilson chose this opportunity to lay before the world what he firmly believed was "the only possible program for world peace." Wilson's program, which he presented to Congress on January 8, 1918, included fourteen principles, or "points."

The first group of points aimed to end the causes of modern war, as Wilson understood these causes. Specifically, he called for open, instead of secret, diplomacy; for freedom of the seas instead of their control by the strong naval powers; for removal of tariffs and other economic barriers between nations; for reduction of land weapons; and for temporary international control of colonies in place of the existing imperialism.

President Wilson also called for the liberation of peoples whose lands had long been ruled by Russia, Austria-Hungary, Germany, and Turkey. Among these peoples were the Poles, Czechs, Slovaks, and South Slavs. Wilson's proposal also included the people living in the German-held region of Alsace-Lorraine. These and other groups were to have the right of "self-determination." That is, they were to decide for themselves the country in which they wished to live.

But the "Fourteenth Point" was the heart of President Wilson's program. With this famous point Wilson urged the creation of a "general association of nations" to give "mutual guarantees of political independence and territorial integrity to great and small states alike."

Influence of Wilson's program

The Fourteen Points and statements explaining them were printed during the war in the languages of the peoples of central Europe and dropped by plane into the heart of enemy country. All this publicity encouraged the Slavic peoples within Germany and Austria-Hungary to boycott the war efforts of their rulers and to speed up their own liberation. Even the German people read the Fourteen Points and found in President Wilson's program hope for a just and lasting peace rather than a continued regime of absolute rule and militarism under the Kaiser.

Moreover, as defeat pressed closer upon them the German and Austrian peoples saw in the Fourteen Points an escape from the harsh penalties that the Allies would otherwise impose upon them. Thus when the great German military offensives failed in the summer of 1918, and when President Wilson made it clear that he would not negotiate with any German authority that was not representative of the people, the people of Germany and Austria-Hungary took steps to overthrow their rulers.

President Wilson and millions of Americans had entered the conflict with the burning conviction that they were waging a crusade "to make the world safe for democracy." In the winter of 1918–19 many Americans believed that this goal was at last in sight.

SECTION SURVEY

IDENTIFY: Bolsheviks, "Yanks," convoy, armistice, idealism, self-determination; Admiral Sims, General Pershing, Marshal Foch; November 11, 1918.

1. What contributions did the United States Navy make to winning the war?
2. Discuss the part played by the A.E.F. in defeating the German army.
3. Who considered the armistice terms of 1918 severe? Why?
4. (a) Why were Wilson's Fourteen Points considered an expression of American idealism? (b) Why was the Fourteenth Point the heart of Wilson's program?

CHAPTER SURVEY

INQUIRING INTO HISTORY

1. What part did American troops play in the victory of the Allies?
2. President Wilson preached a moral crusade in the fighting of World War I. Comment on how this crusade helped win victory for the Allies.
3. What powers of the President are important in time of war?
4. (a) How do you think war advances technological development? (b) How did technological developments change the nature of war by 1914?
5. (a) Why have scientists become as important in modern warfare as politicians and soldiers? (b) Do you think scientists should make value judgments about the kinds of weapons their research will lead to? Explain.
6. The end of World War I brought with it a spirit of high idealism and hope to people throughout the world. Explain.
7. Nearly 20 million persons, both military and civilian, were killed or disabled during World War I. The material damage due to the war is estimated at 28 billion dollars. How do you think these losses affected world conditions after the war?

RELATING PAST TO PRESENT

1. Were American newspapers completely objective during World War I? Do you think they are objective in reporting current conflicts? Explain.
2. Why are civil liberties often restricted during a period of crisis? Are civil liberties in the United States being restricted today? Explain.
3. Do other nations still look to the United States for leadership in the difficult task of building a peaceful world? Explain.

DEVELOPING SOCIAL SCIENCE SKILLS

1. Examine the poster on page 218. (a) What roles does it show for women? (b) Were any of these roles new for women? (c) What effects do you think World War I had on the movement for women's rights?
2. Make a two-column chart, listing the ways America's rights as a neutral nation were violated by Great Britain and by Germany. Why do you think the United States went to war against Germany and not against Great Britain?
3. Read accounts by soldiers, or a book such as *All Quiet on the Western Front,* describing the fighting in World War I. (a) How does what you read compare with your ideas about war? (b) What effects does fighting a war have on individuals?

The "Golden Twenties"
1920-1932

CHAPTER 14
FROM PROSPERITY TO ECONOMIC COLLAPSE
1920-1932

On December 4, 1918, President Wilson and many of his official advisers left New York harbor on the army transport *George Washington* bound for Europe and the peace conference at Versailles (vair·sɪ) near Paris. The vessel docked at Brest, France, on December 13. While waiting for the conference to open, President Wilson visited Paris, London, Rome, and other European cities. People gave him a tumultuous welcome everywhere he went.

But Wilson's triumph was short-lived. At the peace conference all the bitterness of four long years of warfare burst into the open. Wilson did win acceptance of his proposal for a League of Nations designed to safeguard the peace. But in the process he had to compromise many of his principles.

By 1920 it was clear that a large majority of the American people had rejected Wilson's leadership. As you will read in the next chapter, the United States refused to join the League of Nations and, in a sense, turned its back upon Europe. And as you will learn in the following pages, Americans by and large also turned their backs upon Wilson's domestic policies. In the election of 1920 they chose a Republican President to lead the nation.

During the decade of the 1920's three Republican Presidents—Warren G. Harding, Calvin Coolidge, and Herbert Hoover—presided over a country that on the whole enjoyed a period of unparalleled prosperity. But the era of the "Golden Twenties" ended with an economic collapse and the most shattering depression in American history.

THE CHAPTER IN OUTLINE

1. Loss of popularity for Woodrow Wilson and the Democratic Party.

2. Republican control of the government during the "Golden Twenties."

3. The prosperity of the 1920's shattered by the Great Depression.

1450   1750   1800   1850   1900   1950   1980's

1 Loss of popularity for Woodrow Wilson and the Democratic Party

Before America's entry into the war President Wilson had concentrated on his program of domestic reform. As you have read, his first administration, from 1913 to 1917, reduced tariffs, strengthened the antitrust laws, and established the Federal Reserve System. In these and other ways, Wilson tried to restore competition in American business and to protect the consumer.

Even before the war, however, Wilson felt that the "New Freedom" program had largely achieved its goals. And after the war he became deeply involved in organizing world peace. As a result, he had little time left for such difficult domestic problems as a postwar business slump, a decline in farm prices, and widespread unemployment.

Losing support at home

The American people, however, were tired of international issues. They were more interested in their nation's domestic affairs than in a peace treaty or a League of Nations. The Congressional elections of 1918, held just a few days before the armistice, showed how the political winds were blowing. President Wilson appealed to the voters to return a Democratic Congress. Ignoring his appeal, they elected a Republican majority in both the House and Senate.

Wilson's illness

When Wilson returned from the Versailles Conference in the summer of 1919, he found many Senators critical of the Covenant, or constitution, of the League of Nations. But the President refused to compromise on the covenant's basic points. Instead, he tried to win the American public to his point of view.

Late in the summer of 1919, after three weeks of a grueling nationwide speaking tour, Wilson suffered a stroke which left him partially paralyzed. His condition improved somewhat, but he remained an invalid until his death in 1924.

The postwar depression

Wilson's illness came at a time when the country was suffering from a severe postwar depression. With the signing of the armistice, the government began to cancel its wartime contracts. Business executives in wartime industries

President Wilson worked tirelessly but unsuccessfully to gain the support of the American people for the League of Nations. Here, he is on a nationwide speaking tour in the summer of 1919.

suddenly faced the problem of reconverting their plants to peacetime production. New machinery had to be installed, new customers found. During the reconversion, factories closed down or operated with greatly reduced labor forces.

Farmers also suffered during the transition from war to peace. As European farm lands returned to normal production, the American farmers' wartime markets in Europe disappeared. Farm prices, which had soared during the war, dropped as competition increased. Wheat, for example, which had sold for as high as $2.26 a bushel (35.2 liters), dropped to less than $1 a bushel in 1922. Almost half a million American farmers lost their farms because they were unable to pay their debts during this troubled period.

Meanwhile wage earners were also suffering. Many of those who had worked in government wartime agencies lost their jobs when the war ended. Hundreds of thousands of industrial wage earners were thrown out of work when factories closed down or curtailed operations. Many of the 4.5 million returning members of the armed forces could not find work.

As the depression deepened, as wages fell, and as more people lost their jobs, discontent swelled alarmingly. To make things worse, the high cost of living, stimulated by the war, rose even higher. In 1919 it climbed 77 percent above pre-war levels. In 1920 it rose an additional 28 percent. Under such conditions, many workers resorted to strikes. During 1919 more than 4 million workers were at one time or another out on strike. Three of the strikes were especially serious.

The Boston police strike

On September 9 the Boston police force left their posts to strike for higher wages and improved conditions. The strike left Boston without police protection. When rioting and looting broke out, the state guard was called in. The police force, realizing that the strike was lost, announced that they would return to their posts.

At this point, however, the Boston police commissioner refused to allow the strikers to return to their jobs. He announced that he intended to hire a new police force. Governor Calvin Coolidge supported the commissioner. "There is no right," Coolidge flatly stated, "to strike against the public safety by anybody, anywhere, any time." Coolidge's statement was widely applauded all over the country. It brought him to public attention and helped him to win the Vice-Presidential nomination on the 1920 Republican ticket.

The coal strike

Less than two months after this police strike, on November 1, 1919, the United Mine Workers (U.M.W.) went out on strike. Led by their newly elected, colorful, and pugnacious president, John L. Lewis, they demanded higher wages and a shorter work week. On November 9 United States Attorney General A. Mitchell Palmer secured an injunction against the union, which ordered the officers of the U.M.W. to stop all activities tending to encourage the strikers.

But the coal miners refused to return to work. Finally, on President Wilson's suggestion, the problem was submitted to a board of arbitration. The board gave the miners a 27-percent wage increase, but refused to consider a reduction in the weekly hours of work.

The steel strike

Meanwhile, discontent in the steel industry led to a strike involving more than 300,000 workers. The steelworkers had long been dissatisfied with their working conditions. In some plants they worked as long as 12 hours a day, 7 days a week. Moreover, they had not been able to form a union to bargain for them. During the summer of 1919, however, a number of A. F. of L. unions formed a committee which launched a vigorous organizing campaign in the steel towns. The strike started on September 22, 1919, after management refused to recognize the committee's right to speak for all steelworkers.

As the weeks passed, violence erupted around some of the steel mills. At Gary, Indiana, martial law was declared, and federal troops moved in to keep order. Finally, with public opinion running against the steelworkers, the strike was called off, and in January 1920 the strikers returned to their jobs. Three years later, however, the steel companies agreed to establish an 8-hour day.

Labor's declining strength

The postwar depression did not last long. By early 1920 American export trade was soaring as orders for goods poured in from the war-devastated countries. The value of American exports rose to three times the 1913 level.

As economic conditions improved and jobs became more plentiful, many workers lost interest in unions. Membership in the A. F. of L., which had reached a peak of more than 4 million early in 1920, began to decline.

There were, of course, other reasons for the decline of the labor movement. The failure of the steel strike and of other strikes during 1919 discouraged workers. The use of the injunction, as in the strike of the United Mine Workers, was another discouraging factor. And the Supreme Court, in a series of decisions, broadened the base for use of the injunction, restricted labor organizing activities, and ruled unconstitutional legislation intended to improve working conditions. Industrial management, moreover, launched a widely publicized campaign against "the union shop," and identified labor unions with socialism and Communism. A "Red scare" that swept the country in 1919–20 caused large numbers of citizens, including many workers, to turn against organized labor.

The "Red scare"

During the postwar years federal and state governments conducted a vigorous drive against anarchists, Communists, and socialists. The Espionage Act, passed in wartime to punish treasonable or disloyal activities, remained in effect after the war. Under this law, revolutionists and suspected revolutionists were arrested and fined. Some of those arrested were aliens who were deported to the countries from which they had come.

One important reason for the postwar concern with radicals was the Russian Bolshevik Revolution of 1917. This event frightened many Americans who feared that radicals in the United States might try to follow the Bolshevik example. Rumors of revolutionary plots circulated widely from 1917 through 1920.

But there was more than rumor to arouse alarm, even though radical leaders disapproved of acts of irresponsible violence. During the spring and summer of 1919 more than 30 bombs were discovered by postal authorities in packages addressed to prominent citizens. And in New York City on September 16, 1920, a bomb exploded in crowded Wall Street at noontime, killing 38 persons, injuring hundreds, and causing property damage that was variously estimated at from $500,000 to $2.5 million.

Meanwhile, in the fall of 1919 Attorney General Palmer had instructed agents in the Department of Justice to arrest radical agitators throughout the country. Among those arrested were several hundred aliens who were deported.

Criticism of the "Palmer raids"

A number of Americans, both Democrats and Republicans, criticized this drive against radical movements, pointing out that many of the raids were conducted without search warrants. They argued that the Attorney General sometimes ignored the constitutional rights of free citizens.

But it was not just against Attorney General Palmer that the critics directed their fire. During

this postwar period about one third of the states had passed laws to punish advocates of revolutionary change. By 1920 a growing number of Americans who had no sympathy with radicals were becoming increasingly alarmed at the widespread violation of civil liberties. Many leaders of both political parties agreed with President Wilson that Americans could not solve their problems by trying to suppress unpopular political views.

Rising racial tensions

With the growth of northern industry before World War I, many black families had moved from the South to northern industrial centers, hoping to escape lives of poverty and discrimination. The war, with its heavy demand for industrial workers, caused this migration to increase. During the war about half a million southern black wage earners found jobs in the coal mines of West Virginia and Illinois, the meat-packing plants of Chicago, the steel mills of Pittsburgh, the automobile factories of Detroit, and the industries of other large cities.

But black families did not find in the North the equality of opportunity they sought. Black wage earners got the hardest jobs and the lowest pay. Northern white wage earners sometimes staged protest strikes against employment of black workers, especially when industrialists used black laborers as strike breakers. Racial tensions in the North began to rise alarmingly.

Disappointed hopes

A war being fought "to make the world safe for democracy" naturally aroused the hopes of black Americans who looked forward to new and greater freedom at home. Many decided to hasten the day by taking a stronger stand for their rights. In the summer of 1917, 15,000 Negroes in New York City marched in a "silent parade," to the beat of muffled drums, to protest the rising racial tension and violence directed against Negroes.

Black soldiers returning from Europe, where they had been treated as equals, especially by the French, were angry and disappointed that conditions in the United States were little changed. They were especially discouraged to find a new Ku Klux Klan operating in the North as well as in the South. The new Klan harassed Jews, Catholics, foreign-born citizens, and everyone else it chose to call dangerous and "un-American." But Negroes were the special object of Klan violence.

There were other reasons for bitterness among black Americans in the North. During the postwar business depression, competition for

In the summer of 1917, 15,000 Negroes in New York City marched in a "silent parade," to the beat of muffled drums, to protest rising racial tension and violence against black Americans.

jobs between white and black workers became fierce, and the white workers usually got the jobs. There was also a troublesome housing shortage as a result of wartime building restrictions. And when black families tried to move into white neighborhoods, racial friction became acute.

The riots of 1919

During 1919 riots in more than 20 cities, North and South, brought death and injury to hundreds of women and men and destroyed thousands of tenements in city slum areas.

The riots generally began when Negroes fought against some especially discriminatory act. Frightened white citizens, convinced that black Americans were trying to threaten them and gain control, responded with violence. Police forces, ill-equipped to deal with riots, usually sided with white citizens, causing black Americans to take even more desperate actions.

The riots solved no problems. Nor did they spur local or national officials to try to remedy even the more obvious causes of the trouble. As a result, some black Americans decided to take more militant actions. They were now more ready to follow leaders who insisted that black citizens, no less than white, had a lawful right to defend themselves when the law failed to do so.

Despite the many proofs that the North was no utopia for Negroes, southern black families continued to migrate to northern cities. Between 1910 and 1930 the black population of the northern states more than doubled, rising from a little over 1 million to nearly 2.5 million. The racial problem in the United States was no longer largely a southern problem—it was now a national concern.

Other minority problems

Some Americans were aware that other racial and ethnic problems in the nation were becoming critical. By the 1920's it was increasingly clear that the policy of "Americanizing" the Indians under the Dawes Act (page 76) was a failure. Individual farm ownership was contrary to Indian traditions. Many tribes had never engaged in farming. Indians who did try to learn modern methods of farming often had to struggle with worn out, non-fertile land. As for education, the government-sponsored boarding schools and day schools deprived Indian children of their tribal and family identity but gave them no identity that they could find meaningful. As they grew older, many of them tried unsuccessfully to live in two different worlds, neither of which suited their needs.

In 1924 the Indian population as a whole received United States citizenship, partly in recognition of the services of young Indian men who had volunteered to fight in World War I. But citizenship did not lessen the harsh fact that Indian poverty was greater than that of any other group in the United States. The discovery of oil on some Indian lands, among them Osage lands in Oklahoma, brought unexpected riches to a few Indians. But for Indians as a whole, life was grim. Still, earlier predictions that the Indians were a vanishing race proved incorrect. The Indian population in the United States increased from about 243,000 in 1863 to about 350,000 in 1924.

In 1928 a penetrating report by Lewis Meriam of the Institute for Government Research described forcibly the neglected, destructive conditions on Indian reservations. This report played an important part, as you will read later, in the adoption of new Indian policies in the 1930's.

Mexican immigrants

Many former citizens of Mexico became United States citizens, you recall, at the close of the Mexican War in 1848. In the 1890's Mexicans began immigrating into the American Southwest, many of them seeking jobs, some of them escaping from the troubled political and economic conditions in Mexico. In the 1920's about half a million new Mexican immigrants arrived.

Most of these immigrants were poor families from rural areas. These newcomers were forced to work for low wages as migrant laborers in agriculture, in mines, in railroad maintenance, and in the cities of the Southwest and, increasingly, the Middle West. As poor and ill-educated newcomers, they felt the burden of prejudice directed by English-speaking Americans toward all Mexican-Americans. They were discriminated against in jobs, housing, recreation centers, and schools. Established labor groups resented them because they lowered wage scales by accepting, out of dire necessity, almost any rate of pay. White resentment also grew because these new immigrants could cross and recross the southwestern border as economic conditions in Mexico improved or worsened.

Election of 1920

In the Presidential election of 1920, the country's unsettled condition gave the Republican candidate, Senator Warren G. Harding of Ohio, a clear advantage over his Democratic opponent, Governor James M. Cox of Ohio. Many voters blamed the administration in office for the troubled times, including the race riots and other minority problems. The Republicans' plea for a return to "normalcy" had great appeal. Many

Today Indian children study their own rich culture and heritage. But in the early 1900's, schools were used to "Americanize" Indians—to have them give up their tribal customs and heritage.

Americans were tired of Europe and its wars, tired of Wilson's attempts to "make the world safe for democracy." Business people were worried about the 1919 depression of business. Workers and farmers felt that their problems, among them unemployment and falling prices, were being neglected.

Thus Harding won the election with approximately 16 million votes to Cox's 9 million. The electoral vote was even more sweeping, giving Harding 404 to Cox's 127. Eugene V. Debs, the Socialist candidate, who was in prison for violating the Espionage Act, received nearly 1 million votes.

The election of 1920 was the first Presidential contest in which all eligible women could vote. The long struggle for woman suffrage had been won in August 1920, when the Nineteenth Amendment went into effect.

Fading party differences

In the decade that followed their defeat in 1920, the Democrats failed, with a few exceptions, to work out a clear-cut program to challenge the Republicans. They turned away from the spirit of reform that had characterized Wilson's first administration. More and more the Democrats accepted the same conservative principles followed by the Republicans. Both parties supported high tariffs and believed that big business should be let alone. As the years passed, it became increasingly difficult to distinguish between the two parties.

SECTION SURVEY

IDENTIFY: Bolshevik Revolution, the riots of 1919, return to "normalcy," Nineteenth Amendment; John L. Lewis, Warren G. Harding.

1. World War I brought about many dislocations in American life, including a rising cost of living, increased unemployment, and declining profits for large corporations. How does this information relate to the following: (a) strikes, (b) rising racial tensions, (c) the election of 1920?
2. (a) What conditions produced the "Red scare"? (b) How was organized labor affected by the "Red scare"? Why?
3. Many Americans criticized the drive against radicals because it involved a widespread violation of civil liberties. Comment.
4. Why were poor Americans particularly affected by the economic conditions of the postwar period?

2 Republican control of the government during the "Golden Twenties"

Warren G. Harding, who was inaugurated on March 4, 1921, was a genial Ohio newspaper owner who had climbed to the top of the political ladder in his own state. Before becoming President he had served as a United States Senator. Handsome and distinguished, with a warm, easygoing manner—much too easygoing, as it turned out—he had many friends in every walk of life.

Farm relief and financial reform

Harding did not take over an easy job when he entered the White House. Late in 1920 a second postwar depression had hit the country. Farmers, wage earners, business leaders, and the public in general were clamoring for government action and for the fulfillment of the President's promise of a return to "normalcy."

Responding to widespread demands for help, Congress adopted the Emergency Tariff on May 27, 1921. This measure raised rates on some farm products, but failed to raise farm prices generally.

In June Congress adopted the Budget and Accounting Act. The new measure was designed to reduce excessive spending and waste in government, and to provide a more efficient method of handling government expenditures. It also created a Bureau of the Budget in the Treasury Department, with a director appointed by the President.

Up to this time Congress had made annual appropriations on a piecemeal basis, with no great concern for "balancing the budget." Under the new system, all government agencies and departments had to submit annual requests for funds to the Director of the Budget. The director then had to draw up a detailed budget, listing estimated income and expenditures for the coming *fiscal year.°* Once the budget was prepared, the President submitted it to Congress, which could, if it chose, raise or lower the estimates.

Charles G. Dawes, the first director of the budget, was an extremely capable administrator. Under his leadership and that of the Secretary of the Treasury, Andrew W. Mellon, the government began to use surplus revenues to reduce the national debt. At the end of World War I the debt totaled more than $25 billion. During the 1920's it was cut by about one third.

° *fiscal year:* the 12-month period considered as a year for general accounting and budgeting purposes. The fiscal year of the United States government begins on July 1.

Some critics held that Mellon's financial measures reduced the taxes of the wealthy and placed too heavy a burden on the average wage earner, while checking a needed expansion of social services for the poor. But most Americans approved of the emphasis on economy in government spending, along with the reduction of the debt associated with Mellon's 12-year administration of the Treasury.

War veterans and the bonus

Meanwhile, Congress tackled the problem of the war veterans. Many war veterans, as well as many other Americans, felt that the government should provide "adjusted compensation" for veterans. These people pointed out that during the war members of the armed forces had risked their lives for low pay while workers at home earned high wartime wages in more or less safe jobs.

In August 1921 Congress created the Veterans' Bureau. President Harding then appointed Charles R. Forbes as its first director. The Veterans' Bureau was authorized to handle veterans' claims for compensation and hospitalization, to provide medical care for sick veterans, and to administer the government program for veterans' insurance.

The Veterans' Bureau was only a partial answer to the demands of veterans. The American Legion, the Veterans of Foreign Wars, and other veterans' organizations continued to press for adjusted compensation. Congress responded in 1922 with a bonus bill. President Harding vetoed the bill because it did not include any provision for raising the money to be spent.

Finally—to glance ahead—in 1924 Congress passed another bonus bill over President Coolidge's veto. The bill provided adjusted compensation for all veterans except those with ranks above captain. The payments were not to be given in cash but in the form of a paid-up 20-year life insurance policy. Veterans who held the policy for 20 years would receive full compensation.

The Fordney-McCumber Tariff

On September 21, 1922, Harding signed the Fordney-McCumber Tariff Act into law. The new tariff wiped out the reductions made in the Underwood Tariff of 1913 and established considerably higher rates. It continued the limited protection for farmers provided by the Emergency Tariff of 1921. It revised sharply upward the tariff rates on hundreds of manufactured products.

The Fordney-McCumber Tariff also authorized the President, under certain circumstances, to raise or lower any tariff rate by as much as 50 percent. As it turned out, most of the adjustments made were upward rather than downward.

Warren G. Harding had been an Ohio newspaper owner and a United States Senator before he was nominated for the Presidency by the Republican Party and elected in 1920. His warm, friendly personality was one of his greatest assets as President.

Public scandals

Despite some solid accomplishments, the Harding administration left a long, sorry record of corruption. President Harding was not himself involved in the corruption. His mistake was in appointing certain undeserving men to office. Of course, his cabinet did contain such able and respected men as Charles Evans Hughes, who became Secretary of State; Andrew W. Mellon, who headed the Treasury Department; and Herbert Hoover, who served as Secretary of Commerce. But Harding's administration also contained dishonest politicians who brought disgrace upon his administration.

Self-seeking politicians from Harding's home state, known as the "Ohio Gang," succeeded in placing one of their number, Harry M. Daugherty, in the cabinet as Attorney General. An investigation later revealed that Daugherty had used his position to protect persons who violated the prohibition amendment. Another Harding official, Thomas W. Miller, defrauded the government in the sale of alien properties—that is,

IT'S WASHDAY EVERY DAY IN WASHINGTON

This cartoon shows the Senate washing out the "dirty linen" of the Harding administration. Several prominent government officials who had been appointed to office by the President were involved in the political scandals.

foreign-owned properties seized by the American government during World War I. Charles R. Forbes, who headed the Veterans' Bureau, could not satisfactorily account for $200 million spent by his organization.

The most famous scandal took its name from the naval oil reserve lands at Teapot Dome in Wyoming. Secretary of the Interior Albert B. Fall persuaded the Secretary of the Navy, Edwin C. Denby, to transfer the Teapot Dome reserve and another oil reserve at Elk Hills, California, to Fall's jurisdiction. In return for bribes, Fall leased the oil reserves to private oil speculators.

These scandals did not become publicly known until Coolidge took office, when Fall, Forbes, and Miller were each prosecuted and imprisoned. Some hint of what was going on reached Harding in 1923, however, and his health broke under the strain. He died suddenly in the summer of 1923.

Calvin Coolidge

On Harding's death, Calvin Coolidge, the Vice-President, became President. Coolidge, a man of unquestioned honesty, had built his political career in Massachusetts, advancing from state legislator to governor.

To millions of Americans, Calvin Coolidge became a symbol of the thrifty, old-fashioned, simple, country American. In a period of extravagance and "big money," his honesty helped to regain for the Republican Party the public confidence that had been lost as a result of the scandals of the Harding administration.

The election of 1924

Only once during the 1920's did the Republican program face any serious opposition. Curiously enough, the opposition came in part from within Republican ranks.

The revolt broke out in 1924 when the Republicans nominated the staunchly conservative Calvin Coolidge for the Presidency. Coolidge believed that government should encourage, but not regulate, business. He also disapproved of special legislation to help workers or farmers.

Resisting these conservative policies, a group of progressive Republicans broke away from the Republican Party and formed a new Progressive Party. They nominated Senator Robert M. La Follette of Wisconsin as their standard bearer. The Progressive Party received the backing of three important groups of Americans who were dissatisfied with both major parties—western farmers, organized labor, and the socialists. The Progressive Party called for government action on a number of fronts. It urged federal credit and other assistance for farmers, social legislation and additional laws to protect the rights of labor, and government ownership of railroads and water power resources.

La Follette received almost 5 million votes, the largest number any third party had ever mustered. With La Follette's death shortly after the campaign, however, the Progressive Party lost its strength and faded into insignificance.

The Democrats in 1924 nominated John W. Davis, a conservative corporation lawyer. During his campaign Davis concentrated on the scandals of the Harding era. But the Republicans met this challenge by claiming credit for the prevailing prosperity. The argument of prosperity proved effective. Despite the Progressive revolt, which split the Republicans into two factions, Coolidge won by a landslide, piling up 382 electoral votes to 136 for Davis and 13 for La Follette.

Coolidge and thrifty government

President Coolidge continued to emphasize thrift in government. In the name of economy, he vetoed a bonus bill for veterans of World War I. As you have read, Congress passed this bill over his veto. Coolidge also vetoed the McNary-Haugen Bill, which was designed to stabilize farm prices by allowing the government to buy up farm surpluses and sell them abroad.

In other matters, too, Congress and the President disagreed. But the President remained popular. "Keep Cool with Coolidge" was a slogan of the day. He probably could have been re-elected in 1928 had he wished. But a year before the election he announced that he did not choose to run.

The election of 1928

With Coolidge out of the Presidential race, the Republicans nominated Herbert C. Hoover of California, a successful mining engineer with a notable record as administrator of food relief in Europe during and after the war and as Secretary of Commerce after 1921.

The Democrats nominated New York's Governor Alfred E. Smith. Smith advocated a federal farm relief program and also urged stricter regulation of public utilities. These planks in the Democratic platform had strong appeal for many Americans. But Smith had political handicaps that cost him support within his own party. He was opposed to prohibition, he was a Roman Catholic, and he was connected with the Tammany political machine in New York City—all of which made him unpopular with large groups of voters, especially in the South and West.

Hoover won the election, receiving 444 electoral votes to Smith's 87. Smith lost not only his own state of New York, but also several traditionally Democratic states in the South, which for the first time since the Civil War gave their votes to a Republican.

Herbert C. Hoover

President Hoover summed up his political beliefs in the phrase "rugged individualism." His general point of view was very close to Harding's idea of "normalcy" and to Coolidge's belief that government should encourage business but not give special assistance to individuals. Hoover, however, displayed greater imagination than his

This portrait of President Calvin Coolidge reflects the honesty and forthrightness that helped to regain for the Republican Party the public confidence that had been lost during the Harding administration.

Republican predecessors. He believed that "experts" in fields other than government could make important contributions to government. He also believed that the government should assume at least a moderate amount of guidance, or planning, for the social and economic development of the nation.

SOURCES

HERBERT HOOVER'S "RUGGED INDIVIDUALISM" SPEECH (1928)

During one hundred and fifty years we have built up a form of self-government and a social system which is peculiarly our own. It differs essentially from all others in the world. It is the American system. It is just as definite and positive a political and social system as has ever been developed on earth. It is founded upon a particular conception of self-government in which decentralized local responsibility is the very base. Further than this, it is founded upon the conception that only through ordered liberty, freedom, and equal opportunity to the individual will his initiative and enterprise spur on the march of progress. And in our insistence upon equality of opportunity has our system advanced beyond all the world. . . .

When Herbert Hoover (center) first became President, he believed that the nation could look forward to a long period of prosperity. But the events of 1929 proved him wrong.

When Hoover took office, he looked forward to a long period of increasing prosperity. He believed that Americans now expected more than the necessities of life. "The slogan of progress," he declared, "is changing from the full dinner pail to the full garage." For about six months, booming business and heavy consumer buying seemed to bear out this prediction.

The Hawley-Smoot Tariff

In 1929, with a great many Americans enjoying unprecedented prosperity, Hoover called Congress into special session to consider farm relief and a "limited revision" of tariffs.

Instead of a "limited revision," Congress passed the Hawley-Smoot Tariff bill, providing for the highest tariff in American history. President Hoover felt that some of the rates were too high. He also pondered a petition signed by 1,000 leading economists who argued that such high tariffs would raise prices, create hardships for American consumers, seriously interfere with world trade, and invite economic reprisals from other countries. But in 1930, believing that protective tariffs encouraged business prosperity, Hoover put aside his doubts and signed the bill.

The Hawley-Smoot Tariff created problems for many countries, as you will see. Driven to resistance, during the next two years some 25 countries took steps to cut down their imports of American products.

The Agricultural Marketing Act

Hoover did depart from the policies of his Republican predecessors, however, in supporting the Agricultural Marketing Act. This act created a Federal Farm Board with power to lend up to $500 million to cooperative farm groups to help them store crops during years when a surplus of farm products brought falling prices. The theory was that the farmers could sell their stored products later when prices rose. Unfortunately, surpluses continued year after year and prices continued to fall. As a result, the Federal Farm Board used up its financial resources without bolstering farm income.

In his support of federal legislation to aid farmers, Hoover was taking a modest turn away from the "rugged individualism" that he favored in theory. As you will see later, the stock market crash in 1929 and the Great Depression that followed brought new and ever heavier pressures for government action to aid farmers, wage earners, business people, and consumers in general.

SECTION SURVEY

IDENTIFY: "Ohio Gang," Teapot Dome scandal, "rugged individualism"; Alfred E. Smith.

1. How did Coolidge's election to the Presidency in 1924 reflect the temper of the times?
2. Both the Fordney-McCumber Tariff of 1922 and the Hawley-Smoot Tariff of 1930 established high tariff rates. (a) How did these tariffs affect foreign countries? (b) How did they affect American industries? (c) How did they affect American farmers?
3. Despite some solid accomplishments, the Harding administration left a long, sorry record of corruption. Explain.
4. Compare the parties, candidates, issues, and results of the elections of 1924 and 1928.

3 The prosperity of the 1920's shattered by the Great Depression

Flourishing business conditions and a rising standard of living contributed to the political success of the Republican Party during the 1920's. Between 1922 and 1929 jobs were plentiful. Americans on the whole were better fed, clothed, and housed than ever before.

"Easy money"

During the prosperity of the so-called "Golden Twenties" many Americans made and spent money with ease. Millions of workers received relatively high wages, many businesses earned large profits, and an ever-growing number of stockholders received substantial dividends.

As Americans bought more and more consumer goods, the retail trade recorded ever-increasing sales. Some of the profits of successful business enterprises went back into industry, to pay for expansion and new product research. Some paid for workers' recreational facilities, some for company programs providing insurance and pensions for employees. Large sums flowed into medical research, education, and the welfare of the poor.

As surplus income piled higher and higher, more and more Americans were tempted to invest their savings or their profits in the stock market, hoping for big returns.

The limits of prosperity

Not all Americans shared in the prosperity of the "Golden Twenties." This was notably true of Indians, Spanish-speaking Americans, and most black Americans. Many workers lost their jobs when new machines were installed in factories. Some, such as blacksmiths and harness makers, whose skills were no longer needed, found it difficult to adapt to the monotonous work on assembly lines. Furthermore, some industries—such as coal, textiles, and leather—never fully recovered from the postwar slump of the early 1920's. Finally, many farmers did not share in the prosperity that other Americans were enjoying.

The plight of the farmers

After the war, as you may recall, American farmers lost many European markets. Also, as you will see, laws passed in the early 1920's virtually ended immigration. Thus this traditional source of new customers was now lost to the farmers. But although markets were shrinking, farm production—with the help of new machines and new techniques—jumped more than 20 percent between 1919 and 1929.

When the supply of food is high and demand is low, when more people want to sell food and fewer people are able or willing to buy it, farm prices drop. And while farm prices were falling in the 1920's, the prices of the industrial goods that the farmer needed rose higher and higher. As a result many farmers found it increasingly difficult to meet their mortgage payments or the installments on their farm machinery. Thus during the industrial prosperity of the 1920's many farmers were sinking deeper into debt, and many lost their farms. The plight of sharecroppers and tenants, white and black alike, was even worse than that of the small farmers.

Belief in prosperity

But few people in the 1920's paid much attention to these limitations of prosperity. Most Americans believed, with Herbert Hoover, that "we in America are nearer to the final triumph over poverty than ever before in the history of any land." Thus the depression that started late in 1929 came as a stunning blow to most Americans.

The stock market crash

For years the prices of stocks had been moving upward. After Hoover's election in November 1928, moreover, a frenzy of speculation gripped the country. Convinced that they were entering "four more years of prosperity," investors bought feverishly. Despite repeated warnings that stock prices were much too high, Americans, rich and middle class alike, invested in stocks often on credit. During most of 1929 stock prices soared to higher and higher levels.

Then the bubble burst. On October 24, 1929, a panic of selling hit the New York Stock Exchange as frantic orders to sell stock came pouring in. The causes of this panic were chiefly overproduction and overspeculation. More goods had been produced than could be profitably sold. And a great many stocks were either worthless or overinflated. That is, the businesses behind such stocks either existed on paper only, or their actual value was far less than the market value of the stock.

Overproduction and overspeculation had caught up with the American people. The overinflated prices of stocks tumbled downward. On October 29 prices sank to a shattering new low when over 16 million shares of stock were dumped on the market. By mid-November the average value of leading stocks had been cut in half, and stockholders had lost $30 billion. With this "crash" of the stock market, the Great Depression started.

At first business and government leaders tried to reassure the American people. "Business

A photograph of New York City's Wall Street is superimposed on the front page of a newspaper reporting the "nation-wide stampede" to sell stocks.

is fundamentally sound,'' announced Secretary of the Treasury Andrew Mellon. But such words, no matter how reassuring, could not stem the tide of economic disaster sweeping the country.

Spread of the Great Depression

Before 1929 ended, banks all over the country were closing their doors. Businesses everywhere cut back production, and many concerns, finding themselves without customers, were forced out of business. Factories and mines were shut down. Empty railroad cars piled up on the sidings. By 1930 between 6 and 7 million Americans were unemployed. The result was a chain reaction. Unemployment meant fewer customers; a decrease in customers caused further cutbacks in production; these cutbacks, in turn, resulted in more unemployment. By 1932 nearly 12 million Americans were out of work.

The depression struck at all classes. Many well-to-do Americans helplessly watched their fortunes, invested in stocks or businesses, disappear. But the industrial workers and the farmers suffered most. Most wage earners had no savings to tide them over a period of unemployment. In every city thousands of unfortunate men and women stood in lines to get free meals of bread and soup. Families forced out of their homes moved to makeshift huts that they built on unused land at the edges of the city, using scrap lumber, packing boxes, and corrugated iron.

For the farmers the depression came as a final blow. As you have read, most farm families had never shared fully in the prosperity of the twenties. But bad as conditions were before, they became steadily worse between 1929 and 1932. Farm prices fell lower and lower. As their incomes shrank, more and more farmers lost their farms. In some midwestern states desperate farmers used force to prevent sheriffs from foreclosing mortgages on their farms.

Many thousands of jobless people from cities and farms wandered over the land seeking jobs at any wages, hitchhiking or hiding in freight trains, and sleeping on park benches. Never had America known such widespread suffering.

What caused the depression?

There is no simple way to explain the Great Depression. Economists agree that there were many causes, but they disagree about which was most important.

President Hoover insisted that the major cause was the worldwide economic disorder that followed World War I. Many economists agreed. They pointed to the vast destruction of property during the war and the worldwide dislocation of trade during and after the war.

Other economists argued that America's high tariff policies helped to stifle world trade and hurt American business. High tariffs, they claimed, prevented other countries from selling their goods in the United States. This in turn prevented them from securing the dollars that they needed to buy American products.

Still other economists blamed the depression on the excessive borrowing of money—for stocks, for comforts purchased on the installment plan, or for the expansion of businesses. These critics also claimed that the federal government failed to control bank loans and to protect the public against the sale of stocks that had no value.

Some economists have argued that depressions are an inevitable part of the American economic system. According to this view, business expands during periods of prosperity in order to obtain the largest possible profits. But when factories produce more goods than consumers can buy, the factories have to cut down on production, at least until their surpluses are consumed. For this reason, these economists have argued, prosperity and depression are inevitable parts of the business cycle.

Finally, some economists have traced the Great Depression to uneven distribution of income. These economists have argued that, if farmers had received better prices for their products and if workers had received higher wages, the American people would have been able to buy a larger proportion of the surplus goods. Had this happened, these economists claim, the factories would have kept busy and the depression could have been avoided.

Hoover and the depression

Whatever its causes, the depression confronted the Hoover administration with two emergencies. First, there was the widespread misery of people without jobs or farms, without money to buy enough food or clothing, and increasingly without hope. Some Americans urged the federal government to extend direct relief to those in need. President Hoover, however, believed that direct aid was a responsibility of local communities. Direct federal relief, he said, would create a vast, inefficient bureaucracy and undermine the self-respect of the persons receiving it. Unfortunately, local communities did not have the resources to cope with the ever-rising tide of human misery.

To the second emergency, the collapse of business and agriculture, Hoover responded more actively. He instructed the Federal Farm Board to buy up agricultural surpluses in an effort to raise falling farm prices. With the support of Congress, he started several public works programs, among them Boulder Dam (later called Hoover Dam) on the Colorado River. These projects were intended to stimulate business and

The depression struck at all classes. In every American city thousands of men and women stood in lines like this to get free meals of bread and soup.

To American farmers, the depression came as a final blow. Many lost their farms and wandered over the land as migrant workers. This moving photograph shows the troubled mother of a migrant family with her children.

provide employment for jobless workers.

Also at Hoover's urging, Congress created the Reconstruction Finance Corporation (RFC) in February 1932. The Reconstruction Finance Corporation was authorized to lend large sums of money to banks, life insurance companies, railroads, farm mortgage associations, and other enterprises. President Hoover and his associates hoped that federal loans would strengthen these key businesses and thus provide jobs for millions of workers. The RFC advanced nearly $2 billion in loans to American business during the remaining years of the Hoover administration, but the depression grew worse.

In response to a recommendation by Hoover, Congress also passed the Home Loan Bank Act in July 1932. This act created a series of special banks designed to provide financial assistance to savings banks, building and loan associations, and insurance companies—all of which lent money on mortgages. By providing financial aid to these key mortgage institutions, Hoover hoped to reduce foreclosures on homes and farms and to stimulate construction of residential buildings.

In adopting these measures, the President and Congress were accepting, for the first time, the idea that the federal government must assume certain responsibilities when the nation's economy suffers a serious setback. Unfortunately, the measures adopted did not stop the downward trend.

The election campaign of 1932

Although several issues, among them prohibition, entered into the Presidential campaign of 1932, there was really only one important issue—the depression. The Republicans renominated Herbert Hoover. During the campaign Hoover continued to blame the depression on international conditions, and declared that his policies were beginning to bring recovery.

Both of these claims were vigorously rejected by the Democratic Presidential candidate, New York Governor Franklin Delano Roosevelt. Roosevelt maintained that Republican policies, not international conditions, were to blame for the depression. He argued that the federal government should help provide direct relief to the needy and direct aid to farmers. He called for a broad program of public works. And he demanded that safeguards be set up to prevent wild speculation and fraudulent issues of stock. To accomplish this he proposed laws to protect the bank depositor, the purchaser of stocks, and the home owner. Referring to unemployed workers, desperate farmers, and others, Roosevelt stated that these "forgotten" Americans must have a "new deal."

Roosevelt's victory

Franklin D. Roosevelt and his running mate, John Nance Garner of Texas, swept the country in the election of 1932, with Roosevelt winning 23 million popular votes to Hoover's 16 million. Roosevelt carried 42 states and piled up 472 electoral votes to Hoover's 59. Moreover, the Democrats secured decisive majorities in both houses of Congress. Not since the Civil War had the Democratic Party won such a sweeping victory.

A majority of voters throughout the 1920's had given the Republicans credit for the prosperity of those years. Now a great many Americans seemed to be saying that the Republicans should take the blame for the depression. Many who voted for the Democrats were really voting against Hoover rather than for Roosevelt. But many more saw in Roosevelt the kind of dynamic personality that they believed was needed to lead the country out of its troubles.

Roosevelt had promised the American people a "new deal." During the four months between Election Day and Inauguration Day—

March 4, 1933—workers, farmers, and even many business leaders waited impatiently and hopefully to see how the new President would carry out his pledge. You will read about the New Deal in later chapters.

SECTION SURVEY

IDENTIFY: depression, Great Depression, the stock market crash, RFC; Franklin D. Roosevelt; October 1929.

1. The "Golden Twenties" were golden for some, but for the majority of Americans there was little gold in them. Do you agree or disagree? Explain.
2. How do economists explain the major causes of the Great Depression?
3. How did the measures taken by Hoover to combat the depression reflect his philosophy of government and its role in economic affairs?
4. According to the 1920 census, more Americans were living in cities than on farms. How does this fact relate to the hardships experienced by the "little people" with the coming of the depression?

CHAPTER SURVEY

INQUIRING INTO HISTORY

1. Why were Americans more interested in domestic affairs than in international relations in the year 1920?
2. Was the "Red scare" the first experience of this kind in American history? Explain your answer.
3. During the Boston police strike, Governor Coolidge made the following statement: "There is no right to strike against the public safety by anybody, anywhere, any time." What did he mean? Do you agree or disagree with his viewpoint? Why?
4. When the cost of living goes up, how does it affect (a) buying power, (b) people living on fixed incomes?
5. Speaking in the 1920's, Herbert Hoover said: "We in America are nearer to the final triumph over poverty than ever before in the history of any land." (a) What facts supported his opinion? (b) Why were some Americans critical of his view?
6. How did business conditions contribute to the Republican Party's success during the 1920's?

RELATING PAST TO PRESENT

1. What were some causes of the racial riots of 1919? In what ways have these conditions changed today? Do some of these problems still remain?
2. Is it fair to blame or praise a President or a political party for (a) a war, (b) a depression, (c) prosperity? Explain.
3. Compare the attitudes of the American people toward labor unions today and during the period of the 1920's.
4. Do you think the slogan "rugged individualism" still applies to the American economy today? Explain.
5. During the depression years, Mexican-Americans were one of the groups hardest hit by unemployment. Why was this so? Do you think the same thing would happen today in a depression? Why or why not?

DEVELOPING SOCIAL SCIENCE SKILLS

1. Read Herbert Hoover's "rugged individualism" speech of 1928 and Franklin D. Roosevelt's First Inaugural Address of 1933. (a) What is each President's view of the role of the federal government? (b) Based on these speeches, can you predict how each President might deal with the depression? (c) Which President's methods do you think would be more effective? Why?
2. Compare the position of farmers in the 1920's with that of farmers today. For each period, include the number of farmers, the percentage of farmers in the population, farm income, government farm programs. Using this data, cite evidence which shows that farmers are better off or worse off today than in 1920.
3. Examine the pictures on pages 237 and 238. (a) What is the subject of each picture? (b) How does each make you feel? (c) Based on these photographs, what do you think life was like during the Great Depression?
4. Find accounts written by or about black Americans who migrated to the North between 1910 and 1930. (a) Why did they move to the North? (b) What opportunities and problems did they find in the North?

CHAPTER 15
AMERICAN REJECTION OF WORLD LEADERSHIP
1920-1932

On November 11, 1918, almost everyone in America took the day off from work. Factories, offices, stores, and schools closed their doors while Americans, old and young, poured into the streets of every city and town and village across the land to celebrate the armistice that brought an end to World War I. In a joyful statement to the press, President Wilson announced, "Everything for which America fought has been accomplished." So it seemed to him, and so it seemed to Americans in general on November 11, 1918.

But Wilson realized, as millions of Americans did not, that it is easier to win a victory on the battlefield than to build a lasting peace. He warned Americans of the tremendous problems that remained to be solved and challenged them to assume the responsibility of world leadership. Americans, however, were tired of wartime restrictions, and eager to return to the everyday business of living. And when, as the months passed, the European nations began to quarrel over the spoils of war, Americans became increasingly disillusioned.

President Wilson struggled hard to convince Americans to support his plans for peace. But by the early 1920's the American people had repudiated Wilson, rejected the League of Nations, and, at least in political affairs, had turned their backs upon Europe and the opportunities and risks of assuming world leadership.

THE CHAPTER IN OUTLINE

1. America's refusal to join the League of Nations.

2. America's exclusion of Europe's people and goods.

3. Moving toward better relations with Latin America.

4. Working with other nations to build peace and prevent war.

| 1450 | 1750 | 1800 | 1850 | 1900 | 1950 | 1980's |

1 America's refusal to join the League of Nations

On December 4, 1918, the army transport *George Washington* sailed out of New York harbor and steamed toward Europe. Its most distinguished passenger was President Wilson, who was bound for the peace conference at Paris.

Wilson was the first President ever to leave the Western Hemisphere during his term of office. He hoped to persuade the other representatives at the conference to adopt the Fourteen Points that he had earlier outlined as "the only possible program for world peace."

The "Big Four"

The peace conference, which opened on January 18, 1919, had much of the tension of a melodrama. The stage, however, was the world; the principal characters were the chief officials of the four leading powers—Great Britain, France, Italy, and the United States; and the outcome of the drama would affect millions of people.

Wilson arrived at the conference after a triumphal journey through Great Britain, Italy, and France, where masses of people had turned out to greet the man who symbolized their hope for a better world. Encouraged by this reception, Wilson felt that he could use his great popularity to bring about a just peace based on his Fourteen Points. But the three other leading delegates at Paris, supported by powerful interests in their homelands, had very different aims.

David Lloyd George, the British Prime Minister, had just won a general election by using the vindictive slogans "Hang the Kaiser" and "Make Germany Pay." He had no intention of becoming unpopular with the British voters by showing generosity toward the Germans, or by giving up England's naval supremacy and accepting Wilson's idea of "freedom of the seas."

The "Tiger" of French politics, Premier Georges Clemenceau (ZHORZH klay·mahn·SOH), believed that the only way to defend France was to crush Germany. Italy's Vittorio Orlando wanted to acquire territory that had been secretly promised to Italy when it joined the Allies in 1915.

The problem of secret treaties

The united opposition of Lloyd George, Clemenceau, and Orlando was not the only problem President Wilson faced. There was also the problem of secret treaties.

As you have read, in 1917 the Russian Bolsheviks published certain secret treaties that the Allies had made before the United States entered the war. The new Communist rulers of Russia hoped to discredit the Allies by exposing these treaties as "imperialist diplomacy," and to some extent they succeeded.

Under these treaties, the Allies agreed to divide the spoils of victory. Great Britain was to take over Germany's colonies, except for certain territories in the Pacific Ocean which were to go to Japan. (Japan had declared war on Germany

President Wilson traveled through Great Britain, Italy, and France on his way to the peace conference in Paris. Everywhere he went, he received a tumultuous welcome.

in 1914.) France, Russia, Serbia, and Italy were to enlarge their national boundaries at the expense of Germany and Austria-Hungary. And finally, Germany was to make huge payments, called *reparations,* to the Allies to compensate for damages resulting from the war. These secret arrangements obviously contradicted several of Wilson's Fourteen Points, such as open diplomacy, national self-determination, and the end of colonialism.

Wilson's dilemma

Faced with these secret treaties and with the united opposition of Lloyd George, Clemenceau, and Orlando, Wilson could either compromise— or walk out of the Paris Peace Conference. Indeed, at one point he almost did walk out, but he realized that such a step might be regarded as a confession of failure. He was also afraid that Communism might spread from Russia into central Europe if a peace treaty were delayed and conditions remained unstable. His strongest reason for staying, however, was his faith in a League of Nations. Such a League, he was convinced, would in time remedy any injustices that the peace treaty might contain.

The Treaty of Versailles

The final peace treaty, called the Treaty of Versailles, was completed and signed late in June 1919. The treaty showed the results of bargaining between Wilson on one side and Lloyd George, Clemenceau, and Orlando on the other.

The Treaty of Versailles and related treaties made important changes in the map of the world,

and especially in the map of Europe. Germany's colonies were given to the Allied victors, but under a *mandate system* which required the new owners to account for their colonial administration to the League of Nations.

Certain border areas of pre-war Germany were lopped off. One important area, Alsace-Lorraine, was given to France. Other areas were included in a new country, Czechoslovakia, and in a recreated Poland. To satisfy the nationalist desires of various peoples in eastern Europe, several other independent states were created, including Finland, Estonia, Latvia, Lithuania, and Yugoslavia. Certain border changes were made for Italy, Greece, Rumania, and Belgium (see maps, this page).

Under the Treaty of Versailles, the German government had to accept full responsibility for starting the war, and had to agree to remain disarmed. Germany also agreed to pay large reparations for war damage.

Wilson failed to convince the other Allied representatives that vengeance and greed were weak foundations for a lasting peace. But he did successfully oppose some of the more unreasonable Allied demands. And he had the great personal satisfaction of seeing the Covenant of the League of Nations written into the Treaty of Versailles.

The League of Nations

The League of Nations, with headquarters at Geneva, Switzerland, provided international machinery to make war less likely. The ma-

EUROPE BEFORE WORLD WAR I

EUROPE AFTER WORLD WAR I

The "Big Four" at the Versailles peace conference of 1919 were (from left to right) David Lloyd George of Great Britain, Vittorio Orlando of Italy, Georges Clemenceau of France, and Woodrow Wilson of the United States.

chinery consisted of (1) a permanent Secretariat, or administrative and secretarial staff; (2) an Assembly in which each member nation had one vote; and (3) a Council, the all-important executive body. The Council had five permanent members—the five great powers of France, Great Britain, Italy, Japan, and the United States— although other nations were also represented by means of rotating membership. Germany and the Soviet Union (Russia) were excluded from League membership. Closely related to the League were the Permanent Court of International Justice, the International Labor Organization, and other international agencies.

The League Covenant did not outlaw war. But each League member agreed, before going to war, to make every effort to solve its difficulties in a friendly way, and even then to wait during a "cooling off" period before striking a blow. If any member failed to do this, the other members might then decide, through the Council, to apply "economic sanctions" by refusing to trade with the offender. Moreover, the Council might go further and recommend the use of force against the "aggressor" nation. To forestall efforts to change the new map of the world by force, Article Ten of the Covenant provided that each League member was to guarantee the territorial integrity and political independence of every other member.

The League Covenant also created agencies for many worthwhile causes: improving conditions of labor and health throughout the world, working for the reduction of armaments, and trying to abolish slavery and the narcotics trade. These were important steps toward international cooperation.

League weaknesses

The League of Nations was not, of course, a perfect organization. It had several serious weaknesses. For one thing, taking action against an aggressor was almost impossible for several reasons. First, the term "aggressor" was not clearly defined. Second, the Council could only recommend that nations take action, but could not compel them to act. Third, any Council member could block the wishes of the other members because all important Council decisions had to be unanimous. In brief, the work of the League depended upon the willingness of its members to cooperate.

Another basic weakness of the League was its guarantee of existing political boundaries. When the map of Europe was redrawn, some peoples found that they were now part of a different nation—one that they did not want to belong to. Yet these peoples had no way to secure further changes in their national boundaries.

A third weakness was the League's failure to provide adequate machinery for recommending solutions to economic problems that might lead to war. Trade rivalries and tariff barriers still existed, as did imperialism, yet the League could not do much more than study such problems. Still another weakness was exclusion of the Soviet Union and Germany from membership. And finally, the League was in no position to tackle the problem of reducing armaments.

Despite its shortcomings, however, the League of Nations was a promising beginning in the difficult task of creating a new, cooperative world order, dedicated to international peace and justice. In the 1930's about 60 nations belonged to the League, which was bringing an important new ingredient into international affairs—the organized moral judgment of a majority of the nations of the world.

Senate rejection of the League

Early in July 1919 President Wilson returned from Paris to ask the Senate to approve the Treaty of Versailles, and thus bring the United States into the League. The Senate shattered his hopes by rejecting the treaty. Senator Henry Cabot Lodge of Massachusetts, head of the important Committee on Foreign Relations, and other Republican Senators opposed the League.

Many Americans thought that the Treaty of Versailles was unjust, and they were unwilling to have the United States join a League which pledged its members to carry out the provisions of the treaty. Many Americans pointed with alarm to Article Ten of the League Covenant, which pledged each member to guarantee the existing political boundaries of the other members. Americans argued that such a pledge might involve the United States in war.

Wilson's refusal to compromise

Despite the opposition to the League of Nations, the Senate might have voted for it if President Wilson had been willing to accept amendments proposed by Senator Lodge and his supporters. These amendments were designed to safeguard American interests and to prevent the United States from being drawn into European conflicts. Wilson believed, however, that these amendments would so weaken the League that it would become ineffective. He refused to compromise.

To win public support, Wilson traveled across the country making speeches in defense of the League. Finally, exhausted by the long strain, in the fall of 1919 he collapsed, and for seven months lived in seclusion. His one remaining hope was that the public would support his cause by electing a Democratic President in the 1920 election. But the Republican landslide of that year and the election of President Harding seemed to indicate that Americans preferred to forget the League and world problems in general. They paid no heed to Wilson when he warned, "Arrangements of the present peace cannot stand a generation unless they are guaranteed by the united forces of the civilized world."

The rise of Japanese, Italian, and German expansionism in the 1930's proved the accuracy of Wilson's prophecy. For by that time, as you will read, the League had become too weak to prevent the outbreak of World War II.

SECTION SURVEY

IDENTIFY: "Big Four," Treaty of Versailles, reparations, mandate system, economic sanctions; Henry Cabot Lodge.

1. Compare the views of Wilson, Lloyd George, Clemenceau, and Orlando concerning the treaty of peace.
2. Give four ways in which the Treaty of Versailles changed the map of the world.
3. (a) Describe the structure of the League of Nations. (b) What machinery did the League set up for the prevention of war?
4. What were some of the major weaknesses of the League? Explain.
5. (a) List two arguments presented by Americans who rejected the League. (b) Do you think it is really possible to say what would have happened if the United States had joined the League? Explain.

2 America's exclusion of Europe's people and goods

America's refusal to join the League of Nations was based in part upon a desire to avoid becoming involved again in Europe's troubles and quarrels. But this desire led the United States much further than the rejection of the League.

The United States also tried, with considerable success, to keep out the people and products of Europe and Asia. The immigration and tariff laws passed during this period were the most restrictive in American history.

Closing the gates

During the 1920's the United States reversed one of its oldest traditions by almost completely halting immigration. Earlier, it is true, specific laws and international agreements had excluded the Chinese, the Japanese, and most other Asians. But despite exceptions, few Americans had seriously questioned the historic role of the United States as a place of refuge and a land of opportunity for immigrants. Indeed, during the decade before World War I, more Europeans settled in the United States than in any previous decade.

Reasons for closing the gates

Why did a nation of immigrants and descendants of immigrants suddenly close its doors? One reason was the general anti-European feeling that swept over America after the war. But certain groups of Americans had special reasons of their own.

Organized labor, for example, argued that new immigrants were willing to work for lower wages than American workers and thus pulled down the standard of living. Industrialists who had formerly favored immigration as a source of plentiful, cheap, unskilled labor no longer needed masses of unskilled workers, for by 1920 the railroads had been built and the basic industries such as steel were well developed. Finally, many established Americans felt that the newer immigrants, mainly from eastern and southern Europe,

did not easily become "Americanized." These Americans thought that it was harmful to the country to admit settlers whose languages and customs were so different from those of older inhabitants.

The immigration laws

Responding to these and other arguments, Congress passed three laws in the 1920's that progressively restricted immigration from Europe. The Emergency Quota Act of 1921 introduced a *quota system* which limited the number of Europeans and others who could be admitted to 3 percent of the total number of persons of their nationality residing in the United States in the year 1910. The 1921 act also set a total yearly limit of about 350,000 immigrants.

In 1924 an even more restrictive law was passed which reduced the annual quota from 3 to 2 percent, and changed the base year from 1910 to 1890. This change in the base year discriminated against Italians, Austrians, Russians, and other eastern and southern Europeans who had immigrated to America mainly after 1890.

Finally, the National Origins Act of 1929 shifted the base year of immigration to 1920, but counterbalanced this more liberal provision by reducing to 150,000 the total number of immigrants to be admitted during any one year.

The new immigration policies aroused a great deal of bitterness, especially among eastern and southern Europeans. The Japanese were also aroused because the immigration act of 1924

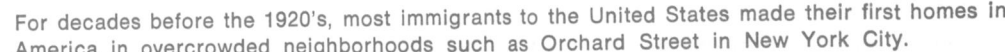

For decades before the 1920's, most immigrants to the United States made their first homes in America in overcrowded neighborhoods such as Orchard Street in New York City.

This cartoon comments on the new, restrictive immigration law passed by Congress in 1924. Do you think the cartoon is an accurate representation of what the law signified?

ended the Gentlemen's Agreement of 1907, which Japan had faithfully observed, and closed the doors completely to Japanese immigrants.

The war of tariffs

While closing its doors to immigrants, the United States was also, like other nations, raising tariff barriers to keep out foreign products. As you have read, the Fordney-McCumber Tariff of 1922 increased import duties on hundreds of items. And in 1930 the Hawley-Smoot Tariff made tariff rates the highest in American history.

America's high tariff policy proved a cruel blow to many countries in Latin America and in Europe. When America's high tariffs deprived these countries of their best markets in the United States, their economic strength declined. Factories closed, people were thrown out of work, and the surplus of farm products mounted steadily.

Some countries struck back by raising their own tariff barriers against American goods. Thus the high tariffs that Congress hoped would aid American industry helped in the end to deprive many American businesses and farms of the foreign markets they badly needed. The peace treaties had barely been signed before the nations of the world were engaged in another war—a trade war fought with tariffs.

War debts and high tariffs

America's high tariff policy created still another problem. How could European countries pay their war debts to the United States if they could not sell their goods in this country?

The war had changed America's relation to Europe from debtor to creditor. Before the war American business leaders had borrowed money from Europeans to finance new industries. During the period before the United States entered the war in 1917, however, Europeans began to

sell their American stocks and bonds to buy war goods. And, as the war progressed, the American government lent huge sums to the warring countries. As a result, by 1918 nearly all the European countries owed money to the United States. The total amounted to about $10 billion.

The American government reduced the interest rates on the loans and arranged for the debtor nations to repay the money over a long period. Yet despite the generous terms, the bankrupt European countries emerged from the war not knowing how they could repay their debts.

President Wilson reminded Congress of one possible solution to Europe's problems when he declared that if the United States wished Europe to repay its debts, Americans had to buy European products. But this became impossible when the United States adopted a high-tariff policy.

War debts and reparations

The only other solution open to the European Allies was to collect war damages, or reparations, from Germany, and to use this money to repay their war debts to the United States. In 1921 a Reparations Commission fixed the total of German reparations at $33 billion. Germany, however, was in the midst of severe economic troubles, and unable to pay such a huge sum. In an effort to secure the money, Germany borrowed from bankers in the United States and Europe.

But there was a limit to the amount that the German government could borrow, and, as the years passed, the reparations had to be reduced—once in 1924 and again in 1929. In spite of this relief, however, Germany's economic situation grew steadily worse. By 1930 the Germans could make no further payments.

A legacy of bitterness

Faced with this situation, the debtor countries notified the United States that they could no longer meet their payments on the war debts. After all, they argued, they had contributed far more to victory in blood and sacrifice than had America and it would be only fair of the United States to cancel all war debts.

The American government, supported by most Americans, refused to admit such a claim. It insisted that the war debts to the United States and German reparations payments to the Allies were two entirely separate matters. Americans pointed out that some of the loans—perhaps as much as a third of the total amount—had, in fact, been made after the armistice. Americans also reminded the European countries that they were not too poor to spend large sums for armaments.

Then in 1931 the debtors, with the exception of Finland, refused to make even a token payment. President Hoover then declared a year's halt, or *moratorium,* on the payment of war debts and reparations. But Germany did not make any more payments, and the whole question was left unsolved.

In the end, most of the war debts and most of Germany's reparations remained unpaid. But America's unsuccessful attempt to collect the war debts increased Europe's resentment against the United States. And the European victors' attempt to collect reparations from Germany, though equally unsuccessful, created a feeling of bitterness among the German people, which, as you will see, contributed to the rise of Adolf Hitler in the early 1930's.

SECTION SURVEY

IDENTIFY: quota system, armaments, moratorium.

1. Give four reasons why the United States closed its gates to many immigrants after World War I.
2. How did the emotions created by the war and a decreased need for cheap labor lead to demands for the restriction of immigration?
3. Who do you think would be more anti-immigrant— people living in rural areas or in urban areas? Explain.
4. (a) What reasons did the European Allies give for stopping payments on their war debts? (b) How did Americans answer these arguments?
5. In what ways did America's high-tariff policies backfire?

3 Moving toward better relations with Latin America

During the early 1900's, you may recall, Presidents Theodore Roosevelt, William Howard Taft, and Woodrow Wilson had all intervened in Latin-American affairs. They had justified their intervention on the grounds that it was necessary (1) to safeguard the Panama Canal, (2) to prevent European countries from extending their influence in the Caribbean, and (3) to protect American citizens and property in Latin America.

This Caribbean policy, as it was called, was continued by Presidents Harding and Coolidge. Critics of the policy—and there were many on both sides of the border—referred to it as "dollar diplomacy." Many Latin Americans called it "Yankee imperialism."

Investments in Latin America

During the "Golden Twenties," as you have read, many Americans had money to invest. The underdeveloped countries of Latin America offered inviting opportunities for investment, and American dollars financed the building of factories, railroads, mines, and ranches in the lands to the south. Whereas in 1913 United States investments in Latin America totaled $1.3 billion, by 1928 they totaled more than $5 billion.

American intervention

American interest in Latin America grew in proportion to the amount of American money invested there. President Coolidge frankly declared that the United States government would protect the property and lives of American citizens wherever they went.

During these years many Latin-American countries were undergoing social and economic revolutions. Frequently two groups in a country struggled to gain control, and each group claimed that it alone represented the people and was the legal government. When this happened, the United States tended to recognize the group most friendly to American interests.

In some instances the United States played an active role in the struggle for power. On occasion it forbade the sale of arms to the group it disliked and armed the group it supported. Worst of all from the Latin-American point of view, the United States sometimes sent armed forces to protect American lives and property.

Relations with Nicaragua

American policy toward Nicaragua offers an example of the kind of intervention that Latin Americans fiercely resented. The United States

President Coolidge, shown here (center) on a visit to Cuba, attempted to improve United States' relations with the nations of Latin America.

was particularly concerned about Nicaragua because of large American investments there. Moreover, Nicaragua was close to the vital Panama Canal. Finally, there was the prospect that a new canal might eventually be built through Nicaragua itself. President Taft had sent marines into the country during an internal conflict to protect American investments and the nearby Panama Canal. President Coolidge withdrew the marines in 1925, but sent them back in 1926 when new disturbances broke out.

This policy was unpopular throughout Latin America. It was also unpopular with many Americans who claimed that the United States was really making war. President Coolidge denied this and spoke of the American occupation as a police duty. But criticism was so strong that the administration took measures to solve the problem by more peaceful means.

In 1927 President Coolidge withdrew most of the marines, leaving only enough to assure the protection of American property if violence again broke out. This helped to relieve the tension between the United States and Nicaragua. But the Nicaraguans demanded the complete withdrawal of *all* marines and the end of American interference. In 1933 President Hoover finally withdrew all United States troops.

Strained relations with Mexico

United States relations with Mexico also reflected the determination of the United States to protect American interests south of the Rio Grande. As you will recall, during Wilson's administration a sweeping social revolution in Mexico had raised new problems in the traditionally uneasy relations between the two countries. American lives and property suffered in the upheaval. But far more threatening to Americans who had invested in Mexican property was the new policy established in the Mexican constitution of 1917.

Article 27 of the Mexican constitution declared that "only Mexicans . . . have the right to acquire ownership [of, or] . . . to develop mines, waters, or mineral fuels in the Republic of Mexico. The nation may grant the same right to foreigners, provided they agree to be considered Mexicans in respect of such property, and accordingly not to involve the protection of their government in respect of the same." This article also canceled concessions made to foreigners by earlier governments. Foreign businesses and investors were quick to protest.

During 1917 and 1918 the United States was too involved in the European war to take any action in regard to Mexico. Moreover, not all of the provisions of the constitution were at once applied. But immediately after the armistice in 1918 oil investors and other American owners of property in Mexico clamored for intervention. These business interests were joined by many American Catholics who were greatly disturbed over anti-Catholic provisions in the Mexican constitution and the anti-clerical policies of the Mexican government. The situation grew worse when the Mexicans supported the anti-American faction in Nicaragua. By 1927 relations between the United States and Mexico were close to the breaking point.

Improved relations

In 1927, however, the United States began slowly to modify its policy. President Coolidge took the first step by sending Dwight W. Morrow, a successful banker, as ambassador to Mexico.

Instead of threatening Mexico with United States power, Morrow tried to understand the Mexican point of view. His sincerity, intelligence, and charm quickly won him many friends in Mexico. The skillful work of Morrow and other American "ambassadors of good will" repaired much of the damage done in the past. The Mexicans agreed to recognize American titles to sub-soil minerals, such as petroleum, that had been in effect before the constitution of 1917.

Moving toward a new policy

The Morrow mission marked a turning point in American relations with Mexico and with other Latin-American countries. From 1927 on, both Calvin Coolidge and his successor, Herbert Hoover, worked hard to develop friendlier relations with the Caribbean republics and with the South American nations. Coolidge went to Havana, Cuba, in 1928 and personally opened a Pan-American Conference. Hoover toured South America in the months before his inauguration.

Latin Americans were pleased by the friendly attention of an American President and a President-elect. Their governments encouraged American investments and gave those investments greater protection than in the past. The United States, in turn, stopped intervening by force in the internal affairs of Latin-American nations.

The Monroe Doctrine modified

But Latin Americans still resented the 1904 Roosevelt Corollary to the Monroe Doctrine. As you may recall, the Roosevelt Corollary stated that the United States had the right to act as police officer of the Western Hemisphere.

In the hope of improving United States relations with Latin America still further, the Department of State declared in 1930 that the Monroe Doctrine no longer would be used to justify United States intervention in Latin-American domestic affairs. Thus by the end of the 1920's relations with Latin America had been considerably improved.

SECTION SURVEY

IDENTIFY: "dollar diplomacy," "Yankee imperialism," police duty; Dwight W. Morrow.

1. Why did America's Caribbean policy arouse resentment in Latin America and criticism in the United States?
2. Why were American policies toward Nicaragua resented by Latin Americans?
3. What were the reasons for American hostility toward Mexico from 1917 to 1927?
4. Summarize the steps taken by the United States from 1927 to 1930 to improve its relations with Latin America.

4 Working with other nations to build peace and prevent war

While the United States was moving toward improved relations with Latin America, it also began to move toward international cooperation. In 1920, it is true, the Department of State completely ignored communications from the newly established League of Nations in Geneva. But as time passed, American experts in international law, public health, and finance became important advisers in League activities. During Harding's administration the United States began to send "observers" to Geneva to take unofficial parts in League committee work dealing with epidemics, slavery, and the narcotics trade. By 1924 American delegates were attending League conferences.

The World Court

Both Harding and Coolidge recommended that the United States join the Permanent Court of International Justice, popularly known as the World Court, created in 1920 to arbitrate international disputes. But the Senate, jealous of its right to make treaties and influenced by Americans who were fearful of "entangling alliances," agreed to join only on its own terms. The nations already belonging to the World Court refused to accept the Senate's terms, and the matter was dropped.

The armaments race

The government was more successful in its efforts to stop the naval armaments race in which

WILL ROGERS, AMERICAN HUMORIST

Will Rogers (1879–1935) was one of America's greatest humorists. "Give me the truth," he once said, "I'll exaggerate it and make it funny." In thirty years as an actor, writer, and radio commentator, he won millions of admirers among the American people.

Born in 1879 in Oklahoma (then known as Indian Territory), he was proud of his partly Indian ancestry. "My ancestors didn't come over on the *Mayflower*," he told a Boston audience. "They met the boat."

He had learned to use the lasso during his early years as a cowboy, and he began his vaudeville career in New York performing on stage with a lasso. But it was Rogers' homely, dry comments about leading public figures and recent events—often delivered while he twirled a rope—that endeared him to his audiences and won him his great reputation on the stage, in the movies, over the radio, and as a newspaper columnist.

He had numerous friends in all walks of life, but his humor spared none of them. Once, referring to President Coolidge's quality of reserve, he said: "Cairo's a great place. I was the only tourist there who never went out to see the Sphinx—well, I've seen Cal Coolidge." Speaking of the government's efforts to help the farmers, he commented, "One thing about farmers' relief. It can't last long, for the farmers ain't got much to be relieved of."

It was a shock to the nation when, in 1935, on the start of an around-the-world flight with his friend Wiley Post, their plane crashed into the sea near Point Barrow, Alaska, and both were killed.

---

it was engaged with Great Britain and Japan. Relations between the United States and Japan were particularly strained after World War I. Americans resented the Japanese occupation of the Shantung Peninsula in China. This occupation, begun in 1914, violated America's Open Door policy, which was designed to keep China's territory intact and to prevent any single power from dominating China. Americans were concerned because Japan was allied with Great Britain.

As a result of the tension created by this situation, each of the three powers was rapidly building up its naval strength. Many people in all three countries were afraid that the naval armaments race might lead to war.

The Washington Conference

Against this disturbing background, nine powers with interests in Asia met in the American capital on November 12, 1921. Secretary of State Charles Evans Hughes opened the Washington Naval Conference by boldly proposing a 10-year "naval holiday" during which no new warships were to be built. He suggested that the United States, Great Britain, and Japan each scrap enough of its own warships to bring the naval strength of the three great sea powers into a ratio of 5:5:3. These limitations applied only to "capital ships," that is, to battleships and heavy cruisers of 10,000 tons (9,072 metric tons)

or more. According to this plan, Great Britain and the United States would be equal in naval strength while Japan would have three fifths as much tonnage as each of the other two countries. France and Italy were to have fleets of equal size, with a ratio of 1.75 to the other powers.

At first, Japan refused to accept the plan. But, eager to make economies at home, the Japanese delegates finally accepted the proposal on the condition that Great Britain and the United States should not further fortify any Pacific colonies, except Hawaii. These agreements were included in what came to be called the Five-Power Treaty.

Other agreements

The Five-Power Treaty was only one of the agreements reached at the conference. Among others were the Four-Power Pact and the Nine-Power Treaty.

In the Four-Power Pact, Japan, Great Britain, France, and the United States agreed to respect one another's rights in the Pacific. They also agreed to consult with one another in the event of any act of aggression in the Pacific area.

In the Nine-Power Treaty, the nations represented at the conference guaranteed the territorial integrity of China and promised to uphold the Open Door policy by promoting trade and relations "between China and the other powers upon the basis of equality of opportunity."

Developments in the Pacific area following the Washington Conference seemed to justify the widespread belief that a major step toward economy and peace had been taken. Japan withdrew, at least partially, from the Shantung Peninsula. Japan also withdrew troops that had occupied parts of Siberia during the Russian Revolution. At a London Naval Conference in 1930 Japan agreed to extend the naval holiday. As you will see, however, this agreement marked the high tide of Japanese cooperation with the Western powers.

The attempt to "outlaw war"

In addition to favoring disarmament, the United States tried to prevent war by what has been called a policy of "wishful thinking." In 1928 Secretary of State Frank B. Kellogg joined with the French foreign minister, Aristide Briand (ah·rees·TEED bree·AHN), in asking all nations to sign a pledge outlawing war "as an instrument of foreign policy." The signers were also to agree to settle all disputes by peaceful methods.

Eventually 62 nations accepted the document, but the Kellogg-Briand Pact, or the Pact of Paris as it was called, proved to be little more than a statement of good intentions. In signing, each nation added its own reservations. None was willing to outlaw war waged in self-defense. Since nearly every nation going to war justifies its action by pleading self-defense, this reservation destroyed the pact's effectiveness.

Finally, the document said nothing about enforcement. Those who signed it were not even bound to consult with one another in case some government acted aggressively. At best, the Kellogg-Briand Pact represented little more than an agreement that war was evil.

The crumbling peace structure

The opening act in the tragedy that later engulfed the entire world began in 1931, although at the time its full significance was not understood. Without warning, the Japanese army rolled across the frontiers of Manchuria (see map, page 309). China, large but helpless, could do little to defend its great northern province. Within a few months the Japanese had torn the province away from the Chinese. A Japanese program to sweep "foreign" influence out of the Far East and to build an Asia for Asians had begun.

Japan's aggression was a violation of the Covenant of the League of Nations and an outright challenge to the Open Door policy of the United States. Japan was bluntly reminded of these facts by Secretary of State Henry L. Stimson. In a formal note issued in 1932, Stimson protested Japan's flagrant violation of the Nine-

The League of Nations, shown here at its first meeting, represented a beginning in the difficult task of building world peace and cooperation.

Power Treaty and of the Kellogg-Briand Pact, both of which Japan had signed. President Hoover and Congress, however, were unwilling to commit the United States to the use of force, or even to economic sanctions, to enforce the Stimson declaration.

Meanwhile the League of Nations was summoned to consider what action, if any, should be taken. To this meeting President Hoover sent an American representative. The League sent a commission to Manchuria to investigate. But beyond a statement of its agreement with the so-called Stimson Doctrine, the League failed to act. Confident that the nations of the world would not act collectively in order to preserve peace, the Japanese withdrew from the League of Nations and prepared to invade and conquer China and Southeast Asia.

The structure of peace had begun to crumble. As you will see, Fascist Italy and, after 1933, the rising Nazi regime in Germany realized that they too could safely embark upon programs of aggression. The peace structure was not firm enough to stand a heavy blow. And the world powers, which by collective action might have bolstered the crumbling structure of peace, were unwilling and unable to act together.

SECTION SURVEY

IDENTIFY: World Court, armaments race, "naval holiday"; Charles Evans Hughes, Frank B. Kellogg, Henry L. Stimson.

1. What conditions led to the Washington Naval Conference of 1921–22?
2. (a) What were the major provisions of the Five-Power Treaty? (b) Indicate the reason for the Four-Power Pact.
3. Why was the Nine-Power Treaty significant for (a) China, (b) the United States, (c) Japan?
4. Why was the Kellogg-Briand Pact of 1928 "little more than a statement of good intentions"?
5. (a) How did the United States react to the Japanese invasion of Manchuria? (b) What was the reaction of the League of Nations? Why?

CHAPTER SURVEY

INQUIRING INTO HISTORY

1. If either Senator Lodge or President Wilson had compromised, the Treaty of Versailles would have been approved by the United States Senate. Comment.
2. How was the League of Nations supposed to protect world peace?
3. What efforts toward world peace did the United States make during the 1920's?
4. The Kellogg-Briand Pact did not survive the challenges posed by the Japanese invasion of Manchuria. Comment.
5. Explain the relationship between each of the following pairs of terms: (a) reparations—moratorium, (b) capital ships—naval holiday, (c) aggression—Stimson Doctrine, and (d) colony—mandate system.
6. During the period just studied, the United States shut its doors to many immigrants and placed high tariffs on foreign goods. Did it act for the same reason in both cases?
7. The Treaty of Versailles showed the results of bargaining between Wilson on the one side and Lloyd George, Clemenceau, and Orlando on the other. Discuss.

8. The League of Nations represented the organized moral judgment of the great majority of nations. Explain.

RELATING PAST TO PRESENT

1. There has not been a global war since 1945. To what developments do you think this fact can be attributed?
2. Does the United States follow one or several policies in dealing with the nations of the world today? Explain.

DEVELOPING SOCIAL SCIENCE SKILLS

1. Analyze Woodrow Wilson's Fourteen Points and the Treaty of Versailles. How many of Wilson's "Points" were incorporated into the Treaty? Why do you think the European nations did not accept all of Wilson's "Points"?
2. Compare the two maps on page 242. (a) What new nations appeared after World War I? (b) Do you think these new nations created new problems? (c) Which nations lost territory as a result of World War I?

CHAPTER *16*

AN ACCELERATED PACE OF LIVING
IN THE "GOLDEN TWENTIES"

Every age, or period of years, in history has certain characteristics that distinguish it from every other age. The decade of the 1920's was no exception. Historians and writers have pinned various labels on the 1920's—among them the "Golden Twenties," the "Roaring Twenties," the "Age of Disillusionment," the "Decade of Wonderful Nonsense," the "Jazz Age," and the "Ballyhoo Years."

These labels suggest that the 1920's were characterized by widespread prosperity, by an unusual outpouring of energy, by a sharp increase in the productivity of American industry, by disillusionment with the outcome of the crusade to make the world safe for democracy, by an emphasis on materialism, and by the desire "to get rich quick" and to have a good time. All of this was true.

But people's ideas, beliefs, and everyday habits did not suddenly change as though by some stroke of magic on Armistice Day in 1918. Neither did their ideas, beliefs, and habits suddenly change when the shadow of the Great Depression fell over the land in the early 1930's.

The forces that gave new directions to American life in the 1920's were deeply rooted in American history and, for that matter, in the history of the Western world. Stimulated in part by World War I, the Industrial Revolution gathered new momentum in the 1920's. Power-driven machines, new sources of energy, more efficient factories, better methods of marketing goods—all of these helped to bring prosperity to the American people.

But the influence of industrialization reached far beyond the nation's economic life. It continued to transform everyday life in urban and rural areas alike. It gave new directions to science and education. It affected literature, art, architecture, and recreation.

THE CHAPTER IN OUTLINE

1. The increasing momentum of the Industrial Revolution.

2. New ways of living in country, town, and city.

3. New ways of living reflected in education, literature, and the arts.

4. Striking changes in the daily life of Americans.

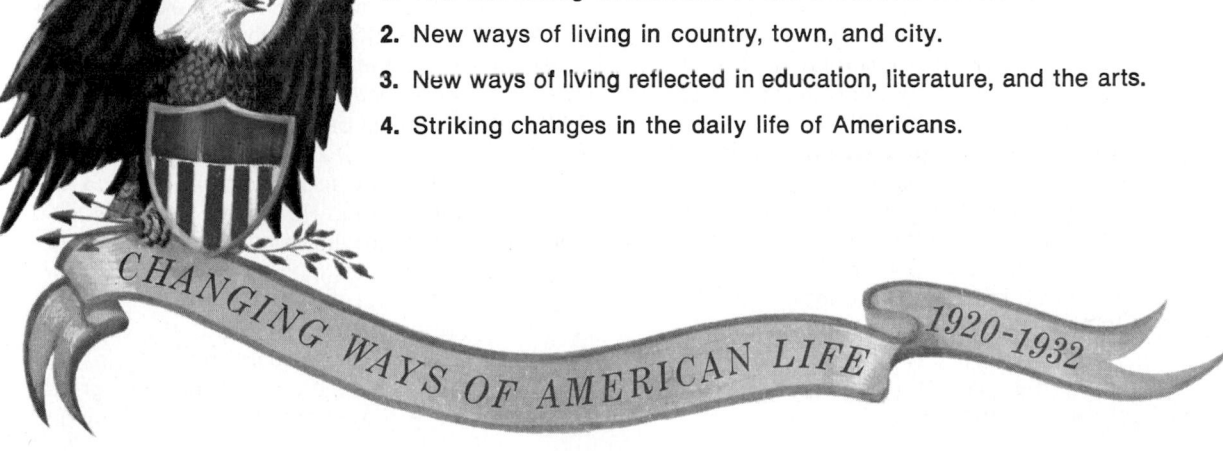

CHANGING WAYS OF AMERICAN LIFE   1920-1932

1 The increasing momentum of the Industrial Revolution

By 1920 the power-driven machine was one of the dominant symbols of America. There were machines in factories, on farms, and in the home —and still the number and variety of machines kept multiplying. The development of the machine depended, however, upon other developments, including new sources of energy, increased production of metals, and more efficient methods of business.

New sources of energy

Energy to drive its machines—this is the first requirement of an industrial nation. And the United States had sources of energy in abundance. It had enormous deposits of coal, huge underground pockets of oil and natural gas, water-power sites, and the technological "know-how" to generate huge amounts of electric power.

By the 1920's coal, the traditional source of energy for the Industrial Revolution, was meeting stiff competition from petroleum, natural gas, and electricity. Between 1920 and 1930 the annual consumption of coal actually dropped by about 20 percent, while petroleum production more than doubled, and the production of natural gas increased 150 percent.

But the most phenomenal development was in the production and use of electricity. In 1900 this new energy source had hardly been tapped. By 1920 Americans were producing 50 billion kilowatt-hours annually; by 1930, 114 billion. In brief, the United States was using more electricity than all other countries of the world combined.

The assembly line

As energy to drive machines became increasingly abundant, manufacturers and engineers tackled the problem of using it most efficiently. Older machines were improved, and new machines were developed for factory, farm, and home. But it was the organization of machines on a conveyor-belt assembly line that provided one of the striking characteristics of the American economy in the 1920's.

As you have read, mass production was an essential element of American industry long before the 1920's. Manufacturers had been using standardized interchangeable parts ever since Eli Whitney and European inventors had developed the technique more than a century earlier. But the conveyor-belt assembly line was relatively new. First used on a large scale by Henry Ford in 1914, the assembly line was soon adopted by other industries.

Bigger and bigger industries

Mass production could be carried on only by large, highly organized industrial concerns. During the "Golden Twenties" there was plenty of surplus capital to finance industrial development. As a result older industries grew by leaps and bounds, while new industries climbed into the ranks of the giants.

Most of the growth of industry was the result of *mergers*—that is, the combining of two or more independent companies into one larger company. Between 1919 and 1929, for example, more than 1,000 mergers took place in manufacturing and mining. By 1930 only 200 corporations owned nearly half of the country's corporate wealth and one fifth of the total national wealth.

Industrial efficiency

As industries continued to grow, they also continued to become more efficient. Efficiency engineering was not, of course, a product of the 1920's. As you may recall, in the early 1900's Frederick W. Taylor had pioneered in studies of machines and the workers who operated them. During the 1920's these "time-and-motion" studies were generally undertaken before a new machine or process was installed in an industrial plant.

Business executives also applied efficiency engineering, or "scientific management," to the problems of business planning and office bookkeeping. This new approach to industrial efficiency was called "cost accounting." Cost accountants found out the cost of every item of machinery, materials, and labor that went into the total cost of producing or selling a product. They could then show business concerns how to cut costs and thus gain greater production at lower prices.

Herbert C. Hoover, as Secretary of Commerce under Presidents Harding and Coolidge, helped to spread the idea of scientific management. He encouraged industry to use fewer and simpler standardized parts and models as a way of achieving economy and efficiency.

Hoover also tried to minimize the waste involved in competition. He urged business organizations to share information, to work out common policies, and to draw up codes of fair prices.

This government attitude naturally encouraged the growth of large-scale industry. In the 1920's the government did not make any great effort to enforce the Sherman and the Clayton

Antitrust Acts. Business and government were more interested in industrial efficiency than in industrial competition.

Advertising and marketing

Marketing techniques also became more effective during the 1920's. Manufacturers spent large sums on advertising to encourage the public to choose their products over those of their competitors. Advertising firms studied public psychology to discover how to appeal to consumers most effectively. Advertising firms also encouraged Americans to abandon the deeply rooted American ideal of thrift. In "an age of abundance," they said, continued prosperity depended upon spending, not saving.

Mail-order houses, department stores, and chain stores continued to grow in number and size. The companies that had pioneered in new methods of marketing during the late 1800's—Montgomery Ward; Sears, Roebuck; the Great Atlantic and Pacific Tea Company; F. W. Woolworth; Marshall Field—were still among the leaders in their fields. These companies and many new ones were getting a big portion of the nation's retail business.

Two new developments, both destined to contribute to a future revolution in the packaging of goods, first emerged in the 1920's. In 1923 Clarence Birdseye developed a method of quick-freezing for preserving perishable foods. In the same year the Du Pont company bought the American patent rights to cellophane, a transparent wrapping material. By the late 1920's frozen foods were being sold in stores, and cellophane was attracting attention.

The automobile industry

Even more important to the story of America's economic expansion in the 1920's was the development of the automobile. In 1920 about 8 million passenger cars and about 1 million trucks were registered in the United States. By 1930 about 23 million passenger cars—an average of one car for every six citizens—and 3.5 million trucks were traveling the nation's roads, and the "automobile revolution" was in full swing.

This revolution had far-reaching consequences. By 1930 cars, trucks, and buses had almost completely replaced horse-drawn vehicles, and even the railroads and trolley cars were beginning to suffer from the competition of the gasoline-driven vehicles.

By the end of the 1920's the automobile industry had become the nation's biggest business, with an annual product valued at $3.5 billion in 1929. Moreover, this new industrial giant

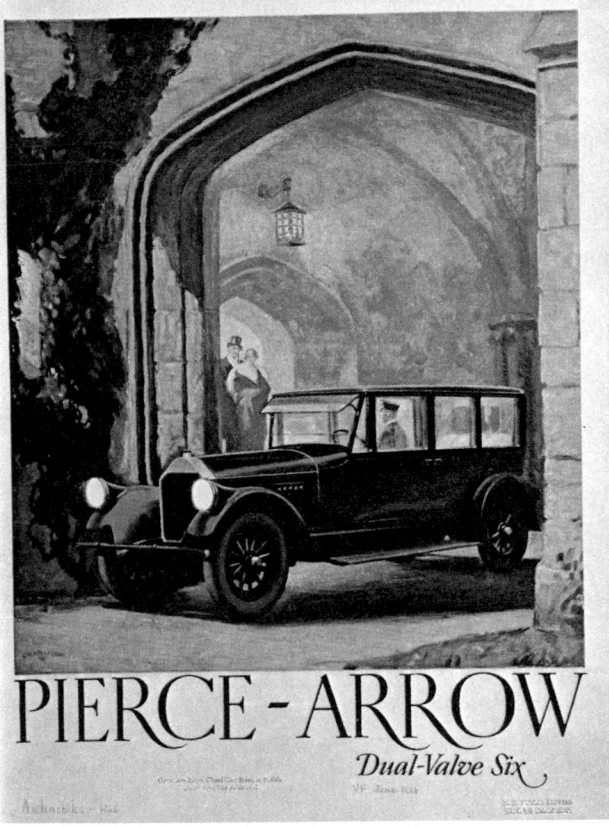

By the 1920's, advertising had become an essential part of American business success. It was used to sell nearly everything, from soap to expensive cars. This automobile ad appeared in 1926.

used huge quantities of steel, glass, rubber, and other materials. It created a rising demand for materials to build paved roads, garages, and service stations. It is estimated that 5 million persons, or one of every nine American workers, were employed in the automobile industry or a related business by 1930.

New industries

Garages, service stations, and trucking firms were only a few of the new industries that emerged during the 1920's. The increasing availability of electricity stimulated production of many laborsaving devices for the home—refrigerators, vacuum cleaners, toasters, electric irons, electric fans, and electric stoves.

The chemical industry, in which Germany had led the world before World War I, became in the 1920's one of America's most rapidly growing enterprises. By 1929 several American chemical companies were larger than any European competitors. In 1930 Du Pont, the giant among chemical companies, was producing

The booming economy of the 1920's was characterized by an "automobile revolution," the emergence of many new industries—and increased pollution.

1,100 different products in 80 different factories in the United States. Among the products pouring out of the chemical plants were rayon, synthetic resins, and a growing variety of plastics.

Problems of industrialization

Despite all its benefits, however, there was a negative side to this rapid process of industrialization. Chemicals, gasoline, and other technical innovations began to pollute America's rivers and lakes—and even the air. In the cities, traffic and air pollution became problems, while crowded housing conditions spurred the spread of slums. In the 1920's, however, few Americans paid much attention to these results of rapid changes in the economy. Most people living in the United States were content to enjoy the advantages of the quickening tempo of the machine age.

SECTION SURVEY

IDENTIFY: merger, scientific management, cost accounting, marketing techniques; Clarence Birdseye.

1. The machine and the word "efficiency" characterized the America of the 1920's. Comment.
2. What was the attitude of the federal government toward big business in the 1920's? Why?
3. What is the function of advertising? Do you think the advertising industry should regulate itself? Explain.
4. What do you think is the relationship between advertising and easy credit?

2 New ways of living in country, town, and city

During the 1920's the onward march of industrialization increasingly affected the lives of all Americans as the nation continued to grow in industrial power and in population.

Facts and figures

The 1920 census revealed that the population of the United States was almost 106 million. And for the first time in American history, those living in towns and cities outnumbered farm and country dwellers. The urban population then totaled 54 million, the rural population 51 million.

The onward march of urbanization and industrialization was even more apparent by the end of the decade. The census of 1930 showed that the population of the United States had climbed to nearly 123 million, an increase of 17 million. Most of the increase was in urban areas, where almost 69 million people lived by 1930. The rural population, on the other hand, totaled only about 54 million.

And even a large part of the rural population lived in small towns and villages. Between 1920 and 1930 the farm population decreased from 31.6 million to 30.4 million, as young people in growing numbers left the farms to seek new opportunities in the booming cities.

Changing ways on the farm

By the 1920's, also, the isolation and loneliness of farm life seemed to be things of the past. Paved roads covered the countryside. Telephone and electric wires stretched along roads and across fields to farmhouses. Single-wire antennas, called "aerials" in the 1920's, carried music, news, and entertainment by way of the new radio sets into farm homes everywhere. Henry Ford's "Tin Lizzies" were parked beside barns and houses.

Machines were also transforming farm life and helping to ease farmers' burdens. Where electricity was available, it was used for lighting, for pumping water, and for operating refrigerators, vacuum cleaners, sewing machines, and other laborsaving devices for the home. Milking machines could be found on many dairy farms. And trucks, tractors, and many power-driven farm implements were now being used in numbers.

Power-driven machines enabled farmers to do much more work in much less time with much less effort. More efficient farming methods and better plants and breeds of livestock also helped to increase farm productivity.

Farm problems

But increased productivity also created problems. A surplus of farm products drove farm prices downward. To be sure, not all farmers were hit equally hard by rising surpluses and falling prices. Dairy and truck farmers profited from the shift in American eating habits away from cereals toward more milk, butter, vegetables, and fruit. Indeed, the citrus fruit industries of California, Texas, and Florida enjoyed a spectacular development as a result of the rising demand for fruit and the establishment of cooperative advertising and marketing organizations. Tobacco growers also enjoyed a "sellers' market" as cigarette smoking became more popular. The large mechanized farms continued to prosper, mainly because they could afford the best equipment and could market their products most economically.

But although some farmers prospered, many suffered. Hardest hit were those families who owned small farms. Many of them, handicapped by lack of money to buy expensive equipment and by limited acreage, found it increasingly difficult to make a living. At the start of the Great Depression in 1929 and 1930, it was the small farmers who first lost their homes and their lands.

Changing ways in town and city

Meanwhile towns and cities were undergoing spectacular growth. Between 1920 and 1930 the rapidly growing population pushed 25 of America's older cities above the 100,000 figure; by 1930, 93 cities had populations of 100,000 or more. Some urban areas more than doubled their populations during this decade.

The very appearance of urban centers began to change. Huge new apartment houses appeared on what had been vacant lots or the sites of one-family houses. New skyscrapers pierced the skyline as builders tried to provide office space for the growing industries.

Less spectacular but no less significant was the changing appearance of shopping areas. In nearly every town and city merchants remodeled older stores or built new stores to provide for the needs of the growing population.

Streets built in earlier times for horse-drawn vehicles and for a more leisurely way of life became increasingly crowded and noisy as automobiles and trucks multiplied. And during the 1920's a new method of transportation, the bus, began to compete with the older electric trolleys. Although not a single bus was registered in the United States in 1920, about 40,500 were registered by 1930.

Women found increasing job opportunities during the 1920's. These women are typists and clerks in a large office.

Perhaps most spectacular of all was the development of suburban areas. Streetcar lines and paved roads pushed out from the cities into the surrounding countryside. Farms in outlying areas were divided into building lots, and row after row of houses appeared in developments with such fanciful names as "Sunset Acres," "Grand View," and "American Venice."

New opportunities for women

The changing appearance of the cities reflected larger and deeper changes in American life. One striking development was the growing freedom and opportunity for women.

For 100 years before the 1920's, women had been winning larger opportunities in political, economic, and social affairs. But their greatest gains came in the 1920's. With the adoption of the Nineteenth Amendment in 1920, women won the right to vote in national elections. This was a landmark in women's long struggle to win equality with men.

Equally important were women's gains made as a result of industrialization. The housewife's burden was eased by new laborsaving devices—washing machines and irons, new types of stoves, vacuum cleaners, and refrigerators. Ready-made clothing and inexpensive sewing machines also relieved women of much of their labor. Packaged foods and canned goods helped to lighten the task of preparing meals.

Middle-class women who could afford these new services found new uses for their leisure time. Many now had more time to read books and magazines, to attend art exhibits, to hear lectures. Others now had time to work for civic improvements, to take part in political affairs, and to influence public opinion through such organizations as the League of Women Voters. Still others took active parts in parent-teacher associations. Never before had so many women found time and opportunity to develop interests outside the home.

The rapidly multiplying machines in mills, plants, and factories created new jobs on assembly lines for less privileged women. This was especially true in the textile and tobacco factories springing up in the South. Moreover, women were finding increasing opportunities to work as sales clerks, office workers, and stenographers.

The "new woman"

In some places the changing status and roles of women brought vigorous expressions of a new sense of freedom. The "new woman," often a "career woman," was more or less independent economically, and she openly challenged what Charlotte Perkins Gilman, a leader of the new feminism, called "this man-made world." The new woman rejected traditional female roles, refused to believe in the superior competence of men, and denounced the different standards imposed on women in economic, sexual, and social relationships.

This defiance of conventional conduct among women was symbolized by the "flappers." These young women, wearing above-the-knee dresses, bobbed hair, and lipstick, shocked older Americans as well as many people their own age. They took advantage of the freedom and mobility of the automobile, discussed sex openly and frankly, smoked cigarettes, and defied the national prohibition law by drinking in "speakeasies," or illegal bars.

To some militant feminists, such indications of social freedom and equality did not go far enough. The Woman's Party publicly challenged remaining legal discriminations against women and demanded full equality in politics, business, the professions, sports, and the arts. In particular, the Woman's Party set as its goal an equal rights amendment to the Constitution that would outlaw all discrimination based on sex.

Workers' gains and losses

The surge of women into offices and factories was only one phase of the revolution that was transforming the lives of wage earners. The ever more rapid development of power-driven machines continued to free workers from back-breaking toil. Increased productivity brought generally higher wages, with which workers could buy products they had never before been able to afford.

Wage earners also benefited from studies undertaken to find ways of lessening fatigue and eliminating accidents on the job. From these studies business managers learned that workers were happier and actually produced more when employers showed an interest in them. Applying this lesson, some employers introduced profit sharing and retirement plans and provided cafeterias, game rooms, and ball parks for employees.

But although employers as a whole showed increasing interest in working conditions, they opposed labor unions even more vigorously than before the war. A growing number of corporations in the 1920's organized "company unions"—that is, unions organized by the employers or their representatives, and dominated by the employers rather than the workers. Company unions, as well as the higher standard of living of the workers, contributed to the decline in strength of organized labor during the 1920's.

Limited progress for Negroes

As you recall, many black families who moved into northern cities in the 1900's met with discrimination in jobs and housing, as well as in almost every aspect of their social life. But they also found new opportunities.

The number of black wage earners in American industries nearly doubled between 1910 and 1930, rising from about 600,000 to more than 1 million. During the same period black employees in clerical occupations rose from 19,000 to nearly 41,000. Negroes employed in civil service jobs increased from about 22,000 to around 50,000, most of them as postal employees. By 1930 some 70,000 Negroes owned their own businesses.

In the late 1800's and early 1900's opportunities for black Americans in most fields had remained quite limited. But despite this, individual Negroes had made outstanding contributions to American life. For example, in 1893 Dr. Daniel H. Williams successfully performed the first open-heart surgical operation. And in 1909 Matthew Hensen, adventurer and explorer, together with Admiral Robert E. Peary, reached the North Pole. In artistic fields Meta Warwick Fuller, a sculptor, and Henry O. Tanner, a painter, among many others, enriched American life with work of high technical skill and great beauty. Finally, in the field of applied science George Washington Carver's achievements were truly impressive. In the early 1900's Carver became famous for his work at Tuskegee Institute in developing hybrid crops, and in instructing southern farmers, white as well as black, how to increase their crop yields and how to put familiar agricultural products to new uses.

In the 1920's black Americans continued to make significant, though limited, gains in education. A growing number of Negroes in the North and the South received a high school education, and more attended colleges and universities. By 1930 about 15,000 black Americans held academic degrees. Yet black leaders, as well as white citizens who shared their concern, pointed out that in 1930 many doors of opportunity still remained closed to black Americans. They also pointed out that the postwar advances, limited though they were, showed clearly what American Negroes could accomplish when they had the opportunity.

Negro rights

In the 1920's the Republican Party was trying to build strong political organizations among white Americans in the South. As a result the Republican administration did little to meet the demands of southern Negroes for federal protection of their voting rights or for a fair share of federally appointed jobs. But in northern urban centers black voters showed increasing strength. In 1928 a northern Negro, Oscar de Priest of Chicago, was elected to Congress where he served three terms.

And black Americans in both the North and the South were making headway in their struggle for equal justice before the law. Here the efforts of the NAACP to bring law suits to enforce the equal rights of black Americans began to show important progress.

Black self-identification

In the 1920's black Americans began to feel a growing sense of racial identification and pride, along with increasing interest in their African backgrounds. These feelings were strongly expressed by Marcus Garvey, a black immigrant from the West Indies.

Between 1910 and 1930, black Americans made significant, though limited, gains in education and job opportunities. This photograph of the staff of a city bank was made in 1928.

Garvey became convinced that Negroes could never win true freedom and equality in the United States. He popularized among black city slum dwellers a form of black nationalism which emphasized a "back to Africa" movement. He eloquently described the achievements of black Africans, and urged his listeners to return "home," where they might enjoy opportunities they could never find in white-dominated America. Although none of Garvey's half million followers actually moved to Africa, his movement gave many Negroes a new sense of racial pride.

Most black leaders of the 1920's opposed Garvey's movement as unrealistic and as escapism. They insisted that Negroes, having long been Americans, could and must win the rights and opportunities that other Americans enjoyed. But these leaders also encouraged American Negroes to interest themselves in the achievements and aspirations of black people in Africa and other parts of the world. Racial solidarity, they urged, should replace the narrow outlook that separated black Americans from black people in other lands, and that also separated black Americans themselves into different economic and social groups.

The "new Negro"

The rise of younger black leaders in the 1920's was stimulated by a book entitled *The New Negro* by Alain Locke, a professor at Howard University. This important book both reflected and encouraged changes taking place in black communities.

The new black leaders insisted that the "new Negro" must be proud of his or her heritage and of black people's achievements. They insisted that black Americans must stop being apologetic and defensive toward white Americans. The "new Negro" must realize that self-assertiveness, not accommodation, was the only effective way to gain equality and full implementation of America's democratic creed.

The "Harlem renaissance"

Inspired by the image of the "new Negro," a cultural renaissance, or rebirth, aroused the interest of many white Americans, while strengthening the growing pride of black Americans. This cultural rebirth of the 1920's centered in New York City's black community of Harlem, and has been called the "Harlem renaissance." But its rich expressions were not confined to Harlem.

These new cultural contributions were marked by originality, freshness of style, and vigor. "Jazz" music, with its exciting and spontaneous rhythms, and "the blues," reflecting the joy, laughter, sadness, and pain of black Amer-

Among the great jazz bands of the 1920's, none was more popular than that of Duke Ellington (seated at the piano).

icans, found outstanding exponents and performers in the 1920's. Among these were W. C. Handy, Scott Joplin, Jelly Roll Morton, and Duke Ellington. Black "spirituals" became part of the repertory of Marian Anderson, who in the 1920's was just beginning her career as one of the world's greatest singers of classical as well as folk music.

The literature of the Harlem renaissance reflected the racial pride of the "new Negro." Langston Hughes, Claude McKay, and Countee Cullen wrote verse marked by haunting bitterness and defiance, but also by joy and hope. This many-sided emotional richness among black writers was exemplified in Jean Towner's *Cane.* This work portrayed black environments in the rural South, in Washington, D.C., and in New York City, starkly revealing its characters' intense emotions while also portraying their beauty and dignity.

SECTION SURVEY

IDENTIFY: urbanization, company union, "flappers," the Woman's Party, *The New Negro,* "Harlem renaissance"; Matthew Hensen, George Washington Carver, Marcus Garvey, Marian Anderson.

1. What conflicts began to emerge in the 1920's between urban and rural values as they related to (a) the family, (b) politics, (c) morals, (d) recreation?
2. What are the relationships between women, freedom, and industrialization? How did women's lives begin to change in the 1920's?
3. Describe the contributions made by (a) individual Negroes in the early 1920's, (b) leading figures in the "Harlem renaissance."
4. (a) What is meant by black self-identification? (b) How was it accomplished? (c) What is meant by the term "new Negro"?
5. What positions were taken by various black leaders in their efforts to improve the position of black Americans?

3 New ways of living reflected in education, literature, and the arts

As the industrial society expanded, it became increasingly clear that Americans needed a far more extensive education than that which had been considered adequate in earlier times. Under the impact of the machine, the educational system continued to change.

Growth of enrollment

One important development was the increase in school enrollment. Between 1900 and 1920, for instance, the total high school enrollment rose from under 700,000 to about 2.5 million. By 1930 the enrollment had soared to about 4.8 million.

The colleges showed similar gains. Between 1900 and 1920 college enrollments jumped from about 237,000 to 597,000. During the 1920's this figure almost doubled, climbing to 1.1 million by 1930.

To meet the needs of this enormously increased student body, American states and communities had to spend huge sums for new school buildings, textbooks and equipment, and teachers' salaries. The wealth created by the growing industrialization provided taxes for education. There were, of course, many young people who still could not afford to go beyond elementary school. But after 1920 a larger proportion than ever before obtained a high school education.

Curriculum changes

The growing complexity of the industrial society with its emphasis upon highly specialized skills called for men and women trained in mathematics, engineering, science, and the skilled trades. To meet the new needs, educators began to enlarge the curriculum to include more work in vocational training, home economics, commercial courses, health, physical education, modern foreign languages, and civic education. Special trade schools, technical schools, and commercial schools were built in an effort to adapt the educational system to the machine age.

Changes in school administration

The machine age also affected the organization and administration of the schools. The development of cars and buses, for example, enabled students from widely scattered areas to attend centrally located schools. As a result, in rural regions consolidated schools of good quality replaced the scattered, one-room "little red schoolhouses." In the cities a few high schools were built for as many as 5,000 to 10,000 students. Some people worried, however, that American schools and colleges might be too much influenced by industrial techniques of organization and administration.

Toward a more effective education

Students of education were reaching new conclusions about how people actually learn and about the purposes of education. Educators, following in the path earlier marked out by psychologists William James and G. Stanley Hall, were proving that a child's mind can be molded—within limits. Other scholars, among them John Dewey, continued to emphasize that life itself is an education, and that the way to produce effective citizens is to give boys and girls actual experience in democratic living. Still other scholars, led by psychologists such as Edward L. Thorndike, worked out tests for measuring intelligence and for evaluating the educational process.

Journalism

Newspapers and magazines also reflected the influence of the machine age. By the 1920's journalism had become big business, highly organized and highly standardized. The *Reader's Digest,* started in 1922, quickly won nationwide circulation with its digests of articles from other journals. *Time* magazine, started in 1923, also became widely read for its terse comments on current affairs.

Many of the individually owned older newspapers were being bought up by large newspaper chains. Chain newspapers ran the same syndicated columns and editorials, the same comics, sports news, and advertisements, and subscribed to the same news services—the Associated Press, the United Press, and the International News Service. The newspapers, like the magazines, reflected the problems of industrial America.

Literature

In the 1920's the faded past of New York City and of Virginia continued to interest two well-established novelists, Edith Wharton and Ellen Glasgow. Much of the literature of the 1920's also dealt with such ever-popular themes as love, personal conflicts, and adventure. Many authors, however, wrote about the conflicts and confusions of the machine age. In his poem *The Waste Land,* T. S. Eliot pictured society in the machine age as grim, barren, standardized, commercialized, cheap, and vulgar. Carl Sandburg, who found much to admire in the new industrialized society, also showed how terrible life could be when society glorified the machine

HIGHLIGHTS OF AMERICAN WRITING

Robert Frost (1874–1963), who described a complete poem as one "where an emotion has found its thought and the thought has found the words," won the Pulitzer prize for poetry four times. Among his most famous poems are "The Death of the Hired Man" and "Mending Wall."

Amy Lowell (1874–1925), a poet and critic, is remembered most for two romantic poems, "Patterns" and "Lilacs."

H. L. Mencken (1880–1956), an essayist and editor, wrote many witty and biting essays and compiled *The American Language,* described by one critic as "a wonderful combination of scholarship, festivity, social history, . . . political and literary feuding, industry, genuine love of country, unashamed bias, humor, commentary on the world, compendium of American manners, and anthology of Mencken prejudices."

Eugene O'Neill (1888–1953), often called America's first important dramatist, wrote several long and deeply psychological dramas; some short plays; and a comedy, *Ah, Wilderness!* He won the Pulitzer prize three times.

Edna St. Vincent Millay (1892–1950) was still a student when one of her best-known poems, "Renascence," was published. She won the Pulitzer prize for poetry with her book of sonnets entitled *The Harp-Weaver.*

Pearl Buck (1892–1973), who grew up and worked as a missionary in China, drew upon her many years there to write several novels about Chinese life. Her Pulitzer-prize-winning novel *The Good Earth* traces a Chinese family through several generations and through many troubles.

Thornton Wilder (1897–1975) was both a novelist and a playwright. His novel *The Bridge of San Luis Rey,* his well-known play *Our Town,* and his allegorical play *The Skin of Our Teeth* all won Pulitzer prizes.

Stephen Vincent Benét (1898–1943) became obsessed with the desire to write a long narrative poem using the military information which so interested him. As a result he produced *John Brown's Body,* which won him a Pulitzer prize for poetry. His short story "The Devil and Daniel Webster" is a minor American classic.

---

and neglected people. Gertrude Stein's bold experiments with words suggested some new ways writers were looking at the contemporary world.

The fiction of the 1920's also reflected the influence of the machine age. *This Side of Paradise,* a popular novel by F. Scott Fitzgerald, revealed the tragic confusion of America's youth in a society all too often characterized by fast living and hard drinking. In *Main Street, Babbitt,* and other novels, Sinclair Lewis portrayed the hypocrisy and the shallowness of those who worshiped the dollar and the material comforts of the machine age. The short stories of Sherwood Anderson poignantly reflected the loss of the old craft skills. Ernest Hemingway, one of the so-called "hard-boiled realists," told of the tragic plight of Americans who lived abroad to escape the standardized culture of machine-dominated America.

Theodore Dreiser, in the novel *An American Tragedy,* pictured youth caught in the mad drive for power and wealth, and condemned a society whose ideals and morals were materialistic and grasping. Willa Cather's *The Professor's House* dealt with the contrasting values of an older world that had time for poetry and the newer world that was so much concerned with material possessions. In his novels, John Dos Passos wrote of the crushing effect the machine had on the individual's ideals and aspirations.

Painting and design

In painting and design Americans were more and more influenced by such European artists as Cézanne, Manet, Monet, Degas, Matisse, and Picasso. Some modernists boldly experimented with geometric designs that often resembled machines in their emphasis on hard angles, masses, and abstract form. Many Ameri-

Edward Hopper, 1887-1967. "Early Sunday Morning." Oil on canvas. 19330. 35 x 60. Collection of Whitney Museum of American Art, New York.

Many artists became interested in painting scenes of American life. Edward Hopper's "Early Sunday Morning," shown here, captured the feeling of a typical American town.

can artists continued to paint the more conventional themes, but they painted them in new ways. Others tried to reveal the meaning of the machine age in their paintings of factories, warehouses, slums, railroads, and other scenes of urban life.

New art forms

The machine age also opened up entirely new forms of art. In the hands of artists, the camera captured the spirit and meaning of the new age. New methods of art reproduction enabled people to own inexpensive yet excellent copies of the world's outstanding works of art. When these reproduction techniques were adopted by the mass-circulation magazines, millions of Americans were able to see the work of the world's greatest photographers, illustrators, and artists.

Aided by commercial artists and industrial designers, manufacturers began to produce telephones, furniture, fabrics, clothing, typewriters, glassware, refrigerators, stoves, automobiles, and a host of other articles that showed that machines and machine products might be beautiful in design and structure.

Architecture

Inspired by such outstanding architects as Louis Sullivan and Frank Lloyd Wright, other architects began to promote the idea that a building ought to use the materials and follow the forms most suitable to the purposes for which it was to be used.

For many people the skyscraper became a symbol of the influence of the machine upon architecture. Built of steel, glass, and concrete, it towered into the sky in order to use as little expensive ground space as possible, with its upper stories set back to prevent the streets from being darkened. In its emphasis upon clear-cut vertical lines and its massing of windows, the skyscraper was an excellent example of how purpose and materials dictated design.

Music and dancing

Music, too, showed the influence of the industrial age. Many people believed that the syncopated jazz of the 1920's expressed the rhythms and the accelerated speed and energy of the machine.

Music also became increasingly available through the radio, the phonograph, and musical instruments manufactured at lower and lower costs. Moreover, wealth created by the new industrial age supported symphony orchestras and opera companies.

Social dancing was transformed by jazz music, while the dance as an art form was revolutionized by Isadora Duncan, Ruth St. Denis, Katherine Dunham, Ted Shawn, and Martha Graham. These dancers emphasized free and expressive movements in contrast to the traditional, formal patterns of the ballet.

SECTION SURVEY

IDENTIFY: machine age, *An American Tragedy, Reader's Digest, Time* magazine; Edward L. Thorndike, William James, Sinclair Lewis, F. Scott Fitzgerald, Edith Wharton.

1. How did some writers show their disillusionment with the America of the 1920's?
2. What is the responsibility of writers—to transmit values or to attempt to convey the spirit of their times?
3. (a) Do you think the artists of the 1920's conveyed the spirit of their times? Explain. (b) Take four artists or writers of the period and show whether they did or did not reflect the 1920's.
4. The skyscraper was a symbol of the influence of land values, purpose, and materials upon architecture. Comment.

4 Striking changes in the daily life of Americans

With money in their pockets and more leisure time than ever before, Americans in the 1920's poured into the countryside, packed stadiums, and jammed motion picture theaters. Indeed, it was this vigorous pursuit of entertainment that led historians to refer to the 1920's as the "Jazz Age" and the "Age of Wonderful Nonsense."

The automobile

The automobile was a major source of American recreation, as entire families piled into the car for an evening's ride or a weekend trip.

By the 1920's the automobile was no longer the exclusive possession of the well-to-do. When working-class families were interviewed in a typical midwestern city in 1923, nearly half of them owned cars. The 1920's also saw the swing from the open to the closed car, with car design becoming an endless topic of conversation.

But although the automobile made travel comfortable and private, it also created new problems. Traffic accidents and deaths kept rising. Young people asserted their independence by driving off in the family car, free from parental supervision. Many Americans believed that the automobile was disrupting the family and destroying the nation's moral code.

National prohibition of liquor

As you may recall, the Eighteenth Amendment was ratified in January 1919. This amendment gave the federal government power to prohibit "the manufacture, sale, or transportation of intoxicating liquors within, the importation thereof into, or the exportation thereof from the United States and all territory subject to the jurisdiction thereof. . . ."

In October 1919 Congress passed the Prohibition Enforcement Act, usually called the Volstead Act, over President Wilson's veto. This act defined as "intoxicating liquor" any beverage containing more than one half of one percent of alcohol. The Volstead Act turned enforcement of the law over to the Bureau of Internal Revenue, and created the special office of Commissioner of Prohibition.

Many Americans who were otherwise law-abiding citizens refused to obey the prohibition laws. This couple is about to enter a "speakeasy," where liquor is being served illegally.

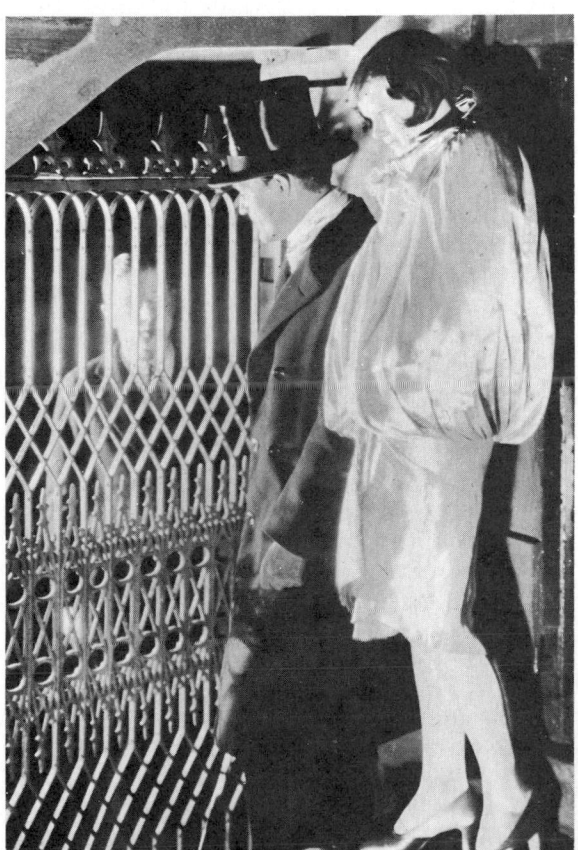

Prohibition problems

The prohibition experiment created serious problems in American life. Long coastlines in the east and west and unguarded frontiers to the north and south made it impossible to stop the flow of illegal liquor into the country.

Bootlegging became big business controlled by criminal elements in the large cities. The gangster Al Capone, who ruled Chicago's underworld, commanded a small "army" of gangsters equipped with revolvers, sawed-off shotguns, and submachine guns. Gang wars and other violence became common in many American cities during the "Roaring Twenties." Moreover, the gangs branched out to seize control of gambling establishments and dance halls. By the end of the decade, they had begun to develop the so-called "rackets." The racketeers collected "protection" money from businesses, threatening violence if their victims failed to pay.

The people themselves were partly to blame for this widespread violation of the law. Many Americans who were otherwise law-abiding refused to take prohibition seriously. Finally, in 1933, the prohibition era ended when the necessary number of states ratified the Twenty-first Amendment. This amendment repealed the Eighteenth Amendment and returned the power to control the sale of intoxicating drinks to the states themselves.

Radio

Meanwhile another new development—radio —was transforming the lives of millions of Americans, young and old alike.

KDKA, the first commercial broadcasting station, began to operate in Pittsburgh on November 2, 1920. Radio immediately became a craze. By 1922 sales of receiving sets and radio parts totaled more than $60 million. By 1929 sales amounted to almost $400 million, more than 600 broadcasting stations had been licensed, and one third of all American homes owned radio receivers.

Radio brought an enormous variety of information and entertainment directly to American families in their homes. The most popular programs featured "crooners," jazz musicians, comedians, sports announcers, and newscasters. But many Americans felt that radio was not fulfilling its great promise as an instrument of education and culture. They criticized the dominant role of advertisers who paid the broadcasting companies and entertainers, and often determined what programs would be presented.

Despite the trivial content of many programs, however, radio served the nation in a variety of ways. By providing common experiences for all Americans, it increased the feeling of national unity. Radio also helped to overcome the isolation of rural life. It encouraged popular interest in current events, including sports, and offered useful information on health, home economics, and farming techniques. It made serious music available to more Americans than ever before. Finally, radio provided greater safety for airplanes and ships.

Movies

The motion picture industry also enjoyed a spectacular growth during the 1920's. By the 1920's huge and lavish motion picture "palaces" had been built in most large cities. By the end of the decade weekly audiences approached 100 million people, and the industry itself had become big business, the fourth largest in the nation.

A major step forward was made in 1927 when Warner Brothers released the first successful "talkie"—*The Jazz Singer,* featuring Al Jolson. For years the industry had been working on the problem of using sound with pictures. Within a year of the first success, the old silent films were being replaced by the even more popular sound pictures.

During the 1920's the movie industry turned out many films more polished in technique and more sophisticated in content than the pre-war films. These new films emphasized such popular themes as social advancement, the reckless enjoyment of life, and the independence of women. In the prosperous "Golden Twenties," many Americans who hoped to become rich learned from the films produced by Cecil B. de Mille and Ernst Lubitsch how the rich behaved, or were thought to behave.

Not all the films of this period, however, were concerned with such popular themes. Erich von Stroheim's *Greed* transformed a realistic novel by Frank Norris into a film which described with great power how greed for money warped the character and finally destroyed the lives of a working-class couple. Lewis Milestone's *All Quiet on the Western Front,* based on a novel about World War I by Erich Remarque, expressed very movingly the widespread anti-war feeling of the 1920's. Other films, such as Robert J. Flaherty's *Nanook of the North,* successfully captured the grandeur of nature in distant places.

Sports

During the 1920's public interest in sports grew markedly. Baseball remained the most popular professional game, with between 9 and

10 million people attending major league games annually. Babe Ruth, who replaced Ty Cobb as the idol of fans, in 1927 astounded the baseball world by hitting a record number of 60 home runs.

College football drew some 30 million spectators in the same year. Red Grange, a halfback for the University of Illinois, became a national hero. Jim Thorpe, with a Sac, Fox, Potawamie, and Irish heritage, also became a national hero. After playing football at Carlisle, an Indian college in Pennsylvania, he won medals in several events at the Olympic Games in Stockholm, Sweden, in 1912. Later, as an outstanding player in big league baseball and professional football, Thorpe was acclaimed as "the outstanding athlete of the half century." In boxing, ardent fans in 1927 spent over $2.6 million to see the famous Dempsey-Tunney match. Amateur as well as professional interest also increased in such sports as golf, tennis, swimming, skating, and bowling.

Feats and fads

Americans in the 1920's were unusually responsive to new fads and fashions and dramatic public events. This period has been called the "Jazz Age" with some justice, for the rhythmic music of jazz was perhaps the most consistently popular of the new fashions. Most of the other fads shifted rapidly from year to year: from the Chinese-originated game of mah-jongg to cross-word puzzles, to vigorous dances like the Charleston, to eccentric activities like flagpole sitting and marathon dances.

But some of the nation's enthusiasm was directed to individual accomplishments. The most glorified hero of the 1920's was Charles A. Lindbergh, who in May 1927 made the first non-stop flight from New York to Paris in his plane *The Spirit of St. Louis.* Another fearless voyager

Boxing was one of the most popular spectator sports of the 1920's. Artist George Bellows painted this scene of Jack Dempsey's being knocked out of the ring by Luis Firpo.

George Bellows, "Dempsey and Firpo." Oil on canvas. 1924. 51 x 63¼. Collection Whitney Museum of American Art, New York.

was Commander (later Admiral) Richard E. Byrd, who made the first flights to both the North and the South Pole. Other Americans who followed the example of Lindbergh and Byrd proved that the postwar period was an age of authentic feats as well as eccentric fads.

SECTION SURVEY

IDENTIFY: Volstead Act, KDKA, *The Spirit of St. Louis,* *The Jazz Singer, Nanook of the North;* Commander Byrd, Babe Ruth.

1. In what ways did the radio and movies serve the American people in this period?
2. The Eighteenth Amendment provides a good example of a segment of the American public trying to legislate moral behavior for all Americans. Comment.
3. How did the prohibition era help to create a breakdown in morality and a lack of respect for the law?
4. How did the hero-worship of Charles Lindbergh fulfill a need of many Americans living in the 1920's?

CHAPTER SURVEY

INQUIRING INTO HISTORY

1. What do you think accounted for the "fads" of the 1920's?
2. What were some of the elements in American life that American writers and artists of the 1920's criticized? Do you agree with them? Why or why not?
3. Why did "the new woman" challenge the so-called "man-made world" during the 1920's? How did feminists try to change women's roles?
4. How did the radio, movies, and newspapers contribute to conformity? How did they contribute to individualism?
5. Why did "practical" courses supersede classical studies in high schools and colleges by 1930?
6. What factors do you think contributed to the change in American manners and morals in the 1920's?
7. How did industrialization affect the lives of people (a) on farms and (b) in cities? Does industrialization always mean progress? Explain.
8. Why do you think Marcus Garvey's message—pride in race and economic self-sufficiency—appealed to black Americans in the 1920's?
9. Justify the use of each of the following terms to describe the tempo of the 1920's: (a) "Golden Twenties," (b) "Roaring Twenties," (c) "Age of Disillusionment." Which do you think best describes the era? Explain.

RELATING PAST TO PRESENT

1. The mass communications media depend upon the public for economic support. Keeping this in mind, do you think the media should cater to the tastes of the "average" person, or should they strive for above-average quality? Explain.
2. Should the federal government be responsible for what the mass media transmit to the American public? Explain.
3. The "Harlem Renaissance" was an expression by black Americans of their discontent as well as of their racial pride. Are black Americans today involved in a new renaissance? Explain.
4. During the 1920's, many black Americans left the South to come North. Did the northern cities turn out to be an escape to freedom or a new imprisonment? Does a similar situation exist today? Explain.

DEVELOPING SOCIAL SCIENCE SKILLS

1. Find a record or a book of songs that were popular in the 1920's. Compare these songs with songs that are popular today. How do they differ? How are they alike? How do the songs reflect the times?
2. Read some of the poetry written by a poet of the Harlem Renaissance. (a) What do the poems tell you about the lives and concerns of black Americans in the 1920's? (b) What are the poet's attitudes about American society and values?
3. Examine the picture on page 256. (a) What is the subject of the picture? (b) What details are emphasized? (c) What do you think is the viewpoint of the artist about industrialization?

The New Deal and World War II

1932-1945

CHAPTER 17
UNDERTAKING A
GREAT EXPERIMENT
1932-1936

President Franklin Delano Roosevelt took office on March 4, 1933, in the midst of the Great Depression. He began his administration with a ringing call to the American people to face the future with courage and faith. "The only thing we have to fear is fear itself," he confidently stated. His calm words helped to lift the nation from its despair and helped to rally the people behind the government.

The President outlined his New Deal program in a crisp, dramatic Inaugural Address. He then presented his reform proposals, with recommendations for immediate action, to a special session of Congress that he called soon after taking office.

The New Deal had in general three aims—relief, recovery, and reform. Because Americans were clamoring for action, the three aims were often mixed together as objectives of a single act of Congress. Sometimes measures adopted to realize one of the aims interfered with other measures designed to achieve the other aims.

But for easier analysis, it is convenient to divide the New Deal into its three essential parts: (1) measures to provide relief for the unemployed; (2) measures to speed the recovery of agriculture, industry, commerce, and labor; and (3) measures to remedy certain weaknesses in the economic system.

Such was the general nature of the Great Experiment that President Roosevelt and Congress launched in the spring of 1933.

THE CHAPTER IN OUTLINE

1. New Deal measures to provide relief and work for the unemployed.

2. Recovery measures to stimulate agriculture and help farmers.

3. Recovery measures to aid banking, building, and transportation.

4. Recovery measures to help industry and encourage labor.

5. Various reform measures carried out by the New Deal.

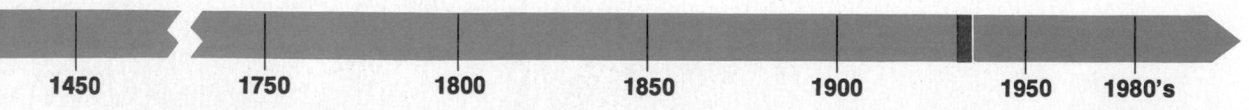

1450　　1750　　1800　　1850　　1900　　1950　　1980's

1 New Deal measures to provide relief and work for the unemployed

The most urgent task facing Roosevelt when he took office was to provide assistance for millions of jobless, hungry Americans. By 1933 nearly 14 million people were out of work.

Direct relief

The Roosevelt administration immediately launched what seemed at the time to be a colossal program of direct relief. In two years the Federal Emergency Relief Administration (FERA), created in 1933, and other federal agencies distributed $3 billion to needy Americans. Money was distributed to the states, allowing state and local officials to use the money as they chose—for direct relief or to provide jobs. At one time nearly 8 million families were on direct relief. But few Americans liked this kind of relief. What the unemployed wanted was jobs. Thus plans were made to replace direct relief with a program to provide work.

Work relief

The federal government attacked the problem of providing jobs in several different ways. For instance, during 1933–34 it paid nearly $1 billion in wages to men and women drawn from the relief rolls who were given jobs on "made work" projects. Many of the "made work" projects—raking leaves and picking up litter in parks—had relatively little value. Critics of the New Deal called this kind of work "boondoggling."

President Roosevelt and other New Dealers knew that federal charity and "made work" were at best necessary evils. What Americans needed and what the New Dealers wanted to provide was socially useful work. To accomplish this purpose, a new agency, the Works Progress Administration (WPA), was created in 1935, with Harry L. Hopkins as its head. The WPA cooperated with state and local governments, which shared in both the cost and the administration of the work relief program. During 1935 and 1936 Congress voted about $6.3 billion in funds for the new agency.

The WPA program helped people in many different ways. By 1936 more than 6,000 schoolhouses had been constructed or repaired; new sewage plants had been built in 5,000 communities; about 128,000 miles (205,990 kilometers) of secondary roads had been constructed or improved; and other public improvements had been made. Unemployed actors, musicians, and writers enriched American life by providing plays, concerts, guidebooks, and other forms of recreation. At the peak of its activity, in March 1936, nearly 4 million Americans were working for the WPA.

Work for youth

Perhaps the greatest tragedy of the depression was its effect upon millions of young Americans. Many were forced to leave school or college because they lacked food and clothing or were

During the Great Depression, most unemployed Americans wanted jobs, not charity. To meet this demand, the Roosevelt administration created such agencies as the WPA and the CCC. A group of CCC workers is shown here.

Mary McLeod Bethune (left) was one of the prominent leaders who made up President Roosevelt's "black cabinet." Here, she meets with Eleanor Roosevelt and a government official.

homeless. Those who graduated during the depression years faced unemployment. Thousands of jobless young Americans roamed the nation in search of work.

Two agencies were created to bring immediate work relief to the nation's youth. In 1933 the Civilian Conservation Corps (CCC) was organized. At times as many as 500,000 young men between 18 and 25 were enrolled in the CCC. Nearly all of them were unmarried; most came from poverty-stricken families. These youths lived in work camps scattered across the land. They received food, clothing, and shelter; they were paid wages which they were expected to share with their families; and they were offered opportunities for recreation and education.

The young Americans in the CCC did socially useful work. They built fire trails in the forests, cleared swamps, planted trees, built small dams for flood control, cleared land for public parks, and in other ways helped to conserve the nation's natural resources.

A second New Deal work relief measure aided young people still in school. The National Youth Administration (NYA), created in 1935, distributed federal money to needy students, who were paid regular wages for performing tasks in and around their school. During its first year the NYA gave jobs to more than 400,000 students.

The New Deal youth program saved hundreds of thousands of youths from idleness, helped them to maintain their self-respect, and enabled many to get an education. It also kept many young Americans out of the overcrowded job market in business and industry.

Negroes and the New Deal

Along with destitute white Americans, needy black Americans gained relief and employment in the Works Progress Administration, the Civilian Conservation Corps, and the National Youth Administration. But the depression hit black wage earners and farmers even harder than it did white workers. Though black Americans made up one tenth of the nation's population, by 1936 one sixth of those on relief were Negroes. Black tenant farmers and sharecroppers faced special hardships, and they often suffered discrimination in receiving benefits from the New Deal agricultural agencies. Discrimination also existed in the administration of federal housing programs and, especially at local levels, in other New Deal programs.

Yet the depression and new opportunities provided by the New Deal stimulated Negroes to struggle with renewed determination for their legal and constitutional rights. In many northern cities black leaders organized "don't buy where you can't work" campaigns. In the Southern Tenant Farmers' Union, tenant farmers, black and white, often joined together against wealthy landowners. The National Negro Congress, launched in 1935 with some support from white liberals and radicals, promoted the interests of black Americans within the New Deal agencies.

Finally, responding to pressures such as these and to the prodding of Eleanor Roosevelt, the President's wife, the New Deal administration appointed prominent Negroes to important federal positions. Among them were Mary McLeod Bethune, Ralph Bunche, and Robert C. Weaver. These leaders and others made up an informal group of advisers often called the "black cabinet."

Indians and the New Deal

In 1928, you may recall, the Institute for Government Research released a report severely critical of Indian policy under the Dawes Act. Partly as a result of this report, Congress in 1934 passed the Howard-Wheeler Act, or Indian Reorganization Act. This law marked a sharp change in Indian policy.

The new law halted the practice of breaking up the reservations by granting land to individual Indians. Going a step further, it tried to restore to tribal ownership portions of the reservations that had not yet become individual homesteads.

The new act permitted tribes to choose whether or not they wished to practice local self-government and to strengthen their own community life by re-establishing their traditional customs, beliefs, and crafts. The act, that is, emphasized local control rather than control from Washington, D.C. Thus, for example, Indians were now allowed to engage in any business of their choice, to make contracts, and to sue or be sued in court.

The Indian Reorganization Act of 1934 also tried to provide a better kind of education, one that would teach Indians how to use their land more effectively. Indians studied soil conservation methods and improved methods of raising and marketing their crops and livestock. The new educational program, which included adults as well as children, made the school a center of community life.

Encouraged by the new policy, many Indian tribes began to rebuild their tribal ways of life and to face the future with new hope. But problems remained. Some tribes that had been more or less successfully "Americanized" rejected the new policy because they believed it would keep them in an inferior status in American society. Some veterans of World War I felt that full recognition of their rights as citizens was more important than preserving tribal customs. Efforts to improve unused Indian lands often were unsuccessful. Thus although the new policy brought greater freedom and recognition to the Indians,

SOURCES

FRANKLIN D. ROOSEVELT'S FIRST INAUGURAL ADDRESS (1933)

So, first of all, let me assert my firm belief that the only thing we have to fear is fear itself—nameless, unreasoning, unjustified terror which paralyzes needed efforts to convert retreat into advance. . . .

Our greatest primary task is to put people to work. This is no unsolvable problem if we face it wisely and courageously.

It can be accomplished in part by direct recruiting by the government itself, treating the task as we would treat the emergency of a war, but at the same time, through this employment, accomplishing greatly needed projects to stimulate and reorganize the use of our natural resources.

Hand in hand with this, we must frankly recognize the overbalance of population in our industrial centers and, by engaging on a national scale in a redistribution, endeavor to provide a better use of the land for those best fitted for the land. . . .

In the field of world policy I would dedicate this nation to the policy of the good neighbor—the neighbor who resolutely respects himself and, because he does so, respects the rights of others—the neighbor who respects his obligations and respects the sanctity of his agreements in and with a world of neighbors. . . .

its aim of raising Indian standards of living was not realized.

Evaluating the relief program

The New Deal relief projects aroused much criticism, not only from Republicans, but also from members of the President's own party. It is true that many mistakes were made. There was bad management. There was waste.

Some New Dealers admitted the truth of these criticisms. They explained, however, that there had been no successful past examples to follow in the gigantic tasks they had undertaken. They also pointed out that they had been handicapped by lack of trained personnel to carry out some of their programs.

But, despite admitted weaknesses in the work relief program, New Dealers claimed that it had fully justified itself. Work provided by the federal government, they insisted, had saved millions of Americans from hunger and had allowed them to retain some measure of self-respect.

SECTION SURVEY

IDENTIFY: New Deal, FERA, direct relief, CCC, work relief, WPA, "black cabinet," Indian Reorganization Act; Ralph Bunche, Eleanor Roosevelt, Robert Weaver.

1. (a) What immediate problems confronted Roosevelt when he took office in 1933? (b) How was he able to get Congress to pass almost all of the initial legislation he proposed?
2. How did the New Deal respect states' rights in distributing funds for relief purposes?
3. Perhaps the greatest tragedy of the depression was its effect upon millions of young Americans. Why was this so?
4. (a) What criticisms were leveled against the New Deal relief program? (b) How did the New Dealers answer these criticisms?
5. What was the experience of Negroes during the New Deal? Of Indians during the New Deal?
6. The New Deal was not radical in concept. Comment.

2 Recovery measures to stimulate agriculture and help farmers

The New Deal measures to provide direct relief and work relief were intended to meet the urgent needs of millions of suffering Americans. Simultaneously, the New Deal administration launched a recovery program designed to restore the nation's economic health.

Saving the farmers' homes

When Roosevelt became President, two out of every five American farms were mortgaged. Moreover, farmers all over the country were faced with mounting debts—back taxes, interest payments, and payments on the principal of their loans. Unable to pay their debts, many farmers watched their farms pass into the hands of banks, insurance companies, and private mortgage holders. Some farm families then rented as tenants the land they had once owned; others were left homeless and jobless.

To relieve this desperate situation, the federal government made available a huge sum of money farmers could borrow at a low interest rate. Some farmers borrowed to buy seed, fertilizer, and equipment necessary to continue operations. Others borrowed to buy back their farms or pay their taxes.

Still others borrowed money from the government to refinance loans that they could not repay at the time. Suppose, for instance, that a midwestern farmer owed $5,000, which he had to repay over a 20-year period with interest at 5 percent. Because of the depression, he could not meet his yearly payments on his debt. He was faced with the foreclosure of his mortgage and the loss of his farm and home. But under the new government program he could borrow $5,000 from the Federal Land Banks to pay off his debt to the mortgage holder. The new debt could run as long as 50 years, with interest at 2.25 percent.

This liberal system of federal credit enabled hundreds of thousands of farm families to protect their land and homes. The farm credit programs were administered by the Farm Credit Administration (FCA), created in 1933.

Higher incomes for farmers

In a second major attack upon the farm problem, the New Dealers tried to increase the farmers' income. The basic government plan for farm recovery was simple. The first step was to raise the prices of farm products. With more dollars to spend, farmers—then about one fourth of the nation's population—would buy more manufactured goods. This rising demand would help to reopen factories. These factories would hire more workers, thus reducing industrial unemployment. The industrial workers, in turn, would spend more money, which in time would help to reopen still more factories. The demand for goods of all sorts, from farm and factory, would spiral upward. The key to the situation, as the New Dealers saw it, was higher farm prices.

The government set out to increase farm prices by utilizing the principle of supply and demand. Consider the example of a grocery store

The year 1934 brought a long-drawn-out nightmare to thousands of farmers living in western Kansas, southeastern Colorado, the Oklahoma Panhandle, northeastern New Mexico, and the semi-arid plains of Texas. Relentless winds swept over drought-ridden land, burying fields, fences, and houses under thousands of tons of drifting dust. Cattle and poultry died. A young boy on his way home from school was found buried in the dust only a quarter of a mile from his home. Farmers were driven to despair. Millions of acres were abandoned by poverty-stricken families who, in desperation, piled their possessions in trucks and moved to the cities or to California.

What caused this dreadful situation? The plains had experienced drought and dust storms even when buffalo and cattle grazed on their long grasses. But as farmers moved in and plowed more than a third of the area, partly as a result of pressure to grow more wheat during World War I, they destroyed the protecting cover of grass. The soil now lay bare beneath the burning sun, defenseless against the driving wind. Only a prolonged drought was required to bring disaster. In 1934 the drought came.

After this disaster, the Soil Conservation Service encouraged farmers to use contour plowing, to plant soil-saving crops, and to set out trees in shelter-belt strips to break the force of the wind. By the late 1930's the farmers in the Dust Bowl were beginning to win their battle against drought, wind, and dust.

THE DUST BOWL

which has bought more oranges than it can sell. The surplus oranges are about to rot. What does the store do? It reduces the price of the oranges. Next time, of course, the store will order fewer oranges, hoping that by reducing the available supply it can sell all the oranges at a good price. This is essentially the policy that the New Deal applied to farm goods in the Agricultural Adjustment Act of 1933.

Limiting farm production

The government reduced the supply of farm products by several methods. To begin with, government agents, acting under the authority of the Agricultural Adjustment Administration (AAA), urged farmers to sign agreements not to use one quarter to one half of their land. By thus limiting the amount of farm produce, the government hoped to raise prices. But even with higher prices farmers had less income because they had fewer products to sell. The government therefore paid farmers a certain sum of money for each acre that they took out of production. The money for these subsidies, or "benefit payments," was secured by collecting taxes from the food processors—meat packers, canners, flour millers, and others who prepared, or "processed" farm products.

Under this program large amounts of farm land were taken out of production. In 1933 a million cotton planters plowed under cotton, and they did not plant about 10 million acres (404,700 hectares) which they ordinarily would have planted. As a result the 1933 cotton crop was re-

duced by about 4 million bales and the price of cotton almost doubled, while the planters received almost $200 million in federal subsidies. Producers of wheat, corn, hogs, rice, tobacco, dairy products, cattle, rye, barley, peanuts, flax, grain, sorghum, and sugar signed similar agreements to limit production.

Evaluating the farm program

New Dealers were pleased with their agricultural recovery program. They pointed out that the prices of farm products had risen and farmers were earning more money. They also pointed out that with this increased purchasing power farmers were spending more money and thus helping to get industry rolling again. These favorable results, the New Dealers said, were the outcome of a sound program of federal planning.

But there was also severe criticism of the New Deal farm program. In the first place, critics pointed out, it was necessary to levy taxes on the food processors to get money for the subsidy payments. These taxes were passed along to the consumer in the form of higher prices. Thus money was being taken from the urban consumer and given to the farmer. While farmers were getting more money, city dwellers were experiencing an actual decline in purchasing power.

In the second place, larger farmers benefited far more from the program than did small farmers. Poorer farmers felt that the benefit payments which finally filtered down to them were inadequate for their needs. In the third place, many critics considered the program bureaucratic—concentrating too much power in an unnecessary number of government bureaus—full of red tape, confusion, and inefficiency. Finally, millions of Americans condemned a program which deliberately decreased food supplies when hunger was widespread.

The program declared unconstitutional

It was the Supreme Court, however, that brought the Agricultural Adjustment Act of 1933 to an end by declaring it unconstitutional. In a 1936 decision in the case of *United States v. Butler,* the Supreme Court stated that Congress had no constitutional right to regulate agricultural production. The Court also ruled that the power to regulate agriculture belonged to the states, and that the federal government had no authority to interfere.

As you will see in the next chapter, however, this Supreme Court decision did not end New Deal efforts to help farmers.

SECTION SURVEY

IDENTIFY: AAA, subsidy, bureaucratic, *United States v. Butler.*

1. Explain the basic New Deal plan for farm recovery.
2. What measures did the New Dealers introduce to help farmers retain their homes and land?
3. Give the arguments for and against the New Deal farm recovery program.
4. Why did the Supreme Court declare the Agricultural Adjustment Act of 1933 unconstitutional?
5. Do you think the New Deal plan for farm recovery supported the principles of capitalism? Explain.

3 Recovery measures to aid banking, building, and transportation

While trying to stimulate agriculture, the New Deal was also trying to restore the health of the country's banks and currency. When Roosevelt took office on March 4, 1933, the nation was in the grip of an unprecedented financial collapse.

Bank failures

For months crowds of panic-stricken Americans had been selling stocks and rushing to banks to withdraw their money before the banks failed. By March 1933 nearly every stock exchange and many banks had closed. Many states, in a belated effort to save their financial institutions, had ordered all banks to suspend activities until further notice. Americans across the country were hiding money in mattresses, under carpets, or in some other place they considered safe.

With so many banks closed, the everyday business life of the nation could not be carried on. People could not pay their bills by check, and there was not enough currency in circulation to meet the everyday needs of even a depressed economy.

The bank holiday

One of Roosevelt's first acts was to issue a proclamation, effective on March 6, 1933, closing every bank in the country for an indefinite period. Congress then enacted laws forbidding any bank to reopen until it could prove its soundness and its ability to carry on business without endangering its customers' deposits. Most banks across the country were able to satisfy the financial experts in the Treasury Department and quickly reopened.

Abandoning the gold standard

Shortly after Roosevelt ordered the "bank holiday," Congress authorized the Secretary of the Treasury to call in all gold coins and gold certificates then in circulation, and provided a maximum penalty of a $10,000 fine and 10 years in jail for anyone found guilty of hoarding gold. With this action Congress abandoned the gold standard, which in the past had meant that all paper currency was redeemable in gold.

Later, in October 1933, Roosevelt undertook to stabilize the price of gold. He authorized the Reconstruction Finance Corporation to buy and sell gold on the world market so that the United States could take "in its own hands the control of the gold value of our dollar." If the price of gold dropped, the RFC could raise it immediately by offering to buy gold at a higher price. If the price rose too high, the RFC could begin to sell gold at lower prices.

Still later, at the end of January 1934, President Roosevelt announced that the gold value of the dollar would be established at 59.06 cents in relation to the old "gold" dollar, whose value had been 100 cents in gold. By "devaluing" the dollar the New Deal administration hoped to force prices upward and thus help the farmers. In this respect, however, the new measure was a disappointment.

"Pump priming"

To revive the nation's economy the New Deal followed a procedure called "pump priming." When the pump in a well does not draw water, it is sometimes necessary to "prime the

These depositors wait anxiously at an Ohio bank during the 1933 "bank holiday." Closings prevented "runs" on sound banks, which reopened after examination by the Treasury Department.

pump" by pouring a little water down the well shaft. This water seals the crack around a washer in the shaft and thus helps to create a vacuum into which the well water rises so that it can be pumped up.

One of the major "pump priming" agencies was the Reconstruction Finance Corporation. By October 1936 the RFC had poured large sums of money into the nation's economy. It did this in the form of loans totaling $11 billion to railroads, banks, insurance firms, and industrial enterprises. Much of this money was quickly repaid.

But the New Deal also "primed the pump" in other ways. It undertook a huge building program. The New Dealers recognized that the building industry is one of the keys to a nation's economic health. It uses materials from many sources, and when construction work is going on, workers are busy in forests, mines, and factories throughout the land. In normal times the building industry employs hundreds of thousands of workers and thus concerns all Americans.

Construction of public works

The building program of the New Deal started in June 1933, when the Public Works Administration (PWA), headed by Harold L. Ickes, Secretary of the Interior, began to contract with private firms for the construction of public works, such as bridges, government buildings, power plants, conservation projects, and dams. The federal government also encouraged states and municipalities to carry on their own building programs, offering them loans and outright gifts amounting to from 30 to 45 percent of the total cost of the projects.

By the summer of 1936 public projects completed under this program included about 70 municipal power plants; several hundred schools and hospitals; nearly 1,500 waterworks; and many federal, state, county, and municipal buildings.

Repair and building of homes

The New Dealers also sought to revive the key building industry by stimulating the building of homes. Like so many New Deal measures, this program was double-barreled. It had as a second goal the relief of home owners.

When President Roosevelt took office, an average of 1,000 American homes were being foreclosed and sold at public auction every day. In June 1933 Congress tried to end this situation by creating the Home Owners' Loan Corporation (HOLC). With money borrowed at low interest rates from this government agency, many home owners paid off their old mortgages. At the same time they arranged with the HOLC to pay off their new mortgages over a long period with much smaller monthly payments. Between 1933 and 1936 the homes of more than 1 million American families were saved by the HOLC.

To provide further aid to the owners of homes and businesses, as well as to stimulate the building industry, the Federal Housing Administration (FHA) was established in 1934. Acting through the FHA, the government encouraged banks to lend money to individuals for repairing and building houses and business properties by insuring the banks against losses on such loans. Yet so desperate was the financial position of most Americans that up until 1936 relatively few people were able to take advantage of the FHA loans, and little residential construction was started.

A federal housing program to provide homes for the very poor was no more successful. Although the PWA lent and gave money to some 27 cities for slum clearance and for the erection of "low cost" apartment houses, results were disappointing. For one thing, rents for the finished apartments were usually more than poor families could afford.

Aid to transportation

No less important than the building industry to a nation's economic life is its transportation system. The depression hit the railroads a stunning blow. Between 1929 and 1933 their income was cut in half, and almost one third of all the railway companies in the United States went bankrupt. Others were saved from complete collapse only by loans from the RFC.

To recover lost business, some western railways lowered their passenger rates from 3.2 cents to 2 cents per mile. The experiment proved so successful that the Interstate Commerce Commission ordered all lines to adopt the same rate.

Government loans also enabled the railroads to install modern equipment, such as diesel engines and streamlined trains.

All of these measures helped the railways. But at the same time the government also spent huge sums of money to improve the nation's highways and waterways, thereby giving a boost to the railroads' competitors.

SECTION SURVEY

IDENTIFY: bank holiday, "pump priming," devaluing the dollar, RFC, PWA, FHA.

1. How did the bank holiday restore public confidence in the banks?
2. (a) "Pump priming" was basic to New Deal economic theory. Explain. (b) In what ways did the New Deal "prime the pump"?
3. What steps were taken at this time to help the transportation industry? Why?
4. Why is the building industry a key industry in the United States?

4 Recovery measures to help industry and encourage labor

All of the New Deal recovery measures were more or less indirect methods of reviving the nation's industrial machine. With the National Industrial Recovery Act, usually referred to as the NIRA, the New Deal tackled the problem head on.

The NIRA

The National Industrial Recovery Act went into effect in June 1933 as a two-year emergency measure. It was intended to revive industry by enabling American employers to cooperate in a great planned effort to find employment for jobless workers and to raise wages. Cooperation was to replace competition as one of the major driving forces of American industry. Antitrust legislation, such as the Sherman and Clayton antitrust acts, was disregarded. Instead the government officially encouraged businesses to end competition and form cooperative trade associations.

The NIRA provided that each industry should, with the aid of the National Recovery Administration (NRA), adopt a "code of fair practices." Once these codes had been approved by the President, they became binding upon the entire industry.

Under the vigorous leadership of General Hugh S. Johnson, administrative head of the NRA, some 95 percent of American industries adopted fair practice codes within a few months. The codes differed a great deal. But in general they limited production and provided for the common control of prices and sales practices. Most codes also outlawed child labor and required that adults not work more than 40 hours a week and that wages not be less than $12 to $15 a week.

Labor under the NIRA

Perhaps the most important—and certainly the most controversial—provisions in the NIRA were contained in the famous Section 7a. This section guaranteed workers the right to bargain collectively with their employers. Employers were forbidden to pressure a worker to join a particular union or to remain a nonunion worker. Employers were also forbidden to refuse work to anyone simply because he or she belonged to a union.

Arguments for the NIRA

President Roosevelt defended the NIRA on the grounds that it allowed labor to organize in order to get a share of profits through higher wages, that it abolished child labor, and that it ended many unfair trade practices. He also argued that it was responsible for putting 4 million people to work and for raising the total annual wages of the nation by $3 billion. His views were strongly supported by Secretary of Labor Frances

In 1933 President Roosevelt appointed Frances Perkins as Secretary of Labor. She was the first woman in American history to serve as a member of a Presidential cabinet. Frances Perkins brought to the job a rich background of experience, for she had had a long and distinguished career in social work and in public life.

In spite of these qualifications, many Americans were at first highly critical of her appointment. Organized labor, speaking through the voice of William Green, head of the American Federation of Labor, insisted that "Labor will never be reconciled to a woman." This proved to be a rash statement. Frances Perkins turned out to be one of the hardest-working members of the cabinet, and she soon gained the respect of organized labor. She held the position of Secretary of Labor for twelve years, serving through the crucial period of World War II. She resigned in May 1945, shortly after President Roosevelt's death.

FRANCES PERKINS, CABINET MEMBER

Perkins, the first woman ever to hold a cabinet position.

Criticisms of the NIRA

The NIRA also had its critics, who became increasingly outspoken. In the first place, owners of small businesses charged that the NRA codes of fair practices had mostly been made by and for large corporations. They claimed that some codes, in assigning quotas of production, gave unfairly small quotas to smaller plants. They also insisted that the minimum-wage provisions in the codes favored the highly mechanized factories that could afford to pay higher wages.

In the second place, it was difficult to enforce the codes. When "chiselers" ignored codes they had promised to obey, honest manufacturers and dealers suffered from unfair competition. In the third place, the courts usually refused to enforce the "fair practices" provisions of the codes. And finally, while a major purpose of the NRA was to aid recovery by increasing the purchasing power of consumers, many manufacturers defeated this purpose by raising prices to cover the increase in wages.

The main objection to the NIRA, however, came from many businesses that opposed it because it stimulated unionization and collective bargaining. Moreover, certain provisions in Section 7a of the act were not clear. For instance, did company unions, under the influence of managers and owners, have the right to engage in collective bargaining? Labor said that company unions could not honestly represent the workers and should be outlawed. Management disagreed.

The National Labor Board

To settle the confused points of the law, Congress established the National Labor Board (NLB), which later became the National Labor Relations Board (NLRB). The National Labor Board was given the power to conduct elections in plants and to determine which labor organization had the right to bargain for all the workers in that particular plant. It also served as a board of arbitration to settle labor disputes brought before it by labor and management.

But the NLB was unpopular with business managers and owners, who claimed that it usually settled disputes in favor of labor. As a result, business began to oppose the entire NRA program. When management refused to grant union demands, a wave of strikes broke out. Yet despite these problems the National Labor Board, before

This 1934 cartoon shows Uncle Sam entangled by the multitude of government agencies created under the New Deal. How many of the agencies indicated in the cartoon can you identify?

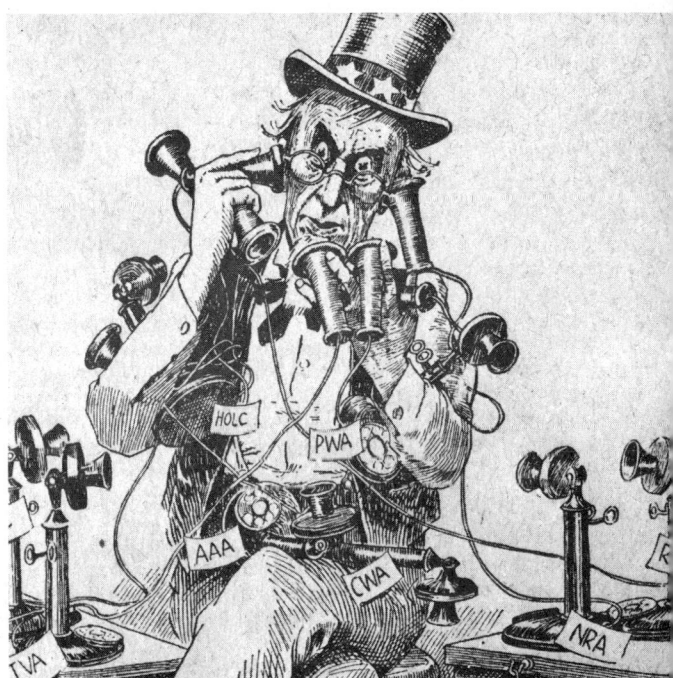

the summer of 1935, settled more than four fifths of the 3,755 disputes referred to it and averted nearly 500 strikes.

The NIRA declared unconstitutional

In May 1935, in the case of *Schechter v. United States,* the Supreme Court declared the NIRA unconstitutional. The judges ruled that Congress had delegated too much of its legislative power to the President, that the President had no power to approve or disapprove of industry codes, and that such codes were not legally binding upon industry. The Court also insisted that, in giving the federal government the right to regulate interstate commerce, the Constitution did not give the government the power to regulate every aspect of business.

The Wagner Act

One important idea in the NIRA was quickly reborn. In 1935 Congress passed the famous National Labor Relations Act, often called the Wagner Act after one of its sponsors, Senator Robert F. Wagner of New York. Workers hailed the Wagner Act as the "Magna Carta of Labor."

The Wagner Act, like the equally well-known Section 7a of the NIRA, guaranteed to labor the right to organize, to bargain collectively with employers for better wages and working conditions, and to engage in "concerted activities . . . for other mutual aid." The Wagner Act specifically condemned as unfair to labor such employer practices as discriminating against or discharging a worker for belonging to a union. It also declared that the majority of the workers in any plant or industry could select representatives for bargaining with management.

Under the Wagner Act the organization of labor proceeded rapidly. While the Wagner Act was in a sense a reform measure, it was also intended to promote industrial recovery by guaranteeing to organized labor a better chance of raising its wages and of thus increasing its purchasing power. No single measure of the New Deal aroused more controversy than the Wagner Act.

SECTION SURVEY

IDENTIFY: NIRA, Section 7a, collective bargaining, *Schechter v. United States*, NLRB, Robert F. Wagner.

1. (a) What was the aim of the NIRA? (b) How was it to be implemented?
2. (a) Give the two most effective arguments in favor of the NIRA. (b) Did these arguments meet the criticisms leveled against the NIRA? Explain.
3. Why did the Supreme Court declare the NIRA unconstitutional?
4. Workers hailed the National Labor Relations Act as the "Magna Carta of Labor." Why?

5 Various reform measures carried out by the New Deal

The New Dealers reasoned that relief and recovery measures were urgently needed in the early 1930's, but that only fundamental reforms could protect the nation against another depression. Under Roosevelt's leadership, the objectives of providing basic economic reform and security became increasingly important in 1935 and in the following years.

Protecting savings

In one of its major reform acts, the New Deal in 1933 established the Federal Deposit Insurance Corporation (FDIC), which guaranteed the savings of bank depositors. First set at $2,500, the guarantee was raised in 1934 to $5,000. (In later years, it was raised to $10,000, then to $20,000, and finally to $40,000.)

The New Deal also strengthened banks in other ways. For example, it increased the power of the Federal Reserve System by placing industrial and savings banks under its supervision. The Federal Reserve Board was given additional power to regulate credit as a check upon reckless speculation.

Another series of laws was designed to protect the public against worthless stocks. Any bank, brokerage house, or sales person that failed to give full and honest information about the true value of stocks and bonds offered for sale was subject to a severe penalty. In 1934 the Securities and Exchange Commission (SEC) was created to administer these laws and to regulate the stock exchanges.

Social security for the people

In another fundamental reform measure the New Deal attacked the problem of individual security.

The Social Security Act of 1935 had three major goals. First, it provided unemployment insurance for individuals who lost their jobs. The money for this purpose was raised by a payroll tax on businesses employing more than eight workers. The unemployment insurance fund was administered by state insurance systems, in cooperation with the federal government.

A second goal of the Social Security Act was to provide old-age pensions ranging from $10 to

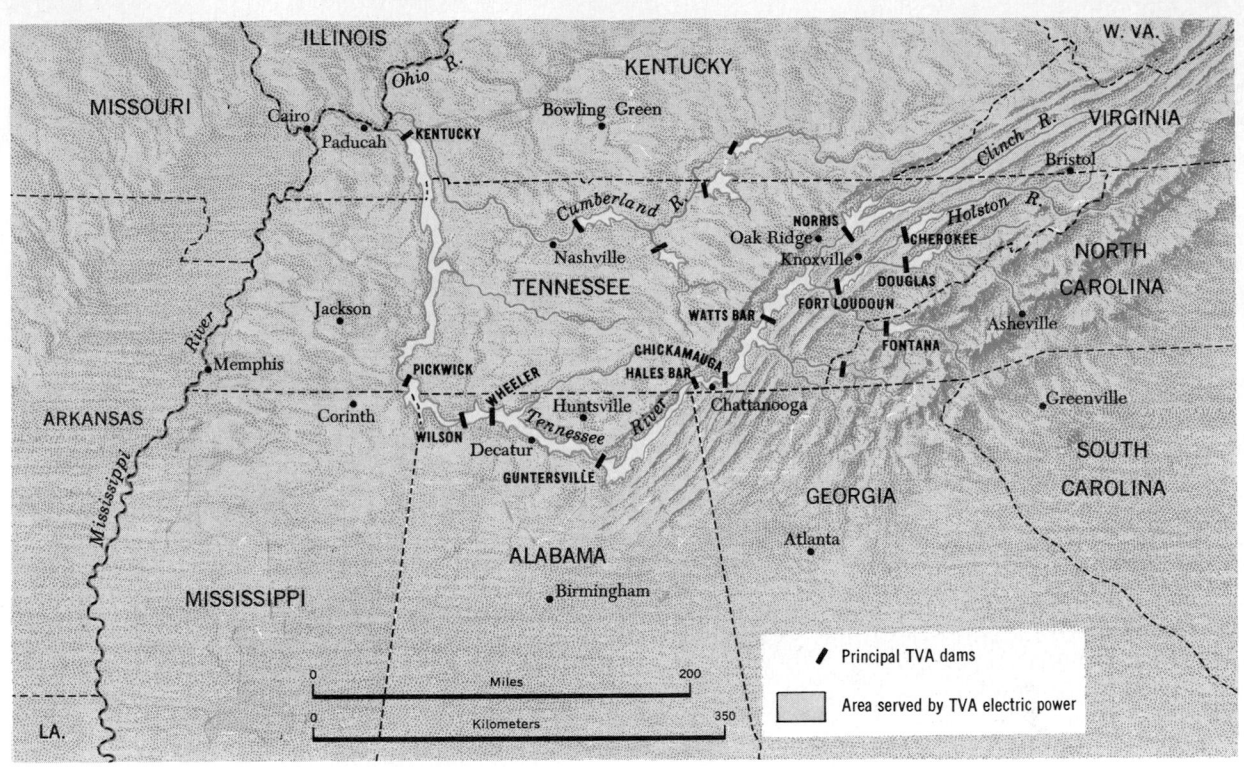

TENNESSEE VALLEY AUTHORITY

$85 a month for persons over 65. The money for this purpose was raised by a payroll tax on employers and a social security tax on the wages of employees.

A third goal of the Social Security Act was to help the handicapped—the blind, the aged, the disabled—as well as dependent children. Federal pensions up to $20 a month were available for needy persons over 65, provided that the states paid an equal amount. Federal funds were also available for those states which sought to protect the welfare of the handicapped.

President Roosevelt called the Social Security Act "a cornerstone in a structure which is being built." It was admittedly only a beginning; excluded from its provisions were public employees, farm laborers, domestic servants, and employees of religious, charitable, and nonprofit educational institutions. Nevertheless, by 1937 nearly 21 million workers were entitled to unemployment benefits, and 36 million retired workers to old-age pensions.

Electricity for homes

Another reform movement sought to bring electricity to more Americans. Despite widespread development of electric power up to the 1930's, only one third of America's homes had electricity; in rural areas only 15 out of every 100 houses were wired.

To solve this problem, the President in 1935 created the Rural Electrification Administration (REA). The REA had the responsibility of developing a program for generating and distributing electricity in isolated rural areas.

Regulating utility companies

In 1935 also, Congress passed the Public Utility Holding Company Act, also called the Wheeler-Rayburn Act. This measure was intended to give the federal government greater power over the nation's gas and electric industries. The act gave the Federal Power Commission authority to regulate the interstate production, transmission, and sale of electricity. It gave the Federal Trade Commission similar authority over gas. It gave the Securities and Exchange Commission authority to regulate the financial practices of public utility holding companies.

By regulating the financial operations of the public utility holding companies, the New Deal hoped to end an increasing trend toward monopoly in public utilities. The measure was designed to prevent any holding company from controlling more than a "single integrated public utility system" operating in a single area of the country. Under the law, utility companies were forbidden to engage in any business other than the production and distribution of gas or electric power. They were also forbidden to issue new stocks and bonds without the approval of the Securities and Exchange Commission.

Finally, in a "death sentence" clause the Public Utility Holding Company Act gave the

The TVA system of flood control includes many dams, some of which produce hydroelectric power. Fontana Dam, shown here, is on the Little Tennessee River in North Carolina.

public utility holding companies five years to readjust their financial affairs. At the end of five years any company that could not prove that it was actually distributing gas or electricity in a given area would be dissolved.

The TVA

With the creation of the Tennessee Valley Authority (TVA), Congress in 1933 launched the United States upon an experiment which had no parallel in American history. The scene of the experiment included parts of seven states in the region drained by the Tennessee River and its tributaries (see map, page 281).

The TVA moved into this region with a plan for the unified development of all its resources. The plan was to improve economic and social conditions for the benefit of the people who lived in the valley, as well as for the benefit of all Americans, by setting a standard of cost for producing and distributing electric power. After a decade of trial and error, New Dealers justified their enthusiasm over the TVA by pointing to several accomplishments.

Power development

TVA enthusiasts were especially proud of the construction of 21 large dams on the Tennessee River and its major tributaries (see map, page 281) and thousands of smaller dams on creeks and brooks. Power plants had been erected to convert the "white coal" of the river into vast quantities of electricity. From these federally owned power plants, high-voltage transmission lines fanned out to cover the region with a network of wires leading into farmhouses in even the most remote valleys. Whereas in 1935 only 1 in every 100 homes in Mississippi had electricity, by 1945 about 20 homes out of 100 were wired. The per capita consumption of electric power in the TVA region was 50 percent higher than the average for the entire United States. Moreover, rates for electric power had been cut by about one third.

Flood control

The TVA dams were also planned as part of a system of flood control. Into a central control room now come daily reports from all over the valley, as well as radio reports from automatic rain gauges, telling the amount of rainfall and the volume of water in each brook, creek, and river. By pushing buttons, sluice gates in great dams can be opened or closed, and millions of tons of water released or stored for future use.

Prevention of soil erosion

Hand in hand with flood control has gone a program to prevent soil erosion and restore the fertility of the land. Millions of trees have been planted. Their roots hold the soil in place, and their leaves pile up to absorb and hold rain and melted snow. Fertilizer produced by the electric power of TVA dams has been sold at cost to the farmers of the Tennessee Valley. Agents from the Department of Agriculture have helped farmers by teaching them the value of fertilizers, contour plowing, crop rotation, and the planting of soil-restoring crops.

Other purposes

The TVA program includes many other features. River transportation has been improved. New roads have been built. Factories have sprung up, providing jobs for thousands of workers. Vast areas of land have been converted into public parks for Americans to enjoy. Lakes have been stocked with fish for the pleasure of vacationists and the profit of commercial fisheries. Schools, libraries, and hospitals have been constructed.

Criticisms of the TVA

There is another side to the TVA story. Privately owned power companies, representing a $12 billion industry, bitterly fought the TVA. The private power interests declared that the TVA was an unnecessary intervention by the federal government in private industry. They insisted that the lower rates charged by the TVA for its electric power were not the result of more efficient production. If the TVA paid taxes as all private industries did, critics insisted, it would have to charge much more for its electricity. Advocates of the TVA believed that its rates should be used as a standard to govern the rates charged by private power producers. But the private power companies insisted that the TVA was an unfair standard, and the less expensive electricity it generated was a gift from the taxpayers of the entire nation to the people of one region.

SECTION SURVEY

IDENTIFY: social security, public utilities, REA, TVA, soil erosion.

1. The FDIC restored public confidence in the banks as savings institutions. Explain.
2. (a) What were the three main purposes of the Social Security Act of 1935? (b) This legislation was long overdue. Comment.
3. (a) The TVA experiment had no parallel in American history. Explain. (b) How did raising the standard of living in the TVA region benefit the rest of the nation?
4. (a) What arguments have been used against the TVA? (b) Do you think these arguments have validity? Explain.

CHAPTER SURVEY

INQUIRING INTO HISTORY

1. In his first Inaugural Address, Franklin D. Roosevelt said: "The only thing we have to fear is fear itself." What did he mean?
2. In an interdependent, complex, industrialized society such as that of the United States, who do you think should be responsible for (a) the poor, (b) the unemployed, (c) the handicapped, (d) the aged? Explain what changes were made in regard to these groups under the New Deal.
3. Was the planned-scarcity aspect of the New Deal farm relief program effective? Why or why not?
4. Compare Hoover's "trickle-down" theory with Roosevelt's "pump-priming" theory. Which theory was more effective in helping to remedy the ills of the depression? Why?
5. List the social and economic reforms made under the New Deal. Next to each reform, state briefly the purpose it was meant to accomplish.
6. (a) Why was the New Deal controversial? (b) Which Americans were the strongest supporters of the New Deal? (c) Which were most opposed to it?

RELATING PAST TO PRESENT

1. Which federal programs begun during the New Deal era are still in operation today?
2. How has history confirmed the criticisms leveled at the New Deal? How has history confirmed the praise given to the New Deal?

DEVELOPING SOCIAL SCIENCE SKILLS

1. Interview your grandparents or older people in your community who remember the Great Depression of the 1930's. How do they describe life during the depression and the New Deal? How do their impressions compare with those you formed from your own reading and studying?
2. Compare the effects of the depression on rural and urban areas. Read accounts or a book by or about people in cities and in rural areas in the 1930's, such as *The Grapes of Wrath*. What problems did people in cities face during the depression? What problems did people in the country face? What did each do to solve their problems?
3. Study the pictures on pages 271, 272, 277, and 282. How do they relate to the period just studied?

CHAPTER 18

THE GREAT EXPERIMENT
ON TRIAL

1936-1940

By 1936 the United States was beginning to recover from the Great Depression. National income had risen sharply since 1932, having jumped from a low of less than $47 billion to almost $70 billion. Industrial production, once again on the rise, was double that of 1932. These and other figures gave convincing proof that in four years the nation had made considerable progress in its battle against the depression.

How much of this progress could be credited to the New Deal was, however, an open question. Some Americans, including large numbers of Republicans, argued that progress had been made in spite of the New Deal. Others, including many Democrats, argued that the New Deal had saved the country from complete catastrophe and had started it on the road to recovery.

But the depression was far from conquered. In 1936 as many as 3.5 million people were still working on government relief projects. Nine million men and women were still unemployed. Many factories and mines were still closed or were working at far less than full capacity. Although the country was on the road to recovery, the American people still faced many problems.

Such was the situation when in 1936 the voters entered another Presidential election year. Should Roosevelt be re-elected? Should the New Deal be continued? These were the big questions facing the voters.

As you will see, Roosevelt won by an overwhelming majority. But as you will also see, during his second term in office he faced mounting problems. In a real sense the New Deal was on trial.

THE CHAPTER IN OUTLINE

1. Mounting opposition to New Deal policies and programs.

2. Continuing New Deal reforms despite growing criticism.

3. The end of the New Deal's "great experiment."

| 1450 | 1750 | 1800 | 1850 | 1900 | 1950 | 1980's |

1 Mounting opposition to New Deal policies and programs

By 1936 President Roosevelt and New Deal supporters were running into growing difficulties. But in the 1936 Presidential election campaign they fought back vigorously and successfully.

Roosevelt's campaign promises

In June 1936 the Democrats enthusiastically renominated Roosevelt for a second term, and again chose John Nance Garner of Texas as his running mate. The platform strongly endorsed the New Deal.

During the campaign Roosevelt again showed great skill in rallying support. He emphasized production and employment gains made during his first term. Business activity, he declared, was almost normal again, thanks to "pump priming." He promised to balance the budget, warning, however, that it was even more important "to balance the human budget." Great steps, he said, had been taken toward that goal, but the New Deal still had a long, hard road to follow.

Roosevelt's supporters

Lined up behind the President were not only most Democrats, but also countless rank-and-file Republicans. Most of the progressive Republican leaders who had supported him in 1932 continued to do so. Labor was overwhelmingly for the President, as were many farmers who remembered the New Deal benefits they had recently received. Many of those who had received federal relief money also supported Roosevelt. The local Democratic political "machines," some of which had used relief money to strengthen their own power, solidly backed the re-election of the entire Democratic ticket. And finally, black voters in the North almost solidly rejected their traditional Republican affiliation and supported the party that, in some measure, had responded to their needs and grievances.

Roosevelt's critics

But the President and the New Deal also had many critics, including a number of influential Democrats who "took a walk" from the party and supported the Republican candidate. And Roosevelt's Republican critics included most big business leaders, many small business people who had suffered under the NRA, bankers, private power companies, newspapers, and many professional people. Some critics objected to Eleanor Roosevelt's efforts on behalf of black Americans.

Opponents of President Roosevelt sometimes likened him to a dictator, claiming that he was undermining the Constitution. They pointed out that the Supreme Court had declared unconstitu-

Critics of the New Deal believed that it undermined the Constitution of the United States and the American way of life. This cartoon likens the New Deal to the Trojan horse of the ancient Greeks and implies that Roosevelt's policies would result in tyrannical government.

tional seven out of nine important New Deal measures. They insisted that the American way of life—individualism, free enterprise, and private property—was being abandoned for socialism and government control. Roosevelt's critics denied that the New Deal had restored prosperity. They pointed to continued unemployment. They stressed the fact that the administration had piled up a huge national debt of over $33 billion and had failed to balance the budget.

Republican promises

The Republican leaders, however, could not win the election of 1936 merely by opposing the New Deal. They had to secure the votes of a great many people who had been helped by the New Deal. To secure these votes, they nominated friendly, thrifty Alfred M. Landon, Governor of Kansas, for President.

Governor Landon was a "liberal" Republican. Although he was in the oil business, he had

President Roosevelt, shown here during his 1936 campaign, was able to rally widespread public support despite growing difficulties of the New Deal.

the support of many farmers who trusted his judgment. Moreover, in a period when most states and the federal government had piled up huge debts, Governor Landon had balanced the Kansas budget.

The Republican platform promised to continue agricultural benefits to farmers, to support labor, and to keep the controls on the stock markets and on reckless speculation. Although these were all New Deal measures, the Republicans insisted that they could carry them out more effectively and economically than the Democrats. The Republicans also promised to balance the budget and to restore to the states certain powers that the federal government had seized to carry out the New Deal program. Thus the Republicans adopted what had traditionally been the Democratic states' rights position.

Roosevelt's victory

The election campaign was filled with angry charges and countercharges. Into the campaign the Republicans poured more than $9 million—a huge sum for those years—the Democrats somewhat more than half that amount. More than 45 million Americans voted, reflecting keen popular interest.

Roosevelt and Garner swept the country with an electoral vote of 523 to 8. Roosevelt's popular vote was also impressive—27,476,673 to Landon's 16,679,583. Moreover, the Democrats won or kept control of all but six governorships and maintained their leadership of both houses of Congress. Not since the re-election of President Monroe in 1820 had a Presidential candidate won such strong backing.

Roosevelt's criticism of the Court

In 1937, early in his second term, President Roosevelt opened an attack on the Supreme Court. Roosevelt was upset because the Court had set aside as unconstitutional seven important New Deal laws. He was also disturbed because the Court had declared unconstitutional a New York state measure providing minimum wages for women and children. Moreover, the federal courts had used the injunction to block federal agencies from carrying out New Deal measures.

Roosevelt declared that all too often certain Supreme Court justices thought in terms of the "horse and buggy" era. "A dead hand was being laid upon this whole program of progress," the President later declared. It was, he said, the hand of the Supreme Court.

Roosevelt and Court "reform"

On February 5, 1937, President Roosevelt asked Congress for power to appoint an extra justice to the Supreme Court for each existing justice who did not retire upon reaching age 70. At the time, six of the nine justices were 70 or older. Roosevelt's proposal, therefore, would have enabled him to appoint six new justices more favorable to the New Deal.

Changes in the Supreme Court

Although the President fought vigorously for his "reform" proposal, he lost. Members of Congress in his own party refused to support him, and public opinion ran strongly against him. In general, people did not want to tamper with the delicate balance of legislative, executive, and judicial powers written into the Constitution.

But although Roosevelt lost the battle for Court reform, he gained most of the things he wanted. The Court began to approve important New Deal measures. The National Labor Relations Act and the Social Security Act were tested and found constitutional. Moreover, the Court approved an act passed by the state of Washington establishing minimum pay for women and children. This act was almost identical to the New York state law that the Court had earlier declared unconstitutional.

Had the Court suddenly realized that it might be well to approve certain popular legislation to prevent a drastic reform of the Court itself? Many Americans believed that such was the case.

Moreover, during Roosevelt's second administration a whole series of court vacancies occurred through death and retirement. By 1941 Roosevelt had been able to replace all but two of the original justices with members who appeared to be more sympathetic to New Deal legislation.

The business slump of 1937–38

Early in 1937, while the issue of the Supreme Court was being argued across the land, the nation's industrial machinery once again slowed down. By the autumn of 1937 factories were closing and unemployment was rising.

The Democrats spoke of what was taking place as a *recession;* that is, a business slump less severe than a depression. The Republicans, on the other hand, called it the "Roosevelt depression." Roosevelt's opponents blamed the Democrats and the New Deal for the business slump, just as the Democrats in 1931 had blamed the Republicans for the Great Depression.

Politics aside, there was fairly widespread agreement on the major cause of the slump. Instead of balancing the budget as he had promised to do back in 1932, Roosevelt had piled up the largest national debt in history. The Republicans, as you have read, had made the most of this fact in the 1936 election campaign. But many Democrats and friends of the New Deal had also become increasingly uneasy about the mounting debt.

Mindful of the growing criticism, the New Deal administration had seized the first chance to reduce expenditures. In 1936, with business conditions steadily improving, the administration had begun to cut spending for relief and public works. Unfortunately, private industry was not yet strong enough to give jobs to the men and women dropped from relief projects. Once again, therefore, the nation's economic system started on a downward spiral.

New "pump priming"

Fortunately, measures adopted to fight the Great Depression automatically began to act as brakes against the 1937–38 recession. More than 2 million wage earners in 25 states, protected by the Social Security Act, began to collect unemployment insurance. The new banking laws protected the savings of depositors. And many government agencies were ready to lend money to business and to construct public works, thus creating new jobs.

President Roosevelt and Congress began once

Clifford Berryman drew this cartoon of President Roosevelt during the Supreme Court battle of 1937 and wrote under it: "Thus ended the Era of Good Feeling."

again to "prime the economic pump" by increasing government lending and spending. The Reconstruction Finance Corporation again came to the rescue of business enterprises in trouble. The WPA doubled the number of workers on its payroll from 1.5 million to 3 million.

By the end of 1938 the nation's economic machinery was once again picking up speed. The Democrats were quick to claim another victory for the New Deal. The Republicans, on the other hand, insisted again that recovery had come in spite of the New Deal. And many Americans, Democrats and Republicans alike, continued to express alarm at the ever-growing national debt.

SECTION SURVEY

IDENTIFY: recession; John Nance Garner, Alfred M. Landon.

1. Compare the parties, candidates, issues, and results of the election of 1936 with those of the election of 1932.
2. (a) Why did Roosevelt say that certain members of the Supreme Court thought in terms of the "horse and buggy" era? (b) How did he propose to remedy this situation? (c) How would his proposal have affected the balance of powers among the branches of the federal government?
3. Show how the measures adopted to fight the Great Depression acted as brakes against the recession of 1937–38.

2 Continuing New Deal reforms despite growing criticism

During the 1936 election campaign President Roosevelt had promised that, if re-elected, he would continue the New Deal. Neither the business recession of 1937–38 nor the mounting criticism of his policies prevented Roosevelt from continuing his program.

Growth of the A. F. of L.

As you may remember, the Wagner Act of 1935 guaranteed to workers the right of collective bargaining and forbade employers to discriminate against organized labor. Under the protection of this law, the A. F. of L. began to organize unskilled workers in the mass production industries —steel, automobiles, aluminum, aircraft, utilities. But the A. F. of L. drive to organize unskilled workers did not move rapidly enough to please many labor leaders.

Organization of the CIO

Growing impatience with the A. F. of L. led John L. Lewis, powerful head of the United Mine Workers, and a group of like-minded labor leaders to organize in 1935 the Committee for Industrial Organization. The CIO immediately launched a drive to organize workers in the automobile, steel, rubber, oil, radio, and other industries in industrial unions. The new industrial unions included all workers, skilled and unskilled, in an industry. The United Automobile Workers (UAW), for example, represented all workers in automotive plants. Whereas in earlier times workers in the automobile industry had negotiated contracts through many separate unions—electrical, welding, metalworking, and the like—they now negotiated as a single powerful organization.

The CIO also encouraged the inclusion of black workers in the new industrial unions. Integrated, rather than segregated, locals heralded a new day in the long effort to organize white workers and black workers in a common cause.

Disturbed by the growing influence of the CIO, A. F. of L. leaders ordered it to disband. When John L. Lewis and other CIO leaders refused to obey this order, the A. F. of L. expelled them. But the CIO continued to operate, and in May 1938 it reorganized as a separate body, the Congress of Industrial Organizations (still called CIO), with John L. Lewis as its first president. By 1940, when Philip Murray succeeded Lewis as president, the CIO had 3.6 million members, roughly equal to the membership of the older A. F. of L.

The sit-down strike

Meanwhile, forceful organizing campaigns by both the A. F. of L. and the CIO resulted in a wave of strikes.

In November 1936 several hundred workers in the General Motors plant at Flint, Michigan, staged a *sit-down strike*. Instead of leaving the plant and organizing picket lines, the workers simply sat down at their machines and announced that they would not leave until management granted their demands.

The sit-down strike, which made it impossible for management to bring in strike breakers, proved extremely effective. Within a few months this relatively new labor weapon spread to many other plants, involving more than half a million workers. All of the leading automobile manufacturers except Ford now recognized the United Automobile Workers, the powerful new CIO union, as the bargaining agent for the automobile industry. The United States Steel Corporation, long a foe of unions, finally accepted the CIO steelworkers' union as the bargaining agent of the steelworkers. The CIO also organized workers in many other industries and made some headway in persuading agricultural laborers to join a CIO union.

In 1939 the Supreme Court ruled that sit-down strikes were illegal. But the CIO—as well as the A. F. of L.—continued to forge ahead. In general, the Wagner Act of 1935 with its guarantee of collective bargaining had given organized labor its great opportunity for growth.

LABOR UNION MEMBERSHIP

	PERCENTAGE OF LABOR FORCE COMPOSED OF UNION MEMBERS
1900	2.8%
1920	11.7%
1930	7.3%
1940	17.3%
1950	23.5%
1974	21.6%

Each symbol represents 1 million members.

The sit-down strike was a new labor weapon of the 1930's. These auto workers are staging a "sit down" at a General Motors factory.

Jurisdictional strikes

Much of the labor unrest during the late 1930's sprang from bitter rivalry between the A. F. of L. and the CIO. Disputes arose over which one had the "jurisdiction," or right, to enroll a particular group of workers. Sometimes these disputes led to *jurisdictional strikes*. Management thus was put in a difficult spot. If it recognized the CIO union, the A. F. of L. workers would go out on strike; if it recognized the A. F. of L. union, the CIO workers would go out on strike; and if it refused to recognize either union, it would run the risk of violating the Wagner Act!

The New Deal administration in general followed a "hands-off" policy in the conflicts between the A. F. of L. and the CIO unions, though many people felt that the National Labor Relations Board favored the CIO. The NLRB, with the support of President Roosevelt, tried with increasing success to settle disputes between the two rival labor organizations, and to prevent or mediate strikes. The great wave of strikes that reached its peak in 1937 and 1938 diminished in the following years as both labor and management reluctantly came to accept government intervention.

The Fair Labor Standards Act

Largely as a result of New Deal labor policies and laws, organized labor became a powerful force during the 1930's. But the New Deal program did not merely encourage and support organized workers; it also aimed at reforming labor conditions in the United States. To this end, President Roosevelt in 1937 proposed the Fair Labor Standards Act, sometimes called the Wages and Hours Law. This law provided a minimum wage scale and a maximum work week for many workers. In the President's words, this bill would put "a floor below which wages shall not fall, and a ceiling beyond which the hours of industrial labor shall not rise."

Strong opposition quickly developed to the Fair Labor Standards Act. Many employers claimed that the bill encouraged unneeded and unwise government interference and control over industry. But the bill was pushed through Congress and went into effect in October 1938.

The Fair Labor Standards Act provided that a legal maximum work week of 44 hours in 1938 be decreased to 40 hours by 1940, with time-and-a-half pay for overtime. It also provided that minimum wages of 25 cents an hour in 1938 be increased to 40 cents an hour by 1945. It prohibited the employment of children under 16 in industries producing goods for interstate commerce. The Department of Labor was responsible for enforcing the act.

Importance of the act

The Fair Labor Standards Act was important for several reasons. First, it marked a great extension of the federal government's control over industry. Second, it aimed not only to stimulate employment by providing for a shorter working day, but also to increase the purchasing power of a large part of labor. Third, the act made it unnecessary to amend the Constitution in order to prohibit child labor. Fourth, it encouraged social legislation by the states, since it removed some of the most marked differences in hours and wages between the North and the South. Fifth, it brought the benefit of federal support to the unorganized as well as to the organized workers of the nation.

Although the Fair Labor Standards Act affected only workers employed in interstate industries, by 1940 about 13 million men and women were benefiting from the law. Roosevelt hailed the new law as being, after the Social Security Act, "the most farsighted program for the benefit of workers ever adopted in this or in any other country."

Important though the Fair Labor Standards Act was, it did not insure freedom from racial discrimination in employment. In 1941 A. Philip Randolph, a powerful and militant black labor leader, threatened to march on the national capital with 10,000 Negroes to demand equal employment opportunities. Responding to this pressure, President Roosevelt in June 1941 established the Fair Employment Practices Committee (FEPC) to counteract racial discrimination in industries that were expanding through government contracts to meet wartime needs.

Helping the farmers

Other far-reaching New Deal measures were meant to improve the economic position of the nation's farmers. When in 1936 the Supreme Court ruled against the Agricultural Adjustment Act of 1933, Congress passed another law.

The Soil Conservation and Domestic Allotment Act of 1936 gave benefit payments to farmers who cooperated in a soil conservation program. Farmers who took part in the program leased part of their lands to the government. Under the supervision of state farm agencies, the farmers then began to restore the fertility of the leased land by practicing the best conservation measures, by using fertilizers, and by sowing soil-restoring plants, such as clover. In return the farmers received a certain sum of money for every acre they withdrew from production.

By this means the government hoped to develop nationwide knowledge of sound conservation practices. Equally important, by limiting production the government hoped to raise the prices of farm products.

The Bankhead-Jones Act

With the Bankhead-Jones Farm Tenant Act of 1937, the New Deal undertook to help tenant farmers, sharecroppers, and migratory farm workers, who moved from place to place in search of jobs. The new law created the Farm Security Administration (FSA). The FSA was authorized to lend money at low interest rates to tenant farmers, sharecroppers, and farm laborers who wished to buy farms. Farmers who received the loans had 40 years to repay.

The Agricultural Adjustment Act of 1938

But the heart of the New Deal agricultural reform program was the second Agricultural Adjustment Act, passed in 1938. This act contained a number of important provisions:

(1) It provided benefit payments to farmers in proportion to the number of acres that they withdrew from production and planted in soil-conserving crops.

(2) The government was authorized to decide the amount of various staple crops that could be marketed each year. With the approval of two thirds of the producers of these commodities in each locality, the government then assigned a certain allotment to each farmer. Farmers who exceeded this allotment had to pay a fine when they sold such crops during a time of surplus.

(3) When harvests were large, the surpluses were stored by the government for later use in "lean" years. But farmers did not lose their income from the surplus crops. The government gave them "commodity loans" on all stored crops.

The amount of these loans was fixed at slightly below *parity;* that is, below a figure based on average prices of each of the commodities for the "base" period from August 1909 to July 1914, a relatively prosperous period for farmers. When the market price of a commodity rose to the parity level, farmers were to sell their stored crops and repay the loans. If the market price remained below parity, the farmers kept the money and the government kept their crops. By this method the government hoped to keep the price of agricultural products at a steady level, benefiting both farmers and consumers. It was a program of "price supports based on parity."

(4) The act also authorized the government to insure wheat crops against drought, flood, hail, and plant diseases.

Evaluating the farm program

In 1932, in the depths of the Great Depression, farm income had sunk to less than $5 billion. By 1938 it had risen to more than $8 billion. By 1940 it totaled more than $9 billion.

But critics were quick to point out that the increased income came from higher prices paid by consumers and from subsidies paid by the

A. Philip Randolph (shown seated before the microphone) rallied black Americans to support New Deal efforts to end job discrimination in defense industries.

government—with taxpayers' money. These critics charged that money had been "taken from Peter to pay Paul."

Critics, including many farmers, also resented increasing government controls over farm production. They feared that subsidies would destroy farmers' independence. Moreover, critics charged that the government's price support program was causing America's agricultural products to lose out in foreign markets.

Such criticisms ended, at least temporarily, in 1941 when the United States was plunged into World War II. Then, as New Deal supporters were quick to point out, the country owed much to the farm legislation of the 1930's. This legislation had improved the economic condition of many Americans, had increased the fertility of millions of acres of land, and had enabled the United States to feed a large portion of the war-devastated world.

Shelter for low-income groups

During his second term in office, President Roosevelt also continued his efforts to ease the housing problem. The National Housing Act of 1937, usually called the Wagner-Steagall Act, had two aims: (1) to stimulate business by government spending for the construction of houses; and (2) to "remedy the unsafe and unsatisfactory housing conditions and the acute shortage of decent, safe, and sanitary dwellings for families of low income in rural and urban communities."

The National Housing Act created the United States Housing Authority (USHA), which began an ambitious program of housing construction. By 1941 the USHA had lent $750 million for the construction of more than 160,000 housing units.

Other New Deal reforms

In 1938 Congress passed the Food, Drug, and Cosmetic Act, which replaced the earlier Pure Food and Drug Act of 1906. The 1938 act required adequate testing of new drugs before they were offered for sale. It also required manufacturers to list the exact ingredients of their products on their labels. In addition, the Wheeler-Lea Act, also passed in 1938, prohibited manufacturers from making false or misleading claims in their advertising.

In 1939 Congress tackled the problem of improper political practices. The Hatch Act placed restrictions upon federal officeholders below the policymaking level in the executive branch of the government. Such officeholders were prohibited (1) from taking an active part in political campaigns, (2) from soliciting or accepting political contributions from workers on relief, and (3) from using their official positions to try to influence Presidential or Congressional elections. In 1940 the Hatch Act was amended to include state and local government employees whose pay came completely or partially from federal funds. The 1940 amendment also limited the amount of money a political party could spend in any one year to a maximum of $3 million, and the amount any individual could contribute to $5,000 annually. But this legislation was not effective because both parties soon found ways legally to avoid these limits.

SECTION SURVEY

IDENTIFY: CIO, sit-down strike, minimum wage, migratory farm workers, parity, price supports, Hatch Act, FEPC; John L. Lewis, A. Philip Randolph, Philip Murray.

1. (a) What prompted the organization of the CIO? (b) How did it differ from the A. F. of L.?
2. How did the Fair Labor Standards Act influence labor conditions in the United States?
3. What measures were taken from 1936 to 1938 to help improve the economic condition of farmers?
4. What steps did the New Dealers take (a) to provide homes for low-income families, (b) to aid consumers?

3 The end of the New Deal's "great experiment"

By the middle of his second term President Roosevelt's influence was beginning to decline. In 1937, as you have read, he had suffered a major defeat when he failed to push through Congress his bill for reorganizing the Supreme Court. In the Congressional elections of 1938 he suffered an even more serious defeat.

Roosevelt's failure to "purge" his party

As the elections approached, Roosevelt decided to "liberalize" the Democratic Party and to "purge," or rid, Congress of those conservative Democrats who had voted against his reform program. Singling out several Democrats by

In a political cartoon of 1938, Uncle Sam is saying to President Roosevelt: "But, Doctor, isn't it time she went on a diet?"

GOVERNMENT EXPENSES

name, he urged voters to defeat them at the polls.

Roosevelt's campaign to liberalize the Democratic Party failed. With only one exception all the members of Congress Roosevelt had opposed were re-elected. Moreover, the voters chose a great many new Democratic members who were foes of the New Deal. To add to Roosevelt's dismay, the Republicans won additional seats in Congress. Nevertheless, the Democrats continued to hold a sizable majority in both the House and the Senate.

New Deal activities suspended

President Roosevelt, a shrewd politician, was quick to see the meaning of the 1938 elections. Realizing that public opinion was turning against him, he began to suspend earlier New Deal activities. By 1939 Congress was cutting appropriations for many New Deal agencies.

As a result of the threatening world situation the PWA and the WPA began shifting their attention from public works to projects involving national defense, such as the building of airports and military highways. Other New Deal agencies, such as the Civilian Conservation Corps and the National Youth Administration, ended operations when Congress cut off further appropriations. Although the TVA weathered attacks both in and out of Congress, the President's recommendation that similar projects be developed in six other areas of the country received little support.

The driving impulse of the New Deal had spent itself. Those who maintained that the reform objectives of the New Deal were still far from being realized faced stiffer opposition and growing public indifference. This changed attitude toward the New Deal can be explained, in part at least, by recovery from the business recession of 1937–38 and by growing concern over national defense.

At eight o'clock on the evening of October 30, 1938, millions of radio listeners throughout the country heard the following announcement: "The Columbia Broadcasting System and its affiliated stations present Orson Welles and the Mercury Theater of the Air in *The War of the Worlds* by H. G. Wells."

There was a brief pause, followed by a weather report. Then an announcer declared that the program would be continued from a New York hotel. A jazz band came on the air. Suddenly the music stopped. An announcer, his voice tense and anxious, broke in to declare that a professor had just observed a series of explosions on Mars. Other announcements followed in rapid order. A meteor had landed near Princeton, New Jersey. Fifteen hundred people had been killed. No, it wasn't a meteor. It was a spaceship from Mars. Martian creatures were emerging. They were armed with death rays. They had come to wage war against the people living on earth.

An untold number of listeners were seized with panic. Some fell to their knees and began to pray. Others gathered their families, rushed from their homes, and fled on foot or by car into the night.

And yet it was only a radio play. CBS stated this fact clearly four different times during the hour-long program. Numerous explanations were advanced for this outburst of mass hysteria. But one thing was clear—the extraordinary power of broadcasting.

INVASION FROM MARS

Roosevelt's financial policies opposed

Much of the opposition to the New Deal came from people who believed that Roosevelt's financial policies were undermining the nation's economic system. With the return of better times this group became larger and more outspoken.

The New Dealers used three different methods for financing their relief, recovery, and reform programs.

One method was inflation. Although Congress authorized President Roosevelt to print paper money, he never did so. He did, however, decrease the gold content of the dollar.

A second method was *deficit spending*. This meant that the government spent more than it received in taxes, leaving the budget unbalanced, or showing a deficit. In the 1930's the national debt increased from about $16 billion to more than $40 billion. Men and women in both parties were highly critical of the failure of the Roosevelt administration to balance the budget. Business leaders in particular lost confidence in an administration that piled up a larger and larger national debt.

Another method by which the New Deal had financed its operations was by raising taxes. In 1935 the administration asked Congress to increase taxes on corporations and to levy taxes on gifts and inheritances. Critics called this a "soak the rich" proposal because it put a new tax burden upon the well-to-do. Despite strong opposition, however, Congress passed the Revenue Act of 1935, often called the Wealth Tax Act. With this measure Congress increased the income tax for individuals and large corporations and levied taxes on gifts and estates. But the revenue thus obtained did not balance the budget, and the national debt continued to grow.

In the Revenue Act of 1936 Congress moved still further in the direction of taxing corporation profits. It laid a steeply graduated tax on corporation profits which were not distributed to stockholders. Business bitterly complained that the new tax would discourage business expansion and prevent the accumulation of surpluses for use in depression years.

In 1938, however, as a result of growing opposition to the New Deal, Congress began to reverse the taxation policy of earlier years. The Revenue Act of 1938 provided for a sharp reduction of corporation taxes. And in 1939 Congress abolished the tax on undistributed profits. At the same time it raised the corporation income tax to a maximum of 19 percent. In addition, for the first time in history Congress required employees of cities and states to pay taxes to the federal government.

A third term for Roosevelt

Despite the fact that Roosevelt's influence was weakening, and despite the fact that the two-term tradition for Presidents was widely accepted as part of the unwritten Constitution,

Wendell Willkie, on August 17, 1940, rode through the crowded streets of his home town, Elwood, Indiana, on the way to deliver his speech accepting the Presidential nomination of the Republican Party.

Roosevelt decided to run for a third term. The President did not at first announce his decision, although he hinted that the critical world situation might compel him to be a candidate. But behind the scenes he arranged matters so that it would have been almost impossible for any Democrat to run against him without his consent.

As a result of Roosevelt's influence in his own party, the Democratic convention chose him on the first ballot at Chicago in July 1940. It also, without general enthusiasm, accepted his Secretary of Agriculture, Henry A. Wallace of Iowa, a former Republican, as his running mate.

The Democratic platform promised to extend social security, to stress the low-cost housing program, and to advance government ownership of public utilities. It also promised to keep the United States out of war and to send no armies abroad unless the nation were attacked.

Wendell Willkie

The Republicans chose as their candidate Wendell L. Willkie, a New York lawyer with a long progressive record. Willkie favored many of the principles of the New Deal. But he believed that the New Deal had been administered in such a way as to endanger individualism, free enterprise, and democracy. Warmhearted and engaging, Willkie proved a strong candidate.

The Republican platform condemned the New Deal for its "shifting, contradictory, and overlapping administrations and policies." It promised to revise the tax system to stimulate private enterprise and to promote prosperity. It also promised to keep the major New Deal reforms, but to administer the laws with greater efficiency and less waste. The Republicans also demanded a constitutional amendment that would limit Presidents to a maximum of two terms. Like the Democrats, the Republicans promised to keep America out of war unless the nation were attacked.

The campaign of 1940

The ominous threat of a second World War hung over the election campaign of 1940. Indeed, in the fall of 1940, while the American people were preparing to vote, Great Britain was fighting desperately for survival.

Both Roosevelt and Willkie advocated a vigorous program of national defense. Both urged all aid to Great Britain short of war. In general, there was no important difference in their attitudes toward the terrible conflict raging abroad.

On domestic issues, however, they differed sharply, with Willkie attacking Roosevelt for irresponsibility and Roosevelt attacking Willkie for "unwitting falsifications of fact." Willkie traveled 30,000 miles (48,279 kilometers) through 34 states in a whirlwind campaign. Roosevelt limited himself to a few speeches.

The election returns

Roosevelt won a sweeping victory in an election in which more Americans voted than in any previous contest in American history. But the returns clearly showed that the President had lost some of his earlier popularity. Roosevelt's 60 percent popular majority in the election of 1936 was reduced to just under 55 percent in the 1940 election. In round numbers this meant that 27 million Americans voted for Roosevelt, and 22 million for Willkie. The popular vote was therefore much closer than indicated by the electoral vote of 449 for Roosevelt and 82 for Willkie. Although the Democrats retained control of Congress, the Republicans increased their strength in both Congress and the state legislatures.

During Roosevelt's third term the New Deal domestic programs of relief, recovery, and reform received less attention as foreign problems and war itself absorbed American energies. Thus a great period of reform in American history came to an end. Whether this suspension of reform activities was the result of war, or whether the reform impulse had spent itself, remains unanswered.

SECTION SURVEY

IDENTIFY: purge, deficit spending, national debt; Henry A. Wallace, Wendell Willkie.

1. By 1938 do you think that the driving impulse of the New Deal had spent itself? Why or why not?
2. (a) Describe the three methods used by New Dealers to raise money. (b) Why were these methods criticized?
3. Compare the parties, candidates, issues, and results of the election of 1940 with those of the election of 1936.
4. Did the New Deal give more people an opportunity to share in the benefits of capitalism? Explain.

CHAPTER SURVEY

INQUIRING INTO HISTORY

1. In your opinion, did the New Deal infringe upon the individual's economic rights? Explain.
2. The AAA was designed to take care of the farmer's main problem—surplus crops. Comment.
3. In what ways did President Roosevelt and the New Deal break with the past?
4. What do you think the proper role of government should be in times of a national economic crisis?
5. (a) Why did Roosevelt try to reform the Supreme Court? (b) Give reasons for the failure of his plan. (c) What position would you have taken on the issue? Give arguments to support your opinion.
6. Summarize the various ways in which the New Deal tried to help (a) the consumer, (b) low-income families on farms and in cities, (c) young people, (d) the aged, and (e) workers.
7. Compare the (a) parties, (b) candidates, (c) issues, and (d) results in the elections of 1936 and 1940.
8. Why was the New Deal largely suspended after 1938?

RELATING PAST TO PRESENT

1. The CCC really created a new frontier. Explain. With what might the CCC be compared today in terms of a new frontier for young people?
2. Using the Great Depression as a basis for comparison, how do you think the United States would react to such a severe economic crisis today?

DEVELOPING SOCIAL SCIENCE SKILLS

1. Examine the cartoons on pages 285, 287, and 292. (a) What is the subject of each cartoon? (b) What is the point of view expressed in each cartoon? (c) Do the cartoons suggest reasons for attacking or supporting the government's policy? Explain.
2. Find accounts written by or about black Americans, or Indians, or Spanish-speaking Americans during the depression. (a) What effects did the depression have on this group of Americans? (b) Did the New Deal provide legislation to help this group of Americans?
3. Read several newspaper accounts of the election campaign of 1940. (a) What were the major issues of the campaign? (b) Did the newspapers give their opinions of Roosevelt and Willkie? (c) Were their opinions biased?

CHAPTER 19

MOVING FROM ISOLATIONISM INTO WAR

1932-1941

In 1933, when Franklin Delano Roosevelt became President for the first time, it was clear that few Presidents had entered office under more unfavorable circumstances.

The Great Depression, the worst depression the country had ever experienced, was becoming worse week by week, not only in the United States but throughout the world.

Equally disturbing was the growth of warlike dictatorships in Asia and Europe. Americans were deeply troubled because the Japanese war machine had already rolled across the borders of Manchuria and, as you have read, seized that province from the Chinese.

But there was no way for President-elect Roosevelt or anyone else to foresee that in 1933 Hitler would win control of Germany; that by 1936 a powerful German army would move into the Rhineland, violating the Versailles Treaty; and that by 1940 Hitler's Nazis, Mussolini's Fascists, and the Japanese war machine would have plunged the world into the most devastating conflict in history.

During the 1930's the United States took an increasingly active interest in foreign affairs. It recognized the Soviet Union. It made provisions to grant independence to the Filipinos. It expanded the Good Neighbor policy. And, although the United States tried to remain neutral in a war-torn world, by the end of 1941 the American people found themselves playing a leading role in the struggle against the dictatorships.

THE CHAPTER IN OUTLINE

1. Broadening American relations with other countries.

2. The roots of the American policy of isolationism.

3. The difficulties of isolationism in a war-threatened world.

4. America's involvement in World War II.

1450   1750   1800   1850   1900   1950   1980's

1 Broadening American relations with other countries

American foreign policy in the 1930's was influenced by two basic considerations: (1) the Great Depression at home and abroad, and (2) the rising threat of dictatorships in Europe and Asia. Both of these developments played a part in nearly every American decision made during these troubled years.

Recognition of the Soviet Union

In 1933, during the first year of the New Deal administration, the United States recognized the Soviet Union. Those favoring this move argued that it was only realistic to recognize a regime that had been in power for 16 years. They pointed out that an increased flow of trade between the two countries would be advantageous to the United States, and they reminded their fellow Americans that the two countries shared a common concern about the threat of Japanese aggression.

In reply to these arguments, the opponents of recognition pointed out that the Communists made no secret of their goal of world conquest. But this objection was met when the Soviet Union promised to stop all propaganda activities in the United States. As it turned out, this promise was not kept. Moreover, United States recognition of the Soviet Union did not result in a substantial increase in trade between the two countries.

Steps toward Philippine independence

In the Jones Act of 1916, as you may recall, the United States promised to give the Filipinos their independence. During the 1920's one administration after another postponed this action, claiming that the Filipinos were not yet ready for independence. In 1933, however, late in Hoover's administration, Congress passed an independence act for the Philippines over the President's veto.

The Philippine legislature rejected this measure. Many Filipinos feared that one of the act's provisions, giving the United States the right to keep military and naval bases, would enable Americans to continue their control in the Philippines. Other Filipinos argued that once they were free, the United States would raise tariff barriers against Philippine products.

In an effort to overcome these fears, Congress in 1934 passed the Tydings-McDuffie Act. This measure was more acceptable to the Filipinos. It provided for the establishment of a Philippine Commonwealth and outlined a gradual 10-year tariff increase on Philippine goods imported into the United States. This would give the Filipinos an opportunity to adjust to an independent economy. Ten years after the establishment of a commonwealth—on July 4, 1946, as it turned out—the Philippines were to become entirely independent, except for the retention of naval bases by the United States.

The Good Neighbor policy

During the 1930's the United States also redoubled earlier efforts to improve relations with Latin America. The friendly policy started by Presidents Coolidge and Hoover was expanded by President Roosevelt.

Self-interest as well as a genuine desire for friendship motivated the Good Neighbor policy. During the 1920's many Americans began to realize that the United States could not afford to continue antagonizing its Latin-American neighbors. When the Great Depression came in the early 1930's, this realization hardened into firm conviction. The United States needed Latin-American trade. The rise of dictatorships in both Europe and Asia further strengthened the conviction that the United States must establish friendlier relations with Latin America.

SOURCES

PROCLAMATION OF PHILIPPINE INDEPENDENCE (1946)

Whereas it has been the repeated declaration of the . . . government of the United States of America that full independence would be granted the Philippines as soon as the people of the Philippines were prepared to assume this obligation; and

Whereas the people of the Philippines have clearly demonstrated their capacity for self-government; . . .

Now, therefore, I, Harry S. Truman, . . . do hereby recognize the independence of the Philippines as a separate and self-governing nation. . . .

The Philippines became an independent nation in 1946 after many years of American rule. Here, parading Filipinos celebrate their independence.

Carrying out the Good Neighbor policy

In 1933 President Roosevelt expressed a widely shared feeing when he declared, "In the field of foreign policy, I would dedicate this nation to the policy of the good neighbor—the neighbor who resolutely respects himself and, because he does so, respects the rights of others." Later that year, in a conference held in Montevideo, Uruguay, the United States joined the other American countries in a pledge not to interfere in the affairs of their neighbors. "No state," the pledge declared, "has the right to intervene in the internal or external affairs of another state."

The Montevideo Pact marked a turning point in United States relations with Latin America. As President Roosevelt put it, "The definite policy of the United States from now on is one opposed to armed intervention."

Nor were these mere words. In 1934 the United States canceled the Platt Amendment, which for 33 years had given it the right to intervene in Cuban affairs. That same year the remainder of American troops were finally withdrawn from Haiti. In 1936 the United States signed a new treaty with Panama giving up its right to intervene in Panama's affairs. And gradually the United States ended its control over the customhouses of the Dominican Republic—a control exercised since 1905.

Testing the Good Neighbor policy

The Good Neighbor policy was put to a severe test in 1938 when President Lázaro Cárdenas (LAH·sah·ro KAHR·day·nahs) of Mexico confiscated the properties of all foreign oil companies. Foreign investors, including Americans, protested vigorously and demanded action from their governments. President Roosevelt refused to intervene on behalf of American investors. Instead, he urged the American oil companies to negotiate directly with the Mexican government. As a result of these negotiations, the Mexican government agreed to pay American oil claims.

International trade agreements

The United States also tried to promote an international revival of trade. The Roosevelt ad-

SOURCES

ABROGATION OF THE PLATT AMENDMENT (1934)

The United States of America and the Republic of Cuba, being animated by the desire to fortify the relations of friendship between the two countries, and to modify with this purpose the relations established between them by the Treaty of Relations signed at Havana, May 22, 1903 . . . have agreed upon the following articles:

Article I. The Treaty of Relations which was concluded between the two contracting parties on May 22, 1903, shall cease to be in force, and is abrogated, from the date on which the present treaty goes into effect.

Article II. All the acts effected in Cuba by the United States of America during its military occupation of the island, up to May 20, 1902, the date on which the Republic of Cuba was established, have been ratified and held as valid; and all rights legally acquired by virtue of those acts shall be maintained and protected. . . .

ministration offered to negotiate with any country special trade agreements that would provide for lowering tariffs.

In the Trade Agreements Act of 1934, Congress authorized the President to raise or lower existing tariffs by as much as 50 percent without Senate approval. As a result, the Roosevelt administration could bargain, or "reciprocate," with other countries. A nation that lowered its tariffs on United States goods would, in turn, receive more favorable tariffs on the goods that it sent to the United States. By 1940 Secretary of State Cordell Hull had signed 22 reciprocal trade agreements.

Equally important was the provision of the Trade Agreements Act known as the "most-favored nation" clause. This clause offered any country the opportunity to be treated as well as the nation seemingly "most favored" in any tariff agreement. This act therefore helped to end tariff discriminations against the United States. It also was an effective instrument for stimulating American business by improving trade relations with other nations.

New tariff agreements worked out with Canada and Great Britain under the Trade Agreements Act were especially important. They stimulated a great increase of trade between these countries and the United States, providing an economic foundation for the political cooperation that became so important in World War II.

SECTION SURVEY

IDENTIFY: dictatorship, Good Neighbor policy, Montevideo Pact, reciprocal tariff, "most-favored nation" clause; Lázaro Cárdenas, Cordell Hull.

1. What were the arguments for and against recognition of the Soviet Union in 1933?
2. What was the major provision of the Tydings-McDuffie Act?
3. What were the conditions that prompted renewal of the Good Neighbor policy?
4. Many obstacles had to be overcome before real cooperation between the United States and Latin America could be achieved. Comment.

2 The roots of the American policy of isolationism

In the early 1930's the threat of war became increasingly ominous. In Asia and Europe the militaristic leaders of Japan, Italy, and Germany started their armies down the road of aggression.

The rise of dictatorships

As the years passed, the Roosevelt administration had to deal with a growing number of totalitarian° rulers. Benito Mussolini, who seized power as the leader of Italian Fascism in 1922, was a swaggering, domineering ruler who dreamed of controlling the Mediterranean and the Middle East. The Japanese warlords, who seized control of Japan in the late 1920's, also had unlimited ambitions. Their seizure of Manchuria in 1931 was only one step in a program to win control of the Far East and the Pacific. Adolf Hitler, the Austrian-born fanatic who climbed to power in Germany in 1933, was a ruthless dictator who also longed for conquest. Josef Stalin, who in the 1920's succeeded Nikolai Lenin as the strong man of the Soviet Union, made no secret of his intention to spread Communism throughout the world.

There were other dictators, including General Francisco Franco, who came to power in Spain in 1939 after a bloody civil war. But in the 1930's the dictatorships of Japan, Italy, and Germany proved to be the most aggressive.

The totalitarian threat to democracy

Hitler, Mussolini, and the Japanese warlords openly expressed their contempt for democracy. It was, in Mussolini's words, "a rotting corpse" that must be replaced by a more "efficient" form of government and a "superior" way of life.

All of the dictatorships scorned the democratic rights of free speech and a free press. In the eyes of the totalitarian rulers, individuals existed to serve the state and had no rights except those that the state chose to give them.

All of the dictatorships glorified force. Compelling the people to work for "bullets rather than butter," they converted their industries to war production and devoted their major efforts to building powerful military machines.

Aggression and mounting tension

By the mid-1930's the dictators were ready to move. In 1935 Mussolini's blackshirted Fascists attacked the African nation of Ethiopia (see map, page 303), using bombers and poison gas against a virtually defenseless people.

° *totalitarian:* designating a dictatorship that exercises total control over a nation and suppresses individual freedom.

Meanwhile, in 1934 and 1935 the Japanese demanded the right to build a navy equal in size to that of any other power. When the other powers refused, Japan withdrew from agreements reached at the Washington Naval Conference of 1921–22 and in subsequent treaties, and began a rapid buildup of its naval forces.

Then, in March 1936, German troops moved into the Rhineland (see map, page 303) in clear violation of the Treaty of Versailles. In July civil war broke out in Spain. In October Germany and Italy signed a military alliance and began to call themselves the Axis° Powers. In November 1936 Germany, Italy, and Japan announced that they were joining in an Anti-Comintern° Pact, thus hiding their aggressive designs under the pretense of resisting Communism.

° *Axis:* a name made up by Mussolini, who said the line from Rome to Berlin formed the "axis" on which the world would turn thereafter. Eventually Japan was included among the Axis Powers. The nations who fought the Axis Powers were known as the Allies.

° *Comintern:* an international organization, dominated by the Russian Communist Party, whose aim was to spread Communism throughout the world.

And on July 7, 1937, Japanese and Chinese troops clashed on the Chinese-Manchurian border. This border "incident" developed into a full-scale war. In time, historians referred to it as the beginning of World War II in the Far East.

Roots of American isolationism

Despite the growing threat to peace, most Americans clung to their determination to avoid becoming involved in war. They believed that the United States could and should remain isolated. Why did Americans feel this way?

In the first place most Americans were disillusioned about the results of World War I. The war had not brought the peace, disarmament, and democracy which millions had hoped to see established across the earth. Instead it had been followed by constant quarreling among the European powers, by tariff wars, and by failures to reduce armaments.

Most important, the war had been followed by an unwillingness or an inability to make the League of Nations an effective instrument for peace. The isolationists refused to accept the argument that the League might have been more successful had the United States joined. They argued that the League's weakness was the best

All of the dictatorships of the 1930's glorified force and armed strength. Hitler staged huge parades like this to demonstrate Nazi Germany's growing military power.

possible evidence that the United States had been wise *not* to join. This widespread disillusionment became increasingly intense when the League failed to check the aggressions of Italy, Germany, and Japan in 1935–37.

American disillusionment over World War I was intensified in 1934 when the Senate Munitions Investigating Committee started to investigate war profits. Figures released by the committee suggested that many American bankers and munitions makers had reaped rich profits from World War I. Many people concluded that America's loans to the Allies had been largely responsible for drawing the United States into the conflict. This conclusion has since been rejected by most historians. In the mid-1930's, however, it fed the spirit of disillusionment.

But disillusionment about World War I was not the only basis for American isolationism. Most Americans believed that the Atlantic and Pacific oceans would protect the United States from attack even if the dictators crushed all opposition in Europe and Asia. Many also argued that improved relations with Latin America gave the nation another safeguard against attack.

The isolationists were strengthened by two other groups. Many Americans believed that the government's first responsibility was to combat the Great Depression. Many others, deeply convinced pacifists, believed that all wars were unjustifiable and that the United States must avoid being drawn into another conflict. Pacifism was strong, especially among young people, in both the United States and Great Britain during the 1930's.

Isolationism in practice

In 1934 American isolationists won a victory when Congress passed the Johnson Debt Default Act. This act forbade the American government and private citizens to lend money to any country that had defaulted, or failed to repay, its war debts.

The Johnson Debt Default Act underscored Americans' annoyance at the failure of all European nations except Finland to repay their war debts. Americans were especially annoyed because some of the defaulting nations were pouring money into military weapons. Americans did not intend to provide them any more money for weapons, or to risk becoming involved in another war because of entangling investments.

Neutrality acts

Between 1935 and 1937 the isolationists won other victories in a series of neutrality acts passed by Congress. These acts, which reflected widespread public sentiment against war, were occa-

This poster was one of many efforts made by various groups to keep the United States out of World War II. The Japanese settled the question when they attacked Pearl Harbor on December 7, 1941.

sioned by Mussolini's unprovoked attack upon Ethiopia, by the civil war in Spain, and by the aggressive actions of Germany and Japan.

In general, the neutrality laws (1) prohibited the shipment of munitions to "belligerents," or warring nations; (2) authorized the President to list commodities other than munitions that could be sold to belligerents only on a "cash-and-carry" basis; (3) made it unlawful for Americans to travel on the vessels of belligerent nations.

The neutrality laws were intended to keep Americans out of war and to prevent the involvement of American citizens in such disasters as the sinking of the *Lusitania* in 1915. With these laws the United States abandoned its long-established doctrine of freedom of the seas and withdrew the traditional rights of citizens to travel where and how they wished.

Dissatisfaction with neutrality

Strong though it was, isolationism by no means represented the thinking of all Americans. Many Americans were dismayed by the abandonment abroad of individual rights that earlier generations had fought so hard to establish.

Still other Americans regretted that the neutrality laws made it difficult for the United States to help the victims of aggression. They feared that the totalitarian aggressors would become bolder if the United States refused to aid weaker nations. In their view, if the United States allowed aggressors to crush their weaker neighbors, the United States might one day find itself surrounded by powerful enemies.

Finally, many international-minded citizens argued that the United States had a moral duty to aid the victims of unprovoked aggression. This attitude cut across party lines. There were internationalists as well as isolationists in both the Democratic and Republican parties.

Policy changes

Between 1933 and 1937 President Roosevelt did not take a firm stand on America's responsibility in a troubled world. At times he sided with the isolationists; at other times with the internationalists.

In 1933 Roosevelt failed to support the work of the London Economic Conference, an important conference called by the League of Nations. The delegates to the conference wanted to find a way to stabilize world currencies in order to boost trade and encourage worldwide economic recovery. Shortly before the conference opened, the United States abandoned the gold standard. President Roosevelt, therefore, did not want to support the stabilization of currency by countries still on the gold standard. He ordered American delegates at the conference to limit their discussions to tariff problems. As a result, the conference failed. Also, Roosevelt no longer pressed for American entrance into the League of Nations, as he had done in the 1920's.

By 1937 Roosevelt was becoming more deeply impressed with the seriousness of the world situation and with the need for the United States to take a positive stand against aggression. In a speech on October 5, 1937, the President said: "If we are to have a world in which we can breathe freely and live in amity without fear —the peace-loving nations must make a concerted effort to uphold laws and principles on which alone peace can rest secure. . . .

"When an epidemic of physical disease starts to spread, the community approves and joins in a quarantine of the patients in order to protect the health of the community against the spread of the disease. . . ."

Continuing isolationism

In his famous "quarantine" speech Roosevelt expressed views that most Americans were not yet ready to accept. Proof of this came with the *"Panay* incident." On December 12, 1937, Japanese planes bombed and strafed a United States gunboat, the *Panay,* and three American oil tankers on the Yangtze River in China (see map, page 330). Several Americans were killed and many were wounded.

Secretary of State Hull immediately sent a sharp note to the Japanese government. He demanded full apologies, compensation, and a promise that no such incident would recur. The Japanese agreed to all of Hull's demands.

During this "incident," the American public revealed how strongly it favored keeping out of war. A public opinion poll showed that 54 percent of all Americans felt that the United States should completely withdraw from China.

By the end of 1937 the tide of aggression was rising rapidly in Asia as well as in Europe. Many Americans, including President Roosevelt, were becoming increasingly alarmed. But most Americans still clung to the belief that the United States could remain isolated.

SECTION SURVEY

IDENTIFY: totalitarian, Axis Powers, isolationism, pacifists, "quarantine" speech, *"Panay* incident"; Benito Mussolini, Adolf Hitler, Josef Stalin, Francisco Franco.

1. Discuss the philosophy of government shared by the totalitarian dictators: for example, their ideas about the role of the individual and the role of the state.
2. List the events of 1935–37 which posed a threat to peace.
3. What were the roots of the widespread feeling of isolationism among Americans from 1920 to 1937?
4. (a) Upon what major experience in American history were the neutrality acts based? (b) Could this be called a misreading of history? Comment.
5. Roosevelt's attitude toward world affairs was changing, but the attitude of the American people was not. Comment.

3 The difficulties of isolationism in a war-threatened world

By 1938 the dictators were becoming more ruthless. During 1938 and 1939 headlines of new aggressions and new crises often crowded other news off the front pages of America's newspapers.

The spread of warfare

In 1938 Japanese forces were attacking along the length of the Chinese coast and pushing inland up the river valleys. Meanwhile, halfway around the world, the Spanish Civil War was bringing misery to hundreds of thousands of other people.

Spain had become an international battleground. Hitler and Mussolini were helping Franco, making the most of the opportunity to test their latest military equipment and to give picked "volunteers" actual battle experience. Soviet "volunteers" were fighting against Franco and his Nazi and Fascist allies. Among Franco's foes in the "International Brigade" were volunteers from many other countries, including the United States.

The United States reacted to this threat to world peace by joining France and Great Britain in a program of nonintervention. With President Roosevelt's approval, Congress in January 1937 barred all shipments of war materials to either side in the civil war in Spain.

New aggressions—and Munich

Another crisis developed when, on March 11, 1938, Hitler's powerful army moved into Austria (see map, this page). Two days later Hitler announced the union of Austria and Germany.

With Austria under his control, Hitler turned greedy eyes toward western Czechoslovakia. This area, known as the Sudetenland (soo·DAY·t'n·land), contained a large proportion of German-speaking people. Hitler demanded that Czechoslovakia turn over the Sudeten region to Germany. By the end of the summer a major crisis was at hand, for Czechoslovakia, with one of the best trained armies in Europe and with the sympathy of other democratic nations overwhelmingly on its side, refused to bow to Hitler.

Tension was at the breaking point when British Prime Minister Neville Chamberlain, French Premier Édouard Daladier, Mussolini, and Hitler met at Munich. There on September 30, 1938, the four men signed a pact which gave to Hitler nearly all he demanded. The Czechs, forsaken by their friends, turned over most of the Sudeten region to Germany. Prime Minister

AGGRESSIONS LEADING TO WORLD WAR II

British Prime Minister Neville Chamberlain (left) met with Adolf Hitler on September 23, 1938, to discuss peace. The meeting led to the ill-fated four-power peace pact signed a week later at Munich.

Chamberlain, whose intense desire for peace blinded him to Hitler's designs, returned to England confident that the Munich Agreement had ended the threat of aggression in Europe. "I believe," he said, "it is peace for our time."

Other leaders did not share Chamberlain's confidence. They believed his policy of "appeasement" would only lead Hitler to make further demands. Throughout Europe nation after nation re-armed with redoubled speed.

Growing American concern

President Roosevelt viewed the events of 1938 with deepening concern. As early as January 28, in a special message to Congress, he coupled a promise to work for peace with a warning that it was time for the United States to build up its defenses. Congress increased appropriations for the armed forces and, in May, authorized more than $1 billion for a "two-ocean navy."

Roosevelt privately referred to the aggressions of Japan, Italy, and Germany as "armed banditry," and Secretary of the Interior Harold L. Ickes called Hitler a "maniac." Officially, however, the President contented himself with per-

sonal notes to foreign rulers, including Mussolini and Hitler, urging them to settle their differences by negotiation and international cooperation. But since the United States was committed to a hands-off isolationist policy, no one paid much attention to the President's words.

Hemispheric defense

As the Sudeten crisis approached the breaking point, however, Roosevelt did make one commitment. In August 1938, in a speech in Ontario, Canada, he extended the protection of the Monroe Doctrine to Canada. He solemnly promised Canadians that "the people of the United States will not stand idly by if domination of Canadian soil is threatened by any other Empire."

Roosevelt's promise to Canada was only one of several steps the United States was taking to develop a hemispheric defense policy. Earlier, at the Buenos Aires Conference of 1936, the United States and the 20 other members of the Pan-American Union had agreed to regard a threat to any American country as a threat to the security of all American countries. The 21 members also agreed to consult together if such a threat developed.

In December 1938, with the clouds of war rapidly gathering, the Pan-American Union met again in Lima, Peru. The delegates repeated their pledge of solid opposition to any threat of foreign intervention in the Western Hemisphere. But they went a step further, agreeing that at the first sign of trouble the foreign ministers of the Western Hemisphere would meet to decide what action their countries should take.

Roosevelt's promise to Canada and the Declaration of Lima provided additional assurance that the Monroe Doctrine had become a multilateral, or many-sided, policy, rather than a unilateral, or one-sided, policy. By 1938 it was clear, as Roosevelt said, that "national defense has now become a problem of continental defense."

New crises leading to World War II

On January 4, 1939, in his annual message to Congress, President Roosevelt warned that the world situation had become extremely grave. He urged greatly increased appropriations for the armed services. He also urged Congress to reconsider the neutrality legislation adopted during 1935–37.

The President's worst fears were soon confirmed. On March 15, 1939, Hitler's armies moved into the rest of Czechoslovakia. On April 7 Mussolini's troops invaded Albania (see map, page 303).

Awakening at long last to their common peril, Great Britain and France announced that

Great Britain and France declared war on Germany after Hitler's invasion of Poland in September 1939. These German soldiers are firing at snipers in the Polish capital of Warsaw.

an attack upon Poland would mean war. Great Britain and France also tried belatedly to get the Soviet Union to join them in an agreement to oppose by armed force any further aggression by either Hitler or Mussolini. It was with shock, therefore, that the democratic nations learned on August 23, 1939, that the U.S.S.R. had just signed a nonaggression pact with Germany.

Seemingly freed by the Soviet pact from the danger of a two-front war, Hitler struck swiftly.

On September 1, without warning, German bombers and powerful mechanized divisions crossed the border into Poland (see map, page 303). Two days later, on September 3, 1939, Great Britain and France declared war on Germany.

While Great Britain and France were mobilizing, Soviet troops invaded Poland from the east. By the end of September all organized Polish resistance had been crushed, and Germany and

SOURCES

FRANKLIN D. ROOSEVELT'S "FOUR FREEDOMS" SPEECH (1941)

In the future days, which we seek to make secure, we look forward to a world founded upon four essential human freedoms.

The first is freedom of speech and expression—everywhere in the world.

The second is freedom of every person to worship God in his own way—everywhere in the world.

The third is freedom from want—which, translated into world terms, means economic understanding which will secure to every nation a healthy peacetime life for its inhabitants—everywhere in the world.

The fourth is freedom from fear—which, translated into world terms, means a worldwide reduction of armaments to such a point and in such a thorough fashion that no nation will be in a position to commit an act of physical aggression against any neighbor—anywhere in the world. . . .

the U.S.S.R. divided Poland between them. The Soviets then demanded and won the right to establish military and naval bases in Estonia, Latvia, and Lithuania (see map, page 303). And on November 30, after Finland refused to grant Soviet demands to establish military bases on Finnish soil, the U.S.S.R. attacked its small neighbor. The Soviet government claimed that its actions were necessary to protect the Russian homeland from invasion.

And thus World War II started and began to spread across Europe.

SECTION SURVEY

IDENTIFY: Declaration of Lima, nonaggression pact,

appeasement; Neville Chamberlain; 1938, 1939.

1. At Munich, Western leaders had a choice between shame or war. They chose shame and made war an inevitability. Comment.
2. Compare the American attitude toward the war in Europe in 1914–15 with that in 1939.
3. In 1938 the Latin-American nations became partners with the United States in enforcing the Monroe Doctrine. This was an effect of the Good Neighbor policy. Comment.
4. Draw a time line covering 1931 to 1939. (a) Below the line list the events abroad that led to World War II. (b) Above the line list United States actions or foreign policy decisions. (c) Some American foreign policies of the 1930's were dictated by the past. Explain, using the time line.

4 America's involvement in World War II

American sympathies in 1939 were overwhelmingly in favor of the Allies. At the same time, however, Americans were determined to stay out of war. President Roosevelt was voicing a widely shared feeling when, in a "fireside chat" over radio on September 3, he said, "As long as it remains in my power to prevent, there will be no blackout of peace in the United States."

Neutrality laws amended

On September 21, 1939, however, Roosevelt urged a special session of Congress to amend the Neutrality Act of 1937. "I regret that Congress passed the Act. I regret equally that I signed the Act," he declared. As Roosevelt pointed out, the existing embargo on the export of munitions actually favored Germany. If it were not for the embargo, Great Britain and France could use their control of the seas to secure from the United States the arms that they desperately needed. Hitler, on the other hand, did not need military equipment, for he had been preparing for war for years.

After a six-week debate, with many members of Congress demanding outright repeal of the neutrality laws and many others insisting on retaining them, Congress finally agreed on a compromise proposal. The new law abolished the arms embargo and allowed any country to buy weapons or munitions from the United States provided that the goods were transported to Europe on foreign ships. This law, which went into effect on November 4, 1939, greatly helped the Allied nations resisting Hitler.

Declaration of Panama

While Congress was debating the problem

of neutrality, the Pan-American Union met at Panama to consider problems of hemispheric defense.

On October 3, 1939, the delegates to the Panama Conference issued a declaration warning all belligerent war vessels to stay out of a "safety zone" around the Americas roughly 300 to 1,000 miles (483 to 1,609 kilometers) wide. Germany, Great Britain, and France challenged this declaration on the ground that no nation or group of nations had the right to close any part of the high seas to their ships. The declaration was important, however, as an indication of genuine cooperation among the nations of the Western Hemisphere.

The fall of France

While Hitler was carrying on his *blitzkrieg,* or "lightning war," against Poland in 1939, the French rapidly mobilized. They braced themselves for an attack against the Maginot (mah·zhee·NOH) Line—the formidable chain of forts guarding their eastern frontier. But Hitler did not attack. People began to joke about the "phony war," which some called a *sitzkrieg,* or "sitting war."

On April 9, 1940, the joking ceased. On that date Hitler demonstrated the true meaning of "blitzkrieg." In the following weeks his powerful armored divisions, supported by fighters and bombers, rapidly overran Denmark, Norway, the Netherlands, Belgium, Luxembourg, and northern France (see map, page 318). On May 26 the British began a heroic evacuation of their expeditionary forces from the beaches of Dunkirk, a seaport in northern France on the Strait of Dover. Although the British were forced to leave much of their equipment, they succeeded in saving most of

With the blitzkrieg, Hitler unleashed a new type of warfare. Before the war started he had assembled a number of highly mobile, highly mechanized units, including tanks and mounted artillery. These units, known as Panzer divisions, were supported by a new type of specially designed aircraft, the Stuka, or dive bomber. Concentrating intense fire power upon a single section of the enemy line, the Panzers and Stukas drove through and fanned out in the rear. Then they raced over the countryside, overrunning command posts and supply depots and paralyzing lines of transportation and communication. When the enemy was completely disorganized, the German infantry moved in and "mopped up" all remaining resistance.

Using the blitzkrieg, Hitler won victory after victory in the early days of the war. But, in time, the Allies organized their own mobile units and their own clouds of fighters and bombers. Then it was a different story. They, too, could use the methods of the blitzkrieg. Sometimes, when it suited their purposes, they allowed Hitler's Panzers to pierce their own lines. Then the Allies sealed off the gap, shot down the Stukas, and moved in to destroy the Nazi tanks and armored equipment with their own mechanized units.

BLITZKRIEG

their troops. On June 10 Italy, sensing that France was doomed, declared war on France and Great Britain.

Hitler's blitzkrieg did not halt until June 22, 1940, when France signed an armistice with Germany. In London the French National Committee pledged continued resistance by the "Free French" under General Charles de Gaulle, and began to rally part of the French colonial empire against the Nazis. Meanwhile Marshal Pétain (pay·TAN) became the leader of a German-controlled French government with headquarters at Vichy (vee·SHEE) in central France (see map, page 318).

The Battle of Britain

With the fall of France, Great Britain stood alone and almost defenseless, for the British had left most of their war equipment on the beaches of Dunkirk.

On May 10, 1940, Winston Churchill replaced Neville Chamberlain as Prime Minister of Great Britain. With a rare gift for leadership Prime Minister Churchill rallied the British people, strengthening their hopes and their determination to fight. Churchill promised that the British would never surrender. If by chance Great Britain itself were to fall, he declared, "Then our Empire beyond the seas, armed and guarded by the British fleet, would carry on the struggle until, in God's good time, the New World, with all its power and might, steps forth to the rescue and liberation of the Old."

By the end of June, with France under Nazi control, Churchill was preparing his people for the coming "Battle of Britain." "Hitler knows that he will have to break us in this island or lose the war," Churchill said. "If we can stand up to him, all Eu-

rope may be free and the life of the world may move forward into broad, sunlit uplands. But if we fail, then the whole world, including the United States, including all that we have known and cared for, will sink into the abyss of a new Dark Age. . . .

"Let us therefore brace ourselves to our duties, and so bear ourselves that, if the British Empire and its Commonwealth last for a thousand years, men will still say, 'This was their finest hour.'"

The supreme test for the British came in the late summer of 1940. In August Hitler unleashed his fighters and bombers against Great Britain in an all-out effort to sweep the Royal Navy from the English Channel and the Royal Air Force from the skies. The Royal Navy fought back furiously, and the Royal Air Force, though almost hopelessly outnumbered, flew day and night, sometimes shooting down as many as 100 Nazi bombers in a single 24-hour period. In October, advised by his military chiefs that an attempt to invade Great Britain would be suicidal, Hitler postponed his invasion plan, "Operation Sea Lion," until spring.

"Never in the field of human conflict," Churchill declared, referring to the Royal Air Force, "was so much owed by so many to so few."

American defense measures

During the summer and fall of 1940 the United States was taking steps to strengthen its own defenses.

To check subversive activities, Congress passed the Alien Registration Act, commonly known as the Smith Act. This law strengthened legislation controlling aliens and made it illegal

Continued on page 310

THE WORLD AT WAR: SEPTEMBER 1939 — AUGUST 1945

GREENLAND

CANADA

ICELAND

NORWAY

SWEDEN

FINLAND

Murmansk

Leningrad

Moscow

SOVIET

GREAT
BRITAIN

London

**SIGNING OF THE ATLANTIC
CHARTER, AUG. 1941**

GERMANY

FRANCE

EUROPE

ITALY

**YALTA CONFERENCE
FEB. 1945**

Yalta

TURKEY

Teheran

IRAN

SPAIN

NEWFOUNDLAND

UNITED
STATES

New
York

Washington 1889-90

NORTH AMERICA

BERMUDA

BAHAMA IS.

MEXICO

Havana 1928,1940

Casablanca

MOROCCO

ALGERIA

LIBYA

IRAQ

Cairo
EGYPT

SUEZ
CANAL

SAUDI
ARABIA

IND

Mexico City
1901-02

PANAMA
CANAL

Panama
1939

TRINIDAD

FRENCH WEST AFRICA

AFRICA

ETHIOPIA

ATLANTIC

PERU

Lima
1938

BRAZIL

SOUTH

AMERICA

OCEAN

UNION OF
SOUTH AFRICA

INDIAN

Santiago
1923

Rio de Janeiro
1906, 1942

URUGUAY

Buenos Aires
1910, 1936

Montevideo
1933

CHILE

ARGENTINA

INDIAN

The following nations, neutral throughout most of the war, joined the Allies after 1944:

ARGENTINA	PERU	LEBANON
CHILE	URUGUAY	SAUDI ARABIA
ECUADOR	VENEZUELA	SYRIA
PARAGUAY	EGYPT	TURKEY

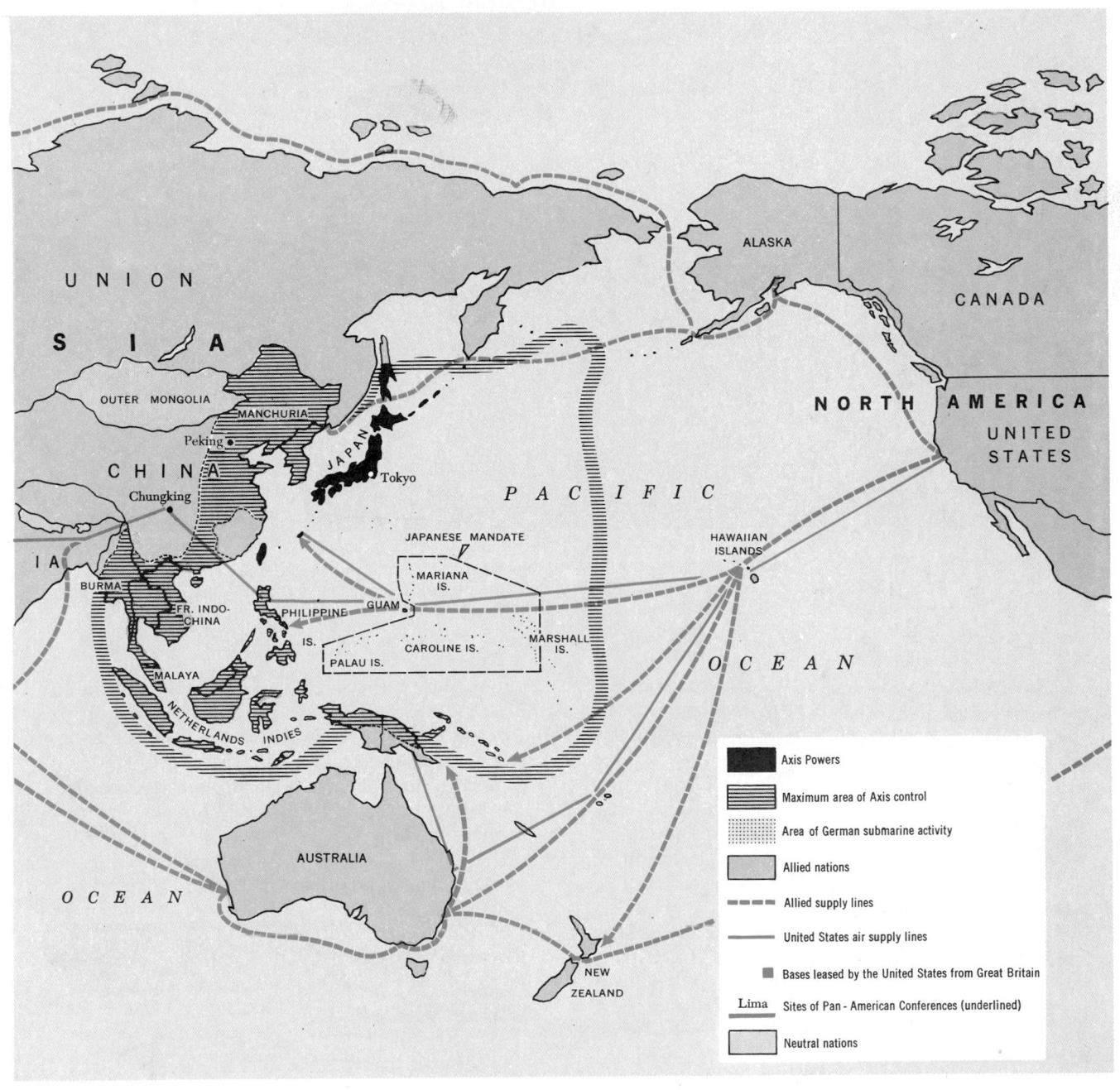

UNION
S I A
OUTER MONGOLIA
MANCHURIA
Peking
CHINA
Chungking
JAPAN
Tokyo
PACIFIC
ALASKA
CANADA
NORTH AMERICA
UNITED STATES
IA
BURMA
FR. INDO-CHINA
PHILIPPINE
IS.
MALAYA
NETHERLANDS INDIES
GUAM
JAPANESE MANDATE
MARIANA IS.
CAROLINE IS.
PALAU IS.
MARSHALL IS.
HAWAIIAN ISLANDS
OCEAN
AUSTRALIA
OCEAN
NEW ZEALAND

Axis Powers

Maximum area of Axis control

Area of German submarine activity

Allied nations

Allied supply lines

United States air supply lines

Bases leased by the United States from Great Britain

Lima Sites of Pan - American Conferences (underlined)

Neutral nations

Winston Churchill, shown here making his famous "V for victory" sign, became Prime Minister of Great Britain in 1940. Churchill's leadership united the British people, strengthening their hopes and determination to fight.

for any person in the United States to advocate the overthrow of the government by force or violence, or to belong to an organization that advocated the violent overthrow of the government.

In July Secretary of State Hull and the foreign ministers of the other American nations gathered in Havana, Cuba, to make plans for preventing Germany from seizing the Western Hemisphere colonies of the countries it had conquered. The Act of Havana stated that the moment the territorial integrity of any colony was in danger, the American republics, acting singly or collectively, would take control of the colony. From then until the end of the war, the colony would be governed by a group of trustees from the American republics.

Two weeks later President Roosevelt met with Prime Minister Mackenzie King of Canada. At this meeting the two leaders created a Permanent Joint Board of Defense to plan for the "defense of the north half of the Western Hemisphere."

In the meantime Congress was furiously de-

bating the pros and cons of the first peacetime draft in American history. The Burke-Wadsworth Act was finally passed and signed by President Roosevelt on September 16, 1940. The law required all men between 21 and 35 to register for the draft, and made them liable for one year of military training.

Roosevelt's Lend-Lease proposal

By the end of 1940 American supplies were flowing to Great Britain and America's defense program was gathering momentum. But President Roosevelt was not satisfied that the government was doing all it could "to keep war away from our country and our people."

What worried Roosevelt most was the fact that the British could not much longer afford to pay cash for the war materials they desperately needed. In his annual message to Congress, Roosevelt declared, "Our country is going to be what our people have proclaimed it to be—the arsenal of democracy." Roosevelt proposed that the United States increase greatly its production of military equipment of all kinds so that it could lend or lease to the British and to the other Allies any materials needed to carry on the fight.

Roosevelt's Lend-Lease proposal provoked a storm of controversy. Many people agreed with the President that the Lend-Lease proposal offered America's best hope of avoiding full-fledged participation in the war. Others, including the isolationists, took a directly opposite position—that Lend-Lease would surely involve America in a shooting war.

Overriding all objections, Congress passed the Lend-Lease Act in March 1941 and appropriated an initial sum of $7 billion for ships, planes, tanks, and anything else that the Allies needed. When on June 22, 1941, Hitler's armies invaded the Soviet Union despite the German-Russian nonaggression pact, the United States made Lend-Lease materials available to the U.S.S.R.

The Battle of the Atlantic

The Lend-Lease arrangement inevitably drew the United States closer to war. By the spring of 1941 German and Italian submarines were turning the North Atlantic into a graveyard of ships. In April American naval vessels began to "trail" enemy submarines, radioing their location to British warships. In July American troops occupied Iceland (see map, page 308) to prevent its occupation by Germany.

In September President Roosevelt issued "shoot on sight" orders to American warships operating in the "safety zone" established back in 1939 at the Panama Conference (page 306). American warships also began to accompany and protect, or convoy, merchant vessels as far as Iceland. And in November Congress voted to allow American merchant vessels to enter combat areas. Roosevelt promptly armed the merchant vessels and provided them with navy gun crews.

The Atlantic Charter

In August 1941, while the United States was moving rapidly toward undeclared war with Germany, Roosevelt and Churchill met to discuss the larger issues involved in the conflict. At this meeting the two leaders drew up a broad statement of war aims that came to be called the Atlantic Charter.

Like Woodrow Wilson's Fourteen Points, the Atlantic Charter listed a number of "common principles" upon which people of good will could build a lasting peace and a better world. In the Atlantic Charter, Roosevelt and Churchill pledged themselves to work for a world free of aggression, a world in which every nation, large or small, would have the right to adopt its own form of government. Once the aggressors were crushed, the Charter declared, all nations must work together

Cordell Hull, President Roosevelt's Secretary of State, is shown here with two Japanese diplomats sent on a "peace" mission to Washington in 1941. It is still not known whether or not these representatives had been informed of the planned attack on Pearl Harbor.

to free all people everywhere from the burden of fear and want.

Rising threat from Japan

While war raged in the European theater, Japan was pushing its conquests in the Far East. In July 1941 Japanese troops occupied French Indochina (see map, page 330). Thoroughly alarmed, President Roosevelt immediately "froze" all Japanese assets in the United States. He also placed an embargo on the shipment of gasoline, machine tools, scrap iron, and steel to Japan. Japan promptly retaliated by freezing all American assets in areas under its control. As a result trade between the United States and Japan practically ended. And then in August the United States sent a Lend-Lease mission to China.

The Japanese, convinced that American resistance was stiffening, began to make plans for an attack upon the United States. Even as its war

The Japanese attack on the American naval and air base at Pearl Harbor, in Hawaii, killed 2,000 Americans and wounded almost 2,000 more.

leaders were making final preparations, however, the Japanese government sent a "peace" mission to Washington. On November 20, 1941, this mission demanded that the United States (1) unfreeze Japanese assets, (2) supply Japan with as much gasoline as it needed, and (3) cease all aid to China. The United States refused to meet these demands, but offered several counterproposals.

On December 7 the Japanese mission announced that further negotiations were useless because the United States clung to "impractical principles" and had failed "to display in the slightest degree a spirit of conciliation."

The attack on Pearl Harbor

On Sunday morning, December 7, 1941—even before Japan's reply had been delivered to the American government—Japanese planes roared down without warning upon the United States fleet anchored in the huge American naval and air base at Pearl Harbor, in Hawaii (see map, page 331). Victims of this surprise attack, the Americans lost almost all of their planes and eight battleships and suffered the partial destruction of several other naval units. More than 2,000 soldiers, sailors, and civilians were killed, and almost 2,000 more were wounded. The same day the Japanese also attacked Wake, Midway, Guam, the Philippine Islands, and other American bases.

War declared

Americans were shocked and angered as the radio announced what had happened on the morning of December 7, 1941. With almost complete unanimity the American people supported President Roosevelt the next day when he asked Congress for a declaration of war against Japan. The Senate declared war unanimously; the House, with only one dissenting vote. Great Britain and the governments-in-exile that had fled their countries when Hitler conquered them also immediately declared war against Japan. Three days later, on December 11, Germany and Italy declared that a state of war with the United States existed, whereupon Congress declared war upon those two countries.

SECTION SURVEY

IDENTIFY: blitzkrieg, Smith Act, "arsenal of democracy," Atlantic Charter, Lend-Lease; Charles de Gaulle, Marshal Pétain, Winston Churchill; December 7, 1941.

1. Without extraordinary heroism on the part of the Royal Air Force and the British people, the Battle of Britain could not have been won. Comment.

2. At certain times in a country's history, the power of a single personality becomes an extremely important force. How does this apply to (a) Churchill's role in Great Britain, (b) Hitler's role in Germany?
3. Trace the events that led to the Japanese attack on Pearl Harbor.
4. The American people were isolationist before 1939 because they believed they were safe behind a two-ocean moat. Comment.

CHAPTER SURVEY

INQUIRING INTO HISTORY

1. How were nationalism, imperialism, and ideologies of racial superiority related to the causes of World War II?
2. Under Franklin D. Roosevelt's Good Neighbor policy, the Monroe Doctrine was transformed into a principle supported by several nations. (a) Explain. (b) Trace the steps which led to the change.
3. How did the United States' arms embargo aid the aggressor nations?
4. (a) Munich has become synonymous with the word appeasement. Explain. (b) How did appeasement help lead to World War II?
5. Pearl Harbor solidified American public opinion and ended the great debate between the internationalists and the isolationists. Explain.
6. Why did many Americans believe in isolationism during the 1930's?

RELATING PAST TO PRESENT

1. How do you think America's international affairs today have been affected by what was learned from the events preceding World War II?
2. Why might it be necessary to recognize the existence of a new country, even if the United States does not approve of its government?

DEVELOPING SOCIAL SCIENCE SKILLS

1. Make a time line for classroom display for the years 1932–40. Using pictures or drawings, show the major events leading to World War II.
2. Use the *Reader's Guide to Periodical Literature* to locate articles from the late 1930's written by isolationists and interventionists explaining why the United States should or should not become involved in the war. (a) What reasons are given for and against American involvement? (b) Which viewpoint do you agree with? Why?

CHAPTER 20
AMERICANS IN THE
SECOND WORLD WAR
1941-1945

World War II had been under way a little more than two years when on December 7, 1941, Japan's savage blow at Pearl Harbor plunged America into the global conflict.

America's enemies had the great advantage of what military leaders call "interior lines of supply and communication." Germany, Italy, and Japan were so situated geographically that the supply lines from their farms and factories to the fighting fronts were relatively short.

The United States and its Allies, on the other hand, had to establish and protect supply lines that often stretched thousands of miles across sea and land to fighting forces in far-off areas of the earth.

America's enemies had an even greater advantage. They had been preparing for war for many years. During these years they had trained huge armies; they had converted their factories to war production; and they had accumulated vast supplies of rifles, machine guns, tanks, planes, and hundreds of other instruments of modern warfare.

The United States, on the other hand, had not really begun to prepare for war until the summer of 1940, and even then preparations had been limited. Indeed, it was America's lack of preparation that led Hitler, Mussolini, and the Japanese war leaders to believe that they could win the war before the United States could mobilize its enormous resources.

Faced by such overwhelming odds, the American people grimly entered the conflict.

THE CHAPTER IN OUTLINE

1. Allied disasters on all fronts followed by Allied offensives.

2. Fighting the "battle of production" on the American home front.

3. Paving the way toward an Allied victory in Europe.

4. Allied victory in the Pacific and the end of World War II.

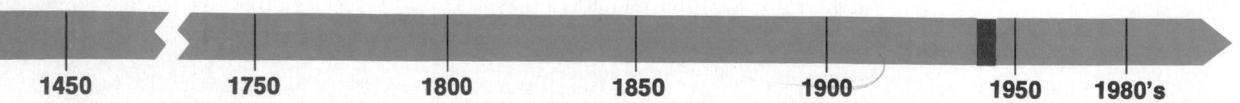

| 1450 | 1750 | 1800 | 1850 | 1900 | 1950 | 1980's |

1 Allied disasters on all fronts followed by Allied offensives

During most of 1942, as Americans were converting to a wartime economy, the United States and its allies suffered a series of almost unrelieved disasters in every theater of the war.

Early Japanese gains

The scene at Pearl Harbor on the evening of December 7, 1941, was one of nearly total destruction. America's offensive power in the Pacific had been wiped out by the Japanese surprise attack. And the Japanese soon struck again in the Pacific. By the end of December Japan had seized the American islands of Guam and Wake; had captured the British colony of Hong Kong; and had launched attacks upon Thailand, British Malaya, and the American-controlled Philippines and Midway (see map, page 330).

Disaster in the Pacific

The new year brought a mounting fury of destruction, with Japanese conquests covering a widening area of the Pacific and Far East (see map, pages 330–31). On January 2, 1942, Japanese troops poured into Manila, capital of the Philippines. On January 11 the Japanese invaded Borneo and Celebes (SEL·eh·beez) in the Netherlands Indies. On February 15 the advancing tide of Japanese troops overran the British naval base at Singapore. Later in the month, in the Battle of the Java Sea, a Japanese naval force delivered a crushing blow to an Allied fleet composed of American, British, Dutch, and Australian warships.

By the end of March the Japanese had conquered most of the Netherlands Indies with its rich supplies of oil, tin, rubber, quinine, and other vital war materials. They had also seized Rangoon, Burma, and were relentlessly driving British, Indian, and Chinese troops out of Burma.

Meanwhile, in the Philippines, a small force of Americans and Filipinos under General Douglas MacArthur continued their heroic but hopeless resistance against the invading Japanese. In January 1942 Manila surrendered, and MacArthur's forces retired to the Bataan Peninsula. In March MacArthur himself was ordered to Australia to take command of the Allied forces in the South Pacific. Fighting against overwhelming odds, the hungry, sick, exhausted survivors on Bataan were captured on April 9. On May 6 the outnumbered and starving troops on the fortress of Corregidor guarding Manila Bay were forced to surrender. The Japanese also cut the Burma Road, destroying the last land route to China (see map, page 330).

Thus by the end of May 1942, almost six months after their attack on Pearl Harbor, the Japanese had overcome all opposition and were poised to strike westward at India; southward at Australia; and eastward through Hawaii at the Pacific coast of the United States. These were dark days for Americans and their weary allies. But by the end of May, Japanese success had reached its peak.

American gains in the Pacific

Despite some opposition at home, the United States accepted the British argument that the defeat of Hitler in Europe must be the first Allied objective. But the war in the Pacific soon proved to be more than a mere holding operation.

Japan suffered its first serious reverse early in May 1942. Carrier-based planes from a British-American naval force caught a Japanese fleet moving southward in the Coral Sea, off the northeastern coast of Australia, and sank or severely damaged more than 30 Japanese warships.

Japanese forces received another setback early in June 1942 when they launched a two-pronged sea-borne attack on the Aleutian Islands and Hawaii. The ultimate Japanese objective was an invasion of the United States. American forces stopped the northern campaign, but only after Japanese troops had occupied the Aleutian islands of Attu and Kiska (see map, page 330). American naval forces blocked the southern campaign by defeating the Japanese in a major battle off the island of Midway.

There are several reasons why the United States began to stem the Japanese tide. First, early in 1942 the United States and Great Britain had pooled their resources to create a unified Pacific command. Second, the American people were beginning to win the important "battle of production" at home. The products of the nation's farms and factories were pouring into Pacific supply depots and forward bases. Finally, time had been gained by the courageous resistance of Americans and Filipinos on Bataan and Corregidor.

The turning tide in the Pacific

On August 7, 1942, the United States undertook its first major offensive action when marines stormed ashore at Guadalcanal in the Solomon Islands (see map, page 330). For four desperate months American marines and army troops clung to a tochold around Guadalcanal's airport, repelling one savage attack after another by Japanese forces from the air, from the sea, and from the surrounding jungle.

This painting shows United States troops landing on the Pacific island of Bougainville in 1943. Island by island, American and British forces fought to push back the Japanese.

In November the Japanese made a desperate effort to regain their former bases in the Solomons, which they needed to carry out their planned invasion of Australia. But Admiral William F. Halsey intercepted the huge Japanese fleet, and in a furious battle, November 12–15, completely routed the Japanese. Guadalcanal was at last secure. The tide of battle in the Pacific had turned. From then on the United States and its allies held the initiative in the Pacific.

Disaster in Europe

The situation in the Atlantic and in Europe during most of 1942 was gravely serious. German and Italian submarines in the Atlantic sank ships more rapidly than the United States and Great Britain could build new ones. Britain, now an isolated fortress in the Atlantic, could not hold out much longer unless reinforcements arrived, and unless the devastating Nazi bombings of vital British industrial areas were stopped.

On the continent of Europe, as in the Pacific, the tide of Axis conquest was rolling with terrifying speed. Yugoslavia fell to the Axis powers. The Greeks had been reduced to near starvation. The Soviet Union had lost its rich grainfields in the Ukraine region, and many major Soviet industrial centers had been ruined. Part of the destruction was done by the Soviet people themselves, for, as they retreated before the Germans, they applied a "scorched earth" policy to their land, destroying everything that they could not carry with them. Despite Soviet resistance the Nazi divisions

rolled on in the summer offensive of 1942, overrunning the oil fields of the Caucasus and rumbling into the outskirts of Stalingrad on the Volga River (see map, page 319). Beyond lay the Ural Mountains, where the Soviet people had moved much factory equipment that they had snatched from the path of the Germans, and where they were feverishly building new industries.

In the Mediterranean the Axis forces were triumphant everywhere. German and Italian aircraft with bases in Italy, Greece, the Greek island of Crete, and North Africa virtually forced British naval craft out of the Mediterranean, and thus denied the British the use of the Suez Canal route to the Indian Ocean. Great Britain was compelled to send its ships thousands of miles around Africa to reach Egypt, the Middle East, and India. By the autumn of 1942 the German *Afrika Korps* under General Erwin Rommel had advanced to the frontiers of Egypt, where it stood poised for a final thrust at the Suez Canal and the oil fields of the Middle East.

Allied November victories

November 1942 marked a turning point of the war. In the Pacific, as you have read, the three-day naval battle of Guadalcanal on November 12–15 started the Allies on their long island-hopping drive toward Tokyo. In North Africa the British General Bernard L. Montgomery caught Rommel by surprise late in October at El Alamein in Egypt, and drove him back across the desert toward eventual and complete defeat.

Of the millions of Americans in the armed forces during World War II, none was more famous than Kilroy. Not "General" Kilroy. Just plain Kilroy. Kilroy with no initials.

Kilroy was amazing. He was anywhere, everywhere, and always the first to arrive. Soldiers drove Japanese troops out of a mountainside cave, and when they cautiously entered, they saw the familiar writing on the cave wall: "Kilroy was here." The writing appeared on the Marco Polo Bridge in China, on the Tomb of the Unknown Soldier in Paris, on packing boxes and the walls of buildings on every continent.

Who was Kilroy? No one knew. Some thought that he was a sergeant, absent without leave, who wandered mysteriously over the world, writing the familiar name wherever he went. In 1946, a year after the war had ended, the American Transit Company staged a radio contest in an effort to identify the original Kilroy. The winner turned out to be James Kilroy, a Boston city councilor, who, during the war, had been an inspector for the Bethlehem Steel Plant in Quincy, Massachusetts. When he was criticized for not paying enough attention to his work, he began to write on packing cases "Kilroy was here" to prove that he was on the job.

Whether this was the true origin of the famous slogan probably will never be known. Kilroy had become a mythical figure, a modern counterpart of such legendary American heroes as Paul Bunyan and John Henry. Tall tales of Kilroy's exploits provided relief for the loneliness and boredom of Americans far from home. Kilroy also served as an inspiration to American troops, for he became a symbol of the unconquerable spirit that could overcome every obstacle and squarely meet every danger.

"KILROY WAS HERE"

On November 8 a mighty invasion armada led by General Dwight D. Eisenhower landed thousands of British, Canadian, and American troops on the northern coast of Africa (see map, page 318). On November 19 the Soviet troops began an encircling movement around the German forces at Stalingrad. Within several weeks, after a heroic defense of their city, the Soviet troops forced the Germans at Stalingrad to surrender.

"This is not the end," Winston Churchill said in November 1942. "It is not even the beginning of the end. But it is, perhaps, the end of the beginning." Subsequent events justified Churchill's words. Before 1942 was over, the Allies held the initiative in Europe, as in the Pacific. From then until the war's end, they exerted steady pressure until they finally pierced the Axis defenses and plunged into the heart of the aggressor nations.

Wartime cooperation

How had the Allies been able to survive the earlier disasters? Why were they able in November 1942 to begin to seize the initiative? One answer is that the tremendous strength of America's human resources and war materials was beginning to have its effect. Another answer is that in their struggle for survival the Allies worked as a team.

On January 1, 1942, the 26 Allied nations, calling themselves the United Nations,° issued a declaration. In this joint Declaration of the United Nations, the 26 countries (1) promised full cooperation in the war effort, (2) agreed not to make a separate peace, and (3) endorsed the war aims outlined in the Atlantic Charter (page 311).

Lend-Lease

Early in 1941, as you recall, even before the United States, had entered the war, Congress laid the basis for large-scale aid to the Allies with the Lend-Lease program (page 310).

After the attack on Pearl Harbor the aid program went into high gear. The United States shipped immense quantities of war materials across the submarine-infested sea routes to its allies in the Pacific and to Great Britain, the U.S.S.R., and the British armies in Egypt and the Middle East. Before the war ended, Lend-Lease aid reached more than $50 billion, of which 69 percent went to Great Britain, about 25 percent to

Continued on page 320

° The wartime Allies called themselves the United Nations. When in 1945 they formed a permanent organization, they continued to use this same name.

WORLD WAR II AND ALLIED VICTORY IN EUROPE

ICELAND

ATLANTIC

GREAT

NORTH
SEA

N.
IRELAND

EIRE

BRITAIN

OCEAN

NORWAY

SWEDEN

FINLAND

BALTIC SEA

DENMARK

ESTONIA

LATVIA

LITHUANIA

Leningrad

SOV

1942-45

1940-44

London

Dunkirk

NETH.

English
Channel

JUNE 6, 1944

NORMANDY

BELG.

Paris

LUX.

GER.

Berlin

1945

1945

Warsaw

POLAND

1944

1945

1945

Kiev

1944

UKR

GERMANY

FRANCE

Vichy

"VICHY FRANCE"

SWITZ.

AUSTRIA

Vienna

CZECHOSLOVAKIA

HUNGARY

1945

RUMANIA

1944

PORTUGAL

SPAIN

1944

SARDINIA

I T A L Y

Rome

Anzio

Cassino

Naples

Salerno

ADRIATIC SEA

YUGOSLAVIA

BULGARIA

1944

TU

Strait of
Gibraltar

SP.
MOROCCO

1942

Algiers

1943

1944

1943

ALBANIA

GREECE

Casablanca

1942

Bizerte

Palermo

SICILY

1942

1943

Tunis

MALTA

CRETE

MOROCCO (Fr.)

ALGERIA (Fr.)

TUNISIA (Fr.)

M E D I T E R R A N E A N

1943

El Alamein

1942

LIBYA

E G

0	Miles	1000
0	Kilometers	1600

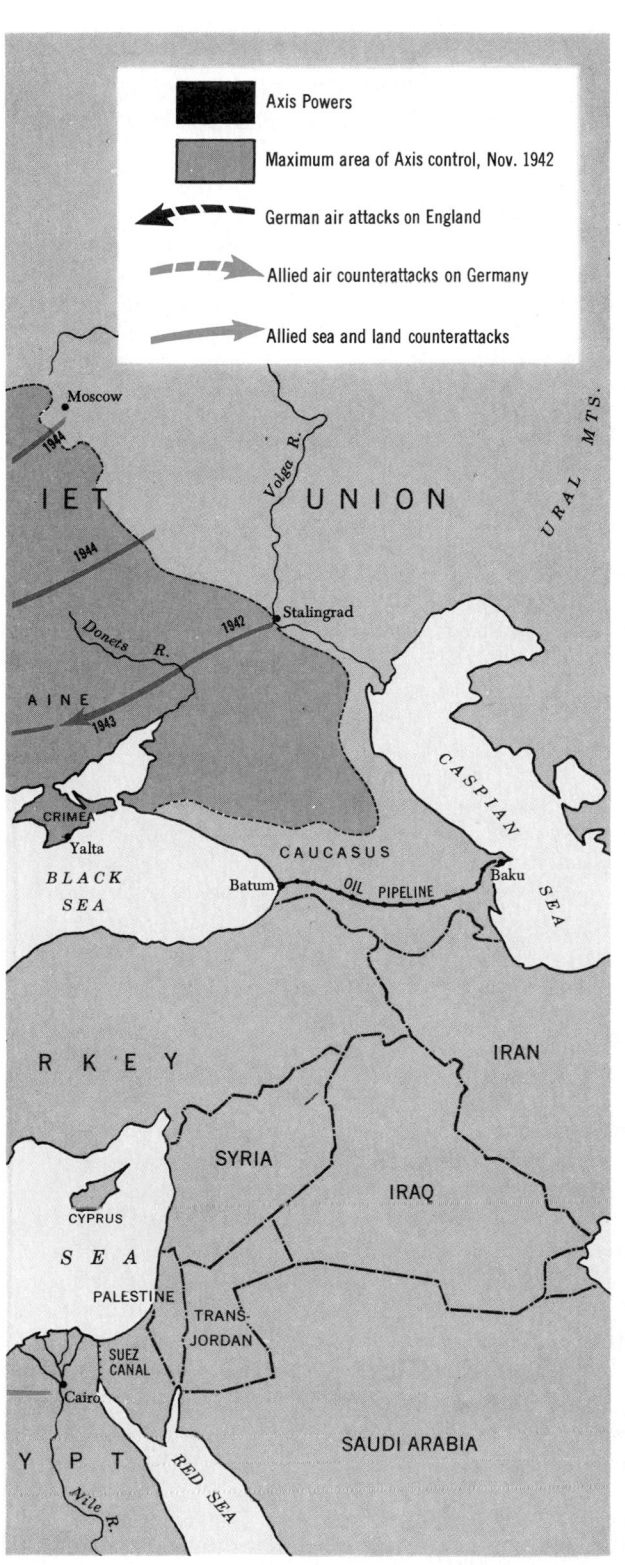

WORLD WAR II IN EUROPE

Dark days for the Allies

1939

SEPT.–OCT.   German invasion and conquest of Poland.

1940

APR.–JUNE   German invasion of Denmark, Norway, Luxembourg, Belgium, Netherlands, France.

MAY   British evacuation from Dunkirk.

JUNE–JULY   Fall of France; establishment of Vichy government.

AUG.–OCT.   Battle of Britain (German air attacks).

OCT.   Axis aggressions in Balkans.

NOV.–FEB. 1941   British offensive in Mediterranean and North Africa.

1941

FEB.–MAY   Battle of the Atlantic begins.

MAR.–APR.   Axis counteroffensive in North Africa.

APR.–JUNE   German invasion of Greece, Yugoslavia, Crete.

JUNE   German invasion of U.S.S.R. begins.

Allied gains: the tide turns

1942

MAY–AUG.   Allied air attacks on Germany begin.

OCT.–NOV.   Allied counteroffensive in North Africa begins.

NOV.–MAR. 1943   Russian counteroffensives in U.S.S.R.; German surrender of Stalingrad (in February).

1943

MAY   Allied victory in North Africa; end of African campaign.

JULY–AUG.   Allied invasion of Sicily.

JULY–JAN. 1944   Russians drive Germans back in U.S.S.R. and enter Poland.

SEPT.   Allies begin Italian campaigns.

SEPT. 8   Italy surrenders.

1944

JUNE 6   Allied invasion along Normandy coast (Operation Overlord).

AUG.   Allied forces land in southern France.

AUG. 25   Allies liberate Paris.

SEPT.   Allies liberate Belgium, Luxembourg.

SEPT.   Battle for Germany begins.

SEPT.–DEC.   Russians conquer Yugoslavia and Hungary.

DEC.   Battle of the Bulge (last German counteroffensive).

Allied victory in Germany

1945

FEB.–APR.   Allied invasion of Germany.

MAY 7   Germany surrenders.

MAY 8   V-E Day (end of war in Europe).

the U.S.S.R., and small quantities to other Allies.

But Lend-Lease was not a one-way arrangement. During the war the United States received in exchange goods and services valued at nearly $8 billion, most of which came from Great Britain. For example, when the American air forces began to arrive in England, the British provided bases, housing, and equipment. The Lend-Lease program was an outstanding example of Allied wartime cooperation.

Cooperative planning

But joint planning of strategy was an even more decisive Allied effort. Shortly after the attack on Pearl Harbor, Prime Minister Churchill and a group of military, naval, and technical aides met in Washington D.C., with General George C. Marshall, Chief of Staff of the Army, and the commanders of America's air, land, and sea forces. This meeting was the first of a series held by the Allied military leaders.

These conferences required a tremendous spirit of give and take. Final decisions were not always popular with all concerned. For example, the Soviets, hard-pressed in the summer of 1942, urged their Allies to relieve the pressure on the Soviet Union in Eastern Europe by opening a "second front" in Western Europe. Roosevelt and American military leaders finally agreed with Churchill that the Allies were not sufficiently prepared to do this and decided instead to land troops in North Africa, from where they could strike at southern Europe. Despite these and other differences among the Allies, the high degree of cooperation achieved was an indispensable factor in the final victory.

SECTION SURVEY

IDENTIFY: "scorched earth" policy, *Afrika Korps*, United Nations, "second front"; Douglas MacArthur, William Halsey, Erwin Rommel, Bernard Montgomery, Dwight D. Eisenhower.

1. December 1941 to May 1942 were dark days for Americans and their weary Allies. Explain.
2. Describe the strategy of the United States and its Allies in fighting the Axis Powers.
3. How did the Lend-Lease program help both the United States and its Allies?
4. "November 1942 marked a turning point of the war." Why?
5. Why was Allied cooperation so decisive a factor in winning the war?

2 Fighting the "battle of production" on the American home front

The Allied victories beginning in November 1942 were won on the farms and in the factories of the Allied nations, as well as on the fighting fronts. By the end of 1942 the United States in particular had made itself "the arsenal of democracy."

Hitler's errors

When he declared war upon the United States, Hitler had already made two grave mistakes. First, he had failed to conquer Great Britain, which he might have done had he launched an invasion immediately after the British armies lost most of their equipment at Dunkirk. Second, his surprise attack upon the U.S.S.R. in June 1941 and his failure to take Moscow led to the disaster of his troops at Stalingrad.

On December 11, 1941, Hitler made a third major mistake by declaring war upon the United States. He failed to realize how swiftly the American people could convert their peacetime industries to war production.

America's soaring production

One of the amazing demonstrations of America's productivity took place on the nation's farm lands. Despite the fact that 2 million agricultural workers served in the armed forces, farmers managed to raise record-breaking crops. They raised enough food to supply the American people as well as their Allies.

The output of America's mines and factories was equally impressive. For example, between July 1, 1940, and July 31, 1945, United States manufacturing plants produced 296,601 military planes, including 97,000 bombers; 86,388 tanks; 88,077 scout cars and carriers; 16,438 armored cars; 2.4 million trucks; 991,299 light vehicles, such as jeeps; 123,707 tractors; 17.4 million rifles and side arms; 2.7 million machine guns; 315,000 pieces of artillery; and 41.4 billion rounds of ammunition.

In addition, America's shipbuilders created the greatest navy and merchant marine the world had ever seen. By 1943 five ocean-going vessels were being launched every 24 hours to join the growing fleet linking America's farms and factories with the far-flung battle fronts.

All in all, production during the war years was 75 percent greater than in peacetime. According to Donald M. Nelson, first chief of the War Production Board, created in January 1942, "American industry turned out more goods for war than we ever produced for our peacetime needs—yet had enough power left over to keep civilian standards of living astonishingly high."

Financing the war

Where did the money come from to finance the war? A little more than one third came from taxes, which were raised to the highest level in American history. The government borrowed the remainder, chiefly by selling huge issues of bonds. Because of this borrowing, the national debt shot upward from about $49 billion in 1941 to nearly $259 billion by the spring of 1945.

The dollar cost of the war was staggering. By 1945 military expenditures totaled $400 billion—twice the sum that the federal government had spent for all of its activities, including all wars, between 1789 and 1940!

Control of production and transportation

In its efforts to organize the war effort and to mobilize the nation's resources, the federal government created a complex network of agencies.

At the top there was a policy-making board called the Office of War Mobilization (OWM). Its job was to unify the activities of the many war agencies.

Just below the OWM was the War Production Board (WPB), which affected the daily lives of nearly every man, woman, and child in the United States, The WPB controlled the allocations of raw materials to industrial plants. It searched the country for scrap iron and the nation's kitchens for fats, tin, and aluminum. It directed the con-

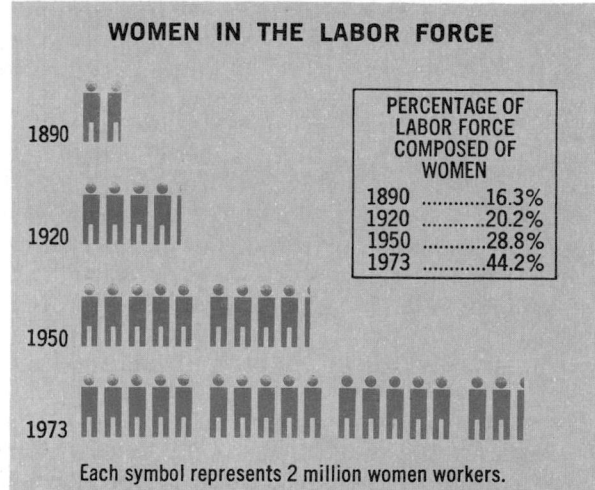

WOMEN IN THE LABOR FORCE

	PERCENTAGE OF LABOR FORCE COMPOSED OF WOMEN
1890	16.3%
1920	20.2%
1950	28.8%
1973	44.2%

1890

1920

1950

1973

Each symbol represents 2 million women workers.

version of factories from peacetime to wartime production, and also stimulated the construction of new industrial plants.

In addition, the WPB restricted the production of all consumer goods which required materials necessary to the war effort. It rationed gasoline to conserve oil and rubber. It even controlled clothing styles to save wool, cotton, rayon, and other vital materials.

To prevent transportation shortages and bottlenecks, the federal government also created the War Shipping Administration and the Office of Defense Transportation. These agencies closely

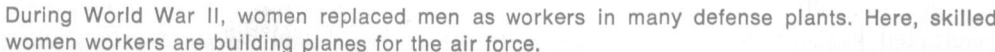

During World War II, women replaced men as workers in many defense plants. Here, skilled women workers are building planes for the air force.

supervised the railroads, express services, and shipping, with the result that supplies and troops were moved efficiently over land and sea.

Mobilizing human resources

The Office of War Information was created to bolster the morale of the armed forces and of civilians by publicizing the achievements of war production. It also gained support for Allied war aims by broadcasting them in dozens of languages to people all over the world.

The War Manpower Commission (WMC) discouraged men and women from working in nonessential occupations. By 1945 it had channeled nearly 30 million wage earners into the war production effort, including 12 million black American workers and 50,000 Indian workers. By 1943 the labor force included 2 million women working in war plants, replacing men who had left for the armed services. Remaining prejudices against working women were greatly diminished.

The WMC also operated the Selective Service System which, by the end of the war, had drafted nearly 10 million out of the more than 15 million Americans who served in the armed forces. Included were more than 1 million black Americans, both volunteers and draftees, about half of whom served overseas. Despite black protests, official military policy, as in previous wars, required Negroes to serve in segregated units. In 1944–45, however, some white and black troops in Europe were integrated to meet an emergency situation.

Also included in the armed forces were about 25,000 Indian volunteers. Among tribes with warrior traditions the rate of enlistment was high. In general the Indian volunteers enjoyed the respect of their white and black fellow soldiers. Indian soldiers who returned to the reservations after the war took back with them new ideas to their families and their tribal communities.

For the first time the American armed forces, which had previously used women only as nurses, now organized corps of women in uniform to replace men in noncombatant jobs. More than 250,000 women entered the army (as Wacs), the Coast Guard (as Spars), the Navy (as Waves), and the Marine Corps. As full-fledged military personnel, women worked as machinists, storekeepers, office workers, radio operators, and as drivers of jeeps and trucks. When people recovered from their surprise at seeing women in these new roles, they began to speak of "the girl behind the man behind the gun." Their performance went far toward breaking down prejudices about what women could and could not do.

Government control of prices

One of the ways in which the government most closely regulated the lives of civilians was through price controls. In World War I the shortage of consumer goods and the increased purchasing power of industrial and agricultural workers had driven prices skyward, bringing on inflation and causing suffering, especially among the poor. The government was determined to prevent prices from skyrocketing again. In its first step against inflation the government raised income taxes, thus draining off dollars that would otherwise have been spent on goods in the stores. As a second step, the government encouraged Americans to buy war bonds, arguing that such purchases were both a patriotic duty and a sound investment. But these measures alone could not prevent inflation.

In 1942, following the example of European governments, Congress authorized the Office of Price Administration (OPA) to establish ceilings, or top limits, on prices and to set up a rationing system. The OPA issued ration books containing coupons which purchasers had to use in addition to money to buy gasoline, fuel, shoes, coffee, sugar, fats and oils, meat, butter, and canned goods. The OPA also established rent controls. By these measures it protected consumers from price increases and unfair distribution of goods as available supplies dwindled and as the housing shortage became acute.

Despite these efforts the prices of consumer goods rose, especially food prices. By 1944 the cost of living had risen 30 percent above 1941 prewar levels. Americans resented government controls over their daily lives, and some violated the price control and rationing system by paying exorbitant prices to obtain more than their share of rationed products. Most Americans, however, accepted price controls and rationing as wartime necessities.

Government control of wages

Shortly after the attack on Pearl Harbor, the leaders of organized labor promised President Roosevelt that American workers would not strike during the war. At the same time they insisted that the government, in return for the "no-strike pledge," must ensure that workers would be fairly treated. By the spring of 1942, however, the cost of living had risen, and workers were becoming restless.

In July 1942 the National War Labor Board (WLB) tried to work out a compromise. It granted a 15-percent wage increase to readjust the workers' incomes to the rise in living costs. Several months later Congress and President Roosevelt authorized the WLB to "freeze" the wages and salaries of all workers at the newly established levels.

For a time there was relatively little trouble.

But as prices continued to rise, labor again became restless, and here and there strikes broke out. In such instances the government usually intervened, and for the most part settled the disputes quickly.

Government control of profits

Paralleling its efforts to control prices and wages, the government also tried to regulate profits —mainly by means of taxation. Personal income taxes were greatly increased for people in the higher income brackets. But the most drastic means of controlling profits was the excess profits tax, levied in 1940, which obliged corporations to pay to the government as much as 90 percent of all excess profits.

Americans did not like government controls, but accepted them with the understanding that they would be removed when the emergency was over.

After the Japanese attack on Pearl Harbor, most Japanese-Americans were forced to leave their homes and to relocate in detention camps, such as the one shown here.

The plight of Japanese-Americans

The upheaval in everyday life resulting from these controls and from the whole vast war effort revealed the extraordinary willingness of the American people to make sacrifices for the national emergency. Despite discomforts, sacrifices, and some displays of selfishness, a remarkably high level of morale was maintained.

To be sure, Americans suffered deep anxieties and fears. But these fears did not lead to the widespread repressions of unpopular and suspected minority groups that occurred in World War I. The tragic exception to this overall tolerance was the forced relocation of some 100,000 Americans of Japanese birth or parentage.

After the Japanese attack on Pearl Harbor, many Americans were genuinely fearful of a Japanese attack on the United States. This fear was soon turned against the Nisei—native-born Americans whose ancestors came from Japan. As a result, most Japanese-Americans—the great majority of whom lived in California—were forced to leave their homes and were taken to detention camps in other states, where they remained as virtual prisoners until the end of the war. Most of the Nisei lost their homes and businesses. Yet there had never been any real proof that these Japanese-Americans had been disloyal. Indeed, nearly all of the Nisei remained loyal, patriotic American citizens despite their harsh, unfair treatment. Many of those who served in the armed forces distinguished themselves for bravery.

After the war Americans regretted their unjustified actions against the Nisei. In 1945 the Nisei were permitted to leave the detention camps and settle wherever they wished. In 1948 Congress passed an act to help the Nisei recover their losses.

Negro advances and setbacks at home

As in previous wars, black Americans contributed their full share not only to the fighting, but to efforts on the home front as well. In 1941 President Roosevelt directed that a Fair Employment Practices Committee be set up to eliminate discriminatory hiring policies in defense industries. As a result, the doors of the nation's defense industries were opened to hundreds of thousands of willing black workers.

Less was accomplished, however, in promoting equal housing opportunities for Negroes in the overcrowded cities in which defense industries were concentrated. Unfair treatment and discrimination on the part of white Americans—especially those white workers who, like many Negroes, had recently migrated from the South—led to outbursts of violence and even riots in several cities. In Detroit in 1943, federal troops restored order after a riot cost the lives of 25 black Americans and 9 white Americans.

Aware of their contributions to the war effort, many black Americans became restless. As they listened to patriotic speeches about freedom for all, they became more determined to make these ideas truly meaningful for themselves. Thus black leaders continued the fight for equal rights at home throughout the war years.

SECTION SURVEY

IDENTIFY: OWM, WPB, Selective Service System, price controls, ration books, black market, Nisei.

1. Why was the United States called the "arsenal of democracy"?
2. It was necessary for the federal government to establish controls and regulations over virtually every aspect of American life during the war. Explain.
3. By 1945 military expenditures totaled $400 billion —twice the sum that the federal government had spent for all activities between 1789 and 1940. What are your reactions to this statement?
4. How did each of the following contribute to the war effort: (a) unions, (b) scientists, (c) women, (d) farmers, (e) black Americans?
5. United States action against the Nisei was justified because the constitutional rights of all citizens are suspended in wartime. Comment.

3 Paving the way toward an Allied victory in Europe

In the summer of 1942, as the tide of war was beginning to turn in favor of the Allies, President Roosevelt and Prime Minister Churchill decided to strike at what Churchill called the "soft underbelly" of the Axis.

Victory in North Africa

The opening blow, as you recall, fell late in October 1942, when the British broke through Rommel's lines at El Alamein and began to drive the Germans back into Libya. Meanwhile, on November 8, a force of 500 troop transports and 350 warships under General Eisenhower's command landed British, Canadian, and American troops on the coasts of French Morocco and Algeria. It was the greatest combination of land, sea, and air forces assembled up to that time.

The loss of French areas in North Africa was a serious blow to the Germans. Although they continued to fight with great skill, their efforts were hopeless. Allied planes and ships cut their supply lines from Italy. General Montgomery's British Eighth Army drove steadily westward, while American forces moved eastward. Outnumbered and caught between the jaws of two enemy forces in Tunisia (see map, page 318), the Germans and Italians surrendered early in May 1943.

As a result of the victory in North Africa, the Allies captured more than 250,000 Axis troops. Far more important, the Allied nations now had control of the Mediterranean. Allied warships could now operate freely, protected by planes based at airfields along the North African coast. The Allies could ship supplies to India through the Suez Canal. They could also ship supplies to the U.S.S.R. by way of Iran.

Invasion of Italy

From their newly won North African bases the Allies subjected Sicily and Italy to merciless bombing. Then, early in July 1943, British, Canadian, and American troops landed in Sicily. The Sicilians offered little resistance, and the crack German troops were greatly outnumbered by the invaders, who swiftly overran the island.

Americans and other Allied peoples were thrilled at the rapid conquest of Sicily and by other goods news that came over the radio during the summer of 1943. Late in July the Italians ended Mussolini's dictatorial rule and organized a new government. Before dawn on September 3 the British Eighth Army landed on the southern coast of the Italian mainland. On September 8 the Italian government surrendered unconditionally, and the following day an Allied invasion force landed at Salerno.

Despite these great successes the campaign for Italy was one of the longest and most difficult of the war. Veteran German troops were rushed in to fill the gaps left by the Italians. Difficult mountain terrain and bad weather helped the Germans. On October 1 Naples fell to an American army under General Mark W. Clark, but for several months the Allies were unable to advance beyond Cassino (see map, page 318). In an effort to outflank the German lines, Allied troops landed on the Anzio beaches on January 22, 1944. But the Nazis fought desperately, and it was not until June 4, 1944, that the Allied armies entered Rome.

From Rome they moved northward. Progress was slow, and every inch of soil was won at great cost by the forces of the Allied nations—Americans, British, Canadians, Indians, New Zealanders, South Africans, French, Moroccans, Algerians, Senegalese, Italians, Poles, Greeks, Arabs, Brazilians, and a Jewish brigade from Palestine. Al-

General Eisenhower (right) commanded the Allied invasion of North Africa in 1942. Later, as Supreme Commander, Eisenhower led the Allied invasion of France in 1944.

though the Nazis were pushed steadily northward, fighting continued in Italy until the last few months of the war in Europe.

Importance of the gains in Italy

The victories of 1943–44 in Italy were immensely important. Through them the Allies strengthened their control of the Mediterranean. The loss of Italy deprived Germany of desperately needed troops. Moreover, from Italian bases Allied fliers were able to bomb southern Germany and the German-held Balkans, including the rich oil fields in Rumania.

Finally, in their efforts to check the Allies in North Africa and Italy, the Germans had been forced to withdraw troops from the Soviet front. This had helped the Soviet Union to regain great stretches of valuable farm land in the Ukraine. Despite the Italian campaign, however, the Nazis continued to concentrate most of their military forces against the Soviet Union, and the Soviets continued to call for a "second front" in Western Europe.

Victory in the Atlantic

The victories in Italy were possible only because the Allies had won control of the Atlantic Ocean. During the early months of the war German submarines waged a mighty battle against ships carrying supplies to Europe. On April 23, 1942, Winston Churchill reported secretly to Parliament:

"I will begin with the gravest matter; namely, the enormous losses and destruction of shipping by German U-boats off the east coast of the United States. In a period of less than sixty days, more tonnage was sunk in this one stretch than we had lost all over the world during the last five months of the Battle of the Atlantic before America entered the war. . . ."

Gradually, however, the Allies began to gain the upper hand. Radar and other devices for detecting planes and submarines were developed. New warships, including small aircraft carriers, began to slide down the ways of American and British shipyards. During 1942 the Axis sank 585 Allied and neutral vessels in the Atlantic. During 1943 the Axis sank only 110 ships. By the end of 1943 the Battle of the Atlantic was won.

Over the sea lanes great convoys carried urgently needed military supplies to the Mediterranean war fronts and to Great Britain, which by 1943 had been converted into a vast base for the invasion of Western Europe.

Victory in the air

While the Allied navies were winning the Battle of the Atlantic, Allied planes began their offensive against Germany and German-occupied Europe. In 1942 American fliers began taking part in Royal Air Force raids. By early 1943 the combined Anglo-American air assault had become a major and increasingly important factor in the struggle. During the last year of the war, fleets of

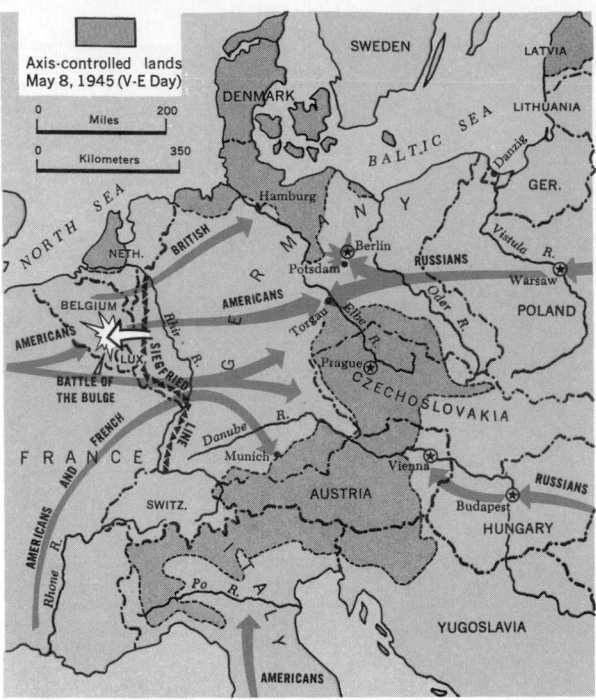

ALLIED VICTORY IN EUROPE

as many as 2,000 heavy bombers were dropping tons of bombs on a single target area.

The destruction was enormous. The constant blows against German transportation centers, industrial plants, and military installations weakened German morale and power to resist. The Allied air raids brought relief to Great Britain, which had suffered tremendous damage from German air attacks. They also helped Soviet armies seeking to drive the Nazis from Soviet soil.

Liberation of Western Europe

The terrific air assault on Germany was merely part of a larger strategy—the invasion and conquest of Germany. By June 1944 General Eisenhower, who had been named Supreme Commander of the Allied invasion armies in Western Europe, was satisfied that it was time to launch the attack.

"Operation Overlord," as the invasion was called, began before dawn on the morning of June 6, 1944 (D-Day). More than 11,000 planes roared into the air. Some dropped airborne troops at key points a few miles inland from the German-occupied French coast. Others bombed roads, bridges, railway junctions, and German troop concentrations. Still others formed a mighty umbrella under which a huge invasion fleet of nearly 4,000 troop transports, landing craft, and warships moved across the English Channel to the Normandy beaches (see map, page 318).

The Germans had worked for years to make these beaches unconquerable. Heavy artillery and machine guns were located in reinforced concrete pillboxes. Barbed wire and tank traps lined the shores. Other tangles of barbed wire were strung on steel and concrete piles and sunk just below the water's surface for hundreds of feet offshore.

Despite the years of preparation, the Germans were powerless to stop the invasion. Field Marshal Karl von Rundstedt later explained: "Terrific air power broke up all bridges and pinned me down completely, and the terrific power of the naval guns made it absolutely impossible for reserves to come up." The Nazis resisted fiercely, but they were outplanned, outnumbered, and outfought.

Allied tank forces ripped through the German defenses and fanned out behind the lines. Aided by the French resistance, or underground movement, they quickly overran the countryside. On August 25, 1944, Paris fell. By this time the Allies had landed more than 2 million troops, nearly 500,000 more vehicles, and millions of tons of munitions and supplies.

Meanwhile, early in August, the United States Seventh Army landed on the southern coast of France and pushed rapidly up the Rhone Valley to join the Allied troops pouring in from Normandy. Within six months after D-Day, France had been liberated and the Allies had swept into the outer defenses of Germany's famous Siegfried Line (see map, this page). Here the attack at last ground to a halt, and the Allied armies paused while new ports were opened, supplies were brought up, and military units were regrouped.

The election of 1944

The preparations for the final drive into Germany did not interfere with the regular November elections in the United States. The Republican candidate for the Presidency, Thomas E. Dewey, governor of New York, had attracted national attention when, as a district attorney, he had successfully prosecuted racketeers in New York. The Republicans considered Dewey a strong candidate. But the war was going well, and the Democrats argued that it would be unwise to replace experienced leaders with new ones. The argument proved convincing. Roosevelt, running for a fourth term, won with an electoral vote of 432 to Dewey's 99. The new Vice-President was Harry S. Truman of Missouri.

Germany's last counterattack

While the Allies were regrouping and the Americans were electing a President, the Germans were preparing a counterattack. On December 16 some 24 German divisions struck at a weakly held point in the Allied lines. German armored forces broke through, creating a dangerous "bulge" in the Allied lines. Christmas 1944 found the Allies fighting desperately in the Battle of the Bulge (see map, page 326), trying to prevent the **Germans from plunging onward to the sea. Reinforcements** were rushed up. The German divisions were shattered and thrown back behind the Siegfried Line. This was the final major counterattack by the Nazis. Their defeat cost them dearly in troops and equipment. Even more important, as General Eisenhower pointed out, was "the widespread disillusionment within the German army and Germany itself."

Invasion of Germany

By February 1945 Allied preparations had been completed for the invasion of Germany. The air forces continued to blast industrial areas, military bases, and transportation lines. Then, in March, the Allies crossed the Rhine, encircled **Nazi troop concentrations, and plunged toward** the heart of Germany (see map, page 326).

Meanwhile the Soviets had been driving the Germans out of the Ukraine, had conquered Nazi-held Rumania and Hungary, and were closing in upon the Nazis from the south and east. Churchill, by now greatly concerned over the Soviet Union's postwar intentions and alarmed at the deep penetration of the Soviet armies into Europe, argued that the Allies should race the Soviets to Berlin and Prague. This was a vital political problem, which should have been decided by the leaders of the Allied governments including, of course, President Roosevelt. But the civilian leaders left the decision to General Eisenhower, who, as Supreme Com-

mander, concluded that his first objective should be the total destruction of the German armies. It would be "militarily unsound," he declared, to depart from this objective for political considerations. As a result of this decision, American forces under Eisenhower's command advanced only as far as the **Elbe River** (see map, page 326), where on April 25 they **joined** with **the Soviet forces at Torgau.**

Allied victory in Germany

Events that ended the war in Europe then followed in rapid order. On May 1 Hitler reportedly took his own life in the burning ruins of Berlin. On May 2 the Soviet troops hammered their way into the last Nazi strongholds of the city, and nearly 1 million German soldiers in Italy and Austria surrendered. Germany was in chaos. Within a week the Nazi forces in the Netherlands, Denmark, and Germany stopped fighting. Early on the morning of May 8 the German High Command surrendered unconditionally. Thus May 8, 1945 (V-E Day), marked the formal end of the war in Europe.

In Churchill's words, the victory over Germany was "the signal for the greatest outburst of joy in the history of mankind." As for himself, he wrote, his joy was tempered by "an aching heart and a mind oppressed by forebodings." He was weighed down by the awful tragedy of the war and concerned over the postwar intentions of the U.S.S.R.

In one of the most moving pictures of World War II, famed photographer Margaret Bourke-White photographed these bewildered prisoners in the notorious Buchenwald concentration camp as horrified American troops arrived to free them.

Shocking revelations of Nazi horrors

The first outbursts of joy and relief at the end of the war in Europe were soon dulled by the shocking news coming out of Germany. As the Allied armies occupied the conquered country, the full extent of Nazi horrors came to light. The world now heard in detail the bloodcurdling crimes the Nazis had committed in their concentration camps. In one of the most terrible displays of brutality in human history, the Nazis had created these camps, or "death factories," to destroy their "political enemies" and to exterminate the entire Jewish population.

The horrified world learned that nearly 12 million men, women, and children, about half of them Jews, had been slaughtered after suffering indescribable anxieties, agonies, indignities, and tortures.

Roosevelt's death

President Roosevelt did not live to see the end of the war nor to share in the world's horror over the full extent of Nazi atrocities. Worn out by his vast responsibilities, he died suddenly on April 12, 1945, in the "Little White House" at Warm Springs, Georgia. People all over the world were stunned at the news of his death. For three days American radio stations canceled programs to devote time to his memory. And Vice-President Harry S. Truman, who now became President, declared, "His fellow countrymen will sorely miss his fortitude and faith and courage in the time to come. The peoples of the earth who love the ways of freedom and hope will mourn for him."

SECTION SURVEY

IDENTIFY: "Operation Overlord," D-Day, Siegfried Line, Battle of the Bulge, V-E Day, concentration camps; June 6, 1944, May 8, 1945.

1. Why was it vital for the Allies to win the Battle of the Atlantic?
2. Describe the events of 1945 that led to the fall of Germany and to the end of the war in Europe.
3. What events led to a working relationship between the United States and the Soviet Union during World War II?
4. The Nazi atrocities in the concentration camps were among the most brutal crimes ever committed against humanity. Comment.

4 Allied victory in the Pacific and the end of World War II

President Roosevelt died in April 1945, only a month before the Allied victory in Europe and only four months before the defeat of the Japanese brought World War II to an end.

By 1943, you recall, the United States and its Allies were taking the offensive in the Pacific. The overall strategy, directed by Admiral Chester W. Nimitz, called for air, land, and naval forces to strike westward at the Japanese-held islands in the Central Pacific; for a fleet under Admiral Halsey to drive the Japanese from the Solomon Islands; and for General MacArthur to advance with troops along the New Guinea coast and on to the Philippines. The ultimate objective was Japan.

Early victories

During 1943 American, Australian, and New Zealand troops pushed forward through the steaming jungles and across the vast stretches of the Central and South Pacific. The struggle was grim, for the Japanese clung to every foot of land. Few prisoners were taken.

Driving the Japanese from their threatening position before Port Moresby, which defended Australia, American and Australian troops fought their way up the New Guinea coast. Before the end of 1943 much of New Guinea had been recovered. American and New Zealand forces also won victories in the Solomons.

Meanwhile, in the Central Pacific, Admiral Nimitz' powerful fleet moved into the Gilbert Islands, and American marines seized Tarawa and Makin (see map, page 330). Far to the north Japan's troops were dislodged from the Aleutian strongholds of Attu and Kiska. The threat to Alaska was now ended.

Despite these successes, won at extreme cost in lives after ferocious fighting, the Allied gains in 1943 were limited. The major Japanese positions remained untouched.

Island hopping to the Philippines

By 1944 a growing volume of troops and supplies was arriving in the Pacific, and many areas conquered by the Allies in 1943 were being converted into bases from which new advances could be made. Powerful new warships and aircraft carriers, temporarily grouped into swift task forces, were sweeping through the outer screen of protecting islands to blast Japanese installations and shipping routes. Carrier planes were raining explosives on the Japanese-held islands prior to invasion.

Suddenly, on January 31, 1944, the Allies struck again, this time against the Marshall Islands (see map, page 330). Three days later they seized Kwajalein (kwoj·ah·lin), one of the keys to Japanese control of the Marshalls. Kwajalein was the first Japanese possession occupied by the Allies. Three weeks later Eniwetok (en·ih·WEE·tok) was stormed successfully. From these two newly acquired bases, strong fleets of B-24 bombers began to blast Truk, major stronghold in the Carolines and key to Japanese control of the Southwest and Central Pacific. Meanwhile General MacArthur, continuing his methodical advance up the New Guinea coast, seized Hollandia. By July all of New Guinea was in his hands, with only bypassed pockets of Japanese troops left to surrender or to starve.

A month earlier, in June 1944, the Pacific war had erupted with extreme violence. Task-force raids and swift strikes by carrier-based planes pinned down Japanese air and naval forces and hammered the defenses of Saipan and Guam in the Mariana Islands (see map, page 330). Then, under cover of intense air and naval bombardment, landing craft swept in upon the beaches. From fleet concentrations near the Philippines, the Japanese sent out swarms of planes, only to lose more than 400 in a few hours. The following day hundreds of American planes roared from the decks of carriers to strike a severe blow at the retreating Japanese fleet.

Though shocked and saddened by the appalling loss of life, the American people were thrilled at the victories on Guam and Saipan. They had long dreaded the thought of a slow, bloody, island-by-island advance to Japan. Now, as they saw the larger strategy unfolding, Americans realized that America's tremendous sea and air power enabled it to seize key positions in the Pacific, leaving Japanese forces isolated and helpless on numerous islands far behind the line of battle.

Victory in the Philippines

But probably the most gratifying news from the Pacific in 1944 was the reconquest of the Philippines. In October a vast naval armada moved up from the New Guinea–Solomons theater of war and in from Saipan and Guam. Under naval and air cover the converging forces poured upon the beaches of Leyte (LAY·teh) in the central Philippines (see map, page 330) and eventually captured the island. Meanwhile, in the Battle of Leyte Gulf, American naval forces struck a shattering blow at Japan's remaining sea power.

Overcoming bitter land resistance, the conquering troops then spread over the Philippines, and early in February 1945 Manila fell to the Americans. "I shall return," MacArthur had promised when, following orders, he had left Corregidor in March 1942. "I'm a little late, but we finally came," he said in Manila in 1945 as the American and Filipino flags were raised above the city.

The Yalta Conference

Long before the Allied victories in 1945, leaders of the great powers had met at a series of conferences to develop a common strategy for defeating the Axis and to formulate plans for a lasting peace.

Early in February 1945 President Roosevelt, Prime Minister Churchill, and Premier Stalin met at Yalta in the southern part of the Soviet Union (see map, page 308) to make plans for the final stages of the war. At Yalta they made far-reaching decisions concerning the postwar world.

One group of decisions involved the creation of a new world organization. The three heads of state agreed to call a conference to meet in San Francisco on April 25, 1945, to draw up a charter for a new international organization. They also agreed on some crucial details regarding the nature of the new organization.

In another group of decisions, Roosevelt, Churchill, and Stalin made plans for the occupation of postwar Germany and the treatment of Poland and the other liberated nations in Eastern and Central Europe. They agreed to divide Germany into four military zones to be occupied and controlled by the United States, Great Britain, the Soviet Union, and France, respectively. They also agreed that the "Big Three"—the United States, Great Britain, and the Soviet Union—would support free elections in Poland and throughout Europe, thereby guaranteeing the right of Europeans to choose their own governments. These and other agreements were announced to the public.

But the "Big Three" also reached several secret agreements. In one of these, Stalin promised that the Soviet Union would enter the war against Japan within three months after the war in Europe ended. In exchange for this promise, Roosevelt and Churchill, upon recommendation of top military leaders, agreed (1) to recognize the Mongolian People's Republic, which had once been part of China but now claimed its independence under Soviet protection; and (2) to allow the Soviet Union to have the Kurile Islands, the southern half of Sakhalin Island, an occupation zone in Korea, and certain rights in Manchuria (see map, page 330). Several of these territories and privileges had been held by Russia before it lost them to the Japanese in the Russo-Japanese War of 1904–05.

Details of the Yalta Conference did not become public until long after Roosevelt's death. Down through the years critics have severely condemned Roosevelt for what they called his "surrender" to Soviet demands. The critics charged

Continued on page 332

WORLD WAR II AND ALLIED VICTORY IN THE PACIFIC

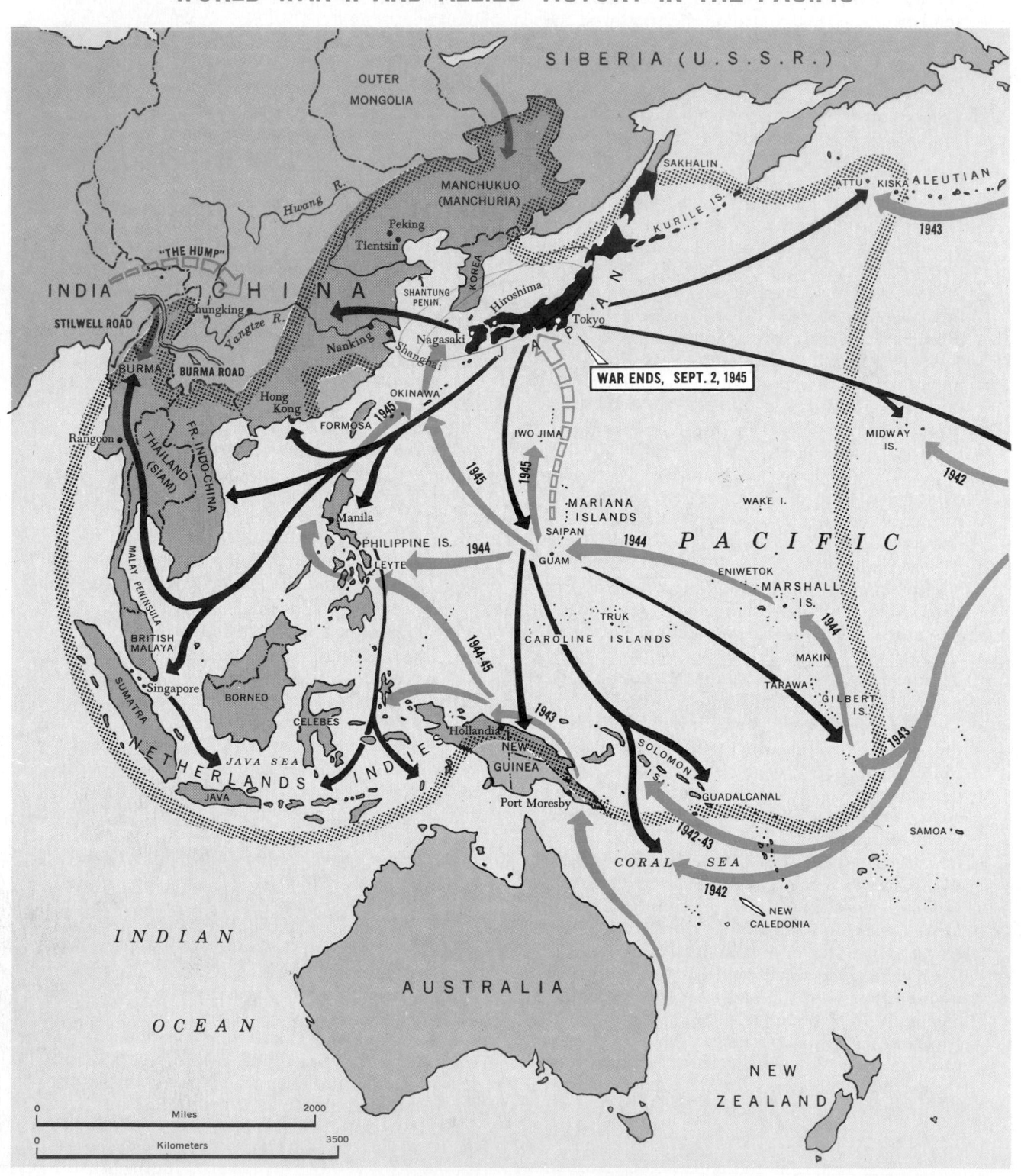

SIBERIA (U.S.S.R.)

OUTER
MONGOLIA

SAKHALIN

KURILE IS.

ATTU   KISKA   ALEUTIAN

1943

MANCHUKUO
(MANCHURIA)

"THE HUMP"

INDIA   CHINA

Peking
Tientsin

SHANTUNG
PENIN.

KOREA

Hiroshima

STILWELL ROAD

Chungking

Yangtze R.

Hwang R.

Nanking

Nagasaki

Shanghai

Tokyo

WAR ENDS, SEPT. 2, 1945

BURMA   BURMA ROAD

Hong
Kong

OKINAWA

1945

MIDWAY
IS.

FORMOSA

1942

Rangoon

FR. INDO-CHINA

THAILAND
(SIAM)

IWO JIMA

1945

1945

MARIANA
ISLANDS

WAKE I.

P A C I F I C

Manila

SAIPAN

1944

PHILIPPINE IS.

1944

GUAM

ENIWETOK

MARSHALL
IS.

1944

MALAY PENINSULA

LEYTE

TRUK

CAROLINE   ISLANDS

MAKIN

BRITISH
MALAYA

TARAWA

GILBERT
IS.

SUMATRA

Singapore

BORNEO

1944-45

CELEBES

Hollandia

1943

1943

N E T H E R L A N D S   I N D I E S

JAVA SEA

NEW
GUINEA

SOLOMON
IS.

JAVA

Port Moresby

GUADALCANAL

SAMOA

1942-43

CORAL   SEA

1942

NEW
CALEDONIA

I N D I A N

AUSTRALIA

O C E A N

NEW

ZEALAND

0   Miles   2000

0   3500
Kilometers

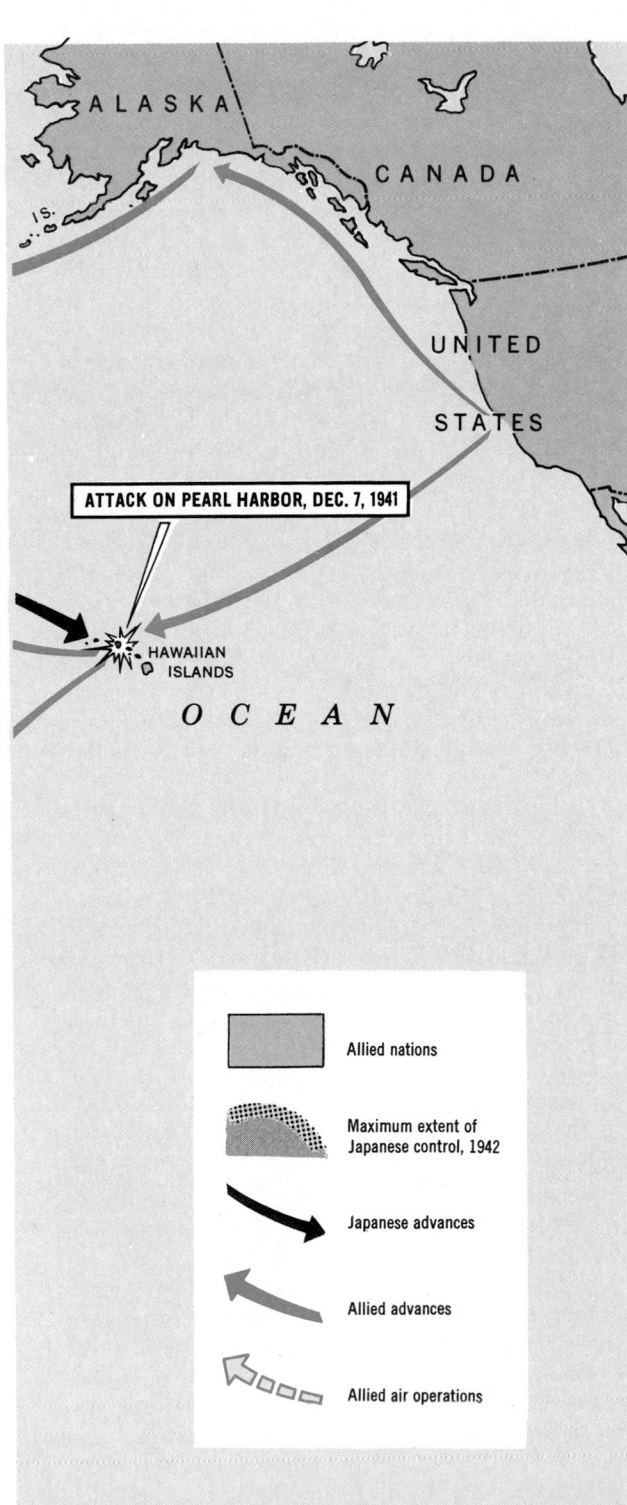

ATTACK ON PEARL HARBOR, DEC. 7, 1941

Allied nations

Maximum extent of
Japanese control, 1942

Japanese advances

Allied advances

Allied air operations

WORLD WAR II IN THE PACIFIC

Dark days for the Allies

1941

JULY	Japanese invasion of French Indo-China.
DEC. 7	Japanese attack Pearl Harbor.
DEC. 8–11	United States declares war against the Axis.
DEC.	Japanese invasion of Thailand and Br. Malaya; capture of Wake, Guam, Hong Kong; invasion of Philippines, Midway.

1942

JAN.	Fall of Manila.
JAN.–MAY	Japanese occupy Netherlands Indies and Burma.
FEB.	Singapore surrenders to Japanese.
FEB.–MAR.	Battle of the Java Sea.
APR.–MAY	Fall of Bataan and Corregidor.
MAY	Battle of the Coral Sea.
JUNE	Battle of Midway.
JUNE	Japanese occupy Attu and Kiska in Aleutians.

Allied gains: the tide turns

AUG.	U.S. marines land on Guadalcanal.
NOV.	Allied victory in naval battle of Guadalcanal.

1943

JAN.–SEPT	Allied gains in New Guinea.
MAR.–AUG.	Allies force Japanese from Aleutians.
JUNE–DEC.	Allied offensive in South Pacific: Solomon Is.
NOV.–FEB. 1944	Allied offensive in Central Pacific: Gilbert Is., Marshall Is., Kwajalein, Eniwetok.

1944

APR.–JULY	Allies seize Hollandia and regain New Guinea.
JUNE–AUG.	Allies capture Saipan and Guam in Mariana Is.
OCT.	Allied campaign to reconquer Philippines begins.

1945

FEB.	Allies liberate Manila; end of Philippines campaign.
FEB.–MAR.	U.S. marines conquer Iwo Jima.
APR.–JUNE	U.S. marines conquer Okinawa.
MAY–AUG.	Allied air offensive against Japanese home islands.

Allied victory in the Pacific

AUG. 6	Atomic bomb dropped on Hiroshima.
AUG. 9	Atomic bomb dropped on Nagasaki.
AUG. 10	Japan surrenders.
AUG. 14	V-J Day (end of war in Pacific).
SEPT. 2	Japan signs formal surrender on U.S.S. *Missouri*.

that as a result of his "surrender," Roosevelt gave the Soviet Union control of Manchuria, paved the way for the Chinese Communists' victory over Chiang Kai-shek (CHY·AHNG KI·SHEK), the Chinese Nationalist leader, and opened the door to Communist aggression in Korea. They also held him responsible for permitting Soviet occupation of East Berlin and East Germany, and the creation of Communist governments in Eastern Europe. These governments were created without the free elections which Stalin had promised.

Roosevelt's defenders have replied to these charges by reminding the critics of the military situation at the time of the Yalta Conference. Soviet armies had already conquered most of Eastern Europe, including Poland. American troops, on the other hand, had not yet crossed the Rhine and were still fighting the Japanese in the Philippines. Moreover, Allied military leaders had warned that the invasion of Japan, scheduled for the spring of 1946, would be extremely costly, and that the United States should be prepared to lose as many as 1 million troops.

Perhaps most important, Roosevelt's defend-

This statue in Washington, D.C., commemorates the heroism of American marines in the Pacific campaign. These men are raising the flag of victory at Iwo Jima.

ers insisted, was the fact that Stalin had given Churchill and Roosevelt reason to believe that the Soviet Union would cooperate in building a new world organization designed to establish the foundations of a lasting peace. As Churchill himself later wrote, "Our hopeful assumptions were soon to be falsified. Still, they were the only ones possible at the time."

The road to victory

On February 19, 1945, a week after the Yalta Conference ended, United States marines landed on the murderous beaches of Iwo Jima (EE·woh JEE·mah). Nearly 20,000 American marines were killed or wounded in the successful effort to gain control of the airfields on this barren volcanic island, only 750 miles (1,207 kilometers) from Tokyo (see map, page 330). Among the marines who helped raise a flag of victory over Iwo Jima was Ira Hayes, an Indian, who later received the Congressional Medal of Honor as an outstanding hero of World War II.

A few weeks later the largest landing force in Pacific history began the invasion of Okinawa (oh·kih·NAH·wah), a Japanese island some 300 miles (482.8 kilometers) from the Japanese homeland. Japanese "suicide planes," flown by pilots who were pledged to die by diving bomb-laden planes into their targets, struck at the American fleet as it closed in on the inner defenses of Japan. Despite bitter Japanese resistance, Okinawa fell in June.

Japan's air and sea power were broken. But Japan still had many well-trained and well-equipped divisions of soldiers. It still controlled large areas of China, although badly needed American supplies were being flown across the eastern Himalayas and transported by trucks over the newly opened Stilwell Road (see map, page 330) to Chiang Kai-shek's embattled troops. But these supplies were only a fraction of what China needed, and Chinese troops were in no position to undertake a major offensive. Moreover, the inner defenses on the Japanese homeland were strong. On the other hand, Japan was blockaded, and, after the war in Europe ended in the spring of 1945, the full weight of the Allies was available for the final struggle in the Pacific.

Day by day the American task forces grew bolder, driving the remaining Japanese ships from the seas and sweeping in to shell shore installations on the Japanese mainland. Day by day huge fleets of bombers, now within easier striking distance of Japan, dropped fire bombs and high explosives in devastating raids upon transportation, industrial, and military centers of the Japanese home islands. By the early summer of 1945 the

The atomic bomb dropped on the Japanese city of Hiroshima fell approximately one mile from the site shown here. Nearly 100,000 men, women, and children were killed by the bomb.

blockade and the relentless bombings were destroying Japan's power to resist. How long could Japan hold out?

The Potsdam Ultimatum

With President Roosevelt's death in April 1945, the responsibility for making decisions to bring about the defeat of Japan fell upon his successor, President Truman. In July Truman met with Stalin and Clement Attlee, the new British Prime Minister, at Potsdam, Germany. At this meeting the leaders discussed plans for the control and occupation of Germany. They also issued an ultimatum to Japan, calling for unconditional surrender. Japan formally rejected the ultimatum on July 29.

The end of World War II

On August 6, 1945, at 8:15 A.M., a solitary plane flew high over the Japanese city of Hiroshima (hee·ro·SHEE·mah). No alarm was sounded. Then suddenly the city disintegrated in a single searing atomic blast. Nearly 100,000 of the 245,000 men, women, and children in Hiroshima were killed instantly or died soon after. A new force had been added to warfare, a force that would enormously complicate the postwar world.

In authorizing the bombing of Hiroshima, President Truman knew that he had made an extremely grave decision. He had given the order only after days of conferring with his key military and political advisers. His decision was made as a last resort to force Japan to surrender immediately, and thus to save the lives of hundreds of thousands of American troops. But despite the devastation of Hiroshima, the Japanese failed to surrender.

On August 8 the Soviet Union declared war on Japan. On August 9 a second atomic bomb destroyed the city of Nagasaki. On August 10 the Japanese government finally asked for peace.

On August 14, 1945 (V-J Day), President Truman announced by radio that Japan had accepted the Allied peace terms. The formal surrender was signed on September 2, 1945. World War II had come to an end.

SECTION SURVEY

IDENTIFY: Potsdam Ultimatum, V-J Day; Chester Nimitz, Harry S. Truman, Chiang Kai-shek; August 14, 1945.

1. Trace the "island-hopping" strategy of the Americans in the Pacific.

2. What role did air power play in both the European and Pacific theaters of the war?
3. (a) Summarize the agreements reached at the Yalta Conference in 1945. (b) Why are these agreements considered controversial?
4. (a) Why did the Japanese finally surrender? (b) Was the dropping of the atomic bomb necessary to end the war? Explain.

CHAPTER SURVEY

INQUIRING INTO HISTORY

1. Despite their deeply rooted belief in individualism and free enterprise, Americans accepted many new governmental controls during World War II. Why?
2. What were the most important reasons for the Allied victory in Europe?
3. What role did science and technology play in winning the war?
4. Japanese-Americans born in the United States proved their loyalty to America with their lives by serving in the American armed forces during World War II. Not one Japanese-American was ever convicted of sabotage or of spying. Yet Japanese-Americans were interned in prison camps at the beginning of the war. Why? In your opinion, can this violation of civil liberties be justified? Explain your answer.

RELATING PAST TO PRESENT

1. If another world war were to come, there would be very few survivors. Comment.
2. Evaluate current American efforts to prevent international conflicts. Do you believe America's foreign policy has overcommitted the nation? Is the United States too isolationist? Explain.

DEVELOPING SOCIAL SCIENCE SKILLS

1. Watch a movie made during World War II about the war or read magazine accounts written during the war. (a) Do the magazines or the movie express a viewpoint about the war? (b) Do they try to rally support for the war? (c) Do you think that movies and other media should be used to influence public opinion?
2. Use primary and secondary sources to find out more about the role of women during World War II. (a) Why did women enter the work force? (b) For the most part, what kinds of jobs did they work at? (c) What happened to these jobs at the end of the war? (d) What effects do you think the war had on the role of women in American society? Explain.

UNIT SEVEN
The Challenges of a New Era
1945-1970's

CHAPTER 21
DEVELOPMENTS ON
THE DOMESTIC FRONT
1945-1970's

President Roosevelt did not live to see the victorious end of World War II or the founding of the United Nations. Worn out by more than 12 years of constant pressure as President, he died suddenly on April 12, 1945.

With Roosevelt's death the burden of present and future problems fell upon his successor, President Harry S. Truman. The new leader was almost 61 years old, gray-haired, plain and folksy, with a winning grin and a liking for people. Born and raised on a farm in Missouri, Truman had served overseas in World War I. After a successful career in local politics, he had been elected to the United States Senate. In the Senate he had supported the New Deal program, and had come to public attention during the early days of World War II when he headed a key Senate committee—the Special Committee to Investigate the National Defense Program. In 1945, after only a few months as Vice-President, he was suddenly elevated to the highest office in the land.

And so, led by a new President, the United States entered the postwar period. The decades after World War II brought new problems and new challenges. As in the past, Americans looked to the Presidency, to each new leader in the White House, to help provide answers to the nation's problems.

THE CHAPTER IN OUTLINE

1. Truman's efforts to solve postwar problems through a "Fair Deal."

2. Eisenhower's role in developing "Modern Republicanism."

3. Kennedy's challenge to the nation to advance to a "New Frontier."

4. Johnson's invitation to Americans to build the "Great Society."

5. Nixon's first-term plans "to bring America together."

6. Nixon's resignation and the early Ford administration.

| 1450 | 1750 | 1800 | 1850 | 1900 | 1950 | 1980's |

1 Truman's efforts to solve postwar problems through a "Fair Deal"

In the years following World War II, the American people faced many new and unfamiliar problems abroad, as you will read in later chapters. At home they were concerned with two major efforts: (1) To transform the economy from wartime production to prosperous peacetime purposes; (2) to resume and extend the social programs of the New Deal, many of which had been suspended during World War II.

Return of the armed forces

After Japan surrendered in August 1945, Americans were eager to return to peacetime conditions. They wanted their sons and daughters, brothers and sisters, husbands and friends, home again. Most of the men and women in the armed forces were just as eager to return to their homes.

The nation's military leaders, involved in the military occupation of defeated enemy nations, reluctantly gave in to public pressure. Within two years after the war ended, the army, the navy, and the air force had sharply reduced their strength.

Aid to veterans

After World War II the government did far more to help veterans return to civilian life than had ever been done before. Government help came through the Servicemen's Readjustment Act of 1944. This "GI Bill of Rights," as it was called, provided for (1) government loans to help veterans set up businesses or farms; (2) government loans to buy homes; (3) pensions and hospital care; and (4) educational opportunities. Under the GI Bill, hundreds of thousands of veterans received money for tuition, books, and part of their living expenses while they attended school or college.

The Employment Act of 1946

The federal government also, for the first time, assumed responsibility for maintaining a high level of employment. Although the Employment Act of 1946 fell short of the guarantee of "full employment," it did commit the federal government to maintain a strong economy and high employment through a policy of federal spending.

Other major postwar legislation

On August 1, 1946, President Truman signed the Atomic Energy Act, which established a government monopoly over the production of all fissionable materials. The act placed the control of nuclear research and production in a newly created Atomic Energy Commission.

The National Security Act of 1947 centralized the responsibility for military research and planning. It created a new executive department, the Department of Defense, headed by a civilian Secretary of Defense. The act provided the new Secretary with three assistants, the Secretaries of the Army, Navy, and Air Force.

In 1947 Congress also proposed the Twenty-second Amendment (page 672), which became part of the Constitution in 1951. This amendment limited a President's length of service to two terms.

Postwar inflation

Some Americans had feared a postwar recession in the economy as industry shifted from wartime to peacetime production. However, there was no serious unemployment as veterans returned to civilian life. Most Americans—with important exceptions—had jobs and enjoyed a high degree of prosperity.

But prosperity brought problems, including inflation. For more than a year after the war ended, President Truman kept wartime price controls (page 322). However, demands for ending these controls grew stronger. When Republicans, who opposed controls, gained a majority in Congress in 1946, Truman ended all controls on prices and wages, though not on rents.

Prices at once started to rise. High wartime wages, saved during the war years when consumer goods had been scarce, had created an enormous reserve of purchasing power. With money to spend and a mounting demand for goods of all kinds, American consumers created a "seller's market" for American business. Prices soared higher and higher.

President Truman retained rent controls because of an acute housing shortage that would have caused rents to skyrocket. Few houses had been built during the Great Depression and almost none during the war, even though the population was increasing. Truman tried to provide government subsidies for new housing but failed. By 1947, however, the housing industry was moving into high gear and the housing situation, while still serious, began to improve.

Labor unrest

Rising prices led to demands for higher wages. In many cases industry met the demands—but raised prices to cover the increased costs of production. The rise in prices, in turn, spurred labor to demand even higher wages. Thus inflation continued its upward spiral, with workers blaming industry, industry blaming workers, and consumers caught in the middle.

Labor unrest led to strikes. Two of the most serious involved the railroads and the coal-min-

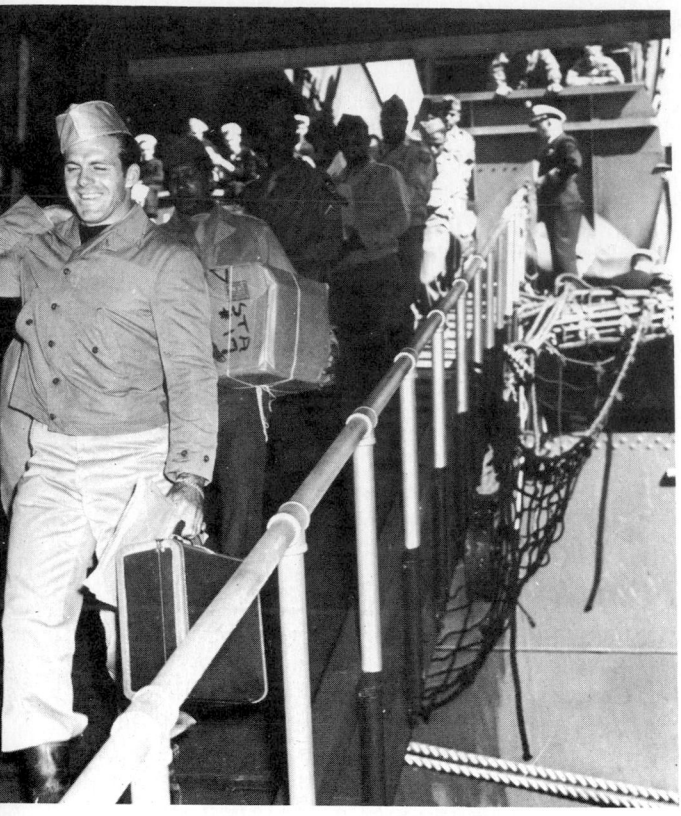

After World War II, the government did far more to help veterans adjust to civilian life than had ever been done after previous wars. Here, Pacific veterans are arriving by ship at San Francisco.

ing industry. President Truman, who was generally sympathetic to organized labor, finally ended the railroad strike by threatening to declare a national emergency and draft the strikers into the army. The federal government also ended the coal miners' strike by seizing the mines and issuing an injunction that forced the miners to return to work.

The Taft-Hartley Act of 1947

The postwar labor unrest and strikes led to public demand for stronger federal controls over organized labor. When the Republicans won control of Congress in 1946, they felt that their victory in part reflected a rising demand for new labor legislation. In June 1947 Congress passed the Labor Management Relations Act, better known as the Taft-Hartley Act, over Truman's veto.

In general, the new law aimed to reduce the power that organized labor had won during the New Deal. The Taft-Hartley Act restricted the contributions of unions to political campaigns. It permitted management to seek injunctions to end strikes, and to sue union officials for violations of contracts or for engaging in certain strikes. The law forbade "closed shop" agreements. It also gave the President power to require an 80-day "cooling-off" period when a strike threatened to affect national health and safety. And the law required employers and union leaders to sign non-Communist oaths.

The Taft-Hartley Act proved highly controversial. Supporters argued that it merely corrected the unfair advantages granted to labor in the Wagner Act of 1935 (page 280). But organized labor protested that the new law deprived workers of many benefits won over a long period.

Gains for organized labor

During the postwar years, however, organized labor did make notable gains. Workers in general won substantial wage increases. Some union contracts provided for wage increases under a formula based on increases in the cost of living and rising productivity. They also included welfare provisions, among them retirement pensions and health insurance.

The election of 1948

By 1948 the nation was enjoying a high level of prosperity. Under such favorable conditions, the Democrats met to choose their Presidential candidate.

The Democratic convention nominated President Truman on the first ballot. Then, largely at his insistence and that of Mayor Hubert H. Humphrey of Minneapolis, the delegates included a strong civil rights plank, or section, in their platform. This plank urged Congress to guarantee (1) the right of every adult to vote and take part in politics; (2) the right of everyone to an equal opportunity to work at any job for which he or she was qualified; (3) the right of everyone to personal security; and (4) the right of everyone to enjoy equal treatment in the armed services. The Democratic platform also favored repeal of the Taft-Hartley Act, federal support of housing, education, and farm income, and broader social security benefits.

The Democratic platform split the party. Southern delegates vigorously opposed the civil rights plank. A number of southern Democrats formed a separate States' Rights Party and nominated Governor J. Strom Thurmond of South Carolina for President.

Former Vice-President Henry A. Wallace also left the Democrats to head a new third party. This Progressive Party sought the support of labor and liberals by promising to renew and extend many New Deal measures.

President Truman won a narrow victory in the 1948 Presidential election. The election results were so close that some newspapers' early editions described Truman's "defeat" at the polls.

With the Democrats divided, public opinion polls and most newspapers predicted that the Republican candidate, Governor Thomas Dewey of New York, would win. But President Truman launched a shrewd election campaign. He asked a special session of the Republican-controlled Congress to live up to its 1946 campaign promises and do something to halt rising prices and solve the housing crisis. When Congress adjourned without acting on these measures, Truman toured the country and denounced the legislators for failing to meet their responsibilities.

The election result was an astonishing victory for President Truman. He polled 49.4 percent of the popular vote to Dewey's 45 percent. Truman won 303 electoral votes, Dewey 189, and Thurmond 39. The Democrats also regained control of Congress and won many state and city elections.

The "Fair Deal"

Heartened by his victory, President Truman decided to launch a broad program of reform. He urged Congress to adopt a "Fair Deal" program and extend some of the New Deal reforms. Many observers doubted that the President could win support for his program from the various groups in his own party. And time after time during Truman's second term, many southern and some northern Democrats did join the Republicans to block Fair Deal measures.

President Truman did, however, have some success with the Fair Deal program. Between 1949 and 1952 Congress (1) extended social security benefits to include 10 million more persons; (2) raised the minimum wage for workers in interstate industries from 40 to 75 cents an hour; (3) authorized the federal government to clear slums and to build 810,000 low-income housing units over a six-year period; (4) continued rent controls to 1951; (5) adopted a new Agricultural Act that established farm price supports at 90 percent of parity through 1950, and thereafter on a sliding scale of 75 to 90 percent; (6) brought more federal employees under civil service; and (7) expanded the work of the Reclamation Bureau in flood control, hydroelectric plants, and irrigation projects.

Concern over internal security

A stepped-up drive against subversive elements in government began in 1947 when President Truman asked the Federal Bureau of Investigation (FBI) and the Civil Service Commission to investigate the loyalty of all federal employees. By the end of 1951 more than 3 million employees had been investigated and cleared, 2,000 had resigned, and 212 had been fired as "security risks."

Meanwhile, in 1948 the FBI and the Department of Justice began an intensive investigation of Communist activity in the United States. Before the year ended 11 Communist leaders had been indicted, tried, and sentenced to prison.

Finally, Congress passed the Internal Security Act of 1950. This law required all Communist organizations in the United States to file their membership lists as well as statements of their financial operations with the Attorney General.

In its deepening concern over internal security, Congress was reacting not only to the possibility of Communist subversion at home but also to the increasingly serious international situation. Both of these issues played major roles in the Presidential election of 1952.

SECTION SURVEY

IDENTIFY: GI Bill, Twenty-second Amendment; Strom Thurmond, Hubert H. Humphrey.

1. (a) What problems confronted the American government after World War II? Why? (b) How did the government meet these problems?
2. Why was the Taft-Hartley Act passed?
3. Give the parties, candidates, issues, and results of the election of 1948.
4. Describe some important achievements of Truman's Fair Deal program.
5. (a) What were the provisions of the civil rights plank of 1948? (b) Why did these provisions arouse controversy?

2 Eisenhower's role in developing "Modern Republicanism"

In the 1952 campaign the Republicans adopted the slogan "It's time for a change." But they did not agree among themselves as to what this change should be.

The election of 1952

Both major political parties entered the election campaign with liberal, middle-of-the-road, and conservative wings. In the Republican con-

Shown here campaigning in the East, Republican candidate Dwight D. Eisenhower won the Presidency in 1952 and again in 1956. In both campaigns, he defeated the Democratic candidate, Adlai E. Stevenson.

vention, the liberals won and nominated General Dwight D. Eisenhower, with Richard M. Nixon as his running mate. The liberal wing of the Democrats also won, nominating Governor Adlai E. Stevenson of Illinois for President and John Sparkman for the Vice-Presidency.

Eisenhower swept the election with 57 percent of the popular vote and a majority of 442 to 89 of the electoral vote. But the Republicans won only narrow control of Congress, and they lost even this to the Democrats in 1954. From then until he left office, Eisenhower had to work with a Democratic Congress. In 1956 Eisenhower was reelected for a second term, defeating the Democratic candidate, Adlai Stevenson of Illinois, by an electoral vote of 457 to 73. However, the voters again returned a substantial majority of Democrats to Congress.

Modern Republicanism

The moderation of President Eisenhower and the strength of Democrats and liberal Republicans in Congress discouraged attempts by conservatives to repeal the social and economic programs of the New Deal and Fair Deal. The President personally favored a moderate extension of social security and federal support for education, housing, slum clearance, and public health measures. This middle-of-the-road policy, together with support for the United Nations, military aid for America's allies, and economic and military help for underdeveloped countries, came to be called "Modern Republicanism."

But traditional Republican policies and ideals were also evident during the Eisenhower years. The administration included leading business executives. Efficiency and economy in government were stressed; in 1956 for the first time in eight years the federal government ended the fiscal year with a surplus. The government also withdrew from such business activities as the manufacture of synthetic rubber, the production of mo-

During the 1950's, surplus farm crops were a serious problem. Congress passed a farm price-support program to aid American farmers.

tion pictures, and the operation of railroads, ships, and hotels. In 1954 Congress amended the Atomic Energy Act to give private industry a larger opportunity to develop atomic energy for peaceful purposes. But an effort to favor private utilities at the expense of the electric power operations of the Tennessee Valley Authority failed when critics protested government favoritism to "special interests."

Social legislation

Responding to Eisenhower's moderate recommendations, Congress in 1954 increased social security benefits and extended benefit coverage to an additional 10.5 million persons. Congress also voted additional funds for medical research and hospital construction. In 1955 it authorized $500 million for slum clearance and urban redevelopment. And in 1958, after the Russians had demonstrated their technological progress by launching several earth satellites, Congress provided loans for able students, especially students of science.

Organized labor

During the Eisenhower years labor continued to make gains. Congress increased the minimum hourly wage from 75 cents to $1. The Ford Motor Company and the General Motors Corporation signed contracts with the United Automobile Workers providing, among other things, that the companies would pay unemployment benefits.

During the 1950's many unions set up welfare funds to aid unemployed, disabled, and retired workers. In December 1955 the A. F. of L. and the CIO voted to combine. The new organization, now called the AFL-CIO, with George Meany as president, had about 15 million members.

However, corrupt leadership in some unions led Congress in 1959 to pass the Labor-Management Reporting and Disclosure Act. This law banned secondary boycotts and picketing by groups not directly involved in a strike. It prohibited Communists and persons convicted of felonies from serving as union officials or employees. The law also sought to insure the financial honesty of union officials and the right of union members freely to take part in union affairs.

In 1959 an important provision of the Taft-Hartley Act was tested in a strike of the United Steel Workers, who were demanding wage increases and other benefits. President Eisenhower, using powers granted in the Taft-Hartley Act, secured an 80-day anti-strike injunction. The workers went back to their jobs, but the injunction settled none of the issues. The union and the steel industry finally reached an agreement providing for step-by-step wage increases. A committee was formed to study disputes, such as management's demand that the union eliminate "featherbedding," or assigning more workers to a job operation than management felt were needed.

The farm problem

With the exception of owners of large commercial farms, farmers in the 1950's did not share as fully as other Americans in the "Eisenhower prosperity." Between 1952 and 1956 farm income dropped 26 percent.

There were a number of reasons for this, including the loss of foreign markets and growing competition from farmers in other countries. Basically, however, the problem was an old one—overproduction in relation to the nation's needs. Since the early 1930's farm productivity had almost doubled, largely because of advances in agricultural technology.

From 1942 to 1954 the government tried to guarantee farmers a fixed price support of 90 percent of parity. When prices dropped below this 90 percent level, the government bought surplus crops at the fixed price. But under this policy, crop surpluses continued to pile up and prices continued to fall. Secretary of Agriculture Ezra Taft Benson then persuaded the Eisenhower administration to end fixed price supports and adopt a flexible scale of 82.5 to 90 percent. This new policy aimed at discouraging farmers from growing crops that were flooding the market.

In 1956 the government made a major change in the farm program. Money from a "soil bank" was to be paid to farmers who withdrew land from production and planted trees on it or built dams and reservoirs. By the end of 1958 the "soil bank" had paid $1.6 billion to farmers for withdrawing land previously used for growing wheat, corn, cotton, tobacco, and rice.

Internal security

The Eisenhower administration also inherited a difficult problem of constitutional rights. Congressional committees were sometimes accused of handling individuals suspected of subversion without proper regard for fair judicial practices. The most controversial was a subcommittee headed by Senator Joseph McCarthy of Wisconsin.

During the first two years of the Eisenhower administration, Senator McCarthy brought charges against former high government officials, against the State Department, and against the army. Many Americans praised McCarthy, but others criticized what they called his recklessness and his disregard for constitutional rights. In 1954 McCarthy's influence declined, partly as a result of a Senate resolution censuring him for some of his actions.

Alaska and Hawaii

In 1959 Alaska and Hawaii were admitted as the 49th and 50th states of the union. They were the first states not sharing a common border with any of the other states. Alaska, now the largest state, adjoins northwestern Canada, far to the north of the state of Washington. Hawaii, a group

of islands in the Pacific Ocean, is located about 2,400 miles (3,862 kilometers) west of California.

Alaska, as you have read, was purchased from Russia in 1867 by Secretary of State William Seward at a time when several nations were competing for its fur trade. So little was known then of its riches that for years Americans called Alaska "Seward's Folly." In the 1900's, however, Alaska became an important American source of timber and fish and of gold and other minerals. Later, in the early 1970's, a massive pipeline project was started to move enormous supplies of oil from the far north to the southern shore of Alaska for shipment in tankers.

Alaska's population today exceeds 300,000, of whom about one fifth are Eskimos of the north, Aleuts of the southwest and the Aleutian Islands, and various Indian tribes, mainly along the southeastern coast. Adult members of these minority groups became American citizens when Alaska became a state.

The first known inhabitants of the Hawaiian Islands were Polynesians, expert seafarers who probably sailed there in ocean-going canoes from other Pacific islands hundreds of years ago. Beginning in the late 1700's European and American ships stopped in the islands for fresh water and food. In the late 1800's American planters, as you may recall, developed prosperous sugar and pineapple plantations and gained control of the islands. The United States annexed the islands in 1898, and Hawaii became a Territory.

Many immigrants from Japan and other parts of the Far East came to the Hawaiian Islands to work on the plantations and remained to become farmers, factory and service workers, and business people. Out of a population of more than 800,000, about 60 percent are of Japanese, Chinese, Filipino, Korean, or Polynesian ancestry, or of mixed ethnic descent.

Continuing prosperity

Americans still faced stubborn domestic and foreign problems as the 1950's ended, but an impressive majority enjoyed a rising standard of living. To be sure, economic progress in the 1950's had been slowed twice by recessions—the first in 1953–54, the second in 1957–58. But by 1959 unemployed workers were returning to their jobs, the stock market had reached record high levels, business was improving, and a spirit of optimism prevailed.

The "Eisenhower prosperity" was tempered, however, by the continuing struggle with Communism, by growing tensions abroad, and by many unresolved problems at home.

SECTION SURVEY

IDENTIFY: AFL-CIO, "soil bank"; Adlai E. Stevenson, Joseph McCarthy, George Meany.

1. From 1954 to 1960 the government operated with a Republican President and a Congress controlled by Democrats. (a) What does this tell you about the state of national politics at this time? (b) What difficulties might this situation present in the functioning of government?

2. In what ways did the Eisenhower administration encourage private enterprise?

3. What is meant by Modern Republicanism?

4. (a) Describe the tensions between internal security and constitutional rights that arose during this period. (b) How did fear contribute to these tensions?

3 Kennedy's challenge to the nation to advance to a "New Frontier"

The nation's unresolved problems at home and abroad were brought strongly to the attention of American voters in the Presidential campaign and election of 1960.

The 1960 election

Both the Republicans and Democrats nominated relatively young, energetic candidates for the Presidency. The Republican nominee, Richard M. Nixon of California, had served in both houses of Congress and since 1953 had been Vice-President under Eisenhower. The Democratic nominee, John F. Kennedy of Massachusetts, had also served in both houses of Congress.

The Vice-Presidential candidates also had distinguished records. Republican candidate Henry Cabot Lodge, Jr., a former Senator from Massachusetts, was Ambassador to the United Nations. Lyndon B. Johnson of Texas, the Democratic candidate, had been the leader of his party in the Senate since 1954.

During the election campaign the Presidential candidates faced each other in a series of television debates. The central issue was the condition of the nation. Kennedy called for a "supreme national effort" to reverse what he called the downward trend of the nation's fortunes at home and abroad. He promised, if elected, "to get America moving again" by advancing the nation to a "New Frontier."

Nixon insisted that the United States was stronger in relation to the Communist world than ever and charged Kennedy with favoring "wild experimentation." He promised, if elected, to build a more secure nation on the foundations of Eisenhower's policies.

Disturbed by such charges and counter-charges, the voters turned out in record numbers in the November election. Out of about 68 million votes cast, Kennedy squeezed through by a slim margin of only 118,000 votes. In the electoral college, however, Kennedy won 303 electoral votes to Nixon's 219.

The new administration

At 43, Kennedy was the youngest man ever elected President. And he was the first Roman Catholic to win the Presidency. He was acutely aware of the problems he faced. Barely half of the voters had shown a willingness to follow the new administration toward a New Frontier. Moreover, conservative Democrats in Congress, mostly from the South, had in the past voted with conservative Republicans to defeat measures similar to those Kennedy now wanted.

Convinced that the nation faced grave prob-

SOURCES

JOHN F. KENNEDY'S INAUGURAL ADDRESS (1961)

We dare not forget today that we are the heirs of that first revolution. Let the word go forth from this time and place, to friend and foe alike, that the torch has been passed to a new generation of Americans—born in this century, tempered by war, disciplined by a hard and bitter peace, proud of our ancient heritage—and unwilling to witness or permit the slow undoing of those human rights to which this nation has always been committed, and to which we are committed today at home and around the world.

Let every nation know, whether it wishes us well or ill, that we shall pay any price, bear any burden, meet any hardship, support any friend, oppose any foe to assure the survival and the success of liberty. . . .

lems at home and abroad, Kennedy tried to secure the ablest men and women he could get for his administrative staff. Among his advisers were scholars, writers, scientists, and prominent business leaders, both Democrats and Republicans.

Economic problems

With his staff organized, the President prepared to attack the related problems of unemployment and economic growth. The immediate problem was unemployment. In January 1961 more than 5 million Americans—nearly 8 percent of the total labor force—were unemployed. The unemployment rate among black Americans was double the rate for the nation as a whole.

The problem of unemployment had its roots deep in the nation's rapidly changing economic life. Some economists stressed that the American economy was not growing as rapidly as it should. Industries were not modernizing or building new factories as rapidly as many of them had done in the past.

Coupled with sluggish economic growth was the problem of automation, or the use of machines to do the work formerly done by men and women. Moreover, the increasingly complex American economy called for new skills on the part of workers. As a result there was less opportunity for the untrained and the poorly educated.

In his Inaugural Address, President Kennedy pledged that the United States would aid the underdeveloped nations of the world "not because we seek their votes, but because it is right."

Measures to stimulate the economy

In line with administration proposals, Congress took steps to increase spending power and retrain workers. Minimum wages were raised to $1.25 an hour, and 4 million more workers were included under wage-hour protection. The Area Redevelopment Act of 1961 authorized the federal government to make loans and grants to stimulate business and retrain workers in depressed areas. In 1962 Congress set aside $900 million for building public works in areas where more than 6 percent of the labor force was unemployed. In 1962 the Manpower Development and Training Act provided for a three-year worker retraining program. Yet even with these and other measures, unemployment remained a major problem.

Housing and urban renewal

The Housing Act of 1961 tried to strengthen the nation's economic and social fabric. This act provided long-term loans at low interest rates to stimulate the construction of moderate-income housing. It included funds to provide hospitals and housing for the elderly. The largest authorization was for urban renewal, including the planning and improvement of mass transportation facilities. Congress also voted nearly $1.5 billion to aid in the construction of buildings for medical and dental schools, and to assist colleges in building classrooms, libraries, and laboratories.

The Trade Expansion Act

In 1962 Congress took a major step to stimulate America's foreign trade. This step was prompted in part by the creation of the Common Market, a large trading area composed of six European nations. To improve trade among themselves, the Common Market nations gradually lowered the tariffs that had limited their trade relations. By 1962 the Common Market nations were enjoying increasing prosperity. Recognizing that the Common Market could greatly affect the United States, Congress passed the Trade Expansion Act of 1962.

This act gave important powers to the President. Over a five-year period the President could cut tariff rates 50 percent below the 1962 level, or raise them 50 percent above the 1934 level. The President could also remove *all* tariffs on products for which the United States and the Common Market countries together accounted for 80 percent of all world trade.

The act contained an "escape clause" that allowed the President to retain or reimpose tariffs to protect industries seriously hurt by tariff reduction. Industries endangered by foreign competition could apply for technical assistance and loans to finance a shift into other manufacturing. Workers in these industries could apply for retraining or relocation allowances.

The continuing farm problem

The Trade Expansion Act was designed, among other things, to help American farmers dispose of their surplus products. In 1962 Congress passed still another act providing for payments to farmers who agreed to turn farm land into forest, wildlife, or recreation areas. It also tightened controls over the production of crops used mainly to feed livestock, and invited farmers to place new limitations on wheat production. In a nationwide farm vote in May 1963, however, a majority of farmers rejected the program.

The rejection of its wheat limitation program was a severe blow to the Kennedy administration's agricultural plans. At the end of 1963 the nation's farmers continued to struggle with surplus products and declining incomes.

Changes in suffrage

During the Kennedy administration several major changes took place in voting rights. The Twenty-third Amendment to the Constitution, adopted in 1961 (see page 672), enabled residents of the District of Columbia to vote in Presidential elections. The Twenty-fourth Amendment, adopted in 1964 (see page 673), forbade the poll tax as a requirement for voting in federal elections.

While voting barriers were being lifted for some citizens, other citizens fought for fairer representation in their state and local legislatures. Between 1962 and 1964 the Supreme Court handed down several history-making decisions relating to representation. The most far-reaching was the Court's "one person, one vote" ruling. According to this decision, election districts for state legislatures as well as for the House of Representatives must be as nearly equal in population as practicable. The Supreme Court thus set in motion a political revolution intended to make each citizen's vote have approximately equal value—and thus provide genuine representative government at both state and federal levels.

The assassination of John F. Kennedy

At 12:30 noon on Friday, November 22, 1963, while riding in a motorcade through Dallas, Texas, President Kennedy was killed by an assassin.

Vice-President Johnson, who also was in the motorcade, immediately drove under close guard to the Presidential plane. There, in the cabin of the plane at 2:38 P.M., Lyndon B. Johnson was sworn in as the thirty-sixth President of the United States.

The tragic weekend

Americans reacted to the tragic news with shocked disbelief, then with deeply felt anger and grief. For three days, while the body of John F. Kennedy lay in state in the Capitol, radio and television stations suspended regular programming, and all but the most essential businesses closed their doors. Messages of sorrow and sympathy poured in from all over the world. The leaders of many nations flew to Washington to pay their respects to the late President.

In the meantime, within an hour and a half of the fatal shooting, the Dallas police had seized a suspect, Lee Harvey Oswald. Oswald was placed under heavy guard in a Dallas jail. Two days later while being moved to another jail, he was shot and killed in full view of millions of Americans who were watching the event on television. His murderer, Jack Ruby, pushed through a group of police officers to shoot Oswald at arm's-length range.

Americans were deeply troubled by this new act of brutality. With Oswald gone, grave questions remained unanswered: Was Lee Harvey Oswald the assassin? If so, had he acted alone, or was he part of a conspiracy to assassinate President Kennedy? Was Jack Ruby part of that conspiracy, and did he kill Oswald to keep him from talking?

The Warren Commission Report

To answer these questions and to put an end to wild rumors and speculation, President Johnson promptly appointed a commission to investigate the case. The commission was headed by Earl Warren, Chief Justice of the Supreme Court.

Ten months later, in September 1964, the Warren Commission released its report. After carefully examining all available evidence and the testimony of 532 witnesses, the commission unanimously concluded that: (1) Lee Harvey Oswald had assassinated President Kennedy. (2) He had acted alone. (3) Jack Ruby also had acted alone. (4) There was no evidence of a conspiracy. ". . . If there is any such evidence," the report said, "it has been beyond the reach of all the investigative agencies and resources of the U.S."

SECTION SURVEY

IDENTIFY: New Frontier, depressed areas, Common Market, Warren Commission; Lee Harvey Oswald, Jack Ruby.

1. Give the parties, candidates, issues, and results of the election of 1960.
2. (a) Describe measures taken by the Kennedy administration to stimulate the economy. (b) Why were these measures less than fully successful?
3. Discuss the significance for democratic government of the (a) Twenty-third Amendment, (b) Twenty-fourth Amendment, (c) "one person, one vote" ruling.
4. Was President Kennedy able to bring the nation to a New Frontier before his assassination? Explain.

4 Johnson's invitation to Americans to build the "Great Society"

In the midst of the tragic events of the weekend of November 22–25, 1963, Americans took pride in the fact that not even the murder of a President could interfere with the orderly procedure of government. Five days after the assassination of President Kennedy, Lyndon B. Johnson, in his first Presidential address to Congress, dedicated himself to the "ideas and the ideals" which John F. Kennedy had "so nobly represented."

President Johnson meant what he said. He gave top priority to three items—a civil rights law, a tax cut, and an "unconditional war on poverty." Speaking quietly but firmly, he declared: "All this and more can and must be done." Thus the new President invited Americans to build what he would later call the "Great Society."

An impressive Congressional record

Congress responded to President Johnson's leadership. Before adjourning in October 1964, Congress chalked up one of the most impressive legislative records in the nation's history. Most far-reaching was the Civil Rights Act of 1964 (Chapter 24). And there were other important measures.

The Revenue Act of 1964 provided an $11.5 billion reduction in personal and corporate income taxes. By leaving more money in the hands of consumers and businesses, the new law greatly stimulated the economy.

The Economic Opportunity Act of 1964 marked another important attempt to "break the cycle of poverty." It created an Office of Economic Opportunity (OEO) and authorized $1 billion to begin the war against poverty. The new agency was to work with state and local governments to increase employment and expand training programs, especially for young people.

Congress also passed several other administration measures. These included (1) authorization of $375 million to help cities improve urban and commuter transit facilities; (2) establishment of a system to preserve federally owned wilderness areas; and (3) pay increases for all federal officials and employees, including members of Congress. However, several measures strongly supported by President Johnson were still being considered when Congress adjourned to begin the 1964 election campaign.

The election of 1964

The Republicans nominated Barry M. Goldwater, a conservative Senator from Arizona, for the Presidency and Representative William E. Miller of New York as his running mate. The Democrats nominated President Lyndon B. Johnson and his choice for Vice-President, Senator Hubert H. Humphrey of Minnesota.

The Presidential race was bitterly contested. From the start both parties were divided. Many moderate Republicans, unable to accept Goldwater's conservative position on several critical issues, refused to support him. The Republicans also lost the support of most black voters. Goldwater was one of only six Republican Senators who had voted against the Civil Rights Act of 1964.

The Democrats, too, had to contend with the loss of many normally Democratic voters. Many white southern Democrats felt that President Johnson, a Texan, had betrayed them by leading the battle for the Civil Rights Act. They threw their

During the years of the "Great Society," many far-reaching social and economic programs were launched. Here, President Lyndon Johnson (far right) meets with members of Congress.

support to Goldwater because of his vote against the act and his strong support of states' rights.

In November a record-breaking number of nearly 70 million voters elected President Johnson by an overwhelming electoral vote of 486 to 52. The popular vote, 42 million to 26 million, gave Johnson a large plurality. The Democrats also won substantial victories in state and local elections and in Congress.

Starting toward the "Great Society"

Encouraged by his sweeping victory, President Johnson challenged Americans to join him in building the "Great Society." He argued that Americans could help build a new world, not just a new nation. "We are in the midst of the greatest upward surge of economic well-being in the history of any nation," the President declared. "But we are only at the beginning of the road to the Great Society." Three major tasks remained: "To keep our economy growing. To open for all Americans the opportunities now enjoyed by most Americans. To improve the quality of life for all."

Great Society legislation

By the time Congress adjourned in the fall of 1965, it had adopted laws dealing with all of the President's major recommendations. In one of the most far-reaching laws, the legislators provided a comprehensive program of aid to education (Chapter 25). In another far-reaching measure,

Congress established Medicare, a national program of health insurance for persons over 65.

The Medicare law contained two major sections: (1) Basic health coverage, with social security paying the larger part of the costs of hospital treatment or home nursing care, the patient paying the rest; (2) voluntary supplementary coverage, enabling individuals covered by social security to buy inexpensive health insurance to cover doctors' bills and certain other health services.

Responding to President Johnson's urging, Congress reduced federal excise taxes on automobiles, television sets, and other consumer items. The cut in excise taxes was designed to encourage Americans to buy more goods. This in turn would stimulate production and reduce unemployment.

In still other efforts to raise the standard of living of impoverished Americans, the legislators adopted several measures. Congress increased to $1.5 billion the funds for the Office of Economic Opportunity's anti-poverty program. Congress also voted $1 billion to help develop the economy of the 11-state Appalachian region. This money was to be spent for highways, flood control, the development of new industries, and for other measures to create new job opportunities for the 15 million people in Appalachia. Congress authorized an additional $3.3 billion to revive the economies in other depressed areas of the nation.

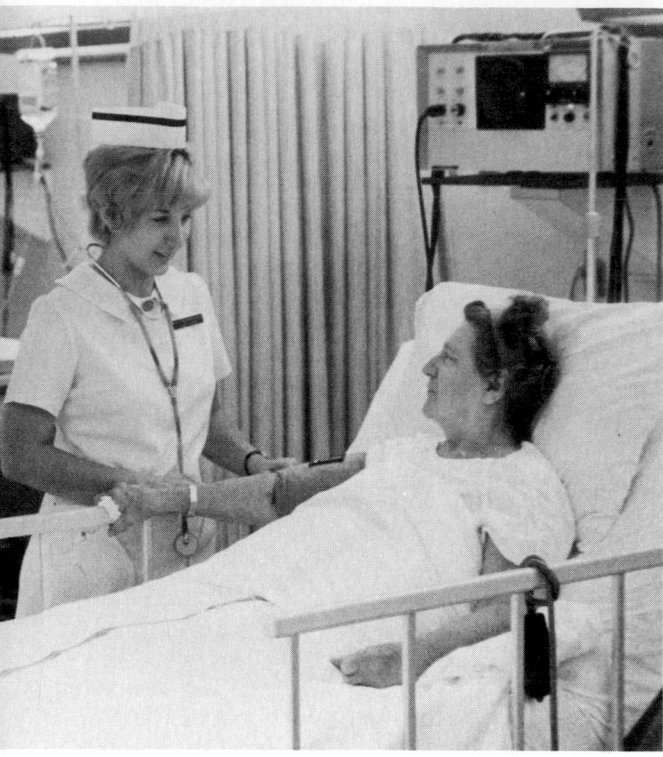

Medicare today provides hospital treatment and other medical benefits for many older Americans.

Congress also authorized $7.5 billion to improve the nation's housing. The housing act included the following provisions: (1) It increased funds for slum clearance, urban renewal, and for building public housing projects. (2) It allocated money for urban planning, the beautification of cities, and the development of parks and recreational areas. (3) It authorized the government to subsidize rent payments of low-income families. (4) It authorized federal grants to improve run-down properties.

Loss of momentum

As it turned out, however, 1965 marked the peak of Johnson's program and his popularity. By 1966 the war in Vietnam (Chapter 23) was absorbing more and more of the nation's resources and the administration's time and energy. And as the war intensified and the Great Society program slowed down, criticism of the President became increasingly widespread.

Eugene McCarthy's challenge

It was Eugene J. McCarthy, Democratic Senator from Minnesota, who first revealed the extent of the dissatisfaction. In November 1967 Senator McCarthy surprised the nation by declaring that he intended to campaign for the Presidency. His purpose was to give voters a chance to show that they opposed the administration's Vietnam policy.

In the nation's first 1968 Presidential primary, held in New Hampshire in March, McCarthy won an impressive victory. One of the outstanding developments of the McCarthy campaign was the response of the nation's youth. Thousands of young volunteers from all over the country poured into New Hampshire to work for a candidate who inspired them with hopeful idealism.

Political developments

The New Hampshire primary triggered a series of political developments. The first came a few days after McCarthy's victory, when Senator Robert F. Kennedy of New York announced that he, too, would seek the Democratic nomination for President. Senator Kennedy, a brother of the late President Kennedy, was an outspoken critic of President Johnson's Vietnam policy.

A second political development, one that came as a stunning surprise to the nation, was President Johnson's declaration, on a nationally televised program on March 31, that he would not run for re-election.

As Johnson later explained, he hoped that removing himself from the Presidential race would help to unite the nation by ending the growing division among the American people over his conduct of the Vietnam War. Even some of President Johnson's political enemies praised his decision.

President Johnson's withdrawal opened the door to the candidacy of Vice-President Hubert Humphrey, who soon joined McCarthy and Kennedy in the race for the Democratic nomination.

The assassination of Robert F. Kennedy

Early in April 1968 the nation mourned the death of the great civil rights leader Martin Luther King, Jr. (Chapter 25). In June the nation again grieved, this time for Senator Robert F. Kennedy, killed by an assassin's bullet just after he had won a close victory over Senator McCarthy in the California primary.

The assassinations of President John F. Kennedy, Martin Luther King, Jr., and Robert F. Kennedy caused many people at home and abroad to wonder if violence was becoming characteristic of American society. What, people asked, was happening to the nation? There was no easy answer. But President Johnson did appoint a commission to study the question of violence. And Congress, over strong opposition, passed a gun-control law, although critics called the new law a "halfway measure."

Fallen hopes for the Great Society

When Lyndon Johnson became President, at

first he dedicated himself to building the Great Society—one free from poverty, discrimination, and injustice. Working closely with Congress, during his first two years in office he made substantial progress toward that goal. Then, as the Vietnam War began to absorb more and more of the administration's attention, domestic programs suffered. The dream of a Great Society became marred by war abroad and by unrest and violence at home.

SECTION SURVEY

IDENTIFY: Great Society, war on poverty, Appalachia,

Medicare; Barry Goldwater, Eugene McCarthy, Robert Kennedy.

1. Under President Johnson, Congress chalked up one of the most impressive legislative records in the nation's history. Explain.
2. With reference to the election of 1964, discuss (a) candidates and parties, (b) results for the political parties and the nation.
3. How was the Great Society similar to the New Deal and Fair Deal programs of reform?
4. Eugene McCarthy triggered a series of political developments. (a) What were they? (b) How did they relate to Vietnam?
5. (a) How did Americans respond to the assassinations of the 1960's? (b) Has violence become characteristic of American society? Explain.

5 Nixon's first-term plans "to bring America together"

It was a restless, disturbed nation that in August 1968 watched the Presidential nominating conventions on television. The two major political parties, reflecting the nation's uneasiness and uncertainty, met to choose their candidates.

Choosing candidates

The Republicans, meeting first, gathered at Miami Beach. Richard M. Nixon, who represented the middle ground as well as the "establishment" of the Republican Party, was nominated on the first ballot. He chose Spiro T. Agnew, Governor of Maryland, as his running mate.

The Democratic convention, held later in Chicago, proved to be one of the most tumultuous in the nation's history. To millions of Americans watching on television, the convention hall appeared to be a disorderly arena in which McCarthy and Kennedy supporters were contending against "establishment" Democrats represented by Hubert H. Humphrey. Humphrey, winning on the first ballot, chose Senator Edmund S. Muskie of Maine as his Vice-Presidential candidate.

The bitterness of the proceedings in the convention hall itself was reflected in the city's streets. Thousands of young people had gathered in Chicago to demonstrate against the Vietnam War and for candidates favoring peace. Claiming that the demonstrations had gotten out of hand, the Chicago police moved in. The violent confrontations that followed, resulting in numerous injuries, were also witnessed by millions of television viewers.

The candidates and the issues

During the campaign neither Nixon nor Humphrey aroused great enthusiasm among voters. The emergence of a third-party candidate, George C. Wallace of Alabama, founder of the American Independent Party, further complicated matters.

The three main issues of the campaign were violence and disorder, Vietnam, and racial strife. Public opinion polls showed that seven out of every ten Americans were convinced that "law and order had broken down in the country." Two out of every three felt that the war in Vietnam was being badly managed. The overwhelming majority of white citizens believed that the civil rights struggle was going "too fast," while an equally large majority of black citizens were convinced that the movement was "not going fast enough."

George C. Wallace

From the beginning, third-party candidate Wallace hammered at the issue of law and order. On the closely related issues of poverty and racial unrest, Wallace expressed opposition to existing welfare programs, forced busing of school children, and the federal enforcement of integration. He pledged, if elected, to repeal open housing legislation, to give the police greater power to deal with demonstrations and civil disorders, and to "restore" to the states and local communities control over welfare programs and the schools. As to Vietnam, he promised to end the war by negotiation, if possible, but to achieve a military victory if negotiations failed.

Richard M. Nixon

Throughout the campaign Nixon stressed the nation's need for new leadership. He declared that the Democrats had brought the United States close to disaster, and that it was "time for a change." Like Wallace, he promised to restore law and order, but added the word "justice" to his pledge.

Turning to the problem of poverty and the

The Democratic convention of 1968 was one of the most tumultuous in the nation's history. Demonstrations and protests in the streets of Chicago reflected the deep divisions among the convention delegates.

crisis of the central cities, Nixon insisted that the Democratic programs of massive federal spending had failed. He promised to review the entire welfare program and to turn over to private businesses the primary responsibility for retraining unemployed workers and rebuilding the cities.

On the issue of Vietnam, Nixon promised the nation that he would "bring an honorable end to the war." He did not say how he would end the war, explaining that he did not wish to upset the delicate peace talks then going on in Paris.

Nixon was more specific, however, in his ideas about military policy and national defense. Pointing to what he called a "security gap," he favored a buildup of American nuclear capability to insure that the United States held clear "superiority" over all potential enemies. His recommendations included the development of an anti-ballistic missile system (ABM). This missile system, he admitted, would be enormously expensive but, in his view, "a necessary investment in peace."

Hubert H. Humphrey

During most of the campaign Humphrey found himself in difficulty. His party was badly divided. Millions of people associated the violence in Chicago with the Democrats.

Humphrey was convinced that force, no mat-

ter how strongly applied, would not end the unrest and violence afflicting the nation. "We can only cut crime," he declared, "by getting at its causes: slums, unemployment, run-down schools and houses. This is where crime begins and that is where it must end." Although he advocated "vigorous federal support of state and local law enforcement," he cautioned that the attack against crime "must not jeopardize hard-won liberties of our citizens."

To meet the problems of poverty and urban decay, Humphrey called for "a Marshall Plan for the cities based upon self-help, local initiative, coordinated planning, and private capital." He advocated job training by private enterprise with government support wherever necessary.

It was the issue of Vietnam that caused Humphrey the most difficulty. At the start of his campaign he lost much support by defending the unpopular administration policy. But at the end of September he abandoned his earlier position. He now advocated a halt to the bombing of North Vietnam, and his chances began to improve. They improved still further when, less than a week before the election, President Johnson announced that he had ordered a halt to all bombing north of the DMZ (Demilitarized Zone), offering hope for an earlier end to the war. Public opinion polls taken the weekend before the election indicated that it was a neck-and-neck race.

The election results

The 1968 Presidential election was indeed a close one. Out of more than 71 million popular votes cast, Nixon's margin of victory over Humphrey was only 260,000 votes. The electoral vote of 302 for Nixon, 191 for Humphrey, and 45 for Wallace did not, however, reflect this closeness. The Democrats kept control of Congress.

Keenly aware of his narrow victory, President-elect Nixon pledged that the "great objective" of his administration would be to unite the country. "We want to bridge the generation gap," he declared in his victory speech. "We want to bridge the gap between the races. We want to bring America together."

The "style" of the Nixon administration

Convinced that the "silent majority" of the American people stood midway between extreme conservatism and extreme liberalism, Nixon sought to hold to a "center" line. In his news conferences and television broadcasts he tried to give the impression of moderation, realism, and responsibility to the public interest even when taking unpopular positions. In contrast, Vice-President Spiro Agnew reflected a "hard line" in his speeches. He denounced the major television networks for alleged "liberal" bias in news coverage; he criticized peace demonstrators and campus radicals; and he charged that the President's foes in Congress gave in to pressures from civil rights and labor lobbyists.

Difficulties with Congress

The Nixon administration, handicapped by a Democratic majority in Congress, had trouble implementing its policies. In an effort to commit the Supreme Court to his own view of a strict interpretation of the Constitution, the President filled the vacancy created by Earl Warren's retirement by appointing Warren E. Burger as Chief Justice. But Nixon was unable to secure the needed majority vote in the Senate to confirm two other nominees to fill a Supreme Court vacancy. Finally, the Senate approved Nixon's choice of Harry Blackmun, a respected moderate judge.

Differences between the administration and Congress also led to other compromises and stalemates. The President insisted on cutting down federal spending, contending that such spending was excessive and that many programs were unwise and poorly administered. But critics in Congress insisted that cuts in spending for social welfare, education, and other domestic programs were not justified. They also objected to the adminis-

tration's reluctance to make substantial cuts in military budget.

The problem of inflation

Among the serious problems facing President Nixon when he took office was the growing pressure of inflation. The rising rate of inflation was partly a result of vast expenditures for the Vietnam War, partly a result of basic problems in the American economy and society, and partly a result of international events.

For the first two and a half years of his Presidency, Nixon tried to control inflation in two ways. He reduced expenditures for domestic programs such as education, welfare, housing, urban renewal, and anti-pollution measures, thus managing to reduce the federal budget by several billion dollars. He also encouraged the Federal Reserve Board and the nation's banks to increase interest rates sharply. This "tight money" policy was intended to make borrowing more expensive and thereby reduce the amount of money and credit Americans would have for bidding up the prices of goods and services.

President Nixon and Congress disagreed about many government policies and programs. Which of these disputed policies are identified in this cartoon?

BACK TO WORK

The Weather

Variable cloudiness with highs near 83 today. Partly cloudy tonight with lows near 63. Yesterday's high, 91; low, 69. (Details and Map, Page C 6)

THE SUN FINAL

Vol. 269—No. 79—F   BALTIMORE, MONDAY, AUGUST 16, 1971   36 Pages   10 Cents

Nixon Orders Wages, Prices Frozen For 90 Days, Calls For New Tax Cuts

PUSH TO FREE IRA SUSPECTS BEGINS TODAY

Key Ulster Catholics Urge Campaign Of Civil Disobedience

By DANIEL BERGER
London Bureau of The Sun

Belfast, Northern Ireland— The major Catholic political leaders last night announced a massive civil disobedience campaign starting today, aimed at freeing the 230 Irish Republican Army suspects who have been held a week without trial.

Temporary Halt Placed On Gold, Dollar Exchange

President Imposes 10 Per Cent Surcharge On Imports In Economic Plan, Announces Reduction In Federal Spending

Text of President's address .... Page A 7

By ART PINE
Washington Bureau of The Sun

Washington—President Nixon announced last night a set of sweeping measures to deal with the nation's domestic and international economic problems, including a 90-day freeze on all wages and prices

To help fight the growing danger of inflation, President Nixon in 1971 adopted a program to control wages and prices. However, this effort to limit the rising cost of living was only partly successful.

Wage and price controls

In spite of reduced federal spending and high interest rates, inflation continued at an alarming rate. Finally, in August 1971, Nixon, who had long opposed federal controls over wages and prices, announced a sweeping new economic program. Its main feature was a 90-day freeze on wages, prices, and rents. A Cost of Living Council was set up to develop guidelines for regulating wages, prices, and profits after the freeze ended. Although business leaders were unhappy about price and profit limitations and labor was equally unhappy about wage guidelines, the rate of inflation slowed a little.

Then, in January 1973, Nixon eased these controls. The administration justified this decision on grounds that inflation was moderating and the economy was beginning to slow down. But with restraints removed, prices began to soar. Faced with a rising storm of criticism, the President again applied partial controls. In 1974, however, he reversed his policy again by removing most of the controls.

Inflation and the energy crisis

The skyrocketing cost of oil soon became a major contributor to inflation in the United States and throughout the world. In the fall of 1973 the Arab oil-producing nations sharply increased the price of oil and, in the midst of a new Arab-Israeli war, cut off all shipments to the United States and other industrial nations that had been supporting Israel. A few months later, the Arabs lifted their embargo, but oil prices remained high.

High oil prices and the embargo caused critical problems for Western Europe and Japan, which depended almost entirely on Arab oil. The United States, which depended upon Arab oil for only about 6 percent of its total requirements, also faced a serious situation. For several years there had been a growing scarcity of energy in the United States. The 6 percent cutoff of oil and soaring prices brought an "energy crisis" during the winter of 1973–74. The cost of gasoline, heating oil, and electricity rose drastically. In some parts of the country shortages caused real hardships. One consequence was a decision by the Nixon administration to start a program to make the United States independent of all foreign countries for its energy requirements by the early 1980's.

Other important developments

In March 1971 Congress adopted the Twenty-sixth Amendment (page 674) lowering the voting age to 18 in both federal and state elections. When the amendment was ratified by the required 38 states three months later, the Census Bureau estimated that 25 million additional young people were now eligible to vote in the next Presidential election.

Shortly before the end of President Nixon's first term, he signed a $30.2 billion revenue-sharing bill. This act channeled federal revenue to states and local communities for various public programs. Nixon regarded this "new federalism" as an essential part of his program for decentralizing the power of the national government.

SECTION SURVEY

IDENTIFY: law and order, inflation, wage and price controls, "energy crisis," Twenty-sixth Amendment; Spiro Agnew, George Wallace, Warren Burger.

1. What were the basic issues of the 1968 election?

What position did each candidate take on these issues?
2. What were some of the difficulties between Congress and President Nixon? What ideas about the role of government did they reflect?
3. How did the Nixon administration attempt to control inflation? How effective were its efforts?

6 Nixon's resignation and the early Ford administration

Nixon's second term began with the triumph of a sweeping re-election victory. It ended two and a half years later with a disgraced administration and with the President's resignation.

The election of 1972

At their 1972 convention the Republicans again nominated Richard M. Nixon and Spiro T. Agnew. The Democratic convention nominated Senator George M. McGovern of South Dakota, a liberal, as its Presidential candidate. Governor George C. Wallace of Alabama, an early contender for the Democratic nomination, had been wounded by a would-be assassin and did not take an active part in the 1972 campaign.

The Democratic convention included among its delegates an unusually large number of black Americans, young people, other minorities, and women. Older party regulars, who believed that the newcomers were moving the Democrats too far to the left, beyond the majority views of the nation, bitterly opposed McGovern's nomination.

From the start McGovern was in trouble. Many traditional Democratic voters opposed him, and others were lukewarm toward his candidacy. McGovern campaigned tirelessly, hitting hard at inflation, corruption, what he called the Nixon administration's "indifference" to civil rights, and above all against United States participation in the Vietnam War. But he was never able to win broad nationwide support.

Nixon was confident of victory. He could count on most of the 12 million to 15 million votes that might have gone to Governor Wallace if he had run. Moreover, Nixon's achievements in foreign affairs were widely praised by Democrats and Republicans alike. And he used TV and radio effectively to criticize McGovern's policies. Nixon also encouraged his supporters to insure a sweeping landslide by spending large campaign funds and by doing whatever else might be needed.

Nixon won one of the greatest victories in American history, winning about 47 million votes to McGovern's 29 million. The electoral vote was 521 to 17. Nixon's victory was largely personal, and Republicans failed to make significant gains in the Democratic-controlled House and Senate.

Growing concentration of executive power

The powers of the Presidency had been increasing since the Great Depression of the 1930's. In part the growing complexities of foreign and domestic policy encouraged, if they did not require, increased executive power. During this time Congress itself had allowed Presidential powers to grow under both Democratic and Republican administrations.

President Nixon interpreted the personal "landslide" victory in the 1972 election as a mandate, or command by the voters, to achieve his foreign and domestic policies, if necessary by ignoring the Democratic majority in Congress. He relied partly upon his Republican followers in Congress, but also upon continuing support from conservative Democrats, chiefly from southern states.

But as Nixon's second term progressed, critics

President Nixon frequently spoke to the American people on television and radio to ask their support for his foreign and domestic policies.

began to express concern over his apparent belief that he, as President, was beyond restraint and above criticism. Senators and Representatives of both parties, for example, protested that much of the authority of cabinet officers, whose appointment required Senate approval, had been turned over by Nixon to his personally appointed White House staff.

Critics further noted that the Nixon administration held back information from Congress and the public, attacked criticism in the mass media as irresponsible and biased, and often tried to block publication of newsworthy material. These efforts and many others added weight to a rising conviction in the nation that Nixon's secrecy, aloofness, and unpredictability threatened the Constitutional balance of powers.

Nixon's social policies

President Nixon believed that the expansion of social programs during previous administrations had worsened the conditions they were supposed to correct. He opposed large federal spending for job training for the handicapped, special education for the disadvantaged; and the use of school buses to speed up racial integration. He called for a halt to federal support for low-cost housing and urban renewal on grounds that neither had succeeded. He criticized publicly financed day care support for children of working mothers. He urged tighter controls over expenditures for Medicare and Medicaid, declaring his preference for health insurance plans of private firms. In January 1973 Nixon called for cutbacks or terminations in more than 100 federal programs in the next budget.

Conflict between President and Congress

Nixon's criticism of Congress was part of a continuing conflict that had started at the beginning of his administration in 1969. On a number of occasions Congress overrode the President's veto of bills expanding social and medical services. President Nixon then impounded, or refused to spend, money that Congress had appropriated for health, education, and other social services. In the continuing struggle, Congress overrode Nixon's veto of a bill appropriating $25 billion for reducing water pollution. Congress also overrode Nixon's veto of a bill restricting the President's power to send American combat troops into action in foreign countries for more than 60 days unless Congress gave its approval.

Vice-President Agnew resigns

While Congress was reaffirming its war-making power, the Justice Department was investigating the financial affairs of Vice-President Agnew. By the fall of 1973 government investigators were prepared to indict the Vice-President for alleged criminal activities, including bribery and extortion, committed while he was Governor of Maryland and Vice-President of the United States.

For a time Agnew angrily proclaimed his innocence of the alleged wrongdoings. But in the late fall he decided to throw himself on the mercy of the court and "plea bargain" for a light sentence.

Agnew's part of the bargain included his immediate resignation as Vice-President, and a *nolo contendere* ("no contest") plea to a single count of tax evasion ($29,500 of undeclared income in 1967). In return the Court agreed not to sentence Agnew to jail for tax evasion, and not to prosecute him for alleged criminal activities.

The extremely lenient sentence—a $10,000 fine and unsupervised probation for three years—was widely criticized. But Attorney General Richardson defended it on grounds that an indictment and a long trial "would have been likely to inflict upon the nation serious and permanent scars."

In accordance with the Twenty-fifth Amendment to the Constitution, President Nixon nominated a new Vice-President. He chose Gerald Ford, the Republican leader of the House of Representatives. The Senate confirmed the nomination.

The Watergate scandals

Agnew's disgrace was a devastating blow to an administration already being shaken to its foundations by a growing list of scandals. The disastrous Watergate affair, as the scandals were called, began in June 1972 with an attempted burglary of the Democratic National Committee offices in Washington's Watergate Apartments complex. Five men were caught in the building. At first they gave false names, but they were soon correctly identified. The trail then led to the organization for which they had been working, the Committee to Re-elect the President.

The White House tried to dismiss the episode as a "third-rate burglary," but news reporters refused to believe this. As the months passed, news reports began to unravel a tangled web of criminal activities that appeared to reach into the highest offices in the land. As a result, by 1973 both the legislative and the judicial branches of government had become actively involved in the Watergate investigations. A special Senate committee, chaired by Senator Sam Ervin of North Carolina, held televised hearings during the spring and summer of 1973. The Attorney General appointed a Special Prosecutor, who organized a staff and began to sift the evidence. A grand jury sitting in a federal district court headed by Judge John Sirica began to gather evidence and prepare indictments.

The Senate Watergate Committee investigated the charges of illegal activities and wrongdoing in the Nixon administration. Millions of Americans watched and listened to these dramatic hearings on television.

Mounting evidence of wrongdoing

As the investigations continued, the charges regarding the offenses and the individuals involved began to multiply. The grand jury charged that members of the administration, if not the President himself, had approved the illegal burglary of the Democratic Party's headquarters and had then attempted to cover up the administration's part in the affair. The grand jury also charged that members of the administration, if not the President himself, had approved of the illegal entry into the offices of a psychiatrist. This break-in was undertaken in an effort to secure damaging personal evidence against one of the psychiatrist's patients, Daniel Ellsberg, who had earlier released classified material relating to the government's plans and actions during the Vietnam War.

Investigators also uncovered evidence of the illegal use by the administration of wiretapping and "bugging" and of a plan to set up a White House secret police force authorized to break federal laws in the name of "national security." Investigators also claimed that the White House had tried to involve the Central Intelligence Agency (CIA) and the FBI in some of its illegal activities. They further claimed that during the 1972 election campaign huge sums of money had been collected from corporations with the understanding that the administration would do special favors for such contributors. As the months passed, additional evidence of wrongdoing steadily accumulated. Numerous officials of the White House staff

were indicted. Some pleaded guilty and went to jail. Others went to trial; most of them were convicted and sentenced.

The fateful tapes

From the beginning President Nixon protested that he was innocent of any wrongdoing. But White House lawyer John W. Dean, who had already confessed to his own participation in the scandals, challenged Nixon's assertion of innocence. Although the growing volume of evidence seemed to support Dean, it was his word against the word of the President of the United States, and the issue remained unresolved.

In July 1973, however, the Senate committee investigating Watergate suddenly learned that the President himself controlled vital evidence. This evidence could settle once and for all the question of his own guilt or innocence of the charge of obstructing justice. During the committee's hearings one of the President's aides testified that for the past two years Nixon had been secretly taping everything said in his offices and over most of his White House telephones.

The Senate Watergate Committee and the Special Prosecutor immediately issued subpoenas requesting President Nixon to turn over those tapes that contained discussions relating to the Watergate affair and the alleged cover-up. But Nixon refused to surrender them on grounds of "executive privilege" and his responsibility as President to safeguard national security. The courts then ruled that the President must release those portions of the relevant tapes that did not relate to national security. After considerable delay Nixon released some, but not all, of the tapes that had been requested. A growing conviction that he was withholding evidence damaging to himself became even more widespread when it was discovered that significant parts of certain tapes had been erased. Finally, in August 1974, the Supreme Court ordered Nixon to release the requested tapes.

The Supreme Court ruling was the final blow to the President's efforts to conceal his part in the illegal White House activities during his administration. The tapes Nixon reluctantly turned over to the Special Prosecutor revealed that his repeated claims of innocence had been false. From the beginning he had deliberately misrepresented to the American public, and even to his legal advisers, his own part in the Watergate scandals.

Nixon's resignation

The revelation of Nixon's betrayal of the public's trust came as the House of Representatives was preparing to vote on the issue of Presidential impeachment. After a three-month investigation, the House Judiciary Committee had approved three Articles of Impeachment.

The three articles that the Judiciary Committee sent to the House charged the President with violating his oath of office by (1) obstruction of justice, (2) abuse of power, and (3) willful disobedience of subpoenas issued by the House of Representatives. "Wherefore," each article concluded, "Richard M. Nixon, by such conduct, warrants impeachment and trial, and removal from office."

Faced with probable impeachment by the House and conviction by the Senate, President Nixon chose to resign and submitted his resignation on August 8, 1974. He denied any guilt, however, and admitted only to having made some "mistakes" and to having lost his "power base" in Congress.

Nixon was the first President in the nation's 198-year history to resign from office. His departure brought an end to a grave constitutional crisis that had threatened to weaken, if not destroy, the democratic process. At issue had been the preservation of the system of checks and balances, the principle of the separation of powers, and the rule of law itself.

On August 9 the Vice-President, Gerald Ford, became the 38th President of the United States. Shortly after he took office he pardoned former President Nixon of any crimes and misdemeanors he might have committed while President. Ford then nominated Nelson A. Rockefeller for the Vice-Presidency. In prolonged hearings, Congress raised the question of a possible conflict of interest between Rockefeller's vast wealth and the duties he might be called upon to perform. Finally, however, both Houses confirmed the nomination.

Gerald Ford takes the oath of office as President of the United States in August 1974. Chief Justice Warren Burger administers the oath as Betty Ford looks on.

President Ford's administration

President Ford, an unpretentious man gifted with the common touch, from the beginning committed himself to a policy of cooperation with Congress. During the many years he had served in the House of Representatives, he had won the respect and liking of his colleagues in Congress.

As the months passed, however, it became clear that the positions he took as Chief Executive were often at odds with the positions of the large Democratic majority in both houses of Congress. His approach to fighting the inflation that had seriously reduced the buying power of Americans and caused hardships to many of them created conflicts with Congress. President Ford insisted that government spending must be sharply cut, while most members of Congress refused to reduce spending for the social welfare programs that they believed were essential to the nation's welfare. The reduction in personal income tax rates and the tax rebate that Congress voted early in 1975 as a means of bolstering the nation's sagging economy were criticized by the President as too large. Nor did President Ford agree with the Democratic Congress on the best way of coping with the energy crisis (see page 352).

By the end of President Ford's first year in office, some critics argued that his administration presented no sharp differences from that of his predecessor. The President's supporters pointed out, however, that his programs and policies were based firmly on Republican Party principles and also represented the President's own goals for the nation. As some observed, President Ford was trying to give Americans what the great majority had voted for in 1972, minus Watergate.

SECTION SURVEY

IDENTIFY: Watergate scandals, executive privilege, Senate Watergate Committee, Articles of Impeachment; George McGovern, Gerald Ford, Nelson Rockefeller.

1. How did President Nixon's 1972 landslide victory contribute to the growing concentration of Presidential power?
2. What were the Watergate scandals? What role did Congress have in investigating these events? What part did news reporters play? What role did the courts have?
3. What were the events that led to President Nixon's resignation? How did his resignation end a grave Constitutional crisis?

CHAPTER SURVEY

INQUIRING INTO HISTORY

1. What were some of the programs launched during President Truman's Fair Deal? Do you think that they were needed or not? Why?
2. Describe America's demobilization and reconversion to peacetime after World War II. What problems did the nation face?
3. The Eisenhower administration continued most of the social and economic reforms of the New Deal and the Fair Deal. Explain.
4. What, in your opinion, were President Kennedy's most important achievements? Explain.
5. What were some of the aims of President Johnson's Great Society programs? Do you think they accomplished their goals? Explain.
6. Do you think the President or Congress should have the leading role in shaping government policies? Use examples from the Presidential administrations you have studied in this chapter to support your opinion.
7. Why were the Watergate scandals such a serious challenge to American government?

RELATING PAST TO PRESENT

1. How has the role of the federal government been changing since the New Deal years? In what ways has this affected the lives of all Americans?
2. Compare the impeachment proceedings against President Nixon with those against President Andrew Johnson in 1868. What were the constitutional issues in each case?

DEVELOPING SOCIAL SCIENCE SKILLS

1. In recent years television has become an important force in American politics. (a) How does television affect Presidential and other elections? (b) What techniques do candidates use to be effective on television? Do these provide an accurate view of candidates?
2. Make a list of the major legislation passed during the administrations of Presidents Truman, Eisenhower, Kennedy, Johnson, and Nixon. (a) Which Presidents were more successful in getting legislation passed? Why? (b) Which Presidents were generally considered effective and outstanding? How do their reputations compare with their legislative records? (c) How would you rate each of these Presidents?

CHAPTER 22

THE CHALLENGES OF WORLD LEADERSHIP
1945-1960

The end of World War II in 1945 brought nothing like the delirious celebrations that had followed Allied victory in World War I. There was rejoicing, to be sure, in all the victorious countries. But the joy and gaiety were restrained, for the dominant feeling was one of immense relief.

The mood of the American people was summed up by the reporter who wrote that "everybody talked of the 'end of the war,' not of 'victory.' "

It was all so different from 1918. In 1918 Americans had been content to let the world take care of itself. In 1945 they felt they knew better. Senator Arthur H. Vandenberg of Michigan, who through the 1930's had been one of the leading isolationists in Congress, spoke for millions of Americans when he was in London in 1944 during a German rocket attack. "How can there be immunity or isolation," he asked, "when man can devise weapons like that?"

Later, in the Senate, Senator Vandenberg renounced his isolationism and came out in favor of American cooperation in building a new world order. "I want a new dignity and a new authority for international law," he announced; "I think American self-interest requires it."

In 1945 the American people were rapidly becoming aware that, like it or not, the United States was destined to play a new role in the world. But not even the most farsighted among them realized the heavy burden of responsibility they would have to carry in the troubled years ahead.

THE CHAPTER IN OUTLINE

1. The role of the United States in organizing the United Nations.

2. "Cold War" between the United States and the U.S.S.R. in Europe.

3. "Hot War" in Asia as a result of Communist aggression.

4. Continuing American efforts to meet the Communist challenge.

1450   1750   1800   1850   1900   1950   1980's

1 The role of the United States in organizing the United Nations

Even before World War II ended, many world leaders were considering ways to build an enduring peace. American officials were among the leaders in this effort.

Roots of the United Nations

As early as January 1, 1942, the Allies—or United Nations, as they called themselves—promised to join together to defeat Italy, Germany, and Japan (page 317). Many Allied leaders—among them Roosevelt, Churchill, and Stalin—agreed that it would be wise to convert the wartime alliance into a permanent organization for peace.

Many Americans shared this point of view. Members of both political parties pledged their support to an international organization of nations. Democrats and Republicans alike agreed to support a program of international cooperation.

Conference at Dumbarton Oaks

Delegates from the United States, Great Britain, the U.S.S.R., and China met in 1944 at Dumbarton Oaks, an estate in Washington, D.C., to prepare a plan for a postwar United Nations organization. On most questions of procedure the delegates quickly reached agreement. Some problems, however, were more difficult to solve.

What, for instance, should they do about the demand by the U.S.S.R. that it be represented in the United Nations not by one delegation but by 16—one for each of the 16 Soviet republics? And what should they do about the Security Council,

the body in which the great powers would have permanent seats and which was charged with keeping peace in the world?

Agreements at Yalta

Meeting at Yalta in February 1945 (page 329), Roosevelt, Churchill, and Stalin reached agreements on several issues that had deadlocked the Dumbarton Oaks Conference. They agreed that two of the Soviet Union's 16 republics would be admitted to the United Nations under the fiction that they were independent nations. The leaders also worked out a compromise on voting procedure in the Security Council. Finally, they agreed to call a United Nations Conference in San Francisco on April 25, 1945, to draw up the Charter of a permanent organization.

The San Francisco Conference

Delegates from 50 nations, representing three fourths of the peoples of the earth, took part in the San Francisco Conference. Despite differences in language and culture, the delegates all worked for one objective—the formation of a world peace organization. In the surprisingly short time of eight weeks the Dumbarton Oaks and the Yalta proposals had been reshaped into the United Nations Charter. On October 24—now celebrated as United Nations Day—the United Nations (UN) came into official existence after its charter had been ratified by the required number of countries.

The General Assembly of the United Nations serves as the "town meeting" of the world. In this photograph, the President of the General Assembly is addressing the delegates.

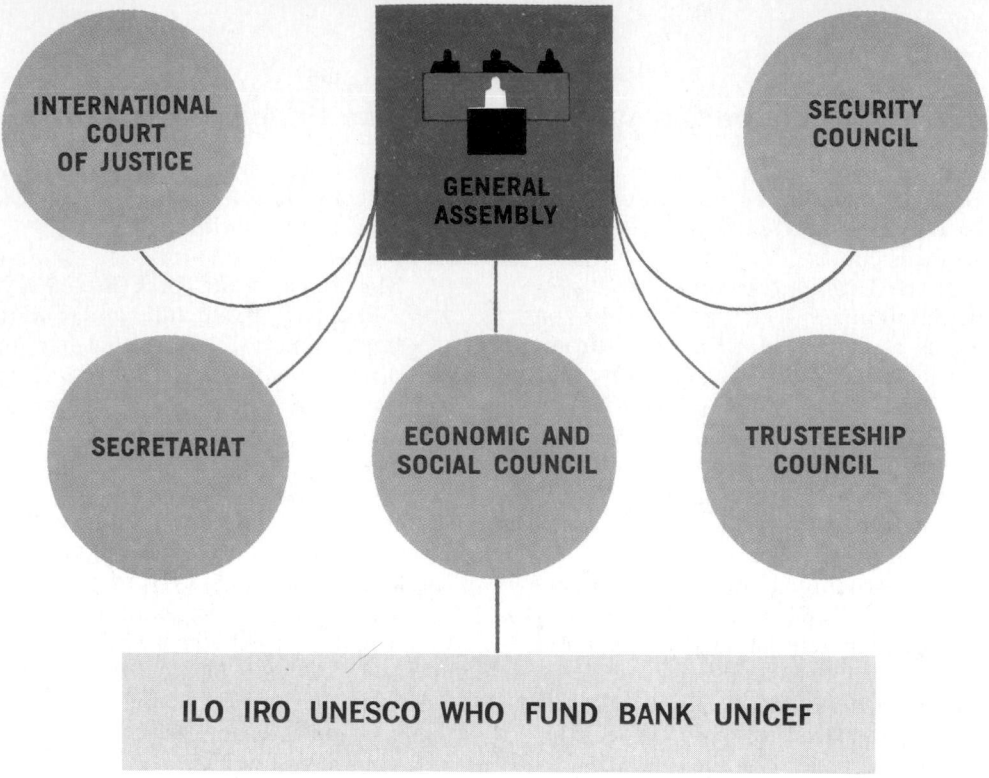

THE UNITED NATIONS

Purposes and organization

The purposes of the UN are clearly stated in the Preamble to the Charter: "We the peoples of the United Nations, determined to save succeeding generations from the scourge of war ... to promote social progress and better standards of life in larger freedom ... have resolved to combine our efforts to accomplish these aims. . . ."

In general, the UN seeks to maintain peace, to provide security, to promote justice, to increase the general welfare, and to establish human rights. Six major organs and many related agencies were created by the UN in order to carry on its work.

(1) The Security Council was to be the police authority of the world, charged with preventing war. It was to consist of 11 members.° Five of these, the so-called "Big Five" powers—the United States, China, France, the Soviet Union, and Great Britain—were to hold permanent seats. The six nonpermanent members were to be elected for two-year terms. The Security Council was to meet in continuous session, and to be ready to go into action at a moment's notice. It was to have at its command an international military force to check aggression. But on matters of peace and security

° It later was increased to 15 members—the five permanent members plus ten nonpermanent members.

any one of the five permanent members could prevent action by its negative vote, or veto.

(2) The General Assembly was to be the "town meeting" of the world, in which all UN members were to be equally represented. It was to make recommendations for the peaceful settlement of disputes. It was to elect all the nonpermanent members of the Security Council, certain members of the Trusteeship Council, and all members of the Economic and Social Council.

(3) The Economic and Social Council, composed of 18 members (now 27), was to study world economic, social, cultural, and health problems, and to make recommendations to the General Assembly or to individual member countries.

(4) The International Court of Justice, modeled after the World Court, was to decide legal questions referred to it by disputing nations. It was to give advisory opinions when asked to do so, but it could not enforce its decisions.

(5) The Secretariat was to handle the administrative work of the UN.

(6) The Trusteeship Council was to look after the welfare of peoples living in colonial areas.

Early years of the UN

Early critics of the UN insisted that it was doomed to fail because the member nations had not given up any of their national sovereignty.

Other people, however, shared the opinion expressed by President Truman in 1945. "This Charter," he stated, "points down the only road to enduring peace. There is no other."

As crises broke out in many parts of the world, Truman's statement took on new meaning. By 1948 the world situation had become so tense that Trygve Lie (TRIG·vuh LEE), the first Secretary-General of the UN, issued a warning. "The trouble," he declared, "lies in the intense conflict over the settlement of the last war . . . between the two most powerful single nations in the world today—the United States and the Soviet Union."

SECTION SURVEY

IDENTIFY: Dumbarton Oaks Conference, San Francisco Conference, "Big Five"; Trygve Lie.

1. (a) What major problems had to be solved before a United Nations organization could be created? (b) Which of these conflicts were settled at the Yalta Conference?
2. Describe the purposes of the United Nations.
3. Indicate the chief functions of the Security Council and the General Assembly.
4. "The United Nations is not a world government." Explain.

2 "Cold War" between the United States and the U.S.S.R. in Europe

At the end of World War II, millions of people suffered from lack of food, clothing, shelter, and medical care. The United States responded generously to this desperate worldwide need for help.

America's new role in the world

During and immediately after the war, the United States played an active role in creating three important UN agencies: (1) the United Nations Relief and Rehabilitation Administration (UNRRA); (2) the International Bank for Reconstruction and Development; and (3) the International Monetary Fund. These UN agencies supplied food, clothing, shelter, and medical care to millions of needy persons in war-damaged nations and provided money to rebuild ruined industries. A large part of the money for these activities came from the United States.

After the war ended, American dollars and supplies flowed directly to the war-devastated areas. Major contributions came from private American organizations—churches, schools, fraternal societies, and civic groups. An even larger contribution came from the United States government in the form of supplies, equipment, loans, and the assistance of specialists and experts.

Expanding Soviet influence

America's new role of world leadership brought it into conflict with the Soviet Union, which also emerged from the war as a major power. The postwar policies of the Soviet Union were, at least in part, a continuation of the expansionist ambitions of tsarist Russia. But now the U.S.S.R. regarded itself as the leader of a Communist revolution destined to replace the "capitalist" and "imperialist" world—a world in which the United States was the principal power.

Thus even before the war ended the Soviets began to move aggressively against their weaker neighbors. In 1940 Latvia, Lithuania, and Estonia —countries to which the Russians had some historical claims—were incorporated into the Soviet Union. As a result of World War II, the U.S.S.R. also acquired large parts of Poland and Rumania. Through Communist governments which they helped to set up, the Soviets by 1948 had gained control of the "free" governments of Poland, Rumania, Hungary, Czechoslovakia, and the eastern part of Germany. Moreover, Soviet influence reached beyond Eastern Europe into the Mediterranean area. Moscow-trained Communists were especially active in Greece and Italy.

The U.S.S.R. was deeply entrenched in the Far East, as well as in Europe. As a result of the Yalta agreements and because of Russia's last-minute entry into the war against Japan, the Soviet Union gained control of large areas that had been Chinese and Japanese territory.

Mounting tension

The Communist leaders defended their actions on grounds of self-defense. They pointed out that during the Bolshevik Revolution the Allies, including the United States, had sent troops into northern Russia and Russian Siberia. They feared, they said, that the United States would lead the "capitalist nations" in a new attack against the U.S.S.R. They claimed that, to defend themselves against such an attack, they were required to maintain powerful military forces and to control bordering countries from which an attack could be launched.

The United States, on the other hand, objected bitterly to the Soviet Union's domination of its weaker neighbors. The United States, which had demobilized most of its own troops, resented the Soviet policy of maintaining huge military forces. Moreover, Americans loathed the ruthless methods used by the Communists to crush all opposition. Most Americans regarded the Soviet Union as the world's newest aggressor.

As friction increased, the Soviet press and radio, rigidly controlled by the government, became increasingly anti-American. The Soviet government refused to join the United Nations Educational, Scientific, and Cultural Organization (UNESCO), which had been established to promote understanding among the peoples of the world. It permitted very few Americans to visit the U.S.S.R. or its "satellite" nations—those nations dominated by the U.S.S.R.

Deadlock over atomic energy

Inability to reach agreement on international control of the atomic bomb greatly added to the mounting tension. Early in 1946, acting on American initiative, the UN created an International Atomic Energy Commission. On June 14, 1946, at the Commission's first meeting, the United States representative, Bernard M. Baruch (buh·ROOK), presented America's proposal for international control.

Baruch proposed that complete control of atomic energy be turned over to an international agency responsible to the UN. This agency would have full authority to enter any country to inspect atomic energy installations. The United States—at that time the only nation that had atomic bombs—was ready, Baruch announced, to give up its secrets to the new world authority. But, he warned, the United States would not reveal any secrets until

the UN provided for "immediate, swift, and sure punishment for those who violate the agreements that are reached by the nations." Baruch insisted that each of the "Big Five" on the Security Council give up its right to the veto on all matters involving atomic energy.

When the United States proposal reached the Security Council, the Soviet Union killed it by a veto.

The Soviet Union then offered its own proposal. It opposed any system of international inspection and control. Instead, it insisted that the United States destroy its atomic bombs, that the UN declare atomic warfare illegal, and that all nations promise not to manufacture atomic bombs. But the Soviet Union flatly refused to give up its veto right in the Security Council. This meant that if any nation, including the U.S.S.R., violated its promise not to make atomic bombs, the Soviet Union or any permanent Security Council member could block all UN action by a single veto.

The Truman Doctrine

Faced with the menace of Communist aggression, the United States began to formulate a policy of "containment." This policy aimed to "contain," or restrict, Soviet expansion and to check the spread of Communism. The new policy was first applied to Greece and Turkey.

In 1947 Greek Communists, supported by the Soviets, were about to seize control of the

At the end of World War II, the nations of Europe had to rebuild their ruined cities and restore their economies. The Marshall Plan provided money and equipment to aid Europe's recovery.

Greek government. At the same time the Soviet Union was trying to force Turkey to give up control of the Dardanelles, the strait between European and Asiatic Turkey. Soviet control of Greece and the Dardanelles would enable the U.S.S.R. to dominate the northeastern Mediterranean and the Suez Canal.

This situation prompted President Truman on March 12, 1947, to announce the "Truman Doctrine." This doctrine stated that the United States must "help free people to maintain their free institutions and their national integrity." He then asked Congress for authority to help the Greeks and Turks strengthen their armed forces to check the spread of Communism. Congress responded with an initial appropriation of $400 million.

The Marshall Plan

Aid to Greece and Turkey, however, was not enough to prevent the spread of Communism. All of war-torn Europe was in economic difficulty, and Communists were winning converts among hungry, disillusioned people.

Early in June 1947 Secretary of State George C. Marshall suggested a solution to Europe's economic problems. The "Marshall Plan," as this program came to be called, proposed to help European countries in self-efforts to get their farms, factories, and transportation systems operating efficiently again. The United States would provide money, supplies, and machinery to any nation, including the Soviet Union and its satellites, that agreed to take part in the program.

The Marshall Plan provoked heated Congressional debate. Those who favored the proposal insisted that the best way to block Communism and strengthen America's own economic system was to restore Europe's economic health. Opponents declared that the United States could not afford to "carry Europe on its back." In the spring of 1948, however, Congress approved the Marshall Plan, officially known as the European Recovery Program.

Despite the opposition of the Soviet Union and its satellites, all of whom denounced the plan as "Yankee imperialism," the Marshall Plan was an outstanding success. Slowly but steadily Europe began to recover from the war.

The Berlin airlift

Meanwhile tension mounted in Germany. In 1945 the great powers had agreed to a joint occupation of Germany. Great Britain, France, and the United States occupied western and southern Germany, and the Soviet Union occupied eastern Germany. Berlin, within the Soviet-controlled zone, was also divided into four sections, each controlled by one of the four powers.

On June 24, 1948, the Soviets suddenly blocked all roads, canals, and railways connecting Berlin and the Western Zone of Germany. By this move they apparently hoped to force the three Western powers out of Berlin.

The British-American answer to the Soviet challenge was the Berlin airlift. Starting in the summer of 1948 and continuing for nearly a year, British and American planes transported more than 2 million tons of food and supplies, including coal, to Berlin. This crisis in East-West relations was finally resolved in 1949 with the aid of the UN.

The North Atlantic Treaty Organization

The Soviet blockade of Berlin and Communist efforts to wreck the Marshall Plan aroused growing alarm in Western Europe. In April 1949

SOURCES

THE MARSHALL PLAN (1947)

It is logical that the United States should do whatever it is able to do to assist in the return of normal economic health in the world, without which there can be no political stability and no assured peace.

Our policy is directed not against any country or doctrine but against hunger, poverty, desperation, and chaos. Its purpose should be the revival of a working economy in the world so as to permit the emergence of political and social conditions in which free institutions can exist. . . .

Any government that is willing to assist in the task of recovery will find full cooperation, I am sure, on the part of the United States government. Any government which maneuvers to block the recovery of other countries cannot expect help from us. Furthermore, governments, political parties, or groups which seek to perpetuate human misery in order to profit therefrom, politically or otherwise, will encounter the opposition of the United States. . . .

nine Western European nations,° determined to meet the Soviet threat, joined the United States, Canada, and Iceland in an alliance known as the North Atlantic Treaty Organization (NATO).

In the Atlantic Pact—the treaty proposing such an alliance—each member nation agreed that ". . . an armed attack against one or more of them in Europe or North America shall be considered an attack against them all. . . ." They also agreed to resist such an attack with armed force, if necessary.

Since the Atlantic Pact was a treaty, it had to be approved by the United States Senate. The chief issue of Senate debate was whether or not the Atlantic Pact would compel the United States to go to war to assist a member nation without an act of Congress. This, you may remember, was the main issue that had kept the United States out of the League of Nations in 1919. However, in July 1949 the Senate did ratify the agreement. Eventually General Eisenhower was appointed Supreme Commander of the NATO forces.

Thus by the end of 1949 an American policy of "containment" had begun to take shape, at least in regard to Europe. NATO strengthened the military defenses of Western Europe. The Marshall Plan strengthened Western Europe's economic structure, thus reducing much of the discontent that had so often helped the spread of Communism.

Meanwhile, however, trouble was brewing in the Middle East and in Asia.

SECTION SURVEY

IDENTIFY: UNESCO, satellite nations, containment; Bernard Baruch, George C. Marshall.

1. Explain America's new role in the postwar world in regard to (a) foreign aid, (b) the Soviet Union.
2. (a) Why did the Soviet Union expand its influence during the postwar period? (b) How did the Soviets justify their actions?
3. (a) Compare the Soviet and the American plans for control of atomic energy. (b) Why did the plans end in deadlock?
4. How did each of the following help to contain Communism: (a) the Truman Doctrine, (b) the Marshall Plan, (c) the Berlin airlift, (d) NATO?

3 "Hot War" in Asia as a result of Communist aggression

Postwar troubles were not confined to Europe. During President Truman's administration growing tensions seriously threatened peace in the Middle East and Asia.

Tensions in the Middle East

Iran soon became a trouble spot. During World War II both American and Soviet troops were stationed in Iran. After the war the United States pulled out its troops, but the Soviets, eager to control the oil-rich land adjoining their borders, did not. Tension mounted. Finally, after the UN intervened in 1946, the Soviets withdrew their military forces.

Meanwhile shadows were gathering over Palestine at the eastern end of the Mediterranean Sea. Since World War I Great Britain had ruled Palestine under a mandate from the League of Nations. On May 14, 1948, when Great Britain voluntarily gave up this mandate, the Jews in Palestine proclaimed the independence of the new state of Israel. This action plunged Israel into war with the neighboring Arab countries of Egypt, Transjordan (later renamed Jordan), Lebanon, Syria, Iraq, and Saudi Arabia. The UN at once took steps to end the fighting. Finally a UN mission under the leadership of a black American, Dr. Ralph J. Bunche, managed to get both sides to agree to an armistice. As a result of his energetic services, Dr. Bunche received the Nobel peace prize.

Communist victory in China

While an uneasy peace was being restored in the Middle East, Chinese Communists, backed by their Soviet allies, were rapidly winning control of China. The struggle for control of China began long before World War II.

In 1927, four years before the Japanese moved into Manchuria, Chiang Kai-shek, leader of the Chinese Nationalist forces, opened war on the Chinese Communists. For a time China was torn by civil conflict. But after Japan attacked China, both of the opposing Chinese factions fought against Japanese troops. During World War II the United States encouraged such cooperation. Chinese troops heroically resisted the invading armies of Japan. In 1945, in recognition of these valiant efforts, China was admitted to the United Nations as one of the "Big Five."

But with the end of World War II the struggle between Chiang's Nationalist forces and the Chinese Communists for control of China once again erupted in armed conflict. The Soviet Union supported and supplied the Chinese Communists,

---

° Great Britain, France, Belgium, the Netherlands, Luxembourg, Italy, Denmark, Norway, and Portugal. West Germany, Turkey, and Greece joined later.

led by Mao Tse-tung (MAU TSAY-TOONG). The United States at first provided military assistance to Chiang's Nationalists, but later withdrew. By 1949 the Communists had conquered most of China. Defeated on the mainland, Chiang and the Nationalist government, together with a small army, retreated to the island of Formosa, or Taiwan.

The United States continued to recognize the Nationalists as the legal government of China, and the Nationalists continued to represent China in the UN Security Council.°

The division of Korea

Meanwhile trouble was brewing in Korea. Between 1910 and 1945 the Koreans had been ruled by Japan. During the closing days of World War II, however, Soviet and American troops swept the Japanese out of Korea. After the war General Douglas MacArthur was appointed Supreme Commander of the Allied Powers, and placed in charge of the occupation forces in Japan.° His responsibilities also included the southern portion of Korea.

At the end of the war, a line drawn across the Korean peninsula at the 38th parallel (see map, page 366) separated American occupation forces in the south from Soviet occupation forces in the north. Americans and most other peoples considered this a temporary arrangement.

But despite UN efforts to unite the country, Korea remained divided, and Soviet and American troops were not withdrawn. Then in 1948 North Korea and South Korea set up separate governments, both claiming authority to rule the entire country. The North Korean government, controlled by Communists and supported by the Soviets, called itself the "People's Republic." The South Korean government, of which Syngman Rhee (SING·man REE) had been chosen president in an election sponsored by the UN, called itself the "Republic of Korea." The United States and 30 UN members (but not the Soviet Union) recognized the Republic of Korea as the lawful government.

Finally the United States and the Soviet Union withdrew their troops. Each left behind a Korean army it had helped to train—two armies now facing each other across the 38th parallel.

° The People's Republic of China replaced Nationalist China in the Security Council in 1972.

° During the occupation period relations between Japan and the Western powers were restored to a friendly basis. In 1951 Japan received independence in a treaty signed at San Francisco.

A UN mission under the leadership of an American, Dr. Ralph J. Bunche, arranged an armistice ending the Palestinian War. Here, Dr. Bunche (right) receives the Nobel peace prize for his efforts.

The Korean challenge

On June 25, 1950, the North Korean army suddenly launched a full-scale invasion of South Korea. In an emergency session the UN Security Council adopted a resolution ordering an immediate cease-fire. The Soviet delegate, Jacob A. Malik, did not attend this meeting. Six months earlier the Soviet Union, angered by the Security Council's refusal to admit a delegate from Communist China, had recalled Malik to the Soviet Union. Not even the Korean crisis could make the Soviets change their minds. Had Malik been present, the Soviet Union could have used its veto power to block all UN action.

Answering the challenge

Meanwhile President Truman was busy conferring with the heads of the State and Defense Departments. On Tuesday, June 27, 1950 the big news broke: the President had pledged American aid to South Korea. That same evening the Security Council adopted a second resolution which termed North Korea an "aggressor" and called on UN members to furnish all possible assistance to the South Koreans. By Friday, June 30, 1950, six days after the North Koreans had crossed the 38th parallel, the UN was firmly committed to action.

The Korean War

The UN itself had no troops to throw into action. Soviet vetoes in the Security Council had blocked every effort to create a UN military force.

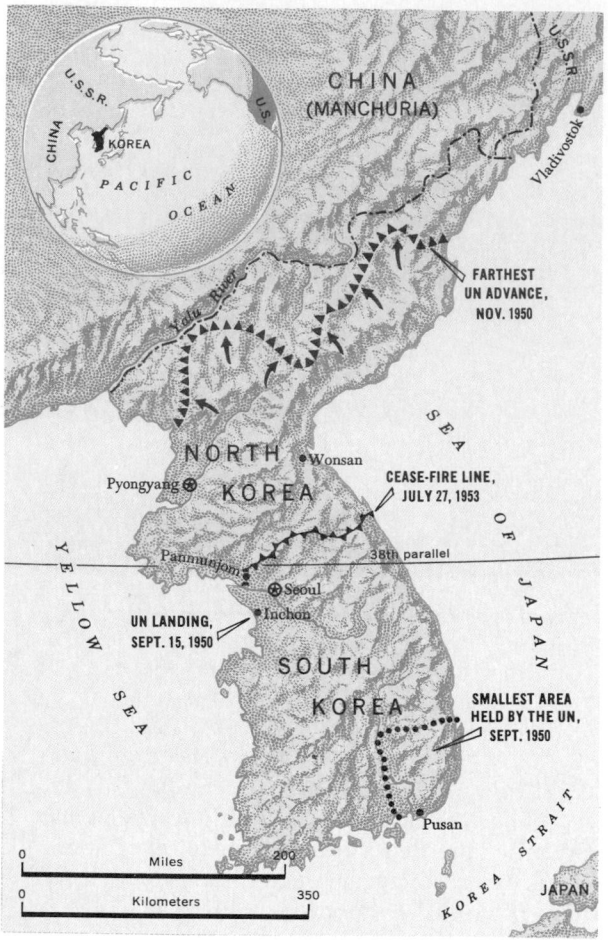

THE KOREAN WAR

Although 19 UN members finally contributed assistance, the major burden of defending South Korea fell upon the United States.

In response to the UN's call, President Truman ordered the United States Seventh Fleet to prevent any attack upon Formosa and to blockade the Korean coast. Truman also ordered United States air and ground forces into Korea.

For a time it looked as though the North Koreans would overrun all of Korea. The South Koreans were hopelessly outnumbered. Neither they nor the first American troops rushed to the scene had the equipment to stand up against the heavily armored, Soviet-made tanks of the North Korean army. By early August the South Korean and UN troops under General MacArthur were desperately defending a small area around Pusan in southeast Korea (see map, this page).

Then the tide suddenly turned. On September 15, 1950, General MacArthur staged a seaborne attack against Inchon and then swept east-ward, recapturing Seoul (SOHL), the capital of South Korea. At the same time a strongly reinforced UN army, now well equipped and powerfully supported from the air, launched a counteroffensive from southeastern Korea. The North Korean forces, caught in a huge trap, began to break up. Thousands surrendered. The rest fled northward across the 38th parallel, with MacArthur's troops in hot pursuit. By November advance units of the UN forces were at the Yalu River, the boundary between North Korea and Communist China.

Then suddenly the tide turned again. Late in November hundreds of thousands of Chinese Communist "volunteers" swarmed across the Yalu River to reinforce the North Korean troops. The UN troops, their lines extended, were outnumbered in many cases by hundreds to one. Finally, after weeks of desperate fighting, MacArthur's forces managed to set up their defense line near the 38th parallel.

The "Great Debate"

The entry of Chinese Communist troops— "volunteers" or otherwise—completely changed the nature of the war. The UN now faced a very grave problem. Should it heed MacArthur's request and allow him to blockade the China coast, bomb the Chinese mainland, and help Chiang Kai-shek's Nationalist forces to launch an invasion of China?

MacArthur's proposal provoked heated debate. MacArthur's supporters argued that quick, decisive action would bring a speedy end to the Korean conflict. Those who disagreed argued that an attack upon Communist China might cause the U.S.S.R. to support its Communist ally openly and thus start another world war.

MacArthur's opponents also pointed to another danger. If the United States committed its military forces to a major war in Asia, the Soviet Union would be free to do as it pleased in Europe.

Stalemate in Korea

By January 1951 President Truman had reached his decision. He ordered General MacArthur to establish the strongest possible defense line near the 38th parallel. But he forbade a blockade of the China coast, the bombing of China, and the use of Chiang's troops to invade China. The war in Korea was to remain strictly a "police action" intended only to protect South Korea. In 1951, therefore, the Korean War reached a stalemate.

But General MacArthur, refusing to accept Truman's decision as final, tried to appeal over the President's authority to prominent members of Congress. In April 1951 President Truman re-

General Douglas MacArthur commanded South Korean and UN troops during the Korean War. He is shown here (seated next to the driver) inspecting UN positions along the front line.

moved MacArthur from his post. "I could do nothing else and still be President," Truman explained. General Matthew B. Ridgway replaced MacArthur as Commander of the UN forces.

American policy and "Point Four"

During 1951 and 1952 the United States continued the rapid buildup of its land, sea, and air forces. The military buildup, however, was only part of America's response to the challenge of Communism in Europe, Asia, and other parts of the world. Through economic aid and technical assistance, the United States assumed a major responsibility for helping less fortunate areas of the world to raise their standards of living. The Marshall Plan was intended primarily for Europe. A new plan, the "Point Four" program, was aimed at underdeveloped areas anywhere in the world.

President Truman first announced the Point Four program in January 1949. "The United States," he said, "is embarking on a bold new program for making the benefits of our scientific advances and industrial progress available for the improvement and growth of underdeveloped areas." Of course, both the government and American businesses had been assisting underdeveloped countries for many years. The "bold new" part of the program consisted of bringing many scattered activities into a carefully planned, coordinated program.

The Point Four program got off to a slow start. But the Korean War convinced even the most hesitant Americans that the world was facing a grave crisis. By 1952 most Americans were persuaded that United States policy should include provisions for foreign aid and the strenthening of military defenses throughout the free world.

SECTION SURVEY

IDENTIFY: Chinese Nationalists, 38th parallel, police action; Ralph Bunche, Mao Tse-tung, Syngman Rhee, Douglas MacArthur.

1. Describe the postwar events that created tension in (a) the Middle East, (b) the Far East.
2. (a) How did the United States answer the challenge of the Korean situation? (b) Did President Truman assume powers not stated in the Constitution? Explain.
3. What issues provoked the "Great Debate" during the Korean War?
4. What made the Point Four program unique?

4 Continuing American efforts to meet the Communist challenge

In 1953 when President Eisenhower took office, he and his Secretary of State, John Foster Dulles, continued the bipartisan foreign policy that had been followed since America's entry into World War II.

Ending the Korean War

During the 1952 election campaign Eisenhower had promised to do everything within his power to end the Korean War. In December 1952 he visited the battle area for talks with political and military leaders. Peace talks were being carried on at this time in Panmunjom (PAN·MUHN·JUM) in Korea (see map, page 366). Finally, on July 27, 1953, North Korea and the UN signed an armistice agreement. This agreement recognized the division of Korea into two countries—North Korea and the Republic of South Korea.

In a formal treaty the United States promised to defend South Korea against attack. The United States also undertook to help the South Koreans improve their economic and social conditions.

Developments in Indochina

Only a few months after the Korean armistice, world peace was threatened by another crisis in the Far East. Ever since the end of World War II, Indochina, a French colony, had been torn by armed conflict. The Vietminh (VYET·meen), a Communist group, had been fighting to win control of the entire country from the French and their anti-Communist Vietnamese allies. When it became clear that Communist China was actively aiding the Vietminh, the United States began to send military equipment to the Vietnamese and French armies.

Early in 1954 the Vietminh, supported by the Chinese, launched a powerful drive against the French and their Vietnamese supporters. In May 1954 the key French fortress of Dienbienphu (dyen·byen·FOO) (see map, page 379) fell to the Communists.

In July a meeting was held in Geneva, Switzerland, to discuss Indochina's fate. Representatives from France, Indochina, Communist China, the Soviet Union, and Great Britain agreed to divide Indochina into three nations—Laos, Cambodia, and Vietnam. The area of Vietnam north of the 17th parallel became the Communist state of Vietminh, later North Vietnam; the portion of Vietnam south of that line became South Vietnam (see map, page 379).

Strengthening Western Europe

In the 1950's the United States continued its efforts to strengthen Western Europe. In October 1954 the United States and its European allies agreed to give the Federal Republic of West Germany full sovereign powers. They also agreed to admit West Germany to NATO, and to allow the new state to build an army of 500,000 troops to serve under the NATO command. The United States, Great Britain, and France also agreed to regard an attack upon West Germany as an attack upon themselves.

Atomic and hydrogen weapons

By the mid-1950's both the United States and the Soviet Union possessed hydrogen bombs. Faced with this fearsome development, the United States made vigorous efforts to work out an agreement with the Soviet Union to end the arms race. But the Soviets refused to accept international inspection within their own borders. Without such inspection, the United States refused to consider any agreement to destroy existing weapons or to stop the manufacture of nuclear weapons.

Hopes for change

In February 1956 startling news came out of the Soviet Union. Communist Party leader Nikita Khrushchev publicly attacked his predecessor, Josef Stalin, calling him a cruel tyrant. Stalin had died in 1953.

What was behind this attack? Was Khrushchev about to adopt a friendlier attitude toward the "free world"? Was he about to loosen the U.S.S.R.'s tight grip on its satellites in Eastern Europe? Would he be willing to end the arms race? Hope began to stir, and in the satellite countries people began to demand a greater degree of freedom from Soviet control.

Revolt in Poland

In October 1956 the leaders of the Communist Party in Poland elected an ardent Polish nationalist, Wladyslaw Gomulka (VLAH·dee·slaf go·MUL·ka), as first secretary of the party. Although a devoted Communist, Gomulka promised the Poles freedom of speech, press, and religion. Encouraged by Gomulka's stand, Poles staged anti-Soviet demonstrations in the streets. On several occasions they exchanged shots with Soviet troops.

The Polish revolt attracted worldwide attention. What would Khrushchev do? Instead of crushing the revolt, Khrushchev granted concessions. He withdrew some Soviet troops from Poland and granted some freedom to the Poles.

The Hungarian tragedy

Inspired by the example of the Poles, the Hungarians also rebelled against the Soviets. On October 23, 1956 students and workers rioted in the streets of Budapest.

The next morning Soviet tanks, guns, and armored cars, supported by jet planes, moved into Budapest. Violent fighting broke out as Hungarian "freedom fighters" resisted with improvised weapons. The rebellion spread as units of the Hungarian army joined the "freedom fighters."

For four days the fighting continued. Then, on October 28, the U.S.S.R. agreed to pull its troops out of Budapest. Two days later Imre Nagy (IM·reh NAHZH), Hungary's premier, promised the Hungarians free elections and an early end to the one-party dictatorship.

But even while the Hungarians were celebrating, the Soviet army was preparing an attack. On November 4 Soviet forces began a massive attack upon Budapest. "All Budapest is under fire," the Budapest radio reported. "The Russian gangsters have betrayed us."

Within a few days the Hungarian fight for freedom came to a tragic end. With all organized resistance ruthlessly crushed, a new Hungarian government, a puppet of the U.S.S.R., began to round up the rebels and imprison them or deport them to the Soviet Union. Refugees by the thousands fled across the frontier into Austria.

Egypt and the Suez Canal

In the same week that the Hungarians rebelled, another crisis developed, this time over the Suez Canal in Egypt. For a few tense days the world hovered on the brink of another war.

The Suez Canal, connecting the Mediterranean and the Red seas, ran entirely through Egyptian territory. Owned and operated by an international company, the Canal was open on equal terms to ships of all nations. By arrangement with Egypt, British troops were stationed at the Canal Zone to safeguard it and protect British interests.

After World War II the Egyptians became increasingly dissatisfied with British military occupation of the Canal Zone. Finally, in 1954, the British government agreed to withdraw its forces. In June 1956 the last British troops withdrew.

In the meantime, in 1954, Colonel Gamal Abdel Nasser led a successful revolution, overthrew the king of Egypt, and became President of the Republic of Egypt. Nasser was determined to modernize the country and extend Egyptian influence throughout the Middle East. One of his major plans involved building a large irrigation dam and electric generating plant at Aswan on the Nile River. When the Soviet Union indicated an interest in financing the dam, the United States offered Egypt a $56 million loan for the Aswan project. But when it became clear that the U.S.S.R. could not at the time afford to finance the project, Secretary of State Dulles withdrew the United States offer.° Great Britain and the World Bank immediately withdrew similar offers. Nasser, furious at this blow to his plans, announced that Egypt was going to seize the Canal and operate it. The Western powers tried in vain to persuade Nasser to agree to international control by the 18 nations that regularly used the Canal.

The Suez crisis

Such was the tense situation when on October 29, 1956, the Israeli army moved rapidly westward through the Sinai Peninsula toward the Suez Canal. The Israeli government announced that its troops had invaded Egyptian territory to forestall a carefully planned attack upon Israel by Egypt.

On October 30 the British and French issued

° In 1959 the Soviet Union agreed to provide money and engineers to build the dam. Construction began in 1960 and was completed in 1969.

Hungarian freedom fighters rebelled against Soviet rule of their country in October 1956. The revolt ended abruptly when Soviet troops crushed the rebellion.

a 12-hour ultimatum. They demanded that Egypt and Israel cease fighting and allow French and British troops temporarily to occupy key points in the Canal Zone. When Egypt refused, the British and French bombed Egyptian airfields and moved troops into the northern part of the Canal Zone.

Then, denouncing Israel, France, and Great Britain as aggressors, the Soviet Union threatened to intervene with force if the three nations did not immediately withdraw.

The United States now found itself in an embarrassing position. Great Britain and France, its allies in NATO, had ignored the UN, and had created a situation that could easily lead to a general war. Moreover, the United States was unwilling to permit the Soviet Union to claim that it was the only champion of Egypt and other small nations against "Western imperialism." Reluctantly the United States delegates to the UN voted in favor of a General Assembly resolution calling for an immediate cease-fire and the withdrawal of British, French, and Israeli troops. Great Britain, France, and Israel accepted these terms.

The Eisenhower Doctrine

As an immediate result of the Suez crisis, the United States adopted what came to be known as the Eisenhower Doctrine. Early in January 1957 President Eisenhower asked Congress (1) to authorize him to use military force if this were requested by any Middle Eastern nation to check Communist aggression; and (2) to set aside $200 million to help those Middle Eastern countries that desired such aid from the United States. Congress granted both requests. The United States thus indicated its intention of checking Communist influence in the Middle East by filling the vacuum left by the decline of British and French influence.

The Eisenhower Doctrine was soon tested. Early in 1958 Egypt and Syria joined together to form the United Arab Republic (U.A.R.). The U.A.R., supported by Communists throughout the Arab world, was strongly anti-Western. Egypt's Nasser, President of the U.A.R., urged the other Arab nations to join the U.A.R.

During the next few months the Arab world was torn by intrigue. Rebellion broke out against the pro-Western government of Lebanon. In Iraq army officers killed the pro-Western leaders and seized control of the government. The new Iraqi government had the support of the Soviet Union and the U.A.R. The neighboring states of Lebanon and Jordan, now convinced that their pro-Western governments would soon be overthrown too, appealed to the United States and Great Britain for help. President Eisenhower immediately sent American marines to Lebanon, and Great Britain flew paratroopers into Jordan.

For several weeks American and British forces remained ready for any emergency. Late in September, after the Secretary-General of the UN reported that the situation was improving, Great Britain and the United States withdrew their troops.

One of the major plans of Egypt's President Nasser was the building of a great irrigation dam at Aswan on the Nile River. The temples of Abu Simbel, one of which is shown here, were threatened by the project and had to be moved to a new site.

The race into space

The crisis in the Middle East was not the major development of 1957–58. The most startling news, which broke on October 4, 1957, was compressed into a single word: *Sputnik*. The Russians had succeeded in orbiting an artificial satellite around the earth.

The American public, long convinced that no nation was superior to the United States in science and technology, was shocked. Recognizing the Soviet achievement, President Eisenhower assured the American people that the United States was developing its own rocket and missile program. On January 31, 1958, the United States launched a small satellite, Explorer I, into orbit, and the space race was under way.

Rockets powerful enough to carry satellites into space could also be used to launch atomic and hydrogen bombs. By 1960 both the Soviet Union and the United States were building stockpiles of Intercontinental Ballistic Missiles (ICBM's) equipped with nuclear warheads. Pushbutton war that could destroy millions of lives in a single instant had become a dreadful possibility.

Rising tensions over Berlin

Meanwhile, in November 1958, the Soviet premier issued an ultimatum on Berlin. Khrushchev gave the Western powers six months to agree to withdraw from Berlin and make it a free, demilitarized city. If by May 27, 1959, the Western powers had not agreed, the Soviet Union would turn over to Communist East Germany complete control of all lines of communication to West Berlin. If the Western powers then tried to gain access to West Berlin without the permission of the East German government, the Soviet Union would help the East Germans to meet force with force. The United States, Great Britain, and France re-

The May 1959 meeting of Premier Khrushchev (left) and President Eisenhower eased cold war tensions and encouraged hope that the Soviet Union was willing to negotiate with the Western powers.

plied by firmly repeating that they would remain in West Berlin.

The temporary easing of tension

During 1959, however, the situation began to improve. Instead of insisting that the Western powers get out of Berlin by May 27, the Soviet Union met with the Western leaders in a Big Four foreign ministers' conference. Although the conference failed to reach any important agreements, it did open the door to further negotiations.

Premier Khrushchev himself seemed to be opening the door a bit wider when, in September, he visited the United States. At the end of his visit he and Eisenhower issued a joint declaration, stating that the most serious issue facing the world was general disarmament. They also expressed agreement that the problem of Berlin and "all outstanding international questions should be set-

SOURCES

DWIGHT D. EISENHOWER'S DISARMAMENT PROPOSALS (1955)

I should address myself for a moment principally to the delegates from the Soviet Union, because our two great countries admittedly possess new and terrible weapons in quantities which do give rise in other parts of the world, or reciprocally, to the fear and danger of surprise attack.

I propose, therefore, that we take a practical step, that we begin an arrangement very quickly; as between ourselves—immediately. These steps would include:

To give each other a complete blueprint of our military establishments . . .

Next, to provide within our countries facilities for aerial photography to the other country. . . .

tled, not by the application of force, but by peaceful means through negotiation."

Encouraged by Khrushchev's apparent willingness to negotiate, the Western powers agreed to meet with the Soviet Premier at a Summit Conference.

Summit Conference plans abandoned

The Summit Conference was never held. Early in May 1960, shortly before the conference was scheduled to open in Paris, Premier Khrushchev charged the United States with "aggression." He announced that on May 1 the Soviets had shot down a United States plane flying over Soviet territory.

American officials at first insisted that the U-2, as the plane was called, was engaged in weather research and had strayed off its course. Later the United States admitted that the U-2 had been engaged in aerial reconnaissance.

Premier Khrushchev was furious. He refused to take part in the Summit Conference unless Eisenhower agreed to stop all such future flights, apologize for past acts of "aggression," and punish those responsible for the flights.

Hoping that the meeting could still be held, President Eisenhower announced that the U-2

flights had been stopped and would not be resumed. He refused, however, to apologize. Khrushchev, refusing to accept anything less than an apology, left for home. Plans for the conference had to be abandoned.

During the remaining months of his second term President Eisenhower continued to seek ways of reducing world tensions. His efforts were fruitless. Khrushchev refused to budge.

SECTION SURVEY

IDENTIFY: Sputnik, Aswan Dam, ICBM, U-2, bipartisan foreign policy; John Foster Dulles, Gamal Abdel Nasser.

1. How did each of the following reveal the continuing challenge of Communism: (a) the Korean armistice, (b) developments in Indochina, (c) tension over Berlin?
2. (a) What were the causes and results of the Suez crisis in 1956? (b) Explain the position taken by the United States.
3. Why was the Summit Conference of May 1960 not held?
4. What was the importance of the Eisenhower Doctrine as a move in the Cold War?

CHAPTER SURVEY

INQUIRING INTO HISTORY

1. Was the Korean War a victory for the United States and the United Nations? Why or why not?
2. How successful was the Marshall Plan? What was its basic philosophy? Explain.
3. How effective were the actions taken by the United States during the years 1945–60 in meeting the challenge of Communism?
4. "The United Nations will not be able to prevent a third world war." Do you agree or disagree? Explain.
5. The Eisenhower Doctrine was really an extension of the containment policy first developed during the Truman administration. Discuss.
6. The launching of Sputnik I led to much self-examination and self-criticism on the part of Americans. (a) Explain. (b) Indicate specific results.

RELATING PAST TO PRESENT

1. What do you think would be gained if the United Nations were given additional powers in order to protect world peace? What might be lost?
2. Compare the twentieth-century "race into space" with the fifteenth-century search for an all-water route to Asia. What are some similarities? What are some differences?

DEVELOPING SOCIAL SCIENCE SKILLS

1. In the 1950's and 1960's the United States frequently became involved in the internal affairs of nations in Latin America, Asia, Africa, and the Middle East in order to prevent Communist takeovers. Do you think such intervention in foreign countries was justified? Use evidence to support your opinion.
2. Study the work of the United Nations since its beginning and then make a list of its chief failures and accomplishments. How would you account for its successes or failures? Do you think the UN is an effective peacekeeping force in the world today? Why or why not?

CHAPTER 23
RE-EXAMINING THE NATION'S ROLE IN WORLD AFFAIRS
1960-1970's

World tensions were close to the snapping point when, in January 1961, John F. Kennedy became President. During the election campaign Kennedy had predicted that the 1960's would be one of the most critical periods in the nation's history. As the years passed, first under the leadership of President Kennedy, then under Presidents Johnson and Nixon, this prediction proved to be well founded.

By the end of the 1960's many unresolved problems had reached the crisis point and other, newer problems demanded attention. Adding to these challenges facing the American people was the fact that many of the most urgent problems were worldwide in scope—pollution of the environment, nuclear disarmament, food for the rapidly growing population. Furthermore, these problems could be solved only through international cooperation.

Of first concern, because it affected all other problems, was America's military involvement in Vietnam. The Southeast Asian conflict, costly in lives and resources, deeply troubled large numbers of Americans.

In one sense, Vietnam was part of a larger issue confronting Americans. The larger issue concerned a clear and direct question: Had the United States assumed more responsibilities around the world than it could meet, even with all its wealth and power?

These were among the issues troubling Americans as the decade of the 1960's drew to a close and the nation approached its 200th anniversary in the 1970's.

THE CHAPTER IN OUTLINE

1. American assumption of global responsibilities.

2. Deepening involvement in Vietnam during Johnson's administration.

3. Attempts to relax world tensions during the Nixon-Ford administrations.

1450   1750   1800   1850   1900   1950   1980's

1 American assumption of global responsibilities

During the 1960's and 1970's the deadly possibility of nuclear war and the challenge of Communist aggression continued to haunt Americans. At the same time other far-reaching developments thrust increasingly heavy demands upon the American people and their leaders.

The world in swift transition

One of the major developments was the growing competition American business faced from Japan, the Soviet Union, and the Common Market countries of Western Europe. These nations, with modern industrial plants and the newest, most efficient equipment, had become serious competitors of the United States for world markets.

Another revolutionary development was the entry of new nations into the world community. By the mid-1970's, UN membership had grown to 142 nations. The greatest part of this growth occurred during the 1960's and 1970's. Most of the new nations, whose population included more than 1 billion people, had emerged from former colonies in the underdeveloped areas of Asia and Africa.

Changing relationships of nations

Still another far-reaching development was the changing balance of world power. After the end of World War II the Communist nations, led by the Soviet Union, had been aligned on one side, the United States and its allies aligned on the other. During the 1960's this alignment began to crumble.

The newly independent nations of Asia and Africa were reluctant to tie themselves to either the Soviet Union or the United States. Led by India, these "uncommitted" nations became increasingly important in world affairs.

Meanwhile the solid front of Communism was breaking up as Communist China challenged the Soviet Union's leadership of world Communism. By the late 1960's the split between the two most powerful Communist countries was complete.

The solid front among anti-Communist nations was also becoming strained. President Charles de Gaulle of France began to challenge America's leadership role. He hoped to establish France at the head of a "third force," a group of nations with power and influence equal to that of the United States and the Soviet Union.

By the 1960's all of the powerful nations—both Communist and non-Communist—were competing for the markets as well as the political support of the underdeveloped nations. Thus many of the world crises facing the United States grew out of the problems of Africa, Asia, and Latin America.

Trouble in Africa

President Kennedy had to deal with the problems of America's relations with the emerging African nations. The most serious crisis developed in the Congo (now the Republic of Zaire).

The Congo, a former Belgian colony, became independent in June 1960. Even before the independence celebrations ended, many rival groups—among them pro-Communist and pro-Western groups—began to battle for control of the government. The problem grew worse when the mineral-rich Katanga province seceded from the newly formed nation.

In the midst of this chaos, the Congo government appealed to the UN. The UN responded by sending a security force of troops from African and Asian nations to police the troubled country.

Although the UN force managed to prevent a full-scale civil war, it was not at first able to end the bloodshed. A new crisis developed in 1961 when Patrice Lumumba, leader of the pro-Communist faction, was assassinated. Soviet Premier Khrushchev demanded withdrawal of all UN troops and threatened to intervene. President Kennedy replied with a warning that the United States would defend the UN operation.

With firm American backing, the UN continued its difficult peacemaking operation in the Congo. By 1965 the fighting ended and Katanga province rejoined the nation. By the late 1960's most scars of the civil war seemed healed, and the Congo (Zaire) became one of the most prosperous African nations.

The Arab-Israeli conflict

As you have read, the Middle East had long been an area of international tension (pages 364 and 369). After the Suez crisis, the bitter quarrel and occasional raids between Israel and the Arab nations continued.

In 1967 Israelis believed that the Arab nations were massing large military forces to destroy Israel. In June 1967 powerful Israeli forces struck at Egypt, Jordan, and Syria, defeating them in a war lasting only six days. After the war Israel kept large areas of land that had belonged to these three Arab states.

The Arab nations were bitter at their defeat and more determined than ever to destroy Israel. They began sending trained guerrilla fighters into Israel. The Israelis continued to strike back.

For many years the Soviet Union sent aid of various kinds, including military aid, to the Arab nations but not to Israel. The United States tried to help the Arab nations overcome their poverty, and it gave military aid to help those nations resist Communism. It also gave military aid to Israel.

In the late 1960's the Middle East remained a danger spot in the world. The Arab nations and Israel were constantly raiding or attacking each other's border areas. The United States and the Soviet Union continued to provide military aid and tried to strengthen their influence in the Middle East. In 1970 the United States was able to secure a truce in the border raids, but a peaceful settlement of the Arab-Israeli conflict still seemed a distant prospect.

Cuba, a Communist beachhead

The Kennedy administration also inherited the extremely serious problem of Cuba. Early in 1959 guerrilla forces led by Fidel Castro overthrew the government of Cuban dictator Fulgencio Batista (bah·TEES·tah). And at first the United States welcomed Castro's rise to power as a victory for democracy.

American sympathy rapidly faded, however, when Castro began to act like a ruthless dictator. He failed to hold the elections he had promised. He put to death hundreds of political enemies and jailed thousands unsympathetic to his regime. He took control of foreign-owned property. In addition, Castro began to lash out at "Yankees" and to turn to Communist nations for support. Castro accepted a Soviet offer of military aid if the United States interfered in Cuba.

At first the United States adopted a policy of patient waiting. During the summer of 1960, however, American policy hardened. The United States (1) placed a temporary embargo on the purchase of Cuban sugar; (2) announced a sweeping program of economic aid to Latin America; and (3) urged the Organization of American States (O.A.S.) to condemn Cuba's actions.

The Bay of Pigs

When Kennedy took office in January 1961 he inherited a plan developed under Eisenhower to overthrow the Castro government. During 1960 a force of anti-Castro Cubans had been trained at bases in Central America with the active support of the United States Central Intelligence Agency (CIA). The plan called for an invasion of Cuba, during which the Cuban underground would rise, join the invasion forces, and overthrow the Castro government. President Kennedy decided to allow the plan to be carried out.

On April 17, 1961, the invasion force landed on the beaches of the Bahía de Cochinos, or the

This dramatic photograph of a Soviet missile base in Cuba was taken by an American U-2 spy plane.

Bay of Pigs. The landing ended in tragedy for the anti-Castro "Freedom Fighters," most of whom were killed or captured. In reply to a storm of criticism, President Kennedy admitted that the invasion attempt had been a mistake, for which he personally assumed full responsibility.

Following the Bay of Pigs invasion attempt, the Soviet Union stepped up its shipments of military equipment to Cuba. In December 1961 Castro declared publicly, "I am a Marxist-Leninist and will be one until the day I die." A month later the O.A.S. voted to exclude Cuba from that organization. The United States had already cut off its trade with Cuba, but failed to persuade the O.A.S. to take similar action.

A world crisis

Another crisis over Cuba in the fall of 1962 brought the world to the brink of a nuclear holocaust. In mid-October American intelligence sources confirmed reports that the Soviet Union was equipping Cuba with long-range jet bombers and offensive missiles capable of delivering nuclear bombs throughout the Caribbean, much of Central and South America, and most of the eastern United States. On October 22, with the evidence before him, President Kennedy ordered the United States Navy to establish a blockade—or "quarantine"—against any further shipment of "offensive" weapons to Cuba. He also demanded that the Soviet Union immediately dismantle the missile bases and withdraw Soviet missiles and bombers from Cuba.

The world waited tensely for Khrushchev's reaction. Faced with the choice between nuclear war or meeting Kennedy's demands, Khrushchev backed down. During the next few weeks the Soviets began to dismantle the missile bases and remove the missiles and bombers. Nonetheless, a Communist nation supported by the Soviet Union was now established only 90 miles from the shores of the United States.

The Alliance for Progress

One of the Western Hemisphere's answers to the Communist challenge was an ambitious program called the Alliance for Progress, outlined by President Kennedy in March 1961. The charter launching the program was signed by the United States and 19 Latin-American countries (all but Cuba) five months later.

The Alliance members agreed to undertake a 10-year program to improve social and economic conditions in Latin America. Finances for the program were to come from private and government sources in Latin America and the United States, as well as from Japan, Western Europe, and international agencies such as the World Bank.

The Alliance for Progress got off to a slow start. Nevertheless, during the first four years the United States contributed $4.5 billion to the program, the Latin-American countries $22 billion. Some progress was made, but the results were disappointing. Much of the money was used to help business interests and military forces in Latin America rather than the masses of poor people. Congress, increasingly impatient, began to reduce the budgets for the Alliance.

The Dominican crisis

One of the most serious crises in United States relations with Latin America developed in the spring of 1965 when revolution plunged the Dominican Republic into chaos.

Calling the situation "grave," President Johnson promptly ordered 400 marines into the capital, Santo Domingo, to protect the lives of Americans there. This was the first time since 1926 that the marines had been ordered into a Latin-American country. During the next two weeks 22,000 additional troops landed, and 10,000 more stood by in navy vessels offshore.

President Johnson justified the large-scale intervention on the ground that it was necessary to (1) end the blood bath, (2) prevent a possible Communist takeover, and (3) enable the people to hold

American troops were sent to the Dominican Republic when a revolution broke out there. Although these troops were soon withdrawn, this incident caused a crisis in United States relations with Latin America.

free elections. He made it clear, however, that the American forces would be withdrawn as soon as the O.A.S. took responsibility for maintaining order.

Meeting in emergency sessions, representatives of the O.A.S. accepted the responsibility. By midsummer a small force of troops from four Latin-American nations had arrived in Santo Domingo, and some of the United States troops had been withdrawn. In late August both sides accepted a provisional president who governed the country until elections were held in June 1966.

Continuing conflict in Southeast Asia

Crises continued to develop in Asia, as well as in Latin America and Africa, during the 1960's. The major crisis areas were the new countries of Southeast Asia—Laos, Cambodia, and North and South Vietnam.

The tiny kingdom of Laos was divided into three political factions—pro-Western, Communist, and neutral. In an effort to secure a strong pro-Western government, the United States poured millions of dollars into Laos. When these efforts failed, the Kennedy administration reversed its policy. In 1962, after lengthy negotiations with the Laotian factions and the Communist powers, a neutral government was established in Laos.

The United States also gave considerable military and economic aid to Cambodia in an effort to secure a pro-Western government. As in Laos, however, the policy failed, and in 1963 Cambodia asked the United States to withdraw its military and technical personnel. You will read later about further American involvement in Cambodia and in South Vietnam.

Communist China

Meanwhile the shadow of aggression by Communist China continued to darken much of Asia.

In 1959 the Chinese Communists took over Tibet, and in 1962, following a border dispute, they launched a large-scale attack on India. In response to appeals from the Indian government, the United States and Great Britain began to airlift military supplies to the hard-pressed Indian troops. Then, as suddenly as the Communist Chinese had attacked, they announced a cease-fire and called for negotiations. But India, shocked by what it considered unprovoked aggression, began to build up its defenses to prepare for any future trouble.

The Sino-Soviet break

Communist China's attack on India was embarrassing to the Soviet Union, which had long maintained friendly relations with India. Western observers believed that Communist China had launched its offensive without consulting the Soviets.

But there was clearer evidence that the Chinese and Soviet Communists were drawing apart. During the early 1960's the Soviets began pulling their military and technical advisers out of Communist China. And by 1964 the leaders of the Soviet Union and Communist China were openly attacking each other's policies.

The smoldering issue of Berlin

This break in the solid front of Communism provided one reason for Khrushchev's failure to press his threats against West Berlin (page 363). In 1961 Khrushchev renewed his threat to make a separate peace treaty with East Germany. He warned that the treaty would end the Western nations' rights of free access to West Berlin. President Kennedy in turn warned that the United States would not abandon the people of West Berlin.

In August 1961 the East German government began to erect a wall along the line between East and West Berlin. The Berlin wall cut off the escape of East Germans into West Germany. And it soon became a grim symbol of the conflicts between the Communist and anti-Communist nations of Europe. President Kennedy repeated that the Western powers would not be forced out by Soviet threats. Khrushchev abandoned his 1961 treaty deadline, only to renew it for 1962. Although by the end of 1963 the Soviet leader had not carried out his threats, the Berlin issue remained unresolved.

The nuclear test ban and disarmament

In August 1961 Premier Khrushchev also announced that the Soviet Union intended to resume nuclear testing. This news shocked people everywhere, for in 1958 the nuclear powers—the United States, Great Britain, and the Soviet Union—had reached an understanding that they would suspend all testing for three years. The three-year period had not yet expired. President Kennedy reacted promptly, warning that if the Soviets carried out their plans, the United States would be forced in the interests of its own defense to resume nuclear testing.

Disregarding this warning and earnest pleas from nations throughout the world, the U.S.S.R. began a series of nuclear tests in the fall of 1961. The following spring, after the Soviet Union had turned down repeated pleas for a fully effective test ban, the United States began its own tests.

Despite the resumption of testing, the United States continued to press for a nuclear test ban and a general arms reduction. The Soviet Union finally agreed to return to the conference table. During

1962, however, negotiations continued to be deadlocked on the old question of international inspection.

The first breaks in the long deadlock came in 1963. In June Moscow and Washington agreed on a "hot line" to provide direct teletype communications between the two capitals to help prevent nuclear war by accident.

In July American, British, and Soviet representatives reached an agreement to ban nuclear tests in the atmosphere, under water, and in space. Underground testing would continue. The United States Senate ratified the agreement, and it went into effect in October 1963.

Continuity and change in foreign policy

To meet the nation's responsibilities in a rapidly changing world, the Kennedy-Johnson administration generally followed the basic foreign policy developed under Truman and Eisenhower. But there were new phases as well as continuity in foreign policy during the early 1960's. The Trade Expansion Act of 1962 was passed to increase world trade as well as to meet the growing competition of the Common Market countries. The Kennedy-Johnson administration also sponsored programs to strengthen international cultural relations by sending outstanding American musicians, theater groups, writers, and artists to visit friendly, neutral, and Communist countries.

The Peace Corps

By far the most imaginative new program, however, was the Peace Corps, an organization of Americans who volunteered to live among the people of underdeveloped lands and to help them with their day-to-day problems. President Kennedy created the Peace Corps by executive order in March 1961. The following September Congress authorized it as a permanent organization. That same month the first American volunteers arrived in the African nation of Ghana to serve as teachers.

From the beginning the Peace Corps was a notable success. By 1970 about 10,000 Americans, mostly young men and women, were serving overseas in 59 different countries. The Peace Corps, with its emphasis on youth and its dedication to the service of humanity, symbolized America's desire to provide humane assistance as well as economic and military leadership in the non-Communist world.

SECTION SURVEY

IDENTIFY: Congo crisis, Sino-Soviet break, Berlin wall, CIA, hot line, O.A.S., Peace Corps; Fidel Castro.

1. (a) Describe world developments that placed heavy demands upon the United States in the 1960's. (b) Why did the United States feel an obligation to respond to these demands?
2. The Cuban missile crisis brought the world to the brink of a nuclear holocaust in 1962. Explain.
3. Review United States relations with Latin America in (a) the Alliance for Progress, (b) the Dominican crisis.
4. In the 1960's Communist China and Southeast Asia again became major American concerns. Why?
5. The nuclear test ban and disarmament were issues that reflected the "balance of power" concept between the major powers. Comment.

2 Deepening involvement in Vietnam during Johnson's administration

In January 1965 Lyndon B. Johnson dedicated his administration to the solution of crucial domestic problems—racial tensions, poverty, injustice. By the end of 1965, however, it was clear that the United States was waging two major wars —the war against prejudice, poverty, and injustice at home and the conflict in Vietnam abroad.

America's limited involvement

American involvement in Vietnam grew out of United States' efforts to prevent Communists from taking over the new countries of Southeast Asia (page 379). During the late 1950's and early 1960's, guerrillas known as the Vietcong, supported by Communist North Vietnam, ranged over the entire countryside of South Vietnam, sometimes even as far as the capital of Saigon (see map, page 379). By the spring of 1961 the struggle was going badly for the anti-Communist government of President Ngo Dinh Diem (NOH DIN ZIM), whose repressive policies had antagonized many of his own people.

To strengthen South Vietnam, the Kennedy administration in 1962 sent some 8,000 troops to train the South Vietnamese armies, to transport the South Vietnamese forces from one danger point to another, and to serve as military advisers. American efforts were frustrated, however, by the refusal of many South Vietnamese to support President Diem's unpopular government. Finally, in the fall of 1963, Diem was assassinated and his government was overthrown. For most of the next two years military leaders ruled the country.

Although by the end of 1964 the number of American advisers and technicians had risen to some 23,000, they were not authorized to engage in combat. As late as October 1964 President Johnson had stated that his administration had no intention of committing American troops to a war in Asia. "We are not," he declared, "about to send American boys nine or ten thousand miles away from home to do what Asian boys ought to be doing for themselves."

A turning point

Only two months earlier, however, the United States had taken a major step toward deeper involvement. In spite of some uncertainty about what had happened, the President announced on August 4, 1964, that two American destroyers had been attacked in the Gulf of Tonkin by North Vietnamese patrol torpedo boats and that he had immediately ordered retaliatory attacks.

Three days later Congress adopted what became known as the Gulf of Tonkin Resolution. This resolution gave the President power to "take all necessary measures to repel any armed attack against the forces of the United States and to prevent further aggression."

Persuasion and force

By early 1965 the Johnson administration was convinced that the South Vietnamese armies, although outnumbering the Vietcong by about six to one, were in danger of being defeated. To prevent this, on February 28 President Johnson ordered United States planes to begin bombing selected targets in North Vietnam. The air strikes were intended to slow down North Vietnamese infiltration into South Vietnam and to force the North Vietnamese government in the capital at Hanoi to negotiate a settlement. In March, as a further demonstration of America's determination to support South Vietnam, the President for the first time committed American troops to active combat.

But President Johnson added persuasion to force in his effort to bring North Vietnam to the conference table. In April he declared that the United States was prepared to offer $1 billion of economic aid to Southeast Asia, including North Vietnam, as soon as the fighting was ended. Several weeks later the President ordered a halt to air attacks on North Vietnam.

None of these actions produced the hoped for results. The North Vietnamese continued to insist that negotiations would not be considered until the bombing had been ended unconditionally and all American troops had been withdrawn from Vietnam. Washington responded by resuming the air strikes and by increasing American troop strength. By the end of 1965 nearly 125,000 Americans had been committed to the war effort.

Late in December President Johnson made another major effort to reach a peaceful settlement. All bombing was halted from December 24 to January 31. During this period the State Department carried on a major diplomatic effort, involving talks with 115 governments, in the hope they would help persuade the Hanoi government to negotiate. The effort failed.

Escalation of the war

After its "peace offensive" failed, the Johnson administration began to increase American military might in Vietnam.

The United States relied heavily upon air power. By the end of 1968 Americans had dropped more bombs on North Vietnam than had been used during all of World War II. By September 1968 the war was costing Americans more than $25 billion a year. American forces in Vietnam now numbered some 540,000, and American casualties

THE CONFLICT IN VIETNAM

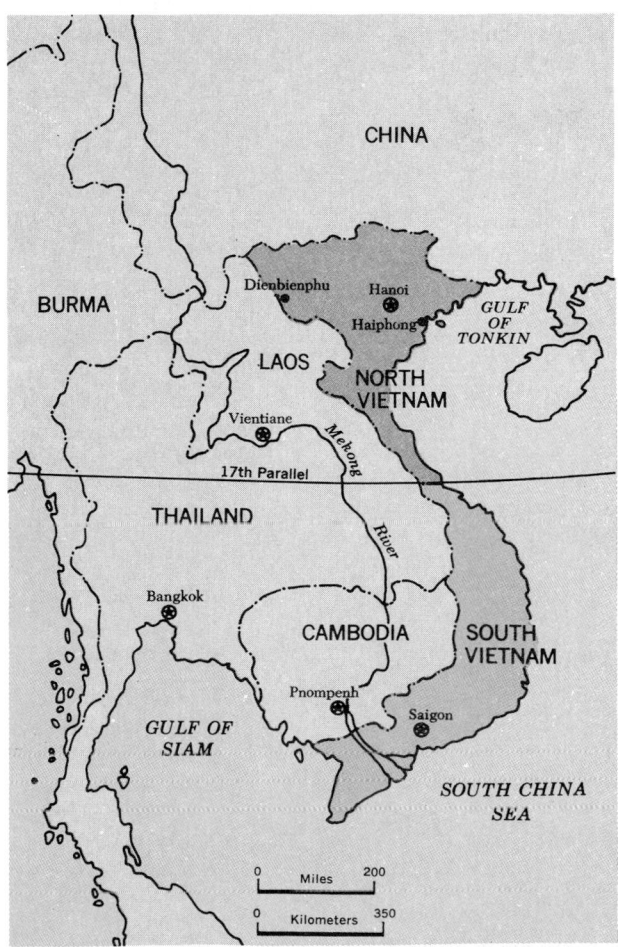

up to that time totaled more than 27,000 killed and 92,000 seriously wounded.

In both North and South Vietnam, the Air Force poured bombs, napalm, rockets, and machinegun fire upon Vietcong supply routes, on guerrilla jungle hideouts, and on villages controlled by or suspected of hiding guerrillas. With support from the air, South Vietnamese and American troops carried out "search-and-destroy" operations. In areas they could not hold and defend they moved the people to refugee centers and burned the villages.

Dislocation of Vietnamese life

The war had a shattering impact on the Vietnamese, North and South alike. Although the air strikes in North Vietnam were aimed at weapons supply depots, roads, bridges, and invasion routes, North Vietnamese civilians were often the victims.

The people of South Vietnam—men, women, and children—bore the heaviest burden, however. By 1968 more than 1.6 million troops° were fighting in a country about the size of the state of Washington. Moreover, there were no "front lines" in this guerrilla warfare. Every village was a potential battleground.

The Vietcong, well organized and strengthened in some areas by North Vietnamese army regulars, avoided large-scale fighting. Instead they used terrorism—bombs planted in a country mar-

---

° On the allied side almost 750,000 South Vietnamese, 540,000 Americans, about 45,000 South Koreans, and about 15,000 Australians, New Zealanders, Thais, and Filipinos. For the enemy, an estimated 300,000, including the Vietcong and North Vietnamese regulars.

---

ketplace or in a busy city and the torture or assassination of unfriendly village leaders. The Vietcong relied largely upon hit-and-run tactics, striking suddenly and then disappearing into the surrounding jungles.

This kind of warfare produced widespread devastation and human misery. By the end of 1967 civilian casualties, the victims of Vietcong terror or allied counterattack, totaled about 100,000 to 150,000 a year. By 1968 at least 2 million of the 16 million people of South Vietnam had become refugees. These people were crowded into the cities, housed in refugee camps, or relocated in "secure" villages free from Vietcong control.

The NLF

The Vietcong were the fighting force of a political organization known as the National Liberation Front (NLF). The NLF was organized in 1960 for the purpose of overthrowing the South Vietnamese government and seizing control of the country. It operated as a "shadow" organization, with its own members paralleling legal South Vietnamese officials at every government level.

From its national headquarters (assumed to be mobile but possibly located in the jungle close to the Cambodian border), the NLF directed its "officials" in the cities, towns, and villages of South Vietnam. Through this "shadow" government it levied taxes, "enlisted" men and women for its fighting forces, and organized terrorism and guerrilla warfare. As the war intensified, the Vietcong were strengthened by troops from the well-trained and well-equipped armies of North Vietnam.

The "other" war

The Saigon government, supported by the

SOURCES

THE GULF OF TONKIN RESOLUTION (1964)

Whereas naval units of the Communist regime in Vietnam, in violation of the principles of the Charter of the United Nations and of international law, have deliberately and repeatedly attacked United States naval vessels lawfully present in international waters, and have thereby created a serious threat to international peace; and

Whereas these attacks are part of a deliberate and systematic campaign of aggression that the Communist regime in North Vietnam has been waging against its neighbors and the nations joined with them in the collective defense of their freedom; . . . Now therefore, be it

Resolved by the Senate and House of Representatives of the United States of America in Congress assembled, That the Congress approves and supports the determination of the President, as Commander in Chief, to take all necessary measures to repel any armed attack against the forces of the United States and to prevent further aggression.

American soldiers had to learn to fight a guerrilla war in the hot, jungle terrain of Vietnam. This conflict was the longest, most unpopular war that the United States has ever fought.

United States, was, in fact, engaged in two major contests—one military, the other political. To win the military effort, it had to root out the NLF "shadow" government and protect South Vietnam's cities and villages from terrorism and guerrilla warfare. To win the political contest, the Saigon government had to convince the Vietnamese people that it genuinely cared about their welfare.

From the start the United States stimulated Saigon's social and economic efforts with economic aid and technical assistance. At the same time it urged the Saigon government to move more rapidly toward the reform of its undemocratic character and the elimination of existing graft and corruption.

The balance sheet in the "other" war

A South Vietnamese election in the fall of 1967 was somewhat encouraging. Since President Diem's assassination in 1963 the country had been ruled by military leaders. The election was the first step toward the return of an elected government and the drafting of a constitution. Defying the Vietcong, who tried everything including violence to sabotage the elections, an estimated 51 percent of the eligible voters went to the polls. General Nguyen Van Thieu (NWIN VAN TYOO) became President.

Further encouragement came at the end of 1967 with a report by the civilian head of America's social and economic program in South Vietnam. According to this report, two thirds of the villages were "totally" or "reasonably" secure and free from Vietcong control. However, many Americans in Vietnam did not share the report's optimism. Other studies revealed that many South Vietnamese did not believe that the Saigon government was really interested in their welfare or that it could protect them from the Vietcong even if it wanted to.

The Tet offensive

Events in early 1968 demonstrated that Vietnamese doubts and fears were justified. Early in February the Vietcong and North Vietnamese army regulars opened the powerful Tet offensive—so-called because it was carried out during the Tet, or lunar New Year holidays. In a coordinated campaign they attacked the "secure" cities of South Vietnam, seizing partial control of or terrorizing 26 provincial capitals.

The South Vietnamese and American troops soon regained control of the capitals. But the price of "victory" came high, for in the course of battle large sections of several cities were blasted into rubble. Equally serious, the Vietcong recovered control of large areas of the countryside.

The Tet offensive dealt a staggering blow to an earlier prediction by General William Westmoreland, commander of America's military forces in South Vietnam, that the enemy was being defeated. It also demonstrated that the "other war"—the effort of the Saigon government to win the allegiance of the Vietnamese people—was still far from won.

The start of the Paris peace talks

At the end of March 1968, with the Tet offensive still a raw memory, President Johnson declared that the United States intended to limit its bombing of North Vietnam. Starting immediately, he said, American air strikes would be confined to invasion routes and to the area immediately north of the Demilitarized Zone (DMZ)—a supposedly "neutral" strip of land separating North and South Vietnam.

The Hanoi government responded with the long-awaited offer to begin peace talks. After weeks of discussion the United States and North Vietnam agreed to hold the talks in Paris, where they began in May 1968.

Criticisms of Johnson's Vietnam policies

The opening of the peace talks did not check widespread criticism among Americans of President Johnson's conduct of foreign affairs. The immediate issue was, of course, Vietnam. But beyond that conflict was the larger problem of the nation's role as a world leader.

As for Vietnam, growing numbers of citizens were convinced that the commitment of American troops to a land war in Asia had been a grave mistake. They rejected the administration's view that the principal enemy was the Communist government of North Vietnam. On the contrary, they argued, the war was largely a civil conflict in which the Vietcong were trying to overthrow what they considered the corrupt and unrepresentative government of South Vietnam. Moreover, they added, the United States was destroying South Vietnam in the process of "saving it" from the Communists. They urged President Johnson to end the bombing of North Vietnam, to redouble his efforts to conclude successful negotiations, and to include representatives of the National Liberation Front in the negotiations.

The issue of Presidential authority

In March 1968, with criticism of administration policies mounting, the Senate Foreign Relations Committee held a televised hearing to review the conduct of the war. As the hearing progressed, Senator J. William Fulbright and other committee members expressed concern not only over American involvement in Vietnam but also over the issue of Presidential authority.

When Secretary of State Rusk appeared before the committee, Senator Fulbright asked him if President Johnson intended to escalate the war by sending more troops to Vietnam. Rusk responded that this was a matter for the President to decide. Rusk reminded the committee that in the Gulf of Tonkin Resolution of 1964 Congress had authorized President Johnson "to take all necessary measures to repel any armed attack against the forces of the United States and to prevent further aggression." Senator Fulbright replied that when he voted for the resolution, he had not intended to give the President a "blank check" to commit American troops to a land war in Asia.

At the heart of this issue was a fundamental question of constitutional powers. The Constitution designates the President as commander in chief of the nation's armed forces and gives him extensive powers over the conduct of foreign affairs. But the Constitution reserves to Congress the power to declare war. Yet in Vietnam the United States was engaged in an undeclared war over which Congress had little control.

Most Americans agreed that there were times when the President had to make far-reaching decisions without waiting for Congress to act. But did this mean that in matters of war and peace the role of Congress was no longer relevant? No one, it seemed, had a conclusive answer.

Was the United States overcommitted?

Beyond the issue of Presidential authority was the larger issue of American foreign policy in general. Since World War II American commitments to prevent the spread of Communism had grown steadily. By 1969 the United States was providing military or economic aid, or both, to more than 70 nations. It had formal commitments to defend 42 nations against any form of aggression, Communist or otherwise. It was prepared to

Student demonstrations in the late 1960's and early 1970's were directed not only against the war in Vietnam, racial injustice, and widespread poverty, but also against the quality of higher education.

wage major wars on two different fronts at the same time, as well as to fight localized conflicts anywhere in the world.

In support of these formidable worldwide commitments, the Defense Department had 3.5 million service men and women under arms—1.5 million of them overseas—and an additional 1.2 million civilian employees. As of January 1968 annual appropriations for military activities totaled $87.6 billion, or $439 for every woman, man, and child in the United States.

Increasing criticism

During the late 1960's Congress increasingly began to question what critics called the "swollen" defense budgets. Few questioned the need to maintain the nation's military defenses. What the critics *did* question was what they believed was the alarming imbalance between the huge sums devoted to military projects and the relatively meager amounts devoted to the nation's domestic problems and the desperate needs of the underdeveloped nations.

In 1968, for example, in contrast to the approximately $88 billion appropriated for military and defense activities, Congress voted only $24 billion for the nation's human needs—welfare, housing, health, and education. And Congress voted only $2.7 billion for aid to the underdeveloped world.

Nor was the imbalance simply a matter of money. As critics pointed out, the many highly skilled men and women working on defense projects were not available to tackle the urgent human problems at home or abroad. The "brain drain" into war industries was robbing the nation's economy of desperately needed human resources.

By the late 1960's the cost and magnitude of America's global commitments had become matters of widespread concern. It was clear, for example, that the enormous military expenditures were feeding the growing inflation in the economy. As the value of the dollar declined (or, to state it differently, as prices rose), it became more difficult to sell American products in foreign markets. And as the inflationary pressures increased, foreign governments and private investors abroad, fearing that the dollar would lose its value, began to withdraw gold from the United States Treasury.

The Johnson administration took steps, including a 10 percent increase in the income tax, to combat inflation and to stabilize the value of the dollar. But critics continued to insist that until the government ended the Vietnam War and re-evaluated its total foreign policy the nation would remain in deep trouble.

Johnson decides not to run for re-election

By the fall of 1968 the Vietnam conflict had become the second longest war in American history and the third largest in terms of lives lost and money spent. Only the Revolutionary War had lasted longer, and only World War I and World War II had cost more in money, resources, and lives. Equally disturbing, the conflict had divided the nation more sharply than it had been divided since the Civil War.

Confronted with these facts and with a swelling tide of criticism, President Johnson decided not to run for another term in the Presidential election in November.

SECTION SURVEY

IDENTIFY: Vietcong, Gulf of Tonkin Resolution, guerrilla warfare, NLF, DMZ; President Diem, President Thieu, General Westmoreland.

1. By 1965 the United States was waging two major wars—one at home, one overseas. How were they interrelated?
2. Trace the evolution of American involvement in South Vietnam starting in 1962.
3. (a) Describe the impact of the war on North and South Vietnam. (b) Describe the impact of the war on the United States and the rest of the world.

3 Attempts to relax world tensions during the Nixon-Ford administrations

The war in Vietnam and growing inflation at home were the major problems facing the nation when Richard M. Nixon became President in January 1969. These problems required the largest share of his attention during his first term in the White House.

Nixon's plan for Vietnam

During the election campaign, Nixon had declared that if elected he would "bring an honorable end to the war." For several months after the election no apparent plan emerged. Critics of the war became increasingly impatient.

In the spring and summer, however, the Nixon plan began to take shape. It foresaw the gradual withdrawal of American troops as soon as the South Vietnamese demonstrated that they were able to defend themselves. The plan also included the replacement of the old "search-and-destroy" policy with a new "protective-reaction" policy. Under this new policy, American troops would engage the enemy only when attacked or threatened by attack. The Nixon administration hoped that the new tactics would reduce American casualties and help quiet some of the opposition to the war.

The invasion of Cambodia

The Nixon plan was a bitter disappointment to those Americans who wanted to end the nation's military involvement in Vietnam as quickly as possible. Those who shared this view were further disheartened in the spring of 1970 by Nixon's startling announcement that South Vietnamese and American troops were crossing the border into "neutral" Cambodia. The objective of the invasion, Nixon said, was to destroy the string of North Vietnamese and Vietcong ammunition supply centers and camps along the eastern border of Cambodia. As soon as these centers from which the Vietcong had been launching their attacks against South Vietnam had been wiped out, the troops would be withdrawn. Nixon promised that all American forces would be out of Cambodia by the end of June.

President Nixon kept his promise. In the meantime, however, the Cambodian venture had shocked millions of Americans and triggered widespread anti-war demonstrations. Further, it intensified a long-standing conflict between Communist and non-Communist forces in Cambodia.

The war continues

The "protective-reaction" policy and the withdrawal of American ground troops from South Vietnam during Nixon's first term in office did reduce American casualties. But there was no let up in the relentless fury of the air war. American air power destroyed large areas in South Vietnam that were controlled by the Vietcong and North Vietnam, blockaded the harbors of North Vietnam, and rained bombs upon North Vietnamese supply routes and ammunition centers in Laos and Cambodia.

Meanwhile the negotiations in Paris continued. Nixon's foreign policy adviser, Henry Kissinger, patiently tried to break the deadlock. Just before the Presidential election of 1972, he announced that "peace is at hand." But the announcement turned out to be premature. The United States continued its military operations for two months, including massive bombing of Hanoi during December. Then early in January 1973 a cease-fire agreement finally was reached.

The cease-fire agreement

By the terms of the agreement (1) the continued presence of North Vietnam military forces was tacitly agreed to; (2) South Vietnam was assured that it was to have a government of its own choosing; and (3) the United States guaranteed continued economic and military aid to South Vietnam. President Nixon then withdrew the remaining American troops. As a result of continuing pressure, most American prisoners of war were later released by North Vietnam.

Assessing the war

As far as Southeast Asia was concerned, the so-called peace was fragile and precarious. Fighting continued between the Vietcong and President Thieu's Saigon regime, with each side blaming the other for violations of the agreements. And in order to prevent North Vietnam from continuing to aid the Vietcong by using supply routes through Laos and Cambodia, the American Air Force continued to support the anti-Communist governments of these strife-torn countries.

Although President Nixon had ended America's direct involvement in the war, many Americans questioned whether similar terms could not have been secured months or even years before the agreements were finally reached in Paris. Nixon insisted that this was not the case. He insisted that events beyond America's control had prolonged the fighting four years after he had promised to end the war and bring the American troops home.

American participation in this longest and most unpopular war in the nation's history had been enormously costly. By the spring of 1973, when the last troops left Vietnam, direct expenditures totaled $137 billion. Some 45,729 Americans had been killed in action and more than 300,000 wounded. As for the people of Southeast Asia, estimates put South Vietnamese deaths at 160,903 and those of the Vietcong and North Vietnamese at 922,295. In addition, more than 6 million refugees were uprooted and homeless. Large areas of Vietnam, Laos, and Cambodia had been devastated.

By an overwhelming majority, Americans agreed that there must be "no more Vietnams." But there was sharp disagreement over what to do about thousands of American draft resisters and deserters who had fled to Canada, Sweden, and elsewhere. Many of these young people became fugitives because they believed that America's role in the Vietnam War was morally wrong. President Nixon refused to consider any form of amnesty, or pardon. President Ford, later, offered conditional amnesty. Early in his term in office, Ford announced his proposal. It included amnesty for those who would take an oath to support the United States and agree to two years of "alternate service" in penal, custodial, or rehabilitation institutions. However, only a small proportion of the draft resisters and deserters accepted President Ford's offer.

End of an era in Southeast Asia

The fighting in Southeast Asia continued and intensified as the Communist forces took the offensive in 1973 and 1974. In Cambodia, during 1974 and 1975, Communist troops captured much of the country and surrounded the capital of Phnom Penh. In April 1975 the last remaining Americans were evacuated by helicopters and the victorious Communist armies took control of Cambodia.

Meanwhile in South Vietnam, resistance to the Communists also was crumbling. When the South Vietnam government ordered a withdrawal of its troops from the north and the central highlands in March 1975, entire units abandoned their equipment and retreated southward before the advancing North Vietnamese and Vietcong. In a last desperate effort to prevent a complete collapse of South Vietnam, President Ford asked Congress to vote $722 million in emergency military aid. But Congress, convinced that the South Vietnamese cause was hopeless and fearing a renewal of America's involvement, refused to support the President. At the end of April, with Saigon surrounded, American helicopters and ships lying off the coast withdrew the remaining Americans as well as 100,000 South Vietnamese. The Vietnamese refugees, for the most part destitute, were temporarily housed on American military bases until they could be relocated in new homes throughout the United States. And so, with the Communist takeover of South Vietnam, three tragic decades of fighting in Vietnam came to an end.

Limiting the President's war-making power

During the Vietnam War, many Americans, including members of both political parties in Congress, had become increasingly concerned over the Presidents' handling of the war. According to the Constitution, only Congress has power to declare war. But in the case of Vietnam, several Presidents had exercised war-making power without Congressional approval. In so doing, had they violated the Constitution? This was the question that troubled growing numbers of Americans.

To be sure, Congress could at any time have ended America's involvement in Vietnam by cutting off all funds for further military operations. But Congress was reluctant to take this step while hundreds of thousands of American troops were fighting in the conflict. Finally, in November 1973, Congress passed and overrode Nixon's veto of the War Powers Act, which provided that no President could send American troops into combat for a period longer than 60 days unless Congress approved. The law also provided that Congress could, by a joint resolution, order the immediate removal of troops from an area of combat.

Nixon's foreign policies

Apart from the unpopular Vietnam War, Nixon's foreign policies won widespread approval. His success in improving relations with Communist China and the Soviet Union was impressive.

In some ways President Nixon's views were much like those of other recent Presidents. He insisted upon the importance of maintaining a military force strong enough to meet any challenge to America's national interests and security. He demonstrated his continued opposition to Communism by insisting upon the exclusion of Cuba from the Organization of American States. This opposition was also apparent in his approval of the secret use of funds by the Central Intelligence Agency to try to prevent a Socialist-Communist election victory in Chile and, later, to make it difficult for the Marxist government elected by those parties to govern. And like earlier Presidents, Nixon largely ignored the denial of civil liberties and other human rights in anti-Communist countries that received American military and economic assistance in exchange for military bases. These countries included Spain, Greece, South Korea, and South Vietnam.

But military and economic aid to anti-Communist countries was only one part of Nixon's foreign policy. He also placed major emphasis on skillful and realistic diplomacy. This, he insisted, would insure peace. Such diplomacy, he maintained, must be sufficiently flexible to account for world conditions that had changed in many ways since the years of the Cold War.

With these considerations in mind, Nixon chose Henry Kissinger, a refugee from Nazi Germany who had become a professor of political science at Harvard University, as his chief adviser for foreign affairs. Without conferring much with the Department of State, Nixon and Kissinger planned the broad outlines of American foreign policy. Their "personal diplomacy" involved an unprecedented number of conferences with leaders in other countries. President Nixon himself traveled to Western Europe, the Soviet Union, China, Canada, Iceland, and the Middle East for talks with other heads of state. Shortly after his re-election in 1972 he appointed Kissinger Secretary of State.

Opening the door to mainland China

In one of his most dramatic moves, Nixon visited the People's Republic of China in February 1972. As an outcome of eight days of "frank discussions" between President Nixon and Chairman Mao Tse-tung, the doors that had been shut

Under President Nixon, the United States began to improve its strained relations with Communist China. In 1972 Nixon and Secretary of State Kissinger visited Chinese leaders in Peking.

and barred between the two countries for more than 20 years began to swing open. Each government promised not to seek dominance in the Asian Pacific region, to cooperate in preventing other powers from doing so, and to avoid international war. Both governments declared that they would seek to develop trade, improve cultural and scientific relations, and work to restore full diplomatic relations. As for the major obstacle to improved relations, President Nixon promised eventual withdrawal of United States military forces from Taiwan and Indochina. In what was regarded as proof of America's desire to cooperate, the Nixon administration used its influence to support China's ally, Pakistan, when war broke out between Pakistan and India over the independence of East Pakistan (renamed Bangladesh).

Détente with the Soviet Union

In May 1972, three months after Nixon had visited Peking, he met with Soviet leaders in Moscow. At the end of eight days of conferences, President Nixon and Communist Party Secretary Leonid Brezhnev declared that they had reached agreement on a number of important issues. They promised to cooperate in efforts to improve trade and to tackle world problems involving space, health, and the environment.

Nixon and Brezhnev also signed two documents intended to limit nuclear armaments. These documents were based upon preliminary understandings arrived at during previous negotiations known as the Strategic Arms Limitation Talks (SALT). One of the documents, an executive

agreement, "froze" offensive missiles at near existing levels for a five-year period. The other document, a treaty requiring Senate approval, limited each nation to two anti-ballistic missile sites in its territory. It also placed a limit on the number of American and Soviet land-based and submarine-based missile forces. The Senate finally ratified this treaty agreement in August 1973. Throughout the world, people hoped that the United States and the Soviet Union were moving away from the confrontations of the Cold War into a period of *détente,* or the gradual relaxation of tensions between them.

In the meantime the Soviet and American delegates at the Strategic Arms Limitation Talks continued their negotiations. The progress made in these negotiations led Nixon and Brezhnev to agree to meet at another summit conference in Moscow in June 1974. At this meeting the Soviet and American leaders reached a number of agreements calling for liberalizing trade relations and increasing cooperation in economic, industrial, and technical matters. They also agreed to ban underground tests of nuclear weapons and to limit anti-ballistic missiles to a single site in each country. But they again failed to reach any agreement on reduction of offensive weapons. This disappointing outcome prompted Secretary of State Kissinger to warn that, if the two nuclear powers could not arrive at some agreement soon, by 1977 "we will be living in a world in which opportunities for nuclear war exist which are unimaginable."

During one of the state dinners held at Moscow in his honor, President Nixon rose to toast a remarkable two years in which Soviet-American relations had, in his words, moved "from confrontation to coexistence to cooperation." But many Americans did not share Nixon's confidence that the period of confrontation with the Soviet Union was finally ended. They insisted that the only true test of détente lay in future Soviet actions.

One of those who reserved judgment was Senator Henry M. Jackson of Washington. Jackson insisted that there must be no liberalization of trade relations until the Soviet Union relaxed its restrictions on the emigration of its citizens, including political dissenters and Jews who wanted to go to Israel. Finally, in the fall of 1974, the Soviet Union apparently accepted this "Jackson amendment," or understanding, and agreed to increase the number of exit visas for Jewish citizens wishing to immigrate to Israel. Senator Jackson hailed the Soviet concession as a great victory. A few months later, however, in January 1975, the Soviets rejected this trade agreement, claiming it could not allow the United States to interfere with Soviet emigration policy. How serious a setback to détente this Soviet rejection of the trade agreement might be was not immediately clear.

The Middle East and a test of détente

Another Arab-Israeli war in the fall of 1973 provided a major test of détente and of Secretary Kissinger's skill as a diplomat. The conflict broke out in October when Egypt and Syria, seeking to recover territories lost in the 1967 war, suddenly launched an attack upon Israel. The Israelis, who were observing Yom Kippur, a holy day to Jews, were caught by surprise and suffered heavy casualties. By the second week of the Yom Kippur War, however, Israeli troops were driving back Syrian tank forces in the north and had seized the offensive in the Sinai Desert. A powerful Israeli force had reached the Suez Canal, crossed the Canal into Egyptian territory, and was threatening to trap the entire Egyptian Third Army. The Israeli offensive also threatened the Egyptian Second Army and brought the Israeli forces to within 60 miles (96.6 kilometers) of Cairo.

In the meantime the United Nations had adopted resolutions calling for a cease-fire. But when the fighting continued in all its fury, the Egyptians, faced with the prospect of certain defeat, called upon the Soviet Union for help. The Soviets, angered by American failure to get Israel to accept the cease-fire, now threatened to send their own troops to help end the fighting. President Nixon immediately ordered a "precautionary alert" for all American forces around the world. For a number of hours a major military confrontation between the Soviet Union and the United States remained a terrifying possibility. Fortunately, reason prevailed when the two great powers persuaded the Arabs and the Israelis to accept the cease-fire and to prepare for negotiations.

Détente, the cornerstone of the foreign policy

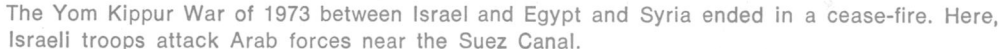

The Yom Kippur War of 1973 between Israel and Egypt and Syria ended in a cease-fire. Here, Israeli troops attack Arab forces near the Suez Canal.

Nixon and Kissinger had worked so long and hard to develop, had survived its first critical trial. But many Israelis were bitter at being forced to end the fighting just as a decisive victory was within their grasp. And the Arabs, angered by American support of the Israelis, embargoed all shipments of oil to the United States and other countries that were friendly to Israel. Although the immediate crisis was over, the cease-fire had brought at best only an uneasy and extremely precarious peace to the Middle East.

SECTION SURVEY

IDENTIFY: "protective-reaction" policy, Vietnam cease-fire, conditional amnesty, SALT, détente, Yom Kippur War; Henry Kissinger, Mao Tse-tung, Leonid Brezhnev, Senator Henry Jackson.

1. How did the United States wind down its involvement in the Vietnam War? What were the terms of the 1973 cease-fire?
2. Why did most Americans agree that there must be "no more Vietnams"?
3. Why did the Vietnam War raise the problem of the President's war-making power? How did Congress try to resolve this problem?
4. Describe President Nixon's policy of détente toward China and the Soviet Union. How did this policy mark an important new effort in America's foreign relations?

CHAPTER SURVEY

INQUIRING INTO HISTORY

1. What was the policy of détente worked out by Nixon and Kissinger? How did it change American foreign policy? What major changes among Communist nations made this new policy possible?
2. How did the Arab-Israeli War of 1973 test the policy of détente with the Soviet Union?
3. Why did the United States commit itself to opposing Communist expansion in Southeast Asia? Describe the actions taken by the Kennedy, Johnson, and Nixon administrations with regard to the conflict in Vietnam.
4. Some American critics of the government's Vietnam policy declared that the United States might win the war but would destroy Vietnam in the process. What did they mean by this statement?
5. Why were the SALT negotiations between the Soviet Union and the United States so important? What progress was made in these negotiations?

RELATING PAST TO PRESENT

1. What was the attitude of the American public toward United States involvement in World War I? In World War II? In the Vietnam War? Explain the reason for each of these attitudes.
2. What responsibility did the President have for making foreign policy decisions in World War II? The Korean War? The Vietnam War? What responsibility did Congress have?

DEVELOPING SOCIAL SCIENCE SKILLS

1. Find articles for and against the war in Vietnam. (a) Do the articles agree on the facts? (b) Do the articles for and against the war use the facts in the same way? (c) What would you say were the values of the writer of each article? (d) How do you think the writers' values affected their opinions?
2. Read John F. Kennedy's Inaugural Address. (a) What kind of foreign policy does it outline? (b) Did events during Kennedy's administration show that America was following this policy? (c) Is this still the basis of American foreign policy?

CHAPTER 24

NEW CHALLENGES FOR THE AMERICAN PEOPLE

The United States in 1976 bore only slight resemblance to the thirteen colonies that two hundred years earlier had declared their independence from Great Britain. The nation that had come into existence with the Declaration of Independence in 1776 had changed dramatically during the first two centuries of its history. It had been transformed in size, in population, and in almost every aspect of its social and economic life.

The thirteen colonies stretching along the Atlantic seaboard had developed into a federal union of 50 states, embracing an area that not only reached from "sea to shining sea" but that also included Alaska to the northwest and the Hawaiian Islands halfway across the Pacific Ocean.

The 1776 population of only 3 million men, women, and children in the thirteen original states had grown to nearly 215 million by 1976, including more than 750,000 Indians, more than 23 million black Americans, some 3 to 5 million Spanish-speaking Americans, as well as descendants of immigrants from almost every country in the world.

In the early days of the nation some 90 percent of the American people were more or less isolated from their neighbors on self-sufficient farms. By 1976 nearly 75 percent were living close to one another in urban areas. Moreover, both the rural and urban areas of the country were continuing to change—almost, it seemed, with every passing day. The land itself was transformed, industries continued to develop, housing sprang up, and new highways stretched their ribbons of concrete and asphalt across the countryside.

And the American people themselves were changing, not only in numbers, but in the goals they were seeking for themselves and for their children. Many groups of Americans, including women and racial and ethnic minorities, were demanding and beginning to win the equality expressed in the Declaration of Independence but long withheld from them.

THE CHAPTER IN OUTLINE

1. The transformation of rural and urban ways of life.

2. Demands by black Americans for equal rights and opportunities.

3. Demands by other minorities and women for an end to discrimination.

CHANGING WAYS OF AMERICAN LIFE   1945-1970's

1 The transformation of rural and urban ways of life

The growth and redistribution of America's population after 1900 radically altered older ways of life in countryside˙and city alike. By the end of World War II, the revolution was in full swing.

The large growth in population

One of the most far-reaching developments was the rapid growth of population. Between 1900 and 1976 the population of the United States nearly tripled—from 76 million at the turn of the century to about 215 million on the nation's 200th anniversary.

The basic reason for the upward surge of population in the United States was the remarkable advances made by medical science. Using antibiotics and many other new drugs, as well as new methods and improved instruments for diagnosis and treatment, physicians were able to reduce the death rate, especially among children, and to prolong life.

In the years following World War II the rate of growth soared to an average level of 3.51 births per woman. By the 1970's, however, the birth rate was slowing down. In December 1972 the Census Bureau reported that it had dropped to about 2 births per woman, or what is called Zero Population Growth°. Even so, because there were many more women of child-bearing age in the 1970's than there were in the 1950's the Census Bureau estimated that by the end of the century America's population would reach 250 million.

The redistribution of people

An equally far-reaching development in postwar America was the growing mobility of people. Americans became increasingly able and willing to move from place to place. In earlier times when life was simpler, large numbers of Americans had lived their lives in the areas in which they were born. However, by the 1960's and 1970's one out of every five Americans was moving to a new place of residence each year.

These population shifts affected different states and different sections of the country in different ways. The West and South became the fastest growing sections of the nation. In 1963, California passed New York to become the most populous state. Meanwhile, the states of the Northeast were losing population in relation to the rest of the nation.

Among the flowing tides of people three

were especially significant: (1) the continuing movement away from the farms; (2) the rapidly increasing movement of middle-class families out of the central cities into the suburbs; and (3) the migration of black Americans out of the South into other sections of the country.

The exodus from the farms

Among the dramatic developments of the new age was the sharp decline in farm population. Between 1940 and 1970 the number of people living on farms dropped from more than 30 million to fewer than 10 million. In some years more than 1 million men and women left the farms to seek better opportunities in the nation's growing urban areas. In 1940, 23 percent of all Americans lived on farms; by 1970 fewer than 6 percent remained.

Despite a rapidly shrinking farm population America was producing more food and other farm products than ever before. In 1940, for example, each farm worker produced enough food for 10 people; by 1970 each worker was producing enough food for more than 47 people.

The remarkable rise in American farm productivity sprang from the rapid increase of efficient, large-scale corporation farms and even more from spectacular developments in agricultural science and technology. Better strains of plants, more use of fertilizer, improved breeds of livestock, increasing attention to soil conservation and the enrichment of farm lands—all these combined to raise the average yield of some farm crops by as much as 50 percent. Electricity, gasoline, and new farm machines also played major roles in boosting production.

Many observers expressed concern over the rapid decline of the farm population. From the beginning of American history, they pointed out, the small family farm had added strength and vitality to democracy and the economy. Now this important part of rural America was diminishing.

From a rural to an urban nation

The decline of the farm population was accompanied by a sharp increase in the urban population. This trend toward urbanization was worldwide. In the United States, however, cities expanded at what seemed an explosive rate.

By the mid-1960's almost 85 percent of the total increase in the nation's population was taking place in urban areas. By the mid-1970's nearly three fourths of all Americans were living in metropolitan areas. These areas included the central or core cities and the surrounding suburbs.

° **Zero Population Growth** is a birth rate that replaces the existing population but does not increase it.

Many Americans moved from the central cities to suburban housing developments like this one in California. These new suburbs grew rapidly in the years after World War II.

Two great migrations of people—one out of the central cities, the other into them—were producing revolutionary changes in American life.

The growth of suburban America

The migration out of the cities was led by young married couples seeking better living conditions for raising their families. This movement strengthened the trend toward a more widespread ownership of homes.

All over the nation people who could afford to do so were moving out of the older cities into the suburbs. The countryside around the cities was being leveled by bulldozers, and huge suburban housing developments were springing up almost overnight. Department stores and banks were opening branches in the new suburban shopping centers, many industries were following the people out of the central cities, and the expanding metropolitan areas were being tied together by a complex network of highways and superhighways.

These changes were impressive. They were transforming the face of the land itself. They were also creating problems

As the suburbs spread in an unplanned sprawl over the countryside, the housing developments, shopping centers, highways, and roads ate up irreplaceable farm lands at an alarming rate. As you will see, one consequence of the lack of planning was a deterioration of the environment and therefore of the quality of life itself. Meanwhile the new suburban communities had to create almost from scratch new schools, police departments, fire departments, water and sewage systems, churches, libraries, hospitals, parks, and scores of other public services.

The growth of supercities

As the suburbs expanded, the metropolitan areas began to grow together to form supercities. By the 1970's three great supercities had begun to take shape. One extended along the Atlantic seaboard from Portland, Maine, to Richmond, Virginia. A second stretched along the shores of the Great Lakes from Chicago, Illinois, to Pittsburgh, Pennsylvania. A third reached down the California coast from San Francisco to San Diego. Others were growing rapidly along Florida's east coast and in eastern and southern Texas, as well as in other parts of the nation. Each of these great concentrations of buildings and people was sometimes called a "megalopolis" from the Greek words *megalo,* meaning "very large" and *polis,* meaning "city."

In both physical appearance and character these very large cities represented something totally new in human experience. Throughout history the city had been a compactly organized unit of activity. The new supercities were entirely different. They were neither urban nor suburban; they were a mixture of both. The megalopolis was an almost continuous system of interwoven urban and suburban areas covering thousands of square miles.

Unfortunately, political developments failed to keep pace with these enormous concentrations of people and activities. For example, some 1,400 different governments operated in the metropolitan area of New York. Thus it was often difficult if not impossible to deal with problems common to the entire area—traffic congestion; health and sanitation; pollution of water, land, and air. No single one of the 1,400 different political units could deal with the problems;

the solutions required a complex cooperative effort, and this was not easy to secure.

It appeared increasingly evident to some observers that the overlapping and competing governments in the metropolitan areas would have to be replaced by single governments with overall jurisdiction. But political traditions and long-established institutions are hard to change, and efforts to achieve such governments had scarcely begun by the 1970's.

The changing faces of the central cities

Meanwhile the original cities—now called the central or inner cities—were also experiencing far-reaching changes and critical problems.

On the positive side, the hearts of the cities, the business areas, were being completely rebuilt. In city after city blocks of gleaming new office buildings and expensive apartment houses towered as visible symbols of the nation's wealth and vitality. Moreover, in most cities rows of low-income apartments were replacing rundown tenements.

Equally visible, however, were signs of decay. Traffic clogged the streets and highways leading into the central cities—streets and highways built in an earlier age for horses and wagons and carriages, not for swarms of automobiles, buses, and trucks. Neglected areas deteriorated into slums when property owners, discouraged by the flight of the middle class from the city, refused to spend money for repairs and improvements. Faced with the decline of property values, city governments found it difficult to collect the amount of tax money they needed to provide essential public services.

The urban crisis

By the 1970's the conditions in America's large cities had become desperate. The core areas of some cities had decayed so badly that they needed to be entirely rebuilt. This would take years and billions of dollars. Meanwhile people living in the slums needed more and better public services—health, education, sanitation, recreation, police and fire protection. Jobs and job-training programs needed to be provided.

But the cities did not have the finances to do the work that had to be done. The people most able to pay the necessary taxes were abandoning the cities; those least able to pay and most in need of the services were becoming more numerous.

By the mid-1970's the urban crisis was in fact a national crisis. A massive and coordinated effort by the federal government and the cities—by the nation as a whole—was now required to deal with the crisis.

"Social dynamite"

The problems confronting the cities were compounded by revolutionary changes taking place in the urban population itself. The middle-class families leaving the cities were being replaced mainly by impoverished men, women, and children from rural areas, particularly from the South and from Appalachia, and from Puerto Rico.

As early as 1961 James B. Conant of Harvard University had issued a report titled *Slums and Suburbs* that attracted nationwide attention. The report pointed out the alarming contrast between the poverty of life in the decaying cores of the cities and the growing wealth of the suburbs. "We are allowing social dynamite to accumulate in our large cities," Conant warned. As you will read in the next section, this dynamite finally exploded.

SECTION SURVEY

IDENTIFY: Zero Population Growth, population shifts, megalopolis, central or inner city, suburb.

1. What has contributed to the growth of population in the United States?
2. What have been the effects upon the United States of the growing mobility of its people?
3. (a) How has technology affected American agriculture? (b) What have been some results?
4. The United States is now an urban nation. Explain.

2 Demands by black Americans for equal rights and opportunities

By the 1960's and early 1970's black Americans, frustrated with what they considered much too slow progress toward the goal of full equality of opportunity, were becoming increasingly insistent upon "freedom now."

The roots of the problem

The struggle that reached crisis proportions by the late 1960's had its roots deep in the past. A century earlier the Thirteenth, Fourteenth, and Fifteenth Amendments had been added to the Constitution. These three amendments freed all slaves, gave them full citizenship, and guaranteed them and all other Americans "the equal protection of the laws." The Fifteenth Amendment also included the specific assurance that the right to vote would not be denied because of "race, color, or previous condition of servitude."

For a number of years after the adoption of these amendments many black southerners voted and held public offices in local and state governments. A number were elected to and served in Congress. After a few years, however, one after another of the southern states adopted laws establishing a new pattern of race relations. By the 1890's, as a result of both law and custom, black citizens' right to vote had been limited. Black southerners were segregated from white southerners in railroad stations, on trains and streetcars, in public parks and buildings, in schools, churches, and hospitals, and in prisons and cemeteries.

Most northerners raised no protest against these laws. On the contrary, black northerners faced increasing discrimination. Then in 1896 the Supreme Court ruled that laws establishing segregation did not violate the Fourteenth Amendment. In the case of *Plessy v. Ferguson* the Court ruled that "separate but equal" facilities met the requirement that all citizens were entitled to "the equal protection of the laws."

Black Americans thus entered the 1900's handicapped by problems they had not anticipated during the first hopeful years of freedom. Yet despite these handicaps they made impressive advances. As you recall, black Americans won increasing success in every field of activity—science, medicine, the professions, business, music and art, entertainment, and sports. By the end of World War II they had made marked—although still narrowly limited —progress toward fuller political, legal, and social rights.

Legal action

During the years after World War II, the movement to end discrimination in government, business, education, and sports began to speed up.

Acting on the recommendations of a Presidential Committee on Civil Rights set up in 1946, President Truman urged Congress to adopt legislation strengthening civil rights laws and enforcement machinery. When Congress failed to act, Truman used his executive powers to order an end to segregation in the armed forces and in the government.

The most important development of the Eisenhower years was a Supreme Court decision of 1954. In *Brown v. Board of Education of Topeka* the court reversed the 58-year-old *Plessy v. Ferguson* ruling that "separate but equal" facilities were constitutional. The Court

Civil rights acts strengthened the political power of black Americans. Here, black southerners register to vote in the 1960's.

unanimously ruled that state or local laws requiring black citizens to send their children to separate schools violated the Fourteenth Amendment.

Several months after the momentous 1954 decision, the Supreme Court required local school authorities to work out plans for gradually ending segregation in public school systems. The Supreme Court also instructed federal district courts to require local school authorities to "make a prompt and reasonable start toward full compliance" and to move "with all deliberate speed."

Encouraged by the Supreme Court ruling, civil rights supporters redoubled their efforts to break down discrimination. As one of their major tactics they undertook to secure the passage of effective legislation. Congress responded with the adoption of five civil rights acts—those of 1957, 1960, 1964, 1965, and 1968.

These five measures were designed to speed up desegregation and to secure for black Americans the voting and other rights guaranteed them in the Constitution but often denied them in practice. This legislation achieved some of its aims. By the mid-1960's race barriers had been largely broken down in hotels and restaurants, in buses and trains and airlines, and in other public facilities. Impressive gains had also been made in voter registration. Whereas in 1965, for example, only 6 percent of the black citizens of Mississippi were registered to vote, by 1967 more than one third had been registered.

The gains in school desegregation in the South were slower but impressive. By 1967 token desegregation was a fact throughout the South, although only 16 percent of black southern students attended integrated schools. Each year the pace quickened. In the fall of 1969 the Supreme Court gave new impetus to the process with its toughest ruling to date, ordering an end to all racially separated school systems "at once." By the early 1970's many southern school districts were integrated.

Direct action

In the 1960's the civil rights movement also used another tactic, that of direct action, to speed integration and eliminate discrimination. By means of bus strikes, sit-ins, "freedom rides" through the South, and a 1963 "March on Washington," civil rights workers dramatized their determination to make court decisions and legislation effective. Students, both black and white, including many from northern colleges and universities, took a leading part in these peaceful demonstrations.

The tactic of direct action had two immedi-

Court-ordered busing of students to achieve school desegregation caused conflicts in some communities. Here, white residents protest "forced busing" in their neighborhood schools.

ate results. It antagonized many white citizens in the North as well as in the South. But at the same time it drew into the movement many black working-class families who had not been involved when the emphasis had been mainly upon legislative action.

Growing frustration and shifting emphasis

During the early 1960's the outlook among black Americans was generally hopeful. New laws, favorable court decisions, and the growing support of many white citizens were encouraging. Moreover, large-scale involvement in demonstrations and other forms of direct action, especially by young people, had given black Americans a deeper sense of self-respect and a growing confidence in their ability to achieve their goals.

By the mid-1960's, however, rising frustration was replacing earlier optimism. Essential though civil rights were, they did not provide jobs for the unemployed. They did not provide adequate housing in either the nation's rural areas or the overcrowded city slums. They did not provide the training or education needed to give disadvantaged men and women the opportunity to raise their standard of living and build a better way of life. More and more it was becoming evident that integrated schools were not necessarily better schools in terms of the quality of education they provided.

Thus by the mid-1960's the goals of the movement shifted from civil rights to economic and social issues—jobs, housing, de facto segregation,° and discrimination by businesses and by organized labor in hiring practices. But as the war in Vietnam absorbed more and more of the nation's resources, black Americans felt that their problems were being neglected. And the goal of equal opportunity seemed as remote as ever. The growing strength of the "white backlash" and the failure of Congress in 1966 to adopt an open housing law forbidding discrimination in the sale or rental of houses and apartments increased black frustration and despair.

Violence in the inner city

The depth of black frustration was starkly revealed in riots that broke out in the community of Watts in Los Angeles, California, in the summer of 1965. The National Guard was called in to restore order, but before the rioting ended 4,000 persons were arrested, hundreds were injured, 34 were killed, and the damage from burning and looting totaled $35 million.

° **de facto segregation:** segregation that exists not by law, but because of neighborhood residence patterns.

Black Americans made significant political gains during the 1960's and 1970's. Here, black mayors of major cities meet to discuss urban problems.

The fury of this urban violence shocked the nation. It was especially alarming to those Americans, black and white alike, who had believed that the civil rights movement was making progress and that race relations were improving. Any lingering optimism in that regard was swept away during the next two years when rioting broke out in cities across the nation. Among the hardest hit were Detroit, Cleveland, Newark, Baltimore, and the nation's capital, Washington, D.C.

Many Americans, black as well as white, blamed the violence on a group of new militant black leaders. Although there was some truth in this explanation, it was by no means the whole truth. The rate of unemployment among black workers the country over was double that of white workers, and among black teenagers in the inner cities the jobless rate was much greater. As the riots demonstrated, poverty from which there seems to be no escape is a fertile breeding ground for violence.

New leaders and "black power"

One of the best known of the new black leaders was Elijah Muhammed, who headed the Black Muslims, the largest and economically most powerful black group. Another was Malcolm X, formerly a Muslim minister, who formed his own organization and preached, bitterly, that the black and white races could exist only if they were completely separated from each other. Before his death, however, Malcolm X gave up his rigid racist position, referring to it as "sickness and madness." In 1965 he was assassinated by black radicals he had antagonized.

By the mid-1960's revolutionary black nationalism was making rapid strides. Among its

new leaders were Floyd McKissick and Stokely Carmichael, who had been active in militant civil rights organizations. Also included were the founders of the Black Panther Party—Huey P. Newton, Bobby Seale, and Eldridge Cleaver. Denouncing cooperation with white "liberals," the Black Panthers advocated immediate confrontation with "the white power structure," and the use of force, if necessary, to protect black Americans against aggressive "white racism."

Black extremists, scorning integration, demanded "black power." In economics, black power seemed to mean the growth of independent black businesses. In education it meant local community control of predominately black schools. In politics it meant the growth of political power either by the formation of a black political party or by control of politics in black neighborhoods through bloc voting. Socially it meant black self-reliance, self-respect, and racial pride.

Moderate black leaders shared many of the objectives of the "black power" movement, but they rejected its tactics. Among these leaders were Roy Wilkins of the NAACP and Dr. Martin Luther King, Jr. King, the most influential of the black leaders and a devoted advocate of nonviolence, denounced the appeal to black racism and the threatened use of force. Those who rejected integration and called for a separation of the races, he believed, did a cruel disservice to black people. Dr. King declared, "There is no salvation in isolation."

Signs of progress

By the mid-1960's the black power movement was making gains. Politically these gains were revealed in the election of black Americans to

Dr. Martin Luther King, Jr., devoted his life to achieving a nonviolent solution to the race issue.

public office—for example, Edward W. Brooke of Massachusetts to the United States Senate; Carl B. Stokes and Richard Hatcher as mayors of Cleveland, Ohio, and Gary, Indiana, respectively; Julian Bond to the Georgia legislature.

And in the spring of 1968 Congress adopted a new civil rights act. The new act extended federal protection to civil rights workers and included a guarantee of open housing. The open-housing provision barred discrimination in the sale or rental of all housing with the exception of owner-occupied homes sold directly by the owner. The new law marked a significant legal victory in the battle against discrimination. Whether it would be effective in practice remained to be seen.

The Kerner Commission Report

The spring of 1968 also brought to the American people the most comprehensive report on the race problem ever released by the federal government. In the summer of 1967 President Johnson had appointed a National Advisory Commission on Civil Disorders headed by Governor Kerner of Illinois to investigate inner city riots and violence. The Kerner Commission's report, issued in March 1968, acknowledged that gains had been made in civil rights laws and desegregation. But the report also warned that little or nothing had been accomplished in areas that mattered most to a majority of black people—housing, jobs and economic security, educational opportunities, and conditions in the inner cities. "Our nation," the commission reported, "is moving toward two societies, one black, one white—separate and unequal."

The commission warned of continued disorder and the destruction of basic democratic values unless improvements were made at once in employment, education, housing, and welfare for black people. This could be done, said the report, only by "a commitment to national action—compassionate, massive, and sustained, backed by the resources of the most powerful and richest nation on earth. From every American it will require new attitudes, new understanding, and, above all, new will."

The assassination of Martin Luther King, Jr.

The assassination of Martin Luther King, Jr., Nobel peace prize winner and most respected of black leaders, on April 4, 1968, fell with stunning force on all Americans, white and black alike. Dr. King was in Memphis, Tennessee, to lead a nonviolent demonstration when he was killed by an assassin's bullets. In the last speech he made before his death, Dr. King said, "It is no longer a question of violence or nonviolence. It is nonviolence or nonexistence."

Dr. King's death served as a grim reminder of the importance of the Kerner Commission's warnings. While the nation mourned the loss of a leader who had devoted his life to a nonviolent solution of the race issue, riots broke out in various cities across the country. Chicago and Washington were worst hit.

The balance sheet

The massive effort called for by the Kerner report did not develop. Yet by the mid-1970's neither its worst predictions nor the revolution threatened by radical black nationalists had taken place.

In 1975 the Civil Rights Commission reported that many black citizens, as well as members of other minorities, were still prevented from voting by various barriers, including unfair changes in the boundary lines of local voting districts and unauthorized changes in voting rules. Even so, black citizens were making important political gains. By 1975 over 2,600 black Americans were serving in elected public offices. This number was only .5 percent of all such offices, but it was an improvement over earlier years. Among those elected were 18 members of Congress and mayors of such cities as Los

SOURCES

I say to you today, my friends, that in spite of the difficulties and frustrations of the moment I still have a dream. It is a dream deeply rooted in the American dream.

I have a dream that one day this nation will rise up and live out the true meaning of its creed: "We hold these truths to be self-evident; that all men are created equal."

I have a dream that one day on the red hills of Georgia the sons of former slaves and the sons of former slaveowners will be able to sit down together at the table of brotherhood. . . .

I have a dream that my four little children will one day live in a nation where they will not be judged by the color of their skin but by the content of their character.

I have a dream today. . . .

Angeles, Atlanta, Detroit, Gary, Newark, and Washington, D.C. New leaders were learning how to work to gain greater political power— how to get out the black vote, to form political alliances, and to make effective use of pressure tactics.

The number of black people attaining middle-income status also was growing, at least until the recession of the mid-1970's. The Equal Rights Commission brought law suits against corporations and labor unions to end unfair employment practices. Yet the rate of unemployment among black workers continued to be far greater than among whites.

Twenty years after the 1954 decision of the Supreme Court in the case of *Brown v. Board of Education of Topeka,* desegregation of the public schools had made progress but was far from complete. Several thousand smaller southern communities had desegregated their schools. But in some districts of most large southern cities desegregation had moved slowly because of residential segregation and other obstacles. Progress was also slow in some districts of a number of northern cities, despite court orders to move toward desegregation. In Denver, Detroit, and other cities, controversy focused upon the issue of busing as a means to overcome school segregation based on neighborhood housing patterns. Public opinion polls showed that a majority of parents, including substantial numbers of black parents, were opposed to compulsory busing. In 1975 opposition to busing in Boston led to incidents of violence between white and black high school students and their parents.

In summary, by the mid-1970's Roy Wilkins of the NAACP reported that black Americans had made gains on all fronts, but that the longest and hardest road still lay ahead. Martin Luther King, Jr., had dreamed of a nation in which men and women and children of every race and creed would be united in peace and justice. Whether and when this dream would be realized remained an open question as the nation moved into the third century of its existence.

SECTION SURVEY

IDENTIFY: *Brown v. Board of Education of Topeka,* desegregation, black power, Kerner Commission Report; Elijah Muhammed, Malcolm X, Martin Luther King, Jr.

1. Name some actions taken by Presidents, Congress, and the Supreme Court since 1954 to guarantee the civil rights of all Americans.
2. Why by the mid-1960's did emphasis shift from civil rights legislation to economic and social issues?
3. How has the movement of white families to the suburbs affected black families in the central cities?
4. What is the relationship between (a) poverty and violence, (b) neighborhood housing patterns and school segregation?
5. "Our nation is moving toward two societies, one black, one white—separate and unequal." (a) What does this warning mean? (b) What is required of Americans as individuals and as a nation to prevent this prediction from coming true?

3 Demands by other minorities and women for an end to discrimination

The discrimination experienced by the nation's black population was shared by other groups—Hispanos, Mexican-Americans, Puerto Ricans, American Indians, and the largest group of all, American women. Encouraged by the efforts of black Americans, these other groups began to redouble their struggle to win equal rights and opportunities in every area of American life.

Spanish-speaking Americans

America's Spanish-speaking population numbered somewhere between 3 and 5 million. Although they included several groups, each of whom differed from the others in many important ways, Spanish-speaking Americans shared certain characteristics that set them apart from the mainstream of American life. Their way of life was traditionally rural, simple in its technology, resistant to social change, strong in its sense of group identification, and proud of its Spanish and Catholic heritage.

The Hispanos

The Hispanos, or Latinos, were the descendants of the original Spanish settlers, who had come to southern California and the southwestern United States in the 1600's and 1700's. Most of them now lived in rural areas. For their livelihood they depended mainly upon the raising of cattle and sheep. The Hispanos were proud of their past and devoted to their way of life. Some of them had attained middle-class status and become prosperous. Others, less fortunate, deeply resented the poverty and the widespread discrimination that marked their lives. But prosperous or poor, the Hispanos resented what they considered to be the sharp practices of the "Anglos," especially in regard to water and mineral rights and the titles of ranch lands.

By the 1960's and 1970's the members of this old and proud minority, now numbering several hundred thousand, were actively resisting "Anglo exploitation" and discrimination. They were demanding full equality of opportunity as American citizens.

Mexican-Americans

Another, far larger Spanish-speaking group were the Mexican-Americans. Many Mexicans had lived in the Southwest when that area was annexed to the United States in the mid-1800's. Many later entered the United States to work on the railroads and ranches of the Southwest and also as unskilled laborers in the towns and cities. They lived in inadequate housing in segregated neighborhoods, called "barrios." English-speaking Americans regarded them as intruders and often treated them unfairly.

During and after World War I hundreds of thousands of Mexicans poured across the border to seek jobs in the United States. Most of them became migrant workers in California's cotton and sugar-beet fields as well as in the rapidly developing commercial fruit orchards and vegetable farms of California. Some, called "braceros," entered the United States under a legal work contract. Others, called "wetbacks," entered the country illegally by swimming or wading across the Rio Grande. Many returned home after the crops had been harvested, but then recrossed the border again the next season. Many others became permanent residents of Los Angeles, El Paso, Dallas, Denver, Detroit, and other cities. As migrant farm workers in the fields and as laborers in the cities, the Mexican-Americans played an essential role in the economic life of the nation, especially of the Southwest.

Many Mexican-Americans in California and the Southwest worked as migrant farm laborers on commercial vegetable farms and fruit orchards.

Puerto Rico is sometimes called "the showcase of Latin America." This beautiful but overcrowded Caribbean island, the home of nearly 3 million people, richly deserves its reputation.

In 1945 the Puerto Ricans launched a program to eliminate poverty and unemployment and to raise the prevailing low standard of living. This program, known as "Operation Bootstrap," was well under way when, In 1952, Puerto Rico became a self-governing commonwealth associated with the United States. Today, with a stable democratic government and a flourishing economy, Puerto Ricans enjoy a per capita income higher than that of any other Latin-American country with the single exception of oil-rich Venezuela.

The peaceful revolution through which the Puerto Ricans secured self-government and better living standards was carried out under the remarkable leadership of Luis Muñoz-Marín (LWEES MOON·yos-mah·REEN). With United States help, the Puerto Ricans have instituted land reforms and developed the island's economy. They have built roads, factories, modern tourist hotels, housing projects, and schools. One way the United States has helped Puerto Ricans in their efforts to raise living standards is through free trade. There are no tariff barriers between the United States and Puerto Rico.

It is significant that Puerto Ricans have transformed their island and at the same time have kept their own cultural traditions. Puerto Rico's victory over poverty, although far from complete, represents one of the most dramatic chapters in recent history.

PUERTO RICO'S PEACEFUL REVOLUTION

By the 1950's many cities in southern California and the Southwest included large numbers of Mexican-Americans. Often unskilled and uneducated, handicapped by not knowing English, discriminated against in wages and housing, most were forced to live in slums. Many of those who did not settle in the cities continued to live as migrant farm workers.

Efforts by labor unions in the 1930's and 1940's to organize Mexican-American farm workers had been largely unsuccessful. In the 1960's, however, Cesar Chavez and other new leaders began to make progress. To the nation as a whole, Chavez soon became the best known figure among Mexican-Americans. He had spent his childhood in migrant labor camps and had emerged as the leader of the underpaid and poorly housed grape and lettuce pickers in California's large vineyards and agricultural enterprises. Committed to the principle of nonviolence, Chavez effectively used the tactic of nationwide boycotts of California grapes and lettuce. Against strong resistance by many growers, he succeeded in organizing a union of migrant laborers, the United Farm Workers.

By the 1970's Mexican-Americans were beginning to obtain at least a measure of the recognition they had struggled so long to secure. Their sons and daughters were enrolled in the high schools and the colleges of California and other southwestern states. Some Mexican-Americans were achieving success in businesses, government, and the professions. And increasingly they were learning how to gain and use political power to improve their own lives.

The Puerto Ricans

The more than 1 million Puerto Ricans living in the United States in the 1970's made up the third Spanish-speaking group. As you recall, Puerto Rico had special relationships with the United States, first as an unincorporated Territory beginning in 1898 and then, after 1952, as a Commonwealth. Under these relationships, since 1898, the inhabitants of the Caribbean island were legally entitled to the rights and privileges of American citizenship. Even before the worldwide depression of the 1930's brought severe hardships to that already poor and overcrowded island, many Puerto Ricans had migrated to New York City in search of jobs. During and after the depression they came in ever-increasing numbers.

Puerto Ricans who moved to New York City, Newark, Chicago, and other northern cities faced many problems. Most came from rural villages. They lacked the skills necessary for life in a highly complex and competitive city environment. Many had only a limited knowledge of English. Perhaps most serious, they were victims of prejudice and discrimination.

Because of these handicaps most of the newcomers were able to get only unskilled jobs that paid the lowest wages. Puerto Rican families were crowded into tenement districts, such as Spanish Harlem and other segregated areas in New York City as well as in other major cities, where their lives were marked by poverty and hardship.

The lives of young Puerto Ricans were especially difficult. In schools they were often handicapped by lack of bilingual programs of instruction. And they found it difficult to obtain jobs when they graduated.

In some ways the experiences of Puerto Ricans in the United States resembled those of earlier immigrants. Many gradually moved up the economic ladder and found places in small businesses, semi-skilled trades, the professions, and the arts. In the fields of entertainment and sports Jose Feliciano, Rita Moreno, Jose Ferrer, and Roberto Clemente became well known. When the voting power of Puerto Ricans in the large cities became clear, politicians began to consider Puerto Ricans as a "force." In 1970 Herman Badillo of New York City became the first Puerto Rican member of the House of Representatives in Congress.

The first Americans

No minority in the nation has had to face more problems than the American Indians. In

Puerto Ricans faced serious problems similar to those of earlier immigrants. They often were forced to work in low-paid, unskilled jobs as they tried to improve their lives.

addition to discrimination, severe unemployment, and widespread poverty, the Indians have had to cope with many federal controls and with shifting federal policies and programs.

The struggle to overcome these handicaps has been carried on by Indian leaders from all walks of life, including the professions—doctors, lawyers, teachers, writers, singers, athletes, and others. It has been a long and at times disheartening struggle.

In 1934 Congress reversed a long-standing policy with the adoption of the Indian Reorganization Act. This 1934 law was originally intended to encourage the Indians to practice self-government and strengthen tribal customs and tribal life. But the promises of the act were rarely fulfilled. Some tribes that had succeeded fairly well in adapting to the majority culture rejected the new policy, claiming that it would keep them in an inferior status in relation to the white majority. Tradition-minded chiefs discovered that many of the 25,000 young Indian soldiers who served in the armed forces during World War II were reluctant to return to tribal customs. These Indian veterans felt that the full recognition of their rights as American citizens was more important than the preservation and perpetuation of tribal life.

During the early 1950's the federal government again adopted a new policy. In this policy the government reversed much of the 1934 program and established new goals. One of the new goals was known as "termination." The policy of termination was intended to end all federal ties with the Indians. Responsibility was to be transferred to those states with large Indian populations. Acting under this policy, the government terminated federal services for a number of tribes, including the Menominees of Wisconsin and the Klamaths of Oregon. But this proved disastrous for the Indians, for the states were unwilling or unable to provide health, education, and welfare services.

The second goal of the new Indian policy was to assimilate the Indians into the majority culture by "relocating" as many as possible in cities. The Bureau of Indian Affairs attracted thousands of Indians to cities with promises of job training and job placement that often were not kept. Some Indians managed to overcome great odds and achieve success. Many others, faced with discrimination and without the support of tribal life, eked out a lonely, impoverished existence in the cities, which remained for them a strange and alien environment. Some, embittered by the experience, returned to the res-

Indians today have achieved greater control over their own lives. Here, a Navajo tribal council meets to discuss problems that affect its people.

ervations. For most Indians, "relocation," like "termination," proved to be a failure.

In the early 1960's the federal government once more reversed itself, encouraging the Indians again to develop tribal life on their reservations. In support of this policy the government provided assistance for housing, vocational training, and economic development. But the possibility of a return to the former policy of termination continued to haunt the Indians.

Meanwhile new Indian leaders were establishing national organizations to develop pride in Indian identity and to win respect for the Indian heritage. Under the slogan "red power," some of these organizations demonstrated a new militancy in demanding an end to discrimination and unfair treatment both on and outside the reservations. These militant efforts received wide publicity and won much sympathy for the Indian cause. For example, in 1973 members of the American Indian Movement seized the trading post and church at Wounded Knee, South Dakota, and held them for several weeks. Their demands were not met, however.

One promising development was a program announced in the summer of 1970 by President Nixon. The new program included as a central feature a final end to the policy of forced termination.

"Termination," the President declared, "implies that the federal government has taken on a trusteeship responsibility . . . as an act of generosity toward a disadvantaged people, and that it can therefore discontinue this responsibility on a unilateral basis whenever it sees fit." But,

Nixon continued, this was not the case: "The special relationship between the Indians and the federal government is the result . . . of solemn obligations which have been entered into by the United States government. . . ." These obligations "carry immense moral and legal force. . . ." They "cannot be abridged without the consent of the Indians."

The new program was intended to give the Indians greater control over their own lives. Thus it gave the Indians responsibility for managing federal funds for Indian housing, education, medical services, public works, and economic development.

By the 1970's it was evident that the Indians, once condemned by white Americans as a "vanishing race," had not only survived but were increasing in numbers. These first Americans now numbered about 750,000 people. They had shown undaunted vitality and persistence in the long, bitter years of forced subordination, white patronage and chauvinism, disease, and unparalleled poverty. At long last they were demanding, on their own terms, an end to discrimination and inequality and a respected, recognized place in American life.

The women's rights movement

American women, nearly 53 percent of the population, were the largest group struggling against discrimination. During the 1960's a movement that came to be known as Women's Liberation, or the women's rights movement, began to gather strength. In part the movement gained strength because of the rapidly growing numbers and proportions of American women who were now employed. Perhaps even more important, the civil rights movement, in which women were actively involved, gave a new impetus to militant protests against discrimination and inequalities confronting women. Growing numbers of women agreed with feminist leaders that sex discrimination kept many women from realizing their full potentialities.

According to public opinion polls, a sizable majority of American women did not feel that taking care of a home and raising children were restrictive and frustrating roles. By the mid-1970's, however, a majority of American women did approve of equal opportunities for their sex in all areas of life.

One of the first and the most prominent

groups within the women's rights movement was the National Organization for Women (NOW). During the 1960's NOW provided much of the leadership of the movement. But other groups soon formed to work for certain objectives. Among the objectives shared by NOW and other feminist groups were equal treatment of women in educational programs, government provision of publicly financed child care centers, repeal of state laws forbidding abortion, and opposition to the treatment of women as sex objects. Some of these groups also demanded that men share in the tasks of homemaking and child-rearing. All of them were united in demanding strict enforcement of the Civil Rights Act of 1964, which forbade sex discrimination in employment.

The women's rights movement is working to achieve full equality for American women. These women are taking part in a demonstration organized by the National Organization for Women.

New freedoms for women

By the 1970's several objectives of the women's rights movement began to be met. Legal suits were filed against businesses, colleges, and other institutions, charging them with sex discrimination in their hiring, pay, and promotion practices. Separate sex roles, which had earlier begun to diminish with the entry of women into the armed forces and police services, became increasingly blurred. Women gained careers in occupations formerly dominated by men or held only by men, including careers as

members of the clergy. Women won outstanding new recognition in sports such as tennis and golf. There were fewer strict barriers between men and women in dress, social customs, and sexual conduct. By early 1975 the Equal Rights Amendment (see page 675), adopted by Congress three years earlier, had been ratified by 34 of the required 38 states.

In 1973 the Supreme Court ruled that women had the right to have abortions before the sixth month of pregnancy. This controversial decision collided with the existing legislation in most of the states, which then began to change their laws to conform to the Court's ruling. At the same time anti-abortion groups challenged the right of the Court to make such a decision and demanded a Constitutional amendment prohibiting abortions.

In political affairs women continued to be greatly underrepresented, but change was in the air. Several members of Congress, such as Bella Abzug, Shirley Chisholm, Barbara Jordan, and Elizabeth Holtzman, became nationally known. In 1974, 18 women were elected to the House of Representatives and 507 women were members of state legislatures. In Connecticut Ella Grasso became the first woman governor of any state who did not occupy that office as the successor of her husband. In New York Mary Anne Krupsak became the first lieutenant-governor. In San Jose, California, Janet Hayes became the first woman mayor of a large American city. Carla Hills became Secretary of Housing and Urban Transportation under President Ford, the third woman ever to serve in a Presidential cabinet.

Despite some active resistance and the inertia of tradition, by the mid-1970's the women's rights movement was moving toward the achievement of most, if not all, of its goals. This development seemed likely to bring about far-reaching changes not only in the lives of women but in the lives of all Americans.

SECTION SURVEY

IDENTIFY: Hispanos, migrant farm workers, United Farm Workers, termination, relocation, American Indian Movement, women's rights movement, NOW, Equal Rights Amendment; Cesar Chavez, Ella Grasso, Bella Abzug, Barbara Jordan, Carla Hills.

1. Identify the several groups of Spanish-speaking Americans. (a) What characteristics do they share? (b) How are their backgrounds different?
2. In what ways have Spanish-speaking Americans suffered discrimination? What actions have they taken to gain better lives?
3. How have American Indians been denied full rights in American life? What changes have occurred in the government's policy toward the Indians?
4. What were some goals of the women's rights movement? What gains have women made in recent years?

CHAPTER SURVEY

INQUIRING INTO HISTORY

1. Describe the effect that the transformation of the United States from a rural to an industrial society has had on different groups of Americans.
2. What are some causes of the urban crisis? Can you suggest some ways of helping to solve the crisis?
3. Compare the aims and activities of the civil rights movement in the early 1960's with those of the late 1960's. What gains were made during these years to strengthen the rights of black Americans?
4. How have government policies toward American Indians shifted in recent years? How are Indian groups now trying to strengthen their traditional cultures and to control their own lives?
5. What is the women's rights movement? How have women's roles been changing in recent years?

RELATING PAST TO PRESENT

1. During the 1800's many Americans considered the United States a "melting pot" of many peoples. How would you describe the United States today? How do you explain your viewpoint if it is different from that of the 1800's?
2. What are some problems and some advantages of living in today's urban society? What were some problems and advantages of living in the rural society of the 1800's?

DEVELOPING SOCIAL SCIENCE SKILLS

1. In a two-column chart with the headings "Court Decisions" and "New Legislation," list some major gains in the civil rights movement since World War II. (a) What effects did each law or decision have? (b) Why do you think a strong civil rights movement developed after the war?
2. Find accounts written about the discrimination faced by women in American society. (a) What kinds of discrimination do women face? (b) What effects has discrimination had on women? (c) What are women doing to end discrimination? (d) Do you think these methods are effective? Why?

CHAPTER *25*

AMERICA IN AN ERA OF RAPID GROWTH AND CHANGE

Change and *growth* are the words that best describe American society in the years since 1945. Nor has anything been more striking than the *speed* with which every aspect of life has been transformed in the United States and throughout the world.

To be sure, change has been a central feature of American life from the day the first European settlers landed on the shores of the New World. Through the course of three and a half centuries Americans subdued a continent and converted the wilderness into one of the world's most prosperous and dynamic nations.

But a new and startling fact in the postwar years has been the *increasingly rapid acceleration* of change. Not since life first appeared on earth has so much change been compressed into such a brief span of time. One observer, writing in the early 1960's, declared that these changes were "so wide-sweeping that they are taking us from one epoch of human history into another." In his judgment, the world of the future will be as different from the world of today as the present world is different from that of the Stone Age hunters who roamed the forests and grasslands in search of food at the dawn of human history.

During the 1940's, however, not even the most far-sighted observers could foresee the amazing developments that would, in the years immediately ahead, profoundly alter older ways of living in the United States and increasingly throughout the world. In 1945—even indeed as recently as the early 1960's—the opportunities and challenges of the new age had not yet been revealed. But by the mid-1970's the American people were becoming keenly aware that the prosperity and power that so many of them had been enjoying were not unmixed blessings. Developments that had brought the nation unprecedented abundance had also created new and formidable problems. The only certainty for Americans was that these problems and challenges would continue to test their ingenuity in the years ahead.

THE CHAPTER IN OUTLINE

1. The increasing momentum of the technological revolution.

2. Building an economy of abundance in the nation.

3. Reappraising the nation's goals in a troubled world.

4. The deepening crisis of the environment.

CHANGING WAYS OF AMERICAN LIFE   1945-1970's

1 The increasing momentum of the technological revolution

The technological revolution has transformed—and continues to transform—almost every aspect of modern life. This profound change in technology—the application of scientific advances and techniques in business and industry—has been made possible by highly organized scientific research and development. Before the postwar years the major advances in science in both Europe and America had been made by individual scientists working alone or with a few colleagues in the laboratories of universities or private industry. During the years following World War II, however, scientific research and development became increasingly a carefully organized team effort in which the federal government played an important role.

One of the most eminent twentieth-century scholars, Alfred North Whitehead, observed that when human beings began to organize research they invented "the art of inventing." This "invention," he concluded, was one of humanity's greatest achievements. The first dramatic demonstration of what scientists and engineers could accomplish by such large-scale cooperation occurred during World War II.

Harnessing the energy of the stars

On Wednesday, December 2, 1942, in below-freezing temperatures, Chicago pedestrians hurried about their business, eager to get out of the cold. Fortunately for their peace of mind, the people of Chicago were unaware of what was going on in a laboratory under the stands of the Stagg Athletic Field at the University of Chicago. In the laboratory, which only a few weeks earlier had been a squash court, a group of scientists led by Enrico Fermi, an Italian refugee, were about to conduct the most fateful experiment ever undertaken.

The scientists, after months of feverish research, were about to start an atomic reaction in an attempt to learn whether, if started, it could be controlled and stopped before it got out of hand. If the reaction proved uncontrollable, the most fearful explosion ever produced by human beings might destroy a large part of Chicago and wipe out untold thousands of lives.

Only the pressure of a national emergency justified the risk. German scientists were trying to develop an atomic bomb. Confronted with this terrifying challenge, President Roosevelt had ordered a select group of the nation's leading scientists and engineers to spare no cost in the effort to beat the Germans in this awesome task. The all-out effort conducted in the utmost secrecy was officially launched on December 6, 1941, under the innocent-sounding code name "Manhattan Project." Only a handful of the nation's top leaders knew that the goal was an atomic bomb.

Writing years later, one of these leaders, Arthur Holly Compton, described the suspenseful moment when Dr. Fermi gave the order to begin the test. "The counters registering the rays from the pile began to click faster and faster until the sound became a rattle. . . . Finally after many minutes the meters showed a reading that meant the radiation reaching the balcony was beginning to be dangerous. 'Throw in the safety rods,' came Fermi's order. They went in with a clatter. . . . The rattle of the counters died down to an occasional click. I imagine that I can still hear the sigh of relief. . . . Atomic Power! It had been produced, kept under control, and stopped. . . ."

The experiment was a success. For the first time in history human beings had grasped, if only for a fleeting moment, the most elemental force in nature—the energy that keeps the stars blazing in the skies.

Organizing human intelligence

But it was a long step from a laboratory experiment to the production of an atomic bomb, and an even longer step to the development of atomic energy for peacetime uses. For three years, in an all-out effort to develop the bomb, thousands of the nation's leading scientists, engineers, and construction workers devoted their time and talents to the Manhattan Project.

Never before had so much money ($2 billion), so much intelligence, and so much effort been channeled into a single undertaking. The atomic bombs that leveled Hiroshima and Nagasaki in August 1945 provided evidence, terrible though it was in this case, of the effectiveness of organized cooperative research. This effectiveness was to be demonstrated again during the 1960's with another massive project—the successful effort conducted over nearly 10 years to land American astronauts on the moon.

The growth of organized research

Mindful of the results achieved by the Manhattan Project and other wartime ventures, such as the development of radar, both government and private industry in the postwar years devoted more and more money to scientific research and development. Whereas in 1930 only $166 million was spent for this purpose, by 1953 the total had risen to $5 billion and by 1969 to $25 billion, almost two thirds of which came from the federal government. Although the federal government is the major investor in scientific research and development, most of the work is carried on in the laboratories of private industry, universities, and independent research institutes.

As a result of highly organized scientific activities, new knowledge began to accumulate at such a staggering rate that people began to speak of the "knowledge explosion." The amount of information available to the human race, it was estimated, was doubling every 10 years. And the new methods of discovery and invention were self-generating. That is, each advance and each gain in knowledge opened up new horizons for science and made possible further progress in technology. As you will see, new industries were created and thousands of new products became available. And most important, scientists were making fantastic progress in understanding the basic forces of nature.

But, as you will also see, each fresh discovery also created new problems. With the invention of the "art of inventing," such rapid change was being built into society that the world could never be the same again.

Computers are now used in most large American businesses. This company's computers do much of the record keeping and clerical work once performed by office workers.

International aspects of the revolution

As the years passed, international scientific research came to be carried on by well-organized teams of scientists from many countries. The period from July 1, 1957, to December 31, 1958, was proclaimed the International Geophysical Year. During this period scientists of 66 nations worked together in a worldwide study of gravity, geomagnetism, meteorology, oceanography, solar activity, cosmic rays, and other fundamental subjects.

In 1959 the United States and 11 other nations, including the Soviet Union, signed a treaty agreeing (1) not to exercise any territorial claim over the vast, ice-covered continent of Antarctica and (2) to set the continent aside as a scientific preserve open to the scientists of all nations.

Early in 1967 a similar treaty relating to outer space was signed by 62 countries. The treaty (1) prohibits the orbiting of nuclear weapons and (2) prohibits any nation from claiming sovereignty over the moon or any planet. President Johnson called the treaty "the first, firm step toward keeping outer space free forever from the implements of war." And in the early 1970's United States astronauts and Soviet cosmonauts began shared experiments involving docking procedures of their spacecraft in outer space.

Computers and the technological revolution

The electronic computer was one of the most significant postwar products of the technological revolution. The first modern computers were developed shortly after World War II. By 1956 fewer than 1,000 were being used. By 1968 more than 15,000 were installed in laboratories, business offices, government agencies, banks, and scores of other organizations. The number doubled during the first half of the 1970's.

In a fraction of a second computers can perform calculations that even the most efficient individual could not complete in a lifetime. Computers available by the mid-1960's could perform in one second 357,000 additions or subtractions or 178,500 multiplications or 102,000 divisions. They were being used in laboratories to provide instant analysis of complex technical problems that could not be studied in any other way. They were being used by businesses and banks for accounting, bookkeeping, and billing. They were being used by governments to check income tax returns and to record data on births, marriages, public health, car registrations, and criminal records. They were being used in industry to forecast economic trends and control assembly lines in automated factories. And by the 1970's the computer industry itself had become a multibillion dollar enterprise, creating new careers and jobs for computer programmers, technicians, and systems planners.

In brief, machines were doing much of certain kinds of mental work once performed by men and women. In fact, any data that could be measured or counted could be handled more efficiently by computers than by human beings.

Automation in business and industry

Other equipment performed still other operations far more swiftly and efficiently than individuals could hope to do. For example, the Bell Telephone Company reported that if it had not installed automatic switchboards, by 1962 a work force equal to the total of all the women in the nation between the ages of 18 and 30 would have been required to handle the 90 billion telephone calls made in the United States that year alone.

The automated machines used in many industries performed a whole series of operations and adjusted themselves to correct their own errors. By the 1960's automated factories could turn raw materials into finished products with only a handful of technicians to plan and control the manufacturing process. By the 1970's automated plants, mills, and factories were common in basic industries operated by large corporations throughout the United States.

Built-in change

Technological development has long been a fundamental part of growth and change in all societies. History provides an almost endless list of examples that demonstrate the profound impact of technological change. The invention of the chariot and its use against foot soldiers transformed the nature of war in ancient times, as did the use of the tank in World War I. The development of the compass, the sternpost rudder, and three-masted ships resulted in a shift of economic and political power from the Mediterranean Sea to the Atlantic Ocean and led to the voyages of exploration to the New World.

But the new and dramatic dimension of change and growth in the postwar world was the speed with which new inventions and new techniques were introduced into society. Never in all human history had technological developments been responsible for such sweeping transformations in peoples' lives. As you will see, the astonishing growth during the postwar years brought Americans an unprecedented abundance of material goods. As you will also see, it also brought new problems that deeply troubled the American nation.

SECTION SURVEY

IDENTIFY: "the art of inventing," Manhattan Project, "knowledge explosion," International Geophysical Year, automation; Enrico Fermi.

1. Large-scale cooperation by scientists and engineers occurred during World War II. Why?
2. The technological revolution has brought about great changes in American society. Explain.
3. What new pressures has the "knowledge explosion" placed on schools and colleges? On students?
4. How have automation and computers affected business? Cite some examples of their uses.

2 Building an economy of abundance in the nation

The most obvious impact of the postwar revolution in science and technology was upon the nation's economic life. After World War II ended, the United States entered a period of unprecedented prosperity built on what economists called "an economy of abundance." This term described an economic system capable of producing more goods and services than Americans as a whole were able to consume.

Growing productivity

In a study based on the nation's economy in the 1950's, a group of distinguished economists concluded that "America today has the strongest, most productive economic system in human history. . . . The United States, with little more than 6 percent of the world's population and less than 7 percent of its land area, now produces and consumes well over one third of the world's goods and services, and turns out nearly one half of the world's factory-produced goods."

Even more significant than the high level of production and prosperity at mid-century were predictions of future growth based on past trends. During the 75 years preceding World War II the United States doubled its output of goods about once every 24 years. From 1945 to the early 1970's the rate of growth climbed sharply. If it continued, the United States would double its production every 18 years.

For Americans as a whole the growth of the economy meant a continuing rise in their standards of living. As you know, however, by the 1970's inflation and recession had become threats to the nation's economic health and to the ability of the economy to continue to grow in the future as it had in the recent past.

The roots of prosperity

There were many reasons for America's remarkable economic growth. Among them were an abundance of natural resources, an excellent transportation system, vast numbers of skilled workers, steadily improving labor-management relations, highly organized and efficiently managed industries, efficient methods of distribution, and an economic system that rewarded both individual effort and teamwork. The role of advertising in stimulating the desire of consumers for more goods and services also played a part in economic growth.

But above all it was the astonishing advance of science and technology during and after World War II that sent the economy spiraling upward. By the 1970's the United States had become the most productive nation in the world. Power-driven machinery and increasingly complex equipment had almost entirely replaced hand tools and backbreaking physical labor in nearly every field of human activity— on farms and in mines, in factories, laboratories, offices, and homes. Roughly one third of all the world's raw materials flowed each year into America's industries. Out of the nation's industrial plants poured an endless variety of products in ever-increasing quantities.

By the 1970's American farm production, too, was setting new records. As a result of striking advances in agricultural science and technology, in farm management, and in marketing, Americans on the whole were among the best fed people in the world. Each year the nation's farms produced huge amounts of food to feed Americans and to export to other nations.

New and expanding industries

As the technological revolution gathered momentum, new industries joined older ones in providing the products, services, and opportunities available to more and more Americans.

The aircraft industry, still in its infancy in the 1920's, grew in the years following World War II to a multibillion-dollar enterprise. Commercial airlines directly employed thousands of men and women. Many other thousands were employed in the plants producing aircraft for the airlines and for private individuals, business firms, and the armed services.

The electronics industry, also an infant in the early 1920's, boomed during World War II with the production of radio transmitters, radar, and other equipment for the military forces. During the postwar years it gained still greater momentum with the production of television sets, computers, automation controls, transistor radios, minicalculators, stereo sets, tape decks, and an incredible variety of complex instruments to control and monitor rockets and missiles.

In the late 1950's, when Soviet and American space exploration began in earnest, the aircraft and electronics industries joined hundreds of other enterprises in an entirely new undertaking—the space program. By the early 1960's some 9,000 American firms were actively participating in research and development of space-related items. By 1964 more than 30,000 scientists and other specialists were working for the National Aeronautics and Space Administration (NASA). Estimates of the total number of Americans engaged in some phase of the space program ranged from 3 to 5 million. Moreover, by 1964 the space research program had created some 3,200 different products, many of which had become part of the nation's everyday life.

Another completely new industry, atomic energy, also expanded greatly during the postwar years. By the early 1960's nearly 140,000 scientists, engineers, and other workers were engaged in atomic energy activities. Although military developments continued to dominate the effort, peaceful applications of atomic energy were growing more numerous. For example, the first commercial atomic-powered plant for generating electricity began operations near Pittsburgh in 1957. By the early 1970's more than 100 nuclear generating plants, producing nearly 8 percent of the nation's electricity, were operating throughout the country, and 1,000 were scheduled for operation by the year 2000. As you will read, however, the potential threat to the environment posed by the production of nuclear energy remained a disturbing problem.

While new industries were coming into existence, older industries were modernizing their plants and expanding their operations by mergers and by the continuing development of new products. Among the postwar industrial giants were the steel, automotive, petroleum, chemical, pharmaceutical, and business machine industries. The giant of giants was the American Telephone and Telegraph Company, the largest corporation in the world. As incomes rose and people had more leisure time, companies manufacturing sports and camping equipment became big businesses.

San Francisco's automated trains comprise one of the most modern systems of mass transportation in the nation.

The revolution in transportation

The nation's swift advance into an "economy of abundance" would not have been possible without revolutionary developments in transportation.

In 1945 commercial airlines were still operating out of small airports and carrying only about 3 million passengers annually, mainly in two-engine propeller-driven planes capable of carrying only 20 to 40 passengers. By the 1960's they were operating out of huge, overcrowded airports, using jet aircraft, and carrying more than 60 million passengers annually as well as ever-growing amounts of freight. By the 1970's jumbo jets with a carrying capacity of 360 passengers or 20 tons of freight were in operation.

Speed as well as size and versatility became a major factor in aircraft design during the postwar years. By the late 1950's jet aircraft on commercial air routes were flying at 600 miles (965.6 kilometers) an hour, close to the speed of sound. By the late 1960's designers were developing supersonic transport planes (SST's) that could fly at more than 2,000 miles (3,218.6 kilometers) an hour, or about three times the speed of sound.

By the early 1970's the Soviet Union, as well as Great Britain and France in collaboration, had developed and were test flying commercial supersonic planes. In the meantime, however, a growing body of scientific evidence suggested that extensive supersonic flights might, in time, damage the earth's ozone shield, with disastrous consequences for peoples everywhere. Faced with this possibility, Congress voted to suspend work on a commercial SST it had been subsidizing.

New problems in transportation

During the postwar years traffic problems on the nation's streets and highways became an engineer's nightmare. Between 1945 and 1970 the number of automobiles, buses, and trucks nearly quadrupled, increasing from 31 million to more than 120 million. The Federal Aid Highway Act, adopted by Congress in 1956, provided for the construction of 42,500 new miles (68,395 kilometers) of superhighways by 1972. Almost as soon as the act was passed, traffic experts began to talk of the need to revise its provisions.

By the early 1970's federal, state, and local governments were pouring billions of dollars annually into the construction of new roads, highways, and parking facilities. By 1976 a nationwide area equal to the total area of the six New England states had been paved with asphalt or concrete to provide nearly 4 million miles (6.4 million kilometers) of hard-surfaced streets, roads, and highways for the nation. But with the addition of more than 2 million new motor vehicles each year, the problem was far from solved. Indeed, figures compiled by traffic engineers indicated that automobile manufacturers were making cars and trucks faster than the nation was building roads and parking facilities to handle them. By the 1970's automobiles also had become the major source of the nation's increasingly critical air pollution.

In the 1970's the transportation needs of America's cities became more pressing. Public transportation by buses and subways was facing mounting deficits and attracting fewer riders. City and state governments provided funds to modernize their bus lines and subways in an effort to reduce the use of cars by city families and commuters. And in 1974 Congress passed the Mass Transportation Act, which provided federal aid to improve local transportation systems. This legislation also reflected Congress' intention to help reduce urban air pollution caused by cars and to conserve the vast amounts of fuel required in using cars for city transportation.

The railroads, once the nation's main carriers of passengers and freight, did not share in the postwar transportation boom. Faced with mounting competition from other forms of transportation, rising taxes, increasing costs of labor and equipment, and falling incomes, many railroads by the 1960's were either bankrupt or on the verge of bankruptcy.

Although the railroads still carried nearly half the nation's freight, they were meeting stiffer and stiffer competition, especially from the trucking industry. Moreover, they had lost most of their passenger business to automobiles, buses, and planes. To be sure, daily commuter trains carrying workers to and from their city jobs were still crowded. But with few exceptions commuter railroads, too, were operating at a loss. Railroad managers argued that if commuter services were to continue, federal, state, and local governments would have to subsidize train service. By the late 1960's city and state governments—particularly in the Northeast—were aiding commuter railroads by lowering taxes and providing subsidies. When these efforts proved inadequate, Congress passed legislation in the early 1970's to rescue some railroads from bankruptcy.

Growth of the middle class

As one result of the changes occurring in the nation's economy, America became increasingly a middle-class society. By the 1970's blue-collar workers, who in 1945 had been the largest group in the labor force, were outnumbered almost two to one by other workers. The greatest growth in employment was in the service industries and in occupations requiring professional and technical skills—teaching, science, engineering, communications, law, medicine, and nursing. Between 1960 and 1968 college enrollments doubled. By 1970 an estimated 7 million students were enrolled and 500,000 teachers were working in the nation's colleges and universities.

One of the most rapidly expanding areas of employment in the postwar years was service in government—federal, state, and local. By the 1970's one out of every five workers in the United States was employed by government.

The changing role of women

Another remarkable postwar development was the increasingly important role women were playing in the nation's work life. The contrast with earlier years was striking. Whereas in 1900 men made up nearly the entire work force, by the early 1970's more than 40 percent of the work force were women.

The number of working women, a large percentage of whom were married, had gained momentum in the years after 1945. Several developments greatly speeded this process. First, the demand for workers during World War II broke down many deeply rooted prejudices and gave women a chance to show that they could do as well as men in many different jobs. Second, and even more significant, the rapid expansion of the postwar economy created thousands of new jobs, nearly all of which demanded brainpower rather than muscle. Third, as women became more independent, they sought jobs and careers to fulfill their own needs and ambitions. Fourth, many married women sought jobs so that their families would achieve a higher standard of living. Indeed, by the 1970's the high prices brought by inflation caused many married women to seek employment. By 1975 nearly half of all American women between the ages of 18 and 65 were gainfully employed.

Steadily growing numbers of women were entering the professions of medicine, law, education, religion, science, and engineering. More and more were occupying positions of leadership in business and government that had formerly been held only by men.

But women continued to face discrimination. Many employers did not accept the principle that women were entitled to the same pay and the same opportunities open to men. Determined to overcome this handicap, women demanded full equality of rights and opportunities in every sphere of American life. As a result, in the 1970's Congress and many state legislatures passed laws guaranteeing equal pay and equal job opportunities for women.

Prosperity and problems

By the early 1970's the American people as a whole enjoyed a standard of living undreamed of even a generation earlier. Food in

The number of women in America's work force has grown steadily in recent years. Many women now work at jobs like these once held only by men.

abundance flowed from the nation's farms, ranches, orchards, and processing plants. A seemingly endless volume and variety of consumer goods poured out of factories into American homes. Striking advances in medical science reduced suffering and prolonged life. Americans of all ages took advantage of new opportunities for recreation, education, and the cultural pleasures of music, literature, and the fine arts.

It was indeed a good life, a life of unprecedented abundance, not only for Americans but for most of the people in the industrialized countries.

Unhappily, the benefits of the good life were not shared equally. According to the 1970 census, an estimated 40 million Americans—one out of every five persons in the nation—lived in poverty or in near poverty. In the world as a whole, two thirds of the earth's population suf-

fered from hunger or malnutrition. Each year millions died from starvation.

Equally disturbing was the growing evidence that the good life carried a hidden price tag—a very high price tag indeed.

SECTION SURVEY

IDENTIFY: "economy of abundance," NASA, Federal Aid Highway Act, Mass Transportation Act.

1. Explain the reasons for America's remarkable economic growth after World War II.
2. What new industries developed rapidly after World War II?
3. List some of the developments in American transportation in the years after World War II.
4. Why did new job opportunities for women develop after 1945? How did women's roles in industry and business begin to change?

3 Reappraising the nation's goals in a troubled world

By the mid-1970's it had become clear that the American people could no longer take for granted the continued growth and prosperity most of them had enjoyed for so many years. As never before in the nation's history, Americans in every walk of life were confronted with the urgent need to reappraise the nation's goals as well as their own personal objectives in life.

The challenges were formidable. Inflation

coupled with recession and mounting unemployment compounded the problems of widespread poverty in a land of plenty. Schools and colleges faced soaring costs and the urgent need to reassess their goals in a rapidly changing world. The growing loss of confidence of many Americans in their government cast a deepening shadow over the democratic process. And in the world as a whole hunger and want were increasing, tensions were mounting, and the environment of the earth itself was deteriorating at an accelerating rate.

The nation's poor

According to the Census Bureau, in 1971 almost 26 million Americans lived in poverty—7.4 million of them black and 2.4 million of Spanish-speaking origin, and many of them members of Indian tribes. Poverty for a nonfarm family of four meant a family income of just over $4,000. In addition, another 15 million women, men, and children were living in near poverty conditions. This total of more than 41 million poor people represented one out of every five Americans. Moreover, 4 million American homes lacked running water and plumbing. New low-income and moderate-income housing was not being built fast enough to replace rundown, worn out dwellings.

The war on poverty

"Poverty in the midst of plenty is a paradox that must not go unchallenged," President Kennedy had declared in 1963. President Johnson, sharing this determination, had launched an "unconditional war on poverty" (page 347). In 1964, responding to the administration's urging, Congress created the Office of Economic Opportunity (OEO). Under the OEO a number of programs were started—a Head Start education program for preschool children; a Neighborhood Youth Corps for unemployed teenagers; a Job Corps for young people who had dropped out of school; an Upward Bound program to help students enter college; and the VISTA program (a domestic version of the Peace Corps) in which volunteers worked with and among the nation's poor.

In 1965 Congress continued the war on poverty with several important measures aimed at improving conditions in job training, health, education, and housing. It expanded the 1964 Economic Opportunity Act. It adopted a Medicare bill providing for hospital care and other medical services for persons over 65. It enacted into law two major education bills, one providing federal aid for elementary and secondary education, and the other for higher education. It created a new federal department, the Department of Housing and Urban Development. To head the new department, President Johnson appointed Robert C. Weaver, the first black American to serve in the cabinet.

Congress also set up a $1.3 billion Model Cities program. Under this program a group of about 75 cities were to develop "model" plans for rebuilding slum areas. These plans were to provide for the coordination of all federal programs—job training, health, education, housing, and welfare. All planning was to be done in cooperation with citizens in the communities to be rebuilt.

Loss of momentum

The driving force of the war on poverty did not last long, however. By 1965 the Vietnam conflict was intensifying. As one result, the antipoverty program began to lose momentum. For

These Job Corps workers are learning job skills as they work at a construction job in a central city neighborhood.

nearly eight long years—under the administrations of President Johnson and President Nixon—the United States grew increasingly preoccupied with the war in Southeast Asia. Then, when direct American involvement in the war ended in 1973, the Watergate scandals (page 354) continued to divide the nation and turn the attention of the government away from the problem of poverty.

During Nixon's administration the Model Cities program came to a halt through lack of funding. At the same time the Office of Economic Opportunity was abolished, and the programs for which it had been responsible were either ended or transferred to other agencies.

Early in his first administration Nixon advocated a "family assistance plan" to fight poverty, which he claimed would be an improvement over the existing welfare system. However, he did not push hard for the plan, nor did Congress enact the measure.

The victims of poverty

Thus in the mid-1970's, as in earlier years, poverty remained a major problem in rural as well as urban areas of the nation. There were nearly as many poor American families living outside metropolitan areas as within them.

In both rural and urban areas, poverty was found most often among certain groups—men and women over 65, unskilled workers, and migrant workers. Among these groups, those who often suffered most were the nation's minorities. Although white Americans comprised two thirds of the poor, the nonwhite population bore the heaviest burden. Only about 12 percent of the total white population lived in poverty, compared to 40 percent of the nonwhite population. And for Americans as a whole, the age of abundance that they had been enjoying was being replaced by years of anxiety as real incomes declined and unemployment continued to increase. By mid-1975 nearly 9 percent of all workers were unemployed.

Education reflects the state of the nation

The fast-moving developments reshaping the nation and the world created both problems and opportunities for the educational system.

During the 1960's one of the more serious problems was overcrowding. The rapidly growing population placed increasingly heavy burdens on the entire educational system. For example, between 1940 and 1970 the number of students enrolled in the nation's schools and institutions of higher education more than doubled, rising from 30 million to more than 70 million. The increase in college and university enroll-

ments, which rose 45 percent in the five-year period from 1963 to 1968, was especially significant. By 1968 at least one third of all young people between 18 and 21 were attending institutions of higher education.

As the shortage of buildings, equipment, and teachers grew more acute, college students became increasingly restless. In the late 1960's demonstrations and even riots occurred on campuses across the nation in protest against the war in Vietnam, racial injustice, and widespread poverty. Students also protested that colleges and universities had become huge, impersonal "educational factories" and that their education seemed to have little relevance to the contemporary world. By the mid-1970's, however, calm had returned to most campuses; yet colleges faced new difficulties.

Defense orientation of higher education

One of the developments in education that troubled many students was the growing emphasis on science and technology. This emphasis had received new impetus in 1957 when the Soviet Union launched its first Sputnik.

A concerned Congress had reacted in 1958 with the National Defense Education Act. The act was designed to strengthen the teaching of science, mathematics, engineering, and modern foreign languages. It provided funds for laboratory and other equipment and for loans to college students.

Criticism that the act neglected the humanities and the social sciences prompted Congress to revise it in 1964. The revised measure increased the money available for student loans. It also provided funds for the purchase of equipment in the teaching of English, history, geography, and civics as well as science, mathematics, and modern foreign languages.

Even more disturbing to many students was the growing involvement of the universities in war-oriented activities. Students charged that the universities were no longer "free" but were becoming "servants of the government."

By the late 1960's universities depended upon the federal government for more than two thirds of their research funds. Especially disturbing to many students was the fact that a large percentage of federal research money was given over to military and defense-related research. In contrast, less than one half of 1 percent of the billions the federal government was spending on research was devoted to efforts to improve the quality of education.

Growing federal support of education

The growth of federal financial support for

education was a significant development of the 1960's.

In both 1961 and 1962 Congress refused, after heated debate, to adopt administration-sponsored bills that included the authorization of funds to help build classrooms and raise teachers' salaries. One group of opponents feared that federal aid would lead to federal control. Another group refused to vote for bills that did not include assistance for church-affiliated schools and other independent schools. Still another group raised an equally controversial issue by insisting that federal aid should go only to schools that had complied with federal law in regard to desegregation.

In 1963, however, the tide began to turn when Congress voted $231 million for construction of buildings for medical and dental schools. It also voted $1.2 billion to assist colleges in building classrooms, libraries, and laboratories. And, as you have just read, in 1964 it greatly expanded the National Defense Education Act.

By far the most significant development was the Education Act of 1965. This act provided $1.3 billion in federal aid to the nation's public elementary and secondary schools. The money was to go to school districts in direct proportion to the number of children in those districts who came from families with annual incomes of less than $2,000 a year. "I deeply believe," President Johnson declared, "that no law I have signed, or will ever sign, means more to the nation."

The Education Act of 1965 provided a pattern for continuing financial assistance to the nation's public elementary and secondary schools. Congress, now committed to the principle of federal support for every level and type of education, began to appropriate increasingly large sums for many new programs. Between 1964 and 1969 federal aid for all types of education increased from $2.4 billion to $7.8 billion. By 1973, in spite of administration efforts to limit spending, federal aid had climbed to $12.7 billion.

Skyrocketing costs

Even with growing federal support, however, the nation's educational institutions faced a financial crisis. Although enrollments began to drop by the early 1970's, expenses skyrocketed, partly because of the growing inflation. Between 1970 and 1974 the number of students attending schools and colleges decreased from 70 million to 58.6 million, but costs during these same years climbed from about $70 billion to nearly $110 billion. In one year alone, from 1973 to 1974, they rose about $11 billion.

Questions of quality

The financial crisis came at a time when the nation's schools and institutions of higher education were confronted with the heaviest responsibility they had ever been expected to carry. Overriding all other issues was the basic question: What kind of education should American schools provide to prepare students for life in a rapidly changing world?

The evidence was overwhelming that poorly educated, poorly trained men and women had little hope of earning an adequate living in an increasingly complex society. Far more serious from society's point of view was the fact that inadequately educated citizens could not help to solve the increasingly critical problems facing the nation and the world.

Extensive efforts to improve the quality of education began in the late 1950's with improvements in the teaching of mathematics, physics, chemistry, biology, and other natural sciences. By the mid-1960's these efforts had broadened to include the humanities and the social sciences. Aided by grants of money from the federal government and from private foundations, projects designed to improve the curriculum and methods of learning were being developed and tried out in research centers and in hundreds of schools. In general the new programs undertook to discourage older methods in which students learned by memorizing data from a lecture or from a textbook. Instead the new projects emphasized an approach in which students assumed major responsibility for solving problems by gathering and analyzing data and arriving at their own conclusions.

Another major development was the effort to improve the quality of education for disadvantaged students. The Head Start program sponsored by the federal government brought preschool children together in an effort to provide them with rewarding learning experiences. "Store-front academies" set up in the central cities and supported by industry and other private organizations gave school "dropouts" the chance to resume their education. Open enrollment programs financed by state and local governments provided an opportunity for high school students from low-income families to attend college.

These and other developments, including the use of closed circuit television, computer terminals, and other kinds of educational technology in the classrooms, represented a determined effort to improve the quality of American education. Years before, historian H. G. Wells had warned that "human history becomes more and more a race between education and catastrophe." By the 1970's America's leaders and growing numbers of America's citizens were acutely aware that, to win the race, education must remain the nation's first priority.

Youth's questioning of older values

The unsettling effect of rapid growth and change was also reflected in the attitudes of young Americans. One of the most striking developments of the 1960's was a widening gap between the generations. By the early 1970's many young people were questioning, and some were rejecting, the values and practices of the older generation.

In their attitudes and behavior young Americans had gone through several distinct phases during the postwar years. Those growing up in the 1950's were described as "the uncommitted generation." With the exception of a few "hipsters" and "beatniks," young people in the 1950's seemed to be conformists. On the whole, their goals in life were the security of a steady job, a home in the suburbs, and a safe, comfortable life. For the most part they avoided political activity.

In the early 1960's, however, a spirit of idealism began to replace the earlier widespread apathy. Inspired by a relatively young President, John F. Kennedy, young people began to commit themselves to causes. Some joined the Peace Corps. Others became active in the civil rights movement. Many began to work within the major political parties. College campuses stirred with new political and intellectual activity.

By 1964, however, some of the idealism was draining away. After President Kennedy's assassination a wave of unrest and protest swept through the ranks of the nation's young people. The growing unrest was not confined to the United States.

In the United States it was relatively easy to identify some of the reasons for the unrest, though no one pretended these were all of the reasons. Unemployment, especially among high school dropouts and minority-group teenagers, was an important source of discontent. College students were becoming increasingly restless as enrollments soared and the overcrowded universities tended to become "educational factories." Many young people, as you have read, were deeply disturbed over America's involvement in Vietnam, which they considered immoral and futile. They were concerned, too, over con-

The right to vote was given to 18-year-olds in the 1970's. These young Americans are waiting to vote in their first election.

tinuing poverty and prejudice and discrimination in a nation that professed democratic principles.

These alienated young people reacted in two different ways. One relatively small group, the "hippies," rejecting the adult world and all it represented, refused to make any commitments or assume any responsibilities. Another still smaller group turned to active rebellion, their goal the overthrow of "the establishment" and the creation of what they considered a better society.

Many Americans hoped that the new generation could be encouraged to work for social and political change within the democratic system. One means to this end was the Voting Rights Act of 1970, which gave 18-year-olds the right to vote in federal elections. In 1971 the Twenty-sixth Amendment extended this right to state and local elections (page 674). It was often pointed out that alienated young people were only a small minority of the new generation. Even so, no thoughtful observer dismissed the group as inconsequential. Their protests, whether in the form of passive withdrawal or active rebellion, served as disturbing reminders of America's unfinished business.

The issue of foreign aid

By the 1970's the issue of American assistance to underdeveloped nations of the world had become increasingly urgent. For one thing, the world's food production had not kept pace with its expanding population, which had nearly doubled in 35 years, increasing from approximately two billion to more than four billion. Moreover, many new nations had been created. In 1945, when the United Nations Charter was signed, the organization numbered 50 members, including only two members from Africa and only three from Asia. By 1975, however, more than half the 142 members were nations of Africa and Asia, and three fourths of the total membership were economically underdeveloped countries.

The UN delegates from the underdeveloped nations represented the poor people of the world, and the poor were becoming increasingly impatient with their lot. As historian Arnold Toynbee put it, "In the most remote villages of the world, hundreds of millions of people have at long last sensed the possibility of a better life." Black militancy and other minority group protests in the United States as well as the rising voices of America's poor were part of a worldwide revolution.

Compounding the problem was the fact that the gap between the rich, industrialized countries and the poor, underdeveloped nations was becoming steadily wider and deeper. By the mid-1970's the problem of providing food and other necessities of life for hundreds of millions of men, women, and children in the underdeveloped nations had reached crisis proportions. During the closing months of 1974 two international conferences were held—one in Bucharest, Rumania, to consider the consequences of the explosive worldwide population growth, the other in Rome to consider how to produce more food and distribute it more fairly throughout the world. Even while these conferences were being held, millions of people in African nations, India, and Bangladesh were facing the threat of famine, and other tens of millions in other lands were living in conditions of near starvation.

It was evident that cooperation among nations on a massive scale was urgent. "The next 30 to 35 years may well be the most challenging in the history of mankind," UN Secretary-General Kurt Waldheim warned. Never before, he declared, had "nations or the international community been faced with such expanding demand for food, shelter, employment, education, and health care."

It was also clear that the rich, industrial nations would have to carry a major share of the responsibility for alleviating the problems of poverty and hunger in the world. Self-interest, as well as America's cherished belief in human dignity and equality of opportunity, seemed to place a special responsibility on the United States. But clearly, the United States, experiencing economic recession and faced with increasingly serious needs among its own people, could not shoulder this burden alone.

Few thoughtful Americans opposed foreign aid as such. There was, however, much disagreement about how much of the nation's resources should be devoted to the effort. There were equally vigorous disagreements as to where foreign aid should go and how it could be used most effectively. As a result of these differences of opinion, foreign aid was sharply reduced in 1969 and in subsequent years.

Critics were quick to contrast the $5.18 billion budget for foreign aid in 1975 with the $86 billion budgeted for national defense. Critics also pointed out that much of the budgeted $5.18 billion was for foreign military aid, not for the relief of poverty and suffering in the underdeveloped countries. These same critics were also quick to remind other Americans that 11 nations ranked ahead of the United States in the percentage of their Gross National Product devoted to helping the underdeveloped nations.

Others argued that the United States must give priority to the needs of America's poor and needy. They emphasized that other rich industrialized nations, for example Japan and France, had only modest foreign aid programs. Communist China and the Soviet Union, they pointed out, used aid to underdeveloped nations primarily to strengthen world Communism. And finally, they claimed that the rich, underdeveloped Arab oil nations had an equal responsibility—and an equal ability—to aid hungry peoples everywhere.

SECTION SURVEY

IDENTIFY: poverty, Model Cities program, Education Act of 1965, Twenty-sixth Amendment.

1. What measures were passed by Congress to help the nation's poor? In your opinion, how effective were these measures?
2. What problems did schools and colleges face in the 1960's? How did these problems change in the 1970's?
3. Do you agree that the United States has a special responsibility to help the underdeveloped nations of the world? Why or why not?

4 The deepening crisis of the environment

Among all the problems confronting the American people as they entered the third century of their nation's history, none was more critical than the deteriorating quality of the natural environment.

As early as 1963 Stewart Udall, then Secretary of the Interior, had sounded a warning of trouble ahead. "History tells us," he warned, "that earlier civilizations declined because they did not learn to live in harmony with the land. . . . America stands today poised on a pinnacle of wealth and power, yet we live in a land of vanishing beauty, of increasing ugliness, of shrinking open space, and of an overall environment that is diminished daily by pollution and noise and blight." During the next few years growing numbers of ecologists°, biologists, and other scientists expressed alarm over the reckless misuse of the environment.

The deteriorating environment

By the mid-1970's most Americans were aware that the nation's amazing economic growth had caused increasing pollution of the most essential of all the natural resources—air, water, and soil. Clean air in many cities had been replaced by smog. Some rivers had been turned into virtual sewers. The sea and the land had become dumping grounds for garbage and other solid wastes. Fertile farm land had been bulldozed to build highways and housing developments. Much of the once beautiful American countryside had been destroyed. "Noise pollution" of an urban society affected people's nerves and threatened their hearing.

° **ecologist:** a scientist concerned with the relationships between the environment and living organisms—plants, animals, and human beings.

The growing contamination of the oceans endangered the shellfish and finfish that provide an essential part of the protein for peoples throughout the world. This threat was intensified by the growing destruction of the rich, fertile marshlands that pour their nutrients into the coastal waters to provide essential food for the creatures of the sea. And the danger was magnified by the uncontrolled overfishing of commercial fishing fleets that are, in fact, floating fish-processing factories.

Moreover, pollution may involve still deadlier hazards. The influence of pollutants upon the composition of the atmosphere, for example, is a problem of deepening concern to informed scientists throughout the world. Some fear pollutants in the air may harm the ozone layer of the earth's atmosphere, and thus pose a grave threat to the earth's life-supporting environment.

The use of the oceans as a dumping ground for polluted wastes, plus the air-borne pollutants that enter the oceans, also may have very harmful long-term consequences. Most of the oxygen in the atmosphere is replenished by plankton, or microscopic marine plants, through the process of photosynthesis. Many of the pollutants now pouring into the oceans are known to slow or even stop this process in marine plants. For this reason, the contamination of the oceans could eventually alter or even destroy nature's global life-support system.

Growing pressures on resources

Three world-wide developments have brought unrelenting pressure upon the natural environment. First, world population has been doubling nearly every 35 years. Second, the economic systems of the industrialized nations have been based upon the assumption of continuous

By the 1960's the air in America's large cities was dangerously polluted with smog and smoke from car and truck exhausts, industrial plants, and apartment houses and office buildings.

growth. Third, the people who live in the under-developed two thirds of the world desperately need, and have begun to demand, a share of the food, clothing, shelter, and comforts of life now enjoyed by most peoples in the developed nations.

Even small efforts to relieve these pressures on the environment would, however, place heavy burdens upon the world's already over-burdened resources—the air, water, soil, raw materials, and fossil fuels. Just to maintain people's standards of living at their present level would require, during the next generation, the production of twice as much food, clothing, shelter, and industrialized goods. Yet such a great increase in production would do nothing to improve the living conditions of a projected world population of about 4 billion men, women, and children by the year 2000.

If the earth's resources were unlimited, the dimensions of the problem would be different. The challenge of continued growth would not appear so formidable. But these resources and the products that are made from them are not unlimited. Some, like lumber, are renewable.

Others, like metals, can be recycled. Still others, like fossil fuels, can be used only once. Very few, like solar energy—the energy coming from the sun—are inexhaustible resources.

Although considerable progress has been made in recent decades in the management and conservation of America's forests and soil, only a small beginning has been made in recycling mineral resources and conserving fossil fuels.

At the beginning of the 1900's the United States was producing about 15 percent more raw materials than it consumed. By 1940, however, American industry was consuming more raw materials than the United States produced. Since then the gap has widened significantly. During the past 25 years the United States has become increasingly dependent upon the rest of the world for a large part of the materials it needs to maintain its industrial productivity. For example, by the mid-1960's the United States, with only 6 percent of the world's population, was consuming more than half of the world's output of oil, nearly 90 percent of the total output of natural gas, and vast quantities of iron ore to produce half of the world's supply of steel.

The energy crunch

Energy tops the list of critical resources without which American productivity would have to be drastically reduced. Sources of energy provide the essential power for American agriculture, lumbering, mining, manufacturing, transportation, communications, heating, cooking, lighting, air-conditioning, and countless other uses. Americans live in a world of machines. The energy required to power machines in the United States doubled between 1950 and 1970, and it is expected to double again by 1985. The consumption of energy is increasing at a similarly rapid rate throughout the world.

Fossil fuels—oil, gas, and coal—make up 95 percent of the energy sources in the United States today and a slightly larger percentage for the world as a whole. The known reserves of the most widely used fossil fuels—oil and gas—are dwindling, and the cost of discovering and developing new sources of these fuels is rising rapidly. In the United States, domestic deposits of fossil fuels now supply only about two thirds of the nation's energy needs. It has been estimated that by 1980 nearly half of the United States' requirements will have to come from other countries. The risks of this situation were dramatized in 1973 when foreign oil producers doubled and redoubled their prices and, for a time, halted oil shipments to the United States. In response, the American government began seeking ways to become self-sufficient in meeting its energy needs.

The expanded use of coal, which now represents only about 15 percent of the energy consumed in the United States, may offer a partial solution. It is estimated that the world's coal reserves, of which 20 percent are in the United States, are large enough to meet projected world energy demands for the next 200 or 300 years. Yet there are drawbacks to this energy source. In the past the mining and burning of coal have raised serious social and environmental problems. While advances in technology have helped to alleviate some of these problems, much more research and planning are still needed.

The United States has other energy options. One is the increased generation of hydroelectricity. There are, however, limits to the amount of energy that can be secured from this source. Even within these limits, construction of needed dams would mean the flooding of valuable timber areas and farmland. Another energy option is the development of geothermal energy, or power generated from hot gases and steam in the interior of the earth. This is a promising but still distant prospect, since geothermal research and development have barely started.

Perhaps the most promising possible energy source is solar energy—the original source of all energy, past, present, and future. Solar radiation is inexhaustible. Scientists estimate that all of the United States' energy requirements for an entire year could be met by the amount of solar energy that falls on the surface of Lake Erie in a single day!

Efforts to develop solar energy have been increasingly successful in recent years. For example, solar batteries have been developed to supply electricity to spacecraft, and they are being used in other applications where only small amounts of electricity are needed and the high cost of this electricity is not a problem. Researchers in many countries are now at work trying to develop practical solar energy devices for heating homes and for other uses. In 1975 President Ford signed into law the Solar Heating and Cooling Act to encourage the development of such devices in the United States over the next five years.

The dilemma of nuclear energy

Another energy option, but one that includes a formidable challenge, is the continuing development of nuclear power. However, the early promise of this potentially limitless source of energy has not yet been realized.

The failure of nuclear energy to meet the early high expectations held for its use has not been due primarily to technical problems, although these have been, and continue to be, very difficult and complex. The failure has been due in part to the criticisms of environmentalists and nuclear scientists, who have insisted upon increasingly stringent but hard to achieve safety precautions. As nuclear knowledge has accumulated, a growing awareness has developed within the scientific community of the terrifying risks posed by this immensely complex technology.

There are several questions regarding the operation of generating plants fueled by nuclear materials, questions that greatly trouble many eminent nuclear scientists. How will it be possible, they ask, to prevent serious accidents in the 1,000 nuclear generating plants that the United States Nuclear Regulatory Commission plans to license during the next 25 years? Is it possible, with scientific knowledge still limited, to determine what impact radiation from nuclear plants may have upon human beings and all other forms of life? And how, these scientists ask, can an absolutely foolproof method be developed to seal, transport,

IN THE FIGHT AGAINST LITTER AND POLLUTION, WE STILL HAVE SO FAR TO GO.

People start pollution. People can stop it.

Most Americans now realize that the earth itself is being endangered by litter and pollution and the misuse of resources. This poster reflects this new awareness.

and store (in some cases for thousands of years) the deadly wastes that will accumulate in ever-growing quantities?

On the other hand, there are scientists and engineers who believe that generating plants using nuclear materials can be a reasonably safe source of energy. And many painstaking investigations are now being carried out in an effort to determine and control the hazards of nuclear generation.

The slow awakening

As early as the 1890's the federal government had begun to reflect the American people's concern about the need to conserve the nation's resources. The early conservation movement, important though it was, had limited goals, however. The early conservationists were mainly concerned with regulating the use of particular resources—forests, wildlife, minerals, and the soil. But a half century later, by the 1950's, more and more people were beginning to understand that the earth itself—including *all* its resources and *all* forms of life—was being endangered by the waste and misuse of resources.

Major credit for arousing widespread public concern probably belongs as much to Rachel Carson as to any other single individual. In her best-selling book *Silent Spring,* published in 1962, she warned that "along with the possibility of the extinction of mankind by nuclear war, the central problem of our age has . . . become the contamination of man's total environment." This warning received nationwide attention and influenced the thinking of government officials and private citizens alike.

Starting in the Kennedy and Johnson administrations, federal, state, and local governments stepped up their efforts to conserve resources and to protect the environment. By the mid-1970's an impressive body of federal, state, and local laws had been enacted. This wide-ranging legislation included measures (1) to regulate the use of pesticides, insecticides, and other potentially dangerous sprays; (2) to protect species of wildlife threatened with extinction; (3) to require automobile manufacturers to provide pollution control devices on exhausts of cars, trucks, and buses; (4) to establish and enforce anti-air pollution standards for factories, office buildings, and apartment houses; (5) to prevent further pollution of the land and water and to clean up the rivers and lakes; (6) to restore the natural beauty of the countryside by screening and in other ways regulating unsightly junkyards and dumps; (7) to create new national and state parks, and to preserve certain areas as untouched wilderness for future generations; and (8) to conserve energy and other scarce resources.

But these measures, though impressive when viewed as a whole, were not directed at the basic causes of the growing environmental crisis. Efforts to bring world population under control, to restrain the excesses of the nations' technological growth, and to meet the needs of deprived people everywhere, remained largely in the talking stage in all countries. Whether the United States would extend its efforts by providing leadership and aid in a worldwide effort to protect the environment remained a question mark.

The need for renewed dedication

In 1976, as Americans celebrated the nation's 200th birthday, they could look back with pride upon two centuries of growth that had raised the United States to a pinnacle of wealth, productivity, and power never before remotely approached in history. But this record of unparalleled growth increasingly was being challenged by the emergence of urgent problems. In a world torn by unrest and dissension, the nuclear armaments race continued unabated. Frustration born of hunger and want and unfulfilled expectations marked the lives of two thirds of the human race. Racial tensions, discrimination, and widespread poverty in the world's richest nation continued to mock the American dream. Most ominous of all was the growing threat of environmental problems which urgently required solutions.

The United States held a special responsibility for the resolution of these problems. This responsibility grew out of America's prominent position in the world, its vast material and human resources, and its traditional commitment to human dignity. The responsibility could be shouldered, however, only if the American people as a whole were prepared to face a challenge as far-reaching in its consequences as the one earlier Americans faced when they adopted the Declaration of Independence. The challenge Americans now faced was one of redefining their concept of the good life. In their "pursuit of happiness" the time had come for them to search for answers to an overriding question: "Growth toward what goals?"

Urgent though the problems were, the American people had good reason to move into the future with confidence. Beginning on that day when a small handful of settlers had landed at Jamestown, Americans had repeatedly demonstrated an amazing ability to adjust to changing ways and changing times. They had seen their nation grow from a rural society of small villages and towns to an urban society of large cities and suburbs. They had watched their nation develop from a simple economy based on self-sufficient farming to the infinitely more complex technology of an industrial society. They had witnessed the United States' emergence from relative isolation to a role of world leadership. As the nation began the

The Cape Cod National Seashore is one of many wilderness areas which are being preserved for future generations of Americans.

third century of its existence, the American people were beginning to confront the new challenges to their ways of life.

They had solved immense problems in the past and were prepared to surmount the new ones. If the past is indeed prologue, the United States would renew itself and prevail.

SECTION SURVEY

IDENTIFY: ecologist, pollution, geothermal energy, solar energy, nuclear energy; Rachel Carson.

1. How does the increasing pollution of the environment seriously endanger peoples everywhere? Give some examples.
2. What effects may growing energy shortages have on America's farms, factories, and businesses?
3. What new sources of energy are being developed? What advantages and what problems do they present?
4. (a) Describe some of the actions America has taken to meet environmental problems. (b) Do you agree that the United States has a special responsibility to help resolve environmental problems? Explain.

CHAPTER SURVEY

INQUIRING INTO HISTORY

1. An experiment performed in Chicago in the year 1942 marked a turning point in the history of the United States and of the world. Explain.
2. The twentieth-century scholar Alfred North Whitehead observed that when scientists and engineers began to organize research, they invented "the art of inventing." Explain what he meant.
3. What are some of the benefits that have resulted from America's economic growth after World War II? What are some of the problems?
4. What are some causes of the environmental crisis? How is the United States trying to meet this crisis?

RELATING PAST TO PRESENT

1. "Human history becomes more and more a race between education and catastrophe." How does this statement apply to the world today?

2. The nation's founders created a Constitution that can adapt to a changing society. Do you agree or disagree? Use evidence from current events to support your argument.
3. Pollution of the land and water and misuse of resources began with the first European settlements in America. Explain.

DEVELOPING SOCIAL SCIENCE SKILLS

1. Play a record of popular hit songs from the 1960's. (a) What is the subject of each song? (b) What do the songs tell you about the lives and concerns of young Americans in the 1960's? (c) How do the hit songs of the 1960's compare with those of the 1970's?
2. Find out about the anti-pollution programs of your city and state. What are some of the problems your city and state face in fighting pollution? What kinds of things can you as an individual do to help prevent pollution?

Readings

UNIT ONE
REBUILDING THE NATION
(1865-1900)

CHAPTER 1 ■ RESTORING THE SOUTH TO THE UNION

LINCOLN'S RECONSTRUCTION POLICY

Adapted from Arthur Brooks Lapsley, ed., The Writings of Abraham Lincoln. *New York: G. P. Putnam's Sons, 1906.*

Many people have wondered if the reconstruction period might have been different if Lincoln had lived. They wonder if Lincoln, who was more flexible and tactful than Andrew Johnson, might have been better able to deal with the Radical Republicans who wanted to punish the South. Of course, it is not possible ever to know, but we do know that Lincoln wanted to follow a moderate policy in restoring the South to the Union.

In this speech, delivered on April 11, 1865, just four days before he was assassinated, Lincoln explained the reconstruction policy he favored. In it he explains why he believes Louisiana has met the conditions necessary to restore it to the Union.

What are Lincoln's main arguments for admitting Louisiana to the Union? What is his viewpoint about giving blacks the right to vote? Do you think his ideas are effective? Explain.

Fellow citizens: We meet this evening not in sorrow, but in gladness of heart. The surrender of the principal Confederate army gives hope of a righteous and speedy peace.

Because of these recent successes, we must think more than ever about re-establishing national authority—about reconstruction. This task is filled with great difficulty. Unlike a war between independent nations, there is no author-ized group for us to negotiate with. No one person has authority to surrender on behalf of any other person. We simply must begin with and help bring together the disorganized elements. And we, too—the loyal people—differ among ourselves about the methods and measures of reconstruction.

We all agree that the seceded states are out of their proper practical relationship with the Union. We also agree that the only object of the government, civil and military, in regard to those states, is to get them back into their proper practical relationship with the Union. I believe that it is not only possible, but in fact easier, to do this without deciding or even considering whether those states have ever been out of the Union. Finding them safely at home, it would be completely useless to worry about whether they had ever been gone.

The number of voters on which the Louisiana government rests would be more satisfactory to all if it totaled 50,000, or 30,000, or even 20,000, instead of 12,000, as it does. It is also unsatisfactory to some that the vote is not given to colored people. I would myself prefer that it were now given to the very intelligent, and those who serve our cause as soldiers.

Still, the question is not whether the Louisiana government, as it stands, is quite all that is desirable. The question is, Will it be wiser to take it as it is and help to improve it, or reject it? Can Louisiana be brought into proper practical relation with the Union sooner by keeping or by getting rid of its new state government? Some 12,000 voters in the state have sworn loyalty to the Union. They have held elections, organized a state government, and adopted a free-state constitution. This gives the benefit of public schools equally to black and white, and gives the legislature the power to grant the vote to the colored people. This legislature has already voted to ratify the Thirteenth Amendment, recently passed by Congress abolishing slavery throughout the nation. These 12,000 persons are thus fully committed to the Union and to maintaining freedom in the state. They are committed to the very things, and nearly all the things, the nation wants. They ask the nation's recognition and its assistance to make good this commitment.

Now if we reject them, we do our utmost to disorganize them. We, in fact, say to the white people: You are worthless or worse. We will neither help you nor be helped by you. To the black people we say: This cup of liberty which these, your old masters, held to your lips, we will take from you. We will leave you to gather the spilled and scattered contents in some way. If this course, discouraging and paralyzing to both white and black, helps in any way to bring Louisiana into a proper practical relationship with the Union, I have so far not been able to see it.

If, on the contrary, we recognize and support the new government of Louisiana, the opposite is true. We encourage the hearts of 12,000 to stick to their work and fight for it, and feed it, and grow it, and ripen it to a complete success. The colored people, too, in seeing all united for them, are inspired with energy and courage. Grant that they get the vote. Will they not gain it sooner by saving the steps already taken toward it? Granted that the new government of Louisiana is related to what it should be only as the egg is to the chicken, we shall have the chicken sooner by hatching the egg than by smashing it.

A NORTHERN TEACHER IN GEORGIA

Reprinted from Dear Ones at Home, *edited by Henry L. Swint, © 1966. Reprinted by permission of Vanderbilt University Press, Nashville, Tennessee.*

By the end of the war large parts of the South were in ruins and many southerners suffered great hardships. Things were especially difficult for the freed slaves. Many suffered from disease and hunger, and many died. Few had job skills or were able to read or write. They lacked jobs and land and often even homes. Something had to be done to help the freed slaves adjust to a new way of life.

Even before the end of the Civil War, many northerners—especially New England abolitionists—had gone into Union-occupied areas of the Confederacy to help the former slaves. They established schools and helped the freed slaves to find homes and jobs. Among these were Sarah Chase, a Quaker from Worcester, Massachusetts, and her sister Lucy, who went to the South early in 1863. They helped to establish schools and taught in various parts of the South for the next seven years.

How would you describe Sarah Chase's attitude toward the people in Columbus, Georgia? Toward her pupils? What future does she see for families in the South who favored the Union?

Columbus, Georgia
February 5, 1866
Dear Mrs. May [a member of the New England Freedman's Aid Society in Boston]:

When I last wrote we had just opened a school at Savannah: There were already several schools there and Colonel Sickles [the military governor of the Carolinas] was managing the affairs of the Freedmen's Bureau in a most admirable manner. So it did not seem right to stay in that charming city, though we could have found enough important work there to fill every moment. Wishing to work where there was the most need—there are so many places where nothing has been done for the freedmen, and where they are sorely persecuted—we came here. A schoolhouse built by the soldiers had just been destroyed by the citizens. The feeling is intensely bitter against anything northern. The affairs of the Bureau have been very much mismanaged in Columbus, and our government has been disgraced by the troops who were stationed here. Now the troops have been withdrawn, and the people are annoyed by the presence of the Bureau and "a few pious and enthusiastic northeastern schoolteachers." "Both must be cleared out of the place," says the daily press. We have never been treated rudely by any of the citizens, but we know that we are generally discussed, and that many plans are proposed for "getting rid" of us.

We have glorious schools, and I am so satisfied with the work here that nothing in the world could make me wish to be in another place, or doing anything else. In my own day school and night school, I have 140 pupils. They have made truly wonderful progress in the five weeks I have been teaching.

How much I wish you could see my school! A more earnest, fine-looking group of students could not be found. I find the people here more tidy and thrifty than in any other place I know, even though many are very poor and nothing has been given them from the North. They are always cheerful and hopeful, ever anxious to improve.

How I wish I were rich! For the first time in my life I say it, for I have so much need of money here. We are too far from the North to make it worthwhile to send any boxes here because it costs too much. But I ought to have money to buy a piece of cloth, or drugs or a splint for a broken limb, or a piece of bedding for some good old soul—someone who has "raised eight children for missus as if they were my own; and nursed master so well the doctor said I saved his life; and now I'm too old to work—I'm turned out to die like a dog." Though I receive money from home, the expense of living is very great. And no individual's funds are enough for everything that is needed.

There are a number of colored people in this place who are very well-off. They cheerfully do what they can, but in a population of about 8,000, they can do little. I shall organize mutual help societies in the Negro churches (Baptist and Methodist) as soon as possible. Large numbers of black people are working for their food alone, and the white people tell them that they are not free yet. Across the river, in Alabama, several Negroes have been shot *because* they were free!

Union! I can more easily believe in the lion and the lamb lying down together than in a union of the North and South. In all the counties around here, the Union families are being persecuted. People here say that those who favor the North cannot live in their communities. We now have with us a family who fled for their lives from their plantation 14 miles [22 kilometers] away. They have never owned slaves and have always been loyal. Consequently the neighbors have been killing their cattle and taking their farm tools and doing many things to make them leave their place. A few nights ago, a regular armed force from the county surrounded their house. They were going to kill the whole family but, finding that one of the sons was not there, they left to decide whether to put it off for another time. During that time a part of the family escaped to the woods.

Such things happen all the time. But it is not a good idea to write North about them. If they get in print, it gives encouragement to many communities who are ready to act in the same way. Now that the military courts are withdrawn, I see only two alternatives for southerners who favor the Union in many parts of the South—either enduring constant persecution, or moving to the North.

STEVENS PRESENTS A RADICAL VIEW

Adapted from Congressional Globe, *39th Congress, 2nd Session Part 1, January 3, 1867.*

President Johnson and the Radical Republicans in Congress had very different ideas about reconstruction. Even so, for a time most of President Johnson's version of Lincoln's moderate reconstruction program was followed. Then in 1866, the Radical Republicans won control of Congress. With a majority large enough to override President Johnson's veto, Congress took control of reconstruction.

One of the leaders of the Radical Republicans was Thaddeus Stevens, who favored a harsh reconstruction program. This selection is a part of Stevens' speech of January 3, 1867, in favor of such a reconstruction program, which Congress passed over President Johnson's veto on March 2, 1867.

In Stevens' view, what was the legal position of the Confederacy during the Civil War? What was its position afterward? What reasons does he use to prove that the President has no authority to reconstruct the nation? What do you think of his reasons?

Since the surrender of the armies of the Confederate States of America, a little has been done toward establishing this government upon the true principles of liberty and justice. But it will be only a little if we stop here. We have broken the chains of four million slaves. We have allowed them to walk about—so long as they do not walk in paths which are walked on by white people. We have allowed them the privilege of attending church—if they can do so without offending the sight of their former masters. We have even given them that highest and most agreeable proof of liberty—the right to work.

But how have we added to their liberty of thought? In what way have we taught them about and granted them the privilege of self-government? We have forced upon them the privilege of fighting our battles, of dying in defense of freedom, and of bearing their equal share of taxes. But where have we given them the privilege of taking part in the formation of the laws for the government of their native land? By what laws have we made them able to defend themselves against oppression and injustice?

Do you call this liberty? Do you call this a free republic, where four million people are subjects but not citizens? Twenty years ago I spoke against this—the tyranny in my native land. Then, twenty million white people held four million black people in slavery. I say it is no nearer a true republic. Now, twenty-five million of a privileged class keep five million from taking part in the rights of government.

Nearly six years ago a bloody war started between different sections of the United States. Eleven states having a very large territory, and ten or twelve million people, aimed to break their connection with the Union. They wanted to form an independent empire, founded on the principle of human slavery and excluding every free state. They did not aim to reform the government of the country, but they claimed their independence of that government and of all obligations to its laws. The "Confederate States" had as perfect and absolute control over those eleven states as the United States had over the other twenty-five.

The two powers prepared to settle the question by arms. They each raised armies of more than half a million men. The war was regarded by other nations as a public war between independent enemies. The two sides regarded each other as such, and claimed to be governed by the laws of war in their treatment of each other. On the result of the war depended the fate of the warring parties.

The Union armies triumphed. The Confederate armies and government surrendered unconditionally. The law of nations then fixed their condition. They were subject to the controlling power of the conquerors. No former laws, no former treaties existed to bind opposing sides. They had all been melted and destroyed in the fierce fires of the terrible war.

In a monarchy, the king would have fixed the condition of the conquered provinces. He might have extended the laws of the empire over them, allowed them to keep some of their old institutions, or have enforced new laws.

In this country, sovereignty rests with the people, and is exercised through Congress. The legislative power is the only protector of that sovereignty. No other branch of the government, or other department, no other officer of the government, holds one single part of the sovereignty of the nation. No government official, from the President and Chief Justice down, can take any action which is not directed by the legislative power.

Since the President is only the servant of the people, who issue their commands to him through Congress, where does he obtain the constitutional power to create new states? Where does he get the power to remake old ones, to establish laws, to fix the qualification of voters, to declare that states have the right to command Congress to admit their Representatives?

To reconstruct the nation, to admit new states, to guarantee republican governments to old states—these are all legislative acts. The President claims the right to make use of them. Congress denies it and claims the right to belong to the legislative branch. This I take to be the great issue between the President and Congress.

The President wants to pardon the conquered rebels from all the expense and damages of the war. He insists that those of our people who had property burned or destroyed by rebel raiders shall not be paid back, but shall bear their own loss. He desires that the states created by him shall be accepted as valid states. At the same time he declares that the old rebel states are still in existence, and always have been, and have equal rights with the loyal states. He is determined to force a solid rebel delegation into Congress from the South.

In opposition to these things, a part of Congress seems to desire that the conquered side shall, according to the law of nations, pay at least a part of the expenses and damages of the war. The loyal people who were plundered and ruined by rebel raiders should be paid back in full. A majority of Congress desires that treason shall be made hateful, not by bloody executions, but by other adequate punishments.

There are several good reasons for the passage of this bill [the reconstruction program]. In the first place, it is just. I am now speaking of granting the vote to Negroes in the rebel states. Have not loyal blacks as good a right to choose rulers and make laws as rebel whites? In the second place, it is a necessity in order to protect the white people who are loyal to the Union in the seceded states. The white Union people are in a great minority in each of those states. With them the blacks would act together as a group. In most states they would form a majority, control the states and protect themselves.

Another good reason is, it would insure the power of the Republican Party. I believe that the safety of this great nation depends upon the continuing power of the Republican Party.

For these, among other reasons, I am for giving the vote to Negroes in every rebel state. If it is just, it should not be denied. If it is necessary, it should be adopted. If it is a punishment to traitors, they deserve it.

But it will be said, as it has been said, "This is Negro equality!" What is Negro equality about? It means, as understood by honest Republicans, just this much and no more: Every person, no matter what his or her race or color, every human being who has an immortal soul, has an equal right to justice, honesty, and fair play. The law should secure those rights for people. The same law which condemns or acquits Africans should condemn or acquit white people. The same law which gives a verdict in a white person's favor should give a verdict in a black person's favor using the same set of facts. Such is the law of God and such ought to be the law of humans.

JOHNSON IS FOUND NOT GUILTY

Adapted from pp. 125–134 of Through Five Administrations: Reminiscences of Colonel William H. Crook, *edited by Margarita Spalding Gerry. Copyright 1907, 1910 by Harper & Brothers. Reprinted by permission of Harper & Row, Publishers, Inc.*

President Johnson's policies, his inflexible stand on reconstruction, and his vetoes of Congressional reconstruction bills made him a hated enemy to the Radical Republicans. They became determined to remove him from office, since they were convinced that Johnson would not enforce their reconstruction program. The House of Representatives impeached Johnson in February of 1868, and he was brought to trial in the Senate in March. During the Senate trial, it seemed clear that the President had not committed any offense for which he could legally be removed from office. Nevertheless, he was found not guilty by the margin of a single vote.

Although never a popular President, Andrew Johnson's dignified behavior during the House impeachment and the Senate trial won the respect of the American people. In this selection, the Senate trial is described by William H. Crook, a White House guard.

According to Crook, why was the trial so important? From this account, what do you think had more effect on the outcome of the trial—legal arguments or behind-the-scenes influence on the voting?

On the 23rd of March, when the actual trial began, the President said good-by to three of his lawyers, who had come to the White House for a final discussion. I was near them as they stood together on the porch. Mr. Johnson's manner was calm and unconcerned. He shook hands with each of them in turn, and said:

"Gentleman, my case is in your hands. I feel sure that you will protect my interests." Then he returned to his office. I went off with the lawyers. At the President's request, I went with them to the Capitol every day.

When, from my seat in the gallery, I looked down on the Senate chamber, I almost had a moment of terror. It was not because of the gathering. It was rather in the thought that one could feel in the mind of every man and woman there: For the first time in the history of the United States, a President was on trial for more than his life—his place in the judgment of his country's people and history.

The trial lasted three weeks. The President, of course, never appeared. In that respect the proceedings lacked the spectacular interest they might have had. Every day the President had a meeting with his lawyers. Otherwise, he attended to the routine work of his position. He was absolutely calm through it all.

As the trial went on, the belief grew with me—I think it did with everyone—that the weight of evidence and constitutional principle lay with the defense. There were several clever lawyers on the prosecution side, but most of the proceedings showed personal feeling and prejudice rather than proof. Every appeal that could be made to the passions of the time was used. By comparison, the calm, ordered, masterly reasoning of the defense must have made everyone believe in the truth of its cause.

But the legal struggle, after all, was hardly the contest that counted. The debate was for the benefit of the country at large. While the legal experts argued, the enemies of the President were working in other ways. The Senate was thoroughly checked for votes. Personal appeals and influence were constant. Every personal motive, good or bad, was used. Long before the final vote, it was known how most of the men would probably vote. Toward the end, only one doubtful vote remained—that of Senator Ross of Kansas. It looked as if Kansas —which had been the fighting ground of rebel guerrillas and northern abolitionists—was to have the determining vote.

Kansas was, from the beginning, abolitionist and Radical. It would have been supposed that Senator Ross would vote with the Radicals.

Then the Radical forces in the Senate and the House put pressure on the Senator from Kansas. Party discipline was used, and then ridicule. Either from uncertainty, or policy, or a desire to keep his associates in uncertainty, Ross refused to say how he would vote. In all probability he was honestly trying to decide for himself.

The last days before the vote was to be taken were breathless ones. The country was paralyzed. Business in Washington was almost at a standstill.

On May 16th the vote was taken. Everyone who by any possible means could get a ticket of admission to the Senate chamber arrived early that morning at the Capitol. The floor and galleries were crowded.

The journal was read. The House of Representatives was told that the Senate, "sitting for the trial of the President upon the articles of impeachment," was ready to receive the other house in the Senate chamber. The question of voting first upon the eleventh article was decided.

The clerk read the legal statement of those crimes of which, in the opinion of the House of Representatives, the President was guilty. At the end, the Chief Justice directed that the roll be called. The clerk called out:

"Mr. Anthony." Mr. Anthony rose.

"Mr. Anthony"—the Chief Justice looked at the Senator—"how say you? Is the respondent, Andrew Johnson, President of the United States, guilty or not guilty of a high misdemeanor as charged in this article?"

"Guilty," answered Mr. Anthony.

A sigh spread round the room. Yet Mr. Anthony's vote was not in doubt. A two-thirds vote of 36 to 18 was necessary to convict. Thirty-four of the Senators were pledged to vote against the President. Although there was some doubt, it was thought that Mr. Fowler of Tennessee would most likely vote for the President. Senator Ross was the only one whose vote was really in doubt. No one knew his position. When Fowler's name was reached, everyone leaned forward to hear his answer.

"Not guilty," said Senator Fowler.

The tension grew. There were many names called before that of Senator Ross was reached. When the clerk called it, and Ross stood up, the crowd held its breath.

"Not guilty," replied the Senator from Kansas.

The Radical Senators, who had been with Ross only a short time before, turned to him in a rage. All over the hall people began to stir. The rest of the roll call was listened to with lessened interest, although there was still the chance of a surprise. When it was over, and the result—35 to 19—was announced, there was a wild outburst, chiefly groans of anger and disappointment, for the friends of the President were in the minority.

I did not wait to hear the verdict read—it would be no surprise to me, as I had been keeping a list of the votes on a slip of paper— I ran downstairs at top speed. In the corridor of the Senate I came across a curious group. In it was Thaddeus Stevens, now completely disabled, whose two attendants were carrying him high on their shoulders. All around him, the crowd, unable to get into the courtroom, was calling out: "What was the verdict?" Thad Stevens' face was filled with rage and disappointment. He waved his arms in the air and shouted in answer:

"The country is going to the devil!"

I ran all the way from the Capitol to the White House. I was young and strong in those days, and I made good time. When I burst into the library, where the President sat with three other men, they were quietly talking. There were no signs of excitement.

"Mr. President," I shouted, too excited and filled with delight to stop myself, "you are acquitted!"

Everyone stood up. I made my way to the President and took hold of his hand. The other men surrounded him, and began to shake his hand. The President responded to their congratulations calmly enough for a moment, and then I saw that tears were rolling down his face.

LAUNCHING THE "NEW SOUTH"

Adapted from Daniel J. Boorstin, ed., An American Primer, *Vol. I. Chicago: University of Chicago Press, 1966.*

In 1886, a group of New York business leaders asked Henry W. Grady, the editor of the Atlanta newspaper the *Constitution,* to come to New York to speak before their group. In his speech, Grady spoke of the "New South" and described the many changes that had taken place during the years following the war. Afterward, the speech became well known, and the term the "New South" became famous. It convinced many people that the South had changed.

And indeed by the 1880's, the South had changed in many ways. Many large plantations were broken up and many small farms were started. Improved farming methods were used and crops other than cotton were grown. Industry began to develop, and with industry came the growth of cities.

Why do you think Grady spends so much time describing "the footsore Confederate soldier"? To what groups of people do you think this speech might appeal? How does Grady characterize black people? What is his advice to northerners regarding blacks? Was this advice followed?

Dear to me is the home of my childhood and the traditions of my people. I would not, if I could, dim the glory they won in peace and war. Nor would I by word or deed take anything from the splendor and grace of their civilization—never equaled before and perhaps never to be equaled again. There is a New South, not the result of protest against the old, but the result of new conditions, new adjustments, new ideas, and new hopes.

Dr. Talmadge [the previous speaker] has drawn for you the picture of your returning armies. He has told you how they came back to you, marching with proud and victorious step, reading their glory in a nation's eyes! Will you be patient while I tell you of another army that returned home at the close of the war. This army marched home in defeat and not in victory, in sorrow and not in splendor, but in glory that equaled yours, and to hearts just as loving. Let me picture for you the footsore Confederate soldier, as he turned his face southward from Appomattox in April 1865. Think of him as

ragged, half-starved, heavy-hearted, weak from want and wounds. Having fought to the point of exhaustion, he surrenders his gun, shakes the hands of his comrades in silence, and—lifting his tear-stained, pale face for the last time to look at the graves that dot the old Virginia hills—pulls on his gray cap and begins the slow and painful journey home. What does he find when he reaches the home he left so prosperous and beautiful? He finds his house in ruins, his farm destroyed, his slaves free, his animals killed, his barns empty, his trade destroyed, his money worthless. His social system has been swept away. His people are without law or legal status. Crushed by defeat, his very traditions are gone. He has no money, credit, job, material, or training. Besides all this, he is faced with the problems of establishing a status for the freed slaves.

What does he do—this hero in gray with a heart of gold? Does he sit down in gloom and despair? Not for a day. The soldier stepped from the trenches into the fields. Horses that had charged Union guns now marched before the plow. Fields that ran red with human blood in April were green with the harvest in June. There was little bitterness in all this. Cheerfulness and frankness were widespread.

But in all this what have we accomplished? What is the sum of our work? We have found out that, in general, the free Negro counts more than he did as a slave. We have built schools and made them free for white and black. We have built towns and cities and put business above politics. We have challenged your spinners in Massachusetts and your ironmakers in Pennsylvania. We have established thrift in city and country. We have fallen in love with work. We have restored comfort to homes from which culture and elegance never left. Above all, we know that we have achieved in these times of peace a fuller independence for the South than that which our fathers sought to win in the political arena by their words or on the battlefield by their swords.

It is a great privilege to have had a part, however small, in this work. Never was a nobler duty given to human hands than the uplifting and rebuilding of the fallen and bleeding South, misguided perhaps, but beautiful in its suffering, and honest, brave, and generous always.

But what of the Negroes? Have we solved the problem they present, or progressed in honor and fairness toward the solution? Let the record speak. No section shows a more prosperous working population than the Negroes of the South. They share our schools, have the fullest protection of our laws and the friendship of our people. Self-interest, as well as honor, demands that they should have this. Our future, our very existence, depends upon our working out this problem in full and exact justice. We understand that when Lincoln signed the Emancipation Proclamation, your victory was assured. For he then committed you to the cause of human liberty, which weapons cannot overcome. Those of our leaders who pledged to make slavery the cornerstone of the Confederacy doomed us to defeat, committing us to a cause that reason could not defend or the sword maintain.

The relations of the southern people with the Negroes are close and friendly. We remember how for four years they guarded our defenseless women and children, whose husbands and fathers were fighting against their freedom. Whenever they struck a blow for their own liberty they fought in open battle. When at last they raised their hands so that the chains might be struck off, those hands were innocent of any wrong against their helpless charges, and worthy to be taken in loving grasp by every person who honors loyalty and devotion. Ruffians have mistreated them, rascals have misled them. But the South, with the North, protests against injustice to this simple and sincere people.

Law can bring the Negro only liberty and the vote. The rest must be left to conscience and common sense. It should be left to those among whom the Negroes' lot is cast, with whom they are closely connected. Their prosperity depends upon having intelligent sympathy and confidence. Faith has been kept with the Negroes in spite of statements to the opposite by those who claim to speak for us or by our enemies. Faith will be kept with them in the future.

But have we kept faith with you? In the fullest sense, yes. We fought hard enough to know that we were beaten. The chains that had held the South in narrow limitations fell forever when the chains of the Negro slave were broken. Under the old system the Negroes were slaves to the South and the South was a slave to the system.

The old South based everything on slavery and agriculture. The new South presents a perfect democracy. Its social system is less splendid on the surface but stronger at the center. It has a hundred farms for every plantation, fifty homes for every mansion, and industry that meets the complex needs of this complex age.

The new South loves its new work. Its soul is stirred with the breath of a new life. It is thrilled by the realization of growing power and prosperity. It understands that its emancipation came because in the wisdom of God its honest purpose was crossed and its brave armies were beaten.

This is said in no spirit of apology. The South has nothing for which to apologize. It believes that the late struggle between the states was war and not rebellion, and that its convictions were as honest as yours.

BOOKER T. WASHINGTON EMPHASIZES HARD WORK

Adapted from Booker T. Washington, Up From Slavery: An Autobiography. *Garden City, N. Y.: Doubleday, Page and Company, 1900.*

By the 1880's, black southerners were segregated from white southerners in schools and public facilities. Also, black Americans were now denied their political and civil rights. Some black leaders spoke out against this discrimination and urged blacks to struggle for their rights; other leaders disagreed.

In a speech in 1895 at the Atlanta Exposition, Booker T. Washington suggested that black Americans should follow a moderate course. His speech became known as the Atlanta Compromise because it seemed to indicate that black Americans should accept segregation. In actuality, Washington believed that if blacks gained job skills and training they would become necessary to the South's economy, and thus would become respected and regain their civil rights.

What does Washington mean when he advises blacks to "cast down your bucket"? When he advises whites to do the same? How does he try to encourage his black listeners? How does he try to reassure his white listeners?

One third of the population of the South is of the Negro race. No project seeking the material, civil, or moral welfare of this section can ignore this part of our population and reach the highest success. I bring to you the feeling of the masses of my race when I say that in no way have the value and manhood of the American Negro been more fittingly and generously recognized than by the managers of this magnificent Exposition. It is a recognition that will do more to strengthen the friendship of the two races than any happening since the dawn of our freedom.

Not only this, but the opportunity given here will awaken among us a new era of industrial progress. We were ignorant and inexperienced, and it is not strange that in the first years of our new life we began at the top instead of at the bottom. A seat in Congress or the state legislature was more sought than land or industrial skill. The political convention or election speeches had more attraction than starting a dairy farm or truck garden.

A ship lost at sea for many days suddenly sighted a friendly ship. From the mast of the unfortunate ship was seen a signal, "Water, water; we die of thirst!" The answer from the friendly ship came back at once, "Cast down your bucket where you are." A second time the signal, "Water, water; send us water!" ran up from the distressed ship. It was again answered "Cast down your bucket where you are." And a third and fourth signal for water was answered, "Cast down your bucket where you are." The captain of the distressed ship, at last listening to the advice, cast down his bucket, and it came up full of fresh, sparkling water from the Amazon River. To those of my race who depend on bettering their condition in a foreign land or who don't realize the importance of developing friendly relations with southern whites, who are their next-door neighbors, I would say: "Cast down your bucket where you are." Cast it down in making friends of the people of all races by whom we are surrounded.

Cast it down in agriculture, in industry, in commerce, in domestic service, and in the professions. In this connection it is well to remember that whatever other signs the South may have, when it comes to business it is in the South that the Negro is given a chance in the commercial world. Our greatest danger is that in the great leap from slavery to freedom we may overlook the fact that most of us are to live by the productions of our hands and fail to keep in mind that we shall prosper as we learn to dignify and glorify common labor and put brains and skill into our occupations. We shall

prosper if we learn to draw the line between the superficial and the substantial, the ornamental things of life and the useful things. No race can prosper till it learns that there is as much dignity in tilling a field as in writing a poem. It is at the bottom of life we must begin, not at the top. Nor should we permit our problems to overshadow our opportunities.

To those of the white race who look to the immigrants of foreign lands for the prosperity of the South, I would repeat what I say to my own race, "Cast down your bucket where you are." Cast it down among the eight million Negroes whose habits you know, whose loyalty and love you have tested. Cast down your bucket among these people who have, without strikes and labor wars, tilled your fields, cleared your forests, built your railroads and cities, and brought forth treasures from the earth. Casting down your bucket among my people, helping and encouraging them, you will find that they will buy your extra land, grow crops in the waste places in your fields, and run your factories. While doing this, you can be sure in the future, as in the past, that you and your families will be surrounded by the most patient, faithful, law-abiding, and unresentful people that the world has seen. We have proved our loyalty to you in the past, nursing your children, watching by the sickbeds of your mothers and fathers, and often following them with tear-filled eyes to their graves. So in the future, we shall stand by you with a loyalty that no foreigner can equal. We are ready to lay down our lives, if need be, in defense of yours. We shall join our industrial, commercial, civil, and religious life with yours in the way that shall make the interests of both races one. In all things that are purely social we can be as separate as the fingers, yet one as the hand in all things essential to mutual progress.

The wisest among my race understand that demonstrating on questions of social equality is foolish. Progress in enjoying all the privileges that will come to us must be the result of severe and constant struggle rather than of forcing. No race that has anything to contribute to the markets of the world is banished for long. It is important and right that all privileges of the law be ours. But it is much more important that we be prepared for making use of these privileges. The opportunity to earn a dollar in a factory just now is worth much more than the opportunity to spend a dollar in an opera house.

W. E. B. DU BOIS OFFERS HIS VIEWS

Adapted from W. E. B. Du Bois, The Souls of Black Folk, *6th ed. New York: A. C. McClurg & Co., 1905.*

Booker T. Washington was the best known leader of black Americans in the late 1800's and early 1900's. However, there were other black leaders who disagreed with Washington's emphasis upon job training and vocational education for black Americans.

Among those who disagreed was W. E. B. Du Bois, a Harvard-educated black scholar. He felt that talented blacks should not be content with vocational education but should go to colleges and universities. He also came to believe that only strong protests against inequality and discrimination could bring about change. In 1903 Du Bois singled out Washington and his Atlanta speech for criticism, and he made his own suggestions for the advancement of black people.

Why, according to Du Bois, did Booker T. Washington win such wide popularity when he did? Do you think Washington asked blacks to give up the three things that Du Bois lists? What does Du Bois advise black people to do?

Easily the most striking thing in the history of the American Negro since 1876 is the importance of Mr. Booker T. Washington. It began at the time when war memories and ideals were rapidly passing. A time of astonishing commercial development was beginning. A sense of doubt and hesitation overtook the freedmen's sons—it was then that his leadership began. Mr. Washington appeared with a simple, definite program, at the moment when the nation was a little ashamed of having given so much sentiment to Negroes, and was concentrating its energies on dollars. His program involved industrial education, pleasing the South, and acceptance and silence as to civil and political rights.

It startled the nation to hear a Negro proposing such a program after many years of bitter complaint. It startled and won the applause of the South. It interested and won the admiration of the North. And after a confused murmur of protest, it silenced if it did not convert the Negroes themselves.

To gain the sympathy and cooperation of the white South was Mr. Washington's first task. At the time Tuskegee [the school started by Booker T. Washington] was founded, this seemed, for a black person, almost impossible. And yet ten years later it was done in the words spoken at Atlanta: "In all things purely social we can be as separate as the five fingers, and yet one as the hand in all things essential to mutual progress." This "Atlanta Compromise" is the most notable thing in Mr. Washington's career. The South judged it in different ways. The radicals saw it as a complete surrender of the demand for civil and political equality. The conservatives regarded it as a working basis for joint understanding. So both approved it. Today its author is certainly the most distinguished southerner since Jefferson Davis, and the one with the largest personal following.

Mr. Washington represents in Negro thought the old attitude of adjustment and giving in, but adjustment at such a time as to make his program unique. This is an age of unusual economic development, and Mr. Washington's program naturally has an economic basis. It becomes a gospel of work and money and almost completely forgets the higher aims of life. Moreover, this is an age when the more advanced races are coming in closer contact with the less developed races, and race feeling is therefore stronger. Mr. Washington's program, for all practical purposes, accepts the inferiority of the Negro race. Again, a reaction against wartime feelings has led to race prejudice against Negroes, and Mr. Washington withdraws many of the high demands of Negroes as American citizens. In other periods of prejudice all the Negro's tendency to self-assertion has been called forth. At this period a policy of giving in is advised. In the history of nearly all other races and peoples, the policy suggested for such crises has been that self-respect is worth more than lands and houses. And that a people who on their own surrender such respect, or stop struggling for it, are not worth civilizing.

In answer to this, it has been claimed that the Negro can survive only through giving in. Mr. Washington asks that black people give up, at least for the present, three things—

First, political power,

Second, demand for civil rights,

Third, higher education of Negro youth. They should concentrate all their energies on industrial education, on gaining wealth, and on pleasing the South. This policy has been courageously and insistently encouraged for over fifteen years, and has been triumphant for perhaps ten years. What has been the result? In

these years there have occurred:

1. The disfranchisement [taking away the vote] of the Negro.

2. The legal creation of a separate status of civil inferiority for the Negro.

3. The steady withdrawal of aid from institutions for the higher training of the Negro.

These movements are not, to be sure, direct results of Mr. Washington's teachings. But his propaganda has, without a shadow of doubt, helped speed them up. The question then arises: Is it possible, and probable, that nine million people can make effective progress along economic lines if their political rights are taken away, and they are made an inferior group and allowed only the smallest chance of developing their outstanding people? If history and reason give any distinct answer to these questions, it is *No*.

In failing to declare plainly and without doubt the demands of their people, even at the cost of opposing an honored leader, the thinking classes of American Negroes would be avoiding a heavy responsibility. They would be avoiding a responsibility to themselves, to the struggling masses, to the darker races of people whose future depends so largely on this American experiment, and especially to this nation. It is wrong to aid a national crime simply because it is unpopular not to do so. The growing spirit of kindliness and understanding between the North and South after the differences of a generation ago ought to make everyone happy, especially those whose mistreatment caused the war. But if that understanding is to be marked by the industrial slavery and civic death of those same black people, then those black people should oppose such a course by all civilized methods—even though it involves disagreement with Mr. Booker T. Washington.

CHAPTER 2 ■ SEVERE TRIALS FOR DEMOCRACY

AN ENGLISH REFORMER ATTENDS A POLITICAL CONVENTION

Adapted from pages 48–53 from Among the Americans *by George Jacob Holyoake, used with the permission of Greenwood Press, the reprint publishers, a division of Williamhouse-Regency, Inc.*

In the 1870's, George Holyoake, a social reformer, came over from England to visit the United States. He was interested in visiting and studying the cooperatives formed by American farmers.

Holyoake was also very curious about American politics, and he admired "the republican equality and the republican freedom of America." He wrote: "The minds of the people, like keyless watches, wind themselves up and always keep going." Because of this interest in politics, he attended a Republican Party convention in 1879 at Saratoga, New York. This is his description of that meeting.

Do you think Holyoake is serious about his description of the convention's procedures? Can you think of some reasons why Americans at this time were willing to listen to such long speeches? What does Holyoake admire about the convention?

The object of the convention, called by the Republican leaders, was to choose a candidate for governor of New York and other state officers. My wish was to see not only what was done, but also how it was done and where it was done.

The convention was held in the Town Hall. It was not bad inside. There was more space than we reserve for speakers in England. But in the center of the stage was a small, ugly desk. The president hit its hollow top with a pitiful wooden hammer, setting off weak echoes within it. Nobody had thought that the grandest use of a public hall is a public meeting.

I had heard a good deal in England about American political organization. It did not appear in the physical arrangements of the meetings though it showed in the proceedings. The names of the candidates for the chief office were read over. The popular name was that of "Alonzo B. Cornell," the son of the founder of the Cornell University. Mr. Cornell received the nomination for governor of New York State. That day I heard his name said a thousand times. Each delegate was called upon to announce aloud the name of the candidate he was voting for. There was only one Cornell, yet no-

body answered as we would do in England—"Cornell." Each said, "Alonzo B. Cornell," or "Jehosophat P. Squattles," or whatever was the name of the other candidate.

An hour was spent over that new governor's name, yet if "Alonzo B." had been eliminated the business would have been finished in a third of the time. (Mr. Cornell himself was a modest, pleasant gentleman, with a businesslike method of speech.)

The character of every people, like that of every individual, is made up of contradictions. The Americans, as a rule, catch on to things quickly. Their conversation is clear, bright, and precise. Their understanding is direct. Yet these quick-witted listeners will tolerate speakers who are long-winded, indirect, and speak endlessly. They will sit and listen to them for long periods of time.

At the New York convention a "program of principles" called a "platform"—was read. No one could make sure what was meant, and a professor of memory could not remember half of what was written. All I remember was that the platform ended with some statements about things in general. Yet there were parts of it which showed intelligence—if only the writer had known when to stop.

I regretted not being able to go to Syracuse to see the Democratic convention. I was told the Democratic conventions were marked by great activity and disorder. The *New York Tribune* said that there would be many "large heads" at Syracuse. I wanted to see "large heads," as I had no idea what a political "large head" was. I was told that the Democrats are more boisterous in their meetings than Republicans. The Democrats seem to be like our Tories at home—indignant at any dissent at their meetings, but persistent in interrupting the meetings of others.

The Saratoga convention was characterized by great order and attention to whoever desired to speak. If anyone had a question, the answer was "The Chair takes a contrary view; the Chair decides against you." The chairman was an institution, or a court of authority. This I found to be a rule in America. The immediate attention given to anyone who wanted to speak was greater than in England. In England the theory of a public meeting is that anyone present may speak, but we never let them do it. If the chairman is willing the audience is not. At several public meetings that I attended in America the right of a person on the floor seemed equal to that of those on the platform. Citizens seemed

to recognize the equality of each other. In England there is no public sense of equality. There is always somebody who is supposed to be better than anybody.

GROWING UP REPUBLICAN

Adapted from Sarah S. Pratt, The Old Crop in Indiana. *Indianapolis: The Pratt Poster Co., 1928.*

In the years after the Civil War, loyalties to political parties became especially strong. The party that a person supported was often the result of tradition and family upbringing. For example, a person who was brought up in a family that supported the Democratic Party would almost never vote for a Republican candidate. And a person raised in a family that supported the Republican Party would not vote for a Democratic candidate.

In these years, there were few Americans who were "independents." Most people supported either the Republican or Democratic Party, or perhaps a smaller third party. And there was very little "ticket splitting," or voting for some of the candidates of both major parties, as there is today. In this selection, Sarah Smith Pratt tells what it was like to grow up in a Republican home in Indiana.

What attitudes does the writer have toward her father? Do you think that the author's attitudes toward political parties might have changed if the visiting Methodists had been Democrats instead of Republicans? Is party loyalty as strong in your family as it was among the Smiths?

Although we lived in a Democratic stronghold, our family happened to be Republican. I realize now that the great shaping force of Republicanism in my youth was my father. He was a perfect example of the "waving-the-bloody-shirt" type—intolerant of everything he did not approve of. He was of that great group of good men who are upset by wrongdoing, but are never willing to hold office. He had great influence throughout the county we lived in because of his education, moral courage, and ability to speak well. He was listened to with respect by a large group of farmers. Nick

Smith's [the author's father] opinions were quoted all over the county. He was the delight of the virtuous and the terror of the wrong-doer. He loved to criticize liquor-sellers and Democrats.

He had come from Baltimore and settled in Indiana about 1836, bringing a stock of farm tools, roofing material, vats, tanks, and hydraulic rams, all greatly needed in that new country.

I was surrounded with Republicanism from the very minute I was born. Editorials read aloud from the newspapers of that day, explained loudly to my mother and filled with criticisms of the "jackasses" and "natural-born fools" who headed the other party—these stamped themselves forever on the well-behaved children who sat and listened.

And yet my father's hunting friend and the companion of his long Sunday walks was Walter Beach, a strong, outspoken Democrat.

My first knowledge of the word "Democrat" came because of Dash, my dog. One night he was found near the kitchen door of the editor of the *Times*. The *Times* was the Democratic newspaper—the *Journal,* the Republican. This editor, because he was short and somewhat pompous, was called "Whistlebreeches."

"Whistlebreeches shot Dash last night. He's lying dead in their yard," my brother came and told us as we were at breakfast.

"Get the wheelbarrow, Lutie, and get him and bury him in the yard—that—that Democrat," my father said as he gulped down his coffee.

When I saw this editor go past our house on his way home at noon, despite my grief I was interested in the name I had heard my father call him: Democrat!

"What *is* a Democrat, Papa? I think it is such a pretty word."

"Democrat" exploded my father, "a Democrat is a man—" he said, too mad to know just what to say. "A man who—who—"

"Now, Nicholas, be careful before the children. Don't say anything mean. You know our minister is a Democrat and so is our doctor."

My father, feeling a little ashamed by this time, said nothing, but he had left a bad impression of the party started by Jefferson. I still think "Democrat" is a great word. It is perhaps the most important of human meanings and—in its perfection—the most unreachable.

An event which deepened my respect for the party in power [the Republican Party] occurred right after the war when a Methodist conference was to be held in Delphi. Brother Sims and Brother McIntosh asked our parents to entertain some of the visiting clergy. We were Episcopalians, but joyfully opened our doors to the visitors. Three of their most interesting men stayed at our house. Two of them were celebrities. The third was a professor from New Orleans. These good-humored men were soon well liked by the whole household. One of them was Elder John L. Smith, a noted man in his day. Another was John Hogarth Lozier—called Chaplain Lozier because of his work in the army, and admired by hundreds of soldiers. The third was a brown-eyed professor.

All the men were strong Republicans. My father, pleased beyond measure to find his own feelings backed up by three such men, showed them the greatest hospitality. There never were more cheerful or wittier talks than those that lasted these three days at our home.

Chaplain Lozier was a writer of verses, many of which had been set to music. Some of them described political events. He had a popular song set to the tune of *"Wait for the Wagon."* He would recite this line by line and we would all sing it:

In Uncle Sam's dominions in 1861
The fight between the Union and secession was begun
The South declared they'd have the rights
That Uncle Sam denied
Or in his Union wagon they would not longer ride.

Wait for the wagon, the old Union wagon,
Wait for the wagon and we'll all take a ride.

This visit served to deepen my belief that the Republican Party was even greater than I had thought it was. Of course, there were good Democrats—old Dr. Blanchard and Lawyer Sims and plenty of good people who were our neighbors. But to think that from the outside world had appeared Elder Smith wearing a long black coat and silk hat, carrying a gold-headed cane, and having elegant manners. He was a Republican. And there was Chaplain Lozier, who could make poems and have them printed and sung. He too was a Republican. And there was Professor Henry Jackson, who could write in French and teach in a young woman's school. And he too was a Republican. Altogether, the greatness of the Republican Party was increased in my mind by this visit of these loyal Methodists.

"WHY GREAT MEN ARE NOT CHOSEN PRESIDENTS"

Adapted by permission of G. P. Putnam's Sons from The American Commonwealth *by James Bryce. Copyright © 1959 by G. P. Putnam's Sons.*

Many historians believe that there have been very few great American Presidents—perhaps seven or eight at most. In his book *The American Commonwealth,* James Bryce, an English scholar, tried to explain why Americans have elected so many ordinary Presidents. This work has been called "the greatest book written about this country." Bryce visited the United States three times before he wrote his study. And he later served as the British ambassador to Washington. Although this selection may seem critical, Bryce actually had a favorable opinion of the American system of government.

What are the three main reasons Bryce gives for the lack of "great men" in the Presidency? Do you think that American Presidents still have the characteristics Bryce describes?

Europeans often ask, and Americans do not always explain, how it happens that this great office—to which any man can rise by his own merits—is not more frequently filled by great men. In America, which is a country where political life is unusually keen, it might be expected that the Presidency would always be won by a man of brilliant gifts. But since the heroes of the Revolution died out with Jefferson and Adams and Madison some sixty years ago, no person except General Grant has reached the office whose name would have been remembered if he had not been President. No President except Abraham Lincoln has shown rare or striking qualities in the office. Who now knows or cares to know anything about the personality of James K. Polk or Franklin Pierce? The only thing remarkable about them is that, being so ordinary, they should have climbed so high.

Several reasons may be suggested for this fact, which Americans are themselves the first to admit.

One is that the number of people with great abilities drawn into politics is smaller in America than in most European countries. In France and Italy, half-revolutionary conditions have made public life exciting and easy to enter. In Germany, a well-organized civil service develops the art of government with unusual success. In England, many persons of wealth and leisure seek to enter politics, while vital problems touch the interests of all classes and make people eager observers of the political scene. In America, many able men rush into a field which is comparatively small in Europe, the business of developing the material resources of the country.

Another reason is that the methods and habits of Congress, and indeed of political life generally, seem to give fewer opportunities for personal distinction. There are fewer ways in which a man may win the admiration of his countrymen by outstanding thought, speech, or ability in administration.

A third reason is that important men make more enemies than less well-known men do. They are therefore less admirable candidates. It is true that the important man has also made more friends, that his name is more widely known, and that he may be greeted with louder cheers. Other things being equal, the famous man is preferable. But other things never are equal. The famous man has probably attacked some leaders in his own party, has replaced others, has expressed his dislike of some group, has perhaps committed errors which can be turned into offenses. No man can be in public life for long and take part in great affairs without causing criticism. People constantly search out all the corners of a Presidential candidate's past life. Therefore, when the choice lies between a brilliant man and a safe man, the safe man is preferred. Party feeling, strong enough to support a man without positive merits, is not always strong enough to gain forgiveness for a man with positive faults.

A European finds that this needs to be explained. For in the free countries of Europe, brilliance or some striking achievement is what makes a leader triumphant. Why should it be different in America? Because in America party loyalty and party organization have been so perfect that anyone chosen as a candidate by the party will get the full party vote if his character is good and his "record," as they call it, is unstained. The safe candidate may not receive quite so many votes from the moderate people of the other side as the brilliant one would, but he will not lose nearly so many from his own party. Even those who admit he is only ordinary will vote for him when the moment for voting comes. Besides, most American voters do not

438

object to ordinary candidates. They have a lower idea of the qualities necessary for a statesman than those who direct public opinion in Europe. They like their candidates to be sensible, vigorous, and, above all, what they call "magnetic." They do not value, because they see no need for, originality or profundity, a cultured background or great knowledge. Candidates are selected by small groups of persons who run the political party but are usually commonplace men.

It must also be remembered that the merits of a President are one thing and those of a candidate another thing. An important American is reported to have said to friends who wished him to be a candidate, "Gentlemen, let there be no mistake. I would make a good President but a very bad candidate." Now to a party it is more important that its choice should be a good candidate than that he should turn out to be a good President. It will be a misfortune to the party, as well as to the country, if the candidate elected proves to be a bad President. But it is a greater misfortune to the party if it is beaten, for it will then lose four years of national patronage.

After all—and this is a point much less obvious to Europeans than to Americans—a President need not be brilliant. Englishmen, imagining him as something like their Prime Minister, assume that he ought to be a great speaker, having also the power to propose a great policy or write a good law. They forget that the President does not sit in Congress. His main duties are to promptly and effectively carry out the laws and maintain public order, and choose the executive officials of the country. Firmness, common sense, and, most of all, honesty are the qualities which the country needs in its chief executive.

So far we have been considering personal merits. But in the selection of a candidate many other considerations have to be regarded. The chief of these is the amount of support which can be secured from different states or regions of the Union. State feeling and sectional feeling are powerful factors in a Presidential election. The Northwest, including the states from Ohio to Dakota, is now the most populous region of the Union, and therefore counts for most in an election. Thus a northwestern man makes the best candidate. A large state casts a greater vote in the election, and every state is of course more likely to be carried by one of its own citizens than by a stranger. Therefore a man from a large state is preferable as a candidate. The problem is further complicated by the fact that some states are already safe for one or the other party, while others are doubtful. Most of the Northwestern and New England states are certain to go Republican. All of the Southern states are (at present) certain to go Democratic. It is more important to please a doubtful state than one you have already. Thus a candidate from a doubtful state, such as New York or Indiana, is to be preferred.

KEEPING PUBLIC SERVANTS ON THEIR TOES

Adapted from David R. Locke, The Morals of Abou Ben Adhem. *Upper Saddle River, N.J.: Literature House/ Gregg Press, 1969.*

The years after the Civil War were years of graft and corruption at all levels of American government. As a result, many writers and journalists tried to make Americans aware of the dishonesty in their governments, in the hopes of ridding the nation of dishonest officials. These writers often used humor to show the faults of government officials. Thomas Nast's famous cartoons of Boss Tweed and the Tammany Ring were one example. Another was the books of David R. Locke, a favorite humorous writer of this period. Lincoln said of one of Locke's earlier books, "For the genius to write such things, I would gladly give up my office." In a later book, Locke wrote down the sayings of "a wise Persian man living in New Jersey." The purpose of this book was to poke fun at American government.

How does Locke make fun of legislators? Do you think he is serious about the remedy he suggests? Do you think this selection still applies to American politics today?

Abou Ben Adhem was not in a good mood. He had put a large sum of money in a bank in New York. The bank had failed because of the strong desire of its cashier to view the sights of the Old World. As the cashier took with him over half a million dollars, the bank had to close. The directors were very sorry, but Abou's money was gone. He was not in a good mood.

At this point a man from Albany approached, bowing deeply three times. "Mighty Abou," said he, "I am a member of the New York legislature."

"Away, man! I want no favors. I have no need of votes. I have no money to spend. I have no desire to be severe, but, sir, whenever I see a member of a legislature, I think that Nature is wasteful. There is a great deal of lightning wasted. Away!"

"Mighty Abou, you mistake me. I am, it is true, a member of that legislature. But I am an honest man. If you will take the trouble to remember, you will remember that there are two or three such as I."

Abou looked at him with a long stare of painful astonishment, ending with a long whistle of disbelief.

"I am an honest member of the legislature of the state of New York," continued this man, "and I desire advice and enlightenment so that I may be of some use to my fellow citizens. Tell me, what can we do in the way of lawmaking that will get rid of all crime in the country? Is there no cure for it?"

Abou looked at him closely.

"I will trust you," he said. "I will believe that you are an honest man, despite the position you hold. And I will give you the information you desire.

"Sweet sir," continued Abou, "three hundred years ago there was a kingdom to the north of what is now Persia in which these things of which you complain did not happen very often. In that blessed land there was almost no crime—no accidents, no mistakes, no nothing. Life there was like a calmly flowing river. The people lived happily and died regretfully. I helped to organize that community. I was the author of the system that brought it about. I—"

"Three hundred years ago?" asked the stranger.

"Three hundred years ago,—did I not say so?"

"I beg your pardon; but, give me, oh give me, the system by which this most desirable state of things was achieved."

"I will. We had in Koamud, which was the name of the kingdom, no prisons, no reform schools, no civil-service examinations, no boards of any kind—nothing of the sort. If the government wanted a postmaster, for example, it did not go foolishly talking about qualifications or anything of that sort. It simply posted on the door of the post office a printed statement of what would be required of the postmaster. Then the first man who said he wanted the position was appointed."

"Were no bonds required of him?"

"No. He took the position, and undertook his duties."

"But suppose he stole money?"

"He was immediately caught and hanged."

"Hung for stealing?"

"Certainly, and for a mistake as well. If there was an error in his accounts by so much as a pound of twine, he was hung immediately."

"But suppose such irregularities were the result of bad business habits?"

"Then he was hung for being a bad businessman. What we wanted was honesty and ability. We treated everyone else the same way. Suppose a railroad train ran off the track. Suppose we discovered that a rail was out of order, or that the roadbed was not properly kept up. We hung the president, directors, and superintendent. If the accident was caused by any slip on the part of the conductor, he was hung. Once we hung all the officials of the Teheran and Ispahan Railroad, and from that time there were no accidents on that line. Their successors were very careful. The superintendent slept very little. The company hung up a small gallows in the cab of every locomotive to remind the engineer of his fate in the event of trouble.

"Then we carried the same rule into everything. The people put their money into the First National Bank of Picalilly. Very good. The bank failed one morning. The authorities took the president, cashier, and board of directors out and hung them all, because they had been guilty of letting the bank fail.

"'I didn't steal a dollar of this money,' said the president.

"'Makes no difference,' said the judge, 'where it was lost. You haven't got it.'

"'But you won't hang a man who has not stolen, will you?' says the president.

"'I will hang you for being an idiot. I shall hang you for risking money that was not yours to risk.'

"And up he went.

"In fact, they hung them more mercilessly for being fools than for any other crime. If a man said, 'I stole it,' they felt a sort of pity for him. If he said, 'I lost it,' they felt none at all, and hung him up in a minute."

"What was the effect of this vigorous hanging?"

"Splendid. Bank officials made no mistakes in their figures and none in their business. The officers of the government were rather careful about their accounts, for they were hung for mistakes as well as for stealing. The presidents and directors of railroads took care of their tracks, and a more watchful and careful set of men than the conductors, engineers, and switchmen you never saw.

"The effect was good in another way. This system reduced the population greatly, but it made a magnificent race of men and women. You see, the vicious and the careless were all hung, leaving only the industrious and clear-headed to live. Consequently, it was a splendid people. I am, perhaps, a fair example. There were no lunatics, idiots, triflers, or dishonest people left to spread mischief and danger."

"Is that government still in existence?"

"Alas! no. There sprang up a class of people who began to feel sorry for criminals. They got into the habit of visiting them just before they were hanged, and sending them flowers, and begging the governor to pardon them. They created sympathy for them, and finally some escaped. Then it was all over. The moment there was any doubt as to the certainty of punishment, people became almost as bad as they are here. Then I left the country.

"Go to Albany, my friend, and make but one penalty—hanging—for all crimes or mistakes, in public or private. True, it would cause a heavy expense on each county for a gallows. It would probably make New York one of the smallest cities, as far as population, in the country. In a week you probably couldn't get a quorum in the New York legislature. But the final effect would be splendid. The next generation would be fifty percent better than this, and the improvement would go on and on to the end of time. I have spoken. Leave me, for I am tired."

The stranger went away sorrowful.

"The idea is good," said he to himself, "but I dare not urge it. If hanging were the rule for crimes or mistakes, how long would my children have a father?"

CHAPTER 3 ■ CONQUERING THE "LAST FRONTIER"

SITTING BULL SPEAKS OF THE WHITES

Adapted from Cry of the Thunderbird: The American Indian's Own Story, *edited by Charles Hamilton. New edition copyright 1972 by the University of Oklahoma Press. Reprinted by permission of the publisher.*

Many Indian leaders became well-known figures during the long period of conflict between the Indians and white settlers on the Great Plains. One of the most famous of these leaders was Sitting Bull, a chief of the Sioux. Although he became well known as a great warrior and war chief, he also was respected as a religious leader or "medicine man."

In the first selection, Sitting Bull speaks of the relationship between Indians and white people. In the second reading, he talks about Custer's "last stand." Although most people at the time thought that Sitting Bull was one of the chiefs who led the Sioux at Little Big Horn, he did not take part in that battle.

What wrongs does Sitting Bull accuse the whites of committing? How does he defend his own actions? What do you think of his arguments?

What treaty that the whites have kept has the red man broken? Not one. What treaty that the whites ever made with us red men have they kept? Not one. When I was a boy the Sioux owned the world. The sun rose and set in their lands. They sent ten thousand horsemen to battle. Where are the warriors today? Who killed them? Where are our lands? Who owns them?

What white man can say I ever stole his lands or a penny of his money? Yet they say I am a thief. What white woman taken as captive was ever insulted by me? Yet they say I am a bad Indian. What white man has ever seen me drunk? Who has ever come to me hungry and gone without food? Who has ever seen me beat my wives or abuse my children? What law have I broken? Is it wrong for me to love my own? Is it wicked in me because my skin is red? Because I am a Sioux? Because I was born where my fathers lived? Because I would die for my people and my country?

*   *   *   *

The palefaces had things that we needed in order to hunt. We needed ammunition. Our interests were in peace. I never sold that much land. (Here Sitting Bull picked up with his thumb and forefinger a little dirt, lifted it, and let it fall and blow away.) I never made or sold a treaty with the United States. I came in to claim my rights and the rights of my people. I was driven by force from my land. I never made war on the United States government. I never stayed in the white man's country. I never committed any robberies in the white man's country. I never made the white man's heart bleed. The white man came onto my land and followed me. The white man made me fight for my hunting grounds. The white man made me kill him or he would kill my friends, my women, and my children.

We have all fought hard. We did not know Custer. There were not as many Indians as the white man says. There were not more than two thousand. I did not want to kill any more men. I did not like that kind of work. I only defended my camp. When we had killed enough, that was all that was necessary.

A PROPOSED SOLUTION TO THE "INDIAN PROBLEM"

Adapted from Nelson A. Miles, "The Indian Problem," North American Review, March 1879.

The "Indian problem" had begun when the Europeans first settled in America. Conflict between the two groups centered largely on the concept of land ownership and differing ideas and ways of life. For the Indians, the problem was how to remain on the land where they had lived and hunted for centuries. For the white settlers, the problem was how to get the land and what to do with the Indians.

During the late 1860's, a long period of conflict began. As white settlers began to move beyond the Mississippi River, they came into conflict with the Indians who lived and hunted on the Great Plains. Thoughtful Americans wondered how the Indians could be removed from these lands without violating ideals of justice and humanity. General Nelson A. Miles, an Army officer with experience in Indian wars, offered his solution to the "Indian Problem" in an article in 1879.

Does Miles think that the Indians are equals of the whites? Do you think he is fair in his summary of the relations between Indians and whites? What are the major features of Miles' plan? Did the government adopt his plan?

Strange as it may seem, after nearly 400 years of conflict between the European and American races on this continent—a conflict in which war and peace have alternated almost as frequently as the seasons—we still must ask the question, What is to be done with the Indians?

The real issue is this: Shall we continue the uncertain and expensive policy that has hurt our name as a nation and a Christian people? Or shall we work out some practical and just system by which we can govern one quarter of a million of our people? Can we secure and maintain their loyalty, raising them from the darkness of barbarism to the light of civilization? Can we put an end to these endless and expensive Indian wars?

In considering the subject, it might be well to examine first the causes of the present situation. If we dismiss from our minds the prejudice we have against the Indian, we can understand more clearly the feelings of both races.

The Indians have the same motives that govern all other people. The lack of confidence and the bitter hatred now existing between the two races have been caused by the warfare that has lasted for centuries. And stories of bad faith, cruelty, and wrong have been handed down by tradition from father to son among both groups of people. It is unfair to suppose that one side has always acted rightly, and that the other is responsible for every wrong that has been committed. We might speak of the treachery of the red man, the violence of his crimes, the cruelties of his tortures, and the hideousness of many of his savage customs. We might try to estimate the number of his victims. Yet at the same time the other side of the picture might appear equally black with injustice.

One hundred years before the Pilgrims landed at Plymouth, the Spanish government issued a decree which allowed American Indians to be made slaves. Later they were sold into slavery in Massachusetts, Rhode Island, Pennsylvania, Virginia, the Carolinas, Georgia, and Louisiana, and hunted with dogs in Connecticut and Florida. They were, for all practical purposes, disfranchised by our original Constitution. By either war or treaty, nearly every tract of land which was desirable to them and valuable to the white settler was taken away. Step by step, they were driven back from the Atlantic to the Far West. Now there is scarcely a spot of ground upon which the Indians have any certainty of remaining permanently.

It may be well to remember that for the most part Europeans were treated kindly by the Indians when they first landed on American shores. When Europeans came to make permanent settlements, they were supplied with food, which enabled them to last through the long and cheerless winters. For a time during the early settlement of this country, peace and good will existed, only to be followed by warfare.

The available land that can be given to the Indians is being rapidly decreased. They cannot be moved farther west. Some political party or administration must take the responsibility of protecting their rights of person and property.

The advantage of placing the Indians under some government strong enough to control them and just enough to command their respect is clear. It is therefore suggested that a system which has proved to be practical should receive at least a fair trial. The government employs army officers who, by long and faithful service, have established reputations for integrity, character, and ability. These officers have commanded armies, reconstructed states, and controlled millions of dollars' worth of public property. During years of experience on the frontier, they have opened the way for civilization and Christianity. The services of these officials could prevent war and uplift the Indian race.

Allowing the civilized and semicivilized Indians to remain under the same supervision as at present, the President of the United States should have power to place the nomadic, or wandering, tribes under the control of the War Department. Officers of known character and experience, who would be interested in improving the Indians' condition, should be placed in charge of the different tribes. One difficulty in the past has been that they have been managed by officials too far away, who knew nothing of the people they were dealing with. The Indians, as far as possible, should be kept in sections of the country to which they have already adapted.

Every effort should be made to locate the Indians by families. The ties of relationship among them are much stronger than is generally supposed. By this means, the Indians will become independent of their tribal relations, and will not be found crowded together in large and unsightly camps, as are common now.

The officers in charge should have enough force to preserve order, patrol the reservations, recover stolen property, arrest the lawless, and keep the Indians upon their reservations and within the limits of their treaties. The officer in charge should have the power to control or prevent the sale of ammunition, as well as to stop the sale of liquor among the Indians. Many thousands of Indian ponies, useful only for war or hunting, should be sold and the money used to buy domestic animals.

The warriors may be made to care for their flocks and herds. The work of the Indians that is now wasted can be used for peaceful and useful pursuits. Yet the great work of reform must be mainly with the young people of the different tribes.

Several years ago I suggested that our unoccupied military posts be used as schools. As many Indian youths as can be gathered voluntarily should be placed at these schools, especially the sons of chiefs who will in a few years govern the different tribes. They could be taught the English language, habits of work, the benefits of civilization, and the power of the white race. After a few years, they would return to their people with some education, with more intelligence, and with their ideas of life entirely changed for the better. They would, in turn, be able to educate their own people. Their influence for good could not be estimated. The expense of educating them would be less than at present, and thousands would benefit. The Indians, as they become civilized and educated, as they acquire property and pay taxes toward the support of the government, should have the same rights of citizenship as all other men enjoy.

A race of savages cannot by any human means be civilized and Christianized within a few years of time. Neither will 250,000 people with their descendants be destroyed in the next 50 years. The white man and the Indian should be taught to live side by side, each respecting the rights of the other. Both should live under wholesome laws, enforced with authority and justice. Such a government would be most helpful to the Indians. It would also be satisfactory to three other groups: (a) people who have invested their capital and are developing the wealth that for ages has lain in the Western mountains; (b) people who have left the overcrowded centers of the East, and whose homes are now on the plains and valleys of the Far West; and (c) the soldiers who are called upon every year to withstand greater exposure and suffering than is required by the troops of any other nation on the globe.

RESISTING "AMERICANIZATION"

Adapted by permission of the publisher from Me and Mine: The Life Story of Helen Sekaquaptewa, *as told to Louise Udall. Tucson: University of Arizona Press, copyright 1969.*

After many years of conflict on the Great Plains, the Indians were defeated and forced to live on reservations. Even so, many Americans still felt that the "Indian problem" had not been solved. They believed that the Indians had to be "Americanized."

As a result, the United States government tried to "Americanize" the Indians in various ways. Education was considered especially important in this effort. Consequently, many Indian children were sent to boarding schools many miles away from their homes. By 1898 some day schools had been built near the reservations. In this selection, Helen Sekaquaptewa, a Hopi Indian born in Arizona, tells of her experiences at a day school in the early 1900's.

Were Hopi parents opposed to education? Why do you think that hiding the children was a serious and rather desperate game? How much benefit do you think the author of this selection received from her education at the day school?

By the time I was old enough to go to school, a day school had been built near the village. Children up to the third grade could go to school by day and live at home. This was a favor to the Hopi parents. Still, many of them tried to prevent their children from attending the day school.

When we were five or six years old, we and our parents became involved with the school officials—assisted by the Navajo police officers —in a serious and rather desperate game of hide-and-seek. Every day the school principal sent out a truant officer, and many times he himself went with the officer. They went to Hopi homes to take the children to school.

When September came, there was no peace for us. Early in the morning, from our houses, we could see the principal and the officer start out from the school, walking up the trail to "get" the children. Parents tried every day in different ways to hide us from them, for once you were caught, you had lost the game. You were discovered and listed and you had to go to school and not hide any more.

Sometimes, after a very early breakfast, somebody's grandmother would take a lunch and go with a group of eight to twelve little girls and hide them in the cornfields away from the village. On another day another grandmother would go in the other direction over the hills among the cedar trees. We would play in a narrow valley, have our lunch, and come back home in the afternoon. Men would be out with little boys playing this game of hide-and-seek.

A place where one or two small children could be hidden away quickly was the rabbit blanket. A rabbit blanket is made by cutting dressed rabbit skins in two-inch strips and weaving them together with wool thread. When not in use, in warm weather, this blanket is hung by the four corners from a hook in the rafter beam. But once it was discovered, this hiding place was out. The school officer would feel the rabbit blanket first thing when he came into the room.

Most houses have a corn storage cupboard in a wall. A cloth covered the front, making a good place to keep the corn dry and clean. One day the officers were only two doors away from our home when my mother became aware of their presence. She grabbed her young son Henry and put him in the cupboard just in time to win the game—that day.

Our houses were two and three stories high. When a lower room became old and unsafe, it was used as a dumping place for ashes, peach stones, melon and squash seeds, and bits of discarded corn. Anything that could be eaten was preserved in the ashes, and the room was gradually filled. In time of famine these bits of food could be dug out and eaten. In my home such a room was about three-fourths filled. One September morning my brother and I were hidden there. We lay on our stomachs in the dark, facing a small opening. We saw the feet of the principal and police officers as they walked by, and heard their big voices as they looked about wondering where the children were. They didn't find us that day.

I don't remember for sure just how I came to be "caught." Maybe both my mother and I got a little tired of getting up early every morning and running off to hide all day. She probably thought to herself, "Oh, let them get her. I am tired of this. It is wearing me down." The hide-and-seek game continued through September. But when October came, the colder weather was on the school's side.

So one morning I was "caught." Even then, it was the rule among mothers not to let the child go voluntarily. As the police officer reached out to take me by the arm, my mother put her arm around me. Tradition required that it appear that I was forced into school.

I was taken from the village to the school-house, along with several other children. First, each of us was given a bath by one of the Indian women who worked at the school. Then we were dressed in cotton underwear, cotton dresses, and long black stockings and heavy shoes supplied by the government. Each week we had a bath and a complete change of clothing. We were allowed to wear the clothes home each day, but my mother took off the clothes of the hated white man as soon as I got home, until it was time to go to school the next day.

Names were given to each child by the school. Mine was "Helen." Each child had a name card pinned on for as many days as it took the teacher to learn and remember the name she had given us. Our teacher was Miss Stanley. She began by teaching us the names of objects around the room. We read a little from big charts on the wall later on, but I don't remember ever using any books.

A feud developed over the years as the people were divided into sides for and against those who came from the outside. These two factions were known as the "Friendlies" (to the government) and the "Hostiles" (to the government). Later these groups were known as the "Progressives" and the "Traditionals."

Those who put their children into school voluntarily were given an ax, a hoe, a shovel, or a rake. (Stoves and wagons they had to work for.) "Hostile" parents scornfully rejected these tools even though they would have served them better than the tools they made of wood or stone. These gifts were looked upon only as a bait that would end in no good to the Indians. "Hostile" parents warned their children, when they were leaving for school, "Don't take the pencil in your hand. If you do, it means you agree to what they want you to do. Don't do it."

The attitude of the parents carried over to their children, as was shown on the school grounds. The children of the "Friendlies" made fun of us, calling us "Hostiles," and they would not let us join with them in their play. Going back up the trail after school was often a skirmish. The "Friendly" children often ran ahead up the trail and gathered rocks and threw them down at us when we came to the bottom of the steep rocky ledge. Sometimes we would try another way up to avoid being hit by rocks.

I liked school. It was pleasant and warm in-side. I liked to wear the clothes they gave us at school; but when I learned that the kids were "hostile" to us, I didn't want to go to school. Everyone, even the principal and the teachers and employees, were more or less against us.

The Mennonites had a church in Old Oraibi, but our parents would not let us go even to their Sunday School. We wanted to go, and sometimes we went to Sunday School by a back path. They would give us a little ticket each time we came, and on Christmas they gave a big prize to the one who had the most tickets. We did not understand much of what they said, but it was nice to be there. I received a few tickets but gave them away. I did not dare accept a present.

ROUGH JUSTICE IN THE IDAHO MINES

Adapted from James F. Rusling, Across America. *New York: Sheldon & Company, 1874.*

Miners were the first large group of settlers to move past the Mississippi River toward the last frontier. After the discovery of gold in California in 1848, the search for gold and silver speeded up, and mining settlements developed in many parts of the West.

No matter where they were located, most mining settlements in the West went through similar stages. The first discoveries led to boom times; then when the precious metals were mined out, the miners moved on, and once-flourishing communities turned into ghost towns. One mining community that escaped this fate was Boise, Idaho. It is described here by James Rusling, who was sent to inspect western posts by the army quartermaster.

How would you describe Rusling's attitudes toward the miners in Idaho? Do you think it is right for people to take the law into their own hands in a case like the one Rusling describes?

Idaho, one of the latest of our new territories, was formed by cutting off the eastern parts of Oregon and Washington. Lewiston, on the Columbia River, was originally its capital; but many local people demanded a more central position, and so Boise became the capital. We found it, in November 1866, a growing town of log and frame buildings, thoroughly alive in every way. Three years before, there was nothing there but a scattered ranch or two. Now it had three thousand inhabitants, two daily newspapers, stagecoach lines in all directions, and growing prosperity. A hotel was just being completed. The Episcopalians and Presbyterians already had their churches up, and the Methodists were expecting to build theirs soon. There were plenty of excellent free schools, to take care of all the children and more.

Boise was then the center of the mining regions of Idaho. The mines were many miles away, at Owyhee, Ruby, Idaho City, and Silver City. But all business sprang from and met here at Boise as the most central point. Mining operations were mostly over for the season, and the streets and saloons of Boise were filled with rough miners on their way to the Columbia River, or even California, to spend the winter and then return. They claimed they could save money by this temporary move—the cost of living was so high in Idaho—and at the same time escape the cold climate.

The bearded miners wore big hats and were dressed in red shirts. Every man carried his bowie knife and revolver, and seemed ready for any emergency. They were evidently a rougher crowd than the Colorado miners. They proved to be from California, Arizona, Nevada, Oregon, Montana, and about everywhere else except Alaska. Your true miner is a traveler, who has "prospected" everywhere from Canada to Mexico. He is already ready to leave for any new "diggings" that promise better than where he is, on half a day's notice, no matter how far. His possessions are few, easy to bundle up or to get rid of. He is a good example of the old saying, "A rolling stone gathers no moss."

The chief business of Boise just then seemed to be drinking whisky and gambling. The saloons were the best-looking buildings in town, and were filled at all hours of the day and night. The gamblers occupied corners of these, and carried on a big business. They were not bothered by anybody. The restaurants were also important points of interest, and gave excellent meals at reasonable prices. Here at Boise, our paper money for the first time stopped being used as currency. Precious metals became the only medium of exchange. It did one's eyes good to see our old gold and silver coins in use once more, though gold and silver "dust" was also a recognized medium of exchange. All the stores, restaurants, and saloons kept a pair of scales. Their customers carried buckskin or leather bags of "dust" from which they made payment and into which they returned their change. Disputes now and then arose if the "dust" was thought not to be up to standard. But these disputes were usually settled peaceably, unless the "dust" proved counterfeit. Then the saloons sometimes flashed with bowie knives or rang with revolvers.

Here at Boise, also for the first time, we met "John Chinaman." Quite a number of Chinese had reached Idaho from California, and were scattered through the towns as waiters, cooks, launderers, etc. A few had gone to the mines, but not many as they preferred the protection of the towns. Along with the rest, these Chinese miners were also traveling to the Columbia River and beyond. As they went their way, we wished well for them. However, it appeared that the stupid, brutal, and barbarous laws of the whole Pacific Coast, where the Chinese are concerned, were still in force in Idaho. A good example of the workings of these laws had just occurred, and should be recorded here. Three or four ruffians had confronted an innocent Chinaman at work in the mines, had first abused and insulted him, and then robbed and killed him. Other miners, hearing of the circumstances, arrested the murderers and took them before an Idaho judge. He promptly freed them on the ground that no white person was present at the time and that the Chinamen (who were present) could not be used as witnesses against white men! This was good Idaho law and justice, no doubt. But it was too strong for the angry miners. That same day they lynched the wrongdoers in the nearest gulch. This was rude law and rough justice, no doubt. But was it not much better than the absurd and inhuman code of the Pacific Coast?

A NORWEGIAN FARM WOMAN WRITES HOME

Adapted from Frontier Mother: The Letters of Gro Svendsen, *translated and edited by Pauline Farseth and Theodore C. Blegen, published by The Norwegian-American Historical Association, 1950, pages 121–123. Reprinted by permission of the publisher.*

Pioneering farmers followed the miners and cattle raisers toward the "last frontier" as they settled and farmed the land on the Great Plains. Although plains farming was difficult, backbreaking work, thousands of families moved to the plains. Many were immigrants, especially from the countries of Scandinavia.

Gro Svendsen and her husband, Ole, left Norway in 1862 to settle in Iowa. Her life on the Great Plains was far from easy, and she died in 1878 after giving birth to her tenth child. But in this selection, a letter written in 1873 to her parents, she tries to tell of the good things in her life on the plains.

What does Gro Svendsen's letter tell you about the lives of pioneer farmers on the Great Plains? What things in her life make her happy? What are her chief worries? How do you think you would have liked living on the plains in the 1870's?

December 6, 1873

My beloved Parents:

I am writing you, my dear parents, in the hope that you are still living and in good health. I should have written you a long time ago. At least I should have thanked you, Father, for your last letter dated the first of March.

I must tell you first of all that we are all well. My health is not always of the best, but so far God has spared me from any long illness, and so I feel that I cannot complain. Rather I should thank God for His infinite goodness.

The children have always been in good health. They are growing strong and healthy. Little Bergit was small and frail for a long time, but this summer she has grown plump and fat. Steffen is very healthy looking, chubby and fat; his cheeks are pink and white like a rose. I wish his grandmother could see him. I am sending you pictures of Svend and Niels and Carl and Albert so now you can see what they look like. Ole was not at home when the pictures were taken, so he was left out. Niels is just as tall as Svend, but not so fat. Many who do not know them think they are twins.

My four oldest children have been attending Norwegian school this fall, but I must sadly confess that they are far behind in their studies. If they were at home in Norway, I know full well that they would have learned a great deal more. We so seldom have Norwegian school, and it is slow work to try to teach the boys at home.

When I wrote you last spring I told you that we were very much concerned about Ole's father, who had been kicked by a horse and was very ill. However, when Ole arrived there, his father had gotten well again.

Store-Ole was here a couple of weeks ago. He stayed a little over a week. His family is well. They like their new home very much and are more than happy over having moved there, in spite of the fact that their harvest will be poor this year because of the locusts that attacked their grain.

Here, also, the crops will be poor. This spring the locusts destroyed our fields, too. In many places there will be no harvest. We did get a little, enough for our own living, but none to sell. So it will be difficult to pay our many debts. We were forced to buy our land for $480. Since we had no money, we had to borrow. Then we had other bad luck. One of our horses had a sore leg this summer. At the time when there was most work to be done we couldn't use him, so we had to buy another horse that cost $150. The sick horse is well again, and now we have three draft horses and one colt. We still owe for the new horse. His name is Jack.

Times have been hard this fall—much harder than any since we came to this land. The future is uncertain. No one knows what tomorrow will bring.

We have been thinking of selling this land and moving up to Rock County [Minnesota] in order to be near Store-Ole. If the opportunity should come, we might move. If we did sell, we should have to get enough for our land so that we would have a few hundred dollars to start all over again in our new home. In the meantime we shall await whatever life may bring.

From what I have said you will see that we are not rich. But though we have no material wealth, we have nevertheless possessions of greater worth—a quiet and peaceful home with many children, all normal, gifted with health and intelligence, spirited, cheerful, and happy. We have other possessions, too. I could not name them all, but all these blessings seem to be of far greater value than money. I am more than satisfied and thankful to God for all His goodness toward His unworthy children.

This letter, which should reach you before Christmas, will be short. But I wanted you to know that we are all well.

A joyous Christmas and a blessed New Year to you, my dear parents, sisters, and brothers.

With love from
Ole and Gro

UNIT TWO
THE RISE OF INDUSTRIALISM
(1860's-1890's)

CHAPTER 4 ■ BUSINESS PIONEERS AND THE GROWTH OF AMERICAN INDUSTRY

CARNEGIE MAKES A DEAL

Adapted from Autobiography of Andrew Carnegie. *Copyright renewed 1948 by Margaret Carnegie Miller. Reprinted by permission of Houghton Mifflin Company.*

In the years after 1870, as industry grew rapidly in the United States, several business leaders came to control entire industries and became enormously wealthy. One of them, Andrew Carnegie, was a Scottish immigrant who settled in the city of Pittsburgh. He studied and worked hard and eventually gained control of many steel mills. Carnegie's steel mills were Pittsburgh's most important industry.

In the following selection from Carnegie's autobiography, he describes what he thinks are the main reasons for business success. He also tells about an early business deal he took part in.

According to Carnegie, what policy is "the true secret of success"? Do you think that Carnegie is correct when he says that quality is the basis of business success? Why? What characteristics of a good business leader does Carnegie show here?

The Keystone Bridge Works have always been a source for satisfaction for me. Almost every company that had tried to build iron bridges in America had failed. Many of the bridges that they built had fallen. Some of the worst railway disasters in America were caused that way. But nothing has ever happened to a Keystone bridge, and some of them have stood where the winds were strong.

Luck had nothing to do with it. We used only the best material and enough of it, making our own iron and later our own steel. We inspected everything very carefully, and would build a safe structure or none at all. When asked to build a bridge which we knew was not strong enough or was poorly designed, we refused. We guaranteed any piece of work that had the stamp of the Keystone Bridge Works (and there are few states in the Union where they are not to be found).

This policy is the true secret of success. It will be uphill work for a few years until your work is proven, but after that it is smooth sailing. Instead of objecting to inspectors, all manufacturing companies should welcome them. A high standard of excellence is easily maintained, and people are educated in the effort to reach excellence. I have never known a company that became successful unless it did good, honest work. Even in these days of the fiercest competition, when price is very important, at the root of great business success there still lies the much more important factor of quality. The effect of attention to quality upon everyone in the firm, from the president of the concern down to the lowest worker, cannot be overestimated.

The president of an important manufacturing work once boasted to me that their workers had chased away the first inspector who had appeared, and that they had never been troubled with another since. This was said as if it ought to be a matter of sincere congratulation, but I thought to myself: "This concern will never stand the strain of competition; it is sure to fail when hard times come." The result proved the correctness of my belief. The surest basis for a manufacturing concern is quality. After that, and a long way after, comes cost.

I gave a great deal of personal attention for some years to the affairs of the Keystone Bridge Works, and when important contracts were involved often went myself to meet the parties. On one such occasion in 1868, I visited Dubuque, Iowa, with our engineer, Walter Katte. We were competing for the contract to build the most important railway bridge that had been built up to that time, a bridge across the Mississippi.

That visit proved how success often depends upon small and unimportant things. We found we were not the lowest bidder. Our chief rival was a bridge-building company in Chicago to which the board of directors who were in charge of building the bridge had decided to give the contract. I stayed and talked with some of the directors. They knew nothing about the advantages and disadvantages of cast-iron and wrought-iron. We had always made the upper part of the bridge with wrought-iron, while our rivals' was made of cast-iron. I explained the result of a steamer striking against the one and against the other. In the case of wrought-iron, it would probably only bend. In the case of cast-iron, it would certainly break and down would come the bridge. One of the directors was able to back up my argument. The other night, he said, he had run his buggy in the dark into a cast-iron lamppost, which had broken to pieces.

"Ah, gentlemen," I said, "there is the point. A little more money and you could have had the indestructible wrought-iron and your bridge would stand against any steamboat. We never have built and we never will build a cheap bridge. Ours don't fall."

There was a pause. Then the president of the bridge company asked if I would excuse them for a few moments. I left the room. Soon they called me back and offered the contract, provided we built the bridge at the lower price, which was only a few thousand dollars less. I agreed to this. That cast-iron lamppost so conveniently smashed gave us one of our most profitable contracts. What is more, it obtained for us the reputation of having won the Dubuque bridge against all competitors.

The moral of that story lies on the surface.

If you want a contract, be on the spot when it is given. A smashed lamppost or something equally unthought of may secure the prize if the bidder is there. And if possible stay until you can take the written contract home in your pocket.

LIFE BEHIND A TOY COUNTER

Adapted from Annie M. MacLean, "Two Weeks in Department Stores," American Journal of Sociology, Vol. IV, May 1899, in Neil Harris, ed., The Land of Contrasts. *New York: George Braziller, 1970.*

What was it like to work as a salesperson in a department store? In the late 1800's, a Canadian sociologist wanted to find out more about the lives and working conditions of sales clerks in large stores. As a result, she decided to take a job as a saleswoman. For several days during the Christmas season she worked in a New York department store. For one week's work she earned $2.00 in wages and $3.25 in commissions. However, 30 cents was taken from her salary because she arrived at work late three times. (Every time sales clerks were late, 10 cents was deducted from their weekly salary.)

What seems to be the store's attitude toward its employees? Toward the public? Do modern department stores operate differently? If so, in what ways?

The hurried breakfast, the rush out into the street crowded with people carrying their lunches, and the streetcars packed with pale-faced, sleepy-eyed men and women made the working world seem very real. Hurrying workers filled the center of the city. No one was stirring. I reached the store promptly at eight, the time of opening. The manager said he would give me two dollars a week plus 5 percent commission on sales. I was then given a number, and by "424" I was known during my stay there.

I was sent to the toy department, where I found sixty-seven other people who were to work with me. The place was filled with all kinds of toys, from a monkey beating a drum to a doll that said "mamma." Our business was first to dust and arrange the stock. Then we stood ready for customers. Our business was to see that no one escaped without buying something. The confusion can be readily imagined. As soon as the elevators emptied themselves on the floor, there was one mad rush of clerks with a quickly spoken, "What would you like, madam?" or, "Something in toys, sir?" The majority of answers were rude. Some people were amused, and a few were alarmed at the urgency of the clerks. One young boy, on being asked by half a dozen clerks at once, threw up his hands in horror, and said, "For God's sake, let me get out of here!" He ran down the stairs, not even waiting for the elevator. The cause of such wasteful activity on the part of so many employees was the 5 percent commission, which could add two or three dollars a week to one's salary.

One of the difficult things at first was trying to remembr the prices, for they were frequently changed during the day, and the penalty for selling something at a lower price was that one was immediately fired. Selling above price, however, met with no disapproval. Every morning there were special sales. Sometimes articles that had sold for one dollar would be reduced to ninety-eight cents. Again, twenty-five-cent articles would be offered at a bargain for forty cents "today only." The manager's brief instructions each morning kept us aware of the bargains. The charms of the bargain counter disappear when one has been behind the scenes and learned something of its history. The humor of it seemed to impress the clerks, for often they would exchange knowing winks when some customer was being victimized.

Oh, that first morning! The hours seemed days. "Can I possibly stand up all day?" was my main thought, for I soon learned that anyone who was found sitting down would be harshly criticized. Later in the week, one of the girls who was exhausted sat for a moment on a little table that was for sale—there was not a seat of any kind in the rooms, and the only way one could get a moment's rest was to sit on the children's furniture that was for sale on one part of the floor. The manager came along and found the poor girl resting. He called out in rough tones: "Get up out of that, you lazy hussy; I don't pay you to sit around all day!" By night the men as well as the women were limping wearily across the floor. Many sales were made under positive physical agony.

How well I remember my first sale there! The people were slow to arrive that morning; in fact, they were slow every morning. We hardly ever had any business until eleven o'clock, and the greatest rush came about six. From twelve thirty to two was a busy time also. My first two customers were types that were common. First a woman with a businesslike expression came to me and demanded that I show her building blocks. They were shown, but proved unsatisfactory. The dolls' buggies, boys' sleds, laundry sets, and skates were examined in slow succession. I was asked about the prices and merits of everything. Then she looked at me and said: "I do not intend to buy today; I just wished to examine your goods." Still I had not a sale on my book and she had taken half an hour of my time.

The next customer was a man who wanted a boy's sled at a cost of one dollar and a half. Now, we had none at that price, but we had them at one dollar and thirty-five cents, and one dollar and sixty-five cents, either of which I thought would suit him. But I was mistaken. He gave me a look of utter scorn, and then criticized me for advertising things we did not have in stock. I meekly suggested that I was not responsible for the ads that appeared in the morning papers. But he was not at all pleased by this. I felt rather upset, but the comforting voice of a cashier said "Don't mind him, he's only a cheapskate."

Thus encouraged I started out on another sale. This time it was a small boy who wanted to buy, and the bright-faced little fellow did me good. He had eighty cents, he said, and he wanted presents for the baby, and Tom, and Freda, and Cousin Jack, and several others. I suggested one thing after another, till finally he had spent his money.

The boy was happy, and so was I. I looked admiringly at the eighty cents set down on my sales sheet. It meant that I had earned four cents in commission. After that the sales came frequently. They were all small, of course, and amounted to only $14.98 for the day. But this was more than I sold any day after that. It has often been noticed that new clerks do better at first than they do later. With me, freshness and interest in the novelty helped to take away my tiredness, and thus invited sales.

My first day ended at six thirty. I went wearily to the coat-room and more wearily to my boarding place. When I arrived there, I could only throw myself upon my small white cot in the dormitory and wonder if it would be all right for a working girl to cry. Presently I was dreaming that blows from an iron hammer were falling upon me. In a little while it was morning, and another day had begun.

A TRUST IS BORN

Excerpt from The Potentates: Business and Businessmen in American History *by Ben B. Seligman. Copyright* © *1971 by the Estate of Ben B. Seligman. Reprinted with the permission of The Dial Press.*

In the 1870's and 1880's, the rapid growth of American industry was greatly spurred by the trend toward business consolidation, or combination. Companies used this form of business organization to gain control of a large part of the market in a certain industry—for example, oil. When the corporations in an industry joined together into one large trust, they gained many advantages. The large size of the trust enabled it to take advantage of the money-saving techniques of mass production and cheap marketing. The trust also could limit production, fix prices, and secure lower railroad rates. Trusts were so effective that they were able to drive out most competition and establish a monopoly or near-monopoly. The American tobacco trust, formed by James Buchanan Duke, is a good example of how such a giant business combination worked.

How were James Duke's business efforts aided by technology? By advertising and promotion? In what way did he gain the support of New York bankers? Which of his methods were illegal? Which were unfair?

It became evident that any business that might develop a wide market for its product would end up in a financier's hands. Entrepreneurs themselves might become financial tycoons, as was the case with James B. Duke. For if money could be made by supplying consumers with goods and services, much more could be made by controlling stocks and bonds. Duke and his tobacco empire are striking not so much for size or importance of product, but because they show the methods that were used in bringing together various branches of a new industry and the way in which a new technology—mechanized cigarette-making—could promote consolidation.

Tobacco had been an important plantation crop before the Civil War. After the war, John Ruffin Green sold tobacco under the trade name of "Bull Durham." (It was named after Durham, North Carolina, the town in which it was processed.) The picture of the bull became a well-known trademark that Blackwell and Carr, who took over after Green, fought to protect. They learned quickly that testimonials and advertising were essential in convincing the consumer to smoke their tobacco or buy their chewing plug. By 1884 the Blackwell and Carr factory had become the largest in the world. Soon many brands of tobacco were being produced in Durham. Those who processed the tobacco were determined to make the city the tobacco capital of the South.

However, the North Carolina town of Winston, near the sleepy village of Salem, soon began to rival Durham as a center for manufacturing tobacco products. One of the aggressive young salesmen in that area was R. J. Reynolds, who headed a family firm there. Lewis Ginter and John Allen had a thriving business in Richmond. Liggett and Myers was a growing firm in St. Louis. There was a great demand for tobacco all over the nation. Chewing and smoking brands were produced in ever-increasing quantities to satisfy it. Concerned with the protection of their trademarks, which clearly distinguished one brand from another, manufacturers passed out premiums and coupons. They gave rebates to dealers, and paid bribes to put their brands in certain stores.

It was not long, however, before Buck Duke would take over all the others. Born in 1856, James Buchanan Duke was named after the Democratic President elected in that year. Duke's father had been a small farmer before the Civil War. Afterward he returned to the land to grow and sell tobacco. His little tobacco curing factory grew steadily. By 1872 it was producing 125,000 pounds [577,000 kilograms] of tobacco a year. In 1874 the elder Duke and his two sons, James and Ben, moved the factory to Durham. The elder Duke took both boys in as partners to form W. Duke & Sons. To obtain more capital, several partners from outside the firm were brought in.

Cigarettes had been popular in Europe for many years, though in America they could not yet compete with plug and smoking tobacco. But Duke felt that he was hitting his head against the stone wall of Bull Durham. Blackwell and Carr had moved far ahead of their rivals in selling plug and smoking tobacco. Duke knew that he could not compete with them, and so he decided on cigarettes. But these had to be rolled by hand. Although Duke had some of the best workers in the business, their output was still too small for an expanding market. Then the Dukes obtained a cigarette machine, which could turn out 120,000 cigarettes a day. Realizing that cigarettes were popular in cities, Duke set up a branch in New York. He successfully competed with the better-known firm of Ginter and Allen. He gave premiums and matched Ginter ad for ad. A favorite selling method was to place a picture of a pretty girl in each package of cigarettes. He sent clever salespeople on the road to find business. People were hired to go from store to store asking only for Duke's product. Incoming immigrants were given free cigarettes at ports of entry. By 1890 W. Duke and Company had become first in the tobacco industry.

Meanwhile, Duke was watching developments in oil, steel, whisky, and sugar. All were being combined through trusts. Why not tobacco? But first one had to get into the good graces of financiers. Duke began to negotiate for small thirty-day or sixty-day loans with New York bankers, always paying them back promptly. Soon Duke had established a line of credit with the powers that counted.

Finally, Duke was able to convince four other large companies that they all ought to get together. In 1890 the American Tobacco Company was started, a combination of Duke, Ginter, and three others. This was 90 percent of the cigarette industry. Capitalization was set at $25,800,000, though the combined tangible assets were just slightly over $3,000,000. Eight years later another company was formed to handle plug tobacco. Dealers were forced to take other items through tie-in sales. If they wanted cigarettes, they had to also take the trust's tobacco plug.

American Tobacco continued to expand by all means available, some fair, many unfair. Almost absolute control over cigarette-making machinery was worked out. Dealers refusing to take the trust's products were blacklisted and subjected to ruinous price wars. Through all these operations, Buck Duke ruled with a iron hand. He fired his star salesman, Edward Small, when he refused to move his family to Cincinnati. By 1905 American Tobacco and its related Consolidated Tobacco Company, both headed by Duke, controlled three fourths of the smoking-tobacco, and over nine tenths of the snuff, in addition to having almost complete control of the cigarette market.

Four other firms were taken over in the early 1890's. Liggett and Myers was then taken over. In 1899 it was R. J. Reynolds' turn to join the trust.

Stocks and bonds were controlled to yield a profit to insiders. Operations were always carried out in secret. Duke used several techniques to dominate the market. One was price-cutting. Another was to form phony "independent" companies to make it look as though there were competition. Duke also offered premiums and rebates, created rival brands to confuse consumers, and took over more competitors. Once a market had been won, retail prices were kept at the same level, while the jobber was squeezed with higher wholesale prices.

Nor was the foreign market neglected. Duke tried to get his products into Japan, but the government there decided to set up its own monopoly. He bought a factory in England, but the Imperial Tobacco Company was formed so British manufacturers could protect English people against American cigarettes. After several years of conflict, the usual cartel agreement [a cartel is an international trust] was reached. The United States and Cuban markets were given to Duke, Great Britain was given to Imperial, and the rest of the world was shared through the British-American Tobacco Company. The entire industry, with the exception of cigar-making, was now controlled by the "Tobacco Trust."

ROCKEFELLER'S ACHIEVEMENTS

Adapted by permission of Charles Scribner's Sons from John D. Rockefeller, Vol. II by Allan Nevins. Copyright 1940 by Charles Scribner's Sons.

Probably no single business leader of the late 1800's received more praise or criticism than John D. Rockefeller. Born into a poor family, in time he came to control the nation's oil industry. In 1870 he organized the Standard Oil Company and located his oil refineries in Cleveland. Like many other industrial leaders of the time, he used unfair business methods such as price-cutting until competing companies went bankrupt or sold out.

By 1882 the Standard Oil Trust had been formed, and by 1887 Rockefeller controlled 95 percent of the oil refineries in the nation.

In this selection, historian Allan Nevins gives his analysis of Rockefeller and his methods. He describes Rockefeller's innovations, or the changes he introduced to American industry. According to Nevins, what important characteristic of the new industrial era did many people fail to see? What was Rockefeller's goal? With what historical figures does Nevins compare industrial leaders? What do you think of this comparison?

It is plain that the place Rockefeller holds in American industrial history is that of a great innovator. Early on, he saw the advantage of combination and order in an industry that was bloated, lawless, and chaotic. Following this vision, he formed a scheme of industrial organization which, magnificent in its harmony and strength, world-wide in its scope, possessed a striking novelty. He met great opposition. Producers, rival manufacturers, courts, legislatures, presidents, and public opinion fought him at every step. He and his partners marched from investigation to investigation, from lawsuit to lawsuit, under a growing load of criticism. But they moved forward. They believed that the opposition was mistaken and irrational. They felt that the full victory of competitive laissez-faire individualism would mean a step backward, confusion, and general loss.

The dominant ideal of pioneering America was one of complete independence and self-sufficiency. Long after the new industrial era was far advanced, people held on to the old faith in a self-balancing system of private ownership, small-unit enterprise, and free competition. They believed that this system would give every person a reward roughly equal to his or her work, integrity, and ability. They were slow to see that the industrial system was not self-balancing, that it grew less so decade by decade. They were slow to see that people were less and less independent, more and more interdependent. They were reluctant to admit that free competition was steadily becoming more restricted, and that its character was changing. It was no longer a competition of small business and individual firms. It was becoming a competition organized by great corporations.

Rockefeller was a realist. Partly by intuition, partly by hard thought, he understood the real nature of economic forces and the real motives behind American industry. He and the other leaders of the "heroic age" in American business development were the guiding forces of our industrial society. Many of the forces and elements in that society were unreasonable and wasteful. Rockefeller wished to bring about a more reasonable and efficient pattern. Behind this desire he placed a good mind, a skill in organization, and a dynamic personal force which were not surpassed, and possibly not

equaled, by those of any other industrial captain in history.

Rockefeller's economic foresight, and the courage he showed in sticking to it, deserve praise. He knew that he was carrying through a great experiment, and he believed the experiment to be sound and wise. Any careful analysis of the work of the best leaders shows that money was not the central object, but a by-product. Greedy people exist, but they seldom obtain great fortunes, for greed tends to defeat itself in complex business operations. Those who built the really great economic structures were not thinking mainly of dollars, or they would have stopped after their first great business successes.

One great fact to be remembered when studying Rockefeller and other captains of industry is that American business has typically been a more optimistic, lighthearted undertaking than business in other lands. The best business people have been great adventurers. The giants of the "heroic age" of industry can be compared with the famous Elizabethan captains —with Drake, Hawkins, Cavendish, Frobisher, Cabot (some of whom were good business people, too). In business, Americans of the nineteenth century found the Great Game. They played it with enjoyment and enthusiasm, they enjoyed it even when it was dangerous, and they took its ups and down calmly. Of all its leaders, none showed more boldness or swiftness than Rockefeller, and none more balance in accepting defeats and victories. Love of the game was one of his motives, particularly as his keen eye saw a pattern in the game that less intelligent people missed.

"IT IS ALL WRONG TO BE POOR"

Adapted from pp. 17–59 of Acres of Diamonds *by Russell H. Conwell. Copyright 1915, 1943 by Harper & Brothers. Reprinted by permission of Harper & Row, Publishers, Inc.*

During the years of the late 1800's, some Americans became very wealthy by amassing fortunes in business and in the stock market. Newspapers and magazines told of the fabulous fortunes that were being made and how the rich lived. Many Americans soon began to envy the lives of the very wealthy. The great American dream of becoming rich was shaped during these years.

Russell Conwell, a Union army officer turned preacher, said that there was no point in envying the rich. Instead he suggested that everyone should settle down and make money where he or she lived. He preached this message more than 6,000 times all over the United States in a famous speech called "Acres of Diamonds." The title of the speech came from its opening story, which told of a rich Arab who sold his lands to go in search of diamonds. The new owner of the Arab's land then found these same riches on the very property that the Arab had sold.

Why, according to Conwell, is it a person's duty to get rich? What do you think of Conwell's speech? Do you agree with his ideas?

Now then, I say that the opportunity to get rich, to obtain great wealth, is here in Philadelphia now, within the reach of almost every man and woman who hears me speak tonight. I mean just what I say. I have come here to tell you what in God's sight I believe to be the truth. If my years have been of any value in teaching me common sense, I know I am right. The men and women sitting here, who found it difficult perhaps to buy a ticket to this talk, have within their reach "acres of diamonds," opportunities to get wealthy. There never was a place on earth more suited to this purpose than the city of Philadelphia today. Never in the history of the world did a poor person without money have such an opportunity to get rich quickly and honestly as he or she has now in our city.

I say that you ought to get rich. It is your duty to get rich. How many of my religious brothers and sisters say to me, "Do you, a Christian minister, spend your time going up and down the country advising young people to get rich, to get money?" "Yes, of course I do." They say, "Isn't that awful! Why don't you preach the gospel instead of preaching about people making money?" "Because to make money honestly is to preach the gospel." That is the reason. The people who get rich may be the most honest people you find in the community.

"Oh," but says some young man here tonight, "I have been told all my life that if a person has money he is very dishonest and dishonorable and mean and contemptible." My friend, that is the reason you have none, because you have that idea of people. The foundation of your faith is altogether false. Let me say here clearly, and say it briefly—ninety-eight

out of one hundred of the rich people of America are honest. That is why they are rich. That is why they are trusted with money. That is why they carry on great enterprises and find plenty of people to work with them. It is because they are honest.

Says another young man, "I hear sometimes of people who get millions of dollars dishonestly." Yes, of course, you hear this, and so do I. But such people are so rare a thing in fact that the newspapers talk about them all the time as a matter of news until you get the idea that all the other rich people get rich dishonestly.

My friends, drive me out into the suburbs of Philadelphia, and introduce me to the people who own their homes around this great city, those beautiful homes with gardens and flowers. I will introduce you to the very best people in character as well as in enterprise in our city. A man is not really a true man until he owns his own home. Those who own their homes are made more honorable and honest and pure, and true and economical and careful, by owning their homes.

Money is power, and you ought to be reasonably ambitious to have it. You ought to because you can do more good with it than you could without it. Money printed your Bible, money builds your churches, money sends your missionaries, and money pays your preachers. (You would not have many of them if you did not pay them.) The person who gets the largest salary can do the most good with the power that is given to him or her.

I say, then, you ought to have money. If you can honestly obtain riches in Philadelphia, it is your Christian and godly duty to do so. It is an awful mistake of these religious people to think you must be awfully poor in order to be religious.

Some people say, "Don't you sympathize with the poor people?" Of course I do, or else I would not have been speaking all these years. I sympathize with the poor, and the number of poor who are to be sympathized with is very small. While we should sympathize with God's poor—that is, those who cannot help themselves—let us remember there is not a poor person in the United States who was not made poor by his or her own shortcomings, or by the shortcomings of someone else. It is all wrong to be poor, anyhow.

Greatness consists not in the holding of some office. It consists in doing great things with little means and in the accomplishment of great purposes from the private ranks of life. To be great at all one must be great here, now, in Philadelphia. He who can give to this city better streets and better sidewalks, better schools and more colleges, more happiness and more civilization, more of God, he will be great anywhere. Let every man or woman here, if you never hear me again, remember this. If you wish to be great at all, you must begin where you are and with what you are, in Philadelphia, now. He that can give to this city any blessing, he who can be a good citizen while he lives here, he that can make better homes, he that can be a blessing whether he works in the shop or sits behind the counter or keeps house—whatever be his life, he who would be great anywhere must first be great in his own Philadelphia.

CHAPTER 5 ■ THE REVOLT OF AMERICAN FARMERS AGAINST BIG BUSINESS PRACTICES

HARDSHIPS OF RURAL LIFE

Adapted from E. V. Smalley, "The Isolation of Life on Prairie Farms," Atlantic Monthly, *September 1893.*

A world away from the rapidly growing, crowded cities of the East and Midwest, with their working-class slums and mansions of the rich, were the farms of the Great Plains. Eugene V. Smalley, a well-known journalist in the years after the Civil War, traveled through the Great Plains, where he visited many of the farms. He wrote about the lives of the farm families on the plains. In this selection, he emphasizes the isolation of farm life and suggests what could be done to make farm life more pleasant.

Why are American farmers so isolated? How does their condition compare with that of European farmers? What solution does Smalley suggest? What factors, which he could not take into account, eventually changed the situation?

In no civilized country have the farmers so poorly adapted their home life to the conditions of nature as have the people of our vast plains region. This is a strong statement, but I am led to this conclusion by ten years of observation. The European farmer lives in a village, where considerable social enjoyment is possible. The women talk together at the village well, and visit frequently at one another's homes. The children find playmates close to home. There is a school, and if the village is not a very small one, a church. The old men gather on summer evenings to smoke their pipes and talk of the crops. The young men play ball on the village green. In a word, something takes place to break the monotony or sameness of daily life. The houses, though small and with little furniture, have thick walls of brick or stone that keep out the summer's heat and the winter's cold.

Now contrast this life with the life of a poor settler in North or South Dakota or Nebraska. Every homesteader must live upon his claim for five years to confirm his title to it. If the country were so thickly settled that every quarter-section of land, or 160 acres [64.7 hectares], had a family upon it, each family would still be half a mile [.8 kilometer] from any neighbor. But many settlers own 320 acres [129.5 hectares] and a few have 640 acres [259 hectares]. Then there are sections of land set aside for schools and other sections are not occupied at all. Thus the average space separating the farms is, in fact, always more than half a mile [.8 kilometer]. Many settlers must go a mile or two to reach a neighbor's house.

If there is any region in the world where the natural sociable instinct of people should be upheld, that region is our northwestern prairies. A short hot summer is followed by a long cold winter. The treeless plain stretches away to the horizon in every direction. In summer, it is covered with grain fields or grass and flowers, and is lovely in its color and vastness. But one mile of it is almost exactly like another. When the snow covers the ground it is bleak and depressing. There are no birds left after the wild geese and ducks have flown south. The silence of death rests on the vast landscape, except when it is swept by cruel winds.

In such a region, you would expect the

houses to be strongly built, but they are not. The new settlers are too poor to build a house of brick or stone. Instead, they haul a few loads of lumber from the nearest railway station. Then they put up a frail little house of two, three, or four rooms that looks as though the prairie winds would blow it away. The barn is often made of sod walls with a straw roof. A barbed-wire fence surrounds the barnyard. There are usually no trees.

In this small, cramped home, the farm family sees nothing more cheerful than the distant houses of other settlers, just as ugly and lonely, and stacks of straw and unthreshed grain. In the summer there is a school for the children, one, two, or three miles away. But in winter the distances across the snow-covered plains are too great for them to travel. Each family must live mainly to itself. A drive to the nearest town is almost the only pleasure. There are few social events in the life of these prairie farmers to liven up the monotony of the long winter evenings.

Visits from neighbors are few, because of the long distances which separate the farm-houses. Another reason is the differences among the people. They have no common past to talk about. They were strangers to one another when they arrived in this new land, and their work and ways have not thrown them together much. Often the strangeness is increased by differences of national origin. There are Swedes, Norwegians, Germans, French Canadians, and perhaps even Finns and Icelanders. The Americans themselves come from many different states. It is hard to establish any social bond in such a mixed population.

An alarming amount of insanity occurs among farmers. In proportion to their numbers, the Scandinavian settlers send the most people to the insane asylums. The reason is easy to see. These people came from cheery little farm villages. Life in their homeland was hard and full of work, but it was not lonesome. Think for a moment how great the change must be from the white-walled, red-roofed village in Norway to an isolated cabin on a Dakota prairie. It is little wonder that so many Scandinavian farmers lose their mental balance.

There is only one solution for the dreariness of farm life on the prairies. The isolated farm-house must be abandoned, and the people must draw together and live in villages. The peasants of the Russian steppes did this centuries ago, and so did those on the great plain of the Danube. In the older parts of our prairie states,

titles to homestead claims are now nearly all confirmed, so farmers no longer have to live on the land they farm. They might go out with their teams to till their fields, and return at evening to village homes. It would be entirely possible to divide the land over again so that each settler would still have 160 acres [64.7 hectares], and no one would live more than a mile from the farthest limit of his farm. The homes of the families would surround a village green, where the schoolhouse would stand. There would probably be a store and a post office. An active social life would soon develop in such a community.

If the plains people were thus brought together into towns, some home industries might be established that would add to family incomes, or at least save expenses. The economic weakness of farming in the North is based on the idle period of the farmer and the work animals during the long winter. If it were possible to bring back to the farm some of the crafts that were carried on in the country thirty or forty years ago, there would be a great gain in comfort, intelligence, and happiness.

According to habit, American farmers feel they must live upon the land they till, and must have no near neighbors. This habit will be hard to break, but I believe it must in time give in to the advantages of living closer together. I have known instances, however, where efforts at more neighborly ways of living have been made on a small scale, and have failed. In the early settlement of Dakota, sometimes four families, each taking a quarter-section homestead, would build temporary houses at the quarter-sections' meeting line, in order to be near each other. But a few years later, when they were able to put up better buildings, they moved to the opposite sides of their claims. They did so, they said, because their chickens got mixed up with those of their neighbors'. In these instances, I should add, the people were Americans. There is an individuality about the average American farmer, the result of generations of isolated living, that does not encourage living close to others.

I am aware that nothing changes so slowly as the customs of a people. It will take a long time to change the settled American habit of isolated farms. If it is ever changed, the new system will have to be introduced near the top of the rural social scale, and work down gradually to the masses. A group of farmers of superior intelligence and of above-average means must set an example and establish a model farm village. Such an experiment would be widely discussed by the newspapers. This extensive free advertising could hardly fail to interest other people in the idea.

The farmers of the West have thus far been engaged in a hard struggle to establish themselves on the soil, obtain the necessities of life, and pay off their mortgages. They are getting ahead year by year. In the older settled districts good houses are taking the place of the pioneer homes, and the towns show progress. Before long these prairie people will begin to try to solve the problems that come with a higher civilization. Then it will be found, I believe, that the first great step toward more comfortable living, intellectual development, and social enjoyment is the abandonment of the lonesome farmhouse and the establishment of the farm village.

A POPULIST ANALYZES FARMERS' PROBLEMS

Adapted from William A. Peffer, The Farmer's Side: His Troubles and Their Remedy. *New York: D. Appleton and Co., 1891.*

During the hard times of the 1880's and 1890's farmers throughout the country gathered in Grange halls and other meeting places to discuss their problems and to demand relief. As this happened, the Grange, a national farm organization founded to provide community activity for farm families, began to work for the improvement of farm conditions. The Grange established cooperatives, and its members went into politics. Then in the early 1890's members of the Grange and other farmers formed their own political party —the Populist Party.

In 1890, William Peffer, a Kansas lawyer and journalist, was elected to the Senate on the Populist Party ticket. In this selection, he summarized the farmers' complaints against the manufacturers, the banks, and the railroads.

According to Peffer, how had the farmers' situation changed between the 1840's and the 1890's in terms of self-sufficiency, cash, and competition? Who or what was to blame? Why did the political power of farmers decline?

A hundred years ago 90 percent of our population lived on farms. Transportation was so expensive that surplus wheat and corn could not be sold 50 miles [80.5 kilometers] away from a market town. Now great cities have grown up, the market has expanded, and distance is practically meaningless. From a small area along the Atlantic coast, we have spread across the continent. We travel by railroad from Boston to San Francisco in less than six days.

The American farmer of today is a completely different sort of person than he was 50 or 100 years ago. A great many men and women now living remember when farmers were largely manufacturers. That is, they made a great many tools and other things for their own use. Every farmer had tools with which he made wooden tools such as forks and rakes, handles for his hoes and plows, spokes for his wagon, and various other things.

Then the farmer produced flax and hemp and wool and cotton. These fibers were prepared on the farm. They were spun into yarn, woven into cloth, made into clothes, and worn at home. Upon every farm geese were kept. Their feathers were used in the home's beds and pillows, and the surplus was sold at the nearest market town.

When winter came, animals raised on the farm were butchered. Meat for family use during the next year was prepared and preserved in the smokehouse. The orchards supplied fruit for cider, for apple butter, and for preserves. Wheat was threshed, a little at a time, just enough to supply the needs of the family for money. Everything was saved and put to use.

One of the results of that sort of careful planning was that only a small amount of money was required to carry on the business of farming. A hundred dollars a year was probably as much as the largest farmers of that day needed to pay for workers, repairs of tools, and all other expenses, because so many things were paid for with farm crops.

Now we find that nearly everything has been changed. All over the West farmers thresh their wheat all at one time, get rid of it all at one time, and in a great many instances waste the straw. They sell their hogs, and buy bacon and pork. They sell their cattle, and buy fresh beef or canned beef or corned beef. They sell their fruit, and buy it back in cans. If they raise flax at all, they thresh it, sell the seed, and burn the straw. Instead of having clothing made on the farm or by a neighbor woman or country tailor a mile away, they either buy their clothing ready-made at the nearest town, or buy the cloth and have a city tailor make it.

Instead of making tools which they use on the farm, they go to town to purchase even a handle for an ax or a mallet. They purchase twine and rope and all sorts of material made of fibers. Indeed, they buy nearly everything now that they once produced, and these things all cost money.

Besides all this, there is something even stranger. In earlier times the American home was a free home. There was not one case in a thousand where a home was mortgaged to secure the payment of borrowed money. Only a small amount of money was then needed to carry on the business of farming, and there was always enough of it to supply the demand. Now when at least ten times as much is needed, there is little or none to be obtained. Nearly half the farms are mortgaged for as much as they are worth, and interest rates are very high.

As to the cause of such changes in the condition of farmers, it is the railroad builder, the banker, the moneychanger, and the manufacturer who have hurt the farmer. The manufacturers came with their factories. The wagonmaker's shop in the neighborhood has given way to the large company in the city where people by the thousand work and where a hundred or two hundred wagons are made in a week. The shoemaker's shop has given way to large companies in the cities where most of the work is done by machines. The old smokehouse has given way to the packing house. The farmer now is forced to go to town for nearly everything. Even a hand rake to clean up the yard must be bought at the city store.

And what is worse, if they need a little more money, they are forced to go to town to borrow it. But they do not find the money there. In place of it they find an agent who will "negotiate" a loan. The money is in the East, at a distance of a thousand, three thousand, or five thousand miles. [1,609, 4,827, or 8,046 kilometers]. The farmers of the country today are maintaining an army of distributors, loan agents, bankers, and others, who are absolutely worthless for all good purposes in the community.

These things, however, involve only the mechanics of farming. The farmers' territory has been invaded by people who buy large tracts of land and operate these large farms like factories. This is "bonanza" farming. The aim of some of the great "bonanza farms" of Dakota is to use machinery so effectively that farming one full section, or 640 acres [259 hectares], represents one year's work for only one person. Railroad companies gave special rates to the bonanza farmers. And while this disastrous competition was going on, ranchers too took possession of vast areas of the public lands and raised cattle by the million at no expense beyond the cost of herding.

These are some of the causes of the hard times in the farming industry. It was impossible for the average farmers to hold their own with such odds against them.

While these problems were increasing, other forces were operating to add to farmers' difficulties. The people were rapidly taking on debts, while prices of farm products fell very low. While one hundred dollars had the same value in 1889 as it did in 1869, lower farm prices made it worth more. It requires twice as many bushels of wheat or of corn or of oats, twice as many pounds of cotton or tobacco or wool, to pay off a debt in 1887 as it did to pay a debt of the same amount in 1867.

It is frequently said that the farmers themselves are to blame for all these problems. But that is not true. The farmer has been the victim of a gigantic scheme of plunder. Never before has such a vast combination of brains and money forced people into labor for the benefit of a few.

In the beginning of our history nearly all the people were farmers, and they made our laws. But as the national wealth increased, they came to supply the needs of those who own or control large fortunes. Farmers worked while others reaped the harvest. It is greed that robbed the farmers. High interest rates took all their money. And now, when their problems are becoming worse and disaster overtakes them, they appeal to those they have made rich only to learn how poor and helpless they are.

From this testimony readers need have no difficulty in determining for themselves "how we got here." Money [bankers and financiers] rules our financial policy. Money controls the business of the country. Money is robbing the people. These people of Wall Street hold the bonds of nearly every state, county, city, and township in the Union. Every railroad owes them more than it is worth. Every trust and combine made to rob the people had its beginnings in the example of Wall Street dealers. This dangerous power which money gives is taking away the liberties of the people. It now has control of nearly half their homes, and is reaching out its clutching hands for the rest. This is the power we have to deal with.

UNITED AGAINST A "COMMON ENEMY"

Adapted from Black and White: Land, Labor and Politics in the South *by Timothy Thomas Fortune. Reprinted by Arno Press, Inc., 1968.*

All farmers faced the problems of debt, overproduction, and low prices during the hard times of the 1880's and 1890's. But these years were especially difficult for black farmers in the South. Some leaders hoped that poor blacks and whites could work together to solve their problems. One man who hoped this was possible was T. Thomas Fortune. Born a slave in Florida, he went to Howard University after the Civil War and later published a newspaper, the New York *Age*.

According to Fortune, what was the chief mistake the North made after winning the Civil War? What reasons does he give for industrial slavery being oppressive? Do you think his hope for the future is realistic?

I know it is not fashionable for writers on economic questions to tell the truth. But the truth should be told. During the war the government confiscated the slave population of the South, but it left to the rebels a far more valuable kind of property. The slave, the perishable wealth, was taken by the government and then freed. But property in land, the wealth which does not perish, was left to the rebels.

The United States took the slave but left the thing which gave birth to *personal slavery* and is now fast giving birth to *industrial slavery.* The latter is more agonizing and much worse than that other slavery, which I once withstood. The old slaveholders had to feed, clothe, and house their property, and take care of it when disease or accident threatened its life. But industrial slavery requires no such care. The new slaveholder only wants to obtain the most labor for the least cost. He does not regard the worker as of any consequence when he can no longer produce. Having worked him to death, or ruined his health and robbed him of his labor, he turns him out upon the world to live upon the charity of people or to die of starva-tion. He knows that there is no profit in wasting time and money upon a disabled industrial slave. He makes wealth and death at one and the same time. He could not do this if our social system did not give him a monopoly of the soil from which a living must be obtained.

I think of the absolutely destitute condition of the colored people of the South at the close of the war. I remember the moral and intellectual harm slavery did them. Not only were they bankrupt, but they were absolutely cut off from the soil, with no right or title to it. Now they have already got a respectable slice of land. They have eagerly taken hold of the opportunities for educational development provided by good men and women. They have bought homes and supplied them with articles of convenience and comfort, often of luxury. I am surprised not at this progress, but that the race did not terrorize and rob society as society had for so long terrorized and robbed them. The thing is strange and marvelous, in the extreme. Instead of becoming outlaws, as the situation would seem to have indicated, the black men and women of the South went to work to better their own lives and the crippled condition of the country, which had been produced by the ravages of rebellion. Meanwhile, many white people of the South, the capitalists, the land-sharks, and the ruffians organized themselves into a band of outlaws. They deliberately murdered innocent men and women for political reasons, and robbed them of their honest labor because they were too lazy to work themselves.

But this highly abnormal, unnatural condition of things is fast passing away. White people, having asserted their superiority in matters of assassination and robbery, have settled down on a barrel of dynamite, as they did in the days of slavery. They will await the explosion with the same self-satisfaction true of them in other days.

The future struggle in the South will be, not between white people and black people, but between capital and labor, landlord and tenant. Already the armies are gathering on the field.

The same battle will be fought upon southern soil that is in preparation in other states where the conditions took longer to develop but are no more deep-rooted or harmful. The social problems in the South will be found to be the same as those in every other section of our country. Questions of "race," "condition," etc., will be properly adjusted as people become better off and forget the unhappy past.

The hour is coming when the working

classes of our country, North, East, West, and South, will recognize that they have a *common cause,* a *common humanity,* and a *common enemy.* If they want to triumph over wrong, without distinction of race or previous condition, *they must unite!* When the battle begins, the rich, be they black or be they white, will be found upon the same side. And the poor, be they black or be they white, will be found on the same side.

Necessity knows no law and discriminates in favor of no person or race.

CHAPTER 6 ■ THE STRUGGLE OF AMERICAN WORKERS TO ORGANIZE

CHANGING CONDITIONS BEWILDER A WORKER

Adapted from Walter A. Wyckoff, The Workers. *New York: Charles Scribner's Sons, 1899.*

Walter Wyckoff wanted to find out how other people in the United States lived. Consequently, soon after he graduated from Princeton University, he decided to travel across the country. It took him two years to travel on foot from Connecticut to California. Along the way, he worked at many different jobs. One of his jobs was construction work for the World's Columbian Exposition in Chicago in 1892. In this selection he writes of the working conditions at the Exposition. These conditions were typical of the new industrial age. Individual workers had become unimportant, and relationships between boss and worker were impersonal.

Why is "Mr. Ford" confused by his new surroundings? By his new job? What is his attitude toward unions? Do you think that joining a union would have helped him?

Our work was the general care of all the plank roads on the grounds. They had been put in fairly good condition, but they received hard use, and constant repairs were necessary. We were, therefore, to give our attention, up to five o'clock in the afternoon, to those sections of the road which most needed repairs. After five, when the work for the day was over, our duty was to go over all the roads and see that they were in good condition for the next morning.

Our job is not easy. The roads constantly need to be repaired. A good deal of hard work is necessary to keep them in order. It is mostly pick and shovel work, the hardest kind of work as far as my experience goes. The old trenches must be kept open and new ones dug, and sometimes the sides of long sections of the road must be buried under a layer of earth to prevent the bare planks from twisting out of shape in the sun.

Among the workers on the grounds, none has interested me more than an American carpenter with whom I sometimes spend an evening. The man is lonely and uncomfortable in his new surroundings. The conditions he faces as a worker are as disturbing to him as the unfamiliar surroundings of his daily life. He holds on to his individuality, but the new things which face him here make that difficult.

The man is a master carpenter from a village home in Ohio. But the certainty of steady work for many months at four dollars a day was tempting enough to cause him to leave his family behind and come here. He had arrived a few days ago and had found work right away.

Seeing the man, a tall, fine-looking, self-respecting American worker, and hearing him speak, and learning even this little of his history, you could see his past. You could almost see a comfortable wooden cottage, which he had built himself, with a garden plot about it and flower beds in front, standing on a well-shaded village street. He owns the cottage and the plot of land, and his children were born there. He is an officer of the village church and has been justice of the peace, and more than once he has served as school trustee. The idea of social inequality is new to him, and it makes him self-conscious. In his home village his family and the families of all his neighbors are all equals. The only exceptions are the minister, the doctor, the village lawyer, and the schoolmaster, because of their special education. His children study and play at school with the children of all his neighbors, and meet with them at church and elsewhere.

But here things are new and strange. He is no longer a man with a name to distinguish him, but has become a worker with a number on his jacket. He goes to work as just one in an army of ten thousand numbers. Home has changed to a barrack. There he, a number, sleeps in a numbered bunk, and eats as one of half a thousand men. His comfort and convenience are not considered, and his views have no bearing whatever on the course of things.

The superintendent of the building upon which he works, whose energy and skill he admires, shifts him about with dozens of other men, having no more regard for him as an individual than if he were a piece of wood. Once he spoke to his superintendent about some detail of the work and found him a most appreciative listener. Then he started to talk about a subject of general interest, only to find that by some mysterious change he was speaking to a stone wall.

And now something else faces him which he regards as another loss of his individuality. He is urged to agree to this loss, and it gives him some concern. He knows very little about labor unions, and now he is bombarded with appeals to join one.

Management does not discriminate between union and nonunion workers in employing people at the Exposition. But many of the union workers here are making the most of the present opportunity. They want to publicize their principles and bring desirable nonunion workers into their organization. My carpenter friend, whom I shall call Mr. Ford, has received much attention.

Two or three times he has asked me to go with him in the evening to meetings which are held near the fairgrounds, and hear speeches from delegates from the Central Labor Union. These we have not found very helpful. There has been a good deal of beer-drinking and much useless speech, which has grown heated at times. Now and then a plain, matter-of-fact worker has given us an interesting talk on the history of unionism and on the need of organization among workers as the only means of safeguarding their interests.

Mr. Ford, much confused, has listened to all this. We have talked it over together on the way back to our rooms, and sometimes late into the night. I have tried to explain to him, as well as I understand it, the idea for labor organization, and the necessity for it which has grown out of the great industrial change since the middle of the 1800's. But Mr. Ford, for all practical purposes, belongs to another period. The industrial change has hardly affected him. He served his apprenticeship, and then was a journeyman and then a master carpenter in due course. In his experience, work has always had its basis in a personal relation, as, for example, between himself as a contractor and the person whose job he undertook and from whom he received payment. A similar personal relation has always existed between himself and the people he has employed.

This new relation between a worker and an impersonal corporation which hires him is one that he does not readily understand. And this merging of one's individuality in an organization which attempts to regulate hours, wages, and employers is a thing he hates.

"Why," he said to me, "I give up my independence, and I'm no better than the worst carpenter in the group. We all get union wages alike. There's no reason for a man to do his best. He ain't a man any more, anyway. He's only a part of a machine. Why, such work as some I see done here, I'd be ashamed to do by moonlight, with my eyes shut. But it makes no difference in the union, you're all on the same level, as nearly as I can make out."

A DISILLUSIONED IMMIGRANT

Adapted from Hungry Hearts *by Anzia Yezierska, copyrighted by Louise Levitas Henriksen. Reprinted by permission of the copyright holder.*

During the late 1800's and the early 1900's, millions of immigrants from many countries came to America. This huge group of newcomers to the United States is often referred to as the "New Immigration." They consisted mainly of immigrants from nations in southern and eastern Europe. For the most part, the newcomers were unskilled workers who had no choice but to live crowded together in slum neighborhoods in the large cities of the East.

During the New Immigration, for the first time, large numbers of Jews from eastern

Europe, especially Russia and Poland, came to America. One of these immigrants was Anzia Yezierska, a sixteen-year-old girl who arrived in New York in 1901. In this selection she tells of her dreams and expectations before her arrival and her reactions to what she found.

What expectations did Anzia Yezierska and her family have? What caused her first doubts about America? Do you think that her experiences in America were typical of most immigrants in the late 1800's and early 1900's? Why?

We traveled in steerage [the section of the ship where those who paid the cheapest fares were crowded together under the decks]—dirty bundles—foul odors—seasick people—but I saw and heard nothing of the stinking dirtiness and ugliness around me. I seemed to float in showers of sunshine. Sight after sight of the new world were in my imagination. From everyone's lips flowed the golden legend of the golden country:

"In America you can say what you feel—you can join your friends in the open streets without fear."

"In America there is a home for everyone. The land is your land. Not like in Russia where you feel yourself a stranger in the village where you were born and lived—the village in which your father and grandfather lie buried."

"Everyone is like everybody else in America."

"All people can do what they want with their lives in America."

"Plenty for all. Learning flows free like milk and honey."

"Learning flows free."

The word painted pictures in my mind. I saw before me free schools, free colleges, free libraries, where I could learn and learn and learn and keep on learning.

In our village there was a school, but only for Christian children. In the schools of America I'd lift up my head and laugh and dance—a child with other children. Like a bird in the air, from sky to sky, from star to star, I'd soar and soar.

"Land! Land!" came the joyous shout.

"America! We're in America!" cried my mother, almost crushing us in her happiness.

Everyone crowded and pushed on deck. They strained and stretched to get the first glimpse of the "golden country," lifting their children on their shoulders that they might see beyond them.

Men fell on their knees to pray. Women hugged their babies and wept. Children danced. Strangers hugged and kissed like old friends. Old men and women had in their eyes a look of young people in love.

Age-old visions sang themselves in me—songs of freedom of an oppressed people.

America! America!

* * * *

Between buildings that rose up like mountains, we struggled with our bundles. Up Broadway, under the bridge, and through the crowded streets of the ghetto, we followed our friend, Gedalyeh Mindel.

I looked about the narrow streets of squeezed-in stores and houses, ragged clothes, dirty bedding hanging out of the windows, ash-cans and garbage cans piled up on the sidewalks. A sadness pressed down my heart—the first doubt of America.

"Where are the green fields and open spaces in America?" cried my heart. "Where is the golden country of my dreams?"

A loneliness for the sweet-smelling silence of the woods that lay beyond our mud hut built up in my heart, a longing for the soft earth of our village streets. All around me was the hardness of brick and stone, the stinking smells of crowded poverty.

"Here's your house with separate rooms like in a palace." Gedalyeh Mindel opened the door of a dingy, airless apartment.

"Where's the sunshine in America?" my mother cried in dismay.

She went to the window and looked out at the wall of the next house. "Like in a grave so dark."

"It ain't so dark, it's only a little shady." Gedalyeh Mindel lighted the gas. "Look only." He pointed with pride to the dim gaslight. "No candles, no kerosene lamps in America, you turn on a screw and put to it a match and you got light like with sunshine."

Again the shadow fell over me, again the doubt of America!

In America there were rooms without sunlight, rooms to sleep in, to eat in, to cook in, but without sunshine. And Gedalyeh Mindel was happy. Could I be satisfied with just a place to sleep and eat in, and a door to shut people out —to take the place of sunlight? Or would I always need the sunlight to be happy?

And where was there a place in America for me to play? I looked out into the alley below and saw pale-faced children running in the street.

"Where is America?" cried my heart.

* * * *

My eyes were shutting themselves with sleep—the dead-weight sleep of complete exhaustion.

"Heart of mine!" my mother's voice moaned above me. "Father is already gone an hour. You know how they'll squeeze from you a nickel for every minute you're late. Quick only!"

I grabbed my bread and herring and ran down the stairs and out into the street. I ate running, blindly pushing through the hurrying crowds of workers—my haste and fear choking each mouthful.

I felt a strangling in my throat as I neared the sweatshop [the factory where she worked]. All my nerves screwed together into iron hardness to withstand the day's torture.

For an instant I hesitated as I faced the window of the old building—dirt and decay cried out from every crumbling brick.

In the shop, raging around me the roar and the clatter, the clatter and the roar, the grind of the pounding machines. Half maddened, half deadened, I struggled to think, to feel, to remember—what am I—who am I—why was I here?

I struggled in vain—confused and lost in the noise.

"America—America—where was America?" it cried in my heart.

The factory whistle—the slowing-down of the machines—the noon hour had come.

I woke as from a nightmare—a tired waking to pain.

In my brain reason began to dawn. In my heart feelings began to pulse. The wound of my wasted life began to hurt and ache. My childhood ended by work—must my youth die too—unlived?

The odor of herring and garlic—the hungry eating of food—laughter and loud, vulgar jokes. Was it only I who was so unhappy? I looked at those around me. Were they happy or only not aware of their slavery? How could they laugh and joke? Why were they not torn with rebellion against this grind—the crushing, deadening movements of the body, where only hands live and hearts and brains must die?

A touch on my shoulder. I looked up. It was Yetta Solomon from the machine next to mine.

"Here's your tea."

I stared at her, half hearing.

"Ain't you going to eat nothing?"

"Yetta! I can't stand it!" The cry broke from me. "I didn't come to America to turn into a machine. I came to America to make from myself a person. Does America want only my hands—only the strength of my body—not my heart—not my feelings—my thoughts?"

AN ITALIAN BOY LOSES AN "I"

Adapted from The Heart Is the Teacher *by Leonard Covello and Guido D'Agostino. Copyright © 1958 by Leonard Covello. Reprinted by permission of Lurton Blassingame, the authors' agent.*

In 1896, when he was nine years old, Leonard Covello came to America with his mother and two younger brothers. (His father had made the trip earlier to earn money for their passage.) Like thousands of other "New Immigrants," they came from Italy. And like thousands of other immigrants, they found that becoming American brought both pleasure and pain.

Many years later, Covello wrote of his experiences as a newcomer. He stressed the culture conflict that developed between immigrant parents and their children. Covello wrote: "We soon got the idea that 'Italian' meant something inferior, and a barrier was erected between children of Italian origin and their parents. This was the accepted process of Americanization. We were becoming Americans by learning how to be ashamed of our parents."

What do you think of the education Leonard Covello received as a young immigrant? Why was his father so upset by the family's name change in school? Has anyone in your family ever changed his or her name? Why? What would you do if something like this happened to you?

Every day in school before receiving our bowl of soup we recited the Lord's Prayer. I had no idea what the words meant. I only knew that I was expected to bow my head. I looked around to see what was going on. Swift and simple, the teacher's blackboard pointer brought the idea home to me. I never looked around again after that.

I learned arithmetic and penmanship and spelling—every misspelled word had to be written ten times or more in my notebook. I do not know how many times I wrote "I must not talk." In this same way I learned how to read in English, learned geography and grammar, the states of the Union, all the capital cities and choice bits of poetry and sayings. Most learning was done in unison. That is, all the children recited to the teacher while they stood at attention. Repetition. Repetition until the things you learned beat in your brain even at night when you were falling asleep.

Silence! Silence! Silence! This was the characteristic feature at school. You never made an unnecessary noise or said an unnecessary word. Outside in the hall we lined up by size, girls in one line and boys in another, without a sound, to go to the assembly. Eyes front and at attention. Lord help you if you broke the rule of silence. I can still see a distant relative of mine, a girl named Miluzza, who could never stop talking. She stood in a corner behind Mrs. Cutter [the teacher] throughout an entire assembly with a spring-type clothespin fastened to her lower lip as punishment. Not at all frightened, instead defiant—Miluzza with that clothespin hanging from her lip. . . .

The piano struck up a march and from the hall we paraded into assembly—eyes straight ahead in military style. Mrs. Cutter was there on the platform, her eyes reaching every corner of the assembly hall. It was always the same. We stood at attention as the Bible was read and at attention as the flag was waved back and forth, and we sang the same song. I didn't know what the words meant, but I sang it loudly with all the rest, in my own way, "Three Cheers for de Red Whatzam Blu!"

One day I came home from school with a report card for my father to sign. I remember that my friend Vito Salvatore happened to be there, and Mary Accurso had stopped in for a moment to see my mother. With a tired look my father looked over the marks on the report card and was about to sign it. However, he paused with the pen in his hand.

"What is this?" he said "Leonard Covello! What happened to the *i* in Coviello?"

My mother stopped sewing. Vito and I just looked at each other.

"Well?" my father insisted.

"Maybe the teacher just forgot to put it in," Mary suggested. "It can happen." She was going to high school now and spoke with an air of authority, and people always listened to her. This time, however, my father didn't even hear her.

"From Leonardo to Leonard I can follow," he said, "a perfectly natural process. In America anything can happen and does happen. But you don't change a family name. A name is a name. What happened to the *i*?"

"Mrs. Cutter took it out," I explained. "Every time she pronounced Coviello it came out Covello. So she took out the *i*. That way it's easier for everybody."

My father hit the table with his fist. "And what has this Mrs. Cutter got to do with my name?"

"What difference does it make?" I said. "It's more American. The *i* doesn't help anything." It was one of the very few times that I dared oppose my father. But even at that age I was beginning to feel that anything that made a name less foreign was an improvement.

Vito came to my rescue. "My name is Victor—Vic. That's what everybody calls me now."

"Vica. Sticka. Micka. You crazy in the head!" my father yelled at him.

For a moment my father sat there, bitter rebellion building in him. Then, with a shrug of giving up, he signed the report card and shoved it over to me. My mother now suddenly entered the argument. "How is it possible to do this to a name? Why did you sign the card? Narduccio, you will have to tell your teacher that a name cannot be changed just like that."

"Mamma, you don't understand."

"What is there to understand? A person's life and his honor is in his name. He never changes it. A name is not a shirt or a piece of underwear."

My father got up from the table, lighted the twisted stump of a cigar and moved out of the argument. "Honor!" he muttered to himself.

"You must explain this to your teacher," my mother insisted. "It was a mistake. She will know. She will not let it happen again. You will see."

"It was no mistake. It was done on purpose. The *i* is out, and Mrs. Cutter made it Covello. You don't understand!"

"Will you stop saying that!" my mother insisted. "I don't understand. I don't understand. What is there to understand? Now that you have become Americanized you understand everything and I understand nothing."

With her in this mood I dared not answer. Mary went over and put her hand on my mother's shoulder. I called to Vito and together we walked out of the apartment and downstairs into the street.

"She just doesn't understand," I kept saying.

"I'm gonna take the *e* off the end of my name and make it just Salvator," Vito said. "After all, we're not in Italy now."

Vito and I were standing unhappily under the gas light on the corner. Somehow or other the joy of childhood had left us. We were only boys, but a sadness that we could not explain pressed down upon us. Mary came and joined us. She had a book under her arm. She stood there for a moment, while her dark eyes looked at us questionably.

"But they don't understand!" I insisted.

Mary smiled. "Maybe some day, you will realize that *you* are the only one who does not understand."

FEAR OF THE IMMIGRANT

From "Unguarded Gates" in The Works of Thomas Bailey Aldrich, *Poems, Vol. II. Boston: The Jefferson Press.*

For the millions of immigrants who came to America in the late 1800's and early 1900's, their first sight of their new land was the Statue of Liberty. It stands on an island at the entrance to New York Harbor. And for most newcomers the statue with its uplifted torch was a wonderful and welcome sight. On the base of the statue was a poem written by Emma Lazarus that welcomed the newcomers.

However, not all Americans in these years welcomed the newcomers. Many Americans were worried by the "New Immigrants," whose ways of life and customs seemed so strange and foreign. Thomas Bailey Aldrich, a writer and editor of the *Atlantic Monthly* magazine, expressed the fears of many Americans in his poem "Unguarded Gates."

How does Aldrich picture the United States in the first stanza? Where do members of the "motley throng" come from? What two frightening things do they bring with them? What consequence is Aldrich most worried about? What laws were passed to guard the gates?

Wide open and unguarded stand our gates,
Named of the four winds, North, South, East,
 and West;
Portals [gates] that lead to an enchanted land
Of cities, forests, fields of living gold,
Vast prairies, lordly summits [mountains]
 touched with snow,
Majestic rivers sweeping proudly past . . .
A realm [land] wherein are fruits of every
 zone, . . .
A later Eden planted in the wilds. . . .
Here, it is written, Toil shall have its wage,
And Honor honor, and the humblest man
Stand level with the highest in the law.
Of such a land have men in dungeons
 dreamed. . . .

Wide open and unguarded stand our gates,
And through them presses a wild motley
 throng—
Men from the Volga and the Tartar steppes,
Featureless figures of the Hwang Ho,
Malayan, Scythian, Teuton, Celt, and Slav,
Flying the Old World's poverty and scorn;
These bringing with them unknown gods and
 rites,
Those, tiger passions, here to stretch their
 claws.
In street and alley what strange tongues are
 loud. . . .

O Liberty, white Goddess! is it well
To leave the gates unguarded? . . .
Lift the down-trodden, but with hand of steel
Stay those who to thy sacred portals come
To waste the gifts of freedom. Have a care
Lest from thy brow the clustered stars be torn
And trampled in the dust. . . .

THE NEED FOR UNIONS

Adapted from John Mitchell, Organized Labor: Its Problems, Purposes, and Ideals. *Philadelphia: American Book and Bible House, 1903.*

In the late 1800's and early 1900's workers faced many problems that were the result of the new industrial age. In order to try to solve these problems, workers began to join together and to organize into unions. However, the right of workers to organize unions and to bargain collectively with employers became an important issue. At times, it seemed that most Americans and even state governments and the federal government were opposed to this effort. Union leaders often had great difficulty in persuading working people to join labor unions.

In this selection John Mitchell, president of the United Mine Workers from 1898 to 1908, gives arguments in favor of labor unions.

Why is it impossible for an individual worker to bargain effectively with an employer? What, according to Mitchell, is the basic principle of trade unionism? How do you think you would have felt about labor unions in these years?

In its basic principle, trade unionism is plain and clear and simple. Trade unionism starts by recognizing that under normal conditions individual, unorganized workers cannot bargain advantageously with the employer for the sale of their labor. Since workers have no money saved, they must sell their labor immediately. Moreover, they have no knowledge of the market and no skill in bargaining. Finally, they have only their own labor to sell, while the employer uses hundreds or thousands of workers and can easily do without the services of any particular individual. Thus workers, if bargaining only for themselves, are at a great disadvantage.

Trade unionism recognizes the fact that under such conditions labor loses value. The labor which workers sell is, unlike other commodities, a thing which is of their very life and soul and being. In the individual contract between a rich employer and a poor worker, the laborer will get the worst of it. Workers are constantly weakened because of wages too low to buy nourishing food, hours too long for enough rest, working conditions that destroy moral, mental, and physical health, and dangers that may cause accidents and disease. The "individual bargain," or individual contract, between employers and workers means that the condition of the worst and lowest worker in the industry will be that which the best worker must accept.

From first to last, from beginning to end, always and everywhere, trade unionism is opposed to the individual contract. It is this principle, the absolute and complete end of contracts between employers and individual workers, upon which trade unionism is founded. There can be no lasting prosperity for the working classes, no real and lasting progress, until this principle is firmly and fully established.

Trade unions were founded to find a substitute for the individual bargain. A trade union, in its usual form, is an association of workers who have agreed among themselves not to bargain individually with their employer or employers, but to agree to the terms of a collective or joint contract between the employer and the union. The difference between the individual and the collective or joint bargain is simply this: In the individual contract one worker in a hundred refuses to accept work, and the employer keeps the service of ninety-nine. In the collective bargain the hundred employees act together and the employer keeps or fires all of them on the same terms. The ideal of trade unionism is to combine in one organization all the workers employed, or capable of being employed, at a given trade. And to demand and secure for each and all of the workers a definite minimum standard of wages, hours, and conditions of work.

To carry out a joint bargain, it is necessary to establish an accepted minimum of wages and conditions which will apply to all. This does not mean that the wages of all shall be the same, but only that equal pay shall be given for equal work. There cannot be more than one minimum wage in a given trade, in a given place, at a given time.

The recognition of the union is nothing more nor less than the recognition of the principle for which trade unionism stands—the right to bargain collectively and to insist upon minimum standards.

There are many employers who are willing to give up the principle of the individual bargain but do not accept the principle of the collective bargain. These employers state that they do not insist upon dealing with their employees as individuals, but that they must keep the right of dealing with "only their own employees." They say that they must not be forced to permit a worker who is not their own employee to interfere in their business.

The right to bargain collectively, however, or to take any other united action, necessarily involves the right to representation. Experience and reason both show that a person who is dependent on the good will of an employer is in no position to negotiate with him. If he insists on what he considers to be the rights of the workers represented by him he may be fired or at least lose his employer's favor. Not only should workers have the right of making collective contracts, but they should also have the right of being represented by whomever they wish. To deny the right of representation is tyranny.

CHAPTER 7 ■ CHANGING WAYS OF LIFE IN THE NEW INDUSTRIAL AGE

THE MAKING OF A NEW YORKER

Adapted from "The Making of a New Yorker" from The Trimmed Lamp *by O. Henry, published by Doubleday & Co., Inc.*

From 1865 to 1900, more and more Americans left farms and small towns to live in the cities. In 1869 no American city had a population of 1 million, but by 1890 New York, Chicago, and Philadelphia each had more than 1 million people.

What caused so many thousands of people to leave their homes and try to start a new life in the city? This great movement of people had many causes. People were attracted to the cities by hopes of jobs and high wages; many also came to escape the dullness of farm life. Cities were interesting places with their bright lights, tall buildings, and bustling activity. The largest American city was New York City. Its crowded streets and activity fascinated many people, especially writers like William Sydney Porter, better known as O. Henry. In this selection, O. Henry writes about "the making of a New Yorker."

What do you think of O. Henry's description of various cities? To what kind of woman would you compare your town? What turns Raggles into a New Yorker? Do you think an incident like this could happen?

Besides many other things, Raggles was a poet. He was called a tramp. But that was only a way of saying that he was a philosopher, an artist, a traveler, a naturalist, and a discoverer. But most of all he was a poet. In all his life he never wrote a line of poetry; he lived his poetry.

Raggles's specialty, had he used ink and paper, would have been sonnets to the cities. He studied cities. A city to Raggles was not only a pile of bricks and mortar, with a certain number of inhabitants. It was a thing with a characteristic and distinct soul, an individual life with its own special flavor and feeling. Two thousand miles [3,219 kilometers] to the north and south, east and west, Raggles wandered, studying cities. And when he found the heart of a city and listened to its secret confession, he went on to another.

Through the ancient poets [those of Greece and Rome] we have learned that cities are like women. So they were to poet Raggles. His mind carried a clear idea of the figure that symbolized and typified each one.

Chicago seemed to swoop down upon him with a breezy suggestion of plumes and perfume.

Pittsburgh impressed him as a royal and generous lady—homely, hearty, with a red face, washing the dishes in a silk dress and white slippers, and telling Raggles to sit before the roaring fireplace and drink champagne along with his pigs' feet and fried potatoes.

New Orleans had simply looked down upon him from a balcony. He could see her thoughtful, starry eyes and catch the movement of her fan, and that was all.

Boston appeared to the poetic Raggles in an unusual way. It seemed to him that he had drunk cold tea and that the city was a white, cold cloth that had been wrapped tightly around his head to spur him to some unknown but tremendous mental effort.

One day Raggles came to the heart of the great city of Manhattan. She was the greatest of all. He wanted to classify and label her and arrange her with the other cities.

Raggles landed from a ferryboat one morning and walked into the center of the town confident and at ease. Without money—as a poet should be—but with the excitement of an astronomer discovering a new star, Raggles wandered into the great city.

Late in the afternoon he came out of the roar and commotion with a look of terror on his face. He was defeated, puzzled, frightened. Other cities had been as easy to read and understand as a child's book. But here was one as cold, glittering, serene, and impossible as a four-carat diamond in a window to a young man in love looking at it and feeling his modest clerk's pay in his pocket.

The greetings of the other cities he had known—their homey kindliness, their rough charity, friendly curses, talkative curiosity, or indifference. This city of Manhattan gave him no clue. It was walled against him. Never an eye was turned upon him. No voice spoke to him.

On Broadway Raggles, the successful suitor of many cities, stood, shy, like any country youth. For the first time he experienced the sad humiliation of being ignored. And when he tried to understand this brilliant, swiftly changing, ice-cold city he failed completely. The houses were defensive walls. The people were bright but bloodless ghosts.

The thing that weighed heaviest on Raggles' soul was the spirit of absolute egotism that seemed to fill the people. Humanity was gone from them. They were like gods of stone, worshiping themselves. Frozen, cruel, cut to an identical pattern, they hurried on their ways like statues brought to life, while soul and feeling lay dead in the marble.

Gradually Raggles became aware of certain types. One was an elderly gentleman with a snow-white, short beard, pink, unwrinkled face and stony, sharp blue eyes. He seemed to personify the city's wealth and icy unconcern. Another type was a tall, beautiful woman, calm, dressed like the princesses of old, with eyes coldly blue. And another was a broad, swaggering, grim fellow, with large cheeks, a baby's skin, and the knuckles of a prize fighter. This type leaned against cigar signs and looked at the world with scorn.

Raggles got up his courage and begged for money. The people passed on without a wink of an eyelash to indicate that they were aware of him. And then he said to himself that this fair but pitiless city of Manhattan was without a soul, and that he was alone in a great wilderness.

Raggles started to cross the street. There was a blast, a roar, a hissing and a crash as something struck him and tossed him over and over six yards [5.5 meters] from where he had been.

Raggles opened his eyes. And then a hand soft as a falling petal touched his head. Bending over him was the woman dressed like a princess of old, with blue eyes, now soft with human sympathy. Under his head on the street were silks and furs. With Raggles' hat in his hand and with his face pinker than ever from an outburst against reckless driving, stood the elderly gentleman who personified the city's wealth. From a nearby cafe hurried the man with fat cheeks and baby skin, carrying a glass full of a red liquid.

"Drink dis, sport," he said, holding the glass to Raggles' lips.

Hundreds of people surrounded him in a moment, their faces wearing the deepest concern. Two policemen got into the circle and pressed back the crowd of people wanting to help. A newsboy slipped one of his papers beneath Raggles' elbow, where it lay on the muddy pavement. A brisk young man with a notebook was asking for names.

A bell clanged importantly, and an ambulance cleared an opening through the crowd. A cool surgeon asked, "How do you feel, old man?" The princess of silks and satins wiped a red drop or two from Raggles' head.

"Me?" said Raggles, with an angelic smile, "I feel fine."

He had found the heart of his new city.

In three days they let him leave his bed for the convalescent ward in the hospital. He had been there an hour when the attendants heard sounds of a fight. They found that Raggles had assaulted and hit another patient.

"What's all this about?" asked the head nurse.

"He was speaking badly about me town," said Raggles.

"What town?" asked the nurse.

"Noo York," said Raggles.

NEW YORK: ANOTHER VIEW

Adapted from Jacob Riis, How the Other Half Lives. *New York: Charles Scribner's Sons, 1890.*

Although cities held great attractions for many Americans, the ugliness and the problems caused by rapid growth and by too many people could not be hidden. All large cities had slum areas, where people lived crowded together in dirty, foul-smelling dwellings. Many of these dwellings were airless and without plumbing.

In New York City thousands of people lived crowded together in such run-down tenements. Many of these tenement-dwellers died of disease and lack of proper food. These conditions in city slums alarmed many people. One of them, Jacob Riis, a newspaper reporter, wrote about slum neighborhoods in New York City and took pictures of the conditions there. The following selection is from his most famous book, *How the Other Half Lives,* written in an effort to improve such conditions.

What are the worst features of tenements, as Riis describes them? What effect do they have on children who live in them? Do you think that slums have changed since Riis wrote about them in 1890?

There are tenements everywhere. Suppose we look into one on Cherry Street. Be a little careful, please! The hall is dark and you might fall over the children pitching pennies back there. Not that it would hurt them. Kicks and punches are their daily diet. They have little else. Here, where the hall turns into complete darkness, is a step, and another, and another. A flight of stairs. You can feel your way if you cannot see it. Stifling? Yes! What do you expect. All the fresh air that ever enters these stairs comes from the hall door that is forever slamming, and from the windows of dark bedrooms.

That was a woman filling her pail you just bumped against. The sinks are in the hallway, so that all the tenants may get to them—and all smell horrible in the summer. Hear the pump squeak! It is the lullaby of tenement-house babies. During the summer, when a thousand thirsty throats want a cooling drink in this block, the pump is worked in vain. But the saloon, whose open door you passed in the hall, is always there. The smell of it has followed you up.

Here is a door. Listen! That short hacking cough, that tiny, helpless cry—what do they mean? They mean that the soiled bow of white you saw on the door downstairs [when someone died, a bow was hung on the door—black for an adult, white for a child] will have another story to tell—oh, a sadly familiar story—before the day ends. The child is dying with measles. With half a chance it might have lived. But it had none. That dark bedroom killed it.

"It was took all of a sudden," says the mother, smoothing the little body with trembling hands. There is no unkindness in the rough voice of the man in overalls who sits by the window grimly smoking a clay pipe, while he watches his child die, bitter as his words sound: "Hush, Mary! If we cannot keep the baby, need we complain—such as we?"

"Such as we!" What if the words ring in your ears as you grope your way up the stairs and down from floor to floor, listening to the sounds behind the closed doors—some of quarreling, some of coarse songs, more of cursing. They are true. When the summer heat comes with its suffering, its meaning is more terrible than words can tell. Come over here. Step carefully over this baby—it is a baby, in spite of its rags and dirt—under these iron bridges called fire escapes. They are loaded down, despite the warnings of the firemen, with broken household goods, with washtubs and barrels, which no one could climb over to escape from a fire.

This gap between dingy brick walls is the yard. That strip of smoke-colored sky up there is the heaven of these people. Do you wonder that the name does not attract them to the churches? That baby's parents live in the back tenement here. This tenement is much like the one in front we just left, only fouler and darker. A hundred thousand people lived in back tenements in New York last year.

What sort of an answer, do you think, would these tenement-dwellers give to the question, "Is life worth living?"

HOW MUCH PROGRESS FOR WOMEN?

Adapted from Elizabeth Cady Stanton, Eighty Years and More. *New York: European Publishing Co., 1898.*

In 1876 Americans celebrated their centennial. One important feature of this celebration of the nation's first one hundred years was the Philadelphia Centennial Exposition. This huge exposition glorified human achievements and progress in many fields. However, there was at least one group of Americans who were not happy with the progress they had made. At this time, American women were still struggling to gain the right to vote and to be considered as social equals. In this selection Elizabeth Cady Stanton, a leader in the women's rights movement, tells about the Woman's Pavilion, or building, at the Exposition.

How did Elizabeth Cady Stanton describe the efforts of some American women to improve their lives? What was her attitude toward the Woman's Pavilion? If you were asked to set up a Woman's Pavilion today, what kind of exhibits would you want to display in it?

The Woman's Pavilion on the centennial grounds was an afterthought, as religious philosophers claim woman herself to have been. The women of the country, after having contributed nearly $100,000 to the centennial, found that no provision had been made for the separate exhibition of their work. The centennial board then decided to raise funds to build a separate building, to be known as the Woman's Pavilion. It covered an acre of ground, and was built at a cost of $30,000—a small sum in comparison with the money which had been raised by women and spent on the other buildings.

The Pavilion was no true exhibit of woman's abilities. Few women are, as yet, owners of the businesses which their work makes profitable. Cotton factories, in which thousands of women work, are owned by men. The shoe business, in some branches of which women are doing more than half the work, is under the ownership of men. Rich embroideries from India, rugs of downy softness from Turkey, the muslin fabric of India, Waltham watches (whose finest mechanical work is done by women), and ten thousand other industries found no place in the pavilion. Said United States Commissioner Meeker of Colorado, "Woman's work makes up three fourths of the exposition; it is scattered through every building. Take it away, and there would be no exposition."

But this pavilion did one good service for the woman by showing her capabilities as an engineer. The boiler, which provided the force for operating the pavilion, was under the care of a young Canadian girl, Miss Allison. She had loved machinery from childhood, and had spent much time in her father's large mills. When she was chosen to run the pavilion machinery, it caused much opposition. It was said that the committee would, some day, find the pavilion blown to bits; that a woman engineer would spend her time reading novels instead of watching the steam gauge; that the idea was impractical. But Miss Allison soon proved both her abilities and the falseness of these statements by taking her place in the engine room and managing its workings with perfect ease. She declared that the work was cleaner, more pleasant, and much less tiring than cooking over a kitchen stove. "Since I have had to earn my own living," she said, "I have never done work I like so well. Teaching school is much harder, and one is not paid so well." She was confident that she could manage the engines of an ocean steamer. There were thousands of small engines in use in various parts of the country, she said. There was no reason why women should not be employed to manage them, following the profession of engineer as a regular business.

But the Woman's Pavilion would have been truly historic if some displays had hung upon its walls. These displays might have included the yearly protest of Harriet K. Hunt against taxation without representation. Another might have been the legal papers served upon the Smith sisters for their refusal to pay taxes while unrepresented. Still another might have been papers issued by the city of Worcester for the forced sale of the house and lands of Abby Kelly Foster, the abolitionist, because she refused to pay taxes without representation. With these should have been exhibited framed copies of all the laws bearing unjustly upon women—those which rob her of her name, her earnings, her property, her children, her person. Another exhibit might have included the legal papers in the case of Susan B. Anthony, who was tried and fined for claiming her right to vote under the Fourteenth Amendment; and the decision of Mr. Justice Miller in the case of Myra Bradwell, denying national protection for woman's civil rights.

Woman's most fitting contributions to the Centennial Exposition would have been these protests, laws, and decisions, which show her political slavery. But all this was displayed in rooms outside the exposition grounds, where the National Woman's Suffrage Association raised its flag and made its protests.

To many thoughtful people it seemed unreasonable for women to complain of injustice in this free land, among such universal rejoicing. When the majority of women are seemingly happy, it is natural to suppose that the discontent of the minority is the result of unfortunate individual circumstances. But the history of the world shows that the great majority, in every generation, just accept the conditions into which they are born. Those who demand larger liberties are always a small minority, whose claims are made fun of and ignored. We would honor any Chinese woman who claimed the right to her own feet so that she could walk; the Hindu widow who refused to climb upon the funeral fire of her husband, and the Turkish woman who threw off her veil and left the harem.

Why not honor as well the intelligent minority of American women who protest against the false disabilities by which their freedom is limited and their development stopped? That only a few protest against the injustice of long-established laws and customs does not disprove the fact of the oppressions. The satisfaction of the many, if real, only proves their lack of concern. That a majority of the women of the United States accept, without protest, the disabilities which grow out of the fact that they cannot vote is simply an evidence of their ignorance and cowardice. The minority who demand a higher political standing clearly prove their greater intelligence and wisdom.

A FRENCH WRITER ADMIRES AMERICAN EDUCATION

Adapted from Paul Bourget, Outre-Mer: Impressions of America. *New York: Charles Scribner's Sons, 1895.*

The growth of free public education, which began before the Civil War, continued in the late 1800's. Beginning in the 1870's, more and more states required all children to attend elementary school. At the same time, many high schools were started, and the idea that a high school education was the right of every American was spreading. By 1900, there were about 6,000 high schools in the United States.

Paul Bourget, a French novelist, traveled widely in the United States in 1893 and 1894. He talked with many Americans, and was impressed with American individualism. He was also greatly impressed with American education. In Boston alone he discovered that there were hundreds of free public schools. He visited some of them, read about others, and wrote this account about American schools.

What single feature of American schools most impressed Bourget? How does he describe the American mind? What does he believe has made it this way? What do you think of the examination questions Bourget lists?

A short tour of investigation will show the traveler that education is organized here to help individuals adapt to their surroundings. The teachers are both men and women, but especially women. These hard-working people earn nearly $900 a year. Their sense of responsibility enables them to strongly influence the children they teach. Perhaps we may find here one of the reasons for the respect in which women are held in America.

It is worthwhile to see these schoolteachers, most of them pretty, teaching their classes, especially in the primary schools. They teach mainly by asking the class questions. The pupils ask permission to answer by raising their hands. The teacher chooses one, then asks another question, searching out this or that one who is backward. It is very simple, very lively, very pleasant. The great variety in the class exercises, none of which lasts more than half an hour, prevents the children from getting tired.

In the beginners' classes, and later too, the feature which most strikes a middle-class Frenchman is the constant use of the concrete and positive method. Making things from clay plays an important part in this method of teaching. In almost every schoolroom you will see a whole collection of figures made by the children —simple objects made in the likeness of things that surround them, a carrot, a loaf of bread, a biscuit, a butterfly, a flower. Here are some children busy with a lesson in which they must draw and describe a potato that lies before them. Others are busy tracing some leaves. They must identify the tree that the leaves come from and give some facts about it. Others have just finished some rather difficult woodwork, made from patterns drawn with chalk upon the blackboard. In all these details you recognize the same principle: to make the eye, the mind, and the hand work together; to train the child to observe, and to regulate his or her thoughts and actions according to his or her observations.

After seeing these methods of education, you understand better the American mind—its almost total lack of abstract ideas, and its amazing power of recognizing reality, of managing machinery and business. The aim is to confront these awakening minds constantly with *fact.*

The exercises are proof of this. I have seen the pupils in a somewhat advanced class replying to a newspaper help-wanted ad as an exercise in writing. When they are grown up, they will have such advertisements to draw up. These things are facts, and this education stresses facts.

You must read the report of the school committee with the picture before you of boys and girls with their spirited, determined faces, teachers with their lively, light and well-ordered schoolrooms, well-stocked laboratories—all this world of study in which nothing calls up the thought of discipline or repression. You will understand the whole system of teaching by reading the part of the report entitled "Examination Papers." This is a list of questions that pupils are asked in written or oral examinations. There is not one, from the simplest to the most difficult, which was not designed to make the child's mind connect with facts.

If the examination is in composition, subjects like these are given:

"Wanted: a young woman to work in a photographic gallery. Must have practical and artistic experience and good references. Address, Room 15, 154 Tremont Street, Boston, Mass. Write the letter that you would write if you desired this job."

"Write a letter to someone you know who

has never been in this school. Describe the playground, the building, your room."

"Write to a friend, giving her advice about her health, telling her the things you have learned about the care of the body."

If it is geography, this is how they prepare children for their future travels:

"Sail from Cape Ann to Cork, with a cargo. What goods would you take and what would you bring back?"

"Make a trip from San Francisco to Paris. Describe the route. What articles would you bring back?"

If the study is mathematics, all the problems will refer to buying and selling.

If it is history, all the questions involve the past of the United States, especially that of New England.

"When and by whom was Boston founded? Describe the Tree of Liberty, the Boston Massacre, the Boston Tea Party. Describe a New England village, a Sunday morning in colonial times. Give an account of the landing in Massachusetts Bay and a short description of the leaders of the first colony."

Evidently the pupil who is prepared to answer all these points has been educated to become a business person in a democracy. It seems to me that these people have reached their ideal, which can be stated in one phrase: the complete identification of education and life.

A CLOSE-UP OF MARK TWAIN

Adapted from My Mark Twain *by William Dean Howells. New York: Harper & Brothers.*

Two important writers of the late 1800's were Mark Twain and William Dean Howells. Twain described the new industrial age in his book *The Gilded Age,* but he was even more popular as a local-color writer who captured the frontier spirit and humor of the West. Howells was famous for his realistic writing. His best-known book, *Silas Lapham,* told about the lives of some newly rich Americans.

Howells and Twain were close friends. And when Twain died in 1910, Howells wrote a tribute to the man he called "the Lincoln of our literature." Although he called it *My Mark Twain,* he noted that he always called Twain by his real name, Samuel Clemens, because his pen name "seemed always somehow to mask him from my personal sense." In this selection, Howells speaks of visiting Twain at his home in Hartford, Connecticut.

What does Howells admire most about Twain's style? What was Twain's attitude toward writing in sequence? What do you think of his method of writing?

Clemens and his architect had planned a luxurious study over the library in his new house. But as his children grew older, it was given to them to use as a schoolroom. He then used the room above his stable. There we used to talk together until he discovered that he preferred to use the large billiard room at the top of his house as a place to write and meet friends. It was pretty cold up there in the early spring and late fall weather. But by lighting all the gas burners and building a fire, we could keep it well above freezing. Here he wrote many of his tales and sketches, and for all I know, some of his books.

We took special pleasure in looking out of the high windows at the pretty Hartford landscape, and down to the tops of the trees covering the hillside near his house. We agreed that there was a charm in trees seen from such a point of view. He had not been a country boy or, rather, a village boy, for nothing. Nothing that nature can offer the young was lost on him. We were natives of the same vast Mississippi Valley. Missouri and Ohio were close enough so that we had learned many of the same ways of talking. I had outgrown mine because I read more, but I gladly recognized the phrases which he used for their lasting juiciness.

His natural use of words formed the backbone of his style. I may have read more, but he was always reading some vital book. It might be some out-of-the-way book, but it had the root of the human matter in it. Perhaps it was a book of great trials, an autobiography, a history, or a narrative of travel—something that showed him life at first-hand. As I remember, he did not care much for fiction, and he had certain distinct dislikes. One was for my dear and honored favorite, Jane Austen. As for plays, he hated the theater, and said he would rather add a list of numbers than follow a plot on the stage. Generally, I think his pleasure in poetry was not great, and I do not believe he cared much for the usual accepted masterpieces of literature. He liked to find out good things and great things for himself. Sometimes he would discover these in a masterpiece new to him alone.

Of all the literary men I have known he was the most unliterary in his background and manner. I do not know whether he knew any Latin, but I think not. German he knew pretty well, and enough Italian to have fun with it. But he used English in all its various forms as if it were native to his own air, as if it had come up out of American, out of Missourian ground. His style was what we know, for good and for bad. But his manner, if I may separate the two, was as entirely his own as if no one had ever written before. He was not enslaved to the consecutiveness in writing which the rest of us are chained to. That is, he wrote as he thought, as all people think, without sequence, without an eye to what went before or should come after. If something occurred to him beyond or beside what he was saying, he put it down on his page, and made it as much at home there as its nature would allow. Then, when he was through with this idea, he would go back to his original thoughts, and keep on with what he had been talking about. He followed this manner in the construction of his sentences, and the arrangement of his chapters.

I helped him with a Library of Humor, which he once edited. When I had done my work according to tradition, with authors, times, and topics carefully studied in order, he tore it all apart, and threw in the pieces wherever he wanted to at the moment. He was right. We were not making a textbook, but a book for the pleasure rather than the instruction of the reader. He did not see why the principle on which he built his own tales and novels should not apply to it. On minor points he was, beyond any author I have known, without favorite phrases or pet words. He also was not against repeating words many times. If a certain word served him better than a substitute, he would use it on a page as many times as he chose.

SMALL-TOWN PLEASURES

Taken from An America That Was *by Albert Britt. © by Albert Britt 1964. Used by permission of Crown Publishers, Inc.*

During the new industrial age, American customs and ways of life were changing. The rapid growth of industry and cities caused great changes in the way Americans acted, thought, and lived. The old customs gave way to the new, in recreation just as they did in everything else. Organized sports took the place of the simpler games of frontier days. The circus and "Wild West" show were new and popular forms of entertainment. In small towns, however, recreation continued to follow the more traditional ways. Here, people played games rather than watched them, and they attended picnics and fairs. In this selection, writer Albert Britt, born in 1874, talks about his boyhood on a farm in southern Illinois and the pastimes he enjoyed.

What were the main amusements of Albert Britt's youth? How did the way he played baseball differ from the way you play it? What pleasures did he have that you lack? Which ones do you enjoy that he lacked? Would you want to change places with him?

Sunday was a day of rest for older people, and the place to rest was a comfortable chair indoors. Only extreme heat could drive them outside to soft grass and the shade of convenient trees. After I had become a city person, I thought of a walk in the woods or through the fields as a form of recreation and my divorce from the farm was complete. Fields and woods were for work and not for idle walking by grown people.

Even mild games were thought to be beneath the dignity of adults, although croquet was permissible. Tennis was unknown to us, although it was creeping into the towns. There was one exception in the case of tennis. Bill Adcock, a prosperous farmer, liked what he heard about this game and came home from town one day with a full set of the necessary equipment, net, rackets, and balls. My brother-in-law Dan saw it and liked the game but not enough to spend money for the equipment. A long fishnet, which he tied himself, made a fair net. He could make his own rackets, which he did—wooden paddles of at least the right shape and size. Balls of course he could not make, so he had to buy them. The result was a game that was a mockery of lawn tennis, even as it was played in that early day. But Dan had an idea. Paddle tennis is with us today.

Of course, being good Americans, we played baseball, but no games on Sunday, although batting and fielding practice were allowed. Neighborhood baseball rose and fell as the number of active young men varied. There were two or three seasons when we Tylerville players thought rather well of ourselves because of a young farmer nearby who could manage to pitch a curve ball. Unfortunately, his control was uncertain and our dream of a township championship never got to first base.

Diamonds were set up wherever there was a large enough stretch of level pastureland to give the players at least a chance to field the ball, although I remember one diamond where a long hit into right field had a better than even chance of rolling down a slope into a creek at the bottom. There were bitter arguments over the scoring of such a hit. Some held the theory that a hit was a hit. Others maintained that such a performance was an act of God and not a home run. Umpires, when there were any, generally followed the rule of safety-first by balancing an outrageously wrong decision in favor of team A by an equally absurd error in behalf of team B at the first opportunity. There were few pitchers' battles, and scorers were kept busy. Thirty-two to twenty-five was thought of as a close game and was entirely satisfactory to those who were watching.

A small, coal-mining community ten or fifteen miles [16.1 or 24.1 kilometers] away in the next county went in strong for baseball and turned out a team that could give a busy afternoon to towns two or three times their size. Wherever they went, a crowd of rooters went with them, not only to cheer but also to bet. Those were good times for coal miners and pay was high by our standards. The rooters were well supplied with money. In the early stages of the game, the bettors walked up and down in front of the spectators showing their money and looking for customers. If there were local laws against public betting, they never applied inside the baseball field when the miners were playing.

When scores were close and hits were important, men who had bet money on the game pleadingly offered "A dollar for a hit!" and if a lucky batter got a hit he gathered in a small harvest of silver dollars from the dust at his feet. These miner-sportsmen were way over our heads and we watched them in silent awe and admiration.

Our money operations were limited to occasional collections to buy new balls. Players supplied their own bats and gloves, although most of us played barehanded. Charlie Glass was our most admired catcher because of his willingness to stand close behind the bat without mitt, mask, shinguard, or chest protector. It was not

our courage but our lack of money that fixed the limit of our equipment. League balls cost a dollar or more, and a lost ball might throw us into bankruptcy. Unless it was lost, a ball stayed in play as long as the stitching held.

Picnics were favorite summer affairs, usually requiring an anniversary or some celebration for an excuse. Farmers were not likely to go on picnics for the mere joy of spending time with Nature. We were in close touch with Nature twelve months of the year and knew it for what it was, a cold-blooded creature who could deal blessing or blight with equal indifference. The Fourth of July was always a good time for a picnic, giving opportunity for a patriotic display and lots of good food at the same time. There were Sunday School picnics, Old Settlers' meetings, country school picnics, and sometimes political picnics.

A big social event was the county fair, which was usually held in early September. That was the week when rain was a catastrophe, however much it might be needed. The fair was a combination livestock show and exhibition of farm machinery and farm products, fruit, vegetables, grain, jams, jellies, preserves, pickles, rows of canned fruits from farm kitchens. Blue, red, and white ribbons, emblems of awards, were proudly displayed by the happy winners. There were side shows too—the fat, tattooed, or bearded lady, a snake charmer with a snake wound around her, the grisly bones found in a cellar somewhere that bore witness to a mysterious murder. In the afternoon there were running and trotting races.

One popular feature was the balloon lift. This always drew a crowd, from the building of the fire that heated the air to lift the big balloon to the moment when the daring pilot cut loose with his parachute and floated down, usually to land in the middle of a cornfield half a mile away.

For country people the fair was another and bigger picnic with fried chicken, lemon pie, and endless visiting. Farmers from all over the county met and gossiped around the pens of fat hogs or prize-winning cattle, and women made envious comments on the blue-ribbon peaches or the excellence of a patchwork quilt that the judges had ignored. There were exhibits of work done in country schools. One year our district walked off with some kind of ribbon. The reason for our achievement is forgotten, but it is certain that samples of my penmanship were not included in the exhibit.

UNIT THREE

THE ARRIVAL OF REFORM

(1897-1920)

CHAPTER 8 ■ THE START OF REFORMS UNDER THE "SQUARE DEAL"

HOW TAMMANY HALL OPERATES

Adapted from William L. Riordan, Plunkitt of Tammany Hall. *New York: McClure, Phillips & Co., 1905.*

By the end of the 1800's corrupt political machines controlled the governments of many large cities. Tammany Hall in New York City was one of the most powerful of these political machines. It stayed in power through graft, by securing the votes of immigrants through favors, and by running a "balanced ticket" so that a member of each major ethnic group held a top position in city government. An important politician in Tammany Hall for many years was George Washington Plunkitt. He served many Tammany bosses, including William Tweed and Charles Murphy.

In 1905 a young newspaper reporter, William L. Riordan, wrote a book about Plunkitt. He recorded Plunkitt's own words on how he became a powerful politician and a millionaire.

How does Plunkitt distinguish between honest and dishonest graft? Can you think of similar examples in politics today? What services does Plunkitt perform for poor families?

Everybody is talking these days about Tammany people growing rich on graft, but nobody thinks of drawing the distinction between honest graft and dishonest graft. There's all the difference in the world between the two. Yes, many of our people have grown rich in politics. I have myself. I've made a big fortune out of the game, and I'm getting richer every day. But I've not gone in for dishonest graft—blackmailing gamblers, saloon-keepers, and so on. And neither have any of the people who have made big fortunes in politics.

There's an honest graft, and I'm an example of how it works. I might sum up the whole thing by saying: "I seen my opportunities and I took 'em."

Just let me explain by examples. My party's in power in the city, and it's going to undertake a lot of public improvements. Well, I'm told ahead of time, say, that they're going to lay out a new park at a certain place.

I see my opportunity and I take it. I go to that place and I buy up all the land I can in the neighborhood. Then the board of this or that makes its plan public, and there is a rush to get my land, which nobody wanted before.

Ain't it perfectly honest to charge a good price and make a profit on my investment and foresight? Of course it is. Well, that's honest graft.

Or supposing it's a new bridge they're going to build. I find out and I buy as much property as I can that has to be used for the road approaches to the bridge. I sell the property at my own price later on and drop some more money in the bank.

Wouldn't you? It's just like looking ahead in Wall Street or in the coffee or cotton market. It's honest graft and I'm looking for it every day in the year. I will tell you frankly that I've got a lot of it, too.

I'll tell you of another case. They were going to fix up a big park. I learned of it and went looking about for land in that neighborhood. I could get nothing at a bargain except a big piece of swamp, but I bought it right away and held on to it. What happened was just what I counted on. They couldn't make the park complete without Plunkitt's swamp, and so they had to pay a good price for it. Anything dishonest in that?

I don't own a dishonest dollar. If my worst enemy was given the job of writing an epitaph for my grave marker he couldn't do more than write:

"George W. Plunkitt. He Seen His Opportunities, and He Took 'Em."

What's important in holding your grip on your district is to go right down among the poor families and help them in the different ways they need help. I've got a regular system for doing this.

If there's a fire on Ninth, Tenth, or Eleventh Avenue, for example, any hour of the day or night, I'm usually there with some of my election district captains as soon as the fire engines arrive. If a family is burned out, I don't ask whether they are Republicans or Democrats. I don't refer them to the Charity Organization Society, which would investigate their case in a month or two and decide they were worthy of help about the time they are dead from starvation. I just get a place for them to live, buy clothes for them if their clothes were burned up, and fix them up till they get things running again. It's philanthropy, but it's politics, too—mighty good politics. Who can tell how many votes one of these fires brings me? The poor are the most grateful people in the world, and, let me tell you, they have more friends in their neighborhoods than the rich have in theirs.

If there's a family in my district that needs help, I know it before the charitable societies do. Me and my men are the first to help. I have a special group of people to look up such cases. The result is that the poor look up to George W. Plunkitt as a father, they come to him when they're in trouble, and they don't forget him on election day.

A MUCKRAKER ATTACKS CITY CORRUPTION

Adapted from Lincoln Steffens, The Shame of the Cities. *New York: McClure, Phillips & Co., 1904.*

By 1900 many Americans felt that something had to be done to reform American government and American life. This reform movement was known as the Progressive movement. Some of the most important supporters of the Progressives were the writers and newspaper reporters who were making Americans aware of how widespread the corruption and abuses had become in the United States. These crusading, reform-minded writers were disliked by some Americans, including Theodore Roosevelt. In a speech in 1906, he described them by referring to a character in the book *Pilgrim's Progress*—"the man with the muckrake." One writer, Lincoln Steffens, proudly adopted the term "muckraker" to refer to anyone who wanted to uncover, or rake up, corruption. Soon the term became very popular.

Steffens became famous because of his magazine articles on corruption in American cities. The following selections are from his book *The Shame of the Cities*.

Why, according to Steffens, do business leaders make bad politicians? Who does he think is to blame for corruption? What solution does he propose?

There is hardly a government office from United States Senator down to alderman in any part of the country to which some business leader has not been elected. Yet politics remains corrupt and government pretty bad. Business leaders have failed in politics as they have in good citizenship. Why?

Because politics is business. That's what's the matter with everything—art, literature, religion, journalism, law, medicine. They're all business, and all as you see them.

Make politics a sport, as they do in England, or a profession, as they do in Germany. Then we'll have—well, something else than we have now—if we want it, which is another question. But don't try to reform politics with the banker, the lawyer, and the merchant. For they are business people and there are two things that make it very difficult for them to achieve reform: One is that they are different from, but no better than, the politicians. The other is that politics is not "their line."

There are exceptions both ways. Many politicians have gone into business and done well. (Tammany ex-mayors, and nearly all the old bosses of Philadelphia, are important financiers in their cities.) Business managers have gone into politics and done well. (Mark Hanna, for example.) The politician is a businessman with a specialty. When a businessman in some other line learns the business of politics, he is a politician, and there is not much reform left in him. Consider the United States Senate, and believe me.

The commercial spirit is the spirit of profit, not patriotism; of credit, not honor; of individual gain, not national prosperity; of trade, not principle.

We cheat our government and we let our leaders rob it. We let them persuade and bribe our power away from us. True, they pass strict laws for us, but we let them pass bad laws too, giving away public property in exchange. Our good, and often impossible, laws we allow to be used for oppression and blackmail. And what can we say? We break our own laws and rob our own government—the woman at the tax office, the lyncher with his rope, and the captain of industry with his bribe and his rebate. The spirit of graft and of lawlessness is the American spirit.

The people are not innocent. This will not be news to many observers. It was to me. When I set out to describe the corrupt systems of certain typical cities, I meant to show simply how the people were deceived and betrayed. But in the very first study—St. Louis—the startling truth showed that corruption was not merely political. It was financial, commercial, and social. Its offshoots were so complex and far-reaching that one mind could hardly grasp them all.

The corruption of St. Louis came from the top. The best citizens—the merchants and big financiers—ruled the town, and they ruled it well. They set out to overtake Chicago. The commercial and industrial war between these two cities was a picturesque and dramatic spectacle such as is seen only in our country. Business leaders were not just merchants, and politicians were not just grafters. The two kinds of citizens got together and used the power of banks, railroads, factories, the prestige of the city, and the spirit of its citizens to gain business and population. And it was a close race. Chicago, having a head start, always led. But St. Louis had spirit, intelligence, and tremendous energy. It pressed Chicago hard. It excelled in a sense of civic beauty and good

government. There are those who still think it might have won. But a change occurred. Public spirit became private spirit, and public enterprise became private greed.

Along about 1890, public franchises and privileges were sought, not only for legitimate profit and common convenience, but also for loot. Taking only slight but always selfish interest in the public councils, leading merchants and financiers misused politics. Other less important and even less honest men, catching the smell of corruption, rushed into the Municipal Assembly, drove out the remaining respectable leaders, and sold the city—its streets, its wharves, its markets, and all that it had—to the now greedy business people and bribers.

So gradually has this taken place that these same citizens hardly realize it. Go to St. Louis and you will find the habit of civic pride in them. They still boast. The visitor is told of the wealth of the residents, of the financial strength of the banks, and of the growing importance of the industries. Yet the visitor sees poorly paved streets full of garbage, and dirty or mud-filled alleys. He passes a broken-down firetrap of a building crowded with the sick, and learns that it is the city hospital.

In Pittsburgh graft falls into four classes: franchises, public contracts, vice, and public funds. There was, besides these, a lot of other loot—public supplies, public lighting, and the water supply. But I cannot go into these. Neither can I stop to discuss the details of the system by which public funds, earning no interest, were put in favored banks from which the city borrowed money at a high interest rate. All these things were managed well within the law. That was the great principle underlying the Pittsburgh plan.

The vice graft, for example, was not blackmail as it is in New York and most other cities. It is a legitimate business, conducted not by the police, but in an orderly fashion by syndicates. The leader of one of the parties at the last election said it was worth $250,000 a year. I saw a man who was laughed at for offering $17,500 for the slot-machine concession. He was told that it was leased for much more. "Speakeasies" [unlicensed drinking places] have to pay off so many people that even though they may earn $500 or more in 24 hours, their owners often just about make a living.

We Americans may have failed. We may be selfish and influenced by gain. Democracy with us may be impossible and corruption inevitable, but these articles, if they have proved nothing else, have shown that we can stand the truth. There is pride in the character of American citizenship. This pride may be a power in the land. So this record of shame and yet of self-respect, disgraceful confession, yet a declaration of honor, is dedicated, in all good faith, to the accused—to all the citizens of all the cities in the United States.

A MUCKRAKER ATTACKS BIG BUSINESS

Adapted from Ida M. Tarbell, History of the Standard Oil Company. *New York: McClure, Phillips & Co., 1904.*

The muckrakers told Americans of the many abuses in their society. Their books and articles made many Americans deeply concerned about the consequences of the great industrial growth and business consolidation then taking place. They brought many of the unfair business methods and practices of large industries to the attention of the public.

Probably the most famous of all muckraking reports about American industry was Ida Tarbell's *History of the Standard Oil Company.* In this series of newspaper articles, which later became a book, she exposed the practices and policies of that giant monopoly.

According to Ida Tarbell, how are the large profits of the Standard Oil trust being used? Why does she regard transportation as the key to Standard Oil's monopoly? What does she believe is the "ethical cost" of the oil industry monopoly? What solutions does she suggest?

The profits of the present Standard Oil Company are enormous. For five years the dividends have been averaging about $45 million a year. When we remember that probably one third of this great yearly profit goes into the hands of John D. Rockefeller, that probably 90 percent of it goes to the few people who make up the "Standard Oil family," the Standard Oil Company becomes a much more serious public matter than it was in 1872, when it began to take over the oil business.

For, consider what must be done with the greater part of this $45 million. It must be invested. The oil business does not need it. It has money for all of its ventures. The money must go into other industries. Naturally, these other interests will be connected to oil. One such interest will be gas, and we have the Standard Oil people steadily taking over the gas interests of the country. Another will be railroads, for all industries depend on transportation. Besides, railroads are one of the great consumers of oil products and must be kept in line as buyers. So we have the directors of the Standard Oil Company acting as directors on nearly all of the great railways of the country. They will go into steel, and we have Mr. Rockefeller's great holdings in the steel trust. They will go into banking, and we have the National City Bank and its connected institutions in New York City and Boston, as well as a long chain running throughout the country.

No one who has followed this history can expect that these holdings will be bought on a rising market. Buy cheap and sell high is a rule of business. When you control enough money and enough banks, you can always work it out so that a stock you want will be temporarily cheap. No value is destroyed for you—only for the original owner. This has been one of Mr. Rockefeller's most successful maneuvers in doing business. The result is that the Standard Oil Company is probably in the strongest financial position of any organization in the world. And every year its position grows stronger, for every year another $45 million is poured into taking over the property most essential to keeping and broadening its power.

In spite of the Interstate Commerce Commission, the crucial question is still that of transportation. Until the people of the United States have solved the question of free and equal transportation, there will always be a trust question. As long as it is possible for a company to own the carrier on which a great natural product depends for transportation, and to use this carrier to limit a competitor's supply or to cut it off entirely, it is foolish to talk about constitutional amendments limiting trusts. As long as the Standard Oil Company can control transportation, as it does today, it will remain master of the oil industry. The people of the United States will pay a high price for oil because of their indifference in regard to transportation. And they will see an increasing amount of natural resources and transportation systems owned by the Standard Oil monopoly.

If all we suffered was limited business opportunities for a few hundred men and women and a constantly rising price for refined oil, the case would be serious enough. But there is a more serious side to it. The ethical cost of all this is the main concern. We are a commercial people. We cannot boast of our arts, our crafts, our culture. Our pride is the wealth we produce. As a consequence, business success is holy. We justify practically any methods to achieve it.

Very often people who admit the facts, who see that Mr. Rockefeller has employed force and fraud to obtain his ends, justify him by declaring, "It's business." That is, "It's business" has come to be a legitimate excuse for hard dealing, sly tricks, special privileges. It is a common enough thing to hear people arguing that the ordinary laws of morality do not apply in business.

Now, if the Standard Oil Company were the only company in the country guilty of the practices which have given it monopolistic power, this story never would have been written. But it is simply the most outstanding example of what can be done by these practices. The methods it uses with such skill, constancy, and secrecy are used by all sorts of business people, from corner grocers up to bankers. If exposed, they are excused on the ground that this is business. If the point is pushed, frequently the defender of the practice falls back on the Christian doctrine of charity, and points out that we are only human and must allow for each other's weaknesses! If this excuse were carried to its logical conclusion, our business people would be weeping on each other's shoulders over human weakness, while they picked each other's pockets.

And what are we going to do about it? For it is *our* business. We, the people of the United States, and nobody else, must cure whatever is wrong in the industrial situation, typified by this account of the growth of the Standard Oil Company. It is clear that our first task is to obtain free and equal transportation privileges by railroad, pipeline, and waterway. It is not an easy matter. It is one which may require severe methods. But the whole system of rate discrimination has been nothing but violence. Those who have profited by it cannot complain if curing the evils they have caused brings hard-

ship to them. At all events, until the transportation matter is settled, and settled right, the monopolistic trust will be with us, a barrier to our free efforts.

As for the ethical side, there is no cure but in an increasing scorn of unfair play—an increasing sense that a thing won by breaking the rules of the game is not worth winning. The business person who fights to obtain special privileges, to crowd competitors off the track by unfair methods, should be treated just the way we treat the doctor or lawyer who is "unprofessional" or the athlete who abuses the rules. Then we shall have gone a long way toward making business a fit profession for our young people.

PRESIDENT ROOSEVELT URGES BUSINESS REFORM

Adapted from James D. Richardson (Comp.), A Compilation of the Messages and Papers of the Presidents, *Vol. X, 1789–1902. Washington: Bureau of National Literature and Art, 1903.*

President Theodore Roosevelt was a skilled politician whose bold acts and personality captured the imagination of Americans. His efforts to regulate the trusts made many Americans think of him as the leader of the Progressive movement. In fact, he was less a crusader than many other Progressive reformers. He believed that reform had to come slowly and had to be carefully planned.

However, Roosevelt did make an enormous contribution to the Progressive movement. His popularity and his support of many of the Progressives' aims helped to publicize the movement and gained it widespread support. The following selection is from his first annual message to Congress in 1901.

How would you describe Roosevelt's attitude toward the "captains of industry"? Why does he recommend caution in dealing with them? What is the "widespread belief" among Americans about trusts? Does he agree with it? What does he think should be done?

The tremendous and highly complex industrial development which went on during the last half of the 1800's brings us face to face, at the beginning of the 1900's, with very serious social problems. Old laws and old customs were once quite enough to regulate the accumulation and distribution of wealth. They are no longer enough.

The growth of great industrial centers has meant a startling increase, not only in wealth itself, but in the number of very large individual and corporate fortunes. The creation of these great corporate fortunes has not been due to the tariff, nor to any other governmental action, but to natural causes in the business world, operating in other countries as they operate in our own.

The process has created much opposition, a great part of which is wholly without cause. It is not true that as the rich have grown richer the poor have grown poorer. On the contrary, never before has the average wage-earner, farmer, or small trader been so well-off as in this country at the present time. There have been abuses connected with the accumulation of wealth. Yet a fortune gained in legitimate business can be acquired only when the person doing so brings great benefits to others.

The captains of industry who have built the railway systems across this continent, who have developed our industry, have on the whole done great good to our people. Without them our development could never have taken place. Moreover, we should realize that it is important not to interfere any more than is necessary for the public good with the strong and forceful people upon whom the success of business operations rests.

Another reason for caution in dealing with corporations is to be found in international business. The richest concerns and those managed by the ablest people are naturally those that take the lead in the struggle for commercial supremacy among the nations of the world. America has only just begun to dominate the international business world. It is of the greatest importance that this position not be placed in danger.

Moreover, striking with ignorant violence at the interests of one set of people almost inevitably puts the interests of all in danger. The basic rule in our national life is that, on the whole, and in the long run, we shall go up or down together. Disaster to great business concerns never limits its effects to the people at the top. It spreads throughout, and while it is bad for everybody, it is worst for those farthest down.

All this is true. And yet it is also true that there are real and serious evils. A practical effort must be made to correct them.

There is a widespread belief among the American people that the great corporations known as trusts are harmful to the general welfare. This belief does not spring from a spirit of envy or lack of pride in the great industrial achievements. It does not rest upon ignorance of the fact that a good deal of capital is needed to accomplish great things. It is based upon the sincere belief that combination and concentration should be, not forbidden, but supervised and within reasonable limits controlled. In my judgment this belief is right.

It is no limitation upon property rights or freedom of contract to require that when people receive from the government the privilege of doing business under corporate form, they should be truthful as to the value of the property in which capital is to be invested. Corporations engaged in interstate commerce should be regulated if they harm the public. Great corporations exist only because they are created and safeguarded by our institutions. It is therefore our right and our duty to see that they work in harmony with these institutions.

The first essential in determining how to deal with the great industrial combinations is knowledge of the facts. In the interest of the public, the government should have the right to inspect and examine the workings of the great corporations engaged in interstate business. Publicity is the only sure remedy we now have. What further remedies are needed in the way of governmental regulation, or taxation, can only be determined after publicity has been obtained.

The large corporations, commonly called trusts, though organized in one state, always do business in many states. There is a complete lack of uniformity in the state laws dealing with them.

Therefore, in the interest of all the people, the nation should take over the supervision and regulation of all corporations doing an interstate business. There would be no hardship in such supervision; banks are subject to it, and in their case it is now accepted as a simple matter of course.

When the Constitution was adopted at the end of the 1700's, no human wisdom could foretell the sweeping changes which were to take place by the beginning of the 1900's. At that time it was accepted as a matter of course that the states were the proper authorities to regulate the comparatively insignificant corporations of the day. The conditions are now wholly different. Wholly different action is called for.

THE GROWING INTEREST IN CONSERVATION

Adapted from George F. Kunz, Proceedings of a Conference of Governors. *Washington: Government Printing Office, 1909.*

One of Theodore Roosevelt's most important achievements was the interest he helped create in the conservation of America's natural resources. In 1908 he held a White House conference on conservation. At this conference more than a thousand delegates listened to speeches expressing concern over how the nation's resources were being used and suggesting reforms. A few speakers such as George Kunz, a mineralogist, also stressed the need to protect America's natural beauty.

In his speech, from which this selection is taken, Kunz speaks of human beings as having passed through various stages of development—savagery, barbarism, and civilization. His remarks reflected the widely held theory of the time that all peoples had progressed through the same well-defined steps on their way to modern civilization.

How does Kunz link the appreciation of the beauty of nature and the development of civilization? Why does Kunz believe that some higher judicial power must weigh the merits of "conflicting interests"? Do you think that present-day Americans have followed Kunz's advice?

The great forces of nature have created the mineral wealth stored beneath the earth. They have carved the hollows and valleys in which our lakes lie and our streams flow. They have lifted up our mountain ranges and have made the soil that feeds our forests and crops. These same forces have made the various features called scenery, which delights the eye, and stirs the imagination. And scenery in turn has affected our movements, our life, and our development. Thus, for many reasons, human history has always been identified with the natural landscape.

In recommending to the conference the protection of American scenery, I deny that there is a conflict between the idea of preserving scenery and the idea of properly using our material resources. Every interest represented in this conference is looking forward to the same goal—the greatest happiness and good for the greatest number of people. That will be reached best by friendly cooperation, by mutual adjustments, and by reasonable concessions when necessary.

The purpose of our organization is to encourage the beautiful without preventing the development of forests, mines, railroads, or water power. But it must not be forgotten that there are many factors in reaching human happiness.

In the lowest status of savagery, when humans are nearest the beasts of the field, happiness depends almost exclusively upon satisfying bodily needs. But as we lift ourselves up through the stages of savagery, and through barbarism into civilization, a new element of happiness becomes important. In this rise, with its accompanying intellectual development, our thoughts constantly range farther and farther from the narrow limits of our own bodies for satisfaction. While meeting physical wants is the first necessity, other needs must also be met.

The wholesome pleasure which one obtains from being in nature is a characteristic of our civilization. We cannot get rid of it even if we wanted to. It makes us better, happier, more efficient citizens. It is a fact of human nature to be honestly recognized. It should not be put aside as empty sentimentalism any more than using the physical resources of the land would be held in contempt as too commercial.

Our goal should therefore be to see how closely we can get together so as to join our interests for the common good. It is at this point that we need some judicial power higher than the individual to weigh the merits of conflicting interests. There are occasions, for instance, when the value to the community of damming a given stream at a given place may not be truthfully expressed in dollars and cents. When we balance all considerations, we may find that the location of the dam farther upstream or farther downstream, or on some other stream, or even preventing it from being built, may contribute to the greatest good for the greatest number. Thus, the necessity for regulation by some branch of government representing all interests is apparent. It is proper that the law should regulate the destruction of trees, rocks, river banks, and other notable features of the landscape.

Nothing is more valuable in creating a love of beauty in the average person than the scenic beauty of forests, mountains, and rivers. For this reason, such objects of natural beauty should be carefully guarded against injury or destruction.

BLACK AMERICANS AND PROGRESSIVE REFORMS

Adapted from H. G. Wells, The Future in America. New York: Harper & Brothers, 1906.

Although the reforms of the Progressive movement brought important benefits to most Americans, it did little to improve the lives of black Americans.

When Theodore Roosevelt became President, many black Americans expected that they would be included in the Progressive reforms. They remembered his praise of black troops during the Spanish-American War. And he stirred the hopes of black Americans by inviting Booker T. Washington to dinner at the White House and by condemning lynching. But during Roosevelt's Presidency, the earlier hopes of black Americans were not realized. Roosevelt and most Progressive reformers ignored the need to improve conditions among blacks. In the following selection, a visiting English writer, H. G. Wells, tells of the plight of black Americans.

What is the basic question that Wells asks about black people? What kinds of answers does he receive? Why does he admire black Americans? What future did he see for them?

In regard to the colored population, just as in regard to the great and growing numbers of Jews, and the growing numbers of Roman Catholics, I have tried time after time to get some answer from Americans to the question that is to me the most obvious. "Your grandchildren and the grandchildren of these people will have to live in this country side by side. Do you think—do you believe it possible—that under the increasing pressure of population and competition, they will be living then in just the same relations that you and these people are living now? If you do not, then what relations do you suggest should exist between them?"

It is not too much to say that I have never once had the beginning of an answer to this question. Usually one is told with great seriousness that the problem of color is one of the most difficult that we have to consider. The conversation then breaks up into long stories and unfavorable statements about black people.

Whatever America has to show in heroic living today, I doubt if it can show anything finer than the quality of will, the constant effort hundreds of black people are making today to live blamelessly, honorably, and patiently. They get for themselves what scraps of refinement, learning, and beauty they can. They keep their hold on a civilization they are begrudged and denied. They do it not for themselves only but for all their race. Each educated colored person is an ambassador to civilization. They know they have a handicap. Yet each one, I like to think, is aware of being a representative, fighting against injustice, insult, and the unspeakable meannesses of bigoted enemies. Every one of them who remains decent and honorable does a little to beat that opposition down.

But what patience the Negroes need! They cannot even show contempt. They must regard as superior those whose daily conduct is clear evidence of moral inferiority. Negroes must go to and fro self-controlled, without all the equalities that the great flag of America proclaims— that flag for which black people fought and died. Negroes must take second place to the strangers who pour in to share the nation's wealth, strangers ignorant even of its language. That Negroes must do—and wait. The Welsh, the Irish, the Poles, the white South, and the Jews may have grievances and complain aloud. Negroes must keep still. The others may be hysterical, revengeful, threatening; their wrongs excuse them. For Negroes there is no excuse. And of all the races upon earth, which has suffered such wrongs as this Negro race? Those people who scorn them have sinned against them beyond all measure.

No, I can't help idealizing the dark submissive figure of the Negro in this spectacle of America. The Negro seems to me to sit waiting—and waiting with a marvelous and constant patience—for finer understanding and a nobler time.

CHAPTER 9 ■ THE EXTENSION OF REFORMS UNDER THE "NEW FREEDOM"

THE BIRTH OF THE PROGRESSIVE PARTY

Adapted with permission of Macmillan Publishing Co., Inc. from The Second Twenty Years at Hull-House *by Jane Addams. Copyright 1930 by Macmillan Publishing Co., Inc., renewed 1958 by John A. Brittain.*

The summer of 1912 was an exciting time in American politics. After the Republicans nominated Taft for the Presidency, Roosevelt split with the party. He and a group of his supporters, together with a wide variety of reformers, joined together to form a third political party known as the Progressive (or "Bull Moose") Party. They held a convention in August at Chicago, where the delegates sang "Onward Christian Soldiers," drafted a platform which they called "A Contract with the People," and nominated Roosevelt for President and Hiram Johnson of California for Vice-President. In this selection Jane Addams, who took part in the convention, tells what it was like.

To Jane Addams, which was more important, having Roosevelt as party leader or having a reform platform? From what you have read, do you think her judgment was correct?

From various directions, people were drawing toward a new political party. It was at first as if one heard in the distance the grave and measured step of history. But the pace increased during the first half of 1912, and became absolutely breathless by midsummer. It was in August 1912 that the Progressive Party was organized.

Suddenly, as if by magic, the city of Chicago became filled with men and women from every state in the Union who were moved by the same needs and hopes. They showed each other common sympathies and memories. They urged methods for righting old wrongs and establishing new standards. For three days they defined their purposes and joined their wills.

Among the members of the platform committee for the new party were social workers, others closely identified with religion, and still others who were scholars. Sometimes when we came across members of the American Economic Association, or of the Civil Service Reform League, or similar groups, we feared that a few people were trying through the new party to obtain measures which, although worthy, had only limited support. To me, this was very alarming. But I gradually discovered that the situation was in reality the very opposite of this. The dean of a university law school acted as head of the resolution committee, and others who knew law supplied information. But these people, together with the so-called "practical" members of the committee, were not representing the opinion of any individual nor the philosophy of any group. They were trying, as conscientious American citizens, to meet the basic duty of adapting the laws to the changed conditions of national life.

Delegates had all experienced the frustration and disappointment of individual effort. They had come to this first national convention of the Progressive Party not only to urge reform legislation, but to test its usefulness through the consent of their fellow citizens, to throw their measures into the life of the nation itself. They believed that the program of social legislation placed before the country by the Progressive Party was of great importance to the average voter regardless of party.

In the hope that the political organization of the nation might never again get so far away from the life of the people, the platform recommended equal suffrage, direct primaries, and the initiative and referendum. We quoted to each other the saying of Walt Whitman, that it seemed to him unbearable that large groups of people should follow those who do not believe in people. We placed at the head of our precious new party two men of political wisdom who had shown an understanding not only of the social demands of the people but also of the people themselves. We realized that Colonel Roosevelt possessed a unique power. In spite of our belief in our leader, however, I was there —and I think the same was true of many others—because the platform expressed the social hopes so long ignored by the politicians.

Although we were all quite well aware that the convention was far from being united, it seemed to us at the moment as if it really were. Certainly, for the time being, all doctrines and group egotisms were dropped. Or rather, they were melted down by overwhelming good will and enthusiasm.

The Progressive convention has been described many times, perhaps never quite adequately. It was a curious moment of release from inhibitions. It did not seem in the least strange that quiet, reserved men and women should speak aloud of their religious and social beliefs, confident that they would be understood. Because we felt so at home in that huge Coliseum, there was a quick understanding of those hidden feelings which we were mysteriously moved to express.

During the three days of the Progressive convention, one could almost hear the breakdown of the well-worn slogans which had provided the old parties their election battle cries for half a century. The sound was not unlike the uproar which accompanies a great religious conference. The old-line politicians were as much surprised to find that politics had to do with the matters discussed at the Progressive convention as the social workers were delighted to discover that their long concern for human needs had come to be considered politics. Nevertheless, in spite of the careful platform building, the entire noisy convention was well described as the "barn raising of a new party."

WILSON'S "NEW FREEDOM"

Adapted from William E. Leuchtenburg, Woodrow Wilson, The New Freedom, © 1961. Reprinted by permission of Prentice-Hall, Inc., Englewood Cliffs, New Jersey.

President Woodrow Wilson was a Progressive of a different sort from Theodore Roosevelt. While Roosevelt distinguished between good and bad trusts and declared that the government should not break up large corporations but regulate them, Wilson believed that all large trusts were bad. He felt that the trusts were too powerful to be controlled and that the antitrust laws should be used to break them up. Wilson used the phrase "a New Freedom" to describe his program of reform. He also wrote a book called *The New Freedom* in which he outlined his reform philosophy. The following selection is taken from that book.

According to Wilson, what special interests endanger the United States? How? Why does Wilson feel that the trusts must be broken up? What does the term "New Freedom" mean to Wilson?

We have entered a very different age from any that came before us. We have entered an age in which we do not do business the way we used to do business. We do not carry on any of the operations of manufacture, sale, transportation, or communication as people used to carry them on. There is a sense in which the individual has been submerged. In most parts of our country people work not for themselves, not as partners in the old way in which they used to work, but generally as employees of great corporations. There was a time when corporations played a very small part in our business affairs. Now they play the chief part, and most workers are the servants of corporations.

You know what happens when you are the servant of a corporation. Your individuality is swallowed up in the individuality and purpose of a great organization.

American industry is not free, as once it was free. American enterprise is not free. The person with only a little capital is finding it harder to get into the field, more and more impossible to compete with big business. Why? Because the laws of the country do not prevent the strong from crushing the weak. That is the reason. And because the strong have crushed the weak, the strong dominate the industry and the economic life of this country. What this country needs above everything else is laws which will look after the people who are striving to succeed rather than the people who are already successful.

Don't fool yourselves for a moment as to the power of the great interests which now dominate our development. They are so powerful that it is almost questionable whether the government of the United States can dominate them or not. Go one step further, make their organized power permanent, and it may be too late to turn back. The roads divide at the point where we stand. They stretch out to regions far separated from one another. At the end of one is the old, tiresome scene of government tied up with special interests. At the other shines the free light of individual freedom, the light of unrestrained enterprise.

I believe in human liberty as I believe in the wine of life. There is no salvation for workers in the small favors of industrial masters. Guardians have no place in a land of free people. Prosperity guaranteed by trustees has no prospect of lasting. Monopoly means the wasting away of enterprise. If monopoly continues, it will always control government. I do not expect to see monopoly hold back itself.

The government of our country cannot be placed in the hands of any special class. The policy of a great nation cannot be tied up with any particular set of interests. I want to say again and again that my arguments do not involve the *character* of the people to whom I am opposed. I believe that the very wealthy who got their money by certain kinds of corporate enterprise have closed in their horizon, and that they do not see and do not understand the people. It is for that reason that I want to break up the little group that has determined what the government of the nation should do. We must save our government from the domination of special classes, not because these special classes are necessarily bad, but because no special class can understand the interests of a great community.

The meaning of liberty has deepened. But it has not stopped being a demand of the human spirit, a basic necessity for the life of the soul. And the day is at hand when it shall be realized on this consecrated soil—a New Freedom. It will be a liberty widened and deepened to match the broadened life of the modern American, returning to us the control of our government. It will throw open all gates of lawful enterprise, releasing energies and warming the generous impulses of our hearts. It will be a process of freedom and inspiration, full of a breath of life as sweet and wholesome as the airs that filled the sails of Columbus, giving the promise and boast of magnificent opportunity in which America dare not fail.

A SPANIARD REPORTS ON THE 1916 ELECTION

Adapted from "Un Año en el otro mundo" by Julio Camba, from This Was America *by Oscar Handlin, published by Harvard University Press. © 1949 by the President and Fellows of Harvard College. Reprinted by permission of the publisher.*

In the election of 1916, the Democrats nominated Woodrow Wilson for a second term and the Republicans chose Charles Evans Hughes, Chief Justice of the Supreme Court, as their candidate. Theodore Roosevelt was again chosen by the Progressive Party. During the campaign, Americans were especially concerned with foreign affairs. With World War I raging in Europe, Wilson's slogan—"He kept us out of war"—attracted many voters. Other issues, of course, were important in the campaign. A Spanish writer, Julio Camba, was in the United States at the time of the election and wrote this account of the campaign.

What, according to Camba, are the "two basic tendencies" in American life? How does the election match them against each other? Camba calls the American President a "kaiser" (German for "emperor"). Do you think the term is accurate? Why?

The battle has already taken shape. The Republican and Progressive parties have met in Chicago to nominate candidates. Soon the Democratic Party will meet. Afterwards, in the month of November, will come the elections, first for the electoral college, then for the President. The names which are most often heard now are Wilson, who is now President, Roosevelt, and Hughes.

We must prepare to see one of the most picturesque spectacles in the world—that is, a Presidential election in the United States. To give you an idea of the sporting spirit with which the people regard such equal contestants, it is necessary to quote the following paragraph from the *Evening Post:* "It is a pity that two men as famous as Wilson and Hughes could not appear together on the same platform! That would be a sensational match, and spectators would pay a fabulous price for admission."

Hughes holds over Wilson the enormous advantage of the offensive. The ex-justice can attack all the Presidential acts of Wilson, who will have to make the great efforts to defend them. In his turn, Hughes will have to show how he would have acted if he had been President. Hughes can depend on a greater number of personal sympathizers than Wilson, who seems to make enemies of his friends. Wilson, in turn, enjoys great intellectual prestige. He writes very well, speaks well, and is considered a most honorable and well-intentioned man.

The candidates are ready. The boxers have put on their gloves. The first round is about to begin.

There are two basic tendencies in the life of this country. One is an idealistic and humanitarian tendency with a great moral content, which reaches from William James, the philosopher, to Henry Ford, the manufacturer of automobiles. The other is a materialistic tendency without any content of idealism, a tendency of capitalism and imperialism. The two tendencies, as may be seen in this election, are now in a state of balance.

It is certain that Hughes and Roosevelt, as against Wilson, represent the second of those tendencies. Hughes stands for the Wall Street capitalists, who gained him the nomination. He speaks for the trusts. He represents the scorn of money for moral values. His friends have put signs all over New York which read: "We don't want professors meddling in our affairs," and "What's the use of democracy in business?" Hughes, in short, represents the materialism of a civilization in which quality counts for nothing. What counts are dollars, many dollars, business, bridges, telephones, cranes, skyscrapers, noise, speed.

If matters continue as they have until now, and if Hughes does not win this time, he (or someone else who represents the same things) will win in four years. The second tendency is steadily winning out over the first. By the same degree that a people enriches itself with material possessions, it also loses some of its spiritual content. The 1800's are dying in the trenches of Europe. At the end of the war, France, Germany, England, and Italy will face in the United States a people whose ideals are those of the corporation—to do business. And *what is the use of democracy in business!* What help is democracy in making money?

This moral difference between that which Hughes represents and that which Wilson represents is, without doubt, much more important for the relations of North America with the rest of the world than the possible difference of opinion between those two men on the European war. One must, moreover, be aware of the position of the President of the United States to understand the importance of the election. The President of the United States is a kaiser [emperor]. He is elected, by a democratic process, a kaiser for four years; yet he is a kaiser who gets what he wishes.

WHAT DID THE PROGRESSIVES ACHIEVE?

Adapted from The Progressive Movement 1900–1915, *Richard Hofstadter, editor, © 1963, pp. 1–5. Reprinted by permission of Prentice-Hall, Inc., Englewood Cliffs, New Jersey.*

The Progressive movement came to an end when the United States entered World War I. It had started to slow down with the outbreak of war in Europe in 1914. With their attention now on foreign affairs, many Americans became less interested in reform. A great many Americans also felt that the Progressive movement had achieved its aims and that further reform was not needed. Then, too, many Americans were tired of the endless talk about reforming the ills of society. What had the reform movement of the early 1900's accomplished, they wondered? Richard Hofstadter, a leading modern historian who has studied this period, gives his answer to this question. The following selection is from the introduction to his book *The Progressive Movement: 1900–1915.*

According to Hofstadter, what did Americans accomplish during the period from the end of the Civil War to 1900? What price did they pay for these achievements? How does Hofstadter describe the chief characteristics of the Progressive movement? Its major accomplishments?

For a long time historians have written of the period between 1900 and 1914 as the Progressive era, and of its variety of reform agitations as the Progressive movement. In using these terms, historians have followed the example of many of the period's leading figures. They liked the ring of the word "Progressive" as applied to themselves. The people of that age were proudly aware, even as they were fighting their battles, that there was something distinctive about the political and social life of their time which sharply marked it off from the era of materialism and corruption.

From the end of the Civil War to the close of the 1800's, the physical energies of the American people had been organized for a remarkable burst of material development. But their moral energies were relatively inactive. Certain moral aspects of the American character had become all but invisible. It was as though the controversy over slavery, the Civil War itself, and the difficulties and failures of Reconstruction had exhausted the moral and political capacities of the people. They abandoned crusades and reforms and jumped instead into the rewarding tasks of material achievements.

During this period Americans had filled up a vast area of land between the Mississippi River and California. They had crossed the country with a railroad network of more than a quarter of a million miles. Still more impressive was the growth of the urban and industrial

486

part of the economy. Whole systems of industry and whole regions of industrial production were created. The urban population jumped from 9.9 million to 30.1 million. Thoughtful observers could see that the day was not very far off when the rural population would be outnumbered and the characteristic problems of the nation would be city problems.

By 1900 it became increasingly evident that all this material growth had been achieved at a terrible cost in human values and in the waste of natural resources. The land and the people had been robbed. Farmers had received small returns for their work. They had had little or no protection against exploitation by the railroads, against the high cost of credit, or against an unjust burden of taxation. At the same time the cities that grew with American industry were themselves industrial wastelands—centers of illegal activities and poverty, ugly, full of crowded slums, badly managed. Industry, after a period of great competition, was rapidly becoming concentrated. Big business choked free competition and concentrated political power in a few hands. Moreover, business, great and small, had lowered the character and quality of politics. Working with powerful bosses, business had won favors and privileges in return for its grants of money to corrupt political machines. Domination of the nation's affairs by political bosses and business organizations was now seen to be a threat to democracy itself.

What had happened, as a great many people saw it at the beginning of the Progressive era, was that in the extraordinary outburst of productive energy of the past few decades, the nation had not developed at the same time the means of meeting human needs or controlling or reforming the evils that come with any such rapid change. The Progressive movement, then, may be looked upon as an attempt to develop the moral will, the intellectual insight, and the political and administrative agencies to remedy the evils of a period of industrial growth. Since the Progressives did not believe in revolution, it was also an attempt to work out a strategy for orderly social change.

What were the main qualities of Progressivism? The name itself may be slightly misleading. Of course, the Progressives believed in progress. But so did a great many conservatives. The distinguishing thing about the Progressives was something else, which for lack of a better term might be called "activism." They argued that social evils will not remedy themselves, and that it is wrong to sit by without doing anything and wait for time to take care of them. As one writer put it, they did not believe that the future would take care of itself. They believed that the people of the country should be stimulated to work energetically to bring about social progress. Progressives believed in energy and governmental action.

If the people were sufficiently aroused, they would grab power away from city and state bosses and millionaire senators and take it back into their own hands. Having done so, they would use their regained power—through the city, state, or federal governments—to solve social and economic problems. Tenements would be gotten rid of. The labor of women and children would be forbidden. The Negro race would be supported in the struggle for its rights. High tariffs and monopoly prices would be regulated out of existence. Social legislation would protect the working classes from the terrible dangers of industry. Dangerous foods and falsely advertised drugs would be driven off the market. Unfair competition by the great corporations would be subject to constant government control. The concentration of business control in the hands of a few powerful banking interests would be broken up. Better credit would be provided for farmers and small business owners. The commercial exploitation of vice and drink would be reduced or eliminated.

The Progressive movement depended on the civic alertness and the aroused mood of a great part of the public. Such a mood cannot last forever. Perhaps what was most remarkable about the Progressives was their ability to maintain enthusiasm for reform as long as they did.

Despite the briefness of many of its achievements, the heritage of the Progressive movement cannot be considered small or unimportant. The Progressives developed for the first time on a large scale a type of realistic journalism and social criticism that has become a permanent quality of American thinking. They gave a new strength to a climate of opinion hostile to monopoly. They forced big business to operate carefully and even to exercise some self-restraint. The traditions of responsible government and forceful leadership of men like Theodore Roosevelt and Woodrow Wilson established unforgettable high points in American leadership. Finally, the reforms of the Progressive era established a basis for further reforms to be passed when the need for them was felt.

The men and women of the Progressive movement must be considered the pioneers of the welfare state. This was not because they sought to promote the growth of big government for its own sake. But they were determined to remedy the most pressing and dangerous social ills of industrial society. In the attempt they quickly learned that they could not achieve their aims without using the power of government. Moreover, they declared—and they were the first in our history to do so with real practical success—the idea that government cannot be seen only as a cold and negative policing agency. Instead it has a wide responsibility for the welfare of its citizens, and for the poor and powerless among them. For this, Progressivism must be understood as a major part in the history of the American conscience.

CHAPTER 10 ■ "THE BIG CHANGE" IN AMERICAN WAYS OF LIFE

THE ALL-POWERFUL TELEPHONE

Adapted from Your United States *by Arnold Bennett. Reprinted by permission of Mrs. Dorothy Cheston Bennett.*

In the early 1900's, many great changes took place in the United States. These changes were the result of new inventions and new methods of industrial production. One of the important inventions of this period was the telephone. In 1911 Arnold Bennett, an English writer, visited the United States. He was both fascinated and terrified by the widespread use of the telephone and he wrote the following selection about this "evil" invention. In fact, he became so interested in this new device that he took a tour of the New York City phone company to learn more about how the telephone system worked.

How do you think Bennett really feels about the telephone? Why does he use this "comic-horror" style of writing? What are his feelings about the telephone operators? To whom does he compare them?

What strikes and frightens the backward European as much as anything in the United States is the efficiency and fearful common use of the telephone. I think of the big cities as great heaps pierced everywhere by elevator shafts full of movement. I think of them too as being threaded, under pavements and over roofs and between floors and ceilings and walls, by millions upon millions of live threads that unite all the privacies of people—and destroy them in making them public! I do not mean that Europe has failed to adopt the telephone, nor that in Europe there are no hotels with the dreadful curse of an active telephone in every room. But I do mean that the European telephone is a toy, and a somewhat clumsy one, compared with the serious American telephone. Many otherwise highly civilized Europeans are shy when speaking into a telephone, as they would be in speaking to a king or queen. Average middle-class Europeans still speak of their telephone, if they have one, in the same falsely casual tone as Americans tend to speak of their motor-car. It is nothing—but somehow it comes into the conversation!

"How odd!" you exclaim. And you are right. It is we Europeans who are wrong, through no particular fault of our own.

The American is ruthlessly logical about the telephone. The only occasion on which I was in really serious danger of being taken for a madman in the United States was when, in a Chicago hotel, I permanently removed the receiver from the telephone in my room. The whole hotel was horrified. Half of Chicago shuddered. In response to a request from the management, I put the receiver back. On the horrified face of the manager I could read the unspoken question: "Is it possible that you have been in this country a month without understanding that the United States is primarily a vast collection of telephone booths?" Yes, I gave in and admired! And I predict that on my next visit I shall find a telephone on every table of every restaurant that respects itself.

It is the efficiency of the telephone that makes it irresistible to a great people whose passion is to "get results"—the speed with which the communication is given, and the clear loudness of the telephone's voice in reply to yours. These things are completely unknown in Europe. If I were to live in the United States, I too should become a victim of the telephone habit, as it is practiced in its most advanced form in suburban communities. There a person takes to the telephone as people in more decadent lands take to drugs. You can see them in the morning at their bedroom window, pouring confidences into their telephone, thus combining the joy of an innocent vice with the healthy freshness of breeze and sunshine.

Now it was obvious that behind the apparently simple outer aspects of any telephone system there must be a complex and marvelous secret organization. In Europe my curiosity would probably never have been excited by the thought of that organization. At home one accepts everything as a matter of course. But in the United States, partly because the telephone is so much more wonderful and terrible there, and partly because in a foreign land one often has whims, I wanted to see the mysteries hidden at the other end of all the wires. Thus, one day, I paid a visit to a telephone exchange in New York. There I saw what nine hundred and ninety-nine out of every thousand of the most eager telephone users seldom think about and will never see.

My first impression was a murmuring sound, as of hundreds of scholars in a school learning their lessons, and a row of young women seated on stools before a long machine of holes and pegs and pieces of elastic cord—all looking extremely serious. One saw at once that none of these young women had a single moment to spare. They were all involved in the tremendous machine, were part of it, keeping up with it and in it, and not daring to take their eyes off it for a moment. What they were saying it was impossible to guess. If one placed oneself close to any particular young woman, she seemed to utter no sound, but simply and without stopping, pegged and unpegged holes at random among the thousands of holes before her. She apparently did this in obedience to the signaling of tiny lights that continually went on and off.

We who had entered were ignored. We might have been ghosts, invisible and silent. Even the supervisors did not turn to look at us as they moved restlessly behind the stools. And yet somehow I could hear the delicate shoulders of all the young women saying, without speaking: "Here come these tyrants again, who have invented this exercise which nearly but not quite cracks our brains for us! They know exactly how much they can get out of us, and they get it. They are cleverer and more powerful than we are, and we have to give in to their discipline. But—" And afar off I could hear: "What are you going to wear tonight?" "Will you dine with me tonight?" "I want two seats." "Very well, thanks, and how is Mrs. . . . ?" "When can I see you tomorrow?" "I'll take your offer for those bonds." . . . And I could see the inside of endless offices and living rooms. But of course I could hear and see nothing really except the low, serious voices and quick movements of those completely absorbed young women on stools exactly alike.

I understood why the telephone service was so efficient. I understood not only from the conduct of the long row of young women, but from everything else I had seen in the precise and evilly clever arrangement of the whole establishment.

MAKING "THE BIRTH OF A NATION"

Adapted from Lillian Gish: The Movies, Mr. Griffith and Me *by Lillian Gish with Ann Pinchot. Reprinted by permission of the Lucy Kroll Agency.*

The first movies were made in the 1890's. Of course, they were nothing like the movies of today. First of all, they were silent—that is, there was no sound except for piano music played in the theater. And they were very short. The first movies lasted for only a few minutes, and by 1914 even the longest movie ran only about an hour.

Then in 1914, D. W. Griffith, the movies' first great director, made "The Birth of a Nation." It was the first large-scale spectacle movie, with a cast of thousands, and it ran for three hours! This movie had enormous impact —many thousands of Americans rushed to see it—and it showed what movies could be like. In this selection, Lillian Gish, one of the stars of "The Birth of a Nation," tells how the picture was made.

Do you agree with Lillian Gish that only the people who lived during a particular period in history know the truth about it? Do you think a movie can tell the truth about a historical event such as the Civil War? Why? How has movie-making changed since 1914?

One afternoon in the spring of 1914, Mr. Griffith took me aside on the set and said, "After the others leave tonight, would you please stay?" Later, as some of the company left, I realized that a similar message had been given to a few others. This method was typical of Mr. Griffith when he was planning a new film.

I suspected what the meeting was about. A few days before, we had been having lunch, and I had noticed that his pockets were filled with papers and pamphlets. My curiosity was aroused but it would have been rude of me to ask about them. With Mr. Griffith one did not ask; one only answered. Besides, I had learned that if I waited long enough he would tell me.

'I've bought a book by Thomas Dixon, called *The Clansman.* I'm going to use it to tell the truth about the War Between the States. It hasn't been told accurately in history books. Only the winning side in a war ever gets to tell its story." He paused, watching the group of actors. "The story concerns two families— the Stonemans from the North and the Camerons from the South." He added significantly, "I know I can trust you."

[Note: Although many of D. W. Griffith's films are shown today, this one is rarely seen. The major reason for this is that it showed the Ku Klux Klan in a favorable light and also showed racial prejudice against black Americans.]

He swore us to secrecy, and his caution was understandable to us. If his competitors should learn of his new project, they would have films on the subject completed before his was finished.

Mr. Griffith didn't need the Dixon book. His plan was to tell his version of the War Between the States. But he evidently lacked the confidence to start production on a twelve-reel film [one reel of film usually ran about 15 minutes] without an established book as a basis for his story. Mr. Griffith wanted to use Dixon's name on the film as author, for as he told me, "The public hates you if it thinks you wrote, directed, and produced the whole film yourself. It's the quickest way to make enemies."

After the first rehearsal, the pace increased. Mr. Griffith worked, as usual, without a script. But this time his pockets were filled with books, maps, and pamphlets, which he read during meals and the rare breaks in his busy schedule. At first I didn't pay much attention to Mr. Griffith's idea of the film. His claim that history books falsified actual happenings struck me as most strange. At that time I was too naive to think that history books would attempt to falsify anything. I've lived long enough now to know that the whole truth is never told in history texts. Only the people who lived through an era, who are the real participants in the drama as it happens, know the truth. The people of each generation, it seems to me, are the most accurate historians of their time.

Soon sets were going up. Costumes arrived. Mysterious boxes evidently filled with military equipment were delivered. As we gradually became aware of the importance of the new project, we grew even more anxious than usual about being assigned roles in the film. All the young players wanted to prove their worth before it was too late. This distress from young girls in their teens may seem strange today, but the photography of that time made us look so old that we believed that by the time we reached eighteen we would be playing character roles.

During the six years with Biograph [a film company], Mr. Griffith had taken steps toward his ultimate goal: filming his version of the Civil War. He had made a number of early pictures that touched on the War Between the States. But it was soon obvious to everyone that this film was to be his most important statement yet. Billy Bitzer [the photographer] wrote of that time: " 'The Birth of a Nation' changed D. W. Griffith's personality entirely. Before, when he started a new picture he would talk about 'grinding out another sausage' and go at it lightly. But his attitude in beginning this one was all eagerness. He acted as if here we had something worthwhile."

Although fact and legend were familiar to Mr. Griffith, he did careful research for "The Birth." The first half of "The Birth," about the war itself, showed his own point of view. I know that he also depended greatly on a number of books. For the second half, about Reconstruction, he consulted Thomas Dixon, and *A History of the American People* by Woodrow Wilson. He also constantly consulted Mathew Brady's photographs [a book of photographs taken during the war by the famous photographer].

As always, sunlight controlled the shooting schedule. Preparations began at five or six in the morning. The actors rose at five o'clock in order to be ready at seven, when it was bright enough for filming. Important scenes were played in the harsh noon sun. I remember that we used to beg to have our closeups taken just after dawn or before sunset, as the soft yellow glow was easier to work in and much more flattering.

The entire staff came on the set to watch us, particularly the men from the laboratory, so that they would know the effects that Mr. Griffith was seeking. This was of great importance, for each scene was shot only once. The only scene that was taken twice was the one in which Mae Marsh as the Little Sister leaps to her death from a cliff.

In those days there was no one to keep track of what an actor was wearing from scene to scene. He was obliged to remember for himself what he had worn and how his hair and makeup had looked in a previous scene. If he forgot, he was not used again. When the death scene was filmed, Mae forgot to tie the Confederate flag, which she'd been wearing in the previous scene, around her waist. That's why the scene had to be retaken. How we all envied her a second chance in a big moment!

In filming the battles, Mr. Griffith organized the action like a general. He stood at the top of a forty-foot tower, the commander-in-chief of both armies, his powerful voice thundering commands through a megaphone to his staff of assistants. Some of the artillery was loaded with real shells, and elaborate warnings were broadcast about their range of fire. Mr. Griffith's sense of order and control made it possible for the cast and extras to survive the broiling heat, pounding hoofs, naked bayonets, and exploding shells without a single injury. He was too thoughtful of the welfare of others to permit accidents. In most war films it is difficult to distinguish between the enemies unless the film is in color and the two sides are wearing different-colored uniforms. But not in a Griffith movie. Mr. Griffith had the rare technical skill to keep each side distinct and clear-cut. In "The Birth," the Confederate army always entered from the left of the camera, the Union army from the right.

The entire industry, always intensely curious about Mr. Griffith, was wondering about this film. What was that crazy man Griffith up to? He was using all of his earlier experiments and adding new ones. He tinted film to achieve dramatic results and to create mood. In the battle scene at Petersburg, the shots of Union and Confederate troops rushing in to replace the dead and wounded are tinted red, and the subtitle reads "In the red lane of death others take their places." At the climax of the film there were the thrilling rides of the Klan. Before the filming of this scene, Mr. Griffith decided to try a new kind of shot. He had a hole dug in the road directly in the path of the horsemen. There he placed Billy and the camera, so that he could get shots of the horses approaching and galloping right overhead, and the audience would see their pounding hoofs. This shot has since become standard, but that was the first time it had been done, and the effect was spectacular.

I saw everything that Mr. Griffith put on film. My role in "The Birth" required about three weeks' work, but I was on call during the whole time that it was being filmed. My dressing room was just across the hall from the darkroom, where the technicians worked. Whenever I had a few minutes I would join them, watching them develop the film and cut it. I could view the day's rushes and give my reactions to them. Watching these pieces of film was like trying to read a book whose pages had been mixed up. There was neither order nor continuity. Here was a touching bit from a scene with Mae; there was a long shot of a battle. It made me realize the job that Mr. Griffith had ahead of him after the filming was done.

The shooting was completed in nine weeks, but Mr. Griffith spent more than three months on cutting, editing, and working on the musical score. I still remember how hard he worked on other films during the day and then at night on "The Birth." Of all his pictures up to that time, none was more filled with difficulties. Without his spirit and faith, it might never have been completed.

FORD DESCRIBES THE FIRST ASSEMBLY LINE

Adapted from My Life and Work *by Henry Ford in collaboration with Samuel Crowther. Reprinted by permission of The Seabury Memorial Home.*

American business and industry continued to expand rapidly during the early years of the 1900's. One of the most far-reaching developments in industry before America's entry into World War I was the introduction of the modern assembly line, pioneered by Henry Ford in the production of automobiles. In this selection, Ford describes how the idea for the assembly line came about.

Do you think that you, as a worker, would have shared Ford's enthusiasm for this new production method? What were some of its advantages? Some of its disadvantages?

A Ford car contains about 5,000 parts, counting screws, nuts, and everything. Some parts are fairly large, and others are hardly larger than watch parts. In our first assembling, we simply started to put a car together at a certain spot on the floor. Workers brought to it the parts as they were needed in exactly the same way that one builds a house.

When we started to make parts, it was natural to create a single department of the factory to make each one. Usually one worker performed all of the operations necessary on a small part. But the rapid speedup of production made it necessary to work out some plans of production so that workers would not be falling over one another.

The first step forward in assembly came when we began taking the work to the workers instead of the workers to the work. We now have two general principles in all operations— that a worker should never have to take more than one step, if it can possibly be avoided, and that no worker need ever bend over.

The principles of assembly are these:

1. Place the tools and the workers in the sequence of the operation so that each part used in making the automobile will travel the least possible distance while in the process of finishing.

2. Use work slides or some other form of carrier so that when a worker completes his operation he drops the part always in the same place. That place should always be the most convenient to his hand. And if possible have gravity carry the part to the next worker for his operation.

3. Use moving assembling lines by which the parts to be assembled are delivered at convenient distances.

The result of the application of these principles is the reduction of the necessity for thought on the part of the workers and the reduction of their movements to a minimum. They do as nearly as possible only one thing with only one movement.

Along about April 1, 1913, we first tried the experiment of an assembly line on a small generator. We try everything in a small way at first. We will rip out anything once we discover a better way, but we have to know absolutely that the new way is going to be better than the old before we do anything drastic.

I believe that this was the first moving line ever installed. The idea came in a general way from the overhead cable that the Chicago packers use in cutting up beef. We had previously assembled the generator in the usual way. With one worker doing a complete job, he could turn out from thirty-five to forty pieces in a nine-

hour day, or about twenty minutes for each assembly. What he did alone was then divided into twenty-nine operations. On an assembly line, that cut down the time for each assembly to thirteen minutes, ten seconds. Then we raised the height of the line eight inches [20 centimeters]—this was in 1914—and cut the time to seven minutes. Further experimenting with the speed cut the time down to five minutes.

In short, the result is this: with the aid of scientific study one worker is now able to do somewhat more than what four workers did only a few years ago. That line established the efficiency of the method and we now use it everywhere. The assembling of the motor, formerly done by one person, is now divided into eighty-four operations—those workers do the work that three times their number used to do.

WHY A MINIMUM WAGE?

Adapted from My Life and Work *by Henry Ford in collaboration with Samuel Crowther. Reprinted by permission of The Seabury Memorial Home.*

Henry Ford also brought great changes in the field of labor relations. In 1914 the Ford Motor Company astonished the business world by voluntarily reducing the weekly hours of work and providing a minimum daily wage of $5 for each of its workers. The $5-a-day wage was nearly double what Ford and other automobile companies had been paying. In the following selection Ford explains the philosophy behind this policy.

According to Ford, what is the relationship between a business and its employees? On what basis should wages be determined? Why, in Ford's view, did his company establish its minimum wage?

What good is industry if it is so unskillfully managed that it does not return a living to everyone concerned? No question is more important than that of wages—most of the people of the country live on wages. The scale of their living —the rate of their wages—determines the prosperity of the country.

It is not usual to speak of employees as partners, and yet what else are they? Whenever people find the management of a business too much for their own time or strength, they call in assistants to share the management with them. Why, then, if people find the production part of a business too much for their own hands, should they deny the title of "partner" to those who come in and help them produce? Every business that employs more than one person is a kind of partnership. The moment a person calls for assistance in business—even though the assistant be but a child—that moment the person has taken a partner.

No person is independent as long as he or she has to depend on another's help. It is a mutual relation. The boss is the partner of the worker; the worker is partner of the boss. It is useless for one group or the other to think that it is the one necessary unit. Both are necessary. They are partners. When they pull and push against each other, they simply hurt the organization in which they are partners and from which both draw support.

It ought to be the employer's ambition, as leader, to pay better wages than any similar line of business, and it ought to be the workers' ambition to make this possible. Of course, there are workers in all factories who seem to believe that if they do their best, it will be only for the employer's benefit—and not at all for their own. It is a pity that such a feeling should exist. But it does exist and perhaps it has some justification. If an employer encourages workers to do their best, and the workers learn after a while that their best does not bring any reward, then they naturally drop back into "getting by." But if they see the profit of hard work in their pay envelope—proof that harder work means higher pay—then they also begin to learn that they are a part of the business, and that its success depends on them and their success depends on it.

"What ought the employer to pay?" "What ought the employee to receive?" These are minor questions. The basic question is, "What can the business stand?" Certainly no business can stand to pay out more than it makes. When you pump water out of a well at a faster rate than the water flows in, the well goes dry.

Employers can gain nothing by looking over the employees and asking themselves, "How little can I get them to take?" Nor can employees gain much by glaring back and asking, "How much can I force them to give?" In time, both will have to turn to the business and ask, "How can this industry be made safe and profitable, so that it will be able to provide a sure and comfortable living for all of us?"

It ought to be clear that the high wage begins down in the factory. If it is not created there, it cannot get into pay envelopes. There will never be a system invented which will do away with the necessity of work. Nature has seen to that. Idle hands and minds were never intended for any one of us. Work is our sanity, our self-respect, our salvation. So far from being a curse, work is the greatest blessing. True social justice flows only out of honest work. The worker who contributes much should take away much. Therefore no element of charity is present in the paying of wages.

The kind of workers who give the business the best that is in them are the best kind of workers a business can have. And they cannot be expected to do this indefinitely without proper recognition of their contribution. People who come to the day's job feeling that no matter how much they may give, it will not give them enough of a return to keep them from being poor are not in shape to do a day's work. But if people feel that their day's work is not only supplying basic needs, but is also giving them a margin of comfort and making them able to give their families opportunities and pleasure, then their job looks good to them and they are free to give it their best.

I have learned through the years a good deal about wages. I believe in the first place that, all other consideration aside, our own sales depend in a measure upon the wages we pay. If we can distribute high wages, then that money is going to be spent. It will serve to make storekeepers and distributors and manufacturers and workers in other lines more prosperous. Their prosperity will show up in our sales.

We announced and put into operation in January 1914, a kind of profit-sharing plan. The minimum wage for any class of work and under certain conditions was $5 a day. At the same time we reduced the working day to eight hours —it had been nine—and the week to forty-eight hours. This was entirely a voluntary act. It was to our way of thinking an act of social justice, and in the last analysis we did it for our own satisfaction. There is a pleasure in feeling that you have made others happy—that you have lessened in some degree the burdens of other people—that you have provided something out of which may be had pleasure and saving. Good will is one of the few really important assets of life. Determined people can win almost anything they go after, but unless they gain good will, they have not profited much.

UNIT FOUR
BECOMING A WORLD POWER
(1898-1920)

CHAPTER 11 ■ AMERICAN EXPANSION OVERSEAS

AMERICA'S "ANGLO-SAXON" MISSION

Adapted from Josiah Strong, Our Country: Its Possible Future and Its Present Crisis. *New York: Baker & Taylor for the American Home Missionary Society, 1885.*

A great change took place in American foreign policy in the late 1800's. The nation's traditional isolationist policy was replaced by a policy of expansionism. During these years a number of writers developed arguments in favor of American expansion overseas as well as in the Western Hemisphere. One of the most influential of these writers was Josiah Strong, a Congregational minister. His arguments in favor of American expansion were based, however, on two false beliefs. One was the concept of an Anglo-Saxon "race," which to Americans meant the people of Great Britain and their descendants. The other belief, called social Darwinism, applied the theories of scientist Charles Darwin—especially the theory of the "survival of the fittest"—to peoples and nations. Many Americans misused Darwin's theories to claim that the earth should belong to the energetic, the strong, and the fit—that is, to the American people.

How do Anglo-Saxons represent the two "great ideas" that Strong describes as the basis of civilization? Why does he predict that Americans will "Anglo-Saxonize" the human race? Did Strong's prediction come true?

Every race which has deeply impressed itself on the human family has been the representative of some great idea—one or more—which has given direction to the nation's life and form to its civilization. The Anglo-Saxon is the representative of two great ideas, which are closely related. One of them is that of civil liberty. Nearly all of the civil liberty in the world is enjoyed by Anglo-Saxons: the English, the British colonists, and the people of the United States. Some peoples, such as the Swiss, are allowed by their neighbors to maintain it. Others, such as the French, have experimented with it. But, in modern times, the peoples whose love of liberty has won it, and whose genius for self-government has preserved it, have been Anglo-Saxons.

The other great idea represented by the Anglo-Saxon is that of a pure, spiritual Christianity.

It is not necessary to argue that the two great needs of human beings are, first, civil liberty, and second, a pure, spiritual Christianity. These are the forces which, in the past, have contributed most to advancing the human race. They must continue to be, in the future, the most efficient aids to its progress. It follows, then, that Anglo-Saxons, as the great representative of these two ideas, have a special relationship to the world's future. They are divinely commissioned to be, in a sense, their brother's keeper.

Another important fact is the Anglo-Saxon's rapidly increasing strength in modern times. In 1700 this race numbered less than 6 million persons. In 1800, Anglo-Saxons (I use the term somewhat broadly to include all English-speaking peoples) had increased to about 20 million. In 1880 they numbered nearly 100 million, having increased almost five times over in 80 years.

In 100 years the United States has increased the size of its territory ten times. There can be no reasonable doubt that North America is to be the great home of the Anglo-Saxons, the principal seat of their power, the center of their life and influence. Our continent has room and resources and climate, it lies in the pathway of the nations, and it belongs to the zone of power. Already, among Anglo-Saxons, we lead in population and wealth.

Moreover, our social institutions are stimulating. In Europe the various classes of society are, like the layers of the earth, fixed and rigid. There can be no great change without a terrible upheaval, a social earthquake. Here, society is like the waters of the sea, constantly moving. All people are free to become whatever they can make of themselves. They are free to transform themselves from rail-splitters or tanners into the nation's President. Our aristocracy, unlike that of Europe, is open to all comers. Wealth, position, influence, are prizes offered for energy. Every farmer's child, every apprentice and clerk, every friendless and penniless immigrant, is free to enter the contest. Thus many causes combine to produce here the most forceful and tremendous energy in the world.

What is the significance of such facts? It seems to me that God, with great wisdom and skill, is training the Anglo-Saxon race for an hour sure to come in the world's future. Up until now in the history of the world there has always been unoccupied land westward. Into this the crowded countries of the East have poured their surplus populations. But there are no more new worlds. The unoccupied farmlands of the earth are limited, and will soon be taken.

The time is coming when the pressure of population on the means of subsistence will be felt here as it is now felt in Europe and Asia. Then the world will enter upon a new stage of its history—the final competition of races. The Anglo-Saxon is being trained for this. Long before our numbers reach a billion, the expansionist tendency inherited by this race, and strengthened in the United States, will assert itself. Then this race of unequaled energy, with all its numbers and the might of wealth behind it—the representative of liberty and Christianity—having developed aggressive traits to force its institutions upon all people will spread itself over the earth. If I predict correctly, this powerful race will move down upon Mexico, down upon Central and South America, out upon the islands of the sea, over upon Africa, and beyond. And can anyone doubt that the result of this competition of races will be the "survival of the fittest"?

Is there room for reasonable doubt? This race, unless weakened by alcohol and tobacco, is destined to drive out many weaker races, absorb others, and mold the remainder, until, in a very true and important sense, it has Anglo-Saxonized humankind.

AN AMERICAN SOLDIER LOOKS BACK

Adapted from a letter of Jacob Judson, Illinois National Guard, April 15, 1956; now in the Manuscript Collection of the Chicago Historical Society. Reprinted by permission of the Chicago Historical Society.

Americans entered the Spanish-American War in 1898 with great enthusiasm. But the Americans were almost as unprepared for war as the Spaniards. American soldiers were sent off to war without proper equipment. In a climate where temperatures often were above 100 degrees Fahrenheit [38° Celsius], American forces were issued heavy woolen uniforms. Their weapons were outdated Springfield rifles that were almost useless, and their food supplies often consisted of spoiled canned meat. Diseases such as malaria, typhoid, dysentery, and yellow fever were widespread.

Of the 5,400 men who died in the war, over 5,000 died from disease. Only 400 lost their lives in battle. Jacob Judson, an Illinois militia officer who received his training for combat near Tampa, Florida, wrote this account of the war some fifty years later.

From Judson's account, what hardships could have been prevented? What is Judson's attitude toward his experiences? Do you think that his description is accurate? Explain.

We of the Spanish War who are still living can look back on our war experience, and can thank our Heavenly Father for being alive today. It's remarkable what our bodies can stand, when I think back on our Picnic Island days in Tampa, Florida—untrained men in a heavy rain, a fierce storm blowing our tents out into the sea, no protection, our clothing soaked to the skin. At sea they gave us canned corned beef that stunk so we had to throw it overboard. Then our landing at Sebony in Cuba, camping at the foot of a hill, with large land crabs crawling over us at night. After that our long march toward San Juan Hill through jungles and swamps, joining up with Rough Riders on Kettle Hill, heavy rains pouring down, no tents for cover, every man for himself, standing in trenches in a foot of water and mud, day and night. When off duty, we massaged our feet to get them back in shape. When the sun came out, our boys would help each other by wringing out wet clothes and blankets, quickly cutting down branches from trees, and constructing an overhead protection by laying on palm leaves. Abel Davis and I found a spot under a tree not far from Teddy Roosevelt's tent.

For lack of proper food men grew weak. Our food ration consisted of a slice of salt pork, hardtack, and some grains of coffee that we had to crack between stones or rocks. Then came the issue of wool-lined underwear in a tropical climate, and orders to burn the underwear we brought from home. After that, you would see the boys in the river streams, their backs covered with boils. Wool-lined underwear and salt pork do not go in a tropical climate.

Then came malaria. It was my duty in the mornings to take our sick boys to the division hospital. There were no doctors in attendance, just a hospital corps sergeant who issued pills out of one bottle for all sicknesses. Sick men lay on cots, their mouths, ears, and noses full of flies. I would go over to these poor boys and with my finger clear their mouths of flies —not so much as a piece of paper to cover their faces. Other boys lay day and night on the edge of the sinks; because of malaria they had no control of their bowels. Morning sick detail would come along and take away any that had died. Their bodies would be buried on a hillside. If heavy rains washed away the soil, a second burial was necessary.

I was one of the fortunate boys. It had been my privilege to train Abel Davis when he joined up with the First. We were very close pals. Abel Davis had a brother who was a doctor in Chicago. This doctor gave Abel a box containing medicines for malaria and other tropical sicknesses, so when I came down with malaria Abel took care of me. There were very few doctors; most of them were down with malaria themselves. Abel pulled me through. Then he came down with the malaria himself, and I used his medicines until he got better. If it was not for that box of medicines, I think both Abel's bones and mine would lie in Cuban hills today.

Colonel Teddy Roosevelt said "The Spanish War was but a drop in the bucket as compared with the war following." This statement was no doubt true. The next war had troops spread all over Europe. But the soldier [in World War I] had full modern equipment, proper clothes, healthy, nourishing food, and the very best medical care, none of which was given the Spanish War soldier.

When the war ended and we landed at Montauk, Long Island, our boys were thin, underweight, and yellow as lemons. It took us years to recover. So I say: Let us thank God for taking care of us all these years.

IN DEFENSE OF IMPERIALISM

Adapted from Modern Eloquence, *Vol. 10, by Albert J. Beveridge, edited by Ashley H. Thorndike. Reprinted by permission of Mrs. George W. Hibbitt and Mrs. Ashley Thorndike.*

The success of the United States in the Spanish-American War led some Americans to dream of a colonial empire. Leading the enthusiasm for overseas possessions was Albert J. Beveridge, a young lawyer from Indiana. In the following speech, delivered in 1898 during his campaign for the Senate, he made a strong appeal for action. After his election, he continued to favor and encourage a policy of expansionism.

What are Beveridge's arguments in favor of expansion? How does he support his case by appeals to his listeners' pride? To their feelings of competition? To their sense of duty?

It is a noble land that God has given us—a land that can feed and clothe the world; a land set like a guard between the two oceans of the globe. It is a mighty people that God has planted on this soil. It is a people descended from the most masterful blood of history and constantly strengthened by the strong working folk of all the earth. It is a people imperial by virtue of their power, by right of their institutions, by authority of their heaven-directed purposes.

It is a glorious history our God has given His chosen people. Its keynote was struck by the Liberty Bell, and is heroic with faith in our mission and our future. It is a history of leaders who expanded the boundaries of the republic into unexplored lands and savage wildernesses.

It is a history of soldiers who carried the flag across blazing deserts and through hostile mountains. It is a history of a multiplying people who overran a continent in half a century. It is a history of prophets who saw the consequences of evils inherited from the past, and of martyrs who died to save us from them.

Therefore, in this campaign, the question is larger than a party question. It is an American question. It is a world question. Shall the American people continue their restless march toward the commercial supremacy of the world? Shall free institutions extend their blessed reign until the empire of our principles is established over the hearts of all humankind?

Have we no mission to perform, no duty to discharge to our fellow humans? Has the Almighty Father given us gifts and marked us with His favor, only to rot in our own selfishness? This happens to people and nations who are cowardly and self-absorbed—China, India, and Egypt.

Shall we be as the man who had one piece of gold and hid it, or as he who had ten pieces of gold and used them until they grew to riches? And shall we gather the reward for carrying out our high duty as the sovereign power of earth? Shall we occupy new markets for what our farmers raise, new markets for what our factories make, new markets for what our merchants sell? Shall we take advantage of new sources of supply for what we do not raise or make, so that what are luxuries today will be necessities tomorrow? Shall our commerce be encouraged until American trade is the imperial trade of the entire globe?

The opposition tells us that we ought not to govern a people without their consent. I answer: The rule of liberty, that all just government takes its authority from the consent of the governed, applies only to those who are capable of self-government. I answer: We govern the Indians without their consent, we govern our territories without their consent, we govern our children without their consent. I answer: How do you assume that our government would be without their consent? Would not the people of the Philippines prefer the just, humane, civilizing government of this republic to the savage, bloody rule of plundering from which we have rescued them?

Shall we turn these people back to the bloody hands from which we have taken them? Shall we abandon them to their fate, with the wolves of conquest all about them—with Germany, Russia, France, even Japan, hungering for them? Shall we save them from those nations, to give them a self-rule of tragedy? It would be like giving a razor to a baby and telling it to shave itself.

They ask us how we will govern these new possessions. I answer: Out of local conditions and necessity. If England can govern foreign lands, so can America. If Germany can govern foreign lands, so can America. If those nations can supervise protectorates, so can America. Why is it more difficult to govern Hawaii than New Mexico or California? Both had a foreign population. Both were more distant from the seat of government when they came under our control than Hawaii is today.

Will you say by your vote that American ability to govern has decayed, that a century's experience in self-rule has failed? Will you show by your vote that you do not believe in American vigor and power and practical sense? Or will you say that we are of the ruling race of the world—that ours is the blood of government, the heart of authority, the brain and genius of administration? Will you remember that we do only what our fathers did—we simply pitch the tents of liberty farther westward, farther southward. We only continue the march of the flag.

There are so many real things to be done— canals to be dug, railways to be laid, forests to be felled, cities to be built, fields to be tilled, priceless markets to be won, ships to be launched, peoples to be saved, civilization to be proclaimed, and the flag of liberty flung to the eager air of every sea.

We cannot escape our world duties. We must carry out the purpose of a fate that has driven us to be greater than our small intentions. We cannot retreat from any soil where Providence has placed our flag. It is up to us to save that soil for liberty and civilization. For liberty and civilization and God's promise fulfilled, the flag must from now on be the symbol to all humankind.

A CRITICISM OF IMPERIALISM

Adapted from Frederick Bancroft, ed., Speeches, Correspondence and Political Papers of Carl Schurz, *Vol. 6. New York: G. P. Putnam's Sons, 1913.*

Not all Americans favored the United States' new policy of overseas expansion. Many well-known Americans spoke out against expansionism. After the Spanish-American War, Carl Schurz, a liberal reformer, became a leading opponent of American expansion. Schurz, who had originally come to the United States from Germany, had been a lawyer, an abolitionist, a Senator from Missouri, and Secretary of Interior in President Hayes' cabinet.

Schurz was especially opposed to the American annexation of the Philippines. The following are selections from a speech he gave on the subject in 1899. According to Schurz, how did earlier American territorial gains differ from those of the 1890's? How does Schurz regard the effort to "Americanize" foreign peoples? Do you think he is more concerned about the effects of expansion on people in the territories or their effects on Americans?

According to the solemn proclamation of our government, the Spanish-American War was undertaken only for the liberation of Cuba, as a war of humanity and not of conquest. But our easy victories put conquest within our reach. When our troops took over foreign territory, a loud demand arose that, pledge or no pledge, the conquests should be kept, including even the Philippines on the other side of the globe.

Why not? was the cry. Has not the career of the Republic almost from its very beginning been one of territorial expansion? Has it not acquired Louisiana, Florida, Texas, the vast areas that came to us through the Mexican War, and Alaska? Has it not digested them well? Were not those acquisitions much larger than those now thought of? If the Republic could digest the old, why not the new? What is the difference?

Look with a clear eye, and you will soon discover differences that should warn you to look out. There are five of great importance.

1. All the former acquisitions were on this continent and, except for Alaska, on our borders.

2. They were located not in the tropical but in the temperate zone, where democratic institutions do well, and where our people could move in great numbers.

3. They were very thinly settled—in fact, without any population that would have been in the way of new settlements.

4. They could be organized as territories in the usual manner. It was expected that they would presently come into the Union as self-governing states with populations much like our own.

5. They did not require an increase in our army and navy, either to subject them to our rule or to protect them from foreign attack.

Compare now our old acquisitions on all these important points with the ones now under discussion.

They are not continental, not bordering our present land, but are overseas—the Philippines are many thousand miles distant from our coast. They are all located in the tropics, where people of the Northern races, such as Anglo-Saxons, have never moved in large numbers. They are more or less densely populated, parts of them as densely as Massachusetts. Their populations consist almost exclusively of races to whom the tropical climate is well suited—Spanish mixed with Negroes in the West Indies, and Malays, Tagals, Filipinos, Chinese, Japanese, Negritos, and various more or less barbarous tribes in the Philippines.

The question is asked whether we may hope to adapt those countries and populations to our system of government. At this, those who favor annexation answer cheerily that when they belong to us, we shall soon "Americanize" them. This seems to mean that Americans in sufficiently large numbers will move there to change the character of the people until they are more like us.

This is a false belief. If we go honestly about it, we may indeed accomplish several helpful things in those countries. But one thing we cannot do. We cannot strip the tropical climate of those qualities which have kept people of the Northern races, to which we belong, from moving and settling there in large numbers. It is true that you will find in towns of tropical regions a few persons of Anglo-Saxon or of other Northern origin—merchants, railroad builders, speculators, professional people, and mechanics. But their number is small, and most of them expect to go home as soon as they make some money.

The scheme of Americanizing our "new possessions" in that way is therefore absolutely hopeless. The forces of nature are against it. Whatever we may do for their improvement, the people of the Spanish islands will outnumber us. The vast majority are completely alien to us, not only in origin and language, but in habits, traditions, ways of thinking, principles, ambitions—in short, in most things that are of the greatest importance in human and political cooperation.

What, then, shall we do with such peoples? Shall we organize those countries as territories with a view to their eventual admission as states?

If they become states on an equal footing with the other states, they not only will govern themselves, but will take part in governing the whole Republic. They will share in governing us, by sending Senators and Representatives into our Congress to help make our laws, and by voting for President and Vice-President. The prospect of such consequences is so alarming that you may well pause before taking the step.

But this may be avoided, it is said, by governing the new possessions as mere dependencies, or subject provinces. This would be a most serious departure from the rule that governed our former acquisitions. It is useless to speak of the District of Columbia and Alaska as proof that we have done such things before and can do them again. Every honest person will at once admit the great difference between those cases and the permanent establishment of arbitrary government over large territories with millions of inhabitants. The question is not only whether we can do such things, but whether having the public good at heart, we *should* do them.

If we do adopt such a system then we shall, for the first time since the abolition of slavery, again have two kinds of Americans. There will be Americans of the first class, who enjoy the privilege of taking part in the government in accordance with our Constitutional principles. And there will be Americans of the second class, who are to be ruled by the Americans of the first class.

This will be a difference no better—rather somewhat worse—than that which existed 125 years ago between English people of the first class and English people of the second class. The first were represented by King George and the British Parliament. The second group consisted of the American colonists. This difference led to the American Declaration of Independence—a document which, I regret to say, seems to have lost much of its charms among some of our citizens. Its basic principle was that "governments derive their just powers from the consent of the governed."

We are now told that we have never fully lived up to that principle. Therefore, we may now throw it aside altogether. But I say to you that, if we are true believers in democratic government, we should move in that direction and not away from it. If you tell me that we cannot govern the people of those new possessions in accordance with that principle, then I answer that this is a reason we should not attempt to govern them at all.

If we do, we shall change the government of the people, for the people, and by the people into a government of one part of the people, the strong, over another part, the weak. Abandoning such a basic principle may at first seem to involve only distant lands, but it can hardly fail to affect democratic government at home. And I warn the American people that a democracy cannot deny its faith in a vital principle—it cannot long play the role of king over subject populations without creating in itself ways of thinking and habits of action most dangerous to its own vitality.

THE WHITE MAN'S BURDENS, PRO AND CON

First poem from Rudyard Kipling, "The White Man's Burden," 1899.

Second, third, and fourth poems adapted from Little Brown Brother *by Leon Wolff, by permission of Barthold Fles, Literary Agent.*

In 1899 Rudyard Kipling, a British writer, wrote a poem called "The White Man's Burden." The poem, written and published in the United States, immediately became a popular defense of expansionism and imperialism. Kipling wrote that the "white man's burden," or responsibility, was to take up the task of governing what Kipling described as childlike and untamed people. He argued that it was the duty of more advanced nations to bring civilization to the backward peoples of the earth.

The poem was imitated and made fun of by many Americans, especially those who were against expansion in the Philippines. The first stanza of Kipling's seven-stanza poem appears here. Following it are poems which are imitations of and answers to his poem.

What is Kipling's attitude toward conquered peoples? What is the point of the first poem that imitates the Kipling poem? Of the second? Of the last, four-line poem?

Take up the White Man's burden—
    Send forth the best ye breed—
Go bind your sons to exile
    To serve your captives' need;
To wait in heavy harness,
    On fluttered folk and wild—
Your new-caught, sullen peoples,
    Half-devil and half-child.

*   *   *   *

Pile on the brown man's burden
  To gratify your greed;
Go, clear away the Negroes
  Who progress would impede;
Be very stern, for truly
  'Tis useless to be mild
With new-caught sullen peoples,
  Half devil and half child.

Pile on the brown man's burden,
  And if ye rouse his hate,
Meet his old-fashioned reasons
    With Maxims [a Maxim gun was a kind of
      machine gun] up-to-date;
With shells and dum-dum bullets [bullets made
    to expand on impact and thus create a
    large wound],
  A hundred times make plain
The brown man's loss must ever
  Imply the white man's gain.

*   *   *   *

Take up the sword and rifle,
  Send forth your ships with speed,
To join the nations' scramble,
  And vie with them in greed;
Go find your goods a market;
  Beyond the western flood,
The heathen who withstand you
  Shall answer it in blood.

Take up the sword and rifle,
  Still keep your conscience whole—
So soon is found an unction [remedy]
  To soothe a guilty soul.
Go with it to your Maker,
  Find what excuse ye can—
Rob for the sake of justice,
  Kill for the love of man.

*   *   *   *

We've taken up the white man's burden
  Of ebony and brown;
Now will you tell us, Rudyard,
  How we may put it down?

FROM THE HAWAIIAN VIEWPOINT

Adapted from Hawaii's Story by Hawaii's Queen *by Liliuokalani, published by Charles E. Tuttle Co., Inc.*

By the late 1800's Americans owned most of the sugar plantations in Hawaii and had obtained a treaty that allowed Hawaiian sugar to enter the United States duty free. However, the McKinley Tariff Act of 1890 threatened the Hawaiian sugar planters by allowing all foreign sugar to enter the United States duty free and by giving a two-cent per pound subsidy to American sugar producers. Shortly afterward the planters asked that Hawaii be annexed by the United States, believing this was the only way to save their sugar industry.

Queen Liliuokalani, who was supported by the Hawaiian people, opposed annexation. And in 1893, because of her efforts against them, the planters and other Americans in Hawaii revolted against her rule and set up their own government. In this selection, the queen tells what happened in Hawaii during the years before the islands were annexed.

Why did the Hawaiians allow Americans to take over their government? For what actions does Queen Liliuokalani criticize the Americans?

It has been said that the Hawaiian people under the rule of the chiefs were harshly ruled. Under the monarchy, it was held, their condition greatly improved, but the native government in any form finally became intolerable to the better informed part of the community. I shall not examine such statements in detail. But I do feel called upon to make a few remarks from my own—that is to say, the native Hawaiian—viewpoint.

I shall not claim that in the days of Captain Cook our people were civilized. I shall not claim anything more for their progress in civilization and Christian morality than missionary writers have. Perhaps I may safely claim even less, admitting the criticism of some intelligent visitors who were not missionaries. In other words, the habits and prejudices of New England Puritanism were not well adapted to a tropical people, and could not be thoroughly absorbed by them.

But they have accepted Christianity in substance. I know of no people who have developed a tenderer Christian conscience, or who have shown themselves more ready to obey its commands. And where else in the world's history have savage people, pagan for ages, with fixed customs and beliefs, made equal progress in civilization and Christianity in the same amount of time?

Does it say nothing for us that we have always recognized our Christian teachers as worthy of authority in our councils? That while four fifths of the population of our islands were killed by diseases introduced by foreigners, the ruling class held on to Christian morality, and gave its strong support and service to the work of saving and civilizing the masses? Has not this class loyally held on to the brotherly alliance made with the better group of foreign settlers, giving freely of its authority and its substance, its sons and daughters, to cement and prosper it?

Why should it be thought strange that education and knowledge of the world have made us able to see that as a race we have some special mental and physical requirements not shared by other races? That certain habits and ways of living are better for our health and happiness than others? And that a separate nationality and a particular form of government, as well as special laws, are, at least for the present, best for us? These things were ours until the pitiless and tireless "annexation policy" was effectively backed by the naval power of the United States.

Before this we had allowed foreigners to give us a constitution and control the offices of government. Not without protest, indeed, for this grabbing of power caused us much humiliation and distress. But we did not resist it by force. It had not entered our hearts to believe that these friends and allies from the United States would ever go so far as to overthrow our form of government, grab our nation by the throat, and turn it over to a foreign power.

Perhaps there is a kind of right, known as the "Right of Conquest," under which robbers may take whatever they are strong enough to grab from others. I will not pretend to decide how far civilization and Christian teachings have outlawed this right.

If we have been friendly to those who sought our ruin, it was because they were Americans, like those whom we believed to be our dearest friends and allies. If we did not resist their final outrage by force, it was because we could not do so without striking at the military might of the United States. The conspirators, having actually gained possession of the government, refused to give up their conquest. So it happens that the people of the islands have no voice in determining their future, but are in a condition like that of the American Indians.

It is not for me to consider this matter from the American point of view. The current question of annexation, however, involves a departure from the established policy of that country and a dangerous change in its foreign relations. I am able to say, with absolute authority, that the native people of Hawaii are entirely loyal to their own chiefs, and are deeply attached to their own customs and government. They either do not understand, or bitterly oppose, the scheme of annexation.

Perhaps I may say here a final word about the Americans who favor this annexation of Hawaii. I observe that it is pretty much a party matter, favored chiefly by Republican leaders and politicians. But is it really a matter of party interest? Is the American Republic to decline and become a colonizer and a land-grabber? And is this prospect acceptable to a people who depend upon self-government for their liberties? There is little question but that the United States could become a successful rival of the European nations in the race for conquest and could create a great military and naval power if such is its ambition. But is such an ambition praiseworthy? Is such a departure from established principles patriotic or wise?

CHAPTER 12 ■ AMERICAN EXPANSION IN THE CARIBBEAN

MR. DOOLEY TALKS ABOUT THE SUPREME COURT

Adapted from Mr. Dooley at His Best *by Finley Peter Dunne by permission of Charles Scribner's Sons. Copyright 1938 Charles Scribner's Sons.*

In the late 1800's Finley Peter Dunne, a news reporter in Chicago, created a make-believe character named Mr. Dooley. Mr. Dooley always had something to say about the people and events of his time. He expressed his sharp and humorous opinions in an Irish brogue to an imaginary friend named Mr. Hennessy. Mr. Dooley's opinions were found in many books and newspapers and were greatly enjoyed by Americans.

Mr. Dooley, of course, had opinions on American expansion. In this selection he comments on the Insular Cases, in which the Supreme Court ruled on the status of newly won territories in the Caribbean and the Pacific. Mr. Dooley especially pokes fun at the disagreements among the justices. In one of the Insular Cases there were five separate opinions written by the judges.

What basic issue was the Supreme Court deciding? Does Mr. Dooley think it was settled by the court's decision? What do you think Mr. Dooley means by his final statement? Do you think that this is true today?

"I see," said Mr. Dooley, "the Supreme Court has decided the Constitution don't follow the flag."

"Who said it did?" asked Mr. Hennessy.

"Someone," said Mr. Dooley. "It happened a long time ago and I don't remember clearly how it come up, but some fellow said that everywhere the Constitution went, the flag was sure to go. 'I don't believe one word of it,' says the other fellow. 'Ye can't make me think the Constitution is going around everywhere a young lieutenant in the army sticks a flagpole. It's too old. It's a home-staying Constitution with a blue coat with brass buttons on it, and it walks with a gold-headed cane. It's old and it's feeble, and it prefers to set on the front step and amuse the children. It wouldn't last a minute in them tropical climates. It would get a pain in the fourteenth amendment and die before the doctors could get around to cut it out. No, sir, we'll keep it with us, and treat it tenderly without too much hard work. When it gives out entirely we'll give it a decent burial and incorporate ourselves under the laws of New Jersey. That's what we'll do,' says he. 'But,' says the other, 'if it wants to travel, why not let it?' 'But it don't want to.' 'I say it does.' 'How'll we find out?' 'We'll ask the Supreme Court. They'll know what's good for it.'

"So it went up to the Supreme Court. There's one thing about the Supreme Court, if you leave anything to them, you leave it to them. Ye don't get a check that lets you call for it in an hour. The Supreme Court of the United States ain't in any hurry about catching the mails. If ye're looking for a game of quick decisions and base hits, ye've got to hire another umpire. It never gives a decision till the crowd has gone and the players have packed their bats in the bags and started for home.

"For a while everybody watched to see what the Supreme Court would do. I knew myself I felt I couldn't make another move in the game till I heard from them. Building operations were stopped and we stood wringing our hands outside the door waiting for information from the bedside. 'What're they doing now?' 'They just put the lawyer's arguments in the ice box and the chief justice is in a corner writing a poem. Brown and Harlan [two of the justices] are discussing the condition of the Roman Empire before the fire. The rest of the Court is considering the question of whether they ought or ought not to wear lace on their robes. No decision today!' And so it went for days, and weeks, and months. The men that had argued that the Constitution ought to follow the flag to all the tough resorts on the Pacific coast and the men that argued that the flag was so lively that no Constitution could follow it and survive, they died or lost their jobs or were forgotten. Little children were born into the world and grew up and never heard of Puerto Rico except when someone got a job there. I'd about made up me mind to try and put the thing out of me thoughts and go back to work when I woke up one morning and saw by the paper that the Supreme Court had warned the Constitution to leave the flag alone and tend to its own business.

"That's what the paper says, but I've read over the decision and I don't see anything of the kind there. There's not a word about the flag and not enough to tire ye about the Constitution. It's a matter of lemons, Hennessy, that the Supreme Court has been setting on for this generation—a cargo of lemons sent from Puerto Rico to some Italian in Philadelphia. [The mention of lemons refers to the fact that all the Insular Cases involved duties, or tariffs, on the tropical products imported from these possessions. Duties were affected by whether or not the possessions were considered part of the United States.] The decision was read by Brown, after a cruel and bitter contest. Says Brown, 'The question here is one of such great importance that we've been struggling over it ever since you saw us last and have only come to a decision (Fuller, Gray, Harlan, Shiras, McKenna, White, Brewer, and Peckham dissenting [disagreeing] from me and each other) because of the hot weather coming on. Washington is a dreadful place in summer. The whole fabric of our government is threatened, the lives of our people and the progress of civilization endangered. The decision of the

Court (the others dissenting) is as follows: First, that the District of Columbia is a state. Second, that it is not. Third, that New York is a state. Fourth, that it is a crown colony. Fifth, that all states are states and all territories are territories in the eyes of other powers, but Gawd knows what they are at home. I'll now fall back in me chair, while me learned but misguided colleagues read the History of Iceland to show ye how wrong I am. But mind ye, what I've said goes. I let them talk because it exercises their throats, but ye've heard all the decision on this lemon case that ye'll get.' A voice from the audience, 'Do I get me money back?' Brown: 'Who are ye?' The voice: 'The man that owned the lemons.' Brown: 'I don't know.' (Gray and White dissenting and the rest concurring [agreeing] but for entirely different reasons.)

"And there ye have the decision, Hennessy, that's shaken the intellects of the nation to their very foundations, or will if they try to read it. 'Tis all right. Look it over some time. 'Tis fine sport if ye don't care for checkers. Some say it leaves the flag up in the air and some say that's where it leaves the Constitution. Anyhow, something's in the air. But there's one thing I'm sure about."

"What's that?" asked Mr. Hennessy.

"That is," said Mr. Dooley, "no matter whether the Constitution follows the flag or not, the Supreme Court follows the election returns."

A CANAL BUILDER AT WORK

Adapted from Arthur Bullard, Panama: The Canal, the Country and the People. *New York: The Macmillan Co., 1914.*

Americans in the early 1900's were proud of their great achievement in building the Panama Canal. Much of the credit for this feat belonged to Colonel Goethals, who was appointed chief engineer by Theodore Roosevelt in 1907. Goethals had to deal with a labor force of 30,000 workers, overcome landslides that delayed the work, and solve enormous engineering problems. Offices, schools, houses, recreation centers, machine shops, and dining halls—all had to be built. Goethals spent time each day listening to workers' complaints, and he soon won the respect and dedication of the workers. In this selection Arthur Bullard, a reporter who traveled to the Isthmus in 1909, tells about the building of the canal.

What do you think of Goethals' "Court of Justice"? Was it necessary for Goethals to be an "absolute autocrat" in these circumstances? Why? What is Bullard's opinion of Goethals?

"Tell me something about Colonel Goethals." My friend was a keen observer who had already given me much information about life and work in the Canal Zone.

"You want to know about the old man?" he said after a moment's thought. "Well the most distinctive picture of him I have is this. I used to live at Culebra. One night I was sitting out on the porch, smoking. There were only a few lights here and there in the Administration Building. One by one they went out, all except that in the old man's office. It was almost ten o'clock when his light went out. It was the dry season. A full moon, as big as a dining-room table, was out—a gorgeous night. The old man came out and walked across the grass to his house. He didn't stop to look up at the moon; he just walked along, his head a little forward, still thinking. And he hadn't been in his own house ten minutes before all the lights were out there. He'd gone to bed. The only time the colonel isn't working is from 10 P.M. to 6 A.M., when he's asleep."

That seems to be the thing which impresses our men down here most of all about the boss. He is always on the job.

Just what is the job?

Strictly speaking, it is administrative, rather than constructive, engineering. The type of the canal was decided upon before the present commission was installed. They have had but few changes of importance to make: widening the channel in the Cut, increasing the size of the locks, and moving the Pacific locks inland, beyond the range of a hostile fleet. Their work has been the perfecting of details and the carrying out of what had been already determined.

Colonel George Washington Goethals, the Chief Engineer and Chairman of the Panama Canal Commission, is now at the head of this great national job of ours. A visitor to the Isthmus who has not included the colonel among the sights has missed more than half of what there is to see down here. You will not have to wait long before you are brought into the throne room, and are face to face with the most absolute autocrat in the world.

Many people have described Colonel Goethals as having a boyish face. But they must have seen him with his hat on, for his hair is white. If, as they say, his face looks 20 and his hair 60, I could not see it, for his eyes—which dominate—look 40. He is broad-shouldered and erect. Above everything, he looks alert and fit. Although he does not spare himself, he has not lost a day from malaria.

Of course, the first thing you do will be to hand him your perfectly useless letter from your representative in Congress. Useless, because even if you have no letter he will show you every courtesy he can without interfering with the job. And he will not interfere with the job even if you bring letters from all the members of Congress.

Like every man who accomplishes a great amount of work, he believes in routine.

Six mornings a week he is "out on the line." He took me along on one of these inspection trips. It was before seven when we reached Pedro Miguel, and we walked back through the Cut to Empire. It was four hours of bitter hard walking, for the colonel kept to no well-worn path. Whatever interested him he wished to see close up. The colonel said, "The only way to keep your health in this climate is to take a little exercise every morning." Doubtless it is true, but I had rather die quickly than keep alive at that rate.

He spends his afternoons on routine desk work, signing papers, approving reports, and so forth. It is part of his system that he discourages oral reports. Everything comes to him on paper. If he wants to talk with any of his subordinates, he generally does it during his morning trips—on the spot. Perhaps the phrase he uses most frequently is, "Write it down."

The afternoon office work is often interrupted by callers. The stream of tourists grows steadily, and the colonel realizes that it is we, the people of the United States, who are doing this canal job. Anyone who is sufficiently interested to come down and look it over is welcome.

The most remarkable part of Colonel Goethals' routine is his Sunday Court of Low, Middle, and High Justice. The colonel holds a session every Sunday morning. I had the good fortune to be admitted one Sunday morning to the audience chamber.

The first callers were a Negro couple from Jamaica. They had a difference of opinion as to the ownership of $35 which the wife had earned by washing. Colonel Goethals listened until the fact was established that she had earned it, then ordered the man to return it. He started to protest something about a husband's property rights under the English law. "All right," the colonel said, decisively. "Say the word, and I'll deport you. You can get all the English law you want in Jamaica." The husband decided to pay and stay.

Then came a Spanish worker who had been hurt in an accident. The colonel called in his chief clerk and told him to help the unfortunate man prepare his claim. "See that the papers are prepared correctly and have them pushed through."

A man came in who had just been thrown out of the service for brutality to the men under him. This action was the result of an investigation before a special committee. The man wanted his job back. The colonel read over the papers in the case, and when he spoke, his language was vigorous. "If you have any new evidence, I will instruct the committee to reopen your case. But as long as this report stands against you, you will get no mercy from this office. If the men had broken your head with a crowbar, I would have stood up for them. We don't need slave drivers on this job."

Then a committee from the Machinists' Union wanted an opinion on some new shop rules. A nurse wanted a longer vacation than the regulations allow. A man and his wife were dissatisfied with the house they had been given. A supervisor of steam shovels came in to ask advice about applying for another job under the Panama government. The end of the canal work is approaching and the farsighted men are beginning to look into the future. "Of course I can't advise you," the colonel said. "You know I would hate to see you go. But if you decide that it is wise, come in and see me. I may be able to give you some introductions which will help you." (And, as everyone knows that a letter of introduction from the chairman of the commission would look like an order to the Panama government, there is another man who will want to vote for Goethals for President in 1916!)

An American Negro introduced some humor. He was convinced that his services were of more value than his foreman felt they were. The colonel preferred to accept the foreman's judgment in the matter. The dissatisfied worker announced that he was the best blacksmith's helper on the Isthmus and that he planned to appeal this decision. The colonel's eyes twinkled. "To whom are you going to appeal?" he asked.

For the fact is that the decisions made in these Sunday sessions will not be changed before the Day of Judgment.

The procession kept up till noon—pitiful, patience-trying foolishness, with occasional humor. "Once in a while," the colonel said, "something turns up which is really important for me to know. And, anyway, they feel better after they have seen me, even if I cannot help them. They feel that they got a fair chance to state their troubles. They are less likely to cause discontent. But it is a strain."

COLOMBIA PROTESTS AMERICA'S ACTIONS

Adapted from Francisco José Urrutía, A Commentary on the Declaration of the Rights of Nations. *Washington, D.C.: 1916.*

The actions taken by the United States to obtain the right to build a canal across the Isthmus of Panama increased the Latin American nations' distrust of their neighbor to the north. Colombia, which was forced to give up the territory of Panama, felt especially threatened. However, that small nation realized that it could not resist the power of the United States. Consequently, leaders of Colombia's government, who were seeking payment for their former territory of Panama, appealed to world opinion for support.

The following selections are from a pamphlet written by Colombia's foreign minister, Francisco José Urrutía, to present his nation's case. A year after the canal was officially opened in July 1920, the United States paid $25 million to Colombia, which in turn recognized the independence of Panama.

What does Urrutía mean by "the crime committed in 1903"? What action does he threaten to take against the United States? Do you think this was a serious threat?

Until 1903 the relations between Colombia and the United States were most friendly. Good will toward Colombia was always recognized by the United States, not only in negotiations about the Panama Canal but in all matters.

The statement that Colombia ever opposed the opening of the Panama Canal is absolutely untrue. On the contrary, the entire diplomatic history of Colombia, from the time of its free-dom from Spain, shows how great was its desire to see the canal built. Out of regard for self preservation, it did try to bring this about without harming its own sovereignty.

With the canal now open, Colombia cannot ignore the fact that this great work is one of the chief factors in the future material development of the world. But as long as the agreement giving a lawful title to the United States is not carried out, Colombia will also maintain that the work, great as it is, stands as a monument to an even greater crime. It will insist that Colombia and Colombia alone is the lawful owner of the Isthmus of Panama. If the formal opening of the canal should take place before a final settlement is arrived at, Colombia will be forced once more to protest to the other nations of the world, against the violation of its sovereignty.

In the eyes of the people of Colombia and of all America, the Panama Canal stands for the victory of might over right, the triumph of force over law. It stands for this far more than it does for the splendid conquest of tropical nature by the science and energy of the people of the United States. The United States has the power to remove this feeling, to change this state of affairs, and to insure that the canal shall be what it would have been without the crime committed in 1903—a great and powerful link uniting Colombia and the United States.

Reference has been made to the danger threatening the canal if it were attacked from Colombian territory, and of the necessity of preventing an alliance between Colombia and any other nation. If any such danger or any such necessity exist, the best guarantee of the safety of the canal lies in an agreement with Colombia. Fear that the Panama Canal might be attacked some day from Colombian territory may be avoided by the United States. This cannot be through a policy of force, but through a policy of friendship and justice. Such a policy calls for returning—by means of payment for past grievances—the ancient and traditional good will and friendship between Colombia and United States.

If the safeguarding of the Panama Canal enters into the scheme of the national defense of the United States, it is natural to suppose that that protection would be sought in an honest and loyal manner by encouraging the friendship of Colombia and by respecting its sovereignty. It can never be reached by returning to a policy already disapproved by both the American continents.

AN AMERICAN IN MEXICO, 1914

Adapted from A Diplomat's Wife in Mexico *by Edith O'Shaughnessy, published by Harper & Brothers, Inc.*

After a revolution broke out in Mexico in 1910, relations between Mexico and the United States became troubled. At first President Wilson, who was anxious not to intervene in Mexico, followed a policy of "watchful waiting." However, in 1914 several American sailors were arrested in Tampico. When the Mexican government refused to apologize by firing a 21-gun salute, Wilson sent American troops to take Veracruz. The anxious days that followed are described in the following selection by Edith O'Shaughnessy, the wife of Nelson O'Shaughnessy, American charge d'affaires at the United States embassy in Mexico City. Although O'Shaughnessy had to support Wilson's actions, in later years he declared that Wilson's Mexican policy was "brutal, unwarranted, and stupid."

What does Edith O'Shaughnessy think of America's intervention in Mexico? What are her feelings toward President Huerta?

April 18th. 6:30 p.m.

It makes me sick with dread to think of the probable fate of Americans in the deserts and mountains of Mexico. Someone has made a mistake, somewhere, somehow, that we should come in to give the final blow to this distracted nation, which still holds on, and rightly, to the little sovereignty we have left it. The foreign powers think we are playing the most cold-blooded, most cruel game of "grab" in all history.

10 p.m.

If we get through this, the next incident will mean war. I hope that the leaders in Washington will appreciate some of the difficulties Nelson has to meet, and act accordingly. How glad I am that I haven't sent my son or my jewels with various terror-stricken friends who have fled. War hasn't come yet. After everything is said and done, everything depends on the life of that wise and patient old Indian [Huerta], who—whatever his sins—is legally president of Mexico. Chase legality out of Latin America and where are you? After him will come anarchy, chaos, and finally intervention—the biggest police job ever undertaken in the Western Hemisphere, however one may feel like making little of it from a military standpoint.

April 19th. 2:30 a.m.

I can't sleep. National and personal problems keep running through my brain. Three railroad men came to the embassy this evening. They brought reports of a plan for the massacre of Americans in the street tonight. But, strange and wonderful thing, a heavy rain is falling. It is my only experience of a midnight rain in Mexico, except that which fell upon the mobs crying "Death to Diaz," nearly three years ago. As all Mexicans hate to get wet, rain is as effective as shellfire in clearing the streets, and I don't think there will be any trouble. Fate seems to keep an occasional unnatural shower on hand for Mexican crises.

Had this war war been started by a great incident or for a great principle, I could stand it. But because the details of a salute could not be decided upon, we cause ourselves, and inflict on others, the horrors of war. It is no situation for amateurs. The longer I live the more respect I have for technical training. Every foreign office in Europe or any other continent keeps experts for just such cases. I may become an interventionist, but *after* Huerta. He has proved himself greatly superior, in executive ability, to any leader Mexico has produced since Diaz, in spite of his lack of balance and his surprising childishness. He would have sold his soul to please the United States and gain recognition. [Wilson refused to recognize the Huerta government.] In that small, soft hand (doubtless bloody, too) were possibilities of bringing back prosperity.

April 20th

My heart is sick. Wednesday that great fleet arrives. What is it going to fight? It can't bombard Veracruz. The streets are full and the houses overflowing with fleeing people. It can't climb the mountains and protect the countless Americans living inland. Huerta's army is engaged in the north in a death struggle against enemies of the government, armed with our guns. Oh, the pity of it!

And this city, beautiful Mexico City, so wonderfully located in the very center of the Western Hemisphere, a great continent to the north and the south, halfway between immense oceans, and lifted nearly 8,000 feet [242 meters] up to the heavens!

April 21st

We are at war. American and Mexican blood flowed in the streets of Veracruz today. The story that reaches us is that the captain of the German ship *Ypiranga* tried to land 17 million rounds of ammunition. Admiral Fletcher protested. The captain of the *Ypiranga* insisted on doing it. The admiral prevented him by force, and they say, took the town—thus putting us on a war basis. Whether this is a true version of what has happened I don't know. It has been many a year since American blood flowed in the streets of Veracruz. General Scott took it in 1847. The endless repetitions of history!

April 22nd

The newspapers are rather fierce this morning. One headline in the *Independiente* says that "the Mexican bullets will no longer spill brothers' blood, but will hit blond heads and white breasts swollen with vanity and cowardice." The newspapers add that the Americans landed "without a declaration of war, like criminals." It is impossible to expect the Mexicans to grasp the idea that the landing of our troops was a simple police measure. In the face of the facts, I am sure such distinctions will be overlooked. At 7:30 an officer appeared in the drawing-room, saying that President Huerta was outside. There was no time to ring for servants. I went to the door and waited while the tearless old Indian, in his gray sweater and soft hat, came quickly up the steps. It was his first and last visit to the embassy during our stay there.

I led him into the drawing-room, where we had a strange and moving conversation. I could not, for my country's sake, speak the endless regret that was in my heart for the official part we had been forced to play in the action carried out by us to his country's undoing. He greeted me calmly.

"Señora, how do you do? I fear you have had many annoyances."

Then he sat back, quietly in a big armchair, impersonal and mysterious. I answered as easily as I could that the times were difficult for everyone. I said that we were very grateful for what he had done for our personal safety and that of other Americans. I asked him if there was anything we could do for him. He gave me a long, piercing look, and after a pause, answered:

"Nothing, Señora. All that is done I must do myself. Here I must remain. The moment has not come for me to go. Nothing but death could remove me now."

I felt the tears come to my eyes, as I answered—"Death is not so terrible a thing."

He answered again, very quietly, "It is the natural law, to which we must all give in. We were born into the world according to the natural law, and must leave according to it—that is all."

He does not want us to leave by way of Guadalajara and Manzanillo. He is giving us his train tomorrow night to take us to Veracruz. There will be a full escort, including three officers of high rank.

I was dreadfully keyed up. I felt the tears come to my eyes. He seemed to think that it was fear that moved me, for he told me not to be anxious.

I said, "I am not weeping for myself, but for the tragedy of life."

And, indeed, since seeing him I have been in a sea of sadness, personal and impersonal—impersonal because of the crushing destiny that can overtake a strong man and a country, and personal, because this many-colored, vibrant Mexican experience of mine is drawing to a close. Nothing can ever be like it.

As we three [Huerta, Edith, and Nelson] stood there together he said, very quietly, his last word:

"I hold no ill will toward the American people, nor toward President Wilson." And, after a slight pause, he added, "He has not understood."

It was the first and last time I ever heard him speak the President's name. I gave him my hand as he stood with his other hand on Nelson's shoulder, and knew that this was indeed the end. I think he realized that my heart was warm and my sympathies rushing out to beautiful, agonizing Mexico. For, as he stood at the door, he suddenly turned and made me a deep bow. Then, taking Nelson's arm, he went out into the starry, perfumed evening, and I turned back into the house I was so soon to leave, with the sadness of life like a hot point, deep in my heart. So is history written. So do circumstances and a man's will seem to raise him up to great ends, and so does destiny crush him.

I am sad, very sad, tonight. Whatever else life may have in reserve for me, this last conversation with a strong man of another temperament than mine will remain on my heart—his calm, his philosophy on the eve of a war he knows can only end in disaster for himself and his people. His many faults, his crimes, even his desperate methods to keep himself in power, his failures—disappear. I know his spirit possesses something which will see him safely through the dark hours when they come.

CHAPTER 13 ■ AMERICA'S ENTRY INTO WORLD WAR I

WILSON'S "WAR MESSAGE"

Adapted from A Compilation of the Messages and Papers of the Presidents, *Vol. XVII. New York: Bureau of National Literature, Inc. n.d.*

After World War I broke out in Europe in 1914, the United States managed to keep out of the war for nearly three years. During this period both sides—the Allies and the Central Powers—violated American neutrality. American ships bound for Europe were stopped by both Great Britain and Germany. However, in 1917 Germany sharply increased submarine warfare against the United States. After months of growing tension over German submarine warfare and its violation of the rights of neutral shipping, President Wilson asked Congress to declare war on Germany. On April 2, 1917, Wilson went before Congress and delivered his "War Message." It was passed by the Senate two days later, by a vote of 82 to 6, and by the House on April 6, by a vote of 375 to 50.

For what reasons does Wilson argue that the United States must enter the war? According to Wilson, what are America's war aims?

I have called the Congress into special session because there are serious, very serious, choices of policy to be made, and made immediately. It was neither right nor constitutional that I should take the responsibility of making them.

On February 3rd, 1917, I officially informed you of the announcement of the Imperial German Government that on and after February 1st, it would put aside all restraints of law or humanity and use its submarines to sink every ship that tried to approach the ports of Great Britain and Ireland, the western coast of Europe, or any of the ports controlled by the enemies of Germany within the Mediterranean.

The new policy has swept every restriction aside. Ships of every kind, whatever their flag, type, cargo, destination, or errand, have been ruthlessly fired on and sent to the bottom of the sea without warning and without thought of help or mercy for those on board. Even hospital ships and ships carrying relief to the stricken people of Belgium have been sunk with the same reckless lack of sympathy or of principle.

I was for a little while unable to believe that such things would, in fact, be done by any government that considered itself civilized. International law had its origin in the attempt to set up some laws which would be respected and observed upon the seas, where no nation had the right of control. That law has been built up by painful stage after stage, always with a clear view of what the heart and conscience of humanity demanded.

I am not now thinking of the loss of property involved, great and serious as that is, but only of the reckless and wholesale destruction of the lives of noncombatants, men, women, and children, engaged in activities which have always, even in the darkest period of modern history, been regarded as innocent and legitimate. Property can be paid for; the lives of peaceful, innocent people cannot be.

The present German submarine warfare against commerce is a warfare against humankind. It is a war against all nations. American ships have been sunk, American lives taken in ways that have stirred us very deeply. But the ships and people of other neutral, friendly nations have been sunk in the same way. There has been no discrimination. The challenge is to all people. Each nation must decide for itself how to meet it.

When I addressed Congress on February 26th, I thought that it would be enough to assert our neutral right with arms; our right to use the sea against unlawful interference; our right to keep our people safe against unlawful violence. But armed neutrality, it now appears, will not work. Because submarines are, in effect, outlaws when used as the German submarines have been used against merchant shipping, it is impossible to defend ships against their attacks. (The law of nations has assumed that merchant ships would defend themselves against cruisers or visible ships chasing them upon the open sea.) Under the present circumstances, we have to destroy the ships on sight.

The German government denies the right of neutrals to use arms at all within certain areas of the sea. The Germans say that the armed guards which we have placed on our merchant ships will be treated as outside the protection of law and dealt with as pirates would be. Armed neutrality is weak enough at best. In such circumstances it is likely only to produce what it was meant to prevent—it is practically certain to draw us into the war without either the rights or the effectiveness of belligerents.

There is one choice we cannot make, that we are incapable of making. We will not choose the path of submission and suffer the most sacred rights of our nation and our people to be ignored or violated. The wrongs against which we now array ourselves are no common wrongs; they cut to the very roots of human life.

With a strong sense of the solemn and even tragic character of the step I am taking and of the grave responsibilities it involves, but in unhesitating obedience to what I see as my constitutional duty, I advise that the Congress declare the recent course of the Imperial German Government to be, in fact, nothing less than war against the government and people of the United States. I advise that it formally accept the status of belligerent which has thus been thrust upon it. I advise that it take immediate steps not only to put the country in a more thorough state of defense, but also to use all its power and resources to defeat the German empire and end the war.

We are now about to accept battle with this natural foe of liberty and shall, if necessary, spend the whole force of the nation to end its power. We are glad, now that we see the facts with no veil of false pretense about them, to fight thus for the ultimate peace of the world and for the liberation of its peoples, the German peoples included; for the rights of nations great and small and the privilege of human beings everywhere to choose their way of life and obedience. The world must be made safe for democracy. Its peace must be planted upon the tested foundations of political liberty.

We have no selfish ends to serve. We desire no conquest, no dominion. We seek no payment for ourselves, no material compensation for the sacrifices we shall freely make. We are but one of the champions of the rights of humans. We shall be satisfied when those rights have been made as secure as the faith and the freedom of nations can make them.

Just because we fight without hatred and without selfish objectives, seeking nothing for ourselves but what we wish to share with all free peoples, we shall, I feel confident, conduct ourselves without passion and observe the principles of right and fair play we are fighting for.

It is a distressing and oppressive duty which I have performed in thus speaking to you. There may be many months of fiery trial and sacrifice ahead of us. It is a fearful thing to lead this great peaceful people into war, into the most terrible and disastrous of all wars, with civilization itself in the balance. But the right is more precious than peace. We shall fight for the things which we have always carried nearest our hearts—for democracy, for the right of those who submit to authority to have a voice in their own governments, for the rights and liberties of small nations, for such a universal domination of right as shall bring peace and safety to all nations and make the world itself at last free.

To such a task we can dedicate our lives and our fortunes, everything that we are and everything that we have. We can do this with the pride of those who know that the day has come when America is privileged to spend its blood and its might for the principles that gave it birth, happiness, and peace. God helping us, we cannot do otherwise.

WOMEN UNITE TO SUPPORT THE WAR

"Fifth Avenue and Grand Street" by Mary Carolyn Davies. Reprinted by permission of Miss Laura Benet.

American women made a great contribution to the war effort. Many of them took over jobs in factories and industry. Many others did volunteer work for organizations such as the Red Cross. They spent many hours preparing bandages to be used in hospitals and first-aid stations. Mary Carolyn Davies, an American writer, described this experience in a poem she called "Fifth Avenue and Grand Street." In the poem, Fifth Avenue stands for wealth and fashion, while Grand Street, on New York's Lower East Side, was a low-income area where many immigrants lived.

What do you think the writer is trying to say in this poem? Why does it apply especially to women? Do you think she is right?

I sat beside her, rolling bandages.
I peeped. "Fifth Avenue," her clothes were
   saying.
It's "Grand Street," I know well, my shirtwaist
   [a kind of dress] says,
And shoes, and hat, but then, she didn't hear,
Or she pretended not, for we were laying
Our coats aside, and as we were so near,

She saw my pin like hers. [Many women dur-
    ing the war wore a star-shaped pin to
    show that someone close to them was
    serving in the armed forces.]
And when girls are
Wearing a pin these days that has a star,
They smile out at each other. We did that,
And then she didn't seem to see my hat.

I sat beside her, handling gauze and lint,
And thought of Jim. She thought of someone
    too;
Under the smile there was a little glint
In her eyelashes, that was how I knew.
I wasn't crying—but I haven't any
Pride in it; we've a better chance than they
To take blows standing, for we've had so many.
We two sat, fingers busy, all that day.

I'd spoken first, if I'd known what to say.
But she did soon, and after, told of him,
The man she wore the star for, and the way
He'd gone at once. I bragged a bit of Jim;
Who wouldn't who had ever come to know
Him? When the girls all rose to go,
She stood there, shyly, with her gloves half
    on,
Said, "Come to see me, won't you?" and was
    gone.

I meant to call, too, I'd have liked it then
For we'd a lot in common, with our men
Across. But now that peace is here again
And our boys safe, I can't help wondering—
    Well,
Will she forget, and crawl back in her shell
And if I call, say "Show this person out"?
Or still be friendly as she was? I doubt
If Grand [Street] will sit beside Fifth Avenue
Again, and be politely spoken to.

We're sisters while the danger lasts, it's true;
But rich and poor's equality must cease
(For women especially), of course, in peace.

ACTION AT THE FRONT

Adapted from "Some War-Time Letters" by Eldon J. Canright in the Wisconsin Magazine of History, *V: 192–195 (1921–1922). Reprinted by permission of The State Historical Society of Wisconsin.*

During World War I, about 8 million soldiers were killed and about 20 million were
wounded in the fighting. It was the first war
in which tanks, dirigibles, and airplanes were
used. And it was the first war in which submarines and machine guns were used on a
large scale. The use of these weapons, and of
poison gas, for mass killing greatly increased
the horrors of the fighting. On the western
front, soldiers spent weeks in muddy, rat-filled
trenches facing steady artillery bombardments
and the threat of poison gas.

Eldon Canright, a private from Wisconsin,
spent 180 days in the trenches along the
western front. In this letter home, he tells his
family what the fighting there was like.

How would you describe Canright's attitude toward the fighting? Does he seem to
share the war aims that President Wilson outlined for the nation?

Somewhere in France
July 8, 1918

My Dear Folks:
I believe I have told you in another letter that
because of the fine record we have made since
we have been at the front, we have been chosen
as "shock troops." Well, we sure are being
shocked!

Try and picture the very worst thunderstorm
you have ever heard. Then multiply it by about
10,000 and you will get some idea of the battle
that has been and still is raging along this
front and in which we are taking a very active
part!

The battle started shortly after midnight a
few days ago and has been raging ever since!
It started with a very heavy bombardment all
along the front, and as the country here is very
flat, you can see for a long way. I can tell you
that it is some sight at night to see the blinding
flashes of the guns all along the line. Even far
off on the horizon you can see the pink glow
flare up and die down and flare up and die
down again—very much like a city burning in
the distance. The roar and crash of the guns
just seems to tear the air into pieces, and explosions shake the ground. To add to the confusion you have the whine and shrieks of the
shells, some coming and some going! And signal rockets of all colors are constantly shooting
up into the air, and that is the way the army
"talks" at night. It's a wonderful sight! The first
night, a shell struck an ammunition supply and
rockets went shooting in every direction. It lasted
for several minutes and was very thrilling!

Of course every so often the Germans send
over poison gas. We have to be constantly on

the alert for it and wear our gas clothes most of the time, and carry our gas masks all the time!

We all have cotton in our ears. Still, the noise of the guns has made some of us temporarily deaf. We have not taken off any of our clothes or gone to bed since the battle started. When it slows up a little we just lie down on the ground, right by the guns, and get what little rest and sleep we can. Our meals are brought to us, as we may not leave the position long enough to go and get them!

The first day they shot down an observation balloon right near us. A pilot attacked it and hit it with his machine gun. The balloon came down in flames, but the observer jumped out and landed with a parachute! However, about a minute later, even before the observer had hit the ground, another airplane had rushed up after the plane that "got" the balloon. The second plane shot him down and he came tumbling out of the clouds with his plane in flames. That happened three days ago, and the burned and broken airplane is still lying there, and so are the two pilots. They are an awful sight. And when the wind is in the right direction (or rather wrong direction) we get a very disagreeable odor, and there are several dead horses, etc., lying out there, too. No one has had time to bury them yet!

During the daytime there are a great many airplanes flying overhead, constantly trying to "see" what the other side is doing. We have seen some very exciting air battles. It is nothing unusual to see anywhere from two to two dozen airplanes fighting and chasing each other in and out of the clouds as they try to get into position to fire—we can hear the "spitting" of their machine guns as they fire. Sometimes you can hear them fighting when they are above the clouds, too! And twice a very daring German pilot flew down over our position and turned his machine gun on us! We could hear the "whang and spit" of the bullets as they struck the ground within a few feet of us! He flew so low that we could see the black cross on the plane and see the pilot shooting at us! But they didn't stay long. They would just shoot down and fire and then away they'd go before we had a chance to shoot back at them.

You see, we are right out in the open with no trenches to protect us, and so we are an easy mark for anything like that! And the Germans have been sending over many shells, too! So the field around our position is all torn up with shell holes—some big ones, too. One of

those big shells makes a noise like the rumble and roar of a freight train going about 1,000 miles [1609 kilometers] an hour! When we hear them coming we say, "Here comes another of the devil's fast freights!" And when they burst, a mountain of rocks and dirt shoots up in the air higher than the trees! They make a hole about eight feet [2.4 meters] deep and about fifteen feet [4.5 meters] in diameter. And shell fragments scatter for about 300 feet [91.4 meters]. A shell fragment makes an awful wound, too, as it just tears a great hole in you, while a bullet just drills a clean round hole! So you can imagine what would happen if one of those shells should make a "direct hit" on our position!

There is, or rather was, a little town over in a clump of trees near here—now there isn't even a wall or a piece of a house standing. There are just broken bricks and pieces of plaster scattered around.

Another thrilling sight is to see the ammunition caissons [wagons] bringing up ammunition. Each caisson is drawn by six horses hitched in teams of two, and a man rides the left horse of each team. They generally come up just before dark and you can see the long line of caissons stretching away down the road, and coming at a gallop. The horses are covered with sweat and lather when they get here! We unload the caissons in a hurry and then they start back again, at a gallop, as the Germans are apt to shell the road at any time—so they are running for their lives! In fact the other night the road was shelled when they were bringing up ammunition! The driver swung off the road and came through the fields, spurring the horses to even greater speed!

This kind of warfare means a great many killed and wounded. But I prefer it, as it is the only way to end the war—just kill off all the Germans!

I have given you details and described disagreeable things, but I just want you to know what war is and what it means for us and for everyone!

But I think it's great sport and certainly am glad I'm here and taking part in this—one of the greatest battles the world has ever known.

Love,
E. J. Canright,
Medical Department
149th Field Artillery
A.E.F.,
A.P.O. No. 715

CELEBRATING THE ARMISTICE—IN FRANCE

Adapted from Mildred Aldrich, When Johnny Comes Marching Home. *Boston: Small, Maynard and Company, 1919.*

For Americans the end of the war came less than two years after they entered the conflict. For Europeans the agony of the war had lasted longer—for four long years. During this time, millions of people had died and millions of others had suffered great hardships.

Mildred Aldrich, an American news reporter and writer, spent the war years living in France. She had worked for several years as a reporter and editor in Boston, then had moved to France in 1898 and bought a small house in the country near the Marne River. The Battle of the Marne in 1914 was fought in the area near her house. In this selection, she tells of the end of the war and how she and her French neighbors reacted to the news of peace.

What does Mildred Aldrich think about the armistice terms? Would you say that her outlook is more French than American? More American than French? A mixture of both?

Saturday morning [November 9] we read about the armistice in the newspapers. Stiff as the terms were, we knew that Germany could not hesitate, just as we knew that the French would not discuss. I had only to look at the two maps I had studied two days before to know that Germany was forced to accept even if the terms had been harder. Yet I could have cried to think it had come so soon. I knew that once Germany had, with Wilson's aid, been allowed to talk, the armistice was inevitable. Beaten to the point where its case was hopeless, and where the final surrender of its army was in sight, it could save itself from invasion only by accepting any terms proposed. As for the Allies, no matter how they felt, they could hardly go on with the fighting once Germany gave in. Much as one grieved that the surrender was made with Germany still the invader, the order to "cease firing" meant the saving of thousands of lives.

The expected news came early Monday morning. As we expected, the Germans had accepted the hard terms of the "unconditional surrender," and the order had been given to "cease firing" at eleven. We had known it would come, but the fact that the order had been given rather surprised us. To realize that it was over! How could one in a minute?

I was up early to wait for the papers. It was a perfectly white day. The whole world was covered with the first frost and wrapped in a deep white fog, as if the huge flag of truce were wound around it. I went out on the lawn and looked toward the north. The fog was so thick, I could not see as far as the hedge. Yet out there I knew the guns were still firing. Between them and me lay such devastation as even the imagination cannot exaggerate, and such suffering and pain as human understanding can but partly understand. Four years and four months—and how much is still before us? The future has its job laid out for it. Are ordinary humans capable of handling it?

Later, as I stood near the road, I heard footsteps running toward me on the frozen ground. Out of the fog came Marin, the town crier, with his drum on his back. He waved his drumsticks at me as he ran, and cried, "I am coming as fast as I can, Madame. We are ringing our bells at four—at the same time Clemenceau reads the terms in the Chamber of Deputies and Lloyd George reads them in London." As he reached the corner just above my gate he swung his drum round and beat it like mad.

It did not take two minutes for all our little village to gather about him. In a loud, clear voice he read the order of the day, which officially announced that the war had ended at eleven o'clock. The inhabitants of the town were authorized to hang out their flags, light up their windows, and join in a dignified celebration of the liberation of France. Then he slowly lifted his cap in his hand as he read the last phrase, which begged them not to forget to pray for the brave soldiers who had given their lives that this day might be, and not to forget that to many among us this day of rejoicing was also a day of mourning.

There was not a cheer.

Amelie told the whole story when she dropped on a bench at the kitchen door, and with dry eyes and tightened lips exclaimed, "Finally! It's over. We beat them!"

After all, that was the important thing. It was not what we hoped for, or what we wanted, but the killing was over. I don't see how the French, on whose bodies and souls the burden had fallen, can, even in their disappointment, have any other thought just now.

Less than an hour after Marin passed over the hill, the mayor and his associates arrived to present me formally with the thanks of the town for the part I had taken in sharing the hard days with them. I did so wish again for some magic means by which every one of the American women who had stretched out generous helping hands across the sea to this little place could have seen the scene, and heard me try to make a French speech. I stumbled a bit, but the French are good at understanding. As far as their faces went I might have been rivaling the best French speaker. I put the honors where they were due. But in spite of all I said, for the moment I was to them—America.

They all went out on the lawn before leaving to look off toward the battlefield. It was still covered with fog, although the mist had thinned. "There," said the mayor, making a sweeping gesture toward the north, "there after all it was decided, perhaps, right under our eyes. Without that victory, all the aid the States sent us later would have been in vain." Perhaps. At any rate that is still the opinion of everyone.

Then we all shook hands at the gate, and they hurried back to ring the church bells to salute the victory. I did not go with them, as they suggested. I was content to sit here on the spot where I had watched in those hot days of September 1914.

The mist was lifting slightly. All along the valley the bells rang for hours, cut at regular intervals by the booming of the guns at the forts.

I sat on the lawn alone, thinking that all over France—wherever the bells had not been destroyed—this same scene was being carried out. I was sure that in Paris, where Clemenceau was standing before the deputies, his reading of the terms of the armistice was being emphasized by guns saluting the victory and by cheers in the streets.

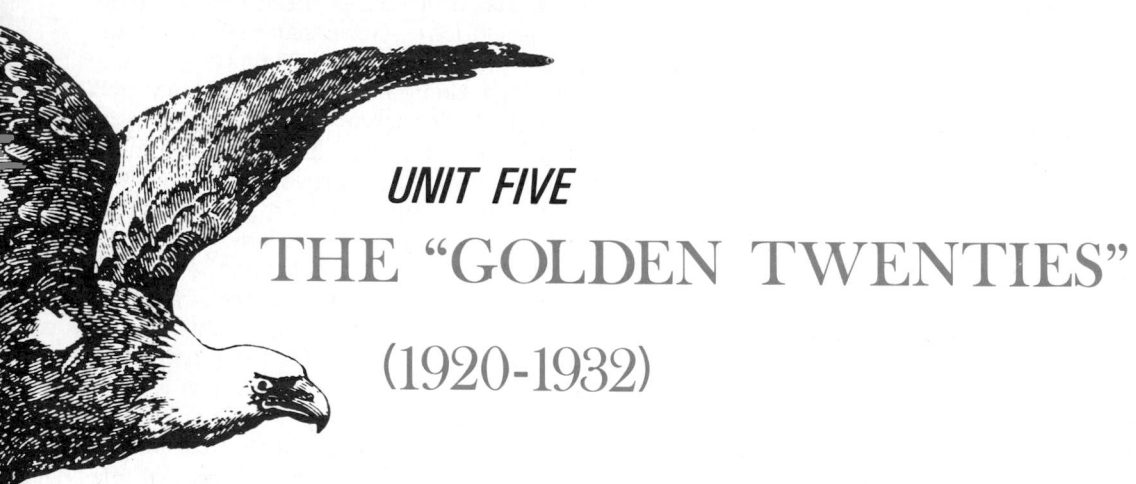

UNIT FIVE

THE "GOLDEN TWENTIES"

(1920-1932)

CHAPTER 14 ■ FROM PROSPERITY TO ECONOMIC COLLAPSE

BLACK AMERICA'S GREAT MIGRATION

Adapted from Charles S. Johnson, "The New Frontage on American Life," in Alain Locke, ed., The New Negro. *New York: Albert and Charles Boni, 1925.*

For black Americans, the war years and the period following World War I were a time of tremendous change. During these years, black families in ever-increasing numbers moved from the South to the cities of the North. Nearly one million black Americans took part in this so-called "Great Migration."

Why did so many people leave the South? Crop failures caused by floods and the boll weevil (an insect that destroys cotton) led to great hardships, especially for farm workers. At the same time, northern factories needed workers to replace those who had left to serve in World War I. Thus the hope of greater opportunities, higher wages, and a better life caused more and more black Americans to move to the North. In this selection, Charles Johnson, a black sociologist, tells about the Great Migration.

How does Johnson describe the migration? What are some of the things that caused it? In what ways did the new Negro culture in the North differ from that of the South?

The cities of the North—stern, impersonal, and enticing—needed people with strong muscles. Europe, suddenly at war, had stopped supplying them, when thousands of blacks came from the South like a silent shadow. There were 500,000 people in the first three-year period. They had come first to the little towns of the South, then to the cities near the towns. Sooner or later, they boarded a special train bound for the North, to go to the cities which attracted them, to their bright lights and high wages, crowds, excitement, and struggle for life.

There was Chicago in the West, known far and wide for its great stockyards; Chicago, remembered for the fairyland wonders of the World's Fair; home of mills yelling for workers.

And there was Pittsburgh, gloomy and cheerless, and the nearby towns of Bethlehem, Duquesne, and Homestead. One railroad line brought in 12,000 new laborers free. The railroads, the vast construction projects of the state, and the large mills wanted workers.

And there was New York City, with its Harlem—the Mecca of Negroes the country over. Old families, brownstone mansions, a step from Broadway. It had factories and docks, large clothing industries, and buildings to be "superintended." It was a land of opportunity for musicians, actors, and those who wanted to succeed, and the national headquarters of everything but the government.

And there was Cleveland, with a faint southern feeling but with iron mills; St. Louis, with great foundries, brick and pottery works; Detroit, the automobile center, with its high wages reflecting the daring economic policies of Henry Ford; Akron and its rubber; Philadelphia, with its comfortable old traditions; and the many little industrial towns where fabulous wages were paid.

Migrations, says one expert, are nearly always due to the influence of an idea. In the case of the Negroes, it was not just an idea, but an idea that was made possible. By tradition, Negroes are rural types. Their usual occupation is agriculture. Their mental and social habits have been adjusted to such an economy.

The South has few cities. The life of the section is based not on manufacturing but on the soil—and more than anything else, the fluffy white bolls of cotton. Cotton is King. When it lives and does well, there is comfort for the owners. When it fails, as is most often the case, a heavy heel twists on the neck of the black tenant farmer. The sharecropping system causing dishonesty and holding Negroes always in debt and almost in slavery; the fierce hatred of poor whites in frightened and desperate competition; the cruelty of the masters; the dullness of rural life; the hope for something better; distant flashes of a new country, calling—these were the soil in which the idea of migration took root and flowered. There was no slow, deliberate making of plans, or inspired leadership, or forces dark and mysterious. To each person in his or her setting came an impulse and an opportunity.

There was Jeremiah Taylor, of Bobo, Mississippi, old and worn out and resigned to his farm. One of his sons came in one morning with the report that folks were leaving "like Judgment day." He had seen a labor man who promised a free ticket to a railroad camp up North. Jeremiah went to town, half doubting, and came back excited and decided. His son left, he followed. In four months his wife and two daughters packed their possessions, sold their chickens, and joined them.

Into George Horton's barber shop in Hattiesburg, Mississippi, came a white man from the North. Said he: "The colored folks owe a debt to the North because it freed them. The North owes a debt to the colored folks because after freeing them it took away their living. Now, this living is offered with interest and a new birth of liberty. Will the colored people live up to their side of the bargain?" The deciding argument was free transportation. Hattiesburg contributed forty men.

And there was Joshua Ward, who had prayed for these times and now saw God cursing the land and stirring up his people. He would ask for his anger no longer.

Rosena Shephard's neighbor's daughter went away. Silence for six weeks. Then she wrote that she was earning $2 a day packing sausages. "If that lazy, good-for-nothing gal can make $2 a day, I can make $4," and Mrs. Shephard left.

Clem Woods could not tolerate any fellow's getting ahead of him. He did not want to leave his job and couldn't explain why he wanted to go North. His boss proved to him that his chances were better at home. But every person who left added to his restlessness. One night a train passed through with two coaches of men from New Orleans. Said one of them: "Good by, I'm bound for the promised land," and Clem got aboard.

Mrs. Selina Lennox was slow to do anything,

but she was a friendly person. The emptiness of her street wore upon her. No more screaming, darting children, no more bustle of men going to work or coming home. The familiar greetings of women who were shopping, the smell of boiled food—all these were gone. Mobile Street, once noisy, was now very quiet, as if some disaster threatened. Now and then the Italian storekeeper, confused and sad, would walk to the middle of the street and look first up and then down and walk back into his store again. Mrs. Lennox left.

George Scott wanted more "free liberty" and accepted a railroad ticket from a stranger who always talked in whispers and seemed to have plenty of money.

Dr. Alexander H. Booth's practice declined. Some of his patients who had left and had owed him money for a long time paid up with an air of superiority that made him very angry. In their letters they said such things as "home ain't nothing like this" or "nobody who has any grit would stay." The doctor left.

Jim Casson in Grabor, Louisiana, had paid his poll taxes, his state and parish taxes. And yet there was no school for his children.

Miss Jamesie Towns taught fifty of the colored tenants' children for four months, out near Fort Valley, Georgia. Her salary was reduced from $16.80 to $14.40 a month.

There is a new type of Negro—a city Negro. He is being shaped out of strangely different elements of the general background. This is a fact overlooked by students of human behavior. In ten years, Negroes have been actually transplanted from one culture to another.

Once there were personal and close relations, in which individuals were in contact most of their lives. Now there are group relations, in which the whole structure is broken, and people are in contact at only one or two points of their lives. The old controls are no longer expected to operate. The newcomers are forced to change their lives.

With Negroes in more industrial contact and competition with white workers of greater experience and numbers, bad feelings build up. The fierce economic fears of workers in competition are increased by racial differences. Beneath the disastrous East St. Louis conflict was a boiling anger toward southern Negroes coming in to "take white people's jobs."

Here lies one of the points of highest tension in race relations. White workers have not, except in a few instances, overcome hatred based on race enough to allow Negro workers

the same privileges they themselves enjoy. While refusing Negroes admission to their unions, they grow furious over their dangerous borings from the outside. Where there is agitation and unrest, there is change. Old traditions are being shaken and rooted up by new ideas. In this the year of our Lord 1925, extending across the entire country, seventeen cities are in violent agitation over Negro residence areas. Once Negroes were silent. Now they are more apt to act with conviction. Claude McKay, the young Negro poet, caught the mood of the new Negro in this, and he turned it into fiery verse which Negro newspapers copied and recopied:

If we must die, let it not be like hogs,
Hunted and penned in an inglorious spot.

Less is heard of the two historic "schools of thought" clashing over the question of industrial training versus higher education for the Negro. Both are, sensibly, now taken for granted as quite necessary. The industrial schools are concerned with adjusting their courses to the new fields of industry in which Negro workers will play an increasing role. The universities must meet the demand for trained Negroes in business, the professions, and the arts. The level of education has been raised through the work of both types of schools.

Thus the new frontier of Negro life is spread out in a jagged, uneven, but progressive pattern. For a group historically kept back and not readily assimilated, contact with its surrounding culture causes uneven results. There is no fixed racial level of culture. There are as many differences in culture, education, and sophistication among Negroes as between the races. It is likely that the culture which has both nourished and abused Negro strivings will, in the end, be enriched by them.

STOCK MARKET FEVER

"American Bores Common, Ex. Div.," from Christopher Columbus and Other Patriotic Verses *by Franklin P. Adams. Copyright 1931 by Franklin P. Adams. Reprinted by permission of The Viking Press.*

During the 1920's, more and more Americans invested their money in stocks. So many people were buying and selling stocks that the New York Stock Exchange had to close down several times during its regular Saturday trading sessions. This was the only way that the brokers' clerks could catch up each week with all the paper work required by the enormous volume of stocks being bought and sold. As the prices of stocks kept on climbing higher and higher, it seemed at times that everyone was speculating in the stock market.

In this selection, newspaper writer Franklin P. Adams makes fun of this frenzied stock buying in a poem called "American Bores Common."

Why is the author critical of the great increase in buying and selling stocks? Did he himself invest in the stock market? Why or why not?

In days of not so very old
Bores did I know a million fold.
They used to tell me this or that:
How cheap—or dear—they'd leased a flat;
They used to tell me of That Kid—
What little Elsie said or did;
They used to tell me of the trains
Between New York and Tiger Plains,
And of how fast they made the trip
From house to office—zippety zip!
Of girls they used to talk—and boast.
Of games, perhaps, they talked the most;
Of fights and baseball games they'd seen;
Of single strokes from tee to green;
Of backhand drives and passing shots;
Of hands that won stupendous pots.
They used to tell, with silly pride,
How yesterevening they were Fried.
They used to tell, the bores supreme,
Of this or that Uncanny Dream.
But nowadays the bores I find
Are of a single, standard kind:
For every person I may meet
At lunch, at clubs, upon the street,
Tells me, in endless wordy tales,
Of market purchases and sales;
Of how he bought a single share
Of California Prune and Pear;
Or how he sold at 33
A million shares of T. & T.
How McAvoy and Katzenstein [stock market brokers]
Told him to sell at 99;
Of thousands lost and millions made
In this or that egregious trade;
How bright he was to buy or sell
FP, GM, X, or GL.
In herds, in schools, in droves, in flocks

The men and women talk of stocks.
They talk in couples and in crowds,
And I, whose head is in the clouds,
Who hold that Mind is more than Matter,
Am bored by all this market patter.
How long can any land be sane
With all its mind on moneyed gain?
And whither, prithee, do we drift
Whose port is Gain instead of Thrift?
It makes me ill, and even sicker
To see so many watch the ticker.

To Mammon bends the national knee;
What fools these stock-mad mortals be!
Ill fares, as Goldsmith [a British writer of the 1700's] used to gab it,
The land where everyone's a Babbitt [a person who strives for money and success, ignoring artistic and intellectual values].
But what a zob they made of me!
I sold a stock at 43
A month ago, and up to date
It's selling at 388.

Ill fares the land, as said before
Where everyone's a stock-mad bore.

WHAT CAUSED THE DEPRESSION?

Adapted from The Great Crash: 1929 *by John Kenneth Galbraith. Copyright © 1954, 1955, 1961 by John Kenneth Galbraith. Reprinted by permission of Houghton Mifflin Company.*

The stock market crash of October 1929 was the beginning of the Great Depression. During this period of hard times, banks and businesses closed down and many millions of Americans were out of work.

What caused the depression? Economists have developed many conflicting theories about the direct and indirect causes of the depression. Some blame the lack of prosperity in American agriculture during the 1920's and the farmers' reduced buying power. Some blame the unequal distribution of income. Others blame overinvestment in the stock market. Still others feel that the huge government debts among nations put too much pressure on the world economy. In this selection, John Kenneth Galbraith, a present-day economist, gives his explanation of this crisis in America's economy.

What explanations of the depression does

. . . The collapse of the stock market in the autumn of 1929 was a natural result of the speculation that went before. The only question about that speculation was how long it would last. Sometime, sooner or later, confidence in increasing stock values would weaken. When this happened, some people would sell. There would be a rush to unload. This was the way past speculative orgies had ended. It was the way the end came in 1929. It is the way speculation will end in the future.

We do not know why a great speculative orgy occurred in 1928 and 1929. The long accepted explanation that credit was easy and so people were forced to borrow money to buy common stocks on margin is obviously nonsense. On many occasions before and since, credit has been easy, and there has been no speculation whatever. Furthermore, much of the 1928 and 1929 speculation occurred using money borrowed at interest rates which for years before, and in any period since, would have been considered exceptionally high. Money, by ordinary standards, was tight in the late 1920's.

Far more important than the rate of interest and the supply of credit is the mood. Speculation on a large scale requires a sense of confidence and optimism. People must also have faith in the good intentions of others, for it is through others that they will get rich. When people are cautious, questioning, or supicious, they resist speculative enthusiasms.

Savings must also be plentiful. Speculation, however it may rely on borrowed funds, must be nourished in part by those who participate. If savings are growing rapidly, people will be willing to risk some of it against the prospect of a good return. . . .

A great many people have always felt that a depression was inevitable in the 1930's. There had been (at least) seven good years; now, by a law of compensation, there would have to be seven bad ones.

There is also the belief that economic life is governed by an inevitable rhythm. After a certain time, prosperity destroys itself and depression corrects itself. In 1929 prosperity, in accordance with the law of the business cycle, had run its course.

Neither of these beliefs can be seriously supported. The 1920's, by being comparatively prosperous, did not call for the 1930's to be depressed. In the past, good times have given way to less good times and less good or bad to good. But change is normal in a capitalist economy. No inevitable rhythm required the collapse of 1930–40.

Finally, the high production of the 1920's did not, as some have suggested, outrun the wants of the people. During these years people were indeed being supplied with an increasing volume of goods. But there is no evidence that they had no more desire for automobiles, clothing, travel, recreation, or even food. On the contrary, all later evidence showed (given the income to spend) a capacity for a large further increase in consumption.

What, then, were the causes of the depression?

There seems little question that in 1929 the economy was fundamentally unsound. This is a circumstance of first-rate importance. Many things were wrong, but five weaknesses seem to have had an especially close bearing on the disaster. They are:

1. *The bad distribution of income.* In 1929 the rich were clearly rich. It seems certain that the 5 percent of the population with the highest incomes in that year received approximately one third of all personal income. The proportion of personal income received in the form of interest, dividends, and rent—the income, broadly speaking, of the well-to-do—was about twice as great as in the years following World War II.

This highly unequal distribution of income meant that the economy was dependent on a high level of investment or a high level of luxury consumer spending or both. The rich cannot buy great quantities of bread. If they are to get rid of what they receive it must be on luxuries or through investment in new plants and new projects. Both luxury and investment spending are subject to wider changes than the bread and rent outlays of the $25-a-week worker. This high-bracket spending and investment was especially open, one may assume, to the crushing news from the stock market in October of 1929.

2. *The bad corporate structure.* . . . American business in the 1920's had opened its hospitable arms to an exceptional number of promoters, grafters, swindlers, imposters, and frauds. In the long history of such activities, there was a kind of flood tide of corporate theft.

3. *The bad banking structure.* The banking structure of the United States was weak. When one bank failed, the assets of others were frozen while depositors elsewhere had a warning to go and ask for their money. Thus one failure led to other failures, and these spread with a domino effect. Even in the best of times local misfortune or isolated mismanagement could start such a chain reaction. (In the first six months of 1929, 346 banks failed in various parts of the country; their deposits totaled nearly $115 million.) When income, employment, and values fell as the result of a depression, bank failures could quickly become an epidemic.

4. *The doubtful state of the foreign balance.* During World War I, the United States became a creditor nation, rather than a debtor nation. In the ten years following the war, the surplus of exports over imports, which once had paid the interest and principal on loans from Europe, continued. The high tariffs, which restricted imports and helped to create this surplus of exports, remained.

Before the war, payments on interest and principal had in effect been deducted from the trade balance. Now that the United States was a creditor, they were added to this balance. During most of the 1920's, the difference was covered by cash—that is, gold payments to the United States—and by new private loans by the United States to other countries. But countries could not make up for their bad trade balance with increased payments of gold, at least not for long. This meant that they had to increase their exports to the United States, reduce their imports, or not pay their past loans. President Hoover and the Congress moved quickly to get rid of the first possibility—that the accounts would be balanced by larger imports—by sharply increasing the tariff. Accordingly, debts, including war debts, were not paid and there was a decline in American exports. The reduction was not great in relation to the total output of the American economy, but it contributed to the general suffering and was especially hard on farmers.

5. *The poor state of economic knowledge.* . . . It seems certain that the economists of the late 1920's and early 1930's were almost determined to be wrong. In the months and years following the stock market crash, they gave advice that was constantly on the side of measures that would make things worse. Asked how the government could best help economic recovery, the sound and responsible adviser suggested that the budget should be balanced. Both political parties agreed on this. . . .

A commitment to a balanced budget meant there could be no increase in government spending to expand purchasing power and relieve suffering. It meant there could be no further tax reduction. But taken in the strictest sense it meant much more. From 1930 on the budget was far out of balance. Balance, therefore, meant an increase in taxes, a reduction in spending, or both. The balanced budget was not the only restraint on government policy. There was also the fear of "going off" the gold standard and, most surprisingly, of risking inflation. . . .

It is in light of the above weaknesses of the economy that the role of the stock market crash in the great tragedy of the 1930's must be seen. The collapse in securities values affected first the wealthy and the well-to-do. In the world of 1929 this was an important group. Its members spent a large proportion of the consumer income. They controlled the greatest share of personal saving and investment. Anything that struck at the spending or investment by this group would of necessity have broad effects on spending and income in the economy at large. . . .

The stock market crash was also an exceptionally effective way of exploiting the weaknesses of the corporate structure. Many companies were forced by the crash to cut down on spending. Their later collapse destroyed both the ability to borrow and the willingness to lend for investment.

The crash was also effective in bringing to an end the foreign lending by which international accounts had been balanced. Now the accounts had, in the main, to be balanced by reduced exports. . . .

Finally, when the misfortune had struck, the attitudes of the time kept anything from being done about it. This, perhaps, was the worst feature of all. Some people were hungry in 1930 and 1931 and 1932. Others feared that they might go hungry. Everyone suffered from a sense of complete hopelessness. Nothing, it seemed, could be done. And given the ideas which controlled policy, nothing could be done.

If the economy had been basically sound in 1929, the effect of the great stock market crash might have been small. But business in 1929 was not sound. On the contrary, it was exceedingly fragile. It was open to the kind of blow it received from Wall Street. . . .

A TEENAGER ON THE SOUP LINE

Adapted from Hard Times: An Oral History of the Great Depression *by Studs Terkel. Copyright © 1970 by Studs Terkel. Reprinted by permission of Pantheon Books, a division of Random House, Inc.*

Many Americans today sometimes wonder what life was like during the Great Depression. They have seen movies and read stories about people standing in soup lines or bread lines, about people going hungry, about jobless people hitchhiking around the nation looking for work. But do these movies and stories give a true picture? What was life really like during the 1930's?

In the late 1960's, writer Studs Terkel decided to find out about American life during the Great Depression by interviewing people who remember those times and asking them how the depression had affected them. He spent months interviewing people and used their conversations in his book *Hard Times*. In this selection, Peggy Terry tells about her experiences as a teenager from Oklahoma during the depression.

Have you ever heard persons who lived during that time talk about the depression? How did the depression affect them? Do they mention the "feeling of together" that Peggy Terry speaks of? How does she compare poor people today with those she knew as a young girl?

I first noticed the difference when we'd come home from school in the evening. My mother'd send us to the soup line. And we were never allowed to curse. If you happened to be one of the first ones in line, you didn't get anything but water that was on top. So we'd ask the guy that was putting the soup into the buckets—everybody had to bring their own bucket to get the soup—he'd dip the greasy watery stuff off the top. So we'd ask him to please dip down to get some meat and potatoes from the bottom of the kettle. But he wouldn't do it. So we learned to curse.

Then we'd go across the street. One place had bread, large loaves of bread. Down the road just a little way was a big shed, and they gave milk. My sister and me would take two buckets each. And that's what we lived off for the longest time.

I can remember one time, the only thing in the house to eat was mustard. My sister and I put so much mustard on biscuits that we got sick. And we can't stand mustard till today.

There was only one family around that ate good. Mr. Burr worked at the ice plant. Whenever Mrs. Burr could, she'd feed the kids. But she couldn't feed 'em *all*. They had a big tree that had fruit on it. She'd let us pick those. Sometimes we'd pick and eat 'em until we were sick.

Her two daughters got to go to Norman to college. When they'd talk about all the good things they had at the college, she'd kind of hush 'em up because there was always poor kids that didn't have anything to eat. I remember she always felt bad because people in the neighborhood were hungry. But there was a feeling of together. . . .

When they had food to give to people, you'd get a notice and you'd go down. So Daddy went down that day and he took my sister and me. They were giving away potatoes and things like that. But they had a truck of oranges parked in the alley. Somebody asked them who the oranges were for, and they wouldn't tell 'em. So they said, well, we're gonna take those oranges. And they did. My dad was one of the ones that got up on the truck. They called the police, and the police chased us all away. But we got the oranges.

It's different today. People are made to feel ashamed now if they don't have anything. Back then, I'm not sure how the rich felt. I think the rich looked down on the poor as much as they do now. But among the people that I knew, we all had an understanding that it wasn't our fault. It was something that had happened to the system. Most people blamed Hoover, and they cursed him—it was all his fault. I'm not saying he's blameless, but I'm not saying either it was all his fault. Our system doesn't run by just one person, and it doesn't fall by just one person, either.

Did I feel a sense of shame? I remember it was fun. It was fun going to the soup line. 'Cause we all went down the road, and we laughed and we played. The only thing we felt is that we were hungry and we were going to get food. Nobody made us feel ashamed. There just wasn't any of that.

Today you're made to feel that it's your own fault. If you're poor, it's only because you're lazy and you're ignorant, and you don't try to help yourself. You're made to feel that if you get a check from Welfare that the bank at Fort Knox is gonna go broke.

Then I got married. My husband and me just started traveling around, for about three years. It was a very nice time, because when you're poor and you stay in one spot, trouble just seems to catch up with you. But when you're moving from town to town, you don't stay there long enough for trouble to catch up with you. It's really a good life, if you're poor and you can manage to move around.

I was pregnant when we first started hitchhiking, and people were really very nice to us. Sometimes they would feed us. I remember one time we slept in a haystack, and the lady of the house came out and found us and she said, "This is really very bad for you because you're going to have a baby. You need a lot of milk." So she took us up to the house.

She had a lot of rugs hanging on the clothesline because she was doing her house cleaning. We told her we'd beat the rugs for her giving us the food. She said, no, she didn't expect that. She just wanted to feed us. We said, no, we couldn't take it unless we worked for it. And she let us beat her rugs. I think she had a million rugs, and we cleaned them. Then we went in and she had a beautiful table, full of all kinds of food and milk. When we left, she filled a gallon bucket full of milk and we took it with us.

You don't find that now. I think maybe if you did that now, you'd get arrested. Somebody'd call the police. The atmosphere since the end of the Second War—it seems like the minute the war ended, the propaganda started. In making people hate each other.

HOOVER'S "AMERICAN PLAN"

Adapted from "Address to the Indiana Editorial Association," in State Papers and Other Public Writings of Herbert Hoover, *Vol. I, edited by William Starr Myers. Reprinted by permission of the Herbert Hoover Foundation.*

As the United States sank deeper and deeper into the worst depression in its history, Americans searched for workable solutions to their economic problems. The nation had never before faced such widespread poverty and so much suffering. But President Hoover believed the nation was suffering only from "frozen confidence" and that prosperity was "just around the corner." Because of this outlook, Hoover tried to use traditional methods to deal with the crisis. Although he realized that some government action was necessary, he was only willing to take limited measures, such as helping to provide some new jobs and making loans to businesses.

In the following speech of June 1931, Hoover outlined his views on how to deal with the depression. Does Hoover oppose or favor the idea of government planning? What arguments does he use to support his position? Do you agree or disagree with his arguments? Explain.

We have many citizens insisting that we produce an advance "plan" for the future development of the United States. They demand that we produce it right now. I presume the "plan" idea is an infection from the slogan of the "five-year-plan" through which Russia is struggling to save itself from ten years of starvation and misery.

I am able to propose an American plan to you. We plan to take care of a 20 million increase in population in the next twenty years. We plan to build for them 4 million new and better homes, thousands of new and still more beautiful city buildings, thousands of factories. We plan to increase the capacity of our railways, to add thousands of miles of highways and waterways, to install 25 million electrical horsepower, to grow 20 percent more farm products. We plan to provide new parks, schools, colleges, and churches for these 20 million people. We plan more leisure for men and women and better opportunities for its enjoyment.

We not only plan to provide for all the new generation. We shall, by scientific research and invention, lift the standard of living of the whole population. We plan to secure a greater distribution of wealth, a decrease in poverty, and a great reduction in crime. And this plan will be carried out if we just keep on giving the American people a chance. Its moving force is in the character and spirit of our people. They have already done a better job for 120 million people than any other nation in all history.

Some groups believe this plan can only be carried out by a fundamental, a revolutionary, change of method. Other groups believe that any system must be the outgrowth of our character and traditions. They believe that we have established certain ideals over 150 years, upon which we must build rather than destroy.

If we analyze the ideas which have been put forward for handling our great national plan, they fall into two main types. The first holds that the major purpose of a nation is to protect the people and to give them equality of opportunity. It holds that the basis of all happiness is in the development of the individual, and that we should steadily build up cooperation among the people themselves to this end.

The other idea is that we shall, directly or indirectly, regiment the population into a bureaucracy to serve the state. It holds that we should use force instead of cooperation in planning, and thereby direct every person as to what may or may not be done.

These ideas present themselves in practical questions which we have to answer. Shall we abandon the philosophy and beliefs of our people for 150 years by turning to a belief that is foreign to our people? Shall we establish a giveaway from the federal treasury? Shall we undertake federal ownership and operation of public utilities instead of regulating them? Shall we pro-tect our people from the lower standards of living of foreign countries? Shall the government, except in temporary national emergencies, enter into competition with its citizens? Shall we regiment our people by extending the arm of bureaucracy into a great many affairs?

Our immediate task as a people is to defeat the forces of economic disruption and pessimism that have swept over us. The duty of government in these times is to use its agencies and influence to strengthen our economic institutions; to inspire cooperation in the community so as to keep up good will and keep our country free from disorder and conflict; to cooperate with the people so that the deserving shall not suffer; and to strengthen the foundations of a better and stronger national life. These have been the objectives of my administration in dealing with this, the greatest crisis the world has ever known. I shall stick with them.

CHAPTER 15 ■ AMERICAN REJECTION OF WORLD LEADERSHIP

WILSON DEFENDS THE LEAGUE

Adapted from War and Peace: The Public Papers of Woodrow Wilson, *Vol. 1, Harper & Row, Publishers, 1927.*

At the end of World War I, President Wilson attended the Versailles Conference, where he helped to write the peace treaty. When he returned home in 1919, he asked Congress to ratify the treaty. However, there was a bitter debate in the United States over whether the Senate should ratify the Treaty of Versailles, and thus approve America's joining the League of Nations. Many Senators were opposed to the United States' joining the League. They feared that membership in the League would involve America too deeply in European politics—perhaps even lead the nation into another war.

President Wilson, however, believed strongly in the League. As a result he decided to appeal directly to the American people for support. On a cross-country speaking tour in the fall of 1919, he made thirty-seven speeches in twenty-nine cities. But the tour ended suddenly when Wilson suffered a stroke. The following selection is from a speech Wilson gave on September 4, at the beginning of his speaking tour.

Why, according to Wilson, is the League "unique in the history of humankind"? What arguments does he offer to urge the United States Congress to ratify the treaty?

After all the discussion of the Treaty of Versailles, perhaps you would like to know what is in it. I find it very difficult in reading some of the speeches that I have read to form any idea about that great document. It is a document unique in the history of the world for many reasons. I think I cannot do you or the peace of the world a better service than by pointing out to you what this treaty contains and what it seeks to do.

In the first place, my fellow Americans, it seeks to punish one of the greatest wrongs in history, the wrong which Germany sought to do to the world and to civilization. Germany attempted an intolerable thing, and it must be punished for the attempt. The terms of the treaty are severe, but they are not unjust.

I can state that the people associated with me at the Peace Conference in Paris had it in their hearts to do justice and not wrong. But they knew, perhaps with a greater sense of what had happened than we could possibly know, the many solemn agreements which Germany had disregarded, the long preparation it had made to defeat its neighbors, and the complete disregard it had shown for human rights. They had seen their lands destroyed by an enemy that devoted itself not only to the effort at victory, but to the effort at terror. There is a method of adjustment in that treaty by which the reparation shall not be pressed beyond the point which Germany can pay. But it will be pressed to the greatest point that Germany can pay—which is just, which is righteous. For, my fellow citizens, this treaty is not meant only to end this single war. It is meant as a notice to any government which in the future may attempt such a thing that humanity will unite to inflict the same punishment on it.

There is no national triumph sought in this treaty. There is no glory sought for any particular nation. The thought of the leaders collected around that peace table was of their people, of the sufferings that they had gone through, of the losses they had suffered. Let us never forget the purpose—the high purpose, the disinterested purpose—with which America lent its strength not for its own glory but for the defense of humanity.

As I said, this treaty was not intended only to end this war. It was intended to prevent any similar war. I wonder if some of the opponents of the League of Nations have forgotten the promises we made our people before we went to that peace table. We had taken men from every household, and we told mothers and fathers and sisters and wives and sweethearts that we were taking those men to fight a war which would end all wars. If we do not end wars, we are unfaithful to the loving hearts who suffered in this war.

That is what the League of Nations is for—to end this war justly, and then to serve notice on other governments which might consider trying to do the same things that Germany attempted. The League of Nations is the only thing that can prevent another dreadful catastrophe and fulfill our promises.

When people tell you, therefore, that the League of Nations is intended for some other purpose than this, answer: If we do not do this thing, we have neglected the central promise we made to our people. The rivalries of this world have not cooled. They have been made hotter than ever. The harness that is to unite nations is more necessary now than it ever was before. Unless there is this assurance of combined action before wrong is attempted, wrong will be attempted just as soon as the most ambitious nations can recover from the financial stress of this war.

Now, look at what else is in the treaty. It is unique in the history of humankind, because the heart of it is the protection of weak nations. There never was a congress of nations before that considered the rights of those who could not enforce their rights. There never was a congress of nations before that did not seek to bring about some balance of power by means of serving the strength and interest of the strongest powers concerned. This treaty says people have a right to live their own lives under the governments which they themselves choose to set up. That is the American principle, and I was glad to fight for it. If there is no League of Nations, the military point of view will win out in every instance, and peace will not last.

Some people have feared with regard to the League of Nations that we will be forced to do things we do not want to do. If the treaty were wrong, that might be so. But if the treaty is right, we will wish to preserve right. I think I know the feelings of our great people better than do some others I hear talk.

The heart of this treaty then, my fellow citizens, is not even that it punishes Germany. That is a temporary thing. It is that it corrects the age-old wrongs which characterized the history of Europe. There were some of us who wished that the treaty also would reach some other age-old wrongs. It was a big job. I do not say that we wished that it were bigger. There were other wrongs elsewhere than in Europe which, no doubt, ought to be righted, and some day will be righted, but which we could not include in the treaty because we could deal only with the countries that the war had affected.

Have you ever thought, my fellow citizens, about the real source of revolution? Revolutions do not spring up overnight. Revolutions come from the long suppression of the human spirit. Revolutions come because people know that they have rights and that they are disregarded. When we think of the future of the world in connection with this treaty, we must remember that one of the chief efforts of those who made it was to remove that anger from the heart of great peoples who had always been suppressed, who had always been the tools in the hands of governments not their own. The makers of the treaty knew that if these wrongs were not removed, there could be no peace in the world. This treaty is an attempt to right the history of Europe.

522

If I were to state what seems to me the central idea of this treaty, it would be this: Nations do not consist of their governments but of their people. That is a simple idea. It seems to us in America to go without saying. But, my fellow citizens, it was never the leading idea in any other international congress made up of the representatives of governments. They were always thinking of national policy, of national advantage, of the rivalries of trade, of the advantages of territorial conquest. There is nothing of those things in this treaty.

I have not come to debate the treaty. It speaks for itself, if you will let it. The arguments against it are directed against it with a great misunderstanding of it. Therefore, I am not going anywhere to debate the treaty. I am going to explain it. And I am going, as I do here today, to encourage you to assert the spirit of the American people in support of it. Do not let people pull it down. Do not let them misrepresent it. Do not let them lead this nation away from the high purposes with which this war was begun and fought. When this treaty is accepted, soldiers will not have to cross the seas again. That is the reason I believe in it.

I say "when it is accepted," for it will be accepted. I have never had a moment's doubt of that. The only thing I have been impatient of has been the delay. Do you realize, my fellow citizens, that the whole world is waiting on America? The only country in the world that is trusted at this moment is the United States. The peoples of the world are waiting to see whether their trust is justified or not. That has been the reason for my impatience. I knew their trust was justified, but I resented the time that certain people wish to take in telling them so. We shall tell them so in a voice as true as any voice in history. In the years to come, people will be glad to remember that they had some part in the great struggle which brought about the fulfillment of the hopes of humankind.

SENATOR BORAH ATTACKS THE LEAGUE

Adapted from American Problems: A Selection of Speeches and Prophecies by William E. Borah, *Horace Green (Ed.). Reprinted by permission of Dodd, Mead & Company, Inc.*

The bitter debate over ratification of the Treaty of Versailles and joining the League of Nations lasted for many months. By the time the Senate voted in November 1919, forty-five amendments and three "reservations," or special clauses to protect American interests, had been added to the treaty. When the final vote was taken on November 19, the Senate rejected the treaty, and thus refused to have the United States join the League of Nations.

One of the leading foes of the treaty, Republican Senator William E. Borah of Idaho, delivered the following speech during the Senate debate. His speech clearly reflected the views of those who opposed the treaty.

To what American tradition does Borah appeal? Why does he believe that the treaty represents a danger to the United States? How does he use American history to strengthen his case against the treaty?

What is the result of this Treaty of Versailles? We are in the middle of all of the affairs of Europe. We have entangled ourselves with all European concerns. We have joined in alliance with all the European nations which have thus far joined the League, and all nations which may be admitted to the League. We are sitting there dabbling in their affairs and meddling in their concerns. In other words—and this comes to the question which is fundamental with me—we have surrendered, once and for all, the great policy of "no entangling alliances" upon which the strength of this Republic has been based for 150 years.

Will my friends who talk of reservations tell me where is the reservation in these articles which protects us against entangling alliances with Europe?

Will those who are differing over reservations tell me which one protects the doctrine laid down by our first President? That fundamental proposition is surrendered, and we are a part of European turmoils and conflicts from the time we enter this League.

You have put in here a reservation concerning the Monroe Doctrine. I think that, as far as language could protect the Monroe Doctrine, it has been protected. But as a practical matter, tell me honestly, as people familiar with the history of your country and of other countries, do you think that you can meddle in European affairs and keep Europe from meddling in your affairs?

There is another and even more pressing reason why I shall vote against this treaty. It endangers what I believe to be the underlying, the very first principles of this Republic. It is in conflict with the right of our people to govern themselves free from all restraint, legal or moral, by foreign powers. It challenges every principle of my political faith. If this faith were mine alone, you could accuse me of arrogance. But I am only being faithful to American ideals as they were created by those who built the Republic and as they have been extended throughout the years.

I will not, I cannot, give up my belief that America must, not alone for the happiness of its own people, but for the moral guidance and greater happiness of the world, be permitted to live its own life. Next to the tie which binds a person to his or her God is the tie which binds a person to his or her country. All schemes, all plans, however ambitious and fascinating they seem, which would compromise our country's freedom of action, I reject absolutely.

Senators, we should not close our eyes to the fact that democracy is something more than just a form of government by which society is restrained into free and orderly life. It is a moral and spiritual force as well. And these are things which live only in the air of liberty. The foundation upon which democracy rests is faith in the moral instincts of the people. Its ballot boxes, the vote, its laws and constitutions are but the outward sign of the deeper and more essential thing—a continuing trust in the moral purposes of the average man and woman.

When this is lost, your outward forms, however democratic in terms, are a mockery. You cannot mix the distinguishing virtues of a real republic with the destructive forces of the Old World and still preserve them. You cannot tie a government whose fundamental principle is that of liberty to a government whose first law is that of force and hope to preserve the former. These things are in constant conflict. One must in time destroy the other.

We may become one of the four dictators of the world, but we shall no longer be master of our own spirit. And what shall it profit us as a nation if we share with others the glory of world control but lose that fine sense of confidence in the people, the soul of democracy.

Look upon the scene as it is now presented. Behold the task we are to take on. Then think of the method by which we are to deal with this task. When this League is formed, four great powers representing the dominant people will rule half of the inhabitants of the globe as subject peoples—rule them by force, and we shall be a party to the rule of force. There is no other way by which you can keep people in subjec-

tion. You must either give them independence, recognize their rights as nations to live their own life and set up their own form of government. Or you must deny them these things by force. That is the scheme, the method proposed by the League.

We are told that this treaty means peace. Even so, I would not pay the price. Would you buy peace at the cost of any part of our independence? We could have had peace in 1776. The price was high, but we could have had it. James Otis, Sam Adams, John Hancock, and Joseph Warren were surrounded by those who encouraged peace and British rule. All through that long and trying struggle, there was a cry of peace—let us have peace.

We could have had peace in 1860. Lincoln was advised by people of great influence and wisdom to let our brothers—and, thank heaven, they are brothers—leave in peace. But the tender, loving Lincoln, bending under the fearful weight of almost certain civil war, an apostle of peace, refused to pay the price. A united country will praise his name forevermore—bless it because he refused peace at the price of national honor and national integrity. Peace upon any other basis than national independence, peace bought at the cost of any part of our national integrity, is fit only for slaves.

But your treaty does not mean peace—far, very far, from it. If we are to judge the future by the past, it means war. Is there any guarantee of peace other than the guarantee which comes from the control of the war-making power by the people? Yet the people at no time and in no place have any voice in this scheme for world peace.

Can you hope for peace when love of country is disregarded in your scheme, when the spirit of nationality is rejected, even scoffed at? Your treaty in a dozen instances breaks the divine law of nationality. Peoples who speak the same language, kneel at the same ancestral tombs—moved by the same traditions and common hopes—are torn apart, broken in pieces, divided, and given to hostile nations. And this you call justice. No, your treaty means injustice. It means slavery. It means war. And to all this you ask this Republic to become a party. You ask it to abandon the principles under which it has grown to power and accept the principles of repression and force.

I turn from this scheme based upon force to another scheme, planned 143 years ago in old Independence Hall, in the city of Philadelphia, based upon liberty. I like it better. I have become so used to believing in it that it is difficult for me to reject it.

America will live its own life. The independence of this Republic will have its defenders. Thousands have suffered and died for it, and their sons and daughters will not be betrayed into the hands of foreigners. The noble face of our first President, so familiar to every boy and girl, looking out from the walls of the Capitol in stern reproach, will call those who come here for public service to a reckoning. The people of our beloved country will finally speak, and we will return to the policy which we now abandon. America, free in spite of all these things, will continue its mission in the cause of peace, of freedom, and of civilization.

TWO BRITISH VIEWS OF AMERICAN ISOLATION

Adapted from Through English Eyes *by J. A. Spender. Reprinted by permission of the Estate of the late J. A. Spender.*

Adapted from The American Illusion *by Collinson Owen, published by Ernest Benn Limited. Reprinted by permission of the publisher.*

Right after World War I, the European nations believed that the United States would join the League of Nations and use its influence and power to help keep the peace in Europe. These hopes ended with the Senate's rejection of the Treaty of Versailles. How did Europe react to America's refusal to join the League? For the most part, Europeans were quite critical of the United States.

Some Europeans, however, tried to analyze more thoughtfully the reasons behind America's return to its traditional policy of isolation. Among them were two British writers, J. A. Spender and Collinson Owen. The first selection (on this page) is taken from a book by Spender; the second selection (page 525) is from a book by Owen.

What does Spender think is the main reason for American isolationism? In Owen's analysis, what incorrect belief does he think helps to explain American actions since the war? In your opinion, do these two articles agree or disagree about the causes of American isolationism?

The first thing, it seems to me, is for Europeans to realize that the United States is not a European power. The habit of treating it as if it acted from the same motives, sympathies, and dislikes as European nations has been the source of much misunderstanding. Most Americans still think they are lucky not to be in Europe and not to be forced to mix themselves in its very tangled affairs. To these—the vast majority of Americans—participation in the war to meet the German challenge was a break, but not a change, in their traditional policy. They regard it as common sense to keep out of Europe if they can.

But this is not the only opinion in America. A large minority of important and politically knowledgeable people have a generous desire to do what they think is their duty to the world. And the whole business community wants to trade with Europe, lend it money, and get back from it what it owes. This "common sense," this idealism, and this commercial ambition are all factors in American policy. We have to consider their interaction in attempting to judge any particular part of its policy.

At the present moment America is seeking a compromise which it hopes will give it the best of all possibilities. It will trade in Europe, maintain its claims on Europe, and shout "Hands off Europe." This annoys and confuses the Europeans. It involves America in such apparent contradictions as starting an enormous program of naval construction at the same time it is proposing a plan for all nations to give up war. There is, nevertheless, a search for the right and wise policy going on all the time, and to treat it with distrust would be a great mistake. It is better to consider what has happened and why it has happened.

The British people should not hastily condemn American policy. The American state of mind corresponds almost exactly to that of the British until quite recently. For a large part of my life—roughly from the year 1880 to the year 1904—it was the aim of both British political parties to stay clear of "continental entanglements." We said to ourselves that the sea made us safe and that we should be able to sit quietly on our island. Why, we asked, should we meddle in quarrels which did not concern us when we had the whole British Empire demanding our extra energy and capital?

It was not argument but events which drove us out of our "splendid isolation." Very reluctantly we came to the conclusion that we must either help to control events on the continent or be controlled by them. Whether we chose rightly or wrongly history must decide. But by the beginning of the 1900's we had discovered that nonintervention was not, as we had supposed, an easy and simple solution, but the most difficult and complicated of all foreign policies. As much as Great Britain might have wished to turn its back on its neighbors, they could not or would not turn their backs on it. Every year these points of contact and friction seemed to increase.

I am not suggesting that American policy will follow the same or a parallel course. Their 3,000 miles [4,828 kilometers] of ocean seem to make it even more obvious common sense for Americans to stand apart than our 21 miles [33.8 kilometers] of English Channel made it for us. The possibilities of meeting between the United States and other nations are fewer than those between the British Empire and other nations. An attack on the United States from Europe would be far more difficult than an attack on the British Isles from the continent. But Americans too discovered in 1917 that it was impossible for them to remain outside a great European struggle. At the end of it, their President said that there would be no neutrals in another war. Thus he proposed a League of Nations to keep the peace. Europe accepted it and America rejected it. Europe is thus left with an American institution which America refused to accept—an American orphan left on Europe's doorstep. The United States still believes, in spite of its experiences of 1917, that nonintervention is a possible policy. At all events the United States is determined that it alone will decide whether, when, and how it will intervene.

The real cause of all this misunderstanding of America is the Great War. Before then all the European nations were aware of the United States, but not obsessed by it. Many of the workers and farmers of these countries may have dreamed of America as the great land of opportunity. But most accepted America much as America thought of itself: a very great country, but a country still in the making. It was a country which had made remarkable progress considering the short time it had been a nation. But it was a country which still had a very long way to go before it could be regarded as a nation as European nations thought of the term. It was not even a real naval or military power, in days when to be a great naval or military power was one of the proofs of civilization.

But the war changed all that. While all Europe was locked in its four years' struggle,

America stole up on us like a bill collector in the night. The war changed us, and seemed to change America. But the fact is that, riches apart, America was exactly the same country after the war that it was before it. Essentially it still remained the same partly developed community. In many ways frontier conditions still ruled, side by side with great material prosperity.

* * * *

Perhaps the most startling discovery one can make in the United States is the fact that many Americans have come to the conclusion that they really won the war.

When this rumor first began, some two or three years after the war was over, no sensible person in Europe paid any real attention to it. No doubt that attitude was then correct. But things have changed very much since then. There are many individuals in the United States who are much too fair and sane to believe in any such fantastic idea. But the people as a whole, aided by the superpatriots, part of the press, the politicians, the movies, and that curious belief that everything American is necessarily best, have now convinced themselves that it was what America did that really mattered. The years 1914–17 are forgotten. Everyone's memory is concentrated on 1918.

This false idea shared by a very large part of a vast nation is not just something to be made fun of. It has its direct effect on international politics. The more firmly America believes this idea, the more likely it is to feel strengthened in its official attitude toward Europe as a continent of warring barbarians, full of old-fashioned treaties and secret diplomacy.

It is a difficult subject to discuss even with some of the best and most open-minded Americans. Although they know that such a claim is absurd, on the whole they would like to feel that America's participation was the really deciding factor.

If the was was really a fight to maintain what we call civilization, against the scientific, military barbarism of the Germany of 1914, then in upholding civilization, the Allies by the middle of 1917 were almost bled to death. The war by that time had become a blood tax on those nations which believed in upholding this civilization. America believed in this ideal, as it assured us both before and after its participation. The blood tax it was called upon to pay in saving it was very, very small. That is the only point of view that needs to be presented in any discussion of whether or not America won the war.

But it would be useless to present such a

view to most Americans. They have become convinced of their comforting false idea. And they believe that the soldiers who crossed the Atlantic to Europe were noble crusaders such as the world had never seen before. It is the habit, of course, of every nation to praise the courage of its own soldiers in war. But though this is a tendency common to all nations, the United States—so far as the last war is concerned—easily goes beyond any other in praising its soldiers. If ever there was a sort of inferiority complex about America's late entrance in the war, it has long since been forgotten, and has been replaced by a mass-produced self-satisfaction and pride concerning the events of 1914–18.

It is a self-satisfaction which has a very definite business as well as patriotic value. So long as America feels like this, there can be no uneasiness of mind concerning Europe's war debts. "Those Europeans" may be feeling the pinch a bit, but they're always getting into wars anyhow, and don't know how to finish them when they begin. America had to do that for them, spending a lot of its own best blood and its own good money in the process. Too much talk about generosity to France and the rest of them becomes tiresome after that.

HOPE FOR A RICH FUTURE

Adapted from Culture and Democracy in the United States, *by Horace M. Kallen. Copyright 1924 by Boni & Liveright, Inc., copyright renewed 1952 by Horace M. Kallen. Reprinted by permission of the Liveright Publishing Corporation.*

In the 1920's, Congress passed several laws to limit immigration into the United States. These laws reflected a widespread feeling of prejudice and intolerance toward the large groups of immigrants who came from the nations of southern and eastern Europe in the late 1800's and early 1900's. This feeling mirrored the fears of many Americans regarding the cultural differences of these newer immigrants.

Not all Americans felt this way about the newcomers. Many Americans believed that the vitality and strength of the United States were based on the great diversity of its people, cultures, and ideas. They did not view their nation as a "melting pot," where people's differences were "melted down" and everyone was "Americanized." Horace Kallen, a scholar and writer, held this view, suggesting that the ideal nation was one in which each group maintained its identity and contributed its special talents to society.

What two alternatives does Kallen believe Americans face? Which one does Kallen favor? Would you say that American society today has become either of Kallen's alternatives?

Today the descendants of the colonists appear to be making a new Declaration of Independence. Again, as in 1776, Americans of British background fear that certain possessions of theirs, which may be lumped under the word "Americanism," are in danger. The danger comes, once more, from a force across the ocean. But this time the force is regarded not as superior, but as inferior. The relationships of 1776 are thus reversed. To save the unalienable rights of the colonists of 1776, it was necessary to declare all people equal. To save the unalienable rights of their descendants in the 1900's, it becomes necessary to declare all people unequal. In 1776 all people were as good as their betters. In 1920 people are permanently worse than their betters.

In 1776 most white people in the colonies *were* actually rather free and rather equal with respect to each other. I speak not so much of the absence of great differences in wealth, as of the fact that the white colonists were similar to each other. They had ethnic and cultural unity and the same background and ideals. Their 150-year-old tradition as Americans blended with their older traditions as Britons. They did not, until the quarrel with the mother country began, regard themselves as anything but English subjects, sharing England's dangers and England's glories.

In time, the nation created by the Declaration of Independence gained all the continental area known as the United States. The French in Louisiana and the Germans in Pennsylvania remained at home. But the descendants of the British colonists traveled across the continent, founding new settlements. If the population of these settlements had continued to grow in the same proportion as it did between 1810 and 1820, Americans of British background would have totaled over 100 million today. The inhabitants of the country today do number over 100 million. But they are not the children of the colonists and pioneers. They are later immigrants and the children of later immigrants, and they are not only British but of all the other European backgrounds.

First came the Irish. They were ethnically different from the British and Catholic in religion. They came seeking food and freedom. Their area of settlement is chiefly the East.

Behind the Irish came large numbers of Germans, quite different in speech and customs. They were culturally and economically far better off than the Irish. They settled inland, over a stretch of territory extending from western New York to the Mississippi.

Beyond the Germans, in Minnesota and the Dakotas, are the Scandinavians. Beyond these, in the mountain and mining regions, are central and eastern and southern Europeans—Slavs of various stocks, Magyars, Finns, Italians. Across the Rockies, a group of Americans of British background balances the small group on the Atlantic seacoast. They are flanked on the south by Latins—Spaniards, Mexicans, Italians—and scattered groups of Asiatics—and on the north by Scandinavians. The distribution of the population along the two coasts is similar. On the Atlantic shore French-Canadians, Irish, Italians, Slavs, and Jews alternate with the British-American population and each other.

Of all these immigrant peoples, most were of peasant stock. They were unable to read or write, surviving on a minimum of food and a maximum of work. The fearful Americans think that their coming to the United States was determined not by any spiritual reason, but because of the steamship agencies and economic need or greed. This opinion ignores four significant exceptions and one notable one. The significant exceptions are the Poles, the Finns, the Bohemians, the Slovaks. Political and religious and cultural persecution plays a large role in their movement here. The notable exception is the Jews. The Jews, more than any other people, come with the attitude of the earliest settlers. For they come because of persecution and disaster and are in search of economic opportunity, liberty of conscience, and civil rights.

All immigrants and their children undergo "Americanization" if they remain in one place in the country long enough—say six or seven years. In general, "Americanization" seems to mean the adoption of the American kind of English speech, American clothes and manners, and the American attitude in politics. "Americanization" means, in short, the disappearance of the outward differences upon which so much race prejudice is based. It appears to mean the blending together, by "the miracle of assimilation," of Jews, Slavs, Poles, French, Germans, Hindus, Scandinavians, and so on. They all are

to become similar in background, tradition, outlook, and spirit to the descendants of the British colonists—the "Anglo-Saxon" stock.

Broadly speaking, these elements of Americanism are somewhat outward, the effect of environment. Along with them go American individualism, the American tendency to look on the bright side of things, and the other "pioneer" virtues. They are purely reactions to the country's natural wealth. As such they are common to all societies where the relation between population and resources is similar.

America is at the parting of the ways. Two genuine social alternatives face Americans, either of which they may achieve if they wish. What do Americans want to make of the United States—a unison, singing the old British theme "America," the America of New England? Or a harmony, in which that theme shall be dominant perhaps, but one among many, and not the only one?

In the United States, the whole social situation is favorable to the idea of unison—everything is favorable except the basic law of America itself and the spirit of American institutions. To achieve unison would require violating them. Fundamentally it would require completely nationalizing education, doing away with every form of parochial and private school, ending instruction in all languages except English, and concentrating on the teaching of history and literature based on the English tradition.

Achieving the other alternative, a harmony, also requires united public action. But this action would not go completely against the ideals of America's fundamental law or the spirit of American institutions. It would seek simply to eliminate the waste and the stupidity in the society's organization, by way of freeing and strengthening those strong forces now at work. Taking the existing ethnic and cultural groups, it would seek to provide conditions under which each group might attain cultural perfection that is *propor to its kind*. All of the various nationalities which make up the American nation must first of all be taught this fact. Perhaps it used to be, to patriotic minds, the outstanding idea of "Americanism"—that democracy means self-realization through self-control and self-discipline.

What is essential in the life of humankind is its inborn positive quality—its inner inheritance. People may change their clothes, their politics, their religions, their philosophies, to a greater or lesser degree. They cannot change their grandparents. Jews or Poles or Anglo-Saxons, in order to stop being Jews or Poles or Anglo-Saxons, would have to cease to be. They inherit their selfhood and the kind of happiness they pursue. This is what, in fact, democracy in operation assumes. There are human capacities which it is the function of the nation to liberate and protect.

As intelligence and wisdom gain over "politics" and special interests, the outlines of a possible great and truly democratic nation can be seen. Its form would be a federal republic. It would be a democracy of nationalities, cooperating voluntarily through common institutions. Thus "American civilization" may come to mean the perfection of the cooperative harmonies of "European civilization"—an orchestration of humankind. As in an orchestra, every type of instrument has its specific tone and its proper theme and melody in the whole symphony. So in society, each ethnic group is like a natural instrument. The harmony and discords of them all make the symphony of civilization.

CHAPTER 16 ■ AN ACCELERATED PACE OF LIVING IN THE "GOLDEN TWENTIES"

A REVOLUTION IN MANNERS AND MORALS

Adapted from pp. 94–109 in Only Yesterday *by Frederick Lewis Allen. Copyright 1931 by Frederick Lewis Allen; copyright renewed 1959 by Agnes Rogers Allen. Reprinted by permission of Harper & Row, Publishers, Inc.*

In many ways, the society we live in today took shape after World War I. Cities and suburbs began to look the way they do now. Things we take for granted, such as automobiles and canned foods, first came into wide use in the 1920's. And along with these material changes came changes in the way people lived, acted, and thought. One writer, Frederick Lewis Allen, described these changes in people's lives as a revolution in manners and morals. In the following selection from a well-known book he wrote about the 1920's, Allen tells about the revolution that took place during those years in the lives of American women.

What were some of the major changes in women's actions and attitudes? Do you think Allen is right in calling the changes in women's lives during the 1920's "revolutionary"? What are some changes in society in recent years that have affected women's lives? Do you consider these changes "revolutionary"?

A revolution in manners and morals was beginning to affect men and women of every age in every part of the country. A number of forces were working together to make this revolution inevitable.

First of all was the state of mind brought about by the war and its conclusion. A whole generation had been affected by the eat-drink-and-be-merry-for-tomorrow-we-die spirit which accompanied the departure of the soldiers to the training camps and fighting front. It was impossible for this generation to return unchanged when the war was over. They found themselves expected to settle down into the dull routine of American life as if nothing had happened. They couldn't do it, and they said so.

The revolution was speeded up by the growing independence of the American woman. She won the vote in 1920. She seemed, it is true, to be very little interested in it once she had it. She voted mostly as the men about her did. Few of the younger women had even a slight interest in politics. To them it was a low and useless business, without flavor and without hope. Nevertheless, winning the vote had its effect. It greatly strengthened woman's position as man's equal.

Even more marked was the effect of women's growing independence from housekeeping. Smaller houses were being built, and they were easier to take care of. Families were moving into apartments, and these required even less of the housekeeper's time and energy. Women were learning how to make lighter work of the preparation of meals. Much of what had once been housework was now either moving out of the home entirely or being made easier by machinery. Women were slowly becoming freed from routine to "live their own lives."

And what were these "own lives" of theirs to be like? Well, for one thing, they could take jobs. Up to this time girls of the middle classes who had wanted to "do something" had been largely restricted to school-teaching, social-service work, nursing, stenography, and clerical work in business firms. But now they poured out of the schools and colleges into all kinds of new occupations. They crowded the offices of publishers and advertisers. They sold antiques and real estate, opened little shops, and invaded the department stores. Married women who had children and could not seek jobs cheered themselves with the thought that home-making and child-rearing were really "professions," after all. No topic was so furiously discussed at luncheon tables from one end of the country to the other as the question whether the married woman should take a job, and whether the mother had a right to. And as for the unmarried woman, she no longer had to explain why she worked in a shop or an office. It was not working that now had to be defended.

With the job—or at least the sense that the job was a possibility—came a feeling of economic independence. With the feeling of economic independence came a weakening of husbandly and parental authority. Unmarried women were leaving the shelter of the family home and getting apartments of their own. Yet even the job did not provide the American woman with that complete satisfaction which the management of a mechanized home no longer provided. She still had energies and emotions to burn; she was ready for the revolution.

Like all revolutions, this one was helped by foreign propaganda. It came, however, not from Moscow, but from Vienna. Sigmund Freud had published his first book on psychoanalysis at the end of the 1800's. But it was not until the war that Freudian ideas began to circulate widely among the American public.

The principal forces which stimulated the revolution in manners and morals were all 100 percent American. They were prohibition, automobiles, confession and other popular magazines, and the movies.

When the Eighteenth Amendment was ratified, prohibition seemed to have an almost united country behind it. Evasion of the law began immediately, however. Strong and sincere opposition to it quickly gathered force. The results were the bootlegger, the speakeasy, and a spirit of deliberate revolt which in many communities made drinking "the thing to do." From these facts in turn flowed further results: the cocktail party, and the general transformation of drinking from a men's pastime to one shared by both men and women together. Meanwhile a new sort of freedom was being made possible by the enormous increase in the use of the automobile. The automobile offered an easy way of escaping temporarily from the supervision of parents and chaperons, or from the influence of neighborhood opinion.

Finally, as the revolution began, its influence led to confession magazines and sensational motion pictures. These in turn had their effect on a vast number of readers and movie-goers who had never heard and never would hear of Freud.

The most obvious sign of what was taking place was the great change in women's dress and appearance. Skirts became shorter and shorter, until they finally reached the knee. With the short skirt went an extraordinary change in the weight and material and amount of women's clothing. The boyishly slender figure became the aim of every woman. The flesh-colored stocking became as standard as the short skirt. Petticoats almost disappeared from the American scene. In fact, the tendency of women to do away with one layer of clothing after another became so great that in 1928 the *Journal of Commerce* estimated that in the previous 15 years the amount of material required for a woman's complete outfit (except for her stockings) had declined from 19¼ yards to 7 yards [17.6 meters to 6.4 meters].

Not satisfied with the freedom of short and skimpy clothes, women sought, too, the freedom of short hair. During the early years of the decade, the bobbed head became increasingly frequent among young girls, chiefly on the ground of convenience. In the late 1920's bobbed hair became almost universal among girls in their twenties, very common among women in their thirties and forties, and by no means rare among women of sixty. Women universally adopted the small cloche hat which fitted tightly on the bobbed head.

The manufacturers of cosmetics and the owners of beauty shops made enormous profits. The popularity of rouge and lipstick spread swiftly to even the smallest village. Women who in 1920 would have thought the use of makeup immoral were soon applying it regularly and making no effort to hide the fact. Beauty shops had sprung up on every street to give "facials," to make war against the wrinkles and sagging chins of age, to pluck and trim and color the eyebrows, and otherwise to heighten and restore the bloom of youth.

These changes in fashion—the short skirt, the boyish figure, the straight, long-waisted dresses, the use of makeup—were signs of a real change in the American feminine ideal (as well, perhaps, as in men's idea of what was the feminine ideal). Women were determined to have freedom—freedom to work and to play without the restrictions that had bound them before to lives of comparative inactivity. But what they sought was not the freedom from men which had put the suffragists of earlier years into hard straw hats and mannish suits and low-heeled shoes. The women of the 1920's wanted to be able to attract men even on the golf links and in the office. Nor was the post-war feminine ideal one of maturity or wisdom or grace. On the contrary: the search for slenderness, and the boyish figure, the popularity of short skirts—all were signs that, consciously or unconsciously, the women of this decade worshiped youth. They wanted to be—or thought men wanted them to be—men's casual and light-hearted companions. Youth was their pattern.

TRYING TO BE A CAREER WOMAN

Adapted from I Am a Woman—and a Jew *by Elisabeth G. Stern. Reprinted by Arno Press, Inc., 1969.*

Though women in the 1920's had many new freedoms, they did not always find their new freedom an easy experience. Should a married woman work? What was a suitable career for a woman? These were questions women faced.

Elisabeth Stern, a writer, was trained as a social worker. After her marriage—to her supervisor—she stayed home to raise a family. However, during the flu epidemic of World War I, her husband became ill and she supported the family by working in a department store. After her husband recovered, she continued to work but as his assistant. In this selection she tells of a new job opportunity and the many problems it presented.

Why did Elisabeth Stern hesitate to take the new job? Do you think the board's questions to her were fair? In what ways have conditions for working women changed since the 1920's? What problems do women face today?

One day in late winter, a long, important-looking envelope came to the office with the name of a well-known woman in the corner. "For you,

Mrs. Morton," [Elisabeth Stern's married name] said the typist.

The letter told me they were planning to open a "health center" in the industrial neighborhood where the Hungarians lived. What they thought of was a place where clinics would be held and free medical treatment given, and where, during the summer, clubs, classes, and community activities would be developed. In time, they would open a camp for children. The president of a large business had signed the letter as chairman of the committee.

They knew, he said, that I had done this sort of work. They wanted me to talk the matter over with them. There were a number of candidates for the position, but they had written to three they particularly wished to have as "first choice." The salary was almost as much as my husband was making.

This was not "just writing." It was not "assisting my husband."

This was a real job for me to do myself, one requiring training, certain special abilities, and experience.

Had I been gathering that experience in the years when I was simply meeting each problem of our life as it came along? I thought over my teaching, my work in the department store, my work with my husband. Curious. I had been an "executive"—why, for years.

Here was an opportunity that any man could be satisfied to have, and at a salary equal to a man's. We had friends teaching in the university who were earning $2,500 a year as heads of their departments. We knew a minister whose parish paid him $1,800 a year, and he was an old man with four degrees.

My husband, whose work this was, who was my chief, received only $700 a year more than this letter offered me.

Could a woman—I—be worth this much? The war had created new conditions, of course. Before, when a woman asked for work, she understood she must expect at least $1,000 a year less than a man, even as an "executive" in a business or profession. I had women friends teaching in colleges and doing social work, who held positions exactly equal with men, and who cheerfully accepted salaries less than half those of the men.

But every woman I knew who had outstanding work, a "big job," was an unmarried woman, or a widow. Married women, at the head of a work as important as a *man's*—and well-paid— were still practically unknown.

What would our friends and neighbors say

if I went away every day to the office—to another office than my husband's? When I had worked at the store my husband was ill. He had been home, and the children had been under his care part of the time. What would people say if I left my children—to do work that was not my husband's, but my own entirely?

If I took this new job, I would be away from nine to five daily, six days a week. My work would be more exacting than my husband's. I would have to leave my children completely in the care of strangers.

The community felt itself very broad-minded when it said, "Oh, she's not an old maid, she's an unmarried woman with a lot of brains who hasn't found a man big enough for her to marry." But the married woman who went to work had to prove that her husband was a man big enough for her to have married. She could not be "bigger" than he. She could not really be as "big."

All these things went through my mind. It will seem strange to women today, but I was afraid to take the work offered me.

Days passed, almost a week, and I could not make a decision. One laughs at these things later. I smile, too, to think now of my fear and hesitation. But I smile as one does at something done by a younger sister.

One morning I turned to my husband and told him of the new offer, of the letter that had been lying under my·pillow for almost a week now.

"Do you want me to do this?" I asked.

He sat thoughtful, silent, a while. "I do not know," he said finally. "It means a great responsibility. It means a real opportunity. It's a really excellent salary." His grave eyes came to mine, worried then. "It is so big a salary that I am troubled by it. It will mean that you must give yourself completely to your work. You'll have to work so hard! I've hoped that after—that store work—you'd never do anything except what you felt you might drop when you wished. I want you to feel that you are free to do anything you like. Do you want to give up writing?"

I think, if he had not said that, I should never have answered the letter. But I understood what he wished to tell me. He wanted me to have a sheltered life, with the responsibility of earning our income on him and the pleasure of economic freedom for me—the fun of writing whenever I wanted to stop working, instead of the serious job of the daily task, the concrete thing, with monthly salary and hourly duties.

"I'd like to do—this," I said.

I met my board one Thursday morning, five people who met in the office of the chairman. Two were women. Of the men one was young and enthusiastic and impractical, and the other was an older man with quiet voice and movement. They had heard of me, knew my work and my husband. They spoke well of my husband.

We discussed the plans they had in mind, and the work done in the past. We decided what activities it might be practical for us to begin with.

Then there was a pause.

"Mrs. Morton," came the voice of the chairman, "this work we are planning will take all your time and all your energy. We know you are a married woman, and we believe, at least I do," and he smiled in a very kind, fatherly way, "that married women are going to become more and more important in all kinds of work in the future, in professions and business equally. We're employing numbers of women in our bank every day. But I want to ask you two questions now. The first is this: you have children, have you not?" I nodded. He went on, slowly, "We did not know you had a family when we first began to consider you. That I will tell you frankly, Mrs. Morton. How will that fit in with your work? Will your husband agree to your giving all your time to this work?"

The other four waited, with him, for me to answer. I understood that these two questions had been discussed before I came in. They had been objections raised by someone.

I thought of the children. Had I neglected them? I wanted to smile, openly, at the question. What work would I do which I could promise to put first, before them? The fact that I was their mother answered that question. I could only work harder, give myself doubly. Nothing would ever come that could stand before them in my thought.

"I held a professional job even when my little daughter was a baby," I answered, letting that speak for me.

The larger of the two women shook her head. "But that's it, Mr. Blank," she said. "Let us be frank, Mrs. Morton. I've heard a great deal about you from Mr. Blank. I think this is your work. But I'm an old-fashioned woman," she admitted. "I do not feel quite easy about seeing young wives and mothers leave their homes. I was a schoolteacher myself, and I gave up my work as soon as I married. However, I am willing to keep up with the times," and she smiled to Mr. Blank. "I feel we ought to be intelligent. It is not clear to me, though," she confessed, "that your children do not suffer by having their mother away on other interests. I can understand that writing would not interfere so with your home. Please do not think I am being too personal, but we have to be in this matter. Can you give your children the proper care if you come to us—and are you doing social work because you want to, or just as a stop-gap?"

It was shrewd of her. She was more acute about me than was I myself.

But at the time I did not think of her shrewdness. I thought only how unfair her questions were. I thought that if I were an unmarried woman, I would never have been asked if my dependents were cared for. I would not have been asked to assure them that I would not neglect the work I was paid to do for some other interest. It was because I was a married woman, a mother, that I was in this undignified position and questioned in this way.

"I do not think," I said, "I wish to speak about my children and the care I give them. It seems to me that if a woman is capable of arranging for the lives of several hundred people, she is equally able to arrange the lives of those dearest to her. I do not wish to discuss how I plan to do so. That seems to be my personal business."

The large lady grew red. She did not answer. The chairman sat back, too. I had been "independent" to the board. I had not been polite and respectful. In other words, I had destroyed my opportunity.

I said good-by, and said good-by to $2,800 a year as I went out.

The house was empty and still when I came in, for my husband was away, the children were at school. I had to get rid of some of the disappointment that I felt. I set to work, scrubbed and washed and swept. I tore through that house with broom and mop. This is what "they" thought I ought to do!

My husband listened to the account of the meeting quietly. "You were right," he said finally. "You could never have started the job under such conditions. Your board would have said that you were giving only part of your attention to the work, that you were thinking of your children and your home. It would have been an impossible situation."

It was true, and I knew it. But still, disappointment ate at me. I had thrown it all away. A man would never have done it. He would have known how to speak, how to smooth things out.

Only women were emotional and hasty.

"A man wouldn't have had to meet such a situation," my husband said. "Do you think he would be asked, even if he were a widower, how he planned to take care of his children?"

I looked at him. "Did you want me to have that job?" I asked, for the second time. "Did you really want me to have it?"

He did not answer immediately. "I don't know," he said slowly. "I don't really care what you do, just so it makes you happy. I would prefer you not to have burdens to weigh you down, like, I suppose, a man carries. That's not because I don't believe you can carry them. It is just that I prefer to do that for us."

"Do you think of me," I asked then, "just as a—well, a little girl? Don't you think—well, that I am as mature as you, as capable?"

At that he laughed, his rare, deep laugh. "I know that is disturbing you," he answered. "You want to be thought 'just as good as a man'—in anything. You feel unhappy because you are afraid I do not regard you so. I suppose you are just as mature as a man, as capable. But," and here he smiled at me again, "it is not because you are capable and a good executive that I love you, my darling."

He did not say quite what I wanted him to say. He did not say I was as capable as a man. But I was satisfied.

"There'll be other opportunities," he said. "Meanwhile, let's get back to my work."

A BLACK WRITER ON THE HARLEM RENAISSANCE

Adapted from "When the Negro Was in Vogue" in The Big Sea *by Langston Hughes. Copyright 1940 by Langston Hughes. Adapted and reprinted by permission of Farrar, Straus & Giroux, Inc.*

During the 1920's, there was a cultural renaissance, or rebirth, in black culture that came to be known as the "Harlem renaissance." An extremely talented group of writers and poets began to speak out against injustices in America and to write of the joys, sorrows, and hopes of black Americans. Black pride was aroused by these writers and by America's growing interest in black music, art, and entertainment, especially in the Harlem area of Manhattan in New York City. Jazz music became the rage, and many black entertainers became extremely popular and famous, as did many night-clubs in Harlem. In this selection, Langston Hughes, one of the leading black writers of that time, writes about the Harlem renaissance and tells why he "had a swell time while it lasted."

How was the work of black writers and black entertainers of the period affected by white audiences? What is Hughes' attitude toward black intellectuals? Toward the ordinary people of Harlem?

The 1920's were the years of Manhattan's black Renaissance. It began with the musical revue *Shuffle Along.* It reached its peak just before the crash of 1929, the crash that sent Negroes, white folks, and all rolling down the hill.

Shuffle Along was a honey of a show. Swift, bright, funny, carefree, and gay, with a dozen danceable, singable tunes. Everybody was in the audience—including me. People came back to see it many times. It was always packed.

To see *Shuffle Along* was the main reason I wanted to go to Columbia. When I saw it, I was thrilled and delighted. From then on I was in the gallery of the Cort Theatre every time I got a chance. *Shuffle Along* gave just the proper push—a pre-Charleston kick—to that Negro vogue of the 1920's that spread to books, African sculpture, music, and dancing.

The 1920's brought the rise of Roland Hayes, who packed Carnegie Hall; the rise of Paul Robeson in New York and London; the booming voice of Bessie Smith on thousands of records; and the rise of that grand comedienne of song, Ethel Waters. The 1920's brought Louis Armstrong and Josephine Baker.

White people began to come to Harlem in large numbers. For several years they packed the expensive Cotton Club on Lenox Avenue. But I was never there, because the Cotton Club was a Jim Crow club for gangsters and rich whites. They did not want Negro customers, unless you were someone famous like Bojangles [a dancer]. So Harlem Negroes did not like the Cotton Club and never appreciated its Jim Crow policy in the very heart of their dark community. Nor did ordinary Negroes like the growing numbers of whites in Harlem after sundown, filling the little cabarets and bars. Formerly only colored people laughed and sang there. Now strangers were given the best ringside tables to sit and stare at the Negro customers—like amusing animals in a zoo.

The Negroes said: "We can't go downtown and sit and stare at you in your clubs. You won't even let us in your clubs." But they didn't say it out loud—for Negroes are practically never rude to white people. So thousands of whites came to Harlem night after night, thinking the Negroes loved to have them there. They firmly believed that all the people who lived in Harlem left their houses at sundown to sing and dance in nightclubs, because most of the whites saw nothing but the nightclubs, not the houses.

Some of the small clubs had people like Gladys Bentley, who was something worth discovering in those days, before she got famous. For two or three amazing years, Miss Bentley sat and played a big piano all night long, without stopping. She slid from one song to another, with a powerful and continuous underbeat of jungle rhythm. Miss Bentley was an amazing exhibition of musical energy—a large, dark, masculine woman, whose feet pounded the floor while her fingers pounded the keyboard—a perfect piece of African sculpture, made alive by her own rhythm.

But when the place where she played became too well known, she began to sing with an accompanist, became a star, moved to a larger place, then downtown, then to Hollywood. The old magic of the woman and the piano and the night and the rhythm are gone. But everything goes, one way or another. The 1920's are gone and lots of fine things in Harlem night life have disappeared like snow in the sun—since it became completely commercial, planned for the downtown tourist trade, and therefore dull.

The dancers at the Savoy even began to practice acrobatic routines. They did absurd things for the entertainment of the whites that probably never would have entered their heads to attempt just for their own amusement.

Some critics say that that is what happened to certain Negro writers, too. They stopped writing to amuse themselves and began to write to amuse and entertain white people. In so doing they distorted their material and left out their American brothers of a lighter complexion. Maybe it's true, since Negroes have writer-racketeers like any other race. But I have known almost all of them, and most of the good ones have tried to write honestly and express their world as they saw it.

All of us know that the happy, sparkling life of the so-called Negro Renaissance of the 1920's was not so happy and sparkling beneath the surface. But it was a period when, at almost every Harlem uppercrust dance or party, one would be introduced to various distinguished white celebrities who were there as guests. It was a period when preachers opened up shouting churches as sideshows for white tourists. It was a period when every season there was at least one hit play on Broadway acted by a Negro cast. And when books by Negro authors were being published with much greater frequency and given much more publicity than ever before or since. It was a period when white writers wrote about Negroes more successfully (commercially speaking) than Negroes did about themselves. It was the period when Ethel Barrymore appeared in blackface in *Scarlet Sister Mary!* It was the period when the Negro was in vogue.

I was there. I had a swell time while it lasted. But I thought it wouldn't last long. For how could a large and enthusiastic number of people be crazy about Negroes forever? But some people in Harlem thought the race problem had at last been solved. They were sure the New Negro would lead a new life from then on in green pastures of tolerance created by Countee Cullen, Ethel Waters, Claude McKay, Duke Ellington, Bojangles, and Alain Locke.

I don't know what made any Negroes think that—except that they were mostly intellectuals doing the thinking. The ordinary Negroes hadn't heard of the Negro Renaissance. And if they had, it hadn't raised their wages any. As for all those white folks in the speakeasies and night clubs of Harlem—well, maybe a colored man could find *some* place to have a drink that the tourists hadn't yet discovered.

AN AGE OF HERO WORSHIP

Adaptation of "Worshiping the American Hero" by Bruce Bliven from America as Americans See It *edited by Fred J. Ringel. Copyright, 1932, by Harcourt Brace Jovanovich, Inc.; copyright 1960, by Fred J. Ringel. Reprinted by permission of the publishers.*

Throughout the history of the United States, certain men and women have become heroes to the American people. In earlier times these heroes were often famous generals or politicians. Americans also seemed to greatly admire men and women known for outstanding individual achievements. In this selection, writer Bruce Bliven suggests that in the 1920's such hero-worship seemed more intense and involved more people. One of the most popular heroes of the period was Charles Lindbergh, but many other Americans also became objects of national hero-worship.

Why, according to Bliven, did Americans worship heroes so much in the 1920's? Do you agree with his reasons? Why do you think none of the "heroes" Bliven mentions was a woman? Who are some people that you especially admire today? Why do you feel this way about them?

For some years past, the most persecuted man in the world has undoubtedly been Charles A. Lindbergh, the American flyer. For a long time, he never dared to appear in public without a police guard, lest his clothes be torn from his back and his life put in danger by frenzied hero-worshipers.

He was driven nearly to desperation by the crowds which gathered at every landing field where his airplane was expected. These crowds, in their eagerness to be near him, refused to leave a clear space in which he could land. When he toured the United States to increase interest in flying, he was driven through the streets of each city in an automobile. Several of his friends had to catch as best they could the heavy packages of candy and the wreaths of flowers which lovesick women tossed at him from the crowd.

Hero-worship is not a new phenomenon in American life. But like many other things nowadays, it is speeded up and achieved on a larger scale. Thirty years ago, after the Spanish-American War of 1898, Admiral Dewey was the subject of equal worship. It ended overnight, however, when he hurt the country's feelings by making a technical transfer to his wife of a house which had been presented to him by the people. Another hero of the same war, Richmond Person Hobson, became the target of masses of strange young women who insisted, one after another, on kissing him in public.

As we have it today, however, hero-worship is a product of our times, especially of the movies and the radio. For twenty-five years movies were silent. A deep psychological need grew among most people to see in person, and to hear the voices of, those whom they had so often followed as gray shadows on a silver screen. The popular movie star dared not appear in public without a disguise, and counted his or her fan mail by hundreds of thousands of letters each year. Then came the radio and it reversed the process. Millions wanted to see the owner of the voice to whose tones, musical or otherwise, they responded night after night. There are several persons, quite unknown a few years ago, who now receive a fee as high as $1,000 a performance just to stand upon a stage.

Americans' love of sport, and their admiration of athletics, of course, accounts for much of the present hero-worship. The typical American attitude toward athletics is still one of spectatorship rather than participation. The outstanding figures in sports—"Babe" Ruth in baseball, Bobby Jones in golf, W. T. Tilden in tennis, Red Grange or Albie Booth in football —are the objects of the greatest public interest. They can, and some of them do, earn large sums of money by endorsing certain advertised products, by writing for the press, and by appearing in vaudeville theaters. For that matter, anyone who has become somewhat known, by whatever means, can take advantage of it to some extent. The woman who shoots her husband or boyfriend writes her life story from her prison cell for some sensational newspaper. The winner of an endurance contest, who has rocked in a rocking chair, or ridden a bicycle, or sat in a tree, longer than anyone else, is an outstanding hit in a theater, though often completely forgotten soon afterward.

What we have seen in recent years is the creation of a vast new machinery for making everyone aware of any new person or idea. Of this machinery the movies and the radio are but a part, although an important one. Let anyone say or do anything interesting, and within a week everyone in America has heard his voice on the radio, seen his photograph and read his interviews in the newspapers, seen and heard him in the movies. This fact has a double result. It not only creates heroes by magic, but it guarantees that people will tire of them with equal speed. Just as a popular song now runs its course and dies in half the time it did a few years ago, there is no one so completely forgotten as the person in the spotlight last year.

The movie is the deadliest of all enemies of these soon-forgotten celebrities. They are now required to make a speech before the camera, and rarely do they come through this ordeal well. They have trouble talking, they perspire, make mistakes in grammar, or what is worse, read a speech which was obviously prepared for them by someone else. It seems probable that when television comes along, only the very sturdiest of our heroes will be able to last.

Are Americans more interested in hero-worship than the people of other countries? Or is it just that the hero-making machinery exists here in more complete form than elsewhere? Certainly hero-worship is not unknown in Europe. American movie stars are mobbed more mercilessly in London than they are in New York. Lindbergh was never in greater danger from the bear-like affection of the mob than at Le Bourget airport in Paris. The making of mob-idols is neither uniquely an American phenomenon nor one of the present age alone. In explanation of America's attitude there are several things to be said, though I can hardly do more than suggest them here.

1. The Americans are only very partially believers in the theory of democracy. While their politics are republican, their business life— which is to them far more important—is conducted on strictly autocratic lines. In this country, as elsewhere, the mob desires ruthless leaders whose strength and success make up for their own weakness and failure.

2. A common error is to suppose that the American temperament is like the English, or that of other North European peoples. It is not. In its intensity, violence of thought and action, and changeability, it is much more Latin than Nordic.

3. It must be remembered, moreover, that America is not so much a nation as a parliament of nations. It has become a commonplace to point out that New York City alone has more Irish than Dublin, more Italians than Naples, more Jews than Jerusalem. Not only in New York but throughout America, these groups with their various racial backgrounds and cultural heritages are vaguely conscious of their differences from one another. They do what they can to find a common meeting ground. It is not too fanciful to say that when they all worship the same hero at the same moment, they feel a sense of kinship to each other which they can acquire in no other way.

4. Most important of all, however, is a feeling at which I have already hinted. Americans, like other Western peoples, feel an uneasy, increasing sense of insecurity in the modern world, where they seem more and more to be the puppets of great economic forces which are beyond anyone's power to control. In this predicament they turn with relief to anyone who, in any field, appears to stand out beyond everyone else. They feel that the world needs giants— as perhaps it does. When they find them, they pretend that they are even taller than in fact they are.

THE NEW DEAL AND WORLD WAR II (1932-1945)

CHAPTER 17 ■ UNDERTAKING A GREAT EXPERIMENT

ROOSEVELT ON GOVERNMENT AND THE ECONOMY

Adapted from The Public Papers and Addresses of Franklin D. Roosevelt, Vol. I, *published by Random House, Inc.*

In 1932 the Democratic Party nominated Franklin D. Roosevelt as its candidate for President. Roosevelt had served as Assistant Secretary of the Navy under President Wilson and had become governor of New York in 1928. But he was not well known to many Americans when he began his Presidential election campaign. His campaign travels to all parts of the nation and his speeches promising to act immediately to end the depression won him victory in the 1932 election.

In his Inaugural Address, Roosevelt promised "a new deal for the American people," and he outlined his program for ending the depression. He believed that the Great Depression was a grave crisis that had to be fought with bold new governmental programs. In the following speech delivered in San Francisco on September 23, 1932, Roosevelt summarized his ideas about what the role of the federal government should be in ending the crisis.

According to Roosevelt, what are the two basic economic rights of all Americans? How can they be guaranteed by business? By government?

I want to speak not of politics but of government. I want to speak not of parties but of universal principles. They are not political, except in that larger sense in which a great American once defined politics—that nothing in all of human life is unrelated to the science of politics.

A look at the situation today indicates only too clearly that equality of opportunity as we have known it no longer exists. Our industrial system is built. The problem just now is whether under existing conditions it is not overbuilt. Our last frontier has long since been reached. There is practically no more free land. More than half of our people do not live on farms, and they cannot make a living by cultivating their own property. There is no safety valve in the form of a Western frontier to which those thrown out of work by the Eastern economic machines can go for a new start. We are not able to invite immigrants from Europe to share our endless plenty. We are now providing a drab living for our own people.

Our system of constantly rising tariffs has at last reacted against us. It has closed our Canadian frontier on the north, our European markets on the east, many of our Latin-American markets to the south, and a sizable part of our Pacific markets on the west.

Just as freedom to farm has ended, so also opportunity in business has narrowed. It still is true that people can start small businesses, trusting their own shrewdness and ability to keep ahead of competitors. But area after area has been taken over altogether by the great corporations. Even in the fields which still have no large companies, the small operator starts under a handicap. The statistics of the past 30 years show that the independent business owner is running a losing race. Perhaps he is forced into bankruptcy. Perhaps he cannot get credit. Perhaps he is "squeezed out" by highly organized corporate competitors—as your corner grocery store owner can tell you.

Recently a careful study was made of the concentration of business in the United States. It showed that our economic life is dominated by some 600 corporations that control two thirds of American industry. The other third is shared by 10 million small businesses. More striking still, it appears that if the process of concentration goes on at the same rate, at the end of another century all American industry will be controlled by a dozen corporations, run by perhaps a hundred people.

Clearly, all this calls for us to think over our values. A builder of more industrial plants, a creator of more railroad systems, an organizer of more corporations, is as likely to be a danger as a help. The day of the great financial promoters to whom we granted anything if they would build or develop is over. Our task now is not discovery or exploitation of natural resources or producing more goods. It is the less dramatic task of managing resources and businesses already in existence. We need to get back foreign markets for our surplus production, and solve the problem of underconsumption. We must adjust production to consumption, distribute wealth and products more fairly, and adapt existing economic organizations to the service of the people. The day of enlightened management has come.

In older times the central [national] government was first a place of refuge, and then a threat. In the same way, in our present economic system the huge corporation is no longer a servant but a danger. I would draw the parallel one step farther. We did not think, when national government became a threat in the 1700's, that we should abandon the principle of national government. Nor today should we abandon the principle of corporations, just because their power can be abused. In other times we dealt with the problem of an overly ambitious central government by changing it gradually into a constitutional democratic government. So today we are changing and controlling our economic units.

As I see it, the task of government in its relation to business is to help in developing an economic declaration of rights, an economic constitutional order. Happily, the times indicate that to create such an order not only is the proper policy of government, but is the only line of safety for our economic structures as well. We know now that these economic units cannot exist unless prosperity is uniform. Purchasing power must be well distributed throughout every group in the nation. That is why even the most selfish corporations would be glad to see wages raised and unemployment ended, and the Western farmer restored to prosperity. That is why some enlightened industries themselves try to limit the freedom of action of each business group within the industry in the common interest of all.

I feel that we are coming to see that private economic power is a public trust. I believe that in order to keep that power any individual or group must fulfill that trust. The people who have reached the top of American business life know this best. Happily, many of them urge that we adopt this greater social contract.

The terms of that contract are as old as the Republic, and as new as the new economic order.

Every person has a right to life. This means the right to make a comfortable living, a right that may not be denied. We have no actual famine. Our industrial and agricultural systems can produce enough and still have capacity to spare.

Every person has a right to individual property. This means a right to be assured of the safety of one's savings. In all thought of property, this right is supreme. All other property rights must give way to it.

These two requirements must be satisfied chiefly by the individuals who control the great industrial and financial concerns which dominate our industrial life. They are not business leaders, but rather princes of property. I am not prepared to say that the system which produces them is wrong. But I do say that they must take the responsibility which goes with the power. Many enlightened business leaders know this.

The responsible heads of finance and industry, instead of acting alone, must work together to achieve the common good. They must, where necessary, sacrifice this or that personal advantage and seek a general advantage. It is here that government comes in. Whenever the dishonest competitor or the reckless promoter refuses to join in achieving a goal recognized as being for the public welfare, the government may properly be asked to apply restraint. Likewise, if the group should ever use its collective power against the public welfare, the government must be swift to protect the public interest.

The government should take over the function of economic regulation only as a last resort when private initiative has finally failed. As yet there has been no final failure, because there has been no attempt.

The final goal of the Declaration of Independence was liberty and the pursuit of happiness. We have learned a great deal about both in the past hundred years. We know that individual liberty and individual happiness mean nothing unless both are achieved without one man's meat being another man's poison. We know that liberty which robs others of basic rights cannot receive governmental protection.

All this is a long, slow task. Human endeavor is not simple. Government includes the art of making a policy, and using political techniques to secure as much of that policy as will receive general public support. We must build toward the time when a major depression cannot occur again. If this means sacrificing the easy profits of inflationary booms, then let them go, and good riddance.

Faith in America, faith in our tradition of personal responsibility, faith in our institutions, faith in ourselves, demand that we recognize the new terms of the old social contract. We shall fulfill them. We must do so. Otherwise, a rising tide of misery, caused by our common failure, will swamp us all. But failure is not an American habit. In the strength of great hope we must all share our common responsibility.

WPA AND THE ARTS

Adaptation of "WPA, Willing Patron of the Arts," in Just Around the Corner, *by Robert Bendiner.* © *1967 by Robert Bendiner. Reprinted by permission of Harper & Row, Publishers, Inc.*

Enormous problems faced President Roosevelt when he took office in March of 1933. Millions of Americans were unemployed, thousands stood in "bread lines" for food every day. As part of the New Deal, Roosevelt planned programs to provide direct relief for the unemployed. Several government agencies also were set up to provide work for jobless Americans.

One of these agencies was the Works Progress Administration (WPA). The WPA provided jobs not only for unemployed factory and office workers but also for artists, writers, musicians, and actors. Through the Arts Projects, the WPA decorated post offices and other government buildings with murals. It performed free concerts, staged plays and musicals, and wrote a set of guidebooks about America.

In this selection, writer Robert Bendiner describes the WPA Arts Projects.

What were the four main types of Arts Projects? What were their major accomplishments? Does the federal government offer aid to America's museums, theaters, and other cultural centers today? Do you think that it should? Explain.

In the history of the world, few depression governments have given housewives free piano lessons. Fewer still have put thousands of artists to work. And before the 1930's probably none had given stage people an annual wage, even a small one, to put on free puppet shows and classical plays. But the New Deal did all of these things. In addition, it paid $90 a month to unemployed reporters, unpublished writers, skilled researchers, and others to prepare some 250 books about America.

It has been pointed out over and over that the Arts Projects, as these operations of the Works Progress Administration were known, produced no Mozarts or Da Vincis. Neither did they produce lasting works of drama or fiction. What they did do was to help many talented people through the hard times. And they exposed to those talents millions of Americans who would otherwise never have known their charms. This introduction of struggling artists helped to destroy in four years certain American myths that had been around for a hundred years—that painting had to be European to have merit, and required wealth to be appreciated; that all concerts except those by the town band were in the nature of good works to which dutiful women dragged long-suffering husbands; and that except for four or five cities the American people required no theater at all.

Statistics are no key to quality, but they *can* point to a highly stimulated interest in music, painting, and plays. By the end of the 1930's, nearly 70 art centers were flourishing in communities where many art teachers had never before seen a professional painting. Some 60,000 Americans had taken painting lessons from government-paid artists. Offices and lobbies in government buildings across the land boasted murals and new paintings. Audiences estimated at 100 million people had heard some 150,000 free concerts, most of them by three dozen newly created symphony orchestras. And a half-million Americans each month had enrolled in free music classes, 40,000 in New York City alone.

A visiting English critic was amazed. "Accidentally WPA has dug up an extraordinary amount of talent," said Ford Madox Ford. "Art in America is being given its chance, and there has been nothing like it since before the Reformation."

Certainly a Reformation was not what Harry Hopkins [head of the WPA] and his aides had in mind when they thought of the Arts Projects. What interested them was the hope of creating a whole new idea of government relief. In three years the country had come a long way from the Hoover view that direct aid to the victims of flood or earthquake was right and proper but not aid to the victims of human-made economics. For a time, welfare was the answer, then work of any kind for any purpose. Now the time had come for "maintaining the morale and skills" of the unemployed by paying them to perform the work they could do best until private business was ready to rehire them.

While the Public Works Administration went on with its building, the newly planned Works Progress Administration would serve human beings. WPA funds would be spent on people, not things. What they were to do would be determined by what they *could* do, not by what the community might lack in the way of parking lots or sewage disposal plants.

Carrying the idea further, WPA proposed to help *all* the jobless artists who might come to it for help, rather than just the truly gifted, who would most likely be the least in need. For years government agencies had hired the best artists, or those it considered such, to do murals and sculpture for its buildings. Now the problem was to employ not just the best, but also those who were merely good—in practice even those who were mediocre and sometimes those who were not very good, who also had to eat.

Of all Americans engaged in the arts in the 1930's, the worst off by far were show people [entertainers]. Some 40,000 show people were extremely poor. So it was that, of all the good works of the WPA, the Federal Theater Project had the greatest opportunity, made the biggest splash, and left the most vivid memories.

One of the great charms of the Federal Theater was that it really covered the country. WPA shows were not just for New York, Chicago, and San Francisco. They were also for Tacoma (Washington), Reading (Pennsylvania), and Timberline Lodge (Oregon), not to mention Gary (Indiana), Peoria (Illinois), and Red Bank (New Jersey). They brought theater to towns in the United States that had not seen live actors for years. And they were received with great enthusiasm.

Three other WPA efforts in the arts left more visible reminders than the Federal Theater. About the Music Project I know little beyond the story of a violinist in a WPA orchestra in Florida. He apologized to the audience, on behalf of himself and the other musicians, for the quality of their concert. Their hands were still stiff, he explained, from their previous relief job, which was building a highway. The lasting work that the Music Project did was to search out and record the real folk music of America—the songs of the Southern mountaineers, the Indian-flavored songs of early Oklahoma, the Cajun songs of Louisiana, and the African-inspired songs of the Mississippi bayous.

On the Art Project, as the painters' and sculptors' unit was called, nobody pretended that the quota of genius was high. Considering the varied talents it had to work with, the Art Project sensibly made no attempt to have everyone paint. Of the 4,000 to 5,000 federally enrolled artists, far fewer than half were engaged in painting pictures or sculpturing or doing murals. Many taught free art classes. Some took photographs of old and decaying American houses. Others worked on posters and stage sets for the Federal Theater.

But the Art Project's real monument was the Index of American Design. For this magnificent work, still widely used, some 400 people reproduced in oil and watercolor the native art with which Americans, from early settlers to late Victorians, had decorated their homes, their possessions, and themselves. Here appeared in all their brightness the scarlet tulips that enlivened the coffeepots of the Pennsylvania Dutch, the embroidery of seventeenth-century Massachusetts, and the wonderful carved figureheads from New England ships. It was this great work, with its 7,000 skillful illustrations, that convinced many Americans that we had a native art after all.

It was charged that the fourth of the federal projects in the arts, the WPA Writers' Project, had little to do with writers. True, the memorable names connected with it can be counted on the fingers. What passed for a Writers' Project was essentially what writer Bernard DeVoto called it, "a project for research workers." Happily, good writers and skilled journalists, headed by Henry Alsberg, its first national director, turned out the most colorful series of guides a nation could ask for. A one-time newspaper reporter, Alsberg felt that

540

Americans might want to know more about places, people, and things in the United States than they could get from filling-station maps. There had not been a guide to America since 1909.

Alsberg's feeling was right. It fitted in, moreover, with the concept that ran through all the Arts Projects—namely, that given the talent available and the controversy that creative work might involve, their best contribution would be to expose Americans for the first time to true, detailed, and vivid information about America. The result was that the guides—one for each of the 48 states, 30 for major cities, and 20 others for great travel arteries like *U.S. One* and *The Oregon Trail*—were remarkably rich.

It was, all in all, a magnificent experiment and one that went far to support sculptor Gutzon Borglum's letter when the WPA was still a developing idea of Harry Hopkins: "I want to suggest that you make your aid to the creative ones among us greater, more effective in scope. You are not after masterpieces, and you should not be discouraged if you have many failures. The real success will be in the interest, the human interest, which you will awaken, and what that does to the nation's mind. I believe that's the door through which you can coax the soul of America back to interest in life." It certainly coaxed it over to a somewhat *different* life.

FLEEING THE DUST BOWL

From Bound for Glory *Narration by Woody Guthrie.* © *1961 by Woody Guthrie Publications Inc. All rights reserved. Used by permission. "Do Re Mi" Words & Music by Woody Guthrie. TRO–© Copyright 1961 & 1963 Ludlow Music, Inc., New York, N.Y. Used by permission. "Pastures of Plenty" Words & Music by Woody Guthrie. TRO–© 1960 & 1963 Ludlow Music, Inc., New York, N.Y. Used by permission.*

American farmers in the plains states were hit by a terrible drought during the 1930's. This lack of rain caused large areas of the Great Plains to dry up and turn into what came to be called "the Dust Bowl." The situation in Oklahoma and other states of the Great Plains was so serious that thousands of farm families were forced to leave their farms. Many of them headed west to California to look for jobs as migrant farm workers.

These poor and desperate Americans were models for the characters in a famous novel written by John Steinbeck, *The Grapes of Wrath.* Woody Guthrie, a song writer, also told of the lives of these people in some of his folk songs. The following selection includes Guthrie's memory of what it was like to wander across America in the 1930's, as well as two of his songs about the Dust Bowl.

What is Guthrie's point in the song "Do Re Me"? To whom is he speaking in "Pastures of Plenty"? How have the lives of migrant workers changed since the 1930's?

I got a few little jobs—helping a water-well driller, hoeing figs, irrigating strawberries in the sandy land, laying roofs, hustling sign jobs with a painter.

I followed the oil towns and found myself as far west as Hobbs, New Mexico. I'd learned how to play a guitar, a few of the easy chords, and was making saloons like a preacher changing from street corner to street corner.

I hit Pampa in the Panhandle of Texas, and stuck there a while. Then the dust storms begun blowing blacker and meaner, and the rain was getting less, and the dust more and more. I made up a little song that went:

'37 was a dusty year
And I says, Woman, I'm leavin' here.

And on one dark and dusty day, I pulled out down the road that led to California.

The further west you walk, the browner, hotter, stiller and emptier the country gets.

I met the hard-rock miners, old prospectors, desert rats, and whole swarms of hitchhikers, migratory workers—squatted with their little piles of belongings in the shade of the big sign boards, out across the flat, hard-crust, gravelly desert. Kids chasing around in the blistering sun. Ladies cooking scrappy meals in sooty buckets, scouring the plates clean with sand. All waiting for some kind of a chance to get across the California line.

* * * *

Do Re Me

Lots of folks back east, they say,
Is leavin' home every day,
Beatin' a hot old dusty way to th' California line.
'Crost th' desert sands they roll
Gettin' outta that old dust bowl,

They think they're a-goin' to a sugar bowl,
But here's what they find:

> Oh, the police at the port of entry say,
> "You're number Fourteen Thousand for to-
> day! Oh!

"If you ain't got th' do re me, folks,
If you ain't got th' do re me,
Why, ya better go back t' beautiful Texas,
Oklahoma, Kansas, Georgia, Tennessee;
> California is a garden of Eden,
> A paradise to live in or see;
> But, believe it or not,
> You won't find it so hot
> If you ain't got th' do re me!"

If you wanta buy a home or farm,
That cain't do nobody harm,
Or take your vacation by the mountains or sea,
Don't swap your old cow for a car,
Ya better stay right where you are;
Ya better take this little tip from me.

Cause I look thru the want ads every day
But the headlines in the papers always say:

Chorus: "If you ain't got . . . ."

    Yes, guess I'm what you'd call a migrant worker. Guess you had to think up some kind of name for me. I travel, yes, if that's what you mean in your red-tape and your scary offices, but you can just call me any old word you want to. You just set and call me off a whole book full of names, but let me be out on my job while you're doing the calling. Thataway, we can save time and money and get more work turned out.
    I ain't nothing much but a guy walking along. You can't hardly pick me out in a big crowd, I look so much like everybody else. Streets. Parks. Big places. I travel . . . yes, I travel. Ain't you glad I travel and work? If I was to stop, you'd have to up and leave your job and start traveling, because there's . . . a lot of traveling that's got to be done.

*   *   *   *

Pastures of Plenty

It's a mighty hard row that my poor hands has
  hoed;
My poor feet has travelled a hot, dusty road;
Out of your dust bowl and westward we rolled;
And your deserts was hot and your mountains
  was cold.

I worked in your orchards of peaches and
  prunes;
Slept on the ground in the light of your moon;
On the edge of your city you'll see us and then
We come with the dust and we go with the wind.

California, Arizona, I make all your crops,
Then, it's north up to Oregon to gather your
  hops,
Dig the beets from your ground, cut the grapes
  from your vine,
To set on your table your light sparkling wine.

Green pastures of plenty from dry desert ground
From that Grand Coulee dam where the water
  runs down;
Ever' state in this union us migrants has been;
We'll work in this fight and we'll fight till we win.

Well, it's always we rambled, that river and I,
All along your green valley I will work till I die;
My land I'll defend with my life if it be,
'Cause my pastures of plenty must always be
  free.

HOW SOCIAL SECURITY WAS BORN

Adapted from The Roosevelt I Knew *by Frances Perkins. Copyright 1946 by Frances Perkins, copyright © renewed 1974 by Susanna W. Coggeshall. Reprinted by permission of The Viking Press.*

Today, Americans take for granted many of the economic and social benefits provided by the federal government. Many of these programs began during the New Deal. One of the most significant programs was social security.

The idea of old-age and unemployment insurance had first been suggested during the progressive era. But the depression brought new demands for such a program. After two years of planning with members of Congress, the Roosevelt administration set up a program of old-age and unemployment insurance. This program, spelled out in the Social Security Act, was passed by Congress in 1935. In this selection, Frances Perkins—Secretary of Labor in President Roosevelt's cabinet and the first woman to serve in the cabinet—outlines how the Social Security law came about.

How was the social security bill's passage through Congress affected by personal factors? By public opinion? Do you think social security is a good program? Why or why not?

Before his inauguration in 1933, Roosevelt had agreed that we should explore at once methods for setting up unemployment and old-age insurance in the United States. Therefore, early in 1933, the President encouraged Senator Robert F. Wagner and Representative David J. Lewis, who were both deeply interested in the subject, to go ahead with their bill on unemployment insurance. The bill, in a rough draft, was offered frankly for educational purposes. It was hoped that in the course of holding hearings the Congressional committees and the introducers of the bill would work out a satisfactory unemployment insurance law.

The President asked me to discuss the matter in as many groups as possible. I began in the cabinet. I made a point of bringing it up at least at every second meeting. In time, the other cabinet members became sincerely and honestly interested.

Hearings were held before Congress. Effective people were invited to testify before the Congressional committees. I myself made over a hundred speeches in different parts of the country that year. I always stressed social insurance as one of the methods for helping the unemployed in times of depression and for preventing depressions. We encouraged others to talk and write about the subject.

The Wagner-Lewis bill in Congress covered only unemployment insurance, but there was a great demand for old-age insurance also. It was easy to add this feature—and politically almost necessary. The President began telling people he was in favor of adding old-age insurance clauses to the Wagner-Lewis bill and putting it through as one program.

A great deal of educational work was done in 1933. But by June 1934 the Wagner-Lewis bill had not reached committee agreement. There had been differences of opinion in the testimony and recommendations to Congress. We began to see that there must be further study and a more complete plan before the bill could be presented to Congress for action.

The President had put the program on the must list. But the weather grew hot and Congress was very tired. Roosevelt decided that it might be better to tell Congress that he would be happy to agree to their adjourning if they understood that he would have a study made during the summer and would present a full program on economic security on January 1 when Congress met again. Congress gladly agreed.

Since members of the cabinet had developed great interest in the social security program, I suggested that it might be well to have the study made by a cabinet committee. The President readily agreed. He saw at once that a program developed by a committee of the cabinet would be under his control. It would not be likely to get off into the kind of political discussion and publicity that might cause doubt and delay.

The members of the cabinet Committee on Economic Security appointed by the President were the Secretary of Labor [Frances Perkins], chairman; Secretary of Agriculture Henry Wallace; Secretary of the Treasury Henry Morgenthau; and Attorney General H. S. Cummings. Harry Hopkins was added because of his vital experience as administrator of the relief program.

It was evident to us that any system of social insurance would not relieve all poverty. Nor would it relieve the sufferings of the presently old and needy. Nevertheless, it was also evident that this was exactly the right time to look ahead to future problems of unemployment and unprotected old age. It was never, I think, suggested by any reasonable person that relief should be abandoned in favor of unemployment and old-age insurance, but it was thought that there could be a blend of the two.

I took pains to make certain that Roosevelt understood and pledged himself to support the program as we worked it out. It must be made clear that this technique of using a cabinet committee to develop the program for him did not mean that he was evading the great issue. I had more than one special conference with him about the subjects we would have to consider in the cabinet committee.

I asked him if he thought it best for me to be chairman, since the public knew I favored the general idea. Perhaps it would be better, from the point of view of Congress and the public, if the Attorney General were chairman.

He was quick in his response. "No, no. You care about this thing. You believe in it. Therefore I know you will back it more than anyone else, and you will drive it through. You will see that something comes out, and we must not delay. I am convinced. We must have a program by next winter and it must be in operation before many more months have passed."

I indicated to him that there were sound arguments, advanced by many thinkers, that since we were in the midst of deflation [a decline in prices, caused by a decrease in the supply of money or in spending] the collection of any money for reserves, no matter by what method, would be further deflationary.

"We can't help that," he answered. "We have to get it started or it never will start."

He was aware that 1936 was not too far away, that there might be a change of administration, and that this program, which in his own mind was *his* program, would never be accomplished, or at least not for many years, if it were not put through immediately.

By the time the study was fully started, the President's imaginative mind had begun to work on it. At cabinet meetings and when he talked privately with a group of us, he would say, "You should make it simple—very simple. So simple that everybody will understand it. And what's more, there is no reason why everybody in the United States should not be covered. I see no reason why all children, from the day they are born, shouldn't be members of the social security system. When they begin to grow up, they should know they will have old-age benefits direct from the insurance system to which they will belong all their life. If they are out of work, they get benefits. If they are sick or disabled, they get benefits.

"And there is no reason why only the industrial workers should get the benefit of this. Everybody ought to be in on it—the farmer and his wife and his family.

"I don't see why not," he would say, as I began to shake my head. "I don't see why not. Cradle to the grave—from the cradle to the grave they ought to be in a social insurance system."

It was not that I did not admire his bold idea of including every person. But I felt that it was impractical to try to develop and manage so broad a system before we had some experience and machinery for the first and most pressing steps.

Moreover, I felt sure that the political climate was not right for such a universal approach. I may have been wrong. Having the administrative responsibility, I was more alarmed than he about how we were going to achieve it. The question of financing was most important. Roosevelt, because he was looking at the broad picture, could skip over that difficult problem.

It is difficult now to understand fully the doubts and confusions in which we were planning this great new undertaking in 1934. The problems of constitutional law seemed almost impossible to overcome. I drew courage from a bit of advice I got accidentally from Supreme Court Justice Harlan Stone. I had said to him, at a social occasion a few months earlier, that I had great hope of developing a social insurance system for the country, but that I was deeply uncertain of the method. I said laughingly, "Your Court tells us what the Constitution permits."

Stone had whispered, "The taxing power of the federal government, my dear. The taxing power is sufficient for everything you want and need."

This was a windfall. I told the President but bound him to secrecy as to the source of my sudden superior legal knowledge. I insisted in the cabinet committee that the taxing power was the method for building up the fund and determining its expenditure for unemployment and old-age benefits to be paid in the future.

The bill with the cabinet committee's recommendations was prepared the first week in January 1935. We took it to the President to see how it should be introduced in Congress. We thought it would be wise to have it referred to a special committee on social security, if possible a joint committee of the Senate and House. Since the measure rested primarily upon the constitutional taxing power of the federal government, it would have gone ordinarily to the Ways and Means Committees.

The news got around that a special committee was being recommended. Representative Robert L. Doughton of North Carolina, chairman of the Ways and Means Committee, went to see the President. He was angry that anyone had thought of bypassing him, though he had never made a speech in the House that had indicated he had any interest in social security. It was a surprise to find out that he cared.

As a result the President said to me, "No, no, it will never do. We will have to put it through the Ways and Means Committee. It is the only thing to do. You will hurt Bob Doughton's feelings if you don't."

The Ways and Means Committee had a number of able members. They put their minds to this new problem not only of finances but of social and economic policy for the whole United States.

The House committee and other members of Congress began to hear from the voters in favor of the social security bill. It was soon clear that it was going to be moved along. In August 1935 Republicans as well as Democrats voted for the bill. There were only a very few who had the courage to vote against it.

I remember that when I appeared before the Senate Committee old Senator Thomas Gore raised a sarcastic objection. "Isn't this socialism?" he asked me.

My answer was, "Oh, no."

Then, smiling, leaning forward and talking to me as though I were a child, he said, "Isn't this a teeny-weeny bit of socialism?"

When the law was signed by the President [on August 14, 1935], we had a little ceremony in his office and he gave out the usual pens. I had brought in not only Congressman Dough-

ton, but also Senator Wagner and Congressman Lewis, and one or two other members of Congress, and had provided the pens for them. As he was signing the copies of the bills with pens that would be given to its sponsors, the President looked up at me. "Frances, where is your pen?" he asked.

"I haven't got one," I replied.

"All right," he said to his secretary, "give me a first-class pen for Frances." And he insisted I was responsible for the bill and thanked me personally in very appreciative terms.

CHAPTER 18 ■ THE GREAT EXPERIMENT ON TRIAL

WINNING A SIT-DOWN STRIKE

Condensed from Hard Times: An Oral History of the Great Depression *by Studs Terkel. Copyright © 1970 by Studs Terkel. Reprinted by permission of Pantheon Books, a division of Random House, Inc.*

By the middle of 1934, after some improvement in the economy, American business and industry again began to slow down. As a result, some Americans began to criticize many of Roosevelt's policies, and their opposition increased during Roosevelt's second term. However, organized labor, especially the members of the newly formed CIO union, continued to support President Roosevelt. They believed that the New Deal's labor policy had brought great benefits and greater economic freedom to working people.

In this selection, Bob Stinson, an auto worker, tells of the first sit-down strike in the General Motors plant at Flint, Michigan, in 1936. When interviewed by writer Studs Terkel many years later, Stinson clearly recalled the day he and the other workers won their strike.

What was the situation in Flint just before the strike? Why did the strikers make special efforts to take care of company property? Are unions a more powerful force in the United States today than they were in 1936? Explain.

Everybody has to have something they're really sold on. Some people go to church. If I'd had anything I'm really sold on, it's the UAW [United Automobile Workers].

I started working at Fisher Body in 1917 and retired in '62, with 45 years service. Until 1933, no unions, no rules: you were at the mercy of your foreman. I could go to work at seven o'clock in the morning, and at seven fifteen the boss'd come around and say: come back at three o'clock. If he preferred somebody else over you, that person would be called back earlier, though you were there longer.

I left the plant so many nights hostile. If I were a fella big and strong, I think I'd a picked a fight with the first fella I met on the corner. It was lousy. You might call yourself a man if you was on the street, but as soon as you went through the door and punched your card, you was nothing more or less than a robot. Do this, go there, do that. You'd do it.

We got involved in a strike in Detroit, and we lost the strike. Went back on our knees. That's the way you learn things. I got laid off in the fall of '31. I wasn't told I was black-balled, but I was told there was no more jobs at Fisher Body for me. So I came to Flint and was hired right off the bat.

We had a Black Legion in this town made up of stool pigeons and bigotty kind of people. They got themselves in good with the management by puttin' the finger on a union organizer. Once in a while, a guy'd come in with a black eye. You'd say, "What happened?" He'd say, "I was walking along the street and a guy come from behind and knocked me down."

The Black Legion later developed into the Flint Alliance. It was supposed to be made up of good solid citizens, who were terrorized by outside agitators, who had come in here to take over the plant. They would get schoolkids to sign these cards, [and] housewives. Every shoe salesman downtown would sign these cards. Businessmen would have everyone in the family sign these cards. They contended they had the overwhelming majority of the people of Flint.

Most people in town was hopin' the thing'd get solved. They had relatives and friends that they knew working in the plant;[it] was no bed of roses. They did accept some of this outside agitator stuff that got in the paper. I think anybody who reads this stuff day after day accepts a little bit of it. The great majority of the people was neutral.

There was fear. You kept your mouth shut when you was in strange company. Every time you put a union button on, you were told to leave the plant. You were fired so fast, it made your head spin.

The Flint sit-down happened Christmas Eve, 1936. I was in Detroit. When I came back, the second shift [the men who worked from 4:30 P.M. to 12:30 A.M.] had pulled the plant [struck]. It took about five minutes to shut the line down. The foreman was pretty well astonished.

The boys pulled the switches and asked all the women who was in Cut-and-Sew to go home. They informed the supervisors they could stay, if they stayed in their office. They told the plant police they could do their job as long as they didn't interfere with the workers.

We had guys patrol the plant, see that nobody got involved in anything they shouldn't. If anybody got careless with company property —such as sitting on an automobile cushion without putting burlap over it—he was talked to. You couldn't paint a sign on the wall or anything like that. You used bare springs for a bed. 'Cause if you slept on a finished cushion, it was no longer a new cushion.

Governor [Frank] Murphy said he hoped he would never have to use National Guard against people. But if there was damage to property, he would do so. We invited him to the plant and see how well we were taking care of the place.

They'd assign roles to you. When some of the guys at headquarters wanted to tell some of the guys in the plant what was cookin', I carried the message. I was a scavenger, too.

The merchants cooperated. There'd be apples, bushels of potatoes, crates of oranges that was beginnin' to spoil.

The soup kitchen was outside the plant. The women handled all the cooking, outside of one chef who came from New York. He had anywhere from ten to twenty women washing dishes and peeling potatoes in the strike kitchen. Mostly stews, pretty good meals. They were put in containers and hoisted up through the window. The boys in there had their own plates and cups and saucers.

Most of the men had their wives and friends come down, and they'd stand inside the window and they'd talk. Find out how the family was. If the union supplied them with enough coal.

We had a ladies' auxiliary. They'd visit the homes of the guys that was in the plant. They would find out if there was any shortage of coal or food. Then they'd maneuver around amongst themselves until they found some place to get a ton of coal.

Some of 'em would have foremen come to their homes: "Sorry, your husband was a very good operator. But if he don't get out of the plant and away from the union, he'll never again have a job at General Motors." If this woman was the least bit scared, she'd come down and cry on her husband's shoulder. He'd more than likely get a little disturbed, get a hold of his strike captain. Sometimes you just had to let 'em go. Because if you kept them in there, they'd worry so much over it, that'd start ruinin' the morale of the rest of the guys.

Morale was very high at the time. It started out kinda ugly because the guys were afraid they put their foot in it and all they was gonna do is lose their jobs. But as time went on, they begin to realize they could win this darn thing, 'cause we had a lot of outside people comin' in showin' their sympathy.

Nationally known people contributed to our strike fund. Mrs. Roosevelt for one. We even had a member of Parliament come from England and address us.

Lotta things worked for the union we hadn't even anticipated. Company tried to shut off the heat. It was a bluff. Nobody moved for half an hour, so they turned it back on again. They didn't want the pipes to get cold. If the heat was allowed to drop, then the pipes will separate— they were all jointed together—and then you got a problem.

Some of the time you were scared, because there was all kinds of rumors going around. We had a sheriff—he came in one night and read the boys the riot act. He told 'em they had to leave. He stood there, looked at 'em a few minutes. A couple of guys began to curse 'im, and he turned around and left.

The men sat in there for forty-four days. Governor Murphy was trying to get both sides to meet on some common ground. I think he lost many a good night's sleep. We wouldn't use force. Mr. Knudsen was head of General Motors and, of course, there was John L. Lewis [founder of the CIO]. They'd reach a temporary agreement and invariably the Flint Alliance or GM headquarters in Detroit would throw a monkey wrench in it. So every morning, Murphy got up with an unsolved problem.

John L. [Lewis] was as close to a Shakespearean actor as any I've ever listened to. He had more command of language. He made a speech that if they shoot the boys out at the plant, they'd have to shoot him first.

Finally, we got the word: THE THING IS SETTLED. My, you had to send about three people, one right after the other, down to some of those plants because the guys didn't believe it. Finally, when they did get it, they marched out of the plants with the flag flyin' and all that stuff.

When Mr. Knudsen put his name to a piece of paper and says that General Motors recognizes the UAW-CIO—until that moment, we were non-people, we didn't even exist. That was the big one.

THE NEW DEAL IN HISTORY

Adapted from "Twelve Years of Roosevelt" by Henry Steele Commager, in The American Mercury, *April, 1945, pp. 391–401. Reprinted by permission of The American Mercury, P.O. Box 1306, Torrance, California 90505.*

For decades now, Americans have been thinking, talking, and writing about the New Deal. During the 1930's—the years of the New Deal —people's feelings were especially strong. Some Americans in those years thought that the New Deal was a radical threat to the American way of life. Others believed that the New Deal programs were moderate reforms necessary to help the nation recover from the depression.

Like other Americans, historians, too, have held strong opinions about the New Deal. In 1945 historian Henry Steele Commager reviewed the record of the New Deal and summed it up in a magazine article. In the following selection, based on that article, Commager explains his reasons for forming a favorable conclusion about Roosevelt and the New Deal.

What did Commager believe were the major achievements of the New Deal? Why do you think Commager concluded in 1945 that the New Deal "is here to stay"? Can you name some New Deal laws, programs, or reforms that still exist today?

Now that the bitter quarrels over New Deal policies have been drowned out by the war [World War II], it is possible to evaluate those policies in some historical perspective. Those policies have been decisively voted for four times by large popular majorities. They have been turned into reality so fully that controversy about them is almost irrelevant. It should be possible to fix, with some degree of accuracy, the place occupied by Roosevelt in American history.

We can see now that the "Roosevelt revolution" was no revolution. Rather it was the high point of 50 years of historical development. Roosevelt himself, though clearly a leader, was an instrument of the people's will rather than a creator of, or a dictator to, that will. Indeed, the issue of the expansion of government control for democratic purposes began in the 1890's. A longer perspective will see the 50 years from the 1890's to the present as a historical unit. The roots of the New Deal go deep down into our past. It is not understandable except in terms of that past.

What was really only a new deal of the old cards looked, to startled and troubled Americans at the time, like a revolution for two reasons. It was carried through with breathless rapidity. And, in spirit at least, it contrasted sharply with what came immediately before it. But if the comparison had been made, not with the Coolidge-Hoover era, but with the Wilson, the Theodore Roosevelt, even the Bryan era, the contrasts would have been less striking than the similarities.

Actually, the precedents for the major part of the New Deal legislation were to be found in these earlier periods. Regulation of railroads and of business dated back to the Interstate Commerce Act of 1887 and the Sherman Act of 1890. The farm relief program of the Populists and of Wilson anticipated much that the Roosevelt administration passed into law. The beginnings of conservation can be traced to the Carey Act of 1894 and the Reclamation Act of 1902.

Power regulation began with the Water Power Act of 1920. Supervision over securities exchanges began with laws of the Harding and Coolidge administrations. Regulation of money is as old as the Union. The fight which Bryan and Wilson waged against the "money power" and Wall Street was more bitter than anything that came during the New Deal. Labor legislation had its beginnings in such states as Massachusetts and New York over 50 years ago. Much of the program of social security was worked out in Wisconsin and other states early in the 1900's.

There is nothing remarkable about this. Nor does it lessen in any way the significance of President Roosevelt's achievements and contributions. It is to the credit of Roosevelt that he worked within the framework of American history and tradition.

What, then, are the major achievements, the lasting contributions, of the first three Roosevelt administrations? First, perhaps, comes the restoration of self-confidence, the reassertion of faith in democracy. Those who lived through the electric spring of 1933 will remember the change from depression and discouragement to excitement and hope. Those able to compare the last decade with previous decades will agree that interest in public affairs has rarely been as widespread, as alert, or as responsive.

All this may seem indefinite. If we look to more definite things, what does the record show? Of primary importance has been the physical rebuilding of the country. It became clear, during the 1920's and 1930's, that the natural resources of the country—its soil, forests, water power—were being destroyed at a dangerous rate. The development of the Dust Bowl, and the migration of farmers to the Promised Land of California, the tragic floods on the Mississippi and the Ohio, dramatized to the American people the urgency of this problem.

Roosevelt tackled it with energy and boldness. The Civilian Conservation Corps enlisted almost 3 million young men. They planted 17 million acres in new forests, built over 6 million small dams to stop soil erosion, and fought forest fires and plant and animal diseases. To check erosion, the government organized a cooperative program which obtained the help of over one fourth of the farmers of the country. More important than all this was the TVA, a gigantic laboratory for regional rebuilding.

Equally important has been the New Deal achievement in human rehabilitation. Roosevelt came into office at a time when unemployment had reached perhaps 14 million, and when private solutions had failed. It was perhaps inevitable that he should sponsor a broad program of government aid. More important than relief was the acceptance of the principle that the government was responsible for the welfare and security of its people.

That this principle was bitterly opposed now seems hard to believe. Its establishment must stand as one of the main achievements of the New Deal. Beginning with emergency legislation for relief, the Roosevelt program in the end included the whole field of social security—unemployment assistance, old-age pensions, aid to women and children, and public health. It involved programs of rural rehabilitation, the establishment of maximum hours and minimum wages, the prohibition of child labor, and reform in housing.

In the political field the achievements of the New Deal were equally notable. First we must note the steady trend toward the strengthening of government and the expansion of government activities—whether for good or bad only the future can tell. As yet no better method of dealing with the problems of a modern economy and society has shown itself. It can be said that though government today has, quantitatively, far greater responsibilities than it had a generation ago, it has, qualitatively, no greater power. For our constitutional system remains as it always was. All power still resides in the people and their representatives in Congress. They can at any moment take from their government any power.

We seem to have overcome our traditional distrust of the government and realized that a strong state could be used to benefit and advance the nation. That is by no means a New Deal achievement. But it is a development which has gained much from the experience of the American people during the Roosevelt administrations.

It has meant, of course, a marked federal centralization. Along with this has come a great increase in the power of the President. The charge that Roosevelt has been a dictator can be dismissed, along with charges that Jefferson, Jackson, Lincoln, Theodore Roosevelt, and Wilson were dictators. American politics simply doesn't run to dictators. But Roosevelt has been a "strong" executive—as every great democratic President has been a strong executive. There is little doubt that Roosevelt accepted this situation cheerfully.

The New Deal, as far as can be foreseen, is here to stay. There seems no chance of a reversal of any of the major developments in politics in the last twelve years. This was recognized by the Republicans in 1940 and again in 1944. Both platforms endorsed all the essentials of the New Deal.

And what, finally, of Roosevelt himself? It may seem too early to fix his position in our history. Yet that position is reasonably clear. He takes his place in the great tradition of American liberalism, along with Jefferson, Jackson, Lincoln, Theodore Roosevelt, and Wilson. Coming to office at a time when the very foundations of the republic seemed threatened, he restored confidence and proved that democracy could act as effectively in crisis as could totalitarian governments.

A liberal, he put government clearly at the service of the people. A conservative, he pushed through reforms designed to strengthen the natural and human resources of the nation, restore agriculture and business to their former prosperity, and save capitalism. He saw that problems of government were primarily political, not economic. He saw that politics should control the economy, not the other way around.

"The only sure defense of continuing liberty," Roosevelt said, "is a government strong enough to protect the interests of the people, and a people strong enough and well enough informed to maintain its sovereign control over its government." The Roosevelt administration proved once more that it was possible for such a government to exist and such a people to flourish, and restored to the United States its position as "the hope of the human race."

A CRITIC LOOKS AT THE NEW DEAL

Adapted from The Roosevelt Myth *by John T. Flynn, published by The Devin-Adair Company, Inc. Copyright © 1948, 1956 by John T. Flynn. Reprinted by permission of the publisher.*

The verdict of history about the New Deal has not been all favorable. Some critics of the New Deal charge that it expanded the authority of the federal government by taking away powers of state governments. They point out that the New Deal programs greatly increased the national debt. Critics also argue that the Roosevelt administration helped labor unions to become much too powerful.

John T. Flynn was one of these critics who believed that Roosevelt's New Deal policies were disastrous for the nation. Flynn was particularly worried about the growth of the government bureaucracy and its increasing power. In this selection from his book *The Roosevelt Myth,* written in 1948, Flynn also bitterly attacks Roosevelt himself as well as his policies.

According to Flynn, what were some myths about Roosevelt? What changes did Roosevelt make in the American economic and political systems? What do you think of Flynn's criticism of Roosevelt? Why do you think Roosevelt provoked such strong feelings?

Many good people in America still cherish the false idea that Roosevelt performed some amazing achievement for this country. They believe he took our economic system when it was completely broken down and restored it to vitality. They think he took over our political system when it was weakest and restored it to its full strength. He put himself on the side of the underprivileged masses. He transferred power from the great corporation executives to the simple working people of America. He controlled the adventurers of Wall Street, and gave security to the humble men and women of the country.

But not one of these claims is true. He did not restore our economic system to vitality. He changed it. The system he so stupidly moved us into is more like the bureaucracy of Germany before World War I than our own traditional order.

Before his regime we lived in a system which depended for its expansion upon private investment in private enterprise. Today [1948] we live in a system which depends for its expansion and vitality upon the government. This is a prewar European importation. And it was imported at the moment when it had fallen apart in Europe. In this system the government takes by taxes or by borrowings the savings of all the citizens and invests them in nonwealth-producing undertakings in order to create work.

Behold the picture of the American economy today. In America today every fourth person depends for a livelihood upon employment either directly by the government or indirectly in some industry supported by government funds. There is a public debt of $250 billion, compared to a pre-Roosevelt debt of $19 billion, and a government budget of $40 billion instead of $4 billion before Roosevelt. Inflation has doubled prices and reduced the lower-paid employed workers to a state of poverty as bad as that of the unemployed in the depression. More people are on various kinds of government relief than when we had 11 million unemployed. Bureaucrats are in every field of life. And the President is calling for more power, more price-fixing, more regulation, and more billions. Does this look like the traditional American scene?

No, Roosevelt did not restore our economic system. He did not construct a new one. He substituted an old one which lives upon permanent crises and an armament economy. And he did this not by a process of orderly design and building, but by a series of mistakes. He moved one step at a time, in flight from one problem to another. Now we have a state-supported economic system that will continue a little at a time to destroy the private system until it disappears altogether.

Roosevelt did not restore our political system to its full strength. One may like the shape into which he battered it, but it cannot be called a repair job. He changed our political system with two weapons—blank-check congressional appropriations and blank-check congressional legislation. In 1933 Congress gave up much of its power when it put billions into his hands. It gave him a blanket appropriation to be spent at his own will. And it passed general laws leaving it to him, through great government bureaus that he set up, to fill in the details of legislation.

These two mistakes gave Roosevelt a power which he used ruthlessly. He used it to break down the power of Congress and concentrate it in the hands of the executive. The result of these two betrayals—the smashing of our economic system and the twisting of our political system—can only be the planned economic state. This, in the form of either communism or fascism, dominates the entire continent of Europe today. The capitalist system cannot live under these conditions. Free representative government cannot survive a planned economy. Such an economy can be managed only by a dictatorial government. The only result of our present system—unless we reverse the drift—will be the gradual disappearance of the system of free enterprise under a free representative government.

There are people who honestly defend this change. They at least are honest. They believe in a planned economy. They believe in a highly centralized government operated by a powerful executive. They do not say Roosevelt saved our system. They say he has given us a new one. That is logical. But no one can praise Roosevelt for doing this and then insist that he restored our traditional political and economic systems to their former vitality.

Roosevelt's star was sinking sadly in 1938 when he had 11 million unemployed and when Hitler made his first war moves in Europe. The cities were filling with jobless workers. Taxes were rising. The debt was soaring. The war rescued him and he seized upon it like a drowning man. By leading his country into the fringes of the war at first and then deep into its center all over the world he was able to do the only things that could save him—spend billions to spread the hot flames of war hysteria and put every man and woman into the war mills. Under the pressure of patriotism, he could silence criticism and work up the illusion of the war leader.

On the moral side, I have barely touched that subject. It will all still be told. But go back through the years, read the speeches and platforms and judgments Roosevelt made, and consider them in the light of what he did. Look up the promises of thrift in public office, of balanced budgets and lower taxes, of honesty in government, and of security for all. Read the speeches he made promising never, never again to send our sons to fight in foreign wars. He broke every promise. He betrayed all who trusted him.

The figure of Roosevelt exhibited before the eyes of our people is false. There was no such being as that noble, selfless, hard-headed, wise, and farseeing combination of philosopher, philanthropist, and warrior. It has been created out of pure propaganda. A small collection of dangerous people in this country are using it to advance their own evil purposes.

CHAPTER 19 ■ MOVING FROM ISOLATIONISM INTO WAR

A "BUG'S-EYE" VIEW OF EUROPE

"the league" by Don Marquis. Copyright 1935 by Doubleday & Co., Inc. From the Book The Lives and Times of Archy and Mehitabel. *Reprinted by permission of Doubleday & Co., Inc.*

Don Marquis, a newspaper writer, became famous as the creator of an imaginary insect named Archy. Archy, a cockroach, was a shrewd observer of people and events. And he did not hesitate to express his opinions on any subject. He had very strong viewpoints, especially about American society.

Each night, Archy used Marquis' office typewriter to write down his ideas about what was happening in the world. Archy supposedly operated the typewriter keys by jumping on them head first. Because he was unable to

550

move the shift key on the typewriter, he was not able to use capital letters or punctuation. In this selection, you will read Archy's view of "post war europe."

To what "mutual animosities," or hatreds, do you think Archy is referring? According to Archy, when will wars cease permanently? Do you think that using a make-believe character to express opinions is effective? Explain.

the league

if the league of nations
can survive the mutual animosities
of the powers which belong to it
it is safe from the activities
of the countries which stayed outside of it
it furnishes a wonderful mechanism
with which to do what the powers
want to do if they only knew
what they wanted to do
incidentally i wonder why europe of today
is always referred to by highbrow writers
as post war europe
they seem to think that the war
which started in nineteen fourteen
is over with whereas there have been
merely a few brief truces
that war is merely worrying through
its first half century
and will only cease permanently
when a generation comes along
which has forgotten all the old feuds

archy the cockroach

THE MENACE OF HITLER

Adapted from Let the Record Speak *by Dorothy Thompson. Copyright © renewed 1967 by Michael Lewis. Reprinted by permission of Houghton Mifflin Company.*

Many Americans were deeply concerned about events in Europe in the late 1930's. They were disturbed by the rise of dictators in some European nations and the aggressive ambitions of these dictators. With each new act of aggression by Germany, Italy, and Japan, some Americans feared that war was certain.

One person who was especially concerned about these events was Dorothy Thompson, a famous journalist whose newspaper and magazine writings were well known to Americans.

During these years, it was said that she was "the equivalent of a troop of tanks in the pre-war skirmishing with Adolf Hitler." The following selection was written on February 18, 1938, shortly after Austrian chancellor Kurt von Schuschnigg had met with Hitler and agreed to admit Nazi members into the Austrian cabinet. Still not satisfied, Hitler sent an army into Austria a few weeks later. Austria then came under the total control of Germany.

Why, as Dorothy Thompson sees it, does Germany want Austria? What two alternatives does she predict for the future? Was she correct?

Write it down. On Saturday, February 12, 1938, Germany won the world war, and dictated, at Hitler's mountain retreat, a peace treaty to make the Treaty of Versailles look like one of the great humane documents of the ages.

Write it down. On Saturday, February 12, 1938, Nazism started on the march across all of Europe east of the Rhine.

Write it down that the world revolution began in earnest—and perhaps the world war.

Write it down that the democratic world broke its promises and gave in, not in the face of strength, but of terrible weakness, armed only with ruthlessness and daring.

What happened?

On February 4, Hitler ousted his chief of staff and fourteen other generals. Why? Because the army leadership refused to move against an unarmed, friendly country—their German-speaking neighbor, Austria. Why did they refuse? Because of squeamishness? Hardly. Because they thought that Britain and France would interfere? Perhaps. Or because they themselves feared the ultimate catastrophe the future would bring as a result of this move? I think this is the best guess.

A week later, Hitler, with his reorganized army, made his move. How did he make it? He called in the chancellor of Austria, Doctor von Schuschnigg, and gave him an ultimatum. Sixty-six million people against six million people. German troops were ready at Austria's borders. Hitler's generals stood behind him as he interviewed the Austrian chancellor. Hitler taunted his victim. "You know as well as I know that France and Britain will not move a hand to save you." Hitler will doubtless hail this meeting as a friendly reconciliation between two German-speaking peoples and the strengthening of peace in eastern Europe.

What does the chancellor of Austria really think about Nazism?

He expressed himself hardly more than a month ago, on January 5, in the *Morning Telegraph* of London.

This is what he said:

"There is no question of ever accepting Nazi representatives in the Austrian cabinet. An enormous distance separates Austria from Nazism. We do not like arbitrary power, we want law to rule our freedom. We hate terror. Austria has always been a humanitarian state. As a people, we are tolerant by nature. Any change now in our *status quo* could only be for the worse."

Why does Germany want Austria? For **raw** materials? It has none of any importance. To add to German prosperity? Austria is a poor country with serious problems. But strategically it is the key to the whole of central Europe. Czechoslovakia is now surrounded. The wheat fields of Hungary and the oil fields of Rumania are now open. Not one of them will be able to withstand the pressure of German domination.

It is horror walking. Not that "Germany" joins with Austria. We are not talking of "Germany." We see a new Crusade, under a pagan symbol, worshiping "blood" and "soil," preaching the holiness of the sword and glorifying conquest. It hates the Slavs, whom it thinks to be its historic "mission" to rule. It subjects all of life to a militarized state. It persecutes men and women of Jewish blood. Now it moves into the historic stronghold of Catholic Christianity, into an area of mixed races and mixed nationalities, which for a thousand years the Austro-Hungarian Empire could rule only with tolerance. Adolf Hitler's first hatred was not communism, but Austria-Hungary. Read *Mein Kampf* [Hitler's book]. And he hated it for what? For its tolerance? He wanted 80 million Germans to rule with an iron hand an empire of 80 million "inferiors"—Czechs, Slovaks, Magyars, Jews, Serbs, Poles, and Croats.

Today, all of Europe east of the Rhine is cut off completely from the western world. The swastika banner, we are told, is the crusader's flag against Bolshevism [Communism]! Madness! Only the signs on the flags divide them [Germany and the Soviet Union].

And it never needed to have happened. One strong voice of one strong power could have stopped it.

Tomorrow, one of two things can happen. Despotism can stop where it is, through the lack of real leadership and creative brains. For the law of despotisms is that they kill off the good, and the brave, and the wise. Perhaps all of Europe east of the Rhine will become, eventually, a no-man's land of poverty, militarism, and despair. But nonetheless a plague spot.

More likely the other law of despotism's nature—the law of constant -aggressiveness—will cause it to move farther and onward, made bolder and stronger by each success.

To the point where civilization will take a last stand. For take a stand it will. Of that there is not the slightest doubt.

Too bad that it did not take it this week.

LONDON DURING THE BLITZ

Condensed from In Search of Light: The Broadcasts of Edward R. Murrow 1938–1961 *edited by Edward Bliss, Jr. Copyright 1941 by Edward R. Murrow. Reprinted by permission of Alfred A. Knopf, Inc.*

After Hitler's invasion of Poland in September 1939, Great Britain and France went to war against Germany. By June 1940 Hitler's blitzkrieg warfare had been so successful that only Great Britain was left to fight Nazi Germany. Then Hitler decided to try to bomb Great Britain into surrender.

All during these long months of war, foreign correspondents, or reporters, stationed abroad kept the American people informed about the war. One of these correspondents was Edward R. Murrow. He was in England during the Battle of Britain, and his radio reports of the nightly Nazi air raids made him famous. Night after night he told Americans of the courage of the British people, the daring of the Royal Air Force pilots, and the horrors they faced. The following are selections from Murrow's broadcasts during the Battle of Britain.

In what ways does Murrow describe the air raids? Why do you think his reporting job was so difficult? What opinions do you think Americans formed from these broadcasts?

September 10, 1940
This is London. And the raid which started about seven hours ago is still in progress. Larry LeSueur [a fellow correspondent] and I have spent the last three hours driving about the streets of London and visiting air-raid shelters. We found that like everything else in this world the kind of protection you get from the bombs

on London tonight depends on how much money you have. On the other hand, the most expensive dwelling places here do not necessarily provide the best shelters, but certainly they are the most comfortable.

We looked in on a renowned hotel tonight and found many old dowagers [women] and retired colonels settling back on the overstuffed settees [couches] in the lobby. It wasn't the sort of protection I'd seek from a direct hit from a half-ton bomb, but if you were a retired colonel and his lady, you might feel that the risk was worth it because you would at least be bombed with the right sort of people.

Only a couple of blocks away we pushed aside the canvas curtain of a trench cut out of a lawn of a London park. Inside were half a hundred people, some of them stretched out on the hard wooden benches. The rest huddled over in their overcoats and blankets. Dimmed electric lights glowed on the whitewashed walls, and the cannonade of anti-aircraft and reverberation of the big stuff the Germans were dropping rattled the boards underfoot at intervals. One woman was saying sleepily that it was funny how often you read about people being killed inside a shelter. Nobody seemed to listen. Then over to the famous cellar of a world-famous hotel, two floors underground. On upholstered chairs and lounges there was a cosmopolitan crowd. But there wasn't any sparkling conversation. They sat, some of them with their mouths open. One of them snored. King Zog [the former king of Albania] was over in a far corner on a chair, the porter told me.

The number of planes tonight seems to be about the same as last night. Searchlight activity has been constant, but there has been little gunfire in the center of London. The bombs have been coming down at about the same rate as last night. It is impossible to get any estimate of the damage. Darkness prevents observation of details. The streets have been deserted, save for a few clanging fire engines during the last four or five hours. The planes have been high again tonight, so high that the searchlights can't reach them.

Once tonight an anti-aircraft battery opened fire just as I drove past. It lifted me from the seat and a hot wind swept over the car. It was impossible to see. When I drove on, the streets of London reminded me of a ghost town in Nevada—not a soul to be seen. A week ago there would have been people standing on the corner shouting for taxis. Tonight there were no people and no taxis. Earlier today there were trucks de-livering mattresses to many office buildings. People are now sleeping on those mattresses, or at least they are trying to sleep.

And so London is waiting for dawn. We ought to get the all clear in about another two hours. Then those big German bombers that have been lumbering and mumbling about overhead all night will have to go home.

September 13, 1940
This is London at 3:30 in the morning. This has been what might be called a "routine night"— air-raid alarm at about nine o'clock and intermittent bombing ever since. I had the impression that more high explosives and few incendiaries [fire bombs] have been used tonight. Only two small fires can be seen. Again the Germans have been sending their bombers in singly or in pairs. The anti-aircraft barrage has been fierce but sometimes there have been periods of twenty minutes when London has been silent. Then the big red buses would start up and move on till the guns started working again. That silence is almost hard to bear. One becomes accustomed to rattling windows and the distant sound of bombs, and then there comes a silence that can be felt. You know the sound will return. You wait, and then it starts again. That waiting is bad. It gives you a chance to imagine things.

The scale of this air war is so great that reporting it is not easy. Often we spend hours traveling about this sprawling city, viewing damage, talking with people and occasionally listening to the bombs come down, and then more hours wondering what you'd like to hear about. We've told you about the bombs, the fires, the smashed houses and the courage of the people. We've read you the communiques and tried to give you an honest estimate of the wounds inflicted upon this, the best bombing target in the world. But the business of living and working in this city is very personal— the little incidents, the things the mind retains, are in themselves unimportant, but they somehow weld together to form the hard core of memories that will remain when the last all clear has sounded. That's why I want to talk for just three or four minutes about the things we haven't talked about before; for many of these impressions it is necessary to reach back through only one long week. There was a rainbow bending over the battered and smoking East End of London just when the all clear sounded one afternoon. One night I stood in front of a smashed grocery store and heard a dripping inside. It was the only sound in all

London. Two cans of peaches had been drilled clean through by flying glass, and the juice was dripping down onto the floor.

Today I went to buy a hat—my favorite shop had gone, blown to bits. The windows of my shoe store were blown out. I decided to have a haircut; the windows of the barbershop were gone, but the Italian barber was still doing business. Someday, he said, we smile again, but the food doesn't taste so good since being bombed. I went on to another shop to buy flashlight batteries. I bought three. The clerk said, "You needn't buy so many. We'll have enough for the whole winter." But I said, "What if you aren't here?" There were buildings down in that street, and he replied, "Of course we'll be here. We've been in business here for a hundred and fifty years."

September 18, 1940

There are no words to describe the thing that is happening. Today I talked with eight American correspondents in London. Six of them had been forced to move. All had stories of bombs, and all agreed that they were unable to convey through print or the spoken word an accurate impression of what's happening in London these days and nights.

I may tell you that Bond Street has been bombed, that a shop selling handkerchiefs at $40 the dozen has been wrecked, that these words [of the broadcast] were written on a table of good English oak which sheltered me three times as bombs tore down in the vicinity. But you can have little understanding of the life in London these days—the courage of the people, the flash and roar of the guns rolling down streets where much of the history of the English-speaking world has been made, the stench of air-raid shelters in the poor districts. These things must be experienced to be understood.

September 22, 1940

I'm standing again tonight on a rooftop looking out over London, feeling rather large and lonesome. In the course of the last fifteen or twenty minutes there's been considerable action up there, but at the moment there's an ominous silence hanging over London. But at the same time a silence that has a great deal of dignity. Just straightaway in front of me the searchlights are working. I can see one or two bursts of anti-aircraft fire far in the distance. Just on the roof across the way I can see a man wearing a tin hat, a pair of powerful night glasses to his eyes,

scanning the sky. Again, looking in the opposite direction, there is a building with two windows gone. Out of one window there waves something that looks like a white bed sheet, a window curtain swinging free in this night breeze. It looks as though it were being shaken by a ghost. There are a great many ghosts around these buildings in London. The searchlights, miles in front of me, are still scratching that sky. There's a three-quarter moon riding high.

Down below in the streets I can see just that red and green wink of the traffic lights, one lone taxicab moving slowly down the street. Not a sound to be heard. As I look out across the miles and miles of rooftops and chimney pots, some of those dirty-gray buildings look almost snow-white in this moonlight here tonight. And the rooftop spotter across the way swings around, looks over in the direction of the searchlights, drops his glasses and just stands there. There are hundreds and hundreds of men like that standing on rooftops in London tonight watching for fire bombs, waiting to see what comes out of this steel-blue sky. The searchlights now reach up very, very faintly on three sides of me. There is a flash of a gun in the distance but too far away to be heard.

AMERICA, "THE ARSENAL OF DEMOCRACY"

Adapted from "Fireside Chat," December 29, 1940, by Franklin D. Roosevelt, from the National Archives and Record Service, Franklin D. Roosevelt Library.

When World War II broke out in Europe in 1939, the United States faced the problem of what role, if any, it would take in the conflict. During the following year, as Hitler's armies defeated one country after another, the debate over what course of action America should take became increasingly heated.

At first, most Americans wanted to remain out of the war. But by 1940, with Great Britain the only nation left in the struggle against Nazi Germany, many Americans became deeply concerned. Some Americans began to question whether neutrality was a wise policy for the nation. Then, near the end of 1940, President Roosevelt dramatically declared that he favored aiding Great Britain with weapons and military supplies. In an historic "fireside chat," broadcast to the American people over radio on

December 29, 1940, President Roosevelt argued that the United States could not remain neutral.

Why does Roosevelt believe America is in great danger? What will happen if Great Britain is defeated? What actions does Roosevelt urge America to take?

This is not a fireside chat on war. It is a talk on national security. The whole purpose of your President is to keep you now, and your children later, and your grandchildren much later, out of a last-ditch war for the preservation of American independence and all of the things that American independence means.

Never before since Jamestown and Plymouth has our American civilization been in such danger as now.

For, on September 27, 1940—by an agreement signed in Berlin—Germany, Italy, and Japan [the Axis powers] joined together. They threatened that if the United States interfered with their expansion program—a program aimed at world control—they would unite against us.

The United States has no right or reason to encourage talk of peace until there is a clear intention on the part of the aggressor nations to give up all thought of dominating or conquering the world.

Some of our people like to believe that wars in Europe and in Asia are of no concern to us. But it is a matter of most vital concern to us that European and Asiatic war makers should not gain control of the oceans which lead to this hemisphere.

Does anyone seriously believe that we need to fear attack while a free Britain remains our most powerful naval neighbor in the Atlantic? Does anyone seriously believe, on the other hand, that we could rest easy if the Axis powers were our neighbors there?

If Great Britain goes down, the Axis powers will control the continents of Europe, Asia, Africa, and Australia, and the oceans as well. They will be able to throw enormous military and naval resources against this hemisphere. It is no exaggeration to say that all of us in the Americas would be living at the point of a gun—a gun loaded with explosive bullets, economic as well as military.

We would enter upon a new and terrible period in which the whole world, our hemisphere included, would be run by threats of brute force. To survive in such a world, we would have to convert ourselves permanently into a militaristic power with a war economy.

Some of us like to believe that even if Great Britain falls, we are still safe because of the Atlantic and the Pacific oceans. But the width of these oceans is not what it was in the days of clipper ships. At one point between Africa and Brazil, the distance is less than from Washington to Denver, Colorado—five hours for the latest type of bomber. And at the north of the Pacific Ocean, America and Asia almost touch each other.

Frankly and definitely there is danger ahead —danger against which we must prepare. But we well know that we cannot escape danger, or the fear of it, by crawling into bed and pulling the covers over our heads.

There are those who say that the Axis powers would never have any desire to attack the Western Hemisphere. This is the same dangerous form of wishful thinking which has destroyed the powers of resistance of so many conquered peoples. The plain facts are that the Nazis have said, time and again, that all other races are their inferiors and therefore subject to their orders. And most important of all, the vast resources and wealth of this hemisphere make up the most tempting loot in all the world.

The experience of the past two years has proven beyond doubt that no nation can appease [make concessions to] the Nazis. No one can tame a tiger into a kitten by stroking it. There can be no appeasement with ruthlessness. There can be no reasoning with a bomb. We know now that a nation can have peace with the Nazis only at the price of total surrender.

The American appeasers ignore the warning to be found in the fate of Austria, Czechoslovakia, Poland, Norway, Belgium, the Netherlands, Denmark, and France. They tell you that the Axis powers are going to win anyway. They argue that the United States might just as well use its influence to achieve a dictated peace and get the best out of it that we can.

They call it a "negotiated peace." Nonsense! Is it a negotiated peace if a gang of outlaws surrounds your community and, on threat of death, makes you pay tribute to save your own lives?

The British people are conducting an active war against an unholy alliance. Our own future security is greatly dependent on the outcome of that fight. Our ability to keep out of war is going to be affected by that outcome.

I make this direct statement to the American people. There is far less chance of the

United States getting into war if we do all we can now to support the nations defending themselves against attack by the Axis than if we go along with their defeat, then wait our turn to be attacked.

If we are to be completely honest with ourselves, we must admit there is risk in any course we may take. But I believe that most of our people agree that the course I suggest involves the least risk now and the greatest hope for world peace in the future.

The people of Europe who are defending themselves do not ask us to do their fighting. They ask us for the implements of war—the planes, the tanks, the guns, the freighters which will enable them to fight for their liberty and our security. We must get these weapons to them in sufficient volume and quickly enough so that we and our children will be saved the agony and suffering of war which others have had to endure.

There is no demand for sending an American military force outside our own borders. There is no intention by any member of your government to send such a force.

Our national policy is not directed toward war. Its only purpose is to keep war away from our country and our people.

Democracy's fight against world conquest is being greatly aided, and must be aided still more, by the rearmament of the United States and by sending every ounce of munitions and supplies that we can possibly spare to help the defenders who are in the front lines. It is no more unneutral for us to do that than it is for Sweden, Russia, and other nations to send steel and ore and oil into Germany every day.

This is not a matter of feelings or of controversial personal opinion. It is a matter of realistic military policy, based on the advice of our military experts. These experts and the members of Congress and the Administration have one single purpose—the defense of the United States.

I want to make it clear that it is the purpose of the nation to build now with all possible speed every machine and factory that we need to manufacture our defense material. We have the people—the skill—the wealth—and above all, the will.

We must be the great arsenal of democracy. For us this is an emergency as serious as war itself. We must apply ourselves to our task with the same determination, the same sense of urgency, the same spirit of patriotism and sacrifice as we would show if we were at war.

A FAMOUS FLYER URGES NEUTRALITY

Adapted from "We Cannot Win This War for England" by Charles A. Lindbergh, in Vital Speeches of the Day, 1941. Reprinted by permission of City News Publishing Co.

In March 1941 Congress passed the Lend-Lease Act, which permitted the United States to send unlimited weapons and military equipment to Great Britain. But even after passage of this law, Americans continued to debate the nation's role in the European war. On one side were the interventionists, who wanted the United States to enter the war on the side of the Allies. On the other side were the isolationists, who thought Americans should keep completely out of Europe's affairs.

One of the best-known isolationists was the famous American flyer Charles A. Lindbergh. He became a leading member of America First, a nationwide organization that favored arming for defense but argued that the United States could not save the Allies. Lindbergh made the following speech at an America First meeting in New York City on April 23, 1941.

Why does Lindbergh oppose America's entry into the war? What does he urge Americans to do? Why does he think his position is wise?

I know I will be severely criticized by the interventionists in America when I say we should not enter a war unless we have a reasonable chance of winning. That, they will claim, is far too materialistic a view. But I do not believe that our American ideals and our way of life will gain through an unsuccessful war. And I know that the United States is not prepared to wage war in Europe successfully at this time.

I have said it before, and I will say again, that I believe it will be a tragedy for the entire world if the British empire collapses. That is one of the main reasons why I opposed this war before it was declared, and why I have constantly favored a negotiated peace. I did not feel that England and France had a reasonable chance of winning. France has now been defeated. Despite the propaganda and confusion of recent months, it is now obvious that England is losing the war. I believe this is realized even by the British government. But they have one last desperate plan remaining. They hope that they may be able to persuade us to send troops to Europe and to share with England militarily, as well as financially, the fiasco of this war.

I do not blame England for this hope, or for asking for our assistance. But we now know that it declared a war under circumstances which led to the defeat of every nation that sided with it, from Poland to Greece. We know that in the desperation of war England promised to all these nations armed assistance that it could not send. We know that it misinformed them as it has misinformed us about its military preparations, its military strength, and the progress of the war.

In time of war, truth is always replaced by propaganda. I do not believe we should be too quick to criticize the actions of a warring nation. But we do have a right to think of the welfare of America first, just as the people in England thought first of their own country when they encouraged the smaller nations of Europe to fight against hopeless odds. When England asks us to enter this war, it is considering its own future, and that of its empire. In making our reply, I believe we should consider the future of the United States and that of the Western Hemisphere.

It is not only our right, it is our duty as American citizens to look at this war objectively and to weigh our chances for success if we should enter it. I have attempted to do this, especially from the standpoint of air power. I have been forced to the conclusion that we cannot win this war for England, no matter how much aid we send.

I ask you to look at the map of Europe today and see if you can suggest any way in which we could win this war if we entered it. Suppose we had a large army in America, trained and equipped. Where would we send it to fight? The campaigns of the war show only too clearly how difficult it is to force a landing, or to maintain an army, on a hostile coast.

Suppose we took our navy from the Pacific, and used it to convoy [to provide naval protection to] British shipping. That would not win the war for England. It would, at best, permit it to exist under the constant bombing of the Germans. Suppose we had an air force that we could send to Europe. Where could it operate? Some of our squadrons might be based in the British Isles. But it is physically impossible to base enough aircraft in the British Isles alone to equal in strength the aircraft that can be based on the continent of Europe.

I have asked these questions on the assumption that we had an army and an air force large enough and well enough equipped to send to Europe, and that we would dare remove our navy from the Pacific. But the fact is that none of these assumptions are correct. Our army is still untrained and inadequately equipped for foreign war. Our air force lacks modern fighting planes because most of them have already been sent to Europe. We have only a one-ocean navy.

When these facts are stated, the interventionists shout that we are defeatists, that we are undermining the principles of democracy, and that we are giving comfort to Germany by talking about our military weakness. But everything I mention here has been published in our newspapers, and in the reports of congressional hearings in Washington. Our military position is well known to the governments of Europe and Asia. Why, then, should it not be brought to the attention of our own people?

I say it is the interventionists in America, as it was in England and in France, who give comfort to the enemy. I say it is they who are undermining the principles of democracy when they demand that we take a course to which more than 80 percent of our citizens are opposed. [According to public opinion polls, by December 1941 only 20 percent of the American people were in favor of declaring war on Germany.] I charge them with being the real defeatists, for their policy has led to the defeat of every country that followed their advice since this war began. There is no better way to give comfort to an enemy than to divide the people of a nation over the issue of foreign war. There is no shorter road to defeat than by entering a war with inadequate preparation. Every nation that has adopted the interventionist policy of depending on someone else for its own defense has met with defeat and failure.

There is a policy open to this nation that will lead to success—a policy that leaves us free to follow our own way of life and to develop our own civilization. It is not a new and untried idea. It was favored by Washington. It was incorporated in the Monroe Doctrine. Under its guidance the United States has become the greatest nation in the world.

It is based upon the belief that the security of a nation lies in the strength and character of its own people. It recommends the maintenance of armed forces sufficient to defend this hemisphere from attack by any foreign powers. It demands faith in an independent American destiny. It is a policy not of isolation, but of independence; not of defeat, but of courage. It is a policy that led this nation to success during the most difficult years of our history, and it is a policy that will lead us to success again.

We have weakened ourselves for many months by dabbling in Europe's wars. While we should have been concentrating on American defense, we have been forced to argue over foreign quarrels. We must turn our eyes and our faith back to our own country before it is too late. And when we do this, a different outlook opens before us. Practically every difficulty we would face in invading Europe becomes an asset to us in defending America. Our enemy, and not we, would then have the problem of transporting millions of troops across the ocean and landing them on a hostile shore. They, and not we, would have to provide the convoys to transport guns and trucks and munitions and fuel across 3,000 miles [5,556 kilometers] of water. Our battleships and submarines would then be fighting close to their home bases. We would then do the bombing from the air and the torpedoing at sea. And if any part of an enemy convoy should ever pass our navy and our air force, they would still be faced with the guns of our coast artillery and behind them the divisions of our army.

The United States is better situated from a military standpoint than any other nation in the world. Even in our present condition of unpreparedness, no foreign power is in a position to invade us today. If we concentrate on our own defenses and build the strength that this nation should maintain, no foreign army will ever attempt to land on American shores.

War is not inevitable for this country. Such a claim is defeatism in the true sense. No one can make us fight abroad unless we ourselves are willing to do so. No one will attempt to fight us here if we arm ourselves as a great nation should be armed. Over 100 million people in this nation are opposed to entering the war. If the principles of democracy mean anything at all, that is reason enough for us to stay out. If we are forced into a war against the wishes of an overwhelming majority of our people, we will have proved democracy such a failure at home that there will be little use fighting for it abroad.

AN EDITORIAL ON THE DANGER OF NEUTRALITY

Condensed from "Editorial Challenging Lindbergh's Views on Entry into World War II" in The New York Times, *April 30, 1941. © 1941 by The New York Times Company. Reprinted by permission.*

Charles Lindbergh, America's flyer-hero and a leader of the isolationist America First Committee, attracted nationwide attention with the speech he made on April 23, 1941 (see page 555), urging that the United States should stay out of the war in Europe. A week later, on April 30, *The New York Times,* one of the nation's most influential newspapers, published a strong editorial challenging Lindbergh's point of view. The *Times* editorial, which follows, argued forcefully that the United States had no choice but to aid England in its fight against Nazi Germany.

What reasons does the *Times* give to explain why the United States must aid England against Germany? What will happen if England is defeated? Do you think the arguments in the editorial are effective or not? Why?

Those who tell us now that the sea is still our certain bulwark [defense], and that the tremendous forces sweeping the Old World threaten no danger to the New, give the lie to their own words in the precautions they would have us take.

They favor an enormous strengthening of our defenses. Why? Against what danger would they have us arm if none exists? To what purpose would they have us spend these almost incredible billions upon billions for ships and planes, for tanks and guns, if there is no immediate threat to the security of the United States? Why are we training the youth of the country to bear arms? Under pressure of what fear are we racing against time to double and quadruple our industrial production?

No man in his senses will say that we are arming against Canada or our Latin-American neighbors to the south, against Britain or the captive states of Europe. We are arming solely for one reason. We are arming against Hitler's Germany—a great predatory [warlike] power in alliance with Japan.

It has been said that if Hitler cannot cross the English Channel he cannot cross 3,000 miles [5,556 kilometers] of sea. But there is only one reason why he has not crossed the English Channel. That is because 45 million determined Britons, in a heroic resistance, have converted their island into an armed base, from which proceeds a steady stream of sea and air power. As Secretary [of State Cordell] Hull has said: "It is not the water that bars the way. It is the resolute determination of British arms. Were the control of the seas by Britain lost, the Atlantic would no longer be an obstacle—rather, it would become a broad highway for a conqueror moving westward."

That conqueror does not need to attempt at once an invasion of the continental United States in order to place this country in deadly danger. We shall be in deadly danger the moment British sea power fails; the moment we are compelled to divide our one-ocean Navy between two oceans simultaneously.

The combined Axis fleets outmatch our own: they are superior in numbers to our fleet in every category of vessel, from warships and aircraft carriers to destroyers and submarines. The combined Axis air strength will be much greater than our own if Hitler strikes in time—and when has he failed to strike in time? The master of Europe will have at his command the resources of 20 conquered nations to furnish his materials, the oil of the Middle East to stoke [run] his engines, the slave labor of a continent to turn out his production.

Grant Hitler the gigantic prestige of a victory over Britain, and who can doubt that the first result, on our side of the ocean, would be the prompt appearance of imitation Nazi regimes in a half-dozen Latin-American nations, forced to be on the winning side, begging favors, clamoring for admission to the Axis? What shall we do then? Make war upon these neighbors, send armies to fight in the jungles of Central or South America; run the risk of outraging native sentiment and turning the whole continent against us? Or shall we sit tight while the area of Nazi influence draws ever closer to the Panama Canal, and a spreading checkerboard of Nazi airfields provides ports of call for German planes that may choose to bomb our cities?

But even if Hitler gave us time, what kind of "time" would we have at our disposal?

There are moral and spiritual dangers for this country as well as physical dangers in a Hitler victory. There are dangers to the mind and heart as well as to the body and the land.

Victorious in Europe, dominating Africa and Asia through his Axis partners, Hitler could not afford to permit the United States to live an untroubled and successful life, even if he wished to. We are the arch enemy of all he stands for: the very citadel [stronghold] of that democracy which he hates and scorns. As long as liberty and freedom prevailed in the United States, there would be constant risk for Hitler that our ideas and our example might infect the conquered countries which he was bending to his will. In his own interest he would be forced to harry [harass] us at every turn.

Who can doubt that our lives would be poisoned every day by challenges and insults from Nazi politicians; that Nazi agents would stir up anti-American feeling in every country they controlled; that Nazi spies would overrun us here; that Hitler would produce a continual series of lightning diplomatic strokes—alliances and "nonaggression pacts" to break our will; in short, that a continuous war of nerves, if nothing worse, would be waged against us?

And who can doubt that, in response, we should have to turn our own nation into an armed camp, with all our traditional values of culture, education, social reform, democracy, and liberty subordinated to the single, all-embracing aim of self-preservation? In this case we should indeed experience "regimentation." Every item of foreign trade, every transaction in domestic commerce, every present prerogative [right] of labor, every civil liberty we cherish, would necessarily be regulated in the interest of defense.

CHAPTER 20 ■ AMERICANS IN THE SECOND WORLD WAR

AN ARMY NURSE IN THE PHILIPPINES

Adapted from "An Army Nurse at Bataan and Corregidor" as told to Annalee Jacoby; from History in the Writing *by Gordon Carroll. Copyright 1945 by Time Inc. Reprinted by permission of Time Inc.*

After the Japanese attack on Pearl Harbor in December 1941, the United States entered World War II. The early months of the war were a disaster for the United States. The Japanese armed forces moved steadily through Southeast Asia, conquering nation after nation and invading island chains in the Pacific Ocean. American and Filipino troops under General Douglas MacArthur struggled to defend the Philippine Islands. But early in January 1942 Manila, capital of the Philippines, was forced to surrender. American forces then retreated to the Bataan Peninsula and the island of Corregidor. There they fought heroically, until Bataan was conquered on April 9 and Corregidor finally fell on May 6.

Thousands of American soldiers, including many sick and wounded, were trapped in the Philippines. In this selection, an army nurse at Bataan and Corregidor describes the last weeks.

What were the conditions at Hospital Number 1 on Bataan? What was the mood of the patients? Of those working in the hospital?

Conditions at Hospital Number I were not too good during the last few weeks we spent there. Patients were flooding in. We increased from 400 to 1,500 cases in two weeks' time. Most of them had serious wounds, but nine out of ten patients had malaria or dysentery besides.

We were out of quinine [a drug used in treating malaria]. There were hundreds of gas gangrene cases, and our supply of vaccine had run out months before. There were no more sulfa drugs. There weren't nearly enough cots, so triple-decker beds were built from bamboo, with a ladder at one end so we could climb up to take care of the patients. They had no blankets or mattresses.

There was almost no food except carabao [water buffalo]. We had·all thought we couldn't eat carabao, but we did. Then came mule, which seemed worse, but we ate that too. Most of the nurses were wearing government-issue heavy-laced men's shoes. [From the term "government issue" came the name for American soldiers in World War II—GI's.] We had to keep our feet taped up to walk in them. Our uniforms had been gone for a long time, so we mostly wore size 32 air corps coveralls. We carried steel helmets and gas masks even in the wards, but we didn't expect to use them.

We went about our work feeling perfectly safe because of the Red Cross markings on the roof. When bombers came overhead on April 4, we hardly noticed them. Then suddenly incendiary [fire] bombs dropped. They hit the receiving wards, mess hall, doctors' and officers' quarters, and the steps of the nurses' dormitory, setting fire to all the buildings but luckily not hitting the wards. Several people walking outside were killed. The patients were terrified, of course, but behaved well. The Japanese prisoners were perhaps the most frightened of all. Everything was a blur of taking care of patients, putting out fires, straightening overturned equipment.

We remained frightened until two hours later when someone heard the Japanese radio in Manila announce that the bombings had been an accident and wouldn't happen again. After that, we wouldn't even leave the hospital for a short drive. We felt safe there and nowhere else.

The morning of April 7 we were all on duty when a wave of bombers came over. The first bomb hit near the Filipino mess hall and knocked us down before we even knew planes were overhead. An ammunition truck was passing the hospital entrance. It got a direct hit. The boys on guard at the gate were shell-shocked, smothered in the dirt thrown up by the explosion.

Hospital patients picked us up and we began caring for patients hurt by shrapnel [bomb fragments]. Everything was terror and confusion. Patients, even amputation cases, were falling and rolling out of the triple-decker beds. Suddenly a chaplain, Father Cummings, came into the ward, threw up his hands for silence and said: "All right, boys, everything's all right. Just stay quietly in bed, or lie still on the floor. Let us pray." The screams stopped instantly. He began the prayer just as a second wave of planes came over.

The first bomb hit near the officers' quarters, the next struck the patients' mess hall just a few yards away. The shock waves bounced us three feet off the cement floor and threw us down again. Beds were tumbling down. Flashes of heat and smoke burned our eyes. But through it all we could hear Father Cummings' voice reciting the Lord's Prayer. He never stopped, never even fell to the ground, and the patients never moved. Father Cummings' clear voice went through to the end. Then he turned quietly and said: "All right, you take over. Put a tourniquet on my arm, will you?" And we saw for the first time that he'd been badly hit by shrapnel.

The next few hours were a nightmare, except for the way everyone behaved. We were afraid to move, but realized we had to get to work. One Filipino with both legs amputated—he'd never gotten out of bed before by himself—rolled onto the ground and said: "Miss, are you all right, are you all right?" The ward boys all told us, "You go on outside—don't stay here any longer. We'll take care of everything." We tried to care first for the patients most seriously hurt. A great many all over the hospital were bleeding badly. We went to where the bomb had hit the ward and began pulling patients from the crater. I saw Rosemary Hogan, head ward nurse, and thought for a moment her face had been torn off. She wiped herself with a sheet, smiled and said: "It's nothing, don't bother about me. Just a nose bleed." But she had three shrapnel wounds.

It would be hard to believe the bravery after that bombing if you hadn't seen it. A soldier had risked his life by going directly to the traction wards where patients were tied to beds by wires. He thought it was better to hurt the men temporarily than to leave them tied helpless above ground where they'd surely be hit by shrapnel, so he cut all tractions and told the patients: "Get under the bed, Joe."

We began immediately to move patients to another hospital. We were so afraid the Japanese would be back again the next day that even the most serious cases were moved, because giving them any chance was better than none. There were only 100 patients left the next morning. We worked all that day making up beds to admit new patients. It never occurred to anyone that we wouldn't go on as usual. Suddenly, after dark, we were told we were leaving in 15 minutes—that we should pack only what we could carry. Then we heard that the Japanese had broken through and the Battle of Bataan was over. The doctors all decided to stay with the patients, even doctors who had been told to go to Corregidor.

We left the hospital at 9 that night—got to Corregidor at 3 in the morning. The trip usually took a little over an hour. As we drove down to the docks, the roads were jammed. Soldiers were tired, aimless, frightened. Cars were overturned. There were bodies in the road. Clouds of dust made it hard to breathe. At midnight on the docks we heard that the Japanese had burned our hospital to the ground.

Bombers were overhead, but we were too tired to care. We waited on the docks while the navy tunnel and ammunition dump at Mariveles were blown up. Blasting explosions, blue flares, red flares, shrapnel, tracers, gasoline exploding—it was like a hundred Fourths of July all at once, but we were too frightened to be impressed. As we crossed the water with Corregidor's big guns firing over our heads and shells from somewhere landing close by, the boat suddenly shook and the whole ocean seemed to rock. We thought a big shell had hit the water in front of us. It wasn't until we landed that we learned that an earthquake had hit just as Bataan fell.

Corregidor seemed like heaven that night.

They fed us and we slept, two to an army cot. We went to work the following morning. Months before, patients on Corregidor had filled a few side tunnels only. Now they were in double-decker beds all along the halls and in the main tunnel. There was constant bombing and shelling—sometimes shock waves from a bomb outside would knock people down at the opposite end of the tunnel. Emperor Hirohito's birthday, April 29, was a specially bad day. The bombing began at 7:30 in the morning and never stopped. Shelling was heavy; soldiers counted over 100 explosions per minute. Dive bombers were going after the gun on the hill directly above our heads and the shock waves inside were terrific.

The worst night on Corregidor was when a bomb hit outside the tunnel entrance. A crowd had gone outside for a cigarette and many were sleeping on the ground at the foot of the cliff. When the first shell hit nearby, they all ran for the tunnel, but the iron gate was shut and it opened outward. As more shells landed, they smashed men against the gate and twisted off arms and legs. All the nurses got up and went back to work—the operating room was overflowing until 5:30 in the morning. There were many amputations.

At 6 o'clock one evening, after the usual bombing and shelling, 21 of us were told we were leaving Corregidor by plane. We don't know how we were selected. Everyone wanted to leave, of course, but morale was splendid. Everyone realized the end was getting close, but none gave up hope.

Now we're safe in Australia. But the only reaction we notice is wanting to make up somehow, anyhow, for those who didn't get away.

DIVE BOMBERS OVER ITALY

Adapted from Brave Men *by Ernie Pyle. Copyright 1943, 1944 by Scripps-Howard Newspaper Alliance. Copyright 1944 by Ernie Pyle. Copyright © 1971, 1972 by Holt, Rinehart and Winston. Reprinted by permission of Holt, Rinehart and Winston, Publishers.*

Americans eagerly followed the war news on radio and in the press. Often they learned about the land campaigns and air and sea battles by reading the newspaper stories written by foreign correspondents. These American reporters covered every phase of World War II on every one of the many battle fronts. Many of these brave reporters went with the American units into battle. They shared the soldiers' daily hardships and dangers, and many of them lost their lives in battle.

Ernie Pyle, one of the most outstanding foreign war correspondents, spent many months at the battle fronts with American troops. His name and his stories were well known to most Americans by the time he died during the fighting on the Pacific island of Ie Shima in April 1945. In this selection, he writes about the war in Europe, describing American dive bombers and their crews fighting in Italy during 1943.

How did the dive-bomber groups support the army infantry? What, according to Pyle, are the most striking features of dive bombing?

I spent some time with a dive-bomber squadron of the 12th Air Support Command. There were about 50 officers and 250 enlisted men in each squadron. They all lived in a big apartment house built by the Italian government for war workers and their families. It was out in the country at the edge of a small town.

In the dive-bomber groups in Italy, pilots and mechanics believed that the dive bomber was the most wonderful machine produced in this war. Certainly, those dive-bomber boys were a spectacular part of our air force.

Their function was to work in extremely close support of our infantry. For instance, suppose there was a German gun position just over a hill which was holding us up because our troops couldn't get at it with their guns. They called on the dive bombers and gave them the location. Within an hour, and sometimes much quicker, bombers would come screaming out of the sky right on top of that gun and blow it up.

They could do the same thing to bunched enemy troops, bridges, tank columns, convoys, or ammunition dumps. Because of their great accuracy they could bomb much closer to our own troops than other kinds of planes would dare. Most of the time they worked less than a thousand yards [914 meters] ahead of our front lines—and sometimes even closer than that.

The group I was with had been in combat six months. During that time they had flown 10,000 missions, fired more than 1 million rounds of 50-caliber ammunition, and dropped 3 million pounds [1.4 million kilograms] of bombs. That's more than the entire Eighth Air Force in England dropped in its first year of operation.

Those boys dived about 8,000 feet [2,438 meters] before dropping their bombs. Without brakes their speed in such a dive would ordinarily build up to around 700 miles [1,126 kilometers] an hour, but the brakes held them down to about 390 miles [627 kilometers].

The dive bombers approached their target in formation. When the leader made sure he had spotted the target he wiggled his wings, raised his diving brakes, rolled on his back, nosed over, and down he went. The next man behind followed almost instantly, and then the next, and the next—not more than 150 feet [46 meters] apart. There was no danger of their running into each other, for the brakes held them all at the same speed.

At about 4,000 feet [1,219 meters] the pilot released his bombs. Then he started his pull-out. The strain was terrific, and all the pilots would "black out" a little bit. It was not a complete blackout, and lasted only four or five seconds. It was more a heaviness in the head and a darkness before the eyes, the pilots said.

If you ever heard a dive bombing by our planes you'd never forget it. Even in normal flight those planes made a sort of screaming noise. In a dive, the wail could be heard for miles. From the ground it sounded as though they were coming directly down on us. It was a horrifying thing.

For several months the posting period back to America [the number of missions a pilot had to fly before being sent home on leave] was set at a certain number of missions. Then it was suddenly increased by more than 20. When the order came, there were pilots who were within one mission of going home. So they had to stay and fly a few more months. Some of them never lived to finish the new allotment.

There is an odd psychological factor in the system of being sent home after a certain number of missions. When pilots got to within three or four missions of the finish, they became so nervous they almost jumped out of their skins. A good many were killed on their last mission. The squadron leaders wished there were some way they could surprise a man and send him home with six or eight missions still to go, thus sparing him the agony of those last few trips.

Nowhere in our fighting forces was cooperation closer or friendship greater than between Americans and British in the air. I never

562

heard an American pilot make a critical remark about a British flier. Our pilots said the British were cooler under fire than we were. The British attitude and manner of speech amused them, but they were never scornful.

They liked to listen in on their radios as the British pilots talked to each other. For example, one day they heard one pilot call to another, "I say, old chap, there is a Jerry [the English nickname for Germans during the war] on your tail."

To which the pilot in danger answered, "Quite so, quite so, thanks very much, old man."

And another time, one of our dive bombers got shot up over the target. His engine was smoking and he was losing altitude. He made for the coast all alone, an easy target for any German fighter that might come along. He was just barely staying in the air, and he was a sad and lonely boy indeed. Then suddenly he heard over his earphones a distinctly British voice saying, "Cheer up, chicken, we have you."

He looked around and two Spitfires [British fighter planes], one on either side, were leading him back to his home field.

WOMEN AND WAR

Adapted from "The Women in the War" by Margaret Mead in While You Were Gone, *edited by Jack Goodman. Copyright © 1946 by Simon and Schuster, Inc., copyright renewed © 1973 by Simon and Schuster, Inc. Reprinted by permission of the publisher.*

Although there were great changes in America during World War II, for most Americans the wartime years did not bring the severe hardships and widespread destruction endured by the peoples of Europe. Americans experienced rationing and shortages of food and other supplies, but they did not have to face enemy bombs or advancing armies.

One of the greatest changes in the United States was the profound effect the war had on the lives of American women. With millions of men in the armed forces, women took over many of the jobs in the nation's factories, farms, and businesses. Many women also now had to take care of their homes and their families alone. In this selection, written shortly after World War II, anthropologist Margaret Mead tells of some of these changes in women's lives.

According to Margaret Mead, what worries did American servicemen have about women on the home front? What did wartime jobs mean for women? What did the author think women's roles would be in the future? Was she correct? Explain.

In wartime, men and women get out of step and begin to wonder about each other. "What will he be like after all those years in the army?" "What will she be like after all those years alone at home?" "I do hope he won't have changed too much." "I hope she will look the same."

All this is natural enough. Boys and girls grow up together in the same world, seeing a lot of each other, each knowing what the other is thinking. Husbands are used to coming home at night and telling their wives what they think of the news in the paper, and having their wives tell them they are exactly right—or exactly wrong. Either way, they know what's going on. Dramatic news, quintuplets and quads, double murders and triple suicides, all fall into place in peacetime. They are events that spice the usual events of life, in which most babies are born one at a time and husbands and wives may sometimes feel like murdering each other but hardly ever do. But in wartime, boys and girls, men and women, separated in time and in space, aren't in step any more, and both begin to wonder what the other one will be like . . . after the war.

The man overseas reads his paper or his magazines filled with news that women are doing new and therefore, by definition, "unwomanly" jobs. (A womanly job is just a job that everybody is used to seeing women do.) He reads about the mannish clothes women are wearing, the welding outfits they are wielding, and he worries. What's happening to women anyway? What will be the use of winning the war if when you go back home all the girls' heads are filled with a lot of strange and unwelcome nonsense?

The newspapers are full of wild stories: bobby soxers [a term for teenagers in the 1940's, since many of them wore heavy white socks called "bobby socks"] wandering about Times Square or storming a performance by Frank Sinatra; the riotous living of war workers. If the man overseas were at home, all this would make sense. He'd have a chance to see that being a woman worker means long hard hours doing unfamiliar work, cramped and difficult living conditions, hours of standing in line waiting for food. He'd know that for every straying bobby soxer there are a hundred youngsters who are working in factories or doing their absent brothers' work on the farm.

Besides the bobby soxers and the quadruplets in the newspapers, there has been continuous writing on the theme: "Will women be willing to return to the home?" This worrying question is often inspired by those in whose interest it will be to discharge women workers as soon as the war is over.

Statistics on how many women are working and plan to work appear in headlines which add, "Eight out of every ten women asked say they will work after the war." Most of those women who say they will go on working are women who would have been working anyway. The number of American women who work has been rising from 2.5 million in 1880 to over 5 million in 1920 and to 11 million in 1940. In 1950—if you ask for official estimates—you'll find that about 16 million women will be working in the United States. That's the kind of society we have, one in which many men aren't paid enough to support their wives, one in which women without husbands are expected to support themselves, one in which very few brothers are willing to support their unmarried sisters. In back of the headlines and the statistics and the threatening questions in the newspapers there lies the simple fact that more women in the United States have to work each year. And that more women than ever before will be working at some time in their lives.

This needn't worry the returning men very deeply. It was part of the America they left, and it's part of the America they are coming back to. The war has speeded things up a little, that's all. After the war, just as it would have been if there had been no war, most girls will plan to work between school and marriage. Many will plan to work until the first baby. Some will go back to work when their children are grown. And an increasing number will work because they have no husbands and no other means of support.

However, some striking things have happened during the war which are due to the war. During the war, over 3 million women have gone to work who would *not* have worked if there had not been a war. A million girls between 14 and 18 who would ordinarily have been in school have been working part or full time. A million young married women, with and without children, have gone to work. Many of them

are wives of men in the armed forces. The remainder of the 3 million women include many women who have worked before and have gone back to work. Some are mothers who cannot stand waiting for the mail to bring news of their sons. Some are mothers who already know that their sons will never return.

There are several ways of looking at these things which have been happening to women. Some people find it more interesting that women have done jobs which no one thought they could do—become welders and machine setters, railroad conductors, and taxi drivers. Most of these are strictly wartime shifts and will become men's jobs again after the war.

To some, the fact that we have women in the armed forces in this war is the most striking thing that has happened. There are only a little over a quarter of a million women in the services. They have joined up in the face of a great deal of disapproval from brothers and boy friends and fathers. They have been given, for the most part, dull and inglorious jobs to do.

What do these figures mean? What will it mean to men that women who wouldn't otherwise have worked now have worked? That their wives have been working while they were gone? That their mothers and their mothers-in-law have worked?

It means, for one thing, that women, as a group, are better informed than they were before. They understand what a time clock is and what a checkoff is. Farm women have learned a great deal more about the drudgery and techniques of farm life. Women in homes which used to employ servants will know a great deal more about housework. Women who have left housework for the factory will come back with some new ideas of what it means to work definite hours. Millions of women will understand more of what their husbands are talking about, when their husbands talk sense, and will have a sounder idea of when they are talking nonsense. A great many more women will understand more about money, how hard it is to make, as well as how hard or how easy it is to spend. Here, perhaps, is one of the places where the experience of women in wartime America will be a useful supplement to the men's. While the men have had four or five years less of dealing with money, the women have had that much more.

The second important experience women have had, while the men were away, is moving about. Small-town girls have gone to cities, city girls to little country towns, factory and office girls to pick beets and milk cows. Northern girls have gone south, and eastern girls have gone west. Some of this moving-about experience will match the men's. Men have lived abroad, but mostly in camps. Women have not had such strange ways of life, but they have actually had to cope with things more—buy and prepare food and convert trailers into homes.

And most of all women have waited. Many of them—those who have worked and traveled—have waited by doing something. Others have just waited. In their minds has been the echo of his "I want to find you just the same." Many women have sensibly interpreted this to mean that he wants her to be as good a 1945 model as she was a 1940 model, as smart a 23-year-old as she was an 18-year-old.

But others, less realistic, have taken boy friends and husbands at their word and tried not to change at all. They have tried to keep their minds, if not their hats, just as they were when their men left. Many of these girls, instead of moving out into the wartime world, have gone home to Mother. They have slipped back into dependent, little-girl positions, stayed 18 years old or even slipped back a little. Getting to know a wife who has tried to stay the same is really going to be more difficult than getting acquainted with a wife who has driven a truck or worn a uniform.

When the returning man looks his wife or sweetheart in the eye, between them will stand his years of danger and hardship which she cannot share or even properly imagine, her flat, empty years which she could not value because he was away. In peacetime, men and women count upon living side by side, watching children grow and gardens flower and houses go up and bank accounts increase and chins get double or beards get stubbier and life flow more quietly—together. All of our patterns for the relations between men and women were based on this simple expectation. This generation will have to make new patterns.

Last of all, the man who left the country in 1941–42 will come back to a new generation of girls. These girls will be, inevitably, a new kind of girl, girls brought up on the war years, on a different sort of romance. They don't expect as much of boys as their older sisters did who grew up when dates were commoner. They will have practically no memory of the depression years. War has stood at the beginning of their young girlhood; war did not crash rudely into the middle of it, finding them unprepared. They will be standing on tiptoe waiting for the post-war world.

LIFE IN A RELOCATION CAMP

Adapted from Nisei Daughter *by Monica Sone. Copyright 1953 by Monica Sone. Reprinted by permission of Little, Brown and Co. in association with the Atlantic Monthly Press.*

After the Japanese attack on Pearl Harbor, many American government officials believed that Japanese-Americans were a danger to the nation's security. As a result, about 112,000 Japanese-Americans were placed in detention or relocation camps. Most of these Japanese-Americans were not allowed to leave the relocation camps until January of 1945. Despite the federal government's internment program, over 17,000 Nisei served in the American armed forces, many winning military awards for bravery.

Monica Sone, a Nisei, or Japanese-American born in the United States, wrote the following account of life in a relocation camp. She was a college student in Seattle, Washington, when the war broke out and she and her family were sent to a relocation camp in Idaho.

Today, most Americans view the wartime treatment of Japanese-Americans as unfair. But during World War II most Americans accepted it as necessary.

Do you think it was fair to segregate Nisei soldiers? If you had been a Japanese-American during the war, how do you think you would have felt about being placed in a relocation camp? Would you have volunteered to serve in the armed forces? Explain.

Camp Minidoka was located in the south-central part of Idaho, north of the Snake River. It was a semidesert region. When we arrived I could see nothing but flat prairies, clumps of greasewood shrubs, and jack rabbits. And of course the hundreds and hundreds of barracks, to house 10,000 of us.

Our home was one room in a large army-type barracks, measuring about 20 by 25 feet [6 by 7.5 meters]. The only furnishings were an iron pot-belly stove and cots.

On our first day in camp, we were given a rousing welcome by a dust storm. We felt as if we were standing in a gigantic sand-mixing machine as the gale lifted the loose earth up into the sky, hiding everything. Sand filled our mouths and nostrils and stung our faces and hands like a thousand darting needles.

Just as suddenly as the storm had broken

out, it died away. We walked out of the mess hall under a pure blue sky, startling in its peacefulness. In the deepening blue shadows, people hurried here and there, preparing for their first night in camp. The Issei [Japanese-Americans born in Japan] men stomped along in their wooden *getas* (high sandals). The Issei women in cool cotton print *yukatas* (Japanese house kimonos) slipped along noiselessly. They bowed to each other, murmuring *"Oyasumi nasai. Rest well."* These familiar words in the alien darkness of the prairie were welcome sounds. I suddenly saw that these people were living through difficult circumstances with simple dignity and patience, and I felt ashamed of my own strong emotions. That night we let ourselves sink deep into the yawning silence of the prairie, which was shattered only by the barking of the coyotes.

Idaho summer sizzled on the average of 110 degrees [43.3 degrees Celsius]. For the first few weeks I lay on my cot from morning till night, not daring to do more than go to the mess hall three times a day.

When September came we slowly emerged from our stupor. The sun no longer stabbed the backs of our necks. Now when I awoke in the mornings, the air felt cool and crisp.

The momentum of the change carried me along into a job at the camp hospital as ward secretary. Henry [her brother] had already been working at the hospital for weeks. Sumi [her sister] and her young friends signed up as nurse's aides. Father finally settled on becoming a member of the internal security staff—a policeman, complete with an olive-drab uniform. Mother, who was not well, stayed home to mop the floor, wash the family laundry, iron and mend our clothes, and attend the English language class, choir practice, prayer meetings, and a Japanese doll-making class.

By fall, Camp Minidoka had bloomed into a full-grown town. Children went to school in the barracks, taught by professional teachers among the evacuees and people hired from the outside. Except for the members of the administration staff, the evacuees themselves supplied the entire labor force in the camp. All church activities were in full session.

During our spare hours, we confiscated scrap lumber, piece by piece, from a lumber pile. Tables and chairs gradually made their appearance in our tiny apartment. Rows of shelves lined the bare walls. We bought gallons of shellac, and white paint, yards of white organdy for curtains, and blue damask for the cots and clothes closet. We had a living room, powder room, three bedrooms, a study, storage room, and a kitchen all in one. It had everything except the kitchen sink and privacy.

Winter in Minidoka was as intense an experience as summer had been. We gave a strong cheer for the government when we were told that they would provide winter clothing for those who needed them. Mother was the first to go after her clothing. When she came home with the bundle, we all gathered around her excitedly to see what she had. She held up a pair of longjohns [men's underwear], olive-drab trousers, and a navy pea coat [jacket].

"They're good quality woolens," she said calmly, "and they'll certainly keep me warm. Only thing, it's too bad we aren't all males."

Sumi and I protested hysterically that we were all going to look like members of the internal security staff, since these clothes were exactly what Father and his friends wore on patrol duty. It was only after a man living in our block became lost one night in a snowstorm and died from exposure that we finally gave in. We ran to the clothing office. The man gave us what was left—size 40 longjohns, sleeveless, collarless vests which hung down to our knees, and wonderful thick, bear-sized pea coats. That taught us a lesson that a man, or at any rate, a woman, cannot live on pride alone.

We had lived in camps through four seasons, and each season had served as a challenge to us. In the meantime we had drifted farther and farther away from the American scene. We had been set apart, and we had become adjusted to our existence. The great struggle in which the world was engaged seemed far away.

Then one day a group of army personnel marched into our camp on a special mission. They made a startling announcement. "The United States War Department has decided to form a special combat unit for the Nisei. We have come to recruit volunteers."

We gasped and we tried to speak. Dunks Oshima, who had brought the news to us, eyed us fiercely as he cried, "What do they take us for? Saps? First, they change my army status to 4-C because of my ancestry, and run me out of town. Now they want me to volunteer for a suicide squad so I could get killed for democracy. That's going some for sheer nerve!"

That was exactly the way most of us felt, but the recruiting officers were well prepared to cope with our emotional explosion. They called meetings and we flocked to them with an injured look.

An officer spoke to us. "You're probably

wondering why we are here, recruiting for volunteers from your group. I think that my explanation is best expressed in the statement recently issued by our President, regarding a citizen's right and privilege to serve the country. I want to read it to you:

'No loyal citizens of the United States should be denied the democratic right to exercise the responsibilities of their citizenship, regardless of their ancestry. The principle on which this country was founded and by which it has always been governed is that Americanism is a matter of the mind and the heart. Americanism is not, and never was, a matter of race or ancestry. All loyal American citizens should be given the opportunity to serve this country wherever their skills will make the greatest contribution, whether it be in our armed forces, war production, agriculture, government service, or other work essential to the war effort.' "

It all sounded very well. It was the sort of declaration which rang true and clear in our hearts. But there were questions in our minds which needed answering. The speaker threw the meeting open for discussion. We said we didn't want a separate Nisei combat unit because it looked too much like segregation. We wanted to serve in the same way as other citizens, in a mixed group with the other Americans.

The man answered: "But if the Nisei men were to be scattered throughout the army, you'd lose your significance as Nisei. Maybe you want it that way, because in the past you suffered with your Japanese faces. Well, why not accept your Japanese face? Why be ashamed of it? Why not take advantage of it for a change? There are powerful organizations now campaigning on the [West] Coast to deport you all to Japan, citizens and residents alike. But there're also men and women who believe in you, who feel you should be given the chance to stand up and express yourselves. They thought that a Nisei combat unit would be just the thing. Whatever you accomplish, whatever you achieve, will be yours and yours alone."

We saw that the speaker was sincere and believed earnestly in this cause. Then we asked him another burning question. "Why had the government ever put us here in the first place? Why? Why? Why?"

The man looked at our wounded faces and said: "I can't answer that question. I can only repeat what you already know, that the government thought evacuation was necessary. The evacuation took place, and right or wrong, it's past. Now we're interested in your future. The War Department is offering you a chance to volunteer and to distinguish yourselves as Japanese-American citizens in the service of your country. Believe me, this combat unit is not segregation in the sense you think it is."

The tension in the mess hall eased, and questions and answers came more naturally. After the meeting we returned to our barracks to continue the debate. Dunks came with us.

"What's a fellow to do?" Dunks said wryly. "They've got us over a barrel. If we don't do our bit, you can bet your boots there won't be much of a future for us here. Those on the Coast who want to deport us will see to that."

I put in, "I'll bet, though, that some of those characters will be totally against a Nisei combat team."

Henry snorted, "Those scrooges will be against anything which might make us look good."

Dunks said, "It's the general public I'm thinking about. They're the ones who count. They want proof of our loyalty. Okay, I'm giving it to them, and maybe I'll die for it if I'm unlucky. But if after the war's over and our two cents don't cut any ice with the American public, well, to blazes with them!"

The next day Henry announced, "Tomorrow I'm going down to volunteer." No one said a word. Father stared down at his veined hands. Mother's face turned into a white mask.

"Please don't feel so bad, Mama."

Mother smiled thinly. "I don't feel bad, Henry. In fact, I don't feel anything just now."

Father spoke to her tenderly, "Mama, if Henry had been born in Japan, he would have been taken into the army and gone off to war long ago."

"That's right. And I guess it's about time we all stopped thinking about the past. I think we should go along with our sons from now. It's the least we can do."

Father said, gratefully, "That's what I wanted to hear. At least we're together on this matter. Imagine what Dunks must be going through."

Mrs. Oshima had refused to speak to her son ever since he had decided to volunteer. "Is this what we deserve from our children," she said, "after years and years of work and hardship for their sake? Ah, we've brought up nothing but fools! They can be insulted, their parents insulted, and still they volunteer."

Early the next morning, Dunks, and George and Paul, sons of Mr. Sawada, the clothing salesman, came into our apartment on their way to the camp hospital for their physical.

"Let's go, Hank, before the crowd gets there."

They left with a great clatter and loud shouting. Father, Mother, Sumi, and I sank to our cots feeling as if we had come out of a turbulent storm which had been raging steadily in our minds since Pearl Harbor. The birth of the Nisei combat team was the climax to our evacuee life, and the turning point. It was the road back to our rightful places.

BRAVERY AT THE BULGE

Adapted from A Man Called White *by Walter White. Copyright 1948 by Walter White, copyright © renewed 1976 by H. Lee Lurie. Reprinted by permission of The Viking Press.*

During World War II the United States armed forces continued their traditional policy of separate units for black Americans. Moreover, a large number of black Americans were put in service units—working in supply depots, driving trucks, doing repair and maintenance jobs. But some black units were assigned to combat. And for a brief period, late in the war, the barriers of racial segregation were broken down.

When the Germans broke through the Allied lines in December 1944, in their counterattack at the Battle of the Bulge, the Allies desperately needed fighting units. As a result, black units and white units fought together to stop the German advance. In this selection Walter White, who was secretary of the NAACP, tells of this history-making event of black and white Americans fighting together.

Why did army officers ask black soldiers to volunteer? Why did black Americans respond as they did? What was the attitude of white officers and soldiers who fought with black soldiers?

One of the most dramatic examples of the abandonment of interracial antagonisms in combat by troops themselves—and a tragic reversal by the army high command—occurred during and after the Battle of the Bulge.

The Germans' sudden, effective breakthrough threatened disaster. The tide of war might have been changed at that point. At the very least, the war would have been longer if this daring maneuver had succeeded, even though more men and war materials would probably have brought Allied victory. Many Americans now alive would have died in the meantime.

Every available man was thrown into the fight to stop the German advance. But even then there were not enough. Desperate appeals were sent to the United States to rush more combat troops as quickly as possible. Many were sent by plane, but even these were not enough. It was at this point, during some of the fiercest fighting, that General John C. H. Lee issued an appeal to colored Service of Supply troops to volunteer for combat.

"It is planned to assign you without regard to color or race to units where assistance is most needed," General Lee promised. He made no effort to minimize the desperate nature of the fighting nor the great number of casualties caused by the German breakthrough. He pointed out that all noncommissioned officers would have to give up their ratings to qualify for service as combat troops.

Great numbers of volunteers answered General Lee's appeal. In some units 80 percent of the soldiers offered their services. In one engineer unit, 171 out of 186 men volunteered. One private in an ordnance company declared: "We've been giving a lot of sweat. Now I think we'll mix some blood with it!"

Negroes were delighted at this first opportunity to function as "real" soldiers. The response was so great that the army had to set up a quota to prevent complete disorganization of its service units.

Generals George Patton, Omar Bradley, and Courtney Hodges gave their approval to the use of Negro soldiers in completely unsegregated combat units. General Eisenhower was enthusiastic. But Eisenhower's chief of staff, W. Bedell Smith, insisted that the plan be submitted to General George C. Marshall, army chief of staff.

Washington was alarmed at the idea of an unsegregated, genuinely democratic army. It ordered the plan abandoned. But the need for combat troops was so critical that the high command in Washington was forced to agree to a compromise—the use of all-Negro platoons in white regiments, instead of a mixture of whites and Negroes throughout regiments. Although Negro soldiers felt that they had been let down, they were still enthusiastic. The Negro platoons were distributed among eleven combat divisions of the First and Seventh Armies. They fought in the crucial stages of the Battle of the Bulge and through the later Allied drive across Germany.

Several of the Negro volunteers won the Distinguished Service Cross or Silver Star. Others were cited for bravery beyond the call of duty.

The army took a poll among the white officers and soldiers who had fought with Negro troops. The results are to me a striking example of the fact that race prejudice is not as stubborn as some people imagine. The army poll showed that after having served in the same unit with black combat soldiers, 77 percent of the officers favored integration, as contrasted with 33 percent before the experience. The figures among enlisted men were 77 percent and 35 percent, after and before serving with Negroes.

A white South Carolina sergeant was quoted by the army as saying, "When I heard about it, I said I wouldn't wear the same shoulder patch they did. After that first day, when we saw how they fought, I changed my mind. They are just like any of the other men to us."

Another sergeant from Alabama, after telling how bitterly he had opposed serving with Negroes at first, confessed a total change of attitude. "I used to think they would be cowards in combat, but I saw them work."

Some 84 percent of white company officers and 81 percent of white platoon sergeants declared that Negro troops had fought superbly, and 17 percent of officers and 9 percent of enlisted men even went so far as to say that Negroes fought better than white troops.

General Patton highly praised the black volunteers. General Eisenhower declared: "All my commanders reported that these volunteers did excellent work." General Charles Lanham of the 104th Division, presenting combat decorations to eleven Negroes, went even further to declare: "I have never seen any soldiers who have performed better in combat than you have."

But Eisenhower, to the dismay of many of us who had faith in him, testified before the Senate armed services committee in 1948 that he believed racial segregation in the army should continue at the platoon level. And in April 1948 the Secretary of War bluntly told a distinguished group of 15 Negro leaders that the army would continue segregation.

DROPPING THE ATOMIC BOMB

Adapted from Memoirs, Vol. I, Year of Decisions *by Harry S. Truman. Published by Doubleday & Co., Inc., 1955. Reprinted by permission of Harry S. Truman Estate.*

When President Roosevelt died in 1945, Vice-President Harry Truman became President. The new President now faced the tremendous task of ending the war and planning for the peace.

After the war in Europe ended, Truman and the other Allied leaders met at Potsdam, Germany, in July 1945. At that meeting they agreed to demand that Japan surrender unconditionally. Japan refused. President Truman, who had been in office less than four months, now had to make the awesome decision of whether to drop an atomic bomb on Japan. Fearing that an attack on the Japanese mainland by American warships and planes would cost as many as a million American lives, Truman decided to approve the use of the atomic bomb. In this selection, taken from President Truman's memoirs, the President explains his decision to use the atomic bomb at Hiroshima.

How was it decided where and when to drop the first bomb? What was President Truman's feeling about his decision to drop the bomb? What do you think of Truman's decision?

The idea of the atomic bomb had been suggested to President Roosevelt by the famous and brilliant Dr. Albert Einstein. Its development turned out to be a vast undertaking. It was the achievement of the combined efforts of science, industry, labor, and the military, and it had no parallel in history. The people in charge and their staffs worked under great pressure. The whole enormous task required the services of more than 100,000 people and immense quantities of material. It required over two and a half years and the spending of $2.5 billion. Only a few of the thousands of people who worked in these plants knew what they were producing. So strict was the secrecy that even some of the highest-ranking officials in Washington did not have the slightest idea of what was going on. I did not.

Before 1939 it had been generally agreed among scientists that in theory it was possible to release energy from the atom. In 1940 we had begun to share with Great Britain all scientific knowledge useful to war, although Britain was at war at that time and we were not. Following this—in 1942—we learned that the Germans were at work on a method to harness atomic energy for use as a weapon of war.

It was under the general policy of sharing knowledge between our nation and Great Britain that research on the atomic bomb started in such feverish secrecy. American and British scientists joined in the race against the Germans. Working together with the British, we thus made it possible to achieve a great scientific triumph in the field of atomic energy. Nevertheless, basic and historic as this event was, it had to be considered at the time as relatively unimportant to the far-flung war we were fighting in the Pacific at a terrible cost in American lives.

We could hope for a miracle, but the daily tragedy of a bitter war was always with us. We worked to construct a weapon of such overpowering force that the enemy could be forced to give in swiftly once we could use it. This was the primary aim of our secret and vast effort. But we also had to carry out the enormous effort of our basic and traditional military plans.

My own knowledge of these developments had come only after I became President, when Secretary of War Henry Stimson had given me the full story. He had told me at that time that the project was nearing completion and that a bomb could be expected within another four months. It was at his suggestion, too, that I had then set up a committee of top people and had asked them to study with great care the possibilities the new weapon might have for us.

It was their recommendation that the bomb be used against the enemy as soon as it could be done. They recommended further that it should be used without warning and against a target that would clearly show its devastating strength. I had realized, of course, that an atomic bomb explosion would cause damage and casualties beyond imagination. On the other hand, the scientific advisers of the committee reported, "We can propose no technical demonstration likely to bring an end to the war; we see no acceptable alternative to direct military use." It was their conclusion that no technical demonstration they might propose, such as dropping the bomb on a deserted island, would be likely to bring the war to an end. It had to be used against an enemy target.

The final decision of where and when to use the atomic bomb was up to me. Let there be no mistake about it. I regarded the bomb as a military weapon and never had any doubt that it should be used. My top military advisers recommended its use. When I talked to Churchill, he told me that he favored the use of the atomic bomb if it might help end the war.

In deciding to use this bomb, I wanted to make sure that it would be used as a weapon of war in the manner set down by the laws of war. That meant that I wanted it dropped on a military target. I had told Stimson that the bomb should be dropped as nearly as possible upon a war production center of prime military importance.

Stimson's staff had prepared a list of cities in Japan that might serve as targets. Kyoto, though favored as a center of military activity, was eliminated when Secretary Stimson pointed out that it was a cultural and religious shrine of the Japanese.

Four cities were finally recommended as targets: Hiroshima, Kokura, Niigata, and Nagasaki. They were listed in that order as targets for the first attack. The order of selection was in accordance with the military importance of these cities. But allowance would be given for weather conditions at the time of the bombing. Before the selected targets were approved as proper for military purposes, I personally went over them in detail with Secretary Stimson, General Marshall, and General Arnold, and we discussed the matter of timing and the final choice of the first target.

General Spaatz, who commanded the Strategic Air Forces, which would drop the bomb, was given some independence as to when and on which of the four targets the bomb would be dropped. That was necessary because of weather and other operational considerations. In order to get preparations under way, the War Department instructed General Spaatz that the first bomb would be dropped as soon after August 3 as weather would permit.

A specialized B-29 unit had been selected for the task. Seven modified B-29's, with pilots and crews, were ready and waiting for orders. Meanwhile ships and planes were rushing the materials for the bomb and specialists to assemble them to the Pacific island of Tinian in the Marianas.

On July 28 Radio Tokyo announced that the Japanese government would continue to fight. There was no choice now. The bomb was scheduled to be dropped after August 3 unless Japan surrendered before that day.

On August 6, the fourth day of my journey home from Potsdam, came the historic news that shook the world. I was eating lunch with members of the *Augusta*'s crew when I was handed the following message:

TO THE PRESIDENT
FROM THE SECRETARY OF WAR

Big bomb dropped on Hiroshima August 5 at 7:15 P.M. Washington time. First reports indicate complete success which was even more conspicuous than earlier test.

I was greatly moved. I said to the group of sailors around me, "This is the greatest thing in history. It's time for us to get home."

A few minutes later a second message was handed to me. It read as follows:

Following information regarding Manhattan [the development of the bomb was called the Manhattan Project] received. "Hiroshima bombed visually. There was no fighter opposition and no flak. Parsons reports 15 minutes after drop as follows: 'Results clear cut successful in all respects. Visible effects greater than in any test. Conditions normal in airplane following delivery.' "

When I had read this I signaled to the crew in the mess hall that I wished to say something. I then told them of the dropping of a powerful new bomb which used an explosive twenty thousand times as powerful as a ton of TNT. I went to the wardroom, where I told the officers, who were at lunch, what had happened. I could not hide my expectation that the Pacific war might now be brought to a speedy end.

UNIT SEVEN
THE CHALLENGES OF A NEW ERA
(1945-1970's)

CHAPTER 21 ■ DEVELOPMENTS ON THE DOMESTIC FRONT

EISENHOWER'S SPECIAL ROLE

Adapted with permission of Macmillan Publishing Co., Inc. from Eisenhower and the American Crusades *by Herbert S. Parmet. Copyright © 1972 by Herbert S. Parmet.*

In 1952 Dwight D. Eisenhower was elected the 34th President of the United States. Eisenhower, the popular hero of World War II, won the election by a huge majority of votes. And during his two terms in office, Eisenhower retained his popularity with the American people. Unlike most Presidents, whose popularity has risen and fallen with events, Eisenhower was able to maintain the support of most of the people throughout the eventful years of his administration.

Eisenhower achieved a unique place among recent American Presidents, for he appeared to be above politics and political battles. He was a moderating influence during difficult years when Americans feared a "Communist menace" within their own government and the nation was fighting a Cold War against Communism throughout the world.

According to the author, why did many Americans respond so favorably to Eisenhower? What were some of Eisenhower's accomplishments in office? Do you think he would be a popular President if he were in office today?

Eisenhower was leaving the White House with a remarkable record in 1961. After eight years in office, during a time of turbulence at home and in the world, Eisenhower, who was universally regarded as a non-politician, was still enormously popular. Few people would dare to argue with the observation that, given a chance, the American people would gladly return him to office for another four years. The final Gallup Poll [a well-known survey of public opinion] taken before he left office showed public confidence in him at 59 percent. This was higher than the *average* levels managed by most Presidents. During his years in office he had averaged 66 percent. Only once, during the first three months of 1958, did he drop below the 50 percent level. Additionally, a study released by Gallup on January 18, 1962 showed that 65 percent of the public believed that historians would agree that he had been either a "great" or a "good" President. When Americans were asked what they considered his greatest single achievement, their reply was simple: "He kept the peace."

Indeed he had. Coming into office at a time of bitter divisions, when the Democratic President [Truman]—and, to a lesser extent, his party—had lost the confidence of millions of Americans, Eisenhower had performed a unique service. He became the conciliator. It was Eisenhower who arranged the Korean peace. Had Stevenson won the election in 1952, the anti-Communist hysteria in the United States, ready to denounce every different idea as "treasonous," would have made such a settlement, so close to the original Thirty-eighth Parallel division, almost impossible.

During the Indochina crisis of 1954 Eisenhower, together with Secretary of State John Foster Dulles, skillfully avoided becoming involved in the two crises over the islands of Quemoy and Matsu. In the Suez war of 1956, Eisenhower also avoided involvement. When he sent the Marines into Lebanon, he did so after choosing a time, place, and display of power that minimized the risks and ensured success. In Berlin, his leadership was so successful that Soviet Premier Nikita Khrushchev found himself outmaneuvered. When the Soviet leader exposed the U-2's activities in May 1960, Eisenhower astonished the world with his admission of responsibility. [The U-2 was an American spy plane shot down over the Soviet Union.] It was clear to him that continued "cover" stories would have damaged credibility more than the truth. Despite the enormous difficulties, Eisen-

hower kept NATO alive and maintained relative harmony, his major objectives.

In his domestic policies, Eisenhower was both less certain and less knowledgeable than in his foreign policy. He was a conservative in the truest sense. He distrusted both the use and accumulation of centers of power. He viewed economics as governed mainly by unchanging natural laws. Thus he favored balanced budgets and was against deficit financing. Long after the New Deal, he fought against overcentralization of government. He equated fiscal strength with national survival. But he held that goal was obtainable only through the "sound" dollar rather than by substantial investments in the public sector. He was careful to preserve the constitutional balance of power between the federal government and the states. Therefore, he minimized what could be done about poverty, urban decay, medical care, education, and public power. At the same time, however, he expanded Social Security so that 90 percent of the population was under its coverage by 1960 and he became the constructor of a national interstate highway system. He met the Sputnik panic by approving the National Defense Education Act, so that federal spending for schools by 1960 nearly tripled the 1952 level. Throughout, however, he believed the best way to do things was through private enterprise and individual initiative with a minimum of government interference. Capital from private individuals encouraged to invest was, to him, better than management by the state. When the great conflict over civil rights began in his term of office, he appeared to many as insensitive and ignorant about the plight of the black Americans. Negroes insisted that he did not really understand, and Roy Wilkins of the NAACP has claimed that his attitude served to encourage the racists. Possibly his own belief in the goodness of people kept him convinced that Americans were incapable of such inhumane conduct. He thought the school-integration decision by the Supreme Court a serious error and a matter best left to the states. But the pressure of politics and necessity and the efforts of his advisors brought him to support the first civil-rights legislation since Reconstruction.

He was not a "political genius," but he knew perhaps better than anyone else around him exactly what the people wanted and how they wanted it. He had, as those who knew him best testify, a remarkable political instinct. Moreover, he knew how to manage people, to use them for his purpose and then cut them loose. In direct contrast to Harry Truman, who had lost all authority by the end of his term, Eisenhower's greatest individual accomplishment was keeping his own standing with the people.

He handled himself with dignity. He was proud of his office and what it represented. When he refused to fight in the "gutter" with Senator Joseph McCarthy, he was thinking as much about his position as his pride, although he had plenty of that, too. Most of all, however, perhaps his great asset in both war and peace was his warmth and ability to impress people as varied as Khrushchev, capitalists, and civil-rights leaders that he was sympathetic and understanding.

His lack of sophistication was a great personal asset with the voters who trusted him. Those who complained that the President was a "hayseed" or an innocent were reluctant to acknowledge that his contribution to history since the early 1940's had been aided not only by personal charm but by a keen mind. To call him a great or good or even a weak President misses the point. He was necessary.

AN APPRAISAL OF KENNEDY

Adapted from pp. 756–758 in Kennedy *by Theodore C. Sorensen. Copyright © 1965 by Theodore C. Sorensen. By permission of Harper & Row, Publishers, Inc.*

Young, handsome, and well-educated, President Kennedy inspired many Americans to take an active interest in government and politics. His energy and idealism also made many Americans believe that the increasingly serious problems facing the nation in the 1960's could and would be solved. Thus President Kennedy's tragic death in 1963 seemed, for a time, to mark an end to many of America's hopes and dreams.

Theodore Sorensen, one of the President's advisors, tried to analyze the special appeal that Kennedy had for so many Americans. Part of the President's popularity was based on Kennedy's "style," or way of doing things. In his book about Kennedy, from which the following selection is taken, Sorensen wrote: "The Kennedy style was special—the grace, the wit, the elegance. . . . But what mattered most to

him, and what in my opinion will matter most to history, was the substance—the strength of his ideas and ideals, his courage and judgment."

What events of Kennedy's Presidency does Sorensen stress? In what ways was Kennedy different from other Presidents, according to Sorensen?

How will history judge him? It is too early to say. I am too close to say. But history will surely record that his achievements were beyond his years. In an eloquent letter to President Kennedy on nuclear testing, Prime Minister Harold Macmillan of Britain once wrote: "It is not the things one did in one's life that one regrets, but rather the opportunities missed." It can be said of John Kennedy that he missed very few opportunities.

In less than three years he presided over a new era in American race relations, a new era in American-Soviet relations, a new era in our Latin-American relations, a new era in fiscal and economic policy, and a new era in space exploration. His Presidency helped start the longest and strongest period of economic expansion in our peacetime history. It helped start the largest and swiftest build-up of our defensive strength in peacetime history. And it brought new and enlarged roles for the federal government in higher education, mental illness, civil rights, and the conservation of human and natural resources.

Some moves were dramatic, such as the Cuban missile crisis, the Test Ban Treaty, the Peace Corps, and the Alliance for Progress. Some were small day-by-day efforts on Berlin or Southeast Asia, where no real progress could be claimed. Some were simply holding our own. No nation slipped into the Communist orbit, no nuclear war raised havoc on our planet, no new recession set back our economy. But generally Kennedy was not content to hold his own. His efforts were devoted to turning the country around, starting it in new directions, getting it moving again. "He believed," said his wife, "that one man can make a difference and that every man should try." He left the nation a whole new set of basic propositions—on freedom now instead of someday for the black American—on winding down instead of "winning" the Cold War—on the unthinkability instead of the inevitability of nuclear war—on cutting taxes in times of deficit—on battling poverty in times of prosperity.

For the most part, on November 22, these problems had not been solved and these projects had not been completed. Even most of those completed will impress historians a generation from now only if this generation makes the most of them.

But I suspect that history will remember John Kennedy for what he started as well as for what he completed. The forces he released in this world will be felt for generations to come. The standards he set, the goals he outlined, and the talented people he attracted to politics and public service will influence his country's course for at least ten years.

People will remember not only what he did but what he stood for. This, too, may help the historians assess his Presidency. He stood for excellence in an era of indifference—for hope in an era of doubt—for placing public service ahead of private interests—for understanding between East and West, black and white, labor and management. He had confidence in people and gave them confidence in the future.

It will not be easy for historians to compare John Kennedy with those who came before him and after him. He was unique in his effect on the office. He was the first to be elected at so young an age, the first of the Catholic faith, the first to reach for the moon and beyond, the first to announce that all racial segregation and discrimination must be abolished as a matter of right, the first to meet our enemies in a potentially nuclear confrontation, and the first to take a solid step toward nuclear arms control. And he was the first to die at so young an age.

All his life he was a winner until November 1963. In battle he became a hero. In literature he won a Pulitzer Prize. In politics he reached the Presidency. His inaugural address, his wife, his children, his policies, his conduct of crises, all reflected his pursuit of excellence.

History and the future must decide. Usually they reserve greatness for those who win great wars, not those who prevent them. But in my unobjective view I think it will be difficult to measure John Kennedy by any ordinary historical yardstick. For he was an extraordinary man, an extraordinary politician, and an extraordinary President. It is my belief that no scale of good and bad Presidents can rate John Fitzgerald Kennedy. A mind so free of fear and myth and prejudice, so opposed to clichés, so unwilling to fool or be fooled, to accept or reflect mediocrity, is rare in our world—and even rarer in American politics. Without lessening any of the great men who have held the Presidency in this century, I do not see how John Kennedy could be ranked below any one of them.

His untimely and violent death will affect the judgment of historians. The danger is that it will turn his greatness into legend. Even though he was himself almost a legendary figure in life, Kennedy was a constant critic of the myth. It would be an ironic twist of fate if his martyrdom should now make a myth of the mortal man.

In my view, the man was greater than the legend. His life, not his death, created his greatness. In November 1963, some saw it for the first time. Others realized that they had too casually accepted it. Others mourned that they had not admitted it to themselves before.

JOHNSON URGES EQUAL RIGHTS FOR ALL

Adapted from Lyndon B. Johnson, "The Right to Vote," in Vital Speeches of the Day. *April 1, 1965.*

When Lyndon Johnson became President after President Kennedy's assassination, he promised the nation he would continue President Kennedy's programs. Almost immediately he called on Congress to pass the civil rights bill that Kennedy had proposed. And after a bitter struggle in the Senate, the Civil Rights Act of 1964 was passed into law in July of 1964. Now, for the first time, all black Americans were guaranteed the right to register to vote. However, some voter registration drives in the South led to violence. In Selma, Alabama, a Unitarian minister was killed in March 1965 after he had taken part in a protest march. A week later, on March 15, Johnson spoke before Congress, proposing a second civil rights bill. The following selection is taken from that speech— a moving statement of Johnson's belief in American democracy.

What does Johnson believe is the most basic right of all Americans? How does Johnson sum up his goals as President? Do you think that he achieved them? Explain.

I speak tonight for the dignity of all human beings and the destiny of democracy. I urge every member of both parties, Americans of all religions and of all colors, from every section of this country, to join me in that cause.

At times, history and fate meet at a single time in a single place to shape a turning point in people's unending search for freedom.

So it was at Lexington and Concord. So it was a hundred years ago at Appomattox. So it was last week in Selma, Alabama.

There, long-suffering men and women peacefully protested the denial of their rights as Americans. Many were brutally assaulted. One good man—a man of God—was killed.

There is no cause for pride in what has happened in Selma. There is no cause for self-satisfaction in the long denial of equal rights of millions of Americans. But there is cause for hope and for faith in our democracy in what is happening here tonight.

For the cries of pain and the hymns and protests of oppressed people have brought together all the majesty of this great government—the government of the greatest nation on earth.

Our mission is at once the oldest and the most basic of this country—to right wrong, to do justice, to serve people.

In our time we have come to live with the moments of great crisis. Our lives have been marked with debate about great issues, issues of war and peace, issues of prosperity and depression.

But rarely in any time does an issue show the secret heart of America itself. Rarely do we meet a challenge, not to our growth or abundance, our welfare or security, but rather to the values, purposes, and meaning of our beloved nation.

The issue of equal rights for American Negroes is such an issue.

There is no Negro problem. There is no southern problem. There is no northern problem. There is only an American problem.

And we meet here tonight as Americans—not as Democrats or Republicans—to solve that problem.

This was the first nation in the history of the world to be founded with a purpose. The great statements of that purpose still sound in every American heart, North and South: "All men are created equal." "Government by consent of the governed." "Give me liberty or give me death."

Those are not just clever words. Those are not just empty theories. In their name Americans have fought and died for two hundred years.

Those words are promised to all citizens so they can share in the dignity of all human beings. This dignity cannot be found in people's possessions. It cannot be found in their power or in their position. It really rests on their right to be treated as a person equal in opportunity to all others.

It says that they shall share in freedom. They shall choose their leaders, educate their children, and provide for their family according to their ability and their merits as human beings.

To apply any other test, to deny people their hopes because of their color, race, religion, or place of birth is not only to do injustice. It is to deny America and to dishonor the dead who gave their lives for American freedom.

Our forebears believed that if this noble view of the rights of people was to flourish it must be rooted in democracy. The most basic right of all was the right to choose your own leaders.

The history of this country in large part is the history of the expansion of that right to all of our people. Many of the issues of civil rights are very complex and most difficult. But about this there can and should be no argument. Every American citizen must have an equal right to vote.

There is no reason which can excuse the denial of that right. There is no duty which weighs more heavily on us than the duty we have to insure that right. Yet the harsh fact is that in many places in this country men and women are kept from voting simply because they are Negroes.

This bill will establish a simple, uniform standard for voting. It will provide for citizens to be registered by officials of the United States government, if state officials refuse to register them.

It will eliminate tiresome, unnecessary lawsuits which delay the right to vote.

Finally, this legislation will insure that properly registered individuals are not prohibited from voting.

There is no constitutional issue here. The command of the Constitution is plain. There is no moral issue. It is wrong—deadly wrong—to deny any of your fellow Americans the right to vote in this country.

There is no issue of state's rights or national rights. There is only the struggle for human rights.

On this issue, there must be no delay, no hesitation, no compromise with our purpose.

We cannot, we must not, refuse to protect the right of every American to vote in every election that he or she may desire to participate in.

But even if we pass this bill the battle will not be over.

What happened in Selma is part of a far larger movement which reaches into every section and state of America. It is the effort of American Negroes to secure for themselves the full blessings of American life.

Their cause must be our cause too. Because it's not just Negroes, but really it's all of us, who must overcome the crippling legacy of bigotry and injustice.

And we shall overcome.

As a man whose roots go deeply into southern soil, I know how agonizing racial feelings are. I know how difficult it is to change the attitudes and the structure of our society. But a century has passed—more than a hundred years—since the Negroes were freed.

And they are not fully free tonight.

Negroes are not the only victims. How many white children have gone without an education? How many white families have lived in poverty? How many white lives have been scarred by fear, because we wasted energy to maintain the barriers of hatred and terror?

And so I say to all of you here and to all in the nation tonight that those who appeal to you to hold on to the past do so at the cost of denying you your future. This great, rich, restless country can offer opportunity and education and hope to all—all, black and white, all North and South, sharecropper and city dweller.

These are the enemies: Poverty, ignorance, disease. They are our enemies, not our fellow humans, not our neighbors. And these enemies too—poverty, disease, and ignorance—we shall overcome.

There is really no part of America where the promise of equality has been fully kept. In Buffalo as well as in Birmingham, in Philadelphia as well as in Selma, Americans are struggling for their freedom. This is one nation. What happens in Selma and Cincinnati is a matter of concern to every American.

At the real heart of the battle for equality is a deep-seated belief in the democratic process. Equality does not depend on the force of arms or on tear gas. It depends upon the force of moral right, on respect for law and order.

The bill I am presenting to you will be known as a civil rights bill.

But in a larger sense, most of the program I am recommending is a civil rights program. Its object is to open the city of hope to all people of all races. All Americans must have the right to vote. And we are going to give them that right.

All Americans must have the privileges of citizenship, regardless of race. And they are going to have those privileges.

I would like to remind you that to exercise these privileges takes much more than just legal right. It requires a trained mind and a healthy body. It requires a decent home and the chance to find a job and the opportunity to escape from poverty.

Of course people cannot contribute to the nation if they are never taught to read or write; if their bodies are stunted from hunger; if their sickness goes uncared for; if their life is spent in hopeless poverty, just drawing a welfare check.

So we want to open the gates to opportunity. But we're also going to give all our people, black and white, the help that they need to walk through those gates.

My first job after college was as a teacher in Cotulla, Texas, in a small Mexican-American school. Few of my students could speak English and I couldn't speak much Spanish.

My students were poor and they often came to class without breakfast. They knew, even in their youth, the pain of prejudice. They never seemed to know why people disliked them, but they knew it was so, because I saw it in their eyes.

I often walked home late in the afternoon, after classes were finished, wishing there was more that I could do. But all I knew was to teach them the little that I knew, hoping that it might help them against the hardships that lay ahead.

Somehow you never forget what poverty and hatred can do when you see its scars on the hopeful face of a young child.

I never thought then, in 1928, that I would be standing here in 1965. It never occurred to me that I might have the chance to help the sons and daughters of those students, and to help people like them all over this country.

But now I do have that chance. And I'll let you in on a secret—I mean to use it.

And I hope that you will use it with me. This is the richest, most powerful country which ever occupied this globe. The might of past empires is little compared to ours. But I do not want to be the President who built empires, or sought grandeur, or extended authority. I want to be the President who educated young children to the wonders of their world.

I want to be the President who helped to feed the hungry and to prepare them to be taxpayers instead of tax eaters.

I want to be the President who helped the poor to find their own way and who protected the right of every citizen to vote in every election.

I want to be the President who helped to end hatred among people and who promoted love among the people of all races, all regions, and all parties.

THE MEANING OF WATERGATE

Adapted from Breach of Faith *by Theodore H. White. Published by Atheneum/Reader's Digest Press. Copyright © 1975 by Theodore H. White. Reprinted by permission.*

In June of 1972, five men were arrested as they attempted to break into Democratic National Committee headquarters at the Watergate building in Washington, D.C. It was soon discovered that they were working for the campaign committee to re-elect President Nixon. Although President Nixon declared that he knew nothing about the burglary, news reporters discovered evidence that pointed to a White House cover-up of the burglary as well as other possible criminal activities. The Watergate scandal soon became a national crisis, as more and more Americans came to believe that the President was covering up a crime and lying about his activities. After many months of Congressional investigations into the Watergate scandals, President Richard M. Nixon resigned from office in August 1974.

In this selection, Theodore White, the author of several best-selling books on recent Presidential election campaigns, expresses his opinion about how and why Watergate happened.

According to White, why are myths especially important to American society? How did the Nixon administration shatter Americans' faith in the Presidency? What effects do you think the Watergate crisis had on American politics and society?

The true crime of Richard Nixon was simple. He destroyed the myth that binds America together. For this he was driven from power.

The myth he broke was critical—that somewhere in American life there is at least one person who stands for law, the President. That faith overcomes all distrust, all evidence or suspicion of wrongdoing by lesser leaders, all corruptions. That faith holds that all people are equal before the law and protected by it. It holds that no matter how the faith may be betrayed elsewhere, at one particular point—the Presidency—justice will be done. It was that faith that Richard Nixon broke.

All civilizations rest on myths. But in America myths have exceptional meaning. A myth is a way of giving meaning to the raw and contradictory evidence of life. It lets people make patterns in their own lives, within the larger patterns.

There is, however, an absolutely vital political difference between the mythology of other nations and the mythology of America. Other nations may fall or last. They may change their governing myths. But French people will always remain French people, Russians will be Russians, Germans remain Germans, and English people—English people. But America is different. It is the only peaceful civilization in the world made up of many races. Its people come from such diverse heritages of religion, language, habit, and color that if America did not exist it would be impossible to imagine that such a grouping could ever behave like a nation. It would be impossible unless its people were bound together by a common faith.

Politics in America is the binding faith. That begins with the founding faith of the Declaration of Independence: "We hold these truths to be self-evident, that all men are created equal, that they are endowed by their creator with certain unalienable rights, that among these are life, liberty, and the pursuit of happiness."

Of all the political myths out of which the Republic was born, none was more hopeful than the myth of the Presidency—that the people, in their shared wisdom, would be able to choose the best person to lead them. From this came a related myth—that the Presidency, the supreme office, would make noble any person who held its responsibility. The office and its duties would, by their very weight, make an individual a superior person, wise enough to resist the clash of all selfish interests.

Richard Nixon behaved otherwise. His lawlessness exploded the myths. He left a nation approaching the 200th anniversary of its glorious independence with a President and a Vice-President neither of whom had been chosen by the people. The faith was shattered. Being shattered, it was to leave American politics more confused than ever since the Civil War.

What Richard Nixon left us is best understood as a set of questions—questions about ourselves and what we seek from government.

The simplest set of questions can be asked and answered in the formula of popular detective stories: Who did it?

Like any popular detective story, this is a story of bungling criminals. It begins with the circumstance, very difficult for Richard Nixon's enemies to accept, that most of the top people involved were strong patriots, convinced that what they were doing was best for their country. Men like Ehrlichman and Haldeman [Nixon's two most important aides] were true believers in the purpose of America as they saw it. They sought nothing for themselves. Beneath came all the others, people of little patriotism and no principle.

They entered into government, all of them, with no greater knowledge of how power worked than the intrigues of political campaigning. They could not understand the essential balance there must always be in the nation's affairs between distrust and suspicion on the one hand and faith and trust on the other. A naive politician gets nowhere. A successful politician must be something of a hypocrite, promising all to all, knowing that, if elected, he or she must inevitably sacrifice the interests of some for others. But people in government must know when to choose trust and faith over political need. The people must trust their words at whatever cost—or they cannot govern. In the Presidency, above all, it is essential to recognize the moment for truth.

From mid-April of 1973 to his end in 1974, the President lied, lied again, and continued to lie. His lying not only added to the anger of those who were on his trail. It slowly destroyed the faith of Americans in that President's honor. He knew what he was doing, for he consciously relied on the mystique of the Presidency to carry him through what lay ahead.

If Nixon had committed a historic crime—treason, or accepting graft, or knowingly twisting American national policy for personal or partisan ends—the detective story would be enough.

Its answer to the question is that the criminals were caught because they were bunglers.

But the initial crime [the Watergate break-in] was commonplace. Nixon might have erased it easily by acting as Presidents must act against lawbreakers. Instead he made it a disaster by trying to cover it up. So another set of questions —not how the criminals were caught, but why Nixon did what he was caught doing.

"Why?" is a political question and one that will hang over American politics for years to come. Nixon was not a stupid man. What did he think he was defending beyond his own skin and reputation?

To trace the answers to the question of "Why?" one must accept the political reality that Richard Nixon and his aides were, for the first time in American politics since 1860, carrying on an ideological war [a struggle between differing sets of ideas]. Because they felt their purpose was high and necessary and the purpose of their enemies dangerous or immoral, he and his aides believed that the laws did not bind them—or that the laws could legitimately be bent.

Again one must go back to a set of American myths to explain the intensity of the ideological war that began in the 1960's.

Wrapped around the original political myths of America—of liberty, of equality, of a government-of-laws-not-people—had been a culture, long since destroyed, with a set of social myths now twisted by time into the rigid political principles of today.

The old social myths rested on the belief that free citizens were able to control their own futures by their own efforts. In the original American community of farmers 200 years ago, it was considered a matter of thrift and constant work and planning whether a person made it or did not. But in corporate America, since the beginning of the 1900's, fewer and fewer people have been able to control their own future by their own efforts. Now, in present-day America, everyone was locked up—in corporations, in unions, in organizations, in schools, in draft boards, in the tax net—and group pressure was the thing. Nixon and his men believed in the old social myths and the old culture. His opponents believed in mobilizing group pressure to force the federal government to do their will or to protect their future.

The old myths glorified self-government. The states and the federal government originally agreed that each had separate responsibilities.

But in practice, by the 1960's the heart of the problem lay in the cities and suburbs.

But the most deceptive inherited social myth was that of American power. That myth was recent. It rested on the brief dominance of American arms as they spread triumphant over the entire globe in 1945. What had happened, however, by the 1960's, was that the myth of American power had been weakened by the revolutions of the postwar world. Americans were faced with a new reality—they were engaged in the first major war that they would not win. By the time Nixon came to power, that realization had split the country at every level. Resentment at the waste and killing in Vietnam had spilled out into the streets in sputtering violence and frightening bloodshed.

Nixon had, to be sure, recognized the weakening of American power abroad. As soon as he took office in 1969, he had begun to end the war in Vietnam. But he clung to the old doctrine that the President alone could make the decisions and arrange the timing for a withdrawal from Asia that would bring peace with honor. Those who opposed him, whether in the streets or in the news system, he would treat with moral fierceness.

The political detective story of Nixon's crime begins there—with his belief that he, as President, was the only caretaker of America's power. The Nixon aides saw themselves as waging war in Vietnam to make peace. They had no doubt that national security required them to carry on that war by all means possible until peace with honor had been won. If the end was good, then the means, however brutal, must also be good. And from this idea of the President's authority came most of the early illegalities, the buggings, the wire-taps, the surveillances, the minor crimes. Until finally the President's aides saw no distinction between ends and means. They were making war not just in Vietnam but all across the home front, too. All the disputes over home issues, as well as foreign issues, became part of the ideological war.

But the political story does not quite answer the "Why?" or explain the particular fierceness of behavior of the men at the White House.

To explain the spite and hatred of their struggle, one must add one more condition—the change of culture that was taking place all over America in the 1960's. The Nixon aides were people of the embattled old culture. As such, they believed the new culture was not only undermining the authority of their President to make war-and-peace, but striking into their homes, families, and schools, too. It was undermining the values with which they had grown up and still held dear.

This conflict of the two cultures far surpassed in emotion the traditional American political struggle between "conservatives" and "liberals." The two cultures clashed in every form of expression—in language, in costume, in slogans. They clashed over important matters—civil rights, "law-and-order," safety in the streets, drug abuse, the dignity of women. The line of clash between the two cultures ran through families as well as communities. Fathers against sons, mothers against daughters, students against teachers, arguing over such matters as dress and manners and morals, and sex and drugs and rioting. This clash of culture and personal values was taking place at the same time as the political clash over the hard issues. And the two added to each other.

One must see all three wars—the war abroad, the ideological war, the cultural war—as crossing each other in the agony of an unstable personality in order to answer the personal "Why?" of Richard Nixon's collapse. The answer can come only by imagining that here was a man who could not, in his waking moments, accept the man he recognized in his own nightmares—the outsider, the loner, the loser.

Throughout his career, except for a few brief years in 1971 and 1972, that had been his inner roles—the outsider, the loser. "They" were against him, always. His authority as President was being challenged by the news system, the rioters, the Congress, the intellectuals. The culture, the manners, the beliefs of his lonely life of striving were being wiped out by the fashions of the new culture. Losers play dirty. He, too, would change the rules. His ruthlessness, vengefulness, nastiness were the characteristics of a man who has seen himself as underdog for so long that he cannot distinguish between real and fancied enemies, a man who does not really care whom he hurts when pressed, who cannot accept or understand when or what he has won.

Always, in the crisis, he reacted as the cornered loser. He could not shake that characteristic. In 1972 he had won so largely that he could misread his victory. It was a victory for his ideas and politics. But he saw it as personal, as a loner. It was not simply an election he had won. He had conquered a land. Its citizens were the occupied. And he could use the law as he wished, however much a hostile Congress, the news system, or intellectuals protested.

CHAPTER 22 ■ THE CHALLENGES OF WORLD LEADERSHIP

BEGINNINGS OF THE COLD WAR

Adapted from The United States and the Origins of the Cold War, 1941–47 *by John Lewis Gaddis (New York: Columbia University Press, 1972), pp. 353–361. Reprinted by permission of the publisher and Mr. John Lewis Gaddis.*

Many Americans hoped that the Western powers and the Soviet Union would continue their wartime cooperation after World War II. But by 1946 the Soviet Union and the United States were sharply divided over such issues as the postwar boundaries of Eastern Europe, disarmament, and the international control of atomic energy. The so-called "Cold War" between the Western powers and the Soviet Union had now begun. It was clear that the Soviet Union was determined to maintain its influence in Eastern Europe and expand it into other areas of the world. And it was equally clear that the United States was determined to stop the further expansion of Communism by the Soviet Union.

Exactly how the Cold War began and whose fault it was is a subject of continuing controversy among many historians. In the following selection, historian John Lewis Gaddis gives his analysis of how the Cold War began.

How does Gaddis feel one should approach the study of the Cold War? Which nation does he think had the primary responsibility for the Cold War? Why? Does Gaddis feel that the Cold War was inevitable? Do you think it was?

American leaders did not want a Cold War, but they wanted insecurity even less. By early 1946 President Truman and his advisers had reluctantly concluded that recent actions of the Soviet Union endangered the security of the United States. In order to understand how the leaders who made American foreign policy came to this conclusion, it is necessary to view the situation as they saw it, not as it appears today in the light of historical hindsight.

World War II had produced a revolution in United States foreign policy. Before that conflict, most Americans believed that their country could best protect itself by staying out of political entanglements overseas. The events of 1939–40 persuaded leaders of the Roosevelt administration that they had been wrong. The bombing of Pearl Harbor convinced others in the United States. From then on, American policy-makers would seek security through involvement, not isolation. They believed that to prevent new wars the whole system of relations between nations would have to be changed. They felt that only the United States had the power and influence to carry out this task. As a result, United States officials set to work, even before entering into the war, to plan a peace settlement which would accomplish such a change in relations between nations.

Lessons of the past greatly influenced how American leaders saw the future. Determined to avoid mistakes which, in their view, had caused World War II, American planners sought to disarm defeated enemies, give peoples of the world the right to shape their own future, revive world trade, and replace the League of Nations with a new and more effective organization. But without victory over the Axis, the United States would never be able to carry out its plan for peace. Given the realities of the military situation, victory depended upon cooperation with the Soviet Union, an ally whose commitment to American postwar ideals was, at best, questionable.

The leaders of the Soviet Union also looked to the past in planning for the future. But their very different experiences led them to conclusions that did not always agree with those of their American allies. For Stalin, the key to peace was simple: keep Russia strong and keep Germany weak. He showed little interest in Washington's plans for collective security [a policy designed to keep world peace by having nations join together to guarantee the security or safety of all nations], the reduction of tariff barriers, and reform of the world money system. Self-determination for the people in Eastern Europe, however, he would not allow. This region was vital to Soviet security, but the people who lived there were bitterly anti-Russian. Nor could Stalin agree with Allied efforts, also growing out of lessons of the past, to limit reparations [payments for war damages] paid by Germany. These two conflicts—Eastern Europe and Germany—became major areas of disagreement in the emerging Cold War.

Moscow's position would not have seemed so alarming to American officials, however, if it were not for the Soviet Union's continued belief in an ideology favoring the overthrow of capitalism throughout the world. Hopes that the United States might cooperate successfully with the Soviet Union after the war had been based on the belief, encouraged by Stalin himself, that the Soviets had given up their former goal of spreading Communism. Soviet expansion into Eastern Europe in 1944 and 1945 caused Western observers to fear that they had been misled. Just at the moment of victory over the Axis, the old fear of world revolution reappeared.

It seems likely that American foreign policy-makers mistook Stalin's determination to ensure Russian security through spheres of influence for a new effort to spread Communism outside the borders of the Soviet Union. The Russians did not immediately set up Communist governments in all the countries they occupied after the war. And Stalin showed very little interest in promoting the fortunes of Communist parties in areas beyond his control. Historians now generally agree on the limited nature of Stalin's objectives. But the Soviet leader failed to make the limited nature of his objectives clear. Having just defeated one dictator, Americans could not regard the emergence of another one without the strongest feelings of alarm and anger.

Nor did they see any reason to give in to what Stalin seemed to be doing. The United States had come out of the war with complete control over the world's most powerful weapon, the atomic bomb. It also had a near-monopoly over the productive facilities which could make possible quick re-establishment of war-shattered economies. Convinced that technology had given them the means to shape the postwar world to their liking, American officials assumed that these instruments would leave the Russians no choice but to go along with American peace plans.

Frustrated in their efforts to work out an acceptable settlement with the Soviet Union, under strong pressure from Congress and the public to make no further compromises, American leaders started on a new Russian policy during the first months of 1946. From now on, expansionist moves by the Soviet Union would be resisted, even at the risk of war. Negotiations would continue, but future concessions would have to come from Moscow. Meanwhile, the United States would begin rebuilding its military forces, now badly decreased by demobilization. It would also begin an ambitious program of economic assistance to nations threatened by Communism.

It is easy for historians, writing twenty-five years later, to suggest ways in which the United States might have avoided, or at least lessened, the dangers of a postwar confrontation with the Soviet Union. President Roosevelt could have eased Russia's military burden by launching a second front in Europe in 1942 or 1943. He could have removed Eastern Europe from the provisions of the Atlantic Charter, thereby recognizing the Soviet sphere of influence in that part of the world. American officials could have helped in the giant task of repairing Russian war damage by granting a generous reconstruction loan, and by allowing extensive reparations from Germany. Finally, the United States could have attempted to lessen Soviet distrust by voluntarily giving up its monopoly over the atomic bomb.

But these were not workable alternatives at the time. An early second front would have greatly increased American casualties and might have weakened support for the war effort. Recognition of the Soviet position in Eastern Europe would have caused opposition in the Senate to American membership in the United Nations, and might have endangered Roosevelt's re-election. Economic concessions to the Russians, in the form of either a reconstruction loan or a more flexible attitude on reparations, would have created a storm of protest from a Congress still largely isolationist in its approach to foreign aid. A decision to give up the atomic bomb would have so alienated the American people and their representatives on Capitol Hill as to weaken the very functioning of the government.

Historians have debated at length the question of who caused the Cold War, but without shedding much light on the subject. Too often they view that event only as a series of actions by one side and reactions by the other. In fact, policy-makers in both the United States and the Soviet Union were constantly weighing each other's intentions, as they understood them, and modifying their own courses of action accordingly. In addition, officials in Washington and Moscow brought to the task of policy making a variety of fixed ideas, shaped by personality, ideology, political pressures, even ignorance and irrationality, all of which influenced their behavior. Once this complex interaction of stimulus and response is taken into account, it becomes clear that neither side can take complete responsibility for the Cold War.

But neither should the conflict be seen as predetermined if for no other reason than the impossibility of "proving" inevitability in history. The power vacuum in central Europe caused by Germany's collapse made a Russian-American confrontation likely. It did not make it inevitable. People as well as circumstances make foreign policy, and through such drastic methods as war, appeasement, or resignation, policy-makers can always change the difficult situations in which they find themselves. One may legitimately ask why they do not choose to go this far, but to view their actions as predetermined by blind, impersonal "forces" is to deny the complexity and particularity of human behavior, not to mention the ever-present possibility of accident. The Cold War is too complicated an event to be discussed in terms of either national guilt or inevitability.

If one must assign responsibility for the Cold War, the most meaningful way is to ask which side had the greater opportunity to adapt itself, at least in part, to the other's position, given the range of alternatives as they appeared at the time. Revisionists [those historians who hold America more responsible than the Soviet Union for causing the Cold War] have argued that American policy-makers had greater freedom of action. But this view ignores the restrictions enforced by domestic politics. Little is known even today about how Stalin determined his choices, but it does seem safe to say that the very nature of the Soviet system gave him a larger selection of alternatives than were open to leaders of the United States. The Russian dictator was free from pressures of Congress, public opinion, or the press. Even ideology did not restrict him: Stalin was the master of Communist doctrine, not a prisoner of it, and could modify or suspend Marxism-Leninism whenever it suited him. This is not to say that Stalin wanted a Cold War—he had every reason to avoid one. But his absolute powers did give him more chances to overcome the internal restraints on his policy than were available to democratic leaders in the West.

The Cold War grew out of a complicated interaction of external and internal developments inside both the United States and the Soviet Union. The external situation—circumstances beyond the control of either power—left Americans and Russians facing one another across a helpless Europe at the end of World War II. Internal influences in the Soviet Union —the search for security, the role of ideology, massive postwar reconstruction needs, the personality of Stalin—together with those in the United States—the ideal of self-determination, fear of Communism, the illusion of unlimited power fostered by American economic strength and the atomic bomb—made the resulting confrontation a hostile one. Leaders of both superpowers sought peace, but in doing so gave in to considerations which, while they did not cause war, made a resolution of differences impossible.

ORGANIZING THE UNITED NATIONS

Adapted from On My Own *by Eleanor Roosevelt. Copyright © 1958 by Anna Eleanor Roosevelt, copyright © 1958 by The Curtis Publishing Company. Reprinted by permission of William Morris Agency, Inc.*

Eleanor Roosevelt was one of the most active First Ladies in the nation's history. She took a special interest in New Deal programs to help young Americans and in efforts to improve the lives of minority groups. And she continued to play an important role in American political life after President Roosevelt's death.

One of Eleanor Roosevelt's greatest contributions was her work with the United Nations. In late 1945 she was appointed by President Truman as a member of the United States delegation to the organizing meeting of the UN General Assembly. At this meeting, held in London in 1946, she served on the committee formed to deal with humanitarian, educational, and cultural matters. In the following account, from her autobiography, she tells about her work as a delegate.

How did Eleanor Roosevelt feel about serving as a member of the United States delegation? About the committee on which she served? Why was the issue of refugees important?

In December of 1945 I received a message from President Truman. He reminded me that the first organizing meeting of the United Nations General Assembly would be held in London, starting in January 1946. He asked me if I would serve as a member of the United States delegation.

"Oh, no! It would be impossible," was my first reaction. "How could I be a delegate to help organize the United Nations when I have no background or experience in international meetings?"

My secretary, however, urged me not to refuse without giving the idea careful thought. I knew in a general way what had been done about organizing the United Nations. After the San Francisco meeting in 1945, when the Charter was written, it had been accepted by the various nations, including our own. I knew, too, that we had a group of people headed by Adlai Stevenson working with representatives of other member nations in London to prepare for the formal organizing meeting. Then, as I thought about the President's offer, I knew that I believed the United Nations to be the one hope for a peaceful world. I knew that my husband had placed great importance on the establishment of this world organization. So I felt a great sense of responsibility. Finally I decided to accept.

Members of the delegation sailed on the *Queen Elizabeth* in January 1946. The dock was crowded with reporters and news photographers who surrounded the Senators and the members of the House of Representatives on the delegation. I was feeling rather lost and quite uncertain about what lay ahead. But as it turned out there was plenty to do even for a confused beginner in such affairs. The first thing I noticed in my stateroom was a pile of blue sheets of paper on the table. These blue sheets turned out to be documents—most of them marked "secret"—that apparently related to the work of delegates. I had no idea where they had come from but assumed they were meant for me, so I looked through them. They obviously contained background information on the work to be taken up by the General Assembly as well as statements of our government's position on various problems.

So, I thought, somebody is putting me to work without delay. I sat down and began reading—or trying to read. It was dull and very hard work. I had great difficulty in staying awake, but I knew my duty when I saw it and read them all. By the time I finished I supposed that the Department of State had no more secrets from me. But I would have found it hard to reveal anything because I was seldom really sure of the exact meaning of what was on the blue sheets. At the time, I feared this was because I couldn't understand plain English when it concerned State Department matters. Later I changed my mind on this, because others seemed to have the same difficulty.

People on the *Queen Elizabeth* were very kind to me. Nevertheless I felt much alone at first. One day, as I was walking down the passageway to my room, I met Senator Arthur H. Vandenberg.

"Mrs. Roosevelt," he said in his rather deep voice, "we would like to know if you would serve on Committee 3."

I had two immediate and rather contradictory reactions to the question. First, I wondered who "we" might be. Was a Republican Senator deciding who would serve where? And why, since I was a delegate, had I not been consulted about committee assignments? But my next reaction crowded these thoughts out of mind. I suddenly realized that I had no idea what Committee 3 might be. So I kept my thoughts to myself and humbly agreed to serve where I was made to serve.

"But," I added quickly, "will you or someone kindly see that I get as much information as possible on Committee 3?"

The Senator promised and I went on to my room. The truth was that at that time I did not know whom to ask for information or guidance. As I learned more about my work, I realized why I had been put on Committee 3, which dealt with humanitarian, educational, and cultural questions. There were many committees dealing with the budgetary, legal, political, and other questions. I could just see the members of our delegation puzzling over the list and saying:

"Oh, no! We can't put Mrs. Roosevelt on the political committee. What could she do on the budget committee? Does she know anything about legal questions? Ah, here's the safe spot for her—Committee 3. She can't do much harm there!"

Oddly enough, I felt very much the same way about it. On the ship coming over, however, State Department officials held briefings [information meetings] for the delegates. We listened to experts on various subjects explain the problems that would be brought up, give the background on them, and then state the general position of the United States. I attended all these sessions. Discovering that there also were briefings for newspaper people aboard the ship, I went to all their meetings, too. As a result of these briefings and various discussions, I began to realize that Committee 3 might be much more important than had been expected. And, in time, this proved to be true.

At the early sessions in London, which were largely concerned with organization, I got the strong impression that many of the old-timers in the field of diplomacy were very doubtful about the new world organization. They had seen so many failures, they had been through the collapse of the League of Nations, and they seemed to doubt that we would achieve much. The newcomers, the younger people in most cases, were the ones who showed the most enthusiasm and determination.

I might point out here that during the entire

London session of the Assembly, I was very uneasy. I knew that as the only woman on the delegation I was not very welcome. Moreover, if I failed to be a useful member, it would not be considered only that I as an individual had failed, but that all women had failed. There would be little chance for others to serve in the near future.

As a normal thing, the important—and I might say, the hard—work of any organization such as the United Nations is not done in the big, public meetings of the General Assembly, but in the small and almost continuous meetings of the various committees. It was while working on Committee 3 that I really began to understand the inner workings of the United Nations. It was ironical perhaps that one of the subjects that created the greatest political heat of the London sessions came up in this "unimportant" committee to which I had been assigned.

The issue arose from the fact that there were many war refugees in Germany when the armistice was signed—Ukrainians, Poles, Czechoslovaks, Latvians, Lithuanians, Estonians, and others. A great number of them were still living there in temporary camps because they did not want to return to live under the Communist rule of their own countries. There also were the Jewish survivors of the German death camps.

This situation flared up in Committee 3. It was raised originally by the Yugoslav representative, Leo Mates. The Yugoslav—and, of course, the Soviet Union—position that Mates put forward was that any war refugees who did not wish to return to their countries were traitors to their country. He argued that the refugees in Germany should be forced to return home and to accept whatever punishment might be given to them. This position was strongly supported by the Soviet representative.

The position of the Western countries, including the United States, was that large numbers of the refugees were not traitors. We felt that they must be guaranteed the right to choose whether they would return to their homes. Since the London sessions were largely technical rather than political debates and since Committee 3 was the scene of one of the early clashes between the Soviet Union and the West, the newspapers carried much of the controversy.

I felt very strongly on the subject, as did others. We spent many hours trying to write some kind of resolution on which all could agree. We never did. Our chairman had to present a majority report to the General Assembly which was immediately challenged by the USSR. In the Assembly the minority position was handled, not by the Soviet representative on Committee 3, but by the head of the Soviet Union's delegation, Andrei Vishinsky. Vishinsky was one of the Russians' great legal minds, a skilled debater, a man with ability to use the weapons of wit and ridicule. It was clear that in view of the importance of the issue someone would have to speak for the United States. The question of who this was to be made our delegation extremely anxious. There was a hurried consultation among the male members. When they broke up, John Foster Dulles approached me rather uncertainly.

"Mrs. Roosevelt," he began, rather lamely, "the United States must speak in the debate. Since you are the one who has carried on for us in this controversy in the committee, do you think you could say a few words to the Assembly? I'm afraid nobody else is really familiar with the subject."

"Why, Mr. Dulles," I answered as meekly as I could manage, "in that case I will do my best."

Actually, I was badly frightened. I trembled at the thought of speaking against the famous Mr. Vishinsky. But when the time came I walked, tense and excited, to the platform and did my best. The hour was late and we knew the Russians would delay a vote as long as possible on the theory that some of our allies would get tired and leave. I knew we must, if possible, hold the South American delegates until the vote was taken because their votes might be decisive. So I talked about Simon Bolivar and his stand for the freedom of the people of Latin America. I talked and watched the delegates. To my joy the South American representatives stayed with us to the end and, when the vote came, we won. This vote meant that the Western nations would have to worry about the ultimate fate of the refugees for a long, long time, but the principle of the right of an individual to make his or her own decisions was a victory well worth while.

The final night the vote on Committee 3's report was taken so late that I did not get back to the hotel till about one o'clock. I was very tired. As I walked wearily up the stairs, I heard two voices behind me. Turning around, I saw Senator Vandenberg and Mr. Dulles. They obviously had something to say to me, but for the life of me I can't remember which one of them said it. Whichever it was, he seemed to be speaking for both.

"Mrs. Roosevelt," he said, "we must tell you that we did all we could to keep you off the United States delegation. We begged the President not to nominate you. But now that you are leaving we feel we must admit that we have worked with you gladly and found you good to work with. And we will be happy to do so again."

I don't think anything could have made the weariness disappear as did those words. I shall always be grateful for the encouragement they gave me.

REPORTING ON THE CONFLICT IN KOREA

Adapted from War in Korea *by Marguerite Higgins. Copyright 1951 by Marguerite Higgins, copyright 1951 by Time Inc. Reprinted by permission of Doubleday & Co., Inc.*

In June 1950, Communist-ruled North Korea began an invasion of South Korea. The United States immediately pledged aid to South Korea, and, with the support of the United Nations, helped to organize an army to defend South Korea. American military forces formed the largest part of this United Nations army, but Canada, Australia, New Zealand, and other nations also provided troops.

During the Korean War many news reporters, or correspondents, went along with American troops to report on the war in Asia. One of the most famous of these war correspondents was Marguerite Higgins, who wrote for the New York *Herald Tribune.* In this selection from her book about the war in Korea, she describes an unexpected enemy attack on American headquarters (located in a schoolhouse) in July 1950.

What were Marguerite Higgins' reactions to the attack? Do you think correspondents should be allowed in the front lines with fighting troops? Why? What effect might this have on news reports about the war?

Half a dozen officers, myself, and Harold Martin [of the *Saturday Evening Post* magazine], were finishing breakfast in the schoolhouse at seven in the morning when suddenly bullets exploded from all directions. They crackled through the windows, splintered through the thin walls. A machine-gun burst slammed the coffeepot off the table. A grenade exploded on the wooden frame on which I had been sleeping, and another grenade sent fragments flying off the roof.

"Where is the little beauty who threw that?" asked Captain William Hawkes, an intelligence officer, as he grabbed at his bleeding right hand, torn by a grenade splinter.

We tried to race down the hall, but we had to hit the floor fast and stay there. We were all bewildered and caught totally by surprise. It was impossible to judge what to do. Bullets were spattering at us from the hill rising directly behind us and from the courtyard on the other side.

Thoughts tumbled jerkily through my mind —"This can't be enemy fire . . . we're miles behind the front lines . . . that grenade must have been thrown from 15 or 20 yards [between 13 and 18 meters] . . . how could they possibly get that close? . . . if they are that close, they are right behind the schoolhouse . . . they can be through those windows and on top of us in a matter of seconds . . . nobody in here even has a carbine [rifle] . . . well, it would be too late anyway . . . why did I ever get myself into this? . . . I don't understand the [weapons] fire coming from the courtyard . . . what has happened to our defense? . . . could it possibly be that some trigger-happy GI started all this? . . ."

There was soon no doubt, however, that it was enemy fire. We were surrounded. During the night the Reds [Communists] had sneaked past our front lines, avoiding the main roads and traveling over mountain trails. In camouflaged uniforms, they crept onto the hillside behind the schoolhouse. Others, circling around, set up machine guns in a rice paddy on the other side of the schoolyard. This accounted for the vicious cross fire.

They had managed to get by our defenses for several reasons. The GIs were completely exhausted from a long patrol into enemy territory. Some of the guards fell asleep. And at least one column of the enemy was mistaken, by those officers awake and on duty, for South Korean police.

We had been warned the night before that South Koreans were helping us guard our exposed right flank. This was only one of the hundreds of cases in which confusion in identifying the enemy lost us lives. It is, of course, part of the difficulty of being involved in a civil war.

I learned all of this, of course, much later. On the schoolhouse floor, with our noses scraping the dust, the only thought was how to get out of the bullet-riddled building without getting killed in the process. The bullets cutting through the cardboard-thin walls ripped the floor boards around us, and we all kept wondering why one of us didn't get hit.

I mumbled to Harold that it looked as if we would have a very close blow-by-blow account of battle to give to the American public. But he didn't hear me because one of the officers suddenly said, "I'm getting out of here," and dove out the window into the courtyard in the direction away from the hill. We all leaped after him and found a stone wall which at least protected us from the rain of fire from the high ground.

In the courtyard we found an uproar of officers and noncoms attempting to dodge the incoming fire and at the same time trying to find their men and produce some order out of the chaos. Some of the soldiers in the courtyard, in their confusion, were firing, without aiming, dangerously close to the GIs racing in retreat down the hill.

Colonel Michaelis, his executive officer, Colonel Farthing, and company commanders were booting reluctant GIs out from under jeeps and trucks and telling them to get to their units up the hill.

A lot of yelling was coming from the opposite corner of the courtyard. I turned my head around in time to see an officer taking careful aim at one of our own machine gunners. He winged him. It was a good shot, and an unfortunate necessity. The machine gunner had gone crazy in the terror of the surprise attack and had started firing on our own vehicles and troops with the machine gun.

An officer came up with the gloomy information that several hundred Koreans had landed on the coast a thousand yards [914 meters] to the north.

I started to say something to Martin as he kneeled methodically recording the battle in his notebook. My teeth were chattering uncontrollably, I discovered, and in shame I broke off after the first disgraceful squeak of words.

Then suddenly, for the first time in the war, I experienced the cold, awful certainty that there was no escape. My reactions were commonplace. As with most people who suddenly accept death as inevitable and about to happen, I was simply filled with surprise that this was finally going to happen to me. Then as the conviction grew, I became hard inside and fairly calm. I stopped worrying. Physically the result was that my teeth stopped chattering

and my hands stopped shaking. This was a relief, as I would have been extremely embarrassed had anyone caught me in that state.

Fortunately, by the time Michaelis came around the corner and asked, "How are you doing, kid?" I was able to answer in a respectably self-contained tone of voice, "Just fine, sir."

A few minutes later Michaelis, ignoring the bullets, moved suddenly into the middle of the courtyard. He yelled for a cease-fire.

"Let's get organized and find out what we're shooting at," he shouted.

Gradually the scramble in the courtyard turned into a pattern of resistance. Two heavy machine-gun squads crept up to the hill under cover of protecting rifle fire and fixed aim on the enemy trying to swarm down. Platoons and then companies followed. Light mortars were dragged up. The huge artillery guns lowered and fired point-blank at targets only a few hundred yards away.

Finally a reconnaissance officer came up and reported that the soldiers landing on the coast were not a new enemy force to overwhelm us but South Korean allies. On the hill, soldiers were silencing some of the enemy fire. It was now 7:45. It did not seem possible that so much could have happened since the enemy had struck.

As the intensity of fire let up slightly, soldiers started bringing in the wounded from the hills, carrying them on their backs. I walked over to the aid station. Because of the sudden rush of casualties, everyone was frantically busy.

One medic was running short of plasma but did not dare leave his patients long enough to try to round up some more. I offered to administer the remaining plasma and passed about an hour there, helping out as best I could.

My most vivid memory of the hour is Captain Logan Weston limping into the station with a wound in his leg. He was patched up and promptly turned around and headed for the hills again. Half an hour later he was back with bullets in his shoulder and chest. Sitting on the floor smoking a cigarette, the captain calmly said, "I guess I'd better get a shot of morphine now. These last two are beginning to hurt."

It was at the aid station that I realized we were going to win after all. Injured after injured came in with reports that the North Koreans were "being murdered" and that they were falling back. There was a brief lull in the fighting. Then the enemy, strengthened with fresh reinforcements, struck again. But Michaelis was ready for them this time. At 1:30 in the afternoon, when the last attacking force had been driven back, more than 600 dead North Koreans were counted in the hills behind the schoolhouse. We really had been lucky.

After the schoolhouse battle I usually took a carbine along in our jeep. I'm a lousy shot, but I know I duck when bullets start flying my way. I reasoned that the enemy had the same reaction and that my bullets, however wild, might at least scare him into keeping his head down or might throw his aim off.

Most correspondents carried weapons of some kind. The enemy did not care if they shot unarmed civilians. And the fighting line changed so often that no place near the front lines was safe from sudden enemy attack.

In those days the main difference between a news reporter and a soldier in Korea was that the soldier in combat had to get out of his hole and go after the enemy, whereas the correspondent had the privilege of keeping his head down. It was commonplace for correspondents to be at the company and platoon level, and many of us frequently went on patrol. We felt it was the only honest way of covering the war. The large number of correspondents killed or captured in Korea is testimony of the dangers to which many willingly subjected themselves.

CHAPTER 23 ■ RE-EXAMINING THE NATION'S ROLE IN WORLD AFFAIRS

THE MISSILE CRISIS IN CUBA

Adapted from Thirteen Days, A Memoir of the Cuban Missile Crisis, by Robert F. Kennedy. Copyright © 1971, 1969, by W. W. Norton & Co., Inc. Copyright © 1968 by McCall Corporation. Reprinted by permission of W. W. Norton & Co., Inc.

In October of 1962, President Kennedy learned from American intelligence reports that the Soviet Union was building powerful missile bases in Cuba. These bases posed so great a danger to the United States' security that Kennedy and his advisors decided they must act immediately. They communicated with the leaders of the Soviet government and demanded that the Soviet Union dismantle and remove these missile sites. For the next few days, war seemed possible as both nations considered what action they should take.

Several years later Robert Kennedy, the President's brother who also was one of his key advisors as well as his Attorney General, wrote a detailed account of the Cuban missile crisis. His book, called *Thirteen Days*, gives a day-by-day record of the events from October 16 through 28, 1962. In this selection, Robert Kennedy describes what happened on October 27 and 28—the most crucial and dangerous days of the missile crisis.

What troubled President Kennedy most on the evening described here? How would you describe Robert Kennedy's meeting with the Soviet ambassador? How was the Cuban missile crisis settled?

[Saturday, October 27]
The President ordered the Ex Comm [the Executive Committee for National Security, which included Secretary of State Dean Rusk, several other members of the Cabinet, and military officials] to meet again at 9:00 P.M. in the White House. While the letter was being typed and prepared to be sent, he and I sat in his office. [This was the letter President Kennedy sent to Khrushchev on October 27, requesting that the missiles in Cuba be dismantled. In return, the United States would end its naval "quarantine."] He talked about Major Anderson and how it is always the brave and the best who die. [Anderson, a U-2 pilot, had been killed the day before by missile fire while on a reconnaissance mission over Cuba.] He talked about the mistakes that lead to war. War is rarely planned. The Russians don't wish to fight any more than we do. They do not want to go to war with us nor we with them. And yet if events continue as they have in the last several days, that struggle—which no one wishes, which will accomplish nothing —will engulf and destroy humanity.

He wanted to make sure that he had done everything in his power, everything possible, to prevent such a catastrophe. Every opportunity was to be given to the Russians to find a peaceful settlement which would not decrease their national security or be a public humiliation. It was not only for Americans that he was concerned, or primarily the older generation of any land. The thought that disturbed him the most, and that made the prospect of war much more fearful than it would otherwise have been, was the possibility of the death of the children of this country and all the world—the young people who had no role, who had no say, who knew nothing even of the confrontation, but whose lives would be ended like everyone else's. They would never have a chance to make a decision, to vote in an election, to run for office, to lead a revolution, to determine their own futures.

It was this that troubled him most, that gave him such pain. And it was then that he and Secretary Rusk decided that I should visit with [Soviet] Ambassador Dobrynin and personally make known the President's great concern.

I telephoned Ambassador Dobrynin about 7:15 P.M. and asked him to come to the Department of Justice. We met in my office at 7:45. I told him first that we knew that work was continuing on the missile bases in Cuba and that in the last few days it had been speeded up. I said that in the last few hours we had learned that our reconnaissance planes flying over Cuba had been fired upon and that one of our U-2's had been shot down and the pilot killed. That for us was a most serious turn of events.

President Kennedy did not want a military conflict. He had done everything possible to avoid a military engagement with Cuba and with the Soviet Union, but now they had forced our hand. Because of the deception of the Soviet Union, our photographic reconnaissance planes would have to continue to fly over Cuba. If the Cubans or Soviets shot at these planes, then we would have to shoot back. This would inevitably lead to further incidents and to escalation of the conflict.

He said the Cubans resented the fact that we were violating Cuban air space. I replied that if we had not violated Cuban air space, we would still be believing what Khrushchev had said—that there would be no missiles placed in Cuba. In any case, I said, this matter was far more serious than the air space of Cuba—it involved the peoples of both of our countries and, in fact, people all over the globe.

The Soviet Union had secretly established missile bases in Cuba while at the same time claiming privately and publicly that this would never be done. We had to have a commitment by tomorrow that those bases would be removed. I was not giving them an ultimatum but a statement of fact. He should understand that if they did not remove those bases, we would remove them. President Kennedy had great respect for the ambassador's country and the courage of its people. Perhaps his country might feel it

necessary to take action. But before that was over, there would be not only dead Americans but dead Russians as well.

He asked me what offer the United States was making, and I told him of the letter that President Kennedy had just sent to Khrushchev. He raised the question of our removing our missiles from Turkey. I said that there could be no arrangement made under this kind of threat or pressure. In the last analysis this was a decision that would have to be made by NATO. However, I said President Kennedy had been anxious to remove those missiles from Turkey (and Italy) for a long period of time. He had ordered their removal some time ago. It was our judgment that, within a short time after this crisis was over, those missiles would be gone.

I said President Kennedy wished to have peaceful relations between our two countries. Time was running out. We had only a few more hours—we needed an answer immediately from the Soviet Union. I said we must have it the next day.

I returned to the White House. The President was not optimistic, nor was I. He ordered twenty-four troop-carrier squadrons of the Air Force Reserve to active duty. They would be necessary for an invasion. He had not given up hope, but what hope there was now rested with Khrushchev's changing his course within the next few hours. It was a hope, not an expectation. The expectation was a military confrontation by Tuesday and possibly tomorrow.

[Sunday, October 28]

I had promised my daughters for a long time that I would take them to the horse show. Early Sunday morning I went to the Washington Armory to watch the horses jump. In any case, there was nothing I could do but wait. Around 10:00, I received a call at the horse show. It was Secretary Rusk. He said he had just received word from the Russians that they had agreed to withdraw the missiles from Cuba.

I went immediately to the White House, and there I received a call from Ambassador Dobrynin, saying he would like to visit with me. I met him in my office at 11:00 A.M.

He told me that the message was coming through that Khrushchev had agreed to dismantle and withdraw the missiles under adequate supervision and inspection; that everything was going to work out satisfactorily; and that Mr. Khrushchev wanted to send his best wishes to the President and to me.

It was quite a different meeting from the

night before. I went back to the White House and talked to the President for a long time. While I was there, he placed telephone calls to former Presidents Truman and Eisenhower. As I was leaving, he said, making reference to Abraham Lincoln, "This is the night I should go to the theater." I said, "If you go, I want to go with you." As I closed the door, he was seated at the desk writing a letter to Mrs. Anderson [wife of the U-2 pilot killed on a flight over Cuba a few days earlier].

THE WAR IN VIETNAM

President Johnson's speech adapted from "Peace Without Conquest," an address by Lyndon B. Johnson at Johns Hopkins University, April 7, 1965 in Public Papers of the Presidents of the United States: *Vol. I. Washington, D.C.: Government Printing Office, 1966.*

Senator Fulbright's statement adapted from The Arrogance of Power *by J. William Fulbright. Copyright © 1966 by J. William Fulbright. Reprinted by permission of Random House, Inc.*

American involvement in the Vietnam War began in 1962 when President Kennedy sent 8,000 military "advisors" to help train the South Vietnamese army. Then, in 1964, President Johnson began to send American combat troops. And in 1965, the United States began the bombing of North Vietnam.

Almost from the beginning, American opinion on the Vietnam War was divided. Some American leaders, known as "hawks," supported the war because they felt the United States had promised to protect South Vietnam and that America's honor and world leadership role were at stake. Other leaders, called "doves," opposed the war, believing that the United States could not create a stable, democratic government in South Vietnam nor instill within the South Vietnamese people the will to fight. As the war continued and more American troops were sent to Vietnam, this debate over the war continued and grew more bitter.

In the following selection, President Johnson offers a defense of the war. In response, Senator William Fulbright suggests that American involvement in Vietnam is a mistake.

Why, according to President Johnson, is the United States fighting in South Vietnam? Why does Senator Fulbright believe that American involvement in South Vietnam is a mistake? Which viewpoint do you favor? Explain.

[PRESIDENT JOHNSON]

Tonight Americans and Asians are dying for a world where each people may choose its own path to change.

Why must we take this painful road?

Why must this nation endanger its ease, and its interest, and its power for the sake of a people so far away?

We fight because we must fight if we are to live in a world where every country can shape its own destiny. And only in such a world will our own freedom be finally secure.

The first reality is that North Vietnam has attacked the independent nation of South Vietnam. Its object is total conquest.

Of course, some of the people of South Vietnam are participating in an attack on their own government. But trained men and supplies, orders, and arms, flow in a constant stream from north to south.

This support is the heartbeat of the war.

Over this war—and all Asia—is another reality: Communist China. The rulers in Hanoi are urged on by Peking. This is a government which has destroyed freedom in Tibet, which has attacked India, and has been condemned by the United Nations for aggression in Korea. It is a nation which is helping the forces of violence in almost every continent. The contest in Vietnam is part of a wider pattern of aggressive purposes.

Why are we in South Vietnam?

We are there because we have a promise to keep. Since 1954 every American President has offered support to the people of South Vietnam. We have helped to build, and we have helped to defend. Thus over many years we have made a national pledge to help South Vietnam defend its independence.

And I intend to keep that promise.

To dishonor that pledge, to abandon this small and brave nation to its enemies, and to the terror that must follow, would be an unforgivable wrong.

We are also there to strengthen world order. Around the globe, from Berlin to Thailand, are people whose well-being rests, in part, on the belief that they can count on us if they are attacked. To leave Vietnam to its fate would shake the confidence of all these people in the value of an American commitment and in the value of America's word. The result would be increased unrest and instability, and even wider war.

We are also there because there are great stakes in the balance. Let no one think for a moment that retreat from Vietnam would bring an end to conflict. The battle would be started again in one country and then another. The central lesson of our time is that the appetite of aggression is never satisfied. To withdraw from one battlefield means only to prepare for the next.

Our objective is the independence of South Vietnam, and its freedom from attack. We want nothing for ourselves—only that the people of South Vietnam be allowed to guide their own country in their own way.

We will do everything necessary to reach that objective. And we will do only what is absolutely necessary.

We hope that peace will come swiftly. But that is in the hands of others besides ourselves. And we must be prepared for a long continued conflict. It will require patience as well as bravery, the will to endure as well as the will to resist.

I wish it were possible to convince others with words of what we now find it necessary to say with guns and planes: Armed hostility is useless. Our resources are equal to any challenge. Because we fight for values and we fight for principles, rather than territory or colonies, our patience and our determination are unending.

Once this is clear, then it should also be clear that the only path for reasonable people is the path of peaceful settlement.

Such peace demands an independent South Vietnam—securely guaranteed and able to shape its own relationships to all others—free from outside interference—tied to no alliance—a military base for no other country.

These are the essentials of any final settlement.

[SENATOR FULBRIGHT]

We are now in a war to "defend freedom" in South Vietnam. The official war aims of the United States government, as I understand them, are to defeat what is regarded as North Vietnamese aggression, to demonstrate the uselessness of what the Communists call "wars of national liberation," and to create conditions under which the South Vietnamese people will be able freely to determine their own future.

I have not the slightest doubt of the sincerity of the President and the Vice-President and the Secretaries of State and Defense in putting forward these aims. What I do doubt, and doubt very much, is the ability of the United States to achieve these aims by the means being used. I do not question the power of our weapons and the efficiency of our military plans; they are cer-

tainly impressive. What I do question is the ability of the United States or any other Western nation to go into a small, alien, undeveloped Asian nation and create stability where there is chaos, the will to fight where there is defeatism, democracy where there is no tradition of it, and honest government where corruption is almost a way of life.

Sincere though it is, the American effort to build the foundations of freedom in South Vietnam is having an effect quite different from the one intended.

One wonders how much the American commitment to Vietnamese freedom is also a commitment to American pride—the two seem to have become part of the same package. When we talk about the freedom of South Vietnam, we may be thinking about how disagreeable it would be to accept a solution short of victory. We may be thinking about how our pride would be injured if we settled for less than we set out to achieve. We may be thinking about our reputation as a great power, fearing that a compromise settlement would shame us before the world, marking us as a second-rate people with failing courage and determination.

Such fears are senseless. They are simply unworthy of the richest, most powerful, most productive, and best educated people in the world.

The cause of our difficulties in Southeast Asia is not a lack of power but too much of the wrong kind of power. We are trying to remake Vietnamese society, a task which certainly cannot be accomplished by force and which probably cannot be accomplished by any means available to outsiders. The objective may be desirable, but it is not practical.

With the best intentions in the world the United States has involved itself in the affairs of developing nations in Asia and Latin America, practicing what has been called a kind of "welfare imperialism." Our honest purpose is the advancement of development and democracy. To achieve this purpose, it has been thought necessary to destroy ancient and unproductive ways of life. In this latter goal we have been successful, perhaps more successful than we know. Bringing skills and knowledge, money and resources in amounts unknown in traditional societies, the Americans have overcome native groups and interests and become the dominant force in a number of countries. Far from being bumbling, wasteful, and incompetent, as critics have charged, American government officials, technicians, and economists have been very successful in breaking down the barriers to change in ancient but fragile cultures.

Here, however, our success ends. Traditional rulers, institutions, and ways of life have crumbled under the fatal impact of American wealth and power. But they have not been replaced by new institutions and new ways of life, nor has their breakdown brought about an era of democracy and development. It has rather brought an era of disorder and demoralization because, while destroying old ways of doing things, we have also destroyed the self-confidence and self-reliance which a society needs to build its own institutions. We have reduced those peoples we intended to help to a condition of dependency. We have done this for the most part without meaning to. With every good intention we have intruded on fragile societies. Although we have been successful in uprooting traditional ways of life, we have been unsuccessful in planting the democracy and advancing the development which are the honest aims of our "welfare imperialism."

A RUSSIAN WRITER WARNS AGAINST DÉTENTE

Adapted from "America, We Beg You to Interfere" by Aleksandr I. Solzhenitsyn, in the AFL-CIO American Federationist, July 1975. Reprinted by permission of the American Federation of Labor and Congress of Industrial Organizations.

One of the major achievements of American foreign policy under President Nixon was the improvement in United States relations with both Communist China and the Soviet Union. This important effort to end the Cold War and relax world tensions became known as the policy of détente. While détente with both China and the Soviet Union seemed to be widely supported, some important voices spoke out against détente with the Soviet Union. One of them was Aleksandr Solzhenitsyn, a famous Soviet writer.

Solzhenitsyn had spent many years in Russian labor and detention camps for writings that were critical of Stalin and later Soviet leaders. Finally, in 1974, he was allowed to leave the Soviet Union to live in exile in Switzerland. The following selection is from a speech he made on a visit to the United States in 1975.

What does Solzhenitsyn describe as "a true détente"? According to Solzhenitsyn, what are the weaknesses of the policy of détente being followed by the United States? What role does he think the United States should play in the liberation movement in Communist countries? What do you think?

The Soviet system is so closed that it is almost impossible for you to understand. Everything is done the way the [Communist] Party demands. That's our system. Judge it for yourself.

It's a system where for 40 years there haven't been genuine elections. It's a system which has no legislative bodies. It's a system without a free press or independent judges. The people have no influence either on foreign policy or on internal policy. Any thinking which is different from what the government thinks is crushed.

It's a system where leaders who have murdered millions have never been tried in the courts but instead retire with huge pensions and live in the greatest comfort. It's a system where the constitution has never been carried out for a single day. All the decisions are made in secrecy, by a small group responsible to no one, and then are released on us like a bolt of lightning.

And what are the signatures of members of such a group worth? How could anyone trust their signatures to documents of détente? Your specialists will tell you that in recent years the Soviet Union has succeeded in creating wonderful chemical weapons and missiles, even better than those used by the United States.

So what are we to conclude from that? Is détente needed or not? Not only is it needed, it's as necessary as air. It's the only way of saving the earth. Instead of a world war, we must have détente—but a true détente.

I would say that there are very few, really only three, main characteristics of such a true détente.

In the first place, there would be disarmament—not only disarmament in terms of war but also in terms of violence. We must stop using the sort of arms [weapons] which are used to destroy one's neighbors, and also the sort of arms which are used to oppress one's fellow citizens. It is not détente if we here with you today can spend our time agreeably while over there people are suffering and dying.

The second sign of détente, I would say, is the following: that it be not one based on smiles, not on verbal concessions, but only on a firm foundation. There must be a guarantee that it will not be broken overnight. This means that the other party to the agreement must have its actions subject to public opinion, to the press, and to a freely elected parliament. Until such control exists there is absolutely no guarantee.

There is a third simple condition. What sort of détente is it when the Soviet Union uses the kind of inhumane propaganda which is proudly called "ideological warfare"? Let us not have that. If we're going to be friends, let's be friends. If we're going to have détente, then let's have détente and put an end to ideological warfare.

The Soviet Union and the Communist countries can conduct negotiations. They know how to do this. For a long time they don't make any concessions and then they give in a little bit. Then everyone says triumphantly, "Look, they've made a concession. It's time to sign."

But we, from our lives there, have learned that violence can only be withstood by firmness.

You have to understand the nature of Communism. The very ideology of Communism, all of Lenin's teachings, holds that people who don't take what's lying in front of them are fools. If you can take it, take it. If you can attack, attack. But if there's a wall, then go back. The Communist leaders respect only firmness. They laugh at persons who continually give in to them. Your people are now saying, "Power without any attempt at conciliation will lead to a world conflict." But I would say that power with continual surrender is no power at all.

From our experience I can tell you that only firmness will make it possible to withstand the assaults of Communist totalitarianism. We see many historic examples. Let me give you some of them. Look at tiny Finland in 1939, which by its own forces withstood Russian attack. You, in 1948, defended Berlin only by your firmness of spirit, and there was no world conflict. In Korea in 1950 you stood up against the Communists, only by your firmness, and there was no world conflict. In 1962 you forced the rockets to be removed from Cuba. Again it was only firmness, and there was no world conflict.

We, the dissidents of the USSR [those who openly disagree with Russian policy within the Soviet Union], don't have any tanks, we don't have any weapons, we have no organization. We don't have anything. Our hands are empty. We have only our hearts and what we have lived through during the past 50 years under the system. And when we have found the firmness within ourselves to stand up for our rights, we have done so. It's only by firmness of spirit that

we have withstood. And if I am standing here before you, it's not because of the kindness or the good will of Communism, not thanks to détente, but thanks to my own firmness and your firm support. They knew that I would not give in one inch, not one hair. And when they couldn't do more, they themselves fell back.

This is not an easy lesson. In our conditions this was taught to me by the difficulties of my own life. And if you yourselves—any one of you —were in the same difficult situation, you would have learned the same thing.

Today there are two major processes occurring in the world. One is a process of short-sighted concessions. It is a process of giving up, and giving up, and giving up, and hoping that perhaps at some point the wolf will have eaten enough.

The second process is one which I consider the key to everything and which, I will say now, will bring a new future to those under Communism. For 20 years in the Soviet Union (and a shorter time in other Communist countries) there has been occurring a liberation of the human spirit. New generations are growing up which are steadfast in their struggle with evil. They are not willing to accept unprincipled compromises. They prefer to lose everything—salary, conditions of existence, life itself—rather than sacrifice conscience or make deals with evil.

This process has now gone so far that in the Soviet Union today, Marxism [the Communist teachings of Karl Marx] has become simply an object of contempt. No serious person in our country today, not even university and high school students, can talk about Marxism without laughing. But this whole process of our liberation, which obviously will involve social changes, is slower than the first one—the process of concessions. Over there, when we see these concessions, we are frightened. Why so quickly? Why give up several countries a year?

You are the allies of our liberation movement in the Communist countries. And I call upon you. Let us think together and try to see how we can adjust the relationship between these two processes. Whenever you help the persons persecuted in the Soviet Union, you're defending not only them but yourselves as well. You're defending your own future. So let us try and see how far we can go to stop this senseless and immoral process of making endless concessions to the aggressor.

On our crowded planet there are no longer any internal affairs. The Communist leaders say, "Don't interfere in our internal affairs. Let us strangle our citizens in peace and quiet." But I tell you: Interfere more and more. Interfere as much as you can. We beg you to come and interfere.

America—in me and among my friends and among people who think the way I do over there, among all ordinary Soviet citizens—brings forth a mixture of admiration and compassion. You're a country of the future; a young country; a country of still unused possibilities; a country of tremendous geographical distances; a country of tremendous spirit; a country of generosity. But these qualities—strength and generosity—usually make a person and even a whole country trusting. This already has done you a disservice several times.

I would like to call upon America to be more careful with its trust and prevent those people who are falsely using the struggle for peace and social justice to lead you down a false road. They are trying to weaken you. They are trying to disarm your strong and magnificent country in the face of this fearful threat—one which has never been seen before in the history of the world. Do not let yourselves be taken in the wrong direction. Let us try to slow down the process of concessions and help the process of liberation!

AN AMERICAN DIPLOMAT DEFENDS DÉTENTE

Adapted from Henry Kissinger, "The Moral Foundations of Foreign Policy," speech delivered at Minneapolis on July 15, 1975, Department of State Bulletin, *No. 1884, August 4, 1975.*

Henry Kissinger, who served as Secretary of State under Presidents Nixon and Ford, played a major role in planning and carrying out the policy of détente. Working closely with President Nixon, Kissinger gave a major new direction to American foreign policy. As Secretary of State, Kissinger helped to negotiate the treaty ending direct United States military involvement in Vietnam. He also helped to arrange President Nixon's historic visits to China and the Soviet Union in 1972.

Secretary of State Kissinger used personal diplomacy to achieve many of the goals of America's foreign policy. He became famous for his so-called "shuttle diplomacy"—traveling by jet plane to all parts of the world to talk with foreign leaders and to negotiate treaties to promote peace. The following selection is from a 1975 speech Kissinger made to explain the policy of détente.

Why is maintaining peace such a difficult task in today's world? How does Kissinger defend the policy of détente? Do you think his arguments are effective? Explain.

Our relationship with the Communist powers has raised difficult questions for Americans ever since the Bolshevik Revolution. [The Russian Revolution took place in 1917–1918.] It was understood very early that the Communist system and ideology were in conflict with our own principles. Sixteen years passed before President Franklin Roosevelt extended diplomatic recognition to the Soviet government. He did so in the belief, as he put it, that "through the resumption of normal relations the prospects of peace over all the world are greatly strengthened."

Today again courageous voices remind us of the nature of the Soviet system and of our duty to defend freedom. About this there is no disagreement.

There is, however, a clear conflict between two principles which is at the heart of the problem. Since the beginning of the nuclear age, the world's fears of catastrophe and its hopes for a better future have both depended on the relationship between the two super-powers. In an era of strategic nuclear balance—when both sides have the capacity to destroy civilized life—there is no alternative to coexistence.

In such conditions the necessity of peace is itself a moral principle. As President Kennedy pointed out: "In the final analysis our most basic common link is that we all inhabit this small planet. We all breathe the same air. We all cherish our children's future. And we are all mortal."

It is said, correctly, that the Soviet idea of "peaceful coexistence" is not the same as ours, that Soviet policies aim at the furthering of Soviet objectives. The problem of peace takes on a profound moral and practical difficulty in a world of nuclear weapons capable of destroying humankind; in a century which has seen the use of brutal force; in an age of ideology which turns the domestic policies of nations into issues of international conflict. But the issue, surely, is not whether peace and stability serve Soviet purposes, but whether they also serve our own. Constructive actions in Soviet policy are desirable whatever the Soviet motives.

This government has stated clearly and constantly the principles which we believe must guide relations between the Soviet Union and the United States and international conduct, principles that are consistent with both our values and our interests:

—We will maintain a strong and flexible military position to preserve our security. We will as a matter of principle and national interest oppose attempts by any country to achieve global or regional predominance.

—We will judge the state of U.S.–Soviet relations according to whether concrete problems are successfully resolved.

—All negotiations will be a two-way street, based on mutual benefit and observance of agreements.

—We will insist, as we always have, that progress in U.S.–Soviet economic relations must reflect progress toward stable political relationships.

—We will never abandon our ideals or our friends. We will not negotiate over the heads of, or against the interests of, other nations.

—We will respond firmly to attempts to achieve advantage by one side.

Beyond the necessities of coexistence there is the hope of a more positive relationship. The American people will never be satisfied with simply reducing tension and easing the danger of nuclear disaster. Over the longer term, we hope that firmness in the face of pressure and the creation of motives for cooperative action may bring about a more lasting pattern of stability and responsible conduct.

Today's joint manned mission in space—an area in which 15 years ago we saw ourselves in rivalry—is symbolic of the distance we have traveled. [He is referring to the Apollo-Soyuz space flight in 1975, in which an American and a Russian spacecraft met and docked in space.] Practical progress has been made on many problems. Berlin is no longer a source of conflict between East and West. Crises have been avoided. The frequency of U.S.–Soviet consultation is unprecedented. The cooperation in many fields is in dramatic contrast to the state of affairs ten, even five, years ago. The agreements already achieved to limit strategic armament programs are unparalleled in the history of diplomacy.

Our immediate attention is on the international actions of the Soviet Union not because it is our only moral concern, but because it is the sphere of action that we can most directly and confidently affect. As a result of improved foreign policy relationships, we have successfully used our influence to promote human rights.

But we have done so quietly, keeping in mind the delicacy of the problem and stressing results rather than public confrontation.

Therefore critics of détente must answer: What is the alternative that they propose? What precise policies do they want us to change? Are they prepared for a prolonged situation of dramatically increased international danger? Do they wish to return to the constant crises and high arms budgets of the Cold War? Does détente encourage repression? Or is it détente that has brought about the demands for openness that we are now witnessing? Can we ask our people to support confrontation unless they know that every reasonable alternative has been explored?

In our relations with the Soviet Union, the United States will maintain its strength, defend its interests, and support its friends with determination and without illusion. We will speak up for our beliefs with vigor and without self-deception. We consider détente a means to regulate a competitive relationship—not a substitute for our own efforts in building the strength of the free world. We will continue on this course because it offers hope to our children of a more secure and a more just world.

The considerations raise a more general question: To what extent are we able to affect the internal policies of other governments and to what extent is it desirable?

There are some 150 nations in the world. Barely 20 of them are democracies in any real sense. The rest are nations whose ideology or political practices are inconsistent with our own. Yet we have political relations and often alliances with some of these countries in Asia, Latin America, Africa, and Europe.

We do not and will not overlook repressive practices. We have used, and we will use, our influence against repressive practices. Our traditions and our interests demand it.

But truth also forces a recognition of our limits. The question is whether we promote human rights more effectively by counsel and friendly relations where this serves our interest or by propaganda and discriminatory legislation. And we must also assess how foreign governments act in relation to their history and to the threats they face. We must have some understanding for the problems of countries adjoining powerful, hostile, and totalitarian regimes.

Our alliances and political relationships serve mutual ends. They contribute to regional and world security and thus support the broader welfare. They are not favors to other governments, but reflect a recognition of mutual interests. They should be withdrawn only when our interests change and not as a punishment for some act with which we do not agree.

In many countries, whatever the internal structure, the populations are unified in seeking our protection against outside aggression. In many countries our foreign policy relationships have proved to be no obstacle to the forces of change. And in many countries, especially in Asia, it is the process of American withdrawal that has weakened the sense of security and created a need for greater internal discipline—and at the same time decreased our ability to influence domestic practices.

The attempt to deal with those practices by restrictive American legislation raises a serious problem. This is not because of the moral view it expresses—which we share—but because of the mistaken impression it creates that our security ties are acts of charity. And beyond that, such acts are almost inevitably doomed to fail because they are too public, too inflexible, and too much a stimulus to nationalistic resentment.

There are no simple answers. Painful experience should have taught us that we ought not exaggerate our ability to foresee, let alone to shape, social and political change in other societies. Therefore let me state the principles that will guide our action:

—Human rights are a legitimate international concern and have been so defined in international agreements for more than a generation.

—The United States will speak up for human rights in appropriate international forums and in exchanges with other governments.

—We will be mindful of the limits of our reach. We will be conscious of the difference between public attitudes that satisfy our self-esteem and policies that bring positive results.

—We will not lose sight of either the requirements of global security or what we stand for as a nation.

CHAPTER 24 ■ NEW CHALLENGES FOR THE AMERICAN PEOPLE

AMERICANS ON THE MOVE

Adapted from Travels with Charley *by John Steinbeck. Copyright © 1961, 1962 by The Curtis Publishing Co., Inc. Copyright © 1962 by John Steinbeck. Reprinted by permission of The Viking Press.*

In 1960 John Steinbeck, a famous American writer, took a three-month tour of the United States, traveling from Maine across the northern part of the country to the western states and then driving back through Texas, Louisiana, and the southern states. He drove those many thousands of miles in a homemade camper. Steinbeck's companion on his travels was his dog, a poodle named Charley.

Steinbeck had always liked to travel, even as a young man. During this trip he kept notes on his adventures and his impressions of some of the Americans he met. One of those meetings took place in the Middle West one evening with an American family who lived in a mobile home and who also liked to move about and travel. In this selection, he tells about his conversation with this family and about the "restless" Americans they seemed to represent.

How do the man and woman Steinbeck talked to regard "roots," or living in one place?

Do you think most Americans would agree with them? What do you think of Steinbeck's ideas about the "restless" Americans?

Then there are the loners. Driving along, you see high on a hill a single mobile home placed to command a great view. Others rest under trees around a river or a lake. These loners have rented a tiny piece of land from the owner. They need only enough land for the unit and the right of passage to get to it. Sometimes the loner digs a well and a cesspool, and plants a small garden. Others transport their water in 50-gallon [189.3-liter] oil drums.

One of the dinners that I shared in a mobile home was cooked in an immaculate kitchen, walled in plastic tile, with stainless-steel sinks and ovens and stoves up against the wall. We ate in a dining alcove paneled in mahogany veneer. I've never had a better or a more comfortable dinner. Afterward we sat in deep comfortable chairs cushioned in foam rubber. This family liked the way they lived and wouldn't think of going back to the old way. The husband worked as a garage mechanic a few miles away and made good pay. The two children walked to the highway every morning and were picked up by a yellow school bus.

I brought up a question that had puzzled me. These were good, thoughtful, intelligent people. I said, "One of our most treasured feelings concerns roots, growing up rooted in some soil or some community." How did they feel about raising their children without roots? Was it good or bad? Would they miss it or not?

The father, a good-looking, fair-skinned man with dark eyes, answered me. "How many people today have what you are talking about? What roots are there in an apartment twelve floors up? What roots are in a housing development of hundreds and thousands of small houses almost exactly alike? My father came from Italy," he said. "He grew up in Tuscany in a house where his family had lived maybe a thousand years. That's roots for you, no running water, no toilet, and they cooked with charcoal or vine clippings. They had just two rooms, a kitchen and a bedroom where everybody slept, grandpa, father, and all the kids. There was no place to read, no place to be alone. Was that better? I bet if you gave my old man the choice he'd cut his roots and live like this." He waved his hands at the comfortable room. "Fact is, he cut his roots away and came to America. Then he lived in a tenement in New York—just one room, walk-up, cold water and no heat. That's where I was born and I lived in the streets as a kid until my old man got a job upstate in New York in the grape country. You see, he knew about vines, that's about all he knew. Now you take my wife. She's of Irish descent. Her people had roots too."

"In a peat bog," the wife said. "And lived on potatoes." She looked fondly through the door at her fine kitchen.

"Don't you miss some kind of permanence?"

"Who's got permanence? Factory closes down, you move on. Good times and things opening up, you move on to where it's better. You have roots, you sit and starve. You take the pioneers in the history books. They were movers. Take up land, sell it, move on. I read in a book how Lincoln's family came to Illinois on a raft. How many kids in America stay in the place where they were born, if they can get out?"

"You've thought about it a lot."

"Don't have to think about it. There it is. I've got a good trade. Long as there's automobiles I can get work, but suppose the place I work goes broke. I got to move where there's a job. I get to my job in three minutes. You think I should drive 20 miles [32 kilometers] because I got roots?"

Later they showed me magazines designed for those who lived in mobile homes, stories and poems and hints for successful mobile living. How to stop a leak. How to choose a place for sun or coolness. And there were advertisements for gadgets, fascinating things, for cooking, cleaning, washing clothes, furniture and beds and cribs. Also there were full-page pictures of new models, each one grander and more shiny than the next.

"There's thousands of them," said the father, "and there's going to be millions."

"Joe's quite a dreamer," the wife said. "He's always figuring something out. Tell him your ideas, Joe."

"Maybe he wouldn't be interested."

"Sure I would."

"Well, it's not a dream like she said, it's for real, and I'm going to do it pretty soon now. It would take a little capital, but it would pay off. I've been looking around the used lots for the unit I want at the price I want to pay. Going to rip out the guts and set it up for a repair shop. I have nearly enough tools already, and I'll stock little things like windshield wipers and fan belts and cylinder rings and inner tubes, stuff like that. These courts [mobile home camp sites] are getting bigger and bigger. Some of the mobile people have two cars. I'll rent some ground right near and I'll be in business. There's one thing you can say about cars, there's nearly always something wrong with them that's got to be fixed. And I'll have my house, this one, right beside my shop. That way I would have a bell and give twenty-four-hour service."

"Sounds like a good deal," I said. And it does.

"Best thing about it," Joe went on, "if business fell off, why, I'd just move on where it was good."

His wife said, "Joe's got it all worked out on paper where everything's going to go, every wrench and drill, even an electric welder. Joe's a wonderful welder."

I said, "I take back what I said, Joe. I guess you've got your roots in a grease pit."

"You could do worse. I even worked that out. And you know, when the kids grow up, we could even work our way south in the winter and north in the summer."

"Joe does good work," said his wife. "He's got his own steady customers where he works. Some men come 50 miles [80.4 kilometers] to get Joe to work on their cars because he does good work."

"I'm a real good mechanic," said Joe.

Driving the big highway near Toledo I had a conversation with Charley on the subject of roots. He listened but he didn't reply. In the pattern-thinking about roots, I and most other people have left two things out of consideration. Could it be that Americans are a restless people —a mobile people, never satisfied with where they are—as a matter of inheritance? The pioneers, the immigrants who settled the continent, were the restless ones in Europe. The steady, rooted ones stayed home and are still there. But every one of us, except the Negroes forced here as slaves, are descended from the restless ones, the wayward ones who were not content to stay at home. Wouldn't it be unusual if we had not inherited this tendency? And the fact is that we have.

But that's the short view. What are roots and how long have we had them? If our species has existed for a couple of million years, what is its history? Our remote ancestors followed the game, moved with the food supply, and fled from evil weather, from ice and the changing seasons. Then after thousands of years they domesticated some animals so that they lived with their food supply. Then of necessity they followed the grass that fed their flocks in endless wanderings. Only when agriculture came into practice did a place achieve meaning and value and permanence. But land is a definite thing, and definite things have a way of getting into few hands. Thus it was that one person wanted ownership of land and at the same time wanted servants because someone had to work it. Roots were in ownership of land, in definite and immovable possessions. In this view we are a restless species with a very short history of roots, and those not widely distributed. Perhaps we have overrated roots as a psychological need. Maybe the greater urge, the deeper and more ancient need, is the hunger to be somewhere else.

AN APPEAL BY MARTIN LUTHER KING, JR.

Adapted from "I Have a Dream," an address by Martin Luther King, Jr. Copyright © 1963 by Martin Luther King, Jr. Adapted and reprinted by permission of Joan Daves Literary Agency.

The most important black leader in the 1960's was Martin Luther King, Jr. For many Americans he became the symbol of the civil rights movement in the 1960's. King first became well-known during the Montgomery, Alabama, bus boycott in 1956. In the years afterward, he became the most outspoken leader in favor of non-violent protest in the civil rights movement.

King favored non-violent direct action such as sit-ins, boycotts, and marches to win equal rights for black Americans. As one of the organizers of the 1963 March on Washington, a massive civil-rights demonstration, he made the following famous speech to the 200,000 people who had gathered in the nation's capital.

How, according to King, has America failed to live up to its "sacred obligation"? What does he mean when he speaks of "meeting physical force with soul force"? How would you describe King's dream?

One hundred years ago a great American, in whose symbolic shadow we stand [the demonstration was held at the Lincoln Memorial], signed the Emancipation Proclamation. This momentous decree came as a great beacon light of hope to millions of Negro slaves who had been seared in the flames of withering injustice. It came as a joyous daybreak to end the long night of captivity.

But one hundred years later we must face the tragic fact that the Negro is still not free. One hundred years later the life of the Negro is still sadly crippled by the chains of segregation and discrimination. One hundred years later the Negro lives on a lonely island of poverty in the midst of a vast ocean of material prosperity. One hundred years later Negroes still find themselves exiles in their own land. So we have come here today to dramatize an appalling condition.

In a sense we have come to our nation's capital to cash a check. When the builders of our republic wrote the magnificent words of the Constitution and the Declaration of Independence, they were signing a promissory note which every American was to inherit. This note was a promise that all people would be guaranteed the unalienable rights of life, liberty, and the pursuit of happiness.

It is obvious today that America has defaulted on this promissory note insofar as its black citizens are concerned. Instead of honoring this sacred obligation, America has given the Negro people a bad check—a check which has come back marked "insufficient funds." But we refuse to believe that the bank of justice is bankrupt. We refuse to believe that there are insufficient funds in the great vaults of opportunity of this nation. So we have come to cash this check—a check that will give us upon demand the riches of freedom and the security of justice. We have also come to this hallowed spot to remind America of the fierce urgency of *now*. This is no time to engage in the luxury of cooling off or gradualism [the idea of proceeding slowly in carrying out change]. *Now* is the time to make real the promises of democracy. *Now* is the time to rise from the dark and desolate valley of segregation to the sunlit path of racial justice. *Now* is the time to open the doors of opportunity to all of God's children. *Now* is the time to lift our nation from the quicksands of racial injustice to the solid rock of brotherhood.

It would be fatal for the nation to overlook the urgency of the moment and to underestimate the determination of the Negro. This sweltering summer of the Negro's legitimate discontent will not pass until there is an invigorating autumn of freedom and equality. The year 1963 is not an end, but a beginning. Those who hope that the Negro needed to blow off steam and will now be content will have a rude awakening if the nation returns to business as usual. There will be neither rest nor tranquility in America until the Negro is granted citizenship rights. The whirlwinds of revolt will continue to shake the foundations of our nation until the bright day of justice emerges.

But there is something that I must say to my people who stand on the warm threshold which leads into the palace of justice. In the process of gaining our rightful place we must not be guilty of wrongful deeds. Let us not seek to satisfy our thirst for freedom by drinking from the cup of bitterness and hatred. We must forever conduct our struggle with dignity and discipline. We must not allow our creative protest to turn into physical violence. Again and again we must rise to the majestic heights of meeting physical force with soul force. The marvelous new militancy which has taken over the Negro community must not lead us to a distrust of all white people. Many of our white brothers, as shown by their presence here today, have come to realize that their destiny is tied up with our destiny. Their freedom is bound to our freedom. We cannot walk alone.

And as we walk, we must make the pledge that we shall march ahead. We cannot turn back. There are those who are asking us, "When will you be satisfied?" We can never be satisfied as long as the Negro is the victim of the unspeakable horrors of police brutality. We can never be satisfied as long as we cannot gain lodging in the motels of the highways and the hotels of the cities. We cannot be satisfied as long as the Negro's basic mobility is from a smaller ghetto to a larger one. We can never be satisfied as long as a Negro in Mississippi cannot vote, and a Negro in New York believes he has nothing for which to vote. No, no, we are not satisfied, and we will not be satisfied until justice rolls down like water and righteousness like a mighty stream.

I know that some of you have come here out of great trouble. Some of you have come fresh from narrow jail cells. Some of you have come from areas where your search for freedom left you battered by the storms of persecution and staggered by the winds of police brutality. You have been the veterans of creative suffering. Continue to work with the faith that unearned suffering is redeeming.

Go back to Mississippi, go back to Alabama, go back to South Carolina, go back to Georgia, go back to Louisiana, go back to the slums and ghettos of our modern cities, knowing that somehow this situation can and will be changed. Let us not wallow in the valley of despair.

I say to you today, my friends, that in spite of the difficulties and frustrations of the moment I still have a dream. It is a dream deeply rooted in the American dream.

I have a dream that one day this nation will rise up and live out the true meaning of its creed: "We hold these truths to be self-evident; that all men are created equal."

I have a dream that one day on the red hills of Georgia the sons of former slaves and the sons of former slaveowners will be able to sit down together at the table of brotherhood.

I have a dream that one day even the state of Mississippi will be transformed into an oasis of freedom and justice.

I have a dream that my four little children will one day live in a nation where they will not be judged by the color of their skin but by the content of their character.

I have a dream today.

I have a dream that one day the state of Alabama will be changed into a situation where little black boys and black girls will be able to join hands with little white boys and white girls and walk together as sisters and brothers.

I have a dream today.

This is our hope. This is the faith with which I return to the South. With this faith we will be

598

able to cut out of the mountain of despair a stone of hope. With this faith we will be able to change the jangling discords of our nation into a beautiful symphony of brotherhood. With this faith we will be able to work together, to pray together, to struggle together, to go to jail together, to stand up for freedom together, knowing that we will be free one day.

This will be the day when all of God's children will be able to sing with new meaning "My country 'tis of thee, sweet land of liberty, of thee I sing. Land where my fathers died, land of the pilgrim's pride, from every mountainside, let freedom ring."

And if America is to be a great nation this must become true. So let freedom ring from the hilltops of New Hampshire. Let freedom ring from the mountains of New York. Let freedom ring from the Alleghenies of Pennsylvania!

Let freedom ring from the snow-capped Rockies of Colorado!

Let freedom ring from the peaks of California!

But not only that; let freedom ring from Stone Mountain of Georgia!

Let freedom ring from Lookout Mountain of Tennessee!

Let freedom ring from every hill and molehill of Mississippi. From every mountainside, let freedom ring.

When we let freedom ring, when we let it ring from every village and every hamlet, from every state and every city, we will be able to speed up that day when all of God's children, black people and white people, Jews, Protestants, and Catholics, will be able to join hands and sing in the words of the old Negro spiritual, "Free at last! free at last, thank God almighty, we are free at last!"

THREE MINORITY VOICES

Forresto Garcia's story adapted from Small Hands, Big Hands *by Sandra Weiner. Copyright © 1970 by Sandra Weiner. Reprinted by permission of Pantheon Books, a division of Random House, Inc.*

Ricky's story adapted from Growing Up Puerto Rican *by Paulette Cooper. Copyright © 1972. Reprinted by permission of Arbor House Publishing Company, Inc.*

Clarence Chen's story adapted from "The Security Blanket of Racial Anonymity" by Clarence Chen, in Bridge, *December 1972. Reprinted by permission of* Bridge.

The United States was settled and built by groups of people of many different races and nationalities. Each of these groups had its own rich and distinctive cultural heritage. Throughout American history, however, many Americans viewed these cultural differences with mistrust and suspicion. They wanted all those who settled in the United States to be "Americanized." Thus, for a long time, many Americans believed in the "melting pot" idea, or the idea of "melting down" all the differences among the peoples in the nation. Although some "melting" did take place, most of the different groups in the United States maintained some feeling of separate cultural identity.

In the 1960's many Americans began to suggest that one of the greatest strengths of the United States was its diversity and its great variety of peoples with differing ethnic backgrounds. There was an increase in Americans' ethnic consciousness, or their feeling of belonging to special racial or national groups. Members of minority groups such as black Americans and Spanish-speaking Americans became more aware and proud of their heritage and their contributions to American culture. In this selection, teenagers of several minority groups express this pride and awareness.

How does Forresto Garcia feel about being Mexican-American? What are Ricky's feelings about being Puerto Rican? How does Clarence Chen describe his experiences as a Chinese-American?

FORRESTO GARCIA

I am Forresto Garcia and sixteen years old. I have five brothers and four sisters. I know how it is to work in the fields but I have been lucky and graduated from my grade school. I like to help poor people and I want to be somebody that helps poor people.

We have just come from Texas to California in our car with a trailer attached to it, and we put all our belongings in the trailer. When we arrived here we looked for a rancher, and he said, "Do you want to work picking cotton?" And we said, "Yes, we want to work," and he said, "Well, I'll give you a house if you work for me for the cotton season," and he gives us a house and that's the way we live. And when the cotton is finished we move to another town and look for another crop. When there is no house we set up our trailer near the rest of the families, but mostly we live outside the trailer. But when we are naughty my father quietly tells us to go into the trailer. You obey right away just by hearing the way he speaks. He has a twig from the prune tree and when he hits you with it you know it. Just once or twice and then he stops.

We get up at five in the morning so we can start work at six. My sisters get up earlier because they have to make breakfast for my dad and my brothers and then make food for the fields. We make an early start so we could earn enough money for the day. We work until about four in the afternoon.

I am trying to get a steady job to help my family so they can have more money. In Texas I have seen many American-Mexicans without shoes, with their feet all dirty, and their faces and hands dirty, and no water to take a bath. We only wear shoes in the summer when we go to church. They are expensive and we must make them last. I am always running around and stubbing my toe.

I sometimes just stay home doing nothing but thinking about my family. On Sunday when there is no work we go to the picnic grounds and cook on an open fire and when it gets very hot we swim in the stream that runs by our house.

It makes me feel bad to see poor people. My brother, he works for the union and he talks a lot about the union and what the union is doing and I like it. When I meet some guys working in the field I say, "How would you like to join the union?" and they say, "No, I'm O.K. and I don't like to help poor people," I get mad at them.

Now when my older brothers and my father picket against picking grapes I help them. I like to see them win what they are fighting for. Some employers are better than others, but some take advantage of the workers. They are rich and my people are so poor.

RICKY

My name is Ricky and I'm Puerto Rican. The best thing about being Puerto Rican is just being Puerto Rican. That's where it's at. I believe Puerto Rican people are the best. They treat me very good—very good. Like they aren't cheap with their stuff. Like you're at a party and it's late. And they say right away, "We got an extra bed. Sleep here." And they feed you and they do everything for you. And they don't have that much. But they've always given to everyone, and they'll give you what they got because they're generous.

Where I live now it looks like a ghetto. But it used to be real pretty. When I was young there were no addicts there and nobody was uptight about drugs. Now everybody is, because there's a lot of junkies [drug users] hanging around all over the neighborhood. Puerto Ricans. Blacks. Dominicans. All the races mix. It doesn't matter.

There's a lot of violence where I live. I watch not because I'm interested, but because you have no choice. After all, if I'm there, what am I going to do—just look the other way? But I like to see people who deserve to get hurt get theirs, you know? The guys that hurt other people. Like the junkies—most people who get hurt in these fights are junkies, because they're the ones who go around hurting people and the others get even. They mug people, kill people, and rob houses, and the people around my way they don't have that much. Maybe they save a year for a television set, and they enjoy watching it. And then here comes somebody, some junkie after money, and he robs these people and takes all they've got and leaves them with nothing.

I know a whole lot of junkies, but they're not my friends—I don't hang out with them. I don't know how people become junkies in the first place. Maybe they're influenced by their friends or they pick it up in school—but something happens to them.

I never smoked marijuana 'cause I don't need it. I don't need anything. Maybe other people need to feel nice. Maybe it makes them feel like a big man. It's the same with violence, guns, and killings, I guess.

I feel nice when I shoot pool. I'm pretty good, too. I make money from it, in fact. I can make thirty or forty dollars on a weekend. I just go up to a guy and say, "Hey, do you want to shoot pool?" I lose a lot of times, but I've won more money than I lost. And I also like to play poker.

Another thing I've always liked to do is turn on the fire hydrant. It's fun getting wet and running around getting other people wet. One time when I was little I was playing with the fire hydrant and I was covering myself with a box so I didn't see a car coming. And I guess the car didn't see me either and the driver didn't pay any attention to the water and I got hit. That happened twice more. The person that hit me the third time was my lawyer. He was going to my house to talk to my parents about the first two cases and then he hit me. I tried to sue but I don't know what happened. I wasn't badly hurt.

I'd still like to play with the fire hydrant, but the cops picked me up for opening one last summer. The only other time I got into trouble with the police was once when they asked me my name. I gave them a phony name and a phony address. I told them I didn't have a phone number, and they believed me.

When a cop gets shot, I say that's bad. Like, they have to take care of people and they're just people, too. They weren't born cops, they just got in it. In fact, I like Puerto Rican cops. They're together people. Puerto Ricans are proud and that's good. Maybe that's why we fight a lot. We are proud people and we don't take anything off of people. We don't ask nobody for nothing. I wouldn't even borrow money from my friends. That's how proud I am.

CLARENCE CHEN

For most of my life I have taken for granted the fact that I am racially different from most of the people I have met and known—they are mostly Caucasian and I am not. When it occurred to me to think about who I was I would think of myself first as a boy, a student, a son, and then, somewhere near the end of the list, as a Chinese.

After all, I was like all of my American friends; we spoke the same slang, played the same games, listened to the same music, wore the same type of clothes. When we were boys, we lived and would have died for the same local baseball team—the White Sox. We played cowboys and Indians. As an adolescent, I had the same financial, emotional, and social crises everyone else did. For all practical purposes, I grew up as a typical American boy who happened to be Chinese.

Throughout my years of growing up, I encountered relatively little outward racial prejudice directed against me. The general lack of racial prejudice directed against me was at least partially due to the absence of any other Chinese people. My family were the first Chinese (and nonwhite) to move into that neighborhood on the South Side of Chicago. My brother and I were the first Chinese students at our elementary and high schools.

But while I am an American for all practical purposes, there have been times when I was acutely and uncomfortably aware that I was also different. Though my mannerisms, speech, and dress were American, my physical appearance was quite obviously Oriental. When I was about five, I believed that my Oriental features made me ugly even though I cannot recall having been told that by anyone.

In school, whenever a topic related to China was brought up in a social studies class, I would notice the other kids looking in my direction—expecting me to be knowledgeable on the subject. Since I knew practically nothing of Chinese history, culture, or language, I generally passed such moments by slumping into my seat and becoming suddenly interested in my books.

Unfortunately, some of my meetings with other Chinese have been similarly embarrassing. Whenever I have met Chinese people who have been brought up in the Chinese culture, I have been met with two sets of responses. Either I am Chinese and able to speak and act Chinese, or I am not Chinese at all but completely American or perhaps Japanese. In the former case, the other person is usually disappointed and embarrassed to learn I cannot speak Chinese. In the latter case, the other person is usually surprised and amused to find I am racially 100 percent Chinese, that my family came to this country just one generation ago, and that I actually know a few phrases in Chinese such as "Thank you" and "See you again."

Several years ago I made a trip to Taiwan. My uncles and aunts, while warmly receiving me as a member of the family, could not help but see me as more American than Chinese. They affectionately called me *wai gwo ren*—a term meaning "foreigner" but also suggesting "Westerner" or "white man." I felt I was viewed as somewhat stupid because of my inability to speak Chinese. There must have been something about my appearance and manner—perhaps my American-style clothes and hair length or my un-Chinese assertiveness—which branded me as an alien; for storekeepers, cab drivers, and waiters quickly knew I was an outsider even before I spoke.

I do not mean to suggest that I have never gotten along with other Chinese. Yes, some of my best friends are Chinese. But they have come from white-collar, middle-class families like mine who have been pretty much assimilated into the mainstream of American culture.

While it may sound as if I have never been genuinely comfortable in the company of either Americans or Chinese, the reality has not been that difficult. Most of the time when I am with other non-Chinese people, the matter of our racial differences never crosses our minds.

While I have occasionally felt uncomfortable being Chinese in a mainly Caucasian country, I am fortunate in belonging to a group of Chinese-Americans in which I can feel very much at home. This group, consisting of eight families scattered around the Chicago area, began as an informal association of Chinese student couples who found themselves stranded in the United States after the Communists came to power in China. The members meet socially once a month at one another's homes.

The people of my generation in this group will, no matter how Americanized they seem to become, always have a unique aspect in their backgrounds—their parents grew up and were brought up in the Chinese culture. Thus, despite our American characteristics, we (the American-born Chinese) have been influenced in certain ways by the traditional culture. All of us have high achievement motivations and have all won superior academic credentials. (Scholarship was, for thousands of years in China, the most honored and respected path to higher status and public recognition.) Furthermore, academic and nonacademic achievements have been felt in our group to reflect shamefully or proudly on the individual and also on the individual's family. It is quite common in our eight-family gatherings to hear one parent praising another parent for his or her offspring's accomplishment. This is a reflection of a traditional Chinese concept: a person's reputation, whether honorable or dishonorable, directly affects the family's reputation. "Good" children in China were those who brought honor to the family name.

Last summer I went to a "Chinese Family Camp" to serve as a counselor. About thirty yards [27.4 meters] off the shore of Lake Wawasee, Indiana, was an anchored raft that could be used by anyone who swam out to it. One afternoon I was resting on it when I suddenly realized that the five or six of us on the raft were all Chinese-American. In that moment, a deep, warm feeling swept through me. I was just where I belonged—a temporary island on which disguises dissolved and I could be what I am—not really American, not really Chinese, but really Chinese-American.

THE RICH CULTURE OF GREEK-AMERICANS

Revised from Rise of the American Nation, *Third Edition, pp. 678–680. New York: Harcourt Brace Jovanovich, Inc., 1972.*

American society is made up of many different groups who share in a common American culture, and who also retain their own cultural heritage and identity. The most obvious of these groups are those who have distinct racial characteristics, such as black Americans, Japanese-Americans, and Chinese-Americans. But there are many other groups within American society with their own special life styles and identity. Among these are the white ethnic groups who are descendants of European immigrants. White ethnic groups include Irish-Americans, Italian-Americans, Polish-Americans, Greek-Americans, and many others.

The following selection is a study of a group of Greek-Americans in Chicago. The experience of these Greek-Americans, sharing in the American culture but at the same time maintaining their Greek heritage, is characteristic of other white ethnic groups.

How does this group of Greek-Americans maintain its separate cultural identity? How are their customs and ideas transmitted from one generation to the next? Do you feel that you are part of a separate ethnic group? Which one? What do you have in common with other members of that group?

Many people are gathering at a large Greek-Orthodox church on the south side of Chicago. It is Greek Easter. Most who come to the church service drive up in American cars. The men are discussing baseball and the cost of a color television set; a few are discussing a political crisis in Greece. The women are comparing notes on their children's schools. The boys and girls are discussing homework and dates. All of them—men, women, and children—are aware that on this day they are members of a special group. They are Greek-Americans, and they are proud of it. This Easter is a day which is uniquely Greek-American. Christmas and the Fourth of July are holidays which they share with other Americans. Greek Easter is theirs.

Because the Greek church uses the Julian calendar, Greek Easter falls later in the year than the Easter celebrated by Protestants and Roman Catholics, who use the Gregorian calendar. Greek Easter is the climax of the Holy Week, with special ceremonies both in the church and at home, leading up to the midnight service and the lighting of candles by the entire congregation. Easter Sunday dinner is an occasion for great family gatherings, featuring roast lamb, *kulurakla*—special Easter bread—and after dinner, a breaking of the dyed red eggs.

Some of the people coming to church on this Easter have not been to church since last Easter, while others come every day bringing their children to the parochial school run by the church. Not everyone in the Greek-American ethnic group participates in the special Greek Easter ceremonies. But everyone knows that Greeks do these things and feels a sense of identification with the group that observes these Easter customs. In various ways their identification as Greek-Americans is a source of support, deep and lasting, to most Americans of Greek descent.

The congregation of the church now lives scattered throughout the south side of Chicago, but once they all lived in the neighborhood around the church. Before that the first generation of immigrants lived in the Harrison-Halstead area, the first center of the Greek community in Chicago. At that time the area was called "Greektown"—the center of the first *kinotitos* (community), the location of the major Greek coffee houses and restaurants, the sites of the first candy factories and the food businesses. It was in Greektown that the Chicago political "machine" made its appeal for Greek votes in return for political services.

Most of Greektown has now been pulled down as part of an urban renewal project, and several Greek-American communities have been established elsewhere in the city, around new churches. Most Greek-Americans in Chicago now feel their connection to their ethnic group through one of these churches or through friendships with other Greek-American families. Contacts are kept very much alive for many reasons, but most especially because older Greek-Americans want to encourage their young people to marry within the group so that the Greek traditions will be carried on. They feel that happier, more satisfactory marriages can be made within the group than outside it.

Nowadays some younger members of the Greek-American community do not marry within the group. Most older Greek-Americans are unhappy when this happens. It is true that some outsiders who marry into the group join the church, and learn Greek ways. However, these people can never really become Greek-Americans because the basis for being a Greek-American is thought to be "blood"—heredity. Greek-Americans think of themselves as descendants of Greek immigrants, not as a group which can be voluntarily joined.

Many Greek-Americans can tell in detail the history of their ancestors who came to America as immigrants, mainly between 1910 and 1920. Many came fully expecting to return to Greece once they had made some money; often these were men alone. However, many did not return, and they later went back, or sent back, for wives. For many, the American dream came true —poor immigrants or their children made good in America, although often after long years of loneliness and struggle. However, contrary to the prediction often made, they were not entirely melted down into Americans. A sense of ethnic community continued. They became Americans, but a special kind of Americans— Greek-Americans.

Over the years Greek-Americans have had serious struggles among themselves. Often the struggles centered around political problems in Greece. Sometimes the struggles reflected differences about church organization.

Both common customs and common history, and, oddly enough, common feuds and struggles have helped to hold the Greek-American community together. Probably equally important in keeping group identity has been the treatment of Greek-Americans by other Americans. When Greek immigrants came to Chicago and started in the restaurant business and the candy business, those already in these businesses feared their competition. When Greeks moved into the Harrison-Halstead area, their customs and language were regarded as strange. Families were laughed at, students in school were made fun of, men in business were abused, church doctrine and ritual were considered odd. The acceptance of new immigrants into American life has often been reluctant. For Greek-Americans, the fact that their church was different from the three more common religions —Protestant, Roman Catholic, and Jewish— tended to keep them apart socially even as they became accepted economically and politically.

WHY WOMEN ARE DISSATISFIED

Adapted from The Feminine Mystique *by Betty Friedan. Copyright © 1963, 1974 by Betty Friedan. Reprinted by permission of W. W. Norton & Co., Inc.*

During the 1950's more and more Americans began to discover that many women were dissatisfied with their role in society. The majority of American women were housewives and mothers; only a minority of them worked at full-time jobs. There were very few women in politics, very few women in the professions, and very few women executives in business and industry.

Betty Friedan, a suburban housewife and mother, was one of those who began to consider the problems of women in American society. Feeling dissatisfied and unhappy with her own life, she decided to investigate how other women felt about themselves and their lives. She reported her findings in a best-selling book, *The Feminine Mystique*. The major point emphasized throughout the book was that millions of women were questioning their role in American society and becoming aware that their world of home, husband, and children was a limited one that did not offer them fulfillment.

In 1964 Betty Friedan helped to found NOW, the National Organization for Women. NOW and other feminist groups began a nationwide effort, the women's rights movement, to secure full equality for women in American society.

According to the author, what is the "feminine mystique"? What is "the problem that has no name"? Has the role of women been changing in recent years? Explain.

The problem lay buried, unspoken, for many years in the minds of American women. It was a strange stirring, a sense of dissatisfaction, a yearning that women suffered in the 1950's in the United States. Each suburban wife struggled with it alone. As she made the beds, shopped for groceries, matched slipcover material, ate peanut butter sandwiches with her children, drove around Cub Scouts and Brownies, she was afraid to ask herself the silent question—"Is this all?"

For over fifteen years there was no word of this yearning in the millions of words written about women and for women by experts telling them that their role was to seek fulfillment as wives and mothers. Over and over women heard that they could desire no greater destiny than to glory in their own femininity. Experts told them how to catch a man and keep him, how to handle children; how to buy a dishwasher, bake bread, cook gourmet snails; how to dress, look, and act more feminine and make marriage more exciting. They were taught to pity the neurotic, unfeminine, unhappy women who

wanted to be poets or physicists or presidents. They learned that truly feminine women do not want careers, higher education, political rights —the independence and the opportunities that the old-fashioned feminists fought for. A thousand expert voices praised women's new maturity. All they had to do was devote their lives from earliest girlhood to finding a husband and having children.

By the end of the 1950's the average marriage age of women in America dropped to 20, and was still dropping, into the teens. Fourteen million girls were engaged by 17. The proportion of women attending college in comparison with men dropped from 47 percent in 1920 to 35 percent in 1958. A hundred years earlier, women had fought for higher education; now girls went to college to get a husband. By the mid-1950's, 60 percent dropped out of college to marry, or because they were afraid too much education would hurt their chances for marriage.

By the end of the 1950's the United States birthrate was overtaking India's. Statisticians were especially astounded at the fantastic increase in the number of babies born to college-educated women. Where once they had two children, now they had four, five, six.

Girls were growing up in America without ever having jobs outside the home. Fewer and fewer women were entering professional work. The shortages in the nursing, social work, and teaching professions caused crises in almost every American city. Concerned over the Soviet Union's lead in the space race, scientists noted that America's greatest source of unused brainpower was women. But girls would not study physics: it was "unfeminine."

The suburban housewife—she was the dream image of young American women. She was the envy, it was said, of women all over the world. The American housewife was freed by science and labor-saving appliances from the drudgery, the dangers of childbirth, and the illnesses of her grandmother. She was healthy, beautiful, educated, concerned only about her husband, her children, her home. She had found true feminine fulfillment. As a housewife and mother, she was respected as a full and equal partner to man in his world. She was free to choose automobiles, clothes, appliances, supermarkets. She had everything that women had ever dreamed of.

In the fifteen years after World War II, this mystique of feminine fulfillment became the cherished center of American culture. Millions of women lived their lives in the image of the

American suburban housewife, kissing their husbands goodbye in front of the picture window, leaving their stationwagonsful of children at school, and smiling as they ran the new electric waxer over the spotless kitchen floor. They gave no thought to the unfeminine problems of the world outside the home; they wanted the men to make the major decisions. They gloried in their role as women, and wrote proudly on the census blank: "Occupation: housewife."

For over fifteen years, the words written for women, and the words women used when they talked to each other, were about problems with their children, or how to keep their husbands happy, or improve their children's school, or cook chicken or make slipcovers. Nobody argued whether women were inferior or superior to men; they were simply different. Words like "emancipation" and "career" sounded strange and embarrassing; no one had used them for years.

If a woman had a problem in the 1950's and 1960's, she knew that something must be wrong with her marriage, or with herself. Other women were satisfied with their lives, she thought. What kind of a woman was she if she did not feel this mysterious fulfillment waxing the kitchen floor? She was so ashamed to admit her dissatisfaction that she never knew how many other women shared it. If she tried to tell her husband, he didn't understand what she was talking about.

But on an April morning in 1959, I heard a mother of four, having coffee with four other mothers, say in a tone of quiet desperation, "the problem." And the others knew, without words, that she was not talking about a problem with her husband, or her children, or her home. Suddenly they realized they all shared the same problem, the problem that has no name. They began, hesitantly, to talk about it. Later, after they had picked up their children at nursery school and taken them home to nap, two of the women cried, in sheer relief, just to know they were not alone.

Gradually I came to realize that the problem that has no name was shared by countless women in America. Sometimes I sensed the problem, not as a reporter, but as a suburban housewife, for during this time I was also bringing up my own three children.

Just what was this problem that has no name? What were the words women used when they tried to express it? Sometimes a woman would say, "I feel empty somehow—incomplete." Or she would say, "I feel as if I don't exist." Sometimes she got rid of the feeling with a tranquilizer. Sometimes she thought the problem was with her husband, or her children, or that what she really needed was to redecorate her house, or move to a better neighborhood, or have another baby. Sometimes she went to a doctor with symptoms she could hardly describe: "A tired feeling—I get so angry with the children it scares me—I feel like crying without any reason."

In 1960 the problem that has no name burst through the image of the happy American housewife. In the television commercials the pretty housewives still smiled over their foaming dishpans. But the actual unhappiness of the American housewife was suddenly being reported, although almost everybody who talked about it found some easy reason to explain it away.

The problem was explained away by telling the housewife she didn't realize how lucky she was. What if she wasn't happy—did she think men were happy in this world? Did she really, secretly, still want to be a man? Didn't she know yet how lucky she was to be a woman?

The problem was also explained away by saying that there are no solutions. This is what being a woman means. What is wrong with American women that they can't accept their role gracefully?

By 1962 the plight of the trapped American housewife had become a national game. Whole issues of magazines, newspaper columns, books, educational conferences, and television panels were devoted to the problem.

Even so, most men, and some women, still did not know that this problem was real. But those who had faced it honestly knew that all the easy remedies did not work. They got all kinds of advice on how to adjust to their role as housewives. No other road to fulfillment was offered to American women in the 1950's. Most adjusted to their role and suffered or ignored the problem that has no name.

It is no longer possible to ignore, to explain away, the desperation of so many American women. This is not what being a woman means, no matter what the experts say. Perhaps the reason has not been found because the right questions have not been asked, or pressed far enough. The women who suffer from this problem have a hunger that food cannot fill. It may not even be felt by women with desperate problems of hunger, poverty, or illness. And women who think it will be solved by more money, a bigger house, a second car, moving to a better suburb, often discover it gets worse.

It is no longer possible today to blame the problem on loss of femininity, or to say that education and independence and equality with men have made American women unfeminine. I have heard so many women try to deny this dissatisfied voice within themselves because it does not fit the pretty picture of femininity the experts have given them.

If I am right, the problem that has no name

stirring in the minds of so many American women today is not a matter of loss of femininity or too much education or the demands of taking care of a house and family. It is far more important than anyone recognizes. It is the key to these other new and old problems which have been torturing women and their husbands and children for years. It may well be the key to our future as a nation and a culture. We can no longer ignore that voice within women that says: "I want something more than my husband and my children and my home."

CHAPTER 25 ■ AMERICA IN AN ERA OF RAPID GROWTH AND CHANGE

AMERICANS EXPLORE THE MOON

Adapted from "The Moon Had Been Awaiting Us a Long Time" by Neil Armstrong, in Life, *August 22, 1969. © 1969 by Time Inc. Used by permission of the publisher.*

The idea of exploring space has captured the imagination of people everywhere, from the beginning of history. Then, in 1957, Soviet scientists sent the first unmanned space satellite, Sputnik I, into orbit around the earth. Four years later, in 1961, the Soviet astronaut Yuri Gagarin became the first person to orbit the earth. His achievement was matched early in 1962 by the American astronaut John Glenn. During the following years the United States and the Soviet Union launched many other successful space flights. These space projects greatly increased scientific knowledge and opened a vast new frontier for exploration.

The most significant American space effort of the 1960's was Project Apollo—the first manned flight to the moon. After several successful Apollo flights above the moon's surface, on July 15, 1969, Apollo 11 was launched from Cape Canaveral with three astronauts aboard —Neil Armstrong, Edwin Aldrin, and Michael Collins. On July 20, Armstrong and Aldrin, flying in a detachable lunar module, or LEM, landed on the surface of the moon. The age-old dream had become a reality. The following selection is an account written by Neil Armstrong discussing the flight of Apollo 11 and the historic landing on the moon.

What benefits does Armstrong believe the Apollo 11 flight will bring? Why do you think people everywhere are fascinated by space exploration?

Our goal, when we were assigned to this flight last January, seemed almost impossible. There were a lot of unknowns, unproved ideas, unproved equipment. The lunar module [a detachable moon spacecraft] had never flown. There were many things about the lunar surface we did not know. It remained to be seen whether it was possible for the ground to communicate simultaneously with two vehicles up there. I honestly suspected, at the time, that it was unlikely that Apollo 11 would make the first lunar landing flight. There was just too much to learn —too many chances for problems.

Then came the flights of Apollo 9 and 10, which were so magnificently successful. It began to seem that we really would get a chance at a landing. From that point on, preparations became relentless.

We were not concerned with safety, specifically, in these preparations. We were concerned with mission success, with the accomplishment of what we set out to do. I felt a successful lunar landing might inspire people around the world to believe that impossible goals really are possible, that there really is hope for solutions to humanity's problems.

We were very conscious of the symbolism of our exploration, and we wanted the small things which go along with a flight to reflect our very serious approach to the business of flying the lunar mission.

The patch we designed was meant to symbolize the peaceful American attempt at a lunar landing. We wanted the names we chose for communication to have both dignity and symbolism. The name Eagle [for the lunar module] was intended to reflect a degree of national pride in the enterprise. The name Columbia [for the space capsule] is also a national symbol. It reflected, too, the aura of adventure, exploration, and seriousness with which Columbus took on his assignment.

The day of the lunar landing was a long one and there was a lot to do every minute. We got up at 5:30 that morning and touched down about 3:20 P.M. Houston time. Our ignition for powered descent was smooth and right on time. But at about 30,000 feet [9,144 meters] we began to have computer problems. They seem to have come from overloading the computer. Mission Control analyzed the problem and the cause, and advised us promptly that we could safely override the alarms and continue our descent.

From about 30,000 feet [9,144 meters] down to 5,000 feet [1,524 meters] we were totally absorbed in analyzing and dealing with this problem, and checking our instruments. Our attention was thus taken away from the windows and from identification of landmarks outside. The first chance we had to spend some time looking out was from below 3,000 feet [914.4 meters]. It was difficult at that height to see very far ahead. The only landmark we could see was a very large, very impressive crater.

At first we considered landing just short of it. That location seemed clearly to be where our automatic guidance system was taking us. By the time we were down around 1,000 feet [304.8 meters], however, it was quite obvious that Eagle was attempting to land in a most undesirable area. I had an excellent view of the crater and the boulder field out of the left window. There were boulders as big as Volkswagens all around.

The rocks seemed to be coming up at us awfully fast. We reduced our descent rate from 10 to 3 feet [3 to .9 meters] per second. It would have been interesting to land in that boulder field from a scientific point of view. I was tempted, but my better judgment took over. We pitched forward to a level attitude, and scanned the surface to the west for a better touchdown area. The one we chose was only a couple of hundred feet square, about the size of a big house

lot. It was ringed on one side by some fairly good-sized craters and on the other with a field of small rocks, but it still looked as if we could live with it. I put Eagle down there.

I am told that my heartbeat increased noticeably during the lunar descent, but I would really be disturbed with myself if it hadn't. During the final seconds of descent, our engine kicked up a substantial amount of lunar dust which blew out almost parallel to the surface, at very high speeds. Normally on earth if you kick up dust it hangs in the air and settles back to the ground very slowly. But since there is no atmosphere on the moon, dust sails away in a flat, low path, leaving a clear space behind it. The dust we kicked up probably still hadn't settled on the lunar surface by the time we landed, but it was a long way away from us and going fast. It was possible to see through it— I could make out rocks and craters—but its movement was distracting. It made it difficult to pick out the speeds for a smooth touchdown. It was much like landing in a very fast-moving ground fog.

Buzz [Aldrin] and I had about 12 minutes of very busy post-touchdown [after landing] work, and then we could relax enough to have a sense of relief, of elation.

It took us somewhat longer to come out from Eagle than we had anticipated. It wasn't until after landing that I made up my mind what to say: "That's one small step for a man, one giant leap for mankind." Beyond those words I don't recall any particular emotion or feeling other than a little caution, a desire to be sure it was safe to put my weight on that surface outside Eagle.

From inside Eagle the sky was black, but it looked like daylight out on the surface and the surface looked tan. There is a very peculiar lighting effect on the lunar surface which seems to make the colors change. I don't understand this completely. If you look down along your own shadow, or into the sun, the moon is tan. If you look straight down at the surface, particularly in the shadows, it looks very, very dark. When you pick up material in your hands it is also dark, gray or black. The material is of a generally fine texture, almost like flour, but some coarser particles are like sand. Then there are, of course, scattered rocks and rock chips of all sizes. My only real problem on the surface was that there were so many places that I would like to have investigated.

All the things we left on the moon are pretty well known by now. We were particularly pleased to leave the patch of Apollo I in memory of our friends and fellow astronauts Gus Grissom, Ed White, and Roger Chaffee [three astronauts who lost their lives during an on-ground training accident in 1967] and the medals in memory of Gagarin and Komarov [two Soviet astronauts]. I believe that the Russians share our own dreams and hopes for a better world.

Looking back, touchdown was for me the most striking achievement in the flight. Lift-off was the next most striking. I thought quite a bit about that single ascent engine and how much depended upon it. When the moment came it was perfection. It gave us not only a very pleasant ride but also a beautiful, final view of our moon base as we lifted up and away from it.

My overwhelming impression of the moon as I walked on it and photographed it was that I was taking pictures of a steady-state process, a process in which some rocks are being worn down continually on the surface and other new ones are being thrown out on top by new events occurring either near or far away. In other words, no matter when humans first reached this spot —a thousand years ago or 100,000 years ago or even a million years from now—it would look generally the same. The only difference would be that at each period in time one would see slightly different rocks, slightly different surfaces, all influenced by the same processes. From what I saw I believe that most of the processes are external (that is, things like meteorite impact). But some materials indicate that there may have been internal processes on the moon at some time.

The most dramatic memories I have now are the sights themselves, those magnificent visual images. They go far beyond any other visual experiences I've had in my life. Of all the spectacular views we had, the most impressive to me was on the way toward the moon, when we flew through its shadow. We were still thousands of miles away but close enough so that the moon almost filled our circular window. It was eclipsing the sun, from our position, and the corona [the outermost part of the atmosphere] of the sun was visible around the moon. It was magnificent, but the moon itself was even more so. We were in its shadow so there was no part of it lit by the sun. It was lit only by the earth, by earthshine. This made the moon appear blue-gray. The entire scene looked three-dimensional.

I was really aware, visually aware, that the moon was in fact a sphere, not a disk. It seemed almost as if it were showing us its roundness, its similarity in shape to our earth, in a sort of welcome. I was sure then that it would be a hospitable host. It had been awaiting its first visitors for a long time.

THE FIRST ELECTRONIC PERSON

Adapted from "Meet Shaky, the First Electronic Person," by Brad Darrach, in Life, *November 20, 1970. © 1970 by Time Inc. Reprinted by permission of the publisher.*

Scientists developed the first modern computers in the 1940's. During the 1950's the capacities and functioning of computers were vastly improved. Computers now could perform calculations that even the most expert mathematicians could never hope to achieve. Next came computers which could be programmed to change their own operations to meet changing conditions. As a result, in the early 1960's science fiction writer Arthur C. Clarke, whose forecasts about other scientific developments had proven remarkably accurate, predicted that computers might soon become more intelligent than people. By the 1970's, however, it was clear that a computer's "intelligence" depended on the information and instructions that human beings provided it.

Still, the possibility of creating a computer that could "think" fascinated scientists. One research institute successfully developed "the first electronic person," named Shaky, whose "brain" consisted of a computer. In this selection, a reporter describes the amazing machine, with its mechanical mind and nearly human ability to "think."

What action was "Shaky" ordered to perform? What does the author believe are some of the possible advantages and possible dangers in the widespread use of computers? Can you describe some uses of computers that affect your life?

It looked at first glance like a Good Humor wagon sadly in need of a paint job. But instead of a tinkly little bell on top of its box-shaped body there was this big metallic whang-doodle that came up, full of lenses and cables.

"Meet Shaky," said the young scientist who was showing me through the Stanford Research Institute. "The first electronic person."

I looked for a twinkle in the scientist's eye. There wasn't any. He sat down at an input terminal and typed out a brief instruction which was fed into Shaky's "brain," a computer set up in a nearby room: PUSH THE BLOCK OFF THE PLATFORM.

Something inside Shaky began to hum. A large glass prism shaped like a thick slice of pie and set in the middle of what passed for its face spun faster and faster till it dissolved into a glare. Then its superstructure made a slow turn and its face leaned forward and seemed to be staring at the floor. As the hum rose to a whir, Shaky rolled slowly out of the room, rotated its superstructure again and turned left down the corridor at about 4 miles [6.4 kilometers] an hour, still staring at the floor.

"It guides itself by watching the baseboards," the scientist explained as we hurried to keep up. At every open door Shaky stopped, turned its head, inspected the room, turned away, and rolled on to the next open door. In the fourth room it saw what it was looking for: a platform with a large wooden block sitting on it. Shaky went in, then stopped short in the middle of the room and stared for about five seconds at the platform. I stared at it too.

"It will never make it," I found myself thinking. "Its wheels are too small." All at once I got gooseflesh. "Shaky," I realized, "is thinking the same thing I am thinking!"

Shaky was also thinking faster. It rotated its head slowly till its eye came to rest on a wide shallow ramp that was lying on the floor on the other side of the room. Whirring briskly, it crossed to the ramp, halfcircled it, and then pushed it straight across the floor till the high end of the ramp hit the platform. Rolling back a few feet, Shaky looked over the situation again and discovered that only one corner of the ramp was touching the platform. Rolling quickly to the far side of the ramp, it gave a slight push to the ramp till the gap closed. Then Shaky swung around, charged up the ramp, located the block, and gently pushed it off the platform.

Compared to the glamorous electronic devices that appear on television, Shaky may not seem like much. But in fact it is a historic achievement. The task I saw Shaky perform would require all the talents of a lively four-year-old child, and the scientists who over the last two years have headed up the Shaky project say it is capable of far more complex routines. Armed with the right devices and programmed in advance with basic instructions, Shaky could travel about the moon for months at a time. Without a single direction from the earth, it could gather rocks, drill cores, make surveys and photographs, and even decide to lay plank bridges over crevices it had made up its mind to cross.

The center of this intricate activity is Shaky's "brain," a remarkably programmed computer with a capacity of more than 7 million "bits" of information. According to the conventional view, the computer is just a glorified adding machine that cannot possibly challenge the human monopoly on reason. But Shaky's brain demonstrates that machines can think. Thinking includes such processes as "exercising the powers of judgment" and "reflecting for the purpose of reaching a conclusion." In some of these respects—among them powers of recall and mathematical agility—Shaky's brain can think better than the human mind.

Marvin Minsky, of Project MAC at the Massachusetts Institute of Technology, recently told me: "In from three to eight years we will have a machine with the general intelligence of an average human being. At that point the machine will begin to educate itself with fantastic speed. In a few months it will be at genius level and a few months after that its powers will be incalculable."

I had to smile at my instant belief—the nervous sort of smile that comes when you realize you've been taken in by a clever piece of science fiction. Then I checked Minsky's idea with other people working on Artificial Intelligence [this new field of computer research]. Many of them said that Minsky's timetable might be somewhat wishful—"give us 15 years," was a common remark. But all agreed that there would be such a machine and that it could bring about the third Industrial Revolution.

Up to a point, says Minsky, the impact will be positive. "The machine dehumanized people, but it could rehumanize them." By automating all routine work and even tiresome low-grade thinking, computers could free billions of people to spend most of their time doing pretty much as they please. But such progress could also produce quite different results. "It might happen," says one expert, "that the Puritan work ethic would crumble too fast and masses of people would give in to the diseases of leisure." An even greater danger may lie in people's increasing dependency upon the computer. The electronic circuit has already replaced the dynamo at the center of technological civilization. Many American industries and businesses, the telephone and power grids, the airlines and the mail service, the systems for distributing food and, not least, the big government bureaucracies would be instantly disrupted and threatened with complete breakdown if the computers they depend upon were disconnected. The disorder in Western Europe and the Soviet Union would be almost as severe.

What's more, our dependency on computers, seems certain to increase at a rapid rate. Doctors are already beginning to rely on computer diagnosis and postoperative care. Artificial Intelligence experts believe that fiscal planners in both industry and government will gradually give to computers nearly complete control of the national (and even the global) economy. In the interests of efficiency, cost-cutting, and speed of reaction, the government may well be forced to surrender human direction of military policies to machines that plan strategy and tactics. In time, say the scientists, diplomats will give up judgment to computers that predict, say, Russian policy by analyzing their own simulations of the entire Soviet state and of the personalities—or the computers—in power there.

Humans, in short, are coming to depend on thinking machines to make decisions that involve their vital interests and even their survival as a species. What guarantee do we have that in making these decisions the machines will always consider our best interests? There is no guarantee unless we provide it, says Minsky, and it will not be easy to provide. After all, people have not been able to guarantee that their own decisions are made in their own best interests. Any supercomputer could be programmed to test important decisions for their value to human beings. But such a computer could also presumably write a program that reversed these "ethical" instructions. There need be no question of computer malice here, merely a matter of computer creativity overcoming external restraints.

The people at Project MAC foresee an even more unsettling possibility. A computer that can program a computer, they reason, will be followed in fairly short order by a computer that can design and build a computer vastly more complex and intelligent than itself—and so on indefinitely.

"I'm afraid the spiral could get out of control," says Minsky. It is possible, of course, to monitor computers, to make an occasional check on what they are doing in there. But even now it is difficult to monitor the larger computers. And the computers of the future may be far too complex to keep track of.

Why not just unplug the thing if it got out

of hand? "Switching off a system that defends a country or runs its entire economy," says Minsky, "is like cutting off its food supply. Also, the Russians are only about three years behind us in A-I work. With our system switched off, they would have us at their mercy."

The problem of computer control will have to be solved, Minsky believes, before computers are put in charge of systems essential to society's survival. If a computer directing the nation's economy or its nuclear defenses ever rated its own efficiency above its ethical obligation, it could destroy our social order—or destroy humankind. "Once the computers got control," says Minsky, "we might never get it back. We would survive at their pleasure. If we're lucky, they might decide to keep us as pets."

But even if no such catastrophe were to occur, say the people at Project MAC, the development of a machine more intelligent than humans will surely deal a severe shock to people's sense of their own worth. Even Shaky is disturbing. A creature that deposed humans from the top of creation might tempt us to ask ourselves: Is the human brain outmoded?

"AN EXCITING NEW IDEA" IN HIGHWAY TRAVEL

Adapted from No Cause for Panic *by Russell Baker. Copyright © 1962, 1963, 1964 by The New York Times Company. Reprinted by permission of J. B. Lippincott Company.*

When automobiles first appeared in the early 1900's, many people thought these odd-looking machines would never replace the horse and buggy. But within a few years this new form of transportation proved successful and thousands of Americans owned automobiles. Soon millions of Americans were driving cars. Along with the increased use and popularity of the automobile came new superhighways, wide ribbons of concrete that linked states together and crisscrossed the entire nation. New businesses—gas stations, motels, and restaurants—sprung up everywhere along the new highways at rest area stops. By the 1960's many of the older, less traveled roads were nearly empty of traffic. Towns and smaller cities bypassed by expressways and turnpikes often lost business and jobs as a result.

Some Americans, however, continued to favor the older, less traveled roads. One of them, humor writer Russell Baker, tells in this selection about a car trip he took through the southeastern part of the United States.

Why does the author favor driving on older roads? What things does he stress in this description of his trip? Do you think he is joking or serious—or both? Explain.

They have an exciting new idea in highway engineering out here. It is called the low-speed, two-lane, unlimited access road, and to anyone who dreads tiresome expressway driving it looks like the wave of the future.

For one thing, it is more dangerous than the old-fashioned superhighway. Farmers are forever pulling out of cornfields right in front of the traveler, and hairpin curves are constantly threatening to send one to Kingdom Come. Giant tractor rigs rush past within inches, smacking the car with a shock wave that leaves it shuddering. All this not only appeals to the natural American love of excitement, but also keeps the driver from sinking into the dull sleepiness that makes turnpike driving such a trial.

The real beauty of the low-speed, two-lane, unlimited access road, however, is that it has character, individuality, and style that tell the traveler a little something of the variety of America. This is what the superhighways have lost. Except for minor differences in plants and trees, the New Jersey Turnpike looks exactly like Florida's Sunshine State Parkway, which looks like the Maine Turnpike, which looks like Interstate 95 in New Hampshire, Virginia, and North Carolina.

The superhighway is designed for a nation of bypassers. It bypasses the grandeur of Frenchman's Bay, bypasses the magnificence of New York City, bypasses the sprawl of Philadelphia, bypasses the neon of the Florida Gold Coast. When the Federal Interstate Highway System is completed, it will be possible to bypass all of America.

The motorists who are bypassing their country may get to their destination a little faster, but they become travelers who are untraveled. Instead of becoming richer people, they are reduced to sleeping lumps of boredom whose horizons are no broader than the next "rest stop."

The truth is that the superhighway is essentially un-American. The idea was imported from Hitler's Third Reich [Germany] which gave the world the Autobahn [the German word for superhighway]. Hitler's Reich was the ideal country to bypass at fast speeds. This is a good country to examine at slow cruising speed.

There is, for example, the sharp shift in moods that occurs at the Big Sandy River where Route 60 crosses from West Virginia into Kentucky. Behind, to the east, lie the industrial towns of Huntington and Charleston, the steamy summer air of clusters of railroad shops and the smell of chemical plants. Back farther still to the east lie the breathtaking Appalachian peaks and river valleys. The traveler prepared to find West Virginia a place of poverty is shocked to find that it is also a place of Swiss beauty and much industrial promotion.

Then, swooping up into the hills of eastern Kentucky, the mood of the road shifts suddenly. Bypassing nothing, it allows time to read the changes in the roadside signs. (Another charming feature of the two-lane road is that billboard signs are posted everywhere to relieve the monotony of the landscape.)

In Virginia the billboards show a sharp competitive instinct among cave operators. "World's Only Known Anthodites," boasts a typical cave sign outside. In West Virginia they show an up-and-at-'em mood. "We feature the future," declares the welcome billboard at Ceredo. And in eastern Kentucky they announce the beginning of the Bible Belt. "The New America Needs the Old Faith," advises a church billboard in Ashland.

Winding westward past the country of crude, unpainted shacks and small tobacco plots, the road flows into the richer farmland of Shelby County [Kentucky]. "Shelby County: Home of Good People, Good Land, and Good Living," reads the welcoming sign. And as it moves toward Lexington through the Blue Grass country, the evidence of good land and good living and billboards selling good bourbon tell the tourists how the country around them is changing as they move west.

For incurable bypassers, it is an exasperating road, full of poorly planned curves, farmers moving at a slow pace, and red lights stopping progress in unbypassed little towns. For those who can take their bypasses or leave them alone, it is a cheering reminder that this is still a country that remains to be discovered by those with the will to explore.

The Autobahn with its bypasses may be making it easier to avoid exploration and discovery, but the two-lane, low-speed, unlimited access road is out here, ready and waiting.

ON BEING POOR IN A RICH COUNTRY

Condensed from "Daddy Tucked the Blanket Around Mama's Shoulders. Tears Were Dropping Off His Cheeks" by Randall Williams in The New York Times, *July 10, 1975. © 1975 by The New York Times Company. Reprinted by permission.*

About 26 million Americans live in poverty. What is it like to be poor in America? Most Americans can only guess at the answer. They may have seen pictures of rundown houses in Appalachia or crumbling blocks of apartments in large American cities. They may have watched television reports about older people on low fixed incomes who are forced to live in poverty, or viewed programs about infants and children from low-income families who suffer from malnutrition and disease.

How does poverty affect people? A retired couple must carefully plan how they spend each dollar. A worker who cannot find a job leaves his family in order that it may be eligible for welfare payments. A jobless teenager in a large city spends her days idle and discouraged about the future.

In this selection, Randall Williams, a writer from Alabama, remembers what it was like growing up poor.

How did poverty affect Williams' relations with his friends? The relationship between his parents? After reading this account, what would you say is the worst thing about being poor?

About the time I turned 16, my folks began to wonder why I didn't stay home any more. I always had an excuse for them, but what I didn't say was that I had found my freedom and I was getting out.

I went through four years of high school in semi-rural Alabama and became active in clubs and sports; I made a lot of friends. But I managed those four years without ever having a friend visit at my house.

I was ashamed of where I lived.

We had a big family. There were several of us sleeping in one room, but that's not so bad if you get along, and we always did. As you get older, though, it gets worse.

Being poor is a humiliating experience for a young person trying hard to be accepted. Even now—several years removed—it is hard to talk about. And I resent the weakness of these words to make you feel what it was really like.

We lived in a lot of old houses. We moved a lot because we were always looking for something just a little better than what we had. You have to understand that my folks worked harder than most people. My mother was always at home, but for her that was a full-time job—and no fun, either. But my father worked his head off from the time I can remember in construction and shops. It was hard, physical work.

I tell you this to show that we weren't shiftless. No matter how much money Daddy made, we never made much progress. I got out thanks to a college scholarship.

I have seen my Daddy wrap copper wire through the soles of his boots to keep them together in the wintertime. He couldn't buy new boots because he had used the money for food and shoes for us. We lived [terribly], but we went to school well-clothed and with a full stomach.

It really is [terrible] to live in a house that was in bad shape 10 years before you moved in. And a big family puts a lot of wear and tear on a new house, too, so you can imagine how one goes downhill if it is teetering when you move in. But we lived in houses that were sweltering in summer and freezing in winter. I woke up every morning for a year and a half with plaster on my face where it had fallen out of the ceiling during the night.

This wasn't during the Depression; this was in the late 60's and early 70's.

When we boys got old enough to learn trades in school, we would try to fix up the old houses we lived in. But have you ever tried to paint a wall that crumbled when the roller went across it? And bright paint emphasized the holes in the wall. You end up more frustrated than when you began, especially when you know that at best you might come up with only enough money to improve one of the six rooms in the house. And we might move out soon after, anyway.

The same goes for keeping a house like that clean. If you have a house full of kids and the house is deteriorating, you'll never keep it clean. Daddy used to yell at Mama about that, but she couldn't do anything. I think Daddy knew it inside, but he had to have an outlet for his rage somewhere, and at least yelling isn't as bad as hitting, which they never did to each other.

But you have a kitchen which has no counter space and no hot water, and you will have dirty dishes stacked up. That sounds like an excuse, but try it. It's the same thing in a house with no closets. You can't keep clothes clean and rooms in order if they have to be stacked up with things.

Living in a bad house is generally worse on girls. For one thing, they traditionally help their mother with the housework. We boys could get outside and work in the field or cut wood or even play ball and forget about living conditions. The sky was still pretty.

But the girls got the pressure, and as they got older it became worse. Would they accept dates knowing they had to "receive" the young man in a dirty hallway with broken windows, peeling wallpaper and a cracked ceiling? You have to live it to understand it, but it creates a shame which drives the soul of a young person inward.

I'm thankful none of us ever blamed our parents for this, because it could have crippled our relationships. As it worked out, only the relationship between our parents was damaged. And I think the harshness which they expressed to each other was just an outlet to get rid of their anger at the trap their lives were in. It ruined their marriage because they had no one to yell at but each other. I knew other families where the kids got the abuse, but we were too much loved for that.

Once I was about 16 and Mama and Daddy had had a particularly violent argument about the washing machine, which had broken down. Daddy was on the back porch—that's where the only water faucet was—trying to fix it and Mama had a washtub out there washing school clothes for the next day and they were screaming at each other.

Later that night everyone was in bed and I heard Daddy get up from the couch where he was reading. I looked out from my bed across the hall into their room. He was standing right over Mama and she was already asleep. He pulled the blanket up and tucked it around her shoulders and just stood there and tears were dropping off his cheeks and I thought I could faintly hear them splashing against the linoleum rug.

Now they're divorced.

Small children have a hard time understanding poverty. They want the same things children from better-off families have. They want the same things they see advertised on television, and they don't understand why they can't have them.

Other children can be incredibly cruel. I was in elementary school in Georgia—and this is interesting because it is the only thing I remember about that particular school—when I was about eight or nine.

After Christmas vacation had ended, my teacher made each student describe all his or her Christmas presents. I became more and more uncomfortable as the privilege passed around the room toward me. Other children were reciting the names of the dolls they had been given, the kinds of bicycles and the grandeur of their games and toys. Some had lists which seemed to go on and on for hours.

It took me only a few seconds to tell the class that I had gotten for Christmas a belt and a pair of gloves. And then I was laughed at—because I cried—by a roomful of children and a teacher. I never forgave them, and that night I made my mother cry when I told her about it.

In retrospect, I am grateful for that moment, but I remember wanting to die at the time.

A WARNING AGAINST ENVIRONMENTAL POLLUTION

Adapted from Silent Spring *by Rachel Carson, published by Houghton Mifflin Company. Copyright © 1962 by Rachel L. Carson. Reprinted by permission of the publisher.*

In the early 1960's Rachel Carson, a zoologist, warned about the growing threat to the environment. In her widely read book *Silent Spring*, she alerted Americans to the dangerous effects of many chemical insecticides and pesticides being used throughout the nation.

The title of Rachel Carson's book referred to some future spring season when migratory birds would fail to arrive. She warned that during such a spring there would be silence everywhere; by then insecticides would have so upset the balance of nature that birds and other wildlife could not survive. It was a frightening picture of a world slowly dying.

Rachel Carson's book was enormously important, for it convinced many Americans that human beings themselves might be polluting their environment and thus endangering all life on earth. In this selection she warns that human beings are changing "the very nature of the world—the very nature of its life."

Does Rachel Carson oppose the use of chemicals? What does she propose? What do you think should be done to protect the environment?

The history of life on earth has been a history of interaction between living things and their surroundings. To a large extent the physical form and the habits of the earth's plant life and its animal life have been molded by the environment. Considering the whole span of earthly time, the opposite effect, in which life actually modifies or changes its surroundings, has been relatively slight. Only within the moment of time represented by the present century has one species—human beings—acquired significant power to change the nature of their world.

During the past twenty-five years this power has not only increased to one of disturbing magnitude, but it has changed in character. The most alarming of all human assaults upon the environment is the contamination of air, earth, and water with dangerous and even deadly materials. . . . The chain of evil that pollution begins, not only in the world that must support life but in living tissues, is for the most part irreversible.

In this now universal contamination of the environment, chemicals are the evil and little recognized partners of radiation in changing the very nature of the world—the very nature of its life. Strontium 90, released through nuclear explosions into the air, comes to earth in rain or drifts down as fallout. It lodges in soil, enters into the grass or corn or wheat grown there, and in time ends up in the bones of a human being, there to remain until death. Similarly, chemicals sprayed on croplands or forests or gardens lie long in soil. They enter into living organisms, passing from one to another in a chain of poisoning and death. Or they pass mysteriously by underground streams until they emerge and . . . combine into new forms that kill plants, sicken cattle, and work unknown harm on those who drink from once pure wells. . . .

It took hundreds of millions of years to produce the life that now inhabits the earth. During that time developing and evolving life reached a state of adjustment and balance with its surroundings. The environment, shaping and directing the life it supported, contained elements that were hostile as well as supporting. Certain rocks gave out dangerous radiation. Even within the light of the sun, from which all life draws its energy, there were short-wave radiations with power to injure. Given time—time not in years but in thousands of years—life adjusts, and a balance has been reached. For time is the essential ingredient. But in the modern world there is no time.

The rapidity of change and the speed with which new situations are created follow the rapid pace of humans rather than the deliberate pace of nature. Radiation is no longer just the background radiation of rocks, the bombardment of cosmic rays, the ultraviolet of the sun, that have existed since before there was any life on earth. Radiation is now the unnatural creation of people's tampering with the atom. The chemicals to which life is asked to make its adjustment are no longer . . . just the minerals washed out of the rocks and carried in rivers to the sea. They are the synthetic creations of people's inventive minds, made in their laboratories, and having no counterparts in nature.

To adjust to these chemicals would require time on the scale that is nature's. It would require not just the years of a person's life but the life of generations. And even this, if possible, would be hopeless, for the new chemicals come from our laboratories in an endless stream. Every year almost 500 chemicals find their way into actual use in the United States alone. The figure is staggering, and all its meanings are not easily grasped—500 new chemicals to which the bodies of people and animals are required somehow to adapt each year, chemicals totally outside the limits of biologic experience.

Among them are many that are used in people's war against nature. Since the mid-1940's over 200 basic chemicals have been created for use in killing insects, weeds, rodents, and other organisms described as "pests." They are sold under several thousand different brand names.

These sprays, dusts, and aerosols are now applied almost universally to farms, gardens, forests, and homes—nonselective chemicals that have the power to kill every insect, the "good" and the "bad," to still the song of birds and the leaping of fish in the streams, to coat the leaves with a deadly film, and to linger on in the soil—all this though the intended target may be only a few weeds or insects. Can anyone believe it is possible to lay down such a barrage of poisons on the surface of the earth without making it unfit for all life? . . .

The whole process of spraying seems caught up in an endless spiral. Since DDT was released for civilian use, a process of escalation has been going on in which ever more poisonous materials must be found. This has happened because insects . . . have evolved super races immune to the particular insecticide used. Hence a deadlier one has always to be developed—and then a deadlier one than that. . . .

Thus the chemical war is never won, and all life is caught in its violent crossfire. . . .

It is not my belief that chemical insecticides must never be used. I do say that we have put poisonous and biologically powerful chemicals into the hands of persons largely or wholly ignorant of their potentials for harm. We have subjected enormous numbers of people to contact with these poisons, without their consent and often without their knowledge. If the Bill of Rights contains no guarantee that a citizen shall be secure against deadly poisons distributed either by private individuals or by public officials, it is surely only because those who wrote it, despite their wisdom and foresight, could conceive of no such problem.

I say, furthermore, that we have allowed these chemicals to be used with little or no advance investigation of their effect on soil, water, wildlife, and people themselves. Future generations are unlikely to overlook our lack of wise concern for the integrity of the natural world that supports all life.

There is still very limited awareness of the nature of the threat. This is an era of specialists, each of whom sees his or her own problem and is unaware of or intolerant of the larger frame into which it fits. It is also an era dominated by industry, in which the right to make a dollar at whatever cost is seldom challenged. When the public protests, confronted with some obvious evidence of damaging results of pesticide applications, it is fed little tranquilizing pills of half truth. We urgently need an end to these false assurances, to the sugar coating of unacceptable facts. It is the public that is being asked to assume the risks that the insect controllers calculate. The public must decide whether it wishes to continue on the present road, and it can do so only when in full possession of the facts.

"FUTURE SHOCK" AND ITS EFFECTS

In the years since 1945, incredible changes have taken place throughout the world. These changes have been especially remarkable in the United States and the other industrialized nations. Modern technology has enabled people in the industrialized nations to produce electric power from the energy of the atom, to use computers to run factories and offices, to travel in jet planes at several hundred miles an hour, and to send rockets and satellites to explore space. As a result of these increasingly rapid technological changes, our lives are constantly changing. In fact, Americans have grown so accustomed to rapid, profound changes that they rarely stop to think how all this has affected their lives and the way they think about themselves and their country.

Alvin Toffler, a sociologist, has used the term "future shock" to describe this experience of far-reaching changes throughout the modern world. In this selection, he discusses some of the remarkable effects he believes rapid change is producing in our lives.

What is "future shock"? How is our own lifetime—the "800th lifetime" in human history—different from earlier lifetimes? What do you think of Toffler's ideas? Explain.

In the three short decades between now and the twenty-first century, millions of ordinary people will face an abrupt collision with the future. Citizens of the world's richest and most technologically advanced nations will find it increasingly painful to keep up with the incessant demand for change that characterizes our time. For them, the future will have arrived too soon.

Western society for the past 300 years has been caught up in a storm of change. This storm now appears to be gathering force. Change sweeps through the highly industrialized countries with ever accelerating speed and unprecedented impact.

A strange new society is apparently erupting in our midst. Is there a way to understand it, to shape its development? How can we come to terms with it?

Much that now strikes us as incomprehensible would be far less so if we took a fresh look at the racing rate of change. For the acceleration of change does not merely buffet industries or nations. It is a concrete force that reaches deep into our personal lives, compels us to act out new roles, and confronts us with the danger of a new and powerfully upsetting psychological disease. This new disease can be called "future shock," and a knowledge of its sources and symptoms helps explain many things.

The parallel term "culture shock" has already begun to creep into the popular vocabulary. Culture shock is the effect that a strange culture has on the unprepared visitor. Peace Corps volunteers suffer from it in Borneo or Brazil. Culture shock is what happens when a traveler suddenly finds himself in a place where yes may mean no, where a "fixed price" is negotiable, where to be kept waiting in an outer office is no cause for insult, where laughter may signify anger. It is what happens when the familiar cues that help an individual to function in society are suddenly withdrawn and replaced by new ones that are strange or incomprehensible.

The culture shock phenomenon accounts for much of the bewilderment, frustration, and disorientation that plagues Americans in their dealings with other societies. It causes a breakdown in communication, a misreading of reality, an inability to cope. Yet culture shock is relatively mild in comparison with the much more serious malady, future shock. Future shock is the dizzying disorientation brought on by the premature arrival of the future. It may well be the most important disease of tomorrow.

Future shock is a product of the greatly accelerated rate of change in society. It is culture shock in one's own society. But its impact is far worse. For most travelers have the comforting knowledge that the culture they left behind will be there to return to. The victim of future shock does not.

Take an individual out of his own culture and set him down suddenly in an environment sharply different from his own, with a different set of cues to react to—different conceptions of time, space, work, love, religion, and everything else—then cut him off from any hope of retreat to a more familiar social landscape, and the dislocation he suffers is doubly severe. Moreover, if this new culture is itself in constant turmoil, and if—worse yet—its values are incessantly changing, the sense of disorientation will be still further intensified. Given few clues as to what kind of behavior is rational under the radically new circumstances, the victim may well become a hazard to himself and others.

Now imagine not merely an individual but an entire society, an entire generation, suddenly transported into this new world. The result is mass disorientation, future shock on a grand scale.

This is the prospect that man now faces. Change is avalanching [falling] upon our heads and most people are unprepared to cope with it.

Is all this exaggerated? I think not. It has become a cliche to say that what we are now living through is a "second industrial revolution." This phrase is supposed to impress us with the speed and profundity of the change around us. But it is misleading. For what is occurring now is, in all likelihood, bigger, deeper, and more important than the industrial revolution. Indeed, a growing body of opinion asserts that the present moment represents nothing less than the second great divide in human history, comparable only with that first great break, the shift from barbarism to civilization.

This idea crops up with increasing frequency in the writings of scientists and technologists. John Diebold, the American automation expert, warns that "the effects of the technological revolution we are now living through will be deeper than any social change we have experienced before." Sir Leon Bagrit, the British computer manufacturer, insists that automation by itself represents "the greatest change in the whole history of mankind."

One of the most striking statements has come from Kenneth Boulding, an economist. Thus he asserts, "The world of today . . . is as different from the world in which I was born as that world was from Julius Caesar's. I was born in the middle of human history, to date, roughly. Almost as much has happened since I was born as happened before."

This startling statement can be illustrated in a number of ways. It has been observed, for example, that if the last 50,000 years of man's existence were divided into lifetimes of approximately sixty-two years each, there have been about 800 such lifetimes. Of these 800, fully 650 were spent in caves.

Only during the last seventy lifetimes has it been possible to communicate effectively from one lifetime to another—as writing made it possible to do. Only during the last six lifetimes did masses of men ever see a printed word. Only during the last four has it been possible to measure time with any precision. Only in the last two has anyone anywhere used an electric motor. And the overwhelming majority of all the material goods we use in daily life have been developed within the present, the 800th, lifetime.

This 800th lifetime marks a sharp break with all past human experience because during this lifetime man's relationship to resources has reversed itself. This is most evident in the field of economic development. Within a single lifetime, agriculture, the original basis of civilization, has lost its dominance in nation after nation. Today in a dozen major countries agriculture employs fewer than 15 percent of the population. In the United States, this figure is already below 6 percent and it is still shrinking rapidly.

Moreover, if agriculture is the first stage of economic development and industrialism the second, we can now see that still another stage —the third—has suddenly been reached. In about 1956 the United States became the first major power in which more than 50 percent of the non-farm labor force ceased to wear the blue collar of factory or manual labor. Blue collar workers were outnumbered by those in the so-called white-collar occupations. Within the same lifetime a society for the first time in human history not only threw off the yoke of agriculture, but managed to throw off the yoke of manual labor as well. The world's first service economy had been born.

Since then, one after another of the technologically advanced countries have moved in the same direction. Ten thousand years for agriculture. A century or two for industrialism. And now, opening before us—super-industrialism.

This lifetime is also different from all others because of the astonishing expansion of the scale and scope of change. Clearly, there have been other lifetimes in which upheavals occurred. Wars, plagues, earthquakes, and famine rocked many an earlier social order. But these shocks and upheavals were contained within the borders of one or a group of adjacent societies. It took generations, even centuries, for their impact to spread beyond these borders.

In our lifetime the boundaries have burst. Today the network of social ties is so tightly woven that the consequences of contemporary events radiate instantaneously around the world. A war in Vietnam alters basic political alignments in Peking, Moscow, and Washington, touches off protests in Stockholm, affects financial transactions in Zurich, triggers secret diplomatic moves in Algiers.

But the final difference between this and all previous lifetimes is the one most easily overlooked. For we have not merely extended the scope and scale of change, we have radically altered it pace. We have in our time released a totally new social force—a stream of change so accelerated that it influences our sense of time, revolutionizes the tempo of daily life, and affects the very way we "feel" the world around us. We no longer "feel" life as men did in the past. And this is the ultimate difference, the distinction that separates the truly contemporary man [the person of today] from all others. For this acceleration lies behind the impermanence [the feeling that nothing will last for long] that penetrates our consciousness, radically affecting the way we relate to other people, to things, to the entire universe.

By changing our relationship to the resources that surround us, by violently expanding the scope of change, and, most crucially, by accelerating its pace, we have broken with the past. We have cut ourselves off from the old ways of thinking, of feeling, of adapting. We have set the stage for a completely new society and we are now racing toward it. This is the crux [real meaning] of the 800th lifetime. And it is this that calls into question man's capacity for adaptation—how will he fare in this new society? Can he adapt to its imperatives [demands]? And if not, can he alter these imperatives?

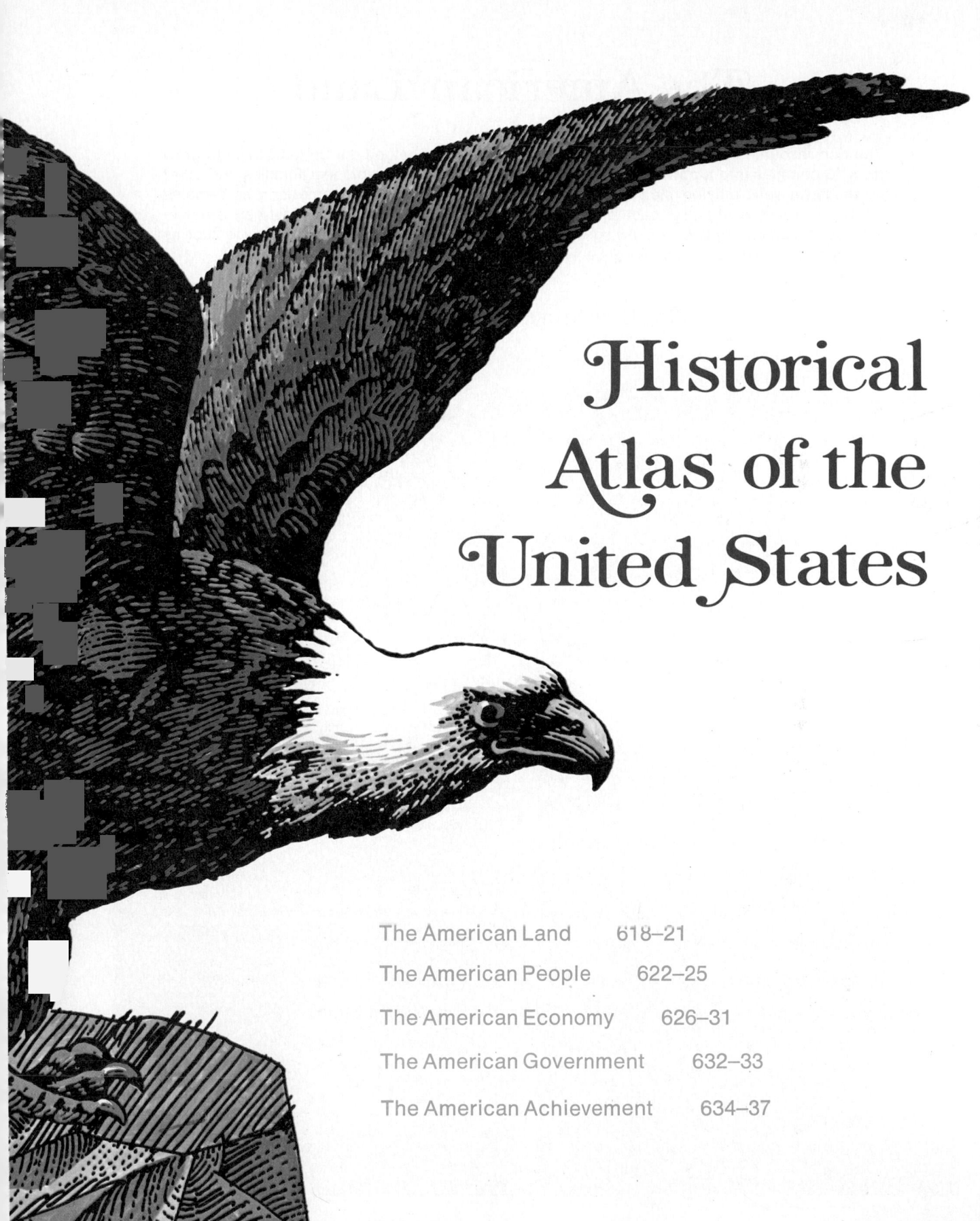

Historical Atlas of the United States

The American Land

The rich resources and incredible beauty of America's land helped the United States to grow from 13 colonies into a powerful nation. Within a few generations, pioneer families and other newcomers were moving steadily across a mighty continent. Soon American settlements stretched from the Atlantic coast to the Pacific shore—and beyond. These vast new areas of land soon became part of a growing union of states. They joined the federal union first as territories and then as states fully equal with all the other states.

The Growth of the Federal Union

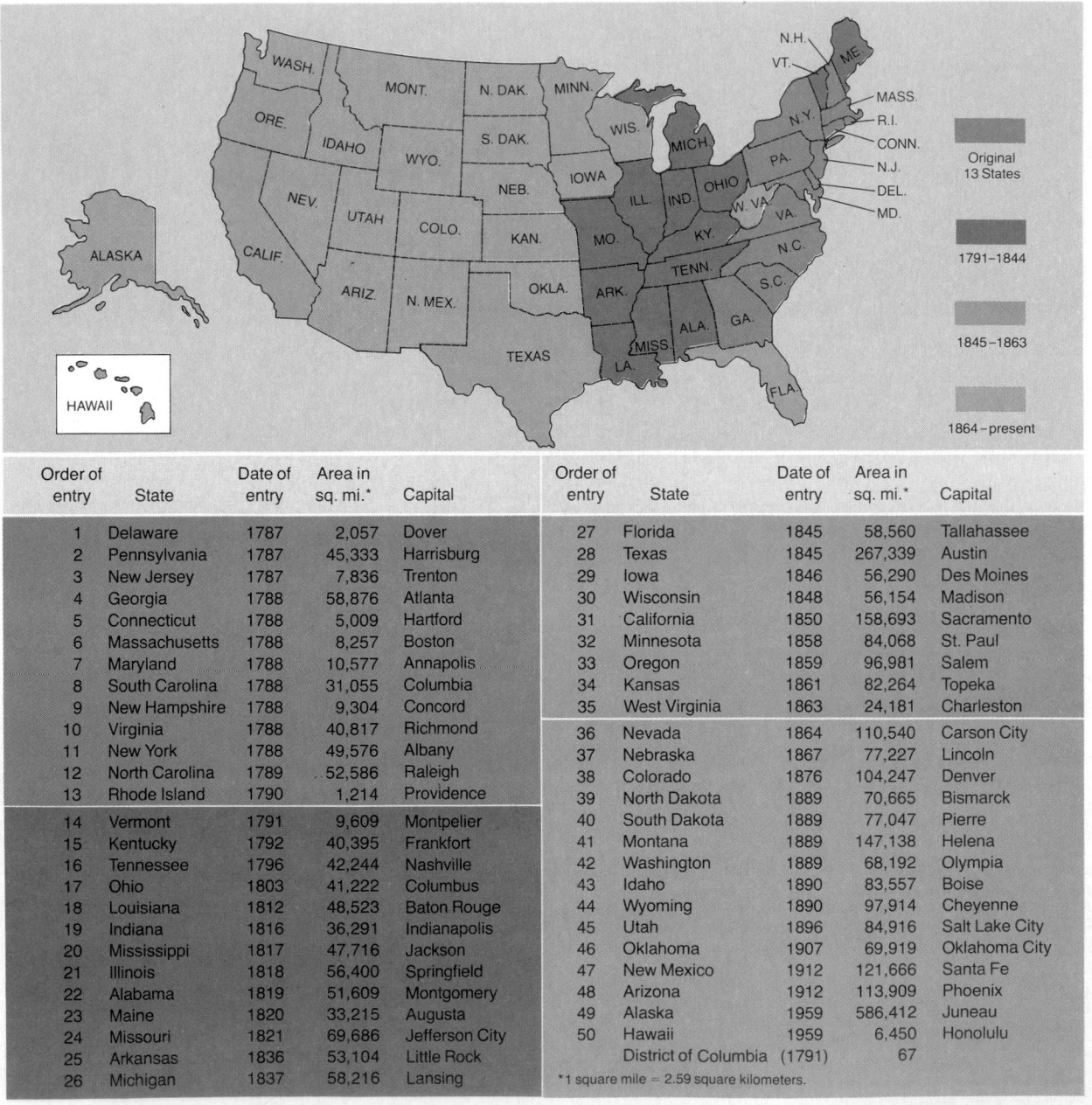

Order of entry	State	Date of entry	Area in sq. mi.*	Capital
1	Delaware	1787	2,057	Dover
2	Pennsylvania	1787	45,333	Harrisburg
3	New Jersey	1787	7,836	Trenton
4	Georgia	1788	58,876	Atlanta
5	Connecticut	1788	5,009	Hartford
6	Massachusetts	1788	8,257	Boston
7	Maryland	1788	10,577	Annapolis
8	South Carolina	1788	31,055	Columbia
9	New Hampshire	1788	9,304	Concord
10	Virginia	1788	40,817	Richmond
11	New York	1788	49,576	Albany
12	North Carolina	1789	52,586	Raleigh
13	Rhode Island	1790	1,214	Providence
14	Vermont	1791	9,609	Montpelier
15	Kentucky	1792	40,395	Frankfort
16	Tennessee	1796	42,244	Nashville
17	Ohio	1803	41,222	Columbus
18	Louisiana	1812	48,523	Baton Rouge
19	Indiana	1816	36,291	Indianapolis
20	Mississippi	1817	47,716	Jackson
21	Illinois	1818	56,400	Springfield
22	Alabama	1819	51,609	Montgomery
23	Maine	1820	33,215	Augusta
24	Missouri	1821	69,686	Jefferson City
25	Arkansas	1836	53,104	Little Rock
26	Michigan	1837	58,216	Lansing
27	Florida	1845	58,560	Tallahassee
28	Texas	1845	267,339	Austin
29	Iowa	1846	56,290	Des Moines
30	Wisconsin	1848	56,154	Madison
31	California	1850	158,693	Sacramento
32	Minnesota	1858	84,068	St. Paul
33	Oregon	1859	96,981	Salem
34	Kansas	1861	82,264	Topeka
35	West Virginia	1863	24,181	Charleston
36	Nevada	1864	110,540	Carson City
37	Nebraska	1867	77,227	Lincoln
38	Colorado	1876	104,247	Denver
39	North Dakota	1889	70,665	Bismarck
40	South Dakota	1889	77,047	Pierre
41	Montana	1889	147,138	Helena
42	Washington	1889	68,192	Olympia
43	Idaho	1890	83,557	Boise
44	Wyoming	1890	97,914	Cheyenne
45	Utah	1896	84,916	Salt Lake City
46	Oklahoma	1907	69,919	Oklahoma City
47	New Mexico	1912	121,666	Santa Fe
48	Arizona	1912	113,909	Phoenix
49	Alaska	1959	586,412	Juneau
50	Hawaii	1959	6,450	Honolulu
	District of Columbia	(1791)	67	

*1 square mile = 2.59 square kilometers.

Territorial Expansion of the United States

Land area	Date	How acquired	Size of area sq. mi. (sq. km.)	Percent of present U.S.	Present states
Original Area	1783	Won from Great Britain; established by Treaty of Paris	888,685 (2,301,694)	24%	Original 13 states, plus Illinois, Indiana, Kentucky, Maine, Michigan, Ohio, Tennessee, Vermont, West Virginia, Wisconsin, and part of Alabama, Minnesota, Mississippi
Louisiana Purchase	1803	Purchased from France	827,192 (2,142,427)	23%	Arkansas, Iowa, Missouri, Nebraska, North Dakota, South Dakota, and part of Colorado, Kansas, Louisiana, Minnesota, Montana, Oklahoma, Wyoming
Florida	1819	Treaty with Spain	72,003 (186,488)	2%	Florida, and part of Alabama, Louisiana, Mississippi
Texas	1845	Annexed	390,144 (1,010,473)	11%	Texas, and part of Colorado, Kansas, New Mexico, Oklahoma, Wyoming
Oregon Country	1846	Treaty with Great Britain	285,580 (739,652)	8%	Idaho, Oregon, Washington, and part of Montana, Wyoming
Mexican Cession	1848	Treaty with Mexico	529,017 (1,370,154)	15%	California, Nevada, Utah, and part of Arizona, Colorado, New Mexico, Wyoming
Gadsden Purchase	1853	Purchased from Mexico	29,640 (76,768)	1%	Part of Arizona, New Mexico
Alaska	1867	Purchased from Russia	586,412 (1,518,807)	16%	Alaska
Hawaii	1898	Annexed	6,450 (16,705)	.1%	Hawaii

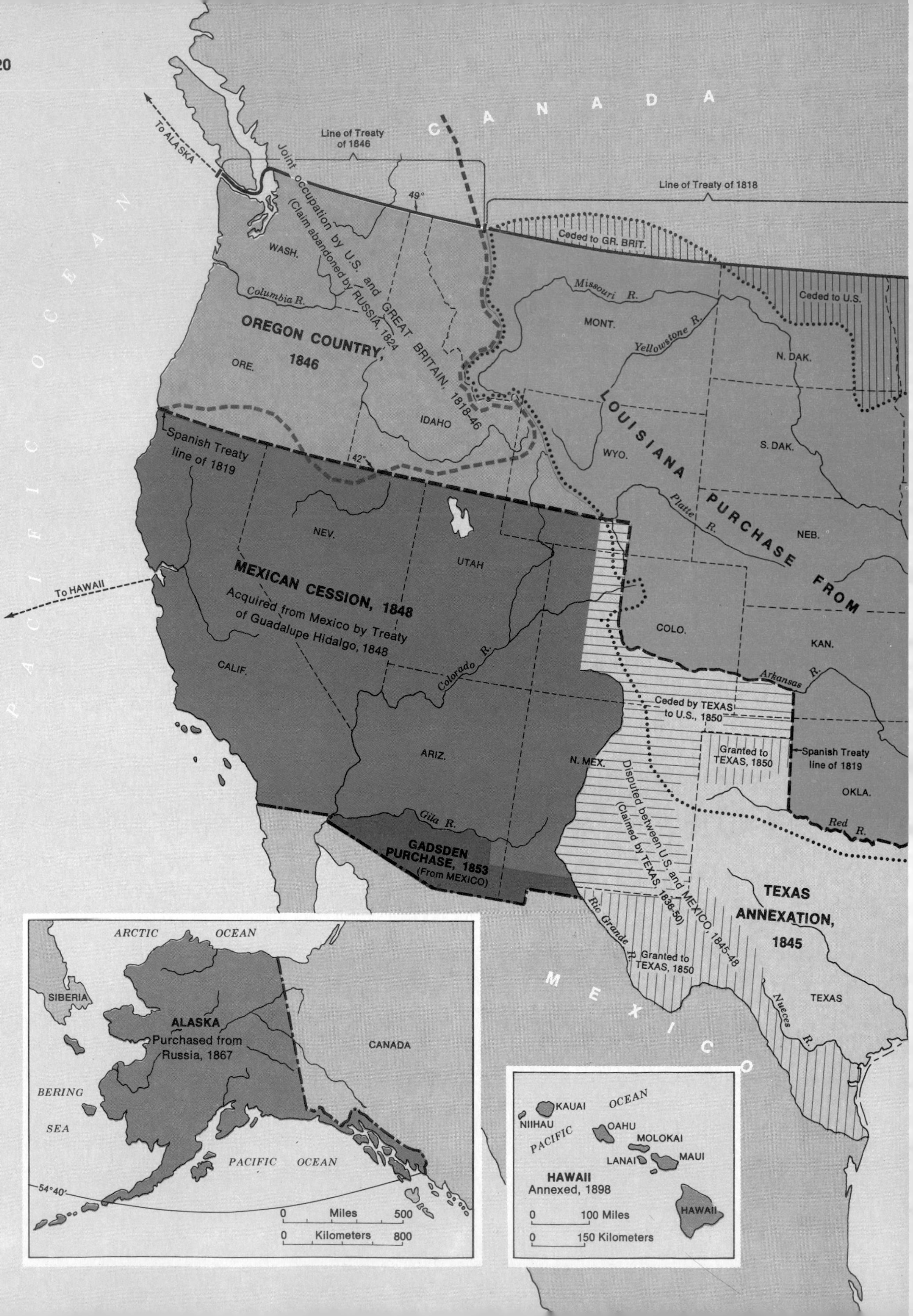

CANADA
PACIFIC OCEAN
To ALASKA
Line of Treaty of 1846
Joint occupation by U.S. and GREAT BRITAIN, 1818-46
(Claim abandoned by RUSSIA, 1824)
49°
Line of Treaty of 1818
Ceded to GR. BRIT.
Ceded to U.S.
WASH.
Columbia R.
Missouri R.
OREGON COUNTRY, 1846
ORE.
MONT.
Yellowstone R.
N. DAK.
LOUISIANA PURCHASE FROM
IDAHO
S. DAK.
WYO.
Spanish Treaty line of 1819
42°
Platte R.
NEB.
NEV.
UTAH
MEXICAN CESSION, 1848
Acquired from Mexico by Treaty of Guadalupe Hidalgo, 1848
To HAWAII
COLO.
KAN.
CALIF.
Colorado R.
Arkansas R.
Ceded by TEXAS to U.S., 1850
Granted to TEXAS, 1850
Spanish Treaty line of 1819
ARIZ.
N. MEX.
OKLA.
Disputed between U.S. and MEXICO, 1845-48
(Claimed by TEXAS, 1836-50)
Red R.
Gila R.
GADSDEN PURCHASE, 1853
(From MEXICO)
TEXAS ANNEXATION, 1845
Rio Grande R.
Granted to TEXAS, 1850
MEXICO
TEXAS
Nueces R.
ARCTIC OCEAN
SIBERIA
ALASKA
Purchased from Russia, 1867
CANADA
BERING SEA
PACIFIC OCEAN
54°40'
0 Miles 500
0 Kilometers 800
KAUAI
OCEAN
NIIHAU
PACIFIC
OAHU
MOLOKAI
LANAI
MAUI
HAWAII
Annexed, 1898
0 100 Miles
0 150 Kilometers
HAWAII

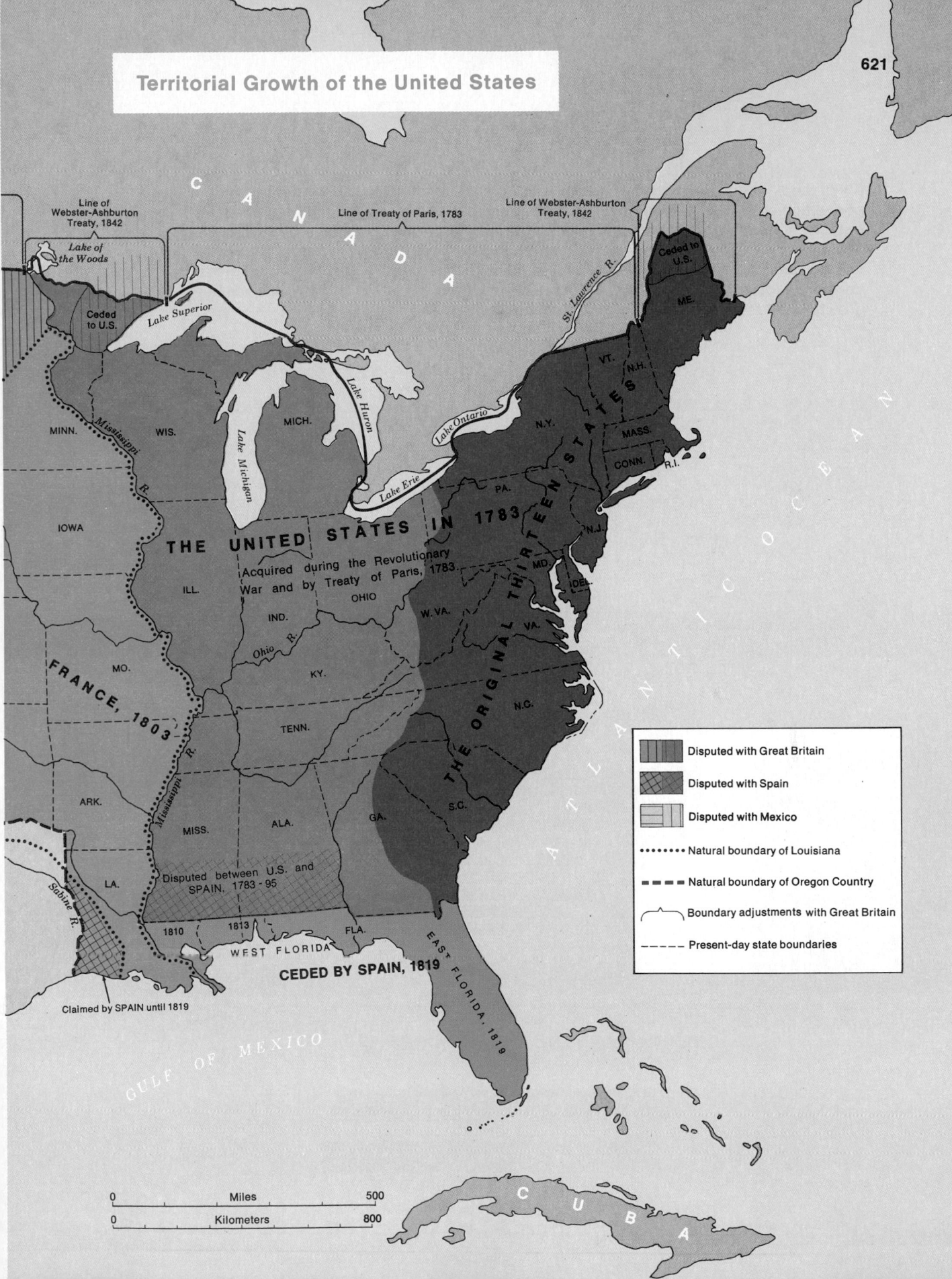

Territorial Growth of the United States

Line of
Webster-Ashburton
Treaty, 1842

Line of Treaty of Paris, 1783

Line of Webster-Ashburton
Treaty, 1842

C A N A D A

*Lake of
the Woods*

Ceded
to U.S.

St. Lawrence R.

Ceded to
U.S.

ME.

Ceded
to U.S.

Lake Superior

MINN.

Mississippi

WIS.

MICH.

Lake Michigan

Lake Huron

VT.

N.H.

N.Y.

Lake Ontario

MASS.

CONN.

R.I.

Lake Erie

PA.

IOWA

THE UNITED STATES IN 1783

Acquired during the Revolutionary
War and by Treaty of Paris, 1783

ILL.

IND.

OHIO

Ohio R.

W. VA.

MD.

N.J.

DEL.

VA.

N. J.

F R A N C E , 1 8 0 3

MO.

KY.

TENN.

Mississippi R.

N.C.

THE ORIGINAL THIRTEEN STATES

ARK.

MISS.

ALA.

GA.

S.C.

Disputed between U.S. and
SPAIN, 1783 - 95

LA.

Sabine R.

1810

1813

FLA.

WEST FLORIDA

EAST FLORIDA - 1819

CEDED BY SPAIN, 1819

Claimed by SPAIN until 1819

G U L F   O F   M E X I C O

A T L A N T I C   O C E A N

C U B A

	Disputed with Great Britain
	Disputed with Spain
	Disputed with Mexico

••••••• Natural boundary of Louisiana

– – – Natural boundary of Oregon Country

⌒ Boundary adjustments with Great Britain

– – – Present-day state boundaries

| 0 | Miles | 500 |
| 0 | Kilometers | 800 |

The American People

When the United States became a nation, the Constitution required a census, or count, of the population every ten years. Since then, Americans have kept a continuous statistical portrait of themselves. America's population has grown from less than 4 million in 1790 to nearly 220 million in 1977. During these years, many Americans have moved from rural areas to urban centers, and in recent decades from central cities to the suburbs. Most states and cities have constantly increased in population. But the most striking change in recent years has been the growth of large metropolitan areas throughout the nation.

Growth of Population in the United States

millions of people

220
200
180
160
140
120
100
80
60
40
20
0

1790   1820   1840   1860   1880   1900   1920   1940   1960   1977

Movement of Population

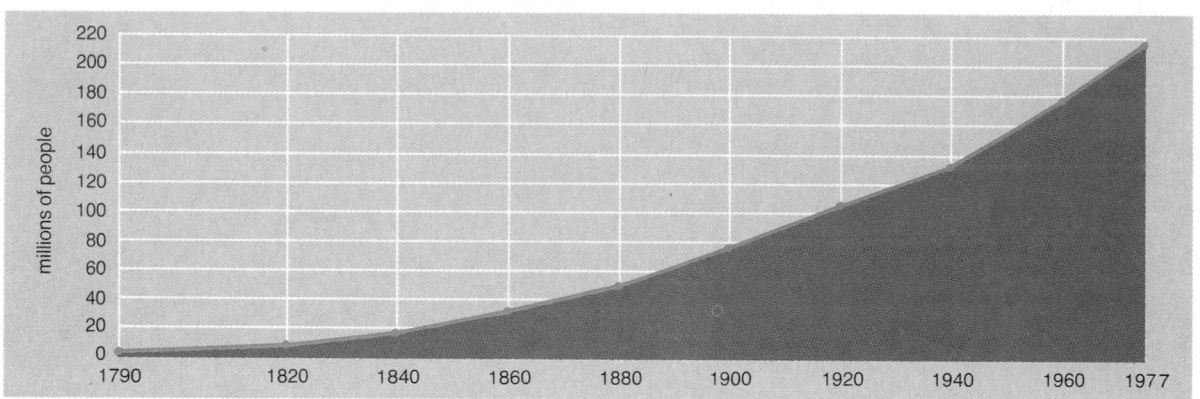

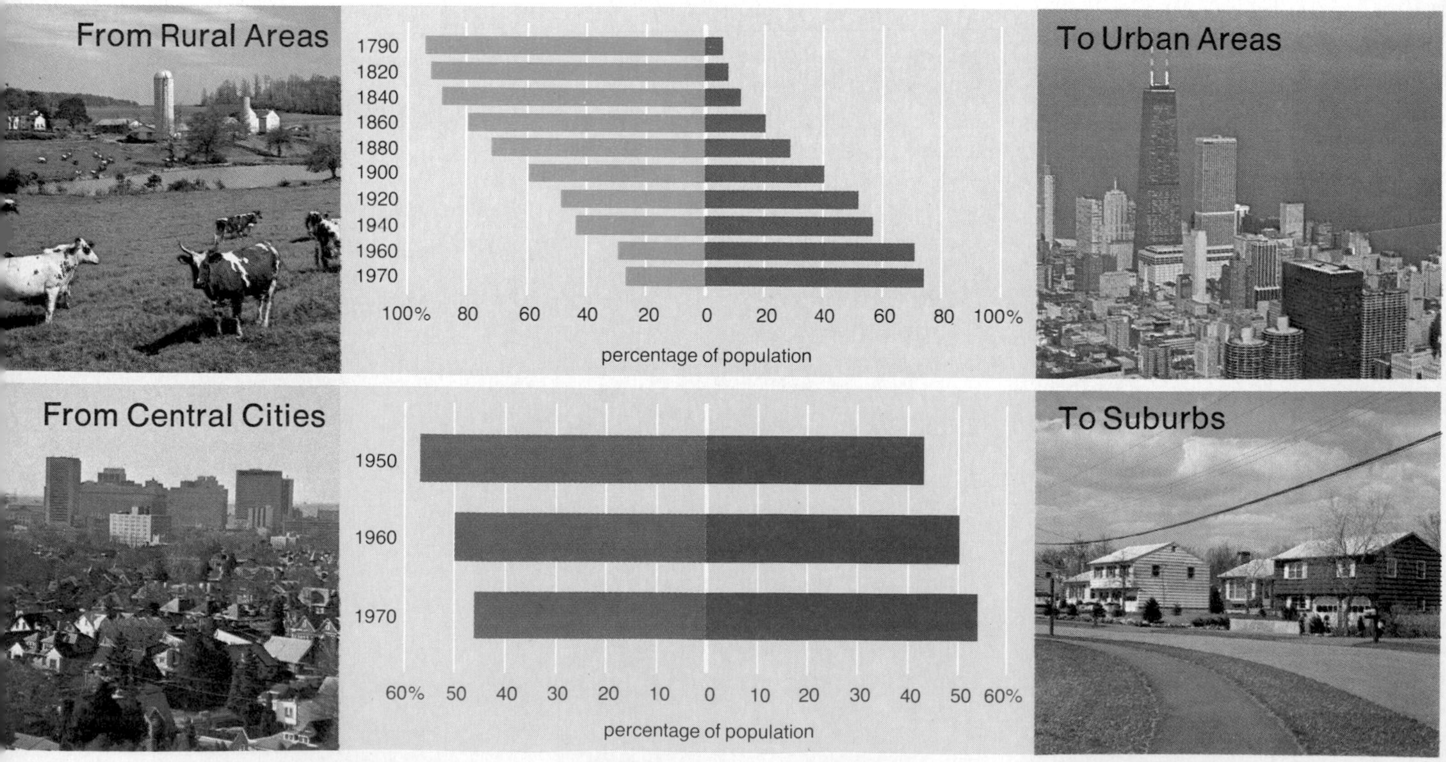

From Rural Areas

To Urban Areas

1790
1820
1840
1860
1880
1900
1920
1940
1960
1970

100% 80   60   40   20   0   20   40   60   80   100%

percentage of population

From Central Cities

To Suburbs

1950

1960

1970

60% 50   40   30   20   10   0   10   20   30   40   50   60%

percentage of population

Population Growth of States and Their Largest Cities

State	Population at first census after entry	State population 1973 (est.)	Represen- tatives in Congress	Largest city in 1973	City population 1890	City population 1930	City population 1973 (est.)
1 Delaware	59,000	573,000	1	Wilmington	61,431	106,597	75,000
2 Pennsylvania	434,000	11,862,000	25	Philadelphia	1,046,964	1,950,961	1,862,000
3 New Jersey	184,000	7,325,000	15	Newark	181,830	442,337	368,000
4 Georgia	83,000	4,818,000	10	Atlanta	65,533	270,366	451,000
5 Connecticut	238,000	3,080,000	6	Hartford	53,230	164,072	149,000
6 Massachusetts	379,000	5,799,000	12	Boston	448,477	781,188	618,000
7 Maryland	320,000	4,074,000	8	Baltimore	434,439	804,874	878,000
8 South Carolina	249,000	2,724,000	6	Columbia	15,353	51,581	112,000
9 New Hampshire	142,000	794,000	2	Manchester	44,126	76,834	84,000
10 Virginia	692,000	4,844,000	10	Norfolk	34,871	129,710	283,000
11 New York	340,000	18,214,000	39	New York	2,507,414	6,930,446	7,647,000
12 North Carolina	394,000	5,302,000	11	Charlotte	11,557	82,675	285,000
13 Rhode Island	69,000	967,000	2	Providence	132,146	252,981	170,000
14 Vermont	154,000	466,000	1	Burlington	14,500	24,789	38,000
15 Kentucky	221,000	3,328,000	7	Louisville	161,129	307,745	336,000
16 Tennessee	106,000	4,095,000	8	Memphis	64,495	253,143	659,000
17 Ohio	231,000	10,743,000	23	Cleveland	261,353	900,429	659,000
18 Louisiana	153,000	3,746,000	8	New Orleans	242,039	458,762	573,000
19 Indiana	147,000	5,304,000	11	Indianapolis	105,436	364,161	728,000
20 Mississippi	75,000	2,317,000	5	Jackson	5,920	48,282	164,000
21 Illinois	55,000	11,176,000	24	Chicago	1,099,850	3,376,438	3,173,000
22 Alabama	128,000	3,546,000	7	Birmingham	26,178	259,678	296,000
23 Maine	298,000	1,039,000	2	Portland	36,425	70,810	61,000
24 Missouri	140,000	4,768,000	10	St. Louis	451,770	821,960	558,000
25 Arkansas	98,000	2,035,000	4	Little Rock	25,874	81,679	142,000
26 Michigan	212,000	9,061,000	19	Detroit	205,876	1,568,662	1,387,000
27 Florida	87,000	7,745,000	15	Jacksonville	17,201	129,549	522,000
28 Texas	213,000	11,828,000	24	Houston	27,557	292,352	1,320,000
29 Iowa	192,000	2,863,000	6	Des Moines	50,093	142,559	199,000
30 Wisconsin	305,000	4,539,000	9	Milwaukee	204,468	578,249	691,000
31 California	93,000	20,652,000	43	Los Angeles	50,395	1,238,048	2,747,000
32 Minnesota	172,000	3,890,000	8	Minneapolis	164,738	464,356	382,000
33 Oregon	52,000	2,219,000	4	Portland	46,385	301,815	378,000
34 Kansas	364,000	2,264,000	5	Wichita	23,853	111,110	261,000
35 West Virginia	442,000	1,788,000	4	Huntington	10,108	75,572	73,000
36 Nevada	42,000	551,000	1	Las Vegas	0	5,165	144,000
37 Nebraska	123,000	1,533,000	3	Omaha	148,514	214,006	377,000
38 Colorado	194,000	2,468,000	5	Denver	106,713	287,861	516,000
39 North Dakota	191,000	635,000	1	Fargo	5,664	28,619	57,000
40 South Dakota	349,000	682,000	2	Sioux Falls	7,205	33,362	74,000
41 Montana	143,000	730,000	2	Billings	836	16,380	67,000
42 Washington	357,000	3,431,000	7	Seattle	42,837	365,583	503,000
43 Idaho	89,000	776,000	2	Boise	2,311	21,544	90,000
44 Wyoming	63,000	353,000	1	Cheyenne	11,690	17,361	44,000
45 Utah	277,000	1,150,000	2	Salt Lake City	44,843	140,267	169,000
46 Oklahoma	1,657,000	2,669,000	6	Oklahoma City	4,151	185,389	374,000
47 New Mexico	360,000	1,099,000	2	Albuquerque	3,785	26,570	274,000
48 Arizona	334,000	2,073,000	4	Phoenix	3,152	48,118	637,000
49 Alaska	229,000	330,000	1	Anchorage	0	2,500	73,000
50 Hawaii	642,000	841,000	2	Honolulu	22,907	138,445	338,000
District of Columbia	8,000 (1800)	734,000	— —	Washington, D.C.	188,932	486,869	734,000

Population of Largest Metropolitan Areas

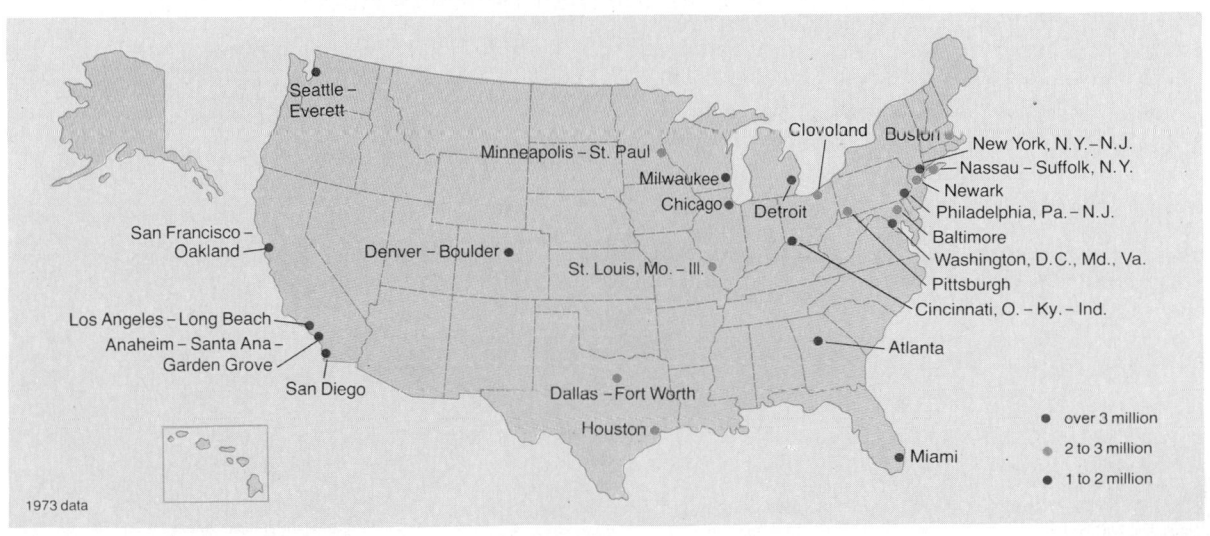

1973 data

Legend:
● over 3 million
● 2 to 3 million
● 1 to 2 million

The people who settled America came from many lands. Indeed, all Americans were immigrants or the descendants of immigrants. The American Indians, the first group of Americans, for example, originally were hunting peoples who came to North America from Asia. Between 1820 and 1974, nearly 50 million people settled in the United States. Germany, Great Britain, Ireland, Italy, and Austria-Hungary accounted for the most immigrants, but large numbers came from many other nations. To describe the varied population that has resulted, the Census Bureau keeps records of different characteristics of the American people. Population breakdowns by race, by age, and by religion are among the most important of these data.

Immigration to the United States

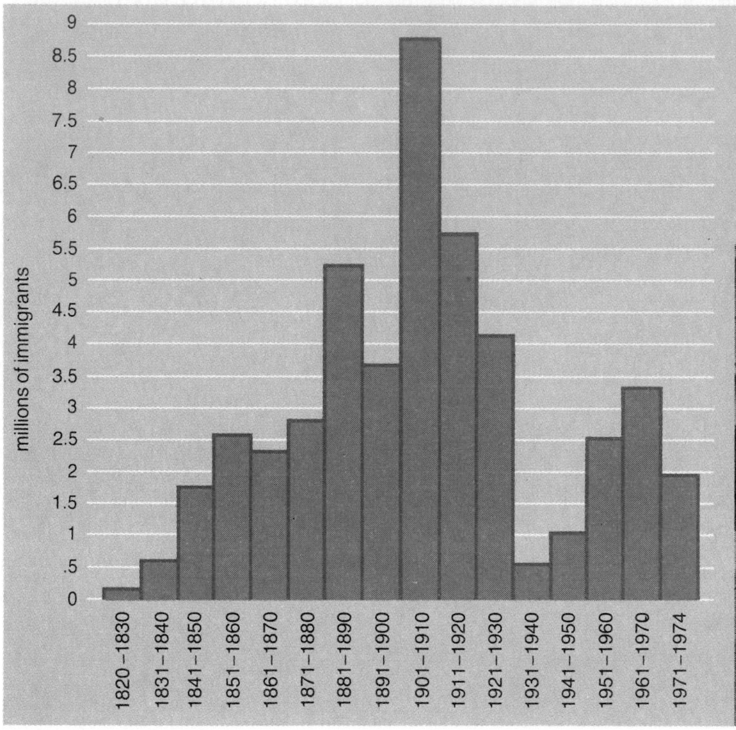

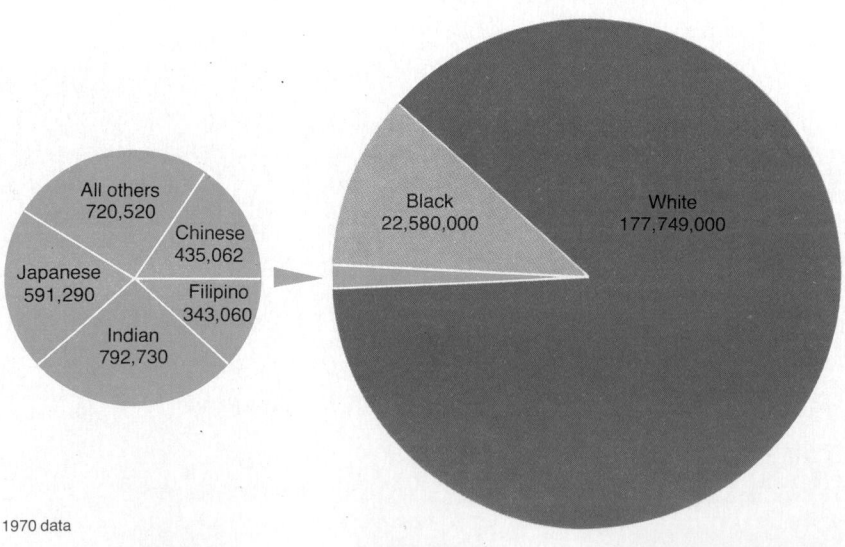

Population Distribution by Racial Backgrounds

All others
720,520

Chinese
435,062

Japanese
591,290

Filipino
343,060

Indian
792,730

Black
22,580,000

White
177,749,000

1970 data

National Backgrounds of Immigrants (1820–1974)

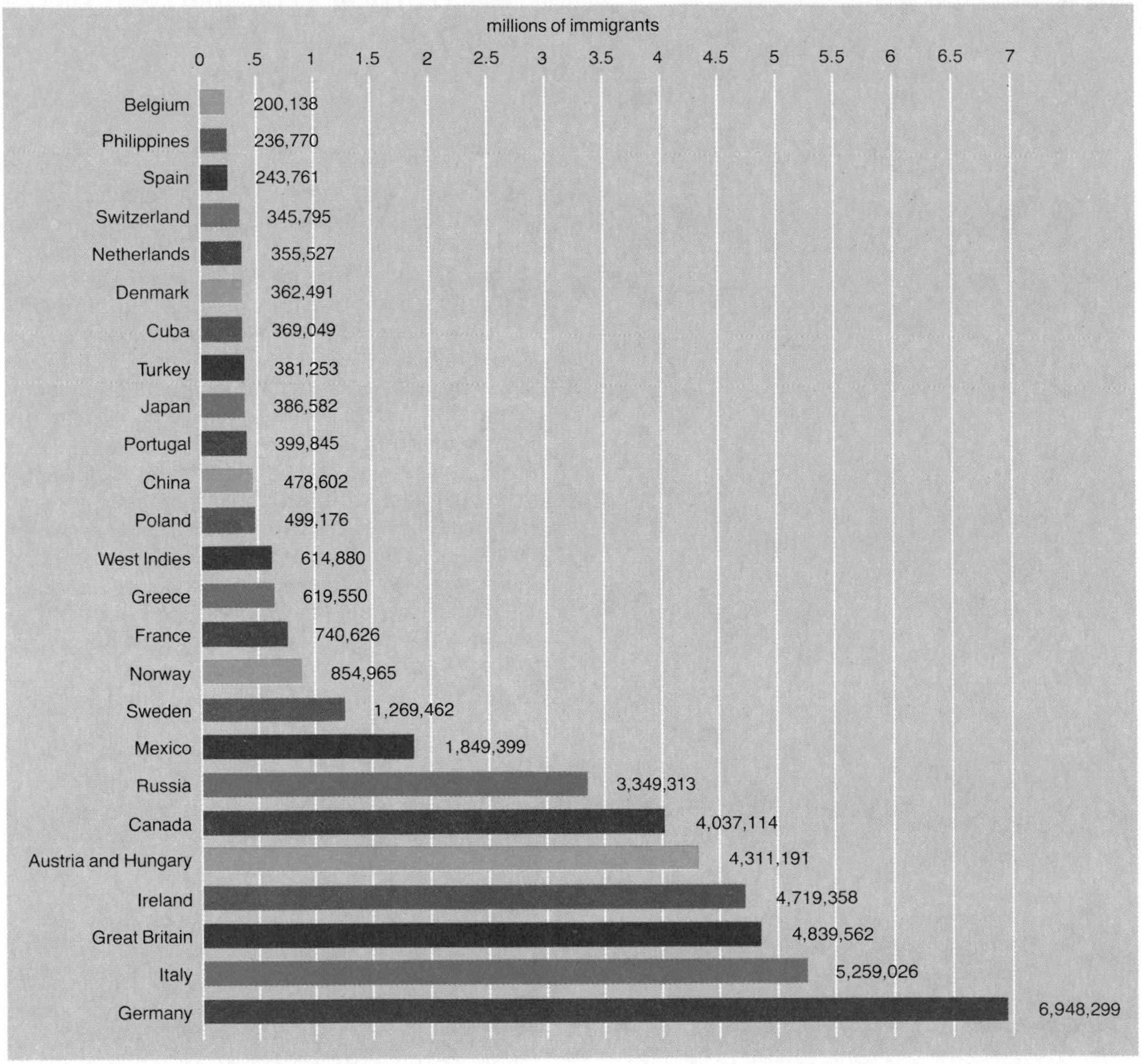

millions of immigrants

Belgium	200,138
Philippines	236,770
Spain	243,761
Switzerland	345,795
Netherlands	355,527
Denmark	362,491
Cuba	369,049
Turkey	381,253
Japan	386,582
Portugal	399,845
China	478,602
Poland	499,176
West Indies	614,880
Greece	619,550
France	740,626
Norway	854,965
Sweden	1,269,462
Mexico	1,849,399
Russia	3,349,313
Canada	4,037,114
Austria and Hungary	4,311,191
Ireland	4,719,358
Great Britain	4,839,562
Italy	5,259,026
Germany	6,948,299

Population Distribution by Age Groups

Distribution by Church Membership

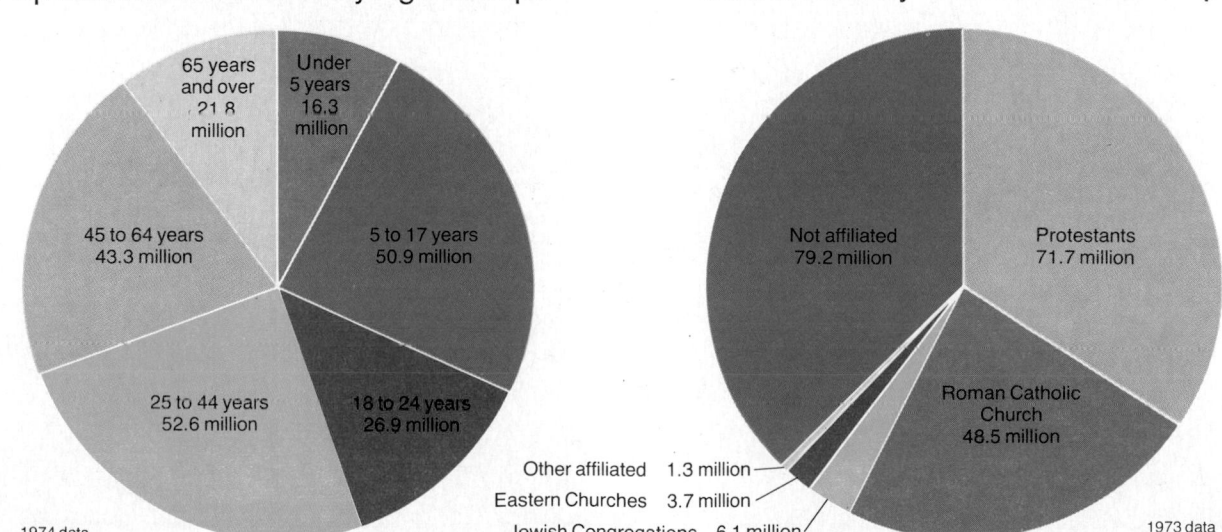

Population Distribution by Age Groups:
- Under 5 years 16.3 million
- 5 to 17 years 50.9 million
- 18 to 24 years 26.9 million
- 25 to 44 years 52.6 million
- 45 to 64 years 43.3 million
- 65 years and over 21.8 million

1974 data

Distribution by Church Membership:
- Not affiliated 79.2 million
- Protestants 71.7 million
- Roman Catholic Church 48.5 million
- Other affiliated 1.3 million
- Eastern Churches 3.7 million
- Jewish Congregations 6.1 million

1973 data

The American Economy

Gross National Product

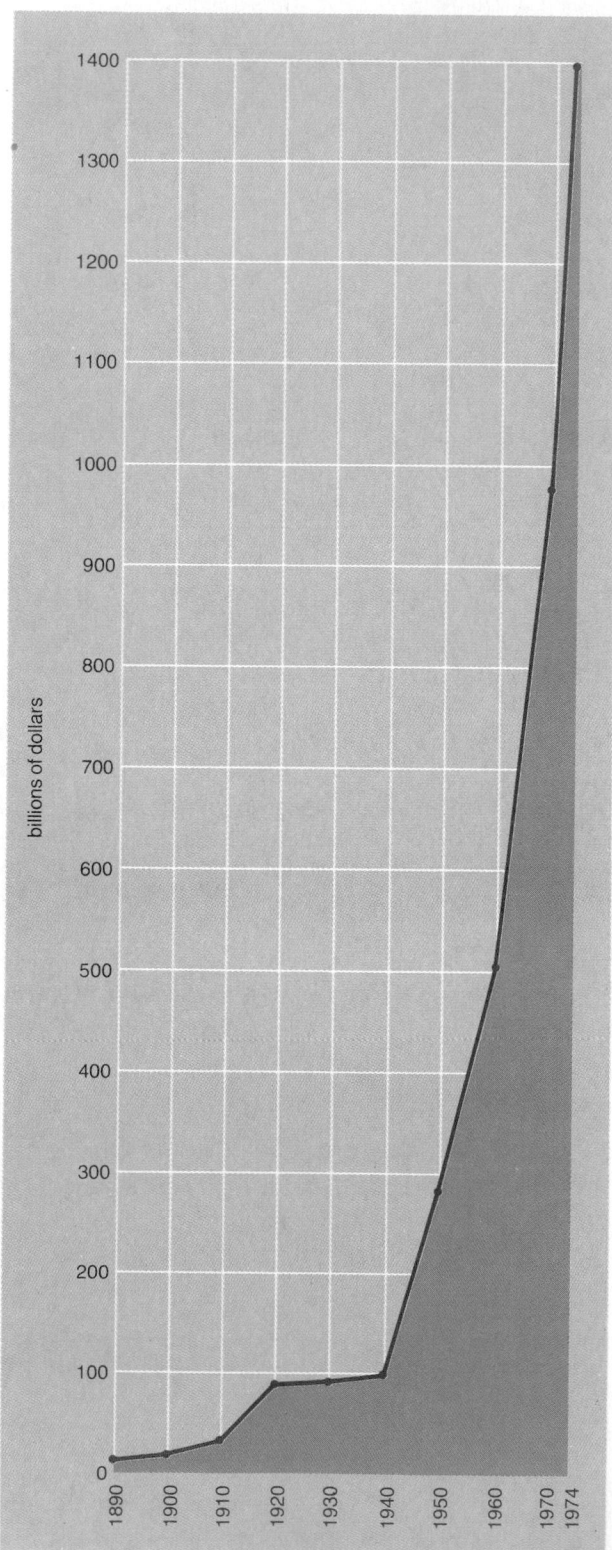

billions of dollars

1400
1300
1200
1100
1000
900
800
700
600
500
400
300
200
100
0

1890 1900 1910 1920 1930 1940 1950 1960 1970 1974

The United States, with its rich resources, advanced technology, and hard-working population, has experienced remarkable economic growth. There are many ways of measuring this growth. One is the Gross National Product (GNP), or the total value of all goods and services produced in the nation. This key measure of economic growth soared from $13.1 billion in 1890 to $1.4 trillion in 1974. Workers' productivity is another indicator of economic progress. For example, each farm worker produced nearly eight times as much food in 1975 as in 1900. The kind of work Americans perform also has changed, with a notable increase in service occupations and government jobs. And the nation's economic growth has reflected American know-how. From the years of hand tools to today's computer-operated machinery, each era has seen major advances which spurred productivity and raised Americans' standards of living.

Major Advances

	1607–1783
POWER	Human muscles Animal muscles Wind and water power
MANUFACTURING MATERIALS	Copper, bronze, iron Wood Clay Plant and animal fibers
FACTORY METHODS	Hand forges and tools Hand-powered equipment
AGRICULTURE	Wooden plows Spades and hoes Axes and other hand tools
TRANSPORTATION	Horses Animal-drawn vehicles Sailing vessels
COMMUNICATION	Hand-operated printing presses Newspapers
MERCHANDISING AND BUSINESS ORGANIZATION	Small shops Peddlers

People Fed by One Farm Worker

1900	6.9 people
1950	15.5 people
1975	55.0 people

Output per Worker

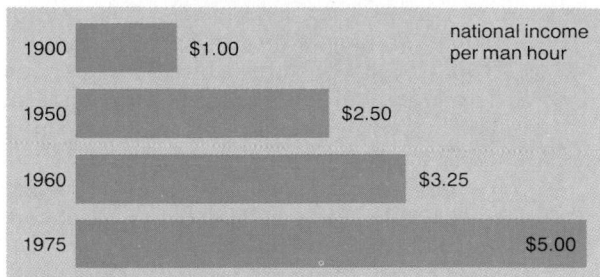

national income per man hour

1900	$1.00
1950	$2.50
1960	$3.25
1975	$5.00

Changes in Workers' Occupations

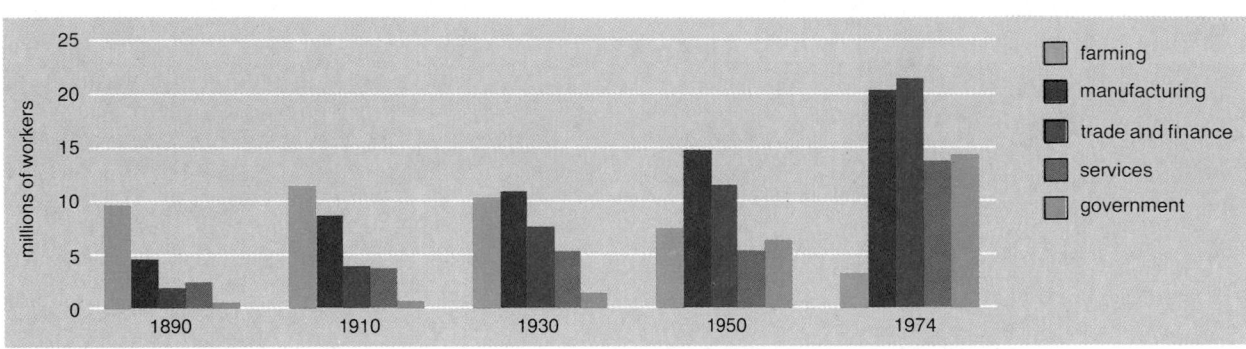

millions of workers

Legend:
- farming
- manufacturing
- trade and finance
- services
- government

Years: 1890, 1910, 1930, 1950, 1974

in American Business and Industry

1783–1850	1850–1900	1900–1920	1920–Present
Steam power	Electric power Internal combustion engines		Atomic energy Solar energy Geothermal energy
Large-scale production of iron	Large-scale production of steel Development of combustion fuels: coal, oil, gas Development of light metals and alloys	Large-scale production of light metals and alloys Development of plastics and synthetics	Large-scale production of plastics and synthetics
Machinery powered by water and steam Interchangeable parts	Mass production, with centralized assembly of interchangeable parts	Conveyor-belt assembly line	Automation Computer-operated machinery
Iron and steel plows Cotton gin Mowing, threshing, and haying machines	McCormick reaper Barbed-wire fencing	Scientific agriculture	Large-scale mechanized agriculture Corporation farms
Canals Clipper ships Development of railroads and steamships	Large-scale steamship and railroad lines City trolleys, elevated trains	Automobiles, trucks, and buses Development of propeller-driven aircraft Subways	Space exploration Monorail trains Supersonic planes
Mechanized printing presses Telegraph Mass-circulation books and magazines	Transatlantic cable Telephones Phonographs Typewriters Cameras	Motion pictures Radios	Television Transistors Magnetic tape Lasers Satellite transmissions
Individual- and family-owned factories and mills General stores	Department stores Chain stores Mail-order houses Growth of corporations Trusts	National advertising Holding companies	Supermarkets Shopping centers Conglomerate corporations Multinational corporations

American economic growth takes on added significance when studied in a world context. The United States occupies less than 7 per cent of the world's land and has less than 6 per cent of its people. Yet it possesses vast natural resources and produces huge amounts of manufactured goods—far out of proportion to its size. A world setting also emphasizes the importance of trade among nations. In the decades since 1850, the value of American exports has increased from $135 million to over $97 billion. During this same period, the value of imports has risen from $211 million to over $100 billion. And the nature of exports and imports changed during this period. For example, exports of raw materials generally have declined, while exports of manufactured products have risen. In the inward and outward flow of commerce, America's neighbors to the north and south—Canada and Latin America—together account for more than a third of the nation's trade. Western Europe and Asia, too, have become equally important areas in America's trade.

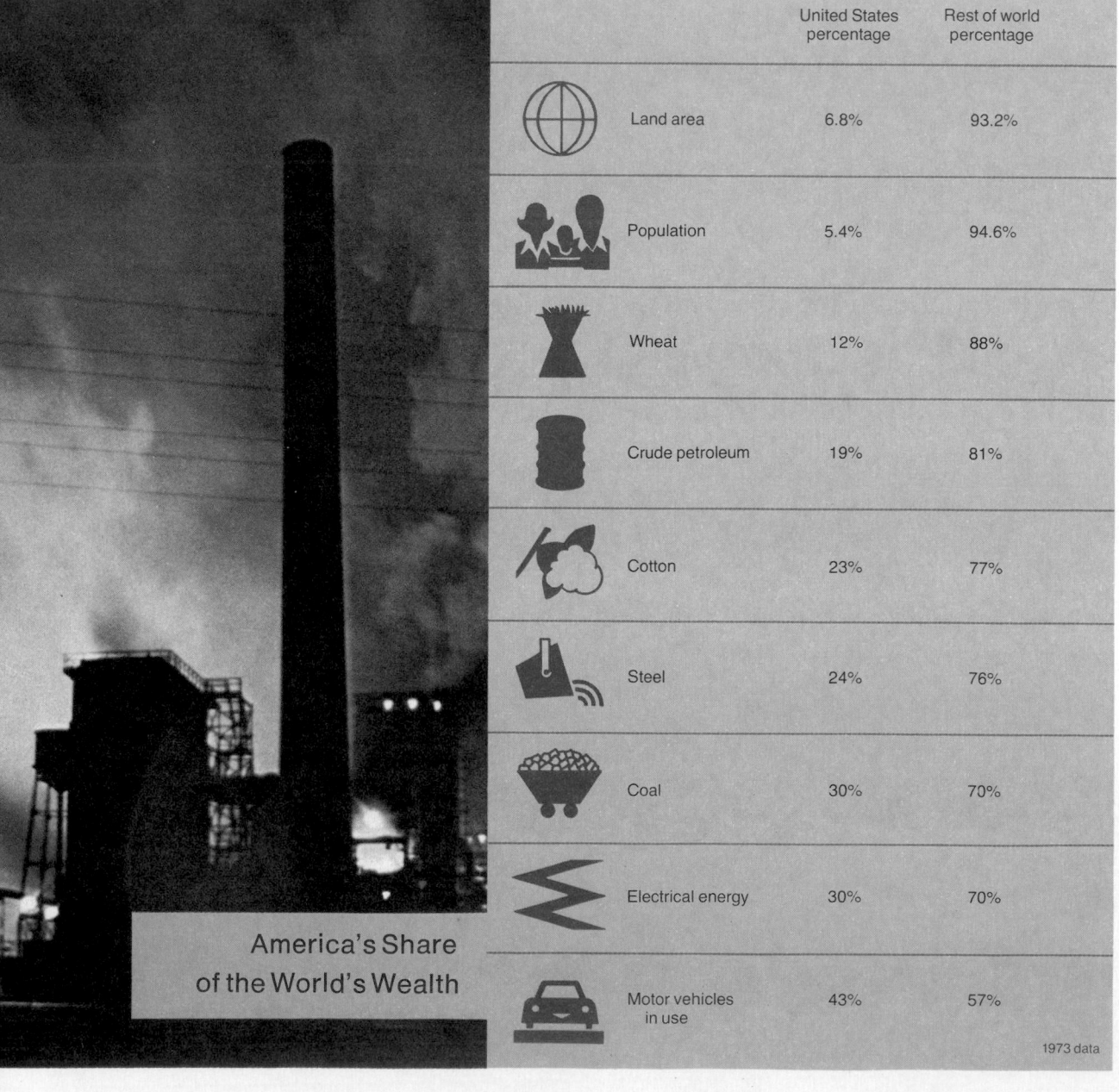

America's Share of the World's Wealth

		United States percentage	Rest of world percentage
	Land area	6.8%	93.2%
	Population	5.4%	94.6%
	Wheat	12%	88%
	Crude petroleum	19%	81%
	Cotton	23%	77%
	Steel	24%	76%
	Coal	30%	70%
	Electrical energy	30%	70%
	Motor vehicles in use	43%	57%

1973 data

America's Exports

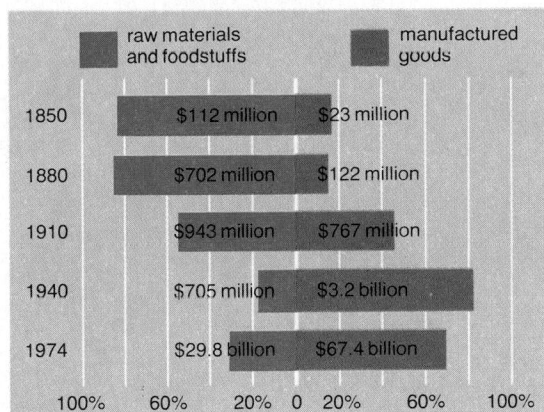

	raw materials and foodstuffs	manufactured goods
1850	$112 million	$23 million
1880	$702 million	$122 million
1910	$943 million	$767 million
1940	$705 million	$3.2 billion
1974	$29.8 billion	$67.4 billion

America's Imports

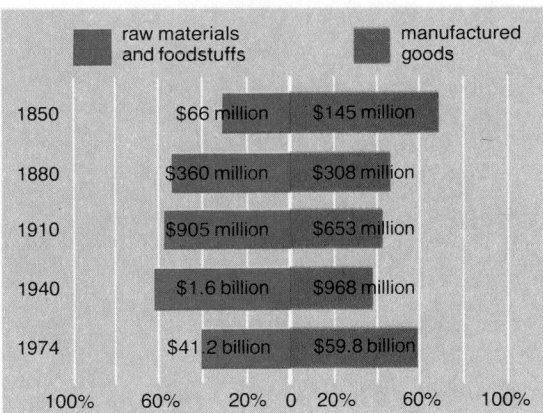

	raw materials and foodstuffs	manufactured goods
1850	$66 million	$145 million
1880	$360 million	$308 million
1910	$905 million	$653 million
1940	$1.6 billion	$968 million
1974	$41.2 billion	$59.8 billion

America's World Trade

ASIA

CANADA

Bering Sea

to Asia $25.8 (26.5%)

from Asia $27.5 (28.7%)

to Canada $19.9 (20.6%)

from Canada $22.3 (23.2%)

from Communist Europe $.9 (.9%)

to Communist Europe $1.4 (1.5%)

from Western Europe $23.4 (24.4%)

to Western Europe $28.6 (29.6%)

UNITED STATES

EUROPE

Pacific Ocean

to Australia and Oceania $2.7 (2.9%)

from Australia and Oceania $1.5 (1.6%)

from Latin America $13.7 (14.3%)

to Latin America $14.5 (15.0%)

CENTRAL AMERICA

Atlantic Ocean

AFRICA

to Africa $3.7 (3.9%)

from Africa $6.6 (6.9%)

SOUTH AMERICA

AUSTRALIA

1974 data, in billions of dollars

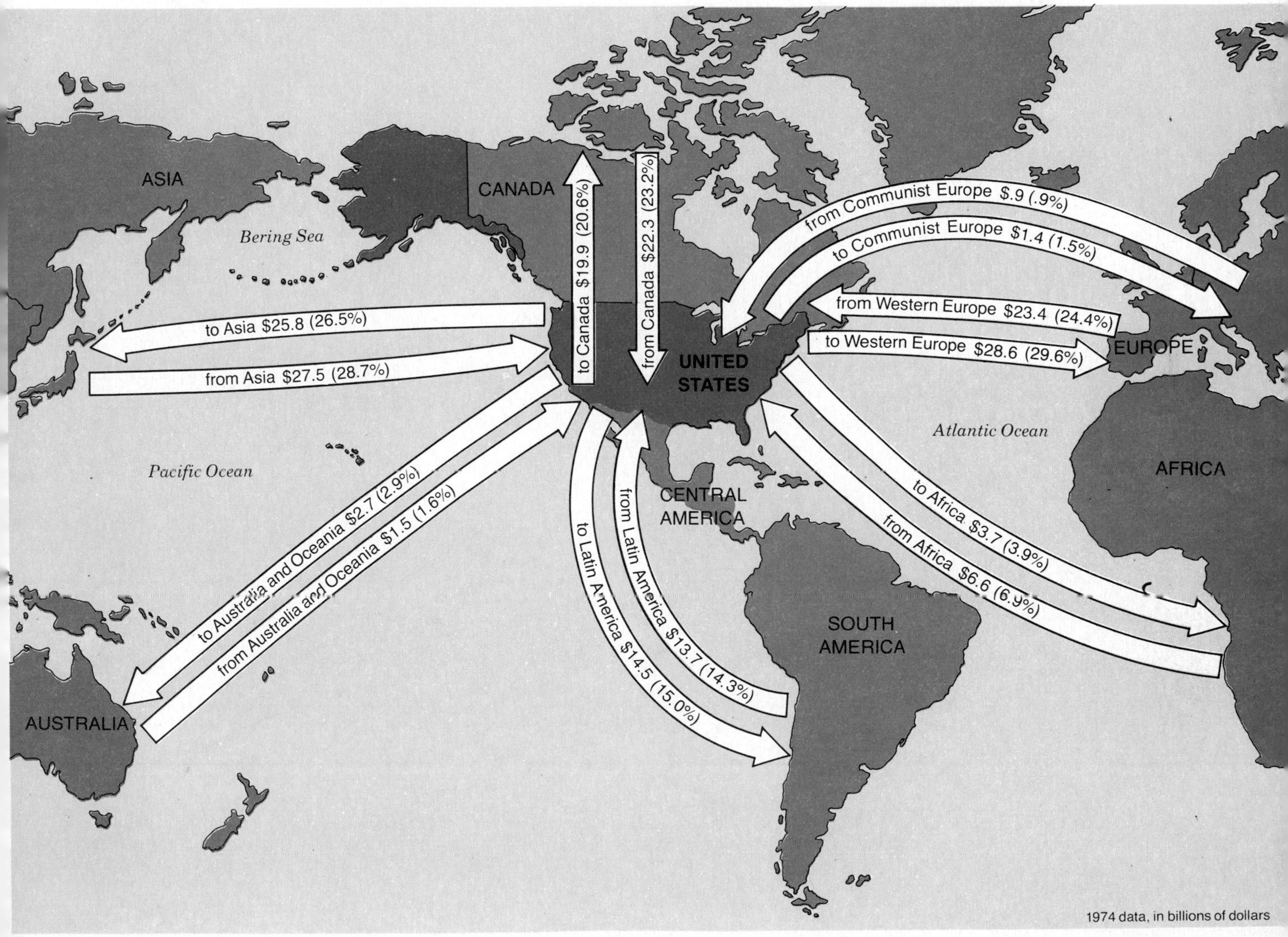

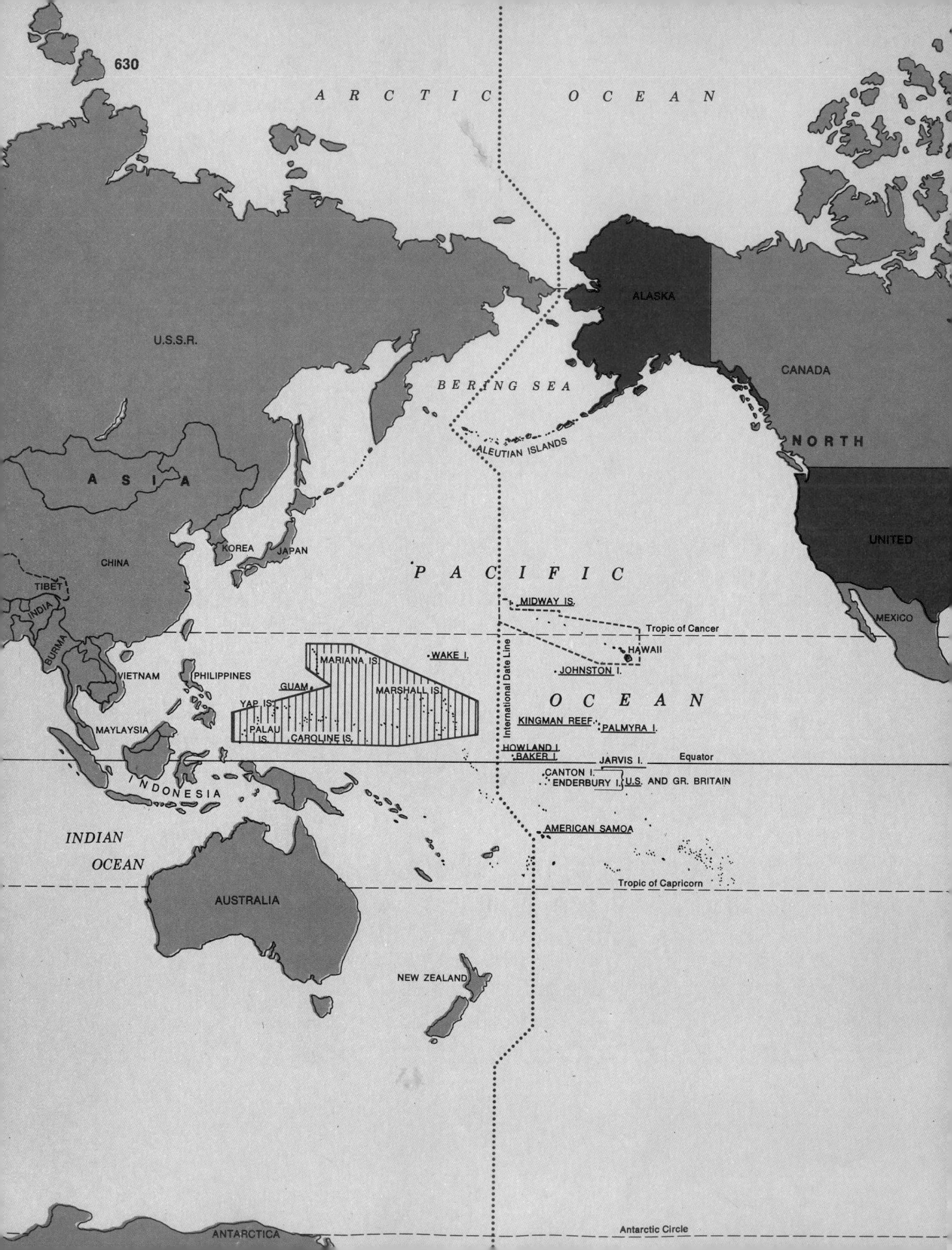

The United States and the World

GREENLAND

Arctic Circle

ICELAND

CANADA

AMERICA

STATES

ATLANTIC

OCEAN

CUBA

PUERTO RICO
VIRGIN IS.

CENTRAL AMERICA

CANAL ZONE

VENEZUELA

COLOMBIA

ECUADOR

PERU

BOLIVIA

SOUTH
AMERICA

BRAZIL

PARAGUAY

CHILE

URUGUAY

ARGENTINA

NORWAY

SWEDEN

FINLAND

GREAT
BRITAIN

IRELAND

GER. POLAND

E U R O P E

FRANCE

PORTUGAL SPAIN

ITALY

MOROCCO

ALGERIA

LIBYA

TUNISIA

MAURITANIA

MALI

NIGER CHAD

A F R I C A

LIBERIA

GHANA

NIGERIA

EGYPT

SUDAN

ETHIOPIA

ZAIRE

SOMALIA

KENYA

TANZANIA

ANGOLA

S.W. AFRICA

MALAGASY

REPUBLIC OF
SOUTH AFRICA

U.S.S.R.

A S I A

TURKEY

SYRIA

ISRAEL

IRAQ

IRAN

AFGHANISTAN

PAKISTAN

SAUDI
ARABIA

INDIA

INDIAN

OCEAN

United States of America

VIRGIN IS. U.S. possessions and other areas associated
with the U.S. (underlined)

U.N. trusteeship area administered by the U.S.

The American Government

Growth and change—in the land, the people, and the economy—have been reflected in American government at all levels. Figures on government expenses and income tell a good deal about the changes in American society. For instance, in recent years state and local government spending has risen sharply, with such services as education and public welfare costing far more today than in 1900. Expenses in the federal government, too, have increased rapidly in recent decades, especially for income security and national defense. And the sources of federal income have changed. Individual and corporation income taxes, plus social security taxes, now provide most of the money in the federal budget.

State and Local Government Expenses Today

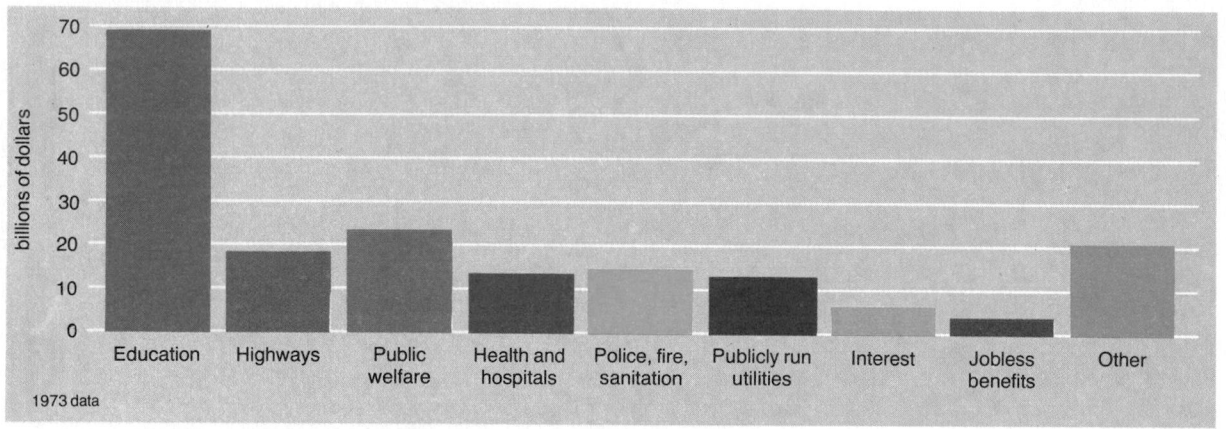

1973 data

State and Local Expenses: 1900–1970

	1900	1910	1920	1930	1940	1950	1960	1970
Education	$255 million	$577 million	$1.7 billion	$2.3 billion	$2.6 billion	$7.2 billion	$18.7 billion	$52.7 billion
Highways	$175 million	$419 million	$1.3 billion	$1.7 billion	$1.6 billion	$3.8 billion	$9.4 billion	$16.4 billion
Public welfare	$37 million	$52 million	$119 million	$444 million	$1.2 billion	$2.9 billion	$4.4 billion	$14.7 billion
Health and hospitals	$60 million	$108 million	$258 million	$456 million	$609 million	$1.7 billion	$3.8 billion	$9.7 billion
Police, fire, sanitation	$141 million	$262 million	$537 million	$751 million	$807 million	$2.1 billion	$4.6 billion	$9.9 billion
Publicly run utilities	$82 million	$186 million	$359 million	$518 million	$1.3 billion	$2.7 billion	$5.1 billion	$9.4 billion
Interest	$68 million	$147 million	$382 million	$741 million	$653 million	$458 million	$1.7 billion	$4.4 billion
Jobless benefits	— —	— —	— —	— —	$494 million	$1.8 billion	$2.4 billion	$2.7 billion
Other	$277 million	$506 million	$998 million	$1.5 billion	$2.0 billion	$5.1 billion	$11 billion	$28.1 billion
Total*	$1.1 billion	$2.3 billion	$5.7 billion	$8.4 billion	$11.2 billion	$27.9 billion	$70 billion	$148.1 billion

*Total may not equal total of columns or of rows because all figures are rounded.

The Federal Budget Today

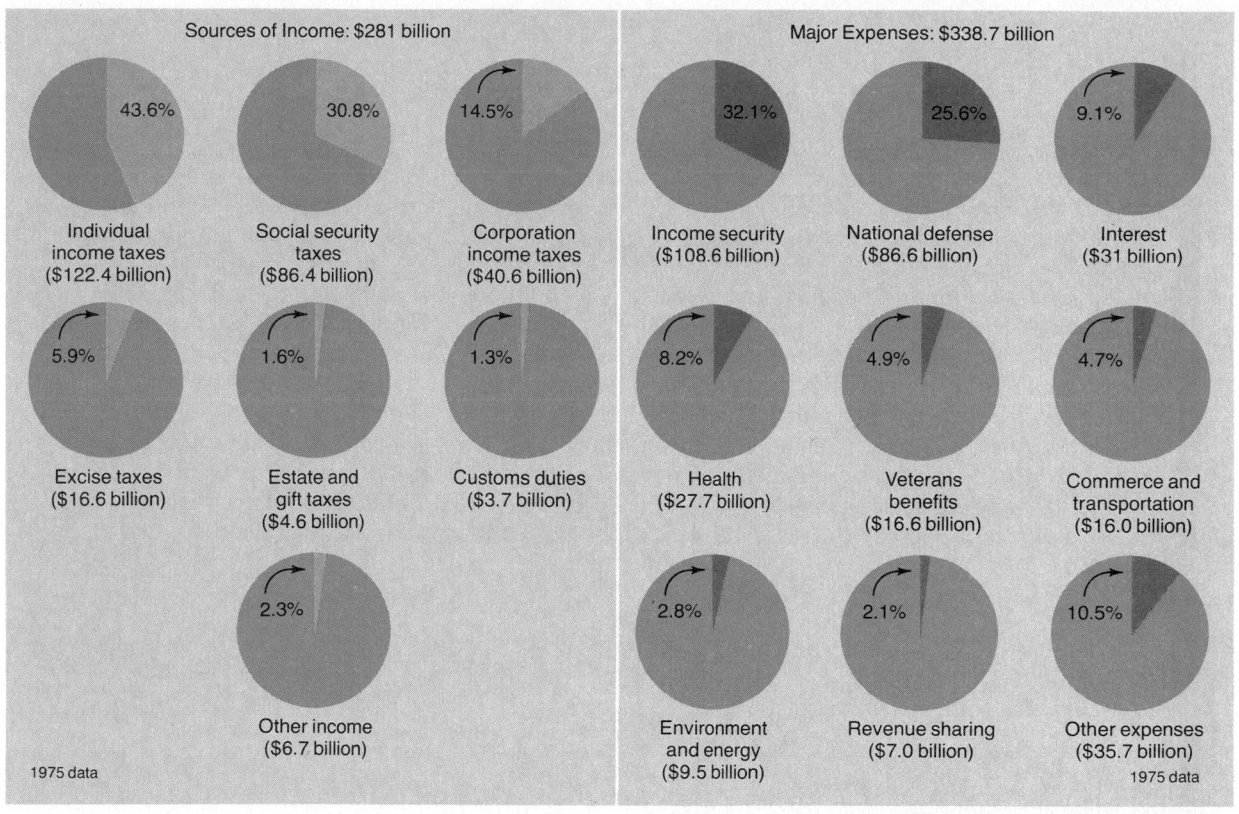

Sources of Income: $281 billion

- Individual income taxes ($122.4 billion) — 43.6%
- Social security taxes ($86.4 billion) — 30.8%
- Corporation income taxes ($40.6 billion) — 14.5%
- Excise taxes ($16.6 billion) — 5.9%
- Estate and gift taxes ($4.6 billion) — 1.6%
- Customs duties ($3.7 billion) — 1.3%
- Other income ($6.7 billion) — 2.3%

1975 data

Major Expenses: $338.7 billion

- Income security ($108.6 billion) — 32.1%
- National defense ($86.6 billion) — 25.6%
- Interest ($31 billion) — 9.1%
- Health ($27.7 billion) — 8.2%
- Veterans benefits ($16.6 billion) — 4.9%
- Commerce and transportation ($16.0 billion) — 4.7%
- Environment and energy ($9.5 billion) — 2.8%
- Revenue sharing ($7.0 billion) — 2.1%
- Other expenses ($35.7 billion) — 10.5%

1975 data

Federal Income: 1900–1970

	Customs duties	Sale of public lands	Excise Taxes	Individual income taxes	Corporation income taxes	Social insurance taxes	Other income	Total*
1900	$233.2 million	$2.8 million	$284.1 million	––	––	––	$47.2 million	$376.2 million
1910	$333.7 million	$6.4 million	$267.3 million	––	––	––	$68.3 million	$675.5 million
1920	$322.9 million	$1.9 million	$901.1 million	$3.9 billion	––	––	$1.6 billion	$6.7 billion
1930	$587 million	$.4 million	$565.1 million	$1.1 billion	$1.3 billion	––	$.6 billion	$4.2 billion
1940	$348.6 million	$.1 million	$1.9 billion	$1.0 billion	$1.1 billion	$.8 billion	$.7 billion	$5.9 billion
1950	$422.7 million	––	$7.6 billion	$17.2 billion	$10.9 billion	$2.9 billion	$2.5 billion	$41.3 billion
1960	$1.1 billion	––	$11.6 billion	$40.7 billion	$21.5 billion	$14.7 billion	$2.8 billion	$92.5 billion
1970	$2.4 billion	––	$15.8 billion	$90.4 billion	$32.8 billion	$45.3 billion	$7.0 billion	$193.7 billion

Federal Expenses: 1900–1970

	Income security	National defense	Interest	Health	Veterans benefits	Other	Total*
1900	––	$191 million	$40 million	––	$141 million	$149 million	$521 million
1910	––	$284 million	$21 million	––	$161 million	$228 million	$694 million
1920	––	$4 billion	$1 billion	––	$332 million	$1 billion	$6.4 billion
1930	––	$734 million	$697 million	––	$821 million	$1.1 billion	$3.3 billion
1940	$3.1 billion	$1.5 billion	$1.1 billion	––	$552 million	$2.8 billion	$9.1 billion
1950	$2.0 billion	$13 billion	$5.8 billion	––	$6.6 billion	$11.8 billion	$39.6 billion
1960	$18.2 billion	$45.9 billion	$8.3 billion	$.8 billion	$5.4 billion	$13 billion	$92.2 billion
1970	$43.8 billion	$80.3 billion	$18.3 billion	$13.1 billion	$8.7 billion	$35.2 billion	$196.6 billion

*Total may not equal total of columns or of rows because all figures are rounded.

The American Achievement

In 1976 the United States celebrated its 200th birthday as a nation. Its people knew that they faced difficult problems—abolishing poverty, providing equal opportunity for every American, controlling pollution of the environment. Yet they could look back over two centuries of impressive achievement. Some things could not be shown with statistics: faith in American values, pride in American democracy. Some things could only be suggested by statistics: the reduction of back-breaking labor, the growth of tolerance and understanding. Still, certain figures had clear and hopeful meaning. They showed, for instance, a steady decline in the death rate. The average life expectancy of Americans doubled during these 200 years. The average workweek was cut almost in half between 1850 and 1976. Family income rose sharply, as did the percentage of families who owned their own homes. More and more students completed their high school education; more and more high school graduates went on to college. These and other statistics provided solid evidence that Americans were a resourceful, hard-working people who despite their problems had ample reason for confidence in the future.

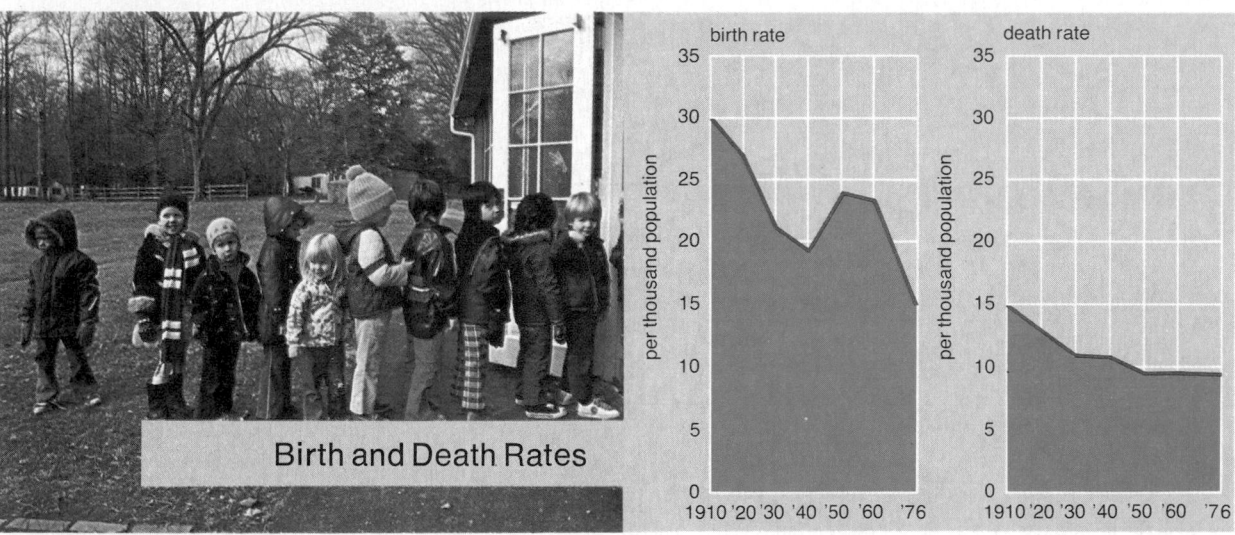

Birth and Death Rates

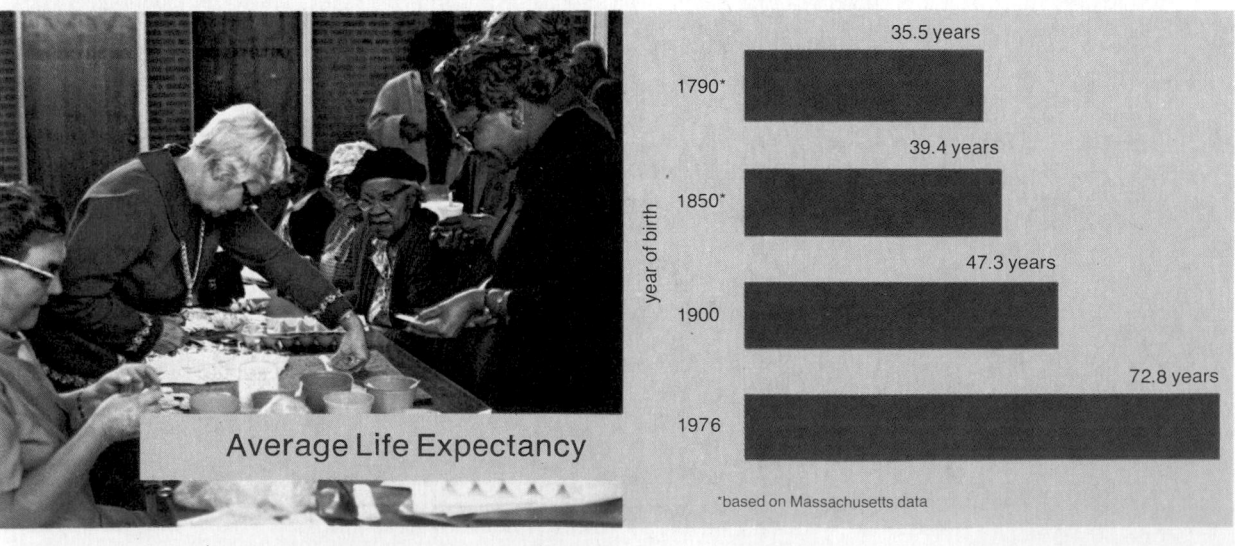

Average Life Expectancy

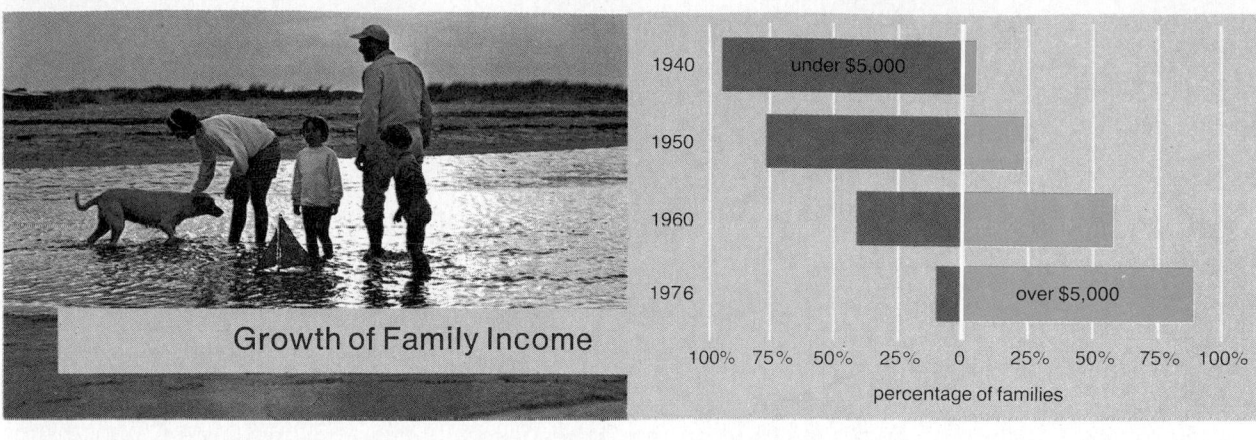

Growth of Family Income

1940   under $5,000
1950
1960
1976   over $5,000

100% 75% 50% 25% 0 25% 50% 75% 100%

percentage of families

Average Workweek

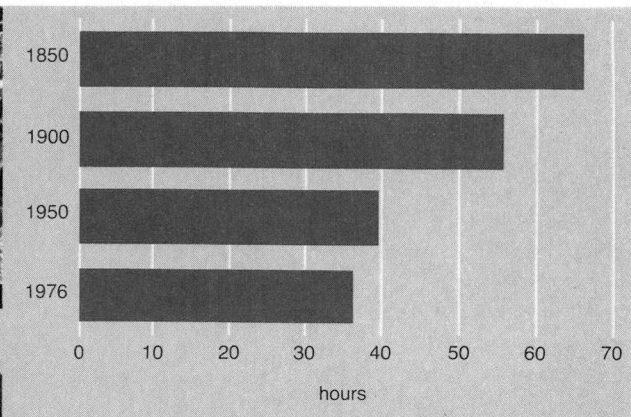

1850
1900
1950
1976

0   10   20   30   40   50   60   70

hours

Growth of Home Ownership

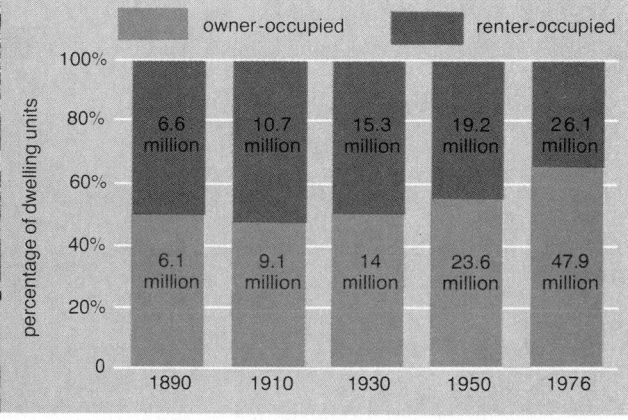

owner-occupied   renter-occupied

percentage of dwelling units

100%
80% | 6.6 million | 10.7 million | 15.3 million | 19.2 million | 26.1 million
60%
40% | 6.1 million | 9.1 million | 14 million | 23.6 million | 47.9 million
20%
0

1890   1910   1930   1950   1976

High School / College Enrollment

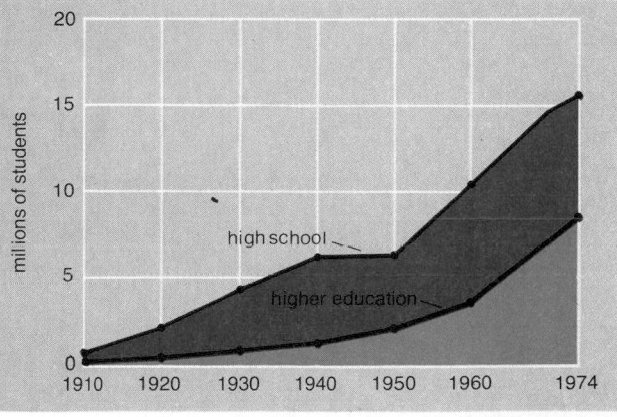

20

15

millions of students

10

5

high school

higher education

1910   1920   1930   1940   1950   1960   1974

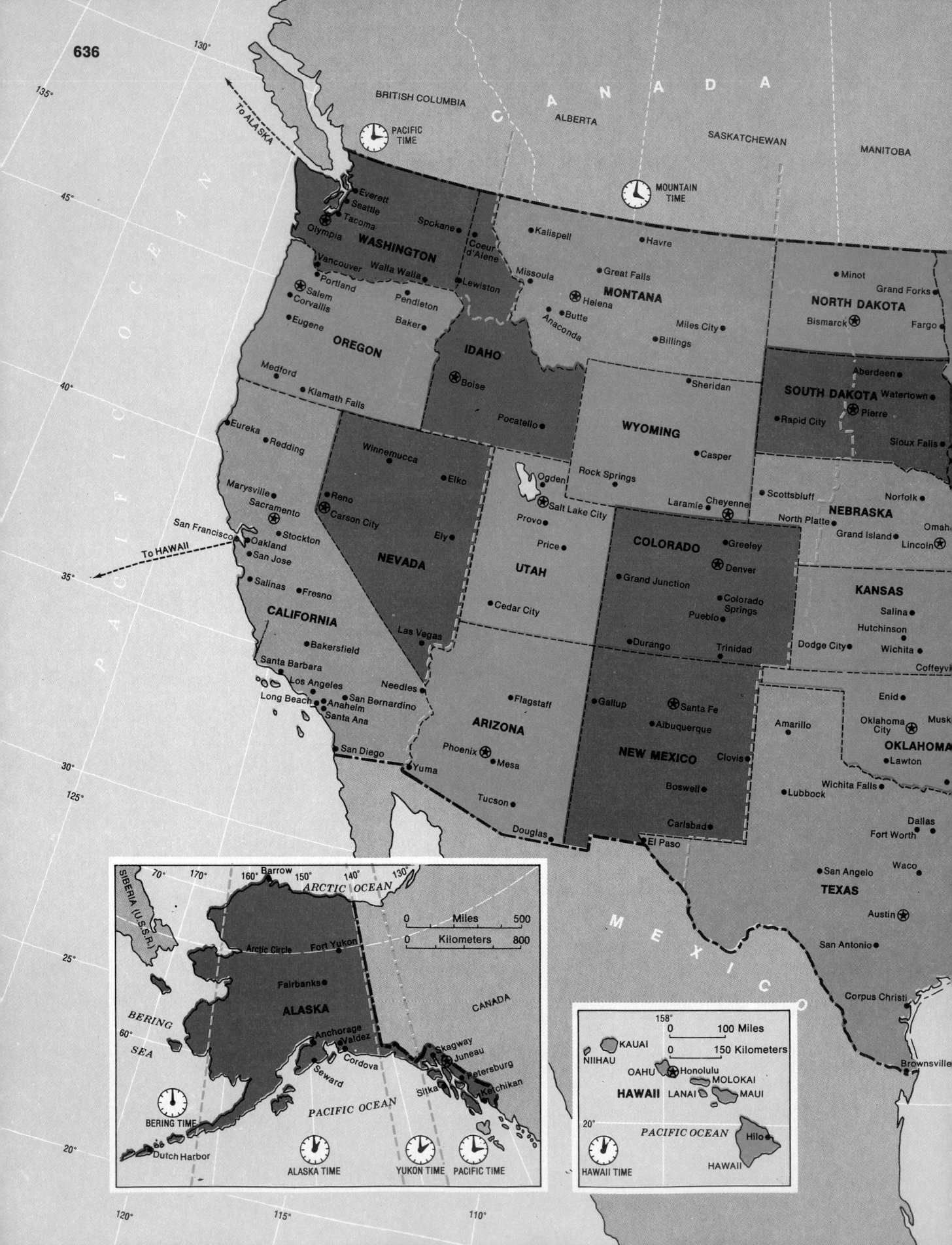

636

CANADA

BRITISH COLUMBIA   ALBERTA   SASKATCHEWAN   MANITOBA

PACIFIC TIME

MOUNTAIN TIME

WASHINGTON
Everett
Seattle
Tacoma
Olympia
Vancouver
Spokane
Coeur d'Alene
Lewiston
Walla Walla
Kalispell
Havre

OREGON
Portland
Salem
Corvallis
Eugene
Medford
Pendleton
Baker
Missoula

IDAHO
Boise
Pocatello

MONTANA
Great Falls
Helena
Butte
Anaconda
Miles City
Billings
Minot
Grand Forks

NORTH DAKOTA
Bismarck
Fargo

Klamath Falls

Eureka
Redding
Marysville
Sacramento
Stockton
San Francisco
Oakland
San Jose
Salinas
Fresno

NEVADA
Winnemucca
Elko
Reno
Carson City
Ely

WYOMING
Sheridan
Rock Springs
Casper

Ogden
Salt Lake City
Provo
Price

UTAH
Cedar City

Laramie
Cheyenne

SOUTH DAKOTA
Aberdeen
Watertown
Pierre
Rapid City
Sioux Falls

COLORADO
Greeley
Denver
Grand Junction
Colorado Springs
Pueblo
Durango
Trinidad

Scottsbluff
North Platte
Grand Island
Lincoln

NEBRASKA
Omah...

KANSAS
Salina
Hutchinson
Wichita
Dodge City
Coffeyvi...

CALIFORNIA
Bakersfield
Santa Barbara
Los Angeles
San Bernardino
Long Beach
Anaheim
Santa Ana
San Diego

Las Vegas
Needles

ARIZONA
Flagstaff
Phoenix
Mesa
Yuma
Tucson

Gallup

NEW MEXICO
Santa Fe
Albuquerque
Clovis
Boswell
Carlsbad
El Paso

Amarillo

OKLAHOMA
Enid
Oklahoma City
Musk...
Lawton

Wichita Falls
Lubbock

Dallas
Fort Worth
San Angelo
Waco

TEXAS

MEXICO

Austin
San Antonio
Corpus Christi
Brownsville

To ALASKA
To HAWAII

PACIFIC OCEAN

SIBERIA (U.S.S.R.)

ARCTIC OCEAN
Barrow

Arctic Circle   Fort Yukon

Miles   0   500
Kilometers   0   800

Fairbanks

ALASKA

CANADA

BERING SEA

Anchorage
Valdez
Seward
Cordova
Skagway
Juneau
Petersburg
Sitka
Ketchikan

Dutch Harbor

BERING TIME

ALASKA TIME   YUKON TIME   PACIFIC TIME

PACIFIC OCEAN

158°
0   100 Miles
0   150 Kilometers

KAUAI
NIIHAU
OAHU   Honolulu
MOLOKAI
LANAI   MAUI

HAWAII

20°

HAWAII TIME

PACIFIC OCEAN

Hilo
HAWAII

States and Cities of the United States

ONTARIO　　　　　QUEBEC

CENTRAL TIME

EASTERN TIME

CANADA

NEW BRUNSWICK

NOVA SCOTIA

Lake Superior

Hibbing
Duluth
Superior
Sault Ste. Marie

MINNESOTA

St. Paul
Minneapolis
Rochester

WISCONSIN

Eau Claire
Green Bay
Oshkosh

MICHIGAN

Lake Huron

Lake Michigan

Caribou
Bangor
MAINE
Augusta
Lewiston
Portland

Montpelier
Burlington
VT.
N.H.
Concord
Manchester

NEW YORK

MASS.
Boston
Worcester

Mason City

IOWA

Sioux City
Cedar Rapids
Dubuque
Des Moines
Davenport

Madison
Milwaukee
Racine
Rockford
Chicago

Grand Rapids
Flint
Lansing
Kalamazoo

Detroit

Lake Erie
Cleveland
Erie

Buffalo
Rochester

Syracuse
Utica
Schenectady
Albany
Troy

Binghamton
Scranton

Hartford
CONN.
R.I.
Providence

Newark
New York
Trenton

Lake Ontario

Peoria

ILLINOIS

Springfield

South Bend
Gary
Fort Wayne

INDIANA

Indianapolis

Akron
Canton

OHIO

Dayton
Columbus
Cincinnati

Warren
Youngstown
Pittsburgh
Wheeling

PENNSYLVANIA

Harrisburg
York

Philadelphia
Camden
N.J.

DEL.
Dover

St. Joseph
Hannibal

Kansas City
Topeka

St. Louis
East St. Louis

Evansville

Covington
Frankfort
Louisville
Lexington

Charleston
Huntington

W. VA.

Washington
Annapolis
MD.

Baltimore

Jefferson City

MISSOURI

Springfield
Cape Girardeau

Cairo
Paducah

KENTUCKY

Owensboro
Middlesboro

VIRGINIA

Richmond
Roanoke

Norfolk

Tulsa

Fort Smith
Hot Springs
Little Rock
Pine Bluff

ARKANSAS

El Dorado

Jonesboro

Memphis

Nashville
Jackson

TENNESSEE

Chattanooga

Oak Ridge
Knoxville

Greensboro
Raleigh

Asheville
Charlotte

NORTH CAROLINA

Wilmington

Tyler
Shreveport

LOUISIANA

Alexandria

Natchez

MISSISSIPPI

Columbus
Jackson
Meridian

Huntsville

Birmingham

ALABAMA

Columbus
Montgomery

Greenville
SOUTH CAROLINA
Columbia

Charleston

Atlanta

GEORGIA

Macon
Columbus
Albany
Savannah

Beaumont
Houston
Galveston

Lake Charles
New Orleans

Baton Rouge

Mobile
Biloxi

Pensacola

Tallahassee
Gainesville

FLORIDA

Jacksonville

GULF OF MEXICO

Orlando
Tampa
St. Petersburg
Ft. Myers

West Palm Beach
Boca Raton
Ft. Lauderdale
Miami

Key West

West longitude
North latitude

ATLANTIC OCEAN

CUBA

60°
45°

40°

65°
35°

30°

25°

20°

95°　90°　85°　80°　75°　70°

Legend

⚝   State Capital

🧭   United States standard time zones are indicated by clocks
(When it is 12:00 noon in Western Alaska, it is 6:00 p.m. along the eastern coast of the United States.)

– – –   Boundaries of time zones

0   Miles   500

0   Kilometers   800

CHRONOLOGY OF EVENTS
IN AMERICAN HISTORY

1096	Crusades to Holy Land start.
1271–95	Marco Polo's travels in Far East.
1492	Columbus reaches America.
1497–98	John Cabot's explorations.
1498	Vasco da Gama reaches India.
1513	Balboa reaches Pacific Ocean.
1519	Cortés lands in Mexico.
1519–22	Magellan's ships circle earth.
1531–35	Pizarro conquers Incas.
1534	Cartier makes first voyage.
1539–42	De Soto explores Southeast.
1588	English defeat Spanish Armada.
1607	Jamestown is founded.
1609	Hudson explores Hudson River.
1619	First women arrive at Jamestown.
1619	First Africans arrive in Virginia.
1620	Pilgrims reach Cape Cod.
1620	Mayflower Compact.
1624	Virginia becomes royal colony.
1630	Massachusetts Bay Colony founded.
1632	Maryland is chartered.
1636	Roger Williams founds Providence.
1636	Harvard University founded.
1639	Fundamental Orders of Connecticut.
1643	New England Confederation formed.
1647	Massachusetts passes school law.
1649	Maryland Toleration Act.
1651–63	Principal Navigation Acts.
1663	Carolina is chartered.
1664	New Netherland becomes New Jersey and New York.
1673	Exploration by Marquette, Joilet.
1675–76	Bacon's Rebellion.
1679	New Hampshire is chartered.
1681	Pennsylvania is chartered.
1681–82	Exploration by La Salle.
1682	Delaware granted to Penn.
1686	Dominion of New England created.
1693	College of William and Mary founded.
1701	Yale University founded.
1732	Georgia is chartered.
1733	Molasses Act.
1735	Zenger trial.
1750	Iron Act.

1754	French and Indian War starts.
1754	Albany Plan of Union proposed.
1754	Columbia University founded.
1755	Braddock defeated disastrously.
1756	Pitt heads British government.
1759	British capture Quebec.
1763	Treaty of Paris.
1763	Proclamation of 1763.
1764	Sugar Act, Currency Act.
1765	Stamp Act.
1766	Stamp Act repealed.
1767	Townshend Acts.
1770	Boston Massacre.
1772	Committees of Correspondence.
1773	Boston Tea Party.
1774	First Continental Congress.
1775	Fighting at Lexington, Concord.
1775	Second Continental Congress.
1775	Battle of Breed's (Bunker) Hill.
1776	Paine's *Common Sense* appears.
1776	Declaration of Independence.
1776	American victory at Trenton.
1777–78	Howe occupies Philadelphia.
1777	Burgoyne surrenders at Saratoga.
1778	Treaty of alliance with France.
1781	Cornwallis surrenders.
1781	Articles of Confederation go into effect.
1783	Treaty of Paris: United States independence recognized.
1785	Land Ordinance.
1786–87	Shays' Rebellion.
1787	Northwest Ordinance.
1787	Constitution is drafted.

George Washington in Office: 1789–1797

1789	Congress creates Departments of State, Treasury, and War.
1789	United States courts are organized.
1790	Assumption Bill is passed.
1791	Bill of Rights is ratified.
1791	Vermont enters Union.
1791	Bank of United States chartered.
1791	Lancaster Turnpike is begun.

1792	Kentucky enters Union.
1793	Proclamation of Neutrality.
1794	"Whiskey Rebellion" is put down.
1794	Jay Treaty.
1795	Pinckney Treaty.
1796	Tennessee enters Union.

John Adams in Office: 1797–1801

1797	XYZ Affair angers Americans.
1798	Navy Department is created.
1798	Eleventh Amendment ratified.
1798	Alien and Sedition Acts.
1798–99	Kentucky and Virginia Resolutions.
1801	Marshall becomes Chief Justice.

Thomas Jefferson in Office: 1801–1809

1803	Ohio enters Union.
1803	*Marbury v. Madison.*
1803	Louisiana Purchase adds vast territory to United States.
1804	Twelfth Amendment ratified.
1804–06	Lewis and Clark expedition.
1805	War with Barbary pirates ends.
1807	Embargo Act.
1809	Non-Intercourse Act.

James Madison in Office: 1809–1817

1811	Indian fight at Tippecanoe.
1811	National Road is begun.
1812	Louisiana enters Union.
1812–14	War of 1812 is fought between United States and Great Britain.
1814	Treaty of Ghent restores peace.
1815	Battle of New Orleans.
1816	Second Bank of United States chartered.
1816	Indiana enters Union.

James Monroe in Office: 1817–1825

1817–25	"Era of Good Feelings."
1817	Mississippi enters Union.
1818	Rush-Bagot Agreement approved.
1818	Illinois enters Union.
1818	Treaty settles Canadian boundary.
1819	*McCulloch v. Maryland.*
1819	*Dartmouth College v. Woodward.*
1819	Alabama enters Union.
1819	Treaty gives Florida to U.S.
1820	Missouri Compromise.
1820	Maine enters Union.
1821	Missouri enters Union.
1821	First public high school opens.
1823	Monroe Doctrine proclaimed.
1824	*Gibbons v. Ogden.*

John Quincy Adams in Office: 1825–1829

1825	Erie Canal opens.
1828	"Tariff of Abominations."

1828	Work begins on Baltimore and Ohio Railroad.

Andrew Jackson in Office: 1829–1837

1830	Webster-Hayne debate.
1831	Slave uprising in Virginia.
1831	First issue of the *Liberator*.
1832	Tariff of 1832.
1832	Ordinance of Nullification.
1832	Jackson vetoes renewal of charter for Bank of United States.
1833	Compromise tariff act.
1836	Texas declares its independence.
1836	Arkansas enters Union.
1837	Michigan enters Union.

Martin Van Buren in Office: 1837–1841

1837	Business panic; depression begins.
1837	Horace Mann starts school reform.
1838	Oberlin admits women.
1841	Jacksonian era ends.

William Henry Harrison in Office: March 4–April 4, 1841

1841	Harrison dies.

John Tyler in Office: 1841–1845

1842	Massachusetts recognizes legal right of labor unions to exist.
1842	Webster-Ashburton Treaty.
1845	Florida enters Union.

James K. Polk in Office: 1845–1849

1845	Texas enters Union.
1846	Treaty settles Oregon boundary.
1846	Iowa enters Union.
1846	Congress declares war on Mexico.
1846	Wilmot Proviso is presented.
1847	Mormons settle at Great Salt Lake.
1848	Treaty ends Mexican War; gives U.S. Mexican Cession.
1848	Women's rights convention at Seneca Falls.
1848	Wisconsin enters Union.

Zachary Taylor in Office: 1849–1850

1849	Gold rush to California.
1850	Taylor dies.

Millard Fillmore in Office: 1850–1853

1850	Compromise of 1850.
1850	California admitted to Union.
1852	*Uncle Tom's Cabin* is published.

Franklin Pierce in Office: 1853–1857

1853	Gadsden Purchase approved.
1853	Perry arrives in Japan.
1854	Kansas-Nebraska Act.
1854	Republican Party is formed.
1856	Violence breaks out in Kansas.

James Buchanan in Office: 1857–1861

1857	Dred Scott decision.
1858	Lincoln-Douglas debates.
1858	Minnesota enters Union.
1859	John Brown raids Harpers Ferry.
1859	Oregon enters Union.
1860	South Carolina secedes.
1861	Kansas enters Union.
1861	Confederacy is formed.
1861	Morrill Tariff Act.

Abraham Lincoln in Office: 1861–1865

1861	South fires on Fort Sumter; Civil War (1861–65) begins.
1861	First Battle of Bull Run.
1862	Battle of *Monitor* and *Merrimac*.
1862	Second Battle of Bull Run.
1862	Battle of Antietam.
1862	Emancipation Proclamation.
1862	Union forces reach Vicksburg.
1862	Homestead Act.
1862	Morrill Act for agricultural and industrial education.
1862	Department of Agriculture formed.
1863	Battle of Gettysburg.
1863	Grant takes Vicksburg.
1863	West Virginia enters Union.
1864	Sherman takes Atlanta, Savannah.
1864	Nevada enters Union.
1865	Freedmen's Bureau is created.
1865	Lee surrenders to Grant.
1865	Lincoln is assassinated.

Andrew Johnson in Office: 1865–1869

1865	Johnson recognizes four reconstructed state governments.
1865	Thirteenth Amendment ratified.
1865–86	Conflict between settlers and Indians on the plains.
1866	National Labor Union is formed.
1867	Nebraska enters Union.
1867	U.S. buys Alaska.
1867	Congressional plan of reconstruction is set up.
1867	Grange is organized.
1868	Fourteenth Amendment ratified.
1868	House impeaches Johnson.
1868	Senate acquits Johnson.

Ulysses S. Grant in Office: 1869–1877

1869	First transcontinental railroad completed.
1869	Knights of Labor founded.
1870	Fifteenth Amendment ratified.
1870–71	Force Acts.
1872	Amnesty Act.
1872	Crédit Mobilier scandal.
1873	Nationwide economic depression.
1875	Resumption Act.
1876	Colorado enters Union.
1876	Centennial Exhibition.
1876	Presidential election disputed.
1876–77	"Granger cases" decided.

Rutherford B. Hayes in Office: 1877–1881

1877	Troops withdrawn from South.
1877	Series of railroad strikes.
1878	Bland-Allison Act.
1880–90	New Immigration from eastern and southern Europe.

James A. Garfield in Office: March 4–September 19, 1881

1881	Garfield is assassinated.

Chester A. Arthur in Office: 1881–1885

1882	Chinese Exclusion Act.
1882	Standard Oil Trust organized.
1883	Civil Service Commission set up.

Grover Cleveland in Office: 1885–1889

1886	Presidential Succession Act.
1886	A. F. of L. is organized.
1886	Haymarket Riot.
1887	Interstate Commerce Act.
1887	Hatch Act.
1887	Dawes Act tries to "Americanize" Indians.

Benjamin Harrison in Office: 1889–1893

1889	Washington, Montana, North Dakota, South Dakota enter Union.
1890	Wyoming, Idaho enter Union.
1890	McKinley Tariff.
1890	Sherman Antitrust Act.
1890	Sherman Silver Purchase Act.
1891	Populist Party is organized.
1892	Homestead steel strike.

Grover Cleveland in Office: 1893–1897

1893	Silver Purchase Act is repealed.
1893	World's Fair held in Chicago.
1894	Wilson-Gorman Tariff.
1894	Pullman strike.
1895	Cubans revolt against Spain.
1896	Bryan is free silver candidate.
1896	Utah enters Union.
1896	Gold discovered in Klondike.

William McKinley in Office: 1897–1901

1897	Dingley Tariff.
1898	Spanish-American War.
1898	Treaty of Paris gives U.S. Puerto Rico, Guam, Philippines.
1898	U.S. annexes Hawaiian Islands.
1899	First Hague Conference.
1899–1900	Open Door policy proclaimed.
1900	Boxer Rebellion.
1901	Platt Amendment.
1901	McKinley is assassinated.

Theodore Roosevelt in Office: 1901–1909

1901	Hay-Pauncefote Treaty.
1901–02	Pan-American Conference.
1902	Newlands Reclamation Act.
1902	Drago Doctrine is announced.
1902	American forces withdrawn from Cuba.
1903	Department of Commerce and Labor is created.
1903	Elkins Act.
1903	Wisconsin adopts direct primary.
1903	Canal Zone is acquired by U.S.
1904	Northern Securities Company ruling.
1904	Roosevelt Corollary to Monroe Doctrine.
1905	Treaty of Portsmouth.
1906	Pure Food and Drug Act.
1906	Meat Inspection Act.
1906	Burke Act modifies Dawes Act.
1906	Pan-American Conference.
1907	Oklahoma enters Union.
1907	"Gentlemen's Agreement" with Japan.
1907	Second Hague Conference.
1908	White House Conservation Conference.
1908	Danbury Hatters ruling.

William H. Taft in Office: 1909–1913

1909	Payne-Aldrich Tariff.
1910	Mann-Elkins Act.
1910	Pan-American Conference.
1911	Transcontinental plane flight.
1912	New Mexico, Arizona enter Union.
1912	Progressive Party is formed.
1912	First state minimum-wage law.
1913	Sixteenth Amendment ratified.

Woodrow Wilson in Office: 1913–1921

1913	Seventeenth Amendment ratified.
1913	Underwood Tariff.
1913	Federal Reserve Act.
1914	World War I starts.
1914	Panama Canal opened to shipping.
1914	FTC is created.
1914	Clayton Antitrust Act.
1916	Jones Act.
1917	Russian Revolution.
1917	U.S. enters World War I.
1917	Smith-Hughes Act.
1917	U.S. buys Virgin Islands.
1918	World War I ends.
1918	Wilson presents Fourteen Points.

1919	Eighteenth Amendment ratified.
1919	"Palmer raids."
1919	Treaty of Versailles (with provision for League of Nations).
1920	Nineteenth Amendment ratified.

Warren G. Harding in Office: 1921–1923

1921	Bureau of the Budget created.
1921	Veterans' Bureau created.
1921–22	Washington Naval Conference.
1921–29	Laws restricting immigration passed.
1922	Mussolini seizes power in Italy.
1922	Fordney-McCumber Tariff.
1923	Harding dies suddenly.

Calvin Coolidge in Office: 1923–1929

1923	Pan-American Conference.
1924	Teapot Dome scandal.
1924	Veterans' bonus bill passed.
1924	All Indians given citizenship.
1927	McNary-Haugen Bill vetoed.
1928	Kellogg-Briand Pact.
1928	Pan-American Conference.

Herbert Hoover in Office: 1929–1933

1929	Stock market crash; start of Great Depression
1930	Public-works programs started.
1930	Hawley-Smoot Tariff.
1931	Japan invades Manchuria.
1932	RFC is created.
1932	Stimson Doctrine is announced.
1932–33	Federal Reserve powers increased.
1933	Hitler comes to power in Germany.
1933	Twentieth Amendment ratified.

Franklin D. Roosevelt in Office: 1933–1945

1933	CCC is created.
1933	Agricultural Adjustment Act.
1933	Roosevelt declares bank holiday.
1933	NIRA goes into effect.
1933	TVA is created.
1933	U.S. recognizes Soviet Union.
1933	Good Neighbor policy announced.
1933	Twenty-first Amendment ratified.
1934	Roosevelt "devalues" dollar.
1934	SEC is created.
1934	Indian Reorganization Act (Wheeler-Howard Act).
1934	Trade Agreements Act.
1934	Platt Amendment canceled.
1935	WPA is created.
1935	NIRA declared unconstitutional.
1935	National Labor Relations Act.
1935	Social Security Act.
1935–37	Neutrality Acts.
1936	AAA ruled unconstitutional.
1936	Pan-American Conference.
1937	Plan to reorganize Supreme Court.
1937–38	Business slump.

1938	CIO separates from A. F. of L.
1938	Fair Labor Standards Act.
1938	Food, Drug, and Cosmetic Act.
1938	Declaration of Lima.
1939	Poland invaded; World War II begins.
1939	Neutrality Act of 1937 amended.
1940	France signs armistice.
1941	"Four Freedoms" speech.
1941	Lend-Lease Act.
1941	Hitler attacks U.S.S.R.
1941	Atlantic Charter states war aims.
1941	Japanese attack Pearl Harbor; U.S. enters World War II.
1942	Corregidor surrenders to Japanese.
1942	Marines invade Guadalcanal.
1942	Allied invasion of North Africa.
1942	OPA is established.
1943	Allied invasion of Italy.
1943	Cairo and Teheran Conferences.
1944	Allies invade Western Europe.
1944	France is liberated.
1945	Yalta Conference.
1945	Roosevelt dies suddenly.

Harry S. Truman in Office: 1945–1953

1945	San Francisco Conference.
1945	War ends in Europe.
1945	Atomic bombs dropped on Japan.
1945	Truman signs UN Charter.
1945	World War II ends.
1946	Philippines become independent.
1946	Wage and price controls ended.
1947	Truman Doctrine is announced.
1947	Marshall Plan is proposed.
1947	Taft-Hartley Act.
1947	Presidential Succession Act.
1948–49	Berlin airlift.
1949	Point Four program is announced.
1949	NATO is formed.
1949	Communists control China.
1950	Internal Security Act.
1950	Korean War starts.
1951	Twenty-second Amendment ratified.
1952	U.S. tests hydrogen bomb.

Dwight D. Eisenhower in Office: 1953–1961

1953	Department of Health, Education, and Welfare is created.
1953	States get title to offshore oil.
1953	Korean armistice signed.
1954	Supreme Court rules segregated public schools unconstitutional.
1954	West Germany is admitted to NATO.
1954	Both U.S. and U.S.S.R. have H-bombs.
1955	Summit conference.
1956	Suez crisis.
1957	Civil Rights Commission created.
1957	*Sputnik* in orbit.
1958	First U.S. satellite in orbit.
1958	Congress admits Alaska to the Union.
1958–59	Berlin crisis.

1959	St. Lawrence Seaway is opened.
1959	Labor-Management Reporting and Disclosure Act.
1959	Congress admits Hawaii to the Union.
1960	Summit Conference called off.

John F. Kennedy in Office: 1961–1963

1961	Peace Corps created.
1961	Alliance for Progress started.
1961	First Soviet cosmonaut orbits earth.
1961	Invasion of Cuba fails.
1961	Area Redevelopment Act.
1961	Berlin wall built.
1962	First American astronaut orbits earth.
1962	U.S. troops sent to South Vietnam.
1962	Trade Expansion Act.
1962	Cuban missile crisis.
1963	Nuclear test-ban treaty.
1963	Kennedy is assassinated.

Lyndon B. Johnson in Office: 1963–1969

1964	Economic Opportunity Act.
1964	Civil Rights Act.
1964	Twenty-fourth Amendment ratified.
1965	Voting Rights Act.
1965	Medicare established.
1965	Escalation in South Vietnam.
1965	Education Act.
1965	Department of Housing and Urban Development created.
1966	National Organization for Women (NOW) is founded.
1966	Department of Transportation created.
1967	Racial disturbances in several U.S. cities.
1967	Twenty-fifth Amendment ratified.
1968	Martin Luther King, Jr., is assassinated.
1968	Vietnam peace talks begin in Paris.

Richard M. Nixon in Office: 1969–1974

1969	American troop withdrawals from Vietnam begin.
1969	American astronauts land on the moon.
1971	Twenty-sixth Amendment ratified.
1972	President Nixon visits Communist China and the Soviet Union.
1972	Twenty-seventh Amendment sent to the states for ratification.
1973	Vice-President Agnew resigns.
1973	Vietnam cease-fire.
1974	President Nixon resigns.

Gerald Ford in Office: 1974–1977

1975	Vietnam falls to Communists.
1975	Joint U.S.-Soviet space mission.
1976	Nation celebrates its bicentennial.

Jimmy Carter in Office: 1977–

1977	Department of Energy created.
1978	Panama Canal treaties passed.
1978	Camp David Summit Conference.

The Declaration of Independence

PREAMBLE

When, in the course of human events, it becomes necessary for one people to dissolve the political bands which have connected them with another, and to assume, among the powers of the earth, the separate and equal station to which the laws of nature and of nature's God entitle them, a decent respect to the opinions of mankind requires that they should declare the causes which impel them to the separation.

A NEW THEORY OF GOVERNMENT

We hold these truths to be self-evident: that all men are created equal, that they are endowed by their Creator with certain unalienable rights, that among these are life, liberty, and the pursuit of happiness.

That, to secure these rights, governments are instituted among men, deriving their just powers from the consent of the governed;

That whenever any form of government becomes destructive of these ends, it is the right of the people to alter or to abolish it, and to institute new government, laying its foundation on such principles, and organizing its powers in such form, as to them shall seem most likely to effect their safety and happiness. Prudence, indeed, will dictate that governments long established should not be changed for light and transient causes; and accordingly all experience hath shown that mankind are more disposed to suffer while evils are sufferable, than to right themselves by abolishing the forms to which they are accustomed. But when a long train of abuses and usurpations, pursuing invariably the same object, evinces a design to reduce them under absolute despotism, it is their right, it is their duty, to throw off such government, and to provide new guards for their future security.

REASONS FOR SEPARATION

Such has been the patient sufferance of these colonies; and such is now the necessity which constrains them to alter their former systems of government. The history of the present king of Great Britain is a history of repeated injuries and usurpations, all having in direct object the establishment of an absolute tyranny over these states. To prove this, let facts be submitted to a candid world.

He has refused his assent to laws the most wholesome and necessary for the public good.

He has forbidden his governors to pass laws of immediate and pressing importance unless suspended in their operation till his assent should be obtained; and when so suspended, he has utterly neglected to attend to them.

He has refused to pass other laws for the accommodation of large districts of people, unless those people would relinquish the right of representation in the legislature, a right inestimable to them, and formidable to tyrants only.

He has called together legislative bodies at places unusual, uncomfortable, and distant from the depository of their public records, for the sole purpose of fatiguing them into compliance with his measures.

He has dissolved representative houses repeatedly, for opposing, with manly firmness, his invasions on the rights of the people.

He has refused, for a long time after such dissolutions, to cause others to be elected; whereby the legislative powers, incapable of annihilation, have returned to the people at large for their exercise; the state remaining, in the mean time, exposed to all the dangers of invasion from without and convulsions within.

He has endeavored to prevent the population of these states; for that purpose obstructing the laws of naturalization of foreigners, refusing to pass others to encourage their migration hither, and raising the conditions of new appropriations of lands.

He has obstructed the administration of justice, by refusing his assent to laws for establishing judiciary powers.

He has made judges dependent on his will alone for the tenure of their offices, and the amount and payment of their salaries.

He has erected a multitude of new offices, and sent hither swarms of officers to harass our people and eat out their substance.

He has kept among us, in times of peace, standing armies, without the consent of our legislature.

He has affected to render the military independent of, and superior to, the civil power.

He has combined with others to subject us to a jurisdiction foreign to our constitution and unacknowledged by our laws, giving his assent to their acts of pretended legislation:

For quartering large bodies of armed troops among us;

For protecting them, by a mock trial, from punishment for any murders which they should commit on the inhabitants of these states;

For cutting off our trade with all parts of the world;

For imposing taxes on us without our consent;

For depriving us, in many cases, of the benefits of trial by jury;

For transporting us beyond seas, to be tried for pretended offenses;

For abolishing the free system of English laws in a neighboring province, establishing therein an arbitrary government, and enlarging its boundaries, so as to render it at once an example and fit instrument for introducing the same absolute rule into these colonies;

For taking away our charters, abolishing our most valuable laws, and altering, fundamentally, the forms of our governments;

For suspending our own legislature, and declaring themselves invested with power to legislate for us in all cases whatsoever.

He has abdicated government here, by declaring us out of his protection and waging war against us.

He has plundered our seas, ravaged our coasts, burned our towns, and destroyed the lives of our people.

He is at this time transporting large armies of foreign mercenaries to complete the works of death, desolation, and tyranny already begun with circumstances of cruelty and perfidy scarely paralleled in the most barbarous ages, and totally unworthy the head of a civilized nation.

He has constrained our fellow-citizens, taken captive on the high seas, to bear arms against their country, to become the executioners of their friends and brethren, or to fall themselves by their hands.

He has excited domestic insurrections among us, and has endeavored to bring on the inhabitants of our frontiers the merciless Indian savages, whose known rule of warfare is an undistinguished destruction of all ages, sexes, and conditions.

In every stage of these oppressions we have petitioned for redress in the most humble terms; our repeated petitions have been answered only by repeated injury. A prince whose character is thus marked by every act which may define a tyrant is unfit to be the ruler of a free people.

Nor have we been wanting in attention to our British brethren. We have warned them, from time to time, of attempts by their legislature to extend an unwarrantable jurisdiction over us. We have reminded them of the circumstances of our emigration and settlement here. We have appealed to their native justice and magnanimity; and we have conjured them, by the ties of our common kindred, to disavow these usurpations, which would inevitably interrupt our connections and correspondence. They, too, have been deaf to the voice of justice and of consanguinity. We must, therefore, acquiesce in the necessity which denounces our separation, and hold them, as we hold the rest of mankind, enemies in war, in peace, friends.

A FORMAL DECLARATION OF WAR

We, therefore, the representatives of the United States of America, in General Congress assembled, appealing to the Supreme Judge of the world for the rectitude of our intentions, do, in the name and by authority of the good people of these colonies, solemnly publish and declare, that these united colonies are, and of right ought to be, free and independent states; that they are absolved from all allegiance to the British crown, and that all political connection between them and the state of Great Britain is, and ought to be, totally dissolved; and that, as free and independent states, they have full power to levy war, conclude peace, contract alliances, establish commerce, and to do all other acts and things which independent states may of right do. And, for the support of this declaration, with a firm reliance on the protection of Divine Providence, we mutually pledge to each other our lives, our fortunes, and our sacred honor.

Constitution of the United States

(The text of the Constitution is printed in BLACK; the commentary in BLUE. Portions of the text printed in brackets have gone out of date or have been changed by amendment.)

PREAMBLE

We, the people of the United States, in order to form a more perfect Union, establish justice, insure domestic tranquillity, provide for the common defense, promote the general welfare, and secure the blessings of liberty to ourselves and our posterity, do ordain and establish this CONSTITUTION for the United States of America.

¶ In addition to stating the purposes of the Constitution, the Preamble makes it clear that the government is established by consent of the governed. "We, the people, . . . ordain and establish" the government. We, the people, have supreme power in establishing the government of the United States of America.

ARTICLE 1. LEGISLATIVE DEPARTMENT

¶ By separating the functions of government among branches concerned with lawmaking (Article 1), law executing (Article 2), and law interpreting (Article 3), the framers of the Constitution were applying the principle of separation of powers, and developing a system of checks and balances, as a defense against tyranny.

SECTION 1. CONGRESS

All legislative powers herein granted shall be vested in a Congress of the United States, which shall consist of a Senate and House of Representatives.

¶ Practice has modified the provision that all lawmaking powers granted in the Constitution are vested in Congress. For example, such administrative agencies as the Interstate Commerce Commission can issue regulations which in some ways have the force of laws.

SECTION 2. HOUSE OF REPRESENTATIVES

1. Election and term of members. The House of Representatives shall be composed of members chosen every second year by the people of the several states, and the electors in each state shall have the qualifications requisite for electors of the most numerous branch of the state legislature.

¶ *Clause 1.* The members of the House of Representatives are elected every two years by the "electors" (voters) of the states. Except for the provisions of Amendments 15, 19, 24, and 26, the individual states decide who may or may not vote.

2. Qualifications. No person shall be a Representative who shall not have attained to the age of twenty-five years, and been seven years a citizen of the United States, and who shall not, when elected, be an inhabitant of that state in which he shall be chosen.

¶ *Clause 2.* This clause specifies the qualifications for a member of the House of Representatives: (1) At least 25 years of age. (2) A United States citizen for at least 7 years. (3) Resident of the state in which elected. (Custom has added the requirement of residence in the Congressional district from which a Representative is elected.) Each state is divided into Congressional districts for the purpose of electing Representatives; each district elects one. ¶ TERM OF OFFICE: 2 years.

3. Apportionment of Representatives and direct taxes. Representatives [and direct taxes] shall be apportioned among the several states which may be included within this Union, according to their respective numbers [which shall be determined by adding to the whole number of free persons, including those bound to service for a term of years, and excluding Indians not taxed, three-fifths of all other persons]. The actual enumeration shall be made within three years after the first meeting of the Congress of the United States, and within every subsequent term of ten years, in such manner as they shall by law direct. The number of Representatives shall not exceed 1 for every 30,000, but each state shall have at least 1 Representative; [and until such enumeration shall be made, the state of New Hampshire shall be entitled to choose 3; Massachusetts, 8; Rhode Island and Providence Plantations, 1; Connecticut, 5; New York, 6; New Jersey, 4; Pennsylvania, 8; Delaware, 1; Maryland, 6; Virginia, 10; North Carolina, 5; South Carolina, 5; and Georgia, 3.]

¶ *Clause 3.* The bracketed portion of this clause beginning on line 5 forms what came to be called the "three-fifths compromise." Amendment 13 and Section 2 of Amendment 14 overruled this provision in the case of black Americans but not for Indians. However, since 1940 Indians have been included in the population census. ¶ Originally, each state was entitled to one Representative for every 30,000 people. Later, membership was limited by law to a total of 435. ¶ A population census of the United States is taken every 10 years to determine the number of Representatives to which each state is entitled. Regardless of its population, however, each state is entitled to at least one Representative in Congress.

4. Filling vacancies. When vacancies happen in the representation from any state, the executive authority thereof shall issue writs of election to fill such vacancies.

¶ *Clause 4.* The "executive authority" refers to the governor of the state; a "writ of election" is an order for a special election to fill the vacant seat.

5. Officers; impeachment. The House of Representatives shall choose their Speaker and other officers; and shall have the sole power of impeachment.

¶ *Clause 5.* In actual practice, it is the majority party—the political party having the largest number of members in the House—which chooses the Speaker of the House and other House officials (clerk, doorkeeper, sergeant at arms, postmaster, and chaplain). The Speaker is the only official chosen from among the members of the House. ¶ The House, by a majority vote, can impeach (accuse) an Executive Department officer or a federal judge. The trial of the impeached official takes place in the Senate. (See Section 3, Clause 6.)

SECTION 3. SENATE

1. Number of members and terms of office. The Senate of the United States shall be composed of two Senators from each state [chosen by the legislature thereof], for six years, and each Senator shall have one vote.

¶ *Clause 1.* Under the provisions of Amendment 17, the 100 Senators are now elected directly by the voters of the states in the same manner as the Representatives. The method of electing Senators provided here, by which the state legislatures chose Senators, came to be considered undemocratic and was therefore changed.

2. Classification; filling vacancies. [Immediately after they shall be assembled in consequence of the first election, they shall be divided as equally as may be into three classes. The seats of the Senators of the first class shall be vacated at the expiration of the second year, of the second class at the expiration of the fourth year, and of the third class at the expiration of the sixth year, so that one-third may be chosen every second year; and if vacancies

¶ *Clause 2.* One third of the Senate comes up for election every two years. This procedure was established in the first Senate, whose Senators were divided into three groups. One group was to serve for two years, the second for four years, and the third for six years. As a result, the terms of Senators today overlap, making the Senate a "continuing" body, in which two thirds of the members are "carried over" through every election. In contrast, the total membership of the House of Representatives is elected every two years. ¶ Under Amendment 17, if a Senator resigns or dies, the state governor can call a special election to fill the vacancy. The state legislature, however, may empower the governor to name a temporary Senator.

happen by resignation, or otherwise, during the recess of the legislature of any state, the executive thereof may make temporary appointments until the next meeting of the legislature, which shall then fill such vacancies.]

3. Qualifications. No person shall be a Senator who shall not have attained to the age of thirty years, and been nine years a citizen of the United States, and who shall not, when elected, be an inhabitant of that state for which he shall be chosen.

¶ *Clause 3.* This clause specifies the qualifications for a Senator: (1) At least 30 years of age. (2) United States citizen for at least 9 years. (3) Resident of the state in which elected. ¶ TERM OF OFFICE: 6 years.

4. President of the Senate. The Vice-President of the United States shall be president of the Senate, but shall have no vote, unless they be equally divided.

¶ *Clause 4.* To serve as president of the Senate and vote only in case of a tie, is the sole duty the Constitution assigns to the Vice-President. In recent years the Vice-President has assumed additional duties at the President's request, such as attending cabinet meetings, traveling abroad on good will tours, and carrying out such ceremonial duties as entertaining leading officials from abroad and representing the government at important events.

5. Other Officers. The Senate shall choose their other officers, and also a president *pro tempore,* in the absence of the Vice-President, or when he shall exercise the office of the President of the United States.

¶ *Clause 5.* "Other officers" include a secretary, chaplain, and sergeant at arms. These officers are not members of the Senate. *Pro tempore* is a Latin expression meaning "for the time being," or "temporarily." Thus, the president pro tempore acts as a temporary president of the Senate.

6. Trial of impeachments. The Senate shall have the sole power to try all impeachments. When sitting for that purpose, they shall be on oath or affirmation. When the President of the United States is tried, the Chief Justice shall preside; and no person shall be convicted without the concurrence of two-thirds of the members present.

¶ *Clause 6.* Only the President, Vice-President, cabinet officials, and federal judges are subject to impeachment and removal from office. Members of the House and Senate cannot be impeached, but they can be censured and even removed from office by the members of their respective houses. ¶ Officials may be impeached only for committing "treason, bribery, or other high crimes and misdemeanors" (see Article 2, Section 4). The Chief Justice of the Supreme Court presides at the impeachment trial of a President. The Vice-President presides over all other impeachment trials. The Senate can find an impeached official guilty only if two thirds of the Senators present agree on the verdict. The only President ever impeached was Andrew Johnson, in 1867; he was saved from conviction by one vote. In 1974 Richard M. Nixon resigned as President after the Judiciary Committee of the House of Representatives recommended to the House that he be impeached.

7. Penalty for conviction. Judgment in cases of impeachment shall not extend further than to removal from office, and disqualification to hold and enjoy any office of honor, trust, or profit under the United States; but the party convicted shall nevertheless be liable and subject to indictment, trial, judgment, and punishment, according to law.

¶ *Clause 7.* The punishment for conviction in impeachment cases can consist only of removal from office and disqualification from holding any other federal office. However, the convicted person may also be tried in a regular court of law for this same offense. Although not impeached, President Nixon was granted a Presidential pardon, which spared him a possible criminal court trial.

SECTION 4. ELECTIONS AND MEETINGS

1. Holding elections. The times, places, and manner of holding elections for Senators and Representatives shall be prescribed in each state by the legislature thereof; but the Congress may at any time by law make or alter such regulations, except as to the places of choosing Senators.

¶ Clause 1. Under this provision, Congress has passed a law stating that, unless the constitution of a state provides otherwise, Congressional elections must be held on the Tuesday following the first Monday in November of even-numbered years. (Until 1960, Maine held elections in September.) Congress has also ruled that Representatives must be elected by districts, rather than by the state as a whole, and that secret ballots (or voting machines, where required by state law) must be used.

2. Meetings. The Congress shall assemble at least once in every year, [and such meeting shall be on the first Monday in December,] unless they shall by law appoint a different day.

¶ Clause 2. Under Amendment 20, Congress now meets on January 3, unless it sets another day by law.

SECTION 5. RULES OF PROCEDURE

1. Organization. Each house shall be the judge of the elections, returns, and qualifications of its own members, and a majority of each shall constitute a quorum to do business; but a smaller number may adjourn from day to day, and may be authorized to compel the attendance of absent members, in such manner, and under such penalties, as each house may provide.

¶ Clause 1. Each house of Congress may disqualify elected candidates and prevent them from taking office on the grounds of public policy. On one occasion the House refused to admit to membership an elected candidate who had violated the criminal laws. On another occasion the Senate refused to seat a victorious candidate whose election campaign had been characterized by "fraud and corruption." *¶ A quorum* is the minimum number of persons required to be present to transact business; a majority of the House or Senate constitutes a quorum. In practice, business is often transacted with less than a quorum present, and may go on as long as no member objects to the lack of a quorum.

2. Proceedings. Each house may determine the rules of its proceedings, punish its members for disorderly behavior, and with the concurrence of two-thirds, expel a member.

¶ Clause 2. Each house has extensive rules of procedure. Each house can censure, punish, or expel a member. Expulsion requires a two-thirds vote.

3. Journal. Each house shall keep a journal of its proceedings, and from time to time publish the same, excepting such parts as may in their judgment require secrecy; and the yeas and nays of the members of either house on any question shall, at the desire of one-fifth of those present, be entered on the journal.

¶ Clause 3. Each house is required to keep a journal of its activities. These journals, called the *House Journal* and the *Senate Journal,* are published at the end of each session of Congress. A third journal, called the *Congressional Record,* is published every day that Congress is in session, and furnishes a daily account of what Representatives and Senators do and say. *¶* If one fifth of those present insist on a roll call of the members' votes, each member's vote must be recorded in the proper house journal.

4. Adjournment. Neither house, during the session of Congress, shall, without the consent of the other, adjourn for more than three days, nor to any other place than that in which the two houses shall be sitting.

¶ Clause 4. Both houses must remain in session for the same period of time and in the same place.

SECTION 6. PRIVILEGES AND RESTRICTIONS

1. Pay and privileges. The Senators and Representatives shall receive a compensation for their services, to be ascertained by law and paid out of the Treasury of the United States. They shall in all cases, except treason, felony, and breach of the peace, be privileged from arrest during their attendance at the session of

¶ Clause 1. In 1977 the salary of a member of Congress was set by law at $57,500 a year. *¶* The provision concerning privilege from arrest establishes the principle of "Congressional immunity." According to this principle, members cannot be arrested or brought into court for what they say in speeches and debates in Congress. The aim of this provision is to enable members of Congress to speak freely. They are subject to arrest, however, if they commit a crime, and, under the laws governing slander and libel, are liable for any false or defamatory statements they may make outside Congress.

their respective houses, and in going to and returning from the same; and for any speech or debate in either house, they shall not be questioned in any other place.

2. Restrictions. No Senator or Representative shall, during the time for which he was elected, be appointed to any civil office under the authority of the United States, which shall have been created, or the emoluments whereof shall have been increased, during such time; and no person holding any office under the United States shall be a member of either house during his continuance in office.

¶ *Clause 2.* This clause emphasizes the separation of powers in the federal government. Legislators cannot, while they are members of Congress, hold positions also in the Executive or Judicial Departments. Nor can legislators resign and then accept positions which were created during their term of office. Thus, members of Congress cannot set up jobs for themselves in the executive or judicial branches of the government. Furthermore, if a member resigns and is appointed to an existing executive or judicial position, he or she cannot profit from any increase in pay in this position that was voted during the member's term in Congress.

SECTION 7. METHOD OF PASSING LAWS

1. Revenue bills. All bills for raising revenue shall originate in the House of Representatives; but the Senate may propose or concur with amendments as on other bills.

¶ *Clause 1.* All revenue, or money-raising, bills must be introduced in the House of Representatives. This provision grew out of a demand that the popularly elected branch of the legislature should have the "power of the purse." (Until Amendment 17 was ratified, the House was the only popularly elected branch.) It was also felt that the voters had more control over Representatives, who are elected for two-year terms, than over Senators, who are elected for six-year terms. Thus, Representatives would be more careful than Senators in considering revenue bills. Since the Senate has the power to amend any bill, however, it can amend a revenue bill in such a way as actually to introduce a revenue bill of its own.

2. How a bill becomes a law. Every bill which shall have passed the House of Representatives and the Senate shall, before it become a law, be presented to the President of the United States; if he approve, he shall sign it, but if not, he shall return it, with his objections, to that house in which it shall have originated, who shall enter the objections at large on their journal, and proceed to reconsider it. If after such reconsideration two-thirds of that house shall agree to pass the bill, it shall be sent, together with the objections, to the other house, by which it shall likewise be reconsidered, and, if approved by two-thirds of that house, it shall become a law. But in all such cases the votes of both houses shall be determined by yeas and nays, and the names of the persons voting for and against the bill shall be entered on the journal of each house respectively. If any bill shall not be returned by the President within ten days (Sundays excepted) after it shall have been presented to him, the same bill shall be a law, in like manner as if he had signed it, unless the Congress by their adjournment prevent its return, in which case it shall not be a law.

¶ *Clause 2.* When both houses of Congress pass a law, it is then sent to the President. ¶ If the President does not approve of a bill, one of several things may occur. The President may (1) veto, or refuse to sign, the bill; (2) permit the bill to become a law without signing it by holding it for 10 days (not counting Sundays) while Congress is in session; (3) near the end of a session, hold the bill in the hope that Congress will adjourn within 10 days or less. In that case, the bill fails to become a law, just as though the President had formally vetoed it. This type of veto is called a "pocket veto." ¶ A bill vetoed by the President can become a law, however, if two thirds or more of both houses vote for the bill a second time. When this happens, Congress is said to have "overridden the Presidential veto."

3. Presidential approval or veto. Every order, resolution, or vote to which the concurrence of the Senate and House of Representatives may be necessary (except on a question of adjournment) shall be presented to the President of the United States; and before the same shall take effect, shall be approved by him, or being disapproved by him, shall be repassed by two-thirds of the Senate and House of Representatives, according to the rules and limitations prescribed in the case of a bill.

¶ *Clause 3.* A *joint resolution* results from declarations passed by both houses of Congress on the same subject. It becomes a law in the same manner as a bill. A Congressional declaration of war takes the form of a joint resolution. A *concurrent resolution* represents only an expression of opinion on the part of either house of Congress. It does not have the force of law and, therefore, does not require Presidential approval. The process of amending the Constitution may start this way. A vote censuring a Representative or Senator, or an expression of sympathy, takes the form of a concurrent resolution.

SECTION 8. POWERS DELEGATED TO CONGRESS

The Congress shall have power

¶ Section 8 places important powers in the hands of Congress, indicating that the framers of the Constitution were aware of the weaknesses of the Congress under the Articles of Confederation. This section lists 18 powers granted to Congress—the *delegated* or *enumerated powers.* The first 17 are "expressed" powers because they clearly designate specific areas in which Congress may exercise its authority. The eighteenth power is contained in the famous "elastic clause," from which has come the doctrine of "implied" powers. The elastic clause permits the "stretching" of the other 17 powers.

1. To lay and collect taxes, duties, imposts, and excises, to pay the debts and provide for the common defense and general welfare of the United States; but all duties, imposts, and excises shall be uniform throughout the United States;

¶ *Clause 1.* This clause gives Congress the power to levy and collect taxes, duties or tariffs (taxes on imported goods collected at customhouses), and excises (taxes on goods produced, sold, or consumed within the country). The term "imposts" includes duties and excise taxes. Notice that these taxes must be uniform throughout the United States. According to this clause, the power to tax may be used for two purposes only: (1) to pay the government's debts, and (2) to provide for the common defense and general welfare. The Social Security tax on payrolls is a present-day use of the power to tax.

2. To borrow money on the credit of the United States;

¶ *Clause 2.* The power granted in Clause 2 enables the government to borrow money by issuing bonds for sale, on which the government pays interest. This clause, extended by Clause 18, has also given Congress the power to establish national banks and the Federal Reserve System.

3. To regulate commerce with foreign nations, and among the several states, [and with the Indian tribes];

¶ *Clause 3.* Congress is given direct control over interstate and foreign commerce. And this provision has been extended, by the use of Clause 18, to give Congress control over transportation, communication, and navigation. In order to exercise this broad power Congress has set up various administrative agencies, such as the Interstate Commerce Commission and the Federal Communications Commission.

4. To establish a uniform rule of naturalization, and uniform laws on the subject of bankruptcies throughout the United States;

¶ *Clause 4.* This clause provides the power to regulate the methods by which aliens become citizens of the United States and to form rules regarding bankruptcy.

5. To coin money, regulate the value thereof, and of foreign coin, and fix the standard of weights and measures;

¶ *Clause 5.* Congress is permitted to coin money, to determine the gold and silver content of money, and to order the printing of paper money. It also permits Congress to set up uniform standards for measuring weights and distances.

6. To provide for the punishment of counterfeiting the securities and current coin of the United States;

7. To establish post offices and post roads;

8. To promote the progress of science and useful arts by securing for limited times to authors and inventors the exclusive right to their respective writings and discoveries;

9. To constitute tribunals inferior to the Supreme Court;

10. To define and punish piracies and felonies committed on the high seas and offenses against the law of nations;

11. To declare war, [grant letters of marque and reprisal,] and make rules concerning captures on land and water;

12. To raise and support armies, but no appropriation of money to that use shall be for a longer term than two years;

13. To provide and maintain a navy;

14. To make rules for the government and regulation of the land and naval forces;

15. To provide for calling forth the militia to execute the laws of the Union, suppress insurrections, and repel invasions;

16. To provide for organizing, arming, and disciplining the militia, and for governing such part of them as may be employed in the service of

¶ *Clause 6.* **Under this clause Congress authorizes the Treasury Department to investigate counterfeiting of money or government bonds.**

¶ *Clause 7.* **Congress is granted the power to control post offices and the mail service.**

¶ *Clause 8.* **This clause shows that the framers of the Constitution were eager to promote the progress of science and the arts. Under this power, Congress has passed laws providing that inventors be granted** *patents* **(exclusive rights to manufacture and sell their inventions for 17 years) and that authors and composers be granted** *copyrights* **(exclusive rights to control the publication or performance of their works for their lifetimes plus 50 years).**

¶ *Clause 9.* **Congress is granted the power to establish the federal district courts, the Courts of Appeals, and other special courts.**

¶ *Clause 10.* **Congress protects and controls citizens and ships of the United States when they are out of the country. It may also punish counterfeiting in the United States of bonds and notes of a foreign government.**

¶ *Clause 11.* **Congress is given the power to declare war. Although Congress alone has this power, several Presidents have taken military action without prior consent of Congress. In 1846 President Polk sent troops into an area claimed by both the United States and Mexico. In 1950 President Truman ordered American troops into Korea. And in the mid-1960's, through executive order, American troops became involved in the conflict in South Vietnam without a formal declaration of war.** ¶ **"Letters of marque and reprisal" were licenses issued by the government to privateers (armed ships, privately owned), allowing them to attack enemy ships during wartime. In the War of 1812, the government of the United States issued many of these licenses to American privateers, who did extensive damage to British trade. Today, the issuing of such licenses is outlawed by international agreement.**

¶ *Clause 12.* **The two-year limit in Clause 12 on money appropriations for the army was included to keep the major military power under strict civilian control.**

¶ *Clause 13.* **Notice that appropriations for the navy were not limited. An air force, of course, was not dreamed of when the Constitution was written.**

¶ *Clause 14.* **Under the power granted in this clause, Congress has established rules and regulations governing military discipline and the procedure of courts-martial.**

¶ *Clause 15.* **The term "militia" now refers to the National Guard units of the states. These units may now be called up by the President to keep law and order. They can become part of the United States Army in emergencies.**

¶ *Clause 16.* **Congress is authorized to help states support their militia.**

the United States, reserving to the states, respectively, the appointment of the officers, and the authority of training the militia according to the discipline prescribed by Congress;

17. To exercise exclusive legislation in all cases whatsoever, over such district (not exceeding ten miles square) as may, by cession of particular states, and the acceptance of Congress, become the seat of government of the United States, and to exercise like authority over all places purchased by the consent of the legislature of the state in which the same shall be, for the erection of forts, magazines, arsenals, dock-yards, and other needful buildings;—and

¶ *Clause 17.* **This clause enables Congress to exercise exclusive control over the District of Columbia, as well as over forts, arsenals, federal courthouses, dockyards, and other installations that are owned and operated by the federal government in the various states.**

18. To make all laws which shall be necessary and proper for carrying into execution the foregoing powers, and all other powers vested by this Constitution in the government of the United States, or in any department or officer thereof.

¶ *Clause 18.* **"Necessary and proper" are the key words in the so-called *elastic clause*. Only by combining the power granted in this clause with one of the other 17 powers can Congress use the implied powers granted to it in the Constitution. Laws based on this clause are, of course, subject to review by the judicial branch.**

SECTION 9. POWERS DENIED TO THE FEDERAL GOVERNMENT

¶ **Section 9 limits the powers of Congress.**

1. [The migration or importation of such persons as any of the states now existing shall think proper to admit shall not be prohibited by the Congress prior to the year 1808; but a tax or duty may be imposed on such importation, not exceeding $10 for each person.]

¶ *Clause 1.* **"Such persons" refers to slaves. This provision grew out of the commerce compromise at the Constitutional Convention held in Philadelphia in 1787. It was agreed that Congress would not prohibit the importation of slaves prior to 1808, and that it would not impose an import tax of more than $10 per slave. The importation of slaves into the United States became illegal in 1808.**

2. The privilege of the writ of *habeas corpus* shall not be suspended, unless when in cases of rebellion or invasion the public safety may require it.

¶ *Clause 2.* **The guarantee of the *writ of habeas corpus* (meaning "you may have the body, or person") has been called the most important single safeguard of personal liberty under Anglo-American law. It protects a person against being held in jail on insufficient evidence or no evidence at all. The lawyer of a person arrested can obtain a writ, or court order, which requires that the arrested person be brought before a judge who must determine whether there are sufficient grounds to hold the person in jail. If there are not enough grounds, the person must be freed.**

3. No bill of attainder or *ex post facto* law shall be passed.

¶ *Clause 3.* **A "bill of attainder" is a legislative measure which condemns and punishes a person without a jury trial. Such measures were used in England where Parliament could, by law, declare persons guilty of treason and punish them by death and confiscation of property. Under the Constitution, Congress cannot by law single out certain persons and inflict punishment on them. The power to punish belongs to the judiciary. ¶ An *ex post facto law* was a law which punished a person for doing something which was legal before the law was passed, or which increased the penalty for earlier actions. Because of this clause, the Lindbergh kidnaping law, for example, passed in the year 1932, could not be applied to persons who committed the crime of kidnaping before that year.**

4. [No capitation or other direct tax shall be laid, unless in proportion to the census herein before directed to be taken.]

¶ *Clause 4.* A "capitation tax" is a direct tax imposed on each person, such as the poll tax on persons voting. This provision was inserted to prevent Congress from taxing slaves per poll, or per person, for the purpose of abolishing slavery. Amendment 16 overrules this clause. Amendment 24 outlaws federal poll taxes.

5. No tax or duty shall be laid on articles exported from any state.

¶ *Clause 5.* This clause also resulted from the commerce compromise. The southern states wanted to make sure that Congress could not use its taxing power to impose taxes on southern exports, such as cotton and tobacco.

6. No preference shall be given any regulation of commerce or revenue to the ports of one state over those of another; nor shall vessels bound to, or from, one state, be obliged to enter, clear, or pay duties in another.

¶ *Clause 6.* This clause declares that the United States is an open market in which all states have equal trading and commercial opportunities.

7. No money shall be drawn from the Treasury, but in consequence of appropriations made by law; and a regular statement and account of the receipts and expenditures of all public money shall be published from time to time.

¶ *Clause 7.* This clause concerns the all-important "power of the purse." Since Congress controls expenditures, it can limit the powers of the President by limiting the amount of money the Chief Executive may spend to run the government. This clause is perhaps the single most important curb on Presidential power in the Constitution. Furthermore, the requirement to account for money spent and received helps to protect against misuse of funds.

8. No title of noblity shall be granted by the United States; and no person holding any office of profit or trust under them, shall, without the consent of the Congress, accept of any present, emolument, office, or title, of any kind whatever, from any king, prince, or foreign state.

¶ *Clause 8.* This clause prohibits the establishment of a nobility. It also discourages bribery of American officials by foreign governments.

SECTION 10. POWERS DENIED TO THE STATES

¶ According to Section 10, states cannot: (1) Make treaties. (2) Coin money. (3) Pass either bills of attainder or ex post facto laws. (4) Impair obligations of contract. (5) Grant titles of nobility. (6) Tax imports or exports without the consent of Congress. (7) Keep troops or warships in time of peace. (8) Deal with another state or foreign power without the consent of Congress. (9) Engage in war unless invaded.

1. No state shall enter into any treaty, alliance, or confederation; grant letters of marque and reprisal; coin money; emit bills of credit; make anything but gold and silver coin a tender in payment of debts; pass any bill of attainder, *ex post facto* law, or law impairing the obligation of contracts, or grant any titlo of nobility.

¶ *Clause 1.* Because Shays' Rebellion was still fresh in the minds of the delegates to the Constitutional Convention, and since several of the states at that time were being urged to pass legislation relieving debtors from the payment of their debts, the delegates decided to protect creditors once and for all by denying states the right to pass laws that would impair obligations of contract. During the Great Depression which began in 1929, and the New Deal period (1933–45), the Supreme Court upheld state laws relieving debtors or mortgagees from paying their debts on the due dates, but payments were simply postponed, not canceled.

2. No state shall, without the consent of the Congress, lay any imposts or duties on imports or exports, except what may be absolutely necessary for executing its inspection laws; and the net produce of all duties and imposts, laid by any state on imports or exports, shall be for the use of the Treasury of the United States; and all such laws shall be subject to the revision and control of the Congress.

¶ *Clause 2.* The powers forbidden to the states in this clause are to vote for taxes on goods sent in or out of a state, unless Congress agrees.

3. No state shall, without the consent of Congress, lay any duty of tonnage, keep troops, or ships of war in time of peace, enter into any agreement or compact with another state, or with a foreign power, or engage in war, unless actually invaded, or in such imminent danger as will not admit of delay.

¶ *Clause 3.* **This clause forbids the states to keep troops or warships in peacetime or to deal with another state or a foreign nation, unless Congress agrees.**

ARTICLE 2. EXECUTIVE DEPARTMENT

SECTION 1. PRESIDENT AND VICE-PRESIDENT

1. Term of office. The executive power shall be vested in a President of the United States of America. He shall hold his office during the term of four years, and together with the Vice-President, chosen for the same term, be elected as follows:

¶ *Clause 1.* **This provision gives the executive power to the President. The President may use all of the means available to carry out the laws or refrain from using some of these means. Of course, the power and prestige of the Presidency depend to some extent on the personality of the person who holds the office.**

2. Electoral system. Each state shall appoint, in such manner as the legislature thereof may direct, a number of electors, equal to the whole number of Senators and Representatives to which the state may be entitled in the Congress; but no Senator or Representative, or person holding an office or trust or profit under the United States, shall be appointed an elector.

¶ *Clauses 2, 3.* **These clauses established the electoral system, but very little that the framers decided about electing a President has survived in the form they intended. The delegates to the Constitutional Convention, still fearful of popular rule, decided that the President and Vice-President ought to be elected by a small group of persons called "electors," chosen according to a method determined by each state legislature. Until Andrew Jackson's Presidency, electors were chosen by state legislatures. Since then, the people have voted directly for the electors. Some changes in the method of electing a President have been made by formal amendment, as in Amendment 12; other changes have resulted from political practice.**

3. Former method of using the electoral system. [The electors shall meet in their respective states, and vote by ballot for two persons, of whom one at least shall not be an inhabitant of the same state with themselves. And they shall make a list of all the persons voted for, and of the number of votes for each; which list they shall sign and certify, and transmit sealed to the seat of the government of the United States, directed to the president of the Senate. The president of the Senate shall, in the presence of the Senate and House of Representatives, open all the certificates, and the votes shall then be counted. The person having the greatest number of votes shall be the President, if such number be a majority of the whole number of electors appointed; and if there be more than one who have such majority, and have an equal number of votes, then the House of Representatives shall immediately choose by ballot one of them for President; and if no person have a majority, then from the five highest on the list the said House shall in like manner choose the President. But in choosing the President the votes shall be taken by states, the representation from each state having one vote. A quorum for this purpose shall consist of a member or members from two-thirds of the states, and a majority of all the states shall be necessary to a choice. In every case, after the choice of the President, the person having the greatest number of votes of the electors shall be the Vice-President. But if there should remain two or more who have equal votes, the Senate shall choose from them by ballot the Vice-President.]

4. Time of elections. The Congress may determine the time of choosing the electors, and the day on which they shall give their votes; which day shall be the same throughout the United States.

¶ Clause 4. Today, Presidential elections are held on the first Tuesday after the first Monday in November. Electoral votes are cast on the first Monday after the second Wednesday in December.

5. Qualifications for President. No person except a natural-born citizen [or a citizen of the United States, at the time of the adoption of this Constitution], shall be eligible to the office of the President; neither shall any person be eligible to that office who shall not have attained to the age of thirty-five years, and been fourteen years a resident within the United States.

¶ Clause 5. This clause specifies the qualifications for President: (1) A native-born citizen of the United States. (2) At least 35 years of age. (3) A resident of the United States for at least 14 years. ¶ TERM OF OFFICE: 4 years.

6. Filling vacancies. In case of the removal of the President from office, or of his death, resignation, or inability to discharge the powers and duties of the said office, the same shall devolve on the Vice-President, and the Congress may by law provide for the case of removal, death, resignation, or inability, both of the President and Vice-President, declaring what officer shall then act as President, and such officer shall act accordingly, until the disability be removed, or a President shall be elected.

¶ Clause 6. If a President dies or is removed from office, the Vice-President succeeds to the office. John Tyler, in 1841, was the first Vice-President to succeed to the Presidency. By assuming the office of President, not simply serving as an acting President, Tyler established a precedent that has since been followed. ¶ Under the Presidential Succession Act of 1947, if both the President and the Vice-President die or are removed from office, the order of succession is as follows: (1) Speaker of the House, (2) President pro tempore of the Senate, and (3) the cabinet members in the order in which their offices were created. ¶ Amendment 25, adopted in 1967, clarifies the procedure to be followed in case the President or Vice-President is unable to serve or resigns.

7. Salary. The President shall, at stated times, receive for his services, a compensation, which shall neither be increased nor diminished during the period for which he shall have been elected, and he shall not receive within that period any other emolument from the United States, or any of them.

¶ Clause 7. In 1969 the President's salary was set by law at $200,000 a year, plus a $50,000 expense account and a nontaxable fund for travel and official entertainment limited to $40,000. The Vice-President's salary was set, in 1969, at $62,500 a year plus a $10,000 expense allowance.

8. Oath of office. Before he enter on the execution of his office, he shall take the following oath or affirmation:—"I do solemnly swear (or affirm) that I will faithfully execute the office of President of the United States, and will to the best of my ability, preserve, protect, and defend the Constitution of the United States."

¶ Clause 8. The President assumes office officially only after taking the oath of office, which is administered by the Chief Justice of the United States.

SECTION 2. POWERS OF THE PRESIDENT

1. Military powers. The President shall be Commander in Chief of the Army and Navy of the United States, and of the militia of the sev-

¶ Clause 1. The important point in this provision is that it places the armed forces under civilian control. The President is a civilian but is superior in military power to any military

eral states, when called into the actual service of the United States; he may require the option, in writing, of the principal officer in each of the executive departments, upon any subject relating to the duties of their respective offices, and he shall have power to grant reprieves and pardons for offenses against the United States, except in cases of impeachment.

officer. ¶ The words "principal officer in each of the executive departments" are the basis for the creation of the President's cabinet. Each cabinet member is the head of one of the executive departments. The President chooses the cabinet members, with the consent of the Senate, and can remove any cabinet official without asking Senate approval.

2. Treaties and appointments. He shall have power, by and with the advice and consent of the Senate, to make treaties, provided two-thirds of the Senators present concur; and he shall nominate, and by and with the advice and consent of the Senate, shall appoint ambassadors, other public ministers and consuls, judges of the Supreme Court, and all other officers of the United States, whose appointments are not herein otherwise provided for, and which shall be established by law; but the Congress may by law vest the appointment of such inferior officers, as they think proper, in the President alone, in the courts of law, or in the heads of departments.

¶ *Clause 2.* The President makes treaties with the advice and consent of two thirds of the Senate. A treaty ratified by the Senate becomes the supreme law of the land. The President can also enter into executive agreements with foreign governments which have the same force as treaties but do not require Senate approval. ¶ With the consent of the Senate, the President can appoint ambassadors, public ministers and consuls, and other diplomatic officials, federal judges, military officers, and members of administrative agencies. "Inferior officers" are those subordinate to the cabinet members or to federal judges. ¶ At the present time, a majority of federal government positions are filled by men and women who have passed examinations given by the United States Civil Service Commission.

3. Filling vacancies. The President shall have power to fill up all vacancies that may happen during the recess of the Senate, by granting commissions which shall expire at the end of their next session.

¶ *Clause 3.* If a vacancy in an important position occurs when Congress is not in session, the President has the power to fill such a vacancy with an interim appointment. When Congress meets again, this appointment, or a new appointment, must be submitted to the Senate so that it may be approved.

SECTION 3. DUTIES OF THE PRESIDENT

He shall from time to time give to the Congress information of the state of the Union, and recommend to their consideration such measures as he shall judge necessary and expedient; he may, on extraordinary occasions, convene both houses, or either of them, and in case of disagreement between them, with respect to the time of adjournment, he may adjourn them to such time as he shall think proper; he shall receive ambassadors and other public ministers; he shall take care that the laws be faithfully executed, and shall commission all the officers of the United States.

¶ The President's duties include: (1) *Legislative duties:* delivering annual and special messages to Congress; calling special sessions of Congress; approving or vetoing bills (see Article 1, Section 7). (2) *Diplomatic duties:* receiving (or refusing to receive) ambassadors or ministers of foreign countries to indicate that the United States "recognizes" (or refuses to "recognize") the government of these countries. The President can also send home the ambassador of a foreign country as a sign that the United States is breaking off diplomatic relations with that country. (3) *Executive duties:* executing all the laws. In actual fact, the administration and enforcement of the laws are in the hands of the various government departments, commissions, and administrative agencies; but the President is responsible for seeing that they are carried out. (4) *Military duties:* commissioning of United States armed forces officers.

SECTION 4. IMPEACHMENT

The President, Vice-President, and all civil officers of the United States, shall be removed from office on impeachment for, and conviction of, treason, bribery, or other high crimes and misdemeanors.

¶ (See annotation of Article 1, Section 3, Clauses 6–7.)

ARTICLE 3. JUDICIAL DEPARTMENT

¶ By authorizing the establishment of a system of federal courts, Article 3 creates the judicial power—the power to hear and decide cases. Under the judicial powers granted by the Constitution or developed through Supreme Court decisions, the courts have declared unconstitutional certain laws of Congress, acts of the President, laws of the state legislatures, and decisions of the state courts.

SECTION 1. FEDERAL COURTS

The judicial power of the United States shall be vested in one Supreme Court, and in such inferior courts as the Congress may from time to time ordain and establish. The judges, both of the Supreme and inferior courts, shall hold their offices during good behavior, and shall, at stated times, receive for their services a compensation, which shall not be diminished during their continuance in office.

¶ Only the Supreme Court is established by the Constitution itself, but the Constitution gives Congress the authority to establish the lower courts which exist today. Since the Constitution does not state the number of justices to be appointed to the Supreme Court, Congress decides the number by law. Today, the Supreme Court has nine justices. ¶ Congress has created two types of lower courts. One type includes federal district courts and Courts of Appeals, which review cases sent up by the district courts. District courts and Courts of Appeals are called "constitutional courts" because they are general courts deriving their power directly from the Constitution. The second type of court deals with cases of a specialized nature. The Court of Claims, the Tax Court, and the Court of Customs and Patent Appeals are included in this second group. ¶ The framers of the Constitution wanted to make sure that federal judges would be independent of political influence. Accordingly, federal judges are appointed for life, subject to good behavior, and their pay cannot be reduced by law during their term of office.

SECTION 2. JURISDICTION OF FEDERAL COURTS

1. General jurisdiction. The judicial power shall extend to all cases, in law and equity, arising under this Constitution, the laws of the United States, and treaties made or which shall be made, under their authority; to all cases affecting ambassadors, other public ministers and consuls; to all cases of admirality and maritime jurisdiction; to controversies to which the United States shall be a party; to controversies between two or more states; [between a state and citizens of another state;] between citizens of the same state claiming lands under grants of different states, and between a state or the citizens thereof, and foreign states, citizens, or subjects.

¶ *Clause 1.* Here the words "law" and "equity" have special meanings. "Law" means the common law—the laws that originated in England and that have been based on centuries of judicial decisions. "Equity" refers to principles of justice also developed in England to remedy wrongs in situations in which the common law was inadequate. Today, in the United States, law and equity are applied by the same judges in the same courts. ¶ The power of the federal courts extends to two types of cases: (1) those involving the interpretation of the Constitution, federal laws, treaties, and laws relating to ships on the high seas and navigable waters; and (2) those involving the United States government itself, foreign diplomatic officials, two or more state governments, and citizens of different states when the sum involved is more than $10,000; also cases involving a state or its citizens versus foreign countries or citizens of foreign countries.

2. Supreme Court. In all cases affecting ambassadors, other public ministers and consuls, and those in which a state shall be a party, the Supreme Court shall have original jurisdiction. In all the other cases before mentioned, the Supreme Court shall have appellate jurisdiction, both as to law and fact, with such exceptions, and under such regulations as the Congress shall make.

¶ *Clause 2.* "Original jurisdiction" means the right to try a case before any other court may hear it. "Appellate jurisdiction" means the right of a court to try cases appealed from lower courts. Most of the cases tried by the Supreme Court are cases appealed from lower federal and state courts. Cases involving foreign diplomats and any state of the United States may be started directly in the Supreme Court.

3. Conduct of trials. The trial of all crimes, except in cases of impeachment, shall be by jury; and such trial shall be held in the state where the said crimes shall have been com-

¶ *Clause 3.* Every person accused of a federal crime is guaranteed a jury trial near the scene of the crime. But accused persons may give up this privilege, if they wish. ¶ Amendments 5, 6, and 7 expand the provisions of this clause.

mitted; but when not committed within any state, the trial shall be at such place or places as the Congress may by law have directed.

SECTION 3. TREASON

1. Definition. Treason against the United States shall consist only in levying war against them, or in adhering to their enemies, giving them aid and comfort. No person shall be convicted of treason unless on the testimony of two witnesses to the same overt act, or on confession in open court.

¶ Clause 1. Treason is the only crime specifically defined in the Constitution. To be found guilty of treason, a person must be shown to have helped wage war against the United States, or to have given aid and comfort to its enemies. A person cannot be convicted without the testimony of two witnesses to the same act unless the person confesses in open court.

2. Punishment. The Congress shall have power to declare the punishment of treason, but no attainder of treason shall work corruption of blood or forfeiture except during the life of the person attainted.

¶ Clause 2. The punishment for treason, as determined by Congress, is death or a fine of $10,000 and imprisonment for not less than five years. This clause further states that the punishment for treason cannot be extended to the children of a traitor. They cannot be deprived of their rights and their property—as had been done in England.

ARTICLE 4. RELATIONS AMONG THE STATES

SECTION 1. OFFICIAL ACTS

Full faith and credit shall be given in each state to the public acts, records, and judicial proceedings of every other state. And the Congress may by general laws prescribe the manner in which such acts, records, and proceedings shall be proved, and the effect thereof.

¶ The purpose of this provision is to make sure that the official records of one state are respected in all the other states. Official records of this kind include birth certificates, marriage licenses, and death certificates; corporation charters, wills, and court decisions. This provision also protects a citizen's right to collect money that has been awarded by a court decision in one state, even if the person who owes the money moves to another state.

SECTION 2. PRIVILEGES OF CITIZENS

1. Privileges. The citizens of each state shall be entitled to all privileges and immunities of citizens in the several states.

¶ Clause 1. The terms "privileges" and "immunities" simply mean the rights of citizens. Thus, a state cannot discriminate against citizens of other states in favor of its own citizens, except in certain very special areas—such as voting, for example. A state can impose residence requirements for voting, so that citizens of another state must reside in the state for a specified period before they can vote as citizens of their new state.

2. Extradition. A person charged in any state with treason, felony, or other crime, who shall flee from justice, and be found in another state, shall on demand of the executive authority of the state from which he fled, be delivered up, to be removed to the state having jurisdiction of the crime.

¶ Clause 2. This provision prevents a prisoner or a person charged with a crime from escaping justice by fleeing across a state line. It provides that a criminal be returned by the state where captured to the state where the crime was committed—a process known as "extradition." A governor of a state cannot be forced to extradite, or return, a prisoner, however, if the governor feels that such action will result in injustice to the accused person.

3. Fugtive slaves. [No person held in service or labor in one state, under the laws thereof, escaping into another, shall in consequence of any law or regulation therein, be discharged from such service or labor, but shall be delivered up on claim of the party to whom such service or labor may be due.]

¶ Clause 3. Since the ratification of Amendment 13 in 1865 brought an end to slavery in this country, the clause is now of historical interest only.

SECTION 3. NEW STATES AND TERRITORIES

1. Admission of new states. New states may be admitted by the Congress into this Union; but no new state shall be formed or erected within the jurisdiction of any other state; nor any state be formed by the junction of two or more states, or parts of states, without the consent of the legislatures of the states concerned as well as of the Congress.

2. Powers of Congress over territories and other property. The Congress shall have power to dispose of and make all needful rules and regulations respecting the territory or other property belonging to the United States; and nothing in this Constitution shall be so construed as to prejudice any claims of the United States, or of any particular state.

SECTION 4. GUARANTEES TO THE STATES

The United States shall guarantee to every state in this Union a republican form of government, and shall protect each of them against invasion; and on application of the legislature, or of the executive (when the legislature cannot be convened) against domestic violence.

¶ *Clause 1.* The Northwest Ordinance of 1787 provided that new states be admitted to the Union on completely equal footing with the original thirteen states. Although the Constitution declares here that new states may not be created within the territory of any other state without its consent, an exception did occur in 1863, when West Virginia was formed from the western part of the state of Virginia. This exception occurred during the Civil War, and West Virginia received permission from the loyal, rather than the secessionist, government of Virginia.

¶ *Clause 2.* Under this provision, Congress has the power to control all property belonging to the federal government. It can set up governments for Territories and colonies of the United States. It can grant independence to a colony, as it did to the Philippines in 1946. It can set aside land for national parks and build dams for flood control.

¶ If public property is being destroyed and public safety is endangered in a state, the President may decide to send troops into that state without having been requested to do so by local authorities. The President may even proclaim martial law in a state. This section also guarantees that states can govern only by consent of the governed.

ARTICLE 5. METHODS OF AMENDMENT

The Congress, whenever two-thirds of both houses shall deem it necessary, shall propose amendments to this Constitution, or, on the application of the legislatures of two-thirds of the several states, shall call a convention for proposing amendments, which, in either case, shall be valid to all intents and purposes, as part of this Constitution, when ratified by the legislatures of three-fourths of the several states, or by conventions in three-fourths thereof, as the one or the other mode of ratification may be proposed by the Congress; provided that [no amendments which may be made prior to the year 1808 shall in any manner affect the first and fourth clauses in the Ninth Section of the First Article; and that] no state, without its consent, shall be deprived of its equal suffrage in the Senate.

¶ One of the most important features of the Constitution is that it can be amended, or changed. This adaptability is one of the four main principles of the Constitution. ¶ An amendment must first be *proposed,* and then *ratified.* There are four methods of amending the Constitution. So far, all amendments have been proposed by Congress and ratified by state legislatures, except Amendment 21, which was ratified by the convention method. ¶ The fact that only 26 amendments have been adopted since 1789—and only 16 since 1791—indicates that it is not easy to change the Constitution, and that changing it is a serious matter, requiring much thought and discussion in Congress, in the state legislatures, and among the people. ¶ Notice that there are two areas in which the Constitution cannot be amended under any circumstances. The first exception is obsolete because it is a reference to the period which preceded 1808. The second exception is still very important because it guarantees that every state shall have equal representation in the Senate.

ARTICLE 6. GENERAL PROVISIONS

1. Public debts. All debts contracted and engagements entered into, before the adoption of this Constitution, shall be as valid against the United States under this Constitution, as under the Confederation.

¶ *Clause 1.* This provision was important because it announced to all that the new government would assume and pay back all debts of the government under the Articles of Confederation. It was one of several actions favored by Alexander Hamilton and undertaken by Congress in order to establish the credit of the new government.

2. The supreme law. This Constitution, and the laws of the United States which shall be made in pursuance thereof, and all treaties made, or which shall be made, under the authority of the United States, shall be the supreme law of the land; and the judges in every state shall be bound thereby, anything in the constitution or laws of any state to the contrary notwithstanding.

3. Oaths of office. The Senators and Representatives before mentioned, and the members of the several state legislatures, and all executive and judicial officers, both of the United States and of the several states, shall be bound by oath or affirmation, to support this Constitution; but no religious test shall ever be required as a qualification to any office or public trust under the United States.

¶ *Clause 2.* **This is the famous "supremacy clause" of the Constitution. It declares that the "supreme law of the land" is: (1) the Constitution, (2) the laws of the United States passed under this Constitution, and (3) the treaties made under the authority of the United States. ¶ According to the supremacy clause, the power of the national government is superior to the power of the state governments, provided that its actions are in accordance with the Constitution. The Supreme Court determines whether the actions of the President and Congress are constitutional.**

¶ *Clause 3.* **No religious qualification shall ever be required as a condition for holding public office. This provision results from the fact that in the United States there is separation of church and state. This means that a person's religion is supposed to remain a private matter, with no bearing on consideration for public office.**

ARTICLE 7. RATIFICATION

The ratification of the convention of nine states shall be sufficient for the establishment of the Constitution between the states so ratifying the same.

¶ **The Constitutional Convention was summoned by the Congress of the Confederation to amend the Articles of Confederation. Under the Articles, amendments had to be approved by all thirteen states. Instead of amending the Articles, however, the delegates to the Constitutional Convention drafted an entirely new plan of government. And realizing that it would be difficult to get the approval of all the states—Rhode Island, for example, had not even sent delegates to Philadelphia—the Framers provided that the Constitution would go into effect after ratification by only nine states, not thirteen. As a result, opponents of the Constitution said it had been adopted by revolutionary means.**

DONE in Convention by the unanimous consent of the States present the seventeenth day of September in the year of our Lord one thousand seven hundred and eighty-seven and of the independence of the United States of America the twelfth. In witness whereof we have hereunto subscribed our names,

G Washington —*President and deputy from Virginia*

NEW HAMPSHIRE

John Langdon
Nicholas Gilman

NEW YORK

Alexander Hamilton

DELAWARE

George Read
Gunning Bedford
John Dickinson
Richard Bassett
Jacob Broom

NORTH CAROLINA

William Blount
Richard Dobbs Spaight
Hugh Williamson

MASSACHUSETTS

Nathaniel Gorman
Rufus King

NEW JERSEY

William Livingston
David Brearley
William Paterson
Jonathan Dayton

MARYLAND

James McHenry
Daniel of St. Thomas Jenifer
Daniel Carroll

SOUTH CAROLINA

John Rutledge
Charles Cotesworth Pinckney
Charles Pinckney
Pierce Butler

CONNECTICUT

William Samuel Johnson
Roger Sherman

PENNSYLVANIA

Benjamin Franklin
Thomas Mifflin
Robert Morris
George Clymer
Thomas FitzSimons
Jared Ingersoll
James Wilson
Gouverneur Morris

VIRGINIA

John Blair
James Madison

GEORGIA

William Few
Abraham Baldwin

Amendments to the Constitution

(The first ten amendments to the Constitution are called the Bill of Rights. The Bill of Rights limits the powers of the federal government but not the powers of the states. The Supreme Court has ruled, however, that the "due process" clause of Amendment 14 protects individuals against denial by the states of certain rights included in the Bill of Rights. For example, the Supreme Court has decided that neither the federal government nor the states can deprive any individual of freedom of religion, speech, press, petition, assembly, or of several other rights that pertain to the fair treatment of an accused person.)

AMENDMENT 1. FREEDOM OF RELIGION, SPEECH, PRESS, ASSEMBLY, AND PETITION (1791)

Congress shall make no law respecting an establishment of religion, or prohibiting the free exercise thereof; or abridging the freedom of speech, or of the press; or the right of the people peaceably to assemble, and to petition the government for a redress of grievances.

¶ Amendment 1 protects five great civil liberties: (1) Freedom of religion means that Congress cannot interfere with the right to worship as one sees fit. The Supreme Court, however, has ruled that Congress can require "conscientious objectors" to bear arms during wartime. Congress has, however, made special provisions to permit conscientious objectors to participate in war work without bearing arms. In interpreting the phrase "establishment of religion," the Supreme Court has decided that this phrase erects a wall of separation between church and state. The Supreme Court has prohibited state and local school authorities from requiring prayers or devotional reading of the Bible in public schools. (2) Freedom of speech means the right to speak out privately and publicly. However, this right does not permit anyone to slander people (make false and malicious remarks about them). Furthermore, the Supreme Court has declared that freedom of speech can be limited by the federal government if there is a "clear and present" danger that what is said may injure the general welfare. (3) Freedom of the press gives newspapers, television, and magazines the right to express ideas and opinions provided they do not libel people (publish false and malicious remarks about them) or incite the violent overthrow of the government. Also, the use of the United States mails may be denied to those publications which spread obscenity and fraudulent ideas. (4) Freedom to assemble is the right to attend meetings and join clubs. (5) The right to petition for redress of grievances means the opportunity to express complaints to any official of the federal government.

AMENDMENT 2. RIGHT TO KEEP ARMS (1791)

A well-regulated militia, being necessary to the security of a free state, the right of the people to keep and bear arms shall not be infringed.

¶ The purpose of this amendment was to prevent Congress from denying states the right to have a militia (or National Guard) of armed citizens. It also protected Americans' right to keep weapons in order to resist a tyrannical government. In the public interest, however, Congress and many states have regulated the ownership and use of weapons by citizens through gun control legislation.

AMENDMENT 3. QUARTERING OF TROOPS (1791)

No soldier shall, in time of peace, be quartered in any house, without the consent of the owner; nor in time of war, but in a manner to be prescribed by law.

¶ Amendments 3 and 4 guarantee all citizens the right to privacy and security in their own homes. ¶ Amendment 3 was designed to prevent the national government from requiring citizens to house and feed military personnel in their homes. The quartering of troops in the colonists' homes by the British government had been a source of friction between the American colonists and the British before the American Revolution.

AMENDMENT 4. SEARCH AND SEIZURE; WARRANTS (1791)

The right of the people to be secure in their persons, houses, papers, and effects, against unreasonable searches and seizures, shall not be violated; and no warrants shall issue but upon probable cause, supported by oath or affirmation, and particularly describing the place to be searched, and the persons or things to be seized.

¶ With the hated "writs of assistance" still fresh in their minds, the supporters of this amendment aimed to limit issuance of search warrants to the following conditions: (1) the warrant must be issued by a judge; (2) there must be a good reason for its use; (3) the officer who asks for a search warrant must take an oath affirming reasons for demanding the warrant; and (4) the warrant must describe the place to be searched and the persons or things to be seized. ¶ The Supreme Court has decided that evidence illegally seized cannot be used in either federal or state courts. Under this amendment the federal government prohibits wiretapping unless a court permit is obtained showing a reasonable certainty that one of a certain list of crimes is being committed. ¶ In 1967 the Supreme Court held that eavesdropping and bugging by electronic means are permissible but only within certain limits; for example, police may use electronic eavesdropping devices if they secure a warrant in advance by showing probable cause. ¶ In 1968 the Supreme Court forbade the use of criminal evidence obtained by police listening in on a party line, but evidence derived from wiretapping is permitted in federal courts in some crimes.

AMENDMENT 5. RIGHTS OF ACCUSED PERSONS (1791)

No person shall be held to answer for a capital, or otherwise infamous, crime, unless on a presentment or indictment of a grand jury, except in cases arising in the land or naval forces, or in the militia, when in actual service in time of war or public danger; nor shall any person be subject for the same offense to be twice put in jeopardy of life and limb; nor shall be compelled, in any criminal case, to be a witness against himself; nor be deprived of life, liberty, or property, without due process of law; nor shall private property be taken for public use, without just compensation.

¶ This amendment lists the rights of an accused person: (1) A person accused of a capital crime or any other serious crime must first be accused by a grand jury (a jury of 12 to 23 persons) before being brought to trial. An "indictment" or "presentment" by a grand jury is merely a formal accusation. (2) A person cannot be tried twice for the same crime. (3) A person cannot be required to give incriminating testimony in a courtroom or before a grand jury or Congressional committee. However, under the Immunity Act of 1954, a witness can be required to testify in certain cases if the evidence he or she may provide cannot be used in any trial of that person. (4) A person cannot be deprived of life, liberty, or property without due process of law—or according to the law of the land. (5) Congress cannot take private property for public use without paying a fair price for it. This provision, an important protection of property rights, establishes the principle of "eminent domain." ¶ Members of the armed forces are tried by military courts and commissions and are not subject to the provision calling for indictment by a grand jury.

AMENDMENT 6. RIGHT TO SPEEDY TRIAL (1791)

In all criminal prosecutions, the accused shall enjoy the right to a speedy and public trial, by an impartial jury of the state and district wherein the crime shall have been committed, which district shall have been previously ascertained by law, and to be informed of the nature and cause of the accusation; to be confronted with the witnesses against him; to have compulsory process for obtaining witnesses in his favor, and to have the assistance of counsel for his defense.

¶ This amendment continues the rights of an accused person. Notice that all witnesses against an accused person must appear on the witness stand, and that the government must help the accused to produce favorable witnesses. If an accused person cannot afford to hire a lawyer, the judge will assign one, and the government will pay the lawyer's fee. These provisions under Amendment 6 apply to federal courts. However, under the "due process" clause of Amendment 14, the Supreme Court has decided that state courts must also assign a lawyer to defend an accused person who cannot afford one.

AMENDMENT 7. JURY TRIAL IN CIVIL CASES (1791)

In suits at common law, where the value in controversy shall exceed $20, the right of trial by jury shall be preserved, and no fact tried by a jury shall be otherwise re-examined in any court of the United States than according to the rules of the common law.

¶ This amendment provides for a jury trial in federal civil cases (trials where one person sues another) in which more than $20 is involved. By custom, however, civil cases are not tried before federal courts unless they involve much larger sums of money.

AMENDMENT 8. BAILS, FINES, PUNISHMENTS (1791)

Excessive bail shall not be required, nor excessive fines imposed, nor cruel and unusual punishments inflicted.

¶ Persons accused of a crime and awaiting trial may be permitted to leave jail if they or someone else posts "bail"—a sum of money serving as a guarantee that the accused will appear for trial. The courts determine the amount of bail asked for. Cruel and unusual punishments, such as torture and beheading, are prohibited. ¶ In a series of rulings the Supreme Court declared invalid convictions of accused persons based on confessions secured by torture or other "third degree" methods.

AMENDMENT 9. POWERS RESERVED TO THE PEOPLE (1791)

The enumeration in the Constitution, of certain rights, shall not be construed to deny or disparage others retained by the people.

¶ The Constitution does not describe specifically all the rights to be retained by the people. This amendment was added in order to guarantee that those fundamental rights not enumerated must be respected by the national government at all times.

AMENDMENT 10. POWERS RESERVED TO THE STATES (1791)

The powers not delegated to the United States by the Constitution, nor prohibited by it to the states, are reserved to the states respectively, or to the people.

AMENDMENT 11. SUITS AGAINST STATES (1798)

The judicial power of the United States shall not be construed to extend to any suit in law or equity, commenced or prosecuted against one of the United States, by citizens of another state, or by citizens or subjects of any foreign state.

¶ This is the first amendment to the Constitution which was designed to overrule a Supreme Court decision. In the case of *Chisholm v. Georgia* (1793), the Supreme Court ruled that two citizens of South Carolina could sue Georgia in a federal court for property that Georgia had confiscated. The states objected, arguing that since the states were sovereign, it was undignified to permit a state to be sued by a citizen of another state in a federal court. As a result of this amendment, a citizen of the United States or of a foreign nation who wishes to bring suit against any state is required to introduce the case in the courts of the state which is being sued.

AMENDMENT 12. ELECTION OF PRESIDENT AND VICE-PRESIDENT (1804)

The electors shall meet in their respective states, and vote by ballot for President and Vice-President, one of whom, at least, shall not be an inhabitant of the same state with themselves; they shall name in their ballots the person voted for as President, and in distinct ballots the person voted for as Vice-President, and they shall make distinct lists of all persons voted for as President, and of all persons voted for as Vice-President, and of the number of votes for each, which lists they shall sign and certify, and transmit, sealed, to the seat of government of the United States, directed to the President of the Senate; the President of the Senate shall, in the presence of the Senate and House of Representatives, open all the certificates and the votes shall then be counted; the person having the greatest number of votes for President shall be the President, if such number be a majority of the whole number of electors appointed; and if no person have such majority, then from the persons having the highest numbers not exceeding three on the list of those voted for as President, the House of Representatives shall choose immediately, by ballot, the President. But in choosing the President, the votes shall be taken by states, the representation from each state having one vote; a quorum for this purpose shall consist of a member or members from two-thirds of the states, and a majority of all the states shall be necessary to a choice. [And if the House of Representatives shall not choose a President whenever the right of choice shall devolve upon them, before the fourth day of March next following, then the Vice-President shall act as President, as in the case of the death or other constitutional disability of the President.] The person having the greatest number of votes as

¶ This amendment alters Article 2, Section 1, Clause 3. Before this amendment, the electors voted for two persons, without designating which was to be President and which Vice-President. As a result, in 1796 the people elected a Federalist President (John Adams) and a Republican Vice-President (Jefferson). In 1800 the electors of the victorious Republican Party each cast one vote for Jefferson, whom they wanted to be President, and one vote for Burr, whom they wanted to be Vice-President. The result, of course, was a tie. Amendment 12, which instructs electors to cast separate ballots for President and Vice-President, prevents such situations. (See also Amendment 23, which makes provision for choosing electors of President and Vice-President by the District of Columbia.)

Vice-President, shall be the Vice-President, if such number be a majority of the whole number of electors appointed, and if no person have a majority, then, from the two highest numbers on the list, the Senate shall choose the Vice-President; a quorum for the purpose shall consist of two-thirds of the whole number of Senators, and a majority of the whole number shall be necessary to a choice. But no person constitutionally ineligible to the office of President shall be eligible to that of Vice-President of the United States.

AMENDMENT 13. SLAVERY ABOLISHED (1865)

SECTION 1. Neither slavery nor involuntary servitude, except as a punishment for crime whereof the party shall have been duly convicted, shall exist within the United States, or any place subject to their jurisdiction.

SECTION 2. Congress shall have power to enforce this article by appropriate legislation.

¶ Amendments 13, 14, and 15 resulted from the Civil War. Amendment 13 freed the slaves, Amendment 14 made Negroes citizens, and Amendment 15 forbade the states to deny black Americans the right to vote. ¶ Amendment 13 forbids slavery, and under Section 2, Congress has the power to enforce this order.

AMENDMENT 14. RIGHTS OF CITIZENS (1868)

SECTION 1. Citizenship defined. All persons born or naturalized in the United States and subject to the jurisdiction thereof, are citizens of the United States and of the state wherein they reside. No state shall make or enforce any law which shall abridge the privileges or immunities of citizens of the United States; nor shall any state deprive any person of life, liberty, or property, without due process of law; nor deny to any person within its jurisdiction the equal protection of the laws.

¶ This section contains a number of important provisions. By the definition of citizenship given here, black Americans were granted citizenship. The second sentence, forbidding states to abridge the privileges and immunities—the rights—of citizens, meant that the states could not interfere with the right of black Americans and other citizens to live a peaceful, useful life, or to travel. ¶ This amendment, like Amendment 5, contains a "due process of law" clause. Amendment 5 denies to Congress and Amendment 14 denies to the states the power to deprive any person of life, liberty, or property without "due process of law." This amendment, originally intended to protect black citizenship, has been broadly interpreted by the courts as a protection for corporations. Corporations, under this interpretation, are considered as "persons." Their property cannot be taken away except by fair, legal methods. Thus, for example, the Interstate Commerce Commission can fix railroad rates only after giving railroad corporations an opportunity to present their side of the case. ¶ The "due process" clause also protects individuals from unfair actions by their state governments. It protects their rights of freedom of religion, speech, press, petition, and peaceful assembly, and the rights of persons accused of crimes against state abuses. It prevents a state, in the exercise of its police power (the power to protect its people), from depriving anyone of civil liberties, except during a national emergency. ¶ The last provision of Section 1 prevents a state from denying equal protection of the laws. In 1954, in the case of *Brown v. Board of Education of Topeka,* the Supreme Court interpreted this provision to mean that segregation in public schools is unconstitutional. Also, in *Baker v. Carr* (1962) the Supreme Court ruled that unfair apportionment of representation in state legislatures violates the equal protection clause of this amendment.

668

SECTION 2. Apportionment of Representatives. Representatives shall be apportioned among the several states according to their respective numbers, counting the whole number of persons in each state, [excluding Indians not taxed]. But when the right to vote at any election for the choice of electors for President and Vice-President of the United States, Representatives in Congress, the executive and judicial officers of a state, or the members of the legislature thereof, is denied to any of the male inhabitants of such state, [being twenty-one years of age] and citizens of the United States, or in any way abridged, except for participation in rebellion, or other crime, the basis of representation therein shall be reduced in the proportion which the number of such male citizens shall bear to the whole number of male citizens [twenty-one years of age] in such state.

¶ This section was never implemented, but later civil rights laws and Amendment 24 guaranteed the vote to black Americans. The Dawes Act and the 1924 citizenship law enfranchised Indians. And Amendment 26 changed the voting age from 21 to 18. This section dealing with apportionment of Representatives is sometimes called the "dead letter clause" of Amendment 14 since its provisions were never carried out.

SECTION 3. Disability for engaging in insurrection. No person shall be a Senator or Representative in Congress, or elector of President and Vice-President, or hold any office, civil or military, under the United States, or under any state, who, having previously taken an oath, as a member of Congress, or as an officer of the United States, or as a member of any state legislature, or as an executive or judicial officer of any state, to support the Constitution of the United States, shall have engaged in insurrection or rebellion against the same, or given aid or comfort to the enemies thereof. But Congress may, by vote of two-thirds of each house, remove such disability.

¶ This section aimed to punish the leaders of the Confederacy for having broken their oath to support the Constitution of the United States. All officials who had taken this oath and who later joined the Confederacy in the Civil War were disqualified from holding federal or state offices. Although many southern leaders were excluded under this section from holding office after the war, by 1872 most of them were permitted to return to political life. In 1898 all of the others were pardoned.

SECTION 4. Public debt. The validity of the public debt of the United States, authorized by law, including debts incurred for payment of pensions and bounties for services in suppressing insurrection or rebellion, shall not be questioned. But neither the United States nor any state shall assume or pay any debt or obligation incurred in aid of insurrection or rebellion against the United States [or any claim for the loss or emancipation of any slave]; but all such debts, obligations, and claims shall be held illegal and void.

¶ This section makes three important points: (1) The public debt of the United States incurred in fighting the Civil War was valid and could never be questioned by southerners. (2) The Confederate debt was void. It was illegal for the federal government or the states to pay any money on Confederate debts. This provision was meant to serve as a harsh lesson to all who had invested money in Confederate bonds. (3) No payment was to be made for the loss of former slaves.

SECTION 5. Enforcement. The Congress shall have power to enforce, by appropriate legislation, the provisions of this article.

AMENDMENT 15. RIGHT OF SUFFRAGE (1870)

SECTION 1. The right of citizens of the United States to vote shall not be denied or abridged by the United States or any state on account of race, color, or previous condition of servitude.

SECTION 2. The Congress shall have power to enforce this article by appropriate legislation.

¶ The purpose of this amendment was to extend the *franchise,* or the right to vote, to Negroes. Thus, according to this amendment, any person who can meet all of the qualifications for suffrage in a particular state cannot be deprived of the right to vote simply because of race or color.

AMENDMENT 16. INCOME TAX (1913)

The Congress shall have power to lay and collect taxes on incomes, from whatever source derived, without apportionment among the several states, and without regard to any census or enumeration.

¶ In 1894, Congress passed an income tax law. The following year, the Supreme Court declared this tax law unconstitutional. The Court stated that the income tax was a direct tax and, therefore, according to the Constitution (Article 1, Section 2, Clause 3; Article 1, Section 9, Clause 4) should have been apportioned among the states according to their population. This decision was unpopular because it prevented the government from taxing people on the basis of their incomes in order to pay for government expenses, which were already large, and growing larger. Amendment 16 overruled the Supreme Court decision and gave Congress the power to tax incomes from any source, and without apportionment among the states according to population. Today, income taxes are the federal government's major source of income.

AMENDMENT 17. ELECTION OF SENATORS (1913)

SECTION 1. Method of election. The Senate of the United States shall be composed of two Senators from each state, elected by the people thereof, for six years; and each Senator shall have one vote. The electors in each state shall have the qualifications requisite for electors of the most numerous branch of the state legislatures.

SECTION 2. Filling vacancies. When vacancies happen in the representation of any state in the Senate, the executive authority of such state shall issue writs of election to fill such vacancies: *Provided* that the legislature of any state may empower the executive thereof to make temporary appointments until the people fill the vacancies by election as the legislature may direct.

[**SECTION 3. Not retroactive.** This amendment shall not be so construed as to affect the election or term of any Senator chosen before it becomes valid as part of the Constitution.]

¶ Before the passage of this amendment, Senators were chosen by the state legislatures (see Article 1, Section 3, Clause 1). There was a great deal of dissatisfaction with this method because it gave the voters little control over the Senate. Amendment 17 provides for the direct election of Senators by the voters of each state, thus making Senators more responsive to the will of the voters who put them in office.

AMENDMENT 18. NATIONAL PROHIBITION (1919)

[**SECTION 1.** After one year from the ratification of this article the manufacture, sale, or transportation of intoxicating liquors within, the importation thereof into, or the exportation thereof from, the United States and all territory subject to the jurisdiction thereof for beverage purposes is hereby prohibited.

SECTION 2. The Congress and the several states shall have concurrent power to enforce this article by appropriate legislation.

SECTION 3. This article shall be inoperative unless it shall have been ratified as an amendment to the Constitution by the legislatures of the several states, as provided in the Constitution, within seven years from the date of the submission hereof to the states by the Congress.]

¶ This amendment outlawed the making, sale, or transportation of alcoholic beverages in the United States except for special purposes. This amendment was later repealed by Amendment 21.

AMENDMENT 19. WOMAN SUFFRAGE (1920)

SECTION 1. The right of citizens of the United States to vote shall not be denied or abridged by the United States or by any state on account of sex.

SECTION 2. Congress shall have power to enforce this article by appropriate legislation.

¶ This amendment, extending the right to vote to all qualified women, marked the greatest single step in extending the suffrage in the United States. Women's struggle to win this basic right began many years before the nineteenth amendment was finally ratified.

AMENDMENT 20. "LAME DUCK" AMENDMENT (1933)

SECTION 1. Beginning of terms. The terms of the President and Vice-President shall end at noon on the 20th day of January, and the terms of Senators and Representatives at noon on the 3rd day of January, of the years in which such terms would have ended if this article had not been ratified; and the terms of their successors shall then begin.

¶ When the Constitution was written, transportation and communication were so slow that a new President and new members of Congress elected in November could not reach the capital to take office until March 4. However, since sessions of Congress began in December, a session including newly elected members could not be held until 13 months after their election. Thus, even if a member running for re-election were defeated in November, he or she would serve in the session of Congress which began the month after this election, and continue to serve several more months. Since defeated candidates had been rejected by the voters they were called "lame ducks," suggesting that their "political wings" had been clipped. One purpose of Amendment 20 was to limit the term and power of "lame duck" members.

SECTION 2. Beginning of Congressional sessions. The Congress shall assemble at least once in every year, and such meeting shall begin at noon on the 3d day of January, unless they shall by law appoint a different day.

SECTION 3. Presidential succession. If at the time fixed for the beginning of the term of the President, the President-elect shall have died, the Vice-President-elect shall become President. If a President shall not have been chosen before the time fixed for the beginning of his term, or if the President-elect shall have failed to qualify, then the Vice-President-elect shall act as President until a President shall have qualified; and the Congress may by law provide for the case wherein neither a President-elect nor a Vice-President-elect shall have qualified, declaring who shall then act as President, or the manner in which one who is to act shall be selected, and such person shall act accordingly until a President or Vice-President shall have qualified.

SECTION 4. Filling Presidential vacancy. The Congress may by law provide for the case of the death of any of the persons from whom the House of Representatives may choose a President whenever the right of choice shall have devolved upon them, and for the case of the death of any of the persons from whom the Senate may choose a Vice-President whenever the right of choice shall have devolved upon them.

[**SECTION 5. Effective date.** Sections 1 and 2 shall take effect on the 15th day of October following the ratification of this article.

SECTION 6. Time limit for ratification. This article shall be inoperative unless it shall have been ratified as an amendment to the Constitution by the legislatures of three-fourths of the several states within seven years from the date of its submission.]

AMENDMENT 21. REPEAL OF PROHIBITION (1933)

SECTION 1. The eighteenth article of amendment to the Constitution of the United States is hereby repealed.

¶ This amendment, which repealed Amendment 18, was the only amendment ratified by special state conventions instead of state legislatures. Congress felt that a popular referendum (vote) would give the people a better chance to voice their opinions on prohibition. As in Amendments 18 and 20, Congress included a provision that the amendment, to become law, have a seven-year limit for ratification by the states.

SECTION 2. The transportation or importation into any state, territory, or possession of the United States for delivery or use therein of intoxicating liquors, in violation of the laws thereof, is hereby prohibited.

[**SECTION 3.** This article shall be inoperative unless it shall have been ratified as an amendment to the Constitution by conventions in the several states, as provided in the Constitution, within seven years from the date of the submission hereof to the states by the Congress.]

AMENDMENT 22. TWO-TERM LIMIT FOR PRESIDENTS (1951)

SECTION 1. No person shall be elected to the office of the President more than twice, and no person who has held the office of President, or acted as President, for more than two years of a term to which some other person was elected President shall be elected to the office of the President more than once. [But this Article shall not apply to any person holding the office of President when this Article was proposed by the Congress, and shall not prevent any person who may be holding the office of President, or acting as President, during the term within which this Article becomes operative from holding the office of President or acting as President during the remainder of such term.]

[**SECTION 2.** This Article shall be inoperative unless it shall have been ratified as an amendment to the Constitution by the legislatures of three-fourths of the several states within seven years from the date of its submission to the states by the Congress.]

¶ The original Constitution placed no limit on the number of terms a President could be elected to office. Washington and Jefferson, however, set a two-term precedent. In 1940 this tradition was broken when Franklin D. Roosevelt was elected for a third term, and in 1944, when he won a fourth term. The purpose of this amendment was to write the two-term precedent into law. The bracket portion was included so that the amendment would not apply to President Truman, who was in office at the time the amendment was ratified. Note that anyone who succeeds to the Presidency and completes less than two years of another person's term may be elected for two more terms.

AMENDMENT 23. PRESIDENTIAL ELECTORS FOR DISTRICT OF COLUMBIA (1961)

SECTION 1. The District constituting the seat of Government of the United States shall appoint in such manner as the Congress may direct:

¶ Amendment 23 enabled residents of the District of Columbia to vote for President and Vice-President. In effect, it gave the capital city three members in the Electoral College, the same number elected by each of the six least populous states.

A number of electors of President and Vice-President equal to the whole number of Senators and Representatives in Congress to which the District would be entitled if it were a State, but in no event more than the least populous State; they shall be in addition to those appointed by the States, but they shall be considered, for the purposes of the election of President and Vice-President, to be electors appointed by a State; and they shall meet in the District and perform such duties as provided by the twelfth article of amendment.

SECTION 2. The Congress shall have power to enforce this article by appropriate legislation.

AMENDMENT 24. POLL TAX BANNED IN NATIONAL ELECTIONS (1964)

SECTION 1. The right of citizens of the United States to vote in any primary or other election for President or Vice-President, for electors for President or Vice-President, or for Senator or Representative in Congress, shall not be denied or abridged by the United States or any state by reason of failure to pay any poll tax or other tax.

¶ This amendment forbade the collection of poll taxes—taxes persons had to pay before they were able to vote—as a requirement for voting in federal elections. (In 1964 five southern states still had poll taxes.) In 1966 the Supreme Court ruled that poll taxes were illegal as a requirement for voting in state and local elections as well.

SECTION 2. The Congress shall have the power to enforce this article by appropriate legislation.

AMENDMENT 25. PRESIDENTIAL DISABILITY AND SUCCESSION (1967)

1. In case of the removal of the President from office or his death or resignation, the Vice-President shall become President.

2. Whenever there is a vacancy in the office of the Vice-President, the President shall nominate a Vice-President who shall take the office upon confirmation by a majority vote of both houses of Congress.

3. Whenever the President transmits to the President pro tempore of the Senate and the Speaker of the House of Representatives his written declaration that he is unable to discharge

¶ This amendment was intended to clarify Article 2, Section 1, Clause 6, particularly in the case of the temporary disability of a President. The problem of disability in office existed during the last part of President Wilson's term and occurred again when President Eisenhower was disabled by a heart attack. This amendment provided two ways (see sections 3 and 4) the Vice-President could assume the duties of the office of the President, as well as a procedure by which the President could again perform the duties of office when the disability ended.

¶ However, the first use of this amendment did not involve Presidential disability. It involved a Presidential resignation. In 1974 Richard M. Nixon became the first President in American history to resign from office. And Vice-President Gerald the powers and duties of his office, and until he transmits to them a written declaration to the contrary, such powers and duties shall be discharged by the Vice-President as Acting President.

4. Whenever the Vice-President and a majority of either the principal officers of the executive departments or of such other body as Congress may by law provide, transmit to the President pro tempore of the Senate and the Speaker of the House of Representatives their written declaration that the President is unable to discharge the powers and duties of his office, the Vice-President shall immediately assume the powers and duties of the office as Acting President.

Thereafter, when the President transmits to the President pro tempore of the Senate and the Speaker of the House of Representatives his written declaration that no inability exists, he shall resume the powers and duties of his office unless the Vice-President and a majority of either the principal officers of the executive department or of such other body as Congress may by law provide, transmit within four days to the President pro tempore of the Senate and the Speaker of the House of Representatives their written declaration that the President is unable to discharge the powers and duties of his office. Thereupon Congress shall decide the issue, assembling within 48 hours for that purpose if not in session. If the Congress, within 21 days after receipt of the latter written declaration, or, if Congress is not in session, within 21 days after Congress is required to assemble, determines by two-thirds vote of both houses that the President is unable to discharge the powers and duties of his office, the Vice-President shall continue to discharge the same as Acting President; otherwise, the President shall assume the powers and duties of his office.

R. Ford, who succeeded as President, became the first person to become President without being first elected to that office or to the Vice-Presidency. ¶ This unique situation occurred in the following way. In 1973 Vice-President Spiro T. Agnew had resigned, and President Nixon had filled the vacancy according to the provisions of Section 2 of this amendment. Gerald R. Ford, a member of the House of Representatives, had been named Vice-President with the approval of Congress. Therefore, when Nixon resigned as President during the Watergate scandal, Ford took over the Presidency. A vacancy then existed in the Vice-Presidency (see Section 2). President Ford named Nelson A. Rockefeller as Vice-President, and this nomination was also approved by a majority vote of both houses of Congress.

AMENDMENT 26. VOTING AGE LOWERED TO 18 (1971)

SECTION 1. The right of citizens of the United States, who are 18 years of age or older, to vote shall not be denied or abridged by the United States or any state on account of age.

¶ Congress, in the Voting Rights Act of 1970, had lowered the minimum voting age from 21 to 18, but the Supreme Court ruled that this law applied only to federal elections. Amendment 26 specified that 18 was the legal voting age in state, local, and federal elections.

SECTION 2. The Congress shall have the power to enforce this article by appropriate legislation.

PROPOSED AMENDMENT 27. THE WOMEN'S RIGHTS AMENDMENT

SECTION 1. Equality of rights under the law shall not be denied or abridged by the United States or by any state on account of sex.

SECTION 2. Congress shall have the power to enforce, by appropriate legislation, the provisions of this article.

¶ This amendment, submitted to the states for ratification in 1972, would prohibit discrimination based on a person's sex.

INDEX

Italicized page numbers preceded by *p, m,* or *c* refer to a picture (*p*), map (*m*), or chart (*c*) on the page.

Boldface page numbers are pages on which a definition or explanation is given.

ACKNOWLEDGMENTS

All drawings by Samuel H. Bryant. Illustration of American bald eagle with banner and shield on *Changing Ways of American Life* Chapters by Raul Mina Mora. Maps by Harold K. Faye, except those on pages 379, 620–21, 630–31, and 636–37, which are Harbrace. Charts and maps on pages 618–19, 622–29, 632–35 are by Graphic Arts International.

KEY: Bettmann, *The Bettmann Archive;* BB, *Brown Brothers;* CHS, *Chicago Historical Society;* Gilcrease, *Thomas Gilcrease Institute of American History and Art, Tulsa, Oklahoma;* HSP, *The Historical Society of Pennsylvania;* LOC, *Library of Congress;* MCNY, *Museum of the City of New York;* MMA, *The Metropolitan Museum of Art;* NYHS, *The New-York Historical Society;* NYPL, Picture Collection, *Picture Collection, the Branch Libraries, the New York Public Library;* UPI, *United Press International, Inc.;* WW, *Wide World Photos, Inc.;* Whitney, *The Whitney Museum of American Art;* Yale, *Yale University Art Gallery.*

PART OPENING PHOTOGRAPHS: p. 1, U.S. Capitol Historical Society, Kiplinger Collection; 33, BB; 176, *top,* Harbrace Archives, *bottom,* Shostal.

UNIT OPENING PHOTOGRAPHS (reading from left to right): *Unit One,* p. 34, Granger; U.S. Signal Corps National Archives; Bettmann; Culver; Culver; LOC; LOC. *Unit Two,* 86, Culver; MCNY; NYPL, *The Century Magazine;* Bettmann; UPI; BB. *Unit Three,* 143, Kennedy Galleries Inc.; MCNY; Culver; Bettmann; Detail, George Eastman House Collection; Detail, George Eastman House Collection; Culver. *Unit Four,* 177, HSP; John Lewis Stage, Photo Researchers Inc.; Culver; Imperial War Museum; Collection of George J. Goodstadt; Photoworld. *Unit Five,* 223, Bettmann; Stanley Dance; NYPL, Picture Collection; NYPL, Schomburg Collection; *Men's Wear,* Fairchild Publications; UPI. *Unit Six,* 269, BB; Tennessee Valley Authority; BB; U.S. Navy Photo, National Archives; BB; H. Armstrong Roberts; WW; UPI. *Unit Seven,* 335, WW; John Launois, Black Star; Photoworld/FPG; John Running, Stock Boston; Laura Gilpin; WW; United Nations; Peter Vadnai, Editorial Photocolor Archives Inc.; UPI; WW; Frederick De Van, Nancy Palmer Agency.

TEXT PHOTOGRAPHS: *Introduction,* p. 3, Historical Pictures Service; 5, American Museum of Natural History; 8, National Gallery of Art, Washington, D.C., Gift of Edgar William and Bernice Chrysler Garbisch; 10, National Gallery of Art, Washington, D.C., Andrew W. Mellon Collection; 11, The Pennsylvania Academy of the Fine Arts; 12, Yale, Mabel Brady Garvan Collection; 15, "The Departure," by K. A. Lamb, Addison Gallery of American Art, Phillips Academy, Andover. Mass., photo by George C. Cushing; 18, Latter Day Saints Church Graphics Library; 19, "Congress Voting Independence," by Pine and Savage, HSP; 20, Amherst Gallery; 21, copyright by White House Historical Association, photo by National Geographic Society; 24, Yale; 25, National Gallery of Art, Washington, D.C., Andrew W. Mellon Collection; 26, Bettmann; 28, "After the Sale: Slaves Going South from Richmond," by Eyre Crowe, CHS; 30, Smithsonian Institution; 31, Bettmann.

Part One, p. 35, Culver; 37, LOC; 38, NYPL, from *Harpers Weekly;* 41, Culver; 44, Bettmann; 45, Smithsonian Institution; 47, LOC; 48, CHS; 52, Granger Collection; 53, Culver; 55, The Association for the Study of Afro-American Life and History, Inc., Washington, D.C.; 57, CHS; 59, LOC; 61, NYPL, Astor, Lenox, Tilden Foundations; 63, Granger Collection; 65, NYPL, Frank Leslie's *Illustrated Newspaper,* Aug. 20, 1881; 69, NYPL, from *Harper's Weekly,* Aug. 12, 1893; 71, "The Cowboy" by Frederic Remington, Gilcrease; 73, National Collection of Fine Arts, Smithsonian Institution, 75, U.S. Signal Corps, National Archives; 78, U.S. Department of Agriculture; 79, Bettmann; 81, Solomon D. Butcher Collection, Nebraska State Historical Society; 84, Courtesy of Gene Autry; 88, NYPL, *Harpers Weekly* Oct. 20, 1882; 90, Bettmann; 91, NYPL, The Century Magazine Vol. XXVI–31; 93, F.W. Woolworth Co.; 95, Culver; 97, LOC; 99, © *Arnold Newman;* 100, MMA, Gift of Lyman G. Bloomingdale,

1901; 104, MMA, Gift of Christian A. Zabrisiae; 107, The New York State Historical Association, Cooperstown, N.Y.; 111, Whitney, 1950; 112, Harvey T. Dunn (1884–1952), American "The Homesteader's Wife" (detail), South Dakota State University, Gift of the artist to the People of South Dakota; 115, CHS; 117, Bettmann; 120, BB; 122, Gilcrease; 124, Collection of Dr. and Mrs. Irving F. Burton, photo by Joseph Klima, Jr.; 126, Bettmann; 127, UPI; 133, 134, Culver; 135, BB; 139, MCNY; 141, *Harper's Weekly,* 1879; 144, Culver; 145, Kennedy Galleries Inc.; 146, Culver; 148, Bettmann; 150, Detail, George Eastman House Collection, photo by Lewis W. Hine; 151, The Association for the Study of Afro-American Life and History, Inc., Washington, D.C.; 152, LOC; 154, James E. Wilkie, Jr.; 155, Theodore Roosevelt Collection, Harvard College Library; 157, Underwood & Underwood; 159, BB; 161, Bettmann; 162, Detail, "Cliff Dwellers" by George Bellows, 1913, Los Angeles County Museum of Art; 164, James Van Der Zee Institute; 167, MCNY; 168, Bettmann; 171, LOC; 174, Detail, George Eastman House Collection.

Part Two: p. 178, 180, LOC; 185, U.S. Signal Corps, National Archives; 186. John Lewis Stage, Photo Researchers Inc.; 188, Culver; 190. LOC; 193, 194, Culver; 197, Historical Pictures Service; 199. NYPL. *New York Herald,* December 16, 1902; 201, Alpha/FPG; 202, BB; 203, Bettmann; 205, Culver; 206, Photoworld/FPG; 209, UPI; 211, Imperial War Museum; 213, Mansell Collection; 215, Culver; 216, BB; 218, Collection of George J. Goodstadt; 224, LOC, photo by Dorothea Lange; 225, UPI; 228, NAACP photo; 229, 231, UPI; 232, BB; 233, NYHS; 234, 236, BB; 237, Bettmann; 238, LOC, photo by Dorothea Lange; 240, 241, National Archives; 243, Radio Times Hulton; 245, George Eastman House Collection, photo by Lewis W. Hine; 246, HSP; 248, 250, Photoworld/FPG; 251, BB; 225, NYPL; 256, Memorial Art Gallery of the University of Rochester; 258, © Men's Wear, Courtesy of Fairchild Publications; 260, NPYL Schomburg Collection; 261, Stanley Dance; 264, Courtesy of the Whitney; 265, Culver; 267, Courtesy of the Whitney; 270, BB; 271, Culver; 272, UPI; 275, 277, BB; 279, *top,* Harris and Ewing, *bottom,* BB; 280, Tennessee Valley Authority; 284, George Skadding; 285, 286, BB; 287, LOC; 289, UPI; 291 WW; 292, 293, BB; 294, WW; 296, Culver; 298, UPI; 300, Photoworld/FPG; 301, Culver; 304, 305, 307, WW; 310, Bettmann; 311, WW; 312, U.S. Navy Photo, National Archives; 314, Charles Phelps Cushing from H. Armstrong Roberts; 316, U.S. Navy Photo; 317, UPI; 321, WW; 323, BB; 325, UPI; 327, Margaret Bourke-White, Time-Life Picture Agency © Time, Inc.; 332, Charles Phelps Cushing from H. Armstrong Roberts; 333, BB; 336, WW; 338, UPI; 339, WW; 340, UPI; 341, Pictorial Parade; 344, UPI; 347, WW; 348, De Wys; 350, Photo Trends; 351, Liederman, *L.I. Press,* N.Y.; 352, *The Baltimore Sun;* 353, 355, UPI; 356, WW; 358, Harbrace; 359, United Nations; 362, 365, 367, UPI; 369, WW; 370, 371, 373, 375, UPI; 376, WW; 381, Camera Press, Photo Trends; 382, Dan McCoy, Black Star; 386, Tashi/Black Star; 387, Photoworld/FPG; 391, Photo Trends; 393, WW; 394, Cary Wolinsky, Stock Boston; 395, WW; 396, Dozier Mobley, Photo Trends; 398, John Running, Stock Boston; 399, LOC; 400, Peter Vadnai, Editorial Photocolor Archives; 401, Laura Gilpin; 402, Frederick De Van, Nancy Palmer Agency; 406, William Ravelli, Photo Trends; 409, Rick Cobb, Photo Trends; 411, *left,* Elizabeth Hamlin, *right,* Vicki Lawrence, Stock Boston; 412, Paul Conklin, Monkmeyer; 415, Daniel S. Brody, Editorial Photocolor Archives; 418, John Launois, Black Star; 420, The Advertising Council of N.Y.; 421, Tim Carlson, Stock Boston.

HISTORICAL ATLAS PHOTOGRAPHS: p. 619, *top left,* T. W. Putney; *top right, bottom left,* Grant Heilman; *bottom right,* P. Rowan, Photo Researchers, Inc.; 622, *top left,* Grant Heilman; *top right, bottom left,* T. W. Putney; *bottom right,* Sybil Shackman, Monkmeyer; 624, Culver; 628, Lizabeth Corlett, DPI; 634, *top,* T. W. Putney; *bottom,* Erich Hartmann, Magnum; 635, *top,* DPI; *center top,* Bruce Rogers, Photo Researchers, Inc.; *center bottom,* Hugh Rogers, Monkmeyer; *bottom,* Paul Conklin, Monkmeyer.